1001 HISTORIC SITES

YOU MUST SEE BEFORE YOU DIE

1001 HISTORIC SITES

YOU MUST SEE BEFORE YOU DIE

GENERAL EDITOR RICHARD CAVENDISH

PREFACE BY KOÏCHIRO MATSUURA
DIRECTOR-GENERAL OF UNESCO

CASSELL
ILLUSTRATED

A Quint**essence** Book

First published in the UK in 2008 by Cassell Illustrated
a division of Octopus Publishing Group Limited
2-4 Heron Quays
London E14 4JP
A Hatchette Livre company
www.octopusbooks.co.uk

A CIP catalogue record for this book is available from the British Library

ISBN-13: 978-1-84403-598-4

QSS.HSI

This book was designed and produced by
Quint**essence**
226 City Road
London EC1V 2TT

Project Editor	Tobias Selin
Editors	Becky Gee, Fiona Plowman, Frank Ritter, Andrew Smith
Art Editor	Rod Teasdale
Designer	Philip Hall
Production	Anna Pauletti
Editorial Director	Jane Laing
Publisher	Tristan de Lancey

Manufactured in Singapore by Pica Digital Pte Ltd.
Printed in China by SNP Leefung Printers Ltd.

Contents

United Nations
Educational, Scientific and
Cultural Organization

In cooperation with UNESCO's
World Heritage Centre

Preface
By Koïchiro Matsuura, Director-General of UNESCO

Anyone who has experienced first-hand the Great Pyramids of Egypt, the Hall of Mirrors of the French royal residence at Versailles, the Palaces of Abomey in Benin, or the remains of the Khmer capital at Angkor, Cambodia, cannot fail to be moved by the extraordinary aura of these irreplaceable treasures that have survived over the centuries.

One of the principal goals of UNESCO (United Nations Educational, Scientific, and Cultural Organization) is to preserve such unique cultural sites around the planet for the enjoyment of present and future generations. This lofty goal is shared by the 185 countries that have signed the international treaty officially named the Convention Concerning the Protection of the World Cultural and Natural Heritage, commonly referred to as the World Heritage Convention.

Since the Convention's adoption in 1972, nations across the globe have formed a growing network of countries dedicated to the protection of World Heritage properties. Underlying this commitment is the fundamental belief that the preservation of our cultural and natural resources, which embody the collective memory of all societies, is the shared responsibility of all. UNESCO believes that by preserving and studying our heritage, we are better equipped to understand who we are, where we come from, and how we can work together to shape a sustainable future.

At present, a total of 851 sites are inscribed on the World Heritage List, and the list gets longer each year. UNESCO is delighted that the publisher of *1001 Historic Sites You Must See Before You Die* has decided to present a selection of these sites for an international readership.

Although the World Heritage List contains a large number of famous sites, we should not overlook lesser known places such as the medieval fortified town of Carcassonne in France; Thingvellir, Iceland's great open-air assembly ground; and the Temple and Tomb of Confucius in China. Moreover, some sites are associated with dark chapters in the history of humankind: the German Nazi concentration and extermination camp of Auschwitz–Birkenau in Poland, the prison complex on Robben Island in South Africa, and Gorée Island in Senegal commemorate horrific events that future generations must never forget.

As you discover the World Heritage sites featured in this handsome publication, it is worth bearing in mind the tremendous ongoing efforts that are required for their preservation. Once a site is inscribed on the List, its care becomes a twofold responsibility; the government of the host country pledges to protect the site, and, on the global level, the international community recognizes its responsibility to assist that government and local people in safeguarding their World Heritage site.

Tourism is now one of the world's largest industries, and experts tell us that its exponential growth will continue. For this reason, tourism-related issues have become increasingly critical in the management of World Heritage sites, especially since the number of visitors to a site climbs dramatically as a result of its inscription on the World Heritage List.

Tourism offers obvious advantages: revenues from entrance fees, concessions, and donations can serve to fund restoration and protection efforts. Tour operators and hotel chains can help by educating their clients in responsible tourism, while visitors can bolster threatened cultural values by supporting local festivities and traditional crafts.

However, increased tourism can also have negative consequences on the social, economic, and environmental context of the site. To meet these challenges, efforts in sustainable tourism must focus on ensuring environmental protection and limiting negative socioeconomic impacts on local communities. In short, sustainability remains the key to the survival of World Heritage.

Tsunamis, earthquakes, and other natural disasters, as well as threats from humans such as looting, warfare, pollution, uncontrolled urbanization, mining, or simple neglect, continue to jeopardize the future of many World Heritage sites. Thirty sites are currently inscribed on UNESCO's List of World Heritage in Danger, which aims to draw world attention to the need to reinforce protection at the national level and through international funding. *1001 Historic Sites* features some of these endangered places, including the marble palaces and splendid terraced gardens of Shalamar in Lahore, Pakistan, which are under threat from urban encroachment, and the fragile remains of the pre-Columbian site of Chan Chan, Peru, whose survival is imperiled by natural erosion.

Through the cooperation and commitment of its signatory countries, the World Heritage Convention has provided the impetus for several successful international safeguarding campaigns. The conservation work on the Old City of Dubrovnik in Croatia after damage sustained during the armed conflict in the 1990s, and the efforts to preserve the deteriorated Wieliczka Salt Mine in Poland, are but two such success stories described in this enlightening publication.

I sincerely hope that *1001 Historic Sites* will open up a new world for you, namely the world of our shared heritage, in which your own commitment to preserve its precious sites can make a difference.

Introduction

By Richard Cavendish, General Editor

History consists of the recorded actions of human beings, and people's actions occur in places. The vast majority of the places no longer exist or have changed out of all recognition or were never of any great interest anyway. In this book we have picked out 1001 sites that can still be rewardingly visited today where important and fascinating things happened in the past. They range all around the world, from the Americas east across the globe to the Pacific, and the history covers a huge span of time—from the development of the earliest human beings millions of years ago to about the middle of the twentieth century, which is as late as we think can yet be sensibly labeled "historic."

We decided that the book should not include scenery and landscape. Mountains, oceans, rivers, and lakes are not in this book, because they are not what we mean by a historic site. Some natural sites do qualify, however, such as Runnymede in England where Magna Carta was signed, Robinson Crusoe's island off Chile where Alexander Selkirk was marooned, Plymouth Rock where the Pilgrim Fathers landed in the New World, and Botany Bay where Captain Cook made his first landing in Australia.

We have ruled out conventional museums and art galleries. You will not find the British Museum or the Smithsonian or the Louvre in the pages that follow. Museums and galleries of that kind contain plenty of historic items, but they are not usually themselves sites where historic events ocurred. In cases where they are, they are included. For example, where a great artist or author, a religious leader, or other historic figure has lived and left a personal imprint, and the place is now preserved as a museum to that person, it qualifies for us as a historic site.

No two people, asked to list 1001 historic sites eminently worth visiting, would come up with the same list—though there are some places in the world so obviously both historic and vividly fascinating that they would almost certainly be included by anyone. It would be difficult to rule out Rome or Athens or Jerusalem, to ignore the Statue of Liberty, the Statue of Christ the Redeemer in Rio de Janeiro, the Leaning Tower of Pisa, or the ruins of Pompeii, or to turn one's back on the Taj Mahal in India, the Great Wall of China, the Egyptian Pyramids, the Sphinx of Giza and Tutankhamen's tomb, Petra and Persepolis, Machu Picchu, or the Maya temples of Mexico and Central America. UNESCO's World Heritage List has been invaluable, and we feature nearly 400 World Heritage sites in the book.

We have tried to make our selection of places cover as wide a range of different types of sites and different aspects of human history as we could.

UNESCO World Heritage sites in this book are indicated by this symbol:

They vary from temples and cathedrals to concentration camps, from the Easter Island statues to battlefields and cemeteries, from the Washington theater where President Lincoln was shot to HMS *Victory* where Lord Nelson breathed his last. They include palaces and grand houses, castles and fortifications, city walls, prisons, caves, mines, bridges, ships, lighthouses, monuments and memorials, theaters and opera houses, fashionable spas, gambling casinos, and one or two quite exceptionally historic hotels, such as the Raffles in Singapore. There is even a bookstore, the City Lights in San Francisco, founded in the 1950s and redolent of the beatniks.

The sites go far back in time to the Sterkfontein Caves in South Africa, the cradle of the human race perhaps 3 million years ago; the site in China, dating back more than 50,000 years, where the remains of Peking Man were discovered; and the caves at Lascaux in France, famed for their cave paintings of perhaps 15,000 years back. Stonehenge is included and Jericho, one of the world's oldest towns, the Saharan rock art at Jebel Acacus in Libya, the standing stones at Carnac, the ruins of Troy, the palace of Knossos in Crete, legendary home of the Minotaur, the Hill of Tara where the high kings of Ireland were crowned, and the site at Wanuskewin where Canada's early peoples stampeded buffalo to their death (and where you can enjoy buffalo sausages in the restaurant).

Moving on from prehistory, historic religious sites stretch across the world and time from ancient Egyptian temples to those of the Greek and Roman era, Christian cathedrals, churches, monasteries and missions, Muslim mosques and Jewish synagogues, Hindu and Buddhist places of worship, and on to Confucian and Taoist temples in China, and Shinto and Zen temples and shrines in Japan. They include the Church of the Holy Sepulchre in Jerusalem, St. Peter's in Rome, St. Mark's in Venice, Notre Dame in Paris, St. Basil's in Moscow, Gaudi's La Sagrada Familia in Barcelona, the Blue Mosque and the Mosque of Suleiman the Magnificent in Istanbul, and the Great Mosque of Cordoba in Spain. The Buddha's sacred bo tree is at Anuradhapura in Sri Lanka. The Ellora caves near Aurangabad in India shelter Hindu, Buddhist, and Jain temples. At Lourdes is the grotto where St. Bernadette saw the Virgin Mary. A church at Aksum in Ethiopia is the traditional hallowed resting place of the Ark of the Covenant, and Echmiadzin Cathedral in Armenia is credited with possessing wood from Noah's Ark. While we were making our selection we decided not to include places that are open only to the adherents of a particular religion, because we want our sites to be visitable by all our readers.

On a tragic note are the twentieth-century concentration and slave labor camps, which include Dachau and Buchenwald, along with others in Austria, Poland, and what was Czechoslovakia. There is the cemetery in Cambodia where many of Pol Pot's victims were buried, and the "Hanoi Hilton" prison in North Vietnam where prisoners were tortured. Perhaps the most famous prison in the world is Devil's Island off the coast of French Guyana, but Alcatraz in San Francisco Bay runs close, and France provides the Citadel of Île Sainte Marguerite where the Man in the Iron Mask was kept prisoner, and the Conciergerie prison in Paris where Marie Antoinette and others were held before they went to the guillotine.

Battlefields and military sites range over Marathon, the great crusader castle of Krak des Chevaliers in Syria, Waterloo, the Alamo, Gettysburg, Gallipoli, World War I trenches near Ypres in Belgium and forts at Verdun, Pearl Harbor in Hawaii, and the Normandy beaches of 1944. There are also the Arlington National Cemetery in the United States, the El Alamein military cemeteries in Egypt, and General MacArthur's headquarters on Corregidor Island in the Philippines. At Kanchanaburi in Thailand are the original bridge on the River Kwai and the graves of prisoners of war who perished building the Japanese "death railway." The A-Bomb Dome in Hiroshima is preserved as it was after the atom bomb blasted it in 1945, and the Yasukuni-jinja in Tokyo is a controversial shrine to Japan's war dead.

Among historic feats in the history of engineering are the Pont du Gard (the beautiful Roman aqueduct in Provence), Hadrian's Wall in Britain, the Eiffel Tower, the Golden Gate Bridge in San Francisco, the Miraflores Locks on the Panama Canal, the Mercedes-Benz and Volkswagen factories in Germany, and the Darjeeling mountain railway that climbs the Himalayas in India. Sites significant in scientific history include the home of Greenwich Mean Time, the place in Canada where Guglielmo Marconi received the first transatlantic wireless signal in 1901 (it consisted simply of the letter "s" in Morse code), and the Kennedy Space Center at Cape Canaveral.

Among a wealth of sites linked with famous figures of the past are the birthplaces of Shakespeare, Mozart, and Mao Zedong, as well as Marie Curie and Martin Luther King. There are Sigmund Freud's home in Vienna, Che Guevara's boyhood home in Argentina, Winston Churchill's country home in England (as well as the cabinet war rooms in London where he ran the war effort), George Washington's beautiful home at Mount Vernon and Thomas Jefferson's at Monticello, the house where Jane Austen lived and wrote, Napoleon Bonaparte's birthplace and childhood home in Corsica, and Pancho Villa's headquarters in Mexico. There are also Hitler's retreat at Berchtesgaden, sites associated with Stalin's youth at Gori in Georgia, the house in Mexico City where Trotsky was murdered, Anne Frank's house in Amsterdam, Salvador Dalí's extraordinary Surrealist residences in Spain, and the warehouse in Dallas from which President Kennedy was shot.

Numerous monuments and memorials to the great include the carved heads of U.S. presidents at Mount Rushmore and the gigantic monument to the great Native American chief Crazy Horse in the Black Hills of South Dakota. Among cemeteries where famous people lie buried are Père Lachaise in Paris, Highgate Cemetery in London with the grave of Karl Marx, the Lenin Mausoleum in Moscow, and the La Recoleta Cemetery in Buenos Aires with the grave of Eva Peron.

Places of learning range from the world's oldest surviving university, founded in Cairo in the tenth century, to the Anatomical Theater at Padua in Italy, where Galileo taught, the Bodleian Library at Oxford, and the Royal Canadian Mounted Police Academy. Sites significant in the history of sport bring in the stadium at Olympia in Greece where the classical Olympic Games were staged, as well as the one built in Athens in 1896 for the first modern Olympics, and the 1936 stadium in Berlin. In addition there are the Istanbul hippodrome, which was the classical world's leading chariot-racing arena, as well as the revered bullring at Ronda in Spain, Wimbledon for lawn tennis, the Royal & Ancient Golf Club in Scotland, Wrigley Field baseball stadium in Chicago, and the Rose Bowl in Pasadena.

Some of the sites have an engaging oddity, quirkiness, or sometimes gruesomeness about them. There is the ancient Zipaquira salt mine in Colombia that has a salt cathedral, or the Partagas cigar factory in Havana, Cuba, or the spectacular stations on the Moscow Metro. The ladies' powder room in the casino at Murcia in Spain is said to be astonishing. The soil for Italy's Camposanto Cemetery was specially brought from the site of Christ's crucifixion, and the Church of Santa Maria Maggiore in Rome numbers the manger from Bethlehem among its relics. There is a chapel built of human bones in the Franciscan church at Evora in Portugal and a tower built of human skulls at Nis in Serbia. Sites in Romania are linked with Vlad the Impaler, who was apparently the inspiration for Dracula, and there is an underground city at Derinkuyu in Turkey. The strange Nazca Lines drawn on the ground in Peru remain profoundly and intriguingly mysterious.

The book is designed to whet your appetite for places where you can still experience history, and that is what we hope it will do.

Index of Historic Sites

Long before European explorers
began to probe the American coasts,
native peoples such as the Incas,
Mayas, and Aztecs had developed
into advanced civilizations, as
evidenced by such sites as Machu
Picchu and Chichén Itzá. European
colonization brought a wealth of
buildings to the Americas, many of
them treasured now, but it also
provoked bloody conflict,
commemorated at sites such as
the Wounded Knee monument
and the Shiloh battlefield.

⇐ Remnants of
the great Mayan
site of Chichén Itzá
in Yucatán, Mexico.

the Americas

Dawson City (Dawson City, Canada)

Birthplace of the world-famous Klondike Gold Rush

> *"There are strange things done in the midnight sun / By the men who moil for gold…"*
>
> Robert Service, *The Cremation of Sam McGee* (1904)

⬆ A colorful street in present-day Dawson City, where visitors can still try their hand at gold panning.

➡ Miners and other locals congregate on Dawson City's busy Front Street during the Gold Rush years.

Built in the wake of the Klondike Gold Rush, Dawson City was a classic boomtown. Founded in 1896, it had 40,000 inhabitants by 1898 but, just a few years later, this had dwindled to 5,000. The surviving buildings, carefully preserved and restored, provide a colorful reminder of those heady days, when adventurers around the world were gripped by gold fever.

The stampede began in August 1896, when George Carmack, Dawson Charlie, and Skookum Jim discovered gold in Rabbit Creek (later renamed Bonanza Creek). As news of the discovery spread, thousands of prospectors flocked to this remote spot, located near the confluence of the Yukon and Klondike rivers. However, while most individuals went in search of their fortune panning for gold, a shrewd character called Joe Ladue (1855–1900) staked out a town-site, well aware that it was the merchants, rather than the miners, who usually got rich. He called the place Dawson City, after George Dawson, the geologist who had originally surveyed the region.

By 1898, Dawson City was in full swing. One contemporary observer summed it up as "[w]ild excitements, misery, riches, debauchery, broken hearts, scurvy, frostbite, suicide." For a brief period, lawlessness reigned. Some got rich, while others were fleeced by the operators of saloons, gambling houses, and brothels, or by suppliers who charged outrageous prices for basic provisions. With all the wooden and canvas structures, fire was a constant hazard. Typically, the first one began after a saloon girl threw an oil lamp at a rival. Disease was rampant. Jack London (1876–1916), who portrayed the Klondike Gold Rush in his writings, was one of many who caught scurvy. Then, just as the town authorities were gaining control, news came of gold finds in Alaska and the prospectors left as suddenly as they had arrived. Today, the city hosts the annual Yukon Gold Panning Championships. **IZ**

Banff Springs Hotel

(Banff, Canada)

Hotel in the Scottish baronial style

Everything in Canada is vast, and the string of super-size hotels built by the Canadian Pacific Railways (CPR) to boost tourism along its Rocky Mountain railway (and so fill their Pullman carriages with travelers) fits in with that enormous scale. The railway was completed in 1885, and a mere three years later on June 1, 1888, the grandest of the grandiose faux Scottish baronial castle-style hotels—The Banff Springs—opened its doors. With 250 rooms and a rotunda it was the world's largest hotel at the time.

Today, the Fairmont Banff Springs Hotel and spa has trebled the number of its rooms; it can accommodate up to 1,700 guests, who can often hear the strains of live bagpipe music. If you balk at the C$900 room fee, you can take a guided tour instead. The hotel, which is massive, can feel like a giant terminus. It is a touch old-fashioned today, but the edifice still stands proud like an alpha-male stag amid the aspen, beneath the shadows of spectacular massifs at the convergence of the Bow and Spray rivers.

From CPR's general manager William Cornelius Van Horne's mission statement, "Since we can't export the scenery, we'll have to import the tourists" to the awful realization by New York architect Bruce Price that the initial building work was 180 degrees off-course—(he allegedly claimed: "You built my hotel backwards!")—there has always been something *mise-en-scène* about the hotel. Price's building was classic late-Victorian architecture—verbose, solid, somber, grand, and so imposing that it became the foundation of Canadian architecture until World War II, and "château style" became the proscribed architectural method for government structures.

Today, the Fairmont Banff Springs Hotel continues to stand in all its dour Gothic splendor as a monument to late-Victorian architectural derring-do. **JH**

Fort Edmonton Park

(Edmonton, Canada)

Historic trading post

Fort Edmonton, the trading post of the Hudson's Bay Company, dominated the fur trade throughout British-controlled North America. Sited in Canada's largest "living-history park," you enter the post via the first of four walk-through historical "streets." Each one showcases white settlement in the history of Edmonton. To move between the seventy-five structures (many of them original) across the 158-acre (64-ha) site, there are various period rides offered including wagon, stagecoach, and streetcar.

The first fort was established in 1794 at the confluence of the Sturgeon and North Saskatchewan

> *"[Buffalo calf] boiled whole, is one of the esteemed dishes amongst the epicures of the interior."*
>
> Paul Kane, artist, on the fort's Christmas dinner

rivers as part of the westward expansion of the fur trade by the Hudson's Bay Company. Three years later, more than 12,500 beaver pelts were being traded. Set inside a high wooden palisade, it was always a commercial stockade rather than a military fort.

The main building—in meticulously re-created woodwork—is Rowand House. It is an impressive, four-story residence with a commanding third-story balcony. Under the chief factor (mercantile agent) John Rowand, the fort became one of the most important in what later became Alberta. The fort was also a place where buffalo meat and other provisions were traded with other posts. It was home to another 130 residents—clerks, artisans, and laborers. Other parts of the post include a forge, stable, and boat shed where square-sailed York boats were built. **JH**

Wanuskewin Heritage Park

(Saskatoon, Canada)

Sacred prairie site of Canada's First Nations

Pronounced "Wah-nus-KAY-win," this is a sacred site full of symbolism, symmetry, and spirits. Like Sydney Opera House's sail or shark fin motif, the tipi encampment "signature" atop the impressive visitor center at the Wanuskewin Heritage Park is a significant landmark on the prairie horizon.

As visitors approach Wanuskewin by car, the four-pointed roof is a highly visible nod to Canada's First Nations, who saw the number four as life enhancing. The circle is the other sacred symbol much in evidence here, from the indoor replica of a circular buffalo pound to the interactive exhibit area shaped like a giant tipi and the ring-shaped amphitheater where "round" and "hoop" dances are still performed. *Wanuskewin*—which means "seeking peace of mind"—was very much a sacred place for First Nation worship and celebration. That spiritual connection to the natural environment is reflected sympathetically in the architecture, landscape, and displays.

With a history dating back more than 6,000 years, this was land used for hunting and occasional wintering by a half dozen Indian tribes of the Northern Plains, including the Cree, Sioux-Assiniboia, and Plains Ojibwa, before they were moved off to the reservations in the 1870s. Reflecting the tribes' dependence on buffalo meat and hides at the site, the visitor center rests at the head of a buffalo jump and "drive lane," where hunters stampeded the animals to the jump. Sculptures of buffalo galloping at full gait greet you outside the entrance, led by an Indian runner decoy disguised as a calf. (The restaurant includes buffalo sausage on the menu.)

Excavations of the Wanuskewin site began in the early 1930s. The archeological remains include a curious boulder alignment (better known as a medicine wheel), tipi rings, and stone cairns. **JH**

"The American Indian is of the soil . . . he belongs just as the buffalo belonged."

Luther Standing Bear, Oglala Sioux chief

Royal Canadian Mounted Police Academy

(Regina, Canada)

Training academy of one of Canada's most recognizable symbols

The square-jawed Mountie in red coat, jodhpurs, and broad-brimmed Stetson hat is as Canadian as maple syrup. It was on the western edge of Regina, capital of the prairie province of Saskatchewan, that the Royal Canadian Mounted Police (RCMP) developed its form and function—a cross between a ceremonial cavalry, national police force, and the FBI.

The site was originally known as Depot Division, but was later renamed RCMP Academy to better reflect its primary function as a training facility (which it has been since 1885, with some 46,000 RCMP cadets graduating), and on a visit here you can see them marching in formation or jogging. The huge 12-acre (5-ha) site has nearly fifty buildings, including the impressive red-roofed headquarters, a mess hall, drill hall, forensic lab, firearms complex, "town site" for simulated policing scenarios, self-defense gym, fitness center, cemetery (where rebel leader-politician Louis Riel is buried), and a chapel set before Sleigh Square —the "heart of the academy" and site of the tourist-attracting Sergeant Major's Parade and the Sunset Retreat Ceremony.

The chapel is the oldest remaining building in Regina and one of the oldest chapels on the prairies. It was built as a mess hall in Ontario and moved here by flatcar, steamer, and ox team. North West Mounted Police carpenters converted it into a chapel, making the altar and pews themselves, and the chapel was dedicated in December 1895.

A futuristic C$40 million, stone-and-glass RCMP Heritage Center replaced the Centennial Museum building on the site in 2007. Exhibit galleries track the history of the force—from 1873, policing the Yukon Gold Rush in the frozen north with the help of dog teams, to modern times, when it cracks cases with the latest DNA technology. **JH**

"There isn't a Force the world over/Like the Scarlet, the Gold, and the Blue."

Bertram Boutlier, "The Recruit" (1945)

Union Station

(Toronto, Canada)

Canada's premier railway station

Even to the jaded twenty-first-century eye, the facade of Toronto's Union Station is still vast and magnificent in its cool proportions, classy decorative stone, and refined Beaux-Arts lines. It may not be as famous as its New York cousin—Grand Central Station—but, to Torontonians, Union Station has served as a great gateway to the city.

Monumental it certainly is because it occupies an entire city block on the south side of Front Street between York and Bay streets. It also recalls a past era of train travel when passengers passed through the lobby or detoured to the station's barbershop and even baths.

The four architects who steered this huge project were friends and admirers of the heroic proportions, sense of drama, and rational planning that constituted Beaux-Arts design. Care in the choice of materials was crucial. The massive 850-foot (260-m) facade is clad in Indiana and Queenston limestone and the centerpiece entranceway comprises a broad colonnade of Bedford limestone, each column weighing 75 tons and rising to 40 feet (12 m). Walk between these huge pillars and you enter the 25-foot- (80-m-) long lobby along marble flooring, laid in a herringbone pattern, which complements the inside walls fashioned in Zumbro (fossilized) stone and echoes the splendidly tiled ceiling. The arching was added to avoid any dark shadows that a flat ceiling would project.

Look halfway up the north and south walls and you will find the names of the cities served by the Canadian Pacific Railway and the former Grand Trunk Railroad (that together formed the "Union"). The list alternates from side to side, naming the cities from east to west. This piece of "Canadiana" came from architect John Lyle's desire to create a decoration expressive of Canada. **JH**

Casa Loma

(Toronto, Canada)

Majestic kitsch monument

Sir Henry Mill Pellatt was the Donald Trump of his day, but instead of building an eponymous tower, this Canadian entrepreneur, who harnessed his fortune to the power of hydroelectricity and Niagara Falls, built a medieval folly called Casa Loma—a sandstone, seven-story, twin-towered Camelot.

You either love it or hate it (depending on how you feel about kitsch), but, like William Randolph Hearst's San Simeon in California, it is a must-see monument to one man (and his wife) "showing the money." Pellatt hired architect Edward Lennox, who incorporated his client's castle sketches into one grand

> *"No one would suspect a freak castle with Saturday night dances. No one did."*
>
> Mary M. Alward, writer

medieval mélange. The Scottish link to all things empirically Canadian is amazing; stonemasons were hired from across the pond in Scotland.

Some three years, C$3 million, and three hundred workers later, what did he get for his money? Aside from twenty-two fireplaces, and the then mod-cons of electric power, a central vacuuming system, a fifty-nine-telephone exchange, and an oven big enough to cook an ox, Pellat could show off, among countless other features, a rather cheerless great hall with a 60-foot (18-m) ceiling hung with flags, chandeliers, and suits of armor and an 800-foot- (250-m-) long secret tunnel linking the house to the fine carriage room and stables. It was here that U-boat sonar detectors were developed during World War II, while Big Band dances were being held inside. **JH**

Parliament Buildings
(Ottawa, Canada)

Canada's historic seat of government

Ottawa was declared capital of the United Province of Canada in 1858 ahead of more obvious candidates such as Toronto, Montréal, and Québec because it was a safe distance from the U.S. border and it was on the border between Québec and Ontario. The location chosen for the new parliament buildings was on the sloping flat top of a limestone cliff above the Ottawa River, which for thousands of years had been a landmark on the river route to the interior of the continent. Britain's Prince of Wales laid the cornerstone in 1860, and six years later the biggest construction project to date in North America was completed.

Placed around a formal lawn and with the great Victoria Tower as the focal point, the Gothic Revival group of buildings was an architectural nod to Britain, although there are definite German and French influences. One year after completion, the buildings were chosen as the seat of government for the new Dominion of Canada, born with a federal government for Ontario, Québec, New Brunswick, and Nova Scotia. Further vast territories to the west were later brought in and, as Canada grew, so did the parliament building. Fires in 1916 and 1952 led to some rebuilding, which aimed to reproduce the original designs, although with different materials and modern techniques. A new addition in the 1920s was the Gothic/Beaux-Arts Peace Tower, which in 1980 was refurbished with the world's first slanting elevator to take visitors around the bells. Like the other buildings, it was heavily decorated with gargoyles, grotesques, and friezes.

Many events of national importance have been marked here over the years: the funerals of statesmen, the coronations, deaths, and visits of British monarchs, and declarations of war and peace. Canadians lying in state here include former Prime Minister Pierre Trudeau and Canada's Unknown Soldier. **AP**

Hôtel-Dieu de Montréal
(Montréal, Canada)

Illustrious Canadian medical institution

The Hôtel-Dieu de Montréal was the first hospital established in Montréal and is one of the oldest in North America. The hospital remains one of the most important teaching hospitals in Canada, and has been the site of many important medical advances.

The founding of the Hôtel-Dieu de Montréal is intimately tied to the foundation of the city itself. On May 17, 1642, Paul Chomedey de Maisonneuve established a small settlement and religious mission called Ville-Marie on the site of Montréal. Among his party was a devout missionary nurse and French settler called Jeanne Mance. She set up a small

"The resolution of [Jeanne Mance] saved not only the island of Montreal but the whole of Canada."

Appleton's Cyclopedia of American Biography

hospital in the settlement in the autumn of 1642, offering care to natives and settlers alike.

On October 8, 1645, the Hôtel-Dieu de Montréal formally came into being. It was staffed by an order of nuns called the Réligieuses Hospitalières de Saint-Joseph. In 1688, the missionary Guillaume Bailly drew up plans for a new stone hospital. From 1695 to 1734, the hospital was damaged three times by fire. In 1861, the Hôtel-Dieu de Montréal was moved from its original site in the old town to its present location near Mount Royal, where it continued to expand and flourish. In 1868, it was the site of the world's first kidney removal, and in 1959 the first-ever transplant of the femur bone took place there. The Hôtel-Dieu de Montréal also houses a museum detailing the history of the foundation. **JF**

Château Ramezay

(Montréal, Canada)

The changing fortunes of the Château Ramezay reflect those of Montréal itself

Château Ramezay is one of the oldest buildings in Montréal, dating from the time of French rule in Québec, and it is the only residence of a French governor still standing in the city.

Claude de Ramezay arrived as Montréal's governor in 1704. The next year, he contracted a local architect and mason to build him a house. After his death in 1724, the Château Ramezay passed to his widow. When the Ramezay family was forced to sell the house because of debts in 1745, it was bought by the French West Indies Company, who used the house as a headquarters and storage depot for furs. In 1755 the house was whitewashed and extended, and cellars were added. After the British commander General James Wolfe conquered Montréal in 1759, the Château Ramezay was used as a residence for the British governor in the city. During the American occupation of the city between 1775 and 1776, the house was the site of a failed attempt by an American delegation, including Benjamin Franklin, to persuade Québec to join the United States. After this, the house was again used as a residence for the British governors until 1854. Subsequently, the Château Ramezay was used as a school, college, and law courts before being opened to the public as a museum in 1895.

In 1929, Château Ramezay became the first building classified as a historical monument by the Québécois government. The house offers examples of original furnishings and paintings, as well as a large garden and costumed actors reenacting life in eighteenth-century Montréal.

The history of the Château Ramezay neatly divides the various phases of Montréal's history—from French trading outpost to part of the British Empire. It stands today as an intimate monument to the three hundred years of the city's history. **JF**

"Join us as brothers in revolt, or risk becoming tools to assist the British."

U.S. manifesto to the people of Québec, 1775

 ◎ # La Citadelle (Québec City, Canada)

Fine fortress from the colonial past of the Americas

Québec City may be the bastion of all things French in Canada (even the stop signs read *Arrêt*, whereas in France they read "Stop"), but the stunning cliff-top fortress of La Citadelle approximately 360 feet (120 m) above the St. Lawrence River atop Cap Diamant is a definite throwback to British Empire rule. The fortress still features guards sporting scarlet tunics and bearskin hats, and it remains the most important fortification built in Canada under British rule. Not surprisingly perhaps, it is referred to locally as the "Gibraltar of America" and is said to be the largest North American fort still working as a military base.

La Citadelle (the French name is used both in English and French) was designed according to a defense system developed by the French military engineer Saint-Léger-Vauban, who refined these star-shaped fortresses to make them virtually impregnable to the assault weapons of the day. Not much of the

original French fortress remains except for the redoubt of 1693 and the powder magazine of 1750 (now a museum). Today the Historic District of Old Québec, including the Citadelle, is a UNESCO World Heritage site representing an eminent example of a fortified colonial town and illustrates a major stage in the populating and growth of the Americas during the modern and contemporary period.

La Citadelle's layout is in the shape of a four-pointed polygon, with each point forming a bastion. Most of the twenty-five buildings on the 37-acre (15-ha) site were erected by the British on the orders of the Duke of Wellington. He anticipated another U.S. attack after the war of 1812. It never happened; in fact there has never been an exchange of fire with an invader and therefore no chance to test the guns protecting the Bastion Prince de Galles, which can fire a shell almost 3 miles (5 km). **JH**

Green Gables House (Cavendish, Canada)

Victorian farmhouse that provided the inspiration for a literary classic

Situated in Prince Edward Island National Park, Canada, Green Gables House is one of the most visited historic sites in the country and where author Lucy Maud Montgomery (1874–1942) set her best-selling novel *Anne of Green Gables* and its sequels. They feature Montgomery's memorable protagonist, Anne Shirley, an imaginative and outspoken redhead.

Built in the mid-nineteenth century, Green Gables House is a typical mid-Victorian farmhouse, deriving its name from the vibrant, dark green paint of the triangular gables on its roof. Montgomery was brought up mainly by her grandparents on rural Prince Edward Island. Their cousins, the Macneills, lived close by in Green Gables House, and Montgomery spent her isolated childhood playing in her cousins' garden. In 1904, while leafing through an old notebook, Montgomery came across a story describing an elderly couple's application for the adoption of an orphan boy, but by mistake a girl was sent instead. This discovery gave the Canadian writer the idea for her literary heroine and *Anne of Green Gables*, the first book in her popular series, was published in 1908.

Prince Edward National Park was set up in the 1930s as a place of natural beauty and as a tourist attraction. A golf course designed by the architect Stanley Thompson runs beside Green Gables House. Lover's Lane and the Haunted Wood—both places Anne haunts in the novels—can also be visited. **LaL**

"There's a lot of different Annes in me. I sometimes think that is why I'm such a troublesome person."

Lucy Maud Montgomery, *Anne of Green Gables* (1908)

 ## L'Anse aux Meadows (Newfoundland, Canada)

The only authentic Viking settlement in the Americas

The subarctic shoreline of L'Anse aux Meadows not only looks like something straight out of a Norse saga, but is straight out of a Norse saga. Archeological digs and carbon dating confirm that this remote spot is the only known Viking settlement in the United States and the earliest recorded European habitation in the New World. The Vikings may have been blown off course on their way from Greenland to Iceland, but they made the best of their new home as a repair and staging post (the local timber was much valued) for probably three winters before skirmishes with native Innuits (and severe winters) forced them to leave.

L'Anse aux Meadows, or Meadow Cove, lies at the northeast tip of the 170-mile- (275-km-) long Great Northern Peninsula on the island of Newfoundland. Here, in 1960, Norwegian writer-explorer Helge Ingstad and his archeologist wife, Anne Stine, were led to a series of overgrown mounds by George Decker.

International excavations supervised by the Ingstads found that these ridges were the lower courses of the walls of eight timber-framed buildings with sod cladding of the same kind used in Iceland and Greenland in the eleventh century. The remains of a small iron smithy suggested possibly the first-known iron smelting in North America.

In the low-level Interpretative Center at L'Anse aux Meadows you can marvel at the artifacts taken from the digs, including the archeological "clincher"—a Norse-designed, ring-headed cloak clasping pin— and a soapstone spindle whorl (flywheel) for clothing and sail repairs. Outside in the meadow, grassy borders outline the original Viking foundations and you can step inside turf-covered reconstructions, including a longhouse. Narrow fire pits were placed at intervals in the middle of the earthenware floor and served for heating, lighting, and cooking. **JH**

Signal Hill (St. John's, Canada)

Historic lookout where the first transatlantic wireless signal was received

Atop Cabot's Tower on Signal Hill, you can clearly see why this site is St. John's most visible landmark. With 525-foot- (160-m-) high cliffs on the north side, this strategic position guards a harbor entrance only 680 feet (207 m) wide and offers uninterrupted panoramic views. From 1704, flag signals were flown from the summit to inform St. John's of approaching friendly or hostile ships—often the latter because Dutch, French, and English forces all vied for this strategic point. In 1762, English and French forces fought the last North American battle of the Seven Years' War on this hill. Signal Hill Tattoo, with its marching drills, muskets, and period battle reenactments, has been a major tourist attraction here since 1967.

Cabot's Tower was built between 1898 and 1900 to commemorate the 400th anniversary of John Cabot's discovery of Newfoundland. It is now the center of Canada's second-largest historic park.

Despite its strategic position, Signal Hill was not properly fortified until the Napoleonic Wars (1803–15). New barracks were built in the 1830s, and the hill was fortified again during the American Civil War. The Newfoundland government turned the barracks into hospitals in 1870. It was in one of these that Guglielmo Marconi received radio signals—the letter *s* in Morse Code—transmitted long distance on December 12, 1901, by electromagnetic waves from Poldu, Cornwall, more than 2,155 miles (3,468 km) away. **JH**

"Every day sees humanity more victorious in the struggle with space and time."

Guglielmo Marconi, inventor

Klondike Gold Rush Historical Park

(Skagway, AK, and Seattle, WA, USA)

Made into a historical park to preserve the routes followed by gold prospectors

The Klondike Gold Rush International Historical Park covers an enormous area, including ground in the United States and Canada, which makes it fairly unique among government-run parks. From 1897 to 1898, the gold rush led prospectors to mines along the Klondike River and Yukon River territory in Canada.

Gold was discovered in August 1896 by a small group of prospectors (one of whom was a woman, Kate Carmack) and word spread rapidly to other mining camps in the Yukon valley. The news first hit the United States when successful prospectors from Canada traveled south to Seattle and San Francisco. It sparked a stampede of people rushing toward Yukon territory and Klondike, journeying along the numerous routes such as the White Pass and Chilkoot Trail. Seattle formed a base for many travelers who set off having outfitted themselves for the long and arduous journey, and the city flourished on the back of the increased revenue. The city's total business receipts went from $300,000 to $25 million between 1896 and 1897. The park consists of a series of units of historical importance that have been preserved, with three around Skagway, one in Seattle, and a further three in Canada. The units cover buildings and parts of the trails, with much of downtown Skagway preserved, including fifteen historic structures.

The international park covers not only areas of outstanding natural beauty, but the original towns built off the back of the gold rush. It preserves an important part of U.S. and Canadian history that saw many fortunes made and lost. **TP**

◩ Bronze sculptures of a Tlingit guide leading a prospector greet vistors to the international park.

◩ Prospectors pause in their frenzied efforts to strike paydirt and win themselves a fortune.

Little Bighorn Battlefield (Bighorn, MT, USA)

This battle was the Indians' greatest victory

The Little Bighorn Battlefield is a windswept swatch of land just beyond the Wyoming–Montana border. It is an area of wide-open country that stretches away into the distance, a country of "big skies" dotted with the occasional band of dark trees and grazing cattle. It was here that the famous Battle of the Little Bighorn was fought, where Colonel George Armstrong Custer and his seventh cavalry were killed, and where the Lakota, Cheyenne, and Arapaho Indians who were fighting to protect their homeland were victorious.

The battle took place on June 25 and 26, 1876, not far from the Little Bighorn River. It was planned to incorporate four separate units of attack: the main one led by Custer, and the others by Major Marcus Reno, Captain Frederick Benteen, and Captain Thomas McDougall. Custer, misjudging the terrain and the numbers of Indian warriors, led his cavalry into the ill-fated attack. He and his men were quickly surrounded and annihilated, then scalped and mutilated (with the exception of Custer's corpse) by the victors. The site of the massacre was first preserved as a national cemetery by the Secretary of War on January 29, 1879, and in 1881 a memorial was erected on Last Stand Hill over the mass grave of the soldiers of the seventh cavalry. In 1991 the U.S. Congress ordered the name of the site to be changed to reflect the Indians' role in the defense of their home territory and, in 1996, a competition was held to design a memorial in their honor. Over time white marble markers have been placed on the spots where the cavalrymen died, and now red granite markers also denote the places where Indian warriors were killed.

The expanse that is the Little Bighorn Battlefield now memorializes one of the Indian's last and greatest efforts to maintain their home territory, and the heroic efforts of a small band of brave cavalrymen. **TP**

Fort Laramie (Goshen County, WY, USA)

Crossroads of a nation moving west

Fort Laramie was pivotal in the expansion and settlement of the west, and was the only civilized supply post and stopping point for an 800-mile (1,287-km) span between Fort Kearney, Nebraska, and Fort Bridger, Wyoming.

Situated at the point where the Laramie and North Platte rivers meet, Fort Laramie was established as a fur trading post around 1834, servicing traveling Cheyenne and Arapaho Native Americans. The post became an important stopping point for people traveling west, drawn by the prospect of gold. As trading developed, Fort Laramie served as a crucial

> *"... the American Fur Company well-nigh monopolizes the Indian trade of this whole region."*
>
> Francis Parkman, historian and author

way station for wagon trains, with a number of the major trails converging here.

In 1849 the fort was purchased by the government and quickly grew to be the largest military outpost in the west. Later the Pony Express and transcontinental telegraph passed through this spot and, with the growth of homesteading, it formed a trading point for ranchers. Within its military capacity, it functioned as a base from which many campaigns were staged, mostly against the Northern Plains tribes who were trying to protect their homeland. It was also here that a number of treaties with the Native Americans were negotiated in an attempt to bring peace between the two factions. As the warring ceased, the importance of the fort decreased. Efforts have been made to preserve the site by National Park Service. **TP**

Mount Rushmore (Keystone, SD, USA)

One of the largest and most famous carved monuments in the world

Mount Rushmore is dedicated to four of the greatest early American presidents. The heads of George Washington (1732–99), Thomas Jefferson (1743–1826), Abraham Lincoln (1809–65), and Theodore Roosevelt (1858–1919), carved into the granite hillside, now gaze across the beautiful South Dakota Black Hills.

A local historian, Doane Robinson, first had the idea for the monument primarily to boost tourism in the area. It was a plan that paid off, with more than two million people now traveling to see the historic monument. Congressional approval was granted and the sculptor, Gutzon Borglum, began to research a suitable location. He settled on Mount Rushmore largely because of the impressive height of the mountain and the good quality of its granite. Work began in 1927, with around 400 sculptors, and continued until 1941, when Borglum unexpectedly died. By this time the four heads had been completed and the funds had all but dried up; the work was stopped, despite Borglum's original idea to represent the four presidents from the waist up.

The choice of Mount Rushmore was a controversial one. The mountain, known as Six Grandfathers by the Lakota Indians, was a sacred place for them. The United States requisitioned the land, allegedly reneging on the Treaty of Fort Laramie, 1868, and many Native Americans saw this and the subsequent carving of the mountain into a monument to American presidents as outrageous. It is not by coincidence that the mammoth mountainside carving of the Crazy Horse Memorial is near Mount Rushmore, and on its completion will dwarf Borglum's work. **TP**

◩ From left to right, George Washington, Thomas Jefferson, Theodore Roosevelt, and Abraham Lincoln.

◪ The heads of George Washington and Thomas Jefferson were the first to near completion.

Crazy Horse Memorial (Black Hills, SD, USA)

On completion the monument will make Mount Rushmore look small in comparison

The unfinished Crazy Horse Memorial is being created on Thunderhead Mountain, a part of the Black Hills in South Dakota considered sacred by many Native Americans. A long winding road leads to the site, where suddenly there unfolds an extraordinary vista: a sculpture being carved from the side of a mountain.

In 1939 Chief Henry Standing Bear wrote to the Polish sculptor Korczak Ziółkowski and asked if he would create a monument to honor the Native Americans. That request sparked what would become one of the largest and most controversial memorial projects. Ziółkowski's vision, which his family has perpetuated, was for a sculpture of Crazy Horse, the Lakota warrior who led his people during the Battle of the Little Bighorn (1876), where Colonel George Armstrong Custer and his men were massacred. Ziółkowski and members of the Lakota tribe chose the location of Thunderhead Mountain, but it is a controversial site and many Lakota people are deeply offended at their sacred ground being destroyed. The sculpture, which on its completion will be the largest in the world, is being carved from the mountainside with a series of controlled explosions. The project also encompasses a comprehensive visitor center, a museum documenting Native American history, and a planned university and medical training center for North American Indians.

The complex is owned by the not-for-profit Crazy Horse Memorial Foundation, and has not had, through choice, any federal funding. It is an enormous and continuing achievement, and an important resource for Native American culture and history. **TP**

↗ The awesome sculpture begins to take shape, hewn from a mountain held sacred by Native Americans.

↘ Ziółkowski's sculpture of Crazy Horse, displayed against the mountain that eventually will embody it.

Wounded Knee Monument (Pine Ridge, SD, USA)

Eternal reminder of the bloody Indian Wars

The simple stone memorial stands against a stark sky on the Pine Ridge Reservation in South Dakota. It is an area of wild beauty, rugged and fierce. The monument marks the site of the massacre of approximately 300 Sioux Indians—men, women, and children—in an episode that marked the end of the physical conflicts of the Indian Wars.

In December 1890, more than 500 U.S. cavalrymen surrounded the fort of the Miniconjou Sioux and Hunkpapa Sioux with orders to confiscate the Indians' arms and to move them to Omaha, Nebraska, to make way for more homesteaders moving on to their territories. Tensions were already running higher than usual with the murder of Chief Sitting Bull a few days previously on the Standing Rock Reservation, and it was his half-brother, Chief Big Foot, who was then surrounded by the U.S. forces. A search was made for weapons, of which few were found, and in the course of the search a gun was fired.

Accounts vary about who fired the first shot and why, but it led to the subsequent slaughter of the Indians, many of whom were women and children and who were greatly outnumbered by the U.S. cavalry, who were armed with Hotchkiss guns, a type of lightweight artillery. (Twenty-five U.S. soldiers also died in the battle, some of whom are believed to have been the victims of "friendly fire.") General Nelson Miles later described the event as a "massacre," and Colonel James Forsyth, who had led the troops, was relieved from duty, although he was later exonerated. The bloody fight effectively marked the end of the Indian Wars, although the resentments continued. **TP**

⬉ Chief Sitting Bull, whose murder proved to be a tragic preface to the massacre at Wounded Knee.

⬀ In its lonely South Dakota site, the Wounded Knee Monument is a lasting reminder of the bloody event.

Deadwood Historic Trail (Deadwood, SD, USA)

Important trading center and one of the most notorious towns in the Wild West

In 1875 gold prospector John Pearson discovered gold along a narrow gulch in the Black Hills of South Dakota. It was a discovery that, combined with Colonel George Armstrong Custer's discovery of gold on French Creek near the present-day town of Custer the year before, led to the mammoth Black Hills Gold Rush. The gulch where Pearson found his gold was lined with dead trees, and the area came to be called Deadwood.

Prospectors, gunslingers, and criminals on the run from the law descended on Deadwood and the town became inherently lawless. In 1876 the problem was compounded when a wagon train trundled up packed with gamblers and prostitutes, along with Wild Bill Hickok and Calamity Jane. The pair now lie alongside other legendary figures such as Potato Creek Johnny, Preacher Smith, and Seth Bullock at the Mount Moriah Cemetery just outside of town. Despite Deadwood's notorious reputation, after the first flush of gold fever had passed the town became a respectable Victorian community, with Main Street boasting traditional rustic wooden buildings, sidewalks, and grand brick residences. In 1878 it became the first town in South Dakota to have a telephone exchange, and the Deadwood Central Railroad was opened in 1879.

Deadwood became an important trading center within the Black Hills but, as the gold dried up, the prospectors moved on to new pastures and the town began to slowly fade. In 1989 limited-wage gambling was legalized in Deadwood, making it one of only three places in the United States at that time to allow it. The effect was immediate, and the tourist trade now flourishes in this historic town of the Wild West. **TP**

⤴ Wild Bill Hickok, Deadwood's most famous resident, was a fearless gunfighter, scout, and lawman.

⤵ Saloon No. 10, where Wild Bill Hickok was killed by a shot to the back of the head while playing poker.

Wrigley Field

(Chicago, IL, USA)

Classic stadium in baseball history

> *"Putting lights in the Wrigley Field is like putting aluminum siding on the Sistine Chapel."*
>
> Roger Simon, journalist

The large expanse of green in the middle of Chicago, Illinois, that makes up the Wrigley Stadium is in actual fact relatively small for a baseball stadium, and the historic site is the fourth-smallest active baseball park in the United States. The well-known stadium is located in the largely residential area of Lakeview, but the neighborhood is more commonly referred to as "Wrigleyville."

Wrigley Field is among the most treasured of baseball parks in the United States, and has a largely indefinable appeal to sports aficionados. It was designed in 1914 by Zachary Taylor Davis, who had worked with Louis Sullivan and Frank Lloyd Wright. The site was originally built for the Federal League baseball team the Chicago Whales, and was called Weeghman Park after Charles Weeghman, who owned the team. The following year the Federal League folded and Weeghman, with nine others (including William Wrigley Jr.), bought the Chicago Cubs. In 1920 the Wrigley family bought the Cubs outright and the park was renamed Cubs Park. It was not called Wrigley Field until 1926. Over the course of the years the stands and layout of the field have been considerably added to, but perhaps the most significant additions were those made in 1937. This was the year that Bill Veeck, the Cubs' treasurer, planted the park's famous ivy on the outfield wall. The ivy thickly covers the wall and if any ball is hit into the ivy and lost, it is ruled a "ground-rule double." Veeck also erected the manual outfield scoreboard, which, amazingly, has never been hit by a ball.

Numerous baseball traditions have started up at Wrigley Field, including singing the national anthem before a game and the song "Take Me Out to the Ballgame." It has also been the scene of many historic sporting moments, making it a national treasure. **TP**

Biograph Theater

(Chicago, IL, USA)

Scene of the killing of John Dillinger

The Biograph Theater is the oldest of Chicago's original theaters and is an excellent example of early movie theater design. The architect Samuel N. Crowen was commissioned in 1914 and devised the simple facade with classical resonance, which has remained largely unchanged over the years. Typical of many small theaters of the period, the entrance lobby is the width of a storefront with a freestanding ticket booth and canopy marquee, the latter of which has been faithfully restored.

Perhaps more compelling than the theater's architecture is its significant place in crime history. Named "Public Enemy No. 1" by the FBI, John Dillinger (1903–34) had been on a rampage of robbery, leaving a number of dead bodies in his wake. He had slipped through the FBI's fingers on numerous occasions, escaped from jail twice, and become a national folk hero in the process—stories, fueled by the widespread poverty of the Great Depression, circulated that he stole from the rich and gave to the poor. He was the thorn in the side of FBI agent Melvin Purvis, who finally "got his man" on the evening of July 22, 1934. Purvis accosted Dillinger as he left the Biograph Theater (having watched the movie *Manhattan Melodrama* with two girlfriends), and shot him. One of Dillinger's girlfriends, Anna Sage, had allegedly set him up and had struck a deal with the FBI ensuring that she would not be deported back to England. However, dark whispers abound that the person gunned down was not in fact Dillinger but another low-life character, Jimmy Lawrence, and that Dillinger had had the last laugh over his would-be nemesis.

The diminutive theater with the big history was designated a Chicago Landmark in 2001, and is still open for moviegoing business. It is without doubt one of the "must-sees" in the Windy City. **TP**

Frank Lloyd Wright's House (Oak Park, IL, USA)

Home of a great U.S. architect

Frank Lloyd Wright (1867–1959) purchased the site for his Oak Park home and studio at the age of just twenty-two, shortly after his marriage to Catherine Tobin. He paid for the property with a $5,000 loan from his employer Louis Sullivan and lived there until 1909, making extensive changes, renovations, and additions to the house. It displays many of the design concepts and experiments that he later developed.

The building served as Wright's family residence, where he raised six children with his wife, and also as his workplace. It was here that he first developed the "prairie style" of architecture, incorporating long, low,

> *"Simplicity and repose are the qualities that measure the true value of any work of art."*
>
> Frank Lloyd Wright, architect

horizontal external lines and open-plan living internally. This was a style that he used frequently in many of the houses he designed in the Chicago area, and it can be seen to best effect in the Robie Residence that was completed in 1909, the year he left his Oak Park home. He extensively remodeled this home in 1895, making changes to the kitchen, dining room, and nursery, adding a two-story polygonal bay on the south side.

One of the most influential and prominent architects of the twentieth century, Frank Lloyd Wright had a long career in which his style developed enormously. His Oak Park residence continues to be important for lovers of architecture because it reflects the germination of so many of his early creative ideas that would later flourish. **TP**

🏛 ⦿ Cahokia Mounds (Collinsville, IL, USA)

Monks Mound formed a focal point for the city and was of ceremonial importance

Cahokia Mounds Historic Site is situated on the vast expanse of the Mississippi River floodplain in Collinsville, Illinois. It is the largest pre-Columbian settlement north of Mexico and was inhabited around 700. The "city" was at its peak from between approximately 1050 to 1150, when it is estimated that the population was a massive 10,000 to 20,000, but by around 1200 the population had started to decline, and by around 1400 the site had been abandoned.

At its height, Cahokia Mounds was an important regional center for the Mississippian culture, with many satellite hamlets and homesteads being built around the main site. The original name of the city is unknown and its inhabitants left no written records; their legacy instead is in the form of their extraordinary building accomplishments. They constructed a series of more than 120 earthen mounds of which 68 are preserved, including the massive Monks Mound; at 100

feet (30 m) high, it is the largest man-made earthen mound in North America. Excavations have uncovered remnants of a huge structure that was originally on top of the mound, probably either a temple or residence for the people's leader. To the west of the mound is Woodhenge, a circle of posts that would have formed a structure for reading astrological signs and times, and to the south of the mound is the vast plaza, an area specifically flattened to form a central gathering point. This, together with Monks Mound, was circled by a wooden stockade with watchtowers that would have separated it from the rest of the city, and indicates the importance of the area to the people.

Today Cahokia Mounds survives as an indelible testament to the astonishing engineering skills and sophistication of the Mississippian culture, and the ongoing archeological excavations continue to uncover North America's indigenous past. **TP**

Harpers Ferry (Jefferson County, WV, USA)

The site has witnessed significant industrial, political, and military events

Harpers Ferry, which is now part of the Harpers Ferry National Historical Park, sits in the valley between the Potomac and Shenandoah rivers, at a point where three states meet: Virginia, West Virginia, and Maryland. It is a geographic location that saw both the establishment and flourishing of the town, and its subsequent virtual destruction.

The area was first settled around 1734 but did not prosper until 1751 when an entrepreneur, Robert Harper, bought a tract of land in the valley and later set up a ferry service crossing the Potomac River. This made the area accessible for settlers who quickly made their way there. Thomas Jefferson visited in 1783 and was struck by the site's natural beauty and resources, and in 1785 George Washington traveled to the town. After his election as president of the United States, Washington proposed the site as the location for the national arsenal and armory. These industries

attracted others and Harpers Ferry flourished, aided by the newly constructed Chesapeake and Ohio Canal that connected it to Washington, DC. In 1859 the town made history when the abolitionist John Brown seized the arsenal and armory hoping to equip his men with weapons to help free the slaves in the South. He was unsuccessful in his quest but it was a move that saw the start of the Civil War inch closer. During the Civil War the town was a center of attack, with its excellent transport networks and arsenal a focal target. Much of Harpers Ferry was destroyed during the war, but it again made history in 1906 as the place where civil rights activists held the first U.S. meeting of the Niagara Movement.

This historic town became part of the National Park Service in 1944. It has seen relatively little new development and many of the original buildings are now listed with the Register of Historic Places. **TP**

🏛 🌐 Monticello (Charlottesville, VA, USA)

Designed, furnished, and lived in by Thomas Jefferson over many decades

Monticello, meaning "little hill" in Italian, is one of the most important private residence buildings in the United States. It was the home of Thomas Jefferson, the president who created the Declaration of Independence and founded the University of Virginia. He was, aside from a politician, an architect, designer, philosopher, inventor, and horticulturist, all of which are demonstrated in Monticello.

The house is situated on an 850-foot- (259-m-) high hill with views down and across the beautiful rolling Virginian landscape. Jefferson was left the land by his father and started work on the house in 1768 along classical Palladian-inspired designs. The house was predominantly finished by 1784, when he set off for Europe, spending five years traveling and absorbing elements of European architecture. On his return he undertook a complete remodeling of Monticello and, among other things, designed a dome for the house;

it was the first of its kind to be seen in Virginia. The house is actually a three-story dwelling, but appears from the outside to have only one story, thanks to the clever arrangement of the upstairs windows. This also makes it appear smaller than it is and enhances the classical beauty of the facade. Unlike the symmetrical exterior, rooms of different shapes, sizes, and heights characterize the interior, and throughout the house are ingenious devices that Jefferson invented. Because of Monticello's hill location, it was possible for Jefferson to build the service buildings into the hillside below the level of the house so that the stunning views were left unobstructed.

Jefferson continued to make small changes to Monticello virtually until his death there in 1826. The house is now open to the public and offers a fascinating perspective of the much-loved home of one of the United States' early presidents. **TP**

Mount Vernon (Mount Vernon, VA, USA)

Beautiful plantation home and final resting place of George Washington

Mount Vernon is situated in the midst of rolling green Virginian countryside, along the banks of the Potomac River. George Washington's father built a house on the site where the current palatial home sits around 1741–42. The home was named Mount Vernon by Lawrence Washington, George's older brother, after Vice Admiral Edward Vernon, who was Lawrence's commanding officer in the Royal British Army. After the death of his brother, George leased the property in 1757 and started to make changes. At this time the huge plantation was virtually self-sufficient and was split into five different farms. He began to enlarge his house, rebuilding the structure on the existing foundations and greatly expanding it. He was an enthusiastic gardener and devoted much time to the layout of the grounds and managing the estate. After his death the estate was sold and it sadly deteriorated, until the Mount Vernon Ladies' Association of the Union purchased it and began restoration work. The association continues to run and maintain the estate and has returned it to its original period character.

The corner of Virginia that is home to Mount Vernon is of immense historical importance with regard to Washington, his life and times, and to plantation life and culture. It is also not without some irony that the president who led the United States to victory over the British lived in a house named after one of Britain's most celebrated military figures. **TP**

"Observe good faith and justice toward all nations. Cultivate peace and harmony with all."

George Washington, former U.S. president

Antietam Battlefield

(near Sharpsburg, MD, USA)

Here the bloodiest single-day battle of the Civil War altered the course of history

The beautiful green rolling Maryland countryside outside Sharpsburg is idyllic, although the tranquility of the scene belies its bloody past. The battle of Antietam took place on September 17, 1862, and was the first fought within the northern states.

The Confederate leader General Robert E. Lee marched his troops into Maryland, taking advantage of an earlier victory and hoping to win over the Maryland people. Abraham Lincoln dispatched the Union leader Major General George B. McClellan to counterattack and prevent Confederates from moving closer to the capital. The fighting started early in the morning of September 17, with the Union soldiers outnumbering the Confederates, but it was poorly coordinated. The Confederates held out against the weak strategies of the attacking soldiers, and after eight hours and thousands of fatalities there was still no major outcome. The battle continued, with Major General Ambrose Burnside deployed to take the stone bridge that now bears his name. As the sun set, both armies held their ground, but Lee then retreated back across the Potomac and into Virginia. The carnage was extreme, and although the Confederates had been stopped, McClellan's leadership was seen as weak. He subsequently refused to follow Lee into Virginia and was later relieved from his command of the army.

The battle was pivotal because it quashed the Confederates' first attempt to take northern territory. It gave Lincoln the opportunity to issue his Emancipation Proclamation and so gave the Civil War another focus alongside restoring the Union. **TP**

◿ Almost 23,000 men were killed at Antietam, ending General Robert E. Lee's first invasion of the North.

◿ Abraham Lincoln towers over his staff following the battle; Major General McClellan stands facing him.

Flag House

(Baltimore, MD, USA)

The flag inspired the U.S. national anthem

The Flag House is one of the oldest buildings in Baltimore, Maryland, and was built around 1793 during a period of growth in the town. The building has been carefully preserved with many of its original features and furniture, but it is not the architecture that makes this house so important; it is the events that occurred within its modest walls.

It was here that Mary Pickersgill, a flag maker and widower, sewed together the Star Spangled Banner that flew over Fort McHenry in 1814 during the American–British War of 1812. The huge flag is well known as the inspiration for Francis Scott Key's poem that became the U.S. national anthem. Mary had been taught flag making by her mother and moved with her mother and daughter to the Flag House in 1807 where she established a flag-making business—dying her silks, designing the flags, and sewing them together. The business supported her family and by 1820 she had made sufficient money to buy the house she had previously been renting.

Apart from the historic flag she made while there, Mary was in all respects a remarkable woman and a trailblazer for early-nineteenth-century women. She was commissioned to make the enormous Star Spangled Banner in 1813, based on her excellent flag-making reputation. The flag measured 30 feet (9 m) by 42 feet (12 m) and now hangs in the National Museum of American History at the Smithsonian Institution. Mary Pickersgill lived in the Flag House until her death in 1857, and in 1927 the house was opened to the public. It is run and preserved by the Star Spangled Banner Flag House Association, which has restored it to its appearance during Pickersgill's time. It now offers a fascinating perspective of nineteenth-century life and documents the humble origins of the world-famous "Star Spangled Banner." **TP**

USS *Constellation*

(Baltimore, MD, USA)

Only surviving Civil War–era vessel

This plucky sloop-of-war ship that serviced the U.S. Navy for more than 100 years enjoyed a $9 million restoration and is now in pristine condition.

The USS *Constellation* was the second ship to bear this name, which led to some degree of confusion, heightened by the fact that she was being built at the same time and in the same dockyard as her predecessor was being broken up. This led to the incorrect assumption that the new USS *Constellation* was simply a rebuild of the old boat and was not a new vessel. The sloop-of-war ship (a small sailing warship with one gun deck) was commissioned in

> *"[To minimize costs], include only such general details as would be noticed by the layman."*
>
> President Roosevelt, on the restoration process

1855, and in 1859 became the flagship for the U.S. African Squadron. In this capacity, she was employed to monitor the slave trade off the coast of Africa, capturing three slave traders. She was active during the Civil War, and after the war shipped supplies to famine-torn Ireland and art exhibits to Paris for the 1878 Exposition Universelle. She later became a training ship and prepared thousands of naval cadets for World War I.

The ship was first decommissioned in 1933, then reassigned by President Franklin D. Roosevelt and used for the U.S. Atlantic Fleet during World War II. After a long and distinguished career the USS *Constellation* was finally decommissioned again in 1955. After an extensive restoration program, she has been opened to the public. **TP**

United States Supreme Court (Washington, DC, USA)

A historic institution and part of the fabric of the United States

This grand building stands magnificently in shining white marble, four stories tall. It forms an integral part of the hub of Washington, DC's seat of power and is the nerve center of judicial equality. Despite the status of the Supreme Court as an institution, it was many years before it was given its own building. The court was first situated in New York City before being moved to Philadelphia in 1790. It was then housed in the State House and later the City Hall. Washington, DC, was made the capital city in 1800 and the Supreme Court was again re-sited. Finally, in 1929, Chief Justice William Howard Taft, the court's former president, persuaded Congress to commission a building for the court.

Work began in 1932 on the magnificent, white, Corinthian-style building, which is constructed mainly from marble. The main entrance is particularly stunning and the decorative detail naturally reflects the theme of justice. The front steps lead to a large oval plaza flanked by two statues, *Contemplation of Justice* and *Guardian of the Law*, carved by James Earle Fraser. Sixteen columns support the pediment, with the architrave above being incised with "Equal Justice Under Law." The grandeur of the building is holistic in its entirety, and, surprisingly in view of the costly materials involved, it was eventually finished under budget. The Supreme Court is one of the most historically important bodies in the United States, and it is housed in a building that emanates power. **TP**

> *"The Republic endures and this is the symbol of its faith."*
>
> Charles Evans Hughes, former chief justice

The White House (Washington, DC, USA)

District of Columbia's oldest public building and symbolic of the power of the United States

The White House needs little introduction. It is the most famous and easily recognizable house in the world, and the private residence and workplace of the president of the United States.

In 1792 a competition was held to design the house and President George Washington (1732–99) chose the winner, James Hoban. The Irishman Hoban modeled his design largely on Leinster House in Dublin, which is now the seat of the Irish Parliament, but Washington called for the plans to be extended. Building began in the autumn of 1792 and by 1800 it was habitable, though not finished. The first president to live there was John Adams. Over the next few years, and under President Thomas Jefferson's directive, the architect Benjamin Henry Latrobe added two small wings that housed the stables and service areas of the building. During the war of 1812, the British set fire to the house, and after the war Latrobe and Hoban were involved in the rebuild, with the most significant additions being Hoban's distinctive north and south porticos, built in 1824 and 1829. Over the years that followed, the White House was added to and altered, but it also suffered from poor maintenance and gradually started to deteriorate. The biggest restoration project was that undertaken by Jacqueline Kennedy, wife of President John F. Kennedy, who added elements of lavish French-style decor. She set a precedent for restoration, and a committee that works closely with the First Lady and aims to retain the historical integrity of the building now oversees the preservation of the White House.

The White House has become virtually iconic of the United States, being one of the country's most photographed buildings, and the Oval Office within has undoubtedly played host to innumerable historic decisions and political events. **TP**

The Capitol (Washington, DC, USA)

A bold architectural experiment that has become symbolic of U.S. government

> "The spirit of this country is totally adverse to a large military force."
>
> Thomas Jefferson, former U.S. president

Near the middle of Washington, DC, rises a hill, Capitol Hill, that stretches eastward, and surmounting this is the Capitol, possibly the most culturally and historically important building in the United States. It has been home to the United States Congress since 1800, with Thomas Jefferson being the first president to be sworn in, in 1801.

Pierre L'Enfant, a French-born architect and planner, chose the site and described it (then called Jenkins Hill) as a "pedestal waiting to happen." The competition to design a building for Congress was held in 1792 and eventually Dr. William Thornton, whose design was inspired by the Louvre, in Paris, won the commission. The building evolved over many years and is now the culmination of several different architects' work. Despite this, the layout has remained essentially true to Thornton's original plans for a central, cube-shaped building topped with a dome and flanked by two wings, although it has been greatly extended. One of the most distinctive features is the massive cast-iron dome that was built by Thomas U. Walter and is three times the size of the original one. Walter also added the wing extensions. The north wing houses the Senate chamber, whereas the south wing accommodates the House of Representatives chamber. Further changes were made to the east front during the twentieth century to correct the proportionate appearance of the building. The pristine Neoclassical beauty and balance of the Capitol also reflects the influence of St. Paul's Cathedral in London and the dome of St. Peter's Basilica, Rome.

The hilltop building is surrounded by the park area of the National Mall, designed by the landscape architect Frederick Law Olmsted. Taken together, the complex is both a symbol of American power and prestige, and an aesthetic triumph. **TP**

Washington Monument (Washington, DC, USA)

One of the tallest freestanding structures in the world

The Washington Monument is situated at the west end of the National Mall in Washington, DC. This landscaped parkland in the middle of the city is home to the U.S. Capitol along with numerous historic monuments and important museums, and is one of the most beautiful of inner city areas. The Washington Memorial, which takes the impressive form of a towering white Egyptian obelisk, is at the far end of an oblong reflecting pool and opposite the Lincoln Memorial. The entire area is of supreme historic importance.

George Washington was the first president of the United States and a man of extraordinary moral fiber. He led his country toward freedom from British rule and established precedents that gained him universal admiration. In this respect the Washington Memorial is one of the most important of its kind, and recognizes and remembers one of the great leaders and a true founding father of the United States. In 1833 John Marshall and former president James Madison formed the Washington National Monument Society. Three years later a competition was held to design the monument, and Robert Mills won with his elaborate Neoclassical plan incorporating a circular Doric colonnade topped with an obelisk and an equestrian statue of Washington. His plans bear little relation to the elegant and moving monument of today. His design was costly and work began on the obelisk first. Construction was delayed by the Civil War and lack of funding, and the monument was not finished until thirty years after the death of Mills.

Today it remains a simple obelisk, without the intended additions, and is more striking because of this. At 555 feet (169 m), it is the tallest building in Washington, DC, and there is an elevator and a staircase within the monument that ascends to a viewing platform that affords a far-reaching panorama across the city. **TP**

"My first wish is to see this plague of mankind, war, banished from the earth."

George Washington, former U.S. president

Ford's Theater (Washington, DC, USA)

Scene of the assassination of President Lincoln, who was shot by actor John Wilkes Booth

Ford's Theater was opened on the site of an old Baptist church and was to have a checkered and terrible history. Shortly after it opened, the theater was destroyed by a fire in 1862, but was totally renovated and reopened a year later. It became a popular venue for theatergoers.

At the same time, John Wilkes Booth, a leading actor, partially retired from the stage and turned his attentions toward supporting the Confederates. A plan was hatched by Booth and his revolutionary contemporaries to snatch the president, Abraham Lincoln, and exchange him for Confederate prisoners. The heist was foiled and in 1865 the Confederates suffered two major defeats. Booth was furious and decided to assassinate the president and various members of his government. He stepped into Lincoln's box at the Ford Theater and shot him in the head with a single-shot Derringer pistol on April 14, 1865. As

Booth made his escape, he broke his leg before mounting a waiting horse and disappearing. He was captured and shot dead twelve days later. Lincoln was carried to the nearby Peterson House, but died early the next morning. The federal government seized the theater from Ford (paying him $100,000) and said it would not be used as a place for entertainment again. The building was instead used for administrative functions until 1893, when the front half of the structure collapsed, killing twenty-two clerks and injuring many others. Although it was repaired, the building fell into decline and was not fully restored until the 1960s, when it returned to being a theater, with a museum dedicated to Lincoln in the basement.

The turbulent past of Ford's Theater has been put to rest, but the grand brick building remains today as a historic monument to one of the United States' great fallen presidents. **TP**

Library of Congress (Washington, DC, USA)

America's national library and one of the world's largest and most important libraries

The Library of Congress is particularly notable for the diversity of its collection and this is primarily because of Thomas Jefferson. The library was established in 1800 after President John Adams passed an act of Congress that moved the seat of government from Philadelphia to Washington, DC. The legislation called for the establishment of a reference library exclusively for Congress and $5,000 was put forward to acquire books. The library was housed in the Capitol until August 1814, when the building was destroyed by invading British troops.

Thomas Jefferson (now retired from his presidency) offered his personal, substantial, and enlightened library to the nation. The diversity of his vast collection, which included philosophy, science, and literature, set the precedent for the subsequent acquisitions of books. The other significant name in the development of the library's collection is Ainsworth Rand Spofford, who was the librarian of Congress from 1864 to 1897. He brought in the copyright law in 1870 that required all copyright applicants to send two copies of their work to the library. This saw the collection rocket in terms of size and diversity, and eventually led to the need for the new building. Authorization was given for the construction of a new library in 1886. The designs were for an Italian Renaissance building that would become one of the grandest and most expensive buildings of the time. It was eventually opened in 1897, and quickly became a well-known and much-loved national monument.

The Library of Congress is now made up of three buildings: the original Thomas Jefferson Building, the John Adams Building that was opened in 1938, and the James Madison Memorial Building, which was opened in 1981 as the library headquarters. **TP**

Lincoln Memorial (Washington, DC, USA)

Regal, Neoclassical monument to one of the greatest of the early U.S. presidents

In the middle of Washington, DC, is a large park area, the National Mall, and dominating the west end of this stands the Lincoln Memorial. From the steps of the monument, a view stretches across the long reflection pond to the obelisk of the Washington Monument, the National World War II Monument, and away in the distance to the U.S. Capitol.

The prolific architect Henry Bacon designed the Lincoln Memorial as his final project and chose as his model the ancient temples of Greece. The gleaming white structure that stands an imposing 190 feet (57 m) long, 119 feet (36 m) wide, and 100 feet (30 m) high comprises a central cella, flanked by two smaller cellas, surrounded by thirty-six massive, fluted Doric columns (a further two columns stand at the entrance behind the colonnade). The magnificent columns correspond to the thirty-six states that formed the Union at that time, and above each column is carved the name of each state. The central cella houses the monumental statue of Lincoln, which was carved over a period of four years under the direction of Daniel Chester French. The sculpture gazes across the reflection pond to the Capitol and was carved from Georgian marble, whereas the building itself was constructed from Indiana limestone and Colorado Yule marble. The two smaller cellas contain the Gettysburg Address and Lincoln's second inaugural address, both inscribed on the wall. Above them are the two large murals *Reunion* and *Emancipation,* by the French artist Jules Guerin.

Lincoln's memorial is the scene of many public gatherings and protests, with one of the most famous addresses being Martin Luther King's "I have a dream" speech in 1963. The memorial is intensely moving and, as a statement of democracy and the first positive steps to freedom, is one of the United States's most important monuments. **TP**

> *"Always bear in mind that your own resolution to succeed is more important than any one thing."*
>
> Abraham Lincoln, former U.S. president

Arlington National Cemetery (Arlington, VA, USA)

The cemetery is recognized as a national place to honor the fallen

Arlington House, home to Arlington National Cemetery, sits atop a rolling green Virginian hillside overlooking the Potomac River, and away from the house spreads row upon row of neatly spaced, gleaming white headstones. The estate of more than 1,100 acres (445 ha) has a turbulent past that is in sharp contrast to the tranquil, spiritual nature of the present-day area. The palatial house was originally built as a memorial to George Washington by his adopted grandson George Washington Parke Custis. It passed to Custis's daughter Mary and her husband, Robert E. Lee, who later became a leading Confederate general. In 1861, at the start of the U.S. Civil War, he ratified allegiance to Virginia and the Confederates, and fearing for his wife's safety urged her to flee from their home. Shortly afterward the house was taken over by Federal troops, and in 1864 Brigadier General Montgomery C. Meigs commissioned the land surrounding the house for use as a war cemetery. Ironically the house was reviled because of its associations with Lee, so what was once a monument to Washington became a rash on the back for the Republicans. By the end of the war in 1865 more than 5,000 bodies had been buried, many of them unidentified, and divided into separate areas for African American troops and Confederates.

By the 1900s North/South antagonisms had been partially laid to rest. The Arlington Memorial Amphitheater was built in 1915 to facilitate funeral services and ceremonies, and in 1932 the Tomb of the Unknowns was inaugurated. There is a longstanding tradition of erecting memorials at Arlington, including the United States Marine Corps Memorial, based on a famous photograph of American troops raising their flag on Iwo Jima, and the recent Pentagon Memorial that honors the 184 people who lost their lives during the September 11, 2001, terrorist attacks. **TP**

"... exactly who the men on the hill are is not as important as the fact that they are there."

John C. Metzler, superintendent

Liberty Bell

(Philadelphia, PA, USA)

Achieved iconic status as the bell that announced the Declaration of Independence

> *"The Liberty Bell is a very significant symbol for the entire democratic world."*

Nelson Mandela, former South African president

The Liberty Bell is the most famous bell in the world and has become a recognized international symbol of freedom. Its name derives from the abolitionists who adopted the bell as their symbol during their lengthy bid to establish freedom from slavery, and it also appeared in their periodical *Liberty* in 1837. It had previously been called the State House Bell, after the building in which it hung (now called Independence Hall). The bell also became symbolic of the American Revolutionary War of 1775 to 1783, and is most famously associated with the United States' independence from the British Empire.

The bell was commissioned by the Pennsylvania Provincial Assembly to hang in the State House. The original bell was made in the Whitechapel Foundry in London and was carefully shipped to Philadelphia in 1752. It was not rung until 1753, and to everyone's dismay cracked. Subsequently it was sent to two Philadelphia Foundry workers, John Stow and John Pass, to be recast, which they did twice. Finally the Whitechapel Foundry was asked to produce a replacement bell, but this proved unpopular, and the bell was relegated to the cupola of the State House. The last Stow and Pass bell remained in the steeple of the State House and became what is known today as the Liberty Bell. The bell was rung on important historic occasions, perhaps most famously on July 8, 1776, to summon the citizens for the first reading of the Declaration of Independence.

The bell cracked on several occasions and was repaired repeatedly over the years. Finally, on George Washington's birthday in February 1846, it cracked beyond repair and was permanently removed from the steeple in 1852. The bell can now be viewed in a pavilion, and serves as a link to the historic events it tolled for during its 100 years of service. **TP**

Eastern State Penitentiary

(Philadelphia, PA, USA)

Marked a revolution in the design of prisons

The Eastern State Penitentiary has provided a model for approximately 300 prison buildings worldwide. During its 142 years of use, it housed some of the United States's most notorious criminals, including the bank robber Willie Sutton and Al Capone.

The penitentiary was based on a Quaker system of reform that aimed to encourage prisoners to reflect on their crimes and thus change their behavior, instead of merely punishing them. This reform was achieved through solitary confinement, which in principle was deemed to encourage inner reflection. All the prisoners were kept in their cells and never allowed to mix. When being moved from their cells to a different area, they were hooded to prevent them from seeing other inmates. It was a system that became increasingly impractical because of rising numbers of prisoners and the proportionate cost involved, and is also thought to have led to profound mental illness. The penitentiary was designed around a radial floor plan that was a departure from traditional prison design. Construction began on the building in 1822, and on October 23, 1829, the penitentiary opened. Because of the impracticality of mass solitary confinement, the system was officially changed in 1913 to operate as a congregate prison until its closure in 1970 (it was used briefly in 1971 after a riot at Holmsburg Prison).

After its closure, the penitentiary was abandoned and fell into ruin, until it was bought in 1980 by the city of Philadelphia from the State of Pennsylvania. In 1988 a task force was formed and a decision made to preserve the building and to restore or modernize it. The penitentiary was opened in 1994 for daily historic tours and is used for hosting a number of events, as well as frequently being filmed as a location in science fiction or horror films. **TP**

Gettysburg Battlefield

(Gettysburg, PA, USA)

The bloodiest clash of the Civil War

The beauty of the area surrounding the town of Gettysburg belies its terrible past. This was the site of the Battle of Gettysburg, 1863, in which thousands of Confederate and Union soldiers were killed, along with their cavalry mounts. It was the single most devastating battle in terms of human and animal cost, and marked a turning point in the war. The Confederates would never recover from their defeat here, and though the war raged on for a further two years, it was at Gettysburg that the tide started to turn.

The town of Gettysburg was situated centrally between a number of other important towns in

> *"The world will little note, nor long remember what we say here, but it cannot forget what they did here."*
>
> Abraham Lincoln, former U.S. president

Pennsylvania and Maryland, and consequently became a focal military point. The sweeping hills and wide-open land around the town, and the town itself, became the scene of the intense battle. To the south of the town is Cemetery Hill, which housed a civilian cemetery, and after the battle it became a military cemetery dedicated by Abraham Lincoln. With its distinctive boulder-strewn landscape, the Union soldiers used the hill as a critical line of defense.

After the battle, a local attorney, David McConaughy, bought 600 acres (243 ha) of land to preserve as a monument, and in 1864 the Gettysburg Battlefield Memorial Association was formed. There has since been a continual effort to prevent urban development and to preserve this piece of ground that is so important in U.S. history. **TP**

National Baseball Hall of Fame (Cooperstown, NY, USA)

Home to the origins of baseball, maybe

The small and scenic Cooperstown is in central New York state and along the south end of the glassy Otsego Lake, made popular through the early writings of James Fenimore Cooper. It is a beautiful setting, and it is here too that the Susquehanna River begins its long, winding journey through New York and Pennsylvania before reaching the sea in the Chesapeake Bay, Maryland.

Cooperstown is a historic district and home to the famous Farmers Museum and the Glimmerglass Opera, but is undoubtedly best known for its National Baseball Hall of Fame and Museum. Here the history of baseball is preserved for perpetuity in unequaled depth and astonishing detail. The museum was established in 1939 by Stephen Carlton Clark initially to try to boost Cooperstown's trade and tourism industry after it had been severely damaged during the Great Depression and by Prohibition. Initially, much of the museum's success was based on a popular story that Cooperstown was in fact the birthplace of baseball, and that the game had been devised by Abner Doubleday, a former Civil War hero, in a cow pasture belonging to Elihu Phinney. This legend, which has done much for the town's fame, has since been brought into question. However, the field where the sport allegedly started was bought by the town and turned into an impressive baseball park, the Doubleday Field, which is now the scene of the annual Hall of Fame game.

Whether or not Cooperstown was the actual birthplace of baseball pales into insignificance against the unmistakable role the sport has played within the town. The place positively breathes baseball; with the tremendous Hall of Fame and Museum, it is possibly the most important baseball town in the United States. **TP**

West Point Military Academy (West Point, NY, USA)

Its military history dates back to 1778

The famous U.S. military academy sits on a high piece of ground overlooking the Hudson River about 50 miles (80 km) north of New York City. It is a beautiful site, but more important it offers a vital military outlook across the river. George Washington first established the area as a military fort to guard the river from the British.

Thomas Jefferson opened the military academy in 1802, and later that year the school was added. Today the West Point campus is one of the largest in the world, covering a staggering 16,000 acres (6,475 ha), and offers all the facilities normally seen on a university

> *"Discipline that makes the soldiers of a free country reliable in battle is not gained by harsh treatment."*
>
> Major General John M. Schofield, general

campus and more. One of the early superintendents at the academy was Colonel Sylvanus Thayer—"father of the military academy." It was Thayer who raised academic standards, basing much of the education around civil engineering, and who introduced the military code of conduct founded on respect, discipline, and honor. Superintendent Douglas MacArthur made significant changes to the academy after World War I, when he increased the bias on physical fitness and training with military procedures as their basis. Today West Point has an unequaled reputation in this respect.

West Point has a visitor center and a museum that provide military history on the area. The museum also houses a large collection of arms and is the oldest and largest military museum in the country. **TP**

Stonewall Inn

(New York, NY, USA)

Marks a turning point in the history of gay liberation

In the heart of New York City in Greenwich Village, and sandwiched between long rows of tall buildings, is the unspectacular facade of the Stonewall Inn. The unstartling nature of the building masks the importance of its place within gay history, for it was here that the gay civil rights movement was born.

In the late 1960s this area of New York was far from salubrious and was home to drug dealers, drag queens, and rundown gay bars. Before the 1960s, police raids on gay bars were commonplace and brutal, but by the time of the Stonewall riots this practice had become less frequent and, as a result, the number of gay bars and nightclubs had risen. However, on June 28, 1969, the police raided the Stonewall Inn, with eight officers descending on the bar at 1:20 A.M. It was an unusually late raid, most being executed in early evening, and excessive force was used. Normally during raids such as this the essentially mild gay community dispersed, but that night saw the culmination of years of repeated abuse and denigration. The recent death of Judy Garland, a gay icon, is also thought to have contributed to the depth of feeling among the community. Rioting broke out within the inn and the surrounding area, and the police at first retreated. Many people were injured and thirteen were arrested in the ensuing furor. Riots continued at the scene until July 3, and by the end of the month the Gay Liberation Movement had been formed. The riots had drawn together a community that had suffered extreme prejudice and discrimination, and the effects were witnessed in the formation of gay rights movements across the world.

Today the restored and reopened Stonewall Inn is the site of many gay pride marches and celebrations, and the month of June and the name *Stonewall* have become synonymous with gay civil rights. **TP**

"The police had set up a boiling pot of water. They should have known that it would bubble over."

Professor Meredith Bacon, political scientist

Empire State Building (New York, NY, USA)

Icon of the architectural and engineering accomplishments of the twentieth century

> *"This building is crystalline and lean, built as much for glory as the Parthenon was."*

Vincent Scully, architecture historian and critic

⊞ Workers, unencumbered by safety equipment, assemble the top of the building's mooring mast.

⊡ Mooring airships to the mast was soon abandoned due to updrafts caused by the skyscraper itself.

The Empire State Building, which for more than forty years was the world's tallest building, is a U.S. national treasure. The architectural firm Shreve, Lamb and Harmon designed the building, with plans being devised in the space of just two weeks.

At this time in New York there was fierce competition to build the tallest building in the world, with the Chrysler Building holding the title before the completion of the Empire State. The Empire State eventually held the "tallest" crown until it was usurped by the North Tower of the World Trade Center in 1972. After September 11, 2001, the Empire State, with 102 floors, again became the tallest structure in New York and the second tallest in the United States, behind the Sears Tower. The building's opening on May 1, 1931, coincided with the Great Depression, resulting in much of the office space remaining unrented, to such an extent that the building was coined "The Empty State Building." It took almost twenty years for it to become profitable, such were the costs of construction, although the observation deck on the eighty-sixth floor proved an instant public draw and initially made more money than the rentals. The elegant Art Deco spire that is so distinctive was intended to be a mooring station for airships, with the top floor being the landing platform with an elevator to transport passengers down to the eighty-sixth floor to check in. The plan proved unworkable, and instead the spire is home to broadcasting antennae that serve the majority of the city's television and radio stations.

The Empire State remains one of the most distinctive and famous buildings in the United States and is one of the best examples of Modernist Art Deco design. At night the top of the building is illuminated with colored floodlights (the colors vary according to season and specific event), and the visual impact is as magnificent in the dark as it is in daylight. **TP**

Brooklyn Bridge (New York, NY, USA)

Iconic image of New York and a testament to architectural progressiveness and power

A population surge in Manhattan and Brooklyn initiated the decision in 1866 to build a bridge over the East River to join the two cities; shortly afterward John Roebling was commissioned for the project. Roebling, an engineer, had invented a twisted wire rope cable in 1841, which became one of the leading constructional components of his bridge designs. He went on to build a series of suspension bridges, including the Cincinnati–Covington Bridge, later renamed the John A. Roebling Suspension Bridge.

The Brooklyn Bridge spans 1,595 feet (486 m) and at the time of its opening in 1883 was the world's longest suspension bridge. The soaring Gothic-style stone towers that lend the bridge its distinctive silhouette were also for many years the tallest structures in the Western Hemisphere. Roebling designed the bridge to be six times stronger than it needed to be, which explains its ability to support the enormous quantity of twenty-first-century traffic. The great bridge has, however, had a troubled past. Roebling died shortly after winning the commission, and his son Washington took over. He in turn developed caisson disease (the bends) while working deep under water in specially designed compartments supervising the digging of the foundations. Semiparalyzed, he retired to his home, where he oversaw construction by relaying messages through his wife. Many of the laborers suffered the same affliction, and numerous other accidents occurred, bringing the death toll to around twenty-seven.

The bridge came to reflect the progressiveness of New York at the end of the nineteenth century. It has since become an essential landmark—an outstanding architectural accomplishment that is still revered across the world, and is also a fundamental symbol of a resilient and powerful city. **TP**

Grand Central Terminal (New York, NY, USA)

The innovative design has proved influential in successive railway station designs

Quite apart from the breathtaking architecture of Grand Central Terminal (often referred to as Grand Central Station), its sheer size is a dramatic and impressive feat of engineering. However, the quality of the structure's design merely complements the site's larger cultural and historical significance.

Grand Central sits on a site that was home to two previous station buildings; the first was built in 1871, and the second between 1899 and 1900. Work began on the present structure in 1903, with the first step being the demolition of the previous station. The firm Reed & Stern oversaw the overall design, whereas the beautiful Beaux-Arts styling and architectural details were handled by Warren and Wetmore. One of the major considerations was the electrification of the railroads, which enabled many of the former tracks approaching the station to be buried. The design incorporated a bi-level station with arriving trains

going underground, under Park Avenue. This in turn created a substantial area above ground for property development and thus raised revenue for the railway company. One of the famous sights at Grand Central is the clock made of Tiffany glass that is surrounded by sculpted figures of Minerva, Hercules, and Mercury, designed by Jules-Alexis Coutan. At the time of its completion, this formed the largest sculptural group in the world, being 48 feet (14 m) high. The ceiling, which was restored in 1998, is also of particular note. It was painted in 1912 by Paul César Helleu and depicts an astronomical sky that is more decorative than accurate.

By the 1950s the popularity of automobiles had superceded the railways and the station fell into decline. However, from the 1980s onward, there has been a series of renovation projects to preserve this extraordinary building. **TP**

Carnegie Hall (New York, NY, USA)

One of the most prestigious music venues in the world and an acoustic gem

Andrew Carnegie (1835–1919), an immensely powerful leader of industry and a philanthropist, commissioned Carnegie Hall in 1890 to create a venue for the Oratorio Society of New York and the New York Symphony Society, on whose boards he sat. It has since become one of the most famous venues in the music world, hosting both classical and popular music events as well as world premieres.

The little-known U.S. architect William Tuthill designed the huge redbrick and brownstone revivalist Italian Renaissance building, whose acoustics were considered second to none. Tuthill's design and his understanding of acoustics were helped by his musical knowledge. He was an amateur cellist and a keen musician, and played on occasion with the Oratorio Society. The hall, which was originally called simply "Music Hall," was one of the last large buildings in New York to be built without the use of a steel frame. It is also particularly noteworthy because of Tuthill's expressive translation of Italian Renaissance features. Unlike contemporary Baroque-inspired theater design, Tuthill chose instead the buildings of Filippo Brunelleschi as his model, and used a simple white and gold scheme on the interior. The exterior is rendered in a soft ocher-colored brick with terra-cotta and brownstone creating decorative details.

In 1893 Carnegie's name was added to that of the hall, and the building stayed in his family until 1925, when it was sold. It was bought by the City of New York in 1960, and two years later its importance was officially recognized when it was designated a National Historic Landmark. **TP**

↖ Andrew Carnegie devoted much of his vast wealth to philanthropical work throughout the world.

← The building contains three music venues: the Main Hall, the Recital Hall, and the Chamber Music Hall.

Ellis Island (New York, NY, USA)

Famous today as the site of the first Federal Immigration Station

Ellis Island is situated in New York Harbor under the watchful presence of the Statue of Liberty. The island, which is often referred to as the Gateway to the New World, was originally little more than 3 acres (1.2 ha) in size, but has been expanded to almost 28 acres (11 ha) through extensive land reclamation projects.

From 1855 to 1890, and before Ellis Island opened as a Federal Immigration Station, immigrants entering New York City were processed at the small Castle Garden Immigration Depot in Manhattan. However, Castle Garden was unable to cope with the increasing numbers of immigrants. The federal government took control, and buildings were constructed on the island to take over the processing. The wooden buildings were opened for business in 1892, but five years later they were razed by fire and all records were lost. The U.S. Treasury ordered a complete rebuild in fireproof materials and in 1900 the new main building was opened. Significantly, the majority of first- and second-class passengers who sailed in were checked only briefly on board and were allowed straight into the city, the assumption being that they had sufficient means to prevent them from becoming a public charge. It was primarily the third-class passengers who had medical and legal checks. The inspection process lasted three to five hours and took place in the Great Hall. The island was also used as a detention center.

After 1924 the island was used only sporadically for immigration and detention, and in 1954 it officially closed. From 1976 it started to open to the public, and in 1984 a major restoration project began that saw the main building reopened to the public in 1990. **TP**

↗ Ellis Island processed nearly twelve million poor immigrants on their way into the United States.

⮕ Redundant from 1954, the 1900 building has since reopened as the Ellis Island Immigration Museum.

New York Public Library (New York, NY, USA)

Comprehensive collection of books of great historical and monetary value

In downtown Manhattan, surrounded by shining glass and steel skyscrapers, is the main research facility of the New York Public Library, a magnificent stone building "guarded" by two sculpted lions. It is considered the crowning achievement of the Beaux-Arts architectural firm Carrère and Hasting, and was the building that propelled them to the forefront of their profession. The impetus for a new public library in New York was generated through a sizable bequest in 1886 by Samuel Jones Tilden, a leading Democratic political figure. There were already two libraries, the Astor Library and the Lenox Library, in New York, but it was decided to combine these with the new proposals and to create a private foundation, which was established in 1895. In 1901 the philanthropist Andrew Carnegie donated a further sum of money for branch libraries, but insisted that the City of New York be responsible for the maintenance of the buildings, making them a combination of private funding and state administration. Carrère and Hasting won the competition for the new library in 1897 and the main building opened on May 24, 1911. The central reading room in the library is a cavernous 78 feet (23 m) wide and 297 feet (90 m) long, with a balcony level to provide more shelf space for the thousands of reference books. Significantly, during the Great Depression of the 1930s, the library became a place where people who had lost their jobs were able to study for higher qualifications that they then used when the economy started to turn. It was also during the Depression that the magnificent stone lions flanking the entrance were coined Patience (to the south) and Fortitude (to the north).

Today the New York Public Library is one of the most important libraries in the world, and many of its works can be accessed online. It is also a fundamental part of the city's early-twentieth-century history. **TP**

"The Public Library's digital gallery is lovely, dark, and deep. Quite eccentric, too."

Sarah Boxer, journalist

St. Patrick's Cathedral (New York, NY, USA)

Largest Gothic Catholic cathedral in the United States

The imposing neo-Gothic St. Patrick's Cathedral sits proudly in the middle of Manhattan, New York, surrounded by high-tech, gleaming skyscrapers and opposite the Rockefeller Center. Farther away is a much smaller, more simple church, which is the Old St. Patrick's, the original seat of the Roman Catholic archdiocese of New York.

In 1850 the diocese of New York was made an archdiocese by Pope Pius IX, and Bishop John Joseph Hughes became the first archbishop. In 1853 he announced his plans to build a new cathedral to replace the Old St. Patrick's, and to create a building reflective of the growing wealth and power of the Catholic Church in the city. The eminent architect James Renwick Jr., who had built several churches in New York, was chosen to design the new St. Patrick's. Archbishop Hughes decided upon a location that at the time was well removed from the center of the city and that subsequently paid off, in light of Manhattan's growth. The Gothic-inspired cathedral is based around the lines of a monumental Latin cross, with the nave running east to west, and the transepts north to south. It is 400 feet (120 m) long and 174 feet (53 m) wide, with a seating capacity of around 2,200, and it is one of the most ornate and inspiring religious buildings in the city. Construction started in 1858, but was stopped during the U.S. Civil War (1861–65), and recommenced in 1865, with the cathedral being dedicated in 1879. Building work continued, however, with the addition of the towers on the west end, the Lady Chapel, and the archbishop's house and rectory.

The striking white marble cathedral is one of the finest religious buildings of the nineteenth century. It is the manifestation of Archbishop Hughes's expansive vision, and reflects the prominent role the Catholic Church plays within the culture of New York and among its inhabitants. **TP**

"The cathedral has come to represent for so many a place of peace and tranquility . . . ."

Reverend Monsignor Ritchie, rector

🏛 ◎ Statue of Liberty (New York, NY, USA)

Iconic landmark that greets all visitors to New York Harbor

The Statue of Liberty, one of the most universally recognized symbols of freedom across the globe, is intrinsically bound to the fabric of the United States. The huge sculpture stands on an imposing pedestal on Liberty Island at the entrance to New York Harbor.

The copper structure was a gift from the French to mark the centennial in 1876 of the United States's Declaration of Independence (July 4, 1776) and to extend the hand of friendship between the two countries. It was also a political move by France, keen to align herself with the republican associations of the United States, and influence her own shaky political stance at the time. French sculptor Frédéric Auguste Bartholdi was commissioned to design the statue. It was shipped from France to New York in 350 pieces and took four months to reassemble. The figure is copper on a steel frame, and her torch flame is gold leaf. Gustave Eiffel, who built the Eiffel Tower, and his assistant were drafted to help with the engineering. American Richard Morris Hunt designed her ten-story pedestal, and this now houses a museum. The figure is richly symbolic: The broken shackles at her feet signify freedom from oppression, the torch symbolizes enlightenment, the tablet in her hand has the date of U.S. independence inscribed on it, and her seven-point crown represents the Seven Seas. Within the pedestal, the poem *New Colossus* by Emma Lazarus is inscribed on a bronze plaque.

After 9/11 the interior of the statue was closed to visitors, although the pedestal and museum remain open and a glass roof allows views up into the framework of the statue. **TP**

◩ For decades, the sight of the Statue of Liberty lifted the hearts of immigrants entering New York.

◱ The steel frame of the statue's left hand takes shape in Frédéric Auguste Bartholdi's studio.

Hancock Shaker Village (Pittsfield, MA, USA)

Former home of a unique religious community

The small town of Hancock, nestled in the beautiful Massachusetts countryside, was first settled around 1767. In approximately 1783 a group of Shakers arrived and gradually built the Hancock Shaker village. The Shakers were a devout and strict Protestant group that had originated in England and spread to the United States, with members of the group arriving in New York in 1774. From there they spread through New York State to Massachusetts and Connecticut. The Hancock Shaker village thrived for a century before starting to decline. In 1960 the Shaker Central Ministry decided to close the community and sold the buildings and land to a private group; it set up the not-for-profit Hancock Shaker Village Inc. This offers a fascinating look at a culture that has largely died out.

Shaker architecture is especially interesting because it is the ultimate expression of efficiency and innovation while retaining a clear and simple beauty of line. The round stone barn at Hancock, built in 1826, is one of the most fascinating Shaker buildings, and the only one of its kind. The central part of the top floor of the building was a hay storage area, with the next level down incorporating stanchions for fifty cattle that fed from a central feed manger. Below this floor was the manure pit that was easily accessible by wagon for cleaning.

Hancock is the largest Shaker museum and village on the east coast of the United States and contains twenty well-preserved buildings set amid gorgeous countryside. The village is particularly important culturally, in the light of the Shakers' almost complete disappearance from modern society. **TP**

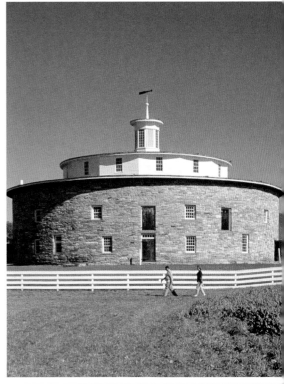

◪ Cattle entered the round stone barn via an earth ramp at the rear that took them directly to the upper floor.

◪ Shakers are so called because they believe in whole-body worship rituals, including communal dancing.

Plymouth Rock

(Pilgrim Memorial State Park, MA, USA)

The site of the first pilgrims' arrival into the "New World"

> *"As one small candle may light a thousand, so the light here kindled hath shone unto many."*

William Bradford, Pilgrim leader

The curving bay of Plymouth, with Cole Hill rising behind the shoreline, is one of the most historic sites in the United States. It was here, in 1620, that the Pilgrims, led by William Bradford, disembarked from their boat *The Mayflower* and set foot on the lands of the New World, going on to establish Plymouth Colony. Today the area, which is Massachusetts's smallest and most visited state park, includes the legendary Plymouth Rock, the Forefathers' Monument, and a replica of *The Mayflower*. Although contemporary accounts of the Pilgrims' landing do not make any reference to the rock, some hundred years later it was heralded as the first place their feet touched—their landing stage—and it has remained venerated as such.

Today the rock is considerably smaller than it once was, having suffered damage from being moved and having had pieces chipped away by souvenir seekers. In 1774 an attempt was made to move the rock, but it split in half in the process, with the bottom half being left where it was. The top half was later transferred to the town square and then to Pilgrim Hall. In 1867 it was moved back to its original location and reunited with the bottom half. The architect Charles Hammatt Billings built an ornate canopy to house the rock, but the structure proved too small, so in 1920 the rock was relocated to its present waterfront location, beneath a new canopy designed by the architects McKim, Mead, and White.

The small, battered, granite chunk is far more than its physical reality. It is an icon of the United States' foundation. The rock's latent symbolism of the bravery and courage of the nation's early settlers is inescapable, and it is no small irony that such an anonymous-looking object occupies such a very important place in U.S. history. **TP**

Old North Bridge

(Concord, MA, USA)

Important and decisive battle site

The small town of Concord has a long and important history stretching back to the first settlers, who were British and established a community here in 1635. The town is set amid beautiful countryside with the snaking Concord River wending its way through the town and on into Worcester County. An anonymous-looking wooden bridge, the Old North Bridge, spans the river and it is on this historic spot that one of the first battles of the American War of Independence (1775–83) was fought. Ironically the battle that was so important was over in a matter of minutes. British troops, who had been in Boston, were sent to Concord to find and destroy the stockpile of ammunition and arms the locals had hidden. The troops' movement was noticed by militia intelligence, and Paul Revere and William Dawes were sent on a midnight ride from Boston to Lexington to warn the colonists.

Meanwhile the British troops had gathered in Concord, and a large number of colonists (known as Minute Men) were making their way there. Seeing smoke rising from the village, the Minute Men assumed the British were torching houses, although it was gun carriages that were burning, and marched toward the Old North Bridge. A shot was fired, which started a volley of gunfire under which the outnumbered British troops retreated, leaving Concord at noon and returning to Boston. It was an unprecedented and surprise victory for the patriots, rather symbolically starting the Revolutionary War with the same outcome that ended it some years—and much bloodshed—later.

The area, including the bridge that has been rebuilt many times, the 5-mile (8-km) Battle Road Trail, and the *Minute Man* statue by the sculptor Daniel Chester French, now forms the Minute Man National Historical Park. **TP**

Sutter's Fort

(Sacramento, CA, USA)

The fort that became a city

In the middle of a commercial area of Sacramento is a big compound, set behind high, white defensive walls. This is Sutter's Fort, originally called New Helvetia (New Switzerland), and it is this historic place that inadvertently gave rise to the city of Sacramento, and the establishment of agriculture in California.

It was established by John Sutter, a Swiss immigrant who received a land grant from the Mexican government of 50,000 acres (20,230 ha) of fertile Sacramento valley. He cultivated the land, growing crops and running herds of cattle. He was the first nonindigenous settler to do so in the area.

> *"We have this one opportunity and if we blow it, we have blown it for good."*
>
> John Sutter, settler

Sutter started his compound in 1840; by the height of his success he owned 150,000 acres (60,700 ha) of rich, cultivated land. In 1847 he famously sent help to the Donner Party, a group of settlers caught in a snowstorm. As a result his fort became known as a temporary shelter for travelers. In 1848, a carpenter named James Marshall found gold. Word traveled rapidly and Sutter's employees left to seek their fortunes in the Californian goldfields. People flocked to the area and Sutter's cultivated lands were destroyed. Despairing, he deeded his remaining acreage to his son, Augustus Sutter, who set about building what would become the city of Sacramento. The old fort compound has been restored to its 1847 appearance, based on a photograph, and is now a California State Historic Landmark. **TP**

Alcatraz Prison (San Francisco Bay, CA, USA)

One of the world's most notorious and sinister prisons

From the middle of the San Francisco Bay rises Alcatraz, or "The Rock." The small island was given its name in 1775 by Spanish explorer Juan de Ayala, who called it La Isla de los Alcatraces, "the island of gannets." A barren and rocky place, it was not used until the 1850s, when a lighthouse was built there.

Around the same time, the U.S. military recognized the value of the island as a fortification and it was turned into a military fortress, later being used to hold captives. By 1912 a large block of cells had been built, and by the 1920s the grim three-story structure was full. On October 12, 1933, the United States Department of Justice acquired the site from the military, and in August 1934 it was turned into the infamous, harsh federal prison.

Over its twenty-nine-year history, it was home to some of the toughest criminals around, including Al Capone, George "Machine Gun" Kelly, and Robert Stroud, the "Birdman of Alcatraz." The prison is perhaps most famous for the fourteen escape attempts that have been made, all of which were deemed "officially" unsuccessful. Of these, the attempt by Frank Morris and John and Clarence Anglin in 1962 was the most daring, and has since been popularized by the Hollywood movie *Escape from Alcatraz*. The three were never caught and were presumed drowned, although their bodies were not recovered. To this day, their fate remains a mystery. **TP**

> *"Alcatraz . . . is a black molar in the jawbone of the nation's prison system."*
>
> Thomas E. Gaddis, author

Golden Gate Bridge (San Francisco, CA, USA)

A feat of engineering once declared impossible

The Golden Gate Bridge, one of the most beautiful suspension bridges in the world, spans the entrance ("the Golden Gate") to San Francisco's bay. The bridge connects San Francisco to Marin County and is the only exit out of San Francisco to the north, being part of the famous U.S. highway Route 101.

Originally, the Golden Gate itself was crossed via a ferry service because it was deemed impossible to span this mammoth stretch with a bridge. It was the tenacity of Joseph Strauss that finally saw a bridge take form. Strauss first came up with plans in 1921, but these were rejected and he spent the next ten years refining his designs. Construction began in 1933 and was finished four years later. Strauss died the year after the bridge was officially opened, and there is now a statue of him near the bridge commemorating the part he played in its inception. The bridge's 4,200-foot (1,280-m) main suspension span is supported by two elegant towers that rise 746 feet (227 m), making them the tallest suspension towers at the time of their completion. The aesthetics of the bridge are unequaled, and the orange vermilion color adds to this. The color was suggested by the consulting architect Irving Morrow, and has a dual function, both fitting in with the surrounding natural scenery and being clearly visible to ships in fog. At night the bridge is floodlit and shines with a golden luminescence that reflects off the waters of the bay and creates a magical effect.

On its completion, the Golden Gate Bridge came to be recognized as a symbol of the United States' power and progress, and set a precedent for suspension-bridge design around the world. It continues to be one of the most frequently photographed bridges, and is one of the most magnificent sights in the United States. **TP**

City Lights Bookstore

(San Francisco, CA, USA)

Legendary independent bookstore that made legal history

City Lights Bookstore was founded in 1953 by poet Lawrence Ferlinghetti and sociologist Peter D. Martin. One of the few independent bookstores remaining in the United States, City Lights has three floors full of books, both familiar and obscure. Freedom of thought, speech, and the written word are hallowed in the store, which plays host to a continuous stream of literary-minded folk from around the world. It was for many years the "literary home of the Beatniks," and remains closely associated with the ethos of freedom, antiauthoritarian politics, and insurgent thinking.

In the 1950s, Ferlinghetti's poetry became the voice of modern expression—his book *The Coney Island of the Mind* remains the most popular poetry book in the United States. In 1955 he opened City Lights Publishers, which produces the Pocket Poetry series. The series' fourth book, Allen Ginsberg's *Howl and Other Poems*, led to Ferlinghetti and his bookstore manager, Shigeyoshi Murao, being imprisoned on obscenity charges, with their trial bringing the Beat Generation to the attention of the media. The pair were acquitted in court, aided by the American Civil Liberties Union and support from literary figures, and the trial became a historic landmark First Amendment case, setting a legal precedent for the right to publish controversial literature.

Together the bookstore and the publishing company continue to contribute to the development of modern thinking. City Lights represents a turning point in legal history through the trial of *Howl* and will remain a significant icon of cultural history. **TP**

⬉ City Lights Bookstore in San Francisco's North Beach neighborhood, a mecca for freethinking readers.

⬅ Beat personalities Bob Donlin, Neal Cassady, Allen Ginsberg, Robert LaVinge, and Lawrence Ferlinghetti.

Mission Dolores
(San Francisco, CA, USA)

The oldest building in San Francisco

Mission Dolores—or Mission San Francisco de Asis— stands on a manicured street in San Francisco, in the shadow of a rebuilt basilica. The original mission was founded not far away, alongside the Laguna Dolores; it was rebuilt in 1782 on its current site. Mission Dolores is San Francisco's oldest surviving structure, having weathered the earthquake of 1906 that devastated much of the rest of the town, including the basilica.

From the end of the eighteenth century, missions were established across California to bring Christianity to what were still primarily Native American lands. The original Mission Dolores was beset with poor weather

> *"Many pagan Indians appeared in a friendly manner and with expressions of joy at our coming."*
>
> Fr. Palou, founder of Mission Dolores, June 27, 1776

and cold fogs from its laguna, causing indigenous people to stay away. This prompted the decision to move the mission to its current location. The small, stout structure was built by Christianized Ohlone Indians who constructed the massively thick and strong walls from adobe bricks arranged in a 10-foot- (3-m-) thick block, all built on a 4-foot (1.2-m) rock foundation. It was a building designed to last. The facade of brilliant white adobe is effortlessly simple, and the interior—of decorated redwood ceiling beams and wooden columns, painted to appear like Italian marble—has remained largely unchanged.

Mission Dolores is still active today. The diminutive building holds a monumental position in the history of San Francisco, being its very first public building and the center around which the city grew up. **TP**

Japanese Internment Camps (Manzanar, CA, USA)

Where hundreds of families were detained

The attack on the U.S. naval base at Pearl Harbor, on December 7, 1941, caused a wave of panic across the country and fears of further Japanese attacks. As a result, President Franklin D. Roosevelt issued Executive Order 9066, resulting in the forced evacuation of more than 120,000 Japanese civilians from their homes in the western coastal states (a similar order was deployed in Canada). The executive order established the Pacific coastline and other areas as military zones, and gave the military the power to exclude any such people it thought necessary. More than two-thirds of the Japanese who were confined to internment camps (relocation centers) were U.S. citizens, and many were children. The orders to rehouse them came before the centers had been properly built, and living conditions were reportedly appalling. Many of the long barrack buildings were without plumbing, heating, or cooking facilities. The detainees were forced to live in close confinement, although some families were forcibly segregated. Many died from illnesses associated with the living conditions and stress.

There were different types of internment centers, with the center at Tule Lake, California, being used for those believed to be a security risk. The order was abolished in January 1945 and the Japanese were allowed to return to their homes, although many chose to leave the United States. A formal apology from the federal government was slow in coming. In 1988 legislation was signed by President Ronald Reagan that saw the surviving detainees—many of whom had lost everything—awarded just $20,000 each.

The internment sites that survive today, of which Manzanar is the best preserved, provide an essential and controversial reminder of U.S. and Japanese history that should not be forgotten. **TP**

Universal Studios (Hollywood, CA, USA)

The first film studios to open to the public

A walk through Universal Studios transports the visitor to the glamorous universe of the movies. The studios are a piece of Hollywood and movie history that stretches back into the past and yet is still in the making; it is a magical experience.

Universal Studios was founded after Carl Laemmle set up a film company in the early 1900s. Laemmle hit upon the idea of opening his company's studios to the public to increase his revenue, the first film company to do so. However, his tours, which began around 1915, were temporarily suspended when "talking" movies started to replace silent films and directors required that sets be free from public noise.

The Universal Studios Film Company has experienced changing fortunes over the years, although it is now one of the major film producers. Public tours began again in earnest in 1962 and were expanded when the Music Corporation of America (MCA) took over Universal Studios. By 1964 the tours had grown to include trips around dressing rooms and various film sets and were further developed to make the company become the enormous theme park it is today. The Hollywood site, the original theme park, is split into two main areas, the Upper Lot and the Lower Lot, connected by a series of escalators. There are now three other Universal Studios parks: one in Florida, one in Japan, and one under construction in Singapore. **TP**

"Hollywood is a place where they'll pay you $1000 for a kiss and 50¢ for your soul."

Marilyn Monroe, film actress

Rose Bowl (Pasadena, CA, USA)

Famous stadium and host to the "grandaddy" of all college football games

Some 10 miles (16 km) northeast of downtown Los Angeles is the town of Pasadena, that juts up against the foothills of the San Gabriel Mountains. The town's name means "of the valley." It is a beautiful area with a thriving tourist season, but is perhaps best known for its annual Tournament of Roses Parade and the Rose Bowl stadium.

The first parade was held on New Year's Day 1890, organized by the Pasadena Valley Hunt Club. Horse-drawn carriages were driven in grand style, with the horses and riders decorated in flowers, in a procession through the local streets. This parade was followed by tug-of-war games, polo matches, and other festivities, all designed to celebrate the clement winter weather of the area. The Rose Bowl stadium was designed in 1921 by the architect Myron Hunt, and was built in 1922, with its opening game being played on New Year's Day 1923. The stadium was originally built in a

horseshoe shape, but has been added to over the years, and is now a complete "bowl." In 1923 the tradition began of holding the annual Rose Bowl college football game after the parade—a game that has become the most famous and historic of bowl games; it is commonly referred to as the "granddaddy of them all." Apart from the historic Rose Bowl college football games, the stadium has hosted numerous other great sporting events, including five Super Bowls. It has also hosted the World Cup Soccer Finals for both men and women, in 1994 and 1999 respectively, as well as the soccer events at the 1932 and 1984 Olympics.

The Rose Bowl stadium has a seating capacity of 92,542 people, and continues to hold prestigious sporting events. It is one of the most historic of the great U.S. stadiums and, despite its great age, remains one of the most elegant. **TP**

Disneyland (Anaheim, CA, USA)

The family theme park that became an international phenomenon

Walt Disney's incredible imagination created a wonderland in films, which he wanted to turn into reality. The idea to build a theme park came to him after visiting a small park in Oakland, California, where he was disappointed with the attractions. He decided to build his own, for his daughters and the children of his employees. His original plan was to build near the Burbank film studios, but the application was denied. He then enlisted the Stanford Research Institute to find a suitable plot. They found an orange grove in rural Anaheim, close to Los Angeles and well served by the Santa Ana Freeway and Harbor Boulevard. It was ideal, and building work started on July 21, 1954, with the opening scheduled for just a year later.

It was an enormous feat of construction, imagination, and finance, and was overseen at every step by Disney. Despite this, the opening day, July 17, 1955, was an unmitigated disaster, later referred to as "Black Sunday." In addition to the 6,000 genuine invitations, tickets were forged and more than 28,000 people showed up, bringing surrounding roads to a standstill. Many of the rides were unfinished or unable to cope with the quantities. In addition there was a heat wave, melting tarmac, a gas leak, and problems with the water fountains.

Since then, Disneyland has become an integral part of U.S. culture, as well as being a national and international phenomenon. **TP**

> *"All our dreams can come true, if we have the courage to pursue them."*
>
> Walt Disney, animation pioneer

Forest Lawn Memorial Parks (Los Angeles, CA, USA)

A pioneering design that created "optimistic" burial grounds

The Forest Lawn Memorial Parks introduced a new type of cemetery, designed to be uplifting and a place of joyous remembrance. The use of themed areas and highly landscaped settings, incorporating sculpture and memorial architecture, set a new precedent in cemetery design.

The original Forest Lawn Memorial Park was in Glendale, California, and was set up in 1906 by a number of businessmen as a nonprofit organization. In 1917 Dr. Hubert Eaton took over the management of the parks and it was under his directorship that they took shape; for this reason he is considered the "founder" of the Forest Lawn Memorial Parks. His vision was for large parklike cemeteries as optimistic places filled with a sense of celebrating life and remembering history. He did away with traditional upright gravestones, and instead introduced plaques and statues, many of which are copies of famous works of art, including Michelangelo's *David* and *Moses*. Many of the statues are for sale and can be purchased to accompany a grave. The parks are dotted with nondenominational chapels and architectural features of a memorial and patriotic nature, including The Court of Liberty, The Hall of Liberty American History Museum, The Lincoln Terrace, and the Monument to Washington. The parks are divided into areas, such as the heart-shaped Babyland (for infants), Eventide, Graceland, and Dawn of Tomorrow. The parks offer different burial "packages," catering for all levels of income. Among those buried here are a number of Hollywood stars.

The beautifully manicured and neatly organized Memorial Parks are quintessentially American in concept; they have created a new chapter in cemetery history, and provide a serene and uplifting setting to help the grieving accept their loss. **TP**

Graumann's Chinese Theater (Los Angeles, CA, USA)

Hollywood Boulevard's most famous theater, home to the handprints of the stars

Grauman's Chinese Theater is perhaps the most famous movie theater in the world, and certainly the most instantly recognizable. The opulent and extravagant Chinese facade is a piece of timeless movie history and has been carefully preserved since the building opened in 1927.

The Chinese Theater was the brainchild of Sid Grauman, a showman and one of the founders of the Academy of Motion Picture Arts and Sciences. He had previously built the Million Dollar Theater and the Egyptian Theater just a few blocks from where the Chinese Theater would eventually stand, but it was the Chinese Theater that would fulfill his dreams. He designed the building, with architect Raymond M. Kennedy, to have the appearance of a huge Chinese pagoda. Two massive coral-colored columns flank the entrance with its bronze roof, and stand either side of a 30-foot- (9-m-) high carved dragon. On either side of the entrance are two giant Heaven dogs that Grauman imported from China, along with temple bells, pagodas, and other Chinese decorative artifacts. The forecourt to the theater is part of the architectural theme and is enclosed by a 40-foot (12-m) curved wall with copper-topped turrets. It is here in the forecourt that the famous collection of footprints, handprints, and autographs of Hollywood greats can be seen, along with the odd hoofprint belonging to Trigger, Tony, and Champion. The interior of the theater is as lavish and exotic as the exterior, and has recently been restored to its original splendor.

Grauman's Chinese Theater is one of the most sought-after locations for Hollywood premieres and was also the venue for the Academy Awards ceremonies between 1944 and 1946. Since its opening night on May 27, 1927, with Cecil B. DeMille's *The King of Kings*, the Grauman Chinese Theater has continued to delight a succession of moviegoers and visitors. **TP**

> "It's an honor. [The Chinese Theater] is the first thing you do when you come to Hollywood."
>
> George Clooney, actor

Union Station (Los Angeles, CA, USA)

One of the last great train stations from the golden age of the railways

The Los Angeles Union Passenger Terminal—now known simply as Union Station—bears deliberate architectural resemblance to the Christian missions, which opened up California to the new settlers. This paid homage to the fact that the railway station was opening up Los Angeles to a new generation of travelers and settlers. The building was designed by the architectural firm Parkinson & Parkinson and opened in May 1939. A highly significant part of railroad history, Union Station provided the meeting point for three important railway lines: the Union Pacific, the Southern Pacific, and the Atchison, Topeka, and Santa Fe railways.

Alongside its necessary tracks, platforms, and other utilitarian buildings, the station comprised well-designed public areas, including gardens, a restaurant designed by the architect Mary Coulter, and an elegant waiting room. Beautifully decorated in marble and terra-cotta, the station's status is an indication of how important the railway was to the United States, before the era of mass air travel. In the 1930s, the railroads allowed everyone to travel and become modern-day pioneers. The building's lavish décor also reflected the glamour that the movie industry had brought to Los Angeles. In 1950, the station achieved cinematic glory itself, as the setting for the movie *Union Station*, a film noir thriller.

Today, the building, which is now considered an emblematic sight in downtown Los Angeles, has become part of the city's subway system. It continues to play its role in everyday life in Hollywood, available for hire not only for films and TV series, but as the setting for weddings and concerts. Although the original structure is small and old-fashioned compared with glossy modern-day terminals, Union Station remains one of the best-loved and most historic train stations in the United States. **LH**

"The people you have to deal with are lice. They never keep their word to anyone about anything."

Insp. Donnelly (Brian Fitzgerald), *Union Station* (1950)

Hoover Dam (border of Nevada and Arizona, USA)

A masterpiece of engineering from the era of the Great Depression

"This morning I came, I saw, and I was conquered ... [by] this great feat of mankind."

President Franklin D. Roosevelt, September 30, 1935

⊡ With the Colorado River diverted through tunnels, the floor of the Black Canyon was prepared for the dam.

⊡ The dam is also called the Boulder Dam because originally its intended site was the Boulder Canyon.

The building of the Hoover Dam was one of the most extraordinary feats of twentieth-century engineering; a feat made all the more remarkable considering the dam was constructed during the Great Depression. The immensely powerful Colorado River had periodically burst its banks, perhaps most devastatingly in 1905 when it flooded Imperial Valley and created a 150-square-mile (388-sq-km) inland sea. This, combined with the need for power and a water supply, contributed to the plans to harness the river.

Before the project could begin, a fair agreement had to be arranged between Arizona, Nevada, California, Utah, Colorado, New Mexico, and Wyoming so that all would benefit. With the Hoover Compromise, construction began. First the river had to be diverted from the proposed site of Black Canyon, which involved blasting four huge tunnels through the canyon walls. More than 8,000 workers then had to clear the now-dry canyon floor of rock before concrete could be poured. The structure itself is a curved gravity dam, with the enormously thick concrete wall shaped like a gentle horseshoe across the canyon. Behind the dam lies Lake Mead, and the force of the lake water pushes against the dam, creating compressive forces that travel the length of the curved concrete wall and into the sides of the canyon, which counteract the forces and effectively "push back." This system creates an immensely strong and rigid structure. The original plans for the facade of the dam were deemed too simple for a structure of such magnitude and importance, so architect Gordon B. Kauffman was enlisted. He designed the elegant and streamlined Art Deco finish.

Hoover Dam is of immense importance both on its critical functional levels, and as an example of the vast scale of the U.S. engineering and architectural achievements of the early twentieth century. **TP**

Virginia City (Storey County, NV, USA)

A city that grew out of the gold rush

In the far west of Nevada, at the base of the Sierra Nevada Mountains, is Virginia City—once the largest, most affluent prospecting town, and the biggest settlement between Denver and San Francisco.

According to legend, the area was first called Old Virginny Town by a drunken miner called James Finney (nicknamed Old Virginny), who dropped a bottle of whiskey outside his tent and named the area in his own honor; this was around 1857. Gold had been discovered at the head of Six-Mile Canyon and the first hopeful prospectors had moved in. The biggest event in the town's history, however, was the discovery of the Comstock Lode, a huge deposit of silver ore on the eastern slope of Mount Davidson. The strike became public in 1859, and as people flooded into the area in the hopes of making their fortunes, the little town grew into a city virtually overnight. So much money was generated through mining that the city of San Francisco was built on the back of it, and the money was said to have financed the Civil War (1861–65). The writer Samuel Langhorne Clemens moved to Virginia City, where he worked for the local newspaper, and as a miner, before adopting the name by which he is best known: Mark Twain.

Production at the Comstock Lode reached its peak in the mid-1870s, but by 1880 structural and engineering problems in the mine led to its decline, and underground mining finally stopped in 1922. The city's prosperity and population similarly suffered, and it became a virtual ghost town until it was restored and turned into a National Historic Landmark—the largest in the United States. **TP**

◩ This part of Virginia City was called Gold Hill, although much of the city's wealth came from silver mining.

◪ Modern cars jostle with vintage jalopies in Virginia City, now repopulating as a booming tourist attraction.

Golden Spike Historic Site (Promontory Summit, UT, USA)

The railroad that joined east and west

At Promontory Summit, in the dry, desert landscape of northern Utah, the east and west United States were joined, forever changing the face of the country and finally breaking down the western frontier. This happened with the completion of the Transcontinental Railroad when the final spike—a symbolic golden one—was driven in on May 10, 1869.

Until the completion of the railroad, the country could be traversed only by stagecoach, horseback, or by sailing from the west coast around South America and up the east coast. In 1862, the U.S. Congress authorized the Central Pacific Railroad to build east from Sacramento, California, and the Union Pacific Railroad to build west from Omaha, Nebraska. Little happened until the end of the Civil War in 1865, when both companies set to the task with renewed vigor. The Central Pacific Railroad encountered the Sierra Nevada Mountains, which greatly impeded their progress, compounded by a shortage of labor, the majority of whom were Chinese immigrants (a Chinese Arch commemorates their contribution to the railroad). The Union Railroad, by contrast, had a large workforce—but of irascible itinerants and drunks. The two railroads came together in 1869, with the Central Pacific engine *Jupiter* and the Union Pacific engine *119* symbolically driven forward to meet each other.

This single event opened up the west to a flood of settlers—and marked the end of the Native Americans' struggle to maintain their homeland and prevent the disintegration of the frontier. It is now celebrated annually, and the area surrounding the spot has been preserved within the Golden Spike Historic Site. **TP**

↗ "Iron horses" of the Union Railroad and the Central Pacific Railroad meet at the completion ceremony.

→ A marker commemorates a record set by the Central Pacific Railroad during the epic construction.

Beehive House

(Salt Lake City, UT, USA)

First Utah home of Brigham Young

The large colonial Beehive House is in the heart of Salt Lake City, Utah, home of the Church of Jesus Christ of Latter-day Saints (LDS), or Mormon, religion. The religion was established in Utah on July 24, 1847, when Brigham Young and a community of followers arrived in the Salt Lake Valley; the date is now a Utah state holiday. Young's actions and the establishment of his colony formed a fundamental part of the foundation of Salt Lake City, and much of the surrounding state of Utah, not least in his election as governor of the state.

In 1857, Young was ousted as governor at the directive of President Buchanan, who sent troops with

> *"I want to live perfectly above the law, and make it my servant instead of my master."*
>
> **Brigham Young, Mormon leader**

a replacement, sparking the "Utah War." Young held out for months, ordering his people to burn their land and property should the soldiers win. Eventually Young backed down but remained a powerful, though unelected, figure.

The Beehive House (named after a sculpture on the roof, representative of industry within the Mormon Church) was the first of his official residences in Salt Lake. The house was built by Young's brother-in-law and designed to accommodate Young and his many wives as well as his office. His second home, The Lion House, was built next door and provided further accommodation for his twenty-seven wives and fifty-six children. Today, the Beehive House is open to the public and has been restored to how it looked during the time of Young's residency. **TP**

Mormon Temple

(Salt Lake City, UT, USA)

The most important Mormon church

The Salt Lake Temple, with its smooth granite exterior and six soaring spires, occupies a central position within Salt Lake City, the capital of Utah, and within the Church of Jesus Christ of Latter-day Saints (Mormon religion). It sits in Temple Square, a downtown oasis of calm, surrounded by other important Mormon buildings such as the headquarters, the Tabernacle, the Joseph Smith Memorial Building, and the conference center. The Mormon religion was first established in New York in 1830 by Joseph Smith Jr., and rapidly spread into Ohio, and then Missouri. In 1838 the so-called Mormon War resulted in the church followers fleeing to Illinois, where they again established a community.

In 1844 Smith and his brother were assassinated, and the leadership of the church came under the Quorum of the Twelve Apostles, fronted by Brigham Young, who led a group of Mormons into Utah to establish a new colony. Salt Lake remains the headquarters of the Mormon church today. The location for the richly symbolic temple was chosen just four days after Young and his party arrived in Salt Lake. The building took more than forty years to complete, with the 1857 to 1858 Utah War (a conflict between the Mormons and the U.S. government) delaying construction, and the interior finally being completed in just a year. Granite from the local Little Cottonwood Canyon was used in the building work, and the exterior is full of symbolism depicting the journey of humankind from life and death to the eternal ever after.

Wilford Woodruff, the church's fourth president, dedicated the temple on April 6, 1893, and it continues to be the most important Mormon church, occupying a crucial role in the history and development of Salt Lake City. **TP**

Gateway Arch

(St. Louis, MO, USA)

Eero Saarinen's stunning memorial sculpture

The compelling Gateway Arch forms part of the Jefferson National Expansion Memorial Park along the Mississippi River at St. Louis, Missouri. Situated near the start of the Lewis and Clark trail, the gleaming archway is a memorial to the Louisiana Purchase in 1803 (made by Thomas Jefferson) and the subsequent opening of the west to settlers following Captain Meriwether Lewis's and Second Lieutenant William Clark's expedition from 1804 to 1806. It also serves to commemorate the establishment of the first civil government west of the Mississippi River, and Dred Scott, a slave who unsuccessfully sued for his freedom in the Old Courthouse and brought the debate over slavery into the public forum.

The arch was designed by Finnish architect Eero Saarinen, who had studied and practiced sculpture before becoming an architect. The Gateway retains a strong sculptural form. The tapered curve of the arch is modeled on the form a chain makes when held at both ends and allowed to fall, which is referred to as a catenary arch. At 630 feet (192 m) high, it is the tallest memorial structure in the United States, and with its legs also being 630 feet (192 m) wide, the arch has a particularly pleasing and balanced form. Within the stainless steel structure is a unique tram system that transports visitors to an observation station at the top, as well as two emergency stairwells. Underneath the arch is a visitor center, museum, theaters, and shops. The observation station offers stunning views across the Mississippi River to the east, and west across St. Louis through narrow windows that are indiscernible from the ground.

Tragically, Saarinen died from a brain tumor before his Gateway Arch was finished, but as a testament to his design, it has become one of the most visited tourist attractions in the United States. **TP**

"Scott and his family ... were, by the laws of Missouri, the property of the defendant."

Summing up of the Dred Scott court case, 1854

🏛 ⑨ **Mesa Verde** (Montezuma County, CO, USA)

The largest number of Pueblo ruins ever discovered

Mesa Verde National Park is one of the most important U.S. parks in terms of cultural significance. Spread over 80 square miles (207 sq km) of Montezuma County in Colorado, it is home to the largest collection of cliff dwellings and ruins of the ancient Pueblo people, who lived here from around 450 to 1300.

Mesa Verde (Green Table) takes its name from the high grass plateaus that characterize the rugged terrain of the area. Much of the park is formed by jagged peaks and valleys with areas of dense forestation interspersed with open country. The park land is quite high, ranging from around 6,000 feet (1,828 m) to 8,500 feet (2,590 m), and was extremely difficult for early settlers to traverse, which partly accounts for the late discovery of the Pueblo villages. Spanish explorers first entered the area while traveling from Santa Fe to California, and they gave the park its name. However, it was not until 1873 that any evidence of the Pueblo villages came to light, and this was through a trapper called John Moss. He took the photographer William Henry Jackson to the area in 1874, which sparked the public's interest. Subsequent explorations revealed numerous ruins of Pueblo villages, and some of the most astonishing cliff dwellings in the world. The Cliff Palace is the most famous of the Mesa Verde dwellings and has around 220 rooms with 23 *kivas* (underground chambers). It is extraordinarily accomplished in design and layout, and is testament to the sophisticated culture of the Ancient Puebloan Indians, who left the area suddenly around 1300, for reasons unknown.

Many of the buildings and artifacts were damaged or stolen before the area was established as a national park in 1906, although there are still innumerable fascinating ruins that survived, and these offer a unique insight to the ancient Puebloan culture. **TP**

Canyon de Chelly (near Chinle, AZ, USA)

An outstanding landscape, home to ruins over two millennia old

Canyon de Chelly is 131 square miles (340 sq km) of breathtaking landscape, situated in the northeast corner of Arizona. It is part of Navajoland, the largest Native American reservation in North America and its stunning geology includes soaring sandstone cliffs and imposing monoliths.

The national monument encompasses three impressive canyons: Canyon de Chelly, Canyon del Muerto, and Monument Canyon, encompassing a wealth of fascinating ancient ruins. The Anasazi, the ancestors of the Pueblo people, settled here around the fourth century, and more than 100 ancient village sites of different ages have since been discovered. Perhaps the most striking aspect of this enormous archeological find is the variety of the buildings that the Anasazi built from simple, single dwellings to multistory and many-roomed houses. Of particular note is the two-story "White House," so called because

of a long wall in the upper reaches that was coated with white plaster. The huge structure is thought to have originally had as many as eighty rooms with four *kivas*—important ceremonial rooms. The Mummy Cave in Canyon del Muerto is another extraordinary site where two mummies were discovered within a three-story tower. The mummies were well preserved by the intense dryness of the desert climate, and it is this aridity that has contributed to the preservation of many of the more fragile ruins.

The Anasazi moved on around the thirteenth century, and approximately 300 years ago the Navajo settled the area and began farming the canyon floor, which they continue to do today. Canyon de Chelly is an area of outstanding natural beauty, a dramatic landscape crafted by nature, shifting rock formations, roaring rivers—now dry—and searing winds, and a place of cultural heritage. **TP**

O.K. Corral

(Tombstone, AZ, USA)

Scene of the Wild West's most famous gunfight

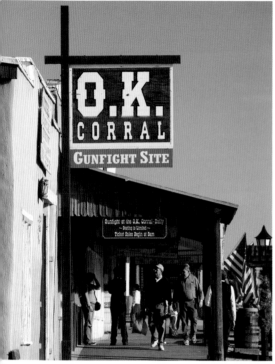

The old western town of Tombstone, Arizona, is home to the O.K. Corral, which has become famous primarily on the strength of a thirty-second gunfight that was actually fought in a small vacant lot just behind the dusty corral. The town of Tombstone was founded in the arid desert in 1877 by scout and prospector Ed Schieffelin, who had struck silver on his travels. As with all the early prospecting towns, Tombstone had a precarious balance of law and lawlessness. In particular there was a large band of outlaws living in the vicinity who were collectively called the Cowboys, and who were involved in a large number of varied crimes.

In 1880 Virgil Earp became town marshal and appointed his brothers, Wyatt and Morgan, his deputies. In 1881 the Earps fell out with the Clanton and McLaury brothers, who were Cowboys, as well as with the sheriff of Cochise County, John Behan. Tension mounted between the two factions, escalated by Doc Holliday picking a fight with Ike Clanton. Virgil Earp and his brothers decided to disarm the Clanton and McLaury brothers (it was illegal to carry arms in the town) and tracked them down to the vacant lot #2. In the ensuing thirty seconds after the first shot was fired, Billy Clanton, Frank McLaury, and Tom McLaury were killed and Virgil and Morgan Earp and Doc Holliday were injured.

The O.K. Corral was the scene of just one of the numerous, colorful incidents of old western life that have been greatly embellished through Hollywood, and form a unique part of U.S. history. **TP**

⬉ Visitors to O.K. Corral do not need to search for the site of the famous gunfight—it is proudly marked.

⬅ The bodies of Tom and Frank McLaury and Bill Clanton are displayed after the brief encounter.

Kit Carson's Home

(Taos, NM, USA)

The marital home of a frontier legend

This unassuming adobe house is where the legendary U.S. frontiersman Christopher ("Kit") Houston Carson lived over a period of twenty-five years. He bought it around 1843 as a wedding present for his young wife, Josefa Jamarillo, who was from a powerful, important local family. The house originally belonged to another member of Josefa's family, and was deemed a suitable purchase for Carson.

Carson had first arrived in New Mexico around 1826 when, using Taos as a base camp, he set off on a number of far-reaching, fur-trapping expeditions. He journeyed as far west as California, and later traveled

> *"We passed the time gloriously, spending our money freely—never thinking our lives were risked."*
>
> Kit Carson, frontiersman

up to the Rocky Mountains of Colorado and across the western frontier. He became friendly with a number of Indian tribes, and his first two wives were from the Arapaho and Cheyenne communities. Carson worked for the military officer and explorer John C. Fremont, whose memoirs propelled Carson to the status of national folk hero. Carson was active during the Mexican–American war and led the forces of U.S. General Stephen Kearney from New Mexico into California. In 1843 he returned to Taos, where he married Josefa and lived in the house on Kit Carson Road (formerly called Taos Canyon Road).

The local Masonic Lodge was determined to preserve the house and in 1910 the Grand Lodge of New Mexico purchased the property. It has since been restored and turned into a museum. **TP**

Governors' Palace

(Santa Fe, NM, USA)

At the heart of New Mexican history

The Governors' Palace in Santa Fe is the oldest continually used building in the United States. This long, low adobe building was at the center of numerous significant historic events involving the struggle over the territorial control of New Mexico. In 1610, Don Pedro de Peralta, the governor of Spanish territory, founded the city of Santa Fe and began work on the Governors' Palace. At this time the powerful "New Spain" consisted of almost the entire southwestern part of the United States, including the states of Texas, Nevada, Utah, Colorado, Arizona, California, and New Mexico. Over the years, the Governors' Palace and the territory of New Mexico came under different ownership, starting in 1680 with the Pueblo Revolt. The Spanish fled in the face of the Pueblo people's uprising and the palace was taken over by the indigenous people, who used it for housing. From 1692 to 1693 Don Diego de Vargas led the Spanish Reconquest back to Santa Fe and the palace once again became the seat of government.

During the Mexican War of Independence (1810–21), the Mexicans took the city and it became the capital of Mexican territory. In 1846 the United States declared war on Mexico, and General Kearny led his troops into Santa Fe to claim the city and New Mexico. The palace saw a further brief change of government during the Civil War (1861–65), when the Confederates took over the building as their regional headquarters of operations.

In 1909 the palace was turned into the Museum of New Mexico, which promotes the rich history and culture of the area and celebrates southwestern Native American arts and crafts. It holds an important place within the history of New Mexico, the development of Santa Fe, and the history of the United States as a whole. **TP**

Dealey Plaza (Dallas, TX, USA)

Where President John F. Kennedy was assassinated

November 22, 1963, is a date few people will forget. It was the day on which Dealey Plaza, in downtown Dallas, Texas, was inadvertently catapulted into the annals of history as the place where President John F. Kennedy was assassinated.

The plaza—which is home to a number of historic statues and monuments—is on land originally acquired by the city in order to build a triple underpass. Three main roads, Elm Street, Main Street, and Commerce Street, were brought together here, where they pass beneath the railroad. The underpass was opened in 1936 and the large park area above it was landscaped and planted with Texas oak trees. The scheme was largely due to George Bannerman Dealey, publisher of the *Dallas Morning News,* and the park was named after him. The area is now partially surrounded by impressive modern skyscrapers, but the plaza itself has remained largely untouched. Following its designation as a Historic Landmark in 1993, there have been plans to further restore it to its appearance of 1963. The north Grassy Knoll—a grass bank that has become the center of numerous conspiracy theories—is bounded by the former Texas School Book Depository, and was above and to the right of Kennedy at the time of his assassination.

In a rather controversial move, the former Texas School Book Depository, the building from which the gunman Lee Harvey Oswald fired his fatal shot, turned its top two floors into the Sixth Floor Museum, dedicated to the life and times of John F. Kennedy. Dealey Plaza has since become home to a continual stream of tourists, as has the Sixth Floor Museum. **TP**

◹ The former Texas School Book Depository now has almost iconic status as Oswald's onetime hiding place.

◁ Minutes before the assassination, the presidential motorcade passes by appreciative Dallas onlookers.

Alamo Mission (San Antonio, TX, USA)

Site of the infamous Battle of the Alamo and the death of David Crockett

In the midst of San Antonio is the Alamo Church, a solid, white, fortified building whose old, thick walls conceal a torturous history laced with irony. It was established as a mission to bring Christianity to the Native Americans and preach peace—but became a military fort and the scene of a bloody battle.

The mission was set up around 1718, with the present site chosen in 1724. The mission initially thrived, but, following a steady decline, it was closed in 1793 and the land was returned to the native people. In 1803 a Spanish cavalry unit took over the buildings, naming them after their hometown of Alamo de Parras, Coahuila, and its cottonwood trees (*álamo* being Spanish for "cottonwood"). Over the ensuing decades the old mission was occupied by Mexican military factions, and in 1836 it played a critical part in the Texas Revolution—the Battle of the Alamo. In December 1835, after five days of fighting, the Texans took control of the Alamo, ousting the Mexican military. In February 1836, however, around 6,000 Mexican troops led by General Antonio López de Santa Anna stormed the Alamo, taking Colonel William B. Travis and his 173 men by surprise. The Texans battled for thirteen days, during which thirty-two volunteers joined them, but they were finally overcome and all slaughtered. Among them was famous frontiersman David Crockett.

After the battle the old mission fell into decay, and its ownership was widely disputed. In 1905 it was bought by the State of Texas and put under the care of the Daughters of the Republic of Texas, who still care for this integral piece of Texan history. **TP**

⬈ More than 6,000 Mexican soldiers were dispatched to wrestle the Alamo from the Texan revolutionaries.

⬈ A plaque exhorts U.S. citizens to remember the men who fought for the independence of Texas.

Fort Sill Military Reservation (Fort Sill, OK, USA)

Site of the infamous Red River campaign

The historic site of Fort Sill in the foothills of the Wichita Mountains, Oklahoma, has had a varied past; today it is home to the U.S. army field artillery. In 1869, Major General Philip H. Sheridan founded the fort. Initially the fort was called Camp Washita, but Sheridan changed it to Fort Sill in honor of his friend Brigadier General Joshua W. Sill, who had been killed in action.

Sheridan used the fort as a base to mount a campaign into Native American territory to try to stop the hostile Southern Plains tribes raiding border settlements in Kansas and Texas. Not long after the fort's foundation, President Ulysses Grant approved a peace policy that restricted the Fort Sill soldiers from taking action against the Native Americans. The tribes' border raids began again almost immediately.

In 1870 stone buildings were erected to replace the original wooden ones; these included a stone corral and other defensive structures. In 1874 the southern Cheyenne, Comanche, and Kiowa tribes went back on the warpath, and there followed the year-long Red River campaign that saw the military overcome the indigenous people. At the end of the campaign, the fort was used for law enforcement, and in 1894 its surrounds were used to house Geronimo and other Apache prisoners. Geronimo later died here. As the frontier disappeared and the West was settled, the fort changed from a cavalry base to field artillery, in which capacity it continues to function. **TP**

"We are all the children of one God. The sun, the darkness, the winds are all listening to what we have to say."

Geronimo, Chiricahua Apache military leader

Shiloh Battlefield (Near Savannah, TN, USA)

Where a fierce Civil War battle raged

Shiloh Battlefield in southwestern Tennessee is the best-preserved of the Civil War battlefields, and was one of the first five military parks to be established in the United States. It spreads over 4,000 acres (1,619 ha) and is home to more than 150 monuments to the different states and regiments involved in the bloody fight. The battlefield's integrity is largely due to the lack of any major roads traversing the park; there is only a 10-mile (16-km) driving tour of the site.

The Battle of Shiloh was two days of fighting that resulted in massive loss of life for both the Confederates, led by Albert Sidney Johnston and Pierre Gustave Toutant de Beauregard, and the victorious Union soldiers, led by Ulysses S. Grant and Don Carlos Buell. It was one of the first major battles of the Civil War in the Western Theater (east of the Mississippi River and west of the Appalachian Mountains). Following the battle, the Union soldiers traveled to Corinth, taking possession of the town and the key railroad junction; this area has been incorporated into the Shiloh National Military Park.

After the battle, the dead were buried where they fell, but on December 27, 1894, the area was designated a National Military Park and the Shiloh National Cemetery was created for the graves of Union soldiers; the Confederate soldiers mostly remain in their original, large mass graves. The park's Hebrew name *Shiloh* means "peace." **TP**

> *"It was a most invigorating, peaceful, quiet Sabbath morning. Not a sound fell upon the ear."*
>
> Capt. James G. Day, 15th Iowa regiment

Graceland (Memphis, TN, USA)

The legendary home of Elvis Presley

Elvis Presley's fame and popularity will never wane. His music changed the face of the twentieth century, and his Hollywood life and death have seen him become one of the most popular and enduring figures in the entertainment industry. Graceland was his primary home for twenty years and the estate became an essential part of the singer's identity.

Elvis purchased the grand, white-columned property in 1957, and moved in along with his parents, Vernon and Gladys Presley. His beloved mother died the following year and is buried at Graceland. Two years later Vernon remarried, moving his new wife, Dee Stanley, into the home. The situation was naturally fraught, and eventually Elvis moved them out and into an adjacent property. Much of Elvis's adult life was played out within the walls of Graceland, and several books detailing his life and times there have been published. In 1967, after five years of their living together at Graceland, he famously married Priscilla Beaulieu.

Following Elvis's death in his bathroom at the house in 1977, Priscilla—who was by that time divorced from the singer—took over the management of the estate, and turned it into a moneymaking enterprise. It was opened to the public in 1982, and in 2006 the couple's daughter, Lisa-Marie, turned over management of Graceland to an entertainment company that now plans to turn it into an even bigger tourist attraction.

As a testament to the cultural significance of Graceland, recent figures reflect that it is the second-most-visited private residence in the United States after the White House. **TP**

↖ Elvis was able to buy Graceland outright with the proceeds of his 1957 No.1 hit, "Heartbreak Hotel."

← Graceland is not so much a mansion as a big Southern colonial house, complete with grand classical portico.

Martin Luther King Jr.'s Birthplace (Atlanta, GA, USA)

Home of one of the world's most important civil rights activists

Martin Luther King Jr. was the most famous leader of the U.S. civil rights movement in the twentieth century. He devoted himself to establishing the Civil Rights Act of 1964 and was awarded the Nobel Peace Prize that year. In 1965 his work for equality and freedom was recognized by the American Jewish Committee, who presented him with the American Liberties Medallion. Tragically, he was assassinated in 1968. The area of Auburn, Georgia, where King was born and spent much of his life has been preserved as a National Historic Site.

King was born on January 15, 1929, on the second floor of a house on Auburn Avenue. The elegant but modest nine-room house was owned by King's grandfather, and was at the heart of a predominantly African-American community. The area became known as Sweet Auburn and was extremely prosperous, with African-American businesses flourishing. Today the area has been preserved, much as it was during King's time. A short walk from his home is the Ebenezer Baptist Church where his father was a preacher, and where King Jr. joined him in the pulpit for eight years. Opposite the church is the Martin Luther King Center for Nonviolent Social Change, which continues King's work. To the east of the church is King's gravesite, in the form of a white marble monument surrounded by a reflection pool.

King's birthplace has been restored to how it would have appeared in the 1930s. It marks the beginning of one of the most important chapters of the civil rights movement, and is a piece of history for all generations and all races. **TP**

↗ Martin Luther King waves to crowds on August 28, 1963, the day he gave his "I Have a Dream" speech.

↘ No. 501 Auburn Avenue in Atlanta is an important part of the city's Martin Luther King National Historic Site.

Wright Brothers National Memorial (Kill Devil Hills, NC, USA)

Site of the world's first airplane flight

> *"... conceived by genius achieved by dauntless resolution and unconquerable faith."*

Inscription on the Wright brothers' memorial

⬆ The Wright Brothers National Memorial on Kill Devil Hill commemorates their ingenuity and daring.

➡ Orville pilots a 1911 glider over the sand dunes at Kill Devil Hills, 4 miles (6.5 km) from Kitty Hawk town.

The town of Kill Devil Hills was established in 1953, but that was many years after the area had witnessed an event of unprecedented importance. Situated along the beautiful North Carolina coast, Kill Devil Hills—named after a fierce moonshine drunk by pirates—sits between the glistening waters of the Atlantic and a series of monumental, rolling sand dunes. It is these dunes that attracted the attention of two pioneering young men—Orville and Wilbur Wright—in the early 1900s.

At this time the area was remote and isolated, and with its sand dunes—some of which are more than 100 feet (30.5 m) high—it provided an ideal location for the brothers to experiment with their gliders as the area's steady winds greatly facilitated flight. Having designed, built, and flown other gliders, in 1903 the brothers built the powered *Wright Flyer*, and on December 17, Orville took the plane on its first flight, creating aviation history. The Wrights had realized that the secret to successful flight lay in mastering control of the aircraft rather than in power.

Both brothers made two short flights each that day, which were witnessed by five onlookers. Ironically, after the final flight, a gust of wind took hold of the grounded plane and hurled it across the ground, causing great damage. The *Wright Flyer* never flew again, although it was restored and put on exhibition, but the brothers soon built her replacement, *Flyer II*.

A granite monument—the Wright Brothers National Memorial—was built in 1932 to commemorate the brothers' achievements and bravery. The Wrights lived in a small wooden shed alongside another wooden structure that became the world's first airplane hangar, and both of these have been reconstructed at the site, based on old photographs. In addition, the flight paths across the dunes are marked out. **TP**

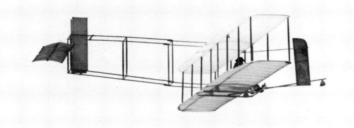

Fort Sumter
(Charleston Harbor, SC, USA)

A piece of Civil War history

Fort Sumter was designed in 1827 as part of the defensive system of Charleston Harbor. It grew partly from the 1812 war with Great Britain, which had highlighted how vulnerable the coastline and harbors were to foreign attack. The fort would witness the start of the American Civil War

Construction began in 1829 with the formation of a human-made island at the harbor entrance. The large fort was built on to this, rising 50 feet (15 m) above the low tide mark and boasting brick-built, 5-foot- (1.5-m-) thick walls. It was a massive project that was still unfinished in December 1860, when Major Armstrong of the U.S. Army moved two companies of men into the structure. Armstrong had been sent with his men to the fort because of the increasingly tense political situation in South Carolina. The Confederates called for the fort's immediate evacuation, but Armstrong refused. On March 5, 1861, the day after President Abraham Lincoln was inaugurated, Armstrong sent a message to the new president that the fort's supplies were running out. Before Lincoln could send a supply ship, the Confederates opened fire on the fort. These were the first shots fired in what would become one of the bloodiest chapters in U.S. history. After thirty-six hours of continuous gunfire, Armstrong and his men surrendered and were evacuated. The Confederates took possession of the fort, and held it for the next four years until the U.S. Army finally overpowered them.

By the end of the nineteenth century, Fort Sumter had been reduced to virtual rubble. It was used for some years as an unmanned lighthouse. Rebuilding and restoration work began around 1898, and it was used by the military during World War I and World War II. Now Fort Sumter is open to the public and is preserved as a U.S. National Monument. **TP**

Ernest Hemingway Home (Key West, FL, USA

Home to the prizewinning author

Ernest Hemingway (1899–1961) won the Pulitzer Prize for his short novel *The Old Man and the Sea* in 1953 and the Nobel Prize in Literature in 1954. A journalist and author, he was known as much for his flamboyant lifestyle as he was for his writing. A war hero and ultimate macho man, Hemingway was noted for his hard drinking, four wives, and love of fishing, boxing, game hunting, bullfighting, and all things Hispanic. His untimely death was as dramatic as his life: He committed suicide using a shotgun at the age of sixty-one.

Hemingway traveled widely; he lived in Paris in the 1920s and later moved between the United States,

> *"All good books are alike in that they are truer than if they had really happened."*
>
> Ernest Hemingway, writer

Cuba, and Spain. With his second wife, fashion journalist Pauline Pfeiffer, he moved to Key West in Florida in 1928. Hemingway's father-in-law bought the house that is now a U.S. National Historic Landmark in 1931, and Hemingway lived there intermittently until 1961. Here he wrote many of his famous works, boxed in a ring he set up in the yard, and fished from his boat *Pilar* in the Florida Keys.

The house was built in 1851 in a Spanish colonial style. The swimming pool, built in 1938 as a present from Pfeiffer to her husband, was the first residential swimming pool built in Key West. The house is packed with Hemingway memorabilia—his typewriter, photos, and animal skins. In addition visitors can see the house's sixty or so many-toed cats descended from Hemingway's own pet tomcat. **CK**

Kennedy Space Center

(Merritt Island, FL, USA)

A place where scientific history is made every day

The Kennedy Space Center is a place where history is made regularly. It serves as a gateway to the future—with the ongoing NASA (National Aeronautics and Space Administration) launch programs and the Space Shuttle—as well as to the past, having played host to one of the most significant moments in modern history, when *Apollo 11* was launched and transported Neil Armstrong to the moon. In 1962, NASA acquired more than 200 square miles (518 sq km) of land on Merritt Island to facilitate the recently announced lunar program of operations. The preceding year, President John F. Kennedy had pledged to get the first man on the moon by 1970, a challenge that was realized a year ahead of target. The area was originally known as Launch Operations Center, but this was changed to honor Kennedy following his assassination in 1963.

Work immediately began on a new launch complex—Launch Complex 39, the current center of NASA's activity. This is the only launch complex the Space Center now uses; all other launch operations happen at Cape Canaveral Air Force Station (CCAFS). It is from Launch Complex 39 that the space shuttle (of which five have so far been built and three remain) is now launched, this being the government's current manned launch vehicle. The Space Center also has a shuttle landing facility. A comprehensive visitor center runs tours of part of the facility.

This small corner of Florida is without doubt one of the most important areas of the United States in terms of furthering the frontiers of space. **TP**

⬈ A space shuttle makes a dramatic takeoff from Launch Complex 39 at Kennedy Space Center.

⬊ The Shuttle Landing Facility at Kennedy Space Center, where the orbiters touch down after their missions.

Pearl Harbor (Oahu, HI, USA)

Where World War II began for the United States

The idyllic island of Oahu is the largest of the Hawaiian islands, and was the first to be discovered by Captain James Cook's crew during his third Pacific expedition in 1778. The island's natural beauty and its rich culture and legends are just a small part of what makes it such an important place. Oahu is also home to Pearl Harbor, the dominant U.S. naval base and shipyard, and the scene of the devastating attack in 1941 by the Japanese, at the height of World War II.

Named after the pearl-producing oysters that were prolific in this bay until the nineteenth century, this area was not initially used as a harbor, due to its shallow waters. However, the location was perfect for a U.S. defensive base and, by 1887, the United States had gained exclusive rights to the area. Dredging work began and in 1908 the naval base and shipyard were established; the shipyard is now one of the largest such naval facilities in the world. The previously little-known Pearl Harbor was thrown into global history on December 7, 1941, when the Japanese launched a "sneak" attack that obliterated the USS *Arizona* and destroyed or damaged twenty-one of the U.S. fleet of battleships, as well as 188 planes. The attack resulted in 2,403 U.S. fatalities, and launched the United States into World War II. Of those who died, almost half were crew members of the USS *Arizona*, whose ammunition compartment exploded after being hit by an armor-piercing bomb. Today the wreckage of the huge warship is clearly visible below the transparent green waters of the harbor and is a ghostly, evocative reminder of the tragic early morning carnage in December 1941.

Pearl Harbor remains an active naval base, shipyard, and sentry box to the Pacific. It is also a graveyard and memorial to the military personnel who lost their lives during the historic event that catapulted the United States into a world war. **TP**

> *"I've asked to be buried at Pearl Harbor. It was a beautiful place, apart from that day."*
>
> Richard Adams, Pearl Harbor survivor

⊞ More than sixty-five years after the Japanese attack, U.S. Navy ships rust away by the Oahu coast.

⊡ The battleships USS *West Virginia* and *Tennessee*, on fire and low in the water after receiving hits.

Kalaupapa Historical Park (Molokai, HI, USA)

The remote haven that became a place of enforced isolation and suffering

"Only one person was in sight ... at Kalaupapa ... a 'patient.' He merely stood and watched."

Ernie Pyle, author and war correspondent

The Kalaupapa Historical Park covers an area of roughly 10 square miles (26 sq km) and spreads across the Kalaupapa Peninsula (Makanalua Peninsula) on the north shore of the Hawaiian island of Molokai. It is a stunningly beautiful place that is totally isolated, being cut off from the rest of the island by sheer cliffs that rise 1,600 feet (488 m), and bordered to the north, east, and west by the brilliant blue Pacific Ocean.

The stunning beauty of Kalaupapa belies its tragic history, which was balanced in turn by astonishing acts of human kindness. The highly contagious Hansen's disease (leprosy) was first seen in Hawaii in 1848, believed to have come from China. It spread quickly, with devastating results that led to the need for isolation procedures. The Kalaupapa Peninsula was chosen as an enforced isolation center, its natural remoteness and fertile land making it a perfect site.

The native residents were forced from their homes in preparation for the new colony. In 1866 King Kamehameha brought in the isolation laws and those suffering from the disease were taken by boat to the peninsula and left with no amentities, caregivers, or supplies. They were expected to become self-sufficient but were too ill and weak to cope alone and suffered dreadfully. In 1873 a Catholic missionary, Father Damien, heard of the plight of the 700 sufferers and traveled with two others to the peninsula, where he set about building houses, churches, and facilities, as well as ministering to their needs. He eventually contracted the disease and died from it in 1889.

The development of sulfone drugs in the 1940s helped to eliminate the disease, and in 1969 the isolation law was repealed. Some former sufferers chose to remain at the site and still live there today. Much of the colony has been preserved as it was; it has become a valuable center of information and a place for quiet contemplation. **TP**

Kawaiahao Church (Honolulu, HI, USA)

The first permanent church to be built in Hawaii

Hawaii's most famous church, Kawaiahao Church, can be found in bustling downtown Honolulu on the Hawaiian island of Oahu. The site is the historic center of Honolulu—itself the commerical and historic heart of the island—and houses many national historic landmarks and places.

In 1824, the history of Christianity in Hawaii was to change forever. In that year, the Queen Regent, Ka'ahumanu, who exercised considerable power during the reigns of King Kamehameha II and King Kamehameha III, announced her conversion to Protestant Christianity. She commissioned the magnificent Kawaiahao Church in 1836. It was designed by Bingham and built using 14,000 slabs of pale pink coral, quarried from the reefs by hand, and timber from locally felled trees. The huge New England–style building, that now seats 4,500 people, was used by visiting dignitaries and influential families in the city, and became the royal place of worship until the Cathedral Church of Saint Andrew was built some years later. It was also in the Kawaiahao Church that King Kamehameha III uttered the phrase "The life of the land is perpetuated in righteousness," which was then taken and used as Hawaii's official motto.

The church, a building of supreme grandeur and importance, is often referred to as the Hawaiian Westminster Abbey. It traces its foundation back to 1820 and the arrival of the first Christian missionaries in the Hawaiian Islands. At first the missionaries, led by the Reverend Hiram Bingham, built four small churches from pili grass on the spot where the current church now stands, and it was in this location that Bingham gave his first sermon.

This historic building, which served for the coronation of King Kamehameha IV and his wedding to Queen Emma in 1843, is of essential cultural importance within the rich history of Honolulu. **TP**

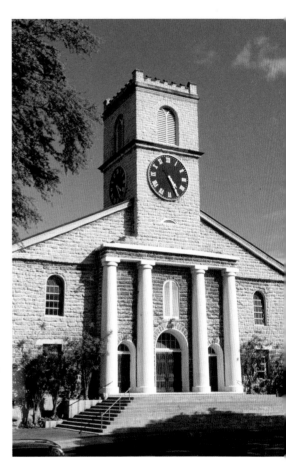

"[In Honolulu] I have had more fun and pleasure of my life these last months than ever before."

Letter from Robert Louis Stevenson, March 1889

Pancho Villa's House

(Chihuahua, Mexico)

Home of the legendary folk hero

The sprawling city of Chihuahua lies in the north of Mexico below the Mexican–U.S. border and in the middle of the desertlike state of Chihuahua. Founded in 1709 by the Spanish, the city has a rich history within Mexico's long, turbulent struggle for independence.

It was during the Mexican Revolution of 1910 to 1917 that Chihuahua became famous thanks to the indomitable Mexican hero Pancho Villa (1878–1923). Born Doroteo Arango Arámbula, his peasant family placed him in an orphanage. As a teenager he killed a man who had raped his sister and fell in with a group of bandits; around this time he changed his name to

> *"Now the Carranzistas beat it/Because Villa's men are coming."*
>
> **Mexican folk song, *La Cucaracha***

Pancho Villa. He has been likened to the folk hero Robin Hood, with tales of his taking from the rich and giving to the poor. After moving to Chihuahua, Villa turned from bandit to revolutionary, supporting Francisco Ignacio Madero (1873–1913) against Porfirio Díaz's (1830–1915) dictatorship. He had a colorful and violent military career, opposing later Mexican leaders, and eventually the United States. In 1920, he "retired" to the home in Chihuahua from where he had planned his attacks, having negotiated a peace agreement with President Huerta (1881–1955). He was assassinated three years later while driving to a baptism.

Villa's house, La Quinta Luz, is now a museum, and remains much as it was, having been preserved by his widow, Luz Corral. The exhibits include the bullet-hole-riddled vehicle in which he died. **TP**

Real de Catorce

(near Matehuala, Mexico)

Unspoiled mountain town

The town of Real de Catorce can be found at the heart of Mexico in one of the most beautiful and highest mountain plateau areas. The small town clings to the mountainside in northwestern San Luis Potosí, with stunning views across the panoramic lowlands, and the location is particularly famed for its breathtaking sunsets. The landscape, wild with large wooded areas and great tracts of desert, is a place that inspires dreams. Perhaps fittingly, the desert is home to peyote cactus, a source of the hallucinogen mescaline.

The Spanish officially founded the town around 1638, and up until the mid-1740s the site was subject to various attacks from Comanche Indians. Real de Catorce's fortunes changed about 1772 when silver was discovered in the area and a number of mines quickly opened. The town rapidly expanded and the economy boomed, which was reflected in the architecture and development of the place, the center of which was rebuilt in 1888. Toward the end of the nineteenth century, a long tunnel was dug to the north, and this now forms the main entryway to the town. During the Mexican Revolution (1910–21), Real de Catorce was virtually abandoned and almost became a ghost town. Latterly, the population has increased with the economy based primarily on tourism and its frequent use as a Hollywood film location. It is also a place of pilgrimage and a center for ceremonial, spiritual gatherings based on the beliefs of the Huichole Indians. Many of these revolve around the sacred and hallucinogenic peyote cactus.

Real de Catorce is a deeply moving place with a fascinating history. The town remains largely as it was in its prime and is essentially untarnished by the trappings of tourism. This, combined with the sublimity of its location, evokes stirrings of spirituality in all but the most blasé of visitors. **TP**

Zacatecas Cathedral

(Zacatecas, Mexico)

Magnificent example of Churrigueresque architecture

Zacatecas is Mexico's second-highest city. Its elevation gives it fantastic views across the land that unfolds beneath, and the location dictated the narrow, winding streets around which the city grew. At the center is the city's true jewel, the cathedral—one of the finest examples of the Spanish–Mexican Baroque (Churrigueresque) style of architecture.

Zacatecas developed on the strength of the silver found in its area. It was officially settled by the Spanish around 1546, after which a huge vein of silver was uncovered and several mines soon opened, including the famous El Edén Mine, which was productive until the middle of the twentieth century. The city flourished, and grand colonial buildings, elaborate houses, churches, and civic structures were erected. Zacatecas has retained much of its historic charm, and the softly colored stone buildings, ornate ironwork, and winding cobbled streets contribute to its appeal.

Standing on the Plaza Hidalgo, the cathedral architecturally dominates the town. The original building was started around 1612, on the site of a former church, but it was completely rebuilt from around 1707 to appear as it does today. The cathedral has three facades, of which the main one is the most decorative and richly ornate, and has carved images of Christ and the apostles and God surrounded by angels making music. To add to its magnificence, the building was constructed with pink cantera stone, which changes color from pink to golden ocher as the bright Mexican sun streams across it.

In recognition of its harmonious design and the Baroque profusion of its facades, where European and indigenous decorative elements are found side by side, the city center was designated a UNESCO World Heritage site in 1993, and it is one of the essential places to visit in Mexico. **TP**

"*[The cathedral] is notable for its harmonious design and the Baroque profusion of its facades*"

UNESCO

El Edén Mine (Zacatecas, Mexico)

Former heart of the world's silver mining industry

North-central Mexico is home to Zacatecas, a small and beautiful Spanish colonial town in the state of the same name, which formed the hub of Mexico's vast silver industry. It is a precipitous and rocky area with the Sierra Madre Occidental mountain range covering the west of the state, the town being situated at a high altitude. It is home to numerous historic buildings and a labyrinth of cobbled streets, and was built into the sides of a steep valley, with stunning views across the countryside.

Spanish conquistadors, who discovered the rich veins of silver in the surrounding hillsides, founded Zacatecas in 1546. Forty years later the El Edén Mine was opened, and was kept in active service until 1960. Although silver is most commonly associated with the area, the mine also produced gold and minerals such as copper, zinc, iron, and lead. It is thanks chiefly to the El Edén Mine and others in the area that Mexico became the world's largest silver producer, and it was the wealth generated through this industry that escalated the growth and development of the country. The El Edén Mine was eventually dug down to seven levels—the conditions for miners were appalling and their life expectancy was greatly truncated. Today, part of the mine is open for guided tours and visitors can experience something of the miners' working environment from the past. Levels five to seven have now been flooded, and the tours are conducted through level four, which is accessed by a train journey through a long, dark tunnel.

The El Edén Mine was one of the most important and productive mines during the sixteenth and seventeenth centuries, and had one of the longest histories for a working mine. It is also in a particularly stunning location, and combined with the historic town of Zacatecas is one of the essential Mexican sites to experience. **TP**

> *"Thousands of laborers lost their lives either quickly in a missed step or slowly in the backbreaking toil."*
>
> Doreen Stevens, travel writer

Alhóndiga de Granaditas (Guanajuato City, Mexico)

Location of catalyst event in Mexico's battle for independence

Set into the hilly terrain of bustling Guanajuato City, the Alhóndiga de Granaditas is a large, rectangular, Neoclassical building with an unadorned exterior. Although it has the appearance of a fortification, its original function was as a granary and trading center for grains.

It was built between 1798 and 1809 and consists of plain, thick stone walls with small windows on the upper level, and just two doors, a small one facing east and the larger main entrance to the north. Inside the granary is an attractive central courtyard, with two staircases leading to the first floor. From the outside the Alhóndiga appears all but impenetrable, and it was this that led the Spanish to shelter here during the early days of the Mexican War of Independence. However, it was the building's wooden doors that would prove catastrophic. Mexican insurgents struggling for their freedom from Spanish colonial rule and guided by the priest Miguel Hidalgo stormed Guanajuato City in 1810. The Spanish Royalists fled to the Alhóndiga, but a local Mexican miner, "El Pípila," tied a stone to his back to protect himself from missiles and rushed to the east door of the building, setting it on fire. The insurgents then poured into the Alhóndiga and massacred those sheltering within. After taking control of the city they marched toward Mexico City, but four of the movement's leaders—Hidalgo, Ignacio Allende, Juan Aldama, and José Mariano Jiménez—were captured and beheaded. As retribution their heads were hung from each corner of the Alhóndiga building as a warning to other revolutionaries.

The plain exterior of this building hides its rather beautiful interior architecture, and belies its bloody past. It is a key site within Mexican history, denoting the bravery of a small group struggling for freedom, and this has been preserved through the conversion of the building into a fascinating museum. **TP**

"Aun hay otras Alhóndigas por incendiar—There are still other Alhóndigas to burn."

Inscription at foot of El Pípila's statue

Juárez Theater

(Guanajuato City, Mexico)

Majestic landmark building in a historic city

The historic city of Guanajuato was founded in the sixteenth century by Spanish conquistadors, who discovered silver in the area. Guanajuato (known as "Place of Frogs" in a local indigenous language) became one of the leading and richest producers of silver and other minerals, its early economic growth being reflected in the grand colonial, Neoclassical, and Baroque style of its architecture.

In 1872, the governor of the state of Guanajuato, General Florencio Antillón, announced plans to build a lavish theater in the town, in honor of his friend the President Benito Juárez (1806–72). Architect José Noriega was commissioned to build the theater on the site of an old monastery and next to the Church of San Pedro Alcantará, and he used elements of the church's ground plan in his design. Work stopped in 1877 when followers of President Porfirio Díaz usurped Antillón from power.

In 1891 work began again, this time under the Díaz administration, and the architect Antonio Rivas Mercado was commissioned to finish the building, giving it its opulent and eclectic look. Díaz opened the theater—named after his political rival—in 1903 to a performance of Giuseppe Verdi's *Aida*. The Neoclassical facade is most striking, particularly the bronze statues lining the portico and bronze lions flanking the entrance. The statues were created by U.S. sculptor W. H. Mullins of Salem, Ohio, who is famous as the designer of the deer that was used by the John Deere tractor company as its logo.

Juárez Theater—with its extravagant architecture and interesting history—is just one of the many magnificent buildings still standing in the historic city of Guanajuato. The city is also well known as the birthplace of Diego Rivera (1886–1957), one of Mexico's best-loved painters. **TP**

Pyramid of Quetzalcóatl

(near Tula, Mexico)

Temple of the feathered serpent god

This great temple—known as "Pyramid B" to archeologists and commonly associated with the feathered serpent god, Quetzalcóatl—is perhaps the most impressive building of the ancient remains at Tula. Built on a limestone ridge, this site is thought to be that of the great capital of the Toltec people, Tollan. Many believe that this was one of the major urban centers of Mesoamerica, flourishing in the ninth and tenth centuries C.E., spreading across an area of around 5 square miles (13 sq km) with a population of 30,000 to 50,000 people. The temple—the ceremonial heart of Tula—is positioned along one side of a large public

> *"All the glory to the godhead/ Had the prophet Quetzalcóatl: All the honor of the people."*
>
> Song dedicated to Quetzalcóatl

plaza. Quetzalcóatl was a major deity in the ancient Americas, worshipped by the Maya and Aztecs, as well as the Toltecs, and seemingly associated at Tula with the morning and evening star.

The sides of this five-stepped pyramid were clad with highly decorative sculptural friezes featuring imagery common to the ancient Americas, such as jaguars, serpents, and eagles. Most striking, however, are the giant warrior figures standing to attention across the temple's summit. These figures and the pyramid—along with the other buildings at Tula—would have once been painted in vivid colors, making the capital a breathtaking sight. Such glories were relatively short-lived, however, as Tula was apparently destroyed in the mid-twelfth century, probably by the Chichimec people. **AK**

La Valenciana Silver Mine

(Guanajuato City, Mexico)

Mine that for 250 years produced a third of the world's silver

The historic, beautiful city of Guanajuato with its mines is the capital of Guanajuato state and clings to the sheer slopes of the Sierra de Guanajuato mountains, approximately 220 miles (355 km) northwest of Mexico City. The town originally developed alongside the River Guanajuato, and ascends steeply up into the mountain in a series of narrow streets, brick stairways, and bridges. Periodically the river would flood the town and in the 1960s it was dammed to prevent further damage. What was once the old riverbed is now a unique subterranean street that allows traffic to pass beneath the city.

The development of Guanajuato City and its fabulous wealth was sparked by the discovery of silver in 1558. By the end of the eighteenth century, the phenomenal amounts of silver being mined had turned Guanajuato into one of the largest silver producers in the world, with the La Valenciana Mine being the most productive. The wealth generated by this industry can be seen in the elaborate buildings of the city, such as the colonial mansions, churches, and theaters, many of which are painted in warm yellows, pinks, and ochers. Close to the La Valenciana Mine is the La Valenciana Church, built by the owner of the silver mine, as the legend goes, to express his gratitude for the mine's success, or as atonement for the exploitation of the miners. It was completed in 1788. The pink cantera stone building is one of the city's most impressive structures, and is a fine example of Churrigueresque Baroque architecture.

The La Valenciana Mine is still active, although the original entrance has been turned into a museum. This is a site of enormous importance because the revenue sparked by the mine largely supported the Spanish Empire and its colonies, and it is located within a city that some argue is the country's most beautiful. **TP**

> *"[Silver mining made] Old Mexico, or New Spain, the brightest jewel in the Spanish crown."*
>
> Philip Wayne Powell, historian

Teotihuacán

(San Juan, Mexico)

Impressive and mysterious ruins of an ancient Mesoamerican city

Lying 25 miles (40 km) north of Mexico City is the site of Teotihuacán, which was once home to an ancient city. Teotihuacán was inhabited from *c.* 200 B.C.E., and had become an economic, political, religious, and trade center by 150 C.E. At its peak from 200 to 400, it was inhabited by 150,000 to 250,000 people, contained 2,000 buildings, and covered more than 11.5 square miles (30 sq km), making it the largest city in the Americas and one of the biggest in the ancient world. The Aztecs gave the city its name—meaning "the place where the gods were created"—but archeologists are unsure which race of people actually founded it; it has been suggested it was the Totonacs.

The vast site is home to the third-largest pyramid in the world, the 215-foot- (65-m-) high Pyramid of the Sun built *c.* 100 C.E. The stepped pyramid is linked by a central avenue, Avenue of the Dead, to the slightly smaller Pyramid of the Moon. Both structures are thought to have been painted red, and would have dominated the city's skyline. The street is flanked by temples and palaces, such as the Palace of the Jaguars with its murals of jaguars in feathered headdresses, and the Palace of the Quetzal with its carved pillars depicting a creature that is half bird, half butterfly.

The city of Teotihuacán fell into disuse *c.* 700 when it was decimated by fire, perhaps the result of an invasion from the rival Toltecs, or even internal unrest. Current opinion leans toward the latter theory, given that it is thought locals had already started to leave the city *c.* 650, possibly because drought and overexploitation of the surrounding agricultural area had depleted the natural resources available. It also appears that many of the structures damaged by fire were civic buildings or those used by the upper classes, which may have become the target of an unruly, and possibly hungry, populace. **CK**

> *"A timeless place, as if it existed from time immemorial and would exist into eternity, outside of history."*
>
> Esther Pasztory, historian

Chapultepec Castle

(Mexico City, Mexico)

Symbol of Mexico's fight for independence

Chapultepec Castle surveys Mexico City from the top of Chapultepec Hill, and sits at one end of the Paseo de la Reforma, a straight 7.5-mile- (12-km-) long avenue. It forms part of Chapultepec Park, an area of forests, lakes, memorials, and museums that was settled around the fourth century. The hill itself, which offers a natural vantage point, was the site of a succession of castles dating back to the pre-Columbian era, prior to the construction of the present one.

The Spanish Viceroy Bernardo de Gálvez commissioned the opulent Baroque castle in 1785. However, the death of the project's engineer and other compounding factors led to the building later being sold to the City of Mexico in 1806. The castle was abandoned at the beginning of the Mexican War of Independence (1810–21), and stood empty until 1833 when it was modified and opened as a military academy. It gained national fame in 1847 when six young army cadets defended it against U.S. Marines during the Mexican-American War of 1846 to 1848, and died in the process. A marble monument near the castle commemorates their heroism.

In 1862 the French, under Napoleon III, invaded Mexico, and two years later Maximilian of Habsburg was crowned Emperor Maximilian of Mexico with his wife, the empress Carlota. They renovated the castle, giving it a Neoclassical finish with strong European detailing. After the fall of the empire in 1867, Chapultepec Castle became a military site before becoming the presidential residence, which is how it remained until 1939 when it became the National Museum of History.

The beautifully restored castle, whose tumultuous past played an important part in Mexican history, is fittingly now devoted to preserving that very history within its capacity as a museum. **TP**

Rivera and Kahlo Studio

(Mexico City, Mexico)

Studio-house of the bohemian artist duo

These brightly painted buildings in the San Angel suburb of Mexico City may seem mundane to the casual observer, but they are important to modern Mexico both for their one-time inhabitants and for their architectural style. The on-off love story of artists and communists Frida Kahlo (1907–54) and Diego Rivera (1886–1957) led to their marriage, divorce, and remarriage, and a turbulent lifestyle. Their romance was at its peak when their friend, the painter and architect Juan O'Gorman, built the structures in 1931.

This was a time when Mexico was keen to establish itself as a modern country with its own

> *"Diego and Frida had open house. . . . There was nothing [they] wouldn't give you."*
>
> Louise Nevelson, artist

identity that no longer looked to Old Europe. Kahlo and Rivera's art was symptomatic of that identity, with its references to the history of its indigenous peoples. So, too, the reinforced concrete structure of the couple's home with its functional style influenced by the French Modernist architect Le Corbusier.

Completed in 1932, the house-studio was the couple's home until they separated in 1934. The large, pink building was Rivera's studio, whereas the smaller blue-and-white one was Kahlo's, and became the salon of Mexico's avant-garde. The studios are linked by a bridge at roof level, so the couple could see each other but have the space to work independently.

Rivera's studio remains largely as it was at his death, with paints, easels, carved wooden masks, and even a denim jacket hung on a coat rack. **CK**

Basilica of Our Lady of Guadalupe (Mexico City, Mexico)

Popular pilgrimage site of revered patron saint of Latin America

Just north of Mexico City, on Tepeyac Hill, lies Latin America's most important Roman Catholic pilgrimage center, the Basilica of Our Lady of Guadalupe. The church was built from 1531 to 1709. Next to the church sits a newer one built in the 1970s because the older church was subsiding. This is the second-most visited pilgrimage site for Roman Catholics after the Vatican in Rome, and the modern basilica is large enough to seat 10,000 worshippers.

The old basilica commemorates a vision to Juan Diego (1474–1548) of the Virgin Mary in 1531. Diego was a poor Indian and Catholic convert. In his vision the Virgin Mary spoke to him in his native language, Nahuatl, and told him that a church should be built on Tepeyac Hill. Diego informed the local bishop, Fray Juan de Zumárraga, who was loath to believe him, and prayed that God would give him a sign as affirmation of the story. Three days later, Diego's uncle was dying

and Diego went in search of a priest to deliver the last rites. The Virgin Mary appeared to him again and told him that his uncle had recovered. She told Diego to gather flowers from the hill and, although it was winter, Diego found flowers, including roses, which he presented to the bishop. As he did so, the roses fell from Diego's cloak, leaving behind a permanent imprint of the image of the Virgin Mary. This time, the bishop believed Diego, and the church was then built to house Diego's cloak, which became a holy relic.

Diego was beatified as a saint in 2002, although he remains a controversial figure, with some skeptics doubting his existence. This is partly because of the lack of documentation affirming Diego's existence, and partly because the story of the vision enabled the Catholic Church to convert the locals. Nonetheless, Our Lady of Guadalupe has become an iconic symbol of national identity for Mexico and its people. **CK**

 ◈ **National Palace** (Mexico City, Mexico)

One of the Mexican nation's most important public buildings

The National Palace is in Mexico City on the Plaza de la Constitución, the second-largest public square in the world, after Moscow's Red Square. Commonly known as El Zócalo—meaning "base" or "plinth"—the square has been at the epicenter of the city since the time of the Aztecs; it was home to several temples and palaces built during the reign of Moctezuma I (1440–69).

Built in 1692, the building was declared the National Palace in 1821 after the Mexican War of Independence (1810–21) against Spain. During the Mexican-U.S. War (1846–48), the military governor of Mexico City, General John Anthony Quitman, became the only U.S. citizen to rule from the palace. It is now home to the offices of the Mexican president, the National Archives, and the Federal Treasury. It also houses a vivid historical mural, depicting the Spanish Conquest of 1520 and Mexico's subsequent struggle for independence, by the painter Diego Rivera.

Above the main gate is the bell rung by the priest Miguel Hidalgo (1753–1811) in 1810 when he gave his *Grito de Dolores* (Cry of Dolores), proclaiming Mexico's independence. He led a 200,000-strong army that marched on Mexico City to attack the Spanish. Hidalgo was executed and is now seen as the father of the Mexican nation. Every September, on the anniversary of Hidalgo's call to arms, locals gather in the square to hear the Mexican president repeat Hidalgo's words: "Mexicans, long live Mexico!" **CK**

> *"[Rivera's] mural is alive with the artist's sweeping defiance and impatience and fury."*

Catherine Keenan, writer

🏛 ◉ Templo Mayor

(Mexico City, Mexico)

Ancient pyramid–temple of the Aztec Empire

"Never was there seen, nor heard, nor even dreamt, anything like that which we then observed."

Bernal Díaz del Castillo, on Tenochtitlán

The archeological site of the Templo Mayor, or the Great Pyramid of Tenochtitlán, is located just off Mexico City's Plaza de la Constitución, also known locally as El Zócalo and one of the city's busiest areas. Remains of the temple were first unearthed in 1978, and since then the area has been excavated. In 1987 a museum was built on the site to store and exhibit the many artifacts uncovered there.

The area has been key to Mexico City's history, and the temple was one of the first sights to greet the Spanish leader of the conquistadors, Hernán Cortés (1485–1547), when he arrived at what was then the Aztec city of Tenochtitlán in 1519. Cortés and his fellow conquistadors had destroyed most of the temple by 1521, after the Spanish Conquest of Mexico.

The temple was first built in 1390, but was rebuilt seven times and enlarged eleven times. It is thought to have been the city's most important building, and is believed to have been a symbolic representation of Coatepec Hill where—according to myth—the god of war and principal Aztec deity, Huitzilopochtli, was born. The 197-foot- (60-m-) high, pyramid-shaped structure had two stairways that allowed access to the summit where there were two shrines, one to the god of water, Tlaloc, and the other to Huitzilopochtli. It would originally have been covered with stucco and polychrome decoration.

Templo Mayor served a number of functions: It is where the Aztecs performed various rites and practiced human sacrifices, including autosacrifices. The latter were regarded as ritual offerings whereby individuals pierced parts of their own bodies, such as an earlobe or tongue, using agave needles or pieces of bone. It is also where the remains of heroic warriors and citizens of high standing were cremated in funerary rituals that may have lasted several days. **CK**

Trotsky's House

(Mexico City, Mexico)

Residence of the Russian revolutionary in exile

Central and South America have long been popular destinations for Europe's political fugitives. For postwar Nazis it would be Argentina, but for Leon Trotsky (1879–1940) it was Mexico. In a story that might be considered too full of drama even for Hollywood, the great architect of the 1917 Russian Revolution would end his days in a quiet, elegant neighborhood of Mexico City. It was there, on August 20, 1940, that he was murdered by Ramón Mercader, a Stalinist agent posing as the author of a pamphlet advocating Trotskyite ideas. Mercader drove the pick of an ice ax through the famous exile's head. It was a gritty end to a life that had never been short of incident.

Trotsky was the intellectual powerhouse behind the Russian Revolution. His relationship with Lenin was fraught but, together, they managed to end the tsarist regime in their country. Trotsky, often disliked by those who perceived arrogance in his sharp, scholarly manner, hoped to take over the leadership of the Communist Party after Lenin's death in 1927. He was, however, not much of a political manipulator and he was easily outmaneuvered by the brutal Stalin.

Trotsky was sent into exile by Stalin in 1929. He lived in Turkey, France, and Norway before arriving in Mexico in 1936. He was warmly welcomed there by President Lázaro Cárdenas, who made special arrangements for his relocation to Mexico City. Trotsky ran with a bohemian crowd, and even lived for a time with the celebrated artists Diego Rivera and Frida Kahlo. In 1939, Trotsky, who by this point had fallen out with Rivera, moved into his own house—known as "the little fortress"—in Coyoacán, a neighborhood peppered with colonial churches and cobblestone streets. It was here that he died. Today, it is a museum, and the bullet holes of an earlier assassination attempt on Trotsky can be seen in the walls of the house. **OR**

San Juan de Ulúa

(Veracruz, Mexico)

Fortress guarding New Spain's treasures

San Juan de Ulúa is an extensive fortress overlooking the city of Veracruz. The fortress was established to protect Veracruz, which was the most important port in Mexico under Spanish rule. Veracruz was founded by conquistador Hernán Cortés (1485–1547), the first Spanish governor of Mexico, in 1519. The port was used to load the annual Spanish fleet with bullion from the Mexican silver mines, and therefore was a target for piracy.

A fortress was constructed on the nearby island of San Juan de Ulúa from 1565. It was a formidable structure, protected by 250 cannons, moats, parapets,

> *"The Indians came on board. They brought presents of fruits and flowers and ornaments of gold."*

William Prescott, historian

and 3-foot- (1-m-) thick walls. In 1568, the English naval adventurers Sir Francis Drake (1540–96) and Sir John Hawkins (1532–95) attempted to unload slaves at San Juan de Ulúa. Although they had been granted a temporary truce, they were attacked by a Spanish convoy and lost all but two ships.

San Juan de Ulúa was the last bastion of Spanish power in Mexico. After Mexico declared independence on September 16, 1810, Spanish forces clung on at the fortress until 1825. During the Mexican–American War (1846–48), U.S. forces bombarded the fortress and took Veracruz. From the nineteenth century, the fortress was used as a prison. Perhaps its most famous prisoner was the bandit Jesús Arriaga (b. 1858), also known as Chucho El Roto, who escaped from the prison in 1885. **JF**

El Tajín
(near Papantla, Mexico)

Capital of the Totonac state and center for an ancient Mesoamerican sport

The Mexican state of Veracruz spreads along the central east coast of the country and is an area of outstanding natural beauty. In the middle of the state is the town of Papantla, outside of which are the remains of the ancient city of El Tajín.

Much of the area has yet to be excavated and the parts that have been uncovered have suffered from plundering. However, it is one of the most fascinating pre-Columbian finds and has a number of unusual and monumental structures. It was originally the capital of the Totonac state and would have been a thriving city during its peak, between 800 and 1150. After this period, the city gradually declined until it was sacked and burned at the beginning of the thirteenth century by warring nomadic Chichimeca peoples. A small population stayed, but it was completely abandoned when the Spanish arrived in the sixteenth century.

The most impressive structure at the site is the Pyramid of Niches. This ceremonial building, which originally had a small temple on top, is a stepped pyramid with six terraces that form 365 niches. It is a masterpiece of Mesoamerican architecture, revealing the astronomical and symbolic significance of the site. The city was famous for its ball games, and there are seventeen ball courts in all at the site. The games were steeped in lavish tradition and extravagance, although nothing is known of their specific rules.

The clues that El Tajín holds to the ancient cultures of Mexico are invaluable. It is a place that resounds with history, and walking along the old streets is a moving and faintly eerie experience. **TP**

◸ The site is called Tajín after one of the names of the Totonac god of thunder, lightning, and rain.

◁ Rituals of human sacrifice often accompanied the ball games at the site, as this stone relief illustrates.

Church of Santa Prisca

(Taxco, Mexico)

Baroque church built on the silver trade

The Church of Santa Prisca is truly the jewel in the crown of Taxco, an old and charming town that was built on the strength of its silver mines. Taxco clings to the steep sides of the western reaches of the Sierra Madre del Sur mountain range, and is made up of winding, narrow cobbled streets lined with rustic whitewashed houses and mellow stone buildings. The town is picturesque and the views are stunning, but it is the Church of Santa Prisca that makes it such a compelling site to visit.

The conquistador Hernán Cortés (1485–1547) and his followers first discovered and settled the area, and began to start mining the silver. The town grew around this industry, but the mines were quickly depleted. Two hundred years later the Frenchman Don José de la Borda traveled to Taxco to join his brother and, as legend has it, his horse struck a rock with its hoof, dislodging it and revealing silver beneath. This vein of silver proved to be huge and the town once again thrived as a mining area, with Don José reaping the financial benefits. He was a deeply religious man and applied for permission to build a church, agreeing to completely fund the construction providing he was given free rein in the design. Don José's ambitious project took seven years to complete, and the lavish Mexican Baroque architecture and opulent interior nearly bankrupted him. Eventually, in time, the silver reserves once more dried up and the mines closed, although the town remains a center for silver jewelry trading.

The Church of Santa Prisca, built on the back of the silver industry, is a permanent reminder of the town's changing fortunes and the vision of one extraordinary man. Its soft pink stone exterior, nine altars, and magnificent decorative scheme make it one of Mexico's most striking churches. **TP**

San Diego Fort

(Acapulco, Mexico)

Main defense of a key shipping center

San Diego Fort defended the port of Acapulco from its construction in the early seventeenth century. Acapulco was a crucial shipping center because it was the embarking point for the annual "Manila Galleon," which ran from 1565 until 1815. For centuries, these ships provided the only direct and reliable trade link between Asia and the Americas.

Acapulco had been a settlement since the Bronze Age, but it was first claimed by Spain in 1528. Located on the Pacific coast, it was the center of Spanish attempts to find a route to Asia. In 1565 Andrés de Urdaneta (1498–1568) found a route from Manila to

> *"Acapulco and her land … where the ships of the south will be built."*
>
> **Spanish Royal decree, 1528**

Acapulco. As a result, Acapulco grew rich, but this attracted attention from buccaneers. In 1587 the English navigator Sir Thomas Cavendish (1555–92) captured a Spanish galleon holding 1.2 million gold pesos. In 1615, after an invasion by a Dutch fleet, the Spanish Viceroy Diego Fernández de Cordoba (1578–1630) commissioned a new modern fort. Located on a hill overlooking the port, it took the shape of a five-pointed star. When it was built, it was the largest fort on the Pacific coast. The fort was nearly destroyed by an earthquake in 1776, but was rebuilt.

The fort now houses Acapulco's History Museum. San Diego Fort is renowned as an example of early modern fort building, and as the main defense of Acapulco—one of the most important ports in the world for more than 200 years. **JF**

Benito Juárez's House (Oaxaca City, Mexico)

Childhood home of a groundbreaking president and national hero

The city of Oaxaca was founded in 1532 in the beautiful Valley of Oaxaca in the Sierra Madre del Sur Mountains by Spanish settlers. The area had been inhabited for many thousands of years prior to this, and close to the city is the ancient pre-Columbian site of Monte Albán. In the city is a small building with brightly colored, thick stone walls. This is the house where Benito Juárez (1806–72), one of Mexico's greatest presidents, spent much of his early life.

Benito Juárez was a Zapotec—one of the indigenous peoples of Mexico—and was born in the village of San Pablo Gueletao. When he was twelve years old, he moved to the city of Oaxaca to find work. There he met Don Antonio Maza, a wealthy citizen who was employing his sister as a servant, and through Maza was introduced to Antonio Salanueva. Salanueva, a devout Catholic, was greatly impressed by Juárez's intelligence and took him in, teaching him to speak Spanish and to read and write. Juárez later abandoned Catholicism and went on to study law before becoming mayor of Oaxaca, senator for Oaxaca, and eventually president of Mexico in 1860. Juárez's period of presidency is called La Reforma (the Reform) based on his system of progressive reforms that, among others, pushed for equal rights for indigenous peoples and sought to reduce the power of the Catholic Church and military in Mexico. His democratic, liberal stance and struggle for equality was partly based on the politics of North America.

The house is now a museum devoted to the great president, and includes furniture and objects from Juárez's time spent living with Antonio Salanueva. **TP**

◩ Portrait of Benito Juárez, the only full-blooded indigenous national to become president of Mexico.

◪ Juárez lived in this house for ten years from December 1818, along with his sister and Don Antonio Maza.

🏛 ◎ Monte Albán (near Oaxaca, Mexico)

The Zapotec capital and one of the earliest cities in Mesoamerica

"Imagine a great isolated hill at the junction of three broad valleys; an island rising nearly a thousand feet from the green sea of fertility beneath it. An astonishing situation." Aldous Huxley wrote this stirring description of Monte Albán—site of the ancient Zapotec capital—in 1934. It still seems extraordinary today that anyone would build a city on top of a mountain, but the Zapotecs were highly advanced in their technical skills, and Monte Albán seems a fittingly breathtaking symbol of their sophistication—even if they did have to flatten a peak and drag supplies and water up from the valley below. The site offers stunning views over the Oaxaca Valley and is best viewed bathed in late afternoon sun.

What remains today is the city's religious and political nerve center. The platforms, pyramids, and sweeping staircases are typical of Zapotec architecture. At the site's heart, a grand central plaza opens out spectacularly. At one end, commanding incredible views, is the huge, many-stepped pyramid called the Southern Platform. At the other end looms the North Platform temple complex, which includes an enclosed altar and fascinating reliefs. An observatory used to observe the skies and time religious rituals is located at the center of the main plaza, and on the plaza's eastern edge is a ball court. On the plaza's west flank lie more platform buildings and reliefs depicting mysterious dancing figures.

Monte Albán seems to have been deserted after 700, when it began to decay. It was then used by the Mixtec peoples, mostly as a royal burial ground, until the Spanish conquest of the 1500s. **AK**

⬈ The city's observatory, shown in the foreground, reflects the use of astronomy in Zapotec religion.

⬈ Violent ball games, much loved by the ancient Mesoamericans, were played in the ball court.

◉ # Palenque (Santo Domingo del Palenque, Mexico)

Ancient Mayan city abandoned in the ninth century

> *"Palenque is an incomparable achievement of Mayan art."*
>
> UNESCO

Palenque is widely regarded as one of the best-preserved examples of a Classical period Mayan sanctuary, and it is remarkable for the quality and profusion of its art and architecture. It is a relatively small city, compared with Copán and Tikal, but it seems to have been the capital of the surrounding Mayan state. The site is still being researched by archeologists, but it is at least 1,600 years old, with inscriptions recording the reign of a king in the early fifth century. It underwent a period of growth during the fifth and sixth centuries before being ransacked on several occasions by nearby cities at the start of the seventh century. These defeats seem to have prompted a wave of reconstruction under a new, powerful leader, Pakal the Great, and it is thought that most of the temples and structures still standing today date from this period. Palenque began to decline around 711, when it was again defeated and ransacked by a rival city, and suffered further defeats over the next century. It had been completely abandoned for several centuries by the time it was discovered in the 1560s by Spanish explorers.

Palenque's central plaza is a considerable engineering achievement, being built directly over the Otulum River, which was redirected through a 165-foot-(50-m-) long vaulted roof canal. Surrounding this public space is the Palace—a complex of interconnected buildings and temples, each positioned at the top of a traditional step pyramid and decorated with a wealth of devotional carvings. Arguably the most important of these buildings is the Temple of the Inscriptions, which contains one of the longest Mayan inscriptions in Central America, chronicling around 180 years of Palenque's history. As well as this wealth of historical information, the temple contains intricate carvings of deities and kings, and the tomb and ornately carved sarcophagus of Pakal the Great himself. **CK**

Catedral de San Ildefonso (Mérida, Mexico)

Colonial cathedral built with the stones of ancient Maya temples

Mérida is the capital of the state of Yucatán in Mexico and is the tenth-oldest city in the country. It was established by Francisco "El Mozo" de Montejo y Léon (1508–65), the son of a Spanish conquistador, on January 6, 1542. Previously the site had been home to a large Maya city known as T'hó that was founded *c.* 1240 by the Maya chief Ah Chan Caan.

The city's cathedral, the Catedral de San Ildefonso, is typical of Mérida, which is also known as The White City, perhaps because of the white facades of some of its buildings. It was the first cathedral built inland in the Americas, and was constructed between *c.* 1556 and 1598 on the east side of Mérida's Plaza Grande.

When the Spanish settlers arrived, they dismantled the existing Maya pyramids and used the large stones to form the foundation of the church. The cathedral was designed by Spanish architect Juan Miguel Aguero in a Renaissance style with two bell towers at the front, and statues of St. Peter and St. Paul at the main entrance. Inside, it has several side chapels, the most notable being the Capilla del Cristo de las Ampollas (Chapel of Christ of the Blisters), which houses a 23-foot- (7-m-) high wooden figure of Christ.

The figure was carved in the 1500s from a tree that was hit by lightning; it burst into flames but did not char. Locals deemed the tree to have miraculous properties, and the wooden figure was placed in a church in the village of Ichmul. When the church burned down, only the Christ figure survived, and it was brought to the cathedral in 1654. The wood was blistered, hence its name. The current figure is a replica of the original that was destroyed in 1915 by revolutionary forces who ransacked the cathedral. The figure has led to the cathedral becoming a pilgrimage site for Roman Catholics, particularly during the Los Gremios religious processions held in September and October, when the figure is carried around Mérida. **CK**

"Wherever Christians have passed, conquering and discovering, it seems as though a fire has gone [too]."

Pedro de Cieza de Léon, conquistador

 ⬡ # Chichén Itzá (Yucatán Peninsula, Mexico)

One of the best-preserved cities of the sophisticated Maya civilization

The vast complex of Chichén Iztá—meaning "at the mouth of the well of the Itzá"—is one of the most notable Maya sites in Mexico's Yucatán Peninsula. It is thought to have been a religious, military, political, and commercial center that at its peak would have been home to 35,000 people. The site first saw settlers in 550, probably drawn there because of the easy access to water in the region via caves and sink holes known as *cenotes*, but it was later abandoned, perhaps because of an invasion by the Toltecs.

The area was settled once more *c*. 1000, before going into decline in the thirteenth century. There is speculation that the city's demise may have been because of famine or a civil war among its inhabitants. The city was also occupied for a short time in 1531, by the Spanish led by conquistador Francisco de Montejo, who intended to make it the Spanish capital of the region, but a native revolt caused the Spanish to flee.

Two of the *cenote* wells still exist at the site. Into these the Maya people would throw offerings of precious items such as pottery, jade, and incense to their rain god, Chaac. During times of drought they may have also made human sacrifices.

The site is known for its well-preserved stone buildings, including The Castle and Temple of the Warriors stepped-pyramids; a large square called the Great Market; the Great Ballcourt with its stone hoops that were used for an ancient ball game; the seat of the ruling government (mistakenly called the Nunnery by the Spanish); and a 74-foot- (22.5-m-) high observatory known as the *Caracol*, or Snail, because of its central domed tower and spiral staircase. The Snail is believed to have been used by the Maya people as an astronomic observatory to chart the heavens and predict when to plant crops, and to decide on the timing of religious ceremonies. **CK**

🏛 ◉ Quiriguá Archeological Park (Izabel, Guatemala)

Maya settlement with some of the world's finest stelae ruins

For some reason, now lost in history, the once-thriving Maya settlement at Quiriguá was abandoned around the tenth century. Until that time, its population lived, worked, and worshipped in an area that is now part of Guatemala. The rulers of Quiriguá became rich from the area's natural resources, the most lucrative of which was jade. The site was rediscovered by Europeans in the eighteenth century and, in the early twentieth century, was bought by the U.S.-owned United Fruit Company. As a result, the ruins, including some of the world's best pre-Columbian stelae, are surrounded by fruit plantations.

The earliest ruins are dated *c.* 550 (although the site was inhabited before then). The name Quiriguá was in existence by the eighth century, and has been found on carvings dating back to that time. Quiriguá had strong links with Copan, in present-day Honduras, and the stonework at both sites exhibits similar attributes. Quiriguá was much smaller than Copan and was therefore considered less important to the Maya world. Copan's dominance over its smaller relation came to an end in the eighth century, however, when its leader was captured by Quiriguá's ruler. The incident earned Quiriguá its independence.

The impressive stone ruins include a plaza around which stand nine ornately carved stelae, the tallest of which is about 36 feet (11 m) tall—26 feet (8 m) of its height projects above ground, whereas the remaining 10 feet (3 m) is buried beneath the earth. Nearby are the remains of a once-mighty pyramid, a ruined acropolis, and stone carvings, believed to have been altars. The stelae and altars are decorated with images of humans (some have beards, an unusual feature in Maya art) and animals, including tortoises, frogs, and jaguars. Quiriguá is famous for its "zoomorphs," depictions of creatures that are part human, part animal. **LH**

  # Tikal (near Flores, Guatemala)

Awe-inspiring ceremonial center of the Maya people

The tips of temple pyramids emerging from a dense canopy of tropical forest hint excitingly at what the great city of Tikal must once have been like. The site was a major urban center of the Maya people, who, with their highly advanced art, architecture, writing, calendars, and astronomical systems created one of the most sophisticated cultures of the ancient Americas. This culture spread across a large swath of Mexico, Guatemala, and Belize, peaking during the region's "classic" era (c. 250–900 C.E.).

Tikal was a very important ceremonial center, with dwellings scattered around its perimeter, although it was also prominent politically and probably controlled the surrounding area. Its ceremonial importance was established around 300 B.C.E. to 100 C.E., when various temples and pyramids were built. From about 600 to 800 C.E., Tikal reached heights that epitomized the Maya's great classic-period achievements. It became

the major center of their steamy southern lowlands, with a prosperous elite class and flourishing artistic life, and at its sacred heart arose complexes of carefully laid-out buildings whose remains are seen today— grand plazas next to stunning palaces, temples, and giant pyramids, all linked by ramps and causeways. There are five huge pyramids, some of which have temples at their apex, such as the Temple of the Jaguar atop "Pyramid I." "Pyramid IV" is the tallest pyramid: Towering over the site at 213 feet (65 m) in height, this was one of the highest buildings of the ancient world. Other remains include tombs, carved stone stelae, water reservoirs, and a possible marketplace. Tikal declined after 800 and faded out in the 900s.

In the 1950s, Tikal National Park was established, and it became a UNESCO World Heritage site in 1979. The remains of a smaller Maya city—Uaxactún—lie around 12 miles (20 km) to the north of Tikal. **AK**

 ⬡ # Casa Popenoe (Antigua, Guatemala)

House in the best-preserved colonial city in Latin America

Once the capital of the Spanish colony of Guatemala, the city of Antigua was designated a UNESCO World Heritage site, being one of the best surviving examples of Spanish Baroque architecture in the Americas. The city—which was built on a grid pattern inspired by the Italian Renaissance—was hit by a devastating earthquake in 1773. Many of the survivors fled to Guatemala City (the present-day capital), although some refused to leave. In time, many of the city's smaller buildings were renovated, although most of the main monuments, such as the huge convents and churches, have been preserved as ruins, being far too costly to rebuild. Despite their ruined state, these buildings still demonstrate their former Spanish colonial grandeur.

Casa Popenoe was built in 1634 by a Spanish nobleman, Don Luis de las Infantas Mendoza. After the earthquake, his house stood empty for a century and a half, until it was bought by a scientist as his family's home. Wilson Popenoe, a North American in Antigua for his job with the U.S.-owned United Fruit Company, bought the house in 1929. He and his wife spent many years and a great deal of money having the house carefully restored to its original seventeenth-century state. Today, their descendants still live in the house, and therefore it is open to the public only for a couple of hours on certain days.

Casa Popenoe is a typically Antiguan house, made of stone and wood. The stone walls and small windows keep the sunlight out, making it cool during sweltering Guatemalan summers. The house is set around a pretty courtyard, replete with brightly colored flowers, a lawn, and idly running water. Large chairs and benches recline around the shady edges of the courtyard. Inside, the house is filled with seventeenth-century art and furniture. **LH**

🏛 ⊚ Church of Our Lady of La Merced (Antigua, Guatemala)

Landmark building of the Spanish colonial city in ruins

The Church of Our Lady of La Merced in Antigua, Guatemala, is all that remains of an enormous religious community, whose buildings were ruined in the devastating earthquake of 1773. The church itself was also damaged, but was subsequently rebuilt and restored. The rest of the buildings, the cloisters, and monastery lie in artistic and evocative ruins all around the church. Today, the ruins are a tourist attraction, famed for their huge fountain—reputedly the largest colonial fountain in Latin America—in the shape of a water lily. It was used by the monks during the seventeenth century as a fish farm in order to keep their table adequately supplied with fresh food.

Visitors cannot fail to be impressed by the intricately ornate moldings on the church's facade, reminiscent of the icing on a wedding cake, as well as its distinctive bright yellow color. Those who look very carefully may be able to discern a nonreligious image worked into the moldings: that of a corn cob, an indication of how important maize was to the Maya people who were hired to work as laborers when the rebuilding work took place. In Guatemala, Catholicism became melded with the local pagan beliefs; many Mayas converted to Catholicism but brought their own interpretation to the religion. This corn cob is a sign of the Maya workers thanking their god for the staple food of their region and perhaps also making a plea for their crops to keep growing. The church had to be restored once again, in the late twentieth century, after the earthquake of 1976, in which 33,000 Guatemalans were killed.

Today, there is frequently a small, local market in the courtyard outside the Church of Our Lady of La Merced. It cannot compare with the huge official market nearby; instead it is a simple collection of makeshift stalls where Maya traders come to sell their vegetables, cooked food, jewelry, and textiles. **LH**

> *"[Antigua is] the most perfect open-air museum of colonial Latin America."*
>
> Pál Kelemen, art historian and archeologist

Remarkable ruined city of the Maya civilization

At the time of the flourishing Maya civilization, the boundaries of what are now known as the countries of Central America were very different from today. The Mayas occupied territories in present-day Mexico, Guatemala, and Honduras, and they left behind some of the most beautiful ancient ruins in the world. Those at Copán, not far from the border between Honduras and Guatemala, are of a settlement that achieved prominence under the fifth-century ruler known as Great Sun Lord Quetzal Macaw (Mah K'ina K'uk Mo'), who was named after two of the area's birds.

The settlement—which is now about a mile outside the town of Copán Ruinas—thrived until the eleventh or twelfth century. Unlike most other former inhabitants of pre-Columbian ruins, the people of Copán were not forced out by the arrival of the Spanish; instead they appear to have moved away at least two centuries prior to the arrival of the conquistadors. Archeologists suggest several theories for why this should have happened, the most widely held being the belief that the land stopped being viable for agriculture. No one has uncovered the original name of this settlement; the name *Copán* dates back only as far as the sixteenth century, and was bestowed upon it by the Spanish settlers.

The site is now run on ecotourism lines. It takes a couple of days to walk around its extent, visiting the ruins of royal homes, middle-class dwellings, servants' quarters, and religious areas. Buried by the Maya beneath the ground lies the uniquely well-preserved, sixth-century Rosalila Temple, with its layers of original paint. Above ground, the temples are decorated with carvings of human faces (some macabre, some humorous), birds, and animals. Today, macaws still fly around the ancient temples and ruined homes, although sadly the quetzal is so endangered that the chances of seeing it are extremely slim. **LH**

"Copán lay before us like a shattered bark in the midst of the ocean."

John Lloyd Stephens, traveler in 1839

Comayagua Cathedral

(Comayagua, Honduras)

Houses the oldest clock in the Americas

Comayagua Cathedral is located in the central plaza of the Honduran town, which is noted for its abundance of Spanish architecture. The cathedral, with its ornate facade, is a fine example of the Spanish colonial style in the New World. However, it is most famed for its clock, which is the oldest in the Americas.

The city of Comayagua was founded by the Spanish on December 8, 1537, and served as the capital of the Honduras district of New Spain from 1540 onward. After Honduras became an independent state in 1838, Comayagua alternated as the capital with Tegucigalpa until 1880, when the latter kept the role permanently.

The construction of Comayagua Cathedral began in 1685, and although it was officially inaugurated on December 8, 1711, it was not fully completed until 1715. Out of the sixteen original altars, only four survive to the present day. The cathedral features one bell tower, with the famous clock located on the third floor. The clock was built by Muslim artisans in southern Spain around 1100, and it rings every fifteen minutes. Its original wooden face was removed as a result of weather damage and replaced with a metal face. The clock, donated by King Philip III of Spain (1578–1621), was installed in Comayagua in 1636 in the city's first cathedral—the Church of Our Lady of La Merced (built 1550–51), which still stands, as do other Spanish colonial structures, including the church of La Caridad and San Francisco, which both date from the later sixteenth century.

Comayagua Cathedral is one of the most important structures in Honduras—a beautiful monument to the nation's Spanish past. The cathedral's clock, which still works today, bridges the wide span of Spanish history—from the era of Moorish conquest to expansion in the Americas. **JF**

Basilica de Suyapa

(Suyapa, Honduras)

Shrine to the national patron saint

This commanding and beautiful basilica, just a few miles from the capital city of Tegucigalpa, dominates the hillside area of Suyapa; its slender square towers and curved domes shoot up through the surrounding greenery announcing the basilica's presence to everyone who comes near. Building work was begun here in 1954, but it seems the basilica may never be completely finished because there is always something more to do. It stands close to the much smaller, nineteenth-century Iglesia de Suyapa, a shrine to the Virgin of Suyapa, the most revered saint not just in this region but in the whole of Honduras.

"The unity that Maria de Suyapa provokes in our people is a strength that we must encourage."

Archbishop of Tegucigalpa

The diminutive statue of the Virgin stands just 2.5 inches (6 cm) tall, but her power is reputed to be prodigious. Large numbers of people who have visited her claim she has worked miracles. The basilica was built so that even more people could benefit from the Virgin's powers; it holds a weeklong celebration dedicated to her every February, and is a place of pilgrimage for Catholics from all over Central America.

The interior of the basilica is decorated with statues, paintings, and giltwork. The famed stained-glass windows disperse brilliantly colored sunlight throughout the interior. During the festival of the Virgin, the area outside the church turns into a fiesta as stallholders sell food, drinks, and religious souvenirs, while people gather patiently in the crowds, waiting for a chance to catch a glimpse of the tiny statue. **LH**

León Viejo

(León, Nicaragua)

Archeological site where Old World meets New World architecture

In the first half of the sixteenth century, Spaniard Francisco Hernández de Córdoba—considered by some to be the founder of Nicaragua—oversaw the building of the city of León. Sited on the shore of Lake Managua, it was well placed for water supplies; however, it also stood in the shadow of the Momotombo volcano. In 1610, the volcano erupted, destroying the city. A new city of León was built about 25 miles (60 km) away and the ruins of León Viejo, or Old León, have since become a tourist attraction.

A Franciscan bishop, Antonio Valdivieso, is credited with bringing Christianity to Nicaragua in the 1540s. The bishop was vocal in upholding the rights of the indigenous people against the Spanish conquistadors and their cruel practices—a stance that led to his murder. For centuries, the whereabouts of his body remained unknown, but in 2000 several tombs were uncovered in the cathedral at León Viejo, one of which is believed to be his; the others are of Franciscan monks. At the time, many people attributed Momotombo's eruption as a reaction to the bishop's brutal murder, and his ghost was said to make regular appearances to the people long after his murder.

León Viejo was a major trading town, popular with gold traders, hence the city was populated with grand buildings. As well as the old cathedral, the ruins include a convent and the old governor's mansion. Although the buildings were almost completely destroyed, the foundations and cellars can still be seen. The crypt at León Viejo also sheltered important archeological finds, including the skeleton of the beheaded Francisco Hernández de Córdoba. The form and nature of early Spanish settlement in the New World, adapting European architectural and planning concepts to the material potential of another region, are uniquely preserved at León Viejo. **LH**

"[H. de Córdoba is] one of the few Spanish conquistadors of whom there are no accounts of atrocities."

Carlos Tunnermann, archeologist

Granada

(Granada, Nicaragua)

Central America's oldest colonial city

Founded in 1524 by Francisco Hernández de Córdoba, Granada in Nicaragua is the oldest colonial city to have been established by the Spanish in Central America. It is important for its rich historic and cultural heritage, which at one point afforded it the moniker "The Jewel of Central America." Granada prospered as a sister city to the impressive colonial center of Antigua, Guatemala. During the colonial era, Nicaragua flourished socially, culturally, and economically. Granada's strategic positioning allowed trade to take place from many different ports simultaneously and it became a center of commerce in the region. At the same time the influx of travelers from both north and south, drawn by its huge colonial influence, enabled the city to thrive.

Granada became so wealthy that it even drew the attention of pirates, privateers, and unofficial military forces. One particular threat came from William Walker (1824–60) in the mid-1850s. He was a U.S. soldier and filibuster who took up residence in Granada, declared himself president, and attempted to gain control of Central America. On failing to do so, he generously decided to set the city ablaze, which destroyed a great deal of the original architecture. To add insult to injury, he reputedly scrawled the words "Granada Was Here" as he abandoned the city. However, Granada was quickly rebuilt and has shown great resilience in the face of continuing adversities.

Today Granada is considered to be one of the most beautiful cities in the whole of Latin America. Its rich colonial heritage has left an indelible mark, in the form of some wonderful colonial-era architecture. Furthermore, there are many museums, galleries, and churches, as well as a large cathedral and Parque Central, where scars from the great fire can still be seen to this day. **KH**

El Castillo

(near San Carlos, Nicaragua)

One of the largest colonial fortresses

The moss-covered fortress El Castillo is situated on the southern shore of the San Juan River in Nicaragua. The fortress was built (1673–75) by the Spanish to guard the confluence between Lake Nicaragua and the San Juan River, and protect Spanish holdings in the region.

At the time of its construction, it was one of the largest fortresses in Central America. It was armed with thirty-two cannons and commanded long views down the river. In addition to its man-made defenses, the waters in front of the fort were shark and crocodile infested. El Castillo was to play an important role in Britain's and Spain's struggle for control of the region.

> "[Nelson's] original force of 200 was swiftly whittled down by disease to only eight men ..."
>
> Edward Marriott, *Wild Shore* (2000)

On July 29, 1762, during the Seven Years' War (1756–63), 2,000 British troops stormed El Castillo. During the fighting the commander of the fortress was killed, but his nineteen-year-old daughter, Rafaela Herrera, took control of the Spanish troops and drove away the British. El Castillo played a part in the early career of Britain's greatest admiral, Horatio Nelson (1758–1805). On April 11, 1780, Nelson launched a surprise attack on El Castillo from land, and captured the fortress. However, he was not able to hold it because he was given no reinforcements or supplies. After nine months the British were forced to leave the fortress.

The fortress of El Castillo continues to loom over the small town that bears its name, demonstrating the former power and glory of the Spanish Empire in the New World. **JF**

Church of Our Lady of the Angels

(Cartago, Costa Rica)

Basilica of Costa Rica's patron saint and the country's most important church

Cartago—the original capital of Costa Rica and now a thriving provincial town—sits in the valley of the Reventazon River, surrounded by the Irazu and Turrialba volcanoes to the north, and the high Cerro de la Muerte and Mount Chirripo to the south. Within the town are two particularly historic churches: the ruins of the first church to be built in Costa Rica and—a few blocks away—the imposing Church of Our Lady of the Angels.

This impressive church is predominantly Byzantine in appearance and has a highly decorative interior. Large stained-glass windows throw sheets of colored light across the equally highly colored tiled floor, and decorated wood columns add to the opulent effect. The church was destroyed in an earthquake in 1926, and was rebuilt as it appears today in 1929. However, it is the story behind this church, rather than its architecture, that makes it so interesting.

According to legend, in 1635 a poor woman called Juana Pereira discovered a stone with an image of a dark-skinned Virgin Mary (*La Negrita* or "the little black one" as the locals named her) lying alongside a path while she was searching for firewood. She took the image home with her, but it disappeared and was found by someone else in the same spot by the path. This happened five times until the locals understood that Our Lady wanted a shrine built there. A shrine was built and it quickly became a place of pilgrimage, especially among the poor. Later, a spring emerged there and its waters were said to have healing powers.

Subsequently, the Church of Our Lady of the Angels was built in 1639, and in 1935 Pope Pius XI declared the shrine a basilica. It continues to be Costa Rica's most important church, and is a place of mass annual pilgrimage to celebrate the appearance of *La Negrita*, who is Costa Rica's patron saint. **TP**

> *"Most holy Mother, send thy angels to defend us and to drive the cruel enemy from us."*
>
> Prayer to Our Lady, Queen of Angels

Panama Canal (near Panama City, Panama)

Separating two continents, joining two oceans, to shorten shipping routes

"The credit belongs to the man whose face is marred by dust and sweat and blood."

Theodore Roosevelt, former U.S. president

⬆ Double gates were installed at the Miraflores Locks, sited where the Panama Canal joins the Pacific Ocean.

➡ Men remove earth from the Cucaracha Slide, a huge landslide caused by heavy rains into the cut channel.

The long, narrow strip of land that is Panama joins together North and South America, and separates the Pacific Ocean to the south from the Caribbean Sea and Atlantic Ocean to the north. The unique location and size of the country make it a natural place for an artificial shipping route, and this was made reality on August 15, 1914, when the Panama Canal was officially opened, with the SS *Ancon* breaking the new waters.

There are three sets of locks along the canal: the Miraflores Locks at the most southerly end, the Pedro Miguel Locks that can just be seen from Miraflores, and the Gatun Locks at the Atlantic end. Miraflores has the tallest lock gates of the three to accommodate the extreme tidal range of the Pacific, and is a two-step lock that covers approximately 1 mile (1.6 km). The lock chambers are monumental concrete structures (built some years before the Hoover Dam) and have to deal with enormous pressures of water, as well as being able to withstand sudden impact in the case of a runaway ship. The consequences of a breach in the gates would be catastrophic, leading to a tidal wave flooding downstream; to prevent this, the gates at both ends of the upper chamber were doubled.

The building and opening of the Panama Canal and its locks was an extraordinary engineering accomplishment, and marked a momentous historic event that changed the shape of shipping and travel. Ships traveling from New York to San Francisco via the canal, for example, now had a journey of less than half the distance required by the previous route around Cape Horn. The building of the canal came at huge human cost, however, with thousands of workers dying from disease and accidents during its construction. Today, more than 14,000 ships pass through the Panama Canal each year. The history of the canal and its locks can be traced at the Miraflores Locks Visitor Center. **TP**

 ⊚ **Old Panama** (Panama City, Panama)

First European settlement on Pacific coast, starting point for expeditions to South America

Built around the entrance to the Panama Canal, Panama City spreads along the Pacific coastline as a glittering mass of skyscrapers and shiny modern architecture—a center of commerce with a rapidly expanding economy. Just a short distance from downtown Panama, however, is a place of an entirely different nature; this is Panama la Vieja, or Old Panama.

Old Panama was the first European settlement on the Pacific coast of the Americas. It is a place of enormous historic interest, reflected in its designation as a UNESCO World Heritage site. The town was founded in 1519 by the Spanish explorer Pedro Arias de Ávila, leader of the first great Spanish expedition to the New World. The city was built on a gridlike plan with a central plaza and the most important buildings facing the shoreline. It was from here that early expeditions traveled to South America, conquering the Inca Empire and establishing gold and silver mines

in Peru. Virtually all the gold and silver leached from South America had to pass back through Old Panama on its way north and to the Portobelo and Nombre de Dios fairs, and the town's extensive colonial buildings were built on the back of this trade. The great quantities of gold in the area attracted hordes of pirates and eventually led to the city's destruction. In 1671, after 150 years of thriving growth, the city was invaded by Henry Morgan, the infamous English pirate, plundering gold and killing those in his way. The powder magazine was set alight, and the whole city was burned and destroyed. The new city was built 2 miles (3 km) to the west and present-day Panama was founded in 1673.

Parts of the old city of Panama remain, with the ruined cathedral and its bell tower among the most impressive of the buildings and a poignant reminder of what Old Panama once was. **TP**

 🏛️ ⦿ **Portobelo** (Colón, Panama)

Once an important port, with fortifications built to protect the Spanish trading routes

In 1502 Christopher Columbus sailed into a beautiful natural harbor on the Caribbean side of Panama. Some ninety years later the spot would become Portobelo, or "beautiful port," and develop into one of Panama's most important trading ports during the seventeenth and eighteenth centuries.

Portobelo was officially founded in 1597, and the site was named San Felipe de Portobelo in honor of King Philip II of Spain. It became the main trading port on the north side of Panama with vast quantities of silver and gold passing through. Such was the extent of the trading at Portobelo that an annual fair was instituted, where merchants could trade over an intense thirty- to sixty-day period and up to seventy boats would sail into port from Spain. The fairs continued until 1738, when they were finally stopped because of constant, bloody attacks from pirates drawn to the vast wealth. The English pirate Henry Morgan attacked the town in 1668, launching a surprise land-based assault and plundering much of the town's wealth after a rampage of murder and rape. Portobelo recovered, but was then taken by the British in 1739 under Admiral Edward Vernon. This led to a change in the Spanish trading routes: Instead of concentrating their fleet and wealth on one or two ports, they started sailing around Cape Horn to use several ports on the west side. As a result, the town fell into gradual decline, which was accelerated by the construction of the Trans-Panama railroad between 1848 and 1855.

Portobelo remains as beautiful as ever, with a number of fascinating historic ruins that bear the scars of its turbulent past. The town was designated a UNESCO World Heritage site in recognition of its supreme importance in Panama's history as an outstanding example of colonial military architecture of this period. **TP**

Castillo de la Real Fuerza

(Havana, Cuba)

Defensive fortress, replacing an earlier fort destroyed by pirates

> *"... our Giraldilla is feminine,*
> *... in profound relationship*
> *with the proximity of the sea."*

Olga López Núñez, art historian

In the sixteenth century, the Spanish-controlled island of Cuba was at the center of a Caribbean plagued by pirates, adventurers, and foreign invaders. The town of Havana and its old fortress, which stood near this site, were attacked several times. In 1555, the Fuerza Vieja (the old fort or, literally, "Old Force") was devastated by a band of French raiders led by Jacques de Sores.

King Philip II of Spain ordered a new fort to be built in a strategically better position (the old fort had been slightly too far from the harbor) and work began in 1558. The new building was dogged by violence and bloodshed before it was even half finished. The land appropriated for the new fortress was private property and its owners were understandably furious; in addition, the architect, the engineer, and the Governor of Cuba fought constantly with one another throughout the building process. It took almost two decades and the deployment of harshly treated slave labor to complete the Castillo de la Real Fuerza (Castle of the Royal Forces) in 1577.

Despite all the time and money spent on the fortress, when it was finally finished the military found it impractical and still too far from the harbor to be effective. In subsequent decades, the fortress became home to a succession of Spanish governors of Cuba, and today it is a national monument, one of several buildings in Old Havana protected by UNESCO. For several years after Fidel Castro came to power in 1959, the fortress was used as revolutionary offices; in more recent times it has served as a museum. Its most famous feature, atop a tower, is a seventeenth-century bronze figurine of a woman known as *La Giraldilla*, which has become symbolic of the city of Havana. (The original is held in the City Museum, with a copy on the tower.) The Castillo de la Real Fuerza is the oldest surviving stone fortress in the Americas. **LH**

Real Fábricas de Tabaco Partagás (Havana, Cuba)

Supplying cigars to aficionados since 1845

Tobacco has been grown commercially in Cuba since 1580 and, by 1700, it was the country's largest export. The Real Fábricas de Tabaco Partagás (Partagás Royal Tobacco Factory) in Havana is one of the largest and oldest cigar factories in Cuba, and is run by the state-owned tobacco company, Habanos SA. It was set up in 1845 by the Spaniard Jaime Partagás Ravelo, who owned many tobacco plantations in the Vuelta Abajo region of the Pinar del Río province. It supplied cigars to the wealthy and noble in Europe and Asia at a time when the pleasures of the Havana cigar had become a topic of conversation for aficionados.

The smell of tobacco permeates the building where 400 workers are involved in the process of producing the cigars—from sorting the leaves, through hand rolling, to packing the final product in cedar-wood boxes. There are more than eighty different stages in making a cigar, and a skilled *tabaquero* (cigar roller) can roll more than 100 cigars a day—frequently smoking a cigar while he or she works. The factory's main room houses workers who sit on benches rolling cigars. Partagás Ravelo is said to have initiated the practice—still continued today—whereby a reader, known as the *lector*, sits at a lectern at the front of the room reading aloud to the cigar rollers from the local newspaper, or maybe from a novel. During the 1880s, poet, writer, and freedom fighter José Martí ensured that workers at the cigar factory were read anti-Spanish propaganda to encourage them to join the independence movement that he led.

The factory continued in private ownership and, by 1958, was the second-largest exporter of Cuban cigars. After the Cuban Revolution in 1959, the tobacco industry was nationalized. The factory has since been renamed the Francisco Pérez Germán. **CK**

Presidential Palace
(Havana, Cuba)

A palace that glorifies a revolution

The grand, wedding cake–like white building that is Havana's Presidential Palace was built from 1913 to 1920. Its lavish interior was decorated by Tiffany & Co. of New York, and it was home to Cuban presidents from Mario García Menocal to Fulgencio Batista. In 1957, the latter survived an assassination attempt here by revolutionary leader Fidel Castro's guerilla fighters.

Following the 1959 revolution, the palace became the Museo de la Revolución. It houses photographs, weaponry, documents, bloodstained clothing, and memorabilia—including Ernesto "Che" Guevara's black beret—relating to the history of the revolution

---

"We cannot be sure of having something to live for, unless we are willing to die for it."

Ernesto "Che" Guevara, revolutionary

---

and its later accomplishments in health, education, and the Angolan War. It attempts to explain why the revolution came about by showing the squalid conditions many ordinary Cubans lived in at that time. The museum also houses El Rincon de los Cretinos (the corner of the cretins), which catalogs the "crimes" committed by such "enemies" as the Central Intelligence Agency, illustrated by satirical cartoons and propaganda. Part of the museum is dedicated to an exhibition concerned with the Cuban War of Independence against Spain.

Outside the building lies the Granma Memorial, a glass casing that houses a replica of *Granma*, the cabin cruiser used by Castro, Guevara, and eighty-one of their revolutionary fighters to sail from Mexico to Cuba in 1956 in their attempt to overthrow Batista. **CK**

Castillo de San Pedro de la Roca del Morro

(Santiago de Cuba, Cuba)

Fortified castle defending the harbor of Cuba's second city

Santiago de Cuba was founded by the Spanish conquistador Diego Velázquez de Cuéllar in 1514, and was the country's capital from 1522 until 1589, when the Spanish moved the government to Havana. The town's large harbor made it the ideal center for Cuba's African slave trade in the 1700s and 1800s, and it was here that Spain surrendered to the United States in 1898, ending the Spanish-American War.

Santiago de Cuba's wealth attracted the attention of pirates and corsairs, eager to grab a share of Spain's riches across the Atlantic, and the Spanish decided to fortify the town with a castle and batteries at Santa Catalina and La Estrella on the opposite side of the bay. Castillo de San Pedro de la Roca del Morro was commissioned by the town's governor, Pedro de la Roca y Borja, in 1638. Italian military engineer Giovanni Bautista Antonelli designed the terraced fortress to sit on the promontory, or *morro*, at the entrance to the town's deep natural harbor. The castle was blown up by English pirate Henry Morgan in 1662, when he and his men captured and destroyed the town. The castle was rebuilt, enlarged, and finally completed around 1669 by a succession of Spanish and Cuban military engineers. The 1740s saw it fend off attacks by the British, but the castle suffered when earthquakes struck the region in 1757 and 1766; it was later restored. Its thick stone walls house a maze of drawbridges, stairways linking its terraces, barracks, a warehouse cut out of the rock, a chapel, and a series of small cells that were used to house slaves in transit. From 1775, Castillo de San Pedro de la Roca del Morro was used as a prison for Cuban political rebels.

Today the castle houses the Museo de la Pirateria (Piracy Museum), which charts the course of piracy in the Caribbean from the 1500s to the days of U.S. imperialism in the 1900s. **CK**

> *"Santiago is to be ours today; American flag will replace Spain's colors at 9 A.M."*
>
> *New York Times*, July 17, 1898

Che Guevara Monument

(Santa Clara, Cuba)

Mausoleum and memorial to Cuban hero

Built to commemorate Cuba's iconic revolutionary Ernesto "Che" Guevara, this monument is a triumph of modern art, the enormous bronze by José Delarra dominating the area. Inside the museum are an exhibition and plaques commemorating Che and his fallen comrades. Since the opening of the memorial, Santa Clara, sometimes known as "the city of Che," has become a mecca for tourists and Che fanatics.

Che was born in 1928 to a wealthy Argentinian family. A young doctor, with a special interest in leprosy, he was drawn into the world of politics and left Argentina to work with Cuban guerillas. Their aim was to overthrow Cuba's right-wing dictator, Fulgencio Batista. Fighting alongside Fidel Castro, Che was soon appointed commander of the rebel army. In 1958, his unit won the battle for Santa Clara—the decisive battle of the revolution. A short distance from the memorial stand the railway carriages used by Che during the operation and in the ensuing weeks when he was in command of this province.

When Fidel Castro became Cuban president, Che was appointed one of his ministers, but in 1965 he left Cuba for the Congo, and a failed campaign. The following year, in Bolivia, planning to overthrow the dictator, Che was captured and shot by a joint CIA and Bolivian unit. Only his hands were sent to Cuba as proof of his death. In 1997, however, his remains and those of his comrades killed in Bolivia were returned to Cuba and interred within the Santa Clara memorial.

Delarra's immensely powerful bronze of Che depicts a man of superhuman strength and physique. Che was, however, a severe asthmatic and photographs show him as a muscular but wiry man. This incredible 82-foot- (25-m-) high statue testifies to the strength and power that Che Guevara represented for his supporters in Cuba. **LH**

Port Royal

(Port Royal, Jamaica)

Jamaican port, once a haven of pirates

For nearly fifty years Port Royal was one of the wealthiest ports in the world, having grown to prominence as a haven for pirates employed by the British to attack rival French and Spanish shipping. Port Royal offered an ideal base for piracy because of its deep harbor and central location on the shipping lanes between Spain and its Caribbean possessions.

Port Royal became an English possession in 1655 after Jamaica was conquered from the Spanish. In 1657, the island's governor, lacking men to defend the city effectively, invited buccaneers into Port Royal to deter Spanish and French attacks. By the 1660s, the

> *"Beneath the . . . adjacent water of Kingston Harbor lies the only sunken city in the New World . . ."*
>
> Donny L. Hamilton, historian

port had become notorious for its depravity, becoming known as "the Sodom of the New World." In 1687, however, antipiracy laws were passed and the city's reputation increasingly became based on the slave and sugar trades. Ironically, Port Royal then became known as a place of execution for pirates. In 1692, Port Royal was devastated by an earthquake that caused two-thirds of the city to sink into the Caribbean Sea and killed half of the city's population. Further natural disasters in the eighteenth century meant that Port Royal never recovered its former prominence.

Today Port Royal is a small fishing village, but it is also one of the most important underwater archeological sites in the world, yielding numerous artifacts from the city's glory days—albeit days built on morally dubious ground. **JF**

Citadelle Laferrière (near Cap-Haïtien, Haiti)

Built entirely by self-liberated slaves as a declaration of independence and freedom

"*The Citadelle reflects the dreams our fathers had for the country . . . of freedom and dignity.*"

Jean-Bertrand Aristide, former Haitian president

Inland from the northern coast of Haiti is the National History Park, containing the monuments of Citadelle Laferrière, the palace of Sans Souci, and the buildings of Ramiers. The significance of these structures, all remarkable in their own right, is that they were built in the early nineteenth century by newly self-liberated black slaves after Haiti's declaration of independence from France in 1804. The buildings, and many others, were ordered by Henri Christophe, King Henri I of Haiti, who was determined that the new Haitian state would face its former colonial master on equal terms.

Of foremost importance to the liberated slaves was security from possible French reprisals. The immense mountaintop fortress of Citadelle Laferrière was built 17 miles (27 km) south of Cap-Haïtien by 20,000 men, driven to work as hard as they had in the plantations. Should the French invade, people who had settled in northern Haiti were instructed to fall back on the citadel, destroying everything of use to their enemy in their wake.

The stone citadel, built between 1805 and 1820 on the summit of the 3,000-foot- (914-m-) high Bonnet à L'Eveque mountain, extended over an area of 108,000 square feet (10,000 sq m). Its walls are a towering 130 feet (40 m) high. Intended to be able to support 5,000 inhabitants under siege for a year, the citadel incorporates food storehouses and huge water cisterns. It was heavily armed with 365 cannons, each dragged with immense effort from the coast; extensive stocks of cannonballs can still be seen, lying piled within the citadel.

The French never laid siege to Citadelle Laferrière, and today the newly restored fortress is one of Haiti's most popular tourist destinations, celebrated by Haitians as a symbol of what their nation can achieve, and by the international community as a symbol of absolute determination to fight for freedom. **FR**

Fortaleza Ozama (Old Santo Domingo, Dominican Republic)

Sixteenth-century fort that witnessed the departure of many great expeditions

Fortaleza Ozama is the oldest and perhaps the most interesting fort in the history of the Americas. During the last five centuries, scores of significant expeditions have set sail from the port, which dates back to 1502. The site was originally constructed by Frey Nicholas de Ovando, the governor of Hispaniola (the original name for the island that is now Haiti and the Dominican Republic). The fort was built to protect the city of Old Santo Domingo from pirates and privateers, but over the decades it became a starting point for many great explorers and their expeditions. Hernán Cortés departed for Mexico from Fortaleza Ozama, and Diego Velázquez set sail to Cuba from this base.

The Fortaleza Ozama is situated on the bank of the Ozama River, where it flows into the Caribbean Sea. The Ozama is considered one of the most important of the 108 rivers in the Dominican Republic, placing the Fortaleza Ozama in a strong strategic position. The fort reached its heyday in the fifteenth century, under the supervision of Gonzalo Fernández de Oviedo, who was despatched from Spain as governor to take control of the fort. Fernández took his duties extremely seriously and when, after twenty-five years in charge of the bastion, he died at his post he was still clutching the keys to the prison. Legend has it that, even in death, it was extremely difficult to prise the keys from his dead fingers. A statue of him stands near the entrance to the fort.

Steeped in history, the fortress is an impressive architectural achievement, never subdued by force of arms. The fort is no longer in use as a military building, but has become a tourist attraction. Visitors can marvel at the Tower of Homage, built to glorify the Spanish conquistadors who sailed from Spain to Santo Domingo to conquer and colonize the Americas. The tower embodies the strength, vitality, and splendor of those first courageous expeditions. **KH**

"The armory was designed to resemble a church in order to trick the pirates."

Danny Aquino, historian

Iglesia de San José (Old San Juan, Puerto Rico, USA)

Second-oldest church in the Americas, in sixteenth-century Spanish-Gothic style

Built by the conquering Spaniards who invaded Puerto Rico in the sixteenth century, the Church of San José is one of the earliest remaining Spanish buildings in this region and the second-oldest church in the Americas. The architect allowed himself free rein with his design, borrowing elements from Gothic cathedrals and the architecture of the Italian Renaissance, melding them together with what would come to be known as the Spanish colonial style. Construction work was begun in 1523 on land given to the church by Juan Ponce de León (*c.* 1460–1521), the first governor of the island.

The first religious order to live here was a group of Dominican friars, who named their church and its monastery in honor of St. Thomas Aquinas. Ponce de León gave the friars a wooden cross, which is still in place today. The church's magnificent altar, which dates back to the fifteenth century, was transported from Cadiz in Spain. In 1532 a Gothic sanctuary was added to the church and Juan Ponce de León was buried here. In 1865, the Jesuits arrived in Puerto Rico and took over both the Dominican order and the Church of St. Thomas Aquinas, which they renamed in honor of San José. The Iglesia de San José is the final resting place of one of Puerto Rico's most famous artists, José Campeche, who died in 1809. Campeche, the mixed-race son of a freed slave, was born in San Juan in 1751 and lived in the city all his life.

In the early twentieth century the body of Juan Ponce de León was moved and reinterred in nearby San Juan Cathedral (a nineteenth-century replacement of the original cathedral, which was older than the Iglesia de San José, but was almost entirely destroyed by a hurricane around 1584). In the square outside the cathedral is a statue of Juan Ponce de León, cast in bronze smelted down from captured British cannons in the late eighteenth century. **LH**

> *"After finding gold on Boriquén (Puerto Rico) . . . he conquered the island and made a fortune."*
>
> The Columbia Encyclopedia, on Juan Ponce de León

Nelson's Dockyard (English Harbour, Antigua and Barbuda)

Georgian dockyard servicing ships of the British Navy, once commanded by Lord Nelson

On the southeastern coast of the Caribbean island of Antigua, near the town of English Harbour, is Nelson's Dockyard—an area known as "hurricane hole" because of the shelter that could be found there from the violent storms that rage along the coastline. The naval station was used during the eighteenth and nineteenth centuries for the maintenance of warships that helped keep the British Empire afloat by ravaging eastern Caribbean islands in order to control the sugar trade. The dockyard and its surrounding area—named Nelson's Dockyard following its restoration in the 1950s—is now part of a national park.

Construction of the dockyard began in 1725. It was abandoned by the Royal Navy in 1889, but during the eighteenth century it was put into service by the British as a base from which to continue the seemingly endless fight against the French. More than 300 men and five officers worked at the dockyard in its heyday. Most of these men were skilled African workers who had been taken into slavery by the British.

Lord Nelson, always keen to play by the book, was disliked during his time in Antigua because he insisted on enforcing the Navigation Act drawn up after the American War of Independence. Prior to the Act, the islanders had been able to trade with Americans, thus providing a good source of revenue. The loss of this revenue was devastating. In 1787, after he had been in the Caribbean for three years, Nelson—possibly to the delight of the locals—became seriously ill and had to be rushed home to England.

Far from being a derelict relic of a bygone age, Nelson's Dockyard has, in the very recent past, received funding from an impressive and disparate range of sources, including the European Union. Private yachts have replaced Nelson's frigates, but English Harbour remains a favorite port for those making the long Atlantic crossing. **OR**

> *"[The Antiguan Colonists] are as great rebels as ever were in America, had they the power to show it."*
>
> Robert Southey, *The Life of Horatio Lord Nelson* (1813)

St. Pierre (St. Pierre, Martinique, France)

The "Paris of the West Indies," destroyed by volcanic disaster

The town of St. Pierre on the Caribbean island of Martinique was the site of the twentieth century's worst volcanic disaster. The town was a thriving outpost of France's colonial empire, grown prosperous on the profits from the island's sugar plantations. Built on a sheltered bay, St. Pierre was hyperbolically celebrated as "the Paris of the West Indies." Its elegant houses, tree-lined squares, fountains, theater, and cathedral all bore the stamp of French culture, although many citizens were descendants of slaves.

St. Pierre was located only 4 miles (7 km) from Mount Pelée, an active volcano. Small eruptions in 1792 and 1851, causing no significant damage, had confirmed a belief that volcanic activity posed no serious threat to the population. When, in April 1902, a series of explosions and emissions of ash and dust from the volcano spread disquiet, the authorities recommended calm. People living in villages close to the volcano were advised to move to the town, which would not be reached by any lava flows. Those who fled in panic as the eruptions worsened throughout the first week of May were the ones to survive.

At 8 A.M. on May 8, 1902—Ascension Day—the volcano exploded, emitting a huge pyroclastic flow, or *nuée ardente*. This massive cloud of hot gas and volcanic rubble rushed toward St. Pierre at a speed of up to 310 miles per hour (500 km/h). Within minutes, almost the entire population of the town was dead and all but a handful of buildings had been destroyed. St. Pierre never recovered its former prosperity after the disaster, and it is now a sleepy small town, dotted with traces of the catastrophe of 1902. **RG**

◱ St. Pierre lies in ruins directly after the volcanic eruption that killed more than 30,000 local people.

◳ St. Pierre, as it exists today, is much smaller than it was before the destruction wrought by Mt. Pelée in 1902.

Monastery of San Francisco (Quito, Ecuador)

Monastery in the "Baroque school of Quito" style, built on the site of an ancient Inca temple

The city of Quito was founded by the Spanish in the 1530s and a monumental church was planned to showcase the city's grandeur. The construction of San Francisco was begun in the first half of the sixteenth century and completed by 1605. The oldest church in South America, the Monasterio de San Francisco—dedicated to St. Francis of Assisi—comprises the church, several chapels, and a monastery. On the plain facade, a carving of St. Francis's rope belt is carved above the large window over the entrance.

The monastery of San Francisco is a pure example of the so-called "Baroque school of Quito," a fusion of Spanish, Italian, Moorish, Flemish, and indigenous art. Visitors should not miss the sculpture of the Winged Virgin—it is one of the few religious works of art in Latin America in which the figure represented resembles the indigenous people, instead of the European conquistadors. The church also contains the tomb of a local stonemason, Cantuña, who built the neighboring chapel. According to local legend, Cantuña was despairing of finishing the chapel when the devil appeared, offering to help him, in return for his soul. Cantuña agreed and was able to finish the chapel quickly—but he left a stone missing. When the devil returned, the missing stone ensured his survival.

The plaza on which the church stands—Plaza de San Francisco—is strangely sloping, a phenomenon that archeologists did not understand until excavations revealed that the monastery was built on the site of an ancient Inca temple. The Incas had, in turn, deposed earlier tribes from the area, who may well have worshipped at this site, too. **LH**

↗ The Monastery of San Francisco was an immense project to undertake in harsh and difficult conditions.

↱ The statue of the *Virgin of Quito* is located atop El Panecillo hill and can be seen from much of the city.

Cartagena Walls

(Cartagena, Colombia)

Extensive fortifications, protecting an important area of an early Spanish settlement

Known locally as Las Murillos, the Cartagena Walls surround the old part of the city, which was designated a UNESCO World Heritage site, due to its military architecture and location on the West Indies way. Because of its wealth and economic importance, the port of Cartagena was frequently attacked by pirates, so the fortifications were constructed to protect the city.

Cartagena was founded in 1533 by the Spanish conquistador Don Pedro de Heredia, and the city almost immediately became a target for pirates. In 1551 the French pirate Jean-François de la Roque de Ruberval forced Heredia to flee the city and pay him a large sum of gold.

In 1585 Sir Francis Drake plundered Cartagena, forcing its inhabitants to seek refuge in a nearby town. In response to this, King Philip II of Spain ordered extensive fortifications to be built to protect the city. It eventually took more than 200 years and fifty million gold pesos to fully complete the fortifications, which feature 90-foot- (27-m-) high walls and several fortresses, including San Sebastián de Pastelillo and San Felipe de Barajas. The walls faced their sternest test in 1741, when Cartegena was attacked by an English fleet led by Admiral Edward Vernon. The English forces of 186 ships and 23,600 men vastly outnumbered the Spanish forces of just six ships and 3,000 men. However, because of the fortifications and the expertise of the Spanish commander Blas de Lezo, the English were eventually repelled.

Cartagena—named after a Spanish port—is one of the most historic cities in South America, its old town preserving its Spanish colonial past. The walls of Cartagena are the most extensive system of defense in South America, and offer stunning views over the town and the Caribbean Sea. **JF**

> *"Cartagena has the most extensive fortifications in South America."*
>
> UNESCO

Quinta de San Pedro Alejandrino (Sta. Marta, Colombia)

Villa where Simón Bolívar spent his last days

The beautiful, early eighteenth-century villa of San Pedro Alejandrino can be found in the oldest established city of continental America, Santa Marta, nestled in the foothills of La Sierra Nevada. It is an area rich in history, notably as the place Simón Bolívar—one of South America's greatest heroes—died.

Bolívar was a great general who fought for independence from the Spanish. He earned the name *El Libertador* for his heroic battles that freed Venezuela, Columbia, Peru, Ecuador, Panama, and Upper Peru (now called Bolivia) from the grip of Spanish rule. In 1826 the Republic of Bolivia was formed, making Bolívar one of a very small number of people to have had a country named after them. His military leadership was not without problems, in part because of the vastness of the countries he freed and their disparate political and cultural heritage. In 1828, in an unpopular move, he made himself dictator in an attempt to unify the region. The widespread unease culminated in an assassination attempt. He stood down in 1830 and planned to leave South America for Europe. Before he could travel, however, he contracted tuberculosis and was invited by Don Joaquin de Mier to rest at his house, the Villa de San Pedro Alejandrino. Bolívar spent his final days at the tranquil villa before succumbing to the disease. He died on December 17, 1830; his body was then removed and buried at Caracas, the capital of Venezuela.

The Villa de San Pedro Alejandrino was a thriving center of agriculture, producing sugarcane, coconuts, honey, and various fruits, as well as boasting a distillery. After Bolívar's death it gradually fell into decline until it was bought in 1891 by the Department of Magdalena and restored. Now it is a museum full of artifacts associated with Bolívar, and dedicated to the art and culture of the six countries he liberated. **TP**

Zipaquira Salt Mine (Zipaquira, Colombia)

Cathedral, carved deep in a salt mine

Amid the hustle and bustle of the old town of Zipaquira in central Colombia, and just a short train ride from Bogotá, is a spot of utter peace and tranquility—the Salt Cathedral.

Inside the salt mountain of Zipaquira, there is a huge, gently winding tunnel that spirals down toward a breathtaking structure. Nearly 600 feet (183 m) inside the mountain is the Salt Cathedral, a church carved from the innermost reaches, with a great towering roof, columns, three naves, a baptismal font, a pulpit, and a crucifix. The whole interior is bathed with the translucent luminosity of its glowing white salt walls,

> *"The darkness wraps you up in yourself ... here people focus and feel closer to God."*
>
> David Rincon, salt miner

and the cavernous space lends itself to extraordinary acoustics. The path wending down to the cathedral has fourteen small chapels leading off it that represent the Stations of the Cross. Miners first carved a sanctuary within the mountain, and in 1954 the first cathedral was created. However, the mine was still active, which caused concerns over the structural safety of the cathedral, and it was closed in 1990. In 1991 a local architect, Jose Maria Gonzalez, began work on a new cathedral, several hundred feet below the original one, and it was completed in 1995. The arduous work involved more than 100 sculptors and miners and four years of hard work.

The cathedral is a work of art, ethereal and inspiring, and a place of infinite serenity that touches all who enter, regardless of creed. **TP**

🏛 ⦿ Valley of the Statues

(San Agustín, Colombia)

Archeological site bringing to light the history and culture of pre-Colombian civilization

The rich, verdant valley of the Magdalena River in Colombia is home to the largest collection of pre-Colombian statuary in South America. It is an area of tremendous beauty, with a history extending back thousands of years—much of it still a mystery. Scattered throughout the area are numerous burial mounds, carved megaliths, and religious statues whose impassive gaze across the green carpets of vegetation is both fascinating and faintly disturbing. The most important sites within the river valley are those around the small town of San Agustín, and this area has now been turned into a 193-square-mile (500-sq-km) park—Parque Arqueológico de San Agustín.

Excavation of the sites began in the 1930s and to date more than 500 statues, dolmens, and tombs have been discovered, with the probability of many more still to be unearthed. The tombs form two groups: those of important people within the early cultures, and those of less importance. The big burial mounds that would have housed prestigious figures are guarded by large and fierce carved figures, mostly anthropomorphic, or by carved animals such as snakes, frogs, and birds. Tombs of "common" people were placed under the floors of their huts, and are less obvious. Some smaller artifacts that have been excavated show signs of color, and would originally have been painted with dyes, primarily in reds and yellows. Other sculptures appear to represent deities that are commonly ascribed as solar gods, which are male figures, and others as lunar gods, female figures.

> *"The equatorial natives worshipped a pantheon of twelve … it included the god of the Moon."*
>
> Zecharia Sitchin, *The Lost Realms* (1990)

The whole area of the Magdalena river valley is of enormous cultural and historical value. Due to the wide date range during which the area was occupied, the tombs and sculptures display the evolution of different early cultures as well as their approach to and perceptions about death. **TP**

National Pantheon
(Caracas, Venezuela)

Monument to Venezuelan heroes

The National Pantheon in Caracas is one of Venezuela's most venerated buildings. Previously a church, it became a National Pantheon in 1874, after President Antonio Guzmán Blanco decreed the transformation of the church of the Santísima Trinidad of Caracas into a site to conserve the remains of heroic comrades. Simón Bolívar is perhaps the most revered person to be laid to rest in this site, and the entire central nave has been dedicated to *El Libertador*. In the niches and under the paving stones are the remains of other well-respected and illustrious Venezuelans.

The building of what is now the Pantheon began in 1812 after an earthquake obliterated the original church that had stood there. This structure was reconstructed slowly, over a period of many years. Between 1853 and 1858, engineer José Gregorio Solano took the first step toward the construction of the building and in the following decades other engineers contributed to its completion. It therefore developed in many different fashions and styles.

In 1910 the Venezuelan government employed Juan Vicente Gómez to lead a major renovation program of the Pantheon, making modifications so that the building would appear more impressive. In 1929 yet another architect was employed to redesign the Pantheon, this time in a neo-colonial/neo-Baroque style. In 1930, with the help of three eminent engineers, another series of alterations was adopted. The entrance stairs were made more monumental, the marble floor was entirely replaced, as was Bolívar's sarcophagus, and the vault was adorned with paintings by the artist Tito Salas. Today the Pantheon is an impressive monument that attests to Venezuela's potency as a nation, and demonstrates a range of architectural styles illustrating the country's historic progression. **KH**

Iglesia de San Francisco
(Caracas, Venezuela)

Where Simón Bolívar was made "Liberator"

This striking church, declared a national monument in the 1950s, is one of Venezuela's best examples of the Latin American colonial style. It was built alongside the San Francisco convent, established here in the 1570s, and began life as a simple adobe structure. In 1593, construction of a more permanent church building began, designed by Antonio Ruiz de Ullán, but an earthquake in 1641 destroyed much of the building. It was replaced by a simple church with a single aisle and side chapels. In 1745, further work by Fray Mateo Veloz reinstated Ruiz de Ullán's original three-aisle plan and added arches.

> *"Judgement comes from experience; and experience comes from bad judgement."*
>
> **Simón Bolívar, revolutionary and statesman**

In 1887 extensive reconstructions, by Stolen Juan Manrique, included replacing the pillars, changing the choir, covering a Mudéjar-style (Moorish-Spanish) paneled ceiling with false vaults, and replacing the main facade with a part-Classical, part-Baroque version. Meanwhile, the church had become the site of major political events, associated especially with Venezuela's national hero, Simón Bolívar, who fought to free his country from Spanish colonial control. It was at this church, in 1813, that he was proclaimed "the Liberator," and here that his spectacular funeral took place in 1842, twelve years after his death.

By the 1950s, the Mudéjar ceiling had been revealed once again and architect Luís Malaussena had supervised other work designed to restore the church to its earlier beauty. **AK**

 ⬡ **Fort Zeelandia** (Paramaribo, Suriname)

Former colonial stronghold that houses the history of Suriname

Dating from the seventeenth century, Paramaribo was the first European settlement in the former colony of Dutch Guiana, now Suriname, on the northern coast of South America. Much of the old town is faded and forlorn—the effect of poverty and three centuries of tropical storms—but today tourist revenues promise regeneration. The town's original Dutch street plan largely survives, and the buildings are a remarkable blend of imported architecture, in the shape of black-and-white Dutch houses arranged around grassy squares, and features deriving from the pre-colonial Indian population and the materials they used.

Fort Zeelandia has its origins in a French stronghold located on a bend by the Suriname River where Spaniards reputedly first set foot in the region in 1499, about 9 miles (15 km) from the sea—and around which the city of Paramaribo is now spread. When the British founded a new colony there in 1651,

some 1,000 Englishmen accompanied by slave labor expanded the fort, naming it Fort Willoughby. The Dutch were ceded the colony in 1667 by the Treaty of Breda, whereupon they completed the fort—consisting of buildings closely clustered within a pentagonal defensive wall with a fortified bastion at each corner—renaming it Fort Zeelandia after the Dutch province of Zeeland.

One of the most historic structures in Suriname, Fort Zeelandia has been fully restored in recent years. Directly on the riverfront and now fronted by the modern building of the National Assembly, it currently houses part of the Suriname Museum, with displays concerning the former colony's past as a slave-dependent coffee and sugarcane producer, the Surinamese indigenous peoples, and the fort itself. Rooms with period décor can be visited in former officers' quarters in the fort grounds. **FR**

Devil's Island (Îles du Salut, French Guiana)

French penal colony established by Napoleon III, immortalized in book and film

The very mention of Devil's Island used to strike fear into the hearts of criminals. For almost a century, it was the French equivalent of banishment—a remote penal colony on the other side of the globe where escape was impossible and a safe return unlikely. Devil's Island is one of the three Îles du Salut (Salvation Isles), located off the coast of French Guiana, in South America. The other islands—Île Royale and Île Saint-Joseph—also housed prisons, as did Kourou, the nearest town on the mainland. The French loosely referred to all of these places as Devil's Island. Prisoners were graded according to the severity of their offenses. The compound on the true Devil's Island—the least accessible of the jails—was reserved mainly for political prisoners and hardened criminals.

The penal settlement was founded in 1852, at a turbulent time in French history. In December 1851, Napoleon III had just staged a coup, and a distant detention center seemed an ideal way of removing his political opponents from the scene. It also provided new settlers to live in a disease-ridden, floundering colony. Convicts with sentences of eight years or less had to spend a similar period of time in the colony; felons with longer sentences were never allowed to return to France.

Devil's Island gained added notoriety from its two most famous inmates—Alfred Dreyfus and Henri Charrière. The former was the victim of a notorious miscarriage of justice (the "Dreyfus Affair," the subject of several films); Charrière wrote a best-selling book, *Papillon* (1970), about his experiences on the island, which was later made into a film starring Steve McQueen and Dustin Hoffman. The prison itself was decommissioned in 1946 and its buildings, now picturesquely overgrown with creepers, have become a tourist attraction. **IZ**

🏛 ◉ Santo Antônio da Barra Fort (Salvador de Bahia, Brazil)

Impressive Portuguese stronghold built to repel Dutch invaders

The striking white fort of Santo Antônio da Barra occupies the windswept tip of a peninsula that juts out into the sea where the waters of the Atlantic meet those of neighboring Todos os Santos (All Saints) bay. Down below, white beaches stretch into the distance; behind, rises the historic center of Brazil's third-largest city, Salvador. Often called Salvador de Bahia, this is now the capital of Bahia state and was once Brazil's capital, founded in 1549 by Portuguese colonizers.

Santo Antônio was the city's most important Portuguese fort, placed strategically to repel the advances of adventurers and colonizers from other countries, jealous of the city's thriving slave-based trade in cotton and, later, tobacco. The Dutch seized the fort and city in 1624, but Portugal took it back in 1625 and it stayed in Portuguese hands until independence in the 1820s. The fort has been remodeled over the years, but the current multisided,

Italian-influenced design dates from the early eighteenth century. Since the 1990s, it has become the home of the Museu Nautico and its collection of nautical maps, instruments, and shipping artifacts.

Above the fort towers the distinctive black-and-white striped lighthouse known as Farol da Barra. Reputed to be the first lighthouse in the Americas, its origins date from the sixteenth century, but it was mostly updated in the nineteenth century. It marks the spot where Italian explorer Amerigo Vespucci, from whom the word America derives, is said to have dropped anchor on All Saints Day (November 1) 1501, thus giving birth to the adjacent harbor's name.

Salvador's history has given it a fascinating heritage mixing indigenous peoples, Europeans, and Africans. A blend of Renaissance, colonial, and local styles are apparent in its old quarter, which includes the fort and lighthouse. **AK**

Estádio do Maracanã (Rio de Janeiro, Brazil)

Built to hold the 1950 World Cup football final, one of the biggest stadiums in the world

The first impression on visiting Rio de Janeiro's Estádio Jornalista Mário Filho—more commonly known as Estádio do Maracanã (Maracanã Stadium) after the Rio de Janeiro neighborhood in which it is located—is its sheer size. It is one of the biggest soccer grounds in the world, with room for 97,000 seated spectators. When it was built for the World Cup in 1950, however, it could hold more than twice that number of standing spectators. The final of that year's World Cup between Uruguay and Brazil officially attracted 173,830 fans, although some estimates put the actual attendance at close to 210,000—a record attendance at a World Cup match and one that is unlikely to be broken. Brazil lost the game in a shock defeat and soccer-mad Brazilians still remember the upset as the *Maracanaço* (the Maracanã blow).

The capacity of the ground has been drastically reduced since then with the multimillion-dollar conversion of the stadium to an all-seated ground, after part of an upper stand collapsed in 1992, killing three fans and injuring another fifty.

The stadium, which was designed by two Brazilian architects, Raphaël Galvão and Pedro Paulo Bernardes Bastos, has also been used for exhibition matches for other sports, as well as for a Mass conducted by Pope John Paul II, and as a regular concert venue. It holds the world record for the largest paying audience for a single band after 198,000 people came to see pop group A-ha in 1991.

The stadium's raison d'être, however, remains soccer and, appropriately, it is inextricably linked with one of Brazil's and, indeed, the world's greatest players, Pelé. It was here that he made his debut for the national team against Argentina in 1957, scored the 1,000th goal of his career in 1969, and played his last game for Brazil against Yugoslavia in 1971. **AS**

Igreja da Ordem Terceira do Carmo (Rio de Janeiro, Brazil)

Baroque church with decorations by master artists

As well as being a vibrant city famed for its heady Carnaval, samba rhythms, and beach culture, Rio de Janeiro, the former capital of Brazil, has a wealth of beautiful churches, many dating back to its time as a Portuguese colony.

The late seventeenth century saw a number of religious orders and their related cultures flourish in Brazil, bringing with them a wave of lavish, distinctively styled Baroque churches. Igreja da Ordem Terceira do Carmo is a stunning example. It was founded by a branch of the Carmelite order and located within the city's historic Centro quarter.

Designed in the eighteenth century by Manuel Alves Setúbal, the church's elegant front facade—a mix of curvaceous Baroque and Neoclassical touches added in the 1800s—is made of granite. The main entrance was crafted in 1761 from limestone brought specially from Lisbon. The tile-covered bell towers were built almost a century later (1847–50), designed by Manuel Joaquim de Melo Real Corte. The interior is filled with opulent Rococo decoration from the 1700s and 1800s—wonderful gilded carving including that by notable master artists Luis da Fonseca and his assistant, Valentim Fonseca e Silva.

The church is part of a historic complex of buildings. Its eighteenth-century neighbor, the Igreja de Nossa Senhora do Carmo da Antiga Sé, was once connected to a Carmelite convent. In 1808, when the Portuguese royal family fled to Brazil in fear of Napoleon and made their home in the city, they turned the convent into a home for Queen Maria I and the Igreja de Nossa Senhora do Carmo da Antiga Sé into a royal chapel. After independence in 1822, Brazil's emperors made the same church their imperial chapel. With the dawn of the republic, in 1889, Igreja de Nossa Senhora do Carmo da Antiga Sé became the Metropolitan Cathedral (until 1976). **AK**

". . . a holy man and a lover of solitude, adopted a solitary lifestyle on Mount Carmel."

From *The Constitutions of the Carmelite Order*

Paço Imperial (Rio de Janeiro, Brazil)

Portuguese Imperial Palace, once a hub of government, now a cultural center

Dating from 1743, the Paço Imperial was a center of colonial political power in Brazil for almost 150 years, until the Republic of Brazil was established in 1889 and new administrative buildings were built. The site was originally the residence of the colonial governor of the region in which Rio de Janeiro is located, before the city was made the capital of Brazil in 1763, at which time the building became the Viceroy's Palace. It became a royal residence in 1808, when King John VI of Portugal fled his homeland, which had been invaded the previous year by the French, under Napoleon. The building finally gained the name it now bears in 1822 when Brazil became an independent empire, and Emperors Pedro I and then Pedro II took up residence. Indeed, it was from one of the balconies here that Pedro I announced to an assembled crowd that he refused to return to Europe, thereby declaring Brazil's independence from its colonial master.

Considering its significant role in the establishment of modern Brazil, the Paço Imperial had to endure a somewhat humbling tenure as Rio's central mail office for most of the twentieth century, before it was renovated in the 1980s and transformed into a cultural center, hosting art exhibitions and theater performances. The palace is one of the best-preserved public buildings in Rio and—as can be seen from the depictions of the Paço Imperial in historical sketches and paintings—its appearance has changed remarkably little since the original architect merged the Royal Mint and various royal warehouses to form a single, Baroque building.

Despite the gradual development of the Praça XV square in which the building stands, the palace retains the feel of a grand Portuguese estate house transplanted to the New World—unsurprising, perhaps, since the architect was a Portuguese military engineer, José Fernandes Pinto Alpoim. **AS**

"By my blood, by my honor, and by God: I will make Brazil free . . . It is time . . . Independence or Death!"

Pedro I, declaration of independence, 1822

Statue of Christ the Redeemer (Rio de Janeiro, Brazil)

Iconic symbol, built on a peak with panoramic views of the city and surroundings

Since 1931, the iconic statue of Christ the Redeemer has towered over Rio de Janeiro, its outstretched arms seen by many as a testament to the warmth of the Brazilian people. Standing 125 feet (38 m) high, and located at the peak of the 2,330-foot (710-m) Corcovado mountain in the Tijuca Forest National Park, the statue is the work of sculptor Paul Landowski, to a design by local engineer Heito da Silva Costa.

The idea for a religious monument on the site was first put forward in 1859 by Pedro Maria Boss. The plan came to fruition, however, only when a monument was proposed to celebrate 100 years of Brazil's independence from Portugal. Constructed from reinforced concrete with outer layers of soapstone, the monument took five years to complete and was unveiled on October 12, 1931.

In 2006, a chapel under the statue was consecrated, allowing Catholics to hold baptisms and weddings there. Access to the statue is now much easier than when it was first built, as the Corcovado railway cuts up from the Rio suburbs, through the jungle, toward the summit, with an elevator and escalator from the station to the peak. It is a truly inspiring site, with panoramic views of one of the world's most exciting and beautifully situated cities. The surrounding Tijuca Forest National Park is one of the last remaining fragments of the Atlantic rain forest, approximately 93 percent of which was cut down by Europeans to make way for coffee plantations. Tijuca Forest was replanted in the second half of the nineteenth century by Major Manuel Gomes Archer, who was appointed the first forest administrator.

Along with the Amazon rain forest, the statue of Christ the Redeemer—one of the largest and most recognizable Art Deco sculptures ever created—has become the key image of Brazil around the world. **AP**

🏛 ◉ São Miguel das Missões (São Miguel das Missões, Brazil)

Mission town that has become one of Brazil's premier archeological sites

São Miguel das Missões was one of the finest "Jesuit reductions"—mission towns created by the Catholic order across the Americas during the seventeenth and eighteenth centuries. São Miguel das Missões, or "St. Michael of the Missions," was the main mission among several clustered together in southern Brazil. Other notable examples flourished relatively nearby in present-day Argentina and Paraguay. At São Miguel das Missões, as elsewhere, the Jesuit missionaries established an entire community, complete with a church and school, devoted to turning the local people—the Guaraní—toward a Christian way of life.

Today, the Jesuits' mission lies in ruins but the remains of its church hint at an impressive township, designed around a large square with the grand church at its heart, encircled by tropical forest. The cathedral standing today in nearby Santo Ângelo is a replica of the church at São Miguel das Missões, a fine Baroque specimen created by Italian Jesuit priest Juan Bautista Prímoli. The sandstone church had three naves, a tower, and a porticoed entrance. Judging by contemporary documents, and remains on show in the museum here, its interior decoration featured gilded altars and attractive carvings and sculptures. These included statues of saints in multicolored wood, carved by both the Jesuits and the Guaraní.

São Miguel das Missões was built at a time when the surrounding region was colonized by both Portugal and Spain. By the 1760s, a conflict of political interests saw the Jesuits expelled from Latin America and recalled to Spain. São Miguel das Missões, along with the other missions, fell into disuse but, over the ensuing years, a large town grew up in its place. In 1940, the famous Brazilian architect Lucio Costa designed an impressive museum at the São Miguel das Missões archeological site. **AK**

Túcume (near Chiclayo, Peru)

Important religious site of well-preserved adobe-brick pyramids

In the Lambeyeque valley in northern Peru stand twenty-six ancient adobe pyramids, known as the site of Túcume. Built around the sacred mountain of La Raya (mountain of the sun's rays), Túcume seems to have been an important place for the Lambeyeque people and then for the Chimú tribe, before the arrival of the Incas. Local legends associate bad spirits with the site and many indigenous people still refuse to visit the pyramids. Some local people refer to Túcume as *purgatorio* or purgatory. This is probably a legacy of rumors started by the Spanish conquistadors in an attempt to keep people away from the site. As a result, Túcume is one of the few ancient archeological sites not to have been damaged by grave robbers.

The Lambeyeque civilization thrived in *c.* 1100 raising crops and animals in the valley, sustained by its natural waterways and man-made watercourses. Archeological evidence suggests that Túcume was a site of religious significance. The recent discovery of 119 bodies seems to prove that ritualized human sacrifice was carried out at one of Túcume's temples, most probably by the Incas in an attempt to ward off the Spanish invasion of 1532. After the arrival of the Spanish, Túcume was razed to the ground. The adobe-brick pyramids were the only buildings that remained more or less intact. After the Spanish conquered Peru, Túcume became a ghost town.

A number of archeological digs have been carried out at Túcume, one of which was led by Norwegian explorer and ethnologist Thor Heyerdahl, in 1988. It was his dig that captured the world's imagination and led to increased interest in this strangely little-known area of Peru. Among the treasures the excavations unearthed were forty tombs and burial chambers, which contained Inca and Chimú artifacts, including textiles, ceramics, and metalwork. **LH**

🏛 ⊚ Chan Chan (near Trujillo, Peru)

The world's largest adobe city

Chan Chan predates the Inca Empire in Peru. It was the capital city of the Chimú tribe, who ruled this part of the region before the arrival of the Incas (*c.* 1470). Chan Chan was home to tens of thousands of people— archeologists' suppositions vary, claiming the site was home to between 30,000 and 100,000 inhabitants— and demonstrates how well ordered and intelligently thought out ancient South American cities were. There were religious buildings, reservoirs, cemetery areas, well-planned houses, communal gardens, and what appear to have been storage facilities, presumably for crops and other commercial items. There were also nine separate living areas or "citadels," perhaps so the different social classes could each be housed in their own district. The buildings are made of a mixture of adobe and mud, decorated with intricate patterns and graphic designs. The majority of the Chimú who lived in Chan Chan worked as

fishermen or potters. Many surviving ceramic artifacts tell the story of their tribe and way of life, depicting people fishing and the animals that were important to their culture, such as monkeys, fish, and dogs. It seems the pottery was traded with other tribes, contributing to a thriving system of bartering.

Chan Chan is the world's largest adobe city and was the largest city ever built in the pre-Columbian Americas. It was a center of Chimú life for several hundred years, before the Chimú were conquered by the Incas. Today, Chan Chan is such a delicate site that it is on UNESCO's World Heritage List. Adobe is easily damaged by natural forces, such as wind and rain; in addition, the site has been sadly neglected and damaged over the last few centuries—particularly by people plundering the site to sell its artifacts to unscrupulous collectors. As such, it needs careful restoration and preservation. **LH**

🏛 ⊚ Church and Convent of San Francisco (Lima, Peru)

Spain's greatest disseminator of Western culture in South America

The historic center of Peru's capital city, founded by Spain in 1535, is second to none in South America. Prominent among its religious monuments are the Cathedral, the Archbishop's Palace, and the Churches and Convents of Santo Domingo and San Francisco.

Now the headquarters of the Museum of Religious Art, the Church and Convent of San Francisco were rebuilt from 1657 to 1674 in the Spanish Baroque style following a disastrous earthquake in the previous year. The site, which had been selected in 1535 by the conquistador Francisco Pizarro himself, is on the bank of the River Rímac; it is the largest area to be occupied by a convent in the New World. Within the complex are the Church of San Francisco, the convent, two small chapels named La Soledad (the Solitude) and El Milagro (the Miracle), and outbuildings. A plaza and secluded communal patios and cloisters integrate the complex; beautiful tiles brought from Seville embellish the cloister walls. Underfoot, an extensive network of catacombs connects the complex to other buildings, including Lima Cathedral. In the catacombs are the skulls and bones of Christians, some of them arranged in neat, if somewhat macabre, wheel-like patterns.

That the rebuilt seventeenth-century complex has survived subsequent earthquakes is thanks to the Portuguese architect appointed to the task, Constantino de Vasconcellos. He used solid pillars to support barrel vaults, and built with wood and *quincha*, a lightweight blend of rushes, mud, and plaster. The only stone elements are the lavishly decorated altarpiece portal and the lateral portal.

The church is a treasure-house of sculpture, carving, furniture, and gold and silver artifacts, paid for by donations from the Spanish gold and silver mines. There is a fine collection of Spanish, Flemish, and Peruvian paintings, and a 25,000-volume library. **FR**

 ## Nazca Lines (near Nazca, Peru)

One of the most puzzling archeological discoveries of the twentieth century

Long before the emergence of the Incas, Peruvian natives had developed a number of sophisticated cultures. The strongest evidence for this can be found in the fascinating Nazca Lines, a series of large, prehistoric images etched into the earth's surface. The purpose of these mysterious drawings is still unknown, although there is no shortage of imaginative theories about their origin and purpose.

The Nazca Lines consist of dozens of different images, spread across the desert floor. Many depict stylized creatures, among them a monkey with a spiral tail, a lizard, a hummingbird, and a whale. Others form geometric shapes, such as triangles and trapezoids. The pictures were created on a high, arid plateau. They were "drawn" by removing surface gravel and brush to reveal the lighter soil underneath. The images have survived for centuries because of the area's unique climate, which is relatively free from rain, wind, and dust, although the images are now coming under threat from modern commercialism.

The Nazca Lines can be seen properly only from above, so it is hardly surprising that they were first spotted in the 1920s when air travel was on the rise. Soon after their discovery, the theorizing began. Among other notions, the lines have been interpreted as open-air, astronomical calendars; alien landing strips; ancient ley lines; oversized versions of textile patterns; and aids for shamanistic visions. The most detailed research was carried out by Dr. Maria Reiche (1903–98), who devoted much of her career to the images. She also set up a viewing platform (*mirador*) and opened a museum and research center. In terms of publicity, however, the greatest impact came from author Erich von Däniken. In his international best seller, *Chariot of the Gods* (1968), he linked the lines with extraterrestrial visitors. **IZ**

 ◎ **Machu Picchu** (near Aguas Calientes, Peru)

Intriguing urban settlement inhabited and abandoned by the Incas

This incredible ruined city is believed to have been founded at the height of the Inca Empire, around 1400 to 1450, and to have been lived in for less than a century. The number of bones found here has led to assumptions that Machu Picchu was a place of sacrifice; the majority of the bones come from young women. The presence of many temples and religious sites seems to prove Machu Picchu had spiritual significance for the Incas. Many modern-day visitors describe Machu Picchu as retaining an atmosphere of religious significance.

Known as "the Lost City of the Incas," it is suggested that Machu Picchu was also the legendary city of El Dorado—searched for fruitlessly by the Spanish conquistadors, but never found. To this day, little is known about Machu Picchu: its original purpose, how the Incas built it, and why they appear to have abandoned it. It was accessible only via a winding, difficult path that takes several days to walk. That path is now known as the Inca Trail, and has become the holy grail of numerous backpackers who hike it every year.

In 1911, Machu Picchu was rediscovered by U.S. explorer Hiram Bingham. Unfortunately, he removed many artifacts and took them back to the United States; discussions are currently ongoing between Peru and the United States about whether the artifacts will be returned. In 1911, the site lay hidden in dense rain forest and Bingham discovered it almost by chance, after hearing from Peruvians about "the last resting place of the Incas." It seems this description was not accurate because the Incas abandoned Machu Picchu before Spanish rule began. Machu Picchu is now a UNESCO World Heritage site, and the number of visitors permitted to hike the Inca Trail each year is regulated by the Peruvian government. **LH**

 ◉ **Sacsayhuamán** (Cuzco, Peru)

A great stone monument of Inca architecture whose purpose remains a mystery

It is impossible to visit this former stronghold of the Incas and not be impressed and humbled by the atmosphere, the history, and the sheer scale of the huge stones used in its construction. Sacsayhuamán stands near the city of Cuzco, whose name means "navel"—the Incas believed Cuzco was situated at the very center of the world. With doorways more than 10 feet (3 m) in height and cornerstones more than 26 feet (8 m) tall, Sacsayhuamán is a feat of human engineering, the story of whose construction causes much discussion among archeologists. Although earthquakes have laid waste to many more modern buildings in the locality, even to those built with the same stone as Sacsayhuamán, incredibly the Inca site itself has remained unshaken by any of the tremors. In the construction of Sacsayhuamán, the stones were laid together without the use of mortar, and they seem to be immovable by nature. The stone used was not local and the story of where it came from, how it was moved to the site, and how the stones were lifted into place is an archeological mystery.

The Incas left no written records and oral history was lost after the Spanish invasion; therefore Sacsayhuamán's original purpose remains uncertain. Many scholars believe it was a fortress, though others suggest it had a religious purpose; perhaps it served as both. In the late twentieth century, archeologists uncovered what appear to be the graves of Inca holy men, adding extra weight to the religious argument, yet Sacsayhuamán is also known to have been the site of a fierce and bloody battle between the invading Spanish and the ruling Incas in 1536, suggesting it had a military purpose. Although the walls appear huge today, it is known that they were originally even more imposing, with many of the stones having been taken by the victorious Spanish to build their homes. **LH**

Cuzco Cathedral (Cuzco, Peru)

A beautiful monument and home to historic art treasures

"The whole structure is magnificent.... Its proportions have unique amplitude."

Héctor Velarde, *Arquitectura Peruana* (1946)

The city of Cuzco's impressive Baroque cathedral stands imposingly on the Plaza de Armas, built over the foundations of what was an important Inca palace, the Palace of Viracocha. This structure was actually the second cathedral to be built in the city; the first was smaller and built very early in the Spanish occupation, in 1536. A couple of decades later, work was begun on the grand new cathedral. The first stone was laid down in 1559, but thanks to erratic funding and a devastating earthquake it took more than 100 years for the new cathedral building to be finished, in 1669. The most talented colonial artists were employed to work on the new cathedral and substantial numbers of indigenous people were temporarily hired as laborers. The original cathedral—on the Inca sacred site—was relegated to the status of a humble church, La Iglesia del Triunfo; it is, however, attached to the newer cathedral and is the oldest church in the city.

Cuzco Cathedral is filled with magnificent regal examples of colonial art, many of which were by members of the renowned local Cuzco School, as well as a portrait of Jesus attributed to Anthony van Dyck. The earliest surviving portrait of the city of Cuzco is also in the church; it shows the city in the 1650 earthquake. There are beautiful examples of stone masonry and skilled metalwork on display, including a solid silver altar. Probably the most famous of all the cathedral's possessions is a painting of the Last Supper, created specially for the cathedral by Marcos Zapata (Cuzco School). It demonstrates how eager the conquistadors were to draw Peruvians into the Catholic religion. The dish placed in front of Christ is not typically associated with Jesus, or the cuisine of the Middle East; instead, Jesus and his disciples are about to feast on *cuy*, the small, skinny carcass of a guinea pig—a Peruvian specialty. **LH**

Convento de Santa Catalina (Arequipa, Peru)

Large convent where the nuns enjoyed a rich lifestyle

The beautiful city of Arequipa, Peru's second-largest city, was a major town in colonial times, and its buildings bear witness to this wealthy history. The Convento de Santa Catalina is not only Arequipa's largest religious building, but one of the largest in all Peru. Its thick walls enclose what amounted to a mini city of its own. The convent took several decades to complete, but by the 1600s was home to around 500 nuns and domestic staff. Despite being a strictly closed convent, life for the nuns here was not at all austere. Convent life was viewed by many young women from aristocratic families as the only alternative to a forced marriage, and it is unlikely that many of them were driven to join the order by a true vocation. The convent was aptly named after St. Catherine of Sienna (1347–80), who defied her parents' attempts to marry her off and instead became a devout nun.

Rich young novices brought extremely large dowries to the convent, and in the seventeenth century, the Convento de Santa Catalina's sleeping quarters bore a far stronger resemblance to the elaborate bedroom suites of so many princesses— furnished with rich draperies and expensive possessions—than humble nuns' cells. The nuns were looked after by an army of servants, who had their own, less elegant, domestic areas.

For four centuries, the Convento de Santa Catalina remained a closed religious order. In 1970, however, it was opened to the public and quickly became a popular visitor attraction. The few remaining nuns have quarters in a separate section, a tranquil refuge from the curious groups of tourists. One of the most popular rooms that tourists can visit on the site is the former cell of Sister Ana de los Angeles, mother superior in the seventeenth century, who was famed for her prophetic visions. **LH**

> *"The nuns were able to invite musicians to perform in the convent [and] have parties."*

Charlotte Beech, journalist

Isla del Sol (Lake Titicaca, Bolivia)

More than 180 Inca ruins can be seen on this tiny island

Isla del Sol is one of thirty-six islands in Lake Titicaca in the otherwise arid Altiplano region of Bolivia, lying 12,506 feet (3,812 m) above sea level. Situated at the southern end of the lake, the island is divided into three parts: Yumani in the south, the sandy beach area of Ch'alla in the east, and Challapampa in the north. The island measures 5.5 square miles (14 sq km), has no cars, and takes approximately three hours to cross on foot. It is populated by 5,000 members of the indigenous Aymara group who call it Titi'kaka, which is thought to stem from the Aymara words *titi* (puma) and *kala* (rock), as the shape of the lake is said to look like a puma hunting a rabbit.

The Aymara live in thatched adobe huts and make a living from farming sheep on the hills, growing maize and potatoes on the island's steep terraces, fishing in the freshwater lake, and from tourists who visit the rocky terrain to see the ruins of Inca shrines and temples. The ruins are thought to date back to the fifteenth century, although archeologists believe the area has been inhabited since 3000 B.C.E. The island was sacred to the Incas because they believed the sun and moon were born on the island itself. They believed that the sun god, Inti, ordered the first Incas to emerge from the lake from whence they headed north to found the Inca capital city of Cuzco.

Among the ruins on the island are the Titiqala caves, where the sun and moon are said to have emerged. At Yumani lie the Inca Steps: 206 steps rising 164 feet (50 m), and leading to a sacred stone fountain with three springs that is said to be a fountain of youth. The Chinkana stone labyrinth complex at Challapampa is thought to have been a seminary for Inca priests. Nearby is an ancient path that runs across the island and is said to bear the footprints of the sun and moon, but the indentations are the effects of natural erosion. **CK**

 🔶 # Tiwanaku (near La Paz, Bolivia)

Spiritual and political center of the Tiwanaku Culture

Tiwanaku (or Tiahuanaco) lies about 9.5 miles (15 km) from Lake Titicaca; its monuments and statues have excited speculation from archeologists and historians for many years. Tiwanaku is claimed by some to be the oldest city in the world; others believe it was a sacred place for Aymara, a tribe that thrived here long before the arrival of the Incas; there are even those who claim the site was built by visitors from another planet, by the same beings who they believe created the Nazca Lines in nearby Peru.

Nestling in the Bolivian Andes, Tiwanaku was built at a height of approximately 2 miles (3.5 km) above sea level, making construction of these massive stone monuments even more of a challenge because the stone had to be transported some distance. The first building work has been dated back to c. 500 C. E., with later additions having been added five or six centuries later. The stones used in the construction of the temples, monoliths, and statues were cut in a specific manner to "lock" them together without the use of any kind of mortar. The heaviest stones weigh around 100 tons. By the time of the Inca arrival in the mid-fifteenth century, the original inhabitants had disappeared. Some historians call this a great mystery; others claim more prosaically that the people of Tiwanaku were agricultural farmers and, as so often happened, once the land was no longer good for cultivation, they simply moved on. The Incas created their own mythology about Tiwanaku, claiming it as the birthplace of humankind.

The importance of this site simply cannot be underestimated and it is astonishing that it is so little known, despite it ranking in importance with such other great monuments as the pyramids in Egypt, the Nazca Lines in Peru, Stonehenge in England, and Petra in Jordan. **LH**

Casa de la Libertad (Sucre, Bolivia)

The university building where Bolivia was officially declared an independent country

> "The freedom of the New World is the hope of the universe."

Simón Bolívar, revolutionary and statesman

The Casa de la Libertad (House of Liberty) on Sucre's main plaza is where the country of Bolivia was born, and it was here in a room at the Jesuit Royal and Pontifical Higher University of San Francisco that the country's Declaration of Independence was signed on August 6, 1825, by Antonio José de Sucre y Álvarez de Peralta (1795–1830). The historic document is on display to visitors in what is now a museum. The university, established in 1624, is one of the oldest in the Americas and had become a significant hotbed of libertarian thought and enlightenment thinking at a time when political revolution had swept Europe and North America.

Formerly known as Upper Peru, the new Republic of Bolivia took its name from its founder, General Simón "The Liberator" Bolívar y Palacios (1783–1830). He was known throughout Latin America as the revolutionary leader of the independence movement that saw the region freed from Spanish colonial rule after Bolívar's War from 1809 to 1825. His leadership led to the creation of the countries now known as Venezuela, Colombia, Ecuador, Peru, Panama, and Bolivia.

The city of Sucre is Bolivia's legislative and constitutional capital and was founded in 1538 by the Spanish, who called it La Plata. Previously it had been known as Chuquisaca by the indigenous Charcas Indians. The new Bolivian republicans renamed the city once more, this time in honor of Bolívar's right-hand man, Antonio José de Sucre. His republican army of 7,000 men defeated the Spanish army of 10,000 at the Battle of Ayacucho in 1824, making him responsible for taking the last Spanish stronghold in the region and ending the Wars of Independence. Bolívar went on to become Bolivia's first president. Paintings of both Bolívar and Sucre adorn the walls of this building. **CK**

◎ # Casa Real de la Moneda (Potosí, Bolivia)

Bolivia's royal mint was built in a town that prospered from mining silver

The Casa Real de la Moneda, or Royal Mint Museum, in Potosí in Bolivia, was originally a mint in what was once one of the richest towns in Latin America. Potosí was founded in 1545 as a mining town and is located high up at an altitude of 13,780 feet (4,200 m) beneath the Cerro de Potosí, sometimes called Cerro Rico (rich mountain), a mountain of silver ore. From 1556 to 1783, at the peak of production, some 45,000 tons of pure silver were mined from Cerro Rico, making Potosí an industrial boom town with 200,000 inhabitants and 86 churches, although most of the wealth made its way across the ocean to the coffers of the Spanish crown. Locals still mine Cerro Rico for silver, iron, zinc, tin, lead, cadmium, and chromium in truly appalling conditions.

During the Bolivian War of Independence from 1809 to 1825, the Casa Real de la Moneda passed back and forth between the hands of the freedom fighters and the army loyal to the crown, and at one point the building was nearly blown up. By the time Bolivia achieved independence in 1825, most of the silver had been depleted and the town has become ever shabbier since then.

In English when someone is rich they are "worth a mint"; in Spanish the equivalent phrase is "worth a *potosí.*" The town's first mint was built in 1672, and then lavishly rebuilt in 1759 under the orders of Spain's new king, Charles III, to modernize coin production techniques. The construction took fourteen years and cost the equivalent of more than $10 million today. Now a museum, the mint is a fascinating place for its history, architecture, and series of galleries that house paintings, silverware, coins, antiques, and machinery once used in the minting process. It is also testament to what was once a vast industrial complex and an eye-opening reminder of colonial exploitation and avarice. **CK**

> *"Working conditions . . . were so appalling that the miners survived no more than six months."*
>
> Allan Taylor, travel writer

🏛 ◈ Misión Jesuítica de San José (San José de Chiquitos, Bolivia)

One of several churches built in the region to promote Christian worship

The Jesuits took control of the Chiquitos region in the 1690s and immediately began building churches for their missions. The Misión Jesuítica de San José was the third of the churches to be built in Chiquitos and one of six that remain today. Settlements were created around each of the churches, inhabited by indigenous people who had converted to Christianity. The Jesuits founded these settlements on sixteenth-century philosophical ideas about what constituted the "ideal city." The churches were all painstakingly restored in the twentieth century, and are now an essential part of a Baroque music festival that takes place here every year.

A surprisingly large church for such a small town, the Misión Jesuítica de San José stands on the edge of a large stone plaza, dominating San José, much as the missionaries intended to dominate the area's indigenous people—although in reality the Jesuits were surrounded by a mass of hostile and well-armed tribes. This particular church was constructed from stone, which was unusual at the time; most other mission churches in this region were constructed from wood and adobe. The church's internal plan was based on the layout of early Christian churches, with four distinct areas separated by three aisles. The decorations were beautifully created by local and Jesuit artisans and include tall columns that were created from single tree trunks.

In the 1760s, when the Jesuits fell out of favor with the authorities and were ordered to leave Spanish-controlled Latin America to return to Spain, the vast majority of their mission buildings were ruthlessly destroyed. However the glorious church at San José de Chiquitos fortunately escaped remarkably unscathed and still serves at the heart of a strong Catholic community. **LH**

 ⬡ **Jesuit Ruins** (Trinidad, Paraguay)

The hilltop ruins are the most impressive and best-preserved of the area's townships

During the seventeenth and eighteenth centuries, present-day Paraguay became one of the major South American regions for Jesuit missionaries seeking to convert local populations to Christianity. To this end they built complete townships (also called reductions) comprising churches, schools, houses, workshops, and farms. Trinidad was one such township and a major mission center.

The hub of Trinidad's layout was a plaza where the local Guaraní people practiced military drills, readying themselves to fight off Spanish landowners and slave traders—Spain colonized the area at this time. Around the plaza stood Guaraní homes and a grand stone church housing the tombs of Guaraní chiefs and fine Guaraní carvings. Other remains include most of the original walls, another church, a bell tower, a schoolhouse, a cemetery, and statuary. Still standing, too, are some of the pillars built to support verandas

that together provided long walkways sheltered from both rain and sun. At its height, this thriving mission exported foodstuffs and artifacts to Peru and Spain—the local people were skilled at raising cattle, growing crops such as corn and rice, and crafting objects from ceramic, bronze, and stone.

Visible on a nearby hill, a few miles northwest of Trinidad, are the ruins of another Jesuit mission—Jesús. Here visitors can see a schoolhouse and a church with a stunning Moorish facade but no roof, its construction left unfinished when the Spanish crown expelled the Jesuits in 1767. After this expulsion, both sites were abandoned and therefore decayed; their Guaraní inhabitants found work on local Spanish estates or made homes in the jungle. In more recent times, much restoration work has been done and the Jesuit Missions were inscribed on the UNESCO World Heritage List in 1993. **AK**

 ⊚ **Colonia del Sacramento** (Colonia del Sacramento, Uruguay)

Strategic site where the Portuguese defended repeated attacks from the Spanish

The Portuguese built this site—originally called the Novo Colonia de Santissimo Sacramento—on Spanish territory, and it became a source of provocation and contention between Portugal and Spain for many years. Shortly after the settlement was founded, it was attacked by the Spanish, who controlled nearby Buenos Aires, and fighting between the two nations ensued for several months. In 1681 the settlement was returned to the Portuguese but remained a thorn in the Spanish side for decades to come, with regular attempts to regain control of it. The political haggling continued until 1731 when, under the Treaty of Utrecht, Novo Colonia de Santissimo Sacramento was finally declared Portuguese.

Novo Colonia de Santissimo Sacramento was founded by Manuel de Lobo, the governor of Brazil. At the time the settlement was built, Uruguay was not a separate country but part of Spanish-controlled Argentina. The settlement was built on a bank of the Rio de la Plata, not far from where the river reaches its confluence with the Uruguay River (a large amount of river traffic traveled regularly by this spot). The Portuguese used the town as an illegal port, thereby avoiding Spanish customs controls—a move welcomed by the British, whose ships were regular visitors to the region. In response, the Spanish built the nearby settlement of Montevideo in an effort to control the smuggling of contraband whose revenue they believed should go to the Spanish crown.

The town is a mixture of Spanish, Portuguese, and vernacular architecture, with the oldest parts bearing a strong resemblance to the oldest areas of Lisbon. The historic center of Colonia del Sacramento, with its colonial houses, churches, and slender, cobbled streets—parts of which are now picturesque ruins—was declared a World Heritage site in 1995. **LH**

Old Government House (Montevideo, Uruguay)

Built as a political headquarters after Uruguay won its independence

Montevideo lies on a natural harbor on the Rio de Plata, on the opposite bank to Buenos Aires in Argentina. For centuries, the small region that would become Uruguay had to fight for independence from Argentina, Brazil, Spain, and Portugal. In 1828, the country of Uruguay was formally created, but its problems were not yet over. Between 1843 and 1852 it was embroiled in war, which led to the devastating siege of Montevideo.

Twenty years after the end of the war, when Uruguay was finally able to govern itself, this cream-colored building was erected as the Government House. Since 1905 it has been known as Palacio Estevez and been used mainly for official ceremonial purposes, but until 1905 it was at the heart of Uruguayan politics. In 1928, U.S. President Herbert Hoover made history when he visited Uruguay and was received by President Campistegui at the Palacio Estevez. Now, in recognition of that event, the Palacio Estevez contains a Museum of the Presidents.

The Plaza Independencia, beside which Palacio Estevez stands, is a chronology of Uruguayan history. Next door to Palacio Estevez is the Palacio Salvo, a twenty-six-story tower built in the 1920s and once the tallest building in South America. Nearby is the old Art Deco Hotel Victoria, now one of the Reverend Moon's Unification churches, and the Solís Theater, named after the Spanish conquistador Juan Diaz de Solís, who came to Uruguay in 1516. In the center of the square stands an equestrian statue of General José Artigas, whose mausoleum lies beneath. Argentinean-born Artigas was a hero of the Uruguayan Independence and one of the founding fathers of South America. A believer in giving power to the people, including the indigenous people, he was driven out of both Uruguay and his homeland, and died in exile in Paraguay. **LH**

Humberstone

(near Iquique, Chile)

Former mining town that had sizable mineral reserves

"*Every building in the center was built from Oregon pine, brought to the desert as ships' ballast.*"

Martin Buckley, journalist

The eerie sense of abandonment is overwhelming at Humberstone. Built to accommodate the workers in the local saltpeter industry, the town was erected quickly and cheaply using many poor quality materials. It was named after the British manager James Humberstone to recognize his contribution of a new ore-refining system to the industry.

It is difficult to imagine the area full of noisy machinery, processing plants, and smoking chimneys but, with a population peak of 3,700, the town was packed full of miners who exploited the extensive natural reserves of sodium nitrate. Used commercially in the manufacture of fertilizers and explosives, the nitrates were transported internationally and the industry contributed significantly to the Chilean economy. Wars were fought with Bolivia and Peru over the mineral reserves, although Chile emerged the victor, taking control of almost all of the nitrate grounds. The country became the leading global producer of natural nitrates. The boom that resulted could not last and the industry was deeply hit by the Great Depression in 1929. The discovery of an artificial method for producing nitrates was the final nail in the coffin. The saltpeter industry dried up, the *pesados* (miners) moved away, and the former industrial town gained the ghostlike and almost magical qualities it still possesses today.

Unlike other former mining towns, Humberstone remains almost in its original entirety. The church, theater, and store all linger as evidence of the once-thriving community, and the rusting remains of machinery and buildings invoke a strong sense of melancholic nostalgia. However, the scorching sun and a recent earthquake, together with the fragile materials and lightweight construction of the deserted town, mean that its future is anything but secure. **KB**

Robinson Crusoe Island

(Isla Robinson Crusoe, Chile)

The island's past inspired the famous book

A tiny island off the coast of Chile, the Isla Robinson Crusoe has the rare distinction of being named after a fictional character. The story of how this came about, though, is firmly grounded in reality. In 1704, privateer Alexander Selkirk had an argument with his captain and was marooned on the island. Marooning was a common punishment among pirates and usually led to a slow death from starvation. Selkirk survived, however, living off wild goats, seals, and berries. He was rescued in 1709, and when he returned to England, his experiences were widely reported. These accounts provided Daniel Defoe with the raw material

"I was a prisoner locked up with the eternal bars ... of the ocean, in an uninhabited wilderness."

Daniel Defoe, *Robinson Crusoe* (1719)

for his celebrated novel, *Robinson Crusoe*.

The island, meanwhile, remained a haven for shipwrecked sailors and castaways, until the Spanish established a fort and a prison to deter visitors. The island remained uninhabited until 1877, when a Swiss émigré, Alfred de Rodt, obtained permission from the Chilean authorities to establish a settlement there. It supported itself by farming and by exporting lobsters to the mainland. The island's change of name was designed to add to this income, by attracting tourists. The community still survives, but it has increasingly been overshadowed by a growing awareness of the island's unique natural habitat. In a bid to preserve this, the Chilean government designated the area as a national park in 1935, and it has since been added to UNESCO's list of World Biosphere Reserves. **IZ**

Casa de Isla Negra

(Isla Negra, Chile)

Pablo Neruda's beachfront house

Poet, communist politician, and a winner of the Nobel Prize for Literature, Pablo Neruda is an iconic figure in the history of Chile, straddling both its political and cultural life. Revered for his outstanding poetry, it was his political activism that made him a controversial figure during his lifetime, leading to his years of exile in Italy.

A supporter of Chile's socialist President Salvador Allende, Neruda was hospitalized with cancer when Allende died during the coup d'état led by General Augusto Pinochet, and passed away himself only days later. His funeral was attended by thousands of Chileans who bravely chose to flout the curfew imposed on them in a gesture against totalitarian rule. Casa de Isla Negra was one of three houses in Chile that Neruda lived in, all of which were vandalized at the time of his death and boarded up by the military government. Neruda's third wife, Matilde Urrutia, campaigned to establish the Fundación Pablo Neruda to preserve the houses, and she is buried at Casa de Isla Negra alongside her husband.

Now a museum administered by the foundation, the beachfront house is as poetic and flamboyant as its owner. A lover of the sea, Neruda bought the stone cottage in 1938 and adapted it to resemble a ship, complete with wooden floors, narrow corridors, and low ceilings. Over the years he also added a roofless tower and a small space complete with a wood and zinc roof that allowed him to hear the rain. The latter was the room he used to write in, looking out of its small window onto the Pacific Ocean. There is a vast collection of books, and each room of the house is a treasure trove packed with maritime memorabilia such as maps, shells, ship figureheads, nautical instruments, paintings, and ships in bottles; there is even an anchor in the garden. **CK**

San Ignacio Miní

(San Ignacio, Argentina)

These ruins are the best example of a Jesuit mission in the country

The mission of San Ignacio Miní was set up by the Jesuits to replace earlier, doomed missions in this region (the earliest of which was also called San Ignacio). The first missions had been set up *c.* 1610 in what is now part of Paraguay. These were terrorized by slave hunters and bandits, forcing the Jesuits to move their mission in the 1630s; that mission also failed. San Ignacio Miní was built in the 1690s and, by the 1730s, there were around 4,000 people living here. In 1767, the Jesuits were out of favor with the Spanish government and were subsequently recalled to Spain; San Ignacio Miní was left to decay and by 1817 it was largely destroyed.

The centerpiece of San Ignacio Miní was an enormous church, sprawling 243 feet (74 m) in length. It was built by local craftsmen using local and imported materials, including sandstone and ceramics. The ruins are a breathtakingly evocative indication of what once stood here, with imposing broken columns, carved stones, and huge, jagged arches made from walls 7 feet (2 m) wide. The few original arches that remain almost intact are a stunning example of a style that has become known as Guaraní Baroque, named after the architecture of this region. The red hue of the sandstone still imparts an impressive warm glow, even though what remains of the church today is a mere memory of the vast, original building.

As well as the church, there were accommodation areas, several workshops, kitchens, dining areas, classrooms, a grand plaza, and of course a cemetery. Significant restoration work on the site started in the 1940s and, in 1983, the glorious ruins of San Ignacio Miní and three other former Jesuit missions in this beautiful rain forest region were added to the World Heritage List. **LH**

> *"Voltaire . . . wrote about the missions, praising the egalitarian impulse behind them."*
>
> Larry Rohter, journalist

Che Guevara's Boyhood Home (Alta Gracia, Argentina)

Now a museum for the political activist

The image of Marxist revolutionary Ernesto "Che" Guevara de la Serna (1928–67) clad in a beret and sporting a beard is one that has come to epitomize the youthful, idealistic rebel. It is also one that visitors to Cuba will see across posters and murals throughout the island, because both the iconic image and the man have achieved an almost saintly status not afforded to Guevara's co-revolutionary, Cuban President Fidel Castro. Such reverence and affection have perhaps been aided by Guevara's death at a young age, when he was executed in Bolivia for his revolutionary guerilla activities in the region.

> *"I will go out with a machine gun in my hand, to the barricades … I'll keep fighting to the end."*
>
> Ernesto "Che" Guevara, revolutionary

The young socialist was born into a middle-class family in Rosario, Argentina, and studied medicine before his beliefs set him to take up political causes instead. The English-style villa in Alta Gracia was built in 1891, and is now a museum dedicated to Guevara's memory and is modeled on his boyhood home. The family came to the region because it was known to have a beneficial climate for those with respiratory diseases, and the young Guevara was an asthma sufferer. The museum has nine rooms containing documents and photographs of Guevara's early life with family and friends. Other items on display include books he read as a child and even a bicycle. The library houses photos of Guevara doing volunteer work, and it was this experience that led to his awareness of social injustice and his eventual political activism. **CK**

Obelisk of Buenos Aires (Buenos Aires, Argentina)

Monument to the city's rich history

The Obelisk of Buenos Aires was built in the staggeringly short time of only four weeks to celebrate the city's 400th anniversary in 1936. The monument lies at the center of the Argentine capital's Plaza de la República square. Standing 220 feet (67 m) high and measuring 527 square feet (49 sq m) at its base, the obelisk is made of white stone from the province of Córdoba and was designed by Argentine Modernist architect Alberto Prebisch. In 2005 it was renovated and covered in an acrylic paint ("Paris stone" color) to protect it against the elements.

The faces of the monument commemorate various historical events in the life of the city: its initial foundation in 1536; its final foundation in 1580; the first time the Argentine flag was flown in the city in 1812 at the Church of Saint Nicholas, where the obelisk itself now stands; and the inauguration of Buenos Aires as the capital of Argentina in 1880. It is possible to go inside the obelisk and climb the 206 stairs to reach its peak, which offers commanding views of the city through four windows.

Yet the obelisk is more than just a monument to the city's past; it has also been a rallying point over the years. Locals gather there to celebrate soccer victories and it has also been the focal point of political and social protests, frequently being defaced by graffiti. During the unpopular Peronist government of 1974 to 1976, a sign was hung on the obelisk saying: "El silencio es salud," meaning "Silence is health." Superficially this was intended as a reminder to motorists not to honk their car horns. But it was also interpreted as a more sinister warning not to express political views in opposition to the government in what was a repressive period in Argentina's history: many anti-Peronists disappeared, and the country was in turmoil with an economy hit by massive inflation. **CK**

Church of San Ignacio de Loyola (Buenos Aires, Argentina)

The oldest church in the city, built to honor the founder of the Jesuits

In Monserrat, one of the historic old quarters in downtown Buenos Aires, the block known as Manzana de las Luces (Block of Enlightenment) can be found. The term comes from the early nineteenth century when important Argentines were educated in the area; the "enlightenment" refers to the wisdom and knowledge they gained. A number of historically significant buildings can be found in this block.

One of these buildings is the Church of San Ignacio, on the corner of Alsina and Bolivar. Built in honor of St. Ignatius Loyola, a noble Basque who went on to found the Society of Jesus, or the Jesuits, the church is said to be the oldest in the city. A temple had previously existed on the site but the construction of a greater place of worship was insisted upon by Jesuit priests. So it was that building began in 1710, and by 1734 the church was completed. It was designed in the shape of a Latin cross with a central vaulted nave and lateral naves with upper galleries and cavernous chapels. The two large Baroque-style corbels of the facade create an illusion of extra space. The right tower, raised in the nineteenth century, housed a bell that had once marked the hour from the Plaza de Mayo, or town hall, which is a five-minute walk away. Of particular note are the hand-carved doors, which open out onto the central nave.

The block housing the church is now included in a program of restoration. In spite of its importance, the Church of San Ignacio had been woefully neglected for many years. The furious protesting of local priests on the streets of the city helped to instigate the repair work. **OR**

◪ St. Ignatius Loyola began life as a soldier; he found his vocation while recuperating from a leg wound.

◨ Within the Baroque interior of the church is a beautiful altar of gilded wood carved by Isidro de Lorea.

La Recoleta Cemetery (Buenos Aires, Argentina)

Where Argentina buries its most illustrious citizens

The area known as La Recoleta was originally the home of a community of monks (Recoletos Descalzos), who built a monastery there in 1716 and a Baroque church in 1732. Today it is home to the city's richest inhabitants. It first became the haunt of the city's wealthy residents after a yellow fever epidemic in 1871 forced them to desert the south of the city and move north. But what makes La Recoleta known worldwide is the cemetery that houses the remains of Argentina's most famous sons and daughters, from presidents to poets, and from lawyers to racing drivers.

The holy ground of the church was annexed as a cemetery in 1822 and now covers 12 acres (5 ha). The cemetery is almost a small town in itself with 4,700 crypts that lie along tree-lined avenues and narrow sidewalks where visitors can wander to gain a feel for Argentina's architecture and history. The entrance is a majestic Neoclassical gate bordered by Doric-style columns, and the various ornate and beautifully crafted stone and marble mausoleums are decorated with statuary and brass or bronze plaques bearing the names of the families and individuals buried there.

The cemetery's most visited grave is the Art Deco monument to Eva Perón, second wife of Argentine President Juan Domingo Perón and the First Lady of Argentina from 1946 until her death in 1952. During her lifetime, the former actress and singer won the affection and support of Argentina's poor and was a vocal supporter of the country's trade unions. Her body lies in a coffin in a compartment under a trapdoor in the marble floor of the tomb in an attempt to fend off grave robbers. **CK**

↗ Eva Perón, in a 1940s photograph, was popularized worldwide by the Andrew Lloyd-Webber musical *Evita*.

⤷ This plaque on Perón's tomb at La Recoleta recalls her as champion of the working people of Argentina.

Metropolitan Cathedral

(Buenos Aires, Argentina)

Burial site of José de San Martín Matorras

The Catedral Metropolitana de Buenos Aires, or Buenos Aires Metropolitan Cathedral, is Argentina's most important Roman Catholic church. It is built on the site where six previous adobe churches had collapsed over two centuries. Building began on the present stone structure, which is designed to a Latin cross plan, in 1753 and it was consecrated as a church in 1804. Construction was finally completed in 1852, although there were some additional embellishments in 1911, and the church is an architectural mix of the Baroque and the Neoclassical styles.

Inside, the cathedral's Santo Cristo de Buenos Aires (Holy Christ of Buenos Aires) chapel contains a wooden carving of Jesus Christ dating to 1671. But the cathedral is most famous for being the burial place of the ashes of the Argentine national hero General José de San Martín Matorras (1778–1850). He led a number of successful military campaigns during the Wars of Independence that raged across South America from 1811 to 1825, that saw him fight in Chile, Peru, and Argentina before eventually retiring to become a farmer. He is regarded as one of the foremost liberators of the region from Spanish rule together with General Simón Bolívar y Palacios (1783–1830).

De San Martín's marble tomb was carved by French sculptor Albert Carrier-Belleuse. It lies in a side chapel, covered by an Argentine flag. However, De San Martín's remains were not housed in the cathedral's mausoleum until thirty years after his death. When his wife died in 1824, De San Martín moved to Europe and spent the rest of his life in Boulogne-sur-Mer in France. His remains were brought back to Argentina and reinterred at the cathedral in 1880.

Also on the site is a tomb dedicated to the unknown soldier of Argentine independence; a perpetual flame burns outside in his memory. **CK**

Teatro Colón

(Buenos Aires, Argentina)

Elegant nineteenth-century opera house

Buenos Aires's Teatro Colón opera house is a sumptuous building and was declared a national historical monument in 1989. The lavishly decorated structure is vast in size and measures 88,285 square feet (8,202 sq m). Its auditorium seats 2,478 spectators and the orchestra pit can house 120 musicians.

A stunning example of Franco-Italian Renaissance architecture, Teatro Colón was not the city's first opera house. One was opened in 1857, but shut down in 1888. Such was the appetite of Buenos Aires for opera that the local government decided the city needed a more modern and larger venue. The city's love for opera

> *"... Italian Renaissance with solid German detail and ... the grace and dash of French architecture."*
>
> **Vittorio Meano, describing the style of the theater**

began in the early nineteenth century, when the first European opera singers arrived to give performances. Buenos Aires began to take its place on the world map for high culture, marking the recognition of the arts in the country. The idea to create an opera house, the majestic grandeur of which would reflect the highbrow nature of its inhabitants and signal its cultural prestige, was a significant move in forming Argentina's national identity post-independence, putting it on a par with the capital cities of Europe.

Building commenced on the current opera house in 1889 and took nineteen years to complete. Three architects were involved in its design: the Italians Francesco Tamburini and Vittorio Meano, followed by the Belgian Jules Dormal. The theater opened in 1908 to the strains of Giuseppe Verdi's *Aida*. **CK**

University of Córdoba

(Córdoba, Argentina)

The oldest university in Argentina and the fourth oldest in the Americas

The colonial town of Córdoba was named after the famous Spanish town of the same name. It was founded, when Argentina was a Spanish colony, by Jerónimo Luis de Cabrera who reputedly named this site as the spot for his city on July 6, 1573. The location was well chosen: it lay in the center of the country, in the foothills of the Sierra Chica Mountains, and beside the Siquia River. Córdoba is not the oldest colonial town in Argentina, but it houses the country's oldest university. The Universidad Nacional de Córdoba was founded by the Jesuit order in the early seventeenth century and was only the second to be founded in the whole of Spanish-controlled Latin America.

When the Jesuits were expelled from the colonies, the university was taken over by the Franciscan order. Control of the university then passed to the national government in 1856. In 1918 the institution saw a student-based movement for the democratization of higher education, called the Reforma Universitaria, which was destined to influence the running of universities in all of Latin America. Nicknamed "La Docta," or "The Learned Lady," the Universidad Nacional de Córdoba continues to be one of the most important universities in Argentina.

The university is located in the center of a block of Jesuitical buildings in the heart of Córdoba that, with its associated estancias (farming estates), was designated a UNESCO World Heritage site in 2000. Other buildings in the old town include the seventeenth-century town hall, a superb museum of history, the old market, the Romanesque-style cathedral, and the church known as the Iglesia Compañia de Jesus, which is the city's oldest surviving building dating from 1622. The city of Córdoba also boasts the oldest remaining school in Argentina, the Monserrat School, which was founded in 1685. **LH**

"... student strikes here in 1918 sparked a nationwide university reform movement ..."

Geoffrey Fox, journalist

From paintings executed in the darkness of caves thousands of years ago, European civilization would reach extraordinary heights of achievement in both culture and science. However, many European historic sites mark clashes between European nation states, with the greatest bloodbath of all time occurring in the early 1900s. Modern Europeans cherish their great heritage, but also recognize that exploitation of distant peoples made much of it possible.

◁ Symbols of Imperial Rome: the Arch of Constantine and the Colosseum.

Europe

🏛 ◉ Thingvellir (Bláskógabyggð, Iceland)

Site of Iceland's first democratic assemblies

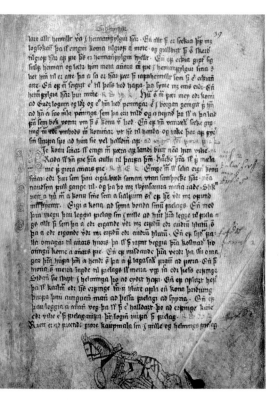

Thingvellir in Iceland is a unique national park that not only offers the visitor landscapes of great natural beauty, but also embodies the very core of Iceland's social, political, and religious history. Thingvellir is one of the oldest parliamentary institutions in the world, and as such has been designated a UNESCO World Heritage site. It is here, on the shores of the largest lake in Iceland, that the general assembly, or Althing, first met in 930 to act as a forum for the Icelandic people. The assembly, comprising chieftains and their advisers, would sit for two weeks a year in the open air of the countryside in order to settle disputes, debate issues, and establish laws.

The Althing meetings took place at Löfbörg (the law rock), and it was from this site that the law speaker proclaimed the laws of the commonwealth. The meetings at the law rock were also used to report news on significant matters, to inaugurate and dissolve the council, and to confirm rulings and laws. The importance of the law rock swiftly disappeared in 1262 when Iceland swore allegiance to its neighbor, Norway. For this reason, the precise location of the rock is uncertain. It is hoped that with further archeological research and resources this mystery may finally be solved.

In addition to being a political monument of great historical interest, the site at Thingvellir is also a place of geological interest. It is part of a fissure zone that runs through Iceland, which is set on the tectonic plate boundaries of the Mid-Atlantic Ridge. The resulting faults and fissures of the area are evident. Fractures the size of canyons traverse the region, and some contain exceptionally clear water. Legend has it that if you drop a coin and watch it fall to the bottom of one of these clefts—Peningagjá (Penny Canyon)—then your dream will come true. This national park is a magical place indeed. **KH**

> *"It will prove true that if we tear apart the laws we will also tear apart the peace."*

Thorgeirr Ljósvetningagoði, lawspeaker, 999

⊞ A sixteenth-century manuscript from the Jónsbók, a code of laws instituted by the Althing in 1281.

⊡ Thingvallakirkja, the church at Thingvellir, and the Thingvallbær, a traditional farmhouse built in 1930.

Alta Rock Carvings (Alta, Norway)

An impressive collection of several thousand prehistoric rock carvings

Nestled away in the north of Norway, just above the Arctic Circle, is an extraordinary series of rock carvings that date from as early as 4200 B.C.E. to around 500 B.C.E. They are part of a large archeological site close to the town of Alta and have survived in remarkable form, given the levels of pollution from industrialization. The wide variety of imagery used in the carvings suggests a culture of hunter-gatherers who are thought to be descendants of the Komsa, a Stone Age society that developed along the Norwegian coast and increased in number during the late Ice Age.

Through their work, the hunter-gatherers who made the Alta carvings have provided us with a great deal of information about their lives. The people who made these carvings were hunters and fishermen, adept at herding animals and building boats. Images of reindeer feature regularly in the carvings, as do those of elk, birds, fish, wolves, bears, and many other species. It is noticeable that bears feature prominently in many of the carvings, often posed in positions that suggest that they were worshipped. Several ancient cultures are thought to have had bear cults and shamanistic rituals.

The history and importance of the Alta carvings is illustrated beautifully throughout the open-air museum constructed around the rocks. A 1.8-mile (3-km) wooden gangway built between the rock carvings makes them immediately accessible, and an exhibition displays photographic documentation of the images. In addition, there is an impressive display of objects that have been found in the area surrounding Alta, an exhibition on Sámi culture (thought to be likely descendants of the Komsa people), and an exhibit about the aurora borealis (the spectacular Northern Lights). The Alta carvings give us a glimpse of what life was like in this region many thousands of years ago. **KH**

> *"The site was holy and the images were imbued with magic."*
>
> Hans-Christian Soeborg, archeologist

⬛ ◉ Urnes Stave Church (near Lustrafjorden, Norway)

An outstanding and highly ornamental example of stave architecture

The church at Urnes has two claims to fame. The wooden structure is one of the oldest surviving examples of a stave church, a traditional style of building that is one of Norway's contributions to the field of architecture. It also boasts some remarkable ornamental details, which have given their name to the style of decoration known as Urnes style. Its antiquity, the exemplary nature of its structure, the quality of its sculpted decor, and its location within a glacial valley are factors that led UNESCO to place the building on its World Heritage List.

Urnes is spectacularly situated in southern Norway, close to the edge of a fjord, with a stunning view of snowcapped mountains in the distance. The building can be dated fairly accurately to around 1130—tests show that the timbers were felled between 1129 and 1131—and was probably built as a private church for a powerful local family, the Ornes. Archeological evidence confirms that there had been two earlier churches on this site, and much of the decoration from the second one was carefully incorporated into Urnes.

This type of architecture takes its name from the staves (upright posts) that formed the framework of the building. The area around the center of the nave is often raised so that the multiple roofs are slightly reminiscent of a pagoda. They may also feature finials, shingle-cladding, and external galleries. The roofing at Urnes is less noteworthy than the extraordinary carvings on its door panels, taken from the previous church. Dating from the late eleventh century, they took the form of a beguiling mix of interlaced ribbon-snakes and dragons. This style was easily adapted to other art forms, such as stonework and metalwork, and it was widely copied in the areas where the Vikings traveled. It proved particularly popular with the Celtic craftsmen of Britain and Ireland. **IZ**

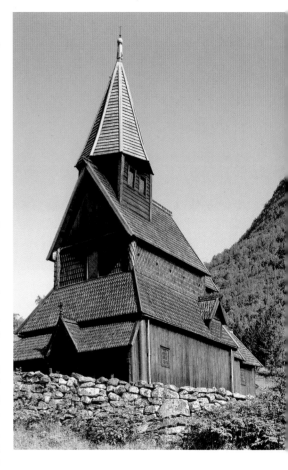

"The church brings together traces of Celtic art, Viking traditions, and Romanesque spatial structures."

UNESCO

Trondheim Cathedral (Trondheim, Norway)

Trondheim is a prosperous setting for one of the most significant churches in Scandinavia

Known also as Nidaros Cathedral, this church became a spiritual and political center from the mid-1100s when it was made the cathedral of the Norwegian archdiocese, which comprised not only Norway but also Iceland, Greenland, the Faeroe Islands, the Isle of Man, and Shetland. The cathedral has long been a pilgrim destination because St. Olav (King Olav Haraldsson), who was responsible for much of Norway's conversion to Christianity, is buried there.

The cathedral has continually been restored and updated since it was first built in 1070. Damage from various plunderings and successive fires in 1327, 1531, 1708, and 1719 has been thoroughly repaired. Most recently, in 1869, a substantial restoration program was set in motion, which continued until 2001. The attentive upkeep of the cathedral has ensured the survival of the Romanesque and Gothic exterior, as well as the delicate ornamentation of the interior. The interior of the cathedral today boasts two grand organs—a Wagner and a Steinmeyer—twentieth-century stained-glass windows, innumerable richly ornamented stone sculptures featuring interesting scenes and inscriptions in Latin and Old Norse, and an added display exhibiting the Crown Regalia. These exhibits have been collected from various coronations that have taken place in the cathedral and it is possible to see impressive crowns, large gold orbs, scepters, an anointment horn, and a "sword of the realm."

The cathedral contains a great deal of information about the history and religious development of Norway. It continues to serve as the local parish church for Trondheim and services are well attended. Indeed the church also attracts numerous visitors to view the fascinating interior, the stunning stained-glass windows, and the beautiful exterior that make it an exceptional Nordic cathedral. **KH**

Troldhaugen (Bergen, Norway)

Where Edvard Grieg lived and died

Edvard Grieg (1843–1907), the composer and pianist, grew up in the impressive Victorian villa, Troldhaugen, and today the house is a museum celebrating his life and work. Grieg, best known for his *Peer Gynt* suites, is considered by many to be Norway's most important composer. Some historians describe him as a nationalist and as a romantic composer, perhaps because he drew much of his inspiration from Norwegian folk songs and dances.

Troldhaugen Museum has been careful to reconstruct Grieg's house in the manner in which he kept it. The attractive exterior boasts a small tower, a rich ornamental veranda, and a balcony spanning the width of the house. The fascinating interior is similarly grand, with a range of rooms that show Grieg's lavish attention to detail. The dining room is adorned with costly silver and the sitting room is dominated by an enormous Steinway grand piano. Every detail suggests a comfortable, even sumptuous, lifestyle. However, Grieg needed to work in complete silence and so built a separate hut in 1891 by the lake, where he could retire from the interruptions of a busy household.

By studying the details and intricacies of the Troldhaugen Museum, both the house itself and the extensive exhibition, it is possible to sense the atmosphere that surrounded Grieg. The environment provides a glimpse not only of Grieg's character, but also of the wellsprings of his inspiration. **KH**

"Grieg referred to his building project [Troldhaugen] as 'my best opus so far.'"

Erling Dahl, museum director

Akershus Fortress (Oslo, Norway)

A strategically important medieval fortress that long kept Oslo safe

King Håkon V Magnusson of Norway (1270–1319) built the impressive Akershus Fortress in 1299 to protect the capital city of Oslo and as a defense against enemies such as Sweden. The strength of the fortress allowed it to resist a great number of sieges. However, in 1624, when an enormous fire raged through Oslo, Akershus was burned to the ground. It was rebuilt soon after by King Christian IV, who redesigned it in the Renaissance style. Once again, the fortress held out against frequent attacks. It was never successfully captured by a foreign enemy, but in 1940 it was surrendered without a struggle to the Germans. When World War II ended in 1945, the castle returned to Norwegian hands and was used to imprison and execute traitors and those who had committed war crimes. Vidkun Quisling, the leading fascist sympathizer, who ruled Norway on behalf of the Nazis, was among those executed at the site.

Akershus's resilience as a fortress was a result of King Håkon's foresight in placing it above the docks of Oslo, facing toward the Oslo fjord. Its proximity to the water meant that the Norwegian army was in a strong position to defend against naval assaults. This was a vital advantage, considering that the majority of Norwegian commerce was conducted by sea. Today the mighty fortress draws many visitors, as well as offering picturesque views across the city to those who walk in its grounds and surrounding park area.

Akershus has not been used solely as a fortress during its lifetime. It has also been occupied as a royal residence and used as a hiding place for royalty and government ministers, as well as a site of National Assemblies, an administrative and educational center, and a venue for cultural performances. The castle's multifaceted history makes it an ideal location for the present museum, which encapsulates the rich and complex history of Oslo. **KH**

> *"Despite having been under siege nine times . . . Akershus has never fallen to an enemy."*

Guardian Unlimited

Ibsen's Home (Oslo, Norway)

Ibsen's home during his twilight years

Today, a century after the playwright's death, Henrik Ibsen (1828–1906) is recognized both as a world-class dramatist and as Norway's finest author. When his plays were first staged, however, they were widely rejected as shocking and scandalous because they stripped bare the hypocrisy of Victorian notions of morality, religion, power, the role of women, and much else. Without Ibsen, the landscape of modern drama might appear very different because many of the issues that we now regard as acceptable subjects for contemporary theater were introduced to the stage for the first time in Ibsen's work.

Restored in 2006, the Ibsen Museum in Kristiania is one of three Ibsen museums in Norway. All three provide insights into the life he led. Great care has been taken to recreate Ibsen's apartment as authentically as possible and, after a lengthy restoration program and intense archeological research, the library, dining room, and parlors are open to the public. The original furniture now stands in place and the interior is decorated as though the author still lived there. Ibsen actually resided in the apartment for the last eleven years before his death. A visit to Ibsen's home takes the visitor backstage to gain a glimpse of the author's private life.

The Ibsen Museum also houses a comprehensive exhibition that celebrates the work of this extraordinary writer, the most widely performed dramatist in the world after Shakespeare. The museum regularly hosts talks, events, readings, and performances to explore Ibsen's work. It was in the study, carefully preserved at the museum, that Ibsen wrote two of his most famous plays: *John Gabriel Borkman* (1896) and *When We Dead Awaken* (1899). The latter play, his final work, is an introspective, psychological drama that explores old age and the final moments of life. **KH**

Kon-Tiki (Oslo, Norway)

Built to establish a link between civilizations

In 1947, the adventurous Norwegian scientist and explorer Thor Heyerdahl and a small crew, set off across the Pacific Ocean on an extraordinary voyage. His purpose was to demonstrate that ancient peoples from South America could have settled the Polynesian islands. To prove the point, he made his journey in a raft built in Peru in what he believed was an ancient Peruvian style and from materials that would have been available at the time. He named it *Kon-Tiki*, after an Inca deity. The raft's basic construction was of balsa tree trunks, tied together with hemp ropes. Its bow, steering oar, deck, mast, main sail, and cabin used mangrove, pine, and fir woods as well as bamboo,

> ## "I knew in my heart that a maritime prehistoric civilization used rafts like the Kon-Tiki."
>
> Thor Heyerdahl, explorer

which also provided tubes for the crew's water supply. A radio was one of his very few concessions to the modern world. After 101 days and about 4,500 miles (7,200 km), the *Kon-Tiki* reached Polynesia only to crash into a reef at Raroia, in the Tuamotu islands.

Today the *Kon-Tiki* can be seen in Oslo's Kon-Tiki Museum, along with the papyrus boat *Ra II*, in which Thor Heyerdahl crossed the Atlantic in 1970 to prove ancient contact between Africa and Central and South America. Here, too, are fascinating finds from Heyerdahl's travels in Polynesia, the Galápagos, and South America. Other exhibits showcasing Norway's seafaring history are close by. These include a museum housing the famous ship of polar exploration, *Fram* (1892), which was involved in Roald Amundsen's race to the South Pole. **AK**

🏛 ◎ **Great Copper Mountain** (Falun, Sweden)

Legendary mining area and the site of the first ever commercial corporation

According to legend, the copper deposits in Falun were discovered in ancient times when a local shepherd noticed how his goat returned from pasture with its horns colored red by the copper-rich soil. Whether you believe the story or not, copper mining in the area is generally thought to have begun as early as the ninth century, and the name Falu Koppargruva (Falu Copper Mine) is mentioned in a written source from 1288. In 1347, Stora Kopparberg (Great Copper Mountain) was granted a charter by King Magnus Eriksson IV, making it the oldest commercial corporation in the world. By the seventeenth century, Falun accounted for one-third of the global copper production, which made the town of Falun the single most important source of income for the Swedish crown. It was during this time, *Stormaktstiden* (the era of great power) that the Swedish Empire was at its strongest, dominating the whole of Northern Europe.

In 1687, the rapid and unplanned exploration of the deposits caused a huge cave-in. Fortunately, this happened on Midsummer Day—one of the few days the miners had off—and no one was killed. But the great pit created by the collapse dominates the site still today. Another famous tale is that of Matts Israelsson. He disappeared in the mine one day prior to his wedding in 1677 and was discovered forty-two years later. His body—almost perfectly preserved in the vitriol-rich air—was put on display in the town square in the hope that someone would be able to identify him. An old, crooked lady soon walked past and immediately cried out: "It's him! My fiancé!"

Although extraction peaked in 1650, it continued uninterrupted until 1992 when the mine was closed. *Falu rödfärg* (Falu red paint), the paint that gives the wooden houses of Sweden their characteristic deep-red color, is still made from the mine's residue. **TS**

Old Uppsala (Uppsala, Sweden)

Last stronghold of paganism in Sweden

Old Uppsala is thought to have been the residence of the kings of Sweden in prehistoric times, and the home of the legendary Yngling dynasty, according to ancient Scandinavian history. Until the Middle Ages it was a site of great political significance because it was the meeting place for the "Ting of all Swedes" (general assembly), which convened annually for the king to summon people to war. By the 1200s and 1300s the area had also become an important trade, economic, and religious center.

Old Uppsala is situated in the valley of the River Fyris, on a cultivated plain surrounded by working farms. It featured in the writings of Adam of Bremen and is considered to be the last stronghold of paganism. The cult center once housed an enormous temple. Christianity arrived in Sweden in the eleventh century, and in the temple's place there now stands a Christian church that was considered sufficiently

important to become the archbishopric of Sweden from 1164 to 1273. The site of this church is very close to the Royal Mounds. Originally there were between 2,000 and 3,000 mounds in the area, but most have now been covered by farmland. More than 1,000 significant archeological finds have been extracted from these mounds, providing important information about the lifestyle of the people who once lived here. The Royal Mounds are thought to have been the royal burial site for the kings in the sixth century, and were established as a "symbol for divinity and power."

Today it is possible to walk around these impressive mounds and to look inside the church, and to visit the Gamla Uppsala museum. The museum's exhibits illustrate the history and myths of Old Uppsala as well as providing a genuine sense of this site as one of the most important historical centers in Sweden. **KH**

Birka Viking Settlement (Island of Björkö, Sweden)

Important archeological site where Christianity was first preached in Sweden

The isolation of the setting of Birka Viking settlement means that the remains are relatively complete and untouched. The site is therefore an important source of information about the Vikings who lived there. First founded in the eighth century, the settlement was occupied until the tenth century. It was deserted around 960 when Sigtuna supplanted Birka as the main trading center.

The Birka settlement was the first real town to be built in Sweden. It was established to control and expand trade, and became a major trading hub because of its strategic position. It provided the Baltic link in the route through Ladoga and Novgorod to the Byzantine Empire and the Abbasid Califate, and consequently became part of a global commercial network. At Birka, Arabic silver and Russian pearls were traded for iron and skins. The trade grew steadily over two centuries along with the power of Christianity. This was first introduced in the 800s when St. Ansgar, a young Benedictine monk, came to Birka to preach the gospel. His mission lasted a year and a half, by which time many people had been baptized. By 831 the first Christian congregation had been established. However, Birka never became an exclusive Christian community; Christians and pagans continued to coexist side by side.

Birka settlement is vital in understanding the complex history of the Viking Age and offers an excellent insight into the lives of its inhabitants. Today, there is a museum that carefully retells the fascinating story of the Birka site, illustrated with numerous archeological remains. **KH**

↗ This cache of coins, jewelry, and a sword was found in the ancient Viking settlement of Birka.

↙ A bronze brooch from a Birka grave represents two animals flanking a symbol of the Norse god, Thor.

Strindberg's House (Stockholm, Sweden)

The home and burial place of the celebrated playwright August Strindberg

The Blue Tower is the only one of August Strindberg's (1849–1912) twenty-four homes in Stockholm that can be seen today. Now a museum, the building has been carefully restored to match Strindberg's original apartment and it offers a fascinating insight into the author's private life. During his prolific, forty-year career, Strindberg wrote more than sixty plays as well as short stories, essays, poetry, historical works, cultural studies, and science books. Throughout his life, he explored different styles of writing, from Naturalism to Symbolism and then Expressionism. A pioneer of the modern theater, he wrote plays such as *Dance of Death* and *Miss Julie*, which scandalized and thrilled audiences with their controversial themes, particularly the hypocrisy of nineteenth-century sexual morality.

The Blue Tower grants the visitor a glimpse into the playwright's everyday existence. His desk betrays his obsessively meticulous nature. Everything is precisely ordered, from his British steel nibs to his handmade paper from the Lessesbo paper mill. Everything remains exactly as it stood when Strindberg died. The author's extensive library holds up to 3,000 books—a sign of his voracious appetite for literature. Even his dining room displays his theatrical tastes, with its garish color scheme of yellows and greens and its carefully staged furniture.

Strindberg's work continues to intrigue audiences because his themes of marital strife, sadism, and violence remain relevant today. He also wrote evocative, mystical dramas that echo his haunting statement: "I dream, therefore I am." The Blue Tower lifts the curtain on August Strindberg. **KH**

↗ Strindberg named the apartment "The Blue Tower" after the famous prison in Copenhagen, Denmark.

→ Strindberg focuses his attention on a game of backgammon at his home in 1900.

🏛 ◎ Drottningholm (Stockholm, Sweden)

A definitive example of Sweden's wealth and power in the 1600s

Drottningholm is a sumptuous Baroque castle, rich in architectural detail. It is one of the royal palaces of Sweden and is currently the private residence of the Swedish royal family. It was built in 1662 by Queen Dowager Hedwig Eleonora. She employed the master architect Nicodemus Tessin the Elder to build the castle, but as he died before being able to finish it, his son, Nicodemus Tessin the Younger, eventually completed the work.

The strong-willed and ruthless Eleonora intended to produce a grand residence that reflected the wealth and power that Sweden had accrued under the Peace of Westphalia. As the protector of the then-underage King Charles XI of Sweden, she was in control of royal affairs and had the power to command the large-scale and impressive construction.

In 1744 Drottningholm passed to Louisa Ulrika of Prussia on her marriage to Adolf Frederick of Sweden. Under her leadership the palace interior was transformed. Attention was given to every room, adding a sophisticated Rococo style. Louisa Ulrika was responsible for rebuilding the Palace Theater in a bold fashion, using stucco, papier mâché decorations, and large paintings. She was also responsible for the Chinese pavilion, built in 1753 in a basic French Rococo style adorned with Chinese and Oriental features that were fashionable in the 1700s.

As well as the theater and Chinese pavilion, the palace has a church (still attended by its congregation) and two beautiful gardens that are mostly accessible to the public—a Baroque garden with wide avenues, and an English garden set with ponds, canals, bridges, and deliberately picturesque vistas. As a whole, Drottningholm is an incomparable seventeenth- and eighteenth-century northern European royal residence, inspired by the Palace of Versailles. **KH**

Regalskeppet *Vasa* (Stockholm, Sweden)

The warship that capsized as she set sail on her maiden voyage

The *Vasa* was meant to be the mightiest warship in the world, carrying sixty-four guns on two gun decks. It was built for King Gustavus Adolphus of Sweden between 1626 and 1628 and cost 100,000 dalers, or 2 percent of Sweden's GNP. It was built according to the specific measurements that Adolphus had given. The ship was 226 feet (69 m) long and 172 feet (52.5 m) from her keel to the top of the mast, with ten sails and three masts, and a capacity for 145 sailors and 300 soldiers. The *Vasa* set sail on her maiden voyage on August 10, 1628, but she sailed only about 400 feet (120 m) before she tipped to her right and water gushed in through the gun ports. To everyone's horror and amazement she sank, and thirty people perished.

At the time there was little understanding of why the *Vasa* sank; however, Adolphus was furious and demanded that the guilty parties be punished. No one was punished, however, because the man responsible for the ship's plans was already dead and the plans had been based upon measurements decreed by the king himself.

The *Vasa* now rests in her museum in Stockholm, having been gloriously resurrected in 1961. She boasts a collection of around 700 sculptures and ornaments, cut in a late Renaissance and early Baroque style. The motifs are taken from Greek mythology, the Bible, and Roman history, all of which make the ship a sumptuous visual display well worth seeing. **KH**

"… had [the sailors] run [back and forth] any more times, she would have gone over."

Admiral Fleming, on the *Vasa*'s stability test

Vadstena Abbey (Vadstena, Sweden)

Motherhouse of the Bridgettine order

Originally a farmhouse, the Abbey of Vadstena was first founded by Saint Bridget in 1346. In 1370 it was approved by Pope Urban V and in 1384 blessed by the Bishop of Linköping—the diocese in which it was based. Saint Bridget was canonized in 1391, thus lending the abbey fame and wealth. In 1523, however, the abbey was plundered by King Gustavus Vasa and later had its land confiscated, the buildings were damaged, and the majority of the abbey's books and valuables were taken. In 1580 King John III restored the abbey, and its community grew stable and contented for a short while—but in 1594 it was again seized and plundered, this time by the Duke of Södermanland, soon to be Charles IX. Some of the abbey's buildings are still standing today but they are no longer used for religious purposes.

The order that Saint Bridget founded is a monastic order of Augustinian canonesses and, during the Middle Ages, both women and men were welcomed into the order, driven collectively by a devotion to the passion of Jesus. The women became nuns and were strictly confined, whereas the men (who became monks) acted as preachers and missionaries, and were particularly effective at advancing Christian culture, especially literature. This may have been because the Bridgettine literary works contained portions of the Bible translated into Swedish, thus making it accessible to the public. The order spread widely and, by 1515, there were twenty-seven houses, thirteen of which were in Scandinavia.

More recently Vadstena Abbey was renovated and modernized and the buildings were assigned new purposes. The brothers' convent became a hospital, and the sisters' convent and the chapter house was a psychiatric hospital (previously Vadstena Lunatic Asylum) up until the 1980s. **KH**

 ## Visby (Island of Gotland, Sweden)

The best-preserved fortified commercial city in northern Europe

Amazingly, many of Visby's original buildings are still standing today; they include churches, dwellings, and schools. The city is set on a well-preserved medieval street grid and is surrounded by a fortified ring wall.

Visby grew into a large town from the twelfth century onward, when Gotland's wealth and prosperity was growing dramatically. The wealth was a direct result of the island's relationship with the Hanseatic League, which had originally been set up by the German ports of Hamburg and Lübeck as a way of protecting Baltic trading ships from piracy, but which eventually dominated most Baltic trade. For mutual protection, Hanseatic ships would travel in convoy, and merchants would together invest in the cargoes of individual ships so that none would be ruined if a ship were lost. Visby was central to trade with the eastern Baltic and Novgorod, and the city grew as more people moved to Gotland. Eventually, the

citizens of Visby built a defensive ring wall around the city that, by the end of the fourteenth century, stood 36 feet (11 m) high, was more than 1.8 miles (3 km) long, and had nearly fifty towers. But then declining trade diminished the city's wealth, Visby was depopulated, and the buildings decayed. Few were actively demolished and consequently most of the ring wall, seventeen medieval churches, and a large number of the original dwelling houses have survived.

Visby's economy began to improve in the mid-nineteenth century and people gravitated back to the city, attracted by the regeneration of Gotland's industry. Now there is a mixture of juxtaposed old and new buildings, and the remains of medieval churches stand alongside contemporary apartment blocks. Today's Visby remarkably combines a small, modern town, no more than one hundred years old, with the remains of a powerful medieval city. **KH**

Kalmar Castle (Kalmar, Sweden)

A medieval defense tower transformed into a stunning Renaissance castle

This legendary castle has a rich history stretching back more than 900 years, to the twelfth century when it was first built. Originally the castle was intended to act as a defense tower, protecting Sweden from the threat of pirates and seafaring enemies, especially Denmark. Kalmar Castle's coastal location close to the Danish border made it of particular strategic importance. The castle also played a fundamental role in Nordic policy-making and was used as the meeting place for the Union of Kalmar in 1397, an agreement that joined the Nordic countries under a common regent. However, in 1658, the castle lost its strategic significance when the Scanian Islands were annexed by Sweden.

Kalmar Castle was first built as a simple round watchtower. Progressively more buildings and towers were added to it; thus, by 1280 it had four towers and a commanding tower connected by a curtain wall. However, it was during the reigns of King Gustav Vasa and his three sons that Kalmar was transformed into a stunning Renaissance castle. They added new buildings, a different church, greater residential quarters, a fresh roof, and large fortification banks. Furthermore, in 1570 the brothers Johan Baptista and Dominic Pahr were employed to carve a detailed well and intricate portals. Sadly, because of a devastating siege and an enormous fire in the 1600s, the castle was severely damaged and afterward neglected. Throughout the 1700s it was used for many purposes: as a storage facility, a royal armory, a prison, and a distillery.

Under the strict supervision of Martin Olsson, a thorough and careful restoration of the building was carried out from 1914 to 1941, using authentic historic construction methods. Today, this beautiful and historic castle is open to the public and is generally recognized as one of Sweden's best preserved Renaissance castles. **KH**

> *"Autocratic, cunning, and with a frightful temper, he shaped the foundation for modern Sweden."*
>
> Björn Hellqvist, writer, on King Gustav Vasa

Lund Cathedral (Lund, Sweden)

One of Sweden's most beautiful cathedrals—an architectural triumph

Lund Cathedral is of huge historical interest and contains many strange artifacts. Some sources suggest it was built in the 1080s; others date it to 1103. Either way, by 1103 the church had become the seat of an archdiocese that hosted the primate of the Nordic countries, and the building was finally consecrated in 1145. The cathedral originally lay under Denmark's rule, but with the Treaty of Roskilde in 1658 the Bishopric of Lund was transferred to Sweden, where it remains today.

The building has undergone many stages of development and restoration in its lifetime, the first of which began in 1234 after a great fire ravaged the building. When the cathedral was rebuilt, the west facade was replaced and many artistic embellishments were added, including new vaults. In the 1370s, glorious Gothic stalls were introduced and in 1398 a Gothic winged altarpiece was built. In 1424 an astronomical clock, the *Horologium mirabile Lundense*, was installed that shows the phases of the moon and where the sun will set. A major renovation by King John I brought fascinating reliefs and a monumental sarcophagus to the cathedral. During the Middle Ages, Lund was a powerful cultural and religious city in the area, but after the Reformation in 1536 the church's influence declined.

The cathedral as it stands today is an impressive piece of architecture. It is a sandstone church built in the Italian Renaissance style, adorned with two 180-foot-(55-m-) high towers that pierce the city's skyline and two heavy bronze entry doors designed by the architect Carl Johan Dyfverman. The elegant interior is structured around three aisles and a transept, and there is a wealth of minute detailing in every corner of the cathedral. Lund Cathedral stands as a remarkable testament to the wealth and power once enjoyed by the church in southern Sweden. **KH**

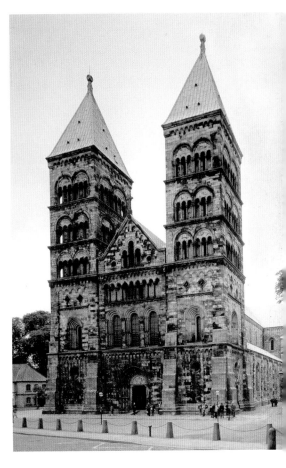

"In dulci jubilo let us our homage show—Our heart's joy reclineth in praesepio."

Carol played by the organ of the astronomical clock

Olavinnlinna Castle (Savonlinna, Finland)

Ownership of this medieval stone castle has been fiercely disputed throughout its history

Olavinlinna Castle was founded in 1475 on the eastern border of Sweden by Erik Axelsson, who was regent of Sweden under the Kalmar Union, which brought together Norway, Sweden, Denmark, and Iceland. Axelsson began construction to protect the kingdom of Sweden from the increasing threat of her adversary, the Grand Duchy of Moscow, which was later to become Russia. Sweden and Russia battled for control of Finnish territory for many years, so the erection of Olavinlinna Castle on the border was hotly contested by the Russians.

The castle was strategically built on a rocky island, close to the shoreline of Lake Saimaa, a location that made it easy to defend. The Russian army repeatedly tried to disrupt the building work, believing that the site was on their side of the border. Disputes over the siting of the castle continued through the centuries and, not long after the Northern War began in 1700,

the Russians took control of the castle. They held Olavinlinna from 1714 to 1721, and again from 1743 to 1809, when Finland became a separate grand duchy under Russia. In 1917, when Finland finally gained its independence, the castle lost its military significance for its warring neighbors.

Today Olavinlinna stands close to Savonlinna, Finland, and consists of a main castle, three large towers, and a noteworthy bailey with an encircling wall, reinforced by still more towers. Two fires in the 1860s caused extensive damage, but the castle was fully restored between 1961 and 1975. The renovations have allowed the castle to be used for a wide range of cultural and social events, and it is now one of Finland's most popular tourist attractions. One important event is the celebrated Savonlinna Opera Festival, hosted every summer, which draws hundreds of thousands of opera lovers to the castle and the town. **KH**

Turku Castle (Turku, Finland)

One of the largest and most imposing medieval castles in Scandinavia

Built in 1280, Turku Castle is steeped in many years of history and its formidable stone walls have witnessed a number of great events in the tumultuous Nordic sagas. Of all the Finnish castles, Turku Castle has taken part in the most dramatic events.

The original structure of the castle first took shape between 1280 and 1310, and was increased in size and strength during the following centuries. The design of the castle began as a simple, square keep with two sturdy gateway towers. A large moat was later built, branching off from the River Aura, effectively placing the castle on an island and thus providing a strong defense. In the fifteenth century, an imposing bailey was built to accompany the keep, and in the sixteenth century, under the rule of Duke Johan, the castle was renovated into the handsome Renaissance building it is today. This was the castle's heyday: It was at the center of the province of Finland Proper and was the administrative center for the whole country. In the seventeenth century, the castle became home to Finland's governors-general and would never again attain the grandeur it had experienced under Duke Johan. By the end of the seventeenth century it had diminished in importance and in the eighteenth century was reduced to being used as a granary. Around the same time, the bailey was turned into a prison, which remained in use until the castle was transformed into a historical museum in the 1890s.

The castle came under fire once again in 1941 in the Continuation War, which raged between Finland and the Soviet Union from 1941 until 1944. The castle was severely damaged by Soviet aircraft; this later led to a thorough and lengthy renovation program, which was finally completed in 1987. Today, the building contains a large exhibition illustrating the castle's rich history and its numerous attacks. **KH**

Suomenlinna Fortress (Helsinki, Finland)

An outstanding example of eighteenth-century European military architecture

Suomenlinna Fortress is an extensive naval base and fortress built across six islands outside Helsinki. It was constructed in the mid-eighteenth century, when Finland was still ruled by Sweden, and the fortress has played a central role in Finnish history since it was first built.

Suomenlinna Fortress was commissioned in 1747 as a response to growing Russian naval power in the Gulf of Finland. Its designer, Count Augustin Ehrensvärd, made use of the most sophisticated contemporary plans for the construction and worked on the fortress until his death. He is also buried there. However, during the Finnish War (1808–09) between Sweden and Russia, Suomenlinna Fortress was surrendered to the Russians with virtually no resistance, and in 1809 Finland was ceded from Sweden and became a semi-autonomous region of the Russian Empire.

During the Crimean War (1854–56) Suomenlinna Fortress was seriously damaged by bombardment from the Anglo-French fleet, but it was repaired and extended after the war. In 1906 the fortress was the center of a brief, and unsuccessful, mutiny against the tsar. More fortifications were added from 1914 to 1917. After World War I, Finland gained independence from Russia, and Suomenlinna Fortress was used as a prison camp for rebels from the Finnish Civil War (1918).

In 1973 Suomenlinna Fortress was turned over to civilian administration. Originally constructed as a military base, the fortress is now a popular picnic and day-trip site, linked to the mainland by frequent ferries. It contains numerous museums as well as an art school, theater, minimum security prison, and the Finnish Naval Academy. The fortress is now an important Finnish landmark and one of the cultural centers of Finland, and in 1991 was designated a UNESCO World Heritage site. **JF**

"Where the Swedish grandee once strode/With silken hose and ceremonial sword . . ."

Joe Brady, "Suomenlinna"

🏛 ◎ Jelling Stones (Jelling, Denmark)

Stepping stones from paganism to Christianity

In the heart of the peaceful countryside of East Jutland, Denmark, is a small town called Jelling, site of two ancient burial mounds, a church, and two impressive rune stones—otherwise known as the Jelling Stones. These are enormous boulders, erected among the burial mounds, with carved inscriptions and illustrative decorations chiseled into them. These stones are of particular significance because they are examples of pagan Nordic culture and they mark the shift from Nordic religious beliefs to Christianity.

The earlier of the two stones (both dating from the middle of the tenth century) was raised by King Gorm the Old, first King of Denmark, in memory of his wife, Thyra, who must have died before him. The two burial mounds may also have been built by him as a funerary monument to Thyra and himself. Their graves have not been discovered, however, and the many more recent graves in the churchyard site have obliterated all traces of earlier tombs. It is likely that originally they were surrounded by a stone circle.

The second of the two Jelling Stones was set up by Gorm's son, Harald Bluetooth. It is larger than Gorm's stone, standing at a height of 8 feet (2.5 m). Its inscription reads, "King Haraldr ordered this monument made in memory of Gormr, his father, and in memory of Thyrvé, his mother; that Haraldr who won for himself all of Denmark and Norway and made the Danes Christian." This illustrates Harald's several intentions when he erected the stone. First, he wanted to honor his mother and father; second, he wished to celebrate his victory over Denmark and Norway, thus emphasizing the foundation of Denmark as a unified kingdom; and finally, he was stressing the transition from Nordic religious beliefs to Christianity. The Jelling Stones therefore comprise a fascinating ancient monument that bears witness to the ending of the pagan era. **KH**

"King Gormr made this monument in memory of Thyrvé, his wife, Denmark's salvation."

Inscription on the older of the two runestones

Ribe Cathedral (Ribe, Denmark)

The first Christian church built in Denmark

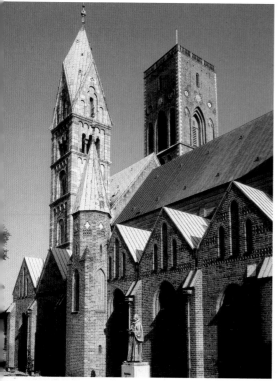

The city of Ribe is said to be the oldest town in Denmark. When the Catholic monk Ansgar brought Christianity to Denmark in 826, he chose Ribe as the site of the first church because of the city's importance as a trading center. In 860 he made a request to the king of Denmark to build the church; however, there is no record of a bishop, or a cathedral, at the site before 948. Before Ansgar arrived, the Danes worshipped the Nordic gods Thor and Odin. Denmark's conversion to Christianity was consequently a major enterprise and Ribe Cathedral was crucial in its success.

The construction of the present-day Ribe Cathedral started around the year 1150 and was finished by about 1250. It was built from sandstone and volcanic tufa, with granite for the foundations and pillars. The cathedral flourished through the ensuing few centuries as the town of Ribe increased in wealth and importance. With the Reformation in 1536, however, the king decided to seize church property, and the bishop of Ribe was deposed. Thereafter, the purpose of the cathedral altered, and around 1600 the cathedral's main tower was installed with cannons and used as a lookout point.

Despite a number of attacks and catastrophic floods, fires, structural failures, and storms, the cathedral still stands as a fine example of Romanesque architecture. It is a beautiful five-aisled edifice with a 170-foot- (52-m-) high watchtower that provides scenic views over the surrounding countryside. Inside the cathedral are countless delicate details, such as a carved bronze door with a lion's head, paintings, mosaics, and stained glass. **KH**

⬉ Ribe Cathedral dominates the town and is visible for miles across the surrounding flat landscape.

⬅ The Romanesque cathedral, built from sandstone and tufa, is the only five-aisled church in Denmark.

Andersen Museum (Odense, Denmark)

Home of Hans Christian Andersen and one of the first museums devoted to a writer

Hans Christian Andersen (1805–75) is a well-loved author of novels, plays, and travelogues, but he is undoubtedly best known for fairy tales such as *The Little Mermaid* and *The Ugly Duckling*. Although his work is often read as children's literature, on closer inspection, Andersen's stories reveal dark, ironic undercurrents clearly aimed at an adult audience.

The Andersen Museum in Odense pays tribute to the writer's achievements and offers a testament to his extraordinary worldwide recognition. The author spent twelve years of his childhood living in the small, rented house—shared with three other families—where the museum is now located. An exhibition retells Andersen's life story, describing his family's bitter struggle against poverty. His father labored to provide for him, while his mother tried to find him an apprenticeship as a weaver, tobacconist, or tailor. Andersen, however, continued to dream of theater and literature and, at the age of fourteen, he set off for Copenhagen where he tried to break into the literary world. After three poverty-stricken years, he was finally discovered by Jonas Collin, director of the Royal Theater. Andersen published his first book of fairy tales at the age of thirty and after that his career went from strength to strength.

The Andersen Museum opened in 1908 and was one of the first museums in the world to be devoted to a writer. It presents a portrait of Andersen the man, his mind, his appearance, and his literary work. The wonderful collection of drawings, documents, garments, and objects on display convey the social world of Andersen's impoverished childhood. **KH**

↗ A stairway offers symbolic deliverance from the poverty Hans Christian Andersen strove to escape.

⇲ Andersen lived in this house in Odense until 1819, when he left to seek fame and fortune in Copenhagen.

🏛 ⟡ **Kronborg Castle**

(Helsingør, Denmark)

Hamlet's Elsinore Castle was modeled on Kronborg Castle

> *"Shakespeare conflated the port, Helsingor, and the castle, Kronborg, into one word: Elsinore."*

Ralph Berry, teacher and author

In the 1420s, a fortress was built on the farthest tip of Zealand in Denmark, at the narrowest point of the sound that lies between Denmark and Sweden, intended as a strong defense against a possible Swedish invasion. Construction was begun by King Eric of Pomerania, who used the fortress as a means of extracting waterway dues from passing ships. In 1585 King Frederick II converted the basic fortress into a magnificent Renaissance castle and named it Kronborg Castle.

Frederick's vision was unique in both outlook and scale. Ornately embellished with marble fireplaces, frescoes, and tapestries, the castle became one of the finest in Europe. Apartments were built for the king and his officials in the north wing, with a chapel and a 187-foot- (57-m-) high trumpeter tower on the south side. The brewery and kitchens were set on the west side at ground level, with numerous guest suites located above. The castle achieved fame outside Denmark as the home of William Shakespeare's Hamlet. Known as Elsinore Castle in the play, Hamlet's castle was based on Kronborg from descriptions given to the playwright by a troupe of traveling actors who had performed there.

After a fire destroyed much of the castle in 1629, successive monarchs attempted to restore the sumptuous decorations. King Christian IV managed to rebuild the splendid exterior, but the interior was never fully refurbished. After a Swedish conquest in 1658, new ramparts were added, making it one of the best defended fortresses in Europe. Today, the royal chambers, chapel, historic suites, and the ballroom are all open to the public and it is possible to walk through the casemates, an extensive underground network of corridors and rooms that could house 1,000 men when the castle was under siege. **KH**

Frederiksborg Castle

(Hillerød, Denmark)

Christian IV's legacy

Frederiksborg Castle is named after King Frederick II of Denmark, who commissioned the building in 1560. However, the impressive design of this palace must be attributed to his son, Christian IV, who continued to build the palace between 1602 and 1620. Frederiksborg was built in the Dutch and French Renaissance styles, which is epitomized by sweeping gables, spiral staircase towers, sandstone decorations, and copper-clad roofs. The distinctive style of Frederiksborg Castle came to be described as the "Christian IV style" because it reflected his architectural tastes and preferences so precisely.

The castle has played many roles and still plays an important part in Danish life. Since 1648 it has been used for ceremonial events, such as the anointing and crowning of new monarchs. The palace chapel is still used for royal weddings, as well as being a Knights' Chapel for the Order of the Elephant and the Order of the Dannebrog.

In 1859, when Frederick VII was in residence, a fire destroyed much of the palace. Reconstruction work began immediately and, by 1864, the exterior had been largely completed. The speed of the reconstruction was made possible partly by large contributions from the prominent philanthropist Jacob Jacobsen.

In 1878 Frederiksborg became the Museum of National History. Today it is also an art gallery, housing Denmark's most important collection of portraits and historic paintings, as well as busts, drawings, and photographs. In 1993 The Modern Collection was also established, after an ancient decree—that had forbidden the display of portraits of living people—was revoked. The combination of fine art, Renaissance architecture, and beautiful Baroque gardens makes Frederiksborg a truly exceptional experience. **KH**

Karen Blixen Museum

(Rungsted, Denmark)

Birthplace and burial place of Karen Blixen

Nestling in the small town of Rungsted is the Karen Blixen Museum, a site dedicated to the life and times of the famous storyteller and novelist. The museum is set in Karen Blixen's family home and introduces the visitor to her social and cultural milieu, granting an insight into her courageous and inspiring personality.

Karen Blixen (1885–1962) traveled across the globe in a period when it was relatively uncommon to do so, especially for a woman. In 1905 her first writings were published in Danish periodicals and, in 1914, she moved to Kenya after marrying her Swedish cousin, Baron Bror von Blixen-Finecke. She lived in Africa for

> *"In the highlands you woke up in the morning and thought: Here I am, where I ought to be."*
>
> Isak Dinesen (Blixen's pseudonym), *Out of Africa* (1937)

seventeen years, during which time her husband left her for long periods while he went away on safaris and military campaigns. This relocation to a foreign climate, culture, and way of life provided fertile ground for Blixen's literary imagination. It became the subject of her second novel, *Out of Africa*. The novel's success gained an impressive reputation for the author and established her in the literary world.

Blixen's life was complex and difficult, but the museum touches on these complications delicately. There is a beguiling blend of cultures and ideas, with decrepit military paraphernalia standing alongside aging African farm furniture. Visitors can wander around this strange collection, trying to figure out how each piece influenced the person who lies behind the much-admired works of literature. **KH**

Amalienborg Palace (Copenhagen, Denmark)

Winter home of the Danish royal family

Amalienborg Palace is the exquisite centerpiece of Frederikstad in Copenhagen. The palace is a superb arrangement of four buildings around an octagonal plaza. In the center of the plaza stands a glorious statue of Frederikstad's founder, Frederik V. Frederik decided to build the district to commemorate the tercentenary of the Oldenburg family's ascent to the throne and Christian I's coronation as king of Denmark. In 1750, the royal architect and adviser, Nicolai Eigtved, was employed to design the district—the intention being to develop a fashionable area for the city's most prestigious citizens.

The four buildings that make up the palace have identical Baroque exteriors, whereas the interiors vary in each case. This is because the buildings originally belonged to four great aristocratic families. Frederik V granted each of them land on which to build, but on certain conditions. The owners were exempt from taxes and duties provided their castles complied precisely with Eigtved's architectural designs and were completed within a time frame. Building began in 1750 and all four structures were finished by 1760. When the royal castle of Christiansborg burned down in 1794 and the royal family became homeless, the four Amalienborg palaces were promptly commandeered by the royal household. The nobles graciously agreed to part with their properties in exchange for wealth and advancement.

Today, Amalienborg stands as a magnificent example of Baroque architecture. A fourteen-year restoration of the beautiful facade began in 1982, which succeeded in returning the palace to its former glory. Frederick IX and Queen Ingrid lived in Frederick VIII's palace, and Christian VII's palace is used today to entertain honored guests to the country and to house special exhibitions. **KH**

Assistens Cemetery (Copenhagen, Denmark)

Burial place of many inspirational and famous figures

In 1711 when a virulent epidemic caused the death of one-third of the inhabitants of Copenhagen, it became necessary to build five new cemeteries. One of these was Assistens Cemetery, situated in the picturesque countryside on the outskirts of Copenhagen. The cemetery was intended to cope with the overcrowding of the city graveyards and to offer families with low incomes an affordable burial place. As a result, Assistens Cemetery was heavily used by working class citizens and avoided by the bourgeoisie. The fashion among the well-off citizens in the early 1700s was to be buried in, or close to, the local parish church.

It was only in 1785 when Johan Samuel Augustin, a wealthy civil servant, decided to be buried in Assistens Cemetery that views began to change. The bourgeoisie started to recognize Assistens as a beautiful and tranquil resting place. Today the site is bursting with trees, shrubs, and flowers, as well as thousands of ornate monuments erected by affluent people to mark their worldly wealth and status. The styles of the graves vary greatly, depending on which century they belong to, but on the whole the emphasis is upon classicism, with some examples of neo-Gothic art.

Today, Assistens Cemetery is part of the Nørrebro section of Copenhagen, which has expanded considerably since 1711. The cemetery now covers an area of 50 acres (20 ha) and has laid to rest more than 250,000 people. The writer Hans Christian Andersen and the existentialist philosopher Søren Kierkegaard are among those buried here. Assistens Cemetery arguably contains more "history" than any other Danish cemetery. The graveyard allows the visitor to trace the development of cultural patterns and social norms over the centuries. **KH**

 ⚙ # Roskilde Cathedral (Roskilde, Denmark)

Haunting burial place of generations of Danish royalty

Roskilde Cathedral is famous for housing the mausoleum of the Danish royal family. Since the fourteenth century, thirty-nine Danish kings and queens have been interred here in their ornamental sepulchres. Depite this, the cathedral has never hosted a royal burial ceremony, only the interments. Its royal connections mean the building has always been meticulously maintained and it continues to serve as the local parish church. Extensions, monuments, and decorations were added at regular intervals, making it an impressive display of shifting fashions in religious art and architecture—a site certainly worth visiting.

There has been a church at this site on Zealand, a small island in eastern Denmark, since the ninth century. The first church to be built here was a simple wooden structure, which was replaced in the eleventh century by a stone church commissioned by Estrid, the sister of King Canute. Bishop Absalon initiated the building of Roskilde Cathedral to replace the little church and create a symbol of the area's growing importance. Construction work began in the 1170s and, in a bold and innovative move, Absalon sponsored the use of expensive new brick materials for this mammoth project. Brick firing had only recently been introduced into Denmark, and Roskilde Cathedral is believed to be the first brick-built Gothic cathedral in northern Europe.

The cathedral was an adventurous building project and used more than three million bricks. It was built over two stories, with a gallery behind the chancel, two towers on either side of the nave, and a particularly wide transept. The main body of the work was completed around 1280, but extensions and decorations continued long afterward. Chapels were added to the cathedral and all the walls were adorned with frescoes and reliefs. **KH**

Skuldelev Ships (Roskilde, Denmark)

Five different ships exhibit the shipbuilding prowess of the Vikings

The Viking ships on display at the marine center in Roskilde, near Copenhagen, are called the Skuldelev ships because they were deliberately sunk at Skuldelev in the Roskilde Fjord. They were scuppered there in 1070 to form a blockade in the waterway, to protect Roskilde, then the capital of Denmark, from attack. It was not until 1962 that they were excavated and archeologists began to piece together their history.

The Skuldelev ships differ enormously from one another in size, shape, timber, and capacity. For example, *Skuldelev 1* is an oceangoing trading vessel with a capacity for six to eight men. In comparison, the *Skuldelev 2* is an oceangoing warship, a longship. Its vast size initially confused archeologists, who thought they had excavated two ships. The vessel would have held a crew of around seventy to eighty men and would have been used by chieftains for war missions. The *Skuldelev 3* is a smaller coastal trader known as a

byrding. It is a trim, elegant merchant vessel, most likely used by a farmer to attend council or to go to market. The *Skuldelev 5* is a small warship and was probably built by the farmers in the Roskilde area under military obligation. Finally, the *Skuldelev 6* is a fishing vessel known as a *ferja*, used for rowing and sailing, and designed specifically for fishing, whaling, and sealing.

The five vessels have collectively provided archeologists with a great deal of information about Viking seafaring and craftsmanship. In addition, the age and type of wood, together with the cut of the planks and the depth of the vessels, provide an insight into Viking existence. The research work that has been undertaken into the story of these archeological shipwrecks has yielded information not only about each individual ship's construction and sailing characteristics, but also about Viking society, culture, and history in general. **KH**

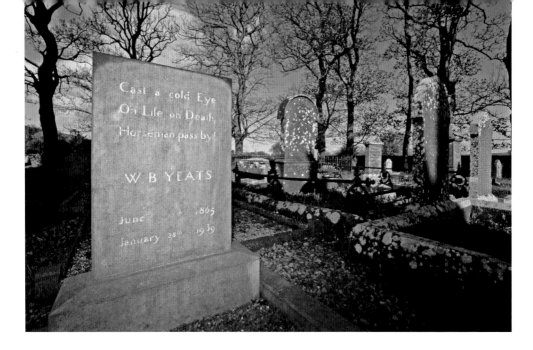

Grave of W. B. Yeats (Drumcliff, Ireland)

Legendary site chosen by the poet for his burial place

William Butler Yeats (1865–1939) is one of Ireland's greatest poets, and admirers of his work continue to flock to his final resting place. This is situated in the tiny village of Drumcliff, in County Sligo. The spot was chosen by Yeats himself. In one of his last poems, "Under Ben Bulben," he described his grave, specifying that the headstone should be made of local limestone rather than marble, and ending with his famously enigmatic epitaph: "Cast a cold Eye, On Life, on Death, Horseman, pass by!"

Yeats had two reasons for choosing to be buried in Drumcliff. On a personal note, one of his ancestors—John Yeats—had been rector there. More important, though, the churchyard lay at the foot of Ben Bulben, an imposing mountain. Throughout his life, the poet had been fascinated by ancient Irish legends, referring to them frequently in his verses, and nowhere in Ireland had more romantic associations for him than

Ben Bulben. Here Diarmaid, the great lover, was slain by a magical boar. Here, too, Ossian the warrior hero was suckled by a doe.

Yeats may have got the tomb that he wanted, but he was unable to exert the same control over his physical remains. He died in the south of France, in January 1939, and was buried in the pretty village of Roquebrune. Yeats left instructions that his body should be transferred to Drumcliff after a year, to minimize the fuss at his funeral. However, his plans were scotched by the outbreak of World War II, and his relatives began the process of repatriation only in 1948. Then, to their horror, they found that the poet's grave had been cleared. In keeping with French practice, the skull was separated from the skeleton and the bones were placed in an ossuary. The body was retrieved, but periodically there are rumors that the wrong bones were shipped back. **IZ**

Hill of Tara (between Navan and Dunshaughlin, Ireland)

Domain of gods and kings sacred to Ireland's early communities

Nowhere in Ireland has richer associations than Temair, the ancient site of Tara. In prehistoric times it was already a major center for ritual, but it assumed even greater importance after the arrival of the Celts. The place featured prominently in early Irish legends and came to be regarded as the seat of the high kings of Ireland. As such, it became a potent symbol and rallying point of Irish unity and patriotism.

Tara is a complex site consisting of at least twenty-four separate monuments. The oldest of these is a passage grave from the Neolithic era (carbon-dated as 3000–2400 B.C.E.), although many of the structures were erected in the Bronze Age or the Iron Age, and not all were tombs. The site also includes a number of *raths* (ring-forts), earthworks, and ritual enclosures. Most of these were later given colorful names, linking them with ancient gods or kings. These include the Mound of the Hostages—a megalithic passage tomb

and probably the oldest monument at the site—the Rath of the Synods, and the Banqueting Hall.

From early times, Tara was regarded as a sacred site because of its links with the high king. The office of high king was usually held by the local ruler and did not signify any great military or territorial power, but it was hugely prestigious. The high king did not reside at Tara, but did participate in its ceremonies. The most important of these was the *feis temrach* (feast of Tara), which symbolized the ritual union between the king and the goddess of sovereignty. Prospective rulers also had to place a hand on the *Lia Fáil* (Stone of Destiny), a mystic pillar stone reputed to shriek whenever it was touched by the rightful king. In later years Christian missionaries sought to exploit the reputation of the site by claiming that St. Patrick's decisive confrontation with the pagan high king took place on the Hill of Tara. **IZ**

Newgrange (Drogheda, Ireland)

Ancient tomb with evidence of an awareness of the universe

The identity of the people who built the finest grave of its kind in Europe in the Stone Age is altogether uncertain. They certainly preceded the Celts, who did not arrive in Ireland until long afterward. The huge mound of stones in the Boyne Valley, some 260 feet (80 m) in diameter and 40 feet (12 m) high, was later surrounded by a ring of thirty-five or more standing stones, of which twelve are still in place. Complicated spirals, zigzags, and other patterns are cut into the stones. Their significance is another mystery, but one theory is that they were connected with the recording of astronomical events, such as the apparent movement of the sun and the phases of the moon, in a society that depended on agriculture and needed an efficient calendar.

From the entrance on the south side, a narrow passage, 60 feet (19 m) long and faced with massive slabs, some of them also incised with complex patterns, leads into a small chamber at the heart of the grave. Here, presumably, the bodies of important people, possibly the local priest-kings, were interred. In midwinter, between December 19 and 23, around the winter solstice, for a few minutes each morning the rising sun shines in along the passage and into the burial chamber deep inside. Whether this was connected with belief in an afterlife is again unknown.

The grave was afterward called the Palace of Oengus, son of the Dagda, the chief god of pre-Christian Ireland. The Vikings raided the monument in the 860s. Since then it has remained brooding and profoundly mysterious, along with the many other prehistoric monuments close by. **RC**

◩ The inner passage, with massive slabs lining the walls and interleaved flat stones making up the floor.

◪ The tomb has a quartz and granite wall at the front, but to the rear it resembles a simple grassy mound.

Clonmacnoise (Athone, Ireland)

Early Irish monastic settlement

In contrast to most other European nations, urban centers were a late development in Ireland. Instead, the local population gravitated toward large monastic communities, which were effectively small towns. Clonmacnoise was one of the earliest and most powerful of these monastic settlements.

Inspired by a vision that he had received, St. Ciarán founded the monastery c. 545 by the banks of the River Shannon. He died of the plague shortly afterward, but his grave became a shrine and Clonmacnoise expanded rapidly as a result. His original wooden church has long since vanished, but the ruins of at least seven others remain. The smallest is the Téampull Chiaráin (Ciarán's Temple), where pilgrims came to visit the saint's grave, whereas the grandest was a cathedral (begun in 909). The latter helped Clonmacnoise to gain the burial rights for a number of local kings. The rights were an important source of patronage and were often fiercely contested by other monastic houses. In 763, for example, the monks of Clonmacnoise fought a pitched battle with their counterparts at Durrow in one such dispute. The site also contains two round towers (lofty watchtowers) and the remains of a castle (c. 1214–20), although none of these protected the settlement from the frequent incursions of Irish, English, and Viking attackers. It was finally abandoned in 1552, following one such raid.

Clonmacnoise was famous for the outstanding quality of its metalwork, its manuscripts, and its stonework. Only the latter can now be appreciated at the site, most notably on the hundreds of decorated grave slabs and on the three magnificent high crosses. The finest of these—the Cross of the Scriptures—was erected by Abbot Colman in memory of his friend King Flann. As the name suggests, it is richly adorned with carvings of biblical scenes. **IZ**

Old Jameson (Dublin, Ireland)

Dublin's historic whiskey distillery

North of the Liffey, Smithfield was once a Viking settlement and later became one of Dublin's principal open spaces, used for regular horse fairs and home to a market. It was there that John Jameson acquired a whiskey distillery. He had arrived from Scotland in the 1770s and was closely linked with the Scotch industry. His wife was a Haig, no less, and his daughter-in-law came from the Stein family, leading grain distillers in Scotland who owned the Bow Street distillery in Dublin, which Jameson bought.

The Irish have been making their own special whiskey from early Celtic times and the word comes from the Celtic *usquebaugh*, meaning "water of life,"

"Whack for my daddy-o
Whack for my daddy-o
There's whiskey in the jar."

Whiskey in the Jar, traditional folk song

---

which turned into *whiskeybae* and was later shortened to *whiskey* (with an "e" in Ireland, but not in Scotland). Jameson's products were "pot still" whiskeys, generally matured in sherry casks for years on end, sometimes for more than twenty years, and mixed to create a variety of distinctive blends of "the hard stuff," greatly admired in Ireland but not widely known abroad. In 1895 a 175-foot- (53-m-) high chimney was added to the distillery, now a tower offering views of Dublin.

Once, two million gallons of Jameson's whiskey were quietly maturing beneath the streets of Dublin, but the distillery closed in 1966 and Jameson's became part of the Irish Distillers Group, with a modern distillery at Midleton in County Cork. The old building was reopened in 1997 as a museum of the history and technology of Irish whiskey. **RC**

Oscar Wilde's House (Dublin, Ireland)

House in a Georgian square where the Wilde family resided from 1855 to 1876

Oscar Wilde (1854–1900) pretended he had been born in Merrion Square, one of Dublin's finest Georgian squares, though his actual birthplace was 21 Westland Road nearby, which was not nearly such a smart address. His elder brother, Willie, had been born there in 1852 and Oscar followed two years later. His mother, who had hoped for a girl, described him as "a great stout creature who minds nothing but growing fat." In 1855 his parents moved to 1 Merrion Square, which had been built when the square was first developed in 1762. The baby Oscar's father, Sir William Wilde, was a distinguished eye and ear surgeon and his mother, Lady Jane Wilde, who called herself "Speranza," was a poet and Irish nationalist who ran a fashionable literary salon. The longed-for daughter, Isola, arrived in 1858.

It was an affluent household, in which Jane Wilde was the dominant figure, and her two boys competed fiercely for her love. She liked to tell them blood-chilling tales of witches and sinister fairies. The house had six servants, there were German, Swiss, and French governesses, and the children were brought up to speak French and German. The boys were both sent to a school their mother considered the Eton of Ireland.

The family stayed at 1 Merrion Square until 1876, when Oscar was in his early twenties. The house was taken over in 1994 by the American College in Dublin, which restored it and opened it to the public. Numerous monuments in the square include one of 1997 to Oscar in the northwest corner, facing his boyhood home and the object of much sardonic comment. Other famous occupants of the square include Daniel O'Connell and W. B. Yeats. **RC**

↖ Wilde subjects the camera to his most challenging stare in this 1882 portrait by Napoleon Sarony.

← Plaques on the wall commemorate the sojourn of Wilde and his family at No. 1 Merrion Square, Dublin.

Trinity College (Dublin, Ireland)

The single college of the historic University of Dublin

Trinity College has several claims to fame. It is Ireland's most distinguished educational establishment, with alumni as diverse as Oscar Wilde, the playwright Samuel Beckett, Bram Stoker, the author of *Dracula*, and Mary McAleese, the current Irish president. Many of its buildings date from the Georgian period—Dublin's architectural golden age. Among the treasures on permanent display in the library is the world-famous Book of Kells.

The college was founded in 1592 by Elizabeth I, mainly for the use of Protestant students. It was built on the site of the ruined abbey of All Hallows. Nothing now remains of this original foundation, although several fine structures date back to the eighteenth century. These include the Rubrics, the Printing House, and the Chapel.

For most visitors, the first port of call is the Old Library with its magnificent Long Room. Measuring 209 feet (64 m), this barrel-vaulted chamber certainly lives up to its name. It is no longer used as a reading room by students, but as a form of museum. The bookcases are lined by a famous collection of marble busts, the finest of which is Louis-François Roubiliac's portrait of Jonathan Swift. There are two medieval harps, one of which may have belonged to the Irish king Brian Boru. Trinity's greatest prize, though, is the Book of Kells. Dating from *c.* 800, this illuminated manuscript is a supreme example of Celtic decoration. It was probably produced on the island of Iona, before being transferred to the monastery at Kells, in County Meath. It was presented to Trinity College in the 1660s by Henry Jones, Bishop of Meath. **IZ**

↗ The Campanile, built in the mid-nineteenth century, stands in the college's quadrangle, Parliament Square.

⊡ In 1860, the roof of the Old Library's Long Room was raised to accommodate the upper tier of bookcases.

Guinness Brewery (Dublin, Ireland)

Some claim that the nearer you are to the brewery, the better the Guinness

Guinness has its own special place in the history of Dublin, Ireland, and beer. The small Rainsford's brewery south of the River Liffey was acquired in 1759 by Arthur Guinness, who took a 9,000-year lease on it, so it still has a while to run. He started brewing ale and, by the 1770s, was producing a brand of dry stout—based on a porter style then popular in London—that became famed for its black color (created by adding roasted barley), creamy head, and distinctive taste. It was so successful that the production of ordinary ale was dropped.

Arthur Guinness built himself a house in Thomas Street, close to the brewery's main gate, but the family dynamo was his son, Sir Benjamin Lee Guinness, who was given a baronetcy and was probably the richest man in Ireland when he died. He was the principal creator of the modern business, and he enlarged the Dublin brewery until it was, for a time, the biggest in the world. It had its own railway and its own fleet of barges to carry consignments to the port of Dublin for shipment abroad. In the 1930s, some 5,000 people worked at the brewery and the firm was the city's biggest employer. The Guinesses themselves joined the English aristocracy as earls of Iveagh and were noted charitable benefactors.

The Guinness Storehouse, opened in 2000 in the heart of the giant brewery complex, tells the story. A special gallery honors John Gilroy, artist and creator of many of the famous 1930s and 1940s advertisements ("My Goodness, My Guinness" and so on). The glass-walled Gravity Bar at the top commands wonderful views over Dublin and rewards visitors with what has been described as "the best pint you will ever experience." Guinness remains the most popular alcoholic beverage in Ireland, and has long been available to aficionados around the world. **RC**

Kilmainham Jail (Dublin, Ireland)

Cold, dark, and violent, Kilmainham was feared and hated for 130 years

Dublin's largest and most notorious prison was closed in 1924, but has been preserved as a memorial. Today, what is often called the Irish Bastille is the largest unoccupied jail in Europe. Many famous figures in the struggle for Irish independence were held there and some were executed. It is a grim place, cramped and cold. There had been a prison at Kilmainham much earlier, in the area known as Gallows Road, but it was in such an abominable state by the 1780s that it was resolved to build a new one nearby. One of the prime movers in the decision was a certain Sir Edward Newenham, who would soon find himself confined in the new prison for debt.

The new jail had fifty-two cells, and from the failed insurrection of 1798 onward it was used for political prisoners as well as common criminals, many of whom were transported to Australia. In the early days, entering the jail was a gruesome experience because public hangings were held at the entrance, from a gibbet above the door. The prison was redesigned and enlarged in the early 1860s, with a high outer wall and a big central hall, and this is the prison that may be seen today with its cells and exercise yards.

When Robert Emmet's rising against the English failed in 1803, he and two hundred of his followers were imprisoned at Kilmainham. He spent his final night on earth there before being hanged and beheaded in front of St. Catherine's Church; on show is the butcher's block on which his head was taken off and to which someone incongruously added piano legs. The cell in which Charles Stewart Parnell was confined in 1881, for close to seven months, is still there, as is the Stonebreaker's Yard in which fourteen leaders of the Easter Rising in Dublin in 1916 were executed. Eamon de Valera was also imprisoned at Kilmainham, in 1923, just before its closure. **RC**

Prospect Cemetery

(Dublin, Ireland)

Prominent figures of Irish history lie in Dublin's enormous Catholic cemetery

Prospect Cemetery, also known as Glasnevin Cemetery, was founded for Roman Catholics by a leading Irish Catholic politician, Daniel O'Connell, and protected with high walls and watchtowers against body-snatching, which was rife at the time. It grew into Ireland's largest cemetery, open to all denominations and covering more than 120 acres (49 ha). It contains more than a million bodies, some of them paupers buried in unmarked graves. The older areas have a suitably melancholy atmosphere of crumbling walls and encroaching ivy, and the cemetery as a whole has a history of styles in funeral monuments from Neoclassical stateliness to Victorian Gothic Medievalism and Celtic Revival.

Some of the most famous figures in Ireland's history since the 1830s lie here. The famous politician Charles Stewart Parnell lies beneath a granite boulder from his estate in County Wicklow, close to the crypt of Daniel O'Connell. The men who carried out the Phoenix Park murders in 1882 lie close to one of their victims, T. H. Burke. Not far away are other political figures: Michael Collins, Countess Markiewicz, Maud Gonne with her son Sean MacBride, and Eamon de Valera with his wife, Sinead. Sir Roger Casement, who was hanged in London for treason, is buried here, and from the world of Irish arts and literature come Erskine Childers and Gerard Manley Hopkins. Brendan Behan, perhaps not inappropriately, rests not far from the Prospect Square entrance, with the famous Grave Diggers pub just outside, and James Joyce's father, John Stanislaus Joyce, is in the cemetery, too. **RC**

⊠ Daniel O'Connell's tomb lies beneath this round tower, some 165 feet (51 m) high, erected in 1861.

⊡ The 1922 funeral procession of revolutionary leader Michael Collins heads toward Prospect Cemetery.

Dublin General Post Office (Dublin, Ireland)

Scene of the Easter Uprising of 1916

This elegant building evokes two very different periods in Ireland's history. Its architecture harks back to the Georgian period when Dublin was one of the leading cities of the British Empire. More significantly, though, the building played a central role in the Easter Uprising of 1916, when Irish rebels courageously launched their bid for independence from British rule.

The General Post Office (GPO) was erected from 1814 to 1818, in a grandiose, Neoclassical style that was frequently reserved for major public buildings. It was designed by Francis Johnston, who had been appointed architect to the board of works and civil buildings in Dublin in 1805. He created the GPO in the Greek Revival style—a branch of Neoclassicism that became popular in Europe and North America in the first half of the nineteenth century.

By the end of the century, the monumentality of the building seemed to epitomize the pretensions of the British establishment. As such, it became a primary target for Irish freedom fighters. On Easter Monday, 1916, the building was occupied by the Irish Volunteers, led by Pádraig Pearse and James Connolly. On the steps outside, they read out a proclamation declaring Irish independence. They continued to hold the GPO for six days, before eventually surrendering to British troops. The building was badly damaged during the fighting, but it was later restored and reopened in 1929. It features two important memorials to the sacrifice of the rebels. Inside, there is a plaque inscribed with the text of the 1916 proclamation. By the door, there is also a poignant statue, *The Death of Cúchulainn* by Oliver Shepherd. Cúchulainn, as the great, legendary hero of Irish literature, was seen as a fitting symbol of nationhood. There are plans to turn the building into a museum, specifically dedicated to the Easter Uprising. **IZ**

Dublin Castle (Dublin, Ireland)

Bastion of British rule for 800 years

Few buildings have had a more varied history than Dublin Castle. Over the years, it has served as a military stronghold, a royal residence, a law court, a prison, a gunpowder store, and a treasury. Even today, it remains versatile, playing host to international conferences and presidential inaugurations, as well as an ever-growing band of tourists.

The Danes had a fortress here during their occupation of Dublin, but the present building dates back to the Anglo-Norman period. In 1204, King John gave orders for the construction of the castle. The building was not solely designed to defend the city; it

> *"I am young yet old in misery. I have never, since my infancy, breathed out of prison."*
>
> **Son of the Earl of Desmond, from his castle cell**

also became the principal base for the administration of British rule in Ireland, functioning until 1922, when it was passed to the Irish Free State.

Most of the grandest parts of the castle date from the Georgian period. These include the attractive Bedford Tower (1761), which dominates the Upper Courtyard, and the magnificent State Apartments, which were designed as living quarters for the viceroy (the royal representative). The most impressive chamber is St. Patrick's Hall (*c.* 1746), which was originally used as a ballroom and for ceremonies relating to the Order of St. Patrick. It is now employed for major state functions. The Chapel Royal, renamed the Church of the Most Holy Trinity in 1943, is a fine example of the Gothic Revival style. It now houses an arts center in its crypt. **IZ**

Jerpoint Abbey (near Thomastown, Ireland)

Ruined Cistercian abbey which made a fortune from sheep

> "The Latin name of the abbey, 'Jeripons,' apparently refers to the bridge over the River Eoir."

Cistercians in Yorkshire Project

Monasticism played a key part in the development of the Irish Church, from the early days of the missionaries to the Middle Ages when monastic foundations were frequently the focal point of local communities. Jerpoint Abbey, now little more than a romantic ruin, is an evocative reminder of the period when the movement was at its peak.

The abbey was founded in the early 1160s by the ruler of Ossory (a small, medieval kingdom in the region of Kilkenny). Originally, the monks appear to have been Benedictines, but by 1180 Jerpoint was a Cistercian house. This religious order, founded in 1098, spread rapidly in the twelfth century and, by 1228, had established thirty-four monasteries in Ireland. Cistercian monks had an austere existence, combining hard manual labor with prayer. The religious houses themselves, however, could amass considerable wealth through their farming activities. With its watermills, its fisheries, and its livestock, Jerpoint fell into this category. Even though the abbey was insolvent for a time, after speculating unwisely on wool prices, by 1540 Jerpoint's annual income had grown to £87—a fortune for the period. This was wealth enough to adorn its buildings with a marvelous array of sculptures and carvings, which remain its most distinctive feature. The finest of these can still be seen in the cloister arcade. Tomb sculpture from the thirteenth to the sixteenth century can be seen in the chapels located by the walls of the abbey's transept.

In common with their counterparts at many other religious houses, the monks of Jerpoint were dispersed when Henry VIII dissolved the monasteries. The abbey and its lands were granted to an influential family, the Earls of Ormond. Over the years, the fabric of the church gradually decayed until, in 1880, it passed into the hands of the Office of Public Works. The ruins are open to the public. **IZ**

Blarney Castle (Cork, Ireland)

Home of the Blarney Stone, where the gift of eloquence can be perilously acquired

The MacCarthy family was a power in Ireland until the last of them, the third Earl of Clancarty, followed James II into exile in the seventeenth century. Their stronghold, Blarney Castle, was built in 1446 by Cormac Laidhir MacCarthy, Lord of Muskerry, as a single tall tower, 85 feet (26 m) high, above the river. There are caves and dungeons beneath it.

The castle is famous for the Blarney Stone. Kissing it while hanging perilously upside down from the battlements, after climbing more than one hundred steps, is said to confer the gift of eloquence, or at least loquacity, and Winston Churchill kissed it in 1912. But where the tradition comes from is a mystery. One explanation traces it to negotiations between Elizabeth I's regime and Cormac MacCarthy, Lord of Blarney, at a time when the queen was seeking to diminish the power of the Irish lords. He was eloquently evasive, and the queen at one point dismissed his latest deceptive protestations as "more Blarney." Enthusiasts for the Celtic revival in the nineteenth century identified the stone as the *Lia Fail*, on which the high kings were crowned at Tara in pagan Celtic times—this stone was said to scream when the rightful successor touched it. It was also allegedly the stone on which Jacob in the Bible rested his head when he saw angels ascending and descending a ladder to heaven.

Nearby Blarney House was built by later owners, the Colthurst family, in a grand and turreted baronial style in 1874. The house was intended as a more comfortable replacement for earlier, outmoded accommodation. In the nineteenth-century gardens are wishing steps, which have to be negotiated with the eyes closed to make a wish come true (another reminiscence of Jacob's Ladder?). The nearby, nineteenth-century woolen mills are also of significant interest for visitors. **RC**

"Thus strong the Blarney influence is shown/E'en upon those most distant from the stone . . ."

John Hogan, "Blarney: A Descriptive Poem" (1842)

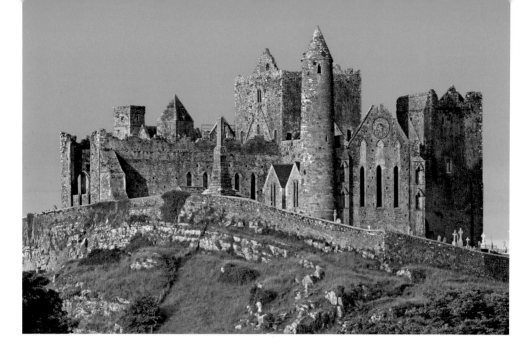

Rock of Cashel (Cashel, Ireland)

Seat of Irish kings, given to the church in the twelfth century

The Rock of Cashel is one of Ireland's most imposing sights. The limestone outcrop dominates the flat, surrounding countryside of the Golden Vale and supports a unique collection of medieval buildings. The location also played a pivotal role in early Irish history, both in the political and the spiritual domain. Cashel was the royal seat of the Eóganacht dynasty, which ruled Munster for centuries.

The stronghold is said to have been founded by Conall Corc after he had a vision of a yew bush growing out of a boulder (Eóganacht means "people born out of the yew"). St. Patrick visited Cashel and converted King Aengus. According to tradition, the saint pierced the king's foot with the spike of his crozier during the baptism, but Aengus bore it unflinchingly, believing it to be part of the ceremony.

The citadel remained the capital of the kings of Munster until 1101, when Muircheartach O'Brien donated the entire site to the Church. This dramatic change of purpose was emphasized ten years later, when Cashel was confirmed as the archbishopric for the southern half of Ireland.

The surviving buildings on the rock all date from the ecclesiastical period. The tallest is the 90-foot- (28-m-) high Round Tower (*c.* 1100), and the finest is Cormac's Chapel (1127–34), which was commissioned by a Munster king, Cormac MacCarthy. This architectural gem is often cited as the first truly Romanesque church in Ireland. Its steep, stone roof, its off-center chancel, and its remarkable wall paintings were all unparalleled at this time. The chapel was eventually dwarfed by the cathedral, which was erected in the thirteenth century and remained in use until 1749, when Archbishop Price transferred the see to St. John's Church in the town of Cashel, apparently because he found the rock too arduous to climb. **RC**

Derry Town Walls (Londonderry, Northern Ireland)

Extreme political conflict characterizes the history of this city on the River Foyle

The story of Northern Ireland's second city goes back to the sixth century and a monastery built among the oak trees on the hilltop (the Irish name Doire means "oak grove"), which was repeatedly attacked by Vikings. The English took the town in 1600 and soon replaced it with a new, planned town, the first of its kind in the country, as part of the Protestant settlement of Ulster that brought in English and Scottish immigrants. The town was put under the control of some of the City of London guilds and Derry became Londonderry. New walls protected it, rather more than 1 mile (1.6 km) long with two watchtowers and four gates leading to the town's central diamond. Other gates were added later. The walls are the only complete town walls in Ireland, and among the very few in Europe not to have been breached.

In 1649 the town was held for Parliament and unsuccessfully besieged by a royalist army for twenty weeks. From 1688 to 1689, held for William of Orange, it was besieged by a French and Irish army fighting for James II. A boom was thrown across the River Foyle to prevent supplies from reaching the defenders, but the starving citizens held out behind their walls, eating horsemeat and cats, dogs, and rats that had fattened on the bodies of the Irish dead, until a ship broke through the boom and the besiegers gave up. The memory was important in the town's subsequent history, and Londonderry became a symbol of Protestant dominance and hatred of "papistry."

A rapid growth of the port, shipping, and commercial enterprises began in the eighteenth century and the town spread beyond its walls. Protests against the treatment of Catholics brought a return of violence in the 1960s and 1970s. Thirteen unarmed civilians were killed in the city on Bloody Sunday, January 30, 1972, by British soldiers. **RC**

 ## Skara Brae (Orkney, Scotland)

Five-thousand-year-old homes with evidence of orderliness and comfort

This Stone Age village was buried beneath sand dunes for centuries until a huge storm blew the sand away, around 1850. What was revealed gives a vivid impression of ordinary life more than 5,000 years ago. Despite their great antiquity the houses are remarkably uniform, so much so that they have been likened to "a group of prehistoric council houses," and there is a strong impression of a regimented community.

Built of stone, the houses would have been roofed with turf or thatch. Their wooden doors opened off an underground maze of narrow passages so low that the inhabitants almost had to crawl through them. Each house, however, had one spacious main room, measuring about 20 square feet (6 sq m). The fitted stone furniture inside included two box beds, possibly one for the man and the other for the woman and their children. The family would have slept on heather or bracken, under blankets of animal skin, and the stone floor would have been made more comfortable with strewn furs and skins.

The Skara Brae families had ornaments and used cosmetics, and each house had the same regulation two-shelf stone dresser, apparently placed to display precious objects to visitors. Stone shelves and cupboards were built into the walls. In the middle of the room was a hearth for burning peat. There are small cells that seem to have been lavatories, with drains, and one of the huts was apparently a workshop. In another, possibly set aside for religious purposes, the bodies of two women had been buried under the floor. The people of the village kept cows, sheep, and pigs, grew cereal crops in their fields, went hunting, and gathered shellfish. The occasional stranded whale would have been a blessing. At about 2,500 B.C.E. sand dunes began to encroach on Skara Brae and the settlement was abandoned. **RC**

Glenfinnan Monument (near Fort William, Scotland)

A lone tower commemorates Bonnie Prince Charlie's doomed bid for the throne

Prince Charles Edward Stuart set foot on the mainland of Scotland for the first time in 1745, in an attempt to reclaim the British throne for the Stuart dynasty. Aged twenty-four, dashing and charming, he was the grandson of the last Stuart king, James II of England (also James VII of Scotland). He had only seven men with him and the chiefs of the Highland clans were reluctant to risk coming out for him. However, some 150 of the local MacDonalds joined him and after some anxious hours the sound of the pipes was heard and Cameron of Lochiel, with 700 fighting men, came down the glen to his side. Cameron had his doubts, but he knew where his loyalties lay and his support was crucial.

Late in the afternoon of August 19, 1745, a big red-and-white banner was unfurled by the prince in the name of his father, James Francis Edward Stuart, who was proclaimed the rightful king of Britain. The adventure would end in tragedy at Culloden and Bonnie Prince Charlie would spend the rest of his life in embittered and futile anger in continental Europe, but the memory of the rebellion has always cast a spell.

At Glenfinnan, the slender battlemented tower, 65 feet (20 m) tall, marks the spot where the Stuart standard was raised. It was erected in 1815 by Alexander MacDonald of Glenaladale, whose great-uncle had loyally supported the prince, in memory of "the generous zeal, the undaunted bravery, and the inviolable fidelity" of his ancestors and "those who fought and bled in that arduous and unfortunate enterprise." The platform at the top of the tower commands wonderful views of Loch Shiel and the surrounding mountains. The statue of a kilted clansman was installed at the top in 1834 and the monument was given to the National Trust for Scotland in 1938. **RC**

Culloden Battlefield (near Inverness, Scotland)

In less than an hour, the last Stuart hopes to regain the throne were extinguished

The last important battle fought on British soil put an end to the Stuart dynasty's final bid to regain the throne, and was also a significant step in the decline of the distinctive culture and way of life of the Scottish Highlands. It pitted an army of some 5,000 Highlanders and Irish led by Prince Charles Edward Stuart—known as the Young Pretender or Bonnie Prince Charlie—against a bigger and better-equipped force under the command of the Duke of Cumberland, a younger son of the Hanoverian king of England, George II. Many of Cumberland's men were Scots, and in fact more Scots fought against the Stuarts than fought for them.

The battle began with an artillery duel, which the Highlanders got the worst of. Eventually Prince Charles Edward ordered a charge. It was carried out with a wild ferocity that broke the Hanoverian front line, but then the charge was held, the impetus ebbed away, and the Highlanders were pushed back and finally overwhelmed. The whole thing took less than an hour. Cumberland ordered no quarter for the wounded, who were slaughtered out of hand. Those who had managed to hide in woods or in farm buildings were searched out and killed. So were some civilians who had come out from Inverness to watch the action.

Cumberland earned himself the nickname "Butcher" for his actions. Prince Charles Edward got away to spend months in hiding, moving about the Highlands, never betrayed despite the substantial price on his head, until he finally escaped to continental Europe on a French warship.

The battle of Culloden remains a powerful event in Scottish national memory. The battlefield site has been gradually acquired since 1944 by the National Trust for Scotland that plans to return the site, as far as possible, to its 1746 state. Walls and trees that would not have been there are to be removed, but a stone cairn memorial from 1881 will remain. **RC**

"Dark, dark was the day when we looked on Culloden/And chill was the mist drop that clung to the tree."

Andrew Lang, "Culloden" (1905)

Jarlshof (Isle of Shetland, Scotland)

Ancient dwellings stripped of their covering by a violent storm

Robert Stewart, Earl of Orkney, a bastard son of King James V of Scotland, built himself a mansion on Shetland in the sixteenth century. Although it was known as the Old House of Sumburgh, Sir Walter Scott coined the name Jarlshof for the isolated house in his 1822 novel *The Pirate*. Its ruins are still there, close to the main runway at Sumburgh airport.

In the 1890s the remains of older settlements going back to the Vikings and thousands of years earlier were revealed just by the house by a fierce storm that blew the concealing sand away. Scott's name of Jarlshof is now also used for these settlements. The remains of huts have survived from about 2,000 B.C.E., with cattle stalls and a metal-working shop that produced axes, swords, and knives. Much later, perhaps in the first century B.C.E., a *broch* was built, a round stone watchtower, apparently as a defense against attacks from the sea. Later still, stone from the broch was used to build wheelhouses—homes with seven or eight rooms surrounding a central hearth. The occupants could have been Picts.

Vikings arrived in the ninth century C.E., first to plunder and then to settle and live by fishing and raising cattle, sheep, and pigs. A Norse stone longhouse was built on the site, 70 feet (21 m) long, containing a living room, kitchen, and bedroom. A path led to outbuildings, thought to have been a cowshed, barn, smithy, and servants' quarters. One small building could have been a temple or a sauna. More buildings were added, and later there was a medieval farm on the site. An artist did drawings of Viking ships and the children had model boats as toys. Shetland was ruled by the Norse earls of Orkney under the sovereignty of Norway until the fifteenth century.

One of Scotland's most important prehistoric archeological sites, Jarlshof has a visitor's center with exhibits detailing Iron Age life. **RC**

> *"I am a daughter of the old dames of Norway, who could send their lovers to battle with a smile."*
>
> Sir Walter Scott, *The Pirate* (1822)

Balmoral Castle (near Crathie, Scotland)

Highland home of Queen Elizabeth II

Balmoral has had a royal connection, on and off, since the time of Robert II of Scots, who had a hunting lodge there in the fourteenth century. The Drummond family built a house in 1390 and the Gordons built a tower house in the sixteenth century. In 1848 Queen Victoria and Prince Albert, who had already fallen in love with the Highlands of Scotland on previous visits, rented the house and liked their "dear paradise" so well that they bought the estate in 1852. They both delighted in the scenery and the solitude of the mountains, and Albert enjoyed the stalking and shooting, and designed a new Balmoral tartan, which the family still wears. They also loved walking, climbing, and sketching, and liked the "simple and straightforward" local people.

In 1853, to the skirl of bagpipes, Victoria laid the foundation stone of a new castle in grand baronial style, with a tower 120 feet (37 m) high from which to fly the royal standard. The old Gordon tower was knocked down in 1855. The architect was William Smith, of Aberdeen, but Prince Albert himself took the lead in the design. The interiors were criticized as suffering from "tartanitis" of the wallpaper, carpets, and curtains, whereas visitors often found the place appallingly cold and not everyone enjoyed nine pipers marching around the table at dinner.

It was at Balmoral that Victoria first encountered John Brown, a Scots servant who was to play an important part in her life. Prince Albert died in 1861 and Balmoral became a shrine to him where the queen could gradually assuage her grief. It has been the royal family's Highlands home ever since. **RC**

◹ Balmoral Castle is not part of the royal estate but a private property owned by the royal family.

◿ John Brown famously encouraged the mourning Queen Victoria to raise her spirts by horse riding.

RRS *Discovery* (Dundee, Scotland)

Now in dry dock in Dundee, RRS Discovery carried Captain Scott to the Antarctic

In 1986, RRS *Discovery* (RRS stands for Royal Research Ship) returned to Dundee and the docks where she was built, to be restored to her appearance when she carried Captain Robert Falcon Scott and his thirty-seven-strong crew in cramped quarters on the national Antarctic expedition of 1901. Dundee was an important shipbuilding center with a tradition of producing sturdy wooden whalers, and *Discovery*, launched in 1901, was one of Britain's last three-masted wooden sailing ships. Fitted with a coal-fired engine, with a displacement of 1,620 tons and a length of 172 feet (52 m), she was commissioned by the Royal Geographical Society.

The ship reached Antarctica in January 1902 and anchored in McMurdo Sound. Her specially reinforced wooden hull was able to cope with the huge pressure of the polar ice, which closed around her and held her fast. It was so cold inside at first that the mattresses were frozen solid to the ship's side, but as storms piled the snow up around *Discovery* it got slightly warmer. In the summer, Scott, Edward Wilson, and Ernest Shackleton, with five sledges pulled by dog teams, set off to try to reach the South Pole. They were 500 miles (800 km) or so from their goal when conditions became so impossibly difficult that they turned back.

The ship remained trapped in the ice for a second winter until relief ships arrived and explosions freed her in February 1904. Scott and his companions returned to England to huge acclaim. It was another Dundee-built ship, the whaler *Terra Nova*, that carried Scott on his fateful 1912 expedition to the South Pole, in which he and his party met their deaths. **RC**

↗ RRS *Discovery* was the last wooden three-masted ship to be built in the British Isles.

→ Captain Scott's South Pole expedition on January 18, 1912; Scott is standing in the middle of the back row.

Glamis Castle (Forfar, Scotland)

Castle legendarily linked to Macbeth, and family seat of the late Queen Mother

"Glamis thou art, and Cawdor; and shalt be/What thou art promis'd; yet I do fear thy nature . . ."

William Shakespeare, *Macbeth* (c. 1605)

⬆ In her earlier years, Elizabeth Bowes-Lyons was known to pour water over visitors to Glamis from a tower.

➡ Glamis Castle is a masterpiece of the Gothic-inspired Scottish Baronial style of architecture.

The family home of Elizabeth Bowes-Lyons, the late Queen Mother, and the birthplace of Princess Margaret, boasts a remarkable collection of chilling legends and ghost stories. For one thing, Glamis Castle is the setting of Shakespeare's *Macbeth*, and the real Macbeth was Thane of Glamis, while the bloodstain to be seen on the floor of King Malcolm's room has been attributed to King Malcolm II, recorded as having been attacked and killed at Glamis in 1034.

The castle's most famous legendary inhabitant is the Monster of Glamis, a child so appallingly deformed that his family kept him locked away in a set of rooms that were bricked up after his death. There is said to be another sealed room where one of the lords of Glamis wanted to play cards on a Sunday, which was strictly forbidden. A stranger appeared and the two settled down to play, but the stranger was said to be the Devil. The same room was perhaps where some of the local Ogilvies, who came to the castle seeking protection from their enemies, the Lindsays, were shut in and left to starve to death. The various ghosts include the "Gray Lady," who haunts the chapel, and a "White Lady," who may be the member of the family who was burned alive as a witch in the sixteenth century.

Romantically turreted and battlemented in red sandstone, the later house began its existence as a royal hunting lodge. In 1372 Robert II gave the building to Sir John Lyon, who had married the king's daughter, Joanna. Their son was made Lord Glamis in 1445 and probably built the original castle, which was massively enlarged in the seventeenth century when the family acquired the earldoms of Strathmore and Kinghorne. They changed their surname to Bowes-Lyon after marrying a rich Bowes heiress from England.

Today, the castle and gardens are open to the public, including the Italian Garden, created in 1910 by Cecilia, mother of the late Queen Mother. **RC**

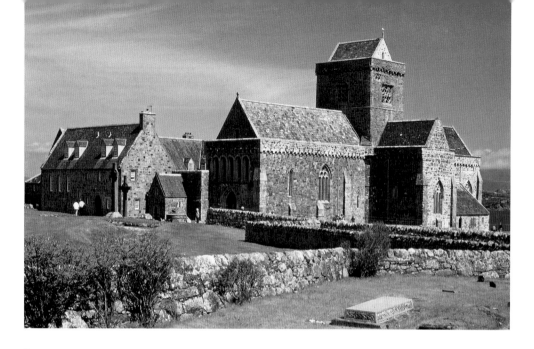

Iona (Iona, Scotland)

The spirit of St. Columba lives on at the abbey he founded on Iona

In 563, St. Columba sailed from his native Ireland for the island of Iona with twelve companions on a mission to convert the pagan inhabitants of Scotland to Christianity. He landed on Iona, where he founded a monastery as his base. Then in his early forties, he was a zealous and formidable man and there is a tradition of him giving the Loch Ness monster such a fearsome telling-off that the creature has seldom been seen since. The saint died on Iona in 597 and his remains are said to rest there in the abbey he founded, in St. Columba's Shrine.

As the cradle of Scottish Christianity, the island became a venerated site of pilgrimage and the burial place of forty-eight of the early kings of the Scots, including Shakespeare's Macbeth. The original abbey was looted and destroyed by Vikings, refounded for Augustinians in about 1080, and rebuilt as a Benedictine community, along with a nunnery,

around 1200. The abbey church was for centuries the cathedral of the bishops of the isles. Most of it today dates from the sixteenth century. Restoration began soon after 1899, when the island's owner, the eighth Duke of Argyll, gave the ruins to the Church of Scotland, and the work was continued by the Iona Community, founded by the Reverend George MacLeod as a pilgrimage center in 1938. The whole island was eventually given to the nation in 1979.

With the abbey and nunnery buildings, there are Celtic crosses, graves of Highland chieftains and important Highland figures, the restored shrine of St. Columba, and a stone called "Columba's pillow" that may have been his gravestone. Iona attracts thousands of pilgrims every year, and some are received as guests at the restored abbey. Dr. Johnson wrote that a man is little to be envied "whose piety would not grow warmer among the ruins of Iona." **RC**

Bannockburn Battlefield (near Stirling, Scotland)

Once-forested site at which Robert Bruce reaffirmed Scottish sovereignty

In 1291 Robert Bruce of Annandale was a leading claimant to the vacant Scottish throne. He did not win it, but his claim passed down to his grandson, the famous Robert the Bruce, who at first supported Edward I of England's attempt to control Scotland, but rebelled in 1306 and had himself crowned King of Scots at Scone. Edward I died the following year and Bruce survived numerous defeats, and an inspiring encounter with a spider in a cave, to conduct a successful guerrilla campaign against the English.

The crunch came in 1314 when Edward II of England marched north with a formidable army of some 18,000 men to encounter Bruce's army of about 5,000 at the Bannock Burn, south of Stirling. The Scots leaders under Bruce included his brother Edward (who was later crowned King of Ireland) and Sir James Douglas. The battle began on June 23 when the English cavalry charged and nearly captured Bruce himself, but were driven back. After an anxious night, fighting resumed the next day when the English cavalry charged again, but were repelled. The Scottish spearmen then advanced in four divisions, gained the advantage, and drove the English pell-mell back into the stream called Bannock Burn in utter confusion. The English king ran for it and most of the English leaders were either killed or taken prisoner. They afterward paid tribute to the humanity with which they were treated. Scottish independence of English rule was confirmed. In 1320, the noblemen of Scotland justified their cause in an impassioned letter to the pope, the Declaration of Arbroath. Bruce remained King of Scots to his death in 1329.

The National Trust for Scotland's guardianship of the battlefield goes back to 1932, and there is an impressive equestrian statue of Bruce near the spot believed to have been his command post. **RC**

Stirling Castle

(Stirling, Scotland)

Childhood home of Mary Queen of Scots

Dominating major east–west and north–south routes, this fortress's strategic importance gave it a key role in Scottish history. Standing 250 feet (76 m) higher than the surrounding terrain on the flat top of an ancient volcano and commanding excellent views in every direction, it was the principal royal stronghold of the Stuart kings from the time of Robert II. Whoever held Stirling, it was said, had the key to Scotland.

The castle has seen its share of violence, having been attacked at least fifteen times in its history. It withstood a siege by Edward I of England in 1304, and another, this time while it was manned by an English garrison, by Robert the Bruce ten years later. A skeleton found in 1797 may have been that of the young eighth Earl of Douglas who, in 1452, was invited to dinner and treacherously stabbed to death on the order of James II. Rebels against James VI seized Stirling Castle in 1584. The Young Pretender tried to take the castle in 1746, but was unsuccessful.

There has been a fortress at Stirling since prehistoric times, but most of the buildings now standing date from the late fifteenth century and later. James IV built the Great Hall—at 138 feet by 47 feet (42 x 14 m), still an awe-inspiring space—c. 1500; Daniel Defoe called it "the noblest I ever saw in Europe." The royal palace, in its Renaissance splendor, was built for James V in the 1540s. It was in the Chapel Royal that his daughter Mary was crowned Queen of Scots when she was nine months old, and she spent much of her childhood at the castle—a little hole in the ramparts is said to have been made especially for her to peep through. Her son, James VI of Scots (and later James I of England), was also baptized in the chapel, later rebuilding it in 1594. The King's Old Building is now home to the regimental museum of the Argyll and Sutherland Highlanders. **RC**

> *"[Mary was crowned] with such solemnitie as they do use in this country, which is not very costlie."*
>
> Sir Ralph Sadler, witness at the Chapel Royal event

Hampden Park

(Glasgow, Scotland)

Scotland's national soccer stadium

In Scotland, as in England, soccer developed out of a ferocious game played across the country by huge numbers. At the first Scotland–England match on record, in 1599, one player was disembowelled and sewn back up again. Modern-style soccer clubs developed in the later nineteenth century and the Glasgow amateur club Queen's Park, founded in 1867, dominated Scottish soccer until eclipsed by the rival professionals of Glasgow Rangers and Glasgow Celtic, founded in the 1870s and 1880s.

The original Hampden Park was the Queen's Park ground opposite Hampden Terrace. In 1884 the club built a new stadium on Cathcart Road. In 1903, in a bold bid to maintain its position in Scottish soccer, the club moved to yet another arena, designed by a specialist stadium architect, Archibald Leitch, in the Mount Florida area in the south of the city. By a long way the country's biggest and best-equipped stadium, it became the accepted place to stage internationals and other major matches. By 1910 it had been enlarged to hold 125,000 spectators, and it was the biggest soccer stadium in the world until the Maracanã Stadium in Rio de Janeiro was opened in 1950. Hampden's north stand was built in 1937 and in that year a Scotland versus England international was watched by 149,500 spectators, the record attendance figure in British soccer.

After 1945, however, the stadium became dismayingly decrepit and in 1980 the Scottish Football Association and the Queen's Park club launched an appeal for money for modernization. The north stand was demolished and other improvements made, which by the early 2000s had reduced the all-seater ground's capacity to 52,000. However, it has remained Scotland's treasured national soccer stadium and is home to the Scottish Football Museum. **RC**

Royal and Ancient Golf Club (St. Andrews, Scotland)

Founding club of the modern game

Named after Scotland's patron saint, St. Andrews was long a place of pilgrimage to the relics of St. Andrew in what is today the ruined cathedral. Today it draws pilgrims to the world's most famous golf club and the Old Course, the most revered in the game. The club's courses—the Old, the New, the Jubilee, the Eden, and the Strathyrum—are on public land and open to anyone to play on, but the clubhouse, built in 1854, is reserved for members only.

The origins of golf are lost in the past. The Romans played a game in which a ball was propelled along with branches of wood. The Dutch had a similar game

> *"Players must not agree to exclude the operation of any Rule or to waive any penalty incurred."*
>
> From *Rules of Golf*, Royal and Ancient Golf Club

in the fifteenth century. Golf was sufficiently popular in Scotland by 1457 for the government to ban it because it took too much time away from archery. From the 1580s there are records of golfers being reproved for playing on Sundays at St. Andrews, Leith, Perth, and elsewhere.

The world's first golf club was founded in Edinburgh in the 1740s, and in 1754 a group of twenty-two "noblemen and gentlemen being admirers of the Ancient and healthful exercise of the Golf" formed the Society of St. Andrews Golfers, which became the Royal and Ancient Golf Club in 1834, when King William IV became its patron. It was gradually recognized as the arbiter on all golfing matters and in 1897 it codified the rules. It is now the game's governing body for most of the world. **RC**

Linlithgow Palace (Linlithgow, Scotland)

Magnificent Stuart residence, reduced by fire to an awe-inspiring ruin

The ruined palace beside Linlithgow Loch is one of the finest Renaissance buildings in Scotland and was a favorite residence of the later Stuart kings. The oldest surviving part of it, oddly enough, is a tower, built by Edward I of England in 1302, that belonged to an earlier royal manor house. Today's palace goes back to James I of Scots, who created a new royal residence there from 1425. James III and James IV added to it, and James V was born there in 1512. He married Mary of Guise at the palace in 1538, and to mark the occasion installed the gorgeous fountain in the main quadrangle, which that day ran with wine. He also rebuilt the south and east sides of the quadrangle. The north side was rebuilt in the seventeenth century.

James IV and his queen, Margaret Tudor, daughter of Henry VII of England, spent much time at Linlithgow, and the room called Queen Margaret's Bower is said to be where she waited anxiously for news of her husband, who was killed in the battle of Flodden against the English in 1513. Her anxiety was the more understandable because he had received a spectral warning from an apparition in the palace's church of St. Michael, rebuilt in the previous century.

James and Margaret's son, James V, was at this point only a baby, not yet two years old. When he died in 1542, his daughter, the future Mary, Queen of Scots, had been born only a week before, at Linlithgow. Two hundred years later, in 1746, the Young Pretender and his army stayed a night at the palace on their retreat northward and, accidentally or otherwise, there followed a fire that left the building in ruins.

Today, it is the huge scale of the roofless and floorless ruin that amazes. Arranged around a central courtyard, it is a towering warren of stone stairways, passages, and chambers. James V's fountain, removed in 2000, was restored and replaced in 2005. **RC**

🏛 ◉ **Edinburgh Castle** (Edinburgh, Scotland)

Aloof on its rocky outcrop, this castle is probably Scotland's most famous site

The castle dominates Edinburgh from the 437-foot (133-m) top of a long-extinct volcano, with steep cliffs leading up to it on three sides. The castle is accessed from the east, where a gentler slope leads to its entrance. Its war-torn history goes back at least to the sixth century, and probably far beyond that.

The castle's oldest surviving building, and perhaps the oldest in Edinburgh, is St. Margaret's Chapel, thought to have been built by King David I of Scots in his saintly mother's memory around 1130. The castle was occupied by the English from 1174 to 1186 and again from 1296 until recovered for Robert the Bruce in 1313. It was used as a royal residence and James IV built the Great Hall, the location of meetings of the Scottish Parliament until 1639. The fortress was frequently besieged in the sixteenth and seventeenth centuries, and was held by the English again from 1650 to 1660 and besieged for William of Orange in 1689.

The esplanade, in front of the castle, is the scene of the annual Military Tattoo. A drawbridge leads in through the portcullis gate and into the castle itself. Many of the buildings today date from the eighteenth century or later. The Honours of Scotland—the Scottish crown, scepter, and sword of state—languished forgotten in a storeroom until rediscovered on Sir Walter Scott's initiative in 1818. The Stone of Destiny, on which the kings of Scots were crowned (if it is the real one), was sent back to Edinburgh from Westminster Abbey in 1996 and the giant cannon Mons Meg was acquired by King James II in 1457.

While hugely important as a tourist attraction, the castle also functions as a British Army headquarters and continues to be garrisoned. The castle holds the regimental museums of the Scots Greys and the Royal Scots, the National War Museum of Scotland, and the Scottish National War Memorial. **RC**

Palace of Holyroodhouse (Edinburgh, Scotland)

Official royal residence and onetime home of Mary, Queen of Scots

The Queen's official residence in Scotland is at the eastern end of Edinburgh's Royal Mile, which leads from Edinburgh Castle, and is used more for official receptions and ceremonies than as a royal home. A new Queen's Gallery for works of art from the royal collection was constructed in the shell of an 1840s building and opened in 2002.

Little is left of the original abbey of the Holy Rood (Holy Cross), which was founded in 1128 by King David I after he saw a vision of a great stag with a shining cross between its horns. By the fifteenth century the abbey guesthouse had been taken over as a more comfortable royal home than Edinburgh's castle and James IV built a new palace there in 1503. A tower was added in the 1530s by James V for himself and his queen, Mary of Guise. It was there that their daughter Mary, Queen of Scots, lived in the 1560s and there that she tried vainly to protect her secretary David Rizzio from a murderous attack by her husband, Lord Darnley, and his accomplices. She had married Darnley in the abbey in 1565, and after he was killed in mysterious circumstances he was buried there in the same vault as James V. Mary later married the Earl of Bothwell in the palace.

Mary's son, James VI of Scots, had Holyroodhouse as his Edinburgh residence, but after he left for England in 1603 it was used only for occasional royal visits. Oliver Cromwell's English troops occupied the building in the 1650s. After a fire, the palace was rebuilt in French château style for Charles II in the 1670s. In the following century the Young Pretender occupied the palace for a few weeks in 1745. **RC**

◹ Surrounded by Holyrood Park, the palace is now used for state ceremonies and official entertaining.

◲ Charles II rebuilt the palace in its present form, tearing down a short-lived one built by Oliver Cromwell.

Forth Railway Bridge (near Edinburgh, Scotland)

Great Victorian engineering feat that spanned the Firth of Forth

Two bridges span the Firth of Forth side by side over the river's narrowest point, the Queensferry Narrows—so called because from 1129 they were crossed by a ferry that David I of Scots named in honor of his mother, Queen Margaret; pilgrims on their way to St. Andrews were carried free. In 1883 work began on building the magnificent Forth railway bridge, more than 1.5 miles (2.5 km) long and one of the great triumphs of Victorian engineering. The bridge carries up to 200 trains a day between Edinburgh and the northeast. Approach spans supported on towers carry the railway tracks from each end to the three enormous double cantilevers in the middle, each 340 feet (104 m) high and themselves connected by suspension spans 345 feet (105 m) long.

The bridge was designed by Sir John Fowler and Sir Benjamin Baker and cost the equivalent of $478 million in today's money. Some 4,600 men worked on it at its peak and nearly 100 were killed in the process. The bridge consumed 55,000 tons of steel and eight million rivets. The last rivet was gold-plated and driven in by the Prince of Wales, the future King Edward VII, when he formally opened the bridge in 1890. One of the bridge's claims to fame, the idea that the repainting process begins again at one end as soon as it reaches the other, seems to be a myth.

There are fine views of the rail bridge from the adjacent suspension road bridge, to the west, which is open to people on foot as well as cars and cycles. The ferries were finally put out of operation when the bridge was completed in 1964. Work began in 1958 and it carried its 250 millionth vehicle in 2002. **RC**

⊿ The Forth Rail Bridge with its three double-cantilevers carries up to 200 train crossings each day.

⊟ The three cantilevers on their massive concrete foundations were the first components to be built.

New Lanark (New Lanark, Scotland)

Industrial village remarkable for its enlightened social management

This cotton-milling company village, cramped in a narrow gorge along the River Clyde southeast of Glasgow, was created in 1785 by the Glasgow businessman David Dale and the English cotton-spinning pioneer Richard Arkwright. Within ten years the mills, the biggest in Britain and powered by river-driven waterwheels, had made it Scotland's largest industrial enterprise. Beside the mills there were workshops and houses for the workers, as well as a school—the workforce included children, generally thought to have been humanely treated, from local orphanages. Of the 1,150 people employed at New Lanark in 1793, almost 800 were children.

In 1798 Dale's son-in-law, Robert Owen (1771–1858), took over the management of New Lanark, and in 1800 Dale sold the village to him. Owen was a pioneering nineteenth-century socialist who believed that decent treatment of workers was the key to a successful business. At New Lanark he saw an opportunity for what he called "the most important experiment for the happiness of the human race" ever attempted. He improved the housing, raised the minimum age for child workers from six to twelve, opened what must have been the world's first day nursery for small children while their mothers worked, and made sure the village shop charged low prices. The sale of alcoholic liquor was restricted, and the young people were taught singing and dancing.

Politicians, intellectuals, and social reformers flocked to see New Lanark, while Owen founded new utopian communities, including New Harmony in the United States. He died aged eighty-seven in 1858. **RC**

◹ For power, the cotton mills at New Lanark at first depended on water wheels driven by the River Clyde.

◺ A contemporary engraving illustrates how the mill buildings were laid out along the riverbank.

Burns Cottage (Alloway, Scotland)

The young Robert Burns absorbed Scottish lore within the walls of this family home

The humble whitewashed cottage, or "auld clay biggin," where Scotland's most famous poet was born in 1759 and spent his first seven years of childhood, is now part of the Burns National Heritage Park and comes with a museum of his life and work. The cottage was built in 1756 by his father, William Burns, a professional gardener from farming stock. A quiet, dour, thoughtful man, in 1757 he married a redheaded, fiery-tempered local girl called Agnes Brown. Robert was their first child. Agnes was illiterate but had a lively knowledge of traditional ballads and songs that she would pass on to her son. Meanwhile, her husband took care to get the best education he could for their four sons and three daughters. For a time he and his neighbors hired a tutor for their children.

A widowed relative of Agnes's called Betty Davidson, also illiterate, lived with the family and, according to the poet, "cultivated the latent seeds of Poesy in the wee boy." She filled his head with what he recalled as "the largest collection in the county of tales and songs concerning devils, ghosts, fairies, brownies, witches, warlocks, spunkies, kelpies, elf-candles, dead-lights, wraiths, apparitions, cantraips, giants, inchanted towers, dragons, and other trumpery." He grew up in an atmosphere rich in the traditional local Scottish culture, while learning to read and write in English.

Across the road from the cottage are the ruins of Alloway Kirk, where William Burns was buried. It is the setting for a scene of orgiastic witchery in Burns's most famous poem, "Tam o'Shanter," written in 1790, which also mentions Brig o'Doon, the bridge over the river nearby. The Burns Monument is close at hand. **RC**

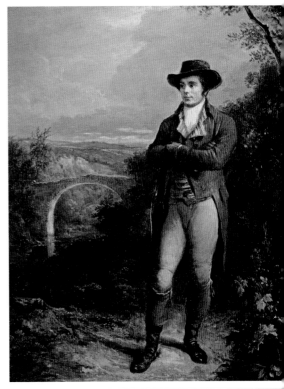

↗ This portrait of Robert Burns features the bridge over the River Doon in his famous poem, "Tam o'Shanter."

→ The plaque above the door of the cottage attests that Robert Burns was born here on January 25, 1759.

Melrose Abbey (Melrose, Scotland)

Great abbey of the Scottish Borders, ransacked by a succession of English invaders

"*Like Melrose Abbey, large cities should especially be viewed by moonlight.*"

Nathaniel Parker Willis, U.S. author and editor

⊞ Robert the Bruce, whose mummified heart is reputed to have been buried at Melrose Abbey.

⊡ Melrose Abbey viewed from the south, where numerous graves cluster close to the walls.

There had been an earlier monastery nearby, founded in the seventh century, but in the twelfth century King David I of Scots persuaded Cistercian monks from Rievaulx in England to come to Melrose, lying 30 miles (50 km) southeast of Edinburgh in Roxburghshire, and found a new abbey, dedicated to the Virgin Mary. The king had set about establishing monasteries to modernize Scottish agriculture and improve education, and he and his successors made sure that the new foundation was amply supplied with land and adequately funded. At his own wish, King Alexander II was buried there after his death in 1249.

In the fourteenth century the Borders abbeys suffered in the Anglo-Scots wars and, in 1385, Melrose was destroyed by an invading English army. The abbey was rebuilt on much the same plan as before, and it is the romantic ruins of this era of construction that can be seen today, described by Sir Walter Scott as "slender shafts of stately stone by foliaged tracery combined." The ruins were all that was left after the English invasion of the 1540s, when Henry VIII was trying to persuade the Scots to betroth the infant Mary, Queen of Scots to his son. After the abbey was wrecked by the English forces, the remains became a local source of building stone.

One legendary event in the history of Melrose occurred after the death of Robert the Bruce in 1329. He had always longed to go on crusade and a party, commanded by Bruce's friend and right-hand man, Sir James Douglas, now set out to take the dead hero's embalmed heart to the Holy Land. On the way they were defeated in battle in Spain and Douglas was killed, but tradition has it that the heart was brought safely back to Scotland and buried at Melrose Abbey. In 1996 a lead casket containing a mummified heart, which may have been that of Bruce, was excavated and placed in the abbey museum. **RC**

Abbotsford (Melrose, Scotland)

Where Sir Walter Scott lived, wrote, and died

In a lovely setting on the bank of the River Tweed below the Eildon Hills, the house is a monument to Sir Walter Scott, one of the most admired writers of his day and a principal creator of the modern romantic view of "bonnie Scotland." In 1811 he bought a farm called Newarthaugh, with 100 acres (40 ha) and a five-room cottage, which he renamed Abbotsford after a ford formerly used by the monks of nearby Melrose Abbey. He moved in the following year with his wife, Charlotte, and their five children, and from 1814 began adding rooms. As well as planting thousands of trees in the grounds, in 1817 he began to build what is now Abbotsford's main block, at considerable expense and in an altogether grander baronial style. The old farmhouse was knocked down in 1822 and the new mansion was finished in 1825. Some of its stones came from historic sites in the Borders.

It was at Abbotsford that Scott wrote some of his best-loved historical novels, including *Rob Roy*, *The Heart of Midlothian*, and *Ivanhoe*. Charlotte died in 1826 and Sir Walter lived on in the house until his death in the dining room in 1832, his bed moved close to a window with a view of the Tweed.

Scott called Abbotsford "a kind of Conundrum Castle to be sure," a mixture of fantasy and solid modern comfort, with up-to-date gas lighting. His descendants still live there and it contains his desk and chair in his study, his library of 20,000 books, and much of his prized collection of historical items, including a crucifix owned by Mary, Queen of Scots and objects that belonged to Rob Roy, Montrose, the Young Pretender, and Flora Macdonald. **RC**

⬉ Scott's popular novels paid for Abbotsford, although for a while the house was held in trust by his creditors.

⬅ Fine furniture and paintings are on display with Scott's collection of books in the spacious library.

Hermitage (Liddesdale, Scotland)

Brooding fortress on the Scottish Borders

If ever there was a grim, bleak stronghold, it is this one. Set on the empty moors near the head of Liddesdale and only 5 miles (8 km) from the border with England, it played a prominent part in the long-running battle for control of disputed border territories.

The castle is said to be haunted, and not without reason. Around 1550 it was described as "an old house not strong, but evil to be won by reason of the strate [difficult] ground about the same." Earlier it had belonged to a family called De Soulis. They had a sinister reputation for cruelty and one of them, William "the Wizard" de Soulis, who was believed to take an unhealthy interest in black magic, apparently lost the estate in 1320 for plotting against Robert the Bruce.

The castle was taken over by the Black Douglases, the most powerful family in the Borders at that time, who built most of the castle as it stands today, with an H-shaped plan consisting of a big keep standing between two massive towers. In 1342 Sir William Douglas shut his enemy Sir Alexander Ramsay in one of the dungeons and left him there to starve to death, though a few unsuspected grains of corn trickling through to him every day from the granary above kept him alive for seventeen days.

In 1492 the castle passed to the Hepburn family, earls of Bothwell. Mary, Queen of Scots fell in love with the fourth earl, even though, or perhaps because, he had murdered her husband. In 1566, while she was staying at Jedburgh, she rode at speed the 25 miles (40 km) to Hermitage with a few companions to be by Bothwell's side after he was injured in a border affray. The ride so exhausted her that on her return to Jedburgh it took her weeks to recover her health.

In the nineteenth century, Sir Walter Scott and other writers reawakened interest in historic castles. Hermitage Castle was duly restored by the Duke of Buccleuch, and given to the nation in 1930. **RC**

Traquair (Innerleithen, Scotland)

Home of Stuarts loyal to the Bonnie Prince

The house by the banks of the River Tweed is one of the most romantic in Britain. Scarcely changed for three hundred years, and dedicated with unyielding loyalty for centuries to the Roman Catholic faith and the Stuart dynasty, it has been visited by no fewer than twenty-seven Scottish and English monarchs since the twelfth century, when it was a hunting lodge in a royal forest. Edward I of England was there in 1304 and Edward II in 1310. In the following century Traquair passed to a younger branch of the royal Stuart (or Stewart) dynasty, whose descendants have lived there ever since. In 1566 Mary, Queen of Scots came visiting with her baby son, the future James VI of Scotland.

> *"On fair Tweed-side, from Berwick to the Bield/Traquair for beauty fairly wins the field ..."*
>
> Imperial Gazette of Scotland, 1868

The present house dates largely from the time of Sir John Stuart, Lord High Treasurer of Scotland under Charles I, who was created Earl of Traquair in 1633. The second earl added the wings and the courtyard around 1700. The fourth earl supported an attempted Jacobite invasion of Scotland in 1708, and had his seventeen children educated by a Catholic priest who was concealed in a room with a secret stairway in case he had to escape. The fifth earl spent time in the Tower of London for supporting the Young Pretender in 1745, and tradition has it that the closed gates at the end of the avenue leading to the house will never be opened until the Stuarts return to the throne. The eighth earl died childless in 1861, when the house passed to the Maxwell Stuarts, who are descended from a sister of the fifth earl. **RC**

Menai Suspension Bridge (Gwynedd–Anglesey, Wales)

Bridge that tamed the unpredictable and dangerous Menai Strait

The project of bridging the Menai Strait between the mainland and Anglesey, to improve the route to Holyhead and the passage to Ireland, was discussed inconclusively from the turn of the nineteenth century. Cattle were swum across, bellowing, but the strait's treacherous currents and strong tides made the ferry crossings difficult and dangerous, and any bridge would need to be high enough to allow vessels to pass beneath. Thomas Telford, the great canal and road engineer, was approached in 1810 and work eventually began in 1819 on a bridge that he designed to carry what became the A5 road from London to Holyhead—a road that he was also building.

The first big suspension bridge in the world, and for some years the longest at 1,000 feet (305 m), it was both practical and beautiful. The single central span, 579 feet (176 m) long between two towers, bears the road and a walkway 100 feet (30 m) above the strait at high tide, suspended on iron chains. By 1825 the stone approach piers had all been built. The chains were anchored in tunnels in solid rock at either end. The central section of chain, weighing more than 23 tons, was floated out on a raft, hauled up into place by a gang of 150 men, and connected to the chains at each end. A fife and drum band played and a substantial crowd cheered lustily as the final connection was made on the Anglesey side.

In a fierce gale the bridge has been described as swinging like a giant hammock, but with some occasional strengthening it has been in use ever since. The iron chains were replaced by steel ones between 1938 and 1940, enabling heavier vehicles to use the bridge. In 1845 another great engineer, Robert Stephenson, built a railway bridge to the west of Telford's bridge. This was destroyed by fire in 1970 and rebuilt as a combined railway and road bridge. **RC**

 ◈ **Caernarfon Castle** (Caernarfon, Wales)

Edward I's declaration of military and political power in North Wales

This tremendous stronghold was in Welsh *Yr Gaer in Arfon*, "The Fortress on the Shore," built on the Menai Strait so that if besieged it could be supplied from the water. The Welsh lords of Gwynedd had a fortress on the site, and the Romans had built a fort centuries earlier nearby, at what they called Segontium, fragments of which have survived. The Roman connection may well have influenced Edward I's decision to build the present castle as a statement of English domination, after the last independent Welsh prince, Llewellyn the Last, was killed in battle in 1282.

The castle was designed by Edward's military architect, James of St. George. Unlike such castles as Harlech and Beaumaris, it was not simply a military stronghold—although its walls were still 20 feet (61 m) thick at the base. Caernarfon Castle was to be the capital and epicenter of English power in Wales. The Welsh settlement on the site was destroyed and a new town was built at the same time as the castle, enjoying its protection as well as its own protective wall.

Edward's son, the future Edward II, was born in Caernarfon (or, in English, Caernarvon) in 1284, apparently in a little room in the Eagle Tower, and his father took the opportunity to show him off triumphantly to the people as their new Prince of Wales. He is said to have announced that he was giving the Welsh a prince born in Wales, who could not speak a word of English.

In 1294 the castle was taken by the Welsh, but was recovered by Edward I. Building work on it did not end until around 1330. Owen Glendower failed to seize it in the 1400s. During the Civil War in the seventeenth century, it was held by Royalists and Roundheads alternately, and it was Parliament that had it reduced to a shell. Prince Charles, oddly garbed, was invested as Prince of Wales at Caernarfon in 1969. **RC**

Dinorwic Slate Quarries (near Llanberis, Wales)

Immense quantities of Welsh slate were once torn from this ravaged ground

"*Quarrymen traveled on foot from as far away as Anglesey each week, crossing the Menai Strait ...*"

Welsh Slate Museum

Slate has been quarried in Snowdonia since Roman times, but in the late eighteenth century demand for roofing slate in Britain, Europe, and North America stimulated what by the 1870s was a major industry, which has left behind it an impressively bleak landscape. A bitter strike in 1900 started the industry on the downward path, and many quarrymen emigrated to South Wales to work in the coal mines.

Quarrying at Dinorwic began in 1787 on land leased from the local landowner, Assheton Smith, but it was after Smith himself took over in 1809 that the business flourished. In 1824 a horse-drawn tramway was constructed to take the slate to Port Dinorwic on the coast for export. This was later replaced by a narrow-gauge railway (part of which is now the Llanberis Lake Railway) and Dinorwic grew into the second-largest slate quarry in the world, outmatched only by the nearby Penrhyn quarry, which produces the same Cambrian slate to this day.

By the late nineteenth century more than three thousand men worked at Dinorwic, quarrying, splitting, and dressing the slate. They worked in gangs and were paid by the amount they produced. Many workers came over from Anglesey and there were barracks to accommodate them until they returned to their families for Sundays. Quarrying was skilled work, but it was a hard life. Workers cut into the rock face with hammers and chisels while dangling in rope cradles that left their hands free. A hospital tried to cope with accidents, but there were only minimal canteen facilities or places to wash and dry clothes.

The quarry closed in 1969 and was taken over for the Welsh Slate Museum, which has preserved many of the buildings and much of the atmosphere. Of special interest is a gravity balance incline, restored to working order to demonstrate how wagons laden with slate were brought up from the quarry. **RC**

Cardiff Castle (Cardiff, Wales)

Victorian medievalist fantasy romantically overshadowing a Norman keep

Cardiff Castle covers the site of a Roman fort of the first century C.E. beside the River Taff, and a stretch of Roman wall is still visible. The Normans built a stronghold there later and the twelfth-century keep, the Black Tower, which is now the entrance gate, and part of the walls have survived. However, what really draws the eye, and some astonished gasps, is the inspired mansion designed and built on the castle grounds by the architect William Burges for the third Marquess of Bute. Possibly the richest British nobleman of his day, he inherited his title from his grandfather, who had transformed Cardiff from a village on the Bristol Channel into a major port, exporting the coal of the South Wales valleys to the world.

Burges and Bute were both fascinated by the Middle Ages, and Burges was an expert on medieval architecture and eagerly grasped the opportunity to create a romantic late-medieval castle on a grand, over-the-top scale in what his contemporaries called Burgesian Gothic. It has a clock tower 150 feet (46 m) high and four other towers, each quite unlike the one before. Every room in the "castle" is decorated with tiles, murals, and carvings, done with superb craftsmanship. Monkeys are fighting over a book at the library entrance, there is a maze on the floor of the Chaucer Room, and nursery rhymes are vividly depicted in the nursery. The castle was given to the city in 1947 by the fifth marquess and is now also home to two Welsh regimental museums.

From 1872 Burges and Bute applied their nineteenth-century medievalist vision to a smaller, but equally romantic Prisoner of Zenda–like castle just outside Cardiff to the north, Castell Coch at Tongwynlais, which they pretended was a hunting lodge. The bedroom for Bute's wife, an amazing realization of everyone's dream of the bedchamber in *Sleeping Beauty*, is a special delight. **RC**

"I was brought up in the thirteenth-century belief and in that belief I intend to die."

William Burges, architect

National Library of Wales (Aberystwyth, Wales)

Unrivaled collection of works in Welsh

Welsh is one of the Celtic group of languages, along with Scots Gaelic, Erse, and Cornish, originally brought to Britain by Celtic invaders before 500 B.C.E. Modern Welsh is descended from Brythonic, which was the native language of England before the invading English (the Anglo-Saxons) arrived after about 500 C.E. Characteristically, the English called the native inhabitants "foreigners," *wealh*, from which the word *Welsh* is derived. Driven westward into what is now Wales, the Welsh language was slowly giving way to English, but nevertheless enjoyed a strong, independent literary tradition from the time of the poet Taliesin around the sixth century.

Revived Welsh nationalism from the eighteenth century onward rescued the language and stimulated a demand for a national library. Cardiff competed as the site with Aberystwyth in the early 1900s, but Aberystwyth won because it has far more Welsh-speakers than Cardiff and it already had a foundation library of 25,000 volumes put together by Sir John Williams, physician to Queen Victoria. The building was designed by the architect Sidney Kyffin Greenslade, and the miners of Wales contributed a shilling each from their pay packets to the cost. Later additions were designed by Sir Charles Holden and the building was finally completed in 1955.

The library's collection of works in Welsh is unrivaled, starting from the oldest surviving Welsh manuscript, the *Black Book of Carmarthen*, and includes the *Book of Taliesin* and the earliest complete text of the *Mabinogion*, as well as the first printed book in Welsh (1546), and the first complete Bible in Welsh (1588). It receives a copy of every book printed in the United Kingdom and the Irish Republic, and now houses more than four million books along with manuscripts, maps, and photographs. **RC**

Caerleon Roman Site (Newport, Wales)

Well-preserved Roman military base

After invading Britain in 43 C.E., it took the Romans around thirty years of fighting to fasten some sort of a grip on Wales and maintain it with military bases and roads. Isca Silurum, founded around 75 C.E. for the Second Legion Augusta, was close to the River Usk. Today called Caerleon (from the Latin *Castra Legionis*) and claimed as the most interesting Roman site in Britain, it was the principal base in southern Wales, the area where Roman culture was to have the most pervasive influence. With an area of 50 acres (20 ha), it was laid out as a rectangle on a neat gridiron pattern with a gate in each of the four sides. The original

> *". . . it was remarkable for royal palaces, so that it imitated Rome in the golden roofs of its buildings."*
>
> **Geoffrey of Monmouth, on Caerleon as Camelot**

earthen walls stood 10 feet (3 m) high with a palisade on top, but in about 120 were replaced with stone walls twice the height. Inside were the barracks blocks, each for about one hundred men, the headquarters building, drill hall, grain store, and hospital. There was a luxurious baths complex and, just outside the walls, a 5,000-seat amphitheater, where gladiators fought.

The Romans moved their base to Cardiff around 300. In the Middle Ages Caerleon was identified with Camelot, where the legendary King Arthur held court with his knights of the Round Table, and a mound on the outskirts of the town gained the name of King Arthur's Round Table. When it was excavated in 1926, it turned out to be the Roman amphitheater. The Legionary Museum has one of the best collections of Roman material in Britain. **RC**

🏛 ◎ Big Pit

(Blaenavon, Wales)

Deep-reaching coal mine created to power the Welsh iron industry

Blaenavon was a quiet country village mainly occupied with sheep farming until the 1780s, when it became one of the cradles of the Industrial Revolution. Three English businessmen leased land from Lord Abergavenny and built an ironworks, which ten years later was the second biggest in Wales. The coal needed for the blast furnaces was dug out from the hillside in tunnels upward of a mile (1.6 km) long, some of which later became part of the Big Pit mine. The ruined Blaenavon ironworks is today open to visitors.

The mine, on the eastern edge of the South Wales coalfield, was opened in 1880. Employing 1,100 people at its peak, it closed in 1980 and was reopened as a museum. The guides were all ex-miners, and it is on tourism that Blaenavon lives today—the colliery now mines visitors instead of coal. It equips them with helmets and lamps, puts them in a cage, and drops them abruptly to 300 feet (91 m) below ground—an experience even seasoned miners never liked—to explore the low galleries and coal seams, the haulage engines, and the pit ponies' stables, and to get a sense of what it must have been like to work there when it might be a walk of 3 miles (5 km) from the shaft to the coal face. Children used to work in the pit, paid twopence for a six-day week, twelve hours a day, spent pulling wagons along tramways. Part of the wage was deducted to pay for their candles. The colliery buildings on the surface include the pithead baths, the winding-engine house, and the blacksmith's forge. It was the depth of the shaft that earned the mine the nickname Big Pit. **RC**

↗ The winding head at Big Pit, used both to bring coal to the surface and to operate the miners' elevator.

➡ Before 1842, there were no laws protecting children working in mines or limiting the age of child labor.

Lindisfarne Priory (Holy Island, England)

Important center of early Christian learning

The buildings at Lindisfarne date from long after the days of St. Cuthbert, the most celebrated of the priory's holy men, but it is the memories of the early days of Christianity in Anglo-Saxon England and the dramatic setting off the Northumbrian coast that give the ruins their evocative appeal. The community was founded by St. Aidan, a Scots missionary to the pagan Saxon kingdom of Northumbria, who was given the island as a base by the Northumbrian king. The monks ranged out from there to a ministry among the local citizens, and the monastery became a center of scholarship and the arts. Its most notable product was the superbly illustrated *Lindisfarne Gospels* of the eighth century (now preserved in the British Museum).

Aidan's most famous successor was the formidable, miracle-working St. Cuthbert, the most revered saint of the north, who spent some time as a solitary hermit on the nearby Farne Islands before becoming abbot in 685, two years before his death. One hundred years or so later, the wealth of the monastery inevitably began attracting the attentions of plundering Vikings, and in 875 the monks finally gave up and fled to the mainland, taking St. Cuthbert's body and the *Lindisfarne Gospels* with them. They wandered about for years on end until finally settling at Durham, where they enshrined St. Cuthbert's remains in the cathedral in 1104.

Nothing is left of the buildings they knew, which were destroyed by the Vikings, but in 1083 a small Benedictine priory was founded at Lindisfarne as an offshoot from Durham. It was closed down by Henry VIII in 1537, but the ruins of the weathered Norman church with its soaring "rainbow" arch and fine west window (restored in the 1850s and later) are still standing, along with ruined domestic buildings of the thirteenth century and after. **RC**

Bamburgh Castle (Bamburgh, England)

Legendary castle on a site of great archeological interest

Rearing up in titanic majesty above the Northumbrian coast, with commanding views of Lindisfarne and the Farne Islands, this castle was in legend the stronghold of Sir Lancelot of the Lake, paladin of the Round Table and the greatest of King Arthur's champions. Ironically, Bamburgh was the first castle of its kind to fall to the newfangled artillery, the nemesis of medieval chivalry, when it was brutally attacked by Edward IV in 1464 during the War of the Roses.

The castle stands on a basalt crag 150 feet (46 m) high, such an obvious point of vantage that it was occupied and fortified before the Romans arrived. The invading Angles took it, and in 547 King Ethelfrith of Northumbria gave it to his wife, Bebba. The name Bamburgh was originally Bebba's burgh. It was a royal palace and many of the Northumbrian kings were crowned there, but it was sacked by the Vikings, taken by the Normans, and rebuilt. The oldest parts of it above ground date from Henry II's time and the principal survivor is the keep.

In the sixteenth and seventeenth centuries the castle was left largely derelict and moldering until it was bought in 1704 by the Bishop of Durham, Lord Crewe. It became the headquarters of a charity, which ran a free school, library, and infirmary, and substantially rebuilt and restored parts of the castle in the 1750s. In 1894 the site was sold to Lord Armstrong, the engineer, inventor, and armaments magnate (creator of the Armstrong gun). As part of his renovation program, Armstrong knocked some of the castle down and turned the rest into a combination of medieval fortress and Victorian mansion, with fascinating effect. His vast King's Hall boasts a fake hammerbeam roof and an array of Fabergé carvings of animals. A fine collection of arms, furniture, tapestries, and porcelain is on display throughout the castle. **RC**

Alnwick Castle (Alnwick, England)

Gloriously preserved medieval castle and stately family home

The Duke of Northumberland's seat in his own shire, in what was in medieval times a walled town (the name is pronounced "Annick"), was the fastness from which the Percy family for centuries held the northeast of England against the Scots. There was already a castle on the site at Alnwick in 1309 when Henry de Percy bought the stronghold from the Bishop of Durham. He and later generations rebuilt and strengthened the structure, and their additions include the impressive barbican and main gate. The stone figures of soldiers keeping a watchful eye out from the battlements were put there in the eighteenth century, when a real garrison was no longer necessary.

The first Henry de Percy took a major role in Edward I's attempted subjugation of Scotland, and his son defeated the Scots in battle and took King David II prisoner. The most famous of the Percy family line was Shakespeare's Hotspur, who rebelled against

Henry IV and was killed in battle in 1408. Later Percys were involved in the Wars of the Roses and in various risings against the Tudors. Some family members spent years imprisoned in the Tower of London, and one was beheaded for treason in 1572.

The direct line died out in 1670. The title went eventually to Sir Hugh Smithson, who married a Percy heiress, took the surname of Percy, and was created Duke of Northumberland in 1766. He had the park landscaped by master gardener Capability Brown with follies by the great Scottish architect Robert Adam. The castle was given its present, grandly baronial appearance by the architect Anthony Salvin in the 1850s, and the interior was sumptuously transformed in Italian Renaissance style. The castle's grandiose appearance led to its use for the filming of some of the Hogwarts School scenes in the early movies of the *Harry Potter* series. **RC**

🏛 ◎ Hadrian's Wall (from Wallsend to the Solway Firth, England)

Most impressive piece of Roman military engineering in northern Europe

Hadrian's Wall was built over a period of approximately eight years across the width of Great Britain at the Roman Empire's northwestern border. It ran east to west for around 70 miles (113 km), from Newcastle to the Solway Firth, to control the frontier with "the barbarians," meaning the Picts to the north. The soldiers and their families attracted local traders, and some of the forts became as much customs posts as military bases. Much of the wall is still an impressive sight, swooping gracefully up and down over the hills, with the best-preserved sections located west of Chesters and east of Birdoswald.

Estimates of the wall's original height range up to 22 feet (7 m). It was built on the orders of the Emperor Hadrian after his visit to Britain in 122 and was subsequently strengthened. Most of the original work was done by Britain's three legions—the second, sixth, and twentieth—but it was auxiliary troops from many parts of the empire who manned the wall. They patrolled it from milecastles, or small forts, built at intervals of a mile (1.6 km) and large enough to accommodate thirty men, and there were two towers between each pair of milecastles.

Running along behind the wall was a massive fortification called the vallum, a broad ditch between earthwork ramparts. Bigger forts with barracks for up to 1,000 men were built at intervals. Points of particular interest today include the fort at Birdoswald with its drill hall; the one at Vindolanda where there was a civilian settlement; the Housesteads fort with barracks, granaries, latrines, and a hospital; and the cavalry fort near Chesters.

After Hadrian's time, the Antonine Wall was built farther north, but it was soon abandoned and the frontier remained along Hadrian's Wall until the Romans pulled out of Britain in 410. **RC**

Dove Cottage (Grasmere, England)

Home of the poet William Wordsworth

This white-walled, slate-floored cottage dates back to the seventeenth century and was once an alehouse, but it is famous because William Wordsworth (1770–1850) and his sister Dorothy, his lifelong companion, lived there from 1799 to 1808. They moved in the year after Wordsworth and his friend Samuel Taylor Coleridge published *Lyrical Ballads*, which set English poetry in a new direction. Wordsworth was then twenty-nine and believed in "plain living but high thinking." He grew peas and beans in the cottage garden, was inspired by the scenery, and did much to attract other writers to the district, and eventually tourists—to his own dismay. He wrote much of his finest poetry at Dove Cottage, including "Daffodils" and "The Prelude."

In 1802 Wordsworth married Mary Hutchinson, and she and her sister Sarah joined the Dove Cottage ménage. Coleridge was a frequent visitor to their home and Dorothy Wordsworth's *Grasmere Journals* shine a light on life there. Wordsworth and Mary had their first three children at the cottage. It was, however, too small for the growing family and they left for other houses in Grasmere and in 1813 for Rydal Mount, not far away, where they spent the rest of their lives. Dove Cottage was taken over for many years by their friend Thomas De Quincey, author of *Confessions of an English Opium Eater*.

Wordsworth died in 1850, and he and Dorothy and Mary all came back to Grasmere in the end; they lie buried in Grasmere churchyard. The Wordsworth Trust opened Dove Cottage, with an excellent Wordsworth collection, to the public in 1981. **RC**

◩ Dove Cottage was originally an inn named the Dove and Olive; it was a public house until 1793.

◩ After moving to the Lake District, Wordsworth and his peers came to be known as the Lake Poets.

Carlisle Castle (Carlisle, England)

The last fortress to be besieged in the history of England

This grim, red stronghold kept a forbidding eye on one end of the Anglo-Scottish border, where there was constant raiding and rustling. As late as 1745 the castle fell to Charles Edward Stuart's ("the Young Pretender") Scots Jacobite army, and the last castle siege in English history took place a year later, when the Jacobite garrison vainly resisted the Duke of Cumberland. Taken prisoner and kept without water, the Jacobites were reduced to licking stones in desperation; the "licking stones" are still there.

On the site of a Roman fort, the castle was built of earth and timber in William Rufus's (1087–1100) time and then reconstructed in stone, probably under his successor, Henry I. Through the succeeding centuries it was strengthened and modernized, and though the twelfth-century keep is the oldest part to survive, the rounded battlements for deflecting cannonballs were not added until about 1540.

The castle changed hands between the English and Scots several times. David I of Scots held it for twenty years from 1135 and Robert the Bruce besieged it in 1315. One of the cells has carvings made by captives in *c.* 1480, but the two most famous prisoners were Mary, Queen of Scots, who was a "guest" in 1568, and border bandit "Kinmont Willie" Armstrong, who escaped in 1596. The fortress was besieged for months in 1644 by the Scots, in alliance with the English Parliament against Charles I. The Royalist garrison surrendered after they had eaten all their dogs and as many of the rats as they could catch. Today the castle contains Roman finds and the museum of the King's Own Royal Border Regiment. **RC**

↗ In 1745 Carlisle Castle was held by Jacobites, only to become their prison when it was recaptured.

➡ Mary Queen of Scots was imprisoned at Carlisle Castle after fleeing from Scotland in 1568.

Durham Cathedral

(Durham, England)

A statement of sheer Norman power

The Prince Bishops of Durham were almost kings in the north and the cathedral in its spectacular setting, towering up on its great rock above a wooded horseshoe bend of the River Wear, is an overwhelming statement of Norman power. St. Cuthbert, the north's most venerated saint, was brought there originally in 995 after his coffin had been moved from one place to another for more than a century by monks originally from Lindisfarne. They were guided to this particular spot, it was said, by the saint himself in a vision.

The saint was duly buried there and the church built over him attracted pilgrims in droves for centuries. Its other attractions included a piece of the baby Jesus's manger and one of the Virgin Mary's ribs. The Normans knocked the church down and their new one is generally considered the finest piece of Norman architecture in the country. The Venerable Bede, historian and biographer of St. Cuthbert, is buried there. The nave and choir were completed around 1130; the nave features massive pillars, every other one of which is carved with a geometric design. A lady chapel was started at the east end for the Virgin Mary, near St. Cuthbert's shrine behind the high altar. However, the walls of the new chapel cracked. Taking this as a sign that the saint disapproved of women, the builders erected the chapel at the other end instead. Until the sixteenth century, a thin slab of black stone set into the floor of the nave was used to mark how far women worshippers were allowed into the church.

The cathedral's twin western towers date from the twelfth and thirteenth centuries; the central tower was rebuilt in the fifteenth after the original tower was brought down by lightning. The lion's head knocker on the north door, used by people seeking sanctuary, is one of Durham's most famous objects and a symbol of safe refuge from the world and its perils. **RC**

> *"Grey towers of Durham . . .*
> *Half church of God, half castle*
> *'gainst the Scot . . ."*

Sir Walter Scott, "Harold the Dauntless" (1817)

Blackpool Tower

(Blackpool, England)

Iconic seaside landmark

Blackpool Tower, rising to a height of 518 feet (158 m), was built in steel and cast iron on the model of the Eiffel Tower in Paris. A company was formed to build it, headed by a local alderman, the future Sir John Bickerstaffe, and the foundation stone was laid in 1891. The tower had the great advantage of providing vacationers with something to do when it rained, and it had a circus tucked between its legs as well as a ballroom, aquarium, and zoo. The tower was built with four viewing platforms, one completely enclosed and another with a glass floor. The platforms were accessible by elevator and commanded views of the surrounding countryside, as far away as the Isle of Man on a clear day.

The seaside vacation was an eighteenth-century creation, when the supposed health-giving powers of seawater were much in vogue and Blackpool's glorious sands began to bring comfortably-off visitors to what was then a pleasant, if obscure, little village on the Irish Sea. By 1830 the site drew about one thousand visitors a year. The arrival of the railway in 1846, however, and Blackpool's nearness to the Lancashire industrial towns transformed it by the 1870s into the country's leading working-class vacation resort. It still claims more visitors than anywhere else in Britain, except London, some seventeen or more million of them a year, to enjoy a traditional mix of amusements, roller coasters, donkey rides, fortune tellers, bingo halls, slot machines, and Blackpool rock. The fall illuminations along the front began in 1912 and have been an annual feature since 1949.

Tea dances are still held in the Edwardian ballroom, with its ornate murals and chandeliers, where the mighty Wurlitzer organ rises majestically from the depths (Reginald Dixon played it for forty years), but the circus no longer has animal acts. **RC**

Haworth Parsonage

(Haworth, England)

The Brontë family home

A small, gray town on the Yorkshire moors, Haworth draws thousands of literary pilgrims to the house where *Jane Eyre* and *Wuthering Heights* were written. The Reverend Patrick Brontë arrived in 1820 with his wife, their young son, Branwell, and five small daughters—Maria, Elizabeth, Charlotte, Emily, and Anne. The family took up residence in the parsonage, a grim, eighteenth-century house looking gloomily and all too prophetically over the graveyard. Mrs. Brontë died in 1821, and Maria and Elizabeth both died in 1825. The other children spent most of their lives in the house. None of them lived to be forty.

> *"All round the horizon there is this line of sinuous wave-like hills; . . . crowned with wild, bleak moors."*

Elizabeth Gaskell, author

Charlotte, Emily, and Anne wrote miniature books about a fantasy world called Gondal, some of which are still in the house. In 1846 they published a volume of poetry under the names Currer, Ellis, and Acton Bell. Branwell drank much of his life away in the nearby Black Bull Hotel and died in 1848. Emily died the same year, lying on a sofa that is still in the house. Charlotte married the Haworth curate in 1854, and died the year after. Patrick Brontë lived on in the parsonage to his death in 1861, and all the family except Anne were buried in the family vault in the church, which was rebuilt apart from the tower around 1880.

The Brontë Society was founded in 1893 and acquired the parsonage in the 1920s. There are many sites on the surrounding moors associated with the sisters' lives and their novels. **RC**

York Minster (York, England)

Early Christian site, today home to dramatic stained-glass windows

"The subdued splendor of the light stealing through the exquisite stained glass … is charming."

L. Valentine, *Picturesque England* (1891)

The impression given by York Minster is one of overwhelming size combined with a light airiness. The cathedral has Britain's richest collection of stained glass. The famous Five Sisters Window is in the north transept and the 1405 East Window, larger than a tennis court, is the biggest stretch of medieval glazing in existence.

York has been effectively the capital of the north of England for centuries, and it has a majestic Gothic church to match, the biggest in England. It was built at a strategic point on the River Ouse that in medieval and earlier days could be reached by seagoing ships. As Eboracum, the site was a major Roman army base and administrative center, and beneath the minster's colossal main tower the remains of the Roman headquarters can be seen. In Anglo-Saxon times the town was an early center of Christianity. A little wooden church was built in 627 for the baptism of the reigning king of Northumbria. This was a historic moment in England's transition from paganism to Christianity and, according to tradition, the font in the minster's crypt marks the spot.

The Anglo-Saxon church was soon rebuilt in stone on a much grander scale, but the building was badly damaged when the Normans besieged and took York in 1069. They replaced it with a new cathedral on a grander scale still, which was rebuilt from the thirteenth century and took 250 years to complete. There was a special dedication service in 1472 when the building was at last almost finished. The twin west towers were completed by 1485, and the enormous Great Peter bell booms out from the northern one every day. The church was restored after serious fires in 1829 and 1840, and there was another blaze in 1984 when lightning struck the south transept. Fortunately the famous Rose Window was not severely damaged and has since been restored and strengthened. **RC**

🏛️ ◎ **Albert Dock** (Liverpool, England)

A triumph of industrial architecture that pioneered the use of enclosed warehouses

Advantageously placed on the north bank of the River Mersey, a few miles inland from the North Sea, the port of Liverpool flourished in the eighteenth century on the slave trade. There were never any slaves in Liverpool itself, or in Britain, but the city exported hardware and cotton items to West Africa, where Africans were bought from the local chiefs and carried across the Atlantic for sale in the Americas. The ships returned to Liverpool with sugar, tobacco, rum, and raw cotton. The port's trade with the rest of the world expanded and, by the end of the nineteenth century, the docks stretched along the Mersey for 7 miles (11 km).

Named in honor of Queen Victoria's consort, Albert Dock's colonnaded, five-story warehouses in red brick were used for storing silk, tea, and tobacco from the Far East. The dock was designed by Jesse Hartley, who ruled the Liverpool waterfront as chief engineer for thirty-six years from 1824 to his death in 1860. It was part of his new system with connecting channels that allowed ships to be moved from dock to dock regardless of the tides. The slave trade was a thing of the past by Hartley's time but, in the hundred years after 1830, nine million people emigrated to America from Liverpool and it was later the home port of the Cunard and White Star liners.

The port declined in the twentieth century and Albert Dock was closed in 1972. It was restored in the 1990s with offices, smart restaurants, and boutiques, and Tate Liverpool, designed by James Stirling for what the guidebooks nervously call "challenging" displays of modern art. The city and the port of Liverpool are an exceptional testimony to the development of maritime mercantile culture in the eighteenth and nineteenth centuries, contributing to the building up of the British Empire and representing the early development of global trading and cultural connections throughout it. **RC**

> *"I have heard of the greatness of Liverpool, but the reality far surpasses the expectation."*

Prince Albert, at the opening of Albert Dock, 1846

Lincoln Cathedral (Lincoln, England)

Historically and architecturally one of the most important medieval cathedrals in Europe

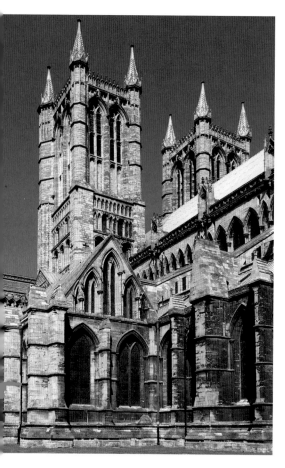

Lincoln Cathedral's central tower, 271 feet (81 m) high, containing the massive bell "Great Tom of Lincoln," originally had a spire, which reputedly made it the highest structure in the world at the time, until a storm destroyed it in the 1540s. The cathedral's magnificent west front provided an uplifting last view on earth for criminals hanged on the wall of one of the towers of Lincoln Castle opposite.

Lincoln Cathedral sits high on its hill, a spectacularly commanding sight for 30 miles (48 km) around. It is held in high esteem by architects past and present, and in the words of Victorian writer John Ruskin "is roughly speaking worth two of any other cathedrals we have." The defensibility of the hill was a key part of Lincoln's strength even in pre-Roman days, and by Norman times it was one of the major cities in the country. It was made the seat of a bishopric in 1072.

A cathedral was duly built, but it was dramatically shattered by an earthquake in 1185 and the future St. Hugh of Lincoln, a Burgundian monk who became bishop the following year, took the opportunity to instigate an extensive rebuilding program. When he died in 1200, he was buried in his cathedral with King John helping to carry the coffin, and his shrine attracted throngs of pilgrims. There was also a shrine to the so-called Little St. Hugh, a boy the city's Jews were falsely accused of murdering. The work of rebuilding went on through the thirteenth century, culminating in the famous Angel Choir, named for its carvings of angels, but also known for the horned "Lincoln imp," which has become the city's best-known emblem. The story goes that the imp was making mischief and sneaked up on an angel, who promptly turned it to stone. Edward I and Queen Eleanor attended the choir's consecration in 1280, and her entrails were buried there when she died ten years later. **RC**

". . . the cathedral of Lincoln is out and out the most precious piece of architecture in the British Isles."

John Ruskin, writer and critic

Boscobel House (Wolverhampton, England)

The secret hiding place of Charles II

All the rest of his life, Charles II loved to tell the story of his adventurous escape from England after his defeat in the Battle of Worcester in 1651 and how he hid in the oak tree in the gardens of Boscobel House. At the time, the house sat amid thick woodland and belonged to a Roman Catholic family, the Giffards. Followers of the Catholic religion feared persecution, and the locals were skilled and experienced at hiding priests and organizing unobtrusive disappearances.

After riding some 40 miles (64 km) from Worcester, Charles arrived in the middle of the night at the nearby estate of Whiteladies. There he was taken under the wing of the five Penderel brothers, servants on the estate, Roman Catholics, and loyal royalists. They dressed him up as a woodman, made him rub soot on his face and hurried him to Boscobel where he met a certain Colonel Carlis, another Worcester fugitive. Carlis and the king spent the Saturday concealed in an oak tree, with bread, cheese, beer, and a pair of pillows for comfort, while Roundhead soldiers searched the area for them. The exhausted Charles eventually went to sleep, but Carlis, afraid his companion might snore or shout out, pinched him awake. When darkness fell, they climbed out of the tree and Charles spent the night in a cramped priest's hole under the attic floor in the house.

From Boscobel, Charles made his way across country in a variety of disguises, helped by many sympathizers. There was a high price on his head, but no one gave him away and he eventually reached the south coast and got away to France.

After Charles's restoration to the throne in 1660, the Penderels were richly rewarded and many an inn took the name The Royal Oak. The original oak tree was torn to bits by souvenir hunters, but a descendant of it grows at Boscobel today and unsurprisingly draws in the crowds. **RC**

> *"By great fortune it rained all the time which hindered them from coming in the wood to search."*
>
> Charles II, on his near capture at Boscobel

Iron Bridge

(Ironbridge, Telford, and Wrekin, England)

The world's first major iron bridge

If any one object marks the beginning of the Industrial Revolution, it is the graceful span of the eye-catching iron bridge in the town and the gorge to which it gave its name. The area in the 1770s was compared with hell for the flames and smoke of its numerous iron foundries. A leading local ironmaster and Quaker, Abraham Darby I, who died in 1717, had invented a new process for smelting iron with coke instead of charcoal, which enabled it to be produced much more cheaply, and his son, Abraham Darby II, had discovered how to forge iron.

A bridge across the river was needed in the town and iron was the logical material for its construction. A single-arched iron bridge was designed by a Shrewsbury architect, Thomas Farnolls Pritchard, but he died in 1777 before it had been built. The existing bridge was cast by the original Abraham Darby's grandson, Abraham Darby III, though the immense cost of it left him in debt until his death in 1789. With a central span of 100 feet (30 m), the bridge was erected in 1779 and was a rapid feat of construction: built within three months, without hampering the passage of boats on the river in the least. Engineers, writers, and painters traveled to the site to admire the bridge and marvel at the local industrial scenery. So many visitors came that the owners of the new Iron Bridge built the Tontine Hotel close by to accommodate them and the village of Ironbridge grew up, with its own market.

Traffic eventually became too much for the bridge and it was closed to vehicles in 1934. In 1986 the Iron Bridge became part of a UNESCO World Heritage site and the local museums have riveting collections on the area's industrial history. Ironbridge Gorge provides a fascinating summary of the development of an industrial region in modern times. **RC**

"The quality of the structure is abysmal. It's shocking how poorly the components fit."

Bill Blake, English Heritage surveyor

Warwick Castle

(Warwick, England)

Heavily fortified medieval castle

Four important families in succession in English history—the Beauchamps, Nevilles, Dudleys, and Grevilles—have owned the castle as earls of Warwick, and it was they who made it one of the country's most impressive baronial strongholds and later inserted a civilized stately home into it. The flawless gardens were designed by master landscape gardener Capability Brown.

Far back in 914, Alfred the Great's daughter Ethelfleda built a fortress to command the River Avon, and the oldest survival on the site now is the mound from William the Conqueror's time. However, today's castle dates back to Thomas Beauchamp, first Earl of Warwick. One of the Order of the Garter's founders, he campaigned for Edward III in France and lavished the ransoms he extracted from captured French noblemen on his stronghold. His grandson Richard, the third earl, was another insatiable paladin who fought for Henry V, carried the baby Henry VI in his arms to his coronation, and watched the trial and execution of Joan of Arc.

The castle passed to a more formidable figure still, Richard Neville, "Warwick the Kingmaker," who played a key role in the Wars of the Roses, switching sides as his interests dictated. Eventually, in 1604, James I gave the castle to Sir Fulke Greville, poet and courtier. After spending a fortune on it, he was murdered by a servant and his ghost allegedly haunts the fortress still. He and his descendants created the splendid staterooms as they are now. The Madame Tussaud's organization, which has owned the castle since 1998, has installed a collection of torture instruments, waxworks, and tableaux, including a scene from a grand 1898 house party given by Daisy, Countess of Warwick. Guests included her lover, the future Edward VII, and the young Winston Churchill. **RC**

Kenilworth Castle

(Kenilworth, England)

Romantic ruins linked with Elizabeth I

The original castle was built by Henry I's treasurer and King John strengthened the defenses with curtain walls and additional towers from about 1210. He surrounded the stronghold with an artificial lake that effectively put it on an island. In 1253 Henry III gave the castle to Simon de Montfort, who subsequently led a civil war in which he was killed in 1265. His men held out in the fortress for the best part of a year before they were starved into surrender.

The fortress was transformed into a civilized palace in the 1390s by John of Gaunt, who had the great hall built and a wing of private quarters. It was in

---

> *"The lordly structure itself . . . was composed of a huge pile of magnificent castellated buildings."*
>
> **Sir Walter Scott, novelist and poet**

---

the sixteenth century, however, that Kenilworth reached the peak of its glory, when it belonged to Robert Dudley, Earl of Leicester, leading supporter, favorite, and perhaps lover of Elizabeth I. He made the place fit for his queen and entertained her there in wildly extravagant splendor. The young William Shakespeare, whose home was not far away, may perhaps have witnessed some of the festivities. In 1575 the queen spent nineteen days there, serenaded with music and enjoying hunting, dancing, and fireworks. The beautiful gatehouse that Dudley built, inhabited as late as the 1930s, has recently been restored.

After Elizabeth, the castle's great days were over. It was partly knocked down after the Civil War in the seventeenth century and its surrounding lake was drained. Kenilworth was given to the nation in 1938. **RC**

Shakespeare's Birthplace (Stratford-upon-Avon, England)

Stratford's premier tourist attraction for more than 250 years

When William Shakespeare was born in 1564, Stratford was a small market town of perhaps some 250 families. It is now possibly England's most popular tourist destination, entirely because the half-timbered house in which he was born is still standing. His father, John Shakespeare, was a prominent citizen of the town who carried on his business in the house from the 1550s and married a local girl, Mary Arden. William was their third child and eldest son. He was baptised in the font in Holy Trinity church and almost certainly sent to the local grammar school, but little is known of his childhood. In 1582 he married Anne Hathaway, who was already pregnant with their first child.

Although he spent his working years as an actor and playwright in London, Shakespeare kept his links with Stratford and in 1597 he bought a house called New Place. He inherited the Henley Street house when John Shakespeare died in 1601 and Mary Shakespeare continued to live there with her sister, Joan Hart. Her son subsequently left London and spent his last years at New Place until his death in 1616, when he was buried in Holy Trinity church, where there is a famous bust of him. The birthplace in Henley Street stayed in the Hart family until the nineteenth century. Part of it became a tavern called the Swan or later the Swan and Maidenhead. It was bought for the nation in 1847, heavily restored, and opened to the public in 1863.

Also open to visitors are other Stratford houses with Shakespeare family connections, and outside the town are Mary Arden's House and Anne Hathaway's Cottage, the girlhood homes of Shakespeare's mother and wife respectively. **RC**

◤ William Shakespeare's father made gloves in the rear of the house and sold them at the front of the property.

◳ Despite his huge success as a London playwright, Shakespeare always regarded Stratford as his home.

Althorp (near Northampton, England)

Family home of Diana, Princess of Wales

Diana Spencer was the daughter of the eighth earl. Born in 1961, and known as Lady Diana from 1975 when her father inherited his title, she married Prince Charles in 1981. After her tragic death in Paris in 1997, her body was taken to Althorp and she lies buried on an island in a lake in the park with the Diana memorial temple close by. The stable block, at one time home to one hundred horses and forty grooms, is now the setting for a comprehensive exhibition on her life.

Althorp (pronounced All-trop or All-thorp) has been the country seat of one of England's most prominent families since the sixteenth century. It sweeps across 14,000 acres (5,665 ha) of countryside and incorporates woodlands, farms, and villages. The Spencers were Warwickshire squires who acquired the Althorp estate in 1508 and made it their main country residence by the 1580s. Royalists in the Civil War, they were earls of Sunderland from 1643 and the second earl was an important political figure in the days of William III, who visited him at Althorp in 1691. The third earl, another major politician, married Anne, daughter of the great Duke of Marlborough, and the fifth earl, Charles Spencer, inherited the Marlborough title.

It was his younger brother John, however, who was one of Sarah, Duchess of Marlborough's favorite companions. On her death, he inherited her fortune as well as Althorp—her art collection is in the house—and was created Earl Spencer in 1765. The family had the original Tudor house extensively remodeled several times, but it was the architect Henry Holland who transformed it, in the 1780s, into the exquisite Georgian mansion of today. **RC**

↗ Behind the mansion is the stable block that now houses an exhibition on the life of Princess Diana.

→ Althorp was the family home of Princess Diana, whose grave and memorial there draw many visitors.

Ely Cathedral (Ely, England)

Founded by the Saxon princess Etheldreda, whose shrine is marked on the site

The cathedral was moored in the marshes of the Isle of Ely like a great ship in a harbor. The name means "island of eels" and the surrounding fenland, before it was drained in the seventeenth century, was almost impenetrable. Its intricate, tussocky paths were known only to the local inhabitants, who did not welcome outsiders, and the Saxon resistance leader Hereward the Wake held out defiantly against the Normans there until 1071. He had his headquarters in the church, which dated back to the seventh century and belonged to a monastery founded on the Isle of Ely in 673 by Etheldreda, daughter of one of the kings of Northumbria. It was rebuilt after it was sacked by the Danes in 870.

Once the Normans gained control, they started to build the present cathedral, the first phase lasting until 1189, when the nave was completed. The structure of the church remains fundamentally a Norman creation to this day, but the choir dates from the thirteenth century and was restored by Sir George Gilbert Scott in the nineteenth century. The most spectacular feature of all, the central octagon rising on arches above the whole width of the nave and supporting the soaring wooden lantern, was built between 1322 and 1346, after the original central tower had fallen in. An extraordinary feat of engineering, it was constructed under the careful eye of Alan de Walsingham, who was sacristan at the time and who also added the delightful lady chapel. The Porta, the impressive great gate into the cathedral off The Gallery, dates from the 1390s.

Oliver Cromwell would have known the community of Ely well. He, his wife and children lived there in the 1630s and 1640s, and their half-timbered house has been refurbished in the Stuart style and is open to visitors. **RC**

Berkeley Castle (Berkeley, England)

Domestic residence of generations of Berkeleys through times of siege and peace

The stronghold where Edward II was brutally murdered, and in which Oliver Cromwell's besieging army bashed a large and still-preserved hole, has been transformed over the centuries into the delightful home of one of England's oldest families. The fine silver, paintings, and furniture in the house today belie a fierce history. Entered across a bridge over the moat, the castle goes back to Henry I's time and commands the flat country east of the River Severn. The Berkeleys themselves are descended from Robert Fitzharding, a rich Bristol merchant who helped to finance Henry II and was rewarded with the lordship of Berkeley. Fitzharding was responsible for the tremendous keep at the site, which was built in the 1150s and includes the dungeon and a holding cell.

The castle's most notorious episode came in 1327 when the deposed Edward II was imprisoned there (unless the theory that he escaped to Italy is believed).

The Lord Berkeley of the day was the son-in-law and trusted supporter of Roger Mortimer, leader of the coup against the king, who was held in the horrible dungeon that can still be seen, before being gruesomely killed with a red-hot poker. Lord Berkeley paid for a black-draped cart to carry the body to Gloucester Cathedral for burial. He fought at Crécy before dying in 1361, and his effigy in the next-door church looks ostentatiously pious.

Later generations of the family liked to hunt their hounds all the way from the castle to London. They also backed their local doctor, Edward Jenner, the pioneer of the vaccination for smallpox, and were among the first families to have their children vaccinated. The Berkeley family have lived in the castle for twenty-four generations and have given their name to both Berkeley Square in London and Berkeley University in California. **RC**

 ⦿ **Blenheim Palace** (Woodstock, England)

Birthplace of Sir Winston Churchill

One of Britain's biggest houses, Blenheim Palace is the only nonroyal residence to be styled a palace. Designed in grand Baroque style by Sir John Vanbrugh, it was built between 1705 and 1722 for John Churchill, first Duke of Marlborough, as a reward from Queen Anne for his victory over the French at the Battle of Blenheim in 1704. Fine paintings and tapestries in the house celebrate the duke's battles. The estate had belonged to the royal family since the Middle Ages and it was there, according to tradition, that Henry II built a retreat for his mistress, Fair Rosamond, and there that the Black Prince was born.

So colossal was the building and so vast the expense that Parliament began to grumble. So did the duke's redoubtable duchess, who began life as Sarah Jennings and became a close friend of Queen Anne. The Duchess of Marlborough was known to be difficult to please and she complained bitterly about the unseemly costliness and showiness of the palace, which was a monument rather than a home. The building was finished in the year of her much-loved husband's death and she erected a column with a statue of him on top on the grounds.

The Marlboroughs left no male heir and the house and estate passed to a branch of the Spencers, who took the additional name of Churchill in 1817. Lord Randolph Churchill was born at Blenheim and played a lively role in the politics of his time. The room in which his son Winston was born in 1874 is on show in the house. Winston proposed to his wife, Clementine, in the park and they are both buried nearby in Bladon churchyard. By their refusal of the French models of classicism, the palace and park illustrate the beginnings of the English Romantic movement, which was characterized by the eclecticism of its inspiration, its return to national sources, and its love of nature. **RC**

Bodleian Library (Oxford, England)

Home to one of the finest collections of literature and music in the world

With approximately 90 miles (145 km) of shelves for considerably more than five million books, one million maps, some 150,000 manuscripts, and a substantial collection of music, the Bodleian Library is the country's second largest library (after the British Library in London) and one of the best stocked in the world. Its collection is constantly growing because it receives a free copy of every single book published in the United Kingdom. This practice has been going on since 1610. The Bodleian Library never lends a book and even King Charles I was once refused permission to borrow one.

Humfrey, Duke of Gloucester, endowed a library for the university Divinity School in the fifteenth century and Duke Humfrey's Library, of 1488, is now one of the Bodleian's showpieces, along with the old Divinity School beneath it. The Bodleian mainly dates, however, from Sir Thomas Bodley's decision to retire from his career as a diplomat and refound the library. One thing he did was to install a series of bookcases, which are now the oldest ones surviving in England. When he died in 1613, he bequeathed most of his money to the library, as well as his collection of medieval manuscripts and hundreds of books. More manuscripts were given by William Laud, future Archbishop of Canterbury, after he was made chancellor of the university in 1629, and he built a new wing for them. The antiquarian John Selden left a notable collection when he died in 1659.

The Bodleian's buildings include those in the Old Schools Quadrangle, which dates from 1619 and has a fine gate tower, the eighteenth-century Clarendon Building by Hawksmoor, and the Baroque, spectacularly domed 1748 Radcliffe Camera by James Gibbs. The New Bodleian across Broad Street dates from the 1930s. **RC**

Hatfield House

(Hatfield, England)

One of England's biggest and grandest Jacobean mansions was built for Robert Cecil

Set close to the Great North Road, in easy reach of London, the house was completed in 1611 and has been occupied ever since by successive generations of Robert Cecil's (chief minister of King James I) descendants, the earls and marquesses of Salisbury.

The Cecils have been prominent in the country's political history since the sixteenth century. Robert Cecil, who died only a year after Hatfield was completed, was the son of Sir William Cecil, chief minister of Elizabeth I. The third Earl of Salisbury spent time imprisoned in the Tower of London, as did the fourth earl, who was so fat he could hardly move. Centuries later, Hatfield was the country seat of the third Marquess of Salisbury, who was prime minister in the 1880s and 1890s, and the fifth marquess, a minister in the Churchill governments. Younger sons included Robert Cecil, who won the Nobel Peace Prize in 1937, and Lord David Cecil, well-known author and critic.

The most fascinating Hatfield personality of all, however, was Elizabeth I. Within the grounds of the main house are the remains of the old royal palace, dating from the 1480s, where she spent much of her youth. There is an oak tree in the grounds, beneath which, so the story goes, she was sitting demurely reading an improving book in 1558, when a delegation came from London to tell her that her sister "Bloody" Mary had died and Elizabeth was now queen. *The Rainbow Portrait* and *The Ermine Portrait* of Elizabeth are in the main house, along with her hat, gloves, and a pair of her silk stockings, thought to be the first hosiery of its kind in England. **RC**

- ⬉ Hatfield House was built by Robert Cecil, loyal chief minister and security adviser of King James I.

- ⬅ Part of the palace in which Queen Elizabeth I spent her childhood survives in the grounds of Hatfield House.

Sutton Hoo

(near Woodbridge, England)

Most complete example of a ship burial

Ship burials are rare in England and this one, discovered among a group of burial barrows in 1939, is the finest. It seems to have been the last resting place of a powerful East Anglian king named Raedwald, who was recognized as high king of the various Anglo-Saxon kingdoms and died in 624 or 625. He straddled paganism and Christianity—both pagan and Christian objects were buried with him—and he was sent into the afterworld in a sturdy rowing galley that was 89 feet (27 m) long, had no mast, and was constructed of overlapping oak planks, fastened with ribs. It was presumably hauled up the River Deben to the site.

The ship rotted away, but it left a clear impression in the ground. There was no body inside, but that had presumably rotted, too. What had survived was an astonishing treasure (now mainly in the British Museum) that gave a new insight into the luxurious style in which a powerful Anglo-Saxon ruler lived and the extent of his people's trading contacts abroad. He had been buried with more than forty pieces of superbly crafted gold jewelry, including a sword with a gold-jeweled pommel and hilt, jeweled shoulder clasps, and a gold buckle. The excavations also unearthed a purse of gold coins as well as more practical items such as silver dishes and drinking horns, cups, spoons, and a large dish from Byzantium. There was a magnificent Swedish-style helmet and a bronze bowl from Egypt as well as a shield, spears and chain mail, leather shoes and a leather bag, and a lyre made of maple wood.

The Sutton Hoo site was given to the National Trust in 1998 and recent excavations revealed remains of a cemetery nearby. On display is a full-scale reconstruction of the original ship burial, and a temporary exhibition displays British Museum items on loan. **RC**

SS *Great Britain*

(Bristol, England)

Once the biggest ship in the world

Perhaps the greatest of all the great British engineers, Isambard Kingdom Brunel (1806–1859) was a key figure in the creation of the nineteenth century's new transport system and in the development of Victorian Bristol, whose merchants backed him as mastermind of the Great Western Railway ("God's Wonderful Railway") from London. He went on to drive farther west still by designing steam-powered ships for Bristol's connections with the New World. The first of them, the *Great Western*, was built in Bristol and launched there in 1838 for the passenger traffic to New York, which she normally reached in fifteen days.

"In typical Brunel style it was an engineering wonder but a financial disaster."

Maev Kennedy, journalist

Brunel went on to build the *Great Britain*, the world's first propeller-driven, iron steamship and, in its day, the biggest ship in existence. The design and engineering of the ocean liner influenced many modern ships and she now lies in the Bristol dock where she was built. Carrying around 250 passengers in unprecedented luxury, she proved too big for the docks in Bristol to cope with. She later sailed from Liverpool and was redesigned to carry emigrants to Australia. She was a troop ship in the 1850s and in 1861 the first English cricket team to tour Australia sailed there aboard her. In 1886 the ship was damaged in a storm when rounding Cape Horn and was abandoned in the Falkland Islands, where she spent years rusting away as a storage hulk until she was rescued and towed back to Bristol in 1970 to be restored. **RC**

 Roman Baths (Bath, England)

Well-preserved religious spa

According to legend, it was King Lear's father, Bladud, who inadvertently discovered the healing properties of the hot springs. Packed off to tend pigs on his own because he had contracted leprosy, he saw that his charges loved wallowing in the water, tried it himself, and was cured.

At the Sacred Spring at Bath, the hot mineral springs bubble up from the ground at temperatures above 104 °F (40 °C) and the main one produces more than 300,000 gallons (1.3 million liters) a day. The spring was known to the pre-Roman Celtic people of Britain and their presiding genius was the Celtic goddess Sulis. When the Romans arrived, they called the site Aquae Sulis, "waters of Sulis," and created a spa that became famous throughout the Roman world. It included a Classical-style temple to the goddess of wisdom, Minerva, with whom the Romans identified Sulis. The bathing complex was unusually extravagant in its use of hot water. The facilities were gradually enlarged to accommodate the numbers of pilgrims who traveled from afar, and the complex remained in use until the fourth or fifth century. The bather would progress through the tepidarium or warm room, and then through a set of increasingly hot "Turkish" baths to a bracing plunge in the cold bath and finally a wallow in the warm, steamy water of the Great Bath.

With four steps along all four sides, the Great Bath in its impressive hall was a place for meeting and chatting as well as bathing. People could stroll along the paved floor around the pool, and there were niches in the walls for sitting and watching the bathers without getting splashed. The baths were abandoned after the Romans withdrew from Britain, but the complex was excavated from the 1870s on. It is below the modern street level and the Great Bath today is open to the sky and visible from the street. **RC**

🏛️ ⊚ **Avebury Stone Circles** (Avebury, England)

Largest of England's prehistoric stone circles

This huge rival to Stonehenge in impressiveness covers an area of 28.5 acres (11.5 ha) that includes much of Avebury village. Two equal-sized stone circles were constructed inside a larger outer circle of one hundred hulking sarsen stones, weighing 15 tons or more each. The whole structure was enclosed in a circular chalk bank, originally at a height of about 55 feet (16.5 m) above the ditch inside it.

The construction of the stone circles was a feat of epic proportions for the locals who dragged the stones to the site from a quarry 2 miles (3 km) away. Laborers using deer antlers as picks and the shoulder blades of oxen as shovels dug 150,000 tons of chalk out of the ditch to make the bank. Gleaming white originally, it separated the sacred area inside it from the ordinary world outside. There were stone structures inside the circles and part of an avenue of stones has survived, apparently a "processional way"

leading in from another sacred site in the southeast, now called the Sanctuary.

Alexander Keiller, of the marmalade dynasty, investigated the site and re-erected some of the fallen stones in the 1930s. The positions of others are marked by concrete pillars. Many of Keiller's finds are in the site museum. Avebury always retained a certain magic and down into the nineteenth century people used to dance around a maypole in one of the circles, perhaps subconsciously echoing fertility rituals of long ago. The many other prehistoric sites nearby, in what has been called a ritual landscape, include the mysterious Silbury Hill of about 2600 B.C.E. The largest man-made prehistoric mound in the British Isles at 130 feet (39 m) high, it must have taken years to build, but what it was for, no one knows. No sign of a burial inside it has been found. One suggestion is that it represented the earth goddess, pregnant with each new year's crops. **RC**

Stonehenge (Salisbury Plain, England)

England's most famous prehistoric monument

Its purpose is unknown, and is likely to remain so. Standing in solitary eeriness on Salisbury Plain, Stonehenge was built and altered over many centuries in a remarkable feat of skill and organization. It is dominated today by a circle of sandstone pillars called sarsens, weighing up to 50 tons each, joined by stone lintels on top and with a horseshoe of the biggest stones inside. They were hauled there from 20 miles (32 km) away to the north. Their surfaces were hammered smooth and some of them have carvings of axes on them. With them are smaller bluestones that originally came from Wales. The complex is surrounded by a ditch and a circular bank of earth, originally 6 feet (1.8 m) high.

The entrance in the northeast points to the sunrise at midsummer over a big pillar, now leaning at an angle, called the Heel Stone. Looking the other way, it points to the midwinter sunset. The circular bank and ditch date back to roughly 3000 B.C.E., but the monument reached its present form during the millennium after about 2000 B.C.E.

Stonehenge was presumably a religious site and an expression of the power and wealth of the chieftains, aristocrats, and priests who had it built— many of whom were buried in the numerous barrows close by. It was aligned on the sun and possibly used for observing the sun and moon, and working out the farming calendar. Or perhaps the site was dedicated to the world of the ancestors, separated off from the world of the living, or was a healing center. Whether it was used by the Druids, the Celtic priests, is doubtful, but the present-day Druids gather there every year to hail midsummer.

In 1986 UNESCO made Stonehenge a World Heritage site jointly with the circles of stones at Avebury, also in Wiltshire, describing them as an incomparable testimony to prehistoric times. **RC**

"Stonehenge . . . presents one of man's first attempts to order his view of the outside world."

Stephen Gardiner, Bishop of Winchester

Eton College (Windsor, England)

Prestigious boys' school with a long line of famous ex-pupils

Eton's roster of famous old boys is unrivaled. Its list of prime ministers runs from Sir Robert Walpole to both the Elder and the Younger Pitt, the great Duke of Wellington, Mr. Gladstone, and more recently Anthony Eden and Harold Macmillan. Besides the poets Shelley, Swinburne, and Robert Bridges, it educated writers as diverse as George Orwell, Aldous Huxley, Henry Greene, Cyril Connolly, and Ian Fleming. Musical figures range from the composer of "Rule Britannia," Thomas Arne, to Sir Hubert Parry of "Jerusalem" fame and the jazz trumpeter Humphrey Lyttelton. Scientists include J. B. S. Haldane, historians include Sir Steven Runciman, and among other celebrated old Etonians are Charles James Fox, the heroic Captain Oates, and lately Prince William and Prince Harry. The school uniform is still a tailcoat and pin-striped trousers.

In almost six hundred years since it was founded by Henry VI, Eton has become the most distinguished school in the country. The king intended it to provide a good education for seventy poor students and choristers. There is a 1719 statue of him in the main school yard, where the appalling toll of life the two World Wars took is also remembered. Some 1,150 Etonians were killed in World War I and close to 750 more in World War II.

Complete with centuries of boyish scrawlings, the original schoolroom has survived. The fine chapel was completed in the 1480s, with wonderful wall paintings of the same period, and a fan vault that was not added until the 1950s. The upper school dates from about 1690. The school playing fields are famous for the assertion, ascribed to the Duke of Wellington by the French author Charles Montalembert, that "The Battle of Waterloo was won on the playing fields of Eton." It was here that the pupils devised the peculiar and often desperately muddy variety of soccer called the Eton wall game. **RC**

"All that rugby puts hair on your chest/What chance have you got against a tie and a crest?"

The Jam, "The Eton Rifles" (1979)

Windsor Castle (Windsor, England)

Largest inhabited castle in the world and one of three official royal residences

Dominating the views for miles around, the castle has been an English royal stronghold since the time of William the Conqueror. Built to command the River Thames, it was reconstructed by Henry II from 1165 and withstood the rebel siege against King John in 1216. Its appearance today, however, is principally the work of Sir Jeffry Wyattville, the architect who rebuilt the fortress in romantic mock-medieval style for George IV in the 1820s and lies buried in St. George's Chapel. The royal family has called itself the House of Windsor since 1917.

The castle has a resident population of around 250 people, including administrators, clergy, and soldiers, and the staterooms with portraits and statues of past sovereigns are used for entertaining distinguished visitors; they were restored after a serious fire in 1992. One of the curiosities on view is the bullet that killed Nelson at the Battle of Trafalgar.

Wyattville created the Waterloo Chamber banqueting hall and St. George's Hall for the Knights of the Garter, whose installation ceremonies have been held at Windsor since the Order was founded by Edward III in 1348. The palace houses numerous royal treasures and works of art by such artists as Holbein, Rubens, and Van Dyck. A favorite item with visitors is Queen Mary's dolls' house, which dates from 1924.

Royals buried in St. George's Chapel, begun in 1475, include Henry VI; Edward IV; Henry VIII with his best-loved wife Jane Seymour; Charles I after his head had been sewn back on; George III; George IV; William IV; Edward VII and Queen Alexandra; George V and Queen Mary; George VI and the Queen Mother; and Princess Margaret. Prince Albert died in the castle in 1861 and he and Queen Victoria were buried in the Frogmore Mausoleum nearby, as later were the Duke and Duchess of Windsor. **RC**

Runnymede (Runnymede, England)

Meeting place where Magna Carta was signed

The meadows by the River Thames belong to a site of special scientific interest today, but their historic interest is as the birthplace of Magna Carta, traditionally considered the founding charter of English liberties. Runnymede was a convenient meeting place for King John and his advisers from Windsor Castle and a group of rebel lords based not far away in Staines. The rebels were bent on reining back the king's tyrannical behavior. His position had been weakened by his military failures in France, and in November 1214 a powerful group of barons had sworn to withdraw their allegiance unless he issued a charter to confirm their accustomed liberties. In May the following year they carried out their threat and advanced on London, which they took without opposition. King John accepted that he had no realistic choice but to give way. He may have signed the document that the barons had prepared on the island now called Magna Carta Island. In it he stated that he was acting "by divine impulse and for the salvation of our soul."

Subsequent monarchs were expected to conform to the charter, though revisions were made and some clauses that pertained to King John in person were dropped. Over the centuries the document was interpreted in ways that none of those present at Runnymede that day would have intended or probably even understood.

Runnymede was given to the National Trust in 1931, and three memorials have been erected on the slope of Cooper's Hill nearby. The Air Forces Memorial of 1953 honors those who "died for freedom" in World War II. The second memorial was given in 1957 by the American Bar Association in honor of Magna Carta and "freedom under law." The third was dedicated in 1965 to the memory of President John F. Kennedy. **RC**

Westminster Abbey (London, England)

Scene of the coronation of almost every English monarch since 1066

> "[The abbey] is well placed to serve the partnership between Church and State in the 21st century."

John Hall, Dean of Westminster

⊡ The far eastern apse of Westminster Abbey contains the Henry VII Lady Chapel, with splendid fan vaulting.

⊡ The two medieval western towers were completed under the direction of Nicholas Hawksmoor in 1745.

William the Conqueror had himself crowned in Westminster Abbey on Christmas Day, 1066, and over the centuries the church has witnessed a succession of royal occasions. A combined national hall of fame and sculpture gallery, it is crowded with the graves, monuments, and memorials of innumerable members of the royal family and famous figures. It all started in a much humbler way with a Benedictine community on what was then an obscure little island in the River Thames. Edward the Confessor took a keen interest and built a new church on the site, which was consecrated just before his death in 1065.

Nothing is left of the building above ground. The great church was rebuilt over centuries on an ever grander scale, as king after king lavished money on it, and most of it now dates from or after Henry III's rebuilding program, which began in 1245. It has a higher nave than any other church in England. Henry IV died in the Jerusalem Chamber in 1413 (it had been predicted he would die in Jerusalem). The spectacularly fan-vaulted Henry VII Lady Chapel, completed in 1519, contains the tombs of the king and many members of his family, including Elizabeth I. Oliver Cromwell was buried in the abbey, but was subsequently and unceremoniously thrown out again.

Not all those remembered in the abbey are actually buried there, but Chaucer, Dr. Johnson, and Tennyson are interred in Poets' Corner, where Ben Jonson was eccentrically buried standing up. Newton and other scientists are commemorated in the Statesman's Aisle. Near the west door are the tomb of the unknown warrior and the memorial to Sir Winston Churchill. Statues of modern martyrs were set across the west front in 1998 and, in the undercroft, a delightful museum of treasures has peculiar wax effigies of Lord Nelson and others. Services are held regularly in this world-famous place of worship. **RC**

Cabinet War Rooms

(London, England)

Underground network of offices for wartime government and personnel

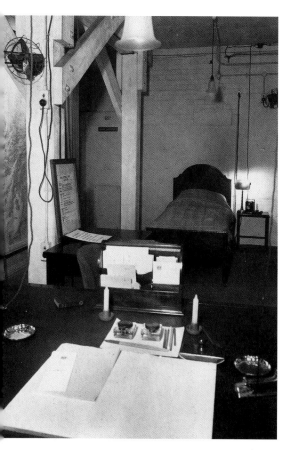

Concealed under Whitehall and the principal government offices is a warren of secret tunnels and underground rooms. In the late 1930s, with a war against Germany threatening and the possible effects of bombing in mind, an enormous subterranean office block was created underneath the Treasury, close to the corner of Horse Guards Road and Great George Street. The complex did not need excavation, being an adaptation and reinforcement of an existing basement area. With more than two hundred rooms, it was roofed over with concrete 17 feet (5 m) thick.

It was in spartan conditions here, from August 1939 until the Japanese surrendered in 1945, that part of the work of the wartime government was carried out, and here that Winston Churchill and his war cabinet, the chiefs of staff of the armed services, and some five hundred civil servants and secretaries lived, worked, and sometimes slept. Abandoned in 1945 and left as it was, the complex was partly opened to the public in the 1980s, and sound effects include air raid warnings and the all-clear sirens.

Among the rooms on view are the war cabinet room; the map room where information about operations was assembled; Churchill's bedroom and office, from which he made some of his wartime broadcasts; and the transatlantic telephone room, from which he spoke directly to President Roosevelt in the White House in Washington. On a lower floor were the canteen, a hospital, a shooting range, and sleeping quarters with ceilings so low that it was impossible to stand upright. Tunnels were built from the war rooms to government offices, with side tunnels leading off. Another tunnel was said, reliably or not, to have been constructed to get the royal family safely away from Buckingham Palace and out of London, in the event of a German invasion. **RC**

"We shall not fail or falter; we shall not weaken or tire. . . . Give us the tools and we will finish the job."

Winston Churchill, radio broadcast, February 9, 1941

Apsley House

(London, England)

Dwelling of the first Duke of Wellington

The great Duke of Wellington's palatial residence at the western end of Piccadilly was popularly known as No. 1 London because it was the first house past the tollgate when entering London from the west. It was originally designed for Lord Apsley in the 1770s by architect Robert Adam and still retains some Adam interiors. From 1807 it belonged to the Marquess Wellesley, eldest brother of Sir Arthur Wellesley, the future Duke of Wellington. The duke lived there from 1816, the year after his final triumph over Napoleon at Waterloo. In 1828 the architect Benjamin Wyatt was engaged to enlarge the house, reface the brick exterior in Bath stone, add the grand Corinthian portico, and redesign the interiors to reflect the duke's prestigious position. Wyatt's furnishings include the long Waterloo Gallery where the duke hosted the annual Waterloo Banquet for officers who had served under him in the wars.

Apsley House was Wellington's London home while he was prime minister from 1828 to 1830, and he used it to display his remarkable collection of paintings, silverware, porcelain, and other loot he either captured or was given by grateful sovereigns and governments. In his wry way he was particularly fond of the heroic nude statue of Napoleon by Canova at the foot of the main staircase, which he liked to pat on the head on his way downstairs.

In 1831 Wellington's windows were broken by rioters and iron shutters were installed for some years. He later chose to spend more time at Walmer Castle in Kent, where he died in 1852. Apsley House was given to the nation in 1947 by the seventh Duke of Wellington and handsomely restored during the 1990s. It looks out over the busy traffic of Hyde Park Corner, the duke's equestrian statue, and the spectacular Wellington Arch. **RC**

Banqueting House

(London, England)

Historic site of court activity

The old royal palace of Whitehall, known to generations of monarchs from Henry VIII onward, burned down in a disastrous fire in 1698, apparently caused by a careless washerwoman. All that is left of it is the Banqueting House. It was built for James I, who scornfully described an earlier building on the site as a rotten shed, and had an impressive replacement designed, in what was then a controversial Neoclassical style, by Inigo Jones. It was completed in 1622, with a gallery from which the citizens could watch their sovereign dine in state. The building was used for various ceremonies, and in 1629 Charles I

> *"I confess that I am, by instinct, better fitted to execute very large works than small curiosities."*
>
> Peter Paul Rubens, artist

commissioned Peter Paul Rubens to produce nine massive ceiling panels, which were painted in Antwerp. Installed by 1635, they glorified the Stuart dynasty and the blessings of its beneficent rule.

Ironically enough, it was from here that Charles I stepped out to his execution through one of the windows on to a scaffold erected outside. The king had been brought under guard from St. James's Palace, where he had spent his last night on earth, and he met the headsman's ax with calm dignity in front of a large crowd. It was also in the Banqueting House that Charles II celebrated his restoration to the throne in 1660, and here that William and Mary were formally offered the throne in 1689. The building later spent time as the Chapel Royal and a museum, until being restored and opened to the public in 1963. **RC**

Bank of England (London, England)

Historic home of the central bank of the United Kingdom

The "Old Lady of Threadneedle Street"—the nickname seems to date from a James Gillray cartoon of 1797—was originally founded in 1694 to provide a sensible mechanism through which the government could raise money. It was the brainchild of a rich City figure, a Scot called William Paterson, and the first governor of the Bank of England, Sir John Houblon, came from a Huguenot family.

From 1708 the bank enjoyed a virtual monopoly on the issue of banknotes and, after first renting offices, in 1734 had a commodious building of its own built in Threadneedle Street. In 1780 the Gordon Rioters tried to storm the bank and were held off by a hastily assembled force of militia and volunteers who made their bullets from melted-down inkwells. From then until 1973, a military guard was placed permanently on duty in the building: hence the saying "as safe as the Bank of England."

In 1788 renowned architect Sir John Soane started on a major rebuilding program that created an impressive Neoclassical edifice that, for security purposes, had no windows, but it was rebuilt between the wars by Sir Herbert Baker to cope with a substantial increase in staff numbers. One of the bank's loyal employees, until 1908, was Kenneth Grahame, the esteemed author of *The Wind in the Willows*. Famous customers once included Sarah, Duchess of Marlborough, George and Martha Washington, and Lord Nelson, but by the end of the nineteenth century the bank had ceased to hold the accounts of any private customers and had become effectively the government's bank. Its trusted duties included guarding the nation's treasure of gold bars. The history of the site is traced in the bank's museum, which was opened by the queen in 1988, in a reconstruction of one of Soane's banking halls. **RC**

 ## 🏛 ◎ **Tower Bridge** (London, England)

Iconic Thames landmark and triumph of Victorian engineering

The spectacle of the two bascules, or drawbridges, rising to allow ships on the River Thames to go through beneath, and then settling back together again, is one of the favorite sights of London. Each of the drawbridges weighs around 1,000 tons and takes a minute and a half for each maneuver. They were originally moved by steam power, but electric motors have been used since the 1970s.

The bascules, which form the roadway for vehicles, were originally kept open for two hours every day at high tide but, since the port of London's decline, they are now raised only by special arrangement. They are suspended from two tall, steel-framed towers, which near the top are connected by a footbridge. Lifts were provided for pedestrians, but the walkway became so infested by thieves and prostitutes that it was closed from 1909 to 1982, when it reopened as part of the Tower Bridge Experience visitor attraction.

There are marvelous views in both directions along the River Thames.

The bridge spanned the upper pool of the Thames, downstream from London Bridge and upstream from the principal London docks. Completed in 1894 and opened by the future Edward VII, the bridge was a remarkable achievement of Victorian engineering and was designed in tandem by the engineer John Wolfe Barry and the architect Horace Jones. It was accepted from the start that the bridge should blend harmoniously with the Tower of London, hence its mock medieval Gothic style, which is vastly impressive though disliked by architectural purists. *The Builder* magazine called it "the most monstrous and preposterous architectural sham that we have ever known," but most people love it and tourists often mistake it for the less eye-catching London Bridge. **RC**

Buckingham Palace (London, England)

Official London residence of the royal family

Buckingham House was built originally for one of the dukes of Buckingham in 1703. George III acquired it in 1762 as a family home for himself and Queen Charlotte, away from the formality of his official St. James's residence. The house filled up with the king's magnificent book collection and many works of art.

The alterations that made the place a palace began in 1825, when George IV's favorite architect, John Nash, began rebuilding it and providing it with suitably grand staterooms and a gorgeous main staircase, at what proved to be stupefying expense. The work was completed by Edward Blore, who, in 1847, added the east front facing The Mall, which is most people's view of the palace and the backdrop to where the changing of the guard takes place.

From her accession in 1837, Queen Victoria was the first sovereign to make Buckingham Palace her main London residence, for official purposes as well as domestic ones. She and Prince Albert lived there, and most of their children were born there. The staterooms have been used ever since for royal entertaining and the reception of official visitors. They also display many of the finest treasures in the royal collection of paintings, sculpture, furniture, and porcelain, put together by previous monarchs—especially Charles I and George IV. The royal standard flies from the flagstaff when the queen is in residence and is hauled down the second she leaves. **RC**

"Foreign countries might indulge in frippery, but England ought to pride herself on her plainness."

Joseph Hume, politician, rues the palace's cost

Highgate Cemetery (London, England)

Landscaped resting place of some of Victorian England's leading figures

London's best-known cemetery, on the slope of Highgate Hill, was created in response to an urgent need for more burial grounds in the capital to relieve the pressure on the earlier ones, which were all too literally bulging with corpses. An Act of Parliament of 1836 provided for the establishment of cemeteries by the London Cemetery Company north, south, and east of the metropolis.

The company's architect, Stephen Geary—he is said to have designed London's first gin palace—planned the cemetery at Highgate, where eventually he would be buried when he died in 1854. The landscaping was beautifully done, with paths winding circuitously among the graves and monuments, Egyptian-style columns and obelisks, abundant trees, and stupendous catacombs. An enormous 1880s specimen was a copy of the Mausoleum of Halicarnassus, one of the original Seven Wonders of the World, erected for Julius Beer, financier and proprietor of the *Observer* newspaper.

Highgate was a tourist attraction from the start. The most famous monument is the brutish one to Karl Marx. Christina Rossetti and most of her family were buried at Highgate, including Dante Gabriel Rossetti's wife, Elizabeth Siddal, with the only copy of his poems to her. (He had her coffin opened in 1869 to retrieve them.) Other celebrated figures range from the philosopher Herbert Spencer to author George Eliot, scientist Michael Faraday, Charles Dickens's wife, Catherine, the actor Sir Ralph Richardson, broadcaster Jacob Bronowski, and TV cook Philip Harben. There are wonderful views over London and monuments adorned with statues and figures, angels, broken violins, draped urns, and other symbols of mortality, as well as animals, including the prizefighter Tom Sayers's pet dog. **RC**

Cutty Sark (London, England)

One of the fastest sailing ships in British maritime history

Why the fast, sharp-bowed, square-rigged merchant sailing ships of the mid-nineteenth century were called clippers is not clear, but the first of them is generally considered to be American, the *Rainbow* of 1845. She was copied by British shipbuilders, especially for the China tea trade because each year's first batch of tea commanded a high price in Europe. The *Thermopylae*, built in Aberdeen in 1868, reached Australia from London in a record sixty-three days on her maiden voyage. The *Cutty Sark* was built on the Clyde in Dumbarton the following year as a rival. In 1871 she made the journey from Shanghai to London in 107 days; however, the clippers were already doomed by the opening in 1869 of the Suez Canal, which gave steam-powered vessels a commanding advantage on the routes to the East.

The *Cutty Sark* plied the Chinese tea trade in the 1870s (carrying a million pounds of tea each voyage), later spent time in the Australian wool trade, was sold to a Portuguese company in 1895, and returned to British ownership in the 1920s. Brought to Greenwich in 1954 and moored in a dry berth beside the Thames, she was restored in all her three-masted glory with her astonishingly complicated rigging—there are more than 10 miles (16 km) of rope in her—as a tribute to the days of sail. She is appropriately close to the Royal Naval College and the National Maritime Museum.

On May 21, 2007, a major fire damaged the center of the ship. Fortunately, the masts, rigging, and many fittings had been removed, and it has been confirmed that the ship can be restored. However, for the present, there is no visitor access to the ship. **RC**

◹ The elegant *Cutty Sark* before the fire of 2007—one of the finest survivors of the days of sail.

◁ The *Cutty Sark*, photographed under full sail in mid ocean while giving service as a wool carrier.

Charles Dickens's House (London, England)

Home of the quintessential London author, now a popular museum

Charles Dickens lived at several London addresses during his life, but this is the only one still standing. The house in Doughty Street stands close to what was Thomas Coram's Foundling Hospital and its beautiful gardens, and is near the legal and commercial areas around High Holborn; many of the locations that feature in his novels are within easy walking distance. The four-story house (plus attic) is in the center of an attractive Georgian terrace. Although now a throughway, when Doughty Street was built it was a private road, blocked at both ends by portered gates.

Charles Dickens and his wife, Catherine, moved into 48 Doughty Street in April 1837, with their first baby, Charles Dickens Junior ("Charley"). They lived here until December 1839 and their two eldest daughters—Mary ("Mamie") and Katey—were born in the house. By the time they moved in, Dickens had already started to achieve fame with *The Pickwick Papers*, which he finished while living at Doughty Street. He also finished writing *Oliver Twist* and wrote the whole of *Nicholas Nickleby* during this time.

In 1902 the Dickens Fellowship was set up to promote the life and works of Charles Dickens worldwide. In 1923, when the Fellowship heard that 48 Doughty Street was threatened with demolition, it began to raise funds to buy the house. The museum opened in 1925, re-creating the home as it would have looked when the Dickens family lived here. Two of the couple's children, Katey and Henry, were still alive when the museum opened. The museum is open almost every day of the year, often opening over Christmas for a truly Dickensian celebration. **LH**

↗ Now home to the Charles Dickens Museum, 48 Doughty Street offers four floors of memorabilia.

↘ Charles Dickens's experience of poverty as a child led to his championing of the poor and oppressed.

Hampton Court (London, England)

Palace loved by royalty, comfortably distant from the smoke of London

> *"The king's court should have the excellence ... but Hampton Court hath pre-eminence!"*
>
> John Skelton, poet

In the old days, Hampton Court, lying about 12 miles (19 km) to the west of London, was reached by boat along the River Thames, a far easier journey than by road. The palace was a favorite of generations of English monarchs who lavished money on the house and grounds, which include the country's most famous maze. Hampton Court was originally built by Cardinal Wolsey, the butcher's son who rose to be chief minister of Henry VIII. The splendor of his hospitality dazzled his contemporaries, but when he fell out of favor with Henry, he handed the palace over to the king in the vain hope of placating him.

Henry made the house bigger and grander still, and added the astronomical clock. He and five of his wives spent time at the palace. Jane Seymour died there after giving birth to the future Edward VI, and the ghost of Catherine Howard is said to haunt the palace, still screaming for mercy from the king after being sentenced to death. Elizabeth I, who liked getting her hands dirty gardening in the grounds—provided that no one important could witness her activity—spent her Christmases at Hampton Court and plays were presented before her in the Great Hall. Shakespeare acted in plays there in James I's time and the conference that led to the King James Bible was held at the palace. Charles II spent his honeymoon there and William III had the buildings substantially enlarged by Sir Christopher Wren.

The early Hanoverians loved Hampton Court, too, and George II employed Sir John Vanbrugh and William Kent to make further improvements. He was the last sovereign to live there because George III had unhappy boyhood memories of the place. From then the palace was largely given over to "grace and favour" residences—apartments awarded to those who had performed some service to the nation. Queen Victoria first opened the palace to the public in 1838. **RC**

Dr. Johnson's House (London, England)

Scene of the creation of the first comprehensive dictionary of English

The grand old man of English literature lived at seventeen or more houses in London after arriving from Lichfield in 1737, but this is the only one to have survived. Built originally about 1700, in 1911 it was threatened with demolition, but the Fleet Street newspaper magnate Cecil Harmsworth came to the rescue and it was preserved and opened to the public.

Johnson was always hard up, but the fee—equivalent to perhaps £150,000 today—offered him to create his *Dictionary of the English Language* allowed him and his wife, Elizabeth ("Tetty"), to rent the substantial house in Gough Square in 1748. Tetty, who was twenty years older than Johnson, died in 1752 and it was a blow from which her husband never recovered. He stayed on in the house until 1759, sharing it with a succession of cats, his young black servant Frank Barber, lodgers including the poet Anna Williams who had gone blind after a cataract operation, and his dictionary assistants. Six of them worked standing up at a long table in the attic. The great work came out in 1755 in two volumes with almost 430,000 entries covering some 80 percent of the language. It was not the first English dictionary but it was by far the most influential until modern times, and it made Johnson's reputation. He was known ever afterward as "Dictionary" Johnson.

Johnson and his friends, including James Boswell, Sir Joshua Reynolds, and the actor David Garrick, liked to meet at the Olde Cheshire Cheese pub (at 145 Fleet Street) near the house. Later it was a favorite haunt of Charles Dickens and was visited by many other famous literary figures, from Tennyson to Mark Twain, W. B. Yeats and Conan Doyle.

The house is of interest, not only because of its connection with Johnson, but also because it is a rare surviving example of a London residential house of the period, restored to how it appeared in 1700. **RC**

"A writer of dictionaries; a harmless drudge [. . .] detailing the signification of words."

Dr. Johnson's definition of "Lexicographer"

Nelson's Column (London, England)

High above London, Lord Nelson's statue faces the Whitehall he served so well

The monument is a statement of triumph over the French and honors the greatest of English naval heroes. Lord Nelson was killed at the Battle of Trafalgar in 1805, in which the Royal Navy destroyed a combined force of thirty-three French and Spanish ships without itself losing a single ship. Lord Nelson's statue, 17 feet (5 m) high, surveys Trafalgar Square from the top of a fluted stone column of 170 feet (52 m). A few days before the statue was hoisted into place, a party of fourteen people ate a perilous steak dinner on top of the column. It is guarded at the bottom by four splendidly formidable lions designed by Sir Edwin Landseer and cast by Carlo Marochetti in 1867, and there are also bronze reliefs of Nelson's naval victories made from captured French cannons.

Although the square itself has been criticized as a thoroughly incompetent piece of town planning, it keeps its hold on Londoners' affections and remains high on the agenda of tourists in the capital. Known for its innumerable pigeons—a few years ago war was declared on them—it is often the scene of political demonstrations. Its history goes back to 1812, when the architect John Nash proposed to clear away a clutter of buildings where the royal mews and stables once stood to create a square at nearby Charing Cross, but it was not constructed until the 1840s, by Sir Charles Barry, architect of the Houses of Parliament. The fountains and the numerous other statues were added later, but the equestrian statue of Charles I, looking down Whitehall to the scene of his execution, has been there since the 1760s. The National Gallery on the square's north side, by William Wilkins, was completed in 1838, several years before the Nelson monument. The church of St. Martin-in-the-Fields by James Gibbs, occupying the northeast corner of the square and known for its immensely grand Classical portico, was constructed in the 1720s. **RC**

> *"If ever man earned his greatness, both by action and by suffering, it was the hero of Trafalgar."*

Illustrated London News, 1843

🏛 ◉ Greenwich Observatory (London, England)

International starting point of accurate measurement of time and space

From the 1420s Greenwich, conveniently positioned on the River Thames and then lying some distance to the east of London, was a favorite residence of English royalty. Henry VI's uncle, the Duke of Gloucester, built the original palace and laid out Greenwich Park, which is the oldest royal park in London. The duke built a watchtower on the top of the hill, looking out over the river and the ships, and this became the site of one of the world's most celebrated observatories. It is particularly famous for the Greenwich Meridian, which runs through it along longitude zero (and is marked on the ground), and for Greenwich Mean Time, which was internationally recognized at a conference in 1884 as the basis of the world's system of time zones.

The observatory was founded by King Charles II, who was interested in science and dabbled in it himself. Sir Christopher Wren was the architect and the first astronomer royal was John Flamsteed, who solemnly cast the new institution's horoscope when he laid the foundation stone. His successor Edmond Halley (of Halley's comet notoriety) was also closely involved. Increasingly sophisticated telescopes and other instruments were added, including John Harrison's new marine chronometers, and extra rooms were built to house them during the following centuries. In 1833 the time ball was put up on one of the turrets to drop every day at 1300 hours precisely as a signal to the ships in the river and local clockmakers.

London's smoke and fogs made the work of the observatory increasingly difficult, and between 1948 and 1957 it was moved to Herstmonceux Castle in Sussex. Part of it was opened as a museum and John Flamsteed's house and other buildings were also put on display. UNESCO inscribed Maritime Greenwich as a World Heritage Site in 1997 for its representation of architecture at an important evolutionary stage, and for its contributions to astronomy and navigation. **RC**

"... to find out the so much desired longitude of places for the perfecting of the art of navigation."

King Charles II, on the purpose of the observatory

St. Paul's Cathedral (London, England)

Masterpiece that rose from the ashes of the Great Fire of London

> *"Scarce ever met . . . so great a perfection, such a mechanical hand, and so philosophical a mind."*

Robert Hooke, architect, praises Wren

⬆ A four-year renovation program, completed in 2005, has revealed many unsuspected decorative details.

➡ The cathedral endures a night of the London blitz in an iconic photograph by Herbert Mason.

Second in prestige only to Westminster Abbey among London's churches, and officially the cathedral of the London diocese, St. Paul's is Sir Christopher Wren's masterpiece. He is buried in the church with a famous epitaph: "If you seek his monument, look around you." The massive dome is outdone in size only by that of St. Peter's Basilica in Rome. Below the dome, inside, is the celebrated Whispering Gallery. St. Paul's was hit by bombs in the blitz of 1941, but was saved from more thorough devastation by its dedicated team of volunteer fire watchers.

The site's religious history goes back to 604, with successive churches culminating in the enormous medieval Old St. Paul's, which concerned itself with business dealings and assignations as well as worship, and was almost completely destroyed in the Great Fire in 1666. As if in revenge, Wren's replacement was mainly paid for by a tax on coal imported into London. The cathedral's first service was held in 1697 and the final stone was put in place in 1710.

The only monument to survive the Great Fire comparatively unscathed is the one to John Donne, the most famous of all deans of St. Paul's. The great Duke of Wellington is buried here and has a gigantic monument in the nave; Lord Nelson lies in the crypt beneath the center of the dome—his body preserved in spirits inside his coffin. Memorials of other famous figures include those of Florence Nightingale, Lawrence of Arabia, and Sir Alexander Fleming, discoverer of penicillin, together with a galaxy of celebrated painters including Sir Joshua Reynolds, J. M. W. Turner, William Blake, Edwin Henry Landseer, William Holman Hunt (his *Light of the World* is in the church), and John Singer Sargent. The church is used for state funerals, national thanksgiving services, and royal occasions. Prince Charles and Diana Spencer were married there in 1981. **RC**

Temple Church

(London, England)

Distinguished by its circular nave, the church was built by the Knights Templar

"*The connection with the law flourished and it is lawyers who today worship in the church.*"

Richard Jones, historian

The Temple is a nest of lawyers south of Fleet Street. The name comes from the Order of Knights Templar, founded in 1118 to protect pilgrims to the Holy Land and the Temple in Jerusalem. The English branch built their headquarters on the north bank of the Thames, which they called the New Temple, with one of their typical round churches. Independent of the London diocese, it is a "royal peculiar" under the crown's control.

Dedicated to the Virgin Mary, the church was consecrated by the patriarch of Jerusalem in 1185 and the chancel was added in the next century. The order's secret initiation ceremonies were conducted in the crypt. Surviving is the penitential cell, where the grand preceptor of Ireland, who had disobeyed the master, was left to starve to death. The Templar Order was suppressed in 1312 and the church passed to the Knights Hospitallers, who leased part of the estate as a hostel for lawyers. James I eventually gave it to the lawyers, requiring them to maintain the church in perpetuity which they did, also using it as a place to meet clients, while a music shop flourished in the porch. Samuel Pepys was one of the customers.

The church was restored three times in the nineteenth century: in the 1820s, 1840s, and 1860s. Much of it was refaced in Bath stone and much was altered. In what may have been a blessing in disguise, the building was severely damaged in the blitz in 1941. From 1947 the architect Walter Godfrey carried out a sensitive restoration, and the damaged figures of the knights who had reposed in the church since medieval times were skillfully repaired. Perhaps most remarkable was the discovery in storage of the wooden interior that Sir Christopher Wren had installed after the Great Fire of 1666—even though the church had not been affected. Wren's woodwork was reinstated, replacing the fire-damaged Victorian chancel interior. **RC**

Lord's Cricket Ground

(London, England)

Revered mecca of English cricket

The world's most famous cricket ground takes its name from Thomas Lord, a competent Yorkshire bowler who in 1787 opened a cricket field in what is now Dorset Square, not far to the south of the present ground. Financial backing came from the newly formed Marylebone Cricket Club (MCC). The first Eton versus Harrow match was played there in 1805, with Lord Byron on the Harrow side. The club moved to another location not far away in 1811, taking the original turf with it, but the site was required for building the new Regent's Canal. Finally, in 1814, Lord and the club leased the present site in St. John's Wood, at the time occupied by a duck pond.

Lord died in 1832 and the MCC, which became recognized as the game's supreme governing authority, bought the Lord's ground outright in 1866. The first grandstand was built in 1867, the Tavern was rebuilt in 1868, and the Middlesex County Cricket Club made Lord's its home ground from 1877. The first "test" or international match at Lord's was won by England against Australia in 1884. Since then all the game's greatest figures have played at Lord's, many of them commemorated by portraits in the famous Long Room in the pavilion. The main gates are a 1923 memorial to the legendary W. G. Grace. The weather vane, made in the shape of Father Time removing a bail from the wicket—a cricketing metaphor for death—dates back to 1926.

Today's ground boasts some striking modern architecture, including the Mound Stand (1987) by Michael Hopkins, the Grand Stand (1999) by Nicholas Grimshaw, and the Media Center (1999) by Future Systems. The museum in the former rackets court has a wonderful collection that includes the urn containing the legendary Ashes, and a stuffed sparrow that got in the way of a cricket ball in 1936. **RC**

Royal Hospital

(London, England)

Home of the Chelsea Pensioners

The Chelsea Pensioners in their blue uniforms and peaked caps—replaced on special occasions by scarlet frock coats and three-cornered cocked hats—are a familiar sight in Chelsea. There are around 400 or so of them, mostly aged fifty-five and upward (in some cases well into their nineties), and one of their special occasions every year is the parade on Oak Apple Day in April when they commemorate the escape from the Roundheads of their founder, Charles II, and his hiding in the oak tree at Boscobel.

According to legend, the idea of creating a home for veteran soldiers came from King Charles's sweet-

> *"[The Royal Hospital is intended for the] succour and relief of veterans broken by age and war."*
>
> **King Charles II**

natured mistress Nell Gwynne, but it is prosaically thought more likely that he got it from Les Invalides in Paris. Sir Christopher Wren was called in to design it, on the site of a theological college founded by James I. The new building was largely paid for by Sir Stephen Fox, who had piled up a fortune as the government's paymaster-general and now gave some of it back. The first pensioners arrived in 1689. Robert Adam and Sir John Soane later made additions to the hospital, but the main buildings remain essentially Wren's.

The spacious grounds, which once ran all the way down to the Thames, draw crowds of visitors to the Chelsea Flower Show every year in May. Buried somewhere in the grounds are two eighteenth-century female soldiers, Christiana Davis and Hannah Snell, who had successfully masqueraded as men. **RC**

Kensington Palace (London, England)

Royal residence associated with the memory of Princess Diana

Originally called Nottingham House, after its former owner, the Earl of Nottingham, Kensington Palace was bought in 1689 by William III who had been finding the old palace of Whitehall by the Thames bad for his asthma. The building was reconstructed by Sir Christopher Wren. The court moved to the palace in Christmas 1689 following the efforts of Queen Mary who, impatient to move in, frequently visited to hurry the workmen along. Soon after one of her visits several people were killed when some newly erected construction work fell down because it had been put up too quickly.

Queen Anne and her husband, Prince George of Denmark, another asthmatic, also liked the palace. So did George I, who had new staterooms constructed, and George II, whose consort, Queen Caroline, had the gardens laid out anew. George III preferred Buckingham Palace, and from then on Kensington Palace was used for junior royals and connections. The Duke and Duchess of Kent moved in and their only child, the future Queen Victoria, was born in one of the ground-floor rooms in 1819. It was her London home all through her girlhood, and it was there in 1837 that she was officially informed of her accession to the throne. She soon moved to Buckingham Palace to get away from her mother. A marble Queen Victoria remains, enthroned in front of the palace.

The Duke and Duchess of Teck lived in Kensington Palace from 1867 and their daughter Mary, future wife of George V, was born there. Queen Victoria's artist daughter, Princess Louise, lived in the palace for years, from 1880 until 1939, and the London Museum was there from 1950 until it moved to its own building in 1975. The palace was home to Princess Alice, Princess Margaret, and Princess Diana, whose funeral procession started from there in 1997. **RC**

🏛 🏵 Tower of London (London, England)

For centuries the impregnable fortress of English royalty

England's most dramatic Norman monument has frowned over the Thames since William the Conqueror built it as a stronghold from which to keep London under his eye. The Tower of London was inscribed as a UNESCO World Heritage Site in 1988 as a typical example of Norman military architecture and the template for many other fortresses built in the medieval period. It was a royal residence until 1603, a military base and barracks, a prison, and a place of execution for those convicted of treason. At times it has sheltered the royal astronomical observatory and the royal zoo. It is still home to the crown jewels, the armories, and the ravens that shuffle about in a sinister manner. Legend has it that the Tower will fall if they ever leave, so their wings are clipped.

The Tower started as a temporary wooden fort, replaced by a massive keep in stone with walls 90 feet (27 m) high and 15 feet (4.5 m) thick, that is still standing as the White Tower. The fortifications were strengthened in the 1190s and the first animals in the menagerie—three leopards—arrived in 1235 and were put on show to the public. Later in the century the outer wall was built, with Traitors' Gate. The mint and the crown jewels were housed in the Tower from the 1300s, and in medieval times the routes of royal coronation processions often started from the Tower.

The Tower has a long record of torture and bloodshed. King Henry VI was murdered there and so were Edward IV's sons, the two "little princes," in the Bloody Tower. Queen Anne Boleyn was beheaded inside the fortress on Tower Green, but most executions were held outside on Tower Hill and the bodies were taken to the Tower's grim chapel of St. Peter ad Vincula ("in chains"). Guy Fawkes and his accomplices were questioned in the Tower in 1605. The place has many ghosts. **RC**

Handel's House (London, England)

Abode of the great German composer and favorite of Hanover King George I

Brook Street, off Grosvenor Square, was built in the 1720s and described in the following decade as "for the most part nobly built and inhabited by People of Quality." George Frideric Handel was the first tenant of No. 25, in 1723, moving in when he was in his thirties. He lived there for the rest of his life, enjoyed a brilliantly successful career in his adopted country, and died in the house in 1759.

Born in Halle, Germany, Handel established himself in charge of music at the court of Hanover. He first came to London in 1710 for the premiere of his opera *Rinaldo*, and the fact that the elector of Hanover succeeded to the English throne, as George I, in 1714 did him no harm at all. His music was immensely popular, and in 1735 he took over the Covent Garden theater and produced six of his operas and numerous oratorios. The Brook Street house was handy for musical events and social circles in Covent Garden and Soho, and for St. James's Palace, where Handel was music master to the royal family and composer to the Chapel Royal. He regularly played the organ in the nearby church of St. George's, Hanover Square. Many of his masterpieces were written in the house, including *Saul*, *Israel in Egypt*, *Messiah*, which had its first English performance in 1743, and *Samson*, as well as the *Water Music* and the music he composed to accompany the royal fireworks.

The great composer was buried in Westminster Abbey. The Brook Street house was suitably restored and opened as a museum to him in 2001. By an odd coincidence, the rock musician Jimi Hendrix lived next door at No. 23 in the 1960s. **RC**

◹ Handel was highly esteemed; J. S. Bach said that he was "the only person I would wish to see before I die."

◸ Blue plaques in Brook Street announce the sojourns of Handel at No. 25 (right) and Hendrix at No. 23.

🏛 ⊚ Westminster Palace (London, England)

House of debate with a 1,000-year-old history of political authority

The palace near Westminster Abbey was a royal residence from Edward the Confessor's time before 1066 until the reign of Henry VIII. It was eventually taken over for the House of Lords and the House of Commons, whose sixteenth-century members faced each other across the choir stalls of St. Stephen's Chapel, with the Speaker in the position of the altar. It was there that figures such as the Elder and Younger Pitts and Charles James Fox debated. In 1834, however, it was decided to burn a lot of unwanted exchequer tally-sticks in a furnace beneath the Lords. By next morning much of the palace was a smoking ruin. Most of today's richly towered and pinnacled edifice dates from the rebuilding.

It was decided to rebuild in "the Gothic or Elizabethan style." The principal architects were Sir Charles Barry and Augustus Welby Pugin, with a committee under Prince Albert overseeing the choice of painting and sculpture. Building work began in 1837, the Lords moved back in 1847, and the new House of Commons, where Gladstone and Disraeli, Lloyd George and Baldwin, Churchill and Attlee, and other famous figures would debate, was opened in 1852. The grand Victoria Tower, through which the sovereign enters the building to open Parliament, was finished in 1860. The most famous single element of the palace is the clock, with its bell, Big Ben. Crowds lined the streets to see the 13.5-ton bell drawn to the site in 1858 and hoisted into the 320-foot- (98-m-) high clock tower. Its sonorous tones have since symbolized both London and Britain. The House of Commons, damaged by bombs in World War II, was rebuilt. **RC**

↗ Westminster Palace, with its soaring vertical lines, is one of the world's finest Gothic Revival buildings.

➡ At the state opening of Parliament the monarch speaks from the throne in the Lords' Chamber.

All England Lawn Tennis and Croquet Club (London, England)

The most prestigious location in international tennis

The club started as the All England Croquet Club with three lawns in Worple Road, Wimbledon, in 1869; the middle one was the original Centre Court. However, in 1874 the new game of lawn tennis was patented by a retired army major named Walter Wingfield and was a hit, not least in Wimbledon. Like croquet, it was played on grass and did not need the expensive courts required for the older "real" tennis. It had gained the upper hand over croquet by 1877, when the first Wimbledon tennis championships were contested. The story goes that they were held to bring in money to pay for the repair of the club's pony-drawn roller.

It was from that point that lawn tennis began to be taken seriously as a sport. In 1882 the club changed its name to the All England Lawn Tennis and Croquet Club. The Lawn Tennis Association was founded in 1888 as the game's governing body in Britain and was closely linked with the Wimbledon club, which moved to the present ground in Church Road, opened by King George V, in 1922. Women played the game successfully from early on and Wimbledon introduced ladies' singles and gentlemen's doubles in 1884, and ladies' doubles and mixed doubles in 1913. Famous Wimbledon players of the 1880s and 1890s included the twin brothers William and Ernest Renshaw, who introduced the overhead service in place of serving underhand. William Renshaw won the singles title seven times. Originally, the Wimbledon championships were open only to amateurs (real or supposed), but in 1968—the start of the "open era"—the distinction was dropped and all players were permitted to play in all tournaments.

The history of the game and the championships is engagingly displayed in the Wimbledon Lawn Tennis Museum, which opened in 1977, the centenary year, and includes the Centre Court in the visit. **RC**

Cenotaph (London, England)

Sobering monument to the fallen of two World Wars

The Great War officially ended at the eleventh hour on the eleventh day of the eleventh month of 1918. A memorial was needed in the capital of the British Empire to those who had been killed fighting in "the war to end wars," and David Lloyd George's government accepted Edwin Lutyens's suggestion for a cenotaph ("empty tomb" in Greek). Emphatically not a Modernist, Lutyens would have much to do with war memorials and cemeteries. The Cenotaph made his reputation, and he became widely regarded outside the profession as the best architect of his day.

Church people wanted a cross as a monument, but "the glorious dead" had not all been Christians and Lutyens kept the Cenotaph free of all religious symbols. The only adornments are wreaths and the flags of the army, navy, merchant navy, and air force. He designed it in 1919 originally as a temporary structure in wood and plaster for a victory parade, to general public approval, and the permanent monument in Portland stone was completed for the formal unveiling by King George V in 1920. The oblong block is topped by a coffin in stone. Its reticent, calm simplicity conceals mathematics of fiendish complexity, involving segments of imaginary circles centered 900 feet (274 m) below ground as well as 1,000 feet (305 m) above ground.

A ceremony is held at the Cenotaph every year on Remembrance Sunday for the dead of both World Wars and a two-minute silence is observed. The monument is appropriately placed in Whitehall, from which England and later Britain and the British Empire were governed for centuries. Close by are many government buildings, the prime minister's house and chancellor's house, both in Downing Street, and the mounted sentries outside the Horse Guards, much photographed by visitors. **RC**

Westminster Hall (London, England)

Magnificent Norman dining hall and scene of many historic trials

When King Edward the Confessor built Westminster Abbey he also built a palace for himself close by, which became the main London residence of the English kings until 1529. Westminster Hall was added by William Rufus, son of William the Conqueror, as a grand banqueting hall. Dissatisfied, he complained that the hall was too small.

From the thirteenth century the hall was used as the home for the principal law courts, and they ceased to meet there only in the nineteenth century. Some of the early parliaments assembled there, too. In 1397, Richard II gave the building a magnificent hammerbeam roof with the widest unsupported span in England. There were shops in the hall along with the courts, lawyers, jurymen, and many spectators. Stalls sold law books, clothes, and toys, and the place in full swing must have been a scene of remarkable noise and confusion.

Perhaps the most dramatic moment in Westminster Hall's history came in 1649, when Charles I was put on trial there and sentenced to death, but there have been many others. William Wallace was condemned to death in the hall in 1305, as was Anne Boleyn in 1536, and Guy Fawkes in 1606, and Oliver Cromwell was installed as Lord Protector there in 1653. His severed head afterward spent years stuck up on the roof, but there is a statue of him outside today. At coronation banquets it was customary for the royal champion to ride into the hall on horseback and challenge to fight to the death anyone who questioned the new sovereign's right to succeed. In the great flood of 1812, three or four boats full of men rowed into the building, which has seen the lying in state of sovereigns and other important figures, including William Gladstone, Edward VII and George VI, Sir Winston Churchill, and Queen Elizabeth, the Queen Mother. **RC**

> *"Thence walked to Westminster Hall, where the King was expected to come to prorogue the House . . ."*
>
> Samuel Pepys, diary entry, May 16, 1664

Statue of Eros (London, England)

Inadvertent symbol of the excitements offered by a London night out

The story of London's best-known and best-loved statue and fountain did not begin with a chorus of acclaim. The statue was criticized as ugly and the basin below it was too small to catch the full flow of the water, so that passersby were sometimes soaked. The fountain was created by the brilliant sculptor Alfred Gilbert and the statue on top is made of aluminum, which was still a novel material at the time.

The winged figure was not intended as a celebration of the Greek god of love—the area around Piccadilly Circus was heavily frequented by prostitutes—but as a memorial to Lord Shaftesbury, the great philanthropist. Perched on one foot on top of the fountain, he was meant to be the Angel of Christian Charity. Originally he aimed his arrow, to "bury his shaft" as was punned, up Shaftesbury Avenue—but this would have become more difficult when he was moved from his original location in the 1980s. Lower down on the fountain is a lively display of fish and marine creatures.

The figure did not remotely resemble an angel and was soon dubbed Eros, which stuck. The monument was supposed to be paid for by public subscription, but Gilbert ended up having to pay much of the cost himself. Although he was immensely highly regarded and almost overwhelmed with commissions, he went bankrupt in 1901 and escaped abroad. However, in 1923 he designed the striking memorial to Queen Alexandria in Marlborough Gate, beside St. James's Palace.

Piccadilly Circus itself was created in 1819 by the architect John Nash as a circular open space linking Regent Street with the shops and malls of Piccadilly. Much altered since then, from 1910 it was dominated by giant advertising signs for Bovril and Schweppes. It came to be regarded as the hub of London, and is one of the world's most famous meeting places. **RC**

"... a striking contrast to the dull ugliness of the generality of our street sculpture ..."

Magazine of Art, on the statue's erection in 1893

Down House (Bromley, England)

Cherished home of Charles Darwin and scene of scientific experimentation

Charles and Emma Darwin lived at Down House for more than forty years and it was there that he wrote his book, *The Origin of Species*. It created an uproar when it was published in 1859, revolutionized scientists' understanding of the natural world and its origins, and has been the subject of argument and counter-argument ever since. Darwin's writing desk and chair are still to be seen in his study, and there are many other family possessions in the house. The grounds where he liked to stroll every day are allegedly haunted by his ghost.

Darwin returned in 1836 from his five-year voyage to South America on the *Beagle* as the ship's unpaid naturalist. In 1839 he married his cousin Emma Wedgwood, granddaughter of the great Josiah Wedgwood, and in 1842 they moved to the village of Downe. They went there for his health, which was frail, and he loved the peacefulness of the quiet little community in Kent. In a letter of 1843 he said that the chief merit of the place was "its extreme rurality" and that "I think I never was in a more perfectly quiet country." He described the house, which dates from the early eighteenth century, as ugly and the garden in its original state as bleak, but he never considered living anywhere else and it was there that he and Emma raised their brood of children. Darwin, who liked to work in his study in short bursts, spent much of his early time there writing a monograph on barnacles. He died at Down House in 1881, aged seventy-three, and was buried in Westminster Abbey. The house was opened to the public in 1929 and is much as it was when Darwin lived there. **RC**

◪ Written at Down House, Darwin's work on barnacles investigated their adaptation to changing conditions.

⊡ The gardens have been restored, with re-creations of experiments made there and in the greenhouse.

Glastonbury Abbey (Glastonbury, England)

Site of Britain's earliest Christian church and reputed hiding place of the Holy Grail

Glastonbury is linked with the beginning of Christianity in England, the Holy Grail, and King Arthur. The story goes that Joseph of Arimathea, who took Christ's body down from the cross, came to England with eleven companions in 63 C.E. They made their way to Glastonbury Tor on the Isle of Avalon, deep among the marshes, and there founded the first Christian church in the British Isles. A tree, the Glastonbury Thorn, grew from Joseph's staff, which he had thrust into the ground. He was said to have brought the Holy Grail, the cup used at the last supper, and possibly concealed it in Chalice Well near the Tor.

The monastery with its original wooden church was allegedly refounded in 166 and visited by St. Patrick in 463. It was rebuilt and enlarged in 708, Abbot Dunstan introduced the Benedictine rule in 940, and three Saxon kings were buried at Glastonbury in the following century. The abbey burned down in 1184 and rebuilding on an imposing scale began immediately. In 1191 the monks claimed to have discovered the grave of King Arthur and Queen Guinevere. Legend has it that Arthur led the Britons during the Saxon invasions of the fifth and sixth centuries, although some historians doubt that he ever existed. However, in 1278 the two bodies were reburied in front of the high altar in the presence of King Edward I and Queen Eleanor. Rebuilding was mainly completed by 1303.

The abbey was closed down in Henry VIII's time and the last abbot, Richard Whiting, was hanged, beheaded, and quartered on the Tor in 1539. The Grail is said to have been smuggled to safety in Wales. **RC**

↗ Glastonbury Abbey was ruined between 1538 and 1541, during Henry VIII's Dissolution of the Monasteries.

➡ This small fountain marks the site of the Chalice Well where the Holy Grail may have been long concealed.

Winchester Cathedral

(Winchester, England)

Church of pilgrimage in the former capital of England

Long before London gained its predominance, Winchester was the capital city of England. King Alfred and his successors had a palace there, and it was at Winchester that the royal treasure was kept and watchfully guarded. The bishops enjoyed special influence and prestige, and several of them have splendid monuments in the cathedral, the city's principal treasure today.

The building with its stumpy tower is unremarkable from the outside, but it is one of the longest churches in the country and the interior has a noble simplicity. The first church was built in the seventh century and among early bishops was St. Swithun, whose name has been linked with rain ever since the monks moved his remains from a humble spot he liked outside the church to a place of honor within—to encourage profitable pilgrimage—and the saint reprovingly pelted them with rain for forty days.

In 1079 the new Norman bishop started a new church and pulled down the old one. The east end was put up in the thirteenth century on ground so boggy that it had to be laid on a giant raft of logs. The rest of the building, including the glorious nave and choir, was rebuilt in the fourteenth century. Reconstruction of the western end ceased for about twenty-five years after the Black Death in 1349.

William Rufus lies buried under a plain block of marble in the choir, where the remains of Canute and other kings are all muddled up together in boxes. Also buried in the cathedral is Jane Austen. The little figure of a diver just outside the lady chapel represents William Walker, who in the early 1900s heroically saved the east end from collapse when the timber raft began giving way. He worked for six years in pitch darkness and black water, single-handedly building a new foundation. **RC**

"an easy way of dawdling away one's time: praying, walking and as little study as your heart would wish"

Canon Edmund Pyle, on visiting the cathedral

Winchester College

(Winchester, England)

Famous boys' school founded in 1382

One of the country's most prestigious boys' schools, Winchester College is thought to be Britain's oldest school with a continuous history, and through Thomas Arnold, a renowned educationalist who was a pupil there, it has influenced all subsequent British public schools. Its founder was William of Wykeham, who was Bishop of Winchester from 1367 to his death in 1404. From humble beginnings, he made his way up in the world in the service of Edward III to a dominating position in the royal council, and it was the king who insisted on his appointment to the Winchester see and then made him chancellor of England.

Wykeham did not forget his own impoverished background. To help other poor boys and train clergy, "having God before their eyes," he founded New College, Oxford, and the Winchester school, which was named St. Mary's College. The colleges were built by the same mason, William Wynford, and the two have enjoyed a close link ever since. In 1382 the bishop bought the site for the college in Winchester and issued its foundation charter for seventy poor scholars under a warden and a staff of teachers, chaplains, and chapel choristers. St. Mary's College opened in 1394.

The school has the atmosphere of an Oxford or Cambridge college. The chapel's famous fourteenth-century wooden roof is an early essay in fan vaulting, and there is a 1680s schoolroom that was probably designed by Sir Christopher Wren. The war memorial cloister, designed by Sir Herbert Baker, movingly commemorates more than 750 Winchester boys who were killed in the two World Wars. Famous old boys include Anthony Trollope and Matthew Arnold, the Labour Party leader Hugh Gaitskell, and the World War II general Lord Wavell, who is buried in the cloister garth. The art historian Sir Kenneth Clark and Tory politician Lord Whitelaw also attended the school. **RC**

Jane Austen's Home

(Chawton, England)

Home of the admired novelist of manners

Jane Austen was born and raised in her father's Hampshire rectory. After his death, she and her sister Cassandra and their widowed mother, with their friend Martha Lloyd, returned to the same county in 1809, settling into the simple redbrick house in Chawton, which dated back 100 years or more and may have been built as an inn. It was there that she revised her early novels and wrote her new ones, and it was while she was at Chawton that her work began to be published, anonymously, from 1811 onward.

Coaches thundering past on the main road outside made the beds in the front rooms upstairs

> *"... a talent for describing the involvements, feelings, and characters of ordinary life ..."*
>
> Sir Walter Scott, praising Jane Austen

shake, and travelers in slower vehicles could see the Austens through the downstairs windows. Jane and Cassandra seem to have shared a bedroom and Jane used to read aloud to her sister at night. Jane got up first and went downstairs to play the piano for a while before making breakfast of tea and toast for the family at 9 A.M. There were occasional visitors, but they led quiet and ordinary lives.

Jane's writing desk is still in the house along with a hoard of letters and other memorabilia, and her donkey carriage is in an old bakehouse. It was at Chawton that she came down with what she called "bile" and suffered from fever and bilious attacks. She resisted bravely, but the illness worsened and she agreed to go for treatment to Winchester, where she died in July. She was forty-one. **RC**

Canterbury Cathedral

(Canterbury, England)

Scene of the infamous murder of Archbishop Thomas Becket in 1170

Sent by Pope Gregory the Great, St. Augustine arrived at the royal court of Kent in Cantwarabyrig in 597 to a welcome from Queen Bertha, who was already a Christian. King Ethelbert was soon converted and Augustine founded a Benedictine abbey, whose ruins have survived. Presently, as "bishop of the English," he built a church that became larger and more imposing over many centuries and would be the mother church of Anglican Christianity. The Norman Archbishop Lanfranc began to rebuild the church in 1070.

Archbishops of Canterbury have played important roles in English politics. A key event occurred in the cathedral in 1170 with the murder of Archbishop Thomas Becket by four knights who thought they were acting on a hint from King Henry II. Miracles were reported from Becket's tomb, he was swiftly canonized, and English and foreign pilgrims came in numbers, substantially increasing both the prestige and the income of the cathedral. Chaucer's *Canterbury Tales* was written in the fourteenth century after he himself had been to the city while the nave was being rebuilt. This was part of a major redevelopment that continued from 1391 until the immense central tower, Bell Harry, was completed in 1505. St. Thomas's shrine behind the high altar was destroyed on the orders of Henry VIII in 1538.

The old pilgrim route to the cathedral runs along the High Street and Mercery Lane to the splendid sixteenth-century Christ Church Gate. The cathedral itself has beautiful stained glass. Other points of interest include the site of Becket's murder in the northwest transept, the crypt where Henry II did penance, and the tomb of the Black Prince.

In 1988 UNESCO inscribed the cathedral as a World Heritage Site for its role in the introduction of Christianity to the Anglo-Saxon kingdoms. **RC**

> *"For the name of Jesus and the protection of the Church I am ready to embrace death."*

Thomas Becket, quoted by Edward Grim, *c.* 1180

Hever Castle

(Hever, England)

Seat of Henry VIII's wife, Anne Boleyn

The house where Henry VIII courted Anne Boleyn is an enjoyable combination of Tudor and Edwardian luxury. The castle was built originally in 1270, with a gatehouse and a walled bailey, or enclosure, but was transformed two hundred years later by the rich Boleyn (they pronounced it Bullen) family, who made themselves a comfortable home inside the protecting outer walls. The head of the family in Henry VIII's time was Sir Thomas Boleyn, two of whose daughters, Mary and Anne, drew the royal eye. Mary was the king's mistress for a while, but Anne, who had grown up at Hever, insisted on marriage in return for her favors. The surprisingly drastic result of her self-assertive stand was the creation of the Church of England and the dissolution of the monasteries.

Anne failed to give Henry a male heir. Accused of adultery with her brother and others, she was beheaded in 1536. The prayer book she carried with her to her death is in the house, with other mementos of both her and Henry. The castle was eventually handed to Anne of Cleves, Henry's fourth wife.

From 1749 to 1895 Hever belonged to a family called Meade-Waldo and grew ever more rundown until it was bought in 1903 by the American multimillionaire William Waldorf Astor. He spent a fortune and hired an army of craftsmen in restoring it, making it opulently comfortable inside and creating beautiful formal gardens with an ample lake. He also built a Tudor-style village just across the moat to make more room for his guests. After his death in 1919, Hever went to his younger son, John Jacob Astor V, owner of *The Times* and subsequently Lord Astor of Hever. He died in 1971 and the family sold the estate twelve years later. The castle has been open to the public since 1983, with numerous exhibits related to Anne Boleyn's time. **RC**

Penshurst Place

(near Tonbridge, England)

Inspiration of Sir Philip Sidney's Arcadia

Penshurst Place is linked with the Sidney family, who acquired the estate in 1552 and from 1618 were earls of Leicester. Their most glamorous figure, Sir Philip Sidney, the Elizabethan poet, courtier, and diplomat, was born there in 1554—his father, Sir William Sidney, planted a nut tree in the grounds to celebrate his arrival. Sir Philip, who was mortally wounded in battle in Holland in 1586, is said to have based the idyllic home he described in his *Arcadia* on Penshurst Place. The family portraits include those of Sir Philip and also Algernon Sidney, who was executed for treason in 1683 and buried at Penshurst.

> *"Fair trees' shade is enough fortification,/Nor danger to thyself if 't be not in thyself."*

Sir Philip Sidney, from *Arcadia* **(1593)**

The Sidneys enlarged the original manor house, which was built in the 1340s by Sir John de Pulteney, a rich wool merchant, four times Lord Mayor of London. The most striking survival from his time is the imposing Barons' Hall. After his death, the house passed to a succession of royal dukes and then to the Duke of Buckingham, who entertained Henry VIII there in 1519, but was executed soon afterward.

The Sidney male line died out in the eighteenth century and John Shelley, a relative of the poet Shelley, succeeded to the estate and took the surname of Sidney in 1793. The family later acquired the title of Lords De L'Isle and Dudley. An arboretum in the grounds commemorates the first Viscount De L'Isle, who won the Victoria Cross in World War II and was Governor General of Australia in the 1960s. **RC**

Dover Castle (Dover, England)

Guardian of the narrowest stretch of the English Channel

Since the English Channel was first formed 10,000 years ago, the White Cliffs of Dover have loomed in front of invaders and travelers from the continent at the crossing's narrowest point. It was an obvious place for a medieval castle, and a particularly large and magnificent one, 375 feet (114 m) above sea level; but the oldest survival is a lighthouse built by the Romans soon after their conquest of Britain in the first century C.E. It is possibly Britain's oldest building still standing.

The Saxons fortified the site with earthwork ramparts, ditches, and wooden palisades. They also used Roman bricks in the seventh century to build the church of St. Mary in Castro, heavily restored in the 1850s. The defenses were improved by William the Conqueror, but the main stone fortifications date from Henry II's time, with a huge keep with walls up to 22 feet (7 m) thick and a double line of encircling walls. In 1216 the castle was held for King John against the rebel lords and an army of French invaders. Later modifications include some made by Henry VIII, and a 23-foot- (7-m-) long bronze cannon that he installed, known as "Queen Elizabeth's Pocket Pistol." Some of the rooms have inscriptions scratched on the walls by foreign prisoners of war held in the castle in the eighteenth century.

Concealed inside the White Cliffs is an intriguing labyrinth of tunnels, first built during the Napoleonic Wars and intended for cannons to repel Napoleon's threatened invasion. This never materialized, but the tunnels came into their own in World War II when they were extended and used as the headquarters of Operation Dynamo, the Dunkirk evacuation. **RC**

↖ The naval headquarters under the castle were used by the commanders of the 1940 Dunkirk evacuation.

← Two concentric walls studded by towers and an immense gatehouse shield the castle's massive keep.

Chartwell (Westerham, England)

Residence of the "British Bulldog," Winston Churchill

Winston and Clementine Churchill were looking for what they called "a country basket" when they found Chartwell Manor, an undistinguished Victorian country house in a thoroughly dilapidated state and riddled with dry rot, but set in delightful countryside with a spring called the Chart Well. He bought it in 1922, without telling her, and they moved in two years later. Clementine was horrified and worried for years about how they could afford it. There were largely unsuccessful attempts to keep cows, sheep, pigs, and chickens. They remodeled the house, but she never became as attached to the place as he was. Used for weekends to begin with, it became their principal home out of London and Sir Winston later said simply that a day away from Chartwell was a day wasted.

Visitors included T. E. Lawrence (Lawrence of Arabia) and the painter Walter Sickert. The Churchills lived at Chartwell when he was Chancellor of the Exchequer in the 1920s, and when he was out of office with his career apparently finished in the 1930s. He also wrote his books and speeches there, and it was to Chartwell that he retired in 1954, spending his last years until his death in 1965 sitting for hours outside on sunny days gazing silently over the lakes and the beautiful landscape.

After the war a group of Churchill's friends bought Chartwell and gave it to the National Trust. The interiors remain as they were and the rooms reflect Clementine Churchill's tastes. Her husband's study is exactly as he left it. There are many of his paintings, and in the garden are the lakes he created and the walls that he built himself. **RC**

↗ Churchill strikes a proprietorial pose before Chartwell Manor, his home, on-and-off, from 1924.

↘ To the original Victorian mansion the Churchills added a large and comfortable garden wing (right).

Charleston Farmhouse (near Lewes, England)

Uniquely decorated home of members of the Bloomsbury Group

Originally an unremarkable farmhouse at the foot of Firle Beacon, a high point of the South Downs, the house was transformed into a country retreat and gathering place for the Bloomsbury group of writers, artists, and intellectuals. It was discovered by Virginia Woolf and her husband, Leonard, and bought in 1916 as a retreat from London by Virginia's sister, the painter Vanessa Bell. She moved in with her lover, Duncan Grant, and the writer David Garnett. An important advantage was that it enabled Grant and Garnett to get work on a local farm, which exempted them from military service in World War I.

The house eventually became Vanessa and Grant's permanent home and over the years they decorated it themselves, in the process painting all the walls and doors as well as everything from the furniture and bookcases to filing boxes and toilet seats. They also acquired fabrics, lamp shades, and other items from

the Omega Workshop in London, founded by their friend, the art critic Roger Fry, and transformed the garden. The result is a vivid, lived-in tribute to Bloomsbury ideals and taste.

Vanessa's sons, Julian and Quentin, recorded the household's doings in the daily Charleston bulletin and Quentin created statues for the garden. Besides the Woolfs, visitors included the writers Lytton Strachey and E. M. Forster, as well as the economist John Maynard Keynes, who spent so much time there that he had his own room.

By the 1950s, however, the Bloomsbury Group was well past its heyday. Vanessa died at Charleston in 1961. Duncan Grant kept the house until his death in 1978 and soon afterward a trust was established to cherish and restore the house. In addition to the permanent display of art by the group, fine and decorative art is shown in an exhibition gallery. **RC**

Royal Pavilion (Brighton, England)

George IV's extravaganza by the sea

The process that turned the obscure fishing village of Brighthelmstone on the Sussex coast into the queen of English seaside resorts started in the 1750s when a certain Dr. Richard Russell settled there and recommended sea bathing and drinking seawater for good health. Wealthy invalids began rolling up to take the cure and in 1783 the Prince of Wales, future Prince Regent and King George IV, paid a visit in the hope of alleviating his gout. He rented a farmhouse near the seafront and in 1787 had the architect Henry Holland build him a substantial Classical-style villa there.

From 1815 to 1822 the house was transformed by John Nash into something resembling the mythical pleasure dome of Kubla Khan, with minarets and domes in the Indian Mogul manner and wildly extravagant Indian and Chinese-style interiors. Even in the kitchen the cooks worked among cast-iron palm trees and it is said that when George first set foot in his new music room, he wept for sheer joy. Brighton quickly acquired a reputation for licentiousness. One of its advantages for George was that he could keep Maria Fitzherbert, whom he had secretly and illegally married in 1785, close by him. She had a house on Old Steine.

George gave Brighton its royal cachet, but the Pavilion was not really Queen Victoria's style and she abandoned it. The furniture and fittings were largely shipped off to London and, in 1849, the pleasure dome was sold to the town council for £53,000 (equivalent to $6 million or more today). It was used variously as a hospital, concert venue, and radar station, and gradually its condition deteriorated. In 1982 an ambitious program of restoration of the structure and stonework was begun, followed by refurbishment of the magnificently exotic interiors. To complete the picture, many of the original items have been returned on loan from the royal family. **RC**

Bateman's (Burwash, England)

Jacobean house and family home of Rudyard Kipling

Rudyard Kipling was already a famous author when he bought Bateman's in 1902. He was only five years away from the Nobel Prize for Literature, he had turned down the poet laureateship, and he had *The Barrack-Room Ballads*, *Stalky & Co*, *Plain Tales from the Hills*, *The Jungle Book*, *The Second Jungle Book*, and much else under his belt. He and his American wife, Carrie Starr Balestier, were driving in Sussex when they first saw the house, built by one of the local ironmasters in 1634. They wanted somewhere quiet to live and raise a family, and the story goes that Kipling instantly cried out, "That's her! The only She! Make an honest woman of her, quick!" Afterward he said, "We have loved it ever since our first sight of it."

Kipling would live there from 1902 for the rest of his life, to his death in 1936. It was there that he wrote *Puck of Pook's Hill* and *Rewards and Fairies*, and his most famous poem, "If"; there that he and Carrie raised their children, John (who was killed in World War I) and Elsie; and there that they entertained friends including Henry James and Rider Haggard. The place remains very much as it was in their time. The study with Kipling's desk, sofa, and books is as he left it, down to the blotting paper. His associations with the East are evident in the many Oriental rugs and curiosities around the house. In the garden is the hollow where two children conjure up Puck in *Puck of Pook's Hill*. Kipling had the watermill converted to generate electricity for the house, and the last of his succession of Rolls-Royce cars, a 1928 Phantom 1, stands in the garage. Carrie survived him by three years, dying in 1939 after leaving the house to the National Trust. **RC**

⬉ Kipling sought seclusion at Bateman's to escape the attention of tourists at his former home of Brighton.

⬋ Bateman's was built of locally quarried sandstone by an ironmaster of the Sussex Weald.

Hastings Battlefield (Battle, England)

Site of Duke William of Normandy's defeat of the Saxons of England

Although the decisive clash in 1066 between the invading Normans and the native English is known as the Battle of Hastings, it was not fought there but several miles to the north. Duke William of Normandy—known in his own time as William the Bastard—believed he had the best claim to succeed Edward the Confessor on the English throne, and he arrived in strength to enforce it. Landing at Pevensey, he moved to Hastings before heading north through the Weald, where on October 14 he encountered the English army under King Harold, drawn up in a strong position along the top of a ridge. The place has been called Battle ever since.

Harold's troops had marched south a long way after defeating Danish invaders at Stamford Bridge in Yorkshire a few days before. They must have been weary, but they had the advantage of the ground and probably had high hopes. Their hopes were too high, in fact, because after hours of repeated charges, William's horsemen succeeded in tempting many of the English down the hill by riding up it and then pretending to run away. Once on the level the English were cut to pieces. Showers of Norman arrows took a heavy toll and Harold himself was killed by an arrow in the eye—at least according to the Bayeux Tapestry—and finally the English army gave in and ran.

Duke William had Battle Abbey built to commemorate his victory, with the high altar placed over the spot where Harold fell, but it was later largely rebuilt; the Great Gate, for instance, dates from the 1330s. The battlefield was preserved as part of the abbey grounds and remains vividly impressive. **RC**

↗ The battlefield as it appears today; the English were unwise to abandon their position on high ground.

➡ In a part of the Bayeux Tapestry, created around 1080, mounted Normans charge the exposed English force.

Mary Rose (Portsmouth, England)

Flagship of Henry VIII, raised from the English Channel after 437 years

The *Mary Rose* is known now for her dramatic sinking in 1545 and her equally dramatic recovery in 1982, but the earliest reference to her is from 1511. She represented a significant advance in the technology of naval warfare in that she was one of the first ships capable of firing a broadside—all the cannons on one side of the ship could be fired simultaneously.

Soon after succeeding to the throne in 1509, Henry VIII ordered the building in Portsmouth dockyard of two new battleships, one of which was the *Mary Rose*. Named after Henry's sister Mary and the Tudor rose, the 500-ton warship was the king's delight and the flagship of the English fleet. For thirty-five years she saw successful service, contributing to the destruction of some of the most powerful French warships of the day. In 1545, however, when a French invasion fleet approached Portsmouth harbor, the *Mary Rose* led the English ships out to fight but sank, under the eye of her royal master watching distraught from the shore. The loss was not a result of enemy gunfire. A row of gunports on one side of the vessel had not been closed after firing and when the ship heeled over in a sudden gust of wind, the water poured in and took her to the bottom. Only forty of the crew of four hundred escaped.

The ship's recovery began with exploration by divers from 1965. The Mary Rose Trust was formed in 1979 to make a survey of the wreck and organize the raising of the ship from her tomb after 437 years. The hull was maneuvered into a cradle, which was lifted up by a crane and lowered on to a barge to be towed ashore. The ship is now in a dry dock, not far from where she was originally built, and is being treated with chemicals for conservation purposes. A hoard of objects recovered with her, on show in the nearby museum, casts a light on life in Henry VIII's time. **RC**

HMS *Victory* (Portsmouth, England)

Nelson's warship at England's most famous naval engagement

HMS *Victory* is the most famous ship in the history of naval warfare, being the flagship of Vice-Admiral Horatio, Lord Nelson at the Battle of Trafalgar. Her keel was laid down in Chatham in 1759. About six thousand trees, mainly oaks, were needed to build her and she cost upward of £5 million in today's money. *Victory* is forever associated with October 21, 1805, the date of the Battle of Trafalgar, and she has since been restored to her appearance on that day.

Weighing 3,500 tons, with 104 guns and a crew of some 800 men, *Victory* was a formidable fighting machine, but her career started quietly, resting for thirteen years on the River Medway with no duties to perform. She did not see action until 1778, when she fought the French in the First Battle of Ushant, and 1797, when she engaged the Spanish in the Battle of Cape St. Vincent. Famous commanders of *Victory* in the 1780s and 1790s included Howe, Hood, and Jervis.

Like Nelson, they occupied the surprisingly elegant admiral's quarters on the upper gun deck.

Victory left Portsmouth in September 1805 and encountered the French and Spanish fleets off Cape Trafalgar. At 11.25 A.M. Nelson sent his famous signal: "England expects that every man will do his duty." The fleets clashed just before noon and the action was at its fiercest at 1.25 P.M. when Nelson, on his quarterdeck, was struck by an enemy sharpshooter's bullet. Carried below and attended by the ship's surgeon, Nelson died three hours later after hearing that the battle was won. His last words, to his flag captain, were either "Kiss me, Hardy" or possibly "Kismet, Hardy." His body was preserved in brandy and taken back to England for his funeral in St. Paul's Cathedral.

Victory has been in her present dock since 1922. The ship's history is told in a special gallery in the Royal Naval Museum close by. **RC**

Corfe Castle

(Corfe, England)

Powerful fortress, ultimately destroyed by an act of treachery

> *"The castle, standing on a very steep, rocky hill, was very strong—almost impregnable."*

Laura Valentine, *Picturesque England* (1894)

Now a spectacular ruin towering on its high mound over a village of the same name, Corfe Castle was a Norman fortification strategically placed to guard a gap through the Purbeck Hills. The Saxon kings had a house on the site earlier, probably a hunting lodge. It was there in 978 that the teenage King Edward was murdered, apparently on the orders of his stepmother Ethelfrith, who wanted her own son, the future Ethelred the Unready, on the throne. Her men stabbed Edward to death as his cupbearer offered him a drink. The body of Edward was buried at Shaftesbury, where miracles were reported from his tomb, and he was canonized as a saint.

The house passed to the Norman kings, who built the castle, and Henry I held his brother Duke Robert of Normandy captive there in 1106. The fortress was enlarged and strengthened over the next two centuries. It was held for the empress Matilda against Stephen, and King John had a comfortable house built inside the battlements and often stayed there.

Much later on, in Charles I's time, the castle and estate were bought by a successful lawyer, Sir John Bankes, who was attorney general to the king. In 1643, with the master of the castle away in the service of the king, his wife, Mary, held the fortress with a small garrison against a siege by parliamentary troops. She and her daughters hurled stones down on the besiegers' heads; after six weeks they slunk off and the redoubtable Lady Bankes seized their cannons. In the winter of 1644 to 1645 a much stronger parliamentary force appeared and, after weeks of stout resistance, a treacherous member of the garrison opened the gates to the enemy. Lady Bankes and her men marched out with the honors of war, but undermining and explosives were then used to destroy the building, with only partial success. **RC**

Tintagel Castle

(near Tintagel, England)

Romantic Cornish redoubt of King Arthur

There could hardly be a more suitable stronghold for the birthplace of the legendary King Arthur, with its dramatic clifftop setting above the rocks and foaming breakers of the north Cornish coast. It was there, the enduring legend has it, that Merlin, the great enchanter, turned King Uther Pendragon into the likeness of the lord of the castle so that the king could enjoy his beautiful wife, Igraine. That night she conceived Arthur. Rocks below the castle have been given names like Arthur's Chair, and, perhaps inevitably, there is also a Merlin's Cave.

Tintagel is home to yet another enduring romantic legend, for by the time Arthur came to his kingdom, the castle was the stronghold of King Mark of Cornwall, husband of an even more beautiful woman, Isolde. Mark's most formidable warrior was his nephew Tristan. He and Isolde fell passionately and tragically in love. Eventually they were buried at Tintagel, where two trees grew from their graves and became entwined above them.

The castle is in a powerful defensive position, almost on an island, linked to the mainland by a narrow rocky ridge and therefore extremely difficult to attack. Today's ruined keep was built in the thirteenth century by Richard, Earl of Cornwall, a younger brother of King Henry III. It is on the site of a stronghold of previous earls going back to the 1140s, and there were buildings on the headland long before that, from perhaps about 500 C.E. These dwellings are thought to have been occupied by Celtic monks. However, the remains of expensive imported pottery have been found there, suggesting an alternative history. Perhaps this was the base of a powerful Romano-British chieftain, ruling at a time when the Britons were fighting the invading Saxons. Could this be the basis for the Arthurian legends? **RC**

Osbourne House

(Cowes, England)

Summer home of Victoria and Albert

Five years after Queen Victoria and Prince Albert were married, they bought Osborne House with an estate of some 340 acres (138 ha) on the Isle of Wight as an enjoyable summer holiday home. They knocked the house down and rebuilt it on a larger scale in Italianate style with two campanile-type towers looking out over the Solent. Their architect was Thomas Cubitt, but Prince Albert himself had much to do with the design of the house, the opulent interiors, and the gardens in which the queen loved to walk. The nine royal children and later innumerable grandchildren were provided with a Swiss cottage in the grounds

"It is impossible to see a prettier place, with woods and valleys and points de vue ..."

Queen Victoria, in a letter to Lord Melbourne

(a grand ancestor of the Wendy house) where they learned cooking, gardening, and domestic skills.

Prince Albert apparently designed the ornate church of St. Mildred nearby at Whippingham, where some of the Mountbattens are buried. After his death in 1861, the grieving Victoria spent more and more time at Osborne House. The Durbar Room was added in 1891 as a grand banqueting hall and the lavish decoration in Indian style was overseen by Rudyard Kipling's father, John Lockwood Kipling. The queen died in her bedroom at Osborne House in 1901, in the arms of one of her grandsons. After her death, the house was given to the nation by Edward VII and from 1903 to 1921 part of it was used as a preparatory training school for the Royal Naval College. Many of the rooms have been kept as they were in her day. **RC**

Anne Frank's House (Amsterdam, Netherlands)

The hiding place of the famous Jewish diarist during World War II

Now a museum, this Dutch town house was the site of a remarkable episode from World War II. German businessman Otto Frank had taken his German-Jewish family—his wife and two daughters—from Germany to Amsterdam, to escape Nazi persecution. However, after the Nazis captured the Netherlands in 1941, Otto and his wife feared that the family might be deported to German labor camps. The family hid in a secluded annex at the back of the building where Otto ran a food products business—263 Prinsengracht. Between 1942 and 1944, the Franks and four other people lived in a set of damp rooms, never going out and relying on provisions brought by friends and some of Otto's workers. His lively teenage daughter Anne kept a vivid diary and her writings went on to become a classic book.

Betrayed by informers, the Franks and their companions in hiding were arrested by the Nazis in August 1944, and sent to concentration camps. Only Otto survived. Anne perished at Bergen-Belsen camp, but her diary had been rescued from the annex and Otto devoted the rest of his life to getting the diary published (first publication, 1947) and setting up a museum at Prinsengracht. Opened in 1960, the museum was renovated and expanded in 1999.

The museum recreates the atmosphere and period of the Franks' experience. Documents and possessions belonging to the eight people who hid here are displayed in the annex, and the front of the house has been restored to its 1940s state. Anne's original diary is displayed in the renovated 265 Prinsengracht, next door to the original hideaway. **AK**

◹ This movable bookcase concealed the entrance to the annex, where eight people hid for more than two years.

◿ Anne Frank began writing her diary on her thirteenth birthday in 1942, weeks before going into hiding.

Rembrandt House Museum (Amsterdam, Netherlands)

Former home and studio of the great Dutch painter and etcher

When Dutch artist Rembrandt van Rijn (1606–69) signed on the dotted line to buy this large, impressive town house in the smart Breestraat area of Amsterdam, it seemed life could not get any better. It was 1639 and his work was celebrated throughout the city. He earned good money, but the purchase price of 13,000 guilders was still an enormous sum for the day and he arranged to pay it off in installments.

Rembrandt lived and worked in this house at Jodenbreestraat 4 between 1639 and 1658. His own work and that of other renowned artists hung on the walls, as he also worked as an art dealer. He used a large, airy room chosen for its unchanging light as his studio, and here produced many of his finest works, aided by assistants preparing paints and canvases. Today, the house is a museum devoted to recreating his life within its walls and celebrating his art—many of the fine etchings he created here are on display. The studio is set up as he might well have had it, as are rooms such as his bedroom and a refined anteroom where he received clients as a dealer.

Sadly, Rembrandt's fortunes turned. His beloved wife, Saskia, died prematurely and—defeated partly by poor money management—Rembrandt slid into bankruptcy and lost the house. For the rest of his life he lived in a small rented house in the humble Rozengracht district. For the next 200 years his former grand home was occupied by a succession of families. In the early 1900s it was purchased by the City of Amsterdam and opened as a museum in 1911. Work to restore the house to its original seventeenth-century glory was not completed until the late 1990s. **AK**

↗ The house, with its distinctive windows and shutters, has been faithfully restored over the years.

→ One of Rembrandt's sixty self-portraits—he is seen as the first artist to study the self through art.

Royal Palace of Amsterdam (Amsterdam, Netherlands)

Elaborate monument to the prestige and prosperity of the Dutch Golden Age

When the Royal Palace of Amsterdam was originally built in 1648 by Jacob van Campen, it was designed to reflect the success of the Dutch Golden Age—the period in which Dutch trade, science, and art flourished—and it succeeded triumphantly. Its enormous size and lavish design reflect the glory of the Dutch Republic and the building became one of the most important monuments of seventeenth-century Holland. At the time it was labeled "The Eighth Wonder of the World" and, for many years, it was the largest administrative building in Europe.

The Royal Palace of Amsterdam went through two very distinct stages in its construction. Originally, when it was first designed by Van Campen, it was not intended to be a palace but an extravagant town hall. His intention was to produce an impressive public building inspired by the administrative palaces in Rome, thus reflecting the opulence of the grand

Amsterdam burgomasters (chief magistrates). For that reason, Van Campen designed a huge building with a central hall more than 98 feet (30 m) long, 59 feet (18 m) wide, and 88 feet (27 m) high. The Construction Master of Amsterdam was employed to install the most contemporary technical fittings and renowned artists were asked to design the interior decorations. The interior is adorned with sculptures and paintings by the leading artists of the day.

With the arrival of Louis Napoleon Bonaparte, created King of Holland by his conquering elder brother in 1806, the town hall was transformed into a royal palace. Louis brought with him an impressive array of furniture, tapestries, clocks, and ornate chandeliers—and it was in this fashion that the palace continued until 1813. In that year Prince William VI returned to power and decided that the town hall should remain a palace. **KH**

Afsluitdijk (near Amsterdam, Netherlands)

A huge feat of engineering, this barrier dam closes off the turbulent Zuider Zee waters

Voltaire once wrote that "God created the earth—except Holland, for the Dutch did that." Few places in Holland demonstrate his point better than the Afsluitdijk (closure dike), which borders the Dutch end of the North Sea, the Waddenzee, and the huge artificial freshwater lake, the Ijsselmeer. However, construction of the dike was a monumental achievement. Ever since the First All Saints' Flood in 1170, when the sea forced its way into what was then a natural freshwater lake, Lake Flavo, turning it into the turbulent Zuider Zee, countless lives have been lost in the centuries of struggle against encroaching storms and floodwaters.

Although the original plan for the dike dates back to 1667, it took the combination of the arrival of modern technology, the urgent need to reclaim farmland to combat severe food shortages after World War I, and heavy storm damage in 1916 for the

government to give the go-ahead to its construction. Following the designs of engineer Cornelius Lely, work got under way in 1927. Boulder clay was dredged from the bottom of the Zuider Zee and initially deposited in two parallel lines across the sea, which were gradually filled with a mixture of sand, more clay, basalt rocks, and mats of willow switch. Massive sluices had to be built at either end to release the outflow of the feeder rivers (notably the Rhone) from what had now become the Ijsselmeer.

There are records of major floods in the old Zuider Zee area three or four times per century throughout the Middle Ages, and the threat of flooding remains a fact of life for the residents of the Netherlands. The massive Afsluitdijk now stands guard over an ever-increasing amount of reclaimed polder land—less picturesque than the old windmills and networks of small dikes, but far more efficient. **AED**

Het Loo Royal Palace

(Apeldoorn, Netherlands)

Favored retreat of the House of Orange

Het Loo was the summer retreat of the Dutch ruling family, the House of Orange, for more than three centuries. It was the creation of one of the house's greatest sons—William III of Orange—who was offered, and accepted, the kingship of England, Ireland, and Scotland in 1689, as well as being the *Stadtholder* (head of state) of the Netherlands from 1672. Het Loo quickly became the favorite retreat of William III and his wife, Mary II Stuart.

William III purchased the site of Het Loo in 1684, intending to build a hunting lodge there. Building began the next year, and the initial house was finished

> *"Nothing makes a gentleman more like a gentleman than living like one."*
>
> **William III of Orange**

in 1686. Het Loo was not as lavish as other Baroque palaces such as Versailles. Indeed, it was not intended to be a palace as such, but a *Lust hof*—literally, a "pleasure house" or retreat. Het Loo was continuously added to in the 1690s. After William III's death in 1702, Het Loo remained in the hands of the House of Orange. There is also a large garden situated behind the house, which nestles in the surrounding woods and is more private than other large Baroque gardens. The original gardens were destroyed in the eighteenth century; they were replaced by a design in the English style, but were restored from 1970 to 1984.

In 1960, Queen Wilhelmina declared that Het Loo would pass to the state after her death. When she died in 1962, the palace became a national museum and the site of a library of the House of Orange. **JF**

Arnhem Bridge

(Arnhem, Netherlands)

Scene of a daring British airborne assault

The Anglo-American assault on the Eindhoven-Arnhem road in September 1944 was an attempt to secure a crossing over the Rhine, and by so doing open a way for a direct invasion of northern Germany. British and U.S. airborne forces would secure key points behind enemy lines and hold them until relieved by the British XXX Corps, advancing overland. British airborne forces were directed to land near the town of Arnhem, and the second battalion of the Parachute Regiment, under Lieutenant-Colonel John Frost, was ordered to capture the road bridge across the Rhine—the key to the entire position.

The plan was overly ambitious (which accounts for the title of the 1977 Richard Attenborough movie of the operation, *A Bridge Too Far*), and from the start things went wrong for the Allies. Although the paratroopers seized one side of the bridge, they were pinned down by the Germans, who reacted with their customary swiftness to the Allied assault. To make matters worse, XXX Corps, far to the south, was making slow progress and was unable to reach the beleaguered British forces in and around Arnhem. Running out of food, water, and ammunition, and heavily outnumbered, Frost's paratroopers were eventually forced to surrender.

The battle was a severe defeat for the Allies but the valiant British defense of Arnhem won the respect of friend and foe alike. Dutch civilians did much to aid the Allies both during and after the battle, helping many men to escape back to their own lines. Since the war there have been annual commemoration services where old veterans and civilians gather to pay their respects to the men killed around the town. The badly damaged bridge over the Rhine was rebuilt to its original design and renamed John Frost Bridge in honor of the British paratroop commander. **AG**

Belfry of Bruges

(Bruges, Belgium

A distinctive symbol and landmark in the medieval heart of Bruges

UNESCO has placed fifty-five belfries in Belgium and northern France on its World Heritage List, recognizing their unique contribution to civic and public architecture. The Belfry of Bruges is one of the oldest and most beautiful of all.

Belfries are bell towers. Many people associate them with churches, but originally they were municipal structures. Their primary purpose was as a watchtower, where bells could be used to sound the alarm but, over the years, they began to serve a wider range of civic purposes. Belfries could contain storage rooms for important charters and documents—the literal meaning of the word is "place of safety or protection"—as well as a conference room, a treasury, or an armory. The Belfry at Bruges formerly housed the city treasury and municipal archives. Similarly, the bells were not used solely in times of danger. They could be rung to inform citizens of the time, notify them of civic activities, and help regulate the working day. As a result, most belfries acquired a set of bells—a carillon—that could chime out different melodies. The carillon at Bruges is particularly elaborate, consisting of no fewer than forty-seven bells.

The 288-foot- (88-m-) high Belfry in Bruges is situated on top of the *Hallen* (the old Cloth Hall), which dates back to *c.* 1240. The original wooden tower burned down in 1280, after being struck by lightning, and it was rebuilt in brick. An elegant, octagonal lantern tower was added in the 1480s. This was once crowned by a wooden spire but it, too, fell victim to a fire and, in the end, the burghers (middle-class citizens) of Bruges decided to settle for a stone parapet instead. This affords a splendid panoramic view of the city and its surroundings for any tourists who feel energetic enough to clamber up the 366 steps, past the clock mechanism, to the summit. **IZ**

"In the market place of Bruges stands the belfry old and brown . . . still it watches o'er the town."

Henry Wadsworth Longfellow, poet

World War I Trenches (Ypres, Belgium)

Trench excavation at one of the most significant battlefields of the Western Front

> *"Sleep impossible. To keep warm is only possible occasionally— to keep dry is a farce."*

Soldier's letter home from Ypres, winter 1915

⊼ World War I shell holes and zigzagging trenches have been exposed at Sanctuary Wood, near Ypres.

⊡ A blasted landscape stretches to the horizon between Boesinghe and Paschendaele after the battles of 1917.

The area around the old Belgian wool city of Ypres was the scene of some of the bloodiest trench fighting of World War I, lasting from October 1914 until the summer of 1918. Despite repeated attempts by the Germans to take Ypres, they were foiled by the Anglo-French armies protecting the city.

The extraordinary power of weaponry in 1914, especially artillery and machine guns, forced armies into elaborate trench networks; by the end of 1914 a trench system was emerging that would stretch from Switzerland to the North Sea. Although there were variations according to terrain, a fairly typical trench line would comprise a winding frontline fire trench, out of which ran a series of saps or tunnels, toward the enemy in no-man's-land. Barbed wire would be staked out in front of the trench. Behind the fire trench ran two or more parallel support lines—where the main frontline troops were stationed—connected to other trenches by communication trenches dug in a zigzag pattern. In vital sections of the line, such as at Ypres, underground dugouts and pill boxes made from reinforced concrete were constructed to protect men from artillery fire.

Conditions in the trenches were often cramped, wet, muddy, and malodorous. Aside from the constant danger of shell or sniper fire, trenches were rat-infested and prone to collapse. Disease was also prevalent. It has been estimated that about one-third of all Allied casualties on the Western Front were sustained in the trenches.

Although most of the trenches around Ypres were ploughed or built over post-1918, archeologists began to uncover trench remains from the late 1980s onward—many of which can be visited by the public. Among these is the "Yorkshire Trench" near the village of Boesinghe (Boezinge), where excavation has been supplemented by careful reconstruction work. **AG**

Canal du Centre Elevators

(La Louvière, Belgium)

Remarkable monument to Belgian engineering and industrialism

Now saddled with an unenviable reputation as the "dirty child of Europe," as it was once described by Greenpeace, Belgium has a long history of industrialization. In the Victorian era, huge coal, iron, and steel industries grew apace with the exploitation of the Congo Basin by the Belgian King Leopold II. The creation of a network of canals to link the major rivers flowing down into France was essential to this development and the Canal du Centre was an important part of this network. It links the Rivers Meuse and Schelde, and provided key transport from nearby mines in the region's industrial heyday.

Heavy industry has now moved up north into the old Flanders region, and the four hydraulic elevators that were originally required to raise heavily laden barges a total of 216 feet (66 m) in the space of just 4 miles (7 km) now service the tourist industry, letting boat trippers appreciate firsthand a remarkable feat of engineering. Their design was much influenced by the British engineer Edwin Clark, although they were constructed by the Belgian John Cockerill Company, beginning in 1888 with a 50-foot- (15.4-m-) high elevator at Houdeng-Goegnies. The remaining three identical elevators are each 55 feet (16.9 m) high.

Inside each superstructure of iron lattice girders there are two water-filled tanks, each just large enough to float a nineteenth-century barge. The tanks rise and fall in turn, supported by central columns that act like pistons in deep, invisible, high-pressure water-filled cylinders below. Gates called "guillotines" control the water flow in and out of the tanks, and ensure that the topmost tank is filled with slightly more water than the bottom one so that the force of gravity can effectively power it back down to the lower level. Only eight lifts of this type were ever built, and these are the only ones still functioning in their original state. **AED**

"... the apogee of the application of engineering technology to the construction of canals."

UNESCO

Rubens's House

(Antwerp, Belgium)

Mansion house of the Flemish master

Even the briefest of glances will confirm that Sir Peter Paul Rubens (1577–1640) was no starving artist, living in a garret. He was the most successful and prolific painter of his day, described by one contemporary as "a prince of painters and painter of princes." Rubens also found time to carry out diplomatic missions for his patrons, which eventually led to him being knighted by Charles I of England. His lavish house was designed to reflect this growing reputation and status.

Work began on the mansion in 1610—just a year after Rubens had gained his first major appointment, as court painter to the Spanish governors of the Netherlands. The artist produced some of the designs himself and, although the exterior facing the street is quite restrained, the inner courtyard was built in a florid, Italianate style. Inside, the chambers included a gallery, housing Rubens's personal art collection, and the great studio, where he received his most distinguished visitors.

Rubens owned more than one house, but this building was the setting for key landmarks in his career. Many of his greatest masterpieces were painted in the studio, and his first wife, Isabella Brandt, died here, as did the artist himself after an attack of gout. In spite of these associations, very little of the original interior has been preserved. After Rubens's death, the house was rented out to William Cavendish, the Marquis of Newcastle, who turned the garden into a riding school for exiled royalists—among them, the future Charles II. Later owners neglected the building, and it was only rescued in 1937 when comprehensive restoration took place. The house is now a museum, displaying an impressive selection of artworks by Rubens, including his *Adam and Eve in Paradise* and *The Annunciation*, and by his contemporaries. **IZ**

Waterloo Battlefield

(Waterloo, Belgium)

Site of one of Europe's pivotal battles

The Battle of Waterloo actually took place at Mont-Saint-Jean, a village 3 miles (5 km) south of Waterloo. Fought on June 18, 1815, it was Napoleon Bonaparte's last battle. Allied forces, led by the British general the Duke of Wellington, and including troops from Britain, Prussia, Hanover, Holland, Nassau, and Brunswick, overcame a 70,000-strong French army in a battle described by Wellington as "the nearest run thing you ever saw in your life." Had the French won, the history of Europe would have been quite different.

The battlefield today is markedly different from the one on which Napoleon and Wellington locked

> *"Nothing except a battle lost can be half so melancholy as a battle won."*
>
> Arthur Wellesley, Duke of Wellington

horns almost 200 years ago. After the battle, the territory of the battlefield was given to the Wellington family by the new state of the United Kingdom of the Netherlands. The main difference between then and now is the presence of a hill, artificially created by the Netherlands's King William I to commemorate the wounding of his son, the Prince of Orange. The monument to the wounded prince is an impressive statue of a lion that sits overlooking the battlefield.

Many of the buildings used by the armies are still intact. The Hougoumont farm—which housed the British—can be visited by the public. It was attacked solidly by the French from midday until six o'clock in the evening, but was never taken. The Haie Sante farm, another Allied fortress, can also be visited, as can Napoleon's headquarters. **OR**

🏛️ ◉ Holstentor (Lübeck, Germany)

Late Gothic city gate, part of the medieval fortifications of Lübeck

The Holstentor presents an almost Disneyland image. Along with more than 1,000 buildings in Lübeck's Altstadt (Old Town), it has been inscribed on the UNESCO World Heritage List. Lübeck was the center of the powerful Hanseatic League, a trading bloc founded in the twelfth century for the mutual defense of trade. It united more than 1,500 merchant cities, from Novgorod to London. The league met for the last time in 1669 and today Lübeck is merely a provincial city, albeit with a fairy-tale appearance.

The gateway comprises two round pointed towers at the north and south sides, with an arched entranceway between them. On one side it bears the Latin inscription *"Concordia Domi Fortis Pax,"* roughly translated as "Harmony Within, Peace Without." The other side is inscribed "SPQL—The Senate and People of Lübeck." The four-story building was erected by the city's master builder, Heinrich Helmsted, between 1464 and 1478, unfortunately on marshy ground. A front gate added in 1585, supposed to improve the city's western defenses, had to be demolished because the Holstentor was sinking and in danger of collapse—by 1863 the lowest arrow slits were found to be about 2 feet (0.6 m) below ground level. Efforts continued unsuccessfully until 1871 to arrest the movement, but by 1934 more advanced techniques were available and further subsidence was finally halted. The two towers, however, still visibly lean toward each other. Further renovation work was carried out in 2005 and 2006 to stabilize the building.

Since 1950 the Holstentor has housed the museum of the city's history and is treasured as a national icon. It appears on the German 2 Euro coin and on the former 50 Deutschmark note, and is also a popular souvenir modeled in marzipan, a centuries-old Lübeck specialty. **CB**

Schwerin Castle (Schwerin, Germany)

Full of charm and strategically located on an island in Schwerin Lake

In 1160 German nobles under Henry the Lion took over a Slav settlement and built a castle on the site. The castle became the seat of the dukes of Mecklenburg, who rebuilt and revised Schwerin, transforming it from a fortification into a palace. In 1765 the ducal residence moved away from Schwerin and did not return until 1837, by which time the building had fallen into a state of disrepair.

Grand Duke Frederick and his successor Frederick Franz II decided to effectively rebuild the castle, using the French Loire château of Chambord as the prime architectural model. After much debate between several architects, work got under way in 1843 under the overall guidance of Georg Adolph Demmler. By 1847 the high main tower had been built, although it was not until 1857 that Frederick Franz and his family were able to move into their fairy-tale castle. In 1913 a fire in the Elizabethzimmer (Elizabeth's room) caused severe damage to Schwerin Castle, and in 1918, with the end of the monarchy in Germany, it was taken over by the state and opened to the public as a museum.

In 1990, after German reunification, Schwerin Castle underwent a massive restoration program; part of the castle was reopened as a museum and the remainder became the seat for the local state government. The staterooms of the dukes of Mecklenburg are on public display, and the extensive grounds that surround the castle can also be admired. **AG**

"Schwerin Castle, splendid as ever but without its previous residents since their abdication in 1918."

Dorothea S. Michelman, historian

St. Pauli Landungsbrücken (Hamburg, Germany)

Hamburg's famous floating dock

The Landungsbrücken (piers) of Hamburg originated in 1839 when a series of pontoons and jetties was built at the edge of the main harbor specifically for steamships. It was considered safer for steamships to operate away from wooden, sail-powered vessels because of the danger of fire from their smokestacks. As Hamburg, which is connected to the North Sea by a 75-mile (120-km) stretch of the great River Elbe, grew into one of Europe's leading oceanic ports in the nineteenth century, millions of passengers passed through the Landungsbrücken.

The whole area was rebuilt between 1906 and 1910, and the Landungsbrücken we see today was constructed during this period. It comprised a floating dock—eventually 2,300 feet (700 m) in length—upon which were built all the facilities needed in the transit of so many passengers. At the same time, the city was developing its underground rail system (U-Bahnhof) and a station was built at the Landungsbrücken to facilitate the transfer of passengers from rail to boat. Distinctive features of the wharf include copper-domed buildings, and a watchtower that has not only clocks on each of its sides but a water level indicator to provide passengers and officials with information on the state of the tides.

The Landungsbrücken was badly damaged in the war and its future seemed in doubt with the decline of transatlantic maritime passenger trade. Growing North Sea trade did, however, prove sufficient to keep the dock afloat, and the area benefited from tourist interest in Hamburg's dockland heritage—more than five million people departed from the Hamburg piers in search of a new life in the United States, Canada, and Australia. In addition to a museum at the Landungsbrücken, there is a sailing ship, the *Rickmer Rickmers* and an old freighter, the *Cap San Diego*, now a maritime museum. **AG**

> *"[A] curious structure . . . a neo-Romanesque line of domes squatting low above the Elbe . . ."*
>
> Michael Gorra, journalist

Volkswagen Factory (Wolfsburg, Germany)

Instrumental in the regeneration of the area and the progress of mass car production

Ferdinand Porsche developed the German "People's Car" (Volkswagen) on the express order of Adolf Hitler to produce a car cheap enough for the working man. The vehicle had to be economical to run, fast, and large enough for two adults and three children to travel in comfort. The project was named the KdF-Wagen, after Hitler's motto of "Kraft durch Freude," or "Strength through Joy." Although several prototype models were made during the late 1930s, the onset of war prevented the car from going into mass production, all manufacturing resources being redirected toward military vehicles.

In 1945 the Wolfsburg plant lay in ruins and came under the jurisdiction of the occupying British army. The factory was intended to be a maintenance depot, but the officer in charge, Major Ivan Hurst, recognized the potential of the Volkswagen car and persuaded the British army to order 20,000 vehicles. More cars were produced for civilian use in Germany and others were exported to Britain. Despite holes in the roof and windows without glass, production had increased to 1,000 cars a month by 1946. New vehicles were bartered for quantities of steel and the other materials used in the car's manufacture.

The plant was offered for sale to British and American car manufacturers, who all rejected the Volkswagen as a vehicle for the future. Wolfsburg was instead handed over to the German government in 1948. During the 1950s, Wolfsburg and Volkswagen became standard bearers of the "German economic miracle" as the new West Germany emerged triumphant from the ruins of war. By 1973 more than sixteen million Volkswagen Beetles had been produced. During the 1970s the company expanded its range of models to become the fourth largest car manufacturer in the world, with the high-tech plant at Wolfsburg covering 2 square miles (5 sq km). **AG**

> *"If you think you're going to build cars in this place, you're a bloody fool, young man."*
>
> British car manufacturer Lord Rootes to Major Hurst

🏛 ◉ **Rammelsberg Mines** (Rammelsberg, Germany)

Mining continued at this site for more than 1,000 years

Although there is some archeological evidence of mining activity dating back to the third and fourth centuries C.E., properly documented mining began at Rammelsberg in the Harz mountain in the tenth century. Silver was the first major discovery but copper, lead, gold, and zinc were also excavated as the complex expanded.

The first mines were simple open pits accessed via ladders. When these sources dried up, the miners began to dig underground shafts using fires to weaken and fracture the rock, which would then be hacked away using picks. Underground water flooding the shafts was a constant problem, but as early as 1250 underground waterwheels were introduced to pump out the water and they were later used as an effective power source. In 1572 a drainage passage, some 7,710 feet (2,350 m) long, was chiseled out of the rock to enable working at the deepest levels. From the seventeenth century onward, gunpowder was used to blast holes in the rock to speed up the mining process.

The nearby town of Goslar grew rich from the Rammelsberg mines and became an important trading center within the Hanseatic League. Reflecting the town's importance, assemblies of the Holy Roman Empire were held in Goslar between 1009 and 1219. Mining continued well into the twentieth century but with seams finally exhausted, commercial excavation ceased in 1988. Since then the mines have become a heritage center and living museum. As well as buildings displaying exhibits from Rammelsberg's past, underground tours are organized on the site, some descending as deep as fourteen levels. **AG**

⬈ Electric railways continue to weave through the mines, now carrying tourists instead of mineral ores.

⬅ The extensive workings of the Rammelsberg mines required a huge complex of processing buildings.

Martin Luther's House (Wittenberg, Germany)

The Reformation influenced the religious and political history of the world

The Protestant reformer Martin Luther (1483–1546) was still a monk when in 1508 he first visited this house, then an Augustinian monastery. The monastery was closed soon after, and when, in 1525, Luther married the former nun Katherina von Bora, the Elector Frederick the Wise allowed them to use the building as a family home. Their union effectively gave a seal of approval to clerical marriages, and Luther and Katherina had six children together.

In keeping with its position as the largest and most important museum devoted to the Reformation, today's Luther House contains an enormous archive that includes 6,000 original manuscripts (some dating back to the eleventh century), 15,000 books and pamphlets (some from Luther's time), and a large collections of coins, medallions, and paintings. There are permanent exhibitions devoted to the spread of Protestantism through Germany.

The museum also contains artifacts directly related to Luther and his family life. They include his monk's robe, his Bible with notes written in the margins, part of the pulpit where he preached his reforming doctrines, a desk, bed, and stove, and some kitchen utensils. The house also contains the majestic *Ten Commandments* painted by Lucas Cranach, a contemporary and supporter of Luther. A newly excavated annex to the house has revealed a stone lavatory thought to have been used by Luther, who suffered from constipation. According to popular belief, it was while on the toilet that he developed the radical idea that salvation is granted by faith and not by deeds. **AG**

↗ Martin Luther wrought radical change by insisting that the Bible, not the Pope, had religious authority.

⊡ Frederick the Wise permitted Luther and his family to live in this elaborately half-timbered house.

Schloss Rheinsberg (Rheinsberg, Germany)

Historic castle and center for the arts

There was a moated castle at Rheinsberg as early as 1335. After a fire damaged the building, it was taken over by Achim von Bredow in 1556 who dispensed with fortifications to build himself a grand house in the Renaissance style. In 1734 King Frederick William I of Prussia bought Rheinsberg and its grounds for his eldest son, Crown Prince Frederick (later Frederick II). Employing the architects Kemmeter and Knobelsdorff, Prince Frederick transformed the building in the latest style. Another floor and a second tower were added to the old building, and the twin towers were joined together by a delightful colonnade. A carefully sited lake—the Grienericksee—set off the beauty of the building, allowing its reflection to shimmer in the tranquil blue waters.

In 1740 Frederick was crowned king and almost immediately he instigated an invasion of Silesia, which led to a series of campaigns that would absorb his attentions for most of his life. In 1744 he gave Rheinsberg to his younger brother, Prince Henry. Living in Rheinsberg from 1753 until his death in 1802, Henry also stamped his own, more artistic, mark on the estate. A patron of the arts, he had the open-air "hedge theater" Heckentheater constructed on the grounds and, in 1774, the Schlosstheater was built, primarily to host musical recitals. As well as being an artistic center for music and painting, Rheinsberg was featured in the work of a number of writers, most notably Theodor Fontane, who wrote glowingly of the beauty of the Schloss and its magnificent lake and landscaped parkland.

After World War II, Rheinsberg was briefly used as a sanatorium before becoming a museum in 1991. The musical connection carries on today: a chamber opera group is associated with the palace and regularly gives concerts that attract large audiences. **AG**

Staatsoper Unter den Linden (Berlin, Germany)

One of the world's great opera houses

Although Berlin enjoys a reputation as a center for fine opera, the art form was relatively slow to develop in Germany; it was not until the music-loving Frederick II came to the throne that an opera house was built in Berlin. The Royal Opera opened in 1742, and quickly established itself as a major venue based on an almost exclusively Italian repertoire. It was only when the rival National Theater opened in 1786 that German-language opera began to be performed on a regular basis, and this Italian-German division lasted until the two theaters were merged in 1807. The combined Royal Theater established a reputation throughout the

> *"One can't judge Wagner's opera … after a first hearing and I don't intend to hear it a second time."*
>
> Gioachino Rossini, composer

nineteenth century as one of the leading opera houses in Europe, coinciding with the heyday of German opera under Richard Wagner.

The opera was renamed the Staatsoper unter den Linden in 1918, and during the 1930s the Nazi party banned several composers' works and prompted the exile of many leading Jewish musicians. The Staatsoper was bombed during World War II and, when it was rebuilt during the 1950s, the partition of Berlin by Allied forces meant it was located within the future East Germany, whereas the Deutsche Oper had the good fortune to be housed in West Germany. Since reunification, the Staatsoper has regained its reputation as a leading classical repertoire opera house, and the Deutsche Oper has specialized in more modern, experimental work. **AS**

Checkpoint
Charlie (Berlin, Germany)

Scene of a standoff between Soviet and U.S. tanks at the height of the Cold War

Despite the postwar division of Berlin into four sectors (Soviet, U.S., British, and French), movement across the city was relatively easy. This came to an abrupt end, however, when on August 13, 1961, the border between East and West Berlin was closed. Initially the division comprised a barricade of barbed wire and roadblocks but it was later consolidated into a high concrete wall.

To facilitate some movement between east and west, checkpoints were set up along the wall; the one in Friederichstadt was called "C," from which it took the better known name of Checkpoint Charlie. It was a crossing point for accredited military personnel, journalists, diplomats, and other dignitaries and consequently became well known, even acquiring a certain glamour when it featured in Cold War spy novels and films. On the eastern side, the checkpoint comprised a barrier pole and zigzag concrete barriers, a watchtower, and a large area where vehicles and their occupants were searched. On the western side stood a simple wooden booth.

Checkpoint Charlie gained fame as the site of several audacious escape attempts. One of the most notorious was a failed attempt by Peter Fechter in 1962; badly wounded while attempting to flee, he was caught on barbed wire and left to bleed to death, watched by the world's media. The collapse of the Berlin Wall in 1989 left Checkpoint Charlie redundant and it was formally closed in 1990. A copy of the booth has been erected where the crossing stood and a private museum—opened in 1963—is situated nearby. **AG**

↗ The booth that stood on the western side is now in the Allied Museum in Zehlendorf; this is a replica.

→ Checkpoint Charlie in operation, controlling an entry point into ideologically isolated East Berlin.

Schloss Charlottenburg (Berlin, Germany)

The Amber Room was described as the eighth wonder of the world

In 1695 Sophie Charlotte, wife of the Elector of Brandenburg, Frederick III, commissioned architect Arnold Nering to build her a modest summerhouse in the Italian Baroque style. On her death in 1705, Frederick named the palace Charlottenburg in her memory. When Frederick was crowned King Frederick I of Prussia in 1700, the building was enlarged into a full-scale palace. It included a distinctive central tower with cupola as well as a large orangery. Today the palace museum's most famous exhibits are antiquities from Troy, excavated by archeologist and treasure hunter Heinrich Schliemann.

The interior of the palace was richly decorated and included the famous Amber Room (its walls were made entirely from Baltic amber), although in 1716 the room was dismantled and sent to Tsar Peter the Great of Russia as a present. After the coronation of Frederick the Great in 1740, further additions were made to the palace, notably the East Wing, although the king's interest waned when he developed a new enthusiasm for the palace of Sanssouci in nearby Potsdam. During the eighteenth century the extensive grounds around the palace were transformed from a French-style formal garden into an exceptionally fine landscaped park, complete with ornamental lake.

Charlottenburg was severely damaged by Allied bombing in 1943 but was subsequently restored and is now the largest palace in Berlin. Within the palace are the Porzellankabinett, which contains an extensive collection of Chinese and Japanese porcelain, and the Galerie der Romantik, a display of paintings from the Romantic movement. **AG**

↖ At the center of the castle is a domed tower, topped by a gilded weathervane of the goddess Fortuna.

← Sophie Charlotte received gifts of Japanese and Chinese porcelain from Dutch seafaring relatives.

The Reichstag (Berlin, Germany)

Soviet soldiers raising the Red Flag over the Reichstag became a symbol of Germany's defeat

The Reichstag, or German Parliament, was built in response to the foundation of the new German Empire in 1871. After a series of architectural competitions, work on the winning design began in 1884 and was completed in ten years. The building was constructed in a conventional Neoclassical style, with a suitably imposing facade and a magnificent cupola engineered in glass and steel.

With the collapse of the German monarchy in 1918, the Reichstag had a new, short-lived importance as the debating chamber of the German Republic. In 1933 it burned down in suspicious circumstances, a disaster that suited the new Nazi government. It had no need for a parliament building and used the fire as an excuse to suppress the communists who were blamed for starting the blaze. Repairs were made to the building, although it was extensively damaged again by Allied bombing and by Soviet artillery in the 1945 battle for Berlin.

Although located in the western part of Berlin, the Reichstag was not used as a parliamentary building post-1945 because the Parliament (Bundestag) of West Germany was moved to the new capital of Bonn. After the reunification of Germany, the Bundestag moved back to Berlin, when the city was reinstated as the capital of Germany. In 1995 work began on the rebuilding of the Reichstag under the direction of Norman Foster. Completed in 1999 the new Reichstag features a vast glass dome over the main debating chamber. Visitors are able to look down on the proceedings, a hopeful symbol of the "transparency" of the new German government. **AG**

↗ Norman Foster's 1990s renovation has restored the Reichstag to the heart of modern Germany.

↘ The Red Army's bitterly resisted push from Russia to Berlin resulted in this scene at the Reichstag.

Berlin Olympic Stadium (Berlin, Germany)

Symbol of Nazi propaganda and site where Jesse Owens made sporting history

The Nazis were determined to make the 1936 Berlin Olympics a memorable showcase for Aryan physical superiority, and with this in mind the architect Werner March was commissioned to build the massive stadium (Olympiastadion), the centerpiece of a sports complex in the Grunewald forest to the west of Berlin. As well as the central Olympic stadium, there was a vast athletics field, the Mayfield (Maifeld), with a capacity of 500,000, the Waldbühne amphitheater that held 25,000 spectators, and more than one hundred other buildings to accommodate the various Olympic sports.

Work on the Olympic stadium began in 1934, and was completed in time for the games in the summer of 1936. Taking the symmetrical form of a large oval, it was built in the monumental Neoclassical style favored by the Nazis and was capable of holding 110,000 spectators. The structure was partially dug into the ground so that the field itself was some 40 feet (12 m) below ground level. Its sheer scale was intended to impress the world and inspire awe, and in this it certainly succeeded. Although Germany topped the medals table, the games were most memorable for the performances of the black American athlete Jesse Owens, who won four gold medals in the track and field events—the myth of Aryan superiority completely undermined.

After World War II, the stadium was taken over by the British and became part of their military occupation headquarters, where it was used for general sporting activities as well as acting as the home for the local football team, Hertha BSC Berlin. After the British withdrawal in 1994, the German authorities decided to redevelop the stadium. The new high-tech stadium was opened in 2004 and used as one of the main venues for soccer's 2006 World Cup. **AG**

Brandenburg Gate (Berlin, Germany)

Iconic gateway between West and East Berlin

One of the great symbols of Berlin—in much the same way as the Eiffel Tower is representative of Paris—the Brandenburg Gate was commissioned by the Prussian king Frederick Wilhelm II. Reflecting a new German interest in Greek antiquity, the building was inspired by the Propylaia, the gate to the Acropolis in Athens. The pediment of the Brandenburg Gate is supported by two pairs of six Doric columns providing five roadways, the slightly wider middle way being the exclusive preserve of the king and his guests.

Above the gate is a classical quadriga—a statue of a goddess drawn in a four-horsed chariot—sculpted originally as a personification of Peace. The quadriga was looted by the French in 1806 and, on its return, the goddess's olive wreath was replaced by an iron cross and the statue became a personification of Victory. During the nineteenth century the Brandenburg Gate came to symbolize Prussian military might, a view endorsed by the Nazis, who made a point of filming German troops marching out to war through the gate.

After the war, it took on further importance as a key gateway between West and East Berlin, ironically underscored when the gate was forced to close in 1961. After the collapse of East Germany in 1989, the Brandenburg Gate reopened and became a symbol of unity; West German chancellor Helmut Kohl walked through it to be welcomed by Hans Modrow, the prime minister of East Germany. **AG**

"The German question will remain open as long as the Brandenburg Gate is closed."

Richard von Weizsäcker, mayor of West Berlin, 1980

 ◎ **Zollverein Coal Mine** (Essen, Germany)

An unashamedly Modernist complex of buildings

Work on the Zollverein mine complex began with the sinking of a shaft in 1847 to supply coal to the iron and steel works of the Ruhr valley. Good rail links also encouraged the mine's development and new shafts were dug during the nineteenth century, eventually making it the largest coal mine in Europe.

In the 1920s the mine was taken over and, to improve productivity, it was transformed by the development of a new shaft "12" and associated facilities. The architects—Fritz Schupp and Martin Kremmer—were influenced by the Bauhaus school and by the concept of "form following function," and designed an outstanding example of Modernist architecture. Work began in 1928 and the new mine was completed four years later. It included a massive, red-painted, A-frame, pit-head tower that became one of the industrial icons of the Ruhr. During the 1980s, however, production went into a terminal decline and

in 1986 the pit closed down, the buildings left derelict.

In the 1990s the huge site was taken over by local government and, following its inscription as a UNESCO World Heritage site, work started to reclaim and restore the complex. Key buildings include the old boiler house—now a design center after a conversion by Norman Foster—and the coal-washing facility, which houses the Ruhr Museum. Other modern businesses are being resited in the Zollverein mine as part of a program of economic regeneration. **AG**

"It constitutes remarkable material evidence of the evolution and decline of an essential industry."

UNESCO

Steinwache Gestapo Prison (Dortmund, Germany)

Notorious torture chamber, interrogation center, and penal institution

In 1906 a large, forbidding police station was built in Dortmund to deal with the increase in crime in the city's expanding northern industrial center, and it soon acquired the nickname of the "stone guard" (Steinwache). Between 1926 and 1927 the police station was extended by the addition of a large cell block that could hold up to 126 prisoners. Ironically, in the light of future use, the cell block was held up as a model for the containment of prisoners. Whereas the three upper floors housed the prisoners, the ground floor had a reception area, several interrogation rooms, a medical center, and living quarters for the police on duty.

After the Nazi assumption of power in early 1933, the Gestapo took over the running of the prison. Some of the cells were transformed into torture chambers and used by the Gestapo to extract confessions from the unfortunate citizens arrested. The first inmates

were political prisoners: social democrats, trade union officials, and communists. They were followed by recalcitrant clergymen, Jews, gypsies, and foreign laborers who committed misdeeds within Germany, as well as German citizens denounced by their neighbors. It is believed that as many as 65,000 people passed through the prison, many on their way to execution or to concentration camps. Even by the vicious standards of Nazi Germany, the prison on Steinstrasse achieved special notoriety.

After the war, the Steinwache remained in use as a prison before becoming a hostel for the homeless. By the 1980s the building was dilapidated and there were calls for its demolition. The prison was given a reprieve by the City of Dortmund in 1987 and preservation work duly commenced. In 1992 the Steinwache Memorial Center was opened as a tribute to those who had suffered at the hands of the Gestapo. **AG**

Aachen Cathedral (Aachen, Germany)

The oldest cathedral in Europe and one of the prototypes of religious architecture

"The collection of the treasury … is of inestimable archeological, aesthetic and historic interest."

UNESCO

The Palatine Chapel was built on the instigation of Charlemagne to act as a religious focal point for his imperial capital city of Aachen. Once finished, the chapel represented a fusion of Byzantine, Roman, and Germanic-Franconian styles, and has since been called a "masterpiece of Carolingian architecture." With its columns of Greek and Italian marble, its bronze doors, and the largest mosaic of its dome (now destroyed), the Palatine Chapel has, from its inception, been perceived as an exceptional artistic creation. It was the first vaulted structure to be built north of the Alps since antiquity. During the Carolingian Renaissance, and even at the beginning of the medieval period, it set a precedent for religious architecture, which led to clear imitations (for example, at Nijmegen in the Netherlands). It is an excellent and distinctive example of the family of aularian chapels based on a central plan with tribunes. In 805 it was consecrated to serve as the imperial church, and for nearly six centuries between 936 and 1531, it was the coronation site for thirty of the emperors of the Holy Roman Empire.

Charlemagne collected many relics during his lifetime and, after his burial in the choir in 814, Aachen became a popular site of pilgrimage throughout Europe. In order to accommodate the vast numbers of pilgrims, the church progressively expanded during the Middle Ages, the most significant and beautiful addition being the glass chapel consecrated exactly 600 years after Charlemagne's death and distinguished by its thirteen magnificent windows. Other additions included a vestibule and several adjoining chapels, which all led to the formal designation of the building as Aachen Cathedral in the fifteenth century.

Unlike many other major buildings in Germany, the cathedral was relatively untouched by the Allied bombing campaign of World War II, and remains today in its original medieval splendor. **AG**

Cologne Cathedral (Cologne, Germany)

Medieval landmark, symbolic of Christianity and perseverance

The foundation stone of Cologne Cathedral was laid in 1248 by Archbishop Konrad of Hochstaden to house the relics of the three magi, plundered from Milan by the Holy Roman Emperor Frederick Barbarossa during the previous century. Although services were being held in the unfinished building by 1265, construction was slow and finally ground to a halt in 1560 with the cathedral only half built. No further construction was carried out until the Gothic Revival of the nineteenth century when, in 1842, King Frederick Wilhelm IV of Prussia ordered the continuation of building work based on the surviving medieval plans and drawings, although the roof was to be of modern steel construction.

Finally completed in 1880—632 years after work had begun—Cologne Cathedral was the largest church in Germany and its prominent double spires were surpassed in height only by the steeple at Ulm. Among the building's treasures are the gilded sarcophagus of the magi (claimed to hold the remains of the three wise men), the "Milan Madonna" (a wooden sculpture from 1290 depicting Mary and Jesus), and the Gero Cross (dating from 970 and the largest wooden cross north of the Alps). The cathedral has twelve bells, the oldest dating back to 1418. The bell of St. Peter (*Petersglocke*) was cast in 1922 and, at 24 tons, it is still the largest free-swinging bell in the world.

Although the twin spires and the west face survived the Allied mass bombing of Cologne during World War II, the cathedral received fourteen direct hits that caused severe damage to other sections of the structure. Restoration work was completed by 1956. When the German Pope Benedict XVI attended the World Youth Day at the cathedral in 2005, it was estimated that one million people visited the cathedral in the ensuing festivities. **AG**

"A superlative symbol of the endurance and steadfastness of Christian faith over seven centuries."

UNESCO

Beethoven's House (Bonn, Germany)

Largest collection of exhibits commemorating the composer's life and works

In 1767 the court tenor of the Elector of Cologne, Johann van Beethoven, and his wife moved into the garden wing of the house at Bonngasse 20, where Ludwig van Beethoven (1770–1827) was born. The accommodation in the house comprised a kitchen and utility room on the ground floor, with a cellar underneath. On the floor above were three rooms in which the family lived. The Beethoven family stayed at this address for a few years before they left to look for larger accommodation in the city.

In 1889 the house was bought by the Beethoven-Haus Society and extensively renovated, to reopen in 1893 as a memorial to the composer. In the 1930s the neighboring house was acquired to hold an archive of documents and memorabilia associated with Beethoven. In the 1990s the house was again renovated and a digital Beethoven-Haus was opened in 2004, providing visitors with an interactive experience of Beethoven's work that included a 3-D production of his opera *Fidelio*.

The house today contains the world's largest private collection of his manuscripts, documents, and diaries. The museum also holds many portraits of Beethoven, as well as musical instruments, furniture, and artifacts used by the composer. Among the musical instruments on display are the organ console from the *Minoritenkirche*, played by Beethoven as a boy, and his last pianoforte, built by the Viennese manufacturer Conrad Graf. The museum is completed by a chamber music hall for the performance of music written by Beethoven and his contemporaries, as well as by more modern composers. **AG**

⬉ Beethoven's famously strong personality is evident in this portrait by Joseph Stieler, painted in 1819–20.

⬅ The salon contains Beethoven's last grand piano, which was loaned to him by the maker, Conrad Graf.

Edersee Reservoir (Waldeck, Germany)

The Edersee achieved unwanted fame when it was attacked by the Dambusters

The damming of the River Eder in northern Hesse began in 1908 and was completed in 1914 to create the Edersee Reservoir. The intention of its designers was to generate hydroelectrical power and regulate the flow of water in order to improve navigation on the River Wesser, downstream of the Eder.

On the night of May 16, 1943, RAF Lancaster bomber aircraft of 617 Squadron launched an attack. Three major dams were chosen as targets—the Eder, the Mohne, and the Sorpe—and the walls of both the Eder and the Mohne were breached in the attack. The raid became a byword for the technological ingenuity of the special "bouncing bombs" developed for the mission, as well as the flying skills and daring of the bomber crews involved. The explosions from the bouncing bombs created a 230-foot- (70-m-) wide and 72-foot- (22-m-) deep breach in the Eder dam's wall, which in turn produced a flood wave 20 to 26 feet (6 to 8 m) in height that tore through the Eder valley for some 18 miles (30 km). The wave caused massive destruction and extensive loss of life, including more than 700 Ukrainian prisoners of war who drowned in their work camp. Despite the scale of the destruction, the dam was rebuilt in a matter of months and hydroelectrical production resumed.

Today the Edersee is an important tourist venue, used by water-sports enthusiasts, and the parkland around the reservoir is popular with hikers and campers. During summer droughts, the villages of Asel, Bringhausen, and Berich, submerged during the dam's construction, become visible again and are visited by descendants of the villagers. **AG**

▣ Rebuilding the Eder dam, successfully breached in the mission, was a top priority of the Nazi war effort.

▣ The Avro Lancaster, Britain's best heavy bomber, was the natural choice for the dambuster mission.

Wilhelmshöhe Palace

(Kassel, Germany)

Large and distinguished collection of art

The Wilhelmshöhe Palace was built for the Landgrave Wilhelm IX of Hesse-Kassel, who financed the ambitious project with money gained from hiring out his Hessian troops to the British crown during the American War of Independence (1776–83). In 1795 construction work began on a classical design that was completed in 1801 and distinguished by a particularly wide and elegant facade. After the Franco-Prussian War (1870–71), Napoleon III was briefly imprisoned in the Wilhelmshöhe, which was also used as the headquarters of the German high command during the latter stages of World War I.

The palace is surrounded by a magnificent landscaped park, one of the finest in Germany. Originally intended as a formal, Baroque garden based on French and Italian models, this changed during the latter part of the eighteenth century when the parkland took on an increasingly informal English aspect. The designers made full use of the garden's steep slopes by incorporating numerous carefully designed water features, including waterfalls, aqueducts, streams, and lakes, as well as a long central cascade similar to that of Chatsworth House in England. A large water tank is hidden within an octagonal castle, itself topped by a pyramid with a huge copper figure of Hercules at its apex. Other elements include a mock ruined medieval castle and a Chinese pagoda.

The palace is now home to a superb gallery of Old Masters that includes famous paintings by Dürer, Rubens, Titian, Rembrandt, and Poussin, as well as an internationally renowned wallpaper collection and a gallery of classical antiquities. During the summer months, when the many water features are in operation, large crowds gather to watch an impressive fluvial display. **AG**

Frankfurt Cathedral

(Frankfurt am Main, Germany)

Coronation site for the Holy Roman Empire

Although ecclesiastically a Catholic parish church, St. Bartholomew's—with a distinctive rosy glow from its sandstone walls—is known as a cathedral because of its size and importance within Germany. There had been a church on the site since at least the ninth century, although in 1239 it was rededicated to St. Bartholomew after the pope sent the saint's skull as a holy relic. A major building program was begun that lasted more than one hundred years.

In 1415 work on the cathedral culminated in the construction of the great octagonal tower, the work of several experienced architects and builders. But in

> *"The young Goethe found the time-honoured ceremony in the cathedral 'deadly boring.'"*
>
> Sabine Hock, historian

1867 a fire swept through St. Bartholomew's, melting the bells in the tower, the structure of which was also badly damaged. Fortunately the cathedral was rebuilt using the original medieval designs. St. Bartholomew's was also hard hit by Allied bombs during World War II, but was once again rebuilt.

Recent archeological excavations have revealed graves from the seventh century, and they include the burial site of a Merovingian girl, along with pottery fragments and gold jewelry. Apart from the reliquaries of St. Bartholomew, the cathedral's treasury contains a fine gold chalice, with engravings in the style of Albrecht Dürer and a gold monstrance. Other items of interest include Van Dyck's oil painting *The Mourning of Christ* and several more modern works, such as Emil Schumacher's *Prophet Job*, painted in 1973. **AG**

Wartburg Castle

(Eisenach, Germany)

Best preserved Romanesque secular building north of the Alps

Founded by Ludwig der Springer, Wartburg Castle developed from a simple military camp into one of Germany's finest fortresses. The earliest part of the castle is the watchtower, constructed by Ludwig in 1067. In 1155 work began on the imposing Great Hall (Palas). Adjoining the Great Hall is the Minstrels' Hall, the scene of a famous contest in the early thirteenth century between Germany's courtly troubadours, which provided the inspiration for Richard Wagner's opera *Tannhäuser*.

Wartburg was the scene of several other important events in German history. In 1521 Protestant reformer Martin Luther was given refuge in the castle by Frederick the Wise, after Luther's excommunication by the pope. While staying there—hidden under the assumed identity of Junker Jörg—he translated the New Testament from Greek into German. In 1817 Wartburg was the location for nationalist celebrations by some 450 members of the German Students' Association, an important first step toward the eventual unification of Germany in 1871.

During the nineteenth century the castle saw a systematic program of restoration that also included a series of frescoes by Moritz von Schwind in the Great Hall. After World War II, the East German government refurbished the castle; the works included restoration of the room used by Luther, complete with its original floor and paneled walls. Of special interest, displayed on a desk he is reputed to have used, is Luther's bible, annotated with comments from the great reformer and his colleagues. Luther's room has become a scene of pilgrimage for Protestant clergy and students of the Reformation, who also visit the Luther House in Eisenach, only a short distance away. Other features of Wartburg Castle include the half-timbered knights' house and the lofty South Tower, built in 1318. **AG**

"Warte, Berg, du sollst mir eine Burg werden!" (Wait, mountain, thou shalt become a castle for me!)

Ludwig der Springer, addressing Warburg's site

Thomaskirche

(Leipzig, Germany)

Immense historical and musical heritage

There has been a church of some description on the site of the Thomaskirche since the twelfth century. The Thomaskirche is most famous for employing Johann Sebastian Bach, the great composer and organist, as its cantor from 1723 to 1750. The church's choir, founded in 1212, is one of the oldest and most famous in Germany and continues to give concerts.

Although the church is now Lutheran, it was consecrated as a Catholic church in 1496. The great reformer Martin Luther was a frequent visitor to Leipzig because it was one of the most important cities in Saxony, and he preached at the church. When the Catholic ruler of the region, George, Duke of

> *"... an open venue in the city, a shelter for everyone longing for consolation and guidance."*
>
> **Christian Wolff, pastor of the Thomaskirche**

Saxony, was succeeded by the Protestant Duke Henry IV, Protestantism became the state religion of Saxony. Luther proclaimed the Reformation of Leipzig at the Thomaskirche on May 25, 1539.

Bach arrived in Leipzig as cantor in 1723. In spite of his music he was relatively underappreciated during his lifetime, and was therefore buried in an unmarked grave. His remains were not recovered until 1894, and they were interred in the Thomaskirche in 1950. Bach is not the only musician associated with the Thomaskirche. Both Wolfgang Amadeus Mozart and Felix Mendelssohn played the organ there, and Richard Wagner was baptized in the church. The Thomaskirche has been recognized as a vital site of world culture by the World Monuments Fund. **JF**

Albrechtsburg

(Meissen, Germany)

The first fine European china was made here

Although constructed in the style of a military fortress, this building—the first of its kind in Germany—was designed as an elegant, stately residence for the brothers Ernst and Albrecht von Wettin (the name Albrechtsburg was not used until 1676). Perched on the slopes of the River Elbe, work on the castle was started in 1471 under the direction of the master builder Arnold von Westfalen. Among the many outstanding architectural features of Albrechtsburg are arched curtain windows, new types of cellular vaulting, and the great spiral stone staircase (Grosser Wendelstein). The staircase uses steps arranged in both concave and convex patterns as well as a concealed newel. Albrechtsburg's time as a royal palace was short-lived, however, as the two Von Wettin brothers decided to divide their lands and build separate royal palaces.

In 1710 the first European porcelain factory was established in the castle, following the discovery by Johann Friederich Bottger of the manufacturing process that had been kept secret by the Chinese. The name Meissen quickly became synonymous with high-quality porcelain china and business was booming. However, the industrial process caused damage to the castle interior, and when production was moved out of the building in 1863 a necessary and extensive program of restoration was begun.

Using money from French reparations after the Franco-Prussian War of 1870 to 1871, a series of enormous murals was commissioned, depicting illustrious scenes from Saxony's history. In 1881 Albrechtsburg castle was opened to the public and today contains an impressive collection of medieval sculptures, and an exhibition that describes the discovery of porcelain and the development of the porcelain industry in Meissen. **AG**

Frauenkirche

(Dresden, Germany)

Reconstruction of an architectural treasure destroyed by wartime bombing

Built between 1726 and 1743, the Frauenkirche was a masterpiece of Baroque architecture. As a Protestant Lutheran church it adopted a radical internal configuration that saw the altar, chancel, baptismal font, and organ placed in view of the congregation. The magnificent organ, built by Gottfried Silbermann, was given its first recital by J. S. Bach. The sandstone dome—known as the "Stone Bell"—dominated the skyline for two centuries when Dresden was considered to be Germany's most beautiful city, and the Frauenkirche the jewel in the crown.

On February 13, 1945, Anglo-American air forces instigated a massive air offensive against Dresden. The center of the city was almost completely destroyed and as many as 35,000 people were killed in the ensuing firestorm. Another casualty was the cathedral itself. Hit repeatedly by high-explosive bombs, the dome finally collapsed in on itself on February 15, the whole cathedral in ruins.

Under the postwar German communist government, the Frauenkirche was left as a pile of rubble, a stark reminder of the horror of modern warfare. During the 1980s the blackened stones became a symbol of the peace movement, which in other major churches in East Germany coalesced into a civil rights protest that marked a step toward the collapse of communism and the reunification of the two Germanys. Immediately after reunification, it was decided to rebuild the Frauenkirche. Work began in 1993 using original drawings and photographs, and the Frauenkirche was reconsecrated in 2005. **AG**

↗ On October 30, 2005, a huge crowd attended the reconsecration ceremony at the Frauenkirche.

⇨ Dresden Town Hall (center) lies in ruins after the 1945 firestorm that destroyed the Frauenkirche.

🏛 ◎ Zwinger Complex (Dresden, Germany)

Cultural center that suffered a harsh bombing campaign during World War II

Sited in the old outer ward (Zwinger) of a former fort, the Zwinger formed a complex of Baroque pavilions and galleries that, along with Dresden's cathedral, became the city's most notable landmarks. Commissioned by the Elector of Saxony, Augustus the Strong, in imitation of Louis XIV's palace at Versailles, the overall design was the work of the master builder and court architect Matthäus Daniel Poppelmann and sculptor Balthasar Permoser.

Construction began in 1710 and was completed some twenty-two years later, although it was officially inaugurated in 1719 to celebrate the marriage of Frederick Augustus to Maria Josepha, the daughter of the Hapsburg emperor. The ornamental stone Crown Gate (Kronentor) was topped by a large decorated crown, and marked the entrance into a large open space around which were clustered six pavilions connected to one another by long galleries. The most notable pavilions were the Rampart Pavilion—with a statue of Hercules—and the Glockenspiel Pavilion, so named after the carillon that was later added to the building. The complex was originally three-sided, the open side leading through landscaped gardens to the River Elbe. This side was, however, enclosed during the 1840s by a gallery designed by Gottfried Semper, which also connected the complex to the newly built Opera House.

The Zwinger Complex was virtually destroyed in the highly controversial Allied bombing raids of February 1945, but was soon rebuilt and later modernized. Today the site houses several museums and galleries. Prominent among these is a gallery of Old Masters that includes artworks by Rubens, Canaletto, and Raphael, an armory that contains a wide range of Saxon weapons and armor, and exhibitions displaying collections of Meissen porcelain, clocks, and scientific instruments. **AG**

" . . . the bombing of German cities simply for the sake of increasing the terror, should be reviewed."

Winston Churchill, former British prime minister

⬆ Part of the gutted Zwinger Gallery is forlornly reflected in an ornamental pool in 1946.

➡ The rebuilt Crown Gate, doubled in height by its crownlike dome, is a High Baroque extravagance.

Goethe's House (Weimar, Germany)

Home of one of the great polymaths of the German Enlightenment

Johann Wolfgang Goethe (1749–1832) was invited to Weimar by the liberal Duke Carl August in 1782, moving into part of a former merchant's house on the Frauenplan. In 1794, the duke gave the entire house to Goethe, who welcomed the extra space for his library, archives, and scientific studies.

Built in the Baroque style in 1709, the house comprised several reception rooms at the front, where Goethe entertained the many guests eager to converse with the great man. At the rear of the house were his workrooms, library, and sleeping quarters. There was also an extensive garden that included a small garden house sometimes used by Goethe. At Weimar he fulfilled a number of commissions for the royal court that included acting as a council member, a director of roads and services, and a financial manager of the courtly finances. In 1789 Christiane Vulpius moved in with Goethe as his mistress and, despite the attendant scandal, lived openly with him until their eventual marriage in 1806.

After the death of Goethe's last grandchild in 1885, the house was taken over by the state as part of a large Goethe museum. The house has been restored as it was in Goethe's time and includes his desk, where he stood to do his work. The regal public rooms are decorated with classical paintings, in contrast to the more homely setting of his workrooms. Other attractions include the nearby White Swan Inn, where he would entertain visitors, and the newly restored Duchess of Anna Amalia Library, which came under Goethe's direction and now contains nearly 10,000 books and 2,000 medieval manuscripts. **AG**

Goethe, as depicted by Joseph Stieler in 1828, contributed to both German literature and science.

Goethe lived in this house from 1782 until his death in 1832; in time he had use of the whole property.

Krämerbrücke (Erfurt, Germany)

The only bridge north of Italy still lined with occupied houses

The Krämerbrücke (Merchants' Bridge) is widely regarded as the centerpiece of the historic town of Erfurt. First mentioned in 742, Erfurt established itself during the Middle Ages as one of the major European centers for the trade in woad—a blue-green dye—and its well-preserved medieval character dates from this period of economic prosperity. The town was also important for its location on a major trading route from the east, and the Krämerbrücke was built at one of the main fords of the Gera River.

The current bridge was preceded by a series of wooden structures that were periodically destroyed by fire, and the bridge, as it stands today, was constructed in 1325 and made of stone to ensure the trade route through the town would remain open. Churches at either end of the bridge were built shortly after the bridge was reconstructed, one of which, the Agidienkirche, still stands. The most remarkable feature of the bridge, however, is the housing that lines both sides of the structure, some of which dates from the fifteenth century and is still inhabited today. Originally the homes were those of some of the town's most important merchants—hence the bridge's name—and they dominate the Krämerbrücke so completely that it is easy to forget that they line a bridge and not an ordinary, bustling street.

Every year, on the third weekend in June, the bridge once again becomes the focus of the town during the popular Krämerbrückefest—a festival that celebrates the town's rich medieval heritage and recreates some of the sights and sounds of Erfurt as it would have appeared during its heyday. **AS**

↗ The houses on the bridge were built by shopkeepers wishing to take advantage of the busy thoroughfare.

→ Only a chance glimpse of the Gera River through a window reminds people that they are on a bridge.

Buchenwald Concentration Camp (Weimar, Germany)

Nearly 250,000 prisoners passed through the camp; at least 56,000 died in captivity

A concentration camp was constructed by the Nazis just outside Weimar in 1937 and given the euphemistic name Buchenwald (beech forest). It contained a wide range of inmates that included not only political prisoners, Jews, and gypsies but a consignment of Norwegian university students and, during 1944, a batch of Anglo-American airmen. Nearly 250,000 prisoners passed through the camp, of whom at least 56,000 were destined to die in captivity.

Although Buchenwald was not an extermination camp—these were sited in Poland—it achieved a particularly grim notoriety. The first commandant of the camp, Karl Koch, and his wife, Ilse, were infamous for their cruelty, and for having prisoners killed on a whim. Ilse Koch had a penchant for the flayed skin of her victims, which she had made into household objects such as book covers and lampshades. Buchenwald was also a site for "medical" experiments, where Soviet prisoners of war were injected with typhus in order to test various vaccines against the disease. The bulk of the prisoners were starved and worked to the point of death in the nearby quarries, or sent east for annihilation in the death camps.

In April 1945, as the Allies began to press toward Buchenwald, the guards fled, leaving the inmates to take over the camp. On April 11, the U.S. Army assumed control of the camp, but shortly afterward it was handed over to the Red Army, because the camp now lay within the zone of Germany occupied by the Soviets. Renamed Camp No. 2, Buchenwald held German prisoners between 1945 and 1950, of whom 7,000 died.

When the camp was closed in 1950, most of the buildings were destroyed, although some of the structures, such as concrete watch towers, remain. A temporary memorial, erected just after the liberation, was supplemented by a stone memorial in 1958. **AG**

"We were incredulous when we saw the American soldiers, smiling at us, making the victory sign."

Dr. Nissim Alhadeff, on Buchenwald's liberation

Burg Rheinfels (St. Goar, Germany)

Largest and most powerful fortification along the River Rhine in the Middle Ages

The castle at Rheinfels was the most successful of the many such fortifications erected along the River Rhine. Count Dieter V. von Katzenelnbogen built the original castle in 1245, primarily to impose heavy toll charges on the boats sailing up and down the Rhine. This naturally caused resentment among the river users: Some twenty-six Rhineland towns combined forces and an army of 1,000 knights and 8,000 men-at-arms, assisted by fifty ships, laid siege to the castle. The siege continued for a year and fourteen weeks, but Burg Rheinfels resisted their best efforts and the Rhennish confederation had no choice but to raise the siege empty-handed.

In 1479 the castle passed to the Landgraves of Hessen, who continued to improve its defenses, which included an extensive tunnel network. Unlike many other medieval castles, Burg Rheinfels was successfully adapted to withstand gunpowder and cannons. It was besieged by Spanish forces in 1626, and it was the only castle on the left bank of the Rhine to withstand assault by the French armies of Louis XIV in 1692. In 1794, however, invading French troops secured the castle and, between 1796 and 1797, the main fortifications were blown up and the stone was taken away for building work.

Today, the castle is a highly picturesque ruin with commanding views over the Rhine. Despite the attentions of the French, about one-third of Burg Rheinfels survived destruction. The ruins were given over to the town of St. Goar in 1925. The extensive underground tunnel network can be explored by the more intrepid tourist. There is also a museum with exhibits on the castle's history, including a large-scale model of the original structure, as well as a collection of folk art from the eighteenth and nineteenth centuries. Part of the castle has been converted into a luxury hotel. **AG**

"... some forty castles were constructed ... as symbols of power and as customs stations ..."

UNESCO, on the Upper Middle Rhine Valley

Porta Nigra

(Trier, Germany)

An impressive projection of Roman power at the fringes of the empire

"… a unique construction that is unlike any of the other preserved Roman city gates."

UNESCO

The city of Trier contains more significant Roman buildings than any other other place north of the Alps. It was designated a World Heritage site by UNESCO in 1981, in recognition of its rich Roman heritage and also because it has two very early Christian church buildings.

The Porta Nigra (Black Gate) was one of four gates built around 180 to 200 C.E. as part of the defenses of the city. Protecting the city from the north, the structure was built from gray sandstone, which by the Middle Ages had blackened to earn the name of Porta Nigra. Trier was an important crossing point over the River Moselle and the gates provided a necessary defensive shield around the site.

At more than 98 feet (30 m) in height, the Porta Nigra consisted of two four-story flanking towers with an entrance of two 23-foot- (7-m-) high carriageways for the passage of traffic. Within the building was a small courtyard. The large sandstone blocks were not held together by mortar but rested one on top of the other, pinned by iron clamps and rods. Although Trier's three other gates were dismantled for house-building purposes during the Middle Ages, the Porta Nigra survived this fate because of the presence of a Greek monk, Simeon, who had lived a hermitlike existence within the building. After his death, a church was built within the Porta Nigra to honor his memory, with the courtyard acting as the nave. Despite some modifications, the original Roman structure remained essentially intact.

In 1802 Trier came under French control and, at the order of Napoleon, the church was dissolved and the Porta Nigra carefully restored as a Roman ruin. Despite the ravages of time and various marauders, the fortified gate remains an impressive sight, the largest such structure north of the Alps, and an eloquent reminder of Rome's imperial past. **AG**

Heidelberg Castle

(Heidelberg, Germany)

Romantic site attracted an artistic following

Although there had been fortifications above the city of Heidelberg since at least 1300, it was not until around 1400 that Ruprecht III built a castle befitting a prince elector. The castle expanded over the next 200 years into a magnificent sandstone edifice rising above the city, looking across to vineyards on the far side of the steep Neckar valley. A particular feature of the castle were the gardens built in 1616 to 1619—the Hortus Palatinus (Palatine Gardens)—considered at the time to be the eighth wonder of the world.

The castle's fortunes then took a turn for the worse. During the Thirty Years' War (1618–48)

> *"It has been victim to everything that has shaken Europe, and now it has collapsed under its weight."*
>
> Victor Hugo, writer

Heidelberg was attacked and taken by forces from both sides and was badly damaged in the process. Subsequent rebuilding work after the war was undone during the campaigns against the French in 1689 and 1693, when much of the castle was left in ruins. Desultory efforts were made to restore the castle but after it was set on fire by lightning in 1764, local people began to carry off the stones from the remains.

By the early nineteenth century, Heidelberg had a reputation as a picturesque ruin, and proved highly popular with the tourists of the day. Among them was English painter J. M. W. Turner, who painted a number of scenes in the Romantic style. The castle remains a popular site and houses the Grosses Fass, the world's largest barrel, 26 feet (8 m) high and capable of holding 55,345 gallons (210,000 liters) of wine. **AG**

Mercedes-Benz Factory

(Stuttgart, Germany)

Eye-catching architecture and engineering

In 1886 Gottlieb Daimler developed the first motor car, a four-wheeled carriage powered by an internal combustion engine with effective transmission to the wheels. Over the next few years Daimler improved the design of the car and combined his business interests with another motoring pioneer, Carl Benz. Emil Jellineck, a wealthy banker and early motor-racing enthusiast, subsequently purchased a controlling interest in the company, and financed a high-performance car in 1900 that was called Mercedes after his daughter. During the 1920s the company took the name Mercedes-Benz.

The original factory at Bad Cannstatt proved too small for the company's expanding production line and, after a fire at the factory, a new plant at nearby Untertürkheim was chosen. Production at this site began in 1904 and cars have been made at Untertürkheim ever since. Despite virtual destruction by severe Allied bombing during World War II, a rebuilt Mercedes-Benz factory was soon up and running and new models were coming off the production lines by 1948. Untertürkheim has been constantly updated and today its high-tech assembly lines are responsible for the production of 4,600 precision-machined engines every day. These and other major units, such as transmissions and axles, are shipped to car plants in Germany and the rest of the world for assembly.

Next to the plant at Untertürkheim is the architecturally renowned Mercedes-Benz Museum, which presents the story of the famous motor car from its invention to present-day technology. The museum showcases the company's achievements and includes the 770 Grand Mercedes owned by Kaiser Wilhelm II, the Silver Arrows racers of the 1930s, the 300SL Gullwing Coupe, and more modern designs such as the A-Class and Smart Car. **AG**

Baden-Baden Kurhaus

(Baden-Baden, Germany)

Elegant site for taking the waters

In the nineteenth century the German spa town of Baden-Baden, on the edge of the Black Forest, was a fashionable gathering place for the rich and famous from across Europe. The desire of the overfed elite of the period to combine leisure activities with a cure for their tortured livers made this and other spas a unique focus of social life.

The existence of medicinal springs at Baden was known to the Romans and had been fitfully exploited through the centuries, but the development of the resort did not begin in earnest until the 1820s. It was then that the colonnaded Kurhaus was designed by German architect Friedrich Weinbrenner and built in the Neoclassical style, combining a spa with gaming rooms. The popular gambling facilities were greatly expanded after Parisian entrepreneur Jacques Bénazet took over the casino in 1838. It was his son Edouard Bénazet who developed Baden to its full potential, adding a new set of gaming rooms decorated in lavish style, modeling them on the rich interiors of French royal palaces.

Baden became an important venue for diplomatic summit meetings, most memorably that of the "Three Emperors"—Franz Joseph of Austria, Alexander II of Russia, and France's Napoleon III—in 1863. It was frequented by the aristocracy and royalty, but also by the nouveaux riches, the professional classes, and many respected citizens on the outskirts of "high society." Russians figured prominently among the numerous visitors to the resort, including novelists Turgenev and Dostoevsky—the latter losing heavily and frequently at the roulette tables. The social world of Baden-Baden's Belle Époque disappeared with World War I, but the resort remains an opulent relic of the leisure pursuits of Europe's privileged elite in a now lost era. **RG**

Haus Wahnfried

(Bayreuth Germany)

Home and resting place of Richard Wagner

Having secured the patronage of Prince Ludwig II of Bavaria, the composer Richard Wagner (1813–83) was able to realize his dream of building a special theater (Festspielhaus) for the performance of his own operas. The Bavarian town of Bayreuth was chosen not only as the site for the opera house but for Wagner's own residence. Wagner moved in on April 28, 1874, with his wife, Cosima (the daughter of Franz Liszt), and their family. Naming it Wahnfried, Wagner would spend the rest of his life there completing the *Ring Cycle* in the house and starting on his final work, *Parsifal*. After Wagner's death in 1883, his family continued to live

> *"Here where my illusion found peace, be this house named by me peace from illusion."*
>
> **Richard Wagner, inscription over front entrance**

there, from where they directed the increasingly important annual Bayreuth Festival.

Many important figures were invited to the composer's house, including the musicians Richard Strauss and Arturo Toscanini and, more controversially, Adolf Hitler. Haus Wahnfried was badly damaged during World War II and taken over by the U.S. forces in the postwar period. When the Americans left, the Wagner family returned to Wahnfried but it was handed over to the town of Bayreuth in 1972. Since then the house has been restored to its former splendor. It contains many artifacts related to Wagner, several of his pianos, a restored library, and a small concert hall. The building also holds an unrivaled archive of Wagner's correspondence and the handwritten scores of his major works. **AG**

Regensburg Old Town

(Regensburg, Germany)

The best-preserved medieval town center in Germany

The medieval centers of many German cities were extensively pulverized by Allied bombing raids in World War II, but fortunately that of Regensburg escaped almost unscathed. The nucleus of the medieval settlement was a Roman fort located on the confluence of the Danube and Regen rivers, to which further areas behind protective walls were gradually added between the eleventh and the late thirteenth century. Space was at a premium and the medieval buildings are tall, separated by dark, narrow lanes. The fortified walls of medieval Regensburg are studded by many towers, built by wealthy families who competed for the prestige of owning the tallest one of all.

Regensburg became preeminent in Bavaria following the construction over the Danube of the Steinerne Brücke, or Stone Bridge, between 1135 and 1146. The first Danube crossing for hundreds of years, the bridge opened the way from northern Europe to Venice. Among the outstanding medieval buildings of Regensburg are the fourteenth-century Town Hall, the early twelfth-century Romanesque Church of St. James, or Schottenkirche, and the nearby Jakobstor city gate: the latter has doors covered by extraordinary carvings. The Dom, or Cathedral of St. Peter, is the city's most prominent landmark; apart from the towers, finished in 1869, it was completed in 1634. Incorporated into the Dom is the Eselsturm, a tower of the eighth-century Romanesque cathedral that previously occupied the site. The cathedral's famous boys' choir, the Regensburger Domspatzen, has thrived for more than a thousand years. **FR**

↗ The Cathedral of St. Peter is the most significant example of Gothic architecture in southern Germany.

→ The city's Old Bridge was a feat of medieval engineering that inspired copies across Europe.

Nuremberg Trials Courtroom (Nuremberg, Germany)

The Nuremberg trials set an important precedent for international jurisdiction

"Voice or no voice, the people can always be brought to the bidding of the leaders. That is easy."

Hermann Göring, at the Nuremberg trials

Despite their many differences, the victorious Allied powers were agreed that the chief Nazi leaders should face trial for their crimes. The Palace of Justice in Nuremberg was chosen as the venue for the trial, largely because the courtroom and its attached prison were among the few suitable places to have escaped damage from Allied bombing. A total of twenty-two Nazi leaders, including Hermann Göring, Rudolf Hess, Karl Dönitz, and Joachim von Ribbentrop, were tried in an extended Court Room 600 (other defendants subsequently faced justice in the Nuremberg "follow-up trials").

The main trials lasted from November 1945 to October 1946, with the defendants charged with crimes against peace and against humanity. The whole procedure was a vast undertaking; evidence taken by the court was sufficient to fill forty-two large volumes. When the verdicts were given, twelve defendants were sentenced to death, three to life imprisonment, four to sentences of ten to twenty years' imprisonment, with just three acquitted. Although Göring had been sentenced to hang, he swallowed poison before his execution. As well as handing out justice to some of the most evil men of the twentieth century, the Nuremberg trials set an important precedent: For the first time in history an international court had passed verdicts on crimes against international criminal law. This was an initial move in the development of international jurisdiction that today holds major wrongdoers to account at The Hague—a recent example being the former president of Serbia and Yugoslavia, Slobodan Milošević.

Once the trials were over, Court Room 600 reverted to its original size and is still used as a criminal court in Nuremberg. Guided tours are conducted by the local state authorities on the weekends, explaining the trials and their international importance. **AG**

Albrecht Dürer's House (Nuremberg, Germany)

Unmissable Nuremberg landmark and home to an innovative artist

German artist Albrecht Dürer (1471–1528) is generally regarded as one of the most important and influential Northern Renaissance artists. Inspired by the new techniques being developed in Italy, Dürer translated these to a Germanic tradition, becoming famous for his sets of woodcuts, although he was also a talented painter in oils and watercolors.

Built *c.* 1420, the four-story house that was to become Dürer's home was greatly enlarged with the addition of gables and large dormer windows in 1502. After much traveling—including two journeys to Italy—Dürer returned to the city of his birth and was at the height of his fame when he bought the house in 1509. He lived in the house until his death and shared it with his mother and his wife, Agnes, along with a collection of pupils and apprentices.

The first two floors were constructed from the sandstone typical of the area, with the other two storeys being half timbered. A large door—wide enough to admit a carriage—led into the ground floor, which acted as a work area and storage space. On the first floor was the kitchen, and above this were the living rooms, and the studio and workshops where Dürer carried out his work.

During the nineteenth century, after a resurgence of interest in the painter, the building was restored as a shrine to Dürer and his art. The house was damaged by bombing in World War II but has undergone a series of repairs and refurbishments that has transformed it into a working museum of the artist's life and works. Located at the end of a street named after the artist, Dürer's home has been carefully restored, complete with the kitchen and rooms displaying the artistic techniques of the time. The top-floor gallery contains three exhibition rooms, while a recently built annex houses a screening room for an audio-visual introduction to the life of the artist. **AG**

"Affection bids us mourn for one who was the best of men. . . . May he rest in peace with his fathers."

Martin Luther, on the death of Albrecht Dürer

Kaiserburg (Nuremberg, Germany)

Castle used by the Holy Roman emperors

Nuremberg is one of the most historically significant cities in Germany, thanks to its close association with the Holy Roman Empire and the Northern Renaissance. During the Middle Ages the city was regarded as the unofficial capital of the empire, sprawling as it did at the foot of the Kaiserburg (Imperial Castle)—a building used periodically by every Holy Roman emperor between 1050 and 1571. Dating from the early eleventh century, it is actually a collection of three smaller structures—the Kaiserburg itself, the Burggrafenburg (Count's Castle), and the Stadtburg (City's Castle). The Stadtburg officially belonged to the city but was maintained at Nuremberg's expense largely for the use of the emperor, whereas the now-ruinous Burggrafenburg was controlled by the local Hohenzollern nobility from 1192 until the mid-fifteenth century, when it was almost completely destroyed by fire and the family left Nuremberg. The Kaiserburg itself was begun by Emperor Conrad III toward the end of the eleventh century and was greatly expanded by Conrad's successor, the legendary Frederick I "Barbarossa," who was responsible for the castle's impressive Doppelkapelle (Double Chapel).

The influence of the emperors was already in decline before the Reformation fractured the empire along a religious divide, with Nuremburg breaking from its Catholic heritage to become a largely Protestant city. The Thirty Years' War reduced the city's importance still further, until Nuremberg was eventually brought within the Kingdom of Bavaria in 1806, becoming something of a provincial backwater.

The Kaiserburg was badly damaged during World War II, and was extensively restored in the 1950s, although the Doppelkapelle and several important towers survived the bombing and remain a powerful reminder of the city's former imperial glory. **AS**

KZ Dachau (Dachau, Germany)

First Nazi concentration camp

In March 1933, Heinrich Himmler ordered Theodore Eicke to establish a concentration camp to hold opponents of the Nazi regime. The first inmates were mainly political prisoners, religious critics of the Nazis, and then Jews. During World War II, the camp population increased dramatically with an influx of prisoners from the East, predominantly Poles, Soviets, and Jews. Prisoners were sent to Dachau for execution and were subject to medical experimentation. Dachau also acted as the central hub for 170 satellite work camps dotted around southern Bavaria. It is thought that some 200,000 prisoners passed through the camp, with an official death toll of 30,000,

---

"Silence encourages the tormentors, never the tormented. Sometimes we must interfere."

Elie Wiesel, Holocaust survivor and writer

---

although thousands of deaths went unrecorded, especially during the typhus epidemic that swept through the camp in 1945. When the U.S. army liberated Dachau on April 29, 1945, it discovered more than 30,000 prisoners living in the most desperate conditions, with a similar number held in the surrounding work camps.

After the war, Dachau was used as an internment camp by the Americans and then as a holding center for refugees. Subsequently, former prisoners set up a memorial for the victims of Dachau and the old prisoners' camp became a museum. One of the wooden barrack huts was rebuilt to show the terrible conditions in which the inmates lived, and concrete foundations of the other thirty-two huts remain to reveal the extent of the camp. **AG**

Hofbräuhaus (Munich, Germany)

One of the most famous breweries in the world

The origins of the Hofbräuhaus date back to 1589 when Duke Wilhelm V founded a brewery on the site of the then royal residence in Munich. By the nineteenth century it comprised a thriving brewery with a tap house attached for use by the public. Demand increased enormously and consequently a new, greatly enlarged beer cellar was opened nearby in 1897—an ornate building in the Bavarian style that has become the now-famous Hofbräuhaus.

Over the years the cellar has been visited by many famous patrons, including Wolfgang Amadeus Mozart, the Empress Elizabeth of Austria, and Lenin and his wife. The latter wrote: "We have especially fond memories of the Hofbräuhaus, where the good beer erases all class differences." Certainly the most notorious visitor was Adolf Hitler, who spoke to a crowd of mixed political opinions in the Hofbräuhaus in November 1921. A full-scale brawl broke out between the rival factions, and in his book, *Mein Kampf,* Hitler recalled fondly how his SA thugs received their "baptism of fire" there.

The Hofbräuhaus has been called the "largest pub in the world" and, with a total capacity of around 3,000 people, this is probably the case. It serves a variety of Bavarian beers—both light and dark in liter steins—accompanied by local specialties that include the Weisswurst or white sausage. It encourages the German sense of *Gemütlichkeit* (geniality) with Bavarian brass bands, waitresses in traditional costume, and loud singing. Although the brewery claims that half the clientele are regulars, it has increasingly become part of Munich's tourist itinerary. **AG**

⬈ The Hofbräuhaus, the royal brewery of the kingdom of Bavaria, was only opened to the public in 1828.

⬊ The calm, tourist-inhabited waterhole of today has famously seen darker and more turbulent times.

Munich Residenz (Munich, Germany)

One of Europe's richest palace interiors, well stocked with fine artifacts

First built as a small, unimposing moated castle in 1385, the Munich Residenz was progressively built up by the Wittelsbach family—the rulers of Bavaria until 1918—who used it as a royal palace and seat of government. As a consequence of the Residenz's development over several centuries, it combines many different styles of architecture and interior decoration, and also contains an interesting variety of artifacts collected by the Wittelsbachs. The style of the buildings ranges from the Renaissance through Baroque and Rococo to the Neoclassical.

Because of the many additions made over time, the Residenz is not so much a single structure as a magnificent complex of buildings—based around ten separate courtyards—that, at times, would resemble a rabbit warren if the scale were not so grand. Important features include the spectacularly painted ceiling of the Antiquarium (the largest Renaissance hall north of

the Alps), the Baroque papal rooms, the Rococo "ornate rooms" designed by François Cuvilliés the Elder, and the Neoclassical Charlotte rooms.

Postwar restoration has enabled the Residenz to take its place as one of the largest and finest palace museums in Germany. A focal point for visitors is the treasury, which contains one of the most important and extensive collections of royal regalia in the world; among the fine exhibits are crowns, ceremonial swords, goblets, and royal insignia, as well as detailed work in bronze, rock crystal, and gold. Of more general historical interest are Charles the Bald's prayer book (from the ninth century), the reliquary of the True Cross, and the statuette of St. George. There are also a significant number of Oriental treasures that include weapons captured from the Turks, intricate ivory work from Sri Lanka, and some fine examples of Chinese porcelain. **AG**

Schloss Nymphenburg (Munich, Germany)

The palace, gardens, and interior decoration constitute a stunning landmark for Munich

The Schloss Nymphenburg was commissioned in 1664 by the Bavarian Elector Ferdinand Maria to celebrate the birth of his son Maximilian Emanuel. Originally little more than an elaborate Italian villa, it gradually developed into the magnificent summer palace of the Bavarian rulers, the Wittelsbach family— a pleasant contrast to the administrative center of the Residenz in Munich.

In the early eighteenth century Max Emanuel added four pavilions, and connected them to the central villa with a series of elegant arcades. The sumptuous interiors demonstrate the Rococo enthusiasm of southern Germany during this period. Particularly noteworthy are the frescoes of Johann Baptist Zimmerman; completed in 1756, they depict scenes from classical mythology with references to the goddess Flora and her many nymphs (from which the Schloss took its name). Rather more controversial

is the "Gallery of Beauties" commissioned by Ludwig I. It displays the portraits of thirty-six of the most beautiful women of the period—painted by J. Stieler between 1827 and 1850—and includes the courtesan Lola Montez, whose relationship with the king understandably aroused fierce scandal.

The nearby court stables now contain a display of historic coaches. They include the Paris Coronation Coach of 1742, and the carriages and sleighs used by Ludwig II on his nighttime dashes between his Bavarian castles. A porcelain factory was built in the palace grounds and a collection of superb items can be seen in the museum. The large landscaped park that surrounds the Nymphenburg contains a hunting lodge (Amalienburg), a decorative pagoda, a magnificent bathing pavilion, and the Magdalenklause, a specially constructed ruin intended as a place for prayer and quiet contemplation. **AG**

Neuschwanstein Castle (Füssen, Germany)

Ludwig II's retreat from reality and a tribute to Richard Wagner

> *"He is unfortunately so beautiful and wise, soulful and lordly, that I fear his life must fade away . . ."*

Richard Wagner, composer, on Ludwig II

⬆ The two-story throne room was inspired by the Byzantine interior of the Hagia Sophia in Istanbul.

▣ In the foreground of this view is the Gateway Building, the first part of the castle to be completed, in 1873.

The mentally unstable King Ludwig II of Bavaria had a fascination with the Middle Ages and the music of Richard Wagner, and these interests were combined in the construction of Neuschwanstein, a mock castle in the Bavarian Alps. Ludwig's obsession with a mythical past was given extra impetus after Bavaria's defeat in the 1866 war with Prussia: Bavaria was absorbed into a Prussia-dominated Germany and was no longer a sovereign state. With no real function to perform as king, Ludwig became more of a recluse and retreated deeper into his fantasies.

Work began in 1869 on the Gateway Building, where Ludwig lived while the rest of the castle was being built. Although scenic, the mountain location of the castle presented many problems for the architectural and construction teams, who often had to work around the clock to meet Ludwig's harsh demands. The exterior was largely complete by 1880, and Ludwig took possession of Neuschwanstein (New Swan Stone Castle) in 1884. The Gothic fantasy, based on ideas by the scene painter Christian Jank, was built in startling white limestone with loving care paid to medieval architectural detail. Within the castle, however, the latest technologies were employed to ensure Ludwig's comfort, including central heating and running hot and cold water throughout the building. The interior featured paintings of the poet Tannhäuser, the swan knight Lohengrin and his father, and the grail king Parsifal—all of whom were represented in Wagner's music.

Ludwig, who had increasingly sought refuge from reality, was deposed and drowned in mysterious circumstances in 1886. The castle—its interiors still unfinished—was taken over by the Bavarian state. The great beauty of its Alpine location and its many romantic associations make Neuschwanstein one of Germany's most popular tourist destinations. **AG**

Oberammergau Theater (Oberammergau, Germany)

World-famous passion plays performed and staged by amateur village residents

The Bavarian village of Oberammergau was severely affected by bubonic plague from 1633 to 1634, and the unfortunate inhabitants vowed that if they could be spared further suffering they would perform a passion play every ten years. The plague abated and the thankful villagers staged their first play in 1634, the stage built over the freshly dug graves of the numerous plague victims. Easter passion plays—usually depicting scenes from Jesus's death and resurrection—were a popular feature of the time, but what distinguishes the plays from Oberammergau is their longevity: They are now performed on the first year of every decade, and the year 2000 marked the village's fortieth performance.

Over time the performances have become more theatrically sophisticated, although they were, and still are, carried out in the open on a wooden stage. Today's audiences, however, are sheltered from the elements. The last of a number of overhauls of the theater took place in 1997, with a refurbished auditorium holding nearly 5,000 covered seats and an improved stage incorporating the latest technical devices. Traditionally the Oberammergau Passion Play lasts for seven hours (with an intermission for food) and comprises a spoken narrative with musical accompaniment and dramatized scenes and tableaux from the Old and New Testaments.

The performances take place over a five-month period and can involve up to 2,000 villagers, who perform all the parts in the play as well as providing musicians, stagehands, and other backstage staff. Popular with outsiders since the eighteenth century, the passion plays have drawn ever-larger crowds, and from the 1930s onward the village has attracted as many as half a million visitors to experience the moving performances. **AG**

Berchtesgaden (Oberbayern, Germany)

The Nazi propaganda machine made much of Hitler's trips to Berchtesgaden

The small Bavarian alpine town of Berchtesgaden was taken over by the German state in the 1930s as a recreational facility for Adolf Hitler and other senior Nazi leaders. Hitler's main house was the Berghof, although in 1939 the Eagle's Nest (Kehlsteinhaus) was built for him as a present; a small house perched high above the town, it offered spectacular panoramic views over the Bavarian Alps.

Under the direction of the Nazi Party secretary Martin Bormann, existing houses were taken over to create an offshoot of the Reichs Chancellory that contained administrative buildings, an SS guard barracks, a hotel for visiting dignitaries, and housing for the large administrative staff serving Hitler. Bormann and other Nazi leaders, such as Hermann Göring and Albert Speer, had their own private houses within the complex. Hitler, however, spent little time there, especially after the outbreak of war in 1939.

Toward the end of the war, the Allies were fearful that Hitler might retreat to Berchtesgaden to form the so-called "Alpine Redoubt" and accordingly bombed the complex on April 25, 1945. What remained was demolished in the early 1950s, with the exception of the Eagle's Nest and parts of the Berghof. Aware of the worldwide fascination with Berchtesgaden's Nazi past, the Bavarian authorities have developed an exhibition center that highlights the Holocaust and the involvement of Berchtesgaden in the Third Reich. **AG**

"[Appreciating] Berchtesgaden ... has to go hand in hand with the memory of the evil."

Linda Pfnuer, head of exhibition center

Normandy Beaches (Normandy, France)

Allied landing zones for the invasion of mainland Europe in World War II

"Your enemy is well trained, well equipped, and battle-hardened. He will fight savagely . . ."

General Eisenhower, D-Day order, June 6, 1944

⬆ The sandy Normandy beaches facilitated landings, but concrete gun emplacements took a heavy toll.

➡ Allied forces come ashore on D-Day; the landing craft are towing balloons to obstruct attacks from the air.

By 1944, with Italy defeated and the Soviet Union pushing the Nazis back from Eastern Europe, the Allied position in World War II had never looked so promising. Allied commanders had been plotting an invasion of France since 1943. The limited range of Allied fighters and the peculiar geography of the French coastline meant that there were only two possible sites for an amphibious attack: Calais and the Normandy coast. Normandy, farther away from Britain but less heavily defended, was chosen for the attack because it offered more options to the invading forces, with the result that it would be harder for the Germans to second-guess their intentions.

The attack was code-named Operation Overlord. Nearly three million troops crossed the channel on June 6, 1944, which makes Overlord the largest invasion of all time. Five major beach sites had been identified on the Normandy coast for the landings of the Allied troops. Sword Beach, the farthest east of the beaches, stretches along 5 miles (8 km) of coast and is only 9 miles (15 km) from Caen. The British came ashore here with relatively few casualties. The Canadian troops, often overlooked in historical accounts, began their assault at Juno Beach, just to the west of Sword beach. Gold Beach was at the center of the invasion and the British had great success there on the first night of the attack. The task was far harder for the Americans on Omaha Beach. They faced the well-trained German 352nd Infantry Division, who engaged them in the fiercest battle of D-Day. The beach farthest to the west was known as Utah, and was the sight of a relatively easy landing.

Today's visitor to the Normandy beaches finds wide, flat, peaceful expanses of sand, although surviving German bunker sytems and rusting barbed wire continue to testify to the momentous invasion and fierce battle of some sixty years ago. **OR**

Lochnagar Crater
(near La Boisselle, France)

Colossal mine crater of World War I

During the early summer of 1916 the British army prepared to make its first great offensive of World War I, an attack against German positions alongside the River Somme. The German line was well defended, but it was thought that a heavy preliminary bombardment would cut through the wire and smash the German trenches. To further diminish resistance to the opening attack, the British had dug a series of tunnels that ran out from their lines to allow explosives to be placed underneath key German positions.

The mine dug near the village of La Boisselle was the largest of all and contained two ammonal charges of 24,000 pounds (10,880 kg) and 30,000 pounds (13,600 kg)—slightly more than 24 tons. The mine detonated successfully at 7.28 A.M. on July 1, 1916, two minutes before the British troops went over the top. The explosion was the largest in history to date. Tons of soil and other debris were flung up into the air—as high as 4,000 feet (1,220 m) according to one observer—and the sound of the explosion could be heard in London. The vast hole made by the explosion—nicknamed the Lochnagar Crater—was 300 feet (90 m) across and 90 feet (27 m) deep. Although it destroyed part of the German front line, allowing British infantry to occupy the crater, the attack elsewhere was a bloody failure, and soon British troops were falling back into the crater as a refuge from German machine-gun fire.

Since the war, many of the craters of the Somme battlefields were gradually filled in by French farmers for agricultural use, but in 1978 the land surrounding the Lochnagar Crater was bought by Richard Dunning so that it would be preserved. Since then it has become an important battlefield memorial site. A ceremony to commemorate the first day of the Somme offensive is held every year on July 1. **AG**

Joan of Arc Memorial Cross (Rouen, France)

Monument of a French national heroine

In the center of Rouen, a modern church—the Église Jeanne d'Arc—marks the spot where Joan of Arc was executed on May 30, 1431. A tall, stark cast-iron cross serves as her memorial; the extraordinary church creates an impression of her execution pyre. Joan of Arc has become a French national heroine, a Catholic saint, and a source of inspiration for politicians, writers, and artists over many centuries. Motivated by religious visions that urged her to drive out the English and bring the Dauphin to Reims for his coronation, Joan's rise and success as a soldier and military leader is an exceptional chapter in history.

> *"To sacrifice what you are and to live without belief, that is a fate more terrible than dying."*
>
> **Joan of Arc, French military leader and martyr**

The challenges she faced were formidable. The Hundred Years' War had started in 1337 when royal succession was disputed and unstable government made France vulnerable to attack. By 1429 the English–Burgundian alliance occupied much of France. Once accepted as a soldier, however, Joan of Arc set about reversing French fortunes by attacking and recapturing occupied fortresses, routing the English, and releasing Orléans from a five-month siege. She regained Reims and then Paris. Joan was captured by Burgundians in May 1430 and, despite dramatic escape attempts, was sold to the English and imprisoned at Rouen. They brought a charge of heresy against her and, found guilty by the corrupt court, Joan of Arc was burned to death. A posthumous trial in 1456 declared her innocence. **EH**

Cathedral of Notre-Dame

(Reims, France)

Setting of every French coronation and survivor of damage in both World Wars

Notre-Dame Cathedral, located at the heart of France's Champagne region and built between 1211 and the early fourteenth century on the site of earlier churches, was the Gothic setting for all the coronations since medieval times, including Charles VII in 1429, with Joan of Arc at his side, and France's last king, Charles X in 1825. The windows were damaged and the rood screen destroyed during the French Revolution, and the cathedral's stonework was severely damaged by bombing during World War I. Restoration work, largely funded by John D. Rockefeller, was undertaken in time for the next war, and subsequent repairs were completed in 1996. Notre-Dame was inscribed a World Heritage site in 1991.

The grace and beauty of this Gothic cathedral gives visitors the impression that it is built of light and air, rather than stone. On the exterior are elegant flying buttresses, crowned by pinnacles sheltering the guardian angels that give rise to the nickname "Cathedral of Angels." Around the chapels of the apse, a delicate openwork gallery is crowned by statues of mythical beasts. The west front is decorated with more than 2,300 statues, including the gallery of fifty-six French kings.

Inside, the cathedral is almost 460 feet (140 m) long and 125 feet (38 m) high, so the nave seems to stretch to infinity. The beautiful, twelve-petaled Great Rose Window, best seen in the evening, depicts the Virgin surrounded by the apostles and angel musicians. The cathedral is full of treasures and surprises from across the centuries: When you visit, seek out the exceptional Flamboyant Gothic organ, paintings by Tintoretto and Poussin, and the astronomical clock. A delightful twentieth-century stained-glass window, designed by Marc Chagall, adorns the axial chapel. **EH**

> *"[It] possesses a monumental character and grace inspired by the silver or goldsmith's art."*
>
> UNESCO, describing the cathedral's sculpture

🏛 ◉ Chartres Cathedral (Chartres, France)

Gothic masterpiece cherished for its stained-glass windows

Chartres Cathedral is widely acclaimed as one of the supreme examples of Gothic architecture and has exerted a considerable influence on the development of Gothic art, both within and outside France. It is renowned, in particular, for the outstanding quality of its sculpture and its stained-glass windows.

The main body of the cathedral was constructed with considerable speed. Work began on the project in 1194 and it was completed in just over twenty-five years. The building replaced an earlier Romanesque structure—itself one of a succession of churches that had existed on this site—that had been the victim of a disastrous fire. However, the west front of the earlier building, with its magnificently carved Royal Portal, and the south tower (on the right when viewed from outside) had survived the blaze and were incorporated into the new design. The second, taller tower was added much later, in the early sixteenth century.

Inside, visitors are immediately struck both by the size of the place (Chartres has the widest nave in France) and by the jewel-like beauty of its medieval stained glass. There are three rose windows, the finest of which is popularly known as "the Rose of France." Equally famous are the Blue Virgin Window close to the south door, and the Tree of Jesse, depicting Christ's descent from the house of King David.

In the Middle Ages, Chartres became a popular pilgrimage center, attracting the faithful from far and wide. Many of these pilgrims were invalids hoping for a miraculous cure. They often made use of the labyrinth (1205) outlined on the nave floor. This unusual feature is a pavement maze, 964 feet (294 m) in length. Pilgrims were expected to pass through it on their knees, while meditating and repenting their sins. This penance was regarded as the symbolic equivalent of a pilgrimage to Jerusalem. **IZ**

🏛 ◉ Palace of Versailles (near Paris, France)

Magnificent court and administrative center of French royalty

The Palace of Versailles is one of the largest, grandest, and most opulent palaces ever built. Built for France's "Sun King," Louis XIV, the vast scale of the building, the grand style of its architecture, the heroic Classical imagery used in its paintings and sculptures, and its extensive gardens were a flagrant display of the wealth and absolute power of the monarchy.

The site was originally a hunting lodge built in what was then a village in 1624 by Louis XIII. His successor, Louis XIV, expanded the lodge from 1660 onward in an effort to escape the pace of central Paris, and he went on to establish his royal court with its attendant town at Versailles in 1682. Perhaps the best known of the thousands of rooms at the palace is the *Galerie des Glaces*, or Hall of Mirrors, begun in 1678, a magnificent confection of elegant mirrors lit by superb chandeliers, reflecting a gallery of tall windows and the gardens outside. The king's move to a location

outside Paris was no mere self-indulgence. By setting up the royal court at Versailles, he gained greater control as monarch, with thousands of government officials living at the palace ready to do his bidding. More important, the greatest of the French nobility were obliged to spend time at the palace, enabling the king to keep a watchful eye on them and ensure they paid homage by observing the deliberately restrictive and often absurd rules of court etiquette. His centralization of rule spoke of his drive for absolute authority and his efforts to prevent the spawning of rival centers of power in the provinces.

The king's successors, Louis XV and Louis XVI, both inhabited the palace. The huge complex fell into disuse after the French Revolution (1789–99). Symbolizing the rule of the toppled monarchy, it was stripped of its priceless contents and left as a hollow shell when political power returned to Paris. **CK**

Château de Malmaison (near Paris, France)

Home of Napoleon and Josephine

Located just a short distance outside Paris, this splendid country retreat has two claims to fame. Historically, it is renowned for its links with Napoleon I and Josephine, its most famous owners. In addition, Malmaison is often cited as a benchmark of interior design because it originated and epitomizes the Empire style, which became characteristic of the entire Napoleonic era.

There has been a house on this site since 1244, although nothing remains of the earlier structures. The present building dates mainly from the eighteenth century. At the time of the Revolution it was owned by a wealthy banker, but in 1799 Napoleon's first wife, Josephine, purchased it from him while her husband was away on a campaign. Upon his return Napoleon engaged two young architects—Charles Percier and Pierre Fontaine—to transform the interior. In doing so, they effectively created the Empire style by

successfully combining ancient, exotic, and imperial elements. The most spectacular effect was achieved in the Tent Room, so called because it resembled the interior of a military commander's tent.

For a brief spell, the Château de Malmaison was dubbed an imperial palace and was used as the seat of government. After Napoleon's move to Saint-Cloud, however, it was mainly used by Josephine. When the couple divorced in 1809, she became its owner and lived there permanently until her death five years later. During this time, her chief delight was the garden and, more specifically, her extensive collection of roses.

The château was later owned by Josephine's grandson Napoleon III but was seriously damaged in the Franco–Prussian conflict (1870), and was briefly used as a military camp. It was finally bequeathed to the State in 1904 and became a museum two years later. It now boasts a small collection of old roses. **IZ**

Basilica of St. Denis (Paris, France)

Burial site of the kings of France

The Basilica of St. Denis has two important claims to fame. It is notable for being one of the earliest masterpieces in the Gothic style. More important, though, the site is believed to be the burial place of St. Denis, France's patron saint, who died *c.* 275. As such, it has long been a focus for French patriotism and pride.

St. Denis (or St. Dionysius) is said to have been the first bishop of Paris and to have been beheaded in the area now known as Montmartre (literally "Martyrs' Mount"). His grave became a place of pilgrimage and a succession of churches was built on the site. These included an abbey, founded by King Dagobert I *c.* 630, and a new church, commissioned by Charlemagne. The town of Saint-Denis—then a short distance north of Paris, but now part of its suburbs—grew up around the site.

The present abbey was begun by Abbot Suger, a powerful cleric who was also Regent of France when Louis VII was away on crusade. Suger's building showed early signs of the new Gothic style, particularly in its vaulting. The chief significance of the abbey, however, is that it became the resting place of the kings of France. This practice dates back as far as the sixth century and became traditional from the tenth century onward. After that, all but three of France's monarchs were interred there. Many of them are commemorated in a remarkable series of carved effigies, commissioned by Louis IX. **IZ**

"A sublime madman who dared to launch such a monument as St. Denis into the air."

Description of Abbot Suger's unnamed architect

🏛 ◉ Eiffel Tower (Paris, France)

Spectacular symbol of Paris and all things French

Designed by the man responsible for the framework of that other great feat of French engineering, the Statue of Liberty, the Eiffel Tower is one of the most famous structures in the world. Instantly recognizable, the tower is a symbol of both France and Paris, as well as an icon of elegance, simplicity, and modernity. The Banks of the Seine, from the Sully Bridge to the Eiffel Tower, and from the Place de la Concorde to the Grand and Petit Palais, were inscribed as a UNESCO World Heritage site in 1991.

Gustave Eiffel's tower takes center stage in every national celebration in France and, fittingly, it was conceived in precisely the same spirit. It was originally commissioned as the focal point of the Exposition Universelle (World Fair) of 1889. The organizers wanted something particularly spectacular because this event coincided with the centenary of the French Revolution. The tower was the ideal solution because, at the time, it was the tallest structure in the world.

The sheer modernity of the tower did not meet with everyone's approval. It was derided as "a tragic street-lamp," "a piece of gymnasium apparatus," "a skinny pyramid of iron ladders," and "an odious column of bolted metal," but, overall, its critics were outnumbered by its admirers. Even so, the tower was still scheduled to be removed when its license expired after twenty years. Ironically, it was saved by the fact that the potential demolition costs were deemed too high.

Since then, the tower has undoubtedly paid its way. It has been used as a radio transmitter since 1903 and is, of course, one of the world's most popular tourist attractions; in 2006, for example, it received more than six million visitors. It is the setting for spectacular firework displays. Other attractions include a skating rink and an interactive "labyrinth" on the first floor. **IZ**

"We protest with all our vigour and indignation against the useless and monstrous Eiffel Tower."

Public letter to a director of the 1889 World Fair

⬆ Gustave Eiffel was an engineer rather than an architect, best known for his bridges and viaducts.

➡ Eiffel's innovative use of metal arches and trusses sparked a revolution in civil engineering and design.

Arc de Triomphe (Paris, France)

Great triumphal arch of the French people that took thirty years to build

Rising up magnificently at the western end of the Avenue des Champs-Élysées, the Arc de Triomphe is one of the world's most famous monuments and a potent symbol of French national pride. Conceived by Emperor Napoleon I as a fitting expression of his imperial rule, its architect, Jean-François-Thérèse Chalgrin, modeled the arch on the triumphal arches of another great imperial age—ancient Rome. It was designed as a pivotal point in a grand city scheme that is still clear and imposing today. The Arc de Triomphe forms the center of a star of radiating avenues that connect it with historic buildings such as the Louvre.

Almost 165 feet (50 m) in height, Chalgrin's design is a milestone in the early nineteenth-century Neoclassical style, a reworking of Classical ideals that dominated public memorial design well into the twentieth century. The arch celebrates Napoleon's military victories with huge sculptural reliefs, showing

The Triumph of 1810 (by Jean-Pierre Cortot), *Resistance* (Antoine Etex), *Peace* (Etex), and, most famous of all, *La Marseillaise* (François Rude).

Today, this is the second largest triumphal arch in the world (the largest was built in North Korea in the 1980s). Traffic swirls terrifyingly around what is, in effect, the first-ever roundabout. A little museum tucked inside the arch tells its story, and a visit to the top offers breathtaking views over this beautiful capital. Beneath the arch lies the Tomb of the Unknown Soldier, commemorating the unidentified war dead of the two World Wars, where an eternal flame is rekindled daily at 6:30 P.M. The iconic status of the Arc de Triomphe is still alive and well. The Tour de France cycle race ends near here each year and the annual military parade marking July 14—known both as French National Day and Bastille Day—begins its journey at the arch. **AK**

🏛 ◈ La Conciergerie (Paris, France)

Former prison on the Île de la Cité, now a historic government building

La Conciergerie is part of the Palais de Justice in Paris, and some sections of the site remain closed to the public because they are still being used for judicial proceedings. This has been an important site since the Roman occupation of Gaul, with the seat of the Roman governors of Paris being located roughly where the Conciergerie stands today. The early French kings also based themselves here, with King Philip IV constructing the palace, of which the Conciergerie formed a part, in the late thirteenth century. The Conciergerie's name dates from this period because it was the official residence of the Comte des Cierges (Count of the Candles)—the palace superintendent in charge of taxes and lodgings.

The royal family moved to the Louvre in the 1350s and, with the palace increasingly being used as a base for the judiciary, the Conciergerie was converted into a prison in the 1390s. The building already had a

sinister reputation, thanks primarily to its torture chamber in the Bonbec Tower, before being used by the Revolutionary Tribunal during the 1790s. The original lofty ideals of the French Revolution had given way to the brutality of the Terror between 1793 and 1795, during which time the Tribunal sent around 2,600 people to the guillotine for real or trumped up crimes against the new republic. The trials were conducted in the Conciergerie's Great Hall and Marie Antoinette, Danton, and Robespierre spent their final days before execution in the cells below.

The building's oldest sections date from the thirteenth century, with the medieval Hall of the Men at Arms a particularly impressive piece of architecture at 209 feet (64 m) long, 90 feet (27 m) wide, and 28 feet (9 m) high. The Conciergerie also contains a chapel dedicated to the memory of Marie Antoinette, a fitting reminder of those claimed by the revolution. **AS**

Montparnasse Cemetery (Paris, France)

Resting place of many celebrities

Paris's Cimetière du Montparnasse is the final resting place of many of France's foremost intellectuals. In the early twentieth century Montparnasse became known as a bohemian area frequented by artists, writers, musicians, intellectuals, and the fast set of the day. The cemetery was the burial place not just of well-known French citizens, but also of a number of foreigners.

Built in 1824, and then known as Le Cimetière du Sud, or the South Cemetery, the graveyard lies in an area previously occupied by three farms. It is one of four important cemeteries built in Paris in the nineteenth century, the others being Montmartre Cemetery in the north, Père-Lachaise Cemetery in the east, and the Passy Cemetery in the present city center. Health concerns had led to a ban on the building of cemeteries in the city in 1786, so they were built outside what was then the city center.

Paris buried—and still buries—its most prestigious citizens in Montparnasse Cemetery, in stylish, ornate mausoleums. Some of the monuments are valuable artworks, too. French sculptor César Baldaccini created a bronze portrait of himself as a minotaur for his tomb, and Romanian sculptor Constantin Brancusi's Cubist stone sculpture *Le Baiser* (*The Kiss*) serves to mark the grave of Russian anarchist Tania Rachevskaïa.

The cemetery's tree-lined avenues are laid out in a grid pattern, and the rue Émile Richard divides it into two sections, known as the large and small cemeteries. Among those buried there are former Mexican president Porfirio Díaz; Spanish Surrealist painter Oscar Domínguez; Irish playwright and Francophile Samuel Beckett; avant-garde French writer, philosopher, and feminist Simone de Beauvoir; French Symbolist poet Charles Baudelaire; French author Guy de Maupassant; and French actor Philippe Noiret. **CK**

Les Invalides (Paris, France)

Military hospital and burial site

At the instigation of Louis XIV, a hospital and home was set up for old and infirm soldiers unable to look after themselves. Its original name of L'Hôpital des Invalides was subsequently shortened to Les Invalides. In keeping with most of the Sun King's projects, this was a "home" on a grand scale.

Les Invalides comprises a series of buildings and some fifteen courtyards, the largest of which was used for military parades. The original chapel—Église St. Louis des Invalides—was the work of Bruant and his successor Mansart, and within it the many enemy flags and standards captured by the French army were

> *"I wish that my ashes rest on the edges of the Seine, [with] these French people that I liked so much."*
>
> Inscription close to Napoleon's tomb

displayed. Shortly afterward, Louis XIV ordered the construction of a second, private chapel, Église du Dôme, distinguished by a magnificent dome based on St. Peter's in Rome. A large esplanade was cleared from the north of the main building to the River Seine and the Pont Alexandre III. Les Invalides became the burial place for many of France's more illustrious military leaders, including Napoleon Bonaparte.

Although assistance is still provided for a few military veterans, most of the buildings are now used to house museums. The most prominent of these is the Musée de l'Armée, which features a superb collection of uniforms, weapons, and other military artifacts from ancient times to World War II. Much space is given over to the Napoleonic Wars, as well as a fine collection of medieval armor. **AG**

Napoleon's Tomb

(Paris, France)

Fitting memorial to France's most famous soldier

The grandeur of the tomb of Napoleon Bonaparte at Les Invalides accords well with his imperial ambitions. The posthumous journey of his remains to their final resting place was a tortuous one, however, and his tomb was only completed forty years after his death. Napoleon died in exile on the island of St. Helena in 1821, six years after his final defeat at the Battle of Waterloo. He was buried on the island because the memories of his campaigns remained fresh for the British and for the new regime in France. Permission to return his remains to France was not granted until 1840, when his body was shipped back to Paris and given a state funeral. It was then placed in a temporary tomb, until Louis Visconti designed his elaborate monument in the Dôme des Invalides. This was not the site that Napoleon had wanted, but Les Invalides had been built as a home for war veterans, and the church was certainly grand enough for an emperor.

Visconti's dramatic concept was to build a crypt without a roof, so that spectators could gaze down at the pillared chamber from ground level. Like a latter-day pharaoh, Napoleon's body was placed in seven coffins, one fitting inside the next. The outermost sarcophagus is made of red porphyry, resting on a base of green granite. Encircling this, the names of his principal battles are inscribed within a laurel crown. Similarly, the twelve statues set against the columns symbolize his major campaigns. Several members of Napoleon's family, including his son, are also in this chamber, together with some of France's most distinguished military leaders. **IZ**

↗ Appropriately for the tomb of a soldier, Napoleon's is surrounded by statues representing his campaigns.

➡ *Napoleon Crossing the Alps* (detail) by Jacques-Louis David (1801) referred to his campaign of 1800.

Père Lachaise Cemetery (Paris, France)

Final resting place of Oscar Wilde and 1960s rock star Jim Morrison

The Cimetière du Père Lachaise was built in 1804 on the site of a former Jesuit retreat, and is the final resting place of many illustrious citizens as well as foreigners such as Irish writer Oscar Wilde and American rock star Jim Morrison. In the year of his coronation, Emperor Napoleon I commissioned architect Alexandre-Theodore Brongniart to design the 42-acre (17-ha) cemetery. Napoleon's actions were truly revolutionary at the time; he declared that "each citizen has the right to be buried whatever his race or his religion." Atheists, non-Christians, and those who committed suicide were previously excluded from being buried in Christian graveyards, deemed to be holy ground.

Brongniart was equally innovative in his design for the cemetery; he conceived it as a garden where visitors could walk along tree-lined avenues admiring statuary and not be distressed by the idea of death. His irregular layout for what he saw as a park shocked his contemporaries, as did his idea that death "would be tamed" by the cemetery's charming ambience.

Also known as the East Cemetery, Père Lachaise is now the largest of four cemeteries built in Paris in the nineteenth century. It has grown to occupy 109 acres (44 ha), and contains more than 300,000 graves, as well as cremated remains. Yet it was unpopular at first, due to its perceived distance from the center of Paris. In a move to encourage people to use the cemetery, the remains of poet Jean de La Fontaine and playwright and actor Molière were transferred there in 1804, followed in 1817 by those of the twelfth-century lovers Pierre Abélard and Héloïse. The plan was successful and the cemetery now houses the remains of many of France's eminent intellectuals, artists, and politicians. Their tombs have been described as "funerary art" and span several art movements, including Gothic, Art Nouveau, and Art Deco. **CK**

Opéra Garnier (Paris, France)

Grand, monumental, sumptuously decorated theater, also known as the Paris Opera

During the reign of Napoleon III, Paris was transformed into Europe's most modern city. Under the guidance of his minister, Baron Haussmann, the narrow, medieval streets were swept away to be replaced by wide boulevards and a series of high-quality public buildings. The Opéra Garnier was one of the finest of these new additions.

The competition for the prestigious commission was won by Charles Garnier, a young and relatively inexperienced architect. His bold, diamond-shaped design was thoroughly eclectic, blending Renaissance and neo-Baroque elements into what one pundit described as a "gigantic wedding-cake." The facade is adorned with statues and other decorative features, including, most famously, *The Dance*—a faintly erotic group of nude sculptures by Jean-Baptiste Carpeaux, which on its first appearance was sprayed with ink by one outraged Parisian.

Inside, the single most impressive feature is the great staircase, with its marble steps and banisters of onyx. The auditorium is scarcely less ornate. Visitors may be distracted by the sight of the massive, 6-ton chandelier, which collapsed during a public performance in 1896, or the false ceiling painted by Marc Chagall, depicting a mélange of opera scenes and local tourist spots.

Fans of musicals are equally intrigued by the basement of the building. Garnier's construction workers were hampered by the watery foundations of the site, which were prone to flooding and required continual pumping. This gave the novelist Gaston Leroux the idea for the subterranean lake that featured so heavily in his work *The Phantom of the Opera*. The phenomenal success of Andrew Lloyd Webber's musical of the same name has ensured that this interest remains as strong as ever. **IZ**

🏛 ◉ Sainte Chapelle (Paris, France)

Glorious showcase of thirteenth-century stained glass

Gothic architecture is often most notable for its size and grandeur, but Sainte Chapelle is a magnificent exception. It may be smaller than the great cathedrals of northern France, but its jewel-like perfection makes it one of the finest examples of the style. Indeed, many people would regard it as one of the nation's most beautiful buildings.

Sainte Chapelle (Holy Chapel) was commissioned by Louis IX, also known as St. Louis, who was undoubtedly France's most pious king. He went on crusades and purchased sacred relics for exorbitant prices. His chapel was specifically designed with the latter in mind. The building was constructed on two levels: The lower chapel was intended for the staff of the royal palace, whereas the upper chapel housed Louis's most precious relics—the Crown of Thorns and a fragment of the True Cross. Fittingly, this chamber resembled a shrine. There were so many windows—

illustrating more than 1,300 biblical scenes—that the walls themselves appeared to be made of glass. One of the windows shows the king receiving the relics.

Later generations did not share Louis's extreme religious fervor and, gradually, the upper chamber fell into disuse. Before the Revolution of 1789 it was used as a storehouse for grain, and afterward it was turned into a legal archive with enormous filing cabinets blocking the stained glass from view. By the nineteenth century, the chapel was in urgent need of restoration and this began in 1837, under the guidance of Eugène-Emmanuel Viollet-le-Duc. The spire, which had been removed, was rebuilt to a new design. The relics were cleared away; the Crown of Thorns is now in the Cathedral of Notre Dame, along with the organ, the altar, and other fittings. Today, the chapel is mainly used for concerts, although mass is held once a year on the feast day of St. Yves. **IZ**

🏛 ⓢ **Pont Neuf** (Paris, France)

Bridge in two spans, linking the Île de la Cité with the banks of the Seine

During the sixteenth century only two bridges crossed the River Seine in Paris; consequently in 1578 King Henri III ordered the construction of a third to ease traffic congestion. The designers he appointed were Baptiste Du Cerceau and Pierre des Illes, and there is some evidence that they made use of an earlier design by Guillaume Marchand. Progress was slow and it was only in 1607 that the bridge, the first to be constructed of stone in Paris, was finished. It was opened by Henri IV, who named it Pont Neuf (New Bridge). The Pont Neuf is the longest bridge in Paris, and it is also the city's oldest bridge still standing.

The Pont Neuf crossed at Île de la Cité—the small island in the Seine at the heart of Paris—and so comprised two separate spans, one of seven arches and the other of five, with the two sections joined by the Parc Vert-Galante on Île de la Cité. An equestrian statue of Henri IV, the "Green Gallant" king, was erected in the Vert-Galante, although this was destroyed in the French Revolution only to be replaced by a replica in 1818—the materials came from two melted-down bronzes of Napoleon. The Pont Neuf—some 760 feet (232 m) in length and 72 feet (22 m) wide—was unusual for its time in that it carried no buildings, and it had wide pavements protecting passengers from horse-drawn traffic. This helped make it a place for people to congregate, and over the years it has become a popular landmark for Parisians, featuring as a subject in paintings, literature, and movies.

The Pont Neuf underwent a major program of renovation in 1994, which was finished in 2007 in time for the 400th anniversary of the bridge's completion. While the bridge was being repaired, it was "wrapped" by the artist Christo in 1995, the whole structure being covered in sheets of a polyamide fabric. **AG**

🏛️ ⊚ Pont Alexandre III (Paris, France)

Elegant bridge epitomizing the aesthetics of the Belle Époque

Widely regarded as Paris's most beautiful bridge, the Pont Alexandre III perfectly represents the spirit of Paris's nineteenth-century rejuvenation. It connects the Hôtel des Invalides with the Grand and Petit Palais—art galleries built for the 1900 World Fair and intended as much to showcase the best of French design and engineering as they were to house fine art. The bridge is within the UNESCO World Heritage site of the Banks of the Seine.

The bridge was planned to provide a suitably attractive approach to the two galleries, and a large part of the bridge's charm comes from its extremely low profile. The designers were given specific instructions that the bridge was not to obstruct the view of either the Champs-Elysées on one bank or the Invalides on the other. Consequently, its single 350-foot (107-m) span is only 20 feet (6 m) high. The bridge can still be seen from a distance, however, thanks to the four 56-foot- (17-m-) high granite pillars at the corners, each topped with gilded statues of the winged-horse Pegasus and an allegorical figure of, alternately, Science, the Arts, Industry, and Commerce. The bridge's allegory of development and achievement is continued in the assortment of lamps, cherubs, and nymphs that adorn its two sides, which together represent France in the Middle Ages, in the Renaissance, under Louis XIV, and in the modern age.

The bridge was named after the Russian tsar Alexander III, and was intended to stand as an emblem of the friendship between Russia and France. The foundation stone was laid in 1896 by Alexander's son, Nicholas II—the last of the tsars—and the bridge was opened in time for the World Fair. Today, the bridge still retains the optimistic, aesthetic spirit of the Belle Époque—an age in which civic development could be as beautiful as it was practical. **AS**

Panthéon (Paris, France)

Mausoleum of some of France's greatest thinkers

The Revolution of 1789 tore apart the fabric of French society, transforming it at every level. The early history of the Panthéon provides a telling illustration of this. It was originally designed to glorify the role of the monarchy and the Catholic Church, but it was put to very different uses by the new regime.

The initial idea for the building came from Louis XV. When he was struck down with a serious illness in 1744, he decided that if he recovered he would give thanks by building a new church in honor of St. Genevieve, the patron saint of Paris. The commission for this was eventually awarded in 1755 to Louis's official architect, Jacques-Germain Soufflot. Soufflot had studied extensively in Italy and used this knowledge to produce an ambitious, Neoclassical design. In essence, this took the form of a building in the shape of a Greek cross, with a huge dome supported by massive Corinthian pillars.

Work began in 1758, but the project was hampered by the Crown's financial problems and progress was very slow. In the end, it was only completed in 1791, after Soufflot's death. The timing could hardly have been worse because the Revolutionary authorities had no interest in a new church. They decided to secularize the building and turn it into a mausoleum for France's national heroes. At the same time, it was renamed the Panthéon (a temple to all the gods), after the Classical rotunda in Rome that was built between 118 and 128.

The task of secularization was entrusted to Soufflot's pupil, Jean-Baptiste Rondelet, who blocked up the windows and gave the place a more funerary character. Since then, the Panthéon has become the final resting place for many celebrities—among them Voltaire, Rousseau, Victor Hugo, Émile Zola, Pierre and Marie Curie, and André Malraux. **IZ**

Victor Hugo's House (Paris, France)

Home of the writer and location of his salon of artists, politicians, and high society

Few writers have become as closely associated with Paris as Victor-Marie Hugo (1802–85). Although born in Besançon, he lived for many years in one of the most historic quarters of the capital, absorbing its spirit and character. This is reflected in two of his most famous works, *Notre-Dame de Paris* (*The Hunchback of Notre-Dame*, 1831) and *Les Misérables* (1862). His principal home is now a museum, dedicated to his life.

From 1832 to 1848, Hugo rented an apartment in the Place des Vosges. Originally called the Place Royale, this elegant square was commissioned by King Henri IV who had intended to live there himself but was assassinated before the project was completed. Hugo's apartment was in the Hôtel de Rohan-Guéménée (in France, the term *hôtel* refers to a large, private residence), named after one of the building's former owners, Louis de Rohan, Prince of Guéménée.

Hugo's home swiftly became a favorite meeting place for writers and artists. Alexandre Dumas, Charles Dickens, and Franz Liszt were all visitors there. Hugo also entertained a string of female admirers who were admitted discreetly by a small, secret stairway; his long-term mistress, Juliette Drouet, was installed in a nearby apartment. The author's stay in the house was cut short during the 1848 Revolution when rioters broke in, prompting him to move to a safer area.

Hugo's house remained in private hands until 1873, when it was acquired by the City of Paris. For a time it was used as a primary school until, in 1903, it was finally opened to the public. The museum covers the full range of Hugo's work, including his mysterious drawings and his very strange furniture designs. **IZ**

◤ This portrait of Victor Hugo in middle age is an exhibit of the Maison de Victor Hugo museum.

◄ Hugo lived with his family in the Place des Vosges for twenty-six years; his mistress lived nearby.

Cathedral of Notre-Dame de Paris (Paris, France)

One of the greatest cathedrals in France and scene of national ceremonies

The Gothic cathedral of Notre-Dame de Paris is situated on the Île de la Cité in the French capital. The Roman Catholic cathedral is France's leading place of Christian worship, and ceremonies such as funeral services for heads of state are held there. The cathedral is a landmark familiar all over the world, partly thanks to the 1831 novel by French author Victor Hugo, *The Hunchback of Notre-Dame.* Hugo wrote the story to raise awareness of the church, which at that time was in disrepair and threatened with demolition. He was successful, a campaign to save the cathedral ensued, and restoration works commenced in 1845.

The cathedral's site was originally that of a Gallic Roman temple to the god Jupiter, and later Paris's first Christian church, Saint-Étienne Basilica. Work began in 1163 under the supervision of the Bishop of Paris, Maurice de Sully, who had the old church torn down. Building was completed in 1345 and various amendments were made over the centuries. From its inception, the church was used by French royalty for religious services and to mark victory celebrations. Even after the storming of the Bastille in 1789, the revolutionaries had a *Te Deum* sung in the cathedral. However, by 1793 Notre-Dame's past associations were frowned upon; many of its statues and artworks were destroyed, religious artifacts were melted down, and the cathedral was used as a warehouse for food. Although Notre-Dame was reconsecrated as a church in 1801, when Napoleon was crowned emperor of the French at a ceremony held there in 1804, its state had become so shoddy that draperies were used to conceal its poor condition. **CK**

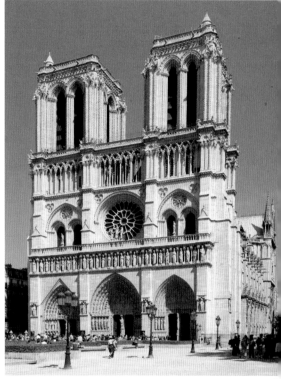

⊿ Work on the towers proceeded in fitful bursts, leading to a blend of styles from bottom to top.

▣ Many of the original chimeras (ornamental gargoyles) were replaced during Viollet-le-Duc's 1845 restoration.

◎ # Château de Fontainebleau

(near Paris, France)

Grandest and most famous of France's royal palaces before Versailles

> *"Continue to serve France; its happiness has been my only thought."*

Napoleon's farewell at the Cour des Adieux

Before the creation of the Palace of Versailles, the Château of Fontainebleau was the grandest and most famous of France's royal palaces. It was built on such a lavish scale, using an international team of artists, that it gave rise to an entirely new style of design—the School of Fontainebleau. The palace and park at Fontainebleau are inscribed as a UNESCO World Heritage site.

The château lies about 40 miles (64 km) to the southeast of Paris. The Forest of Fontainebleau surrounding it was a favorite hunting ground for the cream of French society. Indeed, the château was built on a site previously occupied by an old hunting lodge. In 1528, François I decided to replace the lodge with a palatial country residence. The immense scale of the project stemmed from his desire to increase the prestige of the French monarchy by emulating the princely courts of Renaissance Italy. In order to achieve this status, he imported some of the finest talent from abroad. Sebastiano Serlio advised on the architecture and designed the ballroom, while Rosso Fiorentino and Francesco Primaticcio carried out the decoration in the most spectacular part of the new château—the gallery. Here, the combination of large, elegant murals with elaborate, ornamental stucco pioneered the School of Fontainebleau style.

Fontainebleau remained a favorite residence with later monarchs, many of whom added to its splendor. During the reign of Henri IV, for example, a Second School of Fontainebleau was established. In common with other royal properties, the château suffered during the Revolution, when many of its contents were sold off. However, Napoleon was fond of the place and restored it to its former glory. He signed his first abdication here and took leave of his army in the courtyard (now known as the Cour des Adieux). **IZ**

Château de Vaux-le-Vicomte (Maincy, France)

Prototype of the magnificence of Versailles

The Château of Vaux-le-Vicomte was one of the most influential buildings of its time. It was a precursor of the grandiose architectural style of Louis XIV's France. Vaux-le-Vicomte was the first large-scale collaboration of the architect Louis le Vau, the landscape gardener André le Nôtre, and the painter-decorator Charles le Brun. The three men would later work together to create the ultimate expression of the magnificence of this style, the Palace of Versailles.

Vaux-le-Vicomte was built for Nicolas Fouquet, the superintendent of finances and one of the wealthiest and most powerful men in France. Fouquet had purchased the site for the château in 1641, and by the time Vaux-le-Vicomte was completed in 1661, Fouquet's household was a great focus of French culture and society. The house chef was the great François Vatel, inventor of the Chantilly cream, and the playwright Molière was also a close associate of Fouquet's. Vaux-le-Vicomte became famous for its lavish spectacles. This opulence was not to last. Louis XIV, falsely believing Fouquet's luxurious lifestyle to be funded by embezzled government money, ordered his arrest after a particularly grand fête in 1661. Fouquet was tried and imprisoned for life. After this, Vaux-le-Vicomte passed through a number of owners, eventually falling into disrepair and neglect, until it was rescued by the Sommier family, who purchased it in 1875 and restored it to its former glory.

Vaux-le-Vicomte is a major example of the flowering of French architecture under Louis XIV and, accordingly, it was made a *monument historique* by the French government in 1965. Fouquet, although he enjoyed Vaux-le-Vicomte only for a short time before his fall from power, had helped to create a style where buildings, interiors, and landscape worked together to form a majestic and unified complex. **JF**

Verdun Forts Circuit (Verdun, France)

Germany's attempt to "bleed France white"

If, as Wilfred Owen wrote, World War I exposed as a lie the traditional view that it is a "sweet and honorable thing to die for your country," the battle of Verdun marked the sourest and most dishonorable point in the war. The battle, which began in February 1916, lasted for eleven months and resulted in the deaths of almost a million soldiers.

Before World War I, Verdun in northeastern France was the strongest point in the country, surrounded by a string of mighty forts. The city was a natural target for the Kaiser's armies. Knowing that the French would do all they could to defend their historic forts, the

> *"No battle approach[ed the] duration, artillery fire, and awful sacrifice than the battle [at] Verdun."*
>
> Kelly Miller, sociologist and essayist

Germans poured hundreds and thousands of men into their attack. From February to July 1916, the French were pushed back in some of the bloodiest fighting the war was to see. The other Allies, seeing the trouble the French were in, attacked at the Somme, partly to take German troops away from Verdun. From then on the German forces were stretched and General Pétain and his men were able to recapture the forts from the Germans.

Douaumont and Vaux, two of the main forts, are preserved and may be visited today, as well as tunnels and galleries of the underground citadel. French and German cemeteries and memorials are everywhere on the Verdun battlefield. The Douaumont Ossuary contains the remains of many thousands of soldiers; more remains are found and added every year. **OR**

⛪ ◉ Hôtel de Ville (Nancy, France)

Center of a pioneering example of Baroque town planning

The Hôtel de Ville (town hall) of Nancy in the French province of Lorraine is the centerpiece of an architectural ensemble created around a large square. The square was commissioned by Stanisław Leszczyński, twice former king of Poland, who became the Duke of Lorraine from 1736.

Stanisław arrived in France after losing the crown of Poland to Augustus III. His daughter Maria had married Louis XV in 1725, and the square was designed as a monument to his son-in-law. It was constructed from 1752 to 1755. The square was created to join the medieval part of Nancy to the new town, built in the early seventeenth century, and linked two existing buildings, the Hôtel de Ville and the Hôtel de Gouvernement (seat of regional government). The square is actually rectangular in shape, 410 feet (125 m) by 348 feet (106 m), paved in light ocher stone with two lines of darker stone forming a diagonal cross. The

Hôtel de Ville is located on the south side of the square, facing an Arc de Triomphe. On the east side there is an opera house and on the west side the Museum of Fine Arts (originally a college of medicine). There are also ornamental fountains in the northwest and northeast corners designed by Barthélémy Guibal. The square was first named the Place Royale, but was renamed the Place du Peuple during the Revolution and then the Place Napoleon. In 1831 it was finally renamed the Place Stanislas, and a statue of its creator was placed in the middle of the square.

The complex forms part of a UNESCO World Heritage site that comprises three historic squares in Nancy. The Place Stanislas was restored between 2004 and 2005 in time for its two hundred and fiftieth anniversary. The Hôtel de Ville of Nancy is a centerpiece of one of the finest examples of Baroque town planning in Europe. **JF**

Maginot Line Forts (near Wissembourg, France)

Defensive fortifications on France's border with Germany

In the hope of reducing the massive losses endured by France during World War I, French military thinkers sought defensive solutions to the challenges of modern warfare. After much debate in the 1920s, it was decided to build a defensive shield along France's border with Germany, the barrier taking its name from the then minister of war, André Maginot. Work started in 1930 and the line was broadly complete by 1940, just as the Germans launched their invasion of France.

Despite its name, the Maginot Line was not a simple linear defense but instead consisted of an interlinked series of fortified positions, whose powerful array of artillery and machine guns would bring any German attack to a standstill. The distinguishing feature of the fortifications was their subterranean nature; vast underground complexes housing men, weapons, and machinery were excavated to depths of up to 100 feet (29 m), with only concrete emplacements visible to the enemy. Certain defensive positions, such as Ouvrage Schoenenbourg in Alsace, supported the system. Schoenenbourg was a self-contained underground fortress with its own electrical generator, water tanks, kitchens, and medical facilities. A network of galleries stretching 1.8 miles (3 km) connected the subterranean infantry barracks with the frontline gun emplacements that contained heavy artillery, mortars, and machine guns.

In the event, the Maginot Line repulsed the German assaults of 1940, but unfortunately for the French the main German thrust came through the undefended Belgian Ardennes region, which the French had thought impassable to tanks. Consequently, the entire system was outflanked by the Germans. Although left to decay after the war, some Maginot Line forts, such as Schoenenbourg, have been reopened to the public in recent years. **AG**

🏛 ⬡ Cathedral of Notre-Dame (Strasbourg, France)

Tallest building in the world for more than 200 years

Victor Hugo once described Strasbourg's Notre-Dame Cathedral as a "gigantic and delicate marvel." Built on the site of several earlier churches, the cathedral was constructed between *c.* 1225 and 1439, becoming a Protestant cathedral in 1521 when the Reformation swept through Germany, and returning to the Roman Catholic faith when Strasbourg was brought within France in 1681. The structure varies in style from the Romanesque sections around the choir and south portal through to the High Gothic of the imposing west front—an architectural progression hastened by the introduction in 1225 of a team of innovative architects and masons who had recently gained experience working on the Gothic masterpiece of Chartres Cathedral in northwest France.

Although the cathedral is particularly notable for its stained glass, its High Gothic baptistery, and the literally thousands of sculptures decorating the west front, what is most overwhelming about the building is its sheer size; at 466 feet (142 m) high, the cathedral was the tallest building in the world from 1625 to 1847. The single North Tower commands a view of the Rhine as it flows from the Vosges Mountains, 12.5 miles (20 km) to the east of the city, to the Black Forest, 15.5 miles (25 km) to the west.

The cathedral is also famous for its astronomical clock, which marks not only the time but also the movement of the planets and the zodiac. The clock on display in the cathedral today dates only from the nineteenth century, although much older versions can be seen in the Strasbourg Museum of Decorative Art. The clock, in addition to performing its traditional functions, operates a series of automated figures that are activated every day at 12:30 P.M., including a procession of the ages of man walking past Death, and a procession of the apostles past Christ. **AS**

🏛 ◎ **Palais de Rohan** (Strasbourg, France)

Fortified residence of the Rohan bishops of Strasbourg

The Soubise branch of the Rohan family filled the office of the bishop of Strasbourg for much of the eighteenth century, occupying the seat of the Palais de Rohan for nearly one hundred years, from 1704 to 1803. The Rohan family was also heavily involved in French politics and government, and was one of the most influential in the kingdom.

The family descends from the historic rulers of the duchy of Brittany. Their residence in Strasbourg was designed by the prominent French architect Robert de Cotte. The first Rohan bishop of Strasbourg was Armand Gaston Maximilien de Rohan, who commissioned the construction of the Palais de Rohan. The most famous member of the family was Cardinal Louis René Édouard de Rohan, who became bishop in 1779. Obliged to leave his lavish residence in Strasbourg, Cardinal de Rohan spent most of his time at the royal court in Versailles. He was expelled from court in 1786 after a scandal involving Queen Marie Antoinette, and he eventually returned to Strasbourg. However, after the Revolution he was again forced to move, and he emigrated to Germany in 1791.

The Palais de Rohan now contains three museums: the Musée des Arts Décoratifs, which contains a replica of the apartments occupied by the cardinal; the Musée Archeologique, which details the history of the region and contains artifacts excavated from nearby sites; and the Musée des Beaux Arts, which contains numerous important paintings, including works by Botticelli, Rubens, Rembrandt, Van Dyck, El Greco, Goya, Watteau, Renoir, and Monet.

The Rohans were perhaps the last of the great prince bishop families in European history. They wielded both secular and ecclesiastical influence, and their monumental residence in Strasbourg is a symbol of their power and wealth. **JF**

Standing Stones

(Carnac, France)

Parallel rows of stones, thought to define the routes of prehistoric funeral processions

> *"How it is that the Romans came and disappeared, whilst the race of the rude constructors remains?"*
>
> James Miln, nineteenth-century antiquarian

Clustered around the town of Carnac, in southern Brittany, is the richest concentration of prehistoric monuments in Europe. The area is remarkable not just for the sheer quantity of material—it contains more than 3,000 standing stones—but also for its variety. There are alignments (rows of stones), passage-graves, tumuli (mounds), dolmens (chamber tombs), and decorated stones. Most date back to the late Neolithic era, from *c.* 4,500 B.C.E.

The most striking monuments are the alignments, which are composed of parallel rows of stones. Some of these are very extensive—the alignment of Kermario, for instance, consists of 1,019 stones laid out over a distance of more than 3,000 feet (900 m). There are many legends about the origins of the alignments, but the most popular one describes them as a petrified army of Roman soldiers, turned to stone by a local holy man, St. Kornély (a largely mythical figure). However, their real origins and original purpose are hard to determine. Some archeologists regard them as a kind of open-air calendar, based on astronomical observations. The problem with this idea is that the rows are not entirely straight, and new stones appear to have been added at different periods. More feasible, perhaps, is the theory that the alignments were designed as processional ways, linked with burial rituals. This notion is supported by the fact that the ancient names of two of the principal alignments have strong, funerary associations. Kermario and Kerlescan mean, respectively, "House of the Dead" and "House of Burning."

Carnac has had to confront the problem of conservation. The main alignments have been fenced off and visitors are encouraged to make use of viewing platforms. However, megaliths are so common in this area that many are still easily accessible. **IZ**

Château des Rochers-Sevigné (Vitré, France)

Breton residence of Madame de Sévigné

The Château des Rochers-Sevigné cannot compare with the great châteaux of the Loire, either in terms of size or architectural excellence. Despite its round tower and tall, conical, slate roofs it is closer to a manor house than a grand stately home or a castle, and its charms are homely rather than princely. Instead, it owes its special magic to a long association with one of France's greatest literary figures. Marie de Rabutin-Chantal—better known as Madame de Sévigné (1626–96)—found lasting fame in recognition of her witty and intelligent letters. These works provide a colorful record of French society during a glorious period in the nation's history.

Les Rochers (the Rocks) lies a few miles south of Vitré, in eastern Brittany. Marie's connection with the place began in 1644, when she married the Marquis de Sévigné. His family owned an estate there that dated back to the fourteenth century, although the château itself was largely rebuilt in the seventeenth century. It was not his permanent home but a country retreat, away from the cares of court. The couple's marriage was relatively short-lived. The marquis was killed in a duel in 1651, leaving Marie a widow at the age of twenty-five. She never married again, but visited the château frequently between 1654 and 1690, writing more than 250 of her letters there.

Sévigné is most closely associated with the Cabinet Vert (Green Room), where she always stayed during her visits. The unusual octagonal chapel was built by her uncle, the Abbé de Coulanges, although her real pride and joy were the gardens. These were designed by the renowned André Le Nôtre, who also created the gardens at Versailles, Vaux-le-Vicomte, and Fontainebleau, and Marie herself planted many of the flowers. The château is still owned by her descendants, and parts of it are open to the public. **IZ**

Fort National (St. Malo, France)

Built by Louis XIV to protect his privateers

With its ramparts, forts, towers, and castle, St. Malo in Brittany was one of France's most heavily defended ports. The Fort National stands out among all the military emplacements, partly because it was designed by Marshal Vauban, France's greatest military engineer, but also because it is one of the few historic buildings to have survived relatively intact.

The Fort National was completed in 1689 on a tiny, rocky island, close to the shore. It can be reached by foot at low tide, but is otherwise cut off from the beach. It was built on the orders of Louis XIV, and designed by Vauban. The work was carried out by

> *"It is impossible to have more regard, esteem and friendship than that I have for you."*
>
> King Louis XIV in a letter to Marshal Vauban

Siméon Garengeau, with granite imported from the nearby islands of Chausey. The decision to build a fort was understandable. St. Malo was a well-known haven for privateers (semilegal pirates) and, as such, was often targeted by the victims of their activities. In 1817, the privateer, Robert Surcouf, fought a famous duel outside the walls of the fort, killing eleven Prussian officers, and leaving a twelfth to tell the tale.

St. Malo was heavily bombed in World War II, but its darkest hour came in August 1944 when 380 citizens were imprisoned in the fort by German soldiers. They were left without food for six days while much of the town was destroyed, and eighteen of the prisoners died. Today the fort is a popular tourist site and celebrations to commemorate the tercentenary of Vauban's death were held in 2007. **IZ**

Cathedral of St. Peter and St. Paul (Troyes, France)

One of the most beautiful Gothic cathedrals in France, famed for its stained glass

Troyes's Cathedral of St. Peter and St. Paul is one of the most impressive Gothic cathedrals in France. It is thought that there has been a church of some kind on this site since the fifth century, and a cathedral was built soon after the counts of Champagne chose Troyes as their capital at the end of the ninth century.

The current structure was begun around 1200—the previous cathedrals had been badly damaged by Viking invaders and by fire. Work continued haphazardly over the course of the next 450 years, with the two transepts completed by the beginning of the fourteenth century, the main nave and its four supplementary ones finished toward the end of the fifteenth century, and the extravagant west facade built at the beginning of the sixteenth century by the well-known architect Martin Chambiges.

The bell tower of St. Peter was finished in 1647, but the bell tower of St. Paul was abandoned in 1545, giving the cathedral its distinctive lopsided appearance. The cathedral is built in the Gothic style—an influence particularly apparent in the 93.5-foot- (28.5-m-) high nave and in Chambiges's sculpture on the facade.

The most impressive feature of the cathedral, however, is its use of stained glass. There are almost 5,000 square feet (465 sq m) of stained glass throughout the building, including the magnificent Assumption window (1523–24), the Immaculate Conception (1634), and the Mystical Winepress (1636).

Perhaps the beauty of the windows is to be expected, considering the Champagne region has boasted a reputation for its stained glass since the end of the fifteenth century. Indeed, the local *département* (county) is reputed to have the highest concentration of stained glass in the whole of France with around 29,500 square feet (2740 sq m) in total—some of it dating back to the thirteenth century. **AS**

> *"[On] my architectural excursions ... I found myself in ... this great edifice, one of the finest in Europe."*
>
> Andrew Dickson White, antiquarian, 1905

Ducal Palace of Brittany (Nantes, France)

Home of the dukes of Brittany, from the tenth until the seventeenth century

As its name reveals, this imposing structure was once the official residence of the dukes of Brittany. As such, it had to fulfill a number of different functions: It was a military stronghold and seat of government, as well as a palatial home. These varying needs have left their mark on the architecture of the building, which combines a stark, forbidding facade with a highly elegant interior.

The first defenses on this site were erected after 937, when Alain Barbe-Torte became duke and chose Nantes as his capital. A more substantial castle was begun in 1207, from which only a single tower survives—still known rather confusingly as the "New Tower." At this stage, the military strength of the building remained an important consideration, as the permanent union of Brittany and France did not take place until 1532.

The ducal residence was also used as a prison, with its most notorious inmate being Gilles de Rais, who was condemned for the ritual murders of scores of young children. He was confined at the castle before his execution in 1440. In 1466, Duke François II embarked upon the rebuilding of the castle, a task that was continued by his daughter, Anne of Brittany, one of the castle's most famous residents. In the seventeenth century, the castle became the property of the French royal family.

In the eighteenth century, the building was turned into a garrison. During this period it suffered its most serious damage, when the powder magazine exploded and destroyed one of the towers. The army remained at this site until 1915, when ownership passed to the municipal authorities. For many years the castle housed three small museums, but these have now been amalgamated and, after an extensive fifteen-year restoration program, the castle reopened to the public in February 2007. **IZ**

"Nantes . . . has rather a grand, or at least an eminently well-established, air."

Henry James, *A Little Tour in France* (1884)

🏛 Ⓤ Cathedral of St. Etienne (Bourges, France)

One of the finest examples of Gothic architecture in France

From the mid-twelfth century onward, Europe was caught up in a feverish passion for church building. This was most evident in France, driven by the creation of a new architectural style; the loftier and more graceful appearance of Gothic designs were preferable to the ponderous solidity of the old Romanesque approach. The Cathedral of St. Etienne in Bourges was built when Gothic architecture was reaching maturity and is widely regarded as one of the finest examples of the style.

The existing structure dates from 1195, when Archbishop Henri de Sully decided to build a new cathedral to rival those in the north. His immediate model appears to have been Notre-Dame in Paris. There had been several earlier churches built on his chosen site, the most recent being a Romanesque cathedral deemed too small to reflect the growing wealth and importance of Bourges. Sully died in 1199,

but his successor, Archbishop Guillaume de Dangeon, persisted with the project on the same, ambitious scale. Unwittingly, he also helped to finance the scheme; his canonization, shortly after his death in 1209, resulted in a huge increase in donations.

The bullet-shaped design of the church is unique—it has five aisles, but no transept. The weight of the building is borne on two rows of flying buttresses, one of the great innovations of the Gothic style, yet the size of the towers still caused problems. The south tower—nicknamed the "Mute Tower" because it has no bells—had to be supported by a stone pillar taken from an old prison, and sadly the north tower collapsed in 1506. Despite this, the cathedral is remarkable for the grandeur and unity of its design, for the outstanding quality of its stained-glass windows, and for the carved biblical scenes above its doorways. **IZ**

Château de Chenonceau (Chenonceaux, France)

The most beautiful of all the Loire Valley châteaux

During the Renaissance, a new type of architecture emerged in France. Wealthy aristocrats chose to live on large country estates, in buildings that combined some of the military features of a castle with the elegance and luxury of a palatial mansion. The favorite location for these châteaux was the Loire Valley, not too far from the center of power in Paris, but still far enough away from the city to be a genuine retreat. Chenonceau is widely regarded as the most beautiful of these châteaux.

The main body of the building was constructed on the foundations of an old mill. It was commissioned in 1515 by Thomas Bohier, an inspector of the royal finances. He was frequently absent, carrying out his duties, so the majority of the work was supervised by his wife, Katherine. Chenonceau passed to the Crown in 1535 and, twelve years later, Henri II gave it to his mistress, Diane de Poitiers. She added the arched bridge across the River Cher but, before her plans were completed, Henri died and his widow, Catherine de' Medici, claimed the château for herself. She commissioned the magnificent long gallery on top of the bridge, and staged lavish spectacles in the grounds. These included mock battles, theatrical displays, and fountains of wine. In the eighteenth century, parties of a more sober kind were held by the new mistress, heiress Louise Dupin. Her guests included the philosophers Jean-Jacques Rousseau and Voltaire.

The long tradition of female ownership has inspired *The Ladies of Chenonceau*, a popular son et lumière that is regularly performed at the château. Since 1913, the château has been owned by the Meniers, a famous family of chocolate makers. During World War I they allowed the building to be used as a makeshift hospital. **IZ**

A royal residence and the final home of the great artist Leonardo da Vinci

Le Clos Lucé is situated in the picturesque town of Amboise on the banks of the Loire; it stands 1,600 feet (500 m) from the regal Château d'Amboise. Le Clos Lucé was the home of Leonardo da Vinci (1452–1519) for the last three years of his life.

King Charles VII took control of Château d'Amboise in 1434 and King Charles VIII acquired Le Clos Lucé in 1490. The two royal buildings are allegedly connected by an underground passage. In 1516, King Francis I brought Leonardo da Vinci to Amboise. Francis was well known as a patron of the arts and, encouraged by his sister Marguerite de Navarre, he had turned Le Clos Lucé into a refuge for artists.

Francis had first met Da Vinci in 1515 when the artist had been commissioned to construct a mechanical lion to serve as the centerpiece at peace talks with Pope Leo X. Da Vinci was subsequently invited to the royal residence, and was granted a generous pension. He arrived at his new home with three paintings, including his most well-known work, *Mona Lisa*. Francis grew very close to Da Vinci, and reputedly referred to him as "my father." Da Vinci died in the house, and was buried in a chapel at the Château d'Amboise.

Le Clos Lucé now houses a museum that reflects the rich history of the region and its association with Leonardo da Vinci. It contains several models of machines designed by the artist, and three frescoes that may have been supervised by him. Le Clos Lucé is not only a delightful Renaissance mansion, but also the final home of perhaps the greatest figure of the era—an incomparable artist and a genius. **JF**

◹ A posthumous portrait of Da Vinci completed in 1789 by the renowned Italian engraver Carlo Lasinio.

◸ Da Vinci spent the last three years of his life in Le Clos Lucé and was buried nearby.

Vézelay Abbey (Vézelay, France)

Burgundy's most spectacular church and formerly a famed place of pilgrimage

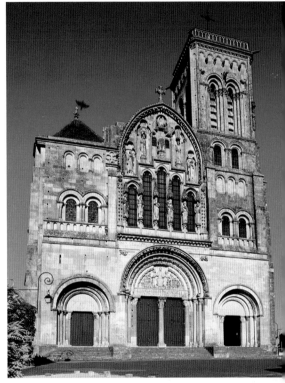

Perched on top of a hill, with a commanding view of the surrounding countryside, is the abbey church of La Madeleine in Vézelay. In architectural terms, it is a gem, perhaps the finest building in Burgundy.

The church at Vézelay was founded in the late ninth century, on the ancient site of a former Roman villa. The church's importance grew during the early eleventh century with the story that Mary Magdalene had spent her final days living as a hermit in Provence, and that her bones had been subsequently brought to Vézelay by a monk. The claim was recognized in a papal letter of 1058 and the church's fortune was assured. It became a place of pilgrimage, and a focus for major religious and political events. Pilgrims, kings, and archbishops flocked to the church. St. Bernard launched the Second Crusade from its pulpit in 1146, and Thomas Becket preached a key sermon there in 1166, threatening Henry II with excommunication.

With its rising reputation, Vézelay needed to expand and Abbot Artaud began the present building in 1096. The cost was prohibitive, however, and the hardship and poverty this created caused furious locals to riot and murder the abbot. The building work was completed, but the abbey's success was short-lived. Ownership of the true relics of Mary Magdalene was disputed and, in 1295, the pope ruled in favor of a rival church. This ushered in a long, slow decline and, when architect Eugène Viollet-le-Duc came to restore the building in the 1830s, it was little more than a shell. Today, Vézelay is considered one of the finest examples of Romanesque architecture, particularly noted for its superb sculptures. **IZ**

↗ Neglect and damage inflicted during the French Revolution brought Vézelay Abbey near to collapse.

➡ The central tympanum of the abbey's narthex (lobby) is thought to represent Christ flanked by his disciples.

Cluny Abbey

(Cluny, France)

The haunting remains of what was once the largest church in the world

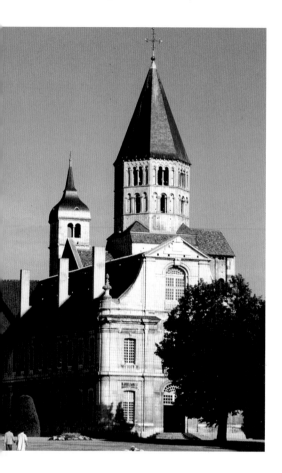

"Cluny no longer echo[es] to the music of psalms and the old abbots lie in nameless graves."

New York Times Magazine, March 4, 1928

A tour around the ruins of Cluny Abbey can be a chastening experience. Looking over the scant remains, it is hard to believe that this church was once the largest in Christendom, and the power and influence of its abbots was second only to the Pope.

Cluny was founded in 910, when the Duke of Aquitaine donated the land surrounding his old hunting lodge for a new Benedictine monastery. The terms of his gift were important: Patrons normally retained some control over the appointment of the abbot—usually so that they could install their own relatives—but the duke's gift had no such strings. The abbots used this independence to retain a firm grip over their own subsidiary houses, structuring the order as a federation. Thus, when the Cluniacs reached the peak of their power, the abbot was effectively the head of around 1,200 monasteries and 10,000 monks. Their organization extended beyond France and included priories in Germany, England, and Spain.

As Cluny's power grew, so too did the size of its church. The original building was replaced in 955, and the last and grandest of the structures was begun by Hugues de Semur (later St. Hugh) *c.* 1088. Eventually, Cluny became a victim of its own success. As it became a bastion of wealth and privilege, the more austere Cistercians took the lead as reformers. Cluny itself was increasingly seen as part of the establishment and, as such, it became an obvious target at the time of the Revolution. The order was suppressed in 1790 and the building was largely demolished. For a time, the remains were used as a stone quarry—it is estimated that 90 percent of the abbey was destroyed. The surviving fragments include a bell tower, a granary, and the stables; smaller items can be seen in the local museum. In recent decades, some restoration work has been carried out. **IZ**

Ducal Palace of Burgundy

(Dijon, France)

Grand palace built by Philip the Good in the fourteenth century

Dijon has been the political center of the Burgundy region ever since the dukes of Burgundy moved their capital here from Beaune in the fourteenth century. At the heart of the city lies the Ducal Palace—a structure that has undergone several phases of reconstruction since the first Duke of Valois, also known as Philip the Good, began building the original palace on the site of an old Roman fortification in 1366.

Notorious for handing over Joan of Arc to the English—and execution—in exchange for 100,000 gold pieces, Philip built a palace that was more a compound than a single structure, with central apartments and reception rooms surrounded by various outer buildings. This loose collection of buildings was extended by successive dukes during the fifteenth century, radiating outward from the cavernous kitchens and the Tour Philippe-le-Bon—a 150-foot- (46-m-) high tower that offers stunning views across Dijon toward the Alps. By the seventeenth century, the palace had become the residence of the governors of Burgundy and the demands placed on the complex, by its new political status as the center of the Burgundian government, led to another period of construction. This organized the palace around a single structure, rebuilding it in the Neoclassical style in which it appears today.

The palace is now home to the city's Musée des Beaux Arts, including a collection of French and Flemish art, begun by the dukes to showcase the artworks collected from their former territories in Flanders and the Netherlands. The museum also houses works by Titian, Rubens, Monet, and Manet, and is well worth visiting for the extravagant tombs of leading Burgundians in the Salle des Gardes (Guard Room)—a grand hall that bears witness to the former power of the city and its leaders. **AS**

> *"The whole history of the house of Burgundy is like an epic of overweening and heroic pride."*
>
> Johan Huizinga, historian

Hôtel-Dieu (Beaune, France)

Charitable hospital set up after the One Hundred Years' War

Few hospitals have the charm of Beaune's Hôtel-Dieu and fewer still have its staying power. This remarkable institution admitted its first patient on New Year's Day, 1452, and signed out its last in 1971. It is now a museum, paying tribute to more than 500 years of medical care.

The Hôtel-Dieu was founded in 1443 by Nicolas Rolin, the powerful chancellor of the dukes of Burgundy, and his wife, Guigone de Salins, to minister to the poor. The hospital's exterior is quite plain, but the cobbled, inner courtyard is delightful. The half-timbered structure is adorned with a fine display of polychrome tiles, formed into geometric patterns, and a series of gables topped with slender pinnacles. The long, covered gallery is a practical feature, enabling the nuns to get about in bad weather, moving between the sickrooms, which were accessible only from outside. The main chamber is the Grande Salle

des Pôvres (Paupers' Ward), which boasts an ornate timber ceiling. In this ward, the beds were arranged to face the altar at the end of the room, so that patients could participate in the services. There was also a smaller ward for wealthier patients (the Salle St-Hugues), and today's visitors can admire the well-preserved kitchen and pharmacy.

For most modern-day visitors, the highlight of a visit to the Hôtel-Dieu will be the Salle St-Louis, which houses Beaune's greatest treasure—a huge altarpiece of *The Last Judgment* (1446–52) by Rogier van der Weyden. A magnifying glass is thoughtfully provided so that tourists can examine the torments of the damned in fine detail.

Today, the site is run by a charitable organization, the Hospices de Beaune. Its principal fund-raising event is an annual wine auction—a reminder that Beaune is the capital of Burgundy's wine region. **IZ**

Chapel of Notre-Dame du Haut (Ronchamp, France)

Le Corbusier's masterpiece of religious architecture

Born in Switzerland, Le Corbusier (real name Charles-Edouard Jeanneret) was one of the giants of twentieth-century architecture, and the Chapel of Notre-Dame du Haut is widely regarded as his masterpiece. Le Corbusier was a pioneer of the machine age, but he also drew inspiration from natural, organic forms. The latter influence became more pronounced after World War II, when the destructive potential of machines had become all too apparent.

This chapel—its roof inspired by a crab shell—is at the top of a hill. The previous church was destroyed in the war and Le Corbusier was commissioned to replace it. As a place of pilgrimage, the chapel occasionally has extremely large congregations. Le Corbusier addressed this by adding an external pulpit and altar for open-air services. Above these, encased in glass, is a statue of the Virgin, rescued from the original church. The chapel's design is asymmetric so that, rather like a sculpture, its appearance changes as the viewer walks around it. The outlines of the outer walls and roof curve and undulate; the chapel's three towers resemble extended ventilation shafts; and, inside, the floor slopes downward toward the altar. The most revolutionary feature, though, is the lighting. Dozens of tiny, irregular windows perforate the walls, while daylight also floods in through a long, horizontal gap at the base of the ceiling so that the roof almost seems to be floating on air. **IZ**

> *"Space and light and order. Those are the things that men need just as much as they need bread."*
>
> Le Corbusier, architect

Tower of the Lantern

(La Rochelle, France)

Part of the medieval town's defensive wall and the scene of a religious massacre

"Monsieur d'Artagnan? . . . He did his whole duty and even more at the siege of Rochelle."

Alexandre Dumas, *Twenty Years After* (1845)

Built between 1445 and 1476, the Tower of the Lantern is one of three medieval towers surrounding La Rochelle's old harbor. Originally, it formed part of the defensive wall around the harbor, linked to the Tower of St. Nicholas and the Tower of the Chain by a massive rampart. At 246 feet (75 m) high, the Tower of the Lantern is the tallest of the three and took its name from its use as a lighthouse. It was subsequently used as a prison and visitors can still see traces of the graffiti carved into the walls by English, Spanish, and Dutch pirates imprisoned there between the seventeenth and nineteenth century.

The tower played a central role in La Rochelle's violent religious history: A Huguenot mob threw thirteen Catholic priests to their death from the spire during the French Wars of Religion, giving the tower its alternative name, the Tower of the Priests. It was in response to such atrocities that the city was besieged by Louis XIII's troops under the command of Cardinal Richelieu in 1627. Richelieu accepted the city's surrender—after famine had killed around 20,000 of its inhabitants. As part of the terms of the surrender, Richelieu demanded the destruction of the city's fortifications, except for the three towers.

The fortifications were later rebuilt, incorporating the towers, although by 1884 they were becoming increasingly dilapidated, as the novelist Henry James recalls appreciatively in *A Little Tour In France*: "The harbor is effective to the eye by reason of three battered old towers which, at different points, overhang it and look infinitely weatherwashed and sea-silvered." In 1879, however, the tower had been named a historic monument and, shortly after James wrote his description, it underwent substantial restoration. The work was carried out between 1900 and 1914, ending with World War I. **AS**

Arch of Germanicus

(Saintes, France)

First-century triumphal Roman arch

Saintes has been an important town in the southwest of France since the Roman occupation, and the Arch of Germanicus is only one of its several Roman ruins. The Roman town of Mediolanum Santonum was founded *c*. 30 B.C.E. at the point where a major road linking Bordeaux and Lyon (then the capital of Gaul) crossed the Charente River.

This arch was built *c*. 20 C.E. and, despite its name, was actually dedicated to a trio of leading Romans—Rome's relatively unpopular second emperor, Tiberius, his natural son Drusus, and Tiberius's adoptive son, Germanicus, who had gained his nickname by his leadership of a string of military campaigns in Germany. The arch is a relatively simple structure compared with other Roman triumphal arches, possibly because it had a practical function as the gateway to the bridge, rather than existing solely as a commemorative structure.

Around the same time, the town gained a public bathhouse and a substantial amphitheater, which seated around 15,000 spectators and can still be seen on the side of a nearby hill. Thanks to these monuments, the town has long been regarded as a must-see historical site for visitors to France. English writer and polymath Sir Thomas Browne wrote in 1662: "There are also still to be seen some remains of Roman magnificence ... above all, two stately and magnificent arches on the bridge, which containeth fourteen arches in all." Sadly the bridge itself was demolished in the nineteenth century to make way for a larger bridge, more suitable for the rapidly expanding town. The Arch of Germanicus's importance was recognized, however, with town officials carefully taking it apart and rebuilding it on the other side of the river. Today the arch stands as a powerful reminder of the Roman influence on French history. **AS**

Cognac Otard

(Cognac, France)

Norman fortress turned cognac distillery

Cognac Otard is a distillery established in 1795 in the Renaissance Château Cognac on the banks of the Charente River. Cognac is a form of brandy made only from the white wines of the Cognac region. The first building on this site was a fortress, built in 950 to defend the region against the Normans. In 1190 it became, by marriage, the property of the Plantagenets—the English kings. Château Cognac was rebuilt during the fifteenth century by the Valois family, and François Valois—later King François I of France—was born here in 1494. In 1517, he extended and redeveloped the château in the Italian style.

> *"Have the goodness to give me a little glass of old cognac, and a mouthful of cool, fresh water."*
>
> Charles Dickens, *A Tale of Two Cities* (1859)

Baron Jean Otard was born near Cognac in 1773; he was the great grandson of James Otard of Scotland who, loyal to the Stuart King James II, had joined him in exile in France. In 1793, Baron Otard narrowly avoided execution in the French Revolution and escaped to England. Returning in 1795, he bought Château Cognac and founded the Otard distillery. The 10-foot- (3-m-) thick walls of the vaulted cellars were ideal for aging the cognac, but the Renaissance chapel was of little use to the business, and was demolished.

As the raw material for cognac, the local white wine is distilled twice, then aged in oak barrels. Much of the wine for Otard cognac comes from two local wine-growing areas, Grande Champagne and Petite Champagne, and so the resulting cognacs are described as fine champagne cognacs. **EH**

Oradour-sur-Glane

(Haute-Vienne, France)

Haunting memorial of World War II

Added to the entrance sign to the old village of Oradour-sur-Glane are three poignant words "Souviens-toi—Remember." In the summer of 1944, Oradour was a village under German occupation, but carrying on daily life much as usual. On June 10, however, soldiers arrived from the SS's Second Panzer Division *Das Reich*. Acting apparently on false information claiming Oradour was involved in Résistance activities, they rounded up the villagers, initially in the largest open space, the Champ de Foire, then kept them under armed guard in half a dozen nearby barns. The women and children were herded into the church—and then the killing began. A bomb was detonated in the church and any survivors were targeted by the SS with grenades or machine-gun fire. The men in the barns were also murdered. After the massacre, the entire village was set on fire. In all, 642 villagers were killed, including more than 200 children. Only one elderly woman and five men survived. (The officer who led the attack as a result of that fatal misinformation was killed in Normandy less than three weeks later.)

After the end of the war, France's General de Gaulle declared Oradour a village martyr. Today, its roofless houses and rusting cars stand as a haunting reminder of a vicious, unprovoked atrocity that shocked even the SS.

Between the Champ de Foire and the cemetery there now stands the Mémorial, or Martyrium, opened in 1974. It bears the names of the dead and displays some poignant souvenirs: a broken watch, identity cards, a child's toy. The name Oradour comes from the Latin *oratorium*, suggesting that the village originally arose around a chapel where people would come to pray for the dead. With tragic irony, Oradour is once more a shrine to the dead. **CB**

Notre-Dame du Port

(Clermont Ferrand, France)

Stunning Auvergnese Romanesque church

The original church in Clermont-Ferrand's Port Quarter (which is named after the market to which local merchants used to *apportait* [or bring] their wares) was built in the sixth century and destroyed by Norman invaders.

At the beginning of the twelfth century, Bishop Saint Avit led the reconstruction of the church; according to legend he insisted that it be built according to the mathematical Golden Ratio, whereby the length of any given section is greater than its width by a ratio of 1:1.6. The church was substantially altered in the nineteenth century with the addition of

> *"The Golden Ratio has inspired thinkers . . . like no other number in the history of mathematics."*
>
> Mario Livio, writer

a clocktower (the previous one having been destroyed in an earthquake in 1476), and the replacement of the roof tiles with slabs of local Volvic stone—a distinctive, jet-black, volcanic rock.

Inside, the church is particularly famous for its detailed sculpture depicting biblical scenes, most notably on the columns' capitals and the lintel of the south doorway. The most famous capital depicts the expulsion of Adam and Eve from the Garden of Eden, with the Archangel Michael seizing Adam by his beard and Eve by her hair. Over the southern doorway is a summary of Christ's life, showing the Adoration of the Magi, the Presentation at the Temple, the Baptism of Christ, and Christ in His Majesty. The church is currently undergoing an extensive restoration program, both internally and externally. **AS**

Notre-Dame du Puy Cathedral

(Le Puy-en-Velay, France)

Enormous Romanesque cathedral that took seven centuries to complete

Le Puy-en-Velay is spectacularly located in the bowl of an ancient volcanic cone—one of many in France's Massif Central region. The town was a rallying point for pilgrims on their way to the holy site of Santiago de Compostela in northern Spain, and much of the medieval town remains today.

Three peaks of volcanic rock defend the town, each of them with a church or statue built on top. On the largest peak stands Notre-Dame Cathedral, a massive Romanesque edifice, built progressively between the fifth and twelfth century. The multiple arches that support the building, the carved leaf and checkerboard decorations, and the six domes above the nave show considerable Byzantine and Moorish influences. The old entrance—still in use today—leads directly into the nave from a steep stairway, reached through huge arches at the top of a cobbled street in the town.

A Black Virgin statue on the altar is a seventeenth-century copy of the original gift to the cathedral from Louis IX, probably acquired during the crusades. The statue is carved from dark walnut wood and has blackened further with age. This sculpture is one of several Black Madonnas in this region. The stately figure is seated and adorned with ornately decorated robes and crown, in the Byzantine style. Embedded in one wall of the cathedral, there is part of an earlier pagan ceremonial stone, paganism being revered at this site before the church was founded. It is known as the "fever stone" and is believed by some to have healing powers.

Crowded with visitors today, it is easy to imagine this huge church full of pilgrims getting ready for the next stage of their journey, uplifted by the grandeur and spirituality of the place and the presence of the Black Madonna. **EH**

"Wherever he destroyed heathen temples, there he used immediately to build churches or monasteries."

Sulpicius Severus, on an early Christian proselytizer

 ## ⊚ **Grand Théâtre** (Bordeaux, France)

Victor Louis's masterpiece of Neoclassical architecture

The Grand Théâtre in Bordeaux was inaugurated on April 17, 1780, ten days after it staged its first production, Jean Racine's *L'Athalie*. It was not the first theater in Bordeaux—an earlier stone theater built in 1738 was destroyed by fire in 1755—but the Grand Théâtre was commissioned as part of a drive to invigorate Bordeaux, transforming it from a medieval city into a modern center of art and learning. Many of the buildings in the center of Bordeaux date from this period, and this program of civic construction was used as a model by Baron Hausmann when he undertook a similar task in Paris in the 1860s. Victor Hugo was so impressed with the city's eventual transformation that he remarked: "Take Versailles, add Antwerp, and you have Bordeaux."

The theater was designed by French Neoclassical architect Victor Louis. In 1755, he had been awarded the highly competitive Grand Prix de Rome. It was in Rome that Louis became inspired by the great Classical and Renaissance architects; this influence is apparent in the Grand Théâtre's portico of Corinthian columns, surmounted with statues of the nine muses and the goddesses Juno, Venus, and Minerva.

In 1871, the theater briefly became the National Assembly for the French Parliament, in recognition of the building's dignified grandeur. It was restored in 1991, and is now home to both the Opéra National de Bordeaux and the Ballet National de Bordeaux. **AS**

> *"I am back from Bordeaux. A grand and fine performance in the theater; a monumental success."*

Hector Berlioz, composer, letter dated June 12, 1859

🏛 ◎ **Monument aux Girondins** (Bordeaux, France)

Memorial to Bordeaux's political martyrs of the Reign of Terror

The Girondists were one of the more militant political factions in the Legislative Assembly during the early years of the French Revolution. Led by an inner group of representatives from the Gironde *département*, of which Bordeaux is the principal city, the faction had been willing to stir up militant patriotic fervor in aid of democratic revolution—a position from which they were seen to retreat as the Revolution began to spiral out of control. As the violence of the Terror took hold, Robespierre accused the Girondists of treachery in seeking to renege on their earlier revolutionary principles. Following a show trial, twenty-one of the leading Girondists were guillotined in October 1793.

In 1881, as the centenary of the storming of the Bastille approached, Bordeaux's authorities decided to erect a monument to these martyrs of the Revolution. Despite these intentions, construction was delayed until 1894 and the monument was not completed until 1902. A collaborative effort between the architect Victor Rich and the sculptors Achille Dumilâtre and Gustave Debrie, the monument is composed of a 121-foot- (43-m-) high central pillar, topped with a statue of Liberty breaking free from her chains.

The grand pillar is surrounded by pools adorned by additional statues of heroic personifications—of the Republic, of Bordeaux, of Eloquence, and of the French cockerel, among others—that together represent the themes of the Triumph of the Republic and the Triumph of the Concorde.

The whole structure forms the focal point of the city's Place des Quinconces—the largest public square in Europe covering around 30 acres (12 ha). During World War II, the bronzes were plundered by the occupying Nazi forces; fittingly, for a monument to French martyrs of freedom, these were recovered and restored to their rightful place in 1983. **AS**

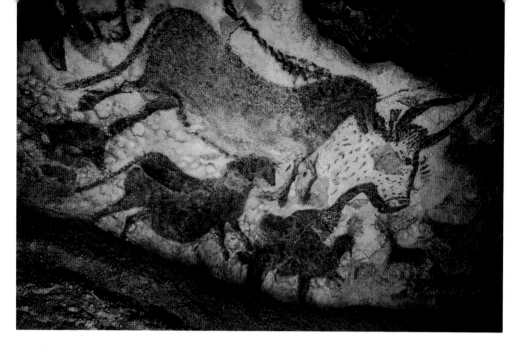

 ## 🏛 ◎ **Lascaux Cave** (near Montignac, France)

One of the most exciting prehistoric discoveries of all time

In September 1940, four boys were playing in the woods when their dog disappeared down a hole—the hole turned out to be the entrance to a cave. Unwittingly, the friends had stumbled across Europe's finest surviving collection of Paleolithic art. The cave at Lascaux is not unique—the Vézère valley alone contains twenty-five decorated caves—but the range and quality of the paintings are unparalleled.

Lascaux contains around 600 paintings and 1,500 engravings, spread across a series of linked chambers. A high proportion of the images depict animals. The most spectacular examples are in the Great Hall of Bulls, which is dominated by four huge beasts measuring up to 18 feet (5.4 m) long. The purpose of the paintings has been much debated. Many are in areas where they could never have been viewed properly, so their function seems to have been religious rather than decorative.

The cave was discovered during wartime so a detailed examination of the site was delayed, but it was opened to the public in 1948. Record crowds came to see it—which rapidly became a problem. The humidity from the visitors' breath, together with the dust and pollen on their shoes, caused a noticeable deterioration in the pictures. The cave was closed in 1963, and a facsimile was created inside a shell of reinforced concrete. Lascaux II opened in 1983 and has proved every bit as popular as the original. **IZ**

"For more than 17,000 years, the bestiary of the Lascaux cave ... survived the ravages of history."

Time, June 11, 2006

Pont Valentré (Cahors, France)

Spectacular fortified bridge dating back to the fourteenth century

A fine example of medieval military architecture, Pont Valentré has presided over seven centuries of history. The fortified bridge, built from local stone, was completed in 1378. Its three-story towers and graceful arches stand 131 feet (40 m) above the River Lot. Two of the towers have parapets allowing defenders to throw rocks and fire arrows at attackers below; the central tower was an observation post.

Pont Valentré withstood all attacks during the One Hundred Years' War (1337–1453) and Cahors successfully resisted English occupation. The town remained resolutely Catholic throughout the Wars of Religion (1562–90) but was taken by Henry of Navarre in 1580. Once king, Henry IV punished Cahors by withdrawing its right to run a wine market, and the town's wealth and power began to decline.

In 1879 the bridge was restored by architect Paul Goût, who added a sculpture to remind visitors of the legend of the bridge's first architect—a man who had asked the devil to help, in exchange for his soul. To outwit the devil, the man gave him an impossible task: to carry the water needed to make the mortar in a sieve. The devil took his revenge: When the stonemasons tried to finish the central tower, they found a corner had been knocked down and it proved impossible to complete. Goût's small statue of the devil is mounted on the summit of the middle tower, his fingers trapped between two slabs of stone. **SC**

"It is an amiable, sturdy, provincial place . . . dominated by its perfect medieval Pont Valentré."

Carmen Callil, *Bad Faith* (2006)

Church of the Jacobins (Toulouse, France)

Home of the Dominican religious order

Architecturally speaking, the Church of the Jacobins is an impressive example of the French Gothic period. Its forbidding redbrick exterior belies a surprising lightness inside, created by the double nave and extremely tall, 72-feet- (22-m-) high pillars, which spread palmlike where they meet the roof.

This striking church is the spiritual home, in Toulouse, of the Jacobins, a religious order more usually known as the Dominicans, founded by Domingo (Dominic) de Guzman. Domingo was a native of Castile but made his name in southern France for his tireless preaching against the Albigensians (also known as Cathars)—a religious sect firmly entrenched in and around Toulouse at the end of the twelfth century. By the mid-thirteenth century, the Albigensians had all but disappeared, brought down not only by Domingo's preaching but also by the Albigensian Crusade—a bloodthirsty war lasting from 1209 to 1229, launched by Pope Innocent III. The Dominicans took on the role of inquisitors among the local populace in a manner that hinted at the ruthless approach they would adopt when subsequently placed in charge of the Spanish Inquisition.

Founded on land acquired by the order in 1229, just as the war against the Albigensians was coming to an end, the sheer size of their church emphasizes the Dominicans' influence in Toulouse. The church was eventually abandoned by the Dominicans during the French Revolution. It became the property of the city of Toulouse in 1810, albeit in a dreadful state of repair; a restoration program was begun in 1920 and was finished only in 1972. Along with the church's architectural highlights and its historic background, it is notable for containing the tomb of St. Thomas Aquinas—one of the Dominicans' and Catholicism's leading theologians. **AS**

Cathedral of Sainte-Cécile (Albi, France)

A cathedral intended to intimidate

The Gothic cathedral at Albi is very different from its northern Gothic counterparts. The most obvious departure, in terms of architecture, is the lack of flying buttresses; at Albi, the supports are built into the wall itself and, from the outside, resemble a series of circular watchtowers. Unlike northern cathedrals, with their slender, tapering spires, Albi's is a solid, massive structure, more reminiscent of a fortress than a church. This was no accident—the new cathedral was designed to intimidate religious rebels.

The town of Albi gave its name to a heretic sect, the Albigensians (or Cathars). A thirteenth-century

> ## "Caedite eos. Novit enim Dominus qui sunt eius. *(Kill them all; the Lord will recognize his own.)*"
>
> **Orders issued to the Albigensian crusaders**

papal war against them was remarkable for its brutality, even by crusading standards. Work began on this new, imposing cathedral in 1282, just a few decades after the Albigensian Crusade. It was commissioned by a Dominican bishop, Bernard de Castanet—head of the Inquisition in Languedoc.

The interior of Albi's cathedral is a colorful contrast to its grim facade, the most spectacular feature being a superb mural of *The Last Judgment* (1474–84). There are also beautiful sixteenth-century frescoes on the ceiling and, around the rood screen, there is a fine collection of polychrome statues, representing various saints and angels. In addition, the cathedral is the proud owner of a magnificent organ, one of the largest organs in France, which was designed by Christophe Moucherel. **IZ**

Carcassonne Walled Town

(Languedoc, France)

Superbly restored fortified town that dates back to Roman times

The hilltop city of Carcassone, in the sun-drenched Languedoc region of southwest France, stands on several ancient trade routes between the Atlantic and Mediterranean and is believed to have been an important trading place since at least the sixth century B.C.E. The Romans fortified the site in *c*. 100 B.C.E., and in 462 C.E. the surrounding kingdom of Septimania was ceded to Visigoth King Theodoric II, who fortified the settlement further.

As a location of strategic economic and military importance, the city has changed hands many times. In 1067 the Trencavel family took control, building the Château Comtal and the Basilica of Saint-Nazaire. Many of the existing fifty-three towers, including the functional yet grand Gothic Trésau Tower and Narbonne Gate, were rebuilt in the thirteenth century on the foundations of ancient towers. In the same era, Carcassonne gained notoriety for its prominent role in the Albigensian Crusades, led by Simon de Montfort. He further fortified the town and it became a border citadel between France and the Kingdom of Aragon.

Along with other châteaux in the region, such as Peyreperteuse and Queribus, the city remained of military importance until the border moved south to the Pyrenees in 1659. The fortifications were gradually abandoned and the city became primarily an economic center for the woolen textile industry. The authorities and leading citizens began moving to the Lower Town (Ville Basse) and the old city became increasingly derelict. After Napoleon formally abandoned it, the once-grand city was due to be demolished but was saved thanks to a furious local uproar. In 1853 architect Eugène Viollet-le-Duc began restoring the city—hence the unauthentic yet fantastic pointed cones, so beloved of filmmakers and artists. **AP**

> *"A means to reestablish [a building] to a finished state, which may in fact never have actually existed."*
>
> Eugène Viollet-le-Duc, on the purpose of restoration

Pont du Gard

(Remoulins, France)

Roman aqueduct that supplied the city of Nîmes with fresh water

The ancient Romans were skillful and inventive engineers. Foremost among their achievements were the immense aqueducts, which they built in many parts of the empire. Reaching a height of 160 feet (49 m), the Pont du Gard is one of the highest and best preserved of these structures.

Aqueducts were designed to supply water to major settlements—in this case, the city of Nîmes (Nemausus). For much of its passage, the water was carried in underground stone channels, but at this site it flowed over the valley of the River Gard (or Gardon). The aqueduct consists of three rows of arches; the water conduit was contained in the uppermost tier. The precise date of the aqueduct's construction is uncertain. For many years it was thought to have been built *c.* 19 B.C.E., under the direction of Marcus Vispanius Agrippa, who also commissioned the first public baths in Rome. Recent excavations suggest, however, that it probably dates from slightly later, around the mid-first century C.E.

After the departure of the Romans, the aqueduct was no longer maintained and gradually fell into disuse. Some of the stone was removed for other construction work, although the structure still proved useful as a conventional bridge. It was only in the eighteenth century that its true historic value was recognized and attempts were made to restore it. In 1743, a new bridge was also erected alongside the lower tier, in order to reduce the traffic traveling over the aqueduct itself.

Since the nineteenth century, there have been a number of restoration programs, the last one taking place in 2000, when the area was pedestrianized and a new museum was created. The aqueduct has also been used as the backdrop for a variety of fairs, exhibitions, and concerts. **IZ**

> *"The Roman architects . . . created a technical as well as an artistic masterpiece."*
>
> UNESCO

Nîmes Roman Arena

(Nîmes, France)

Roman amphitheater, still in use today

Nothing conjures up the lifestyle of the ancient Romans more effectively than the huge amphitheaters, which were built in many parts of the empire. In these oval arenas, they staged their most spectacular entertainments, which included gladiator combats, animal fights, and even naval battles. The arena at Nîmes, in the south of France, is one of the best-preserved examples.

In 121 B.C.E., the town of Nîmes (Nemausus) was taken by the Romans and rapidly forced to adopt their lifestyle. Its arena, with a seating capacity of 16,000, was not particularly large in comparison to other similar sites, but it was hugely popular. The gladiators who fought here were mainly free men rather than slaves, who chose their dangerous profession because it offered high rewards.

Nîmes's amphitheater has survived better than most Roman buildings because it has always been in use. After the departure of the Romans, the Visigoths turned the amphitheater into a fortress, which later passed into the hands of the counts of Toulouse. By the Middle Ages, an entire community had established itself within the walls. At times, there were as many as 700 inhabitants inside the structure, with their own houses and even their own church. The process of clearing away these additions began in the 1780s and accelerated in the following century, when Henri Revoil restored the structure.

In 1853, the arena came full circle when public entertainments were staged there once again. This time it was used for bullfighting and bull-racing. The taste for this type of activity has continued undiminished, and the bullfights staged at Nîmes during the festival period continue unabated. In 1988, a new roof was added to broaden the range of events that can be held there. **IZ**

Cézanne's Studio

(Aix-en-Provence, France)

Final home of the artist Paul Cézanne

Paul Cézanne (1839–1906), one of France's greatest painters, was born in Aix-en-Provence. He owned several houses, but this one has special significance because he designed it himself.

Cézanne came from a wealthy family, and for many years he lived in his parents' home, a large, eighteenth-century manor. This was sold in 1899, after his mother's death, so Cézanne bought an apartment and studio in the center of Aix. When the latter proved unsatisfactory, Cézanne decided to build his own studio, to the north of town. The new studio, which took up the entire first floor, was lit by two large

> *"Painting is damned difficult— you always think you've got it, but you haven't."*
>
> Paul Cézanne, artist

windows to the south and a glass roof to the north. The artist worked here almost every day, for the last few years of his life.

When Cézanne died, his son inherited the property and deliberately left the studio undisturbed. In 1921 it was purchased by Marcel Provence, a passionate champion of Provençal customs and culture. He lived exclusively on the ground floor, determined to preserve "the precious heritage, the spiritual richness attached to these walls, to this garden." After his death, the building was brought into public ownership with funds raised by the Cézanne Memorial Committee. It was turned into a museum, administered by the local university, and opened its doors in 1954. One of its earliest visitors was the Hollywood actress Marilyn Monroe. **IZ**

Château d'If
(Bay of Marseille, France)

Notorious prison made famous in fiction

The Château d'If is situated on a tiny island in the Bay of Marseille. The structure was originally built for military purposes, but it soon became far better known as one of France's most notorious prisons. Many of its inmates were jailed for political reasons—but its most famous resident of all had committed no crime. He was the Count of Monte Cristo, an entirely fictitious character.

The castle was erected as part of Marseille's defenses. It was commissioned by François I, but was never actually put to the test. This may have been fortunate: When Vauban, the famous military engineer, examined it in the early eighteenth century, he considered it crudely built and virtually worthless. By this stage its primary role was already as a gaol rather than a fortress. In the previous century, thousands of religious prisoners had been sent here during the persecution of the Huguenots (French Protestants), and it also became a detention center for political rebels, particularly after the failed uprising of the Paris Commune in 1871.

There is no record of any prisoner ever having escaped from the château, but the character Edmond Dantès managed this feat in *The Count of Monte Cristo*, the novel by Alexandre Dumas, written in 1844. Dantès's adventures were invented, but the author did contrive to weave a genuine prisoner into the story. This was the Abbé Faria, who pioneered the study of hypnotism in France and was imprisoned on the island in 1797.

After 1890 the prison was decommissioned, and the château was opened up to sightseers arriving on boat trips from Marseille. Many were attracted by Dumas's novel, so a suitable cell was prepared, complete with escape hole. Today, the château receives more than 90,000 visitors each year. **IZ**

Citadel of Île Sainte-Marguerite (off Cannes, France)

Home to "the Man in the Iron Mask"

Île Sainte-Marguerite lies half a mile (800 m) from the Riviera town of Cannes. Until the twentieth century, the fort on the island was home to many famous prisoners of the French state. The most well known of these is "The Man in the Iron Mask"—an unknown captive of King Louis XIV.

The fort was built in 1612, when ownership of the island passed to Charles de Lorraine, the Duke of Chevreuse. By the end of the century, it was being used as a barracks and state prison. The prisoner known as "The Man in the Iron Mask" arrived in May 1687. He stayed on the island until 1698, until he was

---

"[He typifies] the sum of all the human misery and suffering ever inflicted by unjust tyranny."

Alexandre Dumas, on *The Man in the Iron Mask*

---

moved to the Bastille in Paris; he died there in 1703. The name of the man was given as Eustache Dauger, but the fact that his face was always covered led to rumors that his identity was more illustrious. The many theories—which still persist—include the rumor that he was the illegitimate older half brother of Louis XIV.

The only man to escape from the island prison is Marshal Bazaine, who surrendered to the Prussians during the Franco-Prussian War (1870–71). He was sentenced to twenty years of exile on the island in 1873, but managed to escape to Italy after only a year. The Algerian rebel leader Abdel Kadir was also held on the island in the mid-nineteenth century.

The fort is now home to a youth hostel and museum. Some of the original cells survive—including that of "The Man in the Iron Mask." **JF**

Musée Picasso, Château Grimaldi

(Antibes, France)

Twelfth-century fortress that became the studio of the artist Pablo Picasso

Château Grimaldi, a substantial fortress, was built in the twelfth century. It was raised on the foundations of the acropolis (high defense point) in what was then the Greek town of Antipolis. It later became the residence of the Bishops of Antibes. In 1383 Luc and Marc Grimaldi from Monaco—crossbowmen in the army of Queen Jeanne of Navarre—were given the fortress and the land around it as a private kingdom. It remained in the Grimaldi family until 1608, when Henri VI bought the land, town, and port of Antibes, and the estate became part of France.

The château has had many uses over the centuries. It has been home to the king's governor, a town hall, and a barracks. In 1925, having become somewhat neglected, Château Grimaldi was recognized as a rich archeological site and bought by Antibes Council for 80,000 francs. Renamed Grimaldi Museum, the château was classified as a historic monument in 1928.

In 1945, the artist Pablo Picasso visited the museum to view an exhibition of children's paintings. He was asked by the curator for "a little drawing for the museum." Picasso was attracted to the place and was invited to use part of the museum as a studio. He produced a great deal of work there between September and November 1946, often using unusual materials such as house paint, fiber cement, reused wood, and plates. Picasso left these works to the town of Antibes, including the famous *La Joie de Vivre*, *Satyr*, *Sea Urchins*, and *The Goat*. These artworks formed the basis for the development of the château into the Picasso Museum as we know it today. **EH**

⊡ One floor of the Château Grimaldi is dedicated to Picasso; work by other artists is displayed elsewhere.

⊡ Picasso gave numerous works to Antibes in 1946; many more were bequested by Jacqueline Picasso in 1990.

Renoir's House, Les Collettes

(Cagnes, France)

The Impressionist's home, created by the artist Pierre-Auguste Renoir

"*A work of art? First, it must be indescribable, and second, it must be inimitable.*"

Pierre-Auguste Renoir, artist

This attractive villa, nestling in a stunning estate renowned for its ancient olive trees, was the final home of the much-loved French Impressionist painter Pierre-Auguste Renoir (1841–1919). Renoir visited the French Riviera increasingly in his later years—hoping its warmth would ease the severe rheumatism that had troubled him since the 1890s—and finally settled permanently at Les Collettes.

He fell in love with the site primarily for its beautiful grounds, where, true to the Impressionists' love of working from nature, he would spend many hours at his easel. One poignant photograph shows Renoir at the end of his life, painting in the garden at Cagnes with an umbrella shading him and a paintbrush strapped to his crippled hand.

Renoir purchased the property in 1907, by which time he was an artist of international stature. He used the site to build a new house, which was completed in 1908 and afforded stunning views of the distant mountains and shoreline. Renoir produced many paintings of the gardens and surrounding area. Today the house is an essential stop-off on the artlovers' trail. It has been preserved much as it was when the artist lived there, with original decoration and furniture and two studios. There are also some original paintings, as well as sculptures, drawings, prints, evocative photographs, and personal possessions. When the artist Henri Matisse visited Renoir in 1917, he was inspired by Les Collettes, and painted the gardens and other scenes around Cagnes.

From 1912 onward, Renoir's ailment forced him to use a wheelchair. Although his health deteriorated steadily, he continued to paint in these lovely surroundings right up until his death, in 1919. Renoir's son, the filmmaker Jean Renoir, said of this site: "The Story of Cagnes and Renoir is a love story." **AK**

La Promenade des Anglais (Nice, France)

A scheme to give employment to the poor

Nice has been an important seaport for centuries but its history stretches back much further: At the foot of Mont Boron, in the area known as Terra Amata above the modern harbor, is the site of a prehistoric settlement believed to be 400,000 years old.

In the fourth century B.C.E., Nice was founded by Phocaeans, a colony of Greek mariners from Marseille, who called their new home Νικαία (victory) to commemorate the defeat of a neighboring colony. In the first century C.E., the Romans arrived, bringing with them their own stone, to build a Roman city on the hill of Cimiez, now a northern neighborhood of Nice, complete with spas, arenas, and shops. In fact, Nice has been owned and occupied by many nations in its long history, and from 1814 to 1860 it belonged to Italy—or, more specifically, to the kingdom of Sardinia. However, on Italian unification in 1860 it was passed back to France for good.

People have always been entranced by the beauty of Nice's shores and temperate climate. From the latter half of the eighteenth century, an English colony took up residence in Nice to escape the harsher northern climate. In 1820, after a particularly cold winter had brought a large number of beggars to Nice, the English, led by the Reverend Lewis Way, decided a project was needed to give employment to the homeless. A path was created that followed the curve of the bay, which the locals immediately christened the "Camin dei Anglès" in the Nissan dialect. When Nice was annexed by France in 1860 this name was changed to its French version, "La Promenade des Anglais." The city of Nice has expanded and enlarged the original 6.5 feet (1.9 m) of pathway so that it now encompasses two wide lanes of traffic, separated by flower beds and palm trees. It stretches for 2.5 miles (4 km) along the beaches of the coast. **RM**

Ephrussi de Rothschild (Cap Ferrat, France)

Renaissance-inspired Rothschild villa

Charlotte Béatrice de Rothschild, born in Paris in 1864, grew up in the luxurious surroundings of Château de Ferrières, which was built in 1859 by her grandfather Baron James de Rothschild. At the age of nineteen, she married Maurice Ephrussi, a Russian banker almost twice her age. An art lover and collector, Béatrice traveled the world in search of treasures, once going so far as to buy a ruin just for the fresco it contained.

She already owned a sumptuous villa in Monaco, but in 1905 discovered Cap Ferrat and bought 17 acres (7 ha) of land on the narrowest part of the peninsula. Fanciful, yet exacting, Béatrice personally oversaw the

> *"…flamboyant Beatrice Rothschild, who never went anywhere without her trunk of fifty wigs…"*
>
> **European Jewish Tours**

seven-year construction of her villa, choosing the color pink as the dominant theme. Béatrice also designed the villa's themed gardens, which include the Florentine, Spanish, Stone, Rose, Japanese, and Provençal areas. The main garden extends from the back of the villa and is designed like a ship's deck, with a Temple of Love on the prow; the sea is visible from all sides. Béatrice named the villa the Île de France in happy memory of a cruise taken on this liner.

When the baroness died in 1934, she bequeathed the villa to the Académie des Beaux-Arts de l'Institute de France. It now contains all the collections she amassed throughout her life and kept in her various homes in Paris and the Côte d'Azur. The villa is open to the public yet retains the atmosphere of a private, intimate, and even occupied residence. **RM**

Maison Bonaparte (Ajaccio, Corsica, France)

Family home of Napoleon Bonaparte

> *"Death is nothing; but to live defeated and inglorious is to die daily."*

Napoleon Bonaparte, military leader and statesman

Corsica became part of the French Republic just a year before Napoleon Bonaparte, whose family was Tuscan in origin, was born on the small island. As a general in the French Revolution, ruler of the French Republic, and, latterly, emperor of France, Napoleon came to dominate Europe for more than a decade. He is now remembered as one of the greatest military tacticians of all time.

Napoleon was born in Ajaccio, the port capital of Corsica, on August 15, 1769. His parents would go on to have six more children. At the age of nine, Napoleon was sent to France to be schooled, and continued his training there as an artillery officer. He did, however, return to his home intermittently and is known to have been there for a few days on returning from Egypt in 1799. After that date, he was destined never to set foot on his homeland again, eventually being exiled, first to Elba, an island off the Tuscan coast, and finally to the island of St. Helena in the south Atlantic. He died here in 1821, after six years of constant guarding by the British.

The house itself—a large building, fairly typical of the region—is now a museum devoted to the Bonaparte family's place in Corsican history and great effort has been put into evoking the spirit of eighteenth-century Corsica. Visitors are shown the rooms used by Napoleon and his family, including the Chambre de l'Alcôve, which is thought—perhaps optimistically—to have been Napoleon's room on returning from Egypt. Napoleon's nephew Napoleon III went on to rule France later in the nineteenth century and a room in the house records this particular period accordingly.

Unsurprisingly, the house is the centerpiece of a town that actively celebrates its famous native son. Streets, squares, cafés, and buildings are all named after Napoleon and information on the great man is readily available. **OR**

Maison Louis XIV (Saint-Jean-de-Luz, France)

Onetime home to the "Sun King," Louis XIV

The Maison Louis XIV is located in the main square of the Basque fishing town of Saint-Jean-de-Luz. It is named after perhaps France's greatest ruler, King Louis XIV (1638–1715), known as the "Sun King," and served as his residence for more than a month during the preparations for his marriage to the Spanish princess Maria Theresa.

When Louis XIV arrived in Saint-Jean-de-Luz in May 1660, the so-called "Long War" (1631–59) between France and Spain had already come to an end, ratified by the Treaty of the Pyrenees (1659). As part of the treaty, Louis XIV was to marry Maria Theresa and the site of the wedding was Saint-Jean-de-Luz. Before the marriage, the town was so thronged by courtiers that it was known as "le Petit Paris."

Louis XIV and his entourage stayed in the house now known as the Maison Louis XIV, which had been built for the Lohobiague family, who were wealthy local shipowners. Maria Theresa stayed in a nearby house now known as the Maison de l'Infante. The royal couple were married in the local church of St. John the Baptist, parts of which date from the fifteenth century. Their reception was held in the town hall, which is adjacent to the Maison Louis XIV.

In the years after the wedding, Louis XIV established himself as an independent ruler—he had become king at the tender age of four, and until 1661 the reins of state had been in the hands of the boy king's adviser, Cardinal Jules Mazarin.

Today, the Maison Louis XIV is preserved as a historic house, open to the public. It houses a collection of memorabilia dating from the time of the wedding, as well as Louis XIV–era furniture. The small town of Saint-Jean-de-Luz, in a sense, saw a turning point in European history, where Spain's status and influence began to diminish, and France began its rise as the major continental power. **JF**

"The Infanta will rest content with the dowry and not thereafter sue for any other of her rights."

Term in Louis XIV's marriage settlement with Spain

Grotte de Massabielle (Lourdes, France)

Famous grotto at Lourdes where the Virgin Mary appeared to the young St. Bernadette

> *"Please go to the priests and tell them that a chapel is to be built here. Let processions come hither."*

An instruction given by the Virgin to St. Bernadette

⬆ Marie Bernadette Soubirous, photographed c. 1860, two years after she received her first vision.

➡ The Basilique du Rosaire et de l'Immaculée Conception was built directly above the grotto.

The Grotto of Massabielle—a simple, shallow cave—was made famous by St. Bernadette in the mid-nineteenth century. Her visions of the Virgin Mary helped to turn the town of Lourdes in southwest France into a major pilgrimage center, attracting more than six million visitors each year.

Marie Bernadette Soubirous was a simple, pious girl—the daughter of a penniless miller. In 1858, when she was just fourteen, she experienced a series of visions at the grotto. The Virgin spoke to Bernadette in the local dialect, instructing her to dig a hole in the ground. On doing so, the girl discovered a spring, which, she was told, could heal the sick. The church authorities questioned her closely, but they could not fault her account. As word of this apparent miracle spread, pilgrims and invalids began to flock to the site, seeking a remedy for their ailments. Bernadette retired to a convent where she spent the remainder of her short life, dying at the age of thirty-five.

In 1862 the visions were officially acknowledged by the church, and the area developed rapidly in response to the burgeoning interest in the site. A statue of the Virgin, based on Bernadette's description of the figure seen in her visions, was placed in the grotto in 1864. A new church, the Basilique du Rosaire et de l'Immaculée Conception (1871–83), was erected for the huge influx of pilgrims and the first national procession was staged in 1873.

The popularity of Lourdes continued unabated in the twentieth century. Bernadette was canonized in 1933, albeit for her piety rather than her visions, and her cult status received fresh impetus from a film of her life. *The Song of Bernadette* (1943), which was an international success, earned the actress Jennifer Jones an Oscar and a Golden Globe Award for her portrayal of the saint. **IZ**

Grand Casino (Monaco)

The world's most famous and glamorous casino

The Grand Casino in Monte Carlo was built in 1878 by Charles III, Prince of Monaco. Designed by Charles Garnier, architect of the Paris Opéra, the building is lavishly and ornately decorated in the opulent Belle Époque style, and stands in formal gardens with a sweeping view over the tiny principality of Monaco.

Charles III built his first casino in 1865, prompted by the imminent threat of bankruptcy. It was so successful that, by 1870, the prince was able to abolish taxation in the principality and, in 1878, to replace it with this commanding, extravagant building. The settlement that grew up around the new casino was named Monte Carlo, in honor of the prince, and the casino became a popular, glamorous destination. The government of Monaco retains a controlling financial interest in the casino—and the principality has remained a tax haven. Citizens of Monaco are, however, forbidden from entering the gaming rooms.

The Grand Casino has inspired a number of books and films, including the first James Bond novel, *Casino Royale*. A music-hall song, "The Man Who Broke the Bank at Monte Carlo," was inspired by the gamblers Joseph Jagger and Charles Wells who swept the board there in the early days by calculating the bias on a roulette wheel. Anyone willing to pay the entrance fees can play in the Salon Blanc or Salons Européans, but the minimum bids in the most exclusive gaming rooms will deter all but the super-rich. **EH**

> *"There was something splendid about the . . . baroque of the Casino Royale."*
>
> Ian Fleming, *Casino Royale* (1953)

Palais Princier (Monaco)

Home of the Grimaldi family since the thirteenth century

The Palais Princier (Prince's Palace) in Monaco occupies the Rocher de Monaco, overlooking the harbor. Exiled from Genoa in the thirteenth century after supporting the losing cause in a long-running dispute between the pope and the Holy Roman emperor, the aristocratic Grimaldi family established themselves in the southeast corner of France, building a number of castles throughout the region.

The Palais Princier was originally founded in 1191 as a fortress, belonging to the Genoese. It was captured by the Grimaldi family in 1297, who have ruled the territory from the same set of buildings almost without pause ever since. Legend has it that François Grimaldi sought shelter in the castle disguised as a monk, then murdered the fortress's guards before opening the gates to let his men in. This story is commemorated on the Grimaldi family crest, which depicts two monks wielding swords, and by a statue

in the palace of François dressed in a monk's habit. Despite several waves of reconstruction throughout the palace's history, reflected in the series of Renaissance staterooms and the subsequent remodeling in the Neoclassical style during the eighteenth century, the underlying theme of the palace is defense, seen in the towers and fortifications. These structures were substantially rebuilt in the nineteenth century, but include some dating back to the Middle Ages. This defensive architecture is an indication of the family's frequently tenuous hold on power over the centuries, with their rule often reliant on the goodwill of their stronger neighbors.

Since Honoré II's reign in the mid-seventeenth century, the family has increasingly concentrated on the aesthetic aspects of palatial life, redesigning the palace to reflect fashionable French styles and building up its impressive art collection. **AS**

Mauthausen Concentration Camp (Mauthausen, Austria)

One of the largest and most brutal of the Nazi camps

In 1938 a group of prisoners from Dachau concentration camp was sent to the village of Mauthausen in Upper Austria to construct a new camp. The camp at Mauthausen would subsequently develop into one of the largest camp complexes in the Nazi system; in addition to other main camps around the nearby village of Gusen, more than one hundred camps were spread throughout Austria.

As a slave labor camp, Mauthausen contributed substantial profits to the SS who ran the system. As well as quarries and tunneling operations around Mauthausen, inmates were used as labor in many German-Austrian industrial concerns, including the Heinkel and Messerschmitt aircraft works, Bayer pharmaceutical company, and the Steyr small arms factory. The original inmates were largely Germans who had resisted the Nazi regime, notably communists, socialists, and religious dissenters. They were joined by Czechs, Poles, and former Spanish Republicans who had fled to France after Franco's victory. It was only near the end of the war that a substantial number of Jews arrived.

Mauthausen was a particularly severe concentration camp, operating under the principle of "extermination by work" (*Vernichtung durch arbeit*). Those too ill to work were starved to death, or from December 1941, gassed. The guards were given free rein to indulge their sadistic impulses: In wintertime, for example, prisoners were stripped, hosed down with water, and left to freeze to death. Estimates of those who died in the complex vary widely, from at least 122,000 to almost one-third of a million. **AG**

⬉ Prisoners were forced to do physically demanding work regardless of their age or state of health.

⬅ Today the entrance to the infamous concentration camp sits amid beautiful and tranquil countryside.

Kaiservilla (Bad Ischl, Austria)

Summer home of the Hapsburg Emperor Franz Joseph I

The Kaiservilla at the fashionable spa resort of Bad Ischl, in Upper Austria, was the summer residence of the penultimate Hapsburg ruler, Emperor Franz Joseph I (1830–1916). It was at Bad Ischl that the young emperor met and fell in love with his beautiful fifteen-year-old Bavarian cousin Elizabeth in 1853. When the couple married the following year, Franz Joseph's mother gave them the villa as a wedding gift.

The Kaiservilla had originally been a modest house, so years of work on the buildings and grounds, supervised by imperial gardener Franz Rauch, were required to transform it into the summer seat of the emperor's court. Yet it remained an essentially domestic dwelling, expressing the typical aspiration of nineteenth-century royalty to a happy family life and private fulfillment. A Tudor-style cottage was built in the gardens for Elizabeth, who also had a gymnasium and riding stables. The emperor indulged his passion for hunting in the surrounding countryside.

Summer idylls at Bad Ischl could not stave off the tide of misfortune that bore down upon the Hapsburgs. Franz Joseph's only son, Crown Prince Rupert, committed suicide with his mistress at Mayerling in 1889; his beloved wife, Elizabeth, was stabbed to death by an anarchist in Geneva in 1898; and in 1914 his designated successor, Archduke Franz Ferdinand, was assassinated in Sarajevo by Serb extremists. It was in the Kaiservilla that Franz Joseph signed Austria's declaration of war on Serbia on July 28, 1914, precipitating a World War that would destroy the Austrian Empire. He left Bad Ischl two days later and never visited it again. **RG**

↗ Elizabeth was a very beautiful and popular empress and her portraits can be seen all over Austria.

→ Franz Joseph described his summer residence as "heaven on earth."

Melk Abbey Church (Melk, Austria)

The centerpiece of one of the world's most historic monasteries

Melk Abbey Church is a fine example of the ornate Baroque school of architecture. The church is located in the historic Benedictine Abbey in the town of Melk, Lower Austria, and is situated overlooking the River Danube. Melk has been a center of spiritual life for nearly a millennium, in continuous use since its foundation, and is one of the best-known monastic sites in the world.

Melk Abbey was founded in 1089 when Leopold II, Margrave of Austria, gave one of his castles to Benedictine monks. In the fifteenth century the abbey was the source of the influential Melk reform movement, which reinvigorated monastic life in the region. In the early eighteenth century a new abbey was constructed in the Baroque style. Originally, the church was meant to be simply modernized, but it was finally decided to build an entirely new structure. Jakob Prandtauer was the architect, and the interior

was decorated by some of the most prominent artists of the time. They include Johnn Michael Rottmayr who added frescoes and altar paintings, Antonio Beduzzi who laid out the interior, and Lorenzo Mattielli who designed the sculptures. The construction was begun in 1702 and completed in 1736.

The abbey church also contains the skeleton of St. Colman, an eleventh-century Irish saint who was martyred near Vienna on his way to Jerusalem. It is contained in a sarcophagus in the left altar. The painting over the high altar depicts the martyrdom of the apostles Peter and Paul, and the fresco over the nave depicts St. Benedict.

The abbey houses an extensive library with a collection of almost 100,000 volumes dating back to the twelfth century. Its school, which was founded in the twelfth century, is still in operation with about 900 pupils of both sexes. **JF**

🏛 ◈ **Semmering Railway** (Semmering Pass, Austria)

Triumph of civil engineering from the early days of steam railways

The Semmering Railway in the Austrian Alps was a spectacular product of the pioneering age of steam rail technology. When work began on the project in 1848, no one had ever attempted to build or operate a railway across a major mountain barrier. At an altitude of 3,184 feet (965 m), the Semmering pass posed a daunting challenge, requiring fresh technology and solutions in tunnel-building, surveying, and steam engine construction.

The architect of the railway was Austrian engineer Carl Ritter von Gegha. He was fortunate to win the backing of the young Austrian emperor Franz Joseph I. With the stability of his realm threatened by restive unemployed laborers, the emperor reasoned that an ambitious mountain railway would provide work for idle hands. In the event, some 20,000 workers were employed on the railway at the peak of its six-year construction period. Along the 25-mile (41-km) route

from Gloggnitz to Mürzzuschlag, they had to build sixteen viaducts, some with double tiers of arches, and fourteen tunnels, including one that was 4,720 feet (1,430 m) long. The track rose at a gradient of one in forty, snaking up the mountainside in curves measuring 623 feet (190 m) in radius that no existing steam engine could negotiate. Trials in 1852 failed to find a suitable locomotive for the track, but a long-boilered engine with eight driving wheels was successfully adopted in the end.

The Semmering railway opened on May 15, 1854, and was still in regular use 150 years later, although it ceased to be steam-powered in 1959. Self-consciously scenic from the start, it is credited with awakening sensitivity to the aesthetics of mountain views in nineteenth-century European culture. In 1998 the Semmering became the first railway to be named a UNESCO World Heritage site. **RG**

Belvedere Palace (Vienna, Austria)

Baroque landmark with a place in Austrian and Hapsburg history

Belvedere is a complex of two palaces and extensive gardens located in Vienna and offering wonderful views of the city. It was constructed for Prince Eugene of Savoy, one of the most successful military commanders of his day, as well as one of the wealthiest people in Europe. After his death, Belvedere became a palace for the Hapsburg emperors.

Eugene acquired the site of Belvedere in 1697, and initially used the land as a large park. The first palace, now known as the Lower Belvedere, was constructed between 1714 and 1716. It was originally designed as a garden villa. Although its architect, Johann Lukas von Hildebrandt, was Austrian, the decoration was mostly carried out by Italian artists. The ceiling of the central Marble Hall depicts Eugene as the new Apollo. A formal French garden was laid out along with the first palace. From 1720 to 1722, the Upper Belvedere was constructed. Originally intended to provide an end to the main garden axis, it was extended to become Eugene's main summer residence. When Eugene died, all of his possessions passed to his niece Princess Victoria of Savoy-Carignan, who sold Belvedere to Empress Maria Theresa in 1752.

Belvedere was extended under the Hapsburgs and, from 1775 to 1890, housed the imperial picture gallery. Its last Hapsburg resident was Archduke Franz Ferdinand, who was assassinated in 1914. Belvedere suffered heavy damage during World War II, but has since been restored. In 1955 the palace was the site of the signing of the Austrian State Treaty, which established the modern state of Austria.

Today the Upper Belvedere houses an art gallery that features paintings by Austrian artists Gustav Klimt, Egon Schiele, and Hans Makart. Belvedere Palace remains a stunning example of the beauty of the Austrian Baroque. **JF**

🏛 ◎ Schönbrunn Palace (Vienna, Austria)

Highly popular imperial palace and gardens

This superb Baroque palace was the summer residence of the ruling Hapsburg family. The distinctive buildings, in a color known as Hapsburg Yellow, house sumptuous interiors: a mass of Rococo swirls, gold decorations, crystal chandeliers, and huge mirrors. Schönbrunn has an incredible 1,441 rooms.

Empress Maria Theresa and her husband, Emperor Franz I, spent their summers at Schönbrunn and, during their reign, the six-year-old Wolfgang Amadeus Mozart was invited to the palace to perform for the empress. Emperor Franz Joseph was born in Schönbrunn in 1830 and was destined to die there at the age of eighty-six. The palace has become famous for its association with Franz Joseph's wife, Empress Elizabeth, known affectionately as Sisi; she loved Schönbrunn and spent much of her married life there.

The Hapsburgs' palace was built in the mid-eighteenth century on the site of a seventeenth-century hunting lodge, which had been destroyed during the Turkish occupation of Vienna. The name *Schönbrunn* means "beautiful spring" because the site included a natural spring that formed the royal family's water supply. Schönbrunn Palace is set in stunning parkland complete with a Neoclassical folly of arches known as the Gloriette, fake Roman ruins, ornate fountains, and an impressive Palm House. There is also a zoo, the legacy of a menagerie begun by Emperor Franz in the 1750s; it is the oldest zoo in Europe still on its original site, but unfortunately because of this the animals' cages are rather small.

In 1918 Emperor Karl I abdicated and Austria became a republic—he gave his abdication speech at Schönbrunn and the palace became the republic's property. Schönbrunn was damaged during World War II and restored in the 1950s. Today it is deservedly one of Vienna's top tourist attractions. **LH**

Kaisergruft

(Vienna, Austria)

Final resting place of the Hapsburgs

The Kaisergruft (Imperial Burial Vault) lies beneath the Kapuzinerkirche (Church of the Capuchins). Since 1633 almost every ruling member of the Hapsburg family has been buried here. Many of the bodies are not complete, however, because tradition insisted that the hearts of the Hapsburgs be buried in the Augustinerkirche. This practice was stopped in 1878, but all Hapsburgs buried here before that time had their hearts removed before their remains were interred in the Imperial Burial Vault. There is only one non-Hapsburg body in the crypt: Countess Fuchs, a close friend of the influential empress Maria Theresa.

The style of the graves varies widely, with some as elaborate as one would expect in such a lavish city and others surprisingly simple. The double tomb of Maria Theresa and Franz I encompasses all the excesses of the Baroque era, yet the humble tomb of their son Joseph II could have been created for another family entirely. Those whose tombs are not here include Emperor Karl I, who abdicated in 1918 and died in exile, and the ill-fated Marie-Antoinette, daughter of Maria Theresa and Franz I, whose grave is in Paris. In 1989 the crypt was reopened for the burial of former Empress Zita, wife of Karl I.

The early twentieth-century Viennese citizens may have wanted to be rid of the Hapsburgs, yet in the twenty-first century the people of Vienna are proud of their heritage. In recent years the popularity of Empress Elizabeth, known as Sisi, has been renewed to iconic status. Sisi was an unconventional empress whose life was saddened by the numerous infidelities of her husband, Franz Joseph, and who was assassinated by an Italian anarchist in Switzerland. It is not unusual when visiting the Imperial Burial Vault to find Sisi's grave adorned with fresh flowers left by modern-day admirers. **LH**

Sigmund Freud's House

(Vienna, Austria)

Freud's home and workplace for four decades

In this large apartment on the second floor of Berggasse 19, in an unassuming area of Vienna, Dr. Sigmund Freud lived and practiced until he was forced to flee Vienna. One of his best-known case studies, a young woman named Dora, lived on the same road, at number 32.

Freud had lived in Vienna since his early childhood; he moved to Berggasse in 1891, when he was in his thirties. It was in this apartment that he completed his most famous book, *The Interpretation of Dreams*, published in Vienna in 1900. Psychoanalysis was controversial yet popular and Freud's waiting room

> *"Civilization began the first time an angry person cast a word instead of a rock."*

Sigmund Freud, psychiatrist

was seldom empty. His practice, however, was seen as degenerative by the Nazi regime—a belief exacerbated because Freud was Jewish.

When Adolf Hitler returned to his native Austria as Führer of Germany in 1938 and announced that Austria had been annexed by its neighbor, many Jews, homosexuals, Roma, and other persecuted groups began to flee Austria, if they were able. The Nazis paid the Freuds a visit, raiding the apartment and stealing a large amount of money; after much consideration and persuasion by friends, Freud decided to leave his beloved city. The family left for London in 1938.

Today the simple apartment has been carefully restored with the help of Freud's children, and houses the Sigmund Freud Museum, complete with the famous doctor's couch. **LH**

Zentralfriedhof

(Vienna, Austria)

Impressive graves and monuments of many of Vienna's luminaries

Zentralfriedhof (Central Cemetery) is the biggest cemetery in Vienna and one of the largest in Europe. More than 2.5 million people have been buried here, and it has become renowned for its many graves of famous Viennese residents. Among the luminaries to have been interred in the cemetery are Beethoven, Brahms, Schubert, both Strausses (father and son), and Mozart's nemesis, Anton Salieri. Mozart is not buried in Zentralfriedhof because he died in poverty and was buried in an unmarked pauper's grave in an unknown location in St. Marx cemetery, but there is a monument to him at Zentralfriedhof. Not all the musicians whose graves are here were buried in the cemetery originally; the remains of Beethoven and Schubert were moved here in 1888, after their neglected graves in the Währinger cemetery began to fall into disrepair.

The cemetery is a surprisingly beautiful, peaceful place to walk around. Not unusually for Vienna, the monuments and architecture are fine examples of sculpture from every featured period; particularly noteworthy is the monument of Johann Strauss Jr. and Anton Hanak's World War I memorial. The main entrance gate, created by Max Hegele in 1905, is a masterpiece of Jugendstil (Art Nouveau). Hegele, a student of Otto Wagner, also designed the magnificent Jugendstil church inside the cemetery, named Dr. Karl Lueger Kirche (after a former mayor of Vienna).

Although Vienna's primary religion was Catholic, the cemetery reflects the diversity of Viennese society and is nondenominational. It is divided into several areas: the Old and New Jewish cemeteries, the Islamic cemetery, the Protestant cemetery, and the Orthodox cemeteries. There is also an area for Austrian presidents and war memorials for the nineteenth and twentieth centuries, including graves for people on both sides of the two World Wars. **LH**

"An old Viennese proverb reflects on death: In life, man pays for everything. Only death is free."

Billie Ann Lopez, travel writer

🏛 ⦿ Staatsoper (Vienna, Austria)

The cultural heart of Vienna for 150 years

In 1857 Emperor Franz Joseph announced grand new plans for Vienna, including boulevards and a number of public buildings. Vienna already had a reputation for musical excellence; therefore the city needed an opera house grand enough to rival those in London and Milan—and the one then being planned in Paris. Work began on the Staatsoper (State Opera House) in 1863 and it was finished by 1869. The Staatsoper was built on the impressive new boulevard that formed a ring around the central district of Vienna; it is now one of many beautiful and elaborate buildings situated along the Ringstrasse.

The Staatsoper was originally known as the Royal Imperial Court Theatre; its architects were Eduard van der Nüll and August Sicard von Sicardsburg, who had won the competition held to design it in 1858. Tragically the two architects were destined never to see their project brought to fruition because they both died in 1868. Their premature deaths happened just after their work had been harshly criticized by a scathing Viennese public who were not happy with the Staatsoper's neo-Renaissance design.

Opening night was May 25, 1869, and the first opera to be performed was Mozart's *Don Giovanni*. The beautiful colonnades that run the length of the Staatsoper were alive with elegantly dressed Viennese eager for a glimpse of the interior. The impressive foyer and the sweeping staircase are breathtaking. A side salon hung with splendid Gobelin tapestries showing scenes from Mozart's *The Magic Flute* was known as the Gobelinsaal, and has been renamed the Gustav Mahler Hall after the Bohemian-Austrian composer. There was also a tearoom, where Franz Joseph would entertain his guests during the interval. The Staatsoper was badly damaged in World War II, but was lovingly restored and reopened on November 5, 1955, with a triumphant performance of Beethoven's *Fidelio*. **LH**

> *"If a composer could say what he had to say in words he would not bother trying to say it in music."*
>
> Gustav Mahler, composer

⬆ One of the stage wings of the Vienna State Opera, reopened in 1955 after war damage was repaired.

➡ The main staircase, a fine example of neo-Renaissance opulence, survived World War II bombing unscathed.

Hofburg Palace (Vienna, Austria)

Grand and extensive former winter palace of the Hapsburgs

The Hofburg was the winter palace of the Hapsburg family. Beginning with Emperor Rudolph I, the Hapsburgs ruled Austria for more than 600 years. This enormous palace was begun in the thirteenth century and added to over the years, as successive rulers strove to prove themselves grander than their predecessors; the most recent additions date from the early 1900s. Surprisingly, this mix of bombastic architectural styles—including neo-Gothic, Renaissance, and Baroque—works well, making the palace an intriguing, complex site to visit.

The oldest part is known as the Schweizerhof or Swiss Courtyard, a name that derives from the emperor of the time being guarded by Swiss soldiers. Its elaborate sixteenth-century gateway is known as the Schweizertor or Swiss Doorway. The vast number of buildings includes a fourteenth-century chapel, two sixteenth-century palaces, and the eighteenth-century Winter Riding School. In 1918 Karl I, the last emperor of Austria, abdicated and the country became a republic. Since that time, the Hofburg Palace has been home to the chapel of the world-famous Vienna Boys' Choir, the Spanish Riding School, the National Library, and the president of Austria's office. In 1938, Adolf Hitler took possession of the Hofburg and it was from the Neue Burg (New Palace) that he announced Germany's annexing of Austria.

The Hofburg's environs are sprawling and it has truly become a palace for the people: There are museums and art galleries, restaurants, cafés, and parks. Most recently the palace's Baroque stables were converted into a major new museum quarter. **LH**

◙ The Dome of the Michaelertrakt is one of the most elaborate features of the palace.

◪ The Hofburg riding hall, built for teaching young aristocrats, is now used by the Spanish Riding School.

Mozart's Birthplace (Salzburg, Austria)

Eighteenth-century birthplace of Mozart, situated on one of Salzburg's busiest streets

Wolfgang Amadeus Mozart was born in the beautiful city of Salzburg at Getreidegasse 9. His name on his birth certificate is Johannes Chrysostomus Wolfgang Theophilus Mozart; unsurprisingly he never used it and changed the name Theophilus to Amadeus. The house in which he was born was owned by the Mozarts' friend and landlord Johann Hagenaeur. The family lived on the third floor from 1747 until 1773, and the house now bears a plaque announcing its association with Salzburg's most famous son.

Mozart's genius was recognized at a very young age. He wrote his first composition at the age of five and was invited to play to the empress of Austria at the age of six. His reputation was instantly assured and he performed in Austria's best houses. Although Salzburg remained his home, it was deemed too isolated for a serious composer—the concert halls and rich patrons were in Vienna—so the family moved to the capital. Mozart spent his adult life alternately adored and derided. He died very prematurely, in Vienna, seven weeks before his thirty-fifth birthday. As he was poverty-stricken at the time of his death, he was buried in an unmarked communal grave.

Today, the house in which Mozart was born is a museum where you can see the child genius's violins, piano, family portraits, and family letters. The museum was opened in 1880 by the International Mozart Foundation; it was extensively remodeled in the late twentieth century and has become an essential sight for all visitors to Salzburg. Getreidegasse is now one of Salzburg's most popular shopping streets, filled with Mozart-related memorabilia. **LH**

↗ Barbara Kraft painted this much-criticized posthumous portrait of Wolfgang Amadeus Mozart in 1819.

→ Mozart's harpsichord is one of several instruments acquired by the International Mozart Foundation.

 ◉ **Graz Zeughaus** (Graz, Austria)

Home to one of the world's finest and most extensive collections of historical weaponry

Graz is a historic and important city, and it was a key military base for centuries. The Graz Zeughaus (provincial armory) houses a vast and comprehensive collection of antique weaponry, a record of the area's rich military heritage. The armory is in the city's Old Town, which in 1999 was added to the UNESCO World Heritage List.

Graz is the capital of the state of Styria, in the southeast of Austria, which was possessed by the Hapsburgs for many centuries from the fourteenth onward. The town was an important base against attacks from the Ottoman Turks, and later successfully held out against numerous incursions from Napoleon. The armory was constructed in the mid-seventeenth century to house the region's weaponry. In the eighteenth century, when the threat of invasion had waned, the empress Maria Theresa sought to close the Zeughaus, but locals lobbied to keep it open as a monument to the military achievements of the region and to its skilled craftsmen and metal workers who produced the weapons.

The collection of weaponry is still housed in the original building, which is five stories high, 26 feet (8 m) wide, and 164 feet (50 m) long. The facade of the building includes sculptures of Mars, god of war, and Minerva, goddess of warriors. The impressive collection of more than 30,000 weapons runs from the fifteenth to the nineteenth centuries. It includes more than 7,800 guns and pistols, 3,300 helmets, 5,400 staffs, and 2,400 swords, as well as numerous examples of intricately decorated suits of armor made for the region's nobles, and even a complete suit of armor for a horse. There is a museum explaining the historical background of the armory on the ground floor, and the collection of weaponry is displayed on the upper floors in purpose-built, wood-paneled rooms. **JF**

Esterházy Palace (Eisenstadt, Austria)

Ornate palace with strong connections to Joseph Haydn

The original palace on this site was a comparatively humble abode, built in the late 1300s in the small village of Zabamortun, in what was then part of Hungary. The land and the palace was bought by King Ludwig of Burgenland in *c.* 1370 and turned into a castle. In the mid-fifteenth century the estate was seized by the ruling Hapsburgs, who had close connections to the Esterházy family. The estate was passed to Earl Nikolaus Esterházy in 1622, although building work did not begin on the palace for more than two decades.

In 1649 the estate was inherited by Paul Esterházy, who began to remodel the medieval castle into a magnificent Baroque palace, suitable for such a high-ranking family. Two architects were commissioned to design the new palace: an Austrian named Filiberto Luchese and an Italian named Carlo Carlone. The two men and the combination of their very different architectural backgrounds created a luxurious mix of Baroque and Classical buildings lavished with elaborate Italian stuccowork. In the early nineteenth century the palace was again partly remodeled, this time under the watchful eye of French architect Charles Moreau. The work, however, was forced to come to an end by the financial losses suffered by the Esterházy family in the Napoleonic Wars.

Today, Esterházy Palace is a popular tourist attraction with special significance for lovers of classical music. The Esterházy family took pride in having its own orchestra and, in 1766, the composer Joseph Haydn was appointed its musical director. In the center of Esterházy Palace is a great hall, built by Carlo Carlone and decorated with Italian frescoes. This room, which has superb acoustics, was renamed Haydn Hall in memory of the composer. A festival of Haydn's music takes place here annually. **LH**

Augusta Raurica

(Augst, Switzerland)

Roman settlement on the Rhine

Augusta Raurica, a Roman provincial capital, is located about 12 miles (20 km) east of Basel, alongside the Rhine. It is the oldest Roman settlement in Switzerland and, named after the Gallic Raurici tribe, was one of the colonies founded by the governor of Gaul, L. Munatius Plancus, in 44 B.C.E. Emperor Augustus renamed the city Colonia Augusta Raurica. During the first and second centuries C.E., it was a prosperous city of approximately 20,000 inhabitants, covering 260 acres (106 ha). Augusta Raurica played an important role in controlling commercial traffic because of its strategic location on the Rhine. Goods in transit through the Roman Empire on the north–south and east–west axis had to cross the Rhine near the settlement. Augusta Raurica remained an important regional, cultural, and economic center until the third century C.E. It was partially destroyed by an earthquake in *c.* 250, and suffered in the years that followed further destruction from the Alamans, a Germanic tribe. This led to the development of two separate settlements that still remain today—Augst and Kaiseraugst.

The Roman town features the best-preserved theater north of the Alps. Other archeological remains include the amphitheater, which had a seating capacity of 6,000, the forum (center of government), the curia (town hall), temples, taverns, bathhouses, residential quarters, an early Christian church with a baptistery, and impressive 14-foot- (4.5-m-) high fortress walls.

The site has been excavated since the sixteenth century, and such is the archeological interest of Augusta Raurica that excavations are still ongoing. There is a small museum and a fully reconstructed Roman house where finds such as ceramics, jewelry, and coins discovered on-site are exhibited. Augusta Raurica is the largest and one of the most important Roman sites in Switzerland. **EP**

Kloster Einsiedeln

(Einsiedeln, Switzerland)

Well-preserved abbey and pilgrimage center

The abbey at Einsiedeln is a hugely popular pilgrimage destination, as it has been since the tenth century when it rivaled Compostela, Loreto, and even Rome. Between 150,000 and 200,000 Catholics from across Europe visit it annually to experience the miraculous statue of Our Lady in the Lady Chapel, which is on the site of the ancient "hermit's chapel." The statue is a "Black Madonna," with a black face and hands.

A monk, Meinrad, first established his hermitage on the slopes of Mount Etzel in the mid-ninth century, taking a statue of the Virgin with him, and other hermits followed. Several years after his death in 861,

---

"The statue is taken to the church, only to return by night to her own place, where a chapel is then built."

Mary Lee Nolan, on the stories of the Black Virgin

Eberhard (previously Provost of Strasbourg) collected these hermits together into a monastic community, and in 934 a Benedictine monastery was founded. The actual abbey was founded in 947 and the monastery flourished until around 1100. From then on it began a decline as a result of tough social and political conditions. However, after the Reformation, prosperity returned, and in the Baroque era it entered a golden age. From the 1600s onward, the monastery has maintained a relatively high level of prosperity.

In recent years Einsiedeln has housed around ninety monks and forty lay brothers, as well as maintaining a seminary and college attached to the abbey. Thus, the abbey buildings (including church, monastic quarters, and an extensive library) have all been beautifully preserved. **KH**

Kapellbrücke

(Lucerne, Switzerland)

Fourteenth-century wooden covered bridge, decorated with historical paintings

Lucerne is built on both sides of the Reuss River where it drains from Lake Lucerne, and the city has several bridges, including Kapellbrücke, or the Chapel Bridge. Originally built in the fourteenth century as part of the city's defenses, this 669-foot- (204-m-) long wooden bridge that runs past a thirteenth-century fortified octagonal water tower is a striking landmark.

The bridge is completely covered with a tiled, pitched roof supported on pillars. The water tower, or Wasserturm, built of brick with a similar tiled roof and standing 140 feet (43 m) above the water, has had many uses during its eighteen centuries, including watchtower, prison, torture chamber, and treasury. The bridge itself has served as a rope factory and housed the weekly market.

Along the length of the bridge, hung in the angles of the roof, there are 120 seventeenth-century paintings on triangular panels, sponsored by wealthy citizens of the city and depicting the history of Lucerne. Hans Wegmann of Zürich was commissioned to do the paintings, but realized that he could not complete the work on schedule by himself and brought in other artists to help. He then complained that the original budget was not adequate, and the cost of the project doubled. The paintings continued to be costly for the people of Lucerne because guards had to be mounted in 1726 to prevent the youth of the city from vandalizing the artwork, and after floods in 1741 when the bridge partly collapsed and the fallen paintings had to be replaced.

The bridge was almost completely destroyed by fire in August 1993. The rebuilding took a matter of months, and the bridge today is an exact replica. Two-thirds of the paintings were also destroyed, and their replacements, by artists working from photographs, took considerably longer. **EH**

> "The [bridge] starts out straight but quickly takes off at a 45-degree angle to reach the other bank."

Jerome Richard, journalist

Palais des Nations (Geneva, Switzerland)

Art Deco home of the United Nations in Geneva

The Palais des Nations (Palace of the Nations), with its 1,969-foot- (600-m-) long Art Deco frontage overlooking the French Alps and Lake Geneva, is the Geneva headquarters of the United Nations. Built between 1929 and 1938, it was designed by leading architects from several European countries: Carlo Broggi of Italy, Julien Flegenheimer of Switzerland, Camille Lefèvre and Henri-Paul Nénot of France, and Josef Vago of Hungary.

The idea for a Society of Nations was first put forward by Marquis Masson in 1771, who suggested that it should be hosted by Switzerland. After the Paris Peace Convention of 1919 to 1920, the League of Nations was created and Masson's vision was finally realized. Its goal was to prevent wars, settle disputes between countries through diplomacy, and improve welfare. The League of Nations became the United Nations after World War II.

The early 1950s saw the addition of two extensions. Three floors were added to the "K" building, and the "D" building was constructed and used as a temporary location for the World Health Organization. The "New" building was constructed in 1973 to provide conference facilities.

The Palais is built in the 111-acre (45-ha) Ariana Park, which was left to the City of Geneva by the Revilliod de Rive family. In the park is a chalet dating from 1668, brought from the Gruyère district, and many trees more than one hundred years old. Under the foundation stone of the Palais, laid on September 7, 1929, is a capsule containing a copy of the Covenant of the League, a document that lists the names of the League of Nations members, and coins of all the countries at the league's Tenth Assembly. The grounds were sold with one condition: that peacocks should roam freely, which they still do today. **LC**

Château de Chillon (Veytaux, Switzerland)

Medieval fortress strategically situated on Lake Geneva

Nestling on the shores of Lake Geneva, the Château de Chillon was once a much-feared stronghold, the power base of the Counts of Savoy. Over the centuries, its power and influence have waned, although its picturesque setting still attracts many sightseers. Estimates suggest that it receives more visitors than any other historic site in Switzerland.

Chillon's dramatic position was the key to its success. Lodged between towering mountains and a sizable lake, it occupied a crucial, strategic location, controlling one of the principal routes between northern and southern Europe. Apart from its military significance, the castle also proved a lucrative source of revenue as costly tolls were levied on passing travelers. The site has been inhabited since Roman times, but the present building was largely constructed by Pierre II, Count of Savoy in the thirteenth century. Prudently, he ensured that the sections by the shore were heavily fortified, and his elegant, princely apartments looked out on to the lake.

From an early stage, Chillon became notorious for its dark, subterranean dungeons. Among the many prisoners who suffered there was François Bonivard, a rebellious sixteenth-century preacher who languished for six years chained to a pillar with his two brothers. He gained posthumous fame in a poem by Lord Byron. In 1816, Lord Byron visited the castle with fellow Romantic poet, Percy Bysshe Shelley, and was deeply moved by the tale of Bonivard's fate. Immediately, he penned *The Prisoner of Chillon* (1816), a powerful meditation on the value of liberty. Byron's signature is scratched on one of the pillars in the dungeon, although doubts have been raised about its authenticity. The castle has proved equally inspiring for artists such as J. M. W. Turner and Gustave Courbet, who produced noteworthy paintings of it. **IZ**

Aosta Roman Remains

(Aosta, Italy)

Roman city from the first century B.C.E.

Tucked up into Italy's northwestern corner, in an Alpine region nudging the Swiss and French borders, Aosta is the principal city of this valley region. Its excellent strategic position, where the Buthier and Dora Baltea rivers meet, was not lost on the ancient Romans. Having ousted the Celtic Salassi people, the Romans made the site their own and founded a town here *c.* 25 B.C.E., during the reign of their first emperor, Augustus. They called it Augusta Praetoria. Today the impressive Roman remains help make this a popular tourist destination.

Aosta is a particularly good example of Roman town planning, its streets laid out according to a very precise rectangular pattern. Notable remains include an amphitheater that once housed thousands of spectators and the triumphal Arch of Augustus. There are also remnants of the ancient walls and the town's impressive eastern gateway, the Porta Praetoria, comprising two arched structures with a small square in between. A major Alpine road, the Great St. Bernard Pass, runs close to the town and was used by the Romans (parts of the original Roman road still exist) as well as by their famous enemy, Hannibal, the legendary Carthaginian general.

As the capital of a province of the Roman Empire, the city of Aosta held a very important position. After the western Roman Empire fell in the late fifth century, Aosta was attacked and fell to a number of successive regimes, from the Germanic Ostrogoths to the great ninth-century ruler Charlemagne. In the tenth century Aosta became part of the kingdom of Burgundy, after which it was ruled by the House of Savoy for centuries. Napoleon arrived in 1800, marching 40,000 troops along the Great St. Bernard Pass, and temporarily ruled the area. In the 1940s Aosta became the regional capital within the new Italian republic. **AK**

Castello di Sarre

(Sarre, Italy)

A millennium-old royal hunting lodge

The castle known as the Castello di Sarre is located in a small town in the Aosta Valley, in northwest Italy. From the eleventh century, the Aosta Valley was ruled by the House of Savoy, which later became the Italian royal family. In the nineteenth century, the Castello di Sarre became the hunting lodge of Victor Emmanuel II of Savoy, the first king of a united Italy. The Castello di Sarre is located on a hill overlooking the Aosta Valley. Its origins are obscure, but its foundations may date from as far back as the eleventh century. The castle passed through the hands of various local aristocrats until in 1708 it was purchased by Baron Jean-François

> *"To be a king all you need to know is how to sign your name, read a newspaper, and mount a horse."*
>
> King Umberto I

Ferrod. He completely rebuilt the castle, leaving only the tower in place from the original structure.

King Victor Emmanuel II purchased the castle in 1869, for 55,000 lire. A keen hunter, the king extended the tower so it could be used as an observatory and added stables. Many of his hunting trophies remain in the castle today. His son, who became King Umberto I, also used Sarre as a hunting lodge and added extensions in 1900. The last king of Italy, King Umberto II, was a frequent visitor until his exile in 1946.

Despite the king's exile, the Castello di Sarre remained the property of the House of Savoy until 1972. Today it is owned by the local government, and houses a museum containing reconstructions of its nineteenth-century furnishings, as well as relics and paintings related to the House of Savoy. **JF**

Turin Cathedral

(Turin, Italy)

Venerable Renaissance cathedral and home to the world-famous Shroud of Turin

Turin Cathedral, constructed in the fifteenth century, is most famous today for being the home of the Shroud of Turin. However, it was also the first major Renaissance building in the city.

The Shroud of Turin is one of the Catholic Church's most holy relics. Believed by some to be the burial cloth of Jesus Christ, it bears the ghostly outline of the back and front of a man. The Shroud passed into the hands of the House of Savoy, the rulers of Turin, in 1453. From 1357 it had been owned by a French knight called Geoffroi de Charny, and although its provenance cannot be reliably traced before this date, it may well have been housed in several locations, including Jerusalem, Edessa, and Constantinople.

The Shroud was brought to Turin Cathedral in 1578 and, since the seventeenth century, has had its own chapel, a fine and dramatic example of Baroque architecture. In 1988 the age of the Shroud's cloth was submitted to carbon dating, which placed it in the period 1260 to 1390. The Catholic Church accepted the results but insists its authenticity has no bearing on its position as an object of veneration. In 1997 the chapel was damaged by fire, although fortunately a fireman was able to carry the Shroud to safety. The Shroud is rarely shown to the public—it was last brought out in 2000, and is next scheduled to be shown in 2025—however, it can be viewed via video link from the Museum of the Shroud in the Chapel. Regardless of the true nature of the Shroud, it has been an object of devotion for centuries and remains an important relic for millions of Christians. **JF**

⬀ Some researchers claim that the carbon dating of the Shroud of Turin merely applied to woven repairs.

⬂ The Cathedral of St. John the Baptist was completed in 1498; the Shroud arrived there in 1578.

Castello Sforzesco

(Milan, Italy)

A fortress built into the city walls

This enormous castle is situated to the northeast of Milan's famous crenellated Duomo. It began life as a defensive fortress, owned by the ruling Visconti family, built across the city's medieval walls. The castle was an integral part of the city's fortifications, growing in size as each successive Visconti added on to it, until the last Visconti, Filippo Maria, turned it into a residence and lived there until his lonely death in 1447.

The Milanese people had had enough of Visconti tyranny, so after Filippo Maria's death they established the Ambrosian Republic and took up any weapon they could find to tear down the walls of the castle. The stones were then used to pay off debts and rebuild the city walls.

Filippo Maria had an only daughter, Bianca Maria, who was illegitimate but was recognized as his heir. She had married Francesco Sforza—a mercenary who had been recruited to defend the dukedom of Milan from its Venetian neighbors. In the three years after Filippo Maria's death, Sforza, a political opportunist, defended the city and the Republic against its greedy neighbors. He then used the situation to his advantage and took power in March of 1450, supported by his wife. He began to rebuild the castle with the idea of making it a symbol of Milan's beauty and power, employing military engineers and the Florentine architect Antonio Averulino.

At the end of the fifteenth century, however, the castle went into a long decline. It was left to fall into partial ruins, before being restored to house the city's art collection in the late 1800s. Today, visitors to the museum can marvel at ceiling frescoes by Leonardo da Vinci, paintings by Filippo Lippi, and a vast collection of Egyptian and prehistoric artifacts—as well as the moving and beautifully unfinished *Pietà Rondanni* by Michelangelo. **RM**

Milan Cathedral

(Milan, Italy)

The second-largest church in Italy

In 1386 work began on an extraordinary Gothic cathedral in central Milan. It was built on a site that had been home to several churches since the fifth century. The huge cathedral—second only to St. Peter's as the largest church in Italy—shows the influence of northern European architecture on Italy at this period. Several of the architects and masons came from north of the Alps, although others were local men. The building reflects the contemporary tensions between north European Gothic and Italian Renaissance styles.

Construction was sporadic, with the initial work completed by around 1420. More work was begun in

> *"So grand, so solemn, so vast ... [yet] a delusion of frostwork that might vanish with a breath!"*
>
> Mark Twain, *Innocents Abroad* (1869)

the late fifteenth century and continued for about a century. The seventeenth and eighteenth centuries saw even more construction, including the impressive Madonna's spire. Before Napoleon's coronation as King of Italy in 1805, he ordered the completion of the facade—work that went on into the nineteenth and twentieth centuries. The architects were careful to respect the building's Gothic origins.

Any visitor to Milan's cathedral will be immediately struck by the size of the central nave, whose height is second only to that of the choir of Beauvais in France. Other features of interest include the magnificent windows—fine examples of "flowery Gothic"—several altars, and the ornate sarcophagi of the church's benefactors, including that of Marco Carelli, who donated 35,000 ducats in the fifteenth century. **AG**

Teatro alla Scala

(Milan, Italy)

The most impressive opera house in Italy—perhaps in the world

In 1776, Milan's main theater, the Teatro Ducale, was destroyed in a fire. The rulers of the city, which was then occupied by Austria, were petitioned by theater shareholders for a replacement and finally decreed that a more impressive theater take its place. The new building was inaugurated in 1778 and named Teatro alla Scala, after the church of the Santa Maria alla Scala, which had been deconsecrated and demolished to make way for the new structure. The cost of the project was defrayed by the sale of private boxes, or *palchi*, to wealthy Milanese, many of whom had previously owned boxes at the old theater.

La Scala, as it soon became known, was built in the Neoclassical style and was distinguished by a handsome facade looking out over a wide square. The auditorium had room for 3,000 spectators: On the main floor (*platea*) the audience stood to watch a performance; above were the individually decorated boxes, the preserve of wealthy patrons; and above the boxes was a large gallery (*loggione*) for the most devoted music lovers, equally quick in lavishing praise or heaping highly vocal scorn on a performance. Although La Scala was a meeting place for high society, its claim to fame has always been its close relationship with great musicians, and, most especially, as a showcase for Italian opera. As well as premiering the works of Rossini, Donizetti, and Bellini, La Scala had a fruitful if stormy relationship with Verdi. In the early twentieth century the conductor Arturo Toscanini also gave premieres of Puccini's works at La Scala, including *Madame Butterfly* and *Turandot*.

Although damaged by bombs in World War II, the refurbished opera house has maintained its close associations with the leading composers of the day, commissioning works from avant-garde musicians, including Berio and Stockhausen. **AG**

"The acoustics of Teatro alla Scala has become a myth and a model for many opera house designers."

Institute of Acoustics

Ducal Palace (Mantua, Italy)

Once home to the region's most powerful family and their unique art collection

This mighty complex of buildings, corridors, courtyards, galleries, and gardens sprawls over 366,000 square feet (34,000 sq m) and has 500 rooms. It is, therefore, a product of centuries of additions and renovations. The palace and the town of Mantua itself are famous for their association with the Gonzaga family, who ruled the area from 1328 to 1707. The oldest buildings in the compound are the Palazzo del Capitano and the Magna Domus, which were built by the Bonacolsi family, rulers of Mantua from 1271 until 1328, when they were ousted by a revolt backed by the Gonzaga. At the end of the fourteenth century one of the foremost military architects of the time, Bartolino da Navara, erected the San Giorgio Castle as part of the palace complex.

The Gonzaga family commissioned and collected many works of art—paintings, sculptures, frescoes, and gardens—during their centuries of reign. Andrea Mantegna, court artist for the Gonzaga from 1460 to 1500, frescoed an entire apartment known as the Camera degli Sposi, or Bridal Chamber. This masterpiece is a series of full compositions showcasing portraits of the Gonzaga in various scenes. Other artists across the years contributed to the splendor of the palace, including Antonio Pisano (Pisanello), Guilio Romano, and Luca Fancelli.

In 1627, the direct line of Gonzaga came to an end with Vincenzo II, an inept and weak man, who had sold many of the works of art to Charles I of England. A French line of the family, the Gonzaga Nevers, came to power but in 1630 Mantua was besieged by a Hapsburg army who looted the palace. When Ferdinand Carlo was finally deposed in 1707 and fled Mantua for Venice, he took more than 1,000 paintings with him. The buildings declined until the twentieth century, when conservation work began and the palace became a museum and art gallery. **RM**

> *"This is no caricature, but a moving document of the human condition."*
>
> Beth Archer Brombert, on the Gonzaga portraits

The imposing fortress home of the ruling Scaliger—or Della Scala—family

Romeo and Juliet's world-famous city is well known not only for its romantic balcony, but also for other remarkable monuments, of which Castelvecchio is one of the most emblematic. Originally it was named St. Martin's, after the old church that was included within its walls in the Middle Ages, but its name was changed to Castelvecchio (Old Castle) when a new manor was erected in the fourteenth century.

Castelvecchio, on the banks of the Adige River, was the fortress of the Scaliger dynasty, which ruled Verona until 1387. It was built by Cangrande II Della Scala in 1354, during a period of turbulent events. Its military aspect is stately and massive towers surround the big parade ground and the main tower. In the case of an assault, the family's escape route was assured northward, fleeing across the Ponte Scaligero. Like the castle, the bridge was constructed in red brick and white marble, and fortified with walls and towers.

When Verona fell under Venetian control in 1404, the castle was used as an arms store; by the eighteenth century it was the seat of the Military Academy of the Venetian Republic. In 1923 the building lost its defensive function, and was restored and converted into Castelvecchio Museum. The castle also hosted a historic trial, in 1944, that sentenced to death the generals who voted to remove Mussolini from office. It was, however, the restoration conducted in 1957 by the architect Carlo Scarpa that turned the museum into a masterpiece of Italian museography, with famous works from the early Christian era through to the eighteenth century. The ensuing archeological excavations brought to light ancient structures and unveiled a forgotten history.

Today Castelvecchio, with its powerful medieval architecture and impressive bridge, is one of the most spectacular tourist attractions in Verona and one of the most interesting museums in the country. **MC**

"Dante stayed with Cangrande ... and under his patronship he composed The Divine Comedy.*"*

Guy Shaked, historian

🏛 ◎ Torre dei Lamberti (Verona, Italy)

A twelfth-century tower that is still the tallest building in Verona

Built in 1172 by the powerful Lamberti family, the tower that still bears their name stands 275 feet (84 m) high and is the tallest building in Verona. Since 1972 it has been open to visitors, who can reach the top via an elevator to enjoy a stunning view of the town. Erected in Romanesque style on the site of the ancient Roman forum, the original tower was much shorter, as one can see by looking at the limit of the lower part, made in bricks and tufa. Its two bells, called Rengo and Marangona, have become famous. The first bell served to call the people to public meetings; the second bell was used to regulate the working hours of the artisans in the nearby square—its name comes from the local dialect for carpenter.

In 1403 a violent thunderbolt struck and caused severe damage to the top of the tower. In the rebuilding, between 1448 and 1464, the structure was raised to its present height, with a refined octagonal belfry set up over elegant windows with three lights. The large clock was added at the end of the eighteenth century. Only a few feet away from the tower, beyond an ancient wrought-iron gate, visitors are immediately drawn to a superb masterpiece of Veronese Gothic sculpture: the Scaliger Tombs (Arche Scaligere). Here rest the bodies of the most renowned members of the Lamberti family who ruled the town for more than a century, such as Cangrande I, Mastino II, Cansignorio, Alberto I, and Giovanni Della Scala. They were buried in engraved monumental sarcophagi, adjacent to the church of Santa Maria Antica, adorned with statues and surmounted by rich pyramidal canopies (the equestrian statue of Cangrande I is now in Castelvecchio Museum).

The Lamberti Tower and the Scaliger Tombs, now, as in the Middle Ages, are sited in the heart of Verona, and with the other monuments constructed around them, they create an atmospheric setting. **MC**

> *"Remember, this is Verona. Suspension of disbelief is your passport to pleasure."*
>
> *New York Times*, May 12, 1996

🏛 ◎ Juliet's House (Verona, Italy)

Reputed family home of the heroine of Romeo and Juliet—*complete with Juliet's balcony*

In an unassuming street stands one of Verona's most visited attractions: Juliet's House (La Casa de Giulietta). Identified as the home of Shakespeare's heroine in the play *Romeo and Juliet*, it has become a shrine for visiting lovers from all over the world. Unfortunately, its iconic status means many visitors feel the need to graffiti their names on the walls—today, the house has become almost as famous for the never-ending graffiti as for its architecture, history, and literary associations.

Although William Shakespeare is not known to have visited Verona, his play was based on an Italian legend about two warring families, whom he called Capulets and Montagues. In reality, what is now known as Juliet's House was once owned by a family with the name of Dell Cappello, a likely source for Shakespeare's Capulets; the Dell Cappello coat of arms is still visible on the keystone. Whether the characters are based on real people is hotly debated, but whether or not Romeo or Juliet ever existed, the story has passed into history as one of the greatest love stories ever written and as such deserves a legendary monument. The house now possesses what is probably the world's most famous balcony. Made from prettily carved stone, the balcony is rumored to be that on which Juliet was standing while Romeo declared his love. In reality, it is a much later addition to the house, built many centuries after Romeo and Juliet are said to have lived. Not far away is Romeo's house and Juliet's supposed tomb (in which archeologists claim there are no bones—and, of course, in the play, Romeo and Juliet are buried together).

Today the house is open as a small museum and it is possible to climb up the stairs to emerge out onto the balcony. There is also a bronze statue of Juliet herself, created in the twentieth century; her right breast is always gleaming, as it has become tradition to stroke it in order to be lucky in love. **LH**

"What's in a name? That which we call a rose by any other name would smell as sweet."

William Shakespeare, *Romeo and Juliet* (c. 1596)

🏛 ◉ Verona Arena (Verona, Italy)

The third-largest amphitheater in Europe—and still in use as a theater today

Verona's Roman Arena is the third-largest amphitheater in Europe after the Colosseum in Rome and the one at Capua, near Naples. Since ancient times, actors have been treading the boards on what is the widest stage in the world. It was built in the first century C.E., under the reign of the emperor Augustus, in a city immortalized by writers ranging from the Latin poet Catullus to Shakespeare.

An enduring symbol of Verona, and an archeological treasure-house, the Arena is a triumph of Roman architecture, originally accommodating 30,000 spectators—a substantial arena even by today's standards. The Romans built their arena outside the city walls, embellishing it with white marble ashlars quarried from the local mountains. In 265, the city walls were extended by the emperor Gallienus and the amphitheater became part of the city. In the twelfth century the outer ring was largely destroyed by an earthquake, but otherwise it has withstood the ravages of time extremely well and is one of the world's best-preserved amphitheaters of the Roman period.

As well as hosting gladiatorial games, a complex drainage system also made spectacular aquatic games possible. In the Middle Ages, the Arena hosted more ritualized combats in the form of jousts and tournaments. By the eighteenth century, the Arena was specifically reserved for theatrical performances, and in 1913 it was chosen for the first time to stage the Lyrical season. The overwhelming success of the event was sealed by a performance of Giuseppe Verdi's *Aida*. Ever since, on summer evenings, the operas performed at the Arena attract thousands of people from all over the world, eager to become part of the history of a monument that, after 2,000 years, continues to amaze its visitors. **MC**

Anatomical Theater, Padua University (Padua, Italy)

The oldest anatomical theater in the world

The University of Padua, founded in 1222, is the second oldest in Italy and is one of the oldest in Europe; its anatomical theater is the oldest still in existence in the world. The university had established a reputation as one of the leading centers for anatomical research, thanks in part to its freedom from church interference. In the sixteenth century, the university's academic independence from the church was preserved by protection given by the Venetian Republic, which allowed important research to take place, despite the church's misgivings.

The university's faculty of medicine, in particular, also benefited from the presence of some of the most important figures in early modern medicine, who began to study the body from an empirical perspective and made pioneering discoveries about basic bodily functions. These included Hieronymous Fabricius, who held the chair in surgery and anatomy

at the university and discovered the valves inside human veins. It was Fabricius who designed the anatomical theater in the shape of a human eye, with a balustrade of wooden balconies around the operating table, and his involvement in establishing the theater was commemorated with the inscription of his name above the theater's doorway. Inaugurated in 1594, operations in the 200-seat theater were open to public view, with special concentration given to procedures where the patient had suffered lacerations as a result of violence. Among Fabricius's students at Padua were the English physician William Harvey, who was a pioneer in the study of blood circulation, and Adriaan van den Spiegel, a Flemish anatomist who was the first to make a thorough study of malaria. In addition to these great medics, Galileo Galilei, the "father of modern astronomy," held the chair of physics at Padua from 1592 to 1610. **JF**

Caffè Pedrocchi

(Padua, Italy)

One of the finest coffeehouses in Italy

At the beginning of the nineteenth century, the entrepreneur Antonio Pedrocchi invested his fortune in founding one of the finest and most beloved coffeehouses in Italy; it still bears his name. Built in 1831 in pure Neoclassical style by the Venetian architect Giuseppe Jappelli, the Caffè Pedrocchi stands in the heart of Padua, near the university and the main squares, where once stagecoaches stopped and deposited their passengers. A few years later Jappelli added a neo-Gothic building—the Pedrocchino—to serve as an offelleria (confectioners' shop), and built the magnificent rooms of the second floor, each in a different style, around a great ballroom dedicated to the composer Rossini. Renowned for its warm hospitality, the Caffè became the hub of Paduan cultural and social life, frequented by nobles, artists, and men of letters, but also by patriots and students. It was a theater for the Risorgimento uprising of 1848, with the tapestries of the three principal rooms of the ground floor boasting the colors of the Italian flag. Originally, this floor also housed the Stock Exchange, in the Octagonal Room.

The Pedrocchi was soon baptized "the Caffè Without Doors" because from 1831 onward it was always open—day and night—for eighty-five years. When Antonio Pedrocchi died in 1852, his coffin was paraded around the squares of Padua as a sign of respect. With the death of his nephew and heir, Domenico Cappellato, in 1891, the Caffè was left to the city; it was clumsily altered at the end of the 1940s, but was completely restored by 1998, with the work carried out to Giuseppe Jappelli's original designs.

The Caffè Without Doors remains a lively focus of literary and musical initiative in Padua and, for those who visit the city, a coffee at Pedrocchi's is a privilege not to be missed. **MC**

Tomb of St. Anthony

(Padua, Italy)

The resting place of Padua's patron saint

St. Anthony, the patron saint of Padua, was born in Lisbon, Portugal. He joined the Franciscan Order in 1220 and devoted his time to helping the poor, to becoming a great preacher, and to fighting heretics. More than fifty miracles have been attributed to him. He died at the age of thirty-six in his beloved Padua, where he had lived and preached for several years. His tomb, in the church of Santa Maria Mater Domini, immediately became a place of pilgrimage.

So many pilgrims arrived that the magnificent St. Anthony's Church was erected, incorporating an earlier structure. The saint's body was moved there in

> *"Actions speak louder than words; let your words teach and your actions speak."*
>
> St. Anthony of Padua

1263 and his tomb opened for the first time; his tongue was found miraculously intact, something that remains a mystery to scientists. His tongue is now displayed inside his church, in the Cappella del Tesoro, a few steps away from the monumental Cappella della tomba di Sant'Antonio. The latter chapel dates back to the sixteenth century, and it is probably the work of Tullio Lombardo; it contains a stunning altar and high reliefs that evoke scenes from St. Anthony's life.

The tomb of St. Anthony remains one of the most important pilgrimage destinations in Italy and, every year on June 13, Padua holds memorial celebrations and processions. St. Anthony's Church also houses works by several great artists, including the sculptor Donatello, whose famous equestrian statue *Gattamelata* (1447) stands in the church's square. **MC**

Teatro Olimpico

(Vicenza, Italy)

Haunting last work of the great architect Andrea Palladio

The Teatro Olimpico is the world's oldest surviving Renaissance theater and probably the world's oldest indoor theater. It is also remarkable as the last work of the renowned architect Andrea Palladio, widely considered to be one of the most influential figures in European architecture.

The Teatro Olimpico was commissioned by the Accademia Olimpica (Olympic Academy) in 1580 and built on the site of an abandoned medieval fortress that had been used as a prison and powder store. Palladio had returned to his home city of Vicenza in 1579, and set about designing a new theater based on classical ideas. He died shortly after construction of the Teatro Olimpico began, so the works were continued using his sketches and drawings. Palladio had not, however, left any designs for the scenes to be placed on the stage. These were produced by Vincenzo Scamozzi. They are constructed of wood and stucco, and although they were only intended to be temporary, they have survived and remain in the theater. Scamozzi also designed two rooms in the theater and the original entrance. On March 3, 1585, the theater was inaugurated with a performance of Sophocles's *Oedipus Rex*. Sadly, only a few more productions were staged before the theater was effectively abandoned.

The Teatro Olimpico is a monument to one of the world's most influential architects and an important site in the history of European theater. Unlike theaters such as the Globe in London, which is a reconstruction of Shakespeare's theater, the Teatro Olimpico survives almost extant in its original form, providing a vital and unique historic link to the Renaissance stage. Today, the theater is used only during the summer because installing a heating system would damage its delicate wooden structures. **JF**

"The Palladian project reconstructed the Roman theater with an archeological precision ..."

Centro di Studi di Architettura Andrea Palladio

🏛 ◈ **Jewish Ghetto** (Venice, Italy)

The world's very first ghetto, dating back to the sixteenth century

"*The Venetian Jewish ghetto ... echoes history and transports tourists back in time.*"

Jewish Journal, November 15, 2002

The Venetian Ghetto was the first to be legally established in the world. It has since bequeathed its name to all similar areas around the globe. In 1516, the Jews of Venice were compelled to live in this area of the Cannaregio district; they remained separate from the rest of the city for more than 250 years.

Until the early sixteenth century, Jews had been relatively tolerated in Venice, compared with the rest of Europe. This was to change after an increasing influx of Jews to Venice, exiled from Spain and Portugal, and because of pressure from the Catholic Church. On March 19, 1516, the Venetian government enforced the segregation of Jews. The area chosen was surrounded on all sides by canals, and linked to the rest of the city by two bridges. Jews had to wear a symbol to differentiate them from Christians and were not permitted to leave the ghetto between midnight and dawn, and during some Christian festivals. In spite of these and other restrictions, the ghetto grew in size, and was enlarged in 1541 and 1637. When Napoleon conquered Venice in 1797, he destroyed the ghetto's gates, ending the legal segregation of the Jews. However, Jews were not granted full Venetian citizenship until 1818, and the ghetto's population declined during the nineteenth century. From 1943 to 1945, two hundred Jews were deported from Venice. Only seven returned from the Holocaust.

The ghetto is still a center of Jewish life in Venice. It houses five synagogues, the oldest of which, the Schola Tedesca, dates from 1528. There is also a yeshiva (religious school), as well as a museum of Jewish culture. The Venetian Ghetto was not the first site of Jewish persecution in Europe, but it was the first time the Jews were officially segregated. Today, the Venetian Ghetto still shows the richness and depth of Jewish life in Venice in the face of centuries of cultural and legal discrimination. **JF**

Bridge of Sighs (Venice, Italy)

One of the world's most iconic bridges, immortalized in poetry and art

The Ponte dei Sospiri, or Bridge of Sighs, one of many bridges built in Venice during the sixteenth and seventeenth centuries, was designed to connect the doges' prison with the interrogation rooms on the third floor of the doges' palace, which stood on the opposite side of a slender canal. A covered bridge built of white limestone, its windows are barred with stone grilles, affording a very limited view of the lagoon and the island of San Giorgio—this, of course, was the last glimpse of freedom for many of the prisoners who were taken on this route. The completely enclosed interior of the bridge is divided into two narrow passageways that are separated by a wall; it is very low and cramped, so that most people led through it would have had to crouch. During the Middle Ages the doges' prison had been used by the Inquisition to interrogate heretics, but by the time the Bridge of Sighs was built, those days were over.

It is often claimed that the bridge's name was born from the idea that prisoners would "sigh" as they glimpsed the beauty of freedom and of Venice for the last time. The actual name "Bridge of Sighs," however, dates from the eighteenth century and Lord Byron's poem "Childe Harold's Pilgrimage," which includes the lines: "I stood in Venice on the Bridge of Sighs, a palace and a prison on each hand." A much more romantic association with the bridge comes from a local legend, which says that lovers will enjoy eternal love if they kiss in a gondola beneath the bridge at sunset.

This icon of Venetian architecture has become renowned around the world, and similar covered bridges have been given the name "Bridge of Sighs" in emulation of it. These include bridges in Oxford and Cambridge, in England, and a bridge in Pennsylvania, in the United States, which connects the Allegheny County Courthouse to the city's prison. **RM**

"Yet I remember . . . the deep midnight, the Bridge of Sighs, the beauty of woman."

Edgar Allan Poe, *The Assignation* (1834)

🏛 ⊚ **Basilica San Marco** (Venice, Italy)

The final resting place of St. Mark and one of the world's most famous churches

Legend has it that in the early ninth century two merchants named Buono (Good Man) of Malamocco and Rustico (Rustic) of Torcello, stole the body of St. Mark from Alexandria in Egypt and carried it back to Venice. Rather than presenting their saintly burden to the head of the Venetian church, they gave the body to the head of the Venetian government, the doge, thereby connecting St. Mark forever to the state. The doge ordered the construction of a church to house the saintly remains, which were placed in a temporary shrine within the doges' palace. A church was completed in 832, but destroyed by fire in a rebellion in 976. It was later rebuilt, forming the basis of the present basilica, which was begun in 1063.

The new church became the official chapel of the doge and, by the fifteenth century, was joined to the doges' palace. The church is immediately recognizable, with its main and subsidiary domes echoing the well-known form of earlier Byzantine churches, and showing influences from Constantine's Church of the Apostles in Constantinople. A mosaic over the far left portal of the basilica, depicting the interment of St. Mark's body, gives an astonishingly accurate portrayal of what the church looked like in the thirteenth century, before the fifteenth-century addition of elaborate white Gothic cresting. Unlike the cathedrals of Florence and Milan, which at the end of the thirteenth century still stood open to the sky, St. Mark's had been structurally complete for many years. Because of this, generations of artists and rulers had already worked a wealth of detail and narrative into the fabric of the church. Designated a cathedral in 1807, St. Mark's stands at the head of one of the most famous European squares, presiding over this public and communal space and giving it a sense of religious and civic history rich in legend and glamor. **RM**

 ⊚ **Rialto Bridge** (Venice, Italy)

Historic bridge that was once the only route across Venice's Grand Canal on foot

One of the greatest feats of Renaissance engineering, this world-famous bridge arches gracefully across the narrowest part of the Grand Canal in the heart of Venice. There had been a succession of bridges at this spot since the 1100s—linked with the important Rialto market on the canal's eastern bank—and more than one collapsed under the weight of large crowds.

The current stone bridge was created by Antonio da Ponte and his nephew Antonio Contino. It is very similar in design to its wooden predecessor, which consisted of two inclined ramps, small shops, and a mobile central section that allowed tall ships to pass through. Da Ponte's design has ramps lined with shops and a covering portico. A large central arch measuring 92 feet (28 m) in width allowed trading ships to sail beneath it, and around 12,000 wooden pilings supported the structure—as they still do today. Being chosen to construct such an ambitious bridge was a major challenge and Da Ponte beat several impressive contenders, including Palladio and Michelangelo.

Until the 1800s, this bridge was the only way to cross the Grand Canal on foot. There are other bridges now, but the Rialto remains an iconic symbol of Venice, despite divided opinions over the centuries about its architectural and design merits. It is still lined with two rows of shops—now selling souvenirs—and gondolas and cruise boats pass beneath just as countless traders have done for centuries. **AK**

"The shadowy Rialto threw its colossal curve slowly forth from behind the palace."

John Ruskin, *The Stones of Venice* (1851–53)

🏛 ◉ Torcello (near Venice, Italy)

Intriguing island in the Venetian lagoon, home to an ancient basilica

Two centuries before building had even begun on the first doge's palace or traders haggled on the Rialto, there existed an established community out on a flat sandbank in the north of the Venetian lagoon: Torcello. Invading Huns and, later, Lombards had driven mainlanders to seek out safety on the lagoon islets during the fifth and sixth centuries, and the permanence and status of Torcello was confirmed when Bishop Mauro of Altino founded the Basilica di Santa Maria Assunta here in 639. It is estimated that by the sixteenth century about 20,000 people lived on Torcello, but its decline had already begun—its silted-up canals and malarial swamps were being progressively abandoned for the growing city of Venice. The basilica, the adjacent church of Santa Fosca, and a few other surviving structures are the last remnants of a once-thriving island city.

The basilica's original layout is largely intact and incorporates several early elements—the circular baptistery forming the entrance (rather than being set to one side as in later churches), the "diaconico" mosaics, and the restored altar table—but its crowning glory, so unexpected in this low-key location, are the mosaics. Extending across the western wall is a *Crucifixion*, a *Resurrection*, and, most dramatically, the *Last Judgement*, completed in the thirteenth century. Most emotive, though, is the glowing, golden *Virgin Mary* above the apse at the eastern end: She is the Madonna Teoteca, the God-bearer, believed to have been the creation of Greek artists more than 700 years ago. Torcello's simple beauty and artistry are a potent reminder of a time and a place when the church was as much a part of Byzantium as it was of Rome.

Today Torcello is, literally, in a backwater, but among its lonely marshlands it is still possible to catch a sense of the watery isolation out of which the city of Venice grew. **CB**

> *"A friend came by in his . . . brightly coloured Torcello fishing boat . . . [and] invited us for a ride."*
>
> Erica Jong, *A City of Love and Death: Venice* (1986)

Scuola di San Rocco (Venice, Italy)

The most complete and exciting examples of the work of Jacopo Tintoretto

The Scuola Grande di San Rocco is the headquarters of a Venetian charitable foundation. The building is best known for its extensive painted interiors by Tintoretto, the best-known painter of the influential Venetian School, and one of the greatest figures of the Italian Renaissance.

The foundation of San Rocco was established in 1478, and named after St. Roch, the saint who was specially invoked against the terrifying plague. The first part of the Scuola to be decorated was the hall (Sala dell'Albergo), and a competition for the commission was opened in 1564. Many artists competed for the commission, but Tintoretto secured it by presenting the Scuola with a finished canvas (*The Glorification of St. Roch*) rather than a sketch, which he donated free of charge.

In 1565 Tintoretto added a depiction of Christ's crucifixion, and he completed the decoration of the hall in 1567. The paintings mostly depict scenes from the Passion of Jesus Christ. From 1576 to 1581 Tintoretto added twenty-five canvases to the ceilings and walls of the Upper Hall. The first work completed in the Upper Hall was the ceiling painting, *The Brazen Serpent* (1577). Finally, from 1582 to 1587, Tintoretto completed eight large canvases in the Ground Floor Hall that depicted scenes from the lives of Jesus and his mother, the Virgin Mary. The artist was paid 100 ducats a year for his work. In effect Tintoretto created an illustrated Bible for the poor and needy who came to the Scuola. The paintings were adapted so they could be viewed in the dim light of the halls. The Scuola di San Rocco is perhaps Tintoretto's major work, and certainly his most extensive. The completion of the decoration of the Scuola includes many of the artist's major works. The Scuola is a monument to one of Italy's greatest artists, and a representation of his faith and artistry. **JF**

"Good drawing can only be brought from the casket of the artist's talent with patient study."

Jacopo Tintoretto, artist

Doge's Palace

(Venice, Italy)

Luxurious seat of the powerful rulers of the Republic of Venice

The Doge's (or Duke's) Palace in Venice was the seat of the State's power during the glorious days of the Venetian Republic. There has been a building on the site since 814, but it was during the fourteenth and fifteenth centuries that a palace reflecting the doge's supreme power in the Republic was constructed.

The original designer may have been the unfortunate Filippo Calendario, who was executed for treason in 1355. The palace was constructed in two distinct phases, made obvious by the height difference between the windows in the southern waterfront facade. The architectural style of the palace is unique, translating high northern Gothic into a style necessary to Venetian geological conditions. It favors squat structures incorporating typical and sometimes exaggerated Gothic features—because tall arches, steeples, and towers would be prone to subsidence.

The northern side of the palace adjoins St. Mark's Cathedral, thus indicating the connection of the basilica (and the patron saint of Venice, St. Mark) to the State rather than the church in Venice. The palace contains many important works of art, including the world's largest oil-on-canvas painting, Tintoretto's *Paradise*, which covers the entire rear wall of the vast Grand Council Chamber. This enormous room, 177 feet (54 m) in length and running almost the entire length of the southern waterfront facade, hosted the meetings of the thousand or so nobles who were the ruling class of the Venetian Republic.

The basement and eaves of the palace were once used to house small-time criminals awaiting trial, including Giacomo Casanova, the famously amorous Venetian—hated by husbands—who escaped from his cell in 1756. The nearby main prison, connected to the Doge's Palace by the Ponte dei Sospiri, or Bridge of Sighs, housed most of the city's criminals. **RM**

> *"...from here the Venetian aristocracy coordinated the conquest of an empire..."*

Francesco da Mosto, *Francesco's Venice* (2004)

Porta Soprana

(Genoa, Italy)

Medieval gateway to the city of Genoa

The Porta Soprana, also called the Porta di Sant'Andrea, is the eastern entrance to the city of Genoa, a medieval gateway enclosed between two battlement towers. It is a twin to the gate at the western entrance to the city, Porta dei Vacca. Between 1155 and 1158, Porta Soprana and the so-called "walls of Barbarossa" were built high and strong as a defense against Genoa's enemies attacking from the sea or land. Genoa was a city-state from before 1100, and day-to-day governing was exercised by a group of elected consuls. Frederick I Barbarossa, Holy Roman Emperor from 1155 to 1190, invaded Italy six times trying to establish his power, which could explain why the Genoese walls are named after him.

The Porta Soprana, constructed of Ligurian stone and fragments of marble, was the first example of Gothic architecture in the city. It is one of the best-known symbols of Genoa, a testament to the city's proud, powerful, and successful history. Carved under the gate's central arch are words in Latin, reading in part: "If you come peacefully, you may touch these gates; if you demand war, you will leave off defeated."

Just inside the gate lies the building known as Casa di Colombo, or Christopher Columbus's House. The present building was actually built in the seventeenth century on the foundations of Columbus's fifteenth-century home (destroyed by French forces in a naval barrage in 1684). It is claimed that Columbus lived in this house during his childhood, the son of a wool weaver who also acted as gatekeeper of the Porta Soprana. Columbus claimed to have gone to sea at the age of ten, where he became an accomplished sailor and map maker. Since being restored, the house has been opened to the public and contains a small museum dedicated to Columbus and marine exploration. **RM**

Verdi's House

(Sant'Agata, Italy)

The home of the great Italian composer

Born in the tiny village of Roncole in Parma, Giuseppe Verdi (1813–1901) became the Italian maestro of opera in the nineteenth century, with works including *Rigoletto*, *Il trovatore*, *La traviata*, *Aida*, *Otello*, *Falstaff*, and *Macbeth*. Verdi appeared on the operatic scene just as the Italian *bel canto* tradition of Rossini, Bellini, and Donizetti was drawing to a close. He took this tradition and transformed it, constantly experimenting and refining to expand the drama, yet all the while giving the audience the melody they loved.

Verdi's first opera was produced at La Scala in Milan in 1839 but tragedy struck soon after when his

"When I am alone with my notes, my heart pounds and the tears stream from my eyes…"

Giuseppe Verdi, on composing

young wife and two infant children became ill and died. This catastrophe, combined with the complete rejection of his next opera, *Un giorno di regno*, served to form Verdi's fatalistic and often harsh character. Throwing himself into his work, he composed prolifically between 1843 and 1849. In 1847 he fell in love again, with prima donna Giuseppina Strepponi. They lived together, but did not marry until 1859.

Verdi's house in Sant'Agata, where he lived sporadically from 1848, has five rooms open to the public, including Giuseppina's bedroom and the canopy bed where she died, Verdi's study, his bedroom, and dressing room. The latter contains the Fritz piano he used from *Rigoletto* to *Aida*. Not only a successful composer, Verdi owned a huge estate, and managed the farm and gardens himself. **RM**

Castello di San Michele

(Ferrara, Italy)

A fortress built to protect a hated ruling family from their people

In 1264, the Guelf family of Este, in a war of dominance for the city of Ferrara, overcame the rival Salinguerra family and finally became lords of the city and its territory—although they would never be accepted or beloved by their subjects. Matters came to a head when the people of Ferrara, worn out by famine and exasperated by endless taxation, rose up against the Este in a bloody rebellion of 1385. Though the rebels were overcome, the event put such fear into Nicolo II d'Este that he commissioned a fortress, the great Castello di San Michele (also known as Castello Estense), to be built around an existing watchtower, the Rocca dei Leoni (Lion's Fortress), in the northern city wall to protect him and his family.

This mighty fortress became the symbol of a despotic and absolute power over a city finally subdued, an indication of the wealth and political and military control of the Este. It was not until 1476, however, after Ercole d'Este defeated a bloody bid for power by his nephew, that the family took up full residence within the castle's environs and works began to improve and expand their apartments. In 1598 Alfonso II, who had already been married three times, faced the fact that he had no legitimate male heir or even a successor who would be recognized by the church. He made various attempts to prevent the end of the house of Este and its property's expected annexation by the church, but the family was finally forced to abandon Ferrara and the castle was taken over by the Papal States, becoming the home of the Cardinal Legates.

Almost 300 years later, the Provincial Administration of Ferrara purchased the fortress at auction for 70,000 lire, and still has its offices there today. The rest of the castle has been restored and is now open to the public. **RM**

> *"Time has begun to thin their ranks, but . . . the people in Ferrara . . . remember Dr. Fadigati."*
>
> Giorgio Bassani, *The Gold-Rimmed Spectacles* (1958)

Arturo Toscanini's Birthplace (Parma, Italy)

The first home of the great conductor

The man whom many consider to be the greatest conductor of his time, Arturo Toscanini (1867–1957), was born in a tiny house in one of the poorest districts of Parma. He spent a year in this house—a very cramped year since his family shared the space with two other families. He was the oldest of four children, and the only son of Claudio and Paola Toscanini.

The young Arturo entered Parma's Royal School of Music on a scholarship at the age of nine. He graduated with the highest honors in cello and composition, and already had a reputation for his photographic memory, wide-ranging musical talents,

> *"To some it is Napoleon, to some it is philosophical struggle; to me it is Allegro con brio."*
>
> Arturo Toscanini, on Beethoven's *Eroica*

and passionately held ideals. He joined an Italian opera company as principal cellist and assistant chorus master, and toured South America. While performing *Aida* in Rio de Janeiro, the conductor was booed off the stage and Toscanini was prevailed upon to take his place. Aged just nineteen, Toscanini conducted the entire opera from memory. This extraordinary effort marked the beginning of his sixty-eight-year career as a conductor. His grasp of a huge range of operatic and orchestral works, and his instinctive musical interpretation allowed him to correct mistakes in scores that had been overlooked for years.

Toscanini's birthplace is now a small museum. The collection includes historic documents, heirlooms, personal mementos, photographs, and a library of Toscanini's recorded works. **RM**

Neptune Fountain (Bologna, Italy)

Giambologna's masterpiece of sculpture

The northern Italian city of Bologna fell to the troops of Pope Julius II in 1506, and remained under papal control until Napoleon Bonaparte invaded Italy in 1796. During this papal period the city flourished. It became known as a place of great learning, a magnet for artists, painters, and craftsmen. The center of the city houses two squares that were once the seat of religious and civic power: the Piazza Maggiore and the adjoining Piazza del Nettuno. Lying between the two stands the Fontana del Nettuno, or Fountain of Neptune. It was made by the Flemish sculptor Jean Boulogne, known as Giambologna.

The artist left his native Flanders for Rome in 1550, before settling in Florence two years later. He was influenced by classical Greek sculpture and the work of Michelangelo, and was eventually recognized as the leading sculptor of the exaggerated style of Italian Mannerism. Giambologna was commissioned to create the bronze sculpture of Neptune, and the subsidiary sculptures that form the fountain, by Pope Pius IV in 1563. Giambologna's interpretation of the god of the sea, carrying a trident while calming the waves, made him famous. Below Neptune lie water-spouts in the shape of fish held by cherubs who sit on a plinth featuring the symbolic papal keys. In a frivolous style common to Mannerism, four mermaids at the base hold a breast in each hand, and each nipple serves as a water spout. In 1564 a block of houses was demolished to make way for the fountain; which was completed in 1566. The fountain's base was designed by Sicilian artist Tomasso Laureti.

The fountain was warmly received, and ensured Giambologna commissions from the powerful Medici family, including work on the Boboli Gardens. As a result, Giambologna's sculptures influenced the design of formal gardens throughout Europe. **CK**

🏛 ◉ Basilica of San Vitale (Ravenna, Italy)

Roman-Byzantine church, home to some of the most famous mosaics in the world

San Vitale dates from the greatest period in Ravenna's history, when it played a pivotal role in the relations between East and West—Constantinople and Rome. The church reflects these very different cultural influences, particularly in its stunning mosaics, which are generally acknowledged as the finest in the Western world.

Situated in northeastern Italy, Ravenna came to the fore as the Roman Empire crumbled. In 402, Ravenna replaced Rome as the capital of the western empire, but by the end of the century the city was in the hands of the Ostrogoths. By 540 the situation had changed again, as Byzantine emperor Justinian took control and made Ravenna the capital of his imperial rule in Italy. San Vitale was built against the backdrop of these upheavals. It was begun by Bishop Ecclesius in 526, during the Ostrogoth period, and was consecrated in 547, under the new regime. The

building was funded privately, by a wealthy banker named Julianus Argentarius, and dedicated to the little-known St. Vitalis.

The church has an unusual octagonal layout, with an outer aisle and galleries. It combines Roman and Byzantine elements, although the influence of the latter is far greater. For this reason, it has been suggested that the plans were produced by a Latin architect who had trained in the East. The mosaics, which consist of biblical scenes and imperial portraits, also have a strong Byzantine flavor. The most famous sections are the two panels showing Justinian and his wife, Theodora, emphasizing the theocratic nature of their rule. Justinian is depicted in the company of twelve attendants—a subtle echo of Jesus Christ and his apostles—and the royal couple present the vessels that will hold the bread and wine, the symbols of the Eucharist. **IZ**

🏛 ⊚ Church of Sant'Apollinare (Ravenna, Italy)

One of the best-preserved churches in Italy, dating back to the sixth century

Sant'Apollinare is one of the best-preserved and most important early Christian churches in Italy. Like the church of San Vitale, it was erected with funds provided by the wealthy patron Julianus Argentarius following the commission of Bishop Ursicinus, and it was consecrated in 549 by the Archbishop Maximian. Its construction took place during a period of major political upheavals in Europe: the fall of the western half of the Roman Empire in 476; the recapture of Italy from the rule of the occupying Goth tribes, carried out by the eastern emperor Justinian between 535 and 552; and the Lombard invasion in 568. At that time, Ravenna was the capital town of the peninsula and therefore one of the main cities of Italy.

When it was built, the church stood close to the sea, at the Roman harbor of Classe. Due to subsequent marsh-draining, however, the waters retreated and this marvelous building now stands proudly in the countryside of Ravenna. The church seems to have been built on the site of an important cemetery, attested to by the imposing sarcophagi that are now displayed along the aisles of the church. It is dedicated to Sant'Apollinare, who was the first bishop of Ravenna and was the first to convert the people of this area to Christianity. His relics were transported from this church to Sant'Apollinare Nuovo in Ravenna in 856.

The church, which is constructed in brick, like the remarkable round bell tower next to it that is believed to date back to the tenth century, is divided into three naves by elegant columns of Greek marble. It also boasts impressive early medieval mosaics in the presbytery and in the apse, where the figure of Sant'Apollinare is set out on a mosaic depicting a delicate green meadow. These remarkable mosaics were made by unknown Byzantine artists and are of inestimable value. **MC**

Puccini's Birthplace (Lucca, Italy)

Family home of the great composer and now a museum dedicated to his life and works

Giacomo Puccini (1858–1924), born in this house in Lucca, composed some of the most popular and well-known operas in the world. A great advocate of operatic realism, much beloved by music enthusiasts, he is considered to be Verdi's musical successor.

Puccini was the last of five generations of musicians who had been musical directors of the San Martino Cathedral for 200 years. His father died when Puccini was five, and the municipality of Lucca supported the family and kept the position of cathedral organist free for him. At the age of eighteen, however, he walked 11 miles (18 km) to Pisa to see a performance of Verdi's *Aida*, which inspired him to become a composer of opera. In 1880 he entered the Milan Conservatory, where he studied with the famous composer and violinist Antonio Bazzini and then Ponchielli, composer of the opera *La Gioconda*. At the age of twenty-five Puccini ran away with a married woman, Elvira, causing an enormous scandal. Elvira and Puccini had one son, Antonio. They finally married in 1904, after the death of Elvira's husband.

Puccini composed a number of operas and his mature works have found international acclaim and respect. They are regularly played in the world's opera houses and include *La bohème*, *Tosca*, *Madame Butterfly*, and *Turandot*. The house in Lucca where Puccini was born is now a small private museum containing memorabilia and documents about his life, including the piano, brought from his house in Viareggio, on which he composed his last opera, *Turandot*. A bronze statue of the composer stands in a piazza close to his home. **RM**

◩ Giacomo Puccini, smoking in a 1913 photograph, was to die after treatment for throat cancer in 1924.

◩ This bronze effigy of Puccini relaxing in a confident, albeit haughty, pose is sited near his birthplace.

🏛 ◉ Camposanto (Pisa, Italy)

Pisa's ancient cemetery, associated by legend with the crucifixion of Jesus Christ

The walled Camposanto, or cemetery, lies at the northern edge of Pisa's grand Campo dei Miracoli (Field of Miracles). It is believed to have been the site of an earlier burial ground. According to legend, this site was created in the twelfth century when the Archbishop of Pisa, Ubaldo de' Lanfranchi, brought back five shiploads of soil from the mount of Golgotha outside Jerusalem, where Christ was crucified. Prominent Pisan citizens were buried here until 1779, sometimes reusing ancient Roman sarcophagi. The cemetery building was begun in 1278 by Giovanni di Simone, constructed on the older cemetery site in the shape of a massive oblong Gothic cloister. The building was not finished until 1464.

The outside walls are lined with forty-three blind arches, and the interior is lit by mullioned and tracery windows that were never glassed in. In the fourteenth century, ancient Roman sculptures and sarcophagi were brought to the cemetery, and the walls covered with frescoes. *The Last Judgement*, *Hell*, and the fantastically realistic *Triumph of Death* are attributed to an unknown artist. Benozzo Gozzoli created another vast series of frescoes, *The Stories of the Old Testament*. He is buried in the Camposanto.

In July 1944 all these great artifacts were virtually destroyed when Allied forces dropped incendiary bombs on the building, melting the lead roof. There are eighty-four remaining—albeit badly damaged—sarcophagi, which mostly date from the third century. Restoration works have been ongoing since 1945, and any frescoes that could be saved have been removed for display elsewhere. **RM**

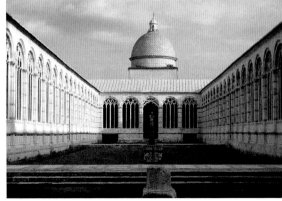

↗ The Camposanto's *Monument to Henry VII* by Tino di Camaino was commissioned by the city of Pisa in 1315.

→ Enclosed by the walls of the Camposanto is a large volume of soil brought from the site of the Crucifixion.

Leaning Tower of Pisa (Pisa, Italy)

One of the world's most instantly recognizable buildings, famous for its imperfection

"*The leaning tower . . . was too small. I felt it keenly. It was nothing like so high . . . as I had hoped.*"

Charles Dickens, *Pictures From Italy* (1846)

⬆ Pisa's Campo dei Miracoli, with the tower, cathedral, and baptistery; the Camposanto lies off to the right.

➡ The Tower of Pisa is a freestanding campanile, or bell tower; it leans at an angle of 5.5 degrees.

Until the twentieth century, the fact that the bell tower of Pisa leans so dramatically was thought to have been the architect's intention—an attention-grabbing, artistic device. After extensive research, however, it is now believed that the tower was originally intended to be vertical. It began to tilt during the initial construction phase because of a defectively laid foundation and the fact that the soil on which it was standing was particularly unstable—a soil made up of mineral deposits and clay, lying on top of a subterranean layer of water.

The identity of the architect remains a mystery, although several names have been suggested at various times. Sixteenth-century art historian and biographer Giorgio Vasari suggested it was Bonnano Pisano; other suggestions include the architects Diotisalvi and Biduino. The evidence is inconclusive, however, and the real identity of the creator of Pisa's famous tower may have been lost forever in history. Construction of the tower began on August 9, 1173, during a time of prosperity and military success. This stability was not to last, and it would be almost 200 years before the tower was finally completed.

Largely unweathered and still extraordinarily beautiful, the tower is a cylindrical body of stone circled around with arcades of arches and columns, topped by a belfry that contains seven bells, tuned to a musical scale. Various works have been carried out on the tower throughout the centuries. Mussolini, irritated by the tilt of the tower, ordered that concrete be poured into its base to return it to the vertical. This only caused it to sink farther into the ground. In 1990, more sensitive restoration was undertaken in a painstaking, decade-long procedure. Because the iconic tilting tower is so important to tourism in Pisa, it is hoped that the works have secured the building at its current angle for the next 300 years at least. **RM**

🏛 ◉ Basilica of the Holy Cross (Florence, Italy)

The Franciscan order's great Florentine church, and final resting place of Michelangelo

In thirteenth-century Florence, the Dominican and Franciscan religious orders grew increasingly powerful and became major rivals. The Franciscans advocated a mystical, personal faith; the Dominicans were more rational and philosophical. Each order's churches reflected their rivalry.

The Franciscans built the basilica (Basilica di Santa Croce) on the site of an earlier church—one that had supposedly been founded by St. Francis himself. It is a massive building, laid out in a series of simple, large rectangular shapes. Originally, the church was quite restrained in its internal and external decoration, but it now contains art by a number of famous painters and sculptors, including Giotto and Donatello.

The church also houses many famous graves, including that of Michelangelo, who, according to legend, wanted his tomb (designed by Giorgio Vasari) placed directly to the right of the church entrance so the first thing he would see on Judgment Day was the dome of the Duomo through Santa Croce's doors. Opposite Michelangelo is Galileo, buried there in 1737, one hundred years after his death. Nicolo Machiavelli and Lorenzo Ghiberti lie inside the church, as does a tomb built for Dante Alighieri, whom the Florentines had exiled from the city in 1301. The town of Ravenna, where Dante actually lies, refused to give back his body, so consequently the tomb in Santa Croce remains an empty monument to the great poet. **RM**

"She watched the tourists; their noses as red as their Baedekers, so cold was Santa Croce."

E. M. Forster, *A Room With A View* (1908)

🏛 ⊚ **Florence Cathedral** (Florence, Italy)

Once the largest church in the world, crowned by Brunelleschi's famous dome

The Basilica di Santa Maria del Fiore, also known as the Duomo, or Florence Cathedral, is now the fourth-largest church in the world—after St. Peter's in Rome, St. Paul's in London, and Milan Cathedral. When it was first built, however, it was the world's largest church, able to house 30,000 worshippers and emblematic of Florence's political and economic dominance.

Building work began on the cathedral in 1296, although it was not consecrated until 1436. It is notable for its stained-glass windows; its ornate green, red, and white marble facade; its collection of paintings and statuary by Renaissance masters; and its world-famous dome. The cathedral has also been the seat of the Council of Florence since 1439, and the place where religious reformer, and instigator of the Bonfire of the Vanities, Girolamo Savonarola, preached. The cathedral has even witnessed murder. In 1478 Giuliano di Piero de' Medici, co-ruler of Florence, was stabbed and killed by men backed by his rivals the Archbishop of Pisa and Pope Sixtus IV. His brother and co-ruler Lorenzo Il Magnifico was also stabbed but escaped and later had the archbishop hanged.

The construction of the building—built on the site of the old cathedral of Santa Reparata—was overseen by several architects, beginning with Arnolfo di Cambio. In 1331 an institution was created to supervise the works, and in 1334 painter and architect Giotto was appointed as master builder, assisted by architect Andrea Pisano. After Giotto's death in 1337, a number of architects took the lead and plans were made to enlarge the original project and build a dome. In 1418 a competition was held to find a designer for the dome; it was won by sculptor and architect Filippo Brunelleschi. His innovative design was self-supporting, requiring no scaffolding. It was completed in 1436 and remains a masterpiece of ingenuity. **CK**

Florence Baptistery Bronze Doors (Florence, Italy)

Exquisite bronze doors dubbed the "Gates of Paradise" by Michelangelo

The Piazza San Giovanni in Florence is home to three important buildings: the cathedral, the campanile, and the baptistery. The octagonal, domed baptistery is covered in eye-catching green and white marble, and its interior is studded with breathtaking mosaics. It is most notable, however, for its three pairs of doors, which were created in the fourteenth and fifteenth centuries and decorated with sculptures depicting scenes from the life of the city's patron saint, St. John the Baptist, and themes of salvation and baptism.

In 1322, the city's powerful wool merchants, the Calimala Guild, decided that the old wooden East Doors should be replaced with bronze. The replacement doors, which have since been repositioned as the South Doors, are fine examples of Gothic craftsmanship. They were designed by Andrea Pisano, and made by Venetian bronzesmith Leonardo d'Avanzo between 1330 and 1336. The casting involved making wax models that were covered with clay and baked. The wax would melt with the heat, leaving a hollow to be filled with the molten metal. The sculptures were then smoothed and engraved.

The Calimala Guild held a competition to replace Pisano's East Doors. The winner was the young Lorenzo Ghiberti, who beat architect and sculptor Filippo Brunelleschi into second place. His doors, since moved to become today's North Doors, were made between 1403 and 1424. Ghiberti's work illustrates the shift to a Renaissance style with its use of perspective and dynamic human sculptures.

Today's East Doors, commissioned by the Calimala Guild, were also made by Ghiberti, from 1425 to 1452. Ghiberti spent most of the rest of his life completing the new East Doors. The gilded doors have become known as the Gates of Paradise, a name bestowed by Michelangelo in tribute to their beauty, and because they mark the entrance to a place of baptism. **CK**

> *"In some of the reliefs I have put as many as a hundred figures, in some more, in others less."*
>
> Lorenzo Ghiberti, sculptor

Palazzo Vecchio (Florence, Italy)

Once the seat of Florentine power, built on an ancient Roman site

Originally called the Palazzo della Signoria (Palace of the Priors), this massive civic structure was commissioned in 1299 by the city council, intended as an appropriate place for the priors to meet. The priors, representatives of the main guilds of Florence, formed the main governing body of the city at that time. Arnolfo di Cambio, already famous for his part in building Florence's cathedral and the church of Santa Croce, turned his hand to the creation of this building. The new palazzo would be the city's main political meeting place until 1565, when it began to lose some of its status to the Uffizi and the Palazzo Pitti.

The building now known as the Palazzo Vecchio (Old Palace) was built on the site of ancient Roman ruins. Into its facade was incorporated an ancient tower in an off-center position; this was intentional as the surrounding piazza itself was not symmetrical. Arnolfo topped the tower with the symbolic Marzocco, or lion, holding up the lily of Florence. The word *marzocco* possibly comes from Mars, the ancient protector of the city before Christian Florence designated St. John as its patron saint. A pair of lions were kept caged in the rear of the palace, until the eighteenth century.

The palazzo went through three successive building stages, reflecting a changing political landscape. Arnolfo's construction was followed by alterations made during the Republic; then a major renovation program was undertaken by Vasari under Cosimo I de' Medici. In 1865, after a 300-year hiatus as the city's main seat of government, the palazzo became the seat of the country's provisional government. In 1872, after the unification of Italy, it returned to its original purpose as the home of the city council, a role that continues today. It is also open to the public, displaying art collections and the private quarters of its occupants throughout history. **SM**

"The dark, sheer front of the Palazzo Vecchio went up like a cliff, to the battlements."

D. H. Lawrence, *Aaron's Rod* (1922)

Monastery of St. Mark (Florence, Italy)

Early medieval church and home to the artist Fra Angelico

> "The one who wanted
> to burn me is now himself
> put to the flames."

Jacopo Nardi, witness of Savonarola's execution

The original building on this site dates from 1100 but became the Church and Monastery of St. Mark in 1299. Early in the fifteenth century the church became an important spiritual center for the Medici family, when Cosimo the Elder began to use it as a regular spiritual retreat and gave it the special protection of the family's name. Michelozzo was commissioned to restore the building and bell tower, and he added sections of architectural importance, such as the sacristy, the library, and the beautiful structuring of the corridors. The monastery was at this time under the Dominicans, who had taken it over from the abolished order of Silvanestri Friars.

Fra Angelico, perhaps the religious order's most famous friar, lived here from 1436 to 1445 and produced some of his finest work in the forty-two cells, cloister, chapter house, and first-floor corridors. The First Cloister is a remarkable example of Renaissance monastic architecture, decorated with flower beds and an enormous cedar of Lebanon, with Fra Angelico's frescoes adorning the walls. The Florentine Humanist Academy met in St. Mark's Gardens, while Cosimo and later Lorenzo the Magnificent used the refectory graced with Ghirlandaio's painting *The Last Supper* to assemble some of the finest intellectual minds of the time. Girolamo Savonarola, instigator of the Bonfire of the Vanities in 1497, was Father Superior here until he was burned at the stake in 1498, and Pico della Mirandola and Agnolo Poliziano are both buried in the church.

The Italian government took control of the church and monastery in 1860 and opened it to the public in 1869. A museum dedicated to Fra Angelico opened in 1920 and displays his delicate, spiritual paintings and frescoes, together with many other important works of art by Ghiberti, Donatello, Ghirlandaio, Pucci, Gherardini, Fra Bartolomeo, and others. **RM**

Medici Palace (Florence, Italy)

A stunning home built for the most powerful family in Florence

Cosimo di Giovanni de' Medici, Cosimo the Elder, commissioned this building from Michelozzo in 1444. It is claimed to be the first Renaissance building in Florence. The historian Vasari related how Cosimo originally rejected a design by Brunelleschi as "too lavish and magnificent," because it would "arouse envy among the citizens, rather than being a grand ornament for the city, and comfortable in itself." The building Michelozzo designed was a cube, elegant and austere, with three clearly delineated floors topped by an overhanging cornice, the top floors displaying a uniform row of arched windows. The ground floor sported a partially closed loggia and two asymmetrical doors opening into a courtyard modeled on a Brunelleschian design, which in turn led into a typical Renaissance garden. The open loggia and courtyard were particularly important as the place where business was transacted and the point of contact between the Medici and the public.

The palace was complete by 1460, and witnessed some of the most dramatic events in Florence's history, including the insurrection led by Savonarola in 1494, when the Republic drove the Medici out of the city and confiscated their property, including the palazzo with its collections and furnishings. Some works of art were transferred to the Piazza Signoria, the new civic seat of government.

In 1512 the Medici returned to the city and regained possession of the palazzo and many of their belongings. The open loggia was closed off because it was no longer necessary for business or politics— and because the Medici had installed four cannons there, insuring against future danger. In 1540, Cosimo I de' Medici, Duke of Florence, moved to the Palazzo Vecchio; the palace was then occupied by lesser members of the Medici family until it was sold to the Riccardi family in 1659. **RM**

" . . . and it became clear that spending money gives me greater pleasure than earning it."

Cosimo di Giovanni de' Medici

 ⊘ **Pitti Palace** (Florence, Italy)

A palace intended to rival that of the Medici, now an outstanding museum

Envious of the Medici, Florentine banker Luca Pitti commissioned a home whose windows would be larger than the entrance of the Palazzo Medici. In the sixteenth century, art historian Giorgio Vasari claimed the architect was Brunelleschi, assisted by his pupil Luca Fancelli, although this has been questioned. The palazzo differs greatly from Brunelleschi's style, and construction began twelve years after his death.

Despite Pitti's hopes, the building was not as impressive in size or content as the Palazzo Medici. Fancelli, as main architect, seemed to favor a utilitarian domestic style for the facade, with rustic stonework fashioned in a triplicated series of seven arched openings, reminiscent of a Roman aqueduct. His design was sustained during renovations of the palazzo and has since been copied numerous times.

Pitti suffered financial difficulties toward the end of his life and died in 1472 without finishing the building. Ironically, in 1549, one of his descendants sold the building to Eleonora di Toledo, Grand Duchess of Tuscany and wife to Cosimo I de' Medici. The palazzo, enlarged and altered, became the official residence of the grand ducal family and took on most of its present appearance.

The Boboli Gardens were built behind the palazzo and provide an oasis of green and cool water in the heart of the city, as well as spectacular views. The Pitti Palace is now an extensive museum. **RM**

"So here we are in the Pitti till April, in small rooms, yellow with sunshine . . . till evening."

Elizabeth Barrett-Browning, letter, December 1847

🏛 ⊚ **Ponte Vecchio** (Florence, Italy)

Fourteenth-century bridge and iconic symbol of the city of Florence

Begun in the fourteenth century, the Ponte Vecchio (Old Bridge) was a popular location for shops, largely due to a supposed tax exemption for premises located here. Until the sixteenth century these were mainly food stalls, especially butchers' stalls. This came to an end after Cosimo de' Medici commissioned Giorgio Vasari in 1565 to build a corridor (Corridoio Vasariano) along the top of the bridge to connect the Palazzo Vecchio with the Palazzo Pitti, eliminating the need to mix with the commoners on his commute between the two. Cosimo could not stand the smell of the butchers' shops and had them removed in 1593. They were replaced with the more upper-class trades of goldsmiths and jewelers.

These types of establishments remain the dominant shops today, their heritage acknowledged by a monument to Benvenuto Cellini, Florence's most famous goldsmith. A modern local tradition symbolizing eternal love involves clamping a padlock on the railings surrounding Cellini's bust and throwing the key in the river; as this damages the bridge, anyone caught taking part in the ritual is now fined.

The Ponte Vecchio is not only the oldest segmental arch bridge in Florence, but the oldest in Europe. Its survival is thanks to a surprisingly merciful order—supposedly from Hitler himself—not to destroy it with all the other bridges in Florence during the German retreat from the city in August 1944. **RM**

"The narrow street . . . which runs up from the Ponte Vecchio to the Piazza, was thickly crowded."

Thomas A. Trollope, *What I Remember* (1887–89)

🏛 ⊚ Medici Tombs (Florence, Italy)

Monuments to members of the illustrious and influential Florentine family

For more than three centuries, the Medici were one of the most powerful families in Italy. They made their fortune from banking and became the ruling family of Florence. The Medici supported many of the key figures of the Renaissance, including Donatello and Michelangelo, both of whom worked on the family's ornate tombs.

Commissioned by Giovanni di Bicci de' Medici, the founder of the banking empire on which the family built their political influence, the tombs are located in the Basilica di San Lorenzo, where they dominate the church. Built between 1419 and 1459, they were designed by Filippo Brunelleschi. The Old Sacristy was built between 1421 and 1440. Donatello, who is buried in the basilica, added decorative details to the structure. Three Medici are memorialized there, including Giovanni Bicci. The New Sacristy, which was begun in 1520 by Michelangelo, houses monuments to four Medici, including Lorenzo II, to whom the now-notorious Florentine statesman Niccolò Machiavelli dedicated *The Prince*, written in 1513. The grandest part of the basilica is the Medici Chapels (completed 1603–04), which were designed by Bernardo Buontalenti. They house monuments to the first six Medici Grand Dukes of Tuscany, as well as the tombs of almost fifty lesser members of the family in its crypt. The first of the many members of the family to rule Florence, Cosimo, is buried in front of the high altar of the basilica.

The Medici tombs display the wealth and influence of an illustrious and powerful family that provided three popes as well as members of the English and French royal families. Perhaps their greatest achievement, however, lay in their patronage of the arts. As such, the Medici tombs include work by many of the world's greatest artists. **JF**

 ⊚ **Palazzo del Popolo** (San Gimignano, Italy)

Communal palace housing Florentine and Sienese art

Visitors to San Gimignano may get the feeling that time has stood still. This enchanting medieval town contains a number of masterpieces of fourteenth- and fifteenth-century Italian art, perfectly preserved in their original architectural settings. The entire town of San Gimignano is protected by UNESCO because of the testimony it bears to medieval civilization.

One of the most important monuments is the Palazzo del Popolo. Completed in 1288, it was probably planned by the great architect Arnolfo di Cambio. It was here that the city council would meet and the *podestà* (chief magistrate) would administer the law. Coats of arms belonging to council officers from different periods are displayed on the walls of the internal courtyard (part of the extension works of 1323). Next to the palace is the imposing Loggia del Popolo, which was built in 1347, where the *podestà* would take the oath of allegiance in front of the townspeople. The Torre Grossa (Big Tower) was constructed next to the palace a few years later. At 177 feet (54 m) high, it is the tallest tower in San Gimignano, whose importance stemmed from its location on the Via Francigena—the traditional pilgrimage route to and from Rome. During the Renaissance, the town boasted around seventy-two tower-houses, which symbolized the power, prestige, and wealth of the families who ruled San Gimignano; only fourteen tower-houses survive today.

The Torre Grossa is open to the public and visitors can enjoy a wonderful panoramic view of the town from the top. Today the Palazzo del Popolo hosts the Musei Civici and the Pinacoteca (picture gallery), which displays works of Florentine and Sienese painters of the fourteenth and fifteenth centuries, such as Domenico Michelino, Pinturricchio, Filippino Lippi, and Coppo di Marcovaldo. **MC**

🏛 ⊚ Siena Cathedral (Siena, Italy)

Spectacular example of Gothic architecture in white and greenish-black marble

By the fifteenth century, the city of Siena had ceded its commercial dominance to Florence but had become a major focus of artistic talent, boasting beautiful art and architecture by some of the greatest figures in the Italian art world. Many of these treasures still exist within the walls of the old town, and perhaps the most spectacular is the cathedral—a fine example of Gothic architecture, with a distinctive Tuscan-Italian spin.

The cathedral that stands today is essentially a thirteenth-century creation, although a Romanesque design was begun in the twelfth century. Striped designs in black and white marble are a major feature, cladding various interior columns and walls. The cathedral's facade, constructed in two main stages starting *c.* 1284, is particularly striking. Much of this was designed by the great Italian artist Giovanni Pisano, who also contributed expressive sculptural decoration that ranks among the finest on any cathedral facade. Between 1265 and 1268, Giovanni's father, Nicola, created a richly carved octagonal marble pulpit for the cathedral, acknowledged as one of his best works. Other highlights include a bell tower; a dome topped by an elegant lantern; stunning marble floors with inlays by Domenico Beccafumi, among many others; sculptures by Bernini and Michelangelo; a font whose carvings include work by Donatello and Lorenzo Ghiberti; and a stained-glass window based on thirteenth-century designs by Duccio—one of the earliest examples of Italian stained glass in existence. In the adjoining Piccolomini Library are vividly colored sixteenth-century frescoes by noted Umbrian artist Pinturicchio.

The cathedral has retained its importance over the years, with artistic additions and restorations made in subsequent centuries, including the bronze door in the facade, which was created in the 1950s. **AK**

 ⬡ **Palazzo Pubblico** (Siena, Italy)

Medieval town hall lavishly decorated with frescoes on themes of governance

Built at the end of the thirteenth century to house the republican government, the Palazzo Pubblico is the town hall of Siena. The building is a fine example of Italian medieval architecture, with Gothic influences. The bell tower, the Torre del Mangia, was built between 1325 and 1344. The Palazzo Pubblico stands at the center of this ancient city on the Piazza del Campo, world famous for Il Pallio, the bareback horse race that circuits the town square twice each summer, each rider and horse representing a city ward. Violent and dangerous, unchanged in centuries, these brief contests bring the center of Siena to life.

The palace is filled with frescoes, including the famous *Allegory of Good Government*, which depicts Justice as a woman gesturing to the symbolic scales. A convicted criminal is beheaded, whereas other figures receive the rewards of justice. Also present is Peace, who is represented as a fashionable, white-clad contemporary female figure with elaborate blonde hair. Other paintings include the *Effects of Good Government*, with prosperous citizens trading and dancing in front of a picturesque countryside, and *Effects of Bad Government*, with rampant crime and disease, framed by a drought-ridden Tuscany.

Some historians have claimed that Siena never fully recovered from the effects of the plague in 1348, which killed about half the city's population. The economy, based around the wool trade and finance, was destroyed and the state declined from its prominent position in Italy, with the ensuing centuries-long comparative lack of growth meaning that Siena did not develop during the Renaissance as did rival Italian cities. The legacy today is one of Italy's best-preserved medieval towns, with narrow streets and ancient building, spared from redevelopment, sprawling growth, and the bombs of World War II. **AP**

Palazzo Ducale
(Urbino, Italy)

Quintessential Renaissance palace, containing an extensive art collection

"It's the only palace in the world that I can go round without feeling oppressed and exhausted."

Kenneth Clark, *Civilisation* (1969)

Duke Federico da Montefeltro (1422–82) was widely recognized as one of the most enlightened leaders of his day, despite his profession as a mercenary with a private army who hired himself out to fight other people's wars. A brilliant military tactician, Federico determined, some ten years or so after being pronounced duke in 1444, to build a residence that would be a gathering place for the greatest thinkers and artists of the mid-fifteenth century.

Originally, the job of designing and building the palace seems to have fallen to the Florentine Maso di Bartolomeo, but it was the architect Luciano Laurana from Dalmatia who took over the work and created the palace that would be his masterpiece. He is responsible for the facade, the light arcaded courtyard, which is a major prototype for a lot of the Renaissance architecture that was to follow, and the Grand Stairway described by Vasari as the most beautiful of its time. The scale of the palace is of human proportions, designed to inspire rather than intimidate. When Laurana left Urbino in 1472, Francesco di Giorgio Martini was hired to complete the works. He had little choice other than to follow the designs laid down by his predecessor, but he is responsible for much of the detail work and decoration to the facade.

The palace is a quintessentially Renaissance residence, built to reflect the ideals of the time and the man who owned it. A visit to the palace, which is considered one of the most important monuments in Italy, reveals a fascinating collection of Renaissance art, including pieces by Raphael, Piero della Francesca, Titian, and Paolo Uccello. Much of the original decoration of the palace has survived, including the duke's tiny *studiolo*. This room showcases intricate inlaid panels of trompe l'oeil woodwork featuring images of art, nature, and war, all richly detailed. **RM**

Palazzo dei Consoli

(Gubbio, Italy)

Important Umbran relics in Gothic palace

A medieval town of narrow streets and somber dark gray stone, Gubbio is dominated by the Palazzo dei Consoli, or Consul's Palace, at the northwest end of the architecturally stunning, red granite, paved "hanging piazza." This flat civic space was built on the side of a very steep hill by creating a massive arched substructure to support and uphold it. The top of the palace, a solid Gothic structure, is adorned with Guelf crenellations and its slender bell tower can be seen for miles around the town. The entrance to the palace, a beautifully arched and sculpted doorway attributed to Angelo da Orvieto, is reached by a graceful staircase from the piazza below. Across the piazza stands the Palazzo Pretorio, completing the compound designed by Gattapone as the town's main seat of government.

The palace houses the town's archeological museum, which holds the biggest collection of Roman artifacts in Umbria. There is also a gallery of paintings and a collection of majolica. By far the most important relics on display are the Eugubine Tablets. These are seven bronze tablets preserving a huge piece of Umbrian history in their ancient language. Having no alphabet of their own, the Umbrian people used Etruscan and then Latin letters to spell out their words phonetically. These tablets date from 200 to 70 B.C.E. and, while they cover some practical matters such as territorial boundaries and information regarding enemy states, they are mostly detailed records of religious instruction to priests about how to discover the will of the gods through animal sacrifice and reading the flight patterns of birds.

The tablets, providing their incomparable insight into ancient life and culture, were discovered by a farmer in 1444 as he plowed his field. He was persuaded by the city to hand them over in exchange for two years' free grazing rights. **RM**

Fontana Maggiore

(Perugia, Italy)

Fountain celebrating the provision of water

This lovely fountain stands in the main piazza of Perugia, which has been the center point of the city since Etruscan times. Perched on a hill, Perugia was easily defended, but the supply of water to the city was a problem for many years. The Fontana Maggiore was built to celebrate the aqueduct that brought water from the mountain springs of Paciano, 5 miles (8 km) from the city, and to provide a place for the water to be collected. The fountain consists of three parts: a foundational basin topped by a smaller basin, both polygonal and made of white and pink stone. These are surmounted by a bronze bowl holding three

> *"Their works in sculpture and in architecture truly deserve to be celebrated."*
>
> Giorgio Vasari, on Nicola and Giovanni Pisano

bronze statues out of which the water pours. Though it does not run constantly, the fountain is still operable.

Nicola Pisano and his son Giovanni sculpted the fountain, embellishing the bottom basin with fifty marble reliefs set in twenty-five field plains, each of these forming a diptych. The diptychs portray Old Testament stories, scenes of political and moral history, the labors of the months, and images of the seven liberal arts; it finishes with the artists' signature diptych—two panels with two eagles, the symbol of the city of Pisa. The panels on the middle basin are plain, but at each connecting angle there is a small statue depicting biblical, symbolic, mythical, and historical figures. The fountain is a monument to the history of humankind, a testament to the necessity of water, and a celebration of its provision. **RM**

Ponte della Torri

(Spoleto, Italy)

Viaduct and aqueduct over Tesino gorge

The mighty ten-arched bridge of Spoleto and the castle to which it leads were built on orders from Cardinal Albornoz around 1364. Pope Innocent VI sent Albornoz to Italy in 1353, charged with restoring papal authority in the Italian states of the church. Later, he paved the way for Pope Urban V to return the seat of the papacy to Rome from Avignon in France, where it was based during the fourteenth century. Spoleto had been gifted to the papacy in the eleventh century, but the town struggled for a long time to maintain its independence. While the papacy was split between Rome and Avignon, it was caught in the struggles between the Guelfs and the Ghibellines. Albornoz brought it once more under papal control in 1354.

Much of the town of Spoleto was constructed on Roman ruins, and it is believed that the bridge was built on an old Roman aqueduct dating from the eighth century. The bridge spans the gorge protecting the Rocca, or fortress, and is protected itself by two towers at either end, which may be the source of its name. However, some think the name is due to the pillars the bridge rests upon, which are hollow with entrance doors, suggesting that they were once easily defensible towers. The bridge consists of a road and a water canal, which still supplies water to the town.

The fortress was rebuilt and strengthened by Albornoz on the foundations of a Roman castle founded by Theodoric the Great around 500. It has six towers that form two separate areas—one for the soldiers and one for the city's ruling governor. This massive fortress resisted many sieges throughout history, and was used as a prison from 1800 until the 1980s. The walls once displayed fine fifteenth-century frescoes but many were whitewashed over. Careful restoration works, however, have brought back much of the original architecture and decoration. **RM**

Forte Michelangelo

(Civitavecchia, Italy)

Fortress with main tower by Michelangelo

One of the largest fortresses of its time, the Forte Michelangelo was built to defend the port of Civitavecchia, which was a vital outlet for the city of Rome. The town had been an important port since the beginning of the second century, when the Emperor Trajan constructed a harbor there.

By the end of the fifteenth century, the port was subjected to frequent attacks and looting by pirates. To defend it, Pope Julius II commissioned Donato Bramante—famous for his designs for St. Peter's Basilica in Rome—to design and build a fortress. It was finished by Bramante's pupils in 1535, during the reign

---

"Michelangelo thus recognized either that Bramante was incapable or else hostile."

Giorgio Vasari, *Life of Michelangelo* (1550)

---

of Pope Paul III. At each corner of the fortress is a defensive tower. One of them, St. Fermina, is named after Civitavecchia's patron saint, and another, St. Sebastian, housed a secret underground exit from the fortress. Parapets topping the walls have openings from which weapons could be fired. The donjon, or octagonal main tower, and its upper part were completed by Michelangelo, who gave his name to the fort. The moat that originally surrounded the fort has now disappeared.

The Forte Michelangelo is a reminder of the time when the papacy was also a secular power that ruled over a large area of Italy. It also reminds us that the great Michelangelo was an accomplished engineer as well as painter, sculptor, poet, and architect—a true Renaissance Man. **JF**

Church of St. Francis of Assisi

(Assisi, Italy)

Sumptuously decorated church built to honor the founder of the Franciscan Order

Thirteenth-century priest St. Francis of Assisi (born Giovanni Bernardone) made a huge impact on the medieval church. His decision to renounce his worldly goods and lead a simple life as a wandering preacher earned him immense respect and helped to counter the widely held belief that many priests were overly privileged and clearly corrupt, and that the church was more interested in accumulating worldly wealth than in the spiritual wellbeing of its followers. Francis felt a special kinship with the poor, so it is ironic that he should have been buried in one of Italy's most sumptuous churches.

Francis was so popular that he was canonized just two years after his death, before he had even received his official funeral. He had hoped to be buried in a pauper's grave on the Colle del Inferno (Hill of Hell, so-called because criminals were executed there), but he could never have envisaged that he would be honored with an enormous double church—the Basilica di San Francesco. The Lower Basilica was completed in just two years (1228–30), although this speed may have been ill-advised because the entire structure had to be underpinned in the 1470s. The dating of the Upper Basilica is less clear, but it was certainly completed by 1253 when both churches were consecrated together.

After Francis's death, his body was held at the church of San Giorgio until it could be interred in the new foundation. Even then, the precise burial place was kept secret for fear that his relics would be stolen—a shocking reminder of the riches that the pilgrimage trade could generate. The saint's remains were rediscovered only in 1818 when they were installed in a new crypt. The church, meanwhile, was lavishly decorated with frescoes by all the major artists of the day, including Giotto. **IZ**

> *"I have been all things unholy. If God can work through me, he can work through anyone."*
>
> St. Francis of Assisi

🏛 ◉ Etruscan Sites at Tarquinia (Tarquinia, Italy)

Remarkable tomb complex with well-preserved murals dating to the seventh century B.C.E.

Before the emergence of the Roman Empire, the Etruscans were the dominant force in the Italian peninsula. Their extensive trading contacts with Greece, Carthage, and the East made them wealthy and helped them to develop a rich, diverse culture. The chief legacy of this can be found in their remarkable tomb complexes. In recognition of this, UNESCO added the two main examples, Cerveteri and Tarquinia, to their list of World Heritage sites.

Cerveteri is a vast necropolis—a true "city of the dead," with streets, squares, and houses carved out of the rock. Tarquinia, on the other hand, is famous for its paintings. Of its six thousand tombs, around two hundred are decorated with murals, dating back as far as the seventh century B.C.E. These are better preserved than others from the same period because the artists took the precaution of coating the walls with a layer of plaster, rather than painting directly onto the rock. The

paintings at Tarquinia cover a wide repertoire of subjects, and are all the more remarkable given that only the immediate family and friends of the deceased would have seen them. There are scenes of feasting and drinking (Tomb of the Lionesses), scenes of hunting, music making (Tomb of the Jugglers), and of mourning (Tomb of the Augurs).

The most famous themes, however, related to the elaborate funeral games that the Etruscans staged in honor of their dead. Some of the sports are familiar—wrestling, boxing, running—but they also enjoyed more cruel pursuits. In the Tomb of the Augurs, for example, a man with a sack over his head (possibly a condemned criminal) is shown fending off a dog, enraged by a nail in its collar biting into its neck. These violent activities are thought to have inspired the gladiatorial combats and wild animal fights that the Romans enjoyed watching in their arenas. **IZ**

🏛 ◉ Arch of Constantine (Rome, Italy)

Triumphal arch dating to 312, incorporating sections from earlier monuments

This imposing arch is one of Rome's leading sights, and is a major monument along the ancient Via Triumphalis—the route taken by Roman emperors on celebratory processions. Along with the Arches of Titus and Septimius Severus, it is one of three commemorative triumphal arches in the city to have survived intact from the days of Classical Rome. The arch was constructed to mark the success of Emperor Constantine I—known as the first Christian Roman Emperor—at the Battle of Milvian Bridge (312), just outside Rome. The victory made him sole ruler of the western Roman empire and was a major marker in the rise of Christianity.

This impressive structure is 69 feet (21 m) high, 84 feet (25.7 m) wide, and 24 feet (7.4 m) deep. The bottom part consists of a massive central arch—through which Constantine would have processed, accompanied by the spoils of his victory—plus side

arches, marble supporting piers, and Corinthian pillars. The Attic section at the top is a frieze of marble panels bearing sculpted scenes, figures, and inscriptions, marking the emperor's campaign and victory against Maxentius.

Constantine's arch is a very early example of inspired recycling, because it incorporates decorative sections taken and adapted from earlier monuments erected in the reigns of Trajan, Hadrian, and Marcus Aurelius. Scholars argue over just how much material was reused and about why this was done. It may simply be that the arch had to be produced hastily in the wake of the Milvian Bridge victory, which is one of the events depicted on it. It may also be a question of deliberately identifying Constantine with earlier much-admired emperors. Major restoration work was carried out in the 1700s, and, more recently, significant work was completed in the late 1990s. **AK**

🏛 ⊚ **Baths of Caracalla** (Rome, Italy)

Second-largest baths complex in ancient Rome, named after the reigning emperor

During the heyday of the Roman Empire, public bath houses were a major civic amenity, offering a variety of leisure activities in congenial surroundings. The baths were also great feats of engineering, particularly after the invention of a system of under-floor heating that provided hot water for the bathers. Rome had several of these establishments, but the Baths of Caracalla were by far the most impressive.

Situated on the Caelian Hill, the baths were begun in 211, during the reign of Emperor Caracalla, and were completed six years later. The buildings could accommodate around 1,600 visitors at a time, and consisted of a number of separate chambers, including the *caldarium*, which had pools with very hot water, the *tepidarium* (lukewarm water), the *frigidarium* (cold water), and the *natatio* (an outdoor swimming pool). The complex also contained a stadium and gymnasium for those who wished to take further exercise, and Greek and Latin libraries for those who preferred to follow more intellectual pursuits.

The baths remained in operation until the sixth century, when invading Goths destroyed the aqueducts that supplied the water. The buildings decayed gradually, and in the sixteenth century the Farnese family removed many of the rich marble fittings to decorate their palace. The baths gained a new lease on life in the twentieth century, when the fascist dictator Benito Mussolini introduced the idea of staging open-air operas there. These concerts have continued, although experts have questioned whether the vibrations from the singers' voices are damaging the structure. **IZ**

◪ *The Baths of Caracalla* (1899) by Sir Lawrence Alma-Tadema, who revelled in fantasies of Roman luxury.

▣ The baths hosted a concert by Pavarotti, Domingo and Carreras on the eve of the soccer World Cup in 1990.

🏛 ◎ Arch of Titus (Rome, Italy)

Oldest surviving example of ancient Rome's triumphal arches celebrating imperial victories

Designed to glorify the memory of individual emperors and their deeds, Rome's monumental arches were also focal points for the magnificent triumphal processions that were staged in the city to welcome home victorious armies after their campaigns. At least thirty-four of these structures were erected in ancient Rome, and the Arch of Titus is the oldest surviving example.

The arch was built shortly after the death of Titus in 81 C.E. and was commissioned by his brother Domitian, who succeeded him as emperor. It is decorated with a series of carvings celebrating Titus's most illustrious victory—the struggle against Jewish rebels that culminated in the capture of Jerusalem in 70 C.E. The sculptures depict Roman soldiers carrying off treasures looted from the temple; they also refer to the emperor's deification after his death. In one scene, the new god parades triumphantly in his celestial chariot and is crowned by Victory; in the vault underneath the arch, Titus is shown ascending into the heavens, borne aloft on the wings of a gigantic eagle.

The appearance of the monument has changed considerably since Roman times. Originally, there was probably a statue of the emperor on the summit, with further sculptures on the facades. These had been lost by the Middle Ages, when new structures were added to the top and the sides of the arch. However, these were removed in 1822 when Giuseppe Valadier undertook a comprehensive restoration of the site. During this process, the arch was completely dismantled and reassembled in its present form. **IZ**

↗ Traditionally, Jews refuse to walk under the arch, given its commemoration of the fall of Jerusalem.

→ Roman soldiers ransack Solomon's Temple in Jerusalem, carrying off the seven-branched menorah.

🏛 ◉ Fountain of the Four Rivers (Rome, Italy)

Masterpiece of Baroque artist Gianlorenzo Bernini and symbol of the papacy's power

"*Bernini was . . . a formative influence as an outstanding exponent of the Italian Baroque.*"

Nicola Hodge and Libby Anson, *The A–Z of Art* (1996)

Situated in the center of the Piazza Navona—one of Rome's most picturesque and famous squares—the Fountain of the Four Rivers (Fontana dei Quattro Fiumi) is a masterpiece of the preeminent Baroque artist Gianlorenzo Bernini. Piazza Navona is also the supposed site of the martyrdom of St. Agnes—the fountain is opposite the Baroque basilica church of Sant'Agnese in Agone. The fountain was built for Pope Innocent X, who was Bernini's patron as well as a member of the powerful Pamphilj family.

The sculptures on the Fountain of the Four Rivers represent the four great rivers of each continent known by contemporary geographers: the Nile from Africa, the Ganges from Asia, the Danube from Europe, and the Río de la Plata from the Americas. Each river is represented by plants and animals from the continent and an allegorical river god semiprostrate before the central tower—an obelisk dating from the first century C.E. The obelisk is surmounted by a dove, the symbol of Innocent X's family, the Pamphilj (whose residence, the Palazzo Pamphilj, was close to the fountain). It is possible that this represents the power of the papacy over the known world.

The Fountain of the Four Rivers is a dynamic, dramatic structure that can be seen from all sides of the Piazza Navona. It is an important political symbol of the power of the papacy, and a symbol of its attempt to reassert its influence after the schism of the Protestant Reformation. As well as serving a propaganda purpose, however, the fountain also provided clean water to the local neighborhood in the days before domestic plumbing. It is also an important work of perhaps the greatest exponents of the Italian Baroque, Gianlorenzo Bernini, who was responsible for earlier fountains in Rome, including the Fountain of the Triton and the Fountain of the Bees, both in the Piazza Barberini. **JF**

Catacombs (Rome, Italy)

Ancient underground burial places of Jews and Christians, dating from the second century

From the first century, Christians, who were considered converted Jews, were often buried in the manner of Jews living in Roman territories—in graves hewn from rock reminiscent of the rock graves of Palestine. These cemeteries were outside the city walls because it was against Roman law to bury the dead within the walls. This is how St. Peter came to be buried in common ground, the great public necropolis on Vatican Hill, and St. Paul in a necropolis along the Via Ostiense.

From the second century, Roman Christians continued this technique and inherited the common underground burial spaces. The belief that their physical bodies would one day be resurrected, and so could not be cremated in accordance with Roman practice, caused a space problem since aboveground cemeteries were scarce and expensive. The solution was to excavate a vast network of galleries, rooms, and interconnecting stairways, with thousands of narrow graves carved into the walls, covering hundreds of miles of corridors. The graves of martyrs were focal points around which Christians wanted to be buried, but it is fiction that the catacombs were secret places for Christians to meet and live during times of persecution. The lack of light and air and, indeed, the thousands of decaying bodies would have made this impossible. The catacombs continued in use until 410 when the Goths laid siege to Rome. In addition, Christianity became the state religion under Constantine in 380, making more conventional means of burial possible.

Over the centuries, the precious relics of the martyrs were transferred from the catacombs to churches of the city, so that eventually even the sacred memory of the catacombs was forgotten. In 1578 a catacomb was discovered by accident, and since then much research and archeological work has been done to recover this invaluable piece of history. **RM**

"There have I often prayed … sick with the corruptions of soul and body, and obtained relief."

Prudentius, describing the catacomb of Hippolytus

🏛 ⊚ Castel Sant'Angelo (Rome, Italy)

Mausoleum converted to a military and then a papal fortress

Built between 135 and 139, Rome's Castel Sant'Angelo was commissioned as a mausoleum for the ashes of the Roman Emperor Hadrian and his family. Later emperors followed suit and the last emperor to rest there was Caracalla, who died in 217. By the fifth century, however, the building had been converted into a military fortress, and further fortifications were added over the next thousand years to make it a papal fortress. The castle has also been used at various points in its history as a prison, housing heretics such as the sixteenth-century philosopher Giordano Bruno and the eighteenth-century occultist Count Alessandro di Cagliostro.

Castel Sant'Angelo received its name from Pope Gregory the Great in 590, after a vision of the archangel St. Michael appeared above the building, symbolically marking the end of a plague in the city. In 1536, to mark this event, a marble statue of St. Michael by

Raffaello da Montelupo was erected on top of the castle. In 1753 this was replaced by a bronze statue by the Flemish sculptor Peter Anton von Verschaffelt. Montelupo's statue can now be seen in an interior courtyard in the castle.

In 1277 a wall and a 2,625-foot- (800-m-) long secret passageway—the Passetto di Borgo—were built by Pope Nicholas III to connect the fortress to the Vatican City and enable popes to escape to safety when under threat. The passage was used in 1494 by Pope Alexander VI when King Charles VIII of France invaded Rome, and again in 1527 when hundreds of people, including Pope Clement VII, took refuge in the fortress for months during the Sack of Rome by the Holy Roman Emperor Charles V. Afterward, Pope Paul III built lavish apartments in the castle for the use of any future pope taking refuge there. The castle now houses the Museo Nazionale di Castel Sant'Angelo. **CK**

🏛 🏵 Church of the Gesù (Rome, Italy)

Mother church of Jesuits, with Baroque facade and ceiling fresco by Giovanni Gauli

The Church of the Gesù (its full name is the Church of the Holy Name of Jesus) is the mother church of the Jesuits (also known as the Society of Jesus)—a Catholic religious order founded by St. Ignatius of Loyola in the mid-sixteenth century. The church is the model for numerous other Jesuit churches across the world.

After two false starts in 1551 and 1554, due to legal and funding problems, construction of the church was finally begun in 1568, with funding provided by Cardinal Alessandro Farnese. The building was designed according to the requirements of the Council of Trent, which had sought to modernize and rationalize Catholicism after the Protestant Reformation had exposed the corrupt practices of the medieval Church. As such, there is no narthex (lobby); instead, the entrance leads straight into the body of the church, with attention focused on the high altar.

There are ten chapels in the church, including one dedicated to St. Ignatius, designed by Andrea Pozzo, which houses the saint's tomb and a statue of the saint designed by Pierre le Gros the Younger. The interior of the church was originally relatively bare until Giovanni Battista Gauli was commissioned to paint it: The main feature is the ceiling fresco, *The Triumph of the Name of Jesus*. The church is also home to the original depiction of *Madonna della Strada* (Our Lady of the Way), the patroness of the Jesuits. The painting is an anonymous late fifteenth-century work of the Roman school.

The Church of the Gesù is in many ways the symbol of the Catholic Reformation. It reflected the new trends in the built structure of the church and housed the most well-known order of this new brand of Catholicism, the Jesuits, who grew to be the largest order in the Church. **JF**

🏛 ⓔ **Basilica of St. John Lateran** (Property of Holy See, Rome)

Cathedral church of Rome and official ecclesiastical seat of the Pope

The first and oldest among the great patriarchal basilicas of Rome, St. John Lateran rests on what used to be the palace of the Laterani family, whose members served as administrators to several emperors. Around 311 it came into the emperor Constantine's hands; he then gave it to the Church and in 313 it hosted a council of bishops who met to declare the Donatist sect as heretics. From then on, the basilica was the center of Christian life in the city, the residence of popes, and the cathedral of Rome.

The original church was probably not very large, and was dedicated to Christ the Savior. It has been rededicated twice—once in the tenth century to St. John the Baptist, and again in the twelfth century to St. John the Evangelist. In popular usage, these subsequent dedications have overtaken the original, though the church remains dedicated to Christ, like all patriarchal cathedrals. In 1309, when the seat of the papacy was moved to Avignon in France, the basilica began to decline. It was ravaged by fires in 1309 and 1361, and, although the structure was rebuilt, the original splendor of the building had been destroyed. Because of this, when the papacy returned to Rome, the Palace of the Vatican was constructed as the new papal seat.

In 1585, Pope Sixtus V ordered the basilica to be torn down and a replacement built—another in a long continuing line of refurbishments and rebuildings of this most important of cathedrals. Despite being bested in architectural terms by St. Peter's, which holds most papal ceremonies thanks to its size and location within the Vatican's walls, St. John Lateran remains the cathedral church of Rome and the official ecclesiastical seat of the pope, as Bishop of Rome. Indeed, it is regarded by Catholics as the mother church of the entire world. **RM**

🏛 ◉ Santa Maria Maggiore (Property of Holy See, Rome)

Basilica of the Virgin Mary, with mosaics dating from the original fourth-century building

Rome may be most famous for the splendor of its imperial past, but it also played a key part in the development of Christianity. From its earliest days, Santa Maria Maggiore has maintained a central role in this process. Its original foundation reflected the growth of the cult of the Virgin Mary and it has always been closely involved in the day-to-day administration of the Catholic Church.

According to tradition, the church was originally founded around 356, after the Virgin appeared to the pope in a vision. Its precise site was indicated by a miraculous snowfall, occurring at the height of summer. This legend is commemorated each year in a special service, during which a shower of white flower petals is dropped from the dome. The present building dates from the following century (432–40). Its dedication to the Virgin was undoubtedly influenced by a crucial decision at the Council of Ephesus in 431,

which confirmed that Mary was the mother of God (and not just Christ's human aspect). The most important survival from this original building is a unique series of mosaics, executed in the old, imperial style, with the Virgin resembling a Roman empress.

Santa Maria is a basilica—an ancient architectural form that the Romans had used for public buildings and that the early Christians adapted for their churches. It is classified as a major basilica because it was, for centuries, the seat of the Patriarch of Antioch—one of the highest-ranking officials in the Catholic Church.

Over the years, there have been many additions. The bell tower is medieval, whereas the elegant facade was designed by Ferdinando Fuga and completed in 1743. There are also two notable chapels, the Sistine Chapel, built for Pope Sixtus V, and the Pauline Chapel, designed for Pope Paul V. **IZ**

🏛 ◉ St. Paul Outside the Walls (Property of Holy See, Rome)

Remains of St. Paul may be contained in a sarcophagus found recently in the basilica

After St. Paul's martyrdom around 62 C.E., his followers built a shrine over his grave. In 324 Constantine ordered a small church to be built on the spot, but in 386 Theodosius demolished this church and began the construction of a much larger and more beautiful basilica. This was consecrated in 390, although the work was not completed until some fifty years later. St. Paul-outside-the-Wall (the name refers to its location outside the main city walls) is considered to be one of the five great ancient basilicas of Rome.

In 1823 a devastating fire destroyed the basilica. This was an appalling loss because, of all the Roman churches, this one had maintained its primitive character for 1,435 years. To restore the basilica, the viceroy of Egypt contributed alabaster pillars and the emperor of Russia sent costly lapis lazuli and malachite for the mosaics. A chronicle of the Benedictine monastery attached to the church mentions that,

during the rebuilding, a large marble sarcophagus was found with the words *"Paolo Apostolo Mart(yri)"* (To Paul the Apostle and Martyr) on the top. Strangely, unlike other tombs found at that time, it was not mentioned in the excavation papers. Almost two hundred years later, in 2006, archeologists discovered perhaps this same sarcophagus under the altar, which may contain the Apostle's remains. It has not yet been excavated, pending a decision on whether it contains human remains, and only one side is visible. **RM**

"I fell unto the ground, and heard a voice saying unto me, Saul, Saul, why persecutest thou me?"

The conversion on the road to Damascus, Acts 22:7

🏛️ ⊚ St. Peter's Basilica (Vatican City)

Most prominent building of Vatican City, with a dome designed by Michelangelo

Lying within Vatican City, St. Peter's Basilica is a center of pilgrimage for Roman Catholics. In 2005 it became the focus of world attention when Pope John Paul II died. Crowds gathered to see him lying in state, and royalty, dignitaries, and world leaders attended his funeral service. The impressive seventeenth-century piazza of the vast church, designed by Gianlorenzo Bernini, and its treasure trove of sculptures and paintings, also make it of interest to art lovers.

The church stands on the site of Emperor Nero's Circo Vaticano, and it is thought that St. Peter and fellow Christian martyrs were killed there between 64 and 67 C.E. The apostle was buried in a grave next to the wall of the stadium; when the stadium was abandoned in 160, a small monument was built to mark the spot. Emperor Constantine ordered a basilica to be built on the site of the saint's tomb in 315, and the church was consecrated in 326.

Pope Nicholas V ordered the reconstruction of the dilapidated church in the fifteenth century, but work began in earnest in 1506 when Pope Julius II commissioned architect Donato Bramante to design a new basilica. Based on a Greek cross plan with a central dome and four smaller domes, the new basilica was completed in 1626.

An aging Michelangelo took over the project in 1547 and designed the 390-foot- (119-m-) high dome above the high altar that was constructed directly above St. Peter's tomb. Architect Carlo Maderno succeeded Michelangelo in masterminding the job, and altered the original plan to resemble a Latin cross by extending the nave toward the piazza. Gianlorenzo Bernini designed the 95-foot- (29-m-) high Baroque canopy that stands in the center of the church, and was made using bronze taken from the Pantheon nearby. **CK**

🏛 ◎ Sistine Chapel (Vatican City)

Private papal chapel, with a legendary ceiling fresco by Michelangelo

Built between 1473 and 1484 for Pope Sixtus IV, the Sistine Chapel lies within the Vatican City. Today it is the private papal chapel and the meeting place of the College of Cardinals when they meet in conclave to elect a new pope. But what draws visitors in droves are the frescoes of the High Renaissance genius Michelangelo Buonarroti.

The barrel-vaulted ceiling of the chapel represents the apex of Michelangelo's career with the nine paintings that make up *God's Creation of the World, God's Relationship with Mankind, and Mankind's Fall from God's Grace* (1508–12) covering 8,610 square feet (800 sq m). Michelangelo was commissioned by Pope Julius II to paint the fresco. Completing the task almost singlehandedly, because the Florentine craftsmen assigned to help him did not meet his exacting standards, it was a feat of endurance for the artist, painting at a fast rate and working from scaffolding. The result is an unrivaled work of art that reinvented the depiction of the human form with the dynamic style of its more than three hundred figures. So arduous was this mammoth undertaking that Michelangelo forswore painting for twenty-three years until he returned to the chapel to paint *The Last Judgment* (1535–41) on the wall behind the altar—this time for Pope Clement VII, although it was completed under the patronage of his successor Pope Paul III. The painting proved controversial at the time for its inclusion of naked male bodies, depicted complete with genitalia.

Although somewhat dwarfed by Michelangelo's masterpieces, the walls of the chapel also contain significant works of art such as Sandro Botticelli's *The Temptation of Christ* (1482) and Domenico Ghirlandaio's *Christ Calling Peter and Andrew to their Apostleship* (1483). On special occasions the chapel is also decorated with tapestries created by Raphael. **CK**

> *"It [is] no work for a papal chapel but rather for public baths and taverns."*

Biagio da Cesena, Clement VII's Master of Ceremonies

⬆ The simple exterior of the Sistine Chapel gives no hint of the extraordinary decorative richness within.

➡ Originally, Michelangelo was to paint only the Apostles, but eventually he painted more than 300 figures.

 ◎ **Colosseum** (Rome, Italy)

Vast Roman amphitheater, scene of gladiatorial contests and spectacles

Construction of Rome's Colosseum was begun around 70 C.E. by Emperor Vespasian, and was completed in 80 C.E. when it was inaugurated by his son, Emperor Titus, in a one-hundred-day-long festival. Constructed of travertine marble, the large circular structure was first known as the Flavian Amphitheater and housed an estimated fifty thousand spectators, who would gather to watch the gladiatorial games that were held there. It was also used for the reenactment of sea battles and for staging classical dramas. Gladiators were usually slaves or prisoners of war known for their athleticism and fighting prowess, who entertained the Roman crowds by fighting each other and hunting various animals. Despite the dangers of such an existence, being a gladiator had benefits—they were trained in military-style schools that offered a better standard of living than that of other slaves, and victorious gladiators were treated as heroes.

Following a gladiatorial contest, the victor would seek a decision from the crowd—or the emperor if he was present—whether the defeated gladiator should be put to death or spared because he had shown bravery. The decision would be made using the now famous gesture of thumbs up or thumbs down. Animals involved in the contests (including lions, leopards, and crocodiles) were kept in cages below the amphitheater and released into the arena via elevators pulled by ropes.

In medieval times, the Colosseum was used as a church, then as a fortress by two prominent Roman families, the Frangipane and the Annibaldi. Time has taken its toll on the building, which has suffered at the hands of earthquakes, robbers plundering its stone, and the effects of modern-day pollution from traffic, but it still stands as a monument to the human appetite for bloody entertainment. **CK**

 ◎ **Pantheon** (Rome, Italy)

Erected as a temple to all the gods, and renowned for its great and still-intact dome

Located on the Piazza della Rotonda, the Pantheon is remarkable for its dome, which is considered to be one of the greatest feats of Roman architecture—not least because it is still intact after two millennia, despite the building having been erected on marshy ground. Within the Pantheon is a large, circular room with a granite and yellow marble floor and a hemispherical dome. The height of the rotunda to the top of the 142-foot (43.3-m) dome exactly matches its diameter, creating a perfect hemisphere. Natural light enters via a circular opening—known as the Great Eye (Oculus)—at the apex of the dome.

The Pantheon was built around 120 by the emperor Hadrian on the site of a temple built by the Roman statesman and general Marcus Agrippa in 27 B.C.E. Agrippa's building was destroyed by fire in 80 C.E., but his name is written above the entrance of Hadrian's elegant building, which was innovative in its day and reminiscent of Greek temples. "Pantheon" means "Temple of all the Gods," and the building was originally dedicated to the planetary gods worshipped by the ancient Romans. The Byzantine emperor Phocas gave the building to Pope Boniface IV in 609, and it became the Christian church of Santa Maria ad Martyres; a column was erected in the Roman Forum in honor of Phocas's gift.

Over the centuries the building was pillaged and damaged, losing its gilded bronze roof tiles when the Byzantine emperor Constans II looted it in 663. Pope Urban VIII removed the bronze ceiling girders on the portico to make cannons for Castel Sant'Angelo as part of his plans to extend the fortifications of the papal fortress. The building has also been used as a tomb, and houses two Italian kings as well as Renaissance painters and architects, including Raphael. **CK**

🏛 ◉ **Spanish Steps** (Rome, Italy)

Celebrated rendezvous, leading from Piazza di Spagna to Piazza Trinità dei Monti

Rome's Piazza di Spagna is home to the Scalinata di Trinità dei Monti (Spanish Steps), built between 1723 and 1725 with a legacy left by a French diplomat, but named after the Bourbon Spanish Embassy to the Holy See. The stairway was designed by Francesco de Sanctis and Alessandro Specchi after much debate regarding how best to build on the steep slope. The idea to build a staircase from the piazza to the church of Trinità dei Monti originated in the seventeenth century. Originally the French wanted to include an equestrian statue of King Louis XIV at the top of stairs. Papal opposition called a halt to the project until a compromise was reached, allowing the building work to continue. The compromise between the papacy and the French is evident on the staircase itself, which contains carvings of the fleurs-de-lis of the Bourbon family along with the checkered eagle coat of arms of Pope Innocent XIII.

The steps have long been a gathering place for the wealthy, the beautiful, and the bohemian; in the eighteenth and nineteenth centuries, they gravitated to the steps, hoping to be chosen as an artist's model. Facing the steps is the house where the English Romantic poet John Keats spent the last months of his life battling with consumption.

At the bottom of the staircase lies the boat-shaped Fontana della Barcaccia (Fountain of the Old Boat) believed to have been designed by Pietro Bernini, father of architect and sculptor Gianlorenzo Bernini. The fountain was inspired by the flooding of the River Tiber in 1588, when a small, flat-bottomed boat used to carry people to safety was found on the spot after the water ebbed. The steps and piazza are the domain of cafés and flower-sellers, making it a relaxing and colorful place, especially in May when the steps are decorated with pots of pink azaleas. **CK**

🏛 ⊚ **Fontana de Trevi** (Rome, Italy)

Baroque fountain where visitors make wishes as they throw coins in the water

Standing 85 feet (26 m) high and 65 feet (20 m) wide, the Fontana di Trevi (Trevi Fountain) dominates the small Palazzo Poli in Rome's Trevi district. The white marble fountain is a fine example of the Baroque style, its dramatic form set against a backdrop of the facade of the Palazzo Poli. The water feeding the fountain comes from the Salone Springs, 13.5 miles (22 km) from Rome and carried by the Aqua Virgo aquaduct, built in 19 B.C.E.

The idea to build the fountain emerged in 1629. Pope Urban VIII commissioned sculptor and architect Gianlorenzo Bernini to come up with some designs. Bernini chose the location in the square opposite what was then the papal residence and is now the official residence of the Italian president. However, the project was abandoned after the pope's death in 1644 and the fountain that was eventually built was designed by Roman architect Nicola Salvi when Pope Clement XII resurrected the idea. Salvi entered a competition organized in 1730 by the pope to design the fountain but lost out to rival Florentine architect Alessandro Galilei. However, Salvi was given the commission in response to public demand that a local man design the project. Work began in 1732 and was completed in 1762 by Giuseppe Pannini after the deaths of both Salvi and the pope.

A statue of Neptune, god of the sea, stands in the fountain's central niche. He is shown driving a shell chariot drawn by sea horses. In the niches on either side stand statues of Abundance and Salubrity. Above the statues lie bas-reliefs depicting the history of Rome's aqueducts. Throwing a coin into the Trevi Fountain is a popular custom, based on traditional legend. One coin thrown over the shoulder ensures a return visit to Rome; a second coin allows the visitor to make a wish. **CK**

Vittorio Emanuele II Monument (Rome, Italy)

Magnificent monument of white marble, celebrating the unification of Italy

This massive structure, designed by Giuseppe Sacconi in 1885 and inaugurated in 1911, celebrates the unification of Italy and honors Vittorio Emanuele II. King of Piedmont, Savoy, and Sardinia from 1849 to 1861, and for many years a leader of the movement toward a united Italy, Vittorio managed in 1860 to annex most of northern and central Italy to his kingdom of Piedmont-Sardinia and the kingdom of Italy was formally established, with Vittorio as its first ruler. Despite his efforts, Venice still remained under the control of Austria, while the Papal States and the kingdom of the Two Sicilies remained separate territories. It was only after several more years of fighting that Venice was ceded by the Austrians and the French armies finally withdrew from Rome, which was declared the capital of the unified Italy in 1871; for the first time in a thousand years the Italian peninsula was free from the presence of a foreign power.

Built of white marble, the monument is visible from most parts of the city. It includes a huge staircase, Corinthian columns, fountains, and two winged Victories surmounting the roofline, each riding a chariot. Vittorio is portrayed in bronze atop a colossal horse. The structure houses the Tomb of the Unknown Soldier as well as the Museum of Italian Reunification.

The monument is often derided as being too large and pretentious, called anything from the "wedding cake" to the "typewriter" (a nickname given by the Americans in 1944). Its origins are also controversial because part of Capitoline Hill and a medieval neighborhood were demolished to make space for it—but it is still a tribute to an important moment in Italian history and attracts many tourists. Mussolini had his official residence in the nearby Palazzo Venezia and made many of his speeches from a balcony overlooking Piazza Venezia. **RM**

🏛 ⊚ **Villa Adriana** (Tivoli, Italy)

Built as a retreat for Emperor Hadrian, whose travels prompted its diversity of styles

Also known as Hadrian's Villa, Villa Adriana is a wonderful example of a Classical Roman residence—and certainly the most spectacularly well-kept Alexandrian garden that remains today. Commissioned by Emperor Hadrian in the second century, the villa was intended as a retreat from his work in Rome, although he eventually came to rule the empire from this complex. Hadrian was a keen patron of the arts and wide-ranging in his tastes, so the villa is an interesting amalgamation of different cultures. Despite his huge effort and investment constructing the retreat, however, the villa went into decline after his death. It was used by various successors but, as the Roman Empire declined, the villa fell into disuse. In the sixteenth century Cardinal Ippolito II d'Este plundered many of the sculptures and ornaments from Villa Adriana to decorate his own home. More recently, great care has been taken to preserve the site. Despite

this, in 2006 the World Monuments Fund placed it on their "100 Most Endangered Sites" list, prompting greater effort to be made to limit the deterioration.

Villa Adriana was originally a complex of more than thirty buildings spanning an area of more than 247 acres (100 ha). The development adopted many different architectural styles, including a Greek maritime theater, a Roman pool, and numerous statues of Egyptian gods. The complex included palaces, bathhouses, temples, Greek and Latin libraries, staterooms, and dwellings for courtiers, guards, and slaves.

In modern times Villa Adriana has become a fascinating cultural and archeological site that offers insight into the lavish lives of the Roman emperors. It also provides us with detailed information on the way that society functioned and cultures evolved two thousand years ago. **KH**

 **Villa d'Este**

(Tivoli, Italy)

Masterpiece of Renaissance design with elaborate terraced gardens

> *"... to stand, sheathed in a grotto/On the reverse side of this shield of water ..."*

Jean Garrigue, *A Water Walk by Villa d'Este* (1959)

The villa and gardens of Villa d'Este, in Tivoli, were constructed for Cardinal Ippolito II d'Este (1509–72), the grandson of the Borgia Pope Alexander VI. The entire estate is a masterpiece of Renaissance design, but the extensive gardens with their numerous fountains and grottoes are particularly impressive.

The construction of the Villa d'Este began in 1550 when Ippolito was made governor of the town of Tivoli—about 18 miles (29 km) from Rome—by Pope Julius III. He ordered the construction of a new villa, featuring paintings by Livio Agresti and other great figures of the late Roman Mannerist school. The highpoint of the Villa d'Este is its elaborate terraced gardens, positioned on the cliffs leading up to the villa. Because of the steep slope, the fountains had to be powered by an elaborate hydraulic system that revived some of the ancient techniques for supplying water that had been used in the nearby Villa Adriana. In the early seventeenth century, Cardinal Alessandro d'Este restored and repaired the gardens and waterworks of the Villa d'Este, which passed into the possession of the House of Hapsburg in the eighteenth century. The gardens were gradually abandoned and fell into disrepair, and the villa's large collection of ancient statues was disassembled and moved to other sites. However, the deterioration of the estate began to be reversed in the nineteenth century when Cardinal Gustav von Hohenlohe obtained the villa and set about restoring it. During his tenure the composer Franz Liszt often visited, and he gave one of his last concerts at the villa.

The Villa d'Este is now owned by the Italian state, and is a UNESCO World Heritage site. It is one of the most beautiful estates in the world, and its fantastical gardens, which were highly influential and copied throughout Europe, are without equal. **JF**

Monte Cassino Abbey

(Cassino, Italy)

Birthplace of the Benedictine order

Located to the south of Rome, the great Abbey of Monte Cassino lies at the top of Mount Cassino, a rocky hill just 1 mile (1.6 km) west of the town that shares its name. The birthplace and bedrock of the Benedictine order, the abbey was founded by Benedict of Nursia in 529 on a site previously used for pagan worship. Benedict razed the image and altar dedicated to the god Apollo, replacing it with a church dedicated to St. John the Baptist. Benedict remained at Monte Cassino until his death. In 784 a new basilica was built over Benedict's tomb and was consecrated by Pope Zachary. The abbey's numbers and reputation for a high state of discipline reached their peak under Abbot Desiderius, who became abbot around 1057. He commissioned the reconstruction of the monastery's buildings by artists brought in from Amalfi, Lombardy, and Constantinople. The site was reconsecrated in 1071 by Pope Alexander II, but the monastery witnessed a steady decline after this date.

The abbey's consecutive courtyards with arcades in the Doric order date from 1515 and are attributed to Bramante. Designed by Cosimo Fansaga, the fourth church to occupy the site was begun in 1649 and consecrated in 1727 by Benedict XIII. A crypt in the eastern portion of the church contains the tomb of St. Benedict, whereas the left transept houses the monument of Lorenzo de' Medici's son Pietro, whose tomb is the work of the architect Antonio di Sangallo.

When the monasteries of Italy were dissolved in 1866, the abbey became a national monument. During World War II, it was destroyed in the four battles of Monte Cassino. Rebuilding took more than a decade and was financed by the Italian government, with the maxim "where and as was," so that the history and importance of the buildings are preserved for the thousands of pilgrims who visit every year. **SM**

Villa Jovis

(Capri, Italy)

Palatial island residence of Emperor Tiberius

Villa Jovis (Jupiter's Villa) was the residence of the Roman emperor Tiberius. It is situated at 1,095 feet (334 m), on the northeastern side of Monte Tiberio on the island of Capri, and is the largest of twelve Tiberian villas on the island. The palatial complex covers 1.7 acres (7,000 sq m) and a considerable portion of the villa remains. Built in the early years of the first century C.E. on a compact square plan, the steep nature of the site required the villa to be built on several levels. It is divided into distinct areas: The north wing contained the emperor's apartments and the south wing the bathhouses; the east wing was used as a reception

> *"He plunged into every wickedness and disgrace … he simply indulged his own inclinations."*
>
> Tacitus, on Tiberius's behavior at the end of his reign

area, and the west wing housed servant quarters.

Near the palace are the remains of an *ambulatio* (open-walled hall) with a striking view over the island, a lighthouse, and a signal tower that enabled Tiberius to rule the empire without leaving Capri. It also functioned as an astronomical observatory. Destroyed after Tiberius's death, it was rebuilt and was operational until the early seventeenth century. Near the palace is the so-called Tiberius's leap (*salto di Tiberio*), an almost vertical cliff from which Tiberius—according to legend—had his victims thrown. The site also features later architectural additions, such as the Church of Santa Maria del Soccorso dating from the eighteenth century. Important archeological finds from Villa Jovis are today housed in the Archaeological Museum of Naples. **EP**

🏛 ◎ **Teatro di San Carlo** (Naples, Italy)

Sumptuously furnished Neapolitan opera house, inaugurated in 1737

In the years after its inauguration in 1737, the Teatro di San Carlo was Europe's most important center of opera. Many of Europe's greatest composers have had their works performed here, and it remains one of the finest opera houses in the world.

The Teatro di San Carlo was built to replace the dilapidated Teatro San Bartolomeo, which dated from the early seventeenth century. The new opera house was commissioned by the king of Naples, Charles III Bourbon. It was intended to be as much an expression of Bourbon wealth and prestige as an opera house with original decoration in gold, with blue upholstery—the colors of the Bourbon family. The theater was inaugurated on November 4, 1737, with a performance of Domenico Sarro's opera *Achille in Sciro*. The theater seated an audience of 3,300, making it the largest opera house in the world at the time. On February 2, 1816, the Teatro di San Carlo was destroyed by fire, but it was rebuilt within ten months on the order of King Ferdinand IV. The current red and gold interior color scheme was fitted in 1854, but otherwise the theater's basic structure went unchanged. After suffering heavy bomb damage during World War II, the theater was repaired by Allied forces and reopened within six months.

Many prominent composers are associated with the Teatro di San Carlo, including Gioacchino Rossini, who was the theater's composer in residence between 1815 and 1822. Giuseppe Verdi wrote three operas for the Teatro di San Carlo, and many of Giacomo Puccini's operas were staged there. The Teatro di San Carlo remains a working opera house, allowing modern listeners to experience the glory days of Neapolitan opera. The building has weathered disaster and war and retained its beauty, remaining an important center of opera. **JF**

🏛 ◎ Castel Nuovo (Naples, Italy)

Thirteenth-century castle with a magnificent fifteenth-century triumphal arch

The New Castle, so named to differentiate it from the old one, Castel dell' Ovo (Egg Castle), was built on orders from Charles I of Anjou after he became king of Sicily in 1266. Before 1266, Palermo was the capital of the kingdom, but Charles moved his base of control to the city of Naples and in 1279 commissioned a mighty fortress to be built there, near the sea. It was completed by 1282 but the events of the Sicilian Vespers in that year—a bloody event in Palermo that triggered a widespread Sicilian rebellion against Charles—prevented the royal family from moving into the palace until after Charles's death in 1285.

The poets Petrarch and Boccaccio were both invited to the court here during King Robert's brilliant reign in the fourteenth century, and Giotto created frescoes (now lost) on the building's walls. The castle was greatly enlarged and embellished under Robert, who was a great patron of the arts. The magnificently carved arch over the west entrance chronicles King Alfonso V of Aragon's triumphal march into Naples in 1443. The bas-reliefs are credited to Francesco Laurana, one of the most important and complex sculptors of the fifteenth century. On a different note, in 1485 Alfonso's son Ferrante I invited a group of barons who were plotting against him to a feast in the octagonal Sala dei Baroni. Some accounts say the doors were locked and the barons arrested, then executed. A more colorful version claims that Ferrante had boiling oil poured over them from the ceiling. The city council of Naples met regularly in this room until 2006.

In 1494 the kingdom was annexed by Spain and the castle demoted from residence to military fortress. Today it contains important artwork, sculpture, and frescoes from the fourteenth and fifteenth centuries, as well as the city's Museo Civico, which displays mostly local artwork from the 1400s to the 1900s. **RM**

🏛 ◎ Pompeii (near Naples, Italy)

Perfectly preserved Greco-Roman city, buried for 1,700 years under a blanket of ash

Around noon, on August 24, 79 C.E., a huge eruption from Mount Vesuvius showered volcanic debris over the city of Pompeii, followed the next day by clouds of blisteringly hot gases. Buildings were destroyed, the population crushed or asphyxiated, and the city was buried beneath a blanket of ash and pumice.

For many centuries Pompeii slept beneath its pall of ash, which perfectly preserved the remains beneath. When these were finally unearthed, in the 1700s, the world was astonished. Here lay a sophisticated Greco-Roman city, home to around twenty thousand people, frozen in time. Grand public buildings included an impressive forum and an amphitheater. Here too were lavish villas and all kinds of houses, dating back to the fourth century B.C.E. Inside were the preserved remains of people sheltering from the eruption; others lay buried as they fled; bakeries were found with loaves still in the ovens. The buildings and their contents revealed day-to-day life in the ancient world—and stirred eighteenth-century interest in all things classical.

Early excavations were haphazard and often damaging, although they constitute the first milestone in the history of modern archeology. More rigorous methods were adopted in the 1800s and even better ones during the 1900s. Each stint brought fresh discoveries and today there is still more to uncover. In 1997, Pompeii, Herculaneum and Torre Anunziata became a combined UNESCO World Heritage site. **AK**

"The sight that met our still terrified eyes was a changed world, buried in ash like snow."

Pliny the Younger, on his escape from Pompeii

🏛 ◎ Paestum (Paestum, Italy)

Three Doric temples and tombs containing well-preserved classical Greek wall paintings

Paestum was originally founded as Poseidonia in the seventh century B.C.E. by colonists from Sybaris—a Greek colony in southern Italy. The site was refounded as the Roman colony Paestum in 273 B.C.E. The site is most notable for its three sturdy sixth-century Doric temples and its still-standing defensive walls.

The oldest temple is that of Hera, built *c.* 550 B.C.E. and mistakenly known as the "Basilica." The temple complex encompassed an inner chamber, a small area housing the cult image or serving as a treasury, and a pit for sacrificial remains. The so-called Temple of Poseidon was also dedicated to Hera, and, in the sacred enclosure of both, thousands of terra-cotta votives of Near Eastern type showing a naked woman have been found. The Temple of Athena was also built in the Doric order, though it incorporated Ionic columns in the porch. There was much construction at Paestum in the Roman period, including a forum, gymnasium, temple to the Capitoline triad (Jupiter, Juno, and Minerva), and a small amphitheater.

The site remained in use after the Roman period, but was abandoned in the Middle Ages, not to be rediscovered until the eighteenth century. Today, the site is also famous for its fifth- and fourth-century painted tombs, which include scenes of a young man diving and guests at a drinking party—the only well-preserved examples of classical Greek wall painting, an art form better known from Etruria. **RF**

> *"Paestum is of especially high value for the creative genius of the builders of its great Doric temples."*
>
> UNESCO

Monreale Cathedral

(Palermo, Sicily, Italy)

Extravagantly furnished Norman cathedral

Monreale Cathedral is commonly regarded as the most impressive monument left by the Norman kings who once ruled in Sicily. The building is a stunning testament to their sumptuous style and illustrates their attention to detail and ornamentation. Built by William II *c.* 1170, the building was originally no more than a church. However, Pope Lucius III elevated its status to that of a metropolitan cathedral in 1182, and it became the seat of the Metropolitan Archbishop of Sicily. Finally, in 1200, the archepiscopal palace and monastic buildings were finished. When King William began the construction of the cathedral, he had a number of objectives. Primarily, he wished to use it to establish himself as sovereign. He also wished to impress on his subjects his power and wealth, and to suppress any thoughts of resistance. Finally, William hoped to use the cathedral to establish Roman Catholicism as the official religion of Sicily—an objective that he managed with some success. Irrespective of his motives, William produced an outstanding cathedral, much of which remains today.

The cathedral itself may seem relatively plain from the outside. Nevertheless, the visitor may begin to get some sense of the grandeur that lies inside from the imposing principal doorways. Designed in a curious mixture of Norman, Byzantine, and Arab styles, the doors are made of bronze and covered in rich carvings and colored inlays. Inside, the structure of the cathedral is built around an impressive central nave and two smaller aisles. The walls are decorated with a cornucopia of meticulous panels and reliefs that depict various scenes from the Old and New Testaments. The intricacy of the craftsmanship and the expense of the materials used in the cathedral offer a sense of the personal style and taste of the Norman kings who once held sway in Sicily. **KH**

Norman Royal Palace

(Palermo, Sicily, Italy)

Palace in Arab-Norman-Byzantine style

This palace complex was begun in the ninth century by the Muslim Emir of Palermo, but with King Roger I's entrance into the city in 1072, it passed into Norman hands, where it remained for the next 122 years. Under Roger II the palace was expanded and enhanced by his commissioning of the Cappella Palatina in 1132. This gorgeous structure, the royal chapel of the Norman dynasty in Sicily, is the best, and perhaps only, surviving example of the Arab-Norman-Byzantine style prevalent in twelfth-century Sicily. Though the palace itself was much rebuilt and altered during the Renaissance and Baroque periods, some of Roger's

> *"The most beautiful [chapel] in the world, the most surprising religious jewel ever dreamt of by man."*
>
> Guy de Maupassant, writer

rooms and work remain, including his bedroom (the *Sala di Ruggero*) and the jewel tower.

The chapel within the palace was consecrated to St. Peter in 1140, and it is glorious in its decoration and detail. Brilliant mosaics cover the walls and floor of the chapel, the oldest of which—on the ceiling, drum, and dome—date from the 1140s. The rest of the mosaic work, dated 1160 to 1170, is somewhat cruder and has Latin rather than Greek inscriptions.

Roger's chapel harmonizes three cultures with its Norman architecture, Arabic arches and script, and Byzantine dome and mosaic work. A perfect example of the fusion of culture in the palace is offered by the traditional Islamic eight-pointed stars on the ceiling of the chapel, which have been clustered together in the shape of a Christian cross. **RM**

Valley of the Temples

(Agrigento, Sicily, Italy)

Great temples of the ancient Greek city of Akragas, dating from the fifth century B.C.E.

The Valley of the Temples is somewhat erroneously named, since the temples actually stand on a rocky ridge south of the acropolis of Agrigento. Constructed mostly in the fifth century B.C.E., the Doric order temples were burned by the invading Carthaginians in 406 B.C.E. and restored by the Romans in the first century B.C.E. All the temples face east in order that the cult statue housed inside the *cella* (inner chamber) might be illuminated by the rising sun. Architecturally, they are of similar design with six columns at the front, save that of Olympian Zeus, which has seven half columns engaged in a wall.

East to west along the scarp, the temples were dedicated to Hera Lacinia, Concord, Heracles, Olympian Zeus, Castor and Pollux, and Hephaistos. The best preserved—including the complete entablature (the frieze above the columns)—is that of Concord, which was converted into a church in the sixth century C.E. The earliest is the Sanctuary of the Chthonic Deities, Persephone and her mother, Demeter, constructed in the seventh or sixth century B.C.E. and comprising a number of small shrines and altars. The largest temple is that of Zeus, constructed in the late sixth century B.C.E. In addition to the unusual half-column construction, the walls of this temple featured giant blocks of stone in the shape of men, supporting the weight from above with raised, bent arms. The two pediments were filled with sculpture, depicting the battle between the gods and giants in the east, and the fall of Troy in the west.

In the absence of local marble, the temples were constructed of local limestone tufa, often in small blocks rather than the large slabs used in marble constructions. This rather rough-looking stone would originally have been covered with a layer of brightly painted stucco. **RF**

"Purely Attic in the dryness, in the dust, and the pale violet haze which swam in the middle distance."

Lawrence Durrell, writer, on visiting the valley

Taormina Amphitheater (Taormina, Sicily, Italy)

Roman amphitheater built on the site of a Greek theater

Following the destruction of the Greek colony of Naxos, Sicily, in 403 B.C.E., exiles reestablished themselves on a steep, rocky hillside 3 miles (5 km) to the north, on the Hill of Taurus. A fortified town was built on the hillside and eventually, when Sicily became a Roman province, the town enjoyed a privileged position as a Roman colony.

Since the late nineteenth century, Taormina has been a popular tourist destination, initially with artists and writers, including Goethe, who extolled its virtues in his book *Flight to Italy*. As well as its spectacular natural beauty, overlooking the Ionian Sea and with Mount Etna—Europe's highest active volcano—in the background, Taormina is scattered with reminders of its ancient history: parts of the old city walls, the Roman *naumachia*, the thirteenth-century cathedral of St. Niccolò—and the remarkably well-preserved amphitheater, which—though not the largest—can

claim to be one of the most beautifully located in Europe. The theater, 350 feet (106 m) in diameter, is built of brick, which suggests that the present structure dates from the Roman period; because of its layout, however, it is probable that it was built on the foundations of an earlier, Greek theater.

The amphitheater is still used today for operatic and theatrical performances, and concerts. It is also the location for the annual Taormina Film Festival, when films are viewed on a screen erected in the theater. **AP**

"the ... smoking mountain of fire enclos[es] the entire scene without in any way being frightening."

Johann Wolfgang von Goethe, *Flight to Italy* (1786)

🏛 ⊚ Ġgantija Temples (Xaghra, Gozo, Malta)

World's oldest stone structures, erected during the Neolithic period

The stone temples of the Maltese archipelago, erected between 3,600 and 2,500 B.C.E., are the oldest free-standing monumental buildings in the world, predating Stonehenge and the Pyramids of Giza by centuries. A total of twenty-three monumental sites grace the islands, seven of which are part of the Megalithic Temples of Malta UNESCO World Heritage site. Of these, the oldest is the temple complex of Ġgantija on the island of Gozo. Set on a hilltop 420 feet (128 m) above sea level, it comprises two temples encircled by a common boundary wall. The two are similar in design, with an entrance passage leading to ovalesque chambers to the left and right, then to three further chambers laid out in trefoil form. Today they are open to the elements, but stone corbelling on the walls suggests they were once roofed with masonry domes. The southern temple, which is larger, older, and the best preserved, has a huge threshold slab on top of which is a stone-cut basin and libation holes to receive liquid offerings. Altars and bone finds suggest animal sacrifices. Two carved heads and a snake in relief were found during clearance in 1827. Although neighboring Malta is famed for its female figurines of abundant proportions, no comparable finds were made at Ġgantija.

The temples are impressive for the sheer size of the building blocks alone, some of which measure 16 feet (5 m) in length and weigh more than 50 tons. It is thought the blocks were moved by rolling them on small stone balls, which are found in some quantity on the site. The temples are also impressive for what they reveal about their builders—settled farmers with a sophisticated social structure and highly developed ritualized belief system. The temples take their name, however, from beliefs of a different kind, for *ġgantija* in Maltese means "belonging to giants." **JB**

Palace of the Grand Masters (Valletta, Malta)

Headquarters of successive rulers of Malta since the late sixteenth century

"*Valletta equals in its noble architecture, if it does not excel, any capital in Europe.*"

Benjamin Disraeli, former British prime minister

The Palace of the Grand Masters in Valletta was the headquarters of one of Europe's oldest military orders, the Knights Hospitaller of St. John. The order arrived in Malta in 1530, having spent eight years without a base after their defeat and expulsion from the island of Rhodes by the Ottomans in 1522. The palace remained the base of the Knights Hospitaller from 1571 to 1798, when Napoleon I conquered the island.

The palace, designed by the Maltese architect Gerolamo Cassar, was built on a site procured by the order in 1571. The site was previously occupied by the nephew of the head of the order, Grand Master Jean Parisot de la Valette, who had a small house there. The palace incorporates this house in its southwest corner. The exterior of the palace is made up of wooden balconies, which replaced the original iron balconies around 1741. The interior is based around two courtyards. The palace was used as the residence of the British governors of Malta after the Royal Navy captured the island from the French in 1800. Malta was granted independence in 1964, and the palace's original council chamber became the permanent home of the island's parliament, the House of Representatives. The room is lined with Gobelins tapestries depicting scenes from the Caribbean and the New World. The palace is also home to the presidential office. Running along the back of the palace is an armory that contains many examples of weaponry used by the knights and their enemies, including the sword of Turgut Reis, the Ottoman admiral and privateer who died at the Siege of Malta in 1565.

The Palace of the Grand Masters has been the base of the rulers of the island of Malta since the late sixteenth century. It also contains a number of items from the island's history, reflecting its changing fortunes over the centuries. **JF**

Cathedral with highly decorated Baroque interior, housing works by Caravaggio

St. John's Co-Cathedral in Malta is the church of the Knights Hospitaller of St. John, a military order founded in the late eleventh century to protect and defend pilgrims traveling to the Holy Land. The order moved to the island of Malta in 1530. It was the head of the order, Grand Master Jean de la Cassière, who commissioned the cathedral in 1573. The cathedral was designed by the Maltese military architect Gerolamo Cassar, and completed between 1573 and 1578. The exterior facade was built after the Great Siege of Malta in 1565, and is a rather severe, almost martial, structure. It stands in stark contrast to the cathedral's highly decorated, Baroque interior, which was the work mostly of the Italian seventeenth-century artist Mattia Pretti.

The carved stone walls and painted ceiling and side altars depict scenes from the life of St. John the Baptist. There are eight chapels in the cathedral, dedicated to the patron saints of the eight langues (sections) of the Knights Hospitaller. Richly decorated marble tombstones of important knights line the nave, with the more important ones placed nearer the front of the cathedral.

St. John's is home to a number of works of art, the most famous of which is *The Beheading of St. John the Baptist* (1608), still preserved in its original setting. It is the most important work of the first great artist of the Italian Baroque period, Michelangelo Merisi da Caravaggio, the only painting the artist actually signed, and a fine example of his dramatic use of chiaroscuro—the use of light and shadow. The painting can still be viewed in the cathedral's oratory. Another work by Caravaggio, *St Jerome II*, is also housed in the cathedral. The cathedral is also a monument to one of the oldest and most illustrious of Europe's military orders, and to its most heroic and important members. **JF**

"The Grandmaster put a gold chain around his neck and made him a gift of two Turkish slaves."

Gian Pietro Bellori, on Caravaggio's success in Malta

Torre de Hércules (La Coruña, Spain)

Oldest lighthouse in operation in the world

There has been a working lighthouse on this craggy cliff top for around 1,900 years. The Torre de Hércules (Tower of Hercules) lighthouse was constructed by the Romans who occupied this part of Spain and called the region Brigantia. It was built in the late first or early second century C.E., in the time of the Emperor Trajan. The architect was a man named Cayo Sergio Lupo and, amazingly, his edifice is still carrying out its original purpose today. The Roman building, which was renovated in the eighteenth century, provides the casing for the workings of a twenty-first-century lighthouse. There are 242 steps inside the tower and the light that blinks out from a height of 367 feet (112 m) above sea level can be seen for an impressive 32 miles (51 km).

The port of La Coruña is the second largest port in Spain, a popular destination for cruise liners and yachts. For hundreds of years, it has been an entry point for Christian pilgrims wanting to walk the sacred route to Santiago de Compostela. The location of the Torre de Hércules on a treacherous stretch of coastline commonly known as the Costa da Morte, or Coast of Death, is significant because the Romans believed that the world was flat and that this coastline marked its perimeter. Responsible for saving the lives of many thousands of sailors, the Torre de Hércules became an internationally famed landmark and remained so throughout the centuries; it can be seen painted on maps dating back to the Middle Ages and earlier.

The name of the lighthouse comes from the Roman myth of the Twelve Labors of Hercules. It was said that Hercules fought and eventually defeated the giant Geryon, then triumphantly buried Geryon's head—supposedly at modern-day La Coruña—and ordered a town to be built above it. The town's coat of arms includes a tower placed over a skull and crossbones, thought to be a reference to this story. **LH**

> *"A very tall lighthouse is erected among a few commemorative works, looking towards Britannia."*
>
> Paulus Orosius, *Historiae Adversum Paganos* (c. 415)

🏛 ◎ **Catedral del Apostol** (Santiago de Compostela, Spain)

Destination of the legendary pilgrim route, Camino de Santiago

The name of Santiago de Compostela is known and revered throughout the Christian world. Its links with the relics of St. James (Santiago in Spanish) have made it the most important destination for pilgrims, after Jerusalem and Rome.

Santiago's cathedral is certainly worthy of a visit in its own right. It has the unusual distinction of being a Romanesque building, concealed within the shell of a Baroque exterior. The original church was founded in the ninth century, but this building was destroyed by the Moors in 997. The present structure dates from the late eleventh century, when the increased number of pilgrims provided ample funds for a new church. Much of the Romanesque building is well preserved in the interior, but the exterior was largely remodeled during the eighteenth century by a local architect, Fernando Casas y Novoa. The architecture, however, must take second place to the medieval legend that provided the raison d'être for the Catedral del Apostol. According to this legend, the apostle St. James the Greater preached throughout Spain before being martyred in Rome. His remains were carried back to Spain and buried in Compostela. His grave was forgotten until 813, when it was rediscovered by a hermit who was led to it by a star. After this event, large numbers of pilgrims began to travel to Compostela to pay homage at his shrine. When they arrived at the cathedral, then as now, their first action was to kiss or touch the saint's statue on the Porch of Glory (Master Mateo's original doorway to the church). They would then touch a similar figure behind the altar and collect their *compostellana* (a confirmation of their pilgrimage).

Pilgrims continue to flock to Santiago to this day. The numbers of visitors are particularly high in "Holy Years," those years when the feast day of St. James—July 25—falls on a Sunday. **IZ**

> "St. James . . . has been given by God to Spain for its patron and protection."
>
> Cervantes, *Don Quixote* (1605)

Influential in the development of religious architecture and home of religious treasures

The Cámara Santa (Holy Chamber) in the Torre de San Miguel, a remaining ruin of the Fruela Palace situated in the heart of Oviedo Cathedral, contains several important Spanish treasures, including the Cross of the Angels, the symbol of the city and one of the finest examples of Asturian art in the world.

The sturdy stone chamber was originally built in the ninth century by King Alfonso II to keep safe precious holy relics rescued from Toledo when it fell to the Moors. Remodeled in the twelfth century, it now forms the inner sanctuary of the cathedral, which was built in 1388 on the well-trodden pilgrim's route to Santiago de Compostela. Taking the form of a pair of linked chapels, the innermost structure is thought to be the original building. The ante-chapel—rebuilt in 1109—is a subtle example of the Spanish Romanesque style. Each of the six columns supporting the vault is sculpted with a lifelike pair of apostles around the Gothic cloisters. The gold Cross of the Angels dates back to 808 and takes its name from the story that it was offered to King Alfonso II by angels disguised as pilgrims. Fashioned by Asturian goldsmiths, it has a splendid core of cherrywood and is lavishly decorated with forty-eight precious stones, including fine rubies and opals.

Other treasures in the Cámara Santa include the tenth-century Victory Cross (a Latin cross covered in gold leaf) and the oak Holy Ark, reputedly originating in Jerusalem and said to have been made by devout followers of the apostles. The chamber contains one intriguing item—the Sudarium, a cloth supposedly used to clean the face of Jesus after the crucifixion. On a gruesome note, research has shown that stains on the cloth, barely visible to the human eye, consist of one part blood and six parts fluid from the lungs of a victim of crucifixion (the blood type also matches that of the Shroud of Turin). **TE**

"The importance of the reign of Alfonso II is fundamental in the history of Asturias."

María Josefa Sanz Fuentes, historian

Covadonga Battlefield (Covadonga, Spain)

The defeat of Muslim forces marked the start of the Christian reconquest of Spain

It is hard to tell where reality ends and myth takes over when it comes to the Battle of Covadonga. What is certain is that this event lies deep within the Spanish national consciousness as a symbol of independence, identity, and a struggle against the odds.

Covadonga village hugs a lower slope of the towering Picos (peaks) de Europa. Pilgrims as well as tourists have long flocked to the village to visit the site where national hero Pelayo, first Christian king of the Asturias region, is said to have decisively defeated Muslim forces in the mountains nearby. Between the eighth and fifteenth centuries, the Iberian Peninsula saw successive bouts of conflict between Muslim conquerors and Christian forces. Christianity finally won the day and the Battle of Covadonga is widely seen as the start of the *reconquista*—the Christian reconquest of Spain after a major Arab invasion of the peninsula in 711. This invasion routed a Visigothic kingdom established in the region and brought the peninsula largely under Arab control by about 713. One pocket of resistance was headed by a Gothic nobleman called Pelayo, who gathered about him in the Asturias Mountains an army that included Visigoths and those fleeing from Muslim strongholds farther south. The battle occurred between 718 and 725. The Spanish-Christian story goes that when Muslim forces decided to crush Asturias, Pelayo's forces withdrew into the mountains, hiding in a narrow pass and a cave and thus gaining the advantage. It is said that, with far fewer fighters, they decimated the Muslim cavalry and released the kingdom of Asturias from Muslim threats forever.

Attractions today include a cave said to be Pelayo's hiding place, which houses his tomb, and a much-restored eighth-century chapel, as well as the impressive nineteenth-century church of Nuestra Señora de las Batallas. **AK**

"We trust in God's mercy and know that from this mountain will emerge the health of Spain."

Pelayo, founder of the kingdom of Asturias

 🏛 🔞 **Altamira Cave** (near Santillana del Mar, Spain)

Contains Paleolithic rock paintings depicting realistic animal images

Altamira belongs to the Franco-Cantabrian belt of decorated caves, which extends from southwest France to northeast Spain. The cave itself had been found by a huntsman in 1868, but it was only eleven years later that a five-year-old girl noticed the paintings. Her father, Marcelino de Sautuola, was the first to excavate the site and publish his findings. His claim that the paintings were Paleolithic was greeted with some skepticism. Some French archeologists even suggested that they were forgeries. Sautuola's theories were eventually vindicated after his death.

The extraordinary paintings are mainly of animals. The finest ones depict bison, but deer, boars, and horses also appear. The artists used just three color pigments—ocher, red, and black—but managed to create remarkably realistic images, particularly in the texture of the manes and fur. The painters also used the uneven surface of the walls to give the animals a sense of volume. In common with the caves at Lascaux and elsewhere, conservation has been a major and ongoing headache. The cave was closed for a time in 1977 and then reopened five years later on a very limited basis (there is a three-year waiting list to view the paintings). Instead, visitors are encouraged to visit one of the replicas of the cave. The first of these was produced by the Deutsches Museum in Munich (1962), but there is another version in Madrid (1964), and a more elaborate one near Altamira itself (2001). **IZ**

"The original cave consisted of a series of rooms and passages in an 'S' shape."

Manuel Franquelo, director of Altamira

🏛 ◈ **Vizcaya Bridge** (Bilbao, Spain)

Architecturally remarkable iron construction and innovative feat of engineering

The Vizcaya Bridge, which crosses the mouth of the Nervión River northwest of Bilbao, is the world's first transporter bridge. Its local name, Puente Colgante, which means "suspension bridge," is something of a misnomer because the structure is quite different from a true suspension bridge.

Designed by Alberto Palacio, the Vizcaya Bridge was the first bridge in the world to carry people and traffic on a high suspended gondola and was used as a model for similar bridges around the world. It saves space and construction costs because it does not have long and bulky access ramps and yet it stands 164 feet (50 m) above the river so that it does not hinder the large ships that operate in and out of the port of Bilbao. The construction of the 538-foot- (164-m-) long bridge brings together traditional nineteenth-century cast iron engineering and more modern lightweight technology using the strength and other properties of twisted steel ropes. Use of the bridge was suspended for four years during the Spanish Civil War, after the upper section was blown up. It is said that the architect, Alberto Palacio, watched the destruction from his house in nearby Portugalete, just before he died. The rebuilt bridge had two high-tech tourist lifts installed in the 164-foot- (50-m-) high pillars, so that visitors can walk over the bridge and enjoy the breathtaking views of the port of Bilbao and the Abra bay. **LC**

"[Construction] entailed the use of what were in their day cutting-edge technologies."

Miren Azkarate, regional culture minister

Monument to Peace

(Guernica, Spain)

Guernica was defenseless against the horrendous attack by the German air force

In a deliberate military attack on unarmed civilians, the little town of Guernica was destroyed by German bombers at the request of General Franco on April 26, 1937, during the Spanish Civil War. Guernica was the home of the Basque parliament, whose rights had been ordained by successive Spanish governments in ceremonies carried out under the Tree of Guernica, an oak tree in the town center. In 1876, the Basque region had been declared a part of Spain and lost its rights to self-government. In the early twentieth century, the move for Basque separatism became a popular cause.

Ostensibly, the Luftwaffe targeted the town for its insignificant arms factory, but in reality it was so General Franco could show the Basques who was boss. On that April afternoon, a busy market day, the Luftwaffe dropped incendiary bombs on thousands of homes and shops. As the streets and their buildings caught fire, those attempting to flee were machine-gunned by the Nazis from above. More than 2,000 people were killed or horrifically maimed. Incredibly, the town's church, parliament building, and the oak tree were not destroyed. Today, the town has been rebuilt and includes a peace monument constructed by Basque sculptor Eduardo Chillida. Work began on the Guernica Peace Museum in 1998 and it opened in 2003. The museum is housed in one of the new buildings, constructed after the tragedy.

Spanish artist Pablo Picasso painted his pain in a mural simply titled *Guernica* (1937). The painting toured Europe and North America; the entrance fees to its exhibition went into a fund for Spanish refugees. So large it covers an entire wall, *Guernica* stood for many years in a New York art gallery because Picasso decreed that the painting should not be exhibited in Spain until the country had thrown off Franco's dictatorship. *Guernica* was returned to Spain in 1981. **LH**

> *"World leaders call this new war a crusade./'Wars end,' said Picasso, 'hostilities go on forever.'"*
>
> Lydia Nibley, "It's Complicated" (2001)

Monumento a los Fueros

(Pamplona, Spain)

Monument to Basque nationalism

Pamplona lies in the heart of Navarra, part of the Basque region of Spain, and the Monumento a los Fueros stands in the town's central square. The *fueros* are the ancient laws and rights of the Basque people that were suppressed by General Franco's nationalist regime, a move that inflamed Basque passion and fueled a determination to retain their culture, language, and laws. After Franco's death in 1975, a Basque parliament was set up, and the Basque people have gained considerable control over their own government and services.

The monument was erected outside Palacio del Gobierno de Navarra in Pamplona in 1903. Paid for by public subscription and designed by Manuel Martinez de Ubago, the monument symbolizes the freedom of Navarra. The monument stands 82 feet (25 m) high and has a pentagonal base, each side of which celebrates five principles: peace, justice, autonomy, history, and work, with inscriptions on bronze plaques. The center section is more ornate, with five marble pillars and statues reflecting the same values. A 16-foot- (5-m-) high statue of a crowned matron is mounted at the top, symbolizing Navarra itself.

Some anthropologists believe that the Basque may be Europe's oldest race, being descended from the Cro-Magnon people who inhabited the Pyrennees and painted the caves in Altamira. The remoteness of their valleys meant that these mountain people remained outside the influence of the rest of Europe. Basque families still inhabit the isolated stone farmhouses, or *caseríos*, and speak Euskera, a language that predates all other European languages and is unique to the region. The traditional music and leaping dances of the region are different from those in any other culture—and they also have sports that are uniquely Basque. **LC**

Federico Paternina

(Haro, Spain)

Largest producer of Rioja

The wine industry in Rioja features consistently in the history of the region in northern Spain, and remains of Roman wineries still exist. During the eighteenth century, wine growers in the Rioja region brought in expertise from France and developed methods for transporting wine, including the use of oak barrels. The wine industry was given a boost in the late nineteenth century when a fungus devastated the vines of Bordeaux, and the wineries in Rioja were able to supply great wines to the rest of Europe.

Federico Paternina Josué founded the bodega in 1896 when he acquired and merged three smaller

> *"Ernest Hemingway was an admirer of this winery and visited Paternina several times."*
>
> Dirk Becker, wine writer

businesses. In 1984 the company was acquired by Marcos Eguizábal Ramírez, a Rioja-born businessman, as part of an initiative to ensure that Spanish wineries remained in Spanish ownership. The company today is one of the few Spanish-owned wineries quoted on the Spanish stock exchange.

Haro, in the center of the Rioja Alta region, is an elegant town with an impressive range of wine bars. Rioja Alta is higher and cooler than the rest of the region, which, with its clay soils, provides the perfect conditions for the tempranillo grape. The geology of the region is also of some considerable interest; dinosaur footprints, 150 million years old, are embedded in rocks throughout the region. There is a fine group of three-toed footprints, up to 11 inches (30 cm) long, near the village of Enciso. **LC**

Salvador Dalí's House

(Figueres, Spain)

Dalí led a secluded life in this apartment

Salvador Dalí (1904–89) spent his final years in his Spanish hometown of Figueres and lived in a tower (Torre Galatea) adjacent to the Old Municipal Theater. The tower is now part of the Dalí Theater-Museum, which pays homage to the artist's brilliance.

Dalí was a talented draftsman with an astoundingly delicate painterly hand—an amazing skill that was frequently attributed to the influence of Old Renaissance Masters. Beyond painting, his repertoire extended into film, photography, animation, and sculpture. Dalí was one of the leaders of the Surrealist art movement, and most of his works were

> *"Surrealism is destructive, but it destroys only what it considers to be shackles limiting our vision."*

Salvador Dalí, artist

produced in this style. Surrealism explored the idea of accessing the unconscious and using it for greater artistic creativity. In Dalí's paintings, such as *The Persistence of Time* or *Self Construction with Boiled Beans (Premonition of Civil War)*, he offers us an insight into his mind, and especially his bizarre subconscious. The paintings reveal a sense of the complex man behind the art, and similar secrets are unveiled in the Dalí Theater-Museum.

The museum stands opposite the church where he was baptized and is also the site of his very first exhibition. It contains the largest and most diverse collection of Dalí works available, even holding some from his personal collection. Everything in the museum has been conceived, designed, and made by the artist. In a sense it is the very heart of Dalí. **KH**

El Banys Arabs

(Girona, Spain)

Well-preserved medieval baths

Girona's Arab Baths (El Banys Arabs) are the best-preserved public baths (after Granada) from medieval Christian Spain. They are accessed through the twin-towered Portal de Sobreportes at the foot of the ninety steps down from the city's St. Felix cathedral. Originally built in 1194 on the site of baths demolished by the French, they were most likely designed by Moorish craftsmen. Although clearly modeled on the template of traditional Roman and Muslim bathhouses, they are actually a twelfth-century Christian structure incorporating elements of both Arab and Romanesque styles.

In 1284 the building was extensively repaired after suffering severe damage during a siege. Closed throughout most of the fifteenth century, the baths eventually went into private ownership until 1617, when they saw service as the laundry room of a convent run by an order of Capuchin nuns. The bathhouses were also used as a pantry and kitchen before they were acquired by the Spanish government in 1929 and completely renovated. Visitors to the baths can enjoy three principal rooms of different temperatures maintained by an underfloor heating system—a hypocaust, literally meaning "heat from below"—based on the traditional Roman system.

The most impressive room is undoubtedly the Apodyterium—or changing room—a delightful space with an octagonal pool in its center that is illuminated by natural light cascading down from a domed skylight supported by eight columns. There are also niches for your clothes and a stone bench for relaxing after the rigors of the hot baths. Next door, in the baths proper, is the frigidarium (cold chamber) to cool down in (traditionally a sort of plunge pool) and bathers also had access to a tepidarium, or warm room, as well as a caldarium, a kind of sauna. **TE**

Castell de Pubol

(Girona, Spain)

Dalí bought and renovated the castle for his estranged wife

This Gothic Renaissance fortress was bought by Spanish Surrealist painter Salvador Dalí as a gift for his Russian wife, Gala, in 1970. Following her death, Dali took up residence in the castle for two years before finally moving to Figueres. Located in the tiny hamlet of Pubol near Girona, the medieval fortress dates back to 1017 but was derelict when Dalí acquired it in 1968. Restoration work and an entire transformation, overseen by Dalí, took more than a year to complete, and the gift was presented to the estranged Gala in the spring on the condition that Dalí never enter the castle unless he was invited in writing (apparently, he seldom was).

The castle—less showy and more sober than his other residences—was furnished with carefully selected pieces of furniture and oddities from antiques dealers in the region. Statues of elephants with vast feet distinguish the garden, and Dalí also built a swimming pool surrounded with busts of the German composer Richard Wagner. There is also a collection of Gala's haute couture dresses. Dalí painted several frescoes inside and later painted two watercolors—*View of Pubol* and *Gala's Castle at Pubol*. In the basement, he built the crypt where Gala was later to be buried after dying at the age of eighty-eight. On the day of her death—June 10, 1982—a grief-stricken Dalí left his home in Port Lligat and went to live in Pubol alongside his muse. During the next two years he painted his last authenticated work—*Kite's Tale and Guitar*—as well as creating his own museum, the Torre Galatea in Figueres. King Juan Carlos also bestowed him with the title Marquis Dalí of Pubol.

In 1984, a severely depressed Dalí was seriously injured in a bedroom fire, which damaged parts of the castle. He moved back to Figueres, where he remained until he died in 1989. **TE**

"Quieter, more serious, and much less surrealistically showy than the houses in Port Lligat and Figueres."

Frommer's Review

Monastery of the Virgin
(Montserrat, Spain)

Pilgrims flock here to see La Moreneta

Montserrat's Monastery of the Virgin is the dramatic home to one of the most revered religious images in the whole of Spain—*La Moreneta*. A Romanesque sculpture carved in wood and dating back to the twelfth century, the Black Virgin—literally translated from Catalan as "the little dark-skinned one"—is an internationally renowned statue of the patron virgin of Catalonia.

The stuff of Catholic legend, the sculpture was reputedly fashioned in Jerusalem by St. Luke around 50 c.e. and brought to Spain by St. Peter, where it was carefully hidden from the Moors in a cave. Local lore claims Benedictine monks could not move it, and therefore a monastery was constructed around it some 4,000 feet (1,219 m) up in the eerily pink mountain peaks. (Montserrat translates as "jagged mountain.") In 1522, Ignatius Loyola, after recovering from battle wounds, visited the shrine before later founding the Jesuit order. Numerous miracles were associated with *La Moreneta* and, in 1592, the grand basilica of the monastery was consecrated to deal with the mass influx of pilgrims to the site. During the Napoleonic invasion, the sanctuary was destroyed in 1812 only to be rebuilt in the nineteenth century, and the Black Virgin was declared Catalonia's patroness by Pope Leo XIII.

La Moreneta—whose dark color is a result of aging wood varnish—is located above the high altar in the basilica next to the monastery. Twice a year thousands of pilgrims flock to the Madonna, and throughout the year honeymoon couples seek its blessing on their marriages. In one version of Arthurian legend, Montserrat was also where Parsifal discovered the Holy Grail. The site was briefly home to German composer Richard Wagner, who used the monastery as a backdrop to the opera *Parsifal*. **TE**

Cathedral of Santa Eulalia (Barcelona, Spain)

Monument to the city's patron saint

Known locally as La Seu, the Cathedral of St. Eulalia is a large Gothic edifice, whose sheer, slender towers seem to pierce the sky. The cathedral took 150 years to complete; it was begun in the thirteenth century but was not finished until the mid-fifteenth century, although much of its impressive Gothic facade was created in the nineteenth century.

The church's interior is stunning, with ornate woodcarvings, paintings, sculpture, marble, and masonry. A plaque dating back to 1493 records the baptism of six indigenous people from the Caribbean, brought to Spain by Christopher Columbus after his

---

"The historian Cirici called [the cathedral] 'the loveliest oasis in Barcelona.'"

Frommer's Review

---

epic journey to the Americas. When wandering around the cloisters, visitors are often surprised to come across a gaggle of white geese. They have been kept here for at least five centuries and are said to represent the purity of St. Eulalia.

St. Eulalia of Barcelona was a young virgin who was martyred at the age of thirteen or fourteen by Roman soldiers. This occurred under the rule of the Emperor Diocletian, who was notorious for his reign of religious persecution. Eulalia died in the city of her birth in 304. Her bones were originally housed in a small church elsewhere in Barcelona. Now they reside in a beautifully ornate tomb inside the crypt of the cathedral that bears her name. Eulalia is a patron saint of mariners, and her name is also invoked in prayers against drought. **LH**

Hospital de Sant Pau

(Barcelona, Spain)

The beauty of Domènech's masterpiece was intended to aid the well-being of its patients

Barcelona's Hospital de la Santa Creu i Sant Pau is a fine example of Catalan Art Nouveau architecture built between 1901 and 1930. The hospital itself was founded in 1401 and its original medieval buildings are now an art school; the twentieth-century structure is still used as a hospital.

The construction of the hospital was funded by local banker Pau Gil, who wanted Barcelona to have a modern hospital that would satisfy the contemporary requirements of the medical profession to the highest level. The original plan was to construct a complex of forty-eight buildings, but only twenty-seven were ever built across the 33-acre site (13.5 ha), and the final complex contains a church, museum, and library. The three-story buildings are interspersed by gardens.

The hospital's architectural flourishes, curvaceous forms, and use of highly colored ceramics, mosaics, and stained glass are reminiscent of those of the famous Catalan architect Antoni Gaudí i Cornet, who was responsible for the city's La Sagrada Familia church. However, the hospital was designed by fellow Catalan architect and contemporary Lluís Domènech i Montaner and completed by his son after the architect's death. Domènech was a politician, architect, and onetime professor and director of Barcelona's school of architecture. He was highly influential in creating a Catalan style of Art Nouveau architecture, both through his own work and his prolific writing on the subject. The hospital is one of his most notable creations and also contains the work of other important Catalan artists and craftsmen of the time, including sculptures by Eusebi Arnau and Pau Gargallo, and paintings and tile work by Francesc Labarta. Domènech's inclusion of artworks and gardens in a hospital was in accordance with his belief that looking at beauty has a therapeutic value. **CK**

"A form of architecture intent on collaboration with all the figurative and decorative arts ..."

Ezio Godoli, art historian

🏛 ◎ La Sagrada Familia (Barcelona, Spain)

Gaudí's labor of love that has yet to reach fruition

> *"The Temple grows slowly, but this has always been the case with things destined to have a long life."*

Antoni Gaudí, architect

⬆ Gaudí in 1878, the year in which he graduated from Barcelona's Escola Tècnica Superior d'Arquitectura.

➦ Barcelona's most famous ecclesiastical building—scaffolding and all.

Building La Sagrada Familia was a labor of love for Catalonia's most famous—and perhaps favorite—son, architect Antoni Gaudí i Cornet. He all but abandoned his commercial work to construct what was intended to be his pièce de résistance, and also an act of religious faith. He designed it to be what he called "a church for the poor," and its construction was—and still is—funded by donations alone.

Despite the fact that building began in 1883, the structure is not yet finished. Some people estimate that it may be complete by the one hundredth anniversary of Gaudí's death, but even this is disputed. Whether the building can ever be completed along Gaudí's original plans, however, remains a moot point, given that during the Spanish Civil War the workshop containing Gaudí's drawings was set on fire. This led to a debate among a group of leading artists, intellectuals, and architects about whether building work should continue. They wanted the church to remain as faithful as possible to Gaudí's original concept, and some even disputed the need for such a large church in what was an increasingly secular society.

That said, La Sagrada Familia is sufficiently complete to be seen as the ultimate expression of Gaudí's unique architectural style. Although he drew on the contemporary vogue for Art Nouveau, Gaudí's individual flourishes stamp his designs with a distinct flavor: organic curves and shapes that echo those found in nature, fantastical almost fairy-tale forms, and highly colored tile work. Fittingly, the architect was buried in a crypt in the basilica after his tragic death caused by falling beneath a tram. Gaudí's disheveled appearance meant no one recognized him when the accident took place, and he was taken to a pauper's hospital nearby to die. When his identity became known, he was offered the chance to move elsewhere, but humbly insisted on staying among the poor. **CK**

🏛 ◎ **Palau Güell** (Barcelona, Spain)

Gaudí's first commission for Güell, built in a limited space but with an unrestrained budget

Few architects have stamped their personality on a city as firmly as Antoni Gaudí i Cornet. A fervent Catalan, he transformed Barcelona—the capital of Catalonia—with a series of extraordinary building projects and architectural innovations.

Gaudí designed the Palau (literally "palace") as a sumptuous town house for Eusebi Güell, the wealthy industrialist who became his chief patron. The site was chosen because the family owned the adjoining property and, for a time, the two buildings were joined. Work began in 1885 and was largely completed by 1888 when the Palau became one of the showpieces of the World Fair. The final flourishes were added during the following year. Much of the construction material came from Güell's own quarries, in nearby Garraf.

Although the palace is one of Gaudí's earlier works, the Palau contains many of the famous signatures of his style. The entrance takes the form of two parabolic arches, one with a ramp leading down to the stables. Wrought ironwork plays a prominent role in the decoration, especially between the arches, where there is a stylized version of the Catalan crest. The interior is reminiscent of ecclesiastical architecture, but the most typical feature is on the roof. Here, Gaudí placed twenty chimneys, each one different and more akin to a sculpture than a functional object. Like stunted, polychrome fir trees, most of them are decorated with trencadís—the fragments of colored ceramics that have become Gaudí's trademark.

Güell lived in the Palau until 1906, when he moved into another of Gaudí's creations, the Parque Güell. The building was owned by the family until 1945, when it passed to the city authorities. Parts of the Palau have since been used as a theater museum, but the building was closed to the public in 2005 to allow for extensive restoration to the stonework. **CK**

"Elegance is the sister of poverty, but one must not confuse poverty with misery."

Antoni Gaudí, architect

Santa María de Poblet (near Tarragona, Spain)

One of the largest and most important monasteries in Spain

The imposing monastery of Santa María de Poblet, in Catalonia, was founded by Cistercian monks from France in the early twelfth century, when the Catalan king Ramon Berenguer IV gave land in La Conca de Barberà to Fontfreda Abbey in France. The first monastic community on the site was led by Abbot Guerau from 1153.

Santa María de Poblet was the first and largest of three sister monasteries to be constructed. They were known collectively as the "Cistercian triangle" and helped consolidate power in Catalonia after the region had been recaptured from the Moors in the twelfth century. The other two monasteries are Vallbona de les Monges and Santes Creus. Poblet Monastery, with the support of the resident kings and nobles, prospered from the twelfth to the eighteenth century, owning substantial areas of land throughout the kingdoms of Catalan and Aragon. In 1835, when the monasteries were acquired by the Spanish state, Santa María de Poblet was ruthlessly plundered and severely damaged by fire. Sadly the monastery lay in ruins until the 1930s, when restoration began, and monks returned to the site in 1940.

This grandiose monastery, enclosed by fortified walls, is a fine example of architecture and design from the Middle Ages. The vaulted cloister, with ornately decorated windows, lies at the heart of the building and at the center of monastic life. The refectory is a vaulted hall with an octagonal fountain; the dormitory, reached only by stairs from the church, is a long, 285-foot (87-m) gallery; and the chapterhouse is a perfect square, with fine columns and a graceful ceiling. The Pantheon of Kings in the abbey church has housed the tombs of kings and nobles since 1359. Behind the stone altar in the church, there is an exceptionally beautiful alabaster *reredos* (decorative screen), carved by sculptor Damià Forment in 1527. **EH**

"The austere, majestic monastery has a fortified royal residence and ... is an impressive sight."

UNESCO

Ebro Battlefields (Ebro, Spain)

Site of the last major battle of the Spanish Civil War

The great Ebro, Spain's longest river, rises in the Cantabrian Mountains of northern Spain and winds southeasterly toward its delta on the Mediterranean coast. It was along a length of the river slicing through the country's Zaragoza and Tarragona provinces, between a point near the inland town of Mequinenza and the delta, that the Republican cause fought its last major offensive of the Spanish Civil War (1936–39).

The civil war was essentially a brutal clash between Spain's ruling Republican regime, under Juan Negrín, and disaffected conservative Nationalists, under the fascist-backed rebel leader, Francisco Franco. Thrown into the complex brew were the ambitions of Spain's communist party. By 1938, the Republican armies were exhausted and the Nationalist troops were pushing on toward the Mediterranean. Negrín decided that immediate action must be taken to stop the rebels from capturing the remaining

Republican strongholds. He planned a massive attack. As Franco's troops advanced toward Valencia, Republican soldiers massed along the Ebro's banks. On the night of July 24, the Republicans crossed the river, taking the Nationalists unawares and seizing a position across the river that let them advance farther into enemy territory. As the summer progressed, the fighting intensified and the Battle of the Ebro struggled on until November 16, 1938, by which time the tables had completely turned. Using their superior air cover and resources, the Nationalists had reversed the Republicans' initial success and eventually stopped them in their tracks, with horrific casualties.

This was essentially the Republicans' last real stand in the civil war. It disastrously depleted their energy, supplies, manpower, and morale, and paved the way for the decisive final victory of Franco on the Catalonia front in January 1939. **AK**

🏛 ◎ Las Médulas (near Ponferrada, Spain)

Mined for gold by the Romans, whose techniques displayed immense engineering prowess

Looking like giant jagged teeth, the pointed rocky crags of this extraordinary, otherworldly landscape glow hot red as the Spanish sun plays over their clay surfaces. Partly covered with chestnut trees, crisscrossed by countless trails, and hiding a honeycomb of tunnels, caves, lakes, and grottoes, these rocks were once the Roman Empire's greatest gold mine. Today they are both a natural wonder and evidence of the Romans' incredibly advanced engineering prowess.

Up to 800 tons of gold were extracted from the area during the first and second centuries C.E., using an ingenious hydraulic system that was a marvel of its time. Roman writer Pliny the Elder described how a *ruina montium* type of mine was created here, whereby staggering amounts of water from nearby mountains were literally flushed through a complex system of specially bored corridors and galleries in order to make the mountains of Las Médulas collapse and expose their treasure more easily. He tells of huge teams of miners spending months at a time shut away from the sunlight, digging tunnels by lamplight, many perishing along the way. After two centuries of intensive mining, the Romans deserted the site.

The natural landscape of Las Médulas may have been ravaged, but the site has been left untouched by industry since the Romans' departure, thus allowing a fascinating insight into their technical ability. Today visitors can walk the many paths and see spectacular caves and grottoes where gold was collected, as well as galleries bearing the marks of miners from thousands of years ago and the remains of villages from this mining age. The nearby Orellán viewpoint provides extraordinary vistas of the landscape. In 1997 UNESCO gave Las Médulas a listing as a uniquely well-preserved showcase for Roman technology. **AK**

🏛 ⊚ **Burgos Cathedral** (Burgos, Spain)

Magnificent Gothic structure—the burial place of El Cid

Northern Spain's Burgos Cathedral is a masterpiece of Gothic architecture dedicated to the Virgin Mary. Laid out to a Latin cross plan, the church is famous for its stained glass windows, artworks, choir stalls, chapels, tombs, statuary, and the fine tracery of its open stonework. It draws its inspiration from churches constructed in northern France during the thirteenth century and is a fine example of how the Spanish adapted the French Gothic style as their own. The dissemination of French Gothic architecture and art was also aided by the fact that Burgos and its cathedral have been a stopping point since medieval times for Christian pilgrims en route from the Pyrenees to Santiago de Compostela in Galicia.

Work began on the church in 1221 with the Bishop of Burgos, Mauricio, at the helm. The bishop had studied in Paris, and it was he who brought in a French master builder to manage the project. A hiatus of 200 years followed before further embellishments were made to the cathedral, including those of German architect Juan de Colonia, who added spires of open stonework tracery to its two frontal towers. The cathedral was completed in 1567, although the Renaissance saw some additions such as the golden staircase known as the Escalera Dorada.

The cathedral is not only notable for its flamboyant architecture, but also houses the remains of members of the Spanish royal house of Castile. But it is most widely known as the burial place of one of Burgos's most eminent sons, the eleventh-century soldier and military leader Rodrigo Díaz de Vivar, known as El Cid, and his wife, Doña Jimena. The couple's remains were interred in the center of the cathedral in 1919. El Cid was a hero of the Spanish *reconquista* of Spain and conquered Valencia in 1094 to regain Spanish control of the city. El Cid went on to govern the city and surrounding region until his death. **CK**

> *"This man [El Cid], the scourge of his time, . . . was one of the miracles of God."*
>
> Ibn Bassam, poet and historian

Monasterio de Santo Domingo de Silos (Burgos, Spain)

Its archive houses the ancient Missal of Silos

El Monasterio de Santo Domingo de Silos in Burgos consists of two juxtaposed monasteries around two cloisters, one medieval and the other Baroque. Its church lies to the north, and its south wing is a collection of Benedictine monks' cells.

The monastery dates from the tenth century and was originally dedicated to St. Sebastian. Today it is dedicated to St. Dominic of Silos, who was abbot here from 1041 to 1073. The saint supervised the renaissance of the monastery after it suffered several raids by the Moors, and it was under his inspired leadership that it became a scholarly center of book illumination and craftsmanship in gold and silver leaf, examples of which can be seen today in the monastery's own museum and library.

The monastery became known for its scriptorium, or place for writing, where the monks copied religious texts by hand. Its library contains the *Missal of Silos*, which is the oldest-known text on paper produced in Christian Western civilization. The eleventh-century text is a Mozarabic rite quarto missal of 154 folios. The text is also important because it shows how rites evolved within the Christian church, since the Mozarabic rites preceded the Latin form of liturgy within the Roman Catholic church. The monastery was also once home to a twelfth-century copy of a commentary on the Apocalypse by the Spanish monk Beatus of Liébana, which was held in high regard by Christians during medieval times. It contains 106 miniatures illustrating biblical scenes and took almost twenty years to produce. It contains one of the oldest Christian maps of the world, showing the routes taken by the early Christian saints and missionaries. The manuscript left the monastery in the eighteenth century and is now housed in London's British Museum, but it remains a testament to the high quality of the monks' craftsmanship. **CK**

"The monastery was in terrible shape, spiritually and materially ... Dominic set about restoring it."

The Reverend Clifford Stevens, author

Valladolid Cathedral (Valladolid, Spain)

Holds a unique archive of music manuscripts

> "... a musical treasure ... unique in Spain: we don't believe there is a superior cathedral archive."

José López Calo, musicologist

King Philip II of Spain commissioned architect Juan de Herrera to design Valladolid Cathedral, or the Catedral de la Nuestra Señora de la Asunción, in the sixteenth century. De Herrera was well known for his austere design of the combined palace and monastery, Royal Monastery of San Lorenzo de El Escorial, which was also commissioned by the king and lies northwest of Madrid. The great Spanish architect was responsible for spearheading a new style (Herreran) of carefully proportioned geometric lines and an absence of decoration, gesturing toward the Classical, whose influence can be seen throughout Spain. But after the death of both king and architect, the church was incomplete, and it was finally opened in 1688 thanks to the efforts of de Herrera's pupil Diego de Praves, who was succeeded by his son. In 1730 the architect Alberto Churriguera finished the work on the facade, aping the style of El Escorial. In 1755 the Great Lisbon Earthquake shook the cathedral, causing damage that resulted in the collapse of a tower in 1841. The tower was rebuilt, but the church remains unfinished.

The cathedral was once home to a work by Greek painter El Greco, and is notable for its ornamental wooden carvings and the reredos (decorative screen) housed in the great chapel. However, it is more famous for its magnificent collection of music manuscripts than for its artworks. The archive contains more than 6,000 original manuscripts dating from the fifteenth century. The church's collection of sixteenth-century manuscripts of polyphonic sacred music, romantic madrigals, and carols, including those by the Franco-Flemish composer Joaquín de Prés and the Spanish composer Juan de Anchieta, is unique. The collection was assembled over the centuries by the cathedral's *maestros de capilla*, or chapel masters, whose duty it was both to supply and compose new music for various religious festivals. **CK**

Atapuerca Caves (Atapuerca, Spain)

Outstanding fossil record of the earliest human beings in Europe

A spectacular cave system near the Spanish town of Atapuerca has provided paleontologists with a rich fossil record of the earliest human beings in Europe. The findings have revealed priceless information about the appearance and way of life of our human ancestors, from almost one million years ago to the present day.

Located in ancient limestone caverns near Burgos, the discovery was fortuitously made when a railway cutting was driven through the site in the late 1890s. Several sites were subsequently excavated, but it was not until 1976 that the significance of Atapuerca was fully realized when a student discovered a human jawbone. Early human remains ranged from *Homo erectus* to the more recently identified species *Homo antecessor*. Excavation work began in earnest and the Sima de los Huesos (Pit of Bones) staked its place on the paleontologist's map. Located at the foot of a 42-foot- (13-m-) high chimney reached by scrambling through the Cueva Mayor cave system, the fossils of bears, wolves, and lions had a minimum age of 350,000 years (corresponding to the Middle Pleistocene period). Among them were remains of about thirty skeletons—the largest hominid collection in the world—of the human species *Homo heidelbergensis*, a direct ancestor of the Neanderthals. A second site, Gran Dolina, revealed layers of sediment rich with fossils and stone tools of the earliest hominids dated between 780,000 and 1 million years ago.

On a more grizzly note, the earliest evidence of cannibalism in the human fossil record was also found. It is believed individuals were consumed under what is termed gastronomic cannibalism—not in a famine or as part of a ritual. These hominids are thought to be part of the first wave of early humans to penetrate the rugged terrain and harsh climates of Western Europe during the ice age 800,000 years ago. **TE**

"The caves of the Sierra de Atapuerca represent an exceptional reserve of data."

UNESCO

🏛 ⊚ Portal of Salamanca University (Salamanca, Spain)

This prestigious institution is Spain's oldest university still in existence

The facade of the University of Salamanca is the official gateway into one of Europe's most venerable educational institutions. The impressive frontage is highly elaborate and decorated in the ornamental Plateresque style, which is native to Spain and originated during the country's Golden Age.

The University of Salamanca is Spain's oldest surviving university and was founded in 1218 by King Alfonso IX of Léon. Many important figures are associated with the university, which has helped boost its reputation as a premier institution. While lobbying for money to fund his voyages, Christopher Columbus made his case to a council of geographers at the university. The conquistador Hernán Cortés and Count Duke Olivares, chief minister of Spain from 1621 to 1640, both attended the university. The poet Fray Luis de León also attended, and taught at, the university, and his statue stands opposite the facade in the Patio de Escuelas. At the center of the richly decorated portal is the coat of arms of Ferdinand II of Aragon and Isabella I of Castile, who united the kingdoms of Spain. It also features the coat of arms of the House of Hapsburg, which ruled Spain from 1516, and a portrayal of the pope discoursing with cardinals. Perhaps the most famous feature of the facade is a representation of a frog on top of a skull, which is supposed to bring luck to anyone who is sharp-eyed enough to find it.

The University of Salamanca has been regarded as a major focus of Spanish culture for nearly eight centuries. Around 1536, Francisco de Vitoria, theologian and scholar of natural law, was appointed chair of theology at the university. Here he established what became known as the School of Salamanca, where innovative thinking on war, economic, practical, and international issues was reflected upon and debated among the prominent intellectuals of the day. **JF**

> *"No business shocks or embarrasses me more than the corrupt profits and affairs of the Indies."*
>
> Francisco de Vitoria, sixteenth-century scholar

La Granja de San Ildefonso (San Ildefonso, Spain)

Spain's equivalent to the Palace of Versailles stands in stunning landscaped gardens

This beautiful Baroque palace, often referred to as "the Versailles of Spain," was built as a summer retreat for King Philip V. The new monarch was actually a Frenchman, the first Bourbon king of Spain, who had been born at the real Versailles and spent much of his life there. Philip began learning Spanish only when he acceded to the throne at the age of seventeen, in 1700. The land on which his summer palace was built had been the site of a royal hunting lodge in the fifteenth century. King Henry IV had later handed the site over to the church, and a monastery dedicated to San Jerónimos was built on it. The name La Granja comes from the word for "farm," because the self-sufficient monks had run a farm on this site. There is still a church here, albeit a grand Baroque edifice very obviously built for royal clients. The church's mausoleum contains the tombs of Philip V and his second wife, Queen Isabella.

La Granja de San Ildefonso stands in spectacular parkland, complete with extensive woodland and formal landscaped gardens, with elegant fountains, statuary, and a large ornamental lake. The vast building is set against the dramatic backdrop of the Guadarrama Mountains. The interiors of the palace were created by an army of the finest artisans, and the furnishings and decor include crystal chandeliers, tapestries, frescoes, Italian Carrara marble, and Japanese lacquerwork.

Close to the palace is a well-known glass factory, also named La Granja, which still produces some of Spain's most exquisite glasswork. In 1918 Philip's grand palace was severely damaged by a fire. It was lovingly restored, with the local glass factory providing many of the replacement fittings, including replicas of the enormous chandeliers. Today, the Bourbon king's summer retreat is one of the region's most popular tourist attractions. **LH**

"[The Baths of Diana fountain] has cost me three millions and amused me three minutes."

Philip V, on one of La Granja's centerpieces

🏛️ ◈ Segovia Aqueduct (Segovia, Spain)

The superb condition of the aqueduct is proof of the quality of the engineering

The granite aqueduct, which stretches across the Spanish city of Segovia, is one of the greatest surviving monuments of Roman engineering. Although now out of use (road vibration and general decay contributed to its decline), the 2,000-year-old span once brought drinking water to the city from the River Frio 10 miles (16 km) away.

Probably built between the second half of the first century and the early part of the second century, it was constructed with 20,400 massive, rough-hewn granite blocks. No mortar, cement, or clamps were used in the aqueduct's construction, and the bricklike blocks are held together by the pressure of keystones. Water was channeled underground and flowed via two tanks—El Caseron (the Big House) and Casa de Aguas (Waterhouse)—to the city. At the latter tank, the water was naturally decanted and coursed down a 1 percent gradient to the Postigo, a rock outcrop above the city. After an abrupt turn, the monument displays its full splendor as it crosses Segovia's Plaza de Azoguejo. Built on two tiers, the tallest section is 98 feet (30 m) high and 984 feet (300 m) long, whereas the whole freestanding span is about 2,625 feet (800 m) long and supported by 166 arches and 120 pillars. A U-shaped channel on the top—or "attic"—of the aqueduct measuring 6 feet (1.8 m) by 5 feet (1.5 m) carried the water to the city, mainly for consumption in Segovia's Alcazar.

Although the aqueduct functioned successfully across the centuries, the structure was severely damaged by the Moors in the eleventh century and was restored in the fifteenth century when thirty-six arches were completely rebuilt in the original style. Since 1997 serious efforts have been made to conserve the aqueduct with traffic rerouted and the Plaza de Azoguejo turned into a pedestrian area. **TE**

🏛 ◎ El Escorial (near Madrid, Spain)

Enormous yet simple architectural monument to a profoundly religious monarch

The Real Monasterio de San Lorenzo de El Escorial (Royal Monastery of San Lorenzo de El Escorial) lies northwest of Madrid and is a vast granite complex that comprises a palace, a church, a monastery, a museum, an art gallery, and a hall of frescoes celebrating Spanish military victories. The colorful library has a ceiling painted by the Italian Mannerist Pellegrino Tibaldi and contains more than 40,000 volumes, including some of Spain's most valuable literary treasures.

King Philip II of Spain commissioned the construction of the complex to commemorate the victory against the French at the Battle of Saint Quentin in 1557. Building began in 1563 under the command of Juan Bautista de Toledo, the architect-in-chief of the royal works. After his death in 1567, his assistant Juan de Herrera took over the project, which was finished in 1584. De Herrera instigated a novel style of architecture, known as Herreran, using carefully proportioned geometric lines and sparse decoration. King Philip II also intended the site to serve as a mausoleum, and it is where many of the Hapsburg and Bourbon Spanish kings from King Charles I of Spain (Holy Roman Emperor Charles V) onward are buried in marble tombs in the Pantheon of Kings. The Pantheon of Princes is the resting place of other members of royalty, such as queens, princes, and princesses. Above the mausoleum lies King Philip II's palace, a series of apartments used by the king, including one with a view to the basilica that allowed him to watch a mass taking place when he was unable to attend because of his problems with gout. The palace's school and monastery are still in use.

The complex also houses one of the largest garden courts in the world, the Cloister of the Evangelists, containing white marble statues of the apostles. **CK**

Plaza de Toros
(Madrid, Spain)

Most important bullring in the world

Bullfighting is more than just a blood sport for the Spanish; rather it is an art form akin to ballet. And nowhere is the spectacle of the bullfighter dressed in his *traje de luces* (suit of lights) more dramatic than in the country's premier bullring in the east of Madrid, the Plaza de Toros Monumental de Las Ventas.

The bullring was built because of the sport's increasing popularity and as a result of the determination of one of Spain's most famous *toreros* (bullfighters), José "Joselito" Gómez Ortega, who wanted to see a national monument of significant size built in the nation's capital. His friend, the architect José Espeliús y Anduaga, started work on it in 1922, but Espeliús died before it was completed. Architect Manuel Muñóz Monasterio then took over the project, which was finished in 1929. A charity bullfight was held in 1931 to inaugurate the bullring, and its popularity proved that the seating around the bullring was still insufficient. It was subsequently enlarged to seat 25,000 spectators and saw its first season in 1935.

A circular brick building with horseshoe-shaped arches, the Mudéjar (neo-Moorish) bullring is decorated with ceramic tiles representing the shields of Spanish provinces. The sand arena is at its center, and the *tendidos* (seating areas) lie around the ring. As is typical for a bullring, some seats are in the shade, and some in the sun—spectators pay extra to have seats in the shade. The tenth *tendido* houses the presidential box, where dignitaries watch the bullfight.

There are many gates around the ring to allow access for the bulls, horses, and the *torero's* assistants. The *puerta de cuadrillas* is where the *toreros* enter the ring, and a victorious *torero* will exit the ring via the *puerta grande*, also known as the Door of Madrid. It is a particular honor to make such an exit during the Fiesta of San Isidro held each May. **CK**

Second of May Memorial (Madrid, Spain)

Scene of a bloody battle for independence

Once the centerpoint of a somewhat down-at-heel neighborhood, this site has played a starring role in Spain's history. On May 2, 1808, heroes of Spain's fight for independence rose up against French domination. Napoleon's forces had been occupying the city for some months as part of his campaign to overrun the Iberian Peninsula. On that fateful May day, French plans to remove further members of the Spanish royal family to France produced an angry mob outside the Royal Palace. When the French fired on them, rebellion spread throughout the city and hours of bloody street fighting ensued. In one spot, the present Plaza de los

> *"It was in Spain that the French army's brutal campaign revealed the ugly face of the new total war."*
>
> David A. Bell, historian

Héroes del dos de Mayo, stood the Spanish artillery barracks of Monteleón. Although most Spanish troops had been confined to barracks, artillery troops at Monteleón defied orders to join the popular struggle.

The French forces crushed the Madrid rebellion, but a fuse had been lit and the events of May 2 sparked uprisings throughout Spain, helped to trigger the bitter Peninsular War, and began the momentum that eventually secured Spanish independence. Hundreds of Madrid citizens perished in that day's fighting. The surrounding area, and a nearby street, is named after Manuela Malasaña, a young local seamstress said to have been executed by the French when the scissors she carried were seen as a malicious weapon. Nowadays May 2 is a public holiday in Madrid and a major fiesta takes place in the square. **AK**

Universidad de Alcalá de Henares

(near Madrid, Spain)

First city to be designed as a university

The area around present-day Alcalá de Henares is one of the oldest settlements in Spain, inhabited for at least 5,000 years; it was colonized by the Romans in the first century and by the Moors in the eighth century. The medieval city of Alcalá de Henares was founded in 1499 by Cardinal Cisneros, one of Spain's premier statesmen, who had a vision of building a great seat of learning.

The first students arrived at the university in 1508 and some of its most famous alumni studied here during the sixteenth and seventeenth centuries, including the playwright Lope de Vega, and Miguel de Cervantes, author of *Don Quixote*, who was also born in Alcalá de Henares. Cervantes's home and place of birth was purchased by the state in 1954 and a museum opened in 1956. Every year, on October 9, Alcalá de Henares celebrates Cervantes's birthday and holds a Cervantes festival. The university is now renowned as the world center for Cervantes studies and awards an annual literary prize in his name.

This medieval center of learning is a truly remarkable achievement of its time, not only as a university, but also as a place of religious acceptance: a harmonious home to Jewish, Christian, and Muslim scholars. Cisnero described his design as the ideal "city of God," and the plans from which Alcalá de Henares was created made their mark across the world after being taken to and recreated in a number of Spanish colonies throughout Latin America. The city suffered damage during the Spanish Civil War and neglect in the difficult years that followed. A resurgence in interest began in the 1980s, and the city was added to UNESCO's World Heritage List in 1998 because it was the first city to be designed and built solely as the seat of a university, and was to serve as the model for other centers of learning in Europe and the Americas. **JF**

"To attain to an eminent degree in learning costs hunger, nakedness, dizziness in the head."

Miguel de Cervantes, novelist

Plaza Mayor (Madrid, Spain)

This huge plaza has a rich history of celebrations, religious ceremonies, and executions

Madrid's Plaza Mayor is a bustling closed square whose bars, cafés, and shops are frequented by tourists and locals alike. Each weekend it plays host to an open-air market of curios, and it is where the annual festival of the city's patron saint, Saint Isidro, takes place. Once a market square, Plaza Mayor was transformed into a Baroque plaza in the sixteenth century, and at 300 by 360 feet (91 by 109 m) is one of the largest public squares in Europe.

The plans for the square were initiated by King Philip II of Spain in 1580 after he had moved the royal court to Madrid in 1561, and they were drawn up by architect Juan de Herrera. De Herrera built the first of the square's buildings, the two-towered Casa de la Panadería (former home to the bakers' guild) in the 1590s; the allegorical murals that now adorn the building were added in 1992. His student, Juan Gómez de Mora, completed the plaza in 1619 during the reign of King Philip III. A bronze equestrian statue of the monarch sculpted in 1616 was moved to the plaza in 1848 and lies at its center. The square was damaged by three fires that occurred in 1631, 1670, and 1790. The reconstruction of the square after the last fire was designed by architect Juan de Villanueva, who added extra floors to the surrounding buildings to reach their current five stories, and installed the many arched porticoes. Work continued on the project after his death and was finished in 1854.

The Plaza Mayor has witnessed bullfights, masked balls, royal marriages, and coronations. But it has not always been a mere social center: It is where saints such as Teresa of Avila, Isidro, and Francis Xavier were canonized, and it was also where executions and acts of faith involving the public procession of those found guilty as heretics under the Spanish Inquisition took place during the seventeenth century. **CK**

Temple of Debod (Madrid, Spain)

The only authentic Egyptian temple outside Egypt

This ancient Egyptian temple, which dates back to the second century B.C.E., originally stood alongside the River Nile; today it can be found in the center of Madrid, in Spain. The temple was moved after its original site was threatened with flooding and destruction during the building of the Aswan Dam. UNESCO made a global appeal for help with saving the great temple of Abu Simbel and many other monuments, including the Temple of Debod, threatened by the intended dam. As Spain had previously been instrumental in providing financial and archeological aid to the people of Egypt (helping conserve many of their most important sites, including the temple of Abu Simbel), the government of Egypt chose to donate the Temple of Debod to Spain.

After more than two millennia of standing in the African dust, the temple was moved to Madrid in 1968. The temple was built on its original site by Pharaoh Moroe Adijalamani in honor of Amon Re, the king of the gods, and Isis, mother of the god Horus and sister-wife of the god Osiris, around whom a dedicated cult grew up. The original structure of the temple was added to several times under subsequent pharaohs and, later, by the Romans, before it was abandoned and began to fall into ruins during the sixth century. What was left of the temple was eventually transplanted to picturesque parkland on the site of a former army barracks close to Madrid's Campo de Moro, where it was restored and partially rebuilt in an attempt to recreate its former architectural glory.

After four years of extensive renovations, the building was opened in 1972 as a tourist attraction with an exhibition of the phases of reconstruction. It is the only genuine Egyptian temple outside Egypt and a truly spectacular site to stumble across in the middle of modern Madrid. **LH**

Lope de Vega's House (Madrid, Spain)

Home of the first Spanish playwright to make a living as a dramatist

Lope de Vega (1562–1635) is one of Spain's greatest writers; a Baroque playwright and poet, he is most well known for his appealing comedies. His output was amazingly prolific, and he is said to have written between 1,500 and 2,500 full-length plays during his lifetime, as well as shorter plays and poems. Many of his works contain a common theme around the conflict between love and honor, and his most popular work is, perhaps, *Fuente Ovejuna* or *The Sheep Well*. The writer was born in Madrid to an undistinguished noble family and lived in the city for most of his life. His family residence from 1610 to 1635 has been preserved as a museum and today contains many original artifacts from his turbulent life.

When Lope de Vega moved to the house in 1610, his literary reputation had already reached its peak. After writing his first play at the age of twelve, he went on to serve in the army and on the Spanish Armada to England, as well as spending eight years in exile from Madrid because of an illicit affair with the daughter of a leading theater owner. In 1600, Lope de Vega married his second wife, Juana de Guardo, but their relationship was damaged by his frequent affairs. After the death of his second wife, he joined the priesthood in 1614, but still continued to enjoy a healthy love life.

Lope de Vega lived on the same street as perhaps the most famous of all Spanish writers, Miguel de Cervantes (1547–1616), author of *Don Quixote*, after whom the street is named. Ironically, the street named for Lope de Vega is a few blocks away. Lope de Vega's House is a faithful reproduction of a typical Madrid family house from the nation's Golden Age. The garden is a reconstruction of one mentioned in one of his poems, and contains several fruit trees dating from his lifetime. The Lope de Vega House is a standing tribute to one of Spain's finest writers. **JF**

🏛 ◎ **Palacio Real de Aranjuez** (Madrid, Spain)

Royal summer residence that marks the development of sophisticated landscape design

Situated near Madrid, the Palacio Real de Aranjuez lies in a valley where the rivers Tagus and Jarama meet. The location was a popular summer resort for the Madrileño nobility, and the palace was built there in the 1380s. King Philip II commissioned the architects responsible for El Escorial, Juan Bautista de Toledo and Juan de Herrera, to build the royal summer residence in 1561. It was largely completed during the reign of Ferdinand VI, although two further wings were added by Charles III. Inside, most of its decorations are from the eighteenth century, and of particular note are the Porcelain Room and the Hall of Mirrors.

But the palace is famed for its gardens and landscape design perhaps more than the architecture of the building. Philip II employed Dutch and French gardeners to create an Italian Renaissance garden with a geometric layout that forms the palace's grounds. A keen botanist, Philip II cultivated both vegetables and plants, and used the latest hydraulic engineering techniques to water the dry landscape. Then in 1660 Philip IV began to create a Baroque-design garden with ornamental fountains such as the Apollo Fountain, statues, and a man-made island, the Jardin de la Isla. It was completed during the reign of Philip V and is the most important garden created in Spain during the Hapsburg period. Its lush greenery and waterways are a contrast to the surrounding arid sierra of the region—the Jardin del Principe contains a network of ditches 19,685 feet (6,000 m) long—and are testament to the interest in agriculture, farming, and botany of a succession of monarchs.

A smaller palace designed by Juan de Villanueva, the Casa del Labrador, stands in the grounds and houses a collection of Neoclassical decorative arts. The palace is also home to the Museo de las Falúas Reales that exhibits Spanish royal pleasure barges. **CK**

Royal Palace

(Madrid, Spain)

Largest palace in Western Europe

The Palacio Real de Madrid, or Royal Palace of Madrid, is the official residence of the Spanish royal family, although the family does not live here but in the Palacio de la Zarzuela on the fringes of Madrid. The Royal Palace of Madrid is, however, used for state functions, and when not in use parts of it are open to the public.

The palace stands on a site first occupied by a ninth-century Islamic fortress built by Mohammed I, Emir of Córdoba that was later used sporadically by the kings of Castile when the Spanish regained control of the city in 1085. King Philip II of Spain moved the royal court there in 1561. The fortress then gave way to a castle known as the Antiguo Alcázar, or Old Castle, in the sixteenth century. When the building burned down in 1734 King Philip V wanted to have a new palace built in the same locale, but this time the structure was made entirely of stone and brick rather than wood, in order to minimize the risk of fire. Building work started in 1738 and was completed in 1755. A number of architects were involved in the project, including renowned Italian architect Francisco Sabatini, and the magnificent gardens that lie to the north of the palace were named in his honor. The building was first used as a royal residence by King Carlos III in 1764.

The vast palace measures 1.5 million square feet (135,000 sq m) and is home to a number of important artworks by painters such as Francisco Goya, Giovanni Battista Tiepolo, Diego Velázquez, and Michelangelo Caravaggio, as well as a collection of musical instruments made by master craftsmen, including the only complete Stradivarius string quintet in the world. The palace is also notable for its collection of armor in La Real Armería, or Royal Armory, which dates back to the thirteenth century. **CK**

Royal Tapestry Factory

(Madrid, Spain)

Handwoven tapestries for royal clients

The Royal Tapestry Factory is a living museum in which carpets and tapestries are still made by hand, using many traditional processes that have scarcely changed since the factory was founded by Philip V, the first Bourbon king of Spain, in the early eighteenth century. The pace with which royal palaces, houses, and hunting lodges were being built and decorated at that time was such that the Bourbons opened several such factories to meet the demand for tapestries, of which this is the only one to survive today.

Tapestries and carpets made at the site can be seen adorning the walls and floors of most of the

> *"Fantasy . . . produces impossible monsters; . . . she is the mother of the arts and the origin of marvels."*
>
> **Francisco de Goya, artist**

Spanish royal palaces. Among the most famous tapestries is a series inspired by cartoons by the artist Francisco de Goya and his brother-in-law Francisco Bayeu. Goya's career as an artist began with the drawings for tapestries and, once appreciated by the royal patrons for whom the rich tapestries were commissioned, he became one of Spain's most celebrated painters.

The original factory was relocated to the present building in the Bourbon district, in 1889, to provide the thriving business with more space. The museum now houses a collection of eighteenth-, nineteenth-, and twentieth-century tapestries, carpets, and paintings, as well as displays explaining modern and traditional tapestry techniques. The royal family still patronizes the factory today. **LC**

Santa María de Guadalupe

(Madrid, Spain)

The most important monastery in Spain for more than four centuries

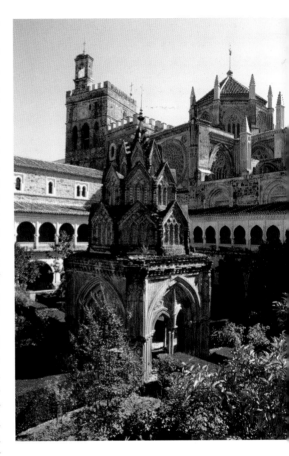

Santa María de Guadalupe stands proudly beside the Guadalupe River in Cácares province. It was founded in 1340 at the spot where a shepherd found a statue of the Madonna that may have been hidden by locals to protect it from Moorish invaders in 714. The monastery, with its fairy-tale turrets, dominates the town of Cácares, which is set in a steep-sided wooded valley.

King Alfonso XI of Castile visited the monastery. Attributing his success in the Battle of Rio Salado against the last African invasion in 1340 to Santa María, he later contributed to the building costs and gave the monastery royal patronage. In 1389, the Hieronymite monks took over and construction work continued. In 1496, some of the first native Caribbeans brought to Europe by Christopher Columbus were baptized here. Santa María de Guadalupe remained the most important cloister in Spain until the secularization of the monasteries in 1835. In the twentieth century the monastery was revived by the Franciscan Order and Pope Pius XII made it a "minor papal basilica" in 1955.

The interior of the monastery is ornately decorated and contains many beautiful works of art, fine embroidered vestments, and illuminated manuscripts. The impressive Baroque sacristy is nicknamed the Spanish Sistine Chapel because of the portraits by Zurbarán hanging on the lavishly decorated walls. Visitors are allowed to touch the dress of the tiny, exquisite statue of Santa María in the ornate chamber behind the altar.

The monastery symbolizes two significant events in world history that occurred in 1492: the reconquest of the Iberian Peninsula by the Catholic kings and Christopher Columbus's historic arrival in the Americas. Its famous statue of the Virgin became a powerful symbol of the Christianization of much of the New World. **LC**

"Columbus found a world, and had no chart, save one that faith deciphered in the skies."

George Santayana, poet

El Greco's House (Toledo, Spain)

Museum dedicated to the artist's unique work in his adopted homeland

Born in Crete, Greece, the painter Doménicos Theotokópoulos (1541–1614), commonly known as El Greco (The Greek), spent more of his life outside of his native country than in it. He left his homeland at the age of twenty-six to study painting in Italy, first in Rome and then Venice, before immigrating to Toledo in 1577, just outside Madrid. El Greco's name is inextricably linked with his adopted city: It was here that he produced his most famous works, which are a synthesis of the Western European and Byzantine styles, with their elongated shapes, mystical feel, almost iconographic faces, and wild use of Fauvist-like color. Although misunderstood by his contemporaries, El Greco was rediscovered as a great artist in the twentieth century by the Expressionists and Cubists who admired his unique flamboyant style.

When El Greco began to receive more commissions and his status grew, he moved in 1585 to rented rooms in the palace of a nobleman, the Marquis de Villena. Here he lived and worked until he died. The house and museum that exist today are not the original palace building, but are next to where the original lay. The museum was created in the nineteenth century by the Marquis Benigno de la Vega-Inclán as a monument and approximation of the environment El Greco inhabited. Every attempt has been made to recreate the furnishings, tile work, woodwork, pottery, furnishings, and general ambience of El Greco's habitat. It also houses many of El Greco's paintings, including *View of Toledo*. The house was opened to the public in 1911, before becoming state property in 1942. **CK**

◪ El Greco was a pupil of Titian but created his own distinctive style of painting.

⊡ The museum's picturesque building and courtyard were built on the ruins of a Renaissance palace.

🏛 ◉ Toledo Cathedral (Toledo, Spain)

One of Europe's finest Gothic buildings and home of major art treasures

This renowned cathedral is one of Spain's most impressive buildings. It was inspired by the vast Gothic cathedrals of northern Europe, such as Chartres, but added an exciting new ingredient—the rich combination of cultural styles that can be found only in the Iberian Peninsula.

The cathedral was begun by a little-known architect, Master Martin, but most of the work was initiated by Petrus Petri, who died in 1291. The predominant style is Gothic, although building took place over such a long period that, inevitably, other influences can be found. There is, for example, the Mozarabic Chapel (1504), which still celebrates mass using the old Visigothic ritual (Mozarabs were Christians living under Moorish rule). Conversely, the cloisters have some Mudéjar features—that is, the Moorish style that survived into the Christian era. The Gothic elements are best demonstrated by the intricate carvings above the three main doorways.

The cathedral is most famous, however, for its two greatest treasures. The first of these is the *Transparente* (1721–32), a marvelously flamboyant marble and alabaster altarpiece by Narciso Tomé. He cut an opening in the vaulting above so that when his sculpted figures are struck by the rays of the sun, they seem to float in a halo of spiritual light. An even greater artwork, perhaps, is *El Espolio* (The Disrobing of Christ), a magnificent painting by El Greco. Although born in Crete, the artist spent most of his career in Toledo, so it is fitting that the cathedral should house one of his greatest works. Such art treasures make the building a museum as well as a church. **IZ**

↗ El Greco's masterpiece *El Espolio* can be seen here in the Toledo Cathedral.

↦ The magnificent cathedral is a treasure-house of stunning artworks.

Sinagoga del Tránsito
(Toledo, Spain)

Important monument to Sephardic Jewish culture in the Iberian Peninsula

During the Middle Ages, Toledo was a sophisticated center for translation and learning, embracing tolerance and a cosmopolitan mixture of Christian, Muslim, and Jewish cultures. Sinagoga del Tránsito embodies this fusion. The plain stone exterior gives little away, but inside is an elaborate and beautiful interior, with decorated pillars supporting keyhole arches of the Mudéjar style, with Gothic influences.

The synagogue was built by Samuel Ha-Leví, who was treasurer to the Castilian king, Pedro the Cruel. It has a high, rectangular prayer hall, ornately decorated with geometric and floral designs and an impressive carved wooden ceiling. It is said that Ha-Leví had cedars imported from Lebanon for its construction, following in the tradition established by Solomon in the building of the First Temple in Jerusalem. Leading from the prayer hall to the north is a separate room for women, and on the eastern wall are three niches used to house scrolls of the Torah. The stucco-work inscriptions include verses in Arabic and Hebrew from the Koran, with psalms along the top of the walls.

The Sephardic (Spanish) Jews were one of the largest Jewish communities in Europe and had flourished under Muslim and Christian rule in Spain since the eighth century. But, from the twelfth century, intolerance of the Jews grew until finally, in 1492, they were expelled from Spain. The synagogue became a Christian church, and a bell tower was added by the Christian religious order of Alcántara, who took over the building. In the eighteenth century, it became a hermitage dedicated to the Tránsito de Nuestra Señora and the building served as a military barracks during the war against Napoleon. In 1971 the synagogue became a museum, and exhibits include manuscripts, costumes, and Hebrew tombstones, some of which date to before 1492. **LC**

> *"It is agreed and resolved that all Jews and Jewesses be ordered to leave our kingdoms."*
>
> Alhambra decree, expelling Jews from Spain

Castillo del Papa Luna
(Peñíscola, Spain)

Castle where Papa Luna took refuge

This formidable fortress-castle crowns the highest point of the lovely old town of Peñíscola, which perches on a high, rocky peninsula lapped by Mediterranean waters—the word *peñíscola* is derived from a word for "peninsula." Today both the town and castle, along with the nearby beach, are major tourist attractions famous for standing in for Valencia in the Charlton Heston movie *El Cid* (1961). Many centuries before that, the site provided the backdrop for some interesting historical events.

Crusading Christian Templar knights built this stronghold, predominantly in the fourteenth century, on the site of a former Arab citadel. Further work continued into the seventeenth century. During the fifteenth century the castle became a player in the drama unfolding around the Great Schism—a fundamental disagreement within the Roman Catholic church. The castle was a home of Benedict XIII, one of the "anti-popes" who set himself up against the recognized pope and turned the castle into a papal palace and library. Benedict was forced to take refuge at Peñíscola in the midst of the drama in the early 1400s and died here in 1423. He was also known as Pedro de Luna, "Luna" being a family of Aragonese nobility, which is how the castle gets its full name of Castillo del Papa Luna. On Papa Luna's death, Peñíscola was the place where another rebel, Benedict XIV, was declared an anti-pope.

The castle's overall style has been variously described as Romanesque and Renaissance. It has a long, impressive facade and is filled with attractive decorative details and frieze work, as well as a monumental staircase that was extensively remodeled in the mid-1600s. These days, the buildings and walled enclosures host a variety of events, from film and music festivals to exhibitions. **AK**

Monastery of San Miguel de Los Reyes (Valencia, Spain)

Religious and cultural seat of learning

Its position alone lends this magnificent complex of buildings an air of atmospheric mystery. It seems almost hidden away on the edge of Valencia, nudging the city's Latin-American district and overlooking a large, quiet square that hints at its original importance.

Few could fail to be struck by the stately Renaissance-style facade of the monastery, with a huge entrance decorated with tiered columns, flanked by twin castellated towers, and offset today by giant palm trees. It was created by the great master mason Alonso de Covarrubias, who was one of the first Spanish architects to make the transition from a

---

"San Miguel de los Reyes's checkered past included housing Franco's political prisoners."

Fiona Dunlop, journalist

Gothic style to an elegant Italian Renaissance approach. This complex was built originally for the Heironymite religious order, which had close ties to nobility and royalty. Standing on the site of a fourteenth-century monastery, San Miguel was designed to be a leading center of religious and cultural learning. Behind its great facade lies a beautiful seventeenth-century church—crowned by a cupola and containing multicolored stonework and an eighteenth-century altar—as well as north and south wings. The older south wing, with a cloister comprising one many-arched gallery above another is an excellent example of Valencian Renaissance architecture. There were also reading rooms and a library with a magnificent collection. Today the monastery is a leading research library. **AK**

⊚ # La Lonja de la Seda

(Valencia, Spain)

A masterpiece of late Gothic architecture and symbol of Mediterranean mercantile wealth

> *"With time and patience the mulberry leaf becomes a silk gown."*
>
> Chinese proverb

During the fifteenth and sixteenth centuries, the Spanish city of Valencia was one of Europe's major centers of trade and culture, and "La Lonja"—as it is often known—is a fittingly lavish expression of that affluent, golden heyday.

La Lonja de la Seda, or the Silk Exchange, comprises several buildings designed as a focal point of the city's thriving commercial life, and together they form a masterpiece of late Gothic civic architecture with a strongly Spanish flavor. Originally, oil was traded on this site before silk took over as the main commodity. Silk merchants gathered to strike their deals in the Sala de Contratación—the magnificent trading hall that is the complex's centerpiece. This vast hall features stunning vaulted ceilings and is supported by beautiful twisted columns spiraling to a height of more than 52 feet (16 m). A second major structure here is the striking crenellated tower, reminiscent of a medieval castle, where debt-ridden merchants were sometimes incarcerated. The third building is the Consulate wing; this houses fine function rooms with beautifully decorated ceilings and provided the meeting place for Spain's first tribunal council of merchants. The rooms contain period furnishings designed to evoke the atmosphere of those heady days. Visitors seeking respite from the summer heat can enjoy the attractive shaded patio garden at La Lonja, complete with orange trees and a fountain.

The Silk Exchange has become one of the major sights of Valencia's old quarter. In 1996, La Lonja de la Seda was inscribed on UNESCO's World Heritage List because the site is of outstanding universal value as a wholly exceptional example of secular building in the late Gothic style, and dramatically illustrates the power and wealth of one of the great Mediterranean mercantile cities. **AK**

Cathedral of Valencia

(Valencia, Spain)

Believed to house the original Holy Grail

Not only is this beautiful cathedral a major part of Valencia's outstanding Gothic architecture, but it also houses what is claimed to be the Holy Grail. This is the chalice often said to have been used at the Last Supper and subsequently by Joseph of Arimathea to catch blood from the wounds of the crucified Christ.

The inspired hand of architect Pere Compte was responsible for the work on the Gothic heart of the cathedral. Although Gothic style dominates, what helps to make the cathedral special is the mix of expertly executed styles showing its evolution over the centuries. One of its entrances is Romanesque

> *"Only the Holy Chalice of Valencia … fits St. Jerome's description of the cup used by Christ."*
>
> Janice Bennett, *St. Laurence and The Holy Grail* (2002)

(the oldest), one Gothic (the Apostles' Door), and one spectacularly Baroque (the most recent).

Valencia was a Moorish kingdom twice in medieval times, and the original cathedral—founded under Catholic monarchs in the mid-thirteenth century—was built on the site of a mosque. The building features grand arches (rounded in the 1700s from their original pointed shape) and an adjoining seventeenth-century domed basilica. Within the cathedral—a Gothic interior with Baroque and Neoclassical additions—the gold and agate Holy Grail lies inside the Santo Cáliz chapel. Also to be seen are valuable paintings by artists such as Zurbarán and Goya. One fascinating oddity of this site is the meeting here of a traditional Water Court where farmers settle disputes surrounding matters of irrigation. **AK**

Palacio Ducal de los Borja (Gandia, Spain)

Glorious example of civic architecture

This grandiose Gothic palace is famous for being the home of the Borjas—the Spanish relatives of the infamous Italian Borgia dynasty. With origins in the late thirteenth century, the palace was reputedly the birthplace of the Duque Francisco de Borja, who was later canonized as St. Francisco of Borja after setting up Jesuit colleges across Europe.

While the Italian clan were debasing the papacy (allegedly serving poisoned wine to their opponents), Duque Francisco, who later became Jesuit General, distanced himself from the murderous intrigues of Rome. Expanded and embellished over the years by his Catholic order, the palace's most sumptuous apartments date from the late eighteenth century. The simple Gothic facade gives no hint of the luxury inside. The elaborately decorated eighteenth-century Baroque Salón de Aguilas showcases a spellbinding fifteenth-century wooden gilded frieze of eagles feasting on fruit. The gilded stucco Galeria Dorada (Gold Gallery) culminates in a stunning ceramic tile mosaic representing the four elements. (The pigment that gives the tiles their luster is now unavailable, as the source plants are extinct.) The arched Cámara de la Duquesa (Duchess Chamber) is where, according to legend, St. Francisco was born in 1510. The majestic sixteenth-century Salón de Coronas (Hall of Crowns) gets its name from the double-crown symbol on the Manises tiles. St. Francisco's office has been transformed into a neo-Gothic chapel boasting a blue vaulted ceiling scattered with golden stars. In the nineteenth century, a simple chapel next to the saint's austere bedroom was transformed into a richly decorated miniature oratory with a series of murals and an exquisite marquetry floor. Outside, the Patio de Armas (Arms Courtyard) is overlooked by well-preserved seventeenth-century balconies. **TE**

Murcia Casino

(Murcia, Spain)

Delightful example of eclectic architecture

The casino in Murcia is one of the finest of its kind in Spain. The eclectic structure, with its rich decoration dating back to the mid-nineteenth century, reflects the fact that historically it has served a city that has prospered thanks to a strong agricultural tradition.

Far from the contemporary conception of a glossy gambling den, the casino is, in fact, an oasislike quasi-social club that combines the functions of a meeting place, concert venue, library, and tearoom. Designed by the architect Francisco Bolarín, it was first opened as a gentlemen's club in 1847. Beyond the decorative Neoclassical facade, completed in 1901, is a Moorish vestibule and Pompeian patio, inspired by Granada's Alhambra and Seville's El Alcázar. Built on two levels, it boasts fourteen Ionic columns and is crowned with a grand glass and iron dome. The impressive covered passage leads to the casino's principal rooms, including an English-style library and reading room, as well as a billiard room.

Architect José Ramón Berenguer designed the sumptuous ballroom in the neo-Baroque style of Louis XIV's Versailles. A focal point for Murcia's social life for more than a century, it can be illuminated by popping a coin in the slot to fire up the 320 lamps of its candelabra. Of particular note is the ladies' powder room, a neo-Baroque confection (open to all) whose ceiling, the work of painter José Marin-Baldo, depicts an allegory of the night represented by the goddess Selene: angels flit about the clouds powdering their noses and tidying their hair. The eyes of a winged woman falling in flames are notorious for an optical illusion, which gives the impression that they are following viewers around the room.

Cool and welcoming, the Murcia Casino is a pleasing respite from the stifling streets of the bustling city. **TE**

Tesoro del Carambolo

(El Carambolo, Spain)

Treasure trove of a lost prehistoric city

In 1958 workmen digging the foundations for a leisure center in Camas, a suburb of Seville, made an incredible discovery. They uncovered a treasure trove of ancient goldwork and jewelry, dating to the sixth century B.C.E. The twenty-one-piece collection, known as the Tesoro del Carambolo (or Carambolo Treasure), has been identified as belonging to the Tartessic era, a culture that flourished in southern Spain c. 700–c. 500 B.C.E and is identified with a city that has become as shrouded in legend as the lost city of Atlantis.

Tartessus is said to have been rich in "gold, silver, ivory, apes, and peacocks," which suggests trading

> *"Tartessus, famous town, receives tin carried by the river from Celtica, as well as gold and bronze."*
>
> Pseudo-Scymnus, *c.* 90 B.C.E.

links with Africa and Asia. It was located somewhere in present-day Andalucía, near the Guadalquivir River. The city was also a major trading point in tin, leading scholars to surmise that the Tartessians had trading links with Cornwall in England. Ancient texts dating back to the sixth and seventh centuries B.C.E. have been discovered in Andalucía, written in the Tartessian language. Little is known of the city's history and, by the sixth century B.C.E., all mention of Tartessus had disappeared from contemporary written history.

Today the Tesoro del Carambolo is safely housed in a bank vault, but a reproduction of the collection is on display at Seville's Museo Arqueológico. The museum identifies the collection as the most significant discovery of prehistoric precious metalwork in the world. **LH**

Great Mosque of Córdoba

(Córdoba, Spain)

Architectural wonder of the medieval world

Situated in Andalucía in southern Spain, Córdoba was once the capital of the Islamic Caliphate of Córdoba that ruled southern Spain and Portugal. At its peak in the tenth century, the town is estimated to have been home to 500,000 people and was the largest city in Western Europe.

The Mezquita, or Great Mosque of Córdoba, is now the Roman Catholic Cathedral of St. Mary of the Assumption after the capture of the city in 1236 by King Ferdinand III of Castile. The site was first home to a Roman temple, and then a church, before the Moors took over the land to build the mosque and a palace. Evidence of the cathedral's Islamic heritage is nonetheless apparent in its prayer niches and its blue-tiled dome covered in stars. Perhaps most striking is the wide open space of the church's interior containing 1,000 red-and-white-striped horseshoe arches made from marble, granite, onyx, and jasper, supported by sculpted columns. The arches were made using pieces taken from the Roman temple.

Built in 784 by the emir of Córdoba, Abd ar-Rahman I, the Mezquita was the second-largest mosque in the Islamic world. It was enlarged by his successors before it was completed in 987. At one point, the mosque was a pilgrimage site for Muslims because it housed an original copy of the Koran, and an arm bone of the prophet Muhammad.

Initially the Spanish consecrated the mosque as a church, and worshipped in it as it stood. It was later adapted to include Christian features, such as the Villaviciosa Chapel, and a Renaissance-style nave at its center. Originally the mosque was an annex to Amir Abd ar-Rahman I's palace connected by a raised walkway; today the palace is home to the current bishop. The Torre del Alminar Baroque belfry is built around what was once the minaret. **CK**

"So near the desert in its tentlike forest of supporting pillars..."

Jan Morris, writer

Torre del Oro

(Seville, Spain)

Attractive symbol of Seville's heyday

The Torre del Oro, or Tower of Gold, was built in the thirteenth century by the occupying Moors, under the Almohad dynasty, and formed part of the city walls of Seville. The twelve-sided watchtower was intended as a fortress to repel attacks from the Moors' Christian enemies, who wanted to claim the land for themselves and their religion.

It was located at a port, on one side of the River Guadalquivir; on the other side of the river a sister tower was built and a chain was stretched between the two to prevent unknown boats from sailing up the river and thereby protecting the port town from enemy attacks. The opposite tower no longer exists. By the sixteenth century, the Torre del Oro had fallen into disuse and was partially ruined. It deteriorated even further with the devastating earthquake of 1755, which laid waste to Lisbon in Portugal and was felt deep inside Spain. In the 1760s, the tower was restored and added to; this is when the battlements around the top were fashioned, to give the tower a more castlelike appearance. In both the eighteenth and nineteenth centuries, the tower was in danger of being razed to the ground by developers—but, on both occasions, the public's opposition was so strong that the tower was saved.

The tower is constructed from pale brick and stone, and opinions differ about how it gained its name. Some suggest the tower was covered in gilded tiles when first built, which glinted in the sun; others claim the tower was used in later years as a gold store, when Spanish ships returned home from the New World, bringing back gold for their monarch. Since the time of the Moors, the Torre del Oro has had a variety of incarnations: as a jail, a chapel, a store for gunpowder, and also as the port's administrative office. Today it houses a small maritime museum. **LH**

Palacio de las Duenas

(Seville, Spain)

Alba family palace set in beautiful gardens

The great Sevillian writer Antonio Machado reminisced in one of his poems about a "courtyard in Seville . . . where the lemon ripens." The courtyard in question belonged to his birthplace, a lovely fifteenth-century palace-house with pretty courtyard gardens shaded by orange and lemon trees. Like the church of San Pedro that stands close by, this palace contains some shining examples of Mudéjar (Christian-Muslim) architecture, for which Seville—the former capital of Muslim Spain—is well known.

The palace buildings are arranged around a series of linked patios, including a large central courtyard.

> *"Each corner is punctuated by a palm tree geometrically positioned, their trunks swathed with roses."*
>
> Di Attenborough, travel writer

Decorative features include white marble columns and fountains planted with arum lilies, formally arranged citrus trees, and tall palms covered with climbing roses. Originally the manor house of the Pineda family, it was later bought by the dukes of Alba. The Albas are a longstanding Spanish family who still play a major part in Seville society. Built in the fifteenth and sixteenth centuries, it is an eclectic mix of Gothic, Mudéjar, and Renaissance elements. It includes a private chapel whose altar is decorated with tile work typical of traditional Sevillian ceramics and a hall with a Renaissance-style paneled ceiling. The palace is surrounded by an impressive boundary wall whose grand, pedimented main entrance bears the coat of arms of the Alba family, created colorfully from Spanish-style tiles. **AK**

Archivo General de Indias

(Seville, Spain)

Valuable historical repository of Spain's extensive colonial empire

An essay in elegant Italianate Renaissance architecture, this imposing building is a records office on a breathtaking scale and a major research center for Spanish history. The General Archives of the Indies houses around eighty million pages of documents charting the history of Spain's colonial empire—especially in the Americas, but also in the Philippines—between the fifteenth and nineteenth century.

Sixteenth-century Seville was a thriving center of burgeoning Spanish power, but its merchants had no suitable meeting place, many of them gathering in the nearby cathedral to conduct their business. In 1572 Philip II commissioned the architect Juan de Herrera—creator of Philip's stunning palace-monastery complex, El Escorial—to design a grand exchange building. It was begun in 1584, and merchants were trading here by 1598, although further building work continued until 1646. What emerged was a restrained, harmonious design with little decoration, its windows recessed between piers and its two main stories defined by attractive balustrades. The building is arranged around a large central courtyard overlooked by finely arched windows. Inside, on the upper floor, are large rooms with beautiful vaulted ceilings.

During the 1600s, the building became the headquarters of Seville's art academy. In 1785, Charles III ordered it to be used to house important colonial records and various structural changes were made, including the building of a glorious main staircase in marble. The building still fulfills this role today, containing documents relating to the Golden Age of the Spanish empire and exploration, including important papers penned by Christopher Columbus and conquistador Hernán Cortés. New restoration work on the building began in 2002, along with a program to digitize the collection. **AK**

"I assure your Highnesses that these lands are the most fertile, level and beautiful countries in the world."

Journal of Christopher Columbus, October 1492

🏛 ◉ Seville Cathedral (Seville, Spain)

Outstanding example of medieval Gothic architecture

In addition to being the world's third-largest church, Seville Cathedral is an excellent example of Gothic architecture. Originally it was the site of an Almohad mosque that was knocked down by the Spanish, who wanted to build a church on a suitably grand scale to reflect the city's position as an affluent trading center.

Construction began *c.* 1400 on the rectangular foundations of the mosque, and the structure took more than 100 years to finish. All that remains of the original mosque is the Patio de los Naranjos (Orange Tree Courtyard) entrance court, where Islamic worshippers once washed their hands and feet in the fountain, and a minaret was built between 1184 and 1196. In 1198 four copper spheres were added on top of the tower, but they were destroyed by an earthquake in 1356. When the cathedral was built, a bell was added to the onetime minaret together with the Christian symbol of the cross, transforming it into

a bell tower. The bell tower was finished in 1568 with the addition of an 11-foot- (3.5-m-) high weather vane of a woman, representing the Christian faith, by Bartolomé Morel. Inside, the cathedral is impressive both for its artworks in the form of paintings, sculptures, and woodcarvings, and for its architectural mix of Gothic, Renaissance, Baroque, and Plateresque styles. One of the cathedral's most notable drawcards is the explorer Christopher Columbus; a nineteenth-century tomb is said to house his remains. **CK**

> *"We shall have a church . . . of such a kind that those who see it built will think we were mad."*

Member of the chapter planning the construction

 ## Alcázar (Seville, Spain)

Beautiful palace with a distinctly Islamic style

The region of Andalucía, in southern Spain, has long been a gateway between Africa and Europe. The Moors invaded Spain in the eighth century and remained the dominant force in the country for more than 300 years. Christian forces launched their "reconquest" of the Iberian Peninsula in the thirteenth century (Seville was regained in 1248), but the lengthy occupation left an indelible imprint on Andalucían history and culture. The Alcázar (from the Arabic word for "palace") in Seville is a perfect example of this fusion of Christian and Islamic styles.

The Moors established a fortress on this site in 712, transforming it into a palace in the ninth century. Some traces of this have survived, but the present building dates mainly from 1364, when Pedro the Cruel commissioned it for his new court. The royal residence was built by Mudéjar craftsmen—that is, Moors who had remained in Spain after the reconquest. Consequently, the style of the building has a strong Arabic flavor—with horseshoe arches, colorful glazed tiles, and courtyards with fountains and sunken gardens—even though it was produced for a Christian monarch.

Later Spanish rulers also left traces of their occupation on the Alcázar. Queen Isabella I founded her Casa de la Contratación (House of Trade) here, in the Sala del Almirante (Admiral's Hall). This was the royal agency that administered Spain's expeditions to the New World. The colonial explorer and navigator Christopher Columbus met the queen here, and his portrait is apparently included in a picture of the Virgin Mary, which is displayed in the chapel. Charles V also made significant additions in contrast to the Islamic design. He was married at the Alcázar in 1525 and subsequently built a series of lavish, Renaissance-style apartments. **IZ**

🏛 ⊙ Alhambra

(Granada, Spain)

One of the Islamic architectural wonders of the world

> *"The Alhambra was described by Moorish poets as 'a pearl set in emeralds.'"*

Mike McDougall, travel writer

Dramatically set, beautifully built, and testament to extraordinary historic cultural diversity, the Alhambra is cherished for its monuments and palaces. Not a single construction but a citadel, it was originally designed in the ninth century as a military area, later becoming the residence of royalty and the court of Granada in the mid-thirteenth century. The mixed-use nature of the Alhambra—as barracks for the royal guard but also, in the *medina* (Arab section), the site of the famous Nasrid palaces and houses of noblemen—helps to explain the profusion of its styles, which are predominantly Renaissance, Italian, and Moorish.

Commanding a wide view of the city and plain of Granada toward the west and north, and of the heights of the Sierra Nevada toward the east and south, the Alhambra was deliberately set on a steep hillside that was difficult to access. With the banks of the River Darro, mountains, and woods as protection, the ramparts prevented outsiders from guessing at the splendor they concealed. The palaces, Casa Real Vieja, Chamber of Comares, Gate of Justice, and the celebrated Chamber of the Lions date back to the fourteenth century and were all the work of two illustrious kings, Yusuf I and his son, Muhammed V. The Upper Alhambra contains baths, ornate bedrooms, and summer rooms, a whispering gallery, and a maze. In 1492 the site became the court of Ferdinand and Isabella after they conquered Granada, and the Church of St. Mary was built upon the site of the royal mosque. Centuries later, Napoleon's troops converted the palaces into barracks and partially destroyed some of the towers.

The bell of the Torre de la Vela is still rung on festive occasions by young girls wishing to ward off spinsterhood. The majesty of the Alhambra is best appreciated by exploring its many legends. **AP**

Royal Chapel

(Granada, Spain)

Memorial to the founders of Spain's empire

The Royal Chapel is the final resting place of the two monarchs who united Spain. Isabella I of Castile's marriage to Ferdinand II of Aragón joined their kingdoms. Their conquest of Granada, the last Muslim territory in Spain, was viewed as the greatest achievement of their reign. It contributed to Pope Alexander VI styling them as "The Catholic Monarchs."

The Gothic design of the chapel reflected Isabella's dislike of the Renaissance style, whereas the neighboring Granada Cathedral, built between 1523 and 1703, is more in the Renaissance mode. The Royal Chapel was originally intended to house the tombs of all Spanish monarchs, although ultimately the palace of El Escorial served this purpose. Isabella was not originally interred in the Royal Chapel; she was first laid to rest in a nearby friary, and Ferdinand joined her in 1516. The following year they were moved to the Royal Chapel by their grandson Charles V. Their tomb and effigies are carved in marble and alabaster by the Florentine Domenico Fancelli. Three other members of the royal family are interred in the chapel: Ferdinand and Isabella's daughter Juana "The Mad"; her husband, Philip I "The Fair," the first Hapsburg ruler of Spain; and Prince Miguel da Paz, their grandson and the Crown Prince of Spain and Portugal. Unsurprisingly, since the capture of Granada in the latter part of the fifteenth century was a triumph for Ferdinand and Isabella, the altarpiece of the Royal Chapel includes four painted wooden panels commemorating the campaign. The chapel also contains Isabella's art collection as well as artifacts from the conquest of Granada.

The Royal Chapel is a monument to two of the founders of Spain. Before Ferdinand and Isabella, Spain was a collection of independent kingdoms. After their reign, Spain was on the road to becoming a unified nation, and a major world power. **JF**

Granada Cathedral

(Granada, Spain)

One of the great Christian-Moorish churches

This historic building took a staggering 180 years to create. Construction began in 1523, but the final stone was not laid until 1704. Part of the reason it took so long was the spread of the Black Death (bubonic plague), which claimed millions of lives across Europe. The cathedral's epic timescale means that it was built by several generations of laborers and artisans from the same families and that it embraces varied architectural styles, from Gothic to Renaissance.

Granada Cathedral was built on the site of the old Grand Mosque, built by the Moors when they ruled this area of Spain. The Moors had arrived in the eighth

> *". . . completely surrounded by a wilderness of roses, among which innumerable nightingales sang."*
>
> **Washington Irving, writer, on Granada**

century, bringing the new religion of Islam with them. Under the Christian Spanish monarchs, the remains of the old Moorish building was turned into one of the finest churches in the kingdom, its interiors forming a masterpiece of Renaissance art, dominated by two huge, ornately gilded, eighteenth-century organs.

The cathedral, which is surrounded by narrow streets and alleys—a memory of the old Moorish *souk* (market)—has five naves and several chapels, including the Capilla Mayor (Main Chapel) and Capilla Real (Royal Chapel). It also houses a number of royal tombs made from Carrara marble, and a royal art collection including masterpieces by Sandro Botticelli, Alonso Cano, and Rogier van der Weyden. The cathedral is a monument to the era when Spain commanded a vast overseas empire. **LH**

La Cartuja (Granada, Spain)

Spain's best example of Baroque style

The Charterhouse—also known as La Cartuja—is a splendid Carthusian monastery and church. Work on this site began shortly after Christianity's final victories in the reconquest of Spain—an achievement that brought to an end centuries of fighting between the Moors and the Christians. La Cartuja is rumored to have been built to rival the splendor of the Alhambra, the grand palace and fortress constructed by the Moors, who were originally Berber tribes from an area now in Algeria and Morocco.

A monastery was first constructed on this site in the sixteenth century. These original buildings were greatly enlarged and adapted in the eighteenth century, making La Cartuja Spain's premier example of the Churrigueresque—a Spanish Baroque style of architectural ornament that is particularly elaborate and sculptural. The initial plans were laid out in 1506, although work did not commence in earnest until 1515. The original charter rooms and accommodation are relatively austere and slightly oppressive, but the other buildings compensate for this in their over-the-top exuberance.

A number of architects, artists, and builders helped to construct La Cartuja, including the great artists Pedro Anastasio Bocanegra and Juan Sánchez Cotán and the renowned sculptors José de Mora and José Risueño. On entering the church, one must look up into the dome to admire the exquisite frescoes by Antonio Palomino. The highly ornate decor is remarkable and lavish, making use of gold, silver, gilt, ivory, marble, mother-of-pearl, and precious stones. The sacristy is particularly noteworthy, a sumptuous indication of the enormous wealth of the church during the Baroque era. Some sense of the scale of the ornamentation can be gleaned from the fact that the decorative work in the sacristy alone took more than half a century to complete. **LH**

> *"Its dynamic interior decoration is a superb example of architecture, painting, and sculpture."*
>
> Spanish Ministry of Culture

Plaza de Toros (Ronda, Spain)

Birthplace of the sport of bullfighting

Ronda's Plaza de Toros is where the sport of bullfighting as it is known today began. Located high up in the mountainous terrain of Ronda, the Plaza de Toros is Spain's oldest surviving bullring. It was built between 1754 and 1784, and saw its first *corrida*, or bullfight, around 1785. The bullring seats more than 5,000 spectators and still hosts occasional bullfights. It is also home to a museum of bullfighting, and is worth visiting for both this and its impressive Neoclassical architecture designed by José Martín de Aldehuela.

The spectacle of pitting man against bull is thought to have its origins in the sixth century, and the practice evolved over centuries to become the formalized ritual known as bullfighting. The *toreros*, or bullfighters, of Ronda played a significant role in developing the sport, as did the bullring itself. Initially, Roman amphitheaters were often used as suitable venues, hence the circular nature of a bullring. But bullfights were also conducted in plazas; thus rectangular shapes were also considered.

The Ronda bullring was one of the first buildings built solely for bullfighting. The skill of its legendary bullfighters contributed to its success as a venue, and led to the adoption of the now common circular shape of a bullring. Preeminent among eighteenth-century bullfighters was Ronda's Romero family, who spawned three generations of leading bullfighters. The most famous was Pedro Romero Martínez, who killed an estimated 6,000 bulls in his career and managed to walk out of the bullring unscathed every time. His then innovative balletic style of fighting came to influence generations of bullfighters. His grandfather Francisco was also influential in what came to be known as the "Ronda School" style of bullfighting when he introduced the use of the *muleta* stick to carry the short red cloak bullfighters had previously draped over one arm. **CK**

"Bullfighting is the only art in which the artist is in danger of death."

Ernest Hemingway, writer

Port of Palos (near Huelva, Spain)

Columbus and his crew set sail from this port

"[I] went to the town of Palos, which is a seaport. There I fitted out three vessels . . ."

Christopher Columbus's log book, May 1492

The port town of Palos has become well known as the place from which the explorer Christopher Columbus set sail on the epic voyage that led him to the New World. His intention was to discover a new route to "the Indies" (southeast Asia) but he happened upon the Americas instead. So convinced was he that he had actually found India, that the indigenous people of the new lands he encountered became known as "Indians."

Columbus was an Italian, a sailor born in Genoa who had long dreamed of discovering new worlds. For some time he lived in Portugal with his Portuguese wife, an acquaintance of King John II. Columbus tried to persuade the Portuguese king to finance his plan to discover a new route to the Indies, but although the king commissioned him to undertake other voyages, he was not interested in Columbus's Indian scheme. After the death of his wife in 1481, Columbus moved to Spain, and King Ferdinand and Queen Isabella agreed to finance his dream. Most people thought Columbus's plan was crazy and royal persuasion had to be used to entice people to accompany him. In addition to the promise of handsome wages, convicts were offered an amnesty in return for joining the crew—only four criminals decided to take up the generous offer.

On August 3, 1492, Columbus and his crew went to the church of San Jorge in Palos to hear Mass, before setting off from Palos harbor on a voyage that was to change the course of world history. The exploration fleet consisted of three ships—the *Santa María* (Columbus's ship), the *Pinta*, and the *Niña*. Palos was the hometown of the other two ships' captains, brothers named Vicente and Martín Pinzón. Today, a statue of Christopher Columbus stands in the town's main square, and visitors interested in exploration can visit the nearby popular Three Ships' Museum. **LH**

Casa del Almirante (Cádiz, Spain)

Home of the admiral of the treasure fleet

Constructed in 1690, the Casa del Almirante is situated near Cádiz's cathedral in the Barrio del Pópulo, and today the building is home to various residential apartments. It was built by Diego de Barrios Leal, admiral of the Spanish treasure fleet.

The sixteenth century saw the port of Cádiz increase in importance; Christopher Columbus set sail from the city on his second and fourth voyages, and Cádiz became home to the Spanish treasure fleet. The fleet consisted of the ships that brought products back to Spain, including gold, silver, gems, and spices from Spanish colonies in the New World. Piracy had become increasingly organized, prolific, and was encouraged by England and France, and so by the 1520s the ships had begun to travel in convoys for their own protection. Two heavily armed fleets carrying manufactured goods and slaves would set sail each year from Spain and make their way to the Caribbean and South America. Once loaded with raw merchandise, the galleons would then meet up in Havana, Cuba, to make the return trip across the Atlantic Ocean. At its peak, the fleet consisted of fifty vessels. The fleet gradually fell into decline, suffering at the hands of natural enemies such as hurricanes, as well as human ones in the form of attacks by rival Dutch and English navies, who were growing in strength.

The lavishness of the Baroque building is testament to the affluence of both the city and of the Barrios family at the time. The house's exterior is covered in red and white marble from Genoa, the Barrios family crest is displayed on the second-floor balcony that lies above a portico entrance flanked by double columns, and the building is crowned by two towers. Inside, the building is home to a majestic staircase crowned by an elliptical cupola, and the ceiling of the main hall is adorned with a painting of the family crest. **CK**

"the more they fill their handes with finding [gold], the more increaseth their covetous desire."

Richard Eden, *Decades of the New Worlde* (1555)

Torre Tavira

(Cádiz, Spain)

Remnant of the port's trans-Atlantic trade

Built in 1778, the Torre Tavira watchtower is a surviving remnant of what was Cádiz's golden era in the eighteenth century when it was one of the wealthiest and most affluent places in Europe. Cádiz's geographical location as a port with access to the Atlantic Ocean was the reason for its prosperity. At this time, it is estimated that as much as 75 percent of Spain's trade was with the Americas, and in 1717 King Philip V made Cádiz the official Spanish entry point for all the commerce arriving from the region. The city's monopoly on trade ended in 1765, but its convenient location and the expertise of its merchants ensured that the city continued to prosper.

Standing 148 feet (45 m) above sea level, the Torre Tavira is one of Cádiz's 126 surviving watchtowers and is named after its first watchman, Antonio Tavira. His job was to record the ships entering and leaving the port. At one time the city was home to 160 watchtowers that were built by the local merchants as overt signs of their success, and sometimes formed part of their own homes. The towers were usually laid out to a square floor plan and were two stories high.

The main function of the towers was to provide vantage points from where merchants could ascertain whether vessels containing their merchandise had arrived. The merchants also used the towers to relay messages to their ships, using flags flown from the roof to control traffic in and out of the port. The towers also served as lookout points to help guard against pirate invasions. But in 1792 the municipal authorities forbade the construction of any more watchtowers, deeming they would no longer be useful. Torre Tavira is now used as a music conservatory and is also home to a camera obscura that was installed in the 1990s. The pinhole camera projects a 360-degree moving picture of the town onto a table. **CK**

Batalla de Guadalete

(near Guadalete River, Spain)

Beginning of Arab domination in Spain

In the eighth century, the area through which the Guadalete River flows, at the southern tip of Spain, was turbulent "frontier" territory that witnessed a new chapter in Spanish-Portuguese history. The frontier lay between Africa's Muslim (Moorish) Arabs and Spain's Visigoth rulers. Controversy surrounds the exact course of events, but one version runs as follows.

When the Visigoth king Witiza died, around 710, his family lost the succession to a prominent Visigoth called Roderick, probably a nobleman or military commander. Witiza's enraged family pursued revenge by seeking help from the powerful Muslim forces of

"Remember that if you suffer these times patiently, you can expect to enjoy all the supreme delights."

Tariq ibn Ziyad, addressing his troops before battle

North Africa, who duly sent a raiding party across the Gibraltar Straits into Spain, driving Roderick south.

Matters then took an unforeseen turn. Tangier's Muslim governor, Tariq ibn Ziyad, brought a much larger army into southern Spain. In July 711 Tariq faced Roderick's army near the banks of the Guadalete, probably close to today's town of Arcos de la Frontera. It seems that Roderick was decisively defeated—although no one actually saw him die—and this opened the floodgates for Muslim domination. The Arabs pushed steadily north, west, and east, and within just eight or so years most of the Iberian Peninsula (modern Spain and Portugal) was under their control. Theories abound about how this happened so easily, one being that virtually the entire Visigoth court was wiped out at Guadalete. **AK**

Pedro Domecq Bodega

(Jerez de la Frontera, Spain)

One of the world's leading sherry houses

The production of sherry is a closely regulated industry and only the sherries produced in and around the Andalucían city of Jerez de la Frontera in southern Spain are legally allowed to use the name. The Pedro Domecq Bodega is perhaps the most prestigious of all the sherry houses in a region also known for its traditions of flamenco dancing and horse breeding.

The Pedro Domecq firm was founded in 1730 by an Irishman called Patrick Murphy. A bachelor who suffered from poor health, Murphy was aided in his business by a local wine grower of French descent called Juan Haurie, who inherited the business when Murphy died in 1762. Haurie divided the business between his five nephews—the most prominent of whom was Juan Carlos Haurie. When Napoleonic forces invaded Spain, Juan Carlos supported them, and was put in charge of sequestering supplies for them during their 1810 to 1812 occupation of Jerez de la Frontera. As a result, he was forced to pay indemnities after the French left, which brought the firm close to bankruptcy. In 1816, however, Pedro Domecq, a relative of Haurie, took over the firm and revitalized it. From 1824 onward, the firm bore the Domecq name and enjoyed great success. In 1823 Fernando VII of Spain made Domecq a supplier to the royal court, and in 1911 the firm was given a royal patent by George V of England. The bodega is located in an airy, whitewashed Moorish building, La Mezquita (The Mosque), next to a cloister dating from the fifteenth century.

The Pedro Domecq Bodega is open to the public for tours that demonstrate how sherry is made. Jerez de la Frontera is the center of one of the most prestigious and historic winemaking areas in Europe, and the Pedro Domecq Bodega is perhaps the most famed and successful house in the region. **JF**

> *"Jerez de la Frontera [lay] between areas ruled by the Moorish caliphs and the Christian monarchs."*

Genevieve McCarthy, wine educator

🏛 ◉ Stock Exchange Palace (Porto, Portugal)

Elegant former center of Porto's finance and commerce

The Palácio da Bolsa, with the amazing Arabian Hall as its centerpiece, is one of Portugal's premier Neoclassical buildings. During the siege of Porto in 1832, fire broke out at the old São Francisco Monastery and the building was razed to the ground. In 1841 Queen Maria II signed the go-ahead for Porto's Chamber of Commerce to build its new headquarters on the site. Joaquim da Costa Lima Júnior was appointed as architect and work began the following year, funded by the merchants themselves.

The design of the palace was influenced by the British Palladian style, particularly John Carr's St. Antonio Hospital and John Whitehead's British Factory House, both also located in Porto. Beyond the austere Doric facade, a vestibule leads to the Hall of Nations, an airy space sheltered by a huge metal and glass dome and decorated with the national coat of arms, as well as those of Portugal's favored trade partners at the end of the nineteenth century (including Britain and the United States). The hall's visually disorientating mosaic floor was inspired by the Greco-Roman style employed at Pompeii. Another notable feature of the palace is the sumptuous stairway, designed in 1868 by Adolfo Gonçalves de Sousa, who took over the Bolsa project in 1860. From the Portraits Room, which contains a highly praised decorated table by cabinetmaker Zeferino José Pinto, visitors enter the palace's architectural pièce de résistance—the Arabian Hall. Modeled by de Sousa after the Alhambra in Granada, Spain, the intricate, Moorish-style structure was begun in 1862 and took eighteen years to complete. Glittering ornaments are enhanced by creative lighting to produce fine chromatic effects.

Today the Stock Exchange Palace—now a national monument—is visited by 200,000 people per year and hosts a broad range of civic functions. **TE**

🏛 ⊚ Batalha Monastery (Batalha, Portugal)

Soaring Gothic monastery

Batalha Monastery is located in central Portugal, and is built in the Portuguese Gothic style. It took more than 150 years to complete and involved the efforts of several architects. Batalha Monastery introduced new architectural techniques and styles to Portugal, and was made a UNESCO World Heritage Site in 1983.

The monastery was started in 1386 by King John I to thank the Virgin Mary for his decisive victory over Castile at the Battle of Aljubarrota (1385). He is buried in the Founder's Chapel (constructed 1426–34) with his wife, Philippa of Lancaster, who had brought with her some English architects who added aspects of the English Perpendicular style. The final structure of the church is narrow at 72 feet (22 m) wide compared with its 106-foot (32-m) height. Stained-glass windows were added in the 1430s, and the monastery was probably the first place for which they were produced in Portugal.

The construction of the monastery went on for the reigns of six more Portuguese rulers, until King John III, in the early sixteenth century, decided to focus his attention on another monastery in Lisbon. This meant that parts of the monastery, namely the "Imperfect Chapels," remained unfinished.

Batalha went into decline when it was twice sacked in 1810 and 1811 by the Napoleonic Marshall André Masséna. In 1834 the Dominican monks who had lived in the site for centuries were ousted, and the complex was abandoned and fell into ruin. However, in 1840, King Ferdinand II began restoration work, which was completed in the early twentieth century.

Batalha Monastery is an important symbol of Portuguese culture, and perhaps the finest example of Gothic architecture in the country. The monastery was made a national monument in 1907. It is a symbol of the piety of the nation's medieval kings, as well as their sophisticated architectural tastes. **TE**

Basilica do Rosário

(Fatima, Portugal)

Popular shrine to the Virgin Mary

The Basilica do Rosário was built in the town of Fatima to commemorate sightings of the Virgin Mary by three shepherd children in 1917. The peasant trio—Lúcia Santos and her two cousins Francisco and Jacinta Marto—were allegedly visited on May 17 in a pasture called Irene's Cove near the village of Aljustrel, about 1 mile (1.6 km) from Fatima. The apparition was said to have told them it was troubled by the fighting tearing Europe apart (this was the penultimate year of World War I). It returned for the next five months and each sighting saw a larger crowd present (although only the children were able to see and hear Mary). Finally, on October 13, it visited for the last time and more than 70,000 people reported seeing storm clouds pass and beams of colored light shoot to earth.

Construction of the basilica, which contains the tombs of the three seers (the last survivor, Lúcia, died in 2005), began on May 13, 1928, and it was consecrated in October 1953. The structure, with a central tower 213 feet (65 m) high, features long Roman-style marble-columned walkways with paintings of Mary on either side of the front entrance. It is flanked by colonnades linking it with a series of buildings, including those housing a convent and hospital. The fifteen altars are dedicated to the fifteen mysteries of the Rosary, and scenes of the apparitions are featured in stained glass. Pilgrims gather in the adjacent Cova, a vast esplanade in which is located a small chapel where the Virgin is believed to have appeared to the children.

In 1970, the Vatican legitimized the Fatima story as part of Christian history. The asphalt esplanade holds 300,000 pilgrims but an audience of more than one million was recorded when the Pope visited. The most popular times to visit are on the thirteenth of each month between May and October. **TE**

Castelo de São Jorge

(Lisbon, Portugal)

Lisbon landmark offering sweeping views

The Castelo de São Jorge is perched on the highest of Lisbon's seven hills and its most famous viewpoint—the "ancient window"—offers spectacular views of the city. The complex consists of the castle proper, as well as the remains of the original royal palace. The nineteenth-century main gate leads to the principal square, Praça D'Armas, whereas the Tower of Ulysses contains a periscope that enables visitors to gain a 360-degree view of Lisbon.

Predating the Romans, the hilltop was originally the site of a fortress to guard the river before the Visigoths took over, and it eventually fell to the

> *"Was then more vice in fallen Lisbon found,/Than Paris where voluptuous joys abound?"*
>
> Voltaire, *Poem on the Disaster of Lisbon*, 1756

Saracens in the early eighth century. The subsequent keepers were the Moors, who were despatched in 1147 during the siege of Lisbon by Portugal's first king, Afonso Henriques. When Lisbon was declared capital of the fledgling Portuguese kingdom in 1255, the castle became the seat of the royal palace. It gained its name in 1371 when it was dedicated to Saint George by King John I, who had married the English princess Philippa of Lancaster. However, with the establishment of a new palace on the banks of the Tagus and damage from the 1531 earthquake, the medieval castle lost its pre-eminence. It suffered incarnations as both a prison and a barracks, and was severely damaged in the great earthquake of 1755. In the 1940s a program of renovation work was started, restoring many of the original buildings and features. **TE**

 ⊕ # Sintra

(near Lisbon, Portugal)

Fairy-tale collection of fascinating and varied buildings amid mountains

Sintra is a Portuguese town crammed with architectural treasures that range from a Moorish castle to wonderful royal palaces, scattered across mountain peaks and punctuated by lavish parks and gardens. Its location, among the craggy Sintra Mountains about 15 miles (24 km) northwest of Lisbon, is spectacular.

Straddling two peaks is a Moorish castle, dating from the eighth or ninth century and restored in the 1800s, whose towers and castellated walls offer breathtaking views. The old quarter of Sintra is dominated by the twin-chimneyed National Palace, one of Portugal's major monuments. Altered and added to from the thirteenth to the sixteenth century, this royal palace brings together Gothic, Portuguese, Moorish, and Renaissance styles, and includes beautiful schemes created from colored glazed tiles.

Perched on another peak is the Pena Palace, created partly from a sixteenth-century monastery and a triumph of nineteenth-century Romanticism. Ferdinand II of Portugal began building this royal residence in the 1830s and concocted a unique castle-palace mixture of Portuguese, Moorish, Gothic, and Bavarian styles. Another Romantic gem is the mid-nineteenth-century Monserrate Palace, with its exotic Mughal decoration and rounded cupolas. All the buildings are offset by an incredible backdrop of gardens and parks. These range from tiny terraces clinging to steep slopes, to the wider bounds of the Sintra-Cascais Natural Park, and give Sintra some of Europe's finest landscaped spaces. In the 1800s the buildings and gardens became a major focus for European Romanticism. In recognition of the town's wide-ranging importance, UNESCO inscribed the "cultural landscape of Sintra" as one of its World Heritage sites in 1995. **AK**

"*The village of Cintra . . . is the most beautiful, perhaps in the world. I am very happy here.*"

Lord Byron, letter to Francis Hodgson, July 16, 1809

🏛 ◉ Jerónimos Monastery (Lisbon, Portugal)

Ornate building created to celebrate Portugal's explorers

The Jerónimos Monastery is in the historic Belém district of Lisbon, and is one of the finest historical monuments in the city. It is the pinnacle of the Manueline style, named after the fifteenth-century king Manuel I, which incorporates elements of Gothic, Italian, Spanish, and Flemish design.

The monastery is located on the site of an earlier religious foundation established by the explorer Henry the Navigator. In 1497, another explorer, Vasco da Gama, and his men stayed there before departing for India. A monastery was built there on the orders of Manuel I to celebrate Da Gama's return in 1499. Construction began in 1502 under Diogo Boitac, and was continued in 1517 by the Spanish architect João de Castilho. Jerónimos Monastery also features elements of Renaissance design, added by the French sculptor Nicolau Chanterene. The construction was funded by a 5 percent tax on certain spices from the

East. Building stopped when Manuel died, but was restarted in 1550. Two Portuguese kings—Manuel and John III—are entombed in the church, as is Vasco da Gama. Adjoining the church is the cloistered monastery, inhabited by monks of the Hieronymite order. The twentieth-century poet Fernando Pessoa is buried in one of the arcades of the cloister. The monastery was extended in 1850, and contains an archeological and a maritime museum. Near Jerónimos Monastery is the Torre de Belém, a large tower on the banks of the River Tagus built between 1515 and 1521 to commemorate the achievements of Vasco da Gama.

Jerónimos Monastery and the Torre de Belém were designated UNESCO World Heritage Sites in 1983 under the heading of Monastery of the Hieronymites and Tower of Belém. The monastery reflects the glory of the Portuguese Age of Discovery. **JF**

🏛 ⊚ Capela dos Ossos (Évora, Portugal)

Memorable chapel decorated with bones

The Capela dos Ossos (Bone Chapel) is a macabre chapel constructed by Franciscan monks to serve as a reminder of life's ephemeral nature. It is one of the best-known parts of the historic centre of the city of Évora, which has been designated as a UNESCO World Heritage Site.

The chapel is adjacent to the large Gothic Church of St. Francis, which was built between 1475 and the 1550s. The Capela dos Ossos is 61.4 feet (18.7 m) long and 36.1 feet (11 m) wide, with three small windows and eight pillars. The chapel is decorated with human bones and skulls held together by cement. It also features two desiccated corpses, one of which is a child. The identities of the bodies are unknown, although it is rumored that they are an adulterous man and his son, cursed by his wife.

It has been estimated that bones from around 5,000 bodies were used to cover the walls and pillars of the chapel. They were probably taken from local graveyards, although local myth has it that they came from plague victims or from combatants who died in a nearby battle. The ceiling is in white brick painted with death motifs.

A reminder of why the chapel was constructed is inscribed above the entrance: *"Nós ossos que aqui estamos pelos vossos esperamos"* ("We bones that are here, for your bones we wait"). The bones of the monks who built the Capela dos Ossos are interred in small white coffins placed in the chapel. The Capela dos Ossos may appear superficially ghoulish, but it was built to serve a religious purpose for the Franciscans who prayed there. In the sixteenth century, life expectancies were shorter and death from disease could come suddenly and unexpectedly. The Capela dos Ossos is a striking and stark product of religious life in the sixteenth century. **JF**

🏛 ◉ Malbork Castle (Malbork, Poland)

Massive fortress and monument to the age of chivalry

One of Europe's largest fortresses, Malbork Castle stands on the banks of the Nogat River, about 25 miles (40 km) south of the coast near Gdańsk. It was built by the Teutonic Knights who invaded the land south of the Baltic Sea in the thirteenth century, initially at the invitation of the Prince of Mazovis to help him control the pagan Prussian tribe. Planned on a grand scale, Malbork was enlarged further when the castle and its settlement became a sovereign monastic state. The headquarters of the Order's Grand Master were moved here from Venice in 1309.

Malbork consisted of three fortified castles, a magnificent palace with several hundred houses, granaries, and other buildings surrounded by a second ring of defensive walls. A formidable stronghold, Malbork was successfully defended against many attempted sieges during the fourteenth century. The Teutonic Knights started as a German Roman Catholic religious order at the end of the twelfth century in Acre, in Palestine. They became a military, crusading force and traveled throughout the Middle East, Hungary, and into the Baltic lands, providing military support, taking possession of land, building towns and forts, and developing strong economies. The Teutonic Order, however, remained loyal to the sovereignty of the pope, which brought them into conflict with their allies. Their crusading ambitions often made enemies of their neighbors. The Teutonic Knights were defeated decisively at the Battle of Grunwald on July 15, 1410, by the armies of Poland and Lithuania, with support from the Tartars. Malbork Castle became a Polish royal residence in 1466.

The castle today is beautifully restored. Its labyrinth of rooms, turrets, stairways, and halls contains a vast collection of amber, armor, paintings, and furnishings. **EH**

Wilanów Palace (Warsaw, Poland)

Important and much-visited royal palace

Wilanów Palace is a wonderfully preserved Baroque residence. It was built for the seventeenth-century king Jan III Sobieski, one of Poland's greatest military leaders, who was responsible for stalling the Turkish advance on Europe at the Battle of Vienna in 1683.

Jan III acquired the small village of Wilanów, on the outskirts of Warsaw, in 1677. The original commission for the palace's design was for a traditional, Polish, ground-floor noble residence. However, the finished palace eventually incorporated a wide range of architectural styles—from an Italian country villa to a Louis XIV–style French palace—while retaining a Polish character. The palace reflected Jan III's military successes and achievements, and he died there. After his death, Wilanów Palace passed through a number of owners from Poland's magnate families and was the residence of King Augustus II the Strong from 1730 to 1733.

In 1805 part of the palace was made into one of Poland's first museums by Count Stanisław Kostka Potocki, exhibiting European and Asian art. The palace's original Baroque garden was supplemented by three other gardens, including one in the English style, and a rose garden, which was added in the mid-nineteenth century. During World War II, much of the collection was stolen by the occupying Nazis. After the war, most of it was returned, and the palace reopened to the public in 1962.

The glory of Wilanów Palace has remained mostly intact in spite of Poland's turbulent history, and particularly World War II. Today the palace still operates as a museum and art gallery, and the palace's rose garden hosts outdoor concerts in the summer. Wilanów Palace is one of Poland's most important cultural and historical sites, and a monument to one of the nation's greatest rulers. **JF**

Wilczy Szianiec (Gierłoz, Poland)

Adolf Hitler's wartime headquarters, and site of a dramatic assassination attempt

"*the German resistance movement must take the plunge before the eyes of the world and of history.*"

Letter to Von Stauffenberg from a co-conspirator

⊡ The dense forest protected the command bunkers in the Wilczy Szianiec complex from aerial observation.

⊡ Adolf Hitler inspects the damage caused by the bomb blast. He suffered only minor injuries.

During World War II, Wilczy Szianiec (Wolfsschanze, or Wolf's Lair) was Adolf Hitler's main field headquarters near Kętrzyn, in the beautiful Mazuria region of northeast Poland. The complex consists of eighty heavily fortified buildings, with its nearby airfield, in 67 acres (27 ha) of woodland. It includes seven massive ferro-concrete bunkers, which are 26 feet (8 m) thick in some places. Although situated in dense woodland, the site was further disguised by artificial greenery suspended on wires and protected by rings of barbed wire and a minefield.

Hitler arrived at Wilczy Szianiec on June 21, 1941, and it was from here, heavily fortified and guarded, that he directed much of World War II. He moved around as little as possible, but this did not prevent the almost successful assassination attempt of July 20, 1944, planned by a group of senior Nazi officers and carried out by one of them. Claus von Stauffenberg attended a meeting with Hitler and twenty other senior officers at Wilczy Szianiec, with a bomb in his briefcase. Four men were killed—but not Hitler himself. The incident provoked vicious reprisals against all those involved, resulting in 5,000 arrests and two hundred executions. Hitler left Wilczy Szianiec for the last time on November 20, 1944. The complex was severely damaged by explosions as the Germans, reportedly using a single plunger, triggered the built-in detonation system to prevent the advancing Soviet army from using it.

"Wolf" was one of Hilter's own nicknames for himself—he began using it in the early 1920s—and the names of his other operational headquarters reflect this. Wilczy Szianiec lacks the grace of most of the fortresses built by earlier warlords and must have created an oppressive atmosphere for Hitler's senior officers. The ruins remain—now a museum, open all year—as a chilling reminder of World War II. **EH**

Marie Curie's Birthplace (Warsaw, Poland)

Birthplace and home of the eminent scientist for twenty-four years

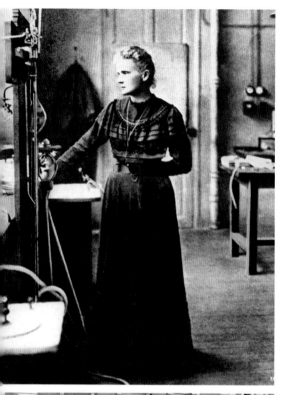

This gracious town house is located in the New Town district of central Warsaw and was among the buildings destroyed by the Germans after the defeat of the Warsaw Uprising in 1944. Originally built in the eighteenth century, the house that stands today is a replica, built after the war.

Marie Skłodowska (1867–1934) was the youngest of five children and her father taught physics at the local secondary school. She went to Paris to study physics and mathematics, and there married the physicist Pierre Curie in 1885. They worked together at the Sorbonne and were jointly awarded the Nobel Prize for Physics in 1903. Marie won the Nobel Prize for Chemistry in 1911. As her exceptional contribution to science and medicine became recognized, Marie was awarded many honorary science, medicine, and law degrees and honorary memberships in learned societies throughout the world. She established radium institutes in Paris and Warsaw. Marie Curie is best known for her discovery of the two radioactive chemical elements polonium and radium, and for her pioneering work in the medical uses of radium.

Marie Curie died in France in 1934 from leukemia probably caused by radiation exposure—she carried test tubes containing radioactive material around in her pocket and kept them in her desk drawer. In her diary, Marie commented on the pretty green-blue light they emitted in the dark! The house in Freta Street is now owned by the Polish Chemical Society and part of the building, containing a museum devoted to the life and work of Marie and Pierre Curie, is open every day. **EH**

↖ A photograph, colored at a later date, of Marie Curie in her laboratory in Paris around 1900.

← The replica of Marie Curie's birthplace in the New Town district—actually one of the older parts of Warsaw.

Chopin's Birthplace (Żelazowa Wola, Poland)

Restored manor where Chopin was born

It is often mistakenly assumed that nineteenth-century composer Frédéric Chopin (1810–1849) was French, but he was actually born in Poland to a French father and Polish mother. Like Mozart, he was a virtuoso performer from a very early age, giving his first public concert at the age of eight; he was sometimes known as the "second Mozart." The simple texture of his Romantic music calls to mind Parisian salons and would go on to inspire French composers such as Debussy and Erik Satie; but Chopin, a patriotic Pole, was the first Western classical composer to use distinctly Slavic elements in his music

The manor house in which Chopin was born can be found in the village of Żelazowa Wola, near Sochaczew, in the region of Masovia. At the time of Chopin's birth, the house belonged to a Count Skarbek, who employed Chopin's father as a tutor. The house is surrounded by a formal garden and is a short walk from the main entrance. By the end of the nineteenth century the house was derelict, but a renewed interest in Chopin's origins has led to renovations. The wooden floors and painted ceiling beams are much as they would have been in Chopin's day. The furnishings are of the period. The rooms are spacious, light streams through the large windows, and the ceilings are high.

While traveling abroad, Chopin heard news of the Russian army's suppression of the November 1830 uprising in Poland. Then twenty years old, he moved to Paris, never to see his homeland again. Today, recitals of his work are given during the summer months at his birthplace. **OR**

↗ Portrait of Frédéric Chopin by B. Franz, painted around 1900 but based on an earlier portrait of the composer.

→ Chopin's birthplace in Żelazowa Wola. The village was also the home to the famous violinist Henryk Szeryng.

Chapel of Skulls

(Czermna, Poland)

Chapel decorated with thousands of bones

The exterior of this small Baroque church looks ordinary enough—in fact, rather plain—but the visitor who ventures inside is in for a shock. The walls and ceiling of the chapel are decorated with 3,000 skulls and other bones, densely and neatly packed together, to create a fascinating, but rather macabre, decorative effect. There are around 20,000 more skulls stored in the vaults.

Created in 1776 by the local Czech parish priest, the chapel serves as a striking memorial to those who perished in the violent religious wars of the seventeenth century and the two Silesian wars of the eighteenth century. It also houses the bones of some of the victims of the many cholera epidemics that plagued the area. Although this display of death is unusual in Christian churches, the practice of storing bones in an ossuary developed in some parts of Europe so that churches could cope when deaths were numerous and frequent—for example, during wars or epidemics of disease—and the graveyards were not large enough for all the dead to be buried. Grave plots were available for a few years, and then the bones were exhumed and stored in the ossuary. There is another famous example at the monastery of Sedlec in the neighboring Czech Republic.

Czermna is situated in what was called the Bohemian Corner, in the old County of Glatz, and is close to Kudowa-Zdrój (Bad Kudowa), one of a string of attractive eighteenth-century spa towns that nestle under the dramatic and beautiful Stołowe (or Table) Mountains in the Silesian region of Poland, close to the border with the Czech Republic. A visit to the Chapel of Skulls would have made an interesting diversion for visitors to the spa at Kudowa-Zdrój—although perhaps not particularly reassuring for those seeking the benefits of a health resort. **EH**

The Black Madonna

(Częstochowa, Poland)

Pilgrimage site with a miraculous icon

The Black Madonna, also known as Our Lady of Częstochowa, is an exceptionally beautiful symbolic painting of the Virgin Mary with Jesus. Mary and Jesus are dark-skinned and their crowns, halos, and robes are elaborately decorated. The icon is located in the chapel of the Virgin Mary in the fortified Baroque Pauline monastery of Jasna Góra, venerated as Poland's most holy place and a pilgrimage destination.

There is documentary evidence that the painting arrived at Jasna Góra from Constantinople (now Istanbul) soon after the monastery's founding in 1382, but the artist and era are disputed. Legend has it that

> *"Its antiquity is so great that its origins are unknown, as if 'dropped from the heavens.'"*
>
> Michael P. Duricy, historian

it was painted in the sixth century by St. Luke; others propose that it was created in the thirteenth or fourteenth century and may overlay an earlier icon. The Black Madonna is credited with numerous miracles, including saving the monastery from the Swedish invasion and siege of 1655, for which she was acclaimed queen and protector of Poland by King Jan Kazimierz in 1656.

The painting is also credited with saving the monastery from fire, and, in the fifteenth century, with the sudden death of a Hussite robber who struck the painting twice with his sword. Attempts to repair the damage have allegedly been unsuccessful because the "scars" reappear. The icon is unveiled twice a day for the many visitors, and thousands visit on August 15, Assumption Day. **EH**

Zamość Old Town

(Zamość, Poland)

Renaissance trading center blending Italian, Dutch, and Polish architectural styles

Set in a highly fertile region of rich black soil in southeastern Poland, the town of Zamość was established in 1580 as a center of trade on the route linking northern and western Europe with the Black Sea. The town's founder, the illustrious diplomat and statesman Jan Zamoyski, commissioned the Italian architect Bernardo Morando to model the town partly on the Italian *città ideale*, or ideal town.

Zamość Old Town, built in the remarkably short time of eighteen years and completed in 1598, is a near-perfect example of late sixteenth-century Renaissance town planning. The style is unusually consistent, marrying the finest traditions of the Italian and Dutch Renaissance to native Polish architecture. The cathedral, the synagogue, the town hall, and the Armenian tenement houses surrounding the grand market square comprise a stylistically unified entity.

While the Old Town is distinguished by beautiful and colorful buildings, it was conceived first of all as a fortress and was built using the latest techniques of military engineering. This is most evident in the fortified wall that surrounds the town, pierced by three entry points. The Old Lublin Gate (Stara Brama Lubelska), from which travelers joined the road to the nearby city of Lublin, is the oldest portal. Beyond the wall, the town was defended by a moat, and just below the Old Lublin Gate, a small pentagonal fortress was constructed in the moat for further protection. At the Battle of Byczyna (1588), Zamoyski defeated and captured the Austrian pretender to the Polish throne—Archduke Maximilian III—and led him through Old Lublin Gate as his prisoner. To commemorate this securing of the throne for the rightful Polish ruler, a patriotic facade was added to the gate. Sadly, today the grand gateway is bricked up and hangs above the now-empty moat. **JF**

> *"The 'ideal town' [Zamość] was ... an economic, cultural and religious center of the region."*
>
> Stanisław Turski, writer

🏛 ◈ Auschwitz-Birkenau Concentration Camp

(Oświęcim, Poland)

Monument to the martyrdom and resistance of millions of men, women, and children

Auschwitz-Birkenau was the principal and most notorious of the six concentration and extermination camps established by Nazi Germany to implement its Final Solution policy which had as its aim the mass murder of the Jewish people in Europe. Built in Poland in 1940 under Nazi German occupation initially as a concentration camp for Poles and later for Soviet prisoners of war, it soon became a prison for a number of other nationalities. Between the years 1942 and 1944 it became the main mass extermination camp where Jews were tortured and killed for their racial origins. The original camp, known as Auschwitz I, was initially built for Polish political prisoners and over time developed into the administrative center for the other camps. Auschwitz II (Birkenau) was the main extermination (Vernichtungslager) camp, and it was here that at least 800,000 Jews were sent to their deaths. Auschwitz III (Monowitz) was a special work camp that supplied forced labor for the I. G. Farben synthetic rubber and oil extraction plant.

More than 1.2 million people were annihilated, 90 percent of whom were Jews. The poison gas Zyklon-B was the major agent of death in the camp, although overwork, starvation, beatings, and random shootings accounted for the demise of many other inmates. Of particular horror were the medical experiments conducted by Dr. Josef Mengele—the "Angel of Death." The camp was closed at the end of 1944, in the face of the advancing Red Army. Today what remains of the camp has been made into a memorial site. its inscription on the World Heritage List serves as a beacon of warning to uphold the human values and ideals that are part of the UNESCO constitution declared out of the ashes of World War II in 1945. **AG**

🏛 ⊚ Wieliczka Salt Mines

(Cracow, Poland)

Labyrinthine medieval salt-manufacturing site featuring intricate salt carvings

Wieliczka is one of the oldest documented salt-manufacturing sites in Europe. Rock salt was first discovered in Wieliczka in the thirteenth century, and it was mined continuously from the Middle Ages until 1992. The mine is spread over nine levels, and reaches 1,072 feet (327 m) below the surface. It includes 2,040 chambers, and more than 186 miles (300 km) of galleries, 26 surface shafts, and around 180 shafts connecting caverns across its nine levels. In addition to its well-preserved mining chambers, what is most remarkable is that the mine contains chapels, sacred artworks, and statues sculpted in salt by local miners, as well as salt lakes on which it is possible to row in small dinghies. Much of it is now open to visitors.

Of the several chapels in the mine, the oldest preserved is the Baroque St. Anthony Chapel where mass was first celebrated in 1698. In addition to its altars and many detailed bas-reliefs, the chapel is also home to several freestanding statues carved from salt blocks, including those of the Virgin Mary and the infant St. Anthony, the patron saint of metal miners. The largest of the chapels is that of the patron saint of the local miners, St. Kinga. Work began on the chapel in 1896, and continued sporadically until 1963. It is completely carved from salt, from floor to ceiling, including the altar and other decorations, the most remarkable being the large chandeliers made from salt crystals that were adapted for electricity in 1918.

Various other chambers are dedicated to religious and Polish historical figures; the most frivolous is the small Kunegunda Pit Bottom that contains carved figures of gnomes imitating miners at work, in a playful nod to the efforts of the miners, and also to Polish folklore. **CK**

🏛️ ◎ **Royal Castle** (Cracow, Poland)

Historic seat of the Polish monarchy

> "In the tunnels of a certain rock there lived an immensely dreadful monster..."

Master Vincent, on the Dragon of Wawel

The Royal Castle is located on Wawel Hill, Cracow, on the left bank of the River Vistula. It has been an important center of power in Polish history from as early as the ninth century. The current castle on the hill was built in the Renaissance style using architects and artists from across Europe, and it is one of the most important buildings of its type in Central Europe.

The castle on Wawel Hill was the Polish royal residence from 1038 to 1596, and was built on the same site as previous Romanesque and Gothic structures. The history of the current Renaissance castle dates back to 1504, when King Alexander Jagiellon began to rebuild the castle using Italian and German architects. His brother King Sigismund I "The Old" continued the work, and the castle was completed in 1540. The final structure was spread over three floors surrounding a very impressive arcaded courtyard. King Sigismund II Augustus added to the decor of the castle by acquiring a fine set of Flemish tapestries, which are still preserved in the castle. After a fire in 1595, King Sigismund III Vasa added a wing in the early Baroque style, designed by Italian architects.

The castle fell out of use as the royal court moved to Warsaw, so the monarchs visited Cracow only infrequently. After Poland lost independence in 1795 it eventually fell into the hands of the Austrians, who used it as a military hospital. During World War II, it was the residence of the Nazi governor general Hans Frank. After World War II, the castle became a museum of Polish history, displaying many unique artifacts including the Polish coronation sword, the "Szczerbiec"; the castle now houses part of the Polish National Art Collection. The beautifully restored royal chambers and private apartments are open to the public. It is also possible to visit the "Dragon's Den," home to the legendary Dragon of Wawel; the cavern in the western slope of Wawel Hill is 886 feet (270 m) long. **JF**

Wawel Cathedral (Cracow, Poland)

Important Polish church, and resting place of Polish kings and queens

The Polish Cathedral Basilica of Saints Stanisław and Vaclav, more commonly known as Wawel Cathedral, lies on Cracow's Wawel Hill, and was built in 1320. The church is home to a number of ecclesiastical artworks in Gothic, Renaissance, Baroque, and Romanesque styles, but it is best known as the coronation and burial site of the Polish monarchy for several centuries. It houses the marble tombs of the thirteenth century's King Vladislav I the Short, King Casimir III the Great and Queen-Saint Jadwiga, and the fourteenth century's King Vladislav II Jagiello and King Casimir IV Jagiello. It also has memorials to various historical figures such as clergymen, poets, national heroes, and three other saints, including the country's patron saint St. Stanisław, an eleventh-century Cracow bishop who was killed by King Boleslav II.

By the sixteenth century, monarchs broke with the tradition of being buried in the cathedral and were laid to rest in crypts such as the opulent, golden-domed, Renaissance-style Sigismund Chapel that houses the sarcophagi of King Sigismund I the Old, his wife, and his successor, who was the last of the Jagellion dynasty. The interior of the chapel is lavishly decorated. The cathedral is also famous for the Sigismund Bell cast in 1520 that measures 9 feet (2.7 m) across and weighs 18.5 tons. It hangs in the fourteenth-century church belfry, and local superstition says that those who touch the bell's clapper and make a wish will have their wish granted. Visitors can climb to the top of the belfry.

Yet perhaps what is most notable about the cathedral is that it contains the 13-foot- (4-m-) high Gothic Crucifix of the Black Christ. According to tradition, the devoted young Queen Jadwiga often prayed before the crucifix, and during these frequent hours of prayer Christ spoke to her several times. Queen Jadwiga was canonized as a saint in 1997. **CK**

"We wish to learn from [Saint Jadwiga] how to put that lesson [of love] into practice in our time."

Pope John Paul II, on the canonization of St. Jadwiga

Spas of Karlovy Vary

(Carlsbad, Czech Republic)

Famous spa town attracting visitors from all over Europe

Karlovy Vary is an attractive spa town, nestling within wooded hills at the confluence of two rivers—the Ohře and the warm Teplá. Hot mineral springs, thought by many to have medicinal properties, rise in the town and the twelve main springs have been harnessed to provide the town with its spas. The gracious public and private buildings of the resort were largely built during the eighteenth and nineteenth centuries, but Karlovy Vary was founded much earlier, in 1370, by King Charles IV. Karlovy Vary literally means "Charles's Spa"—the king allegedly discovered the springs while out hunting. Carlsbad is the English version of its German name, Karlsbad. The town and its springs attracted visitors from all over Europe for three centuries until its tourist trade was curtailed between 1582 and 1664 by a sequence of floods, fire, and war.

It experienced a revival, enjoying its heyday in the nineteenth century, during which its many visitors from all over Europe included Goethe, Beethoven, Karl Marx, Tsar Peter the Great, Bismarck, and Chopin. However, most of the permanent population of Karlovy Vary was German, and tensions arose after the Czech declaration of independence in 1918. By 1935 the German-speaking population of the region, who called themselves the Sudeten Germans, had formed political parties and movements that sympathized and collaborated with the Nazis. Adolf Hitler visited Karlovy Vary in 1938, during the Nazi occupation of the Sudetenlands. The Germans were expelled from the town when the Czechoslovakian state was restored at the end of the war.

Karlovy Vary today retains its Bohemian fairy-tale quality and attracts many visitors to its spas. It is frequently used as a film set—most recently for parts of the James Bond film *Casino Royale*. **EH**

> *"Visits of celebrities have . . . had an important impact on the cultural history of the city."*
>
> Dr. Stanislav Burachovič, historian

Mariánské Lázně

(Marienbad, Czech Republic)

Nineteenth-century spa town

The small spa town of Mariánske Lázně in the northwest Czech Republic was founded by Karel Kašpar Reitenberger, the abbot of the nearby Teplá Monastery, in the early nineteenth century. His friends, doctor Jan Nehr, architect Jiří Fischer, builder Anton Turner, and gardener Václav Skalník helped him turn a large area of unpromising marshland into a grand town with baths, Neoclassical pavilions, terraces, parks, a promenade, and a Baroque-style cast-iron colonnade to which the spring water is piped. A "singing fountain" in front of the colonnade plays music every two hours. Reitenberger was banished to Austria, accused of spending too much of the monastery's money on the project, before the success of the scheme became apparent. As its popularity grew, the town, which belonged to the monastery, became its most important source of income.

During the last years of the nineteenth century and the first part of the twentieth, Mariánske Lázně—then known as Marienbad—became one of the most fashionable places to be seen. The list of visitors is long and distinguished, including Tsar Nicholas II, Emperor Franz Joseph II, Goethe, Kafka, Edison, Mark Twain, Dvořák, Strauss, Nobel, Freud, Ibsen, Chopin, and Wagner. King Edward VII of Britain made nine visits, staying at the Weimar Hotel, and he opened the royal golf course just outside the town in 1905. The spring waters and treatments derived from them have been credited with curative properties for many disorders.

Mariánske Lázně is a gracious town surrounded by the beautiful wooded hills of the Slavkovský Forest. It remained popular with visitors between World War I and World War II but was inaccessible to foreign visitors during the communist era. Following the return of democracy in 1989, the town has been restored and once again attracts visitors. **EH**

Terezín Fortress

(Terezín, Czech Republic)

Fortress used as a Nazi concentration camp

Construction of a fortress to defend Prague from a potential Prussian invasion was begun in 1780, using a design by the military engineer General Karl Clemens, and it was completed ten years later. Named after the former empress Maria Theresa, Terezín was built in the style developed by the great French engineer Vauban, and was one of the last important bastion fortresses to be built in Europe. Unlike many other forts of a similar scale and type, Terezín is particularly well preserved.

Terezín was built with eight main bastions plus an earth rampart and a moat. The garrison consisted of 5,655 men, whose numbers could be doubled in times

> *"Terezín will always be linked to the disaster that befell the ... Jewish communities of Czechoslovakia."*
>
> Detlef Mühlberger, historian

of war. To house the garrison, and attendant warehouses, armories, and shops, a small town was built within the fortress walls, based on a classical grid system. From the 1880s it was used mainly as a prison.

The fortress achieved special notoriety during World War II, when it was taken over by the Nazis and used as a concentration camp under its Germanized name, Theresienstadt. Most of the inmates were Jews, who included many scholars, artists, and musicians. Parts were given over to lawns and flower beds, and concerts and exhibitions were held as a masquerade to deceive Red Cross inspectors that the inmates were being humanely treated. Theresienstadt was, in fact, primarily a holding camp: Of the 144,000 people sent there, 33,000 died in the camp, and another 88,000 were deported to extermination camps. **AG**

🏛 ◉ Karlův Most (Prague, Czech Republic)

Prague's most familiar monument

Karlův Most (Charles Bridge) was commissioned by Charles IV to replace Judith Bridge (constructed 1158–1172), a narrower construction that had been unable to withstand a flood in 1342. The cornerstone for the new bridge was laid in 1357. The architect was the German Peter Parler, who also designed St. Vitus's Cathedral. Two towers—one built in the Renaissance style dating from the sixteenth century, and the other late Gothic and dating from 1464—flank the entrance and offer good views along the bridge and over the many spires for which Prague is famous.

In the mid-seventeenth century, the bridge began its evolution from Gothic stone crossing to the enigmatic avenue of statues seen today. The Baroque statue of John of Nepomuk, erected in 1683, remains a somber depiction of the country's patron saint. Between the sixth and seventh pillars sits a cross that legend holds marks the place where St. John was thrown into the Vltava on the orders of King Wenceslas (Václav IV) of Bohemia in 1393. Eventually, all pillars were occupied—a total of thirty statues, mostly Baroque. During the twentieth century, the city has undertaken a gradual replacing of the flood-damaged Baroque statues with modern stone replicas. The originals now rest in the National Museum. All traffic is barred from the bridge to ensure its longevity.

Although damaged by a number of floods over the six and a half centuries it has stood, the bridge was, until 1741, the only crossing over the Vltava and remains a point of focus for visitors and residents of the medieval city of Prague. Perhaps most impressive after dark when street lamps light the way and the statues become silhouettes, Karlův Most is an important and inspiring centerpiece to Central Europe's finest medieval city. **AP**

🏛 ◉ Old Jewish Cemetery (Prague, Czech Republic)

Crowded and poignant reminder of the rich history of Jews in Prague

Prague had a thriving Jewish community from the twelfth century until the late nineteenth century, when a large section of the Jewish district was demolished by the municipal authorities to make way for new four-story Art Nouveau tenements intended to give Prague a more cosmopolitan appearance. The diminished Jewish population was then virtually eliminated by the Holocaust in World War II and only a few families lived here during the communist era. Since the democratic reforms of 1989, the Jewish population has grown, but there are probably no more than 2,000 Jews in Prague today.

The Old Jewish Cemetery is at the heart of the Josefov district, which had been the Jewish Quarter, north of the Old Town Square. In use from the mid-fifteenth century (the oldest tomb dates from 1439) until 1787, the walled cemetery, partially shaded by dark trees, is literally crammed with headstones with fading Hebrew inscriptions. The number of people buried here far exceeds the 12,000 or so headstones. As the area of the cemetery was fixed, earth was brought in and new graves were created on top of the existing layers. The older headstones are of sandstone and the newer stones are of white and pink marble, and they seem to tumble over one another like crystals in a cavern.

Among the sixteenth-century graves are those of Rabbi Löw, creator of the Golem legend, the mathematician David Gaus, and Mordechai Maisel, a Jewish mayor responsible for substantially extending the Jewish quarter. The cemetery is atmospheric and peaceful and stands as a poignant memorial to the thriving Jewish communities of earlier centuries.

The cemetery is open to the public every day, and is near Prague's five remaining synagogues and the Jewish Museum. **EH**

🏛️ ◈ **Prague Castle** (Prague, Czech Republic)

Hilltop complex that dominates the city of Prague

A castle in Prague was built by Prince Borivoj toward the end of the ninth century, comprising a simple rampart of clay and stones, surrounded by a moat. Over the years a series of additions would make Prague Castle the largest medieval fortified complex in Europe. The castle became the seat of government for the kingdom of Bohemia, and subsequently that of Czechoslovakia and the Czech Republic.

As well as the cathedral of St. Vitus and a convent, the castle grounds include the remains of the Romanesque royal palace from the twelfth century, rebuilt in the Gothic style two centuries later at the instigation of Charles IV. After the disruptions of the fifteenth-century Hussite Wars, a major rebuilding program was begun by Ladislaus II in 1485. The incorporation of Bohemia within the Hapsburg Empire saw further changes, especially during the reign of Rudolph II, who made the castle his primary residence during the latter part of the sixteenth century. Rebuilding took on a Renaissance character, with several new additions such as the Royal Gardens, the Spanish Hall, a shooting range, and a ball court. The depredations of the Thirty Years' War (1618–48) led to a decline in Prague's fortunes, and although there was some rebuilding during the eighteenth century, Prague became just a provincial city competing against the imperial splendor of Vienna.

During the twentieth century, the castle in Prague achieved a new prominence as a physical expression of Czech nationalism, especially after the foundation of the Czechoslovak Republic in 1918. Since the Velvet Revolution of 1989, Prague Castle has undergone a program of renovation, and is now being opened up to the public. There are several museums within the castle complex, including Rudolf II's collection of Czech and European art. **AG**

🏛 ◈ St. Vitus's Cathedral (Prague, Czech Republic)

Soaring cathedral inside Prague Castle

As the site of the coronation and interment of Bohemia's monarchs, the Cathedral of St. Vitus is not only the largest church in Prague, but also the most important. The origins of the cathedral go back to 925 when Duke Wenceslas I (Václav) built a church to house a holy relic—the Arm of St. Vitus—given him by the Holy Roman Emperor.

Although there was an expansion of the church in 1060, it was not until 1344 that work began on the great Gothic edifice we see today. The building was laid down in the French Gothic style by Matthias of Arras, but after his death in 1352 work continued under the supervision of the German architect Peter Parler and his family workshop. Parler was a great innovator, and the vaults in St. Vitus's ceiling are masterpieces of Gothic construction. Of particular interest is the chapel of St. Wenceslas, where the relics of the saint—who was martyred introducing Christianity to Bohemia—

are kept. The chapel is magnificently decorated with semiprecious stones and includes scenes from the Passion of Christ and St. Wenceslas's life.

Despite the efforts of Matthias and the Parlers, the cathedral was far from complete, however, and apart from some Renaissance and Baroque additions it remained in its unfinished state until the nineteenth century. In 1844, the Union for the Completion of the Cathedral of St. Vitus was formed with the aim of finishing the cathedral in Gothic style and removing non-Gothic decorations. The process was slow and it was not until 1929 that the cathedral was complete—nearly 600 years after work began.

Inside the cathedral are 22 side chapels, including the richly decorated Chapel of St. Wenceslas. The twentieth-century stained glass in the nave is also particularly striking. The chancel and crypt contain many royal tombs and sarcophagi. **AG**

Capuchin Church

(Brno, Czech Republic)

Baroque church with fascinating crypt

The Capuchin Church in Brno is famed for its crypt, which contains mummified bodies of the friars who lived and prayed in the monastery and church. It is also a glorious Baroque church.

The first Capuchin monastery was built in Brno in 1604, but the monks who inhabited it were forced out by the invading Swedish army. From 1648 to 1651 a new monastery was constructed. It conformed to the traditional design of Capuchin churches used across the world. Its exterior is plain and white, and its facade features a mosaic of St. Francis of Assisi. The interior is more ornate and typically Baroque, featuring an altar

> *"What we are, they once were; what they are, we will be."*
>
> **Inscription in crypt of Capuchin Church**

picture by the Dutchman Joachim Sandrat, and paintings added in the eighteenth century by the local artist Josef Rottr. In the mid-eighteenth century the church was partially rebuilt by Moric Grimm, who was later buried there.

In the underground crypt the atmospheric conditions allowed corpses to dry out and become mummified. More than 150 friars were buried here, as well as rich supporters and donors to the church. The crypt was used between 1658 and 1787, when the Emperor Joseph II forbade burials inside the walls of towns. There are now twenty-four mummified friars remaining in the crypt. They are laid out on the floor, fully clothed, with a few bricks behind their heads and their final facial expressions often visible; some hold religious objects. **JF**

Battlefield of Austerlitz

(Slavkov, Czech Republic)

Scene of Napoleon's great tactical victory

Fought in 1805 in open farmland between the towns of Slavkov (Austerlitz) and Brno in the former Austrian Empire, the Battle of Austerlitz was Napoleon's great tactical masterpiece. Napoleon's French army destroyed an allied army under the command of Tsar Alexander I of Russia and Francis II of Austria; the battle is also known as the Battle of the Three Emperors.

Having captured Vienna in the autumn of 1805, Napoleon advanced northward to take on a combined Russo-Austrian force on December 2. The French army was slightly outnumbered, and Napoleon's extended position seemed vulnerable. But Napoleon had foreseen this, and he deliberately weakened his right wing to encourage the allies to attack him there. The allies fell into his trap. While Marshall Davout's corps valiantly defended the French right from the main allied advance, Napoleon launched Marshall Soult's corps against the flank of the main allied attacking force, which fell back in disarray. Marshall Bernadotte's corps exploited the gap in the allied line while Marshalls Lannes and Murat on the French left flank pushed forward successfully. By nightfall the allied army had ceased to exist as a fighting entity, and the Austrians agreed to an unconditional surrender while the Russians fell back to their possessions in Poland.

Although the battlefield has suffered from road building and urban encroachment, much of the course of the engagement can be followed by military enthusiasts. In 1911 an unusual memorial chapel was built on the Pratzen plateau—scene of the counterattack against the allied flank led by Marshall Soult—its pyramidal steeple rising high above the chapel, which contains many bones found on the battlefield. On the anniversary of Austerlitz there are processions across the battlefield and various re-enactments of scenes from the battle. **AG**

Čachtice Castle

(Čachtice, Slovakia)

Castle ruins that were the site of many bloody murders

Čachtice Castle is located in the Carpathian Mountains in Slovakia. It was first constructed to act as a sentry post on the road to Moravia. It gained its present infamy as the home of Countess Elizabeth Báthory, who murdered numerous people in the castle and surrounding areas and became known as the Bloody Lady of Čachtice.

The castle was constructed in the Romanesque style for a local noble house of Hunt-Poznan. It later belonged to Matthew Csák III of Trenčín, a powerful local magnate. It was renovated in both the Gothic and Renaissance styles from the fifteenth to the seventeenth century. In 1575 it was given to Elizabeth Báthory as a wedding gift by her husband, Ferencz Nádasdy, who was a general.

While her husband was away campaigning, Elizabeth was in charge of running the estate at Čachtice. From 1585 Elizabeth began her series of tortures and murders. The initial victims were local peasant girls who were often employed at the castle, then daughters of nearby gentry families. The murders escalated after her husband's death, and she became involved with some accomplices. Their deeds eventually attracted official attention. In 1610 Emperor Matthias ordered an investigation and Elizabeth's crimes were uncovered. As a result of her noble status and family ties, Elizabeth was not executed but sentenced to house arrest. She died four years later in the castle on August 21, 1614. The estimate of the number of victims varies widely—from thirty-six to as many as 650. In 1708 Čachtice Castle was captured and plundered by Hungarian rebels from the army of Francis II Rákóczi, and it started to decay.

Čachtice Castle has now fallen into ruin, although it is a national reserve because the hill it is on contains many rare plants. **JF**

"You, Elizabeth . . . do not deserve to breathe the air on earth, nor to see the light of the Lord."

Count Thurzo, ordering house arrest for Elizabeth

🏛 ⬡ Fisherman's Bastion (Budapest, Hungary)

Important part of the urban development in the old Castle Hill quarter

> *"Fisherman's Bastion provides sweeping views of the seven bridges spanning the Danube."*
>
> Helena Bachmann, journalist

Fisherman's Bastion, or Halászbástya, is a viewing terrace that extends some 590 feet (180 m) along the eastern side of the old Castle Hill, providing magnificent views across the River Danube to the parliament buildings and the nineteenth-century Pest area of the city.

Comprising a series of walkways punctuated by seven stone towers, the structure has been described as "sugary," "fairy tale," and even "Disneyesque"—and not without reason. Neo-Gothic and neo-Romanesque in style, it was designed by Hungarian architect Frigyes Schulek, who was also responsible for the creative restoration and rebuilding of the nearby medieval Gothic Church of Our Blessed Lady (more commonly known as Matthias Church). The Bastion's sweeping stairways, paved terraces, and conical turrets, all carved from white limestone, were intended to showcase this newly restored ecclesiastical gem and complement its flamboyant style. The curious name (the Bastion is neither close to the water nor serves any defensive purpose) comes from the old castle walls that the modern terrace was built on—a stretch that was close to the medieval fish market and consequently defended by the Guild of Fishermen. The seven towers have their own historical meaning, too, and are said to represent the seven Hungarian tribes that settled in the vast plain known as the Carpathian Basin in 896.

A popular symbol of the city of Budapest that features on almost all its promotional literature, the Bastion is—as intended—a perfect place to stroll, sit, and take in the glorious river vista. By day there is a small charge levied on each staircase for access to the terraces; after dusk the view of the city lights is free. Budapest, including the banks of the Danube, the Buda Castle Quarter, and Andrássy Avenue, was inscribed on the World Heritage List in 1987. **JB**

Parliament Buildings (Budapest, Hungary)

The high dome defines the city skyline around one of Europe's oldest legislative buildings

When Hungarian craftsman and architect Imre Steindl won the national competition to design Budapest's new Országház, or parliament buildings, in 1882, his main intention was to "humbly and carefully" combine "splendid medieval style with national and personal features." The resulting Gothic Revival building, home to the National Assembly of Hungary, the offices of the prime minister, and the president of the Republic, is a triumph of Hungarian eclecticism. The buildings—which look not unlike London's Houses of Parliament—stand in the Lipót district on the banks of the River Danube. Carved from white limestone with needle-fine pinnacles, ninety stone statues of famous figures and military leaders, and a central cupola, the structure is a spectacular feature of the Pest side of the city, especially when viewed from Castle Hill on the river's distant shore.

The official entrance stair on Kossuth Square is flanked by a pair of magnificent lions and leads through the front door to the vast main staircase—considered to be one of Steindl's finest creations. Nearly 90 pounds (40 kg) of 23-karat gold and thousands of precious gems cover the building's interior, and the halls and chambers glister with honeyed opulence. There are many fine frescoes and paintings, stained-glass artworks, tapestries, and statues throughout, as well as small, considered touches—most notably the numbered ashtrays in the corridor of the Delegation Room where the deputies left their cigars while voting in the council chamber.

The parliament buildings were under construction for seventeen years, and toward the end of that time Steindl was so ill he had to be carried on-site in a chair to direct the work. He lived until the buildings' completion but unfortunately was blind by this time. Visitors can view his bearded bronze bust in a niche on the main staircase. **JB**

> *"The building was self-consciously intended to be one of the world's great houses of Parliament."*
>
> Frommer's Review

Early Christian Necropolis

(Pécs, Hungary)

Many of these early Christian tombs have survived centuries of turbulent history

In the fourth century, Pécs was a Roman town known as Sopianae, whose inhabitants buried their dead in a nearby cemetery or "necropolis." Today this ancient Christian burial site is a popular tourist attraction and protected by UNESCO as part of its World Heritage List. The tombs themselves are in underground chambers; on the ground above these chambers some memorials to the dead still remain.

By the fourth century, Christians were no longer persecuted by Rome. The Emperor Constantine had converted to Christianity and the Edict of Milan in 312 C.E. led to a flowering of this new religion. The emperor's conversion meant that those who would have been persecuted for their beliefs by previous rulers were promoted to the highest ranks of society. Christianity spread throughout the Roman Empire and Sopianae became one of the most important centers in the early Christian world.

For many centuries, the ancient tombs of modern-day Pécs lay undisturbed; this was to change with the arrival of archeologists in the eighteenth century, and the work they began has continued to the present day. Hundreds of tombs have been found, as well as a number of burial chambers. The necropolis is remarkably well preserved, its tombs still resplendent with murals. The paintings depict biblical stories, scenes from everyday life, and images of contemporary Christian rituals. They are a rich source of information about the earliest days of Christianity. Many of the tombs lie beneath the stunning Basilica of St. Peter, parts of which date back to the eleventh century. This elegant, ornate church with its four tapering steeples continues the tradition of a Christian place of worship on this site—a site that also exhibits signs of human occupation stretching back several millennia before the birth of Christ. **LH**

". . . sepulchral art and architecture of the Roman provinces is . . . fully illustrated by Sopianae cemetery."

UNESCO

Putna Monastery

(Bukovina, Romania)

Religious site inspired by Prince Stephen

Prince Stephen the Great, ruler of Moldavia from 1457 until 1504, took just three years to build the Romanian Orthodox Putna Monastery on land bordering the Putna River in Bukovina. As well as its importance as a religious site, Bukovina was a key medieval cultural and artistic center with a scriptorium, trilingual (Greek-Slavonic-Romanian) schools, and several craft workshops. Prince Stephen was instrumental in the building and style of a number of churches and monasteries across Moldavia, many of them dedicated to him, but it was at Putna Monastery where he was laid to rest. His tomb has remained a site of pilgrimage to the current day.

A cross marks the hilltop site where he fired an arrow, and the spot where it landed determined the site of the monastery. A section of tree trunk containing the arrow hole is kept in the museum. Within a few years of completion, a fierce fire destroyed most of the church, Stephen's home, and much of the site's outer walls. The church was rebuilt and subsequently demolished again by both fire and earthquake. The present church was completed in 1761 and exhibits many architectural and decorative features of that period.

Putna Monastery museum contains a valuable collection of embroideries dating back to the time of Stephen the Great, including a rich collection of priests' clothes and shawls, iconostasis curtains, and coverings. There are examples of decorated religious texts, most notably the sumptuous *Four Gospels* and items typical of those made in the highly skilled workshops of the embroiderers, weavers, icon makers, miniature painters, wood carvers, silversmiths, bookbinders, and sculptors. Putna Monastery represents a period of remarkable economic, social, and political progress in the history of Romania. **LH**

Black Church

(Brasov, Romania)

Largest Gothic monument in Romania

In 1384 building work on the Black Church was begun by the German community who lived in the city of Brasov. Originally a Roman Catholic cathedral, the church was converted to Lutheranism in the sixteenth century by the great Transylvanian reformer Johannes Honter. It was partially destroyed by fire in 1689 when Hapsburg forces invaded the city during the Great Turkish War; the walls became charred and blackened due to smoke damage, and thereafter the church was known as the Black Church.

The bell tower is 123 feet (37 m) high and houses one bell weighing 6 tons, the biggest bell in Romania.

> *"Now the time has come in which the Lord will awaken a new people unto himself."*
>
> Johannes Honter, on the Reformation in Transylvania

The impressive organ was finished in 1839, has 4,000 pipes, and is still played at concerts and at the Lutheran services that are regularly held here. The Black Church measures nearly 290 feet (88 m) in length and has three naves of equal height. Special attention should be given to the oak door of the southern portal, which bears the date 1477; the locally crafted bronze font, which was donated in 1472; and the wall painting in the southern entrance area, painted in 1476. The old pews in the side naves are a splendid example of Baroque wood carving and date from the first half of the eighteenth century. Possibly the most valuable treasure, though, is the Black Church collection of Anatolian carpets, protected from the sun's ultraviolet rays by the installation of special glass in the high windows that let in the natural sunlight. **LH**

Dracula's Castle (Bran, Romania)

The unique architecture is a perfect backdrop for the myth associated with the fortress

Sometimes fact and fiction become so closely intertwined that it is hard to separate them. The castle at Bran is a case in point. It is now popularly known as Dracula's Castle, in the same way that Sherwood Forest is popularly regarded as the home of Robin Hood, even though the connections between the site and the character are highly dubious.

The evil vampire of the movies originates from a novel by Irish writer Bram Stoker. Written in 1897, his *Dracula* was inspired by a genuine, historical figure—Vlad Țepeș (*d.* 1476), better known as Vlad the Impaler. Vlad also used the name Dracula (Son of Dracul), because his father was Vlad Dracul. Vlad was a suitably bloodthirsty model for the fictional character, but his links with the castle are tenuous at best. He may briefly have been a guest there; he may even have been imprisoned there, though it is equally possible that he never set foot in the place. None of these uncertainties

discourages the tourists or the souvenir sellers, who find the castle's imposing appearance an admirable setting for the creepy legend.

The origins of Bran Castle itself are uncertain. Some historians believe that it was built in the early thirteenth century by the Teutonic Knights (a military and religious order), but there is no documentary record of the structure before 1377, when it was identified as part of the border defenses between Wallachia and Transylvania. The castle has had several owners over the centuries, among them Mircea the Wise, Vlad's grandfather. In the 1920s it was the favorite home of Marie, the British-born Queen of Romania, and it remained in royal hands until 1948, when it was confiscated by the communist authorities. For many years the castle was used as a museum and attracted a continuous stream of visitors but, in 2006, it was returned to Marie's heirs. **IZ**

Peleş Castle (Sinaia, Romania)

Built as a summer residence by Carol I, the castle is his final resting place

Born at Sigmaringen, south of present-day Germany, Carol I became the first king of the newly formed kingdom of Romania in 1881. Under the rule of the communist Ceausescu regime, the whole area was closed and the beautiful castle was rarely used. After the December 1989 Revolution when Ceausescu was overthrown, Peleş Castle was reopened for tourists with many of its spectacular rooms and valuable collections made accessible to the public.

Set in the superb Carpathian Mountains amid breathtaking scenery and small-scale farming, the castle is built of wood, stone, bricks, and marble in the German neo-Renaissance style. German architect Wilhem Dodere, and later Czech architect Karel Liman, designed a royal palace with more than 160 rooms, fairy-tale turrets, and pointed spires. A separate building houses the electrical power plant that enabled Peleş Castle to be the first European castle entirely lit by electricity, and it was also the first to have central heating. The Peleş brook, from which the castle takes its name, passes through the courtyard, which also has a fountain. The interior holds two armories, a collection of almost 2,000 paintings, rich stained-glass windows, Murano crystal chandeliers, gold and silver plates, Meissen and Sèvres porcelain, and ebony and ivory sculptures. Peleş is surrounded by seven terraces with statues by the Italian artist, Romanelli, stone wells, vases, and Carrara marble. There are many rooms of note with some, such as the Florentine Room and the Turkish Room, being quite outstanding.

The Romanian authorities have recently returned Peleş Castle to the former king of Romania, King Michael, the last living European leader who was in power during World War II. And so this remarkable and romantic castle once more belongs to the Romanian monarchy. **LH**

Snagov Monastery, Church, and Palace

(Ilfov, Romania)

Legendary burial site of Vlad the Impaler but archeologists have failed to find his remains

> *"It was like a miracle, . . . the whole body crumbled into dust and passed from our sight."*

Bram Stoker, *Dracula* (1897)

Snagov Monastery is built on an islet in Snagov Lake, some 25 miles (40 km) north of Bucharest, and the structure dates back to medieval times. The first written record of Snagov is documented in 1408 in the Court Charter issued during the reign of Mircea cel Batran. During this reign, the first buildings were erected and porches from this era can be seen in the museum. The present church was built in the early sixteenth century when Neagoe Basarab was Prince of Wallachia, with further development undertaken when Constantin Brancoveanu came to the throne in 1688.

Built of stone and brick, Snagov Monastery was surrounded by defense walls and a lookout tower, which doubled as a bell tower. The monastery was rebuilt in 1521 and the tower remains intact, together with a church and the ruins of some of the cells. Tools and pottery from the Bronze and Iron Ages have been found at the site, as have Roman and Byzantine coins indicating that this small island had been inhabited long before the monastery was built. The church was painted in 1563 by Dobromir the Young, and the paintings are considered to be among the greatest examples of mural painting in Romania. Snagov Monastery is closely associated with Prince Vlad the Impaler, son of Vlad Dracul and the inspiration for Bram Stoker's novel *Dracula*. Vlad the Impaler was mysteriously killed in a battle in 1476, and legend says that his head was sent to the sultan as a gift and that his decapitated body was subsequently buried near the altar inside the monastery church.

More recently, the magnificent Snagov Palace was used as one of the residences enjoyed by Nikolae and Elena Ceausescu during their rule of Romania. Notorious for their extravagant lifestyle, the Ceausescus amassed a huge collection of gifts, including many paintings. **LH**

Mogosoaia Palace

(Lake Mogosoaia, Romania)

Fine example of native Romanian design

Situated a little more than 6 miles (10 km) from the Romanian capital, Bucharest, this architectural monument joins its Renaissance, Romanian, Byzantine, and Baroque features to form a unique and stately whole. Mogosoaia Palace was built for Constantin Brâncoveanu, who was Prince of Wallachia (present-day southern Romania) from 1689 to 1714. He was also a great patron of the arts. Constantin acquired the land for the site of the palace in 1681, and began building there from 1698. The magnificent structure was completed four years later. The prince was able to enjoy his palace for only a few years, though, because in 1714 he was imprisoned by the Ottomans in Istanbul, and then tortured and executed.

One facade of the palace features traditional Romanian staircase balconies and has a columned arcade surrounding the central courtyard. On the facade overlooking Lake Mogosoaia is a loggia (columned gallery open to the air on one side) fashioned in the Venetian style. In 1912, the palace was given to the great Romanian writer and socialite Marthe Bibesco by her husband, Prince George III Valentin Bibesco. In the 1920s Marthe restored the palace and wrote many of her well-known novels there. The palace soon became an important social hub and she received numerous visitors from European high society. However, Marthe left Romania in 1945 and Mogosoaia Palace was seized by the communist authorities in 1948.

The palace building and its beautiful landscaped grounds are now open to the public. The palace itself houses the Brancovenesc Museum, which exhibits paintings, sculptures, and rare books and manuscripts. Furthermore it reflects Romania's rich cultural heritage, expressed in the unique "Brancovenesc" style of design. **JF**

Histria Archeological Site (near Constanta, Romania)

Ancient settlement, rich in treasures

Sometimes known as the Romanian Pompeii, Histria stands on the shores of Lake Sinoe. Originally a port, this important fortress enclosing some 86 acres (35 ha) has Greek, Roman, and Byzantine connections. The first Greek colonists arrived in 657 B.C.E. and their skill at working with metals, glass, and ceramics brought prosperity. The harbor gradually became sand locked, causing it to be abandoned in the seventh century B.C.E. and it was not discovered for another 1,400 years, with archeological work beginning in 1914.

Artifacts have been found that reflect the turbulent history of the site, which included numerous

> *"Eight decades of archeological research led to the accumulation of a huge amount of data."*
>
> Alexandru Suceveanu, archeologist

barbarian attacks, two Roman invasions, and rule by the Dacian King Burebista, who was assassinated in 44 B.C.E. There are several exposed areas of the walls that enclosed this large city, and mosaics and paved roads where visitors can walk freely. As well as two Roman baths, there are the remains of a limestone Greek temple. There are also eight basilicas, including a Christian basilica built with stones from the old theater in the sixth century C.E. In addition to the religious and civil ruins, the living, trade, and workshop areas can also be identified. On display at the museum are Greek amphorae, Latin inscriptions, jewelry, tools, and guns. The earliest documented currency in Romania was the 0.28 ounce (8 g) silver drachma, issued in Histria in 480 B.C.E., contributing to Histria's claim to be the oldest settlement in Romania. **LH**

🏛️ 🔷 Madara Rider (near Madara, Bulgaria)

Loved by all Bulgarians, the Madara Rider has become an evocative symbol of the country

Sited high on a cliff face in the Madara Plateau of northeastern Bulgaria, the Madara Rider is a unique and exceptional bas-relief carving depicting a life-size horseman spearing a lion. The lion is being trampled by the horse and a dog is trailing behind. On both sides of the carving are Greek inscriptions that express the early history of the Bulgarian state and the reigns of three famous Khans. These constitute some of the earliest surviving written words on Bulgarian history.

In 681 the nomadic tribe of the Bulgars was victorious in a battle against Byzantium. In alliance with the local Slavs they established the Bulgarian state and it was formally recognized by the Byzantine Empire. The iconic Madara Rider was carved around thirty years later in celebration. Khan Tervel was chosen as the ruler of the new state, and some scholars believe that the horseman is intended to be a portrait of this victorious leader. Madara continued to serve as a major site of pagan worship during the First Bulgarian State and, in addition to the Rider, visitors can also visit caves at the foot of the cliffs where religious practices occurred. At a height of 246 feet (75 m) above ground, the inaccessibility of the site makes the resulting carving all the more extraordinary. The realism of the scene by the unknown sculptor is also remarkable for the period. Including the inscription, the work covers an area of 1,400 square feet (130 sq m) on an almost vertical 328-foot- (100-m-) high cliff face.

This sacred monument to victory survives as a dynamic and timeless tribute to the early Bulgarians and has no parallel in European cultural history. Yet despite existing for more than 2,000 years, the future of the Madara Rider is now severely threatened by its relentless exposure to the natural elements and by local earth tremors. **KB**

Aleksander Nevski Church (Sofia, Bulgaria)

A monument to the troops who sacrificed their lives to the liberation of Bulgaria

Between 1877 and 1878, some 200,000 Russian troops were killed while fighting to liberate Bulgaria from its Turkish occupiers; this neo-Byzantine church in the heart of Sofia is dedicated to their memory. The saint from whom the church takes its name was aptly chosen, as Aleksander Nevski is the patron saint of Russian regiments and tsars. Nevski was a thirteenth-century Russian general whose acumen and bravery saved his troops from fierce Scandinavian hordes in a battle *c.* 1240.

Today, Aleksander Nevski Church sits at the center of a bustling square, around which a continual frenzied din of traffic hurls itself over the cobbled roads. In the nearby park is a lively market at which stallholders peddle an assortment of goods from nineteenth-century coins to twentieth-century Russian helmets and twenty-first-century paintings. In the midst of all this mayhem, the church remains an oasis of peace.

Behind the ornate exterior, the church's crypt houses a rich collection of icons, which span a millennium of history; the oldest dates back to the ninth century.

The church's foundations were begun in the nineteenth century but the magnificent building was not completed until 1912. Lavish building materials used in the church's construction were sourced from all over the world and include African alabaster, Italian marble, and Brazilian onyx; atop these are splendid copper and gilded domes that sparkle invitingly in the sun. The outside of the church is a masterpiece of Byzantine excess, hiding a slightly disappointing interior. The church has three altars: one dedicated to St. Aleksander Nevski; one to St. Methodius and St. Cyril, who are credited with inventing the Cyrillic alphabet; and one to St. Boris, without whom this church would never have been built—he introduced Christianity to Bulgaria in the ninth century. **LH**

🏛 ⬡ Tomb of Kazanlak (Kazanlak, Bulgaria)

The outstanding murals are masterpieces of Hellenistic art

Dating from the fourth century B.C.E., this ancient tomb is probably that of an important chieftain of the Odrysae—a tribe that occupied the southern part of the ancient Thracian territory in what is now central Bulgaria—and it is located only 5 miles (8 km) from the Thracian capital of Seuthopolis. The site was discovered by chance and was not excavated until 1944. The tomb is a *tholos*—also known as a beehive tomb because of its resemblance to a traditional tapered dome beehive—and it is likely to have been inspired by the earlier Mycenean *tholos* tombs on the Greek mainland, of which the so-called Treasury of Atreus at Mycenae itself is the best-known example.

The Thracian Tomb is on a much smaller scale, however, with the main burial chamber only 10.5 feet (3.2 m) high, compared with the Treasury of Atreus, which reaches 42.6 feet (13 m) at its highest point. As with the other Thracian *tholoi* in the area, this well-preserved tomb is divided into three main areas—an antechamber, a main burial chamber, and a corridor connecting the two—but it is unique for the incredibly detailed murals that cover the walls of all three sections, depicting geometric patterns, battles, prancing horses, and a touching farewell banquet for a dead man and his wife. As well as their beauty, these murals are celebrated for their near-pristine condition and are regarded as some of the best-preserved artworks from the Hellenistic world.

Such is the importance of the treasured murals that the entire tomb is housed within a protective enclosure with entry restricted to scholars who can show a specific need to study the murals themselves. Most visitors experience the tomb through an exact replica that has been constructed nearby. The tomb was designated a UNESCO World Heritage site in 1979. **AS**

🏛 ◉ Rila Monastery (Rila Mountains, Bulgaria)

The monastery has survived years of foreign occupation and intervention

Flanked by rivers amid spectacular mountain scenery, Rila Monastery, fortresslike from the outside, is clearly an impressive place. Its history lives up to its appearance. The monastery's eventful existence began with Ivan Rilski, who was the leader of a monastic colony of hermits. He was famous for having healing powers and his bones later became much in demand among medieval rulers—the bones were moved in 1183 to Esztergom, until eventually, after both Byzantine and Bulgarian interventions, they were returned to the monastery in 1469. The buildings themselves have had no less of an adventurous time, being regularly sacked and rebuilt.

The current buildings date from the 1830s, a period of strong national revival. Once inside the forbidding walls, the visitor is likely to be amazed by the charm and the size of the structure. The magnificent Nativity church is the largest monastic

church in Bulgaria and the irregular-shaped courtyard is bounded by four levels of delightfully striped and checkered colonnaded balconies. Higgledy-piggledy, red-tiled roofs and scattered domes add to the overall impression. There is more to the place than charm, however. The museum contains the remarkable Rila Cross, a double-sided crucifix carved by Brother Raphael between 1790 and 1802. The main church is covered with dramatic and colorful frescoes, graphically depicting the different fates awaiting the saved and the sinners.

Proclaimed as a national museum in 1961 by the Bulgarian government and included on UNESCO's list of World Heritage sites in 1983, Rila Monastery nonetheless remains a working monastery where guests may stay in sparsely furnished "guest cells." The abbot is determined that it remain the place of pilgrimage it has been for more than 1,000 years. **AED**

Temple-Sanctuary of the Great Gods (Samothráki, Greece)

Temple to the gods, open to all

The earliest stages of this temple complex—one of the principal pan-Hellenic sanctuaries, built to honor a variety of gods—were created by the ancient Greeks around the seventh century B.C.E.

The temple-sanctuary was the center of the powerful, influential, sacred cult. The cult, its rituals, and the specific gods involved were shrouded in mystery—adherents were forbidden to utter the deities' names. Details are still unclear today, but a "great mother" figure was at the heart of the cult. What was unusual for the time was that the cult seems to have been open to everyone. The main buildings to be seen today include a large rotunda, an open court famed for its frieze of dancing figures, and the Hiéron, a splendid structure with a beautifully decorated facade, where the most sacred rites seem to have been performed.

The complex thrived during the times of the Macedonian kings; this was reputed to be where Philip II met his future wife Olympias. The Romans then seized the island and kept the cult alive until it faded in medieval times, with some revived interest in its mysteries in the 1600s and 1700s. By this time the island was ruled by the Turks, until it came under Greek rule after World War I. Organized archeological work began in the 1800s, when the famous third- or second-century B.C.E. statue known as the "Winged Victory of Samothrace" was unearthed at the site. **AK**

"Philip, . . . initiated into the mysteries of Samothrace at the same time with Olympias, fell in love with her."

Plutarch, *Life of Alexander* (79 C.E.)

Achilleion Palace (Gatsouri, Corfu, Greece)

Homage to ancient Greece

Built near the town of Gatsouri, 6 miles (10km) southwest of Corfu city, the Achilleion Palace was commissioned by Elizabeth, Empress of Austria. The empress was an extraordinarily independent woman who spent much of her adult life traveling through Europe. She studied the classics and became fluent in modern Greek. Her life was marred by tragedy, including the suicide of her only son, Crown Prince Rudolf of Austria, in 1889. Shortly after his death, Elizabeth began planning to build a palace on her beloved Corfu. The palace became her summer refuge and was designed with the Greek hero Achilles as its primary theme. It is a sumptously classical structure full of sculptures and paintings modeled on ancient Greek mythology and set within lavish gardens. Elizabeth visited the magnificent palace often until her assassination in Geneva in 1898.

In 1907 the German kaiser Wilhelm II bought the palace and made several changes to the building and gardens. During World War I it was used as a military hospital and was then handed over to the Greeks, who used it as a government building. During World War II, it served as a military headquarters.

The palace has been greatly restored and is sometimes used in a diplomatic capacity for European Summit meetings. It is an important and compelling building and is a significant component of "modern" Greek culture and history. **TP**

"O swallow lend me your wings,
Take me along to far-off fields; …
gladly would I loose my chains."

Poem written by Elizabeth of Austria (1854)

🏛 ◉ Meteora Monasteries (Kalambaka, Greece)

Fourteenth-century clifftop monasteries, keeping alive the Greek Orthodox tradition

> *"In a region of almost inaccessible sandstone peaks, monks settled on these 'columns of the sky'."*

UNESCO

⬆ Monastic cells at the Megalo Meteoro. This monastery is built on the highest outcrop of all those at Meteora.

➡ The Monastery of Agios Nikolaos Anapafsa was founded in the fourteenth century.

In the northwest of Thessaly, fertile plains spread into the hazy blue distance, with the eastern Pindus Mountains in the background and the great Pinios River cutting a swath. In the foothills of the mountains there is an extraordinary landscape of craggy, gray rock pinnacles soaring up into the sky like a stone forest. It is here, in these remote rock towers, that the Meteora Monasteries can be found.

Monks first came to inhabit the naturally formed caves within the rocks in the ninth century, but it was not until the fourteenth century that construction began on the monasteries themselves. At this time the Byzantine empire was starting to fade and the opposing Turks were repeatedly attacking monastic communities. Seeking isolation and safety, a group of monks established a small community in the rock towers near Kalambaka. Around 1356 a gift from the Serbian emperor Symeon Uros allowed them to build the Church of the Transfiguration there. Over the years more buildings were added, the complex becoming known as Megalo Meteoro, or Grand Meteoro, and developing into the richest and most powerful of the monasteries. The community eventually encompassed twenty-four monasteries, which were reached by suspended rope nets and retractable wooden ladders. Each monastery was independent, with its own wealth and crops or herds of sheep and goats. Through these monasteries, Hellenic traditions were perpetrated during the Turkish occupation of Greece and saved from being consumed by the Ottoman Empire and lost forever.

There are six monasteries at Kalambaka (one is a nunnery) that are open to the public, and a further one that has been restored recently. They are full of artwork and artifacts, and are still occupied by a few monks and nuns who preserve the ancient culture and traditions of Orthodox life. **TP**

🏛 ◉ Tomb of Philip of Macedon (Vergina, Greece)

Family tomb of Macedonian royal family, dating from the third century B.C.E.

The small farming village of Vergina in northern Greece is at first largely unremarkable, but it is just outside here, in the foothills of Mount Pieria, that an amazing archeological find was made in 1977.

The area surrounding Vergina was the site of the ancient royal capital city of Macedon, Aigai, and had been inhabited since the Bronze Age. It flourished for centuries and became the seat of the wealthy Macedonian kings. In 1977 the Greek archeologist Manolis Andronikos discovered a number of tombs and, in particular, an impressive tumuli believed to contain the remains of the great Macedonian king Philip II, father of Alexander the Great. Within the two-chambered tomb was a golden chest bearing the emblem of the Macedonian royal family and containing the skeleton of a man. In the adjacent chamber were the remains of a female figure in a similar chest. Further excavations revealed another tomb of similar state thought to be that of Alexander IV of Macedon, Alexander the Great's son. Dating of the first tomb to 317 B.C.E., however, has shed some doubt on the identification of Philip II, and the remains are now believed to be those of Philip III, the bastard son of Philip II.

Despite the controversy, nothing can detract from the enormous importance of this find, added to which the tomb contains numerous artifacts and exquisite wall paintings in brilliant colors that shed light on Greek painting techniques.

The excavations at this site, and the continued finds in the area, are some of the most important of modern times. The site represents an exceptional testimony to a significant development in European civilization, at the transition from classical city-state to the imperial structure of the Hellenistic and Roman periods. In respect of this, the site was designated a UNESCO World Heritage site in 1996. **TP**

"Of the Greeks, some were well disposed to the Macedonians, others remained neutral."

Diodorus Siculus, historian

⚲ ◈ Sanctuary of Athena Pronaea (Delphi, Greece)

Dedicated to the Greek goddess of wisdom and protector of the city of Athens

Athena's temple-sanctuary sits on a terrace overlooking breathtaking mountain views. Evidence suggests that the first temple to Athena—the Greek goddess of wisdom and protector of the city of Athens—was built here in the seventh century B.C.E. When this was destroyed, a second temple was constructed nearby, during the fourth century. There is a tradition that in 480 B.C.E., when the Persians who were attacking Delphi reached the sanctuary, a great storm arose and dreadful cries emanated from the temple, sending the attackers into a terrified retreat.

Today's remains provide one of ancient Delphi's most distinctive sights, thanks to the striking and elegant fourth-century building known as the *tholos* (circular building). The architect of the *tholos*, Theodorus, who wrote a treatise on its design, created an elegant structure of multicolored marble and limestone that blended several styles of Greek classical architecture. The *tholos* stood on a three-stepped podium, with an outer formation of twenty graceful Doric columns supporting a frieze decorated with relief sculpture. Inside were ten Corinthian columns and a coffered ceiling. The roof may have been conical in shape, but details of its structure are contentious. The purpose of this building remains puzzling, though it may have been built simply to house an impressive statue of the goddess herself.

An inhabited village stood on the site of the Delphic remains until the late nineteenth century, when some of the buildings on Athena's terrace were still being used as village houses. This village was moved in the 1890s to make way for major excavations. The most distinctive of the remains of the *tholos* that can be seen today—three outer columns, topped by their entablature—were re-erected and restored in 1938. UNESCO added Delphi to its World Heritage List in 1987. **AK**

"Two crags split off from Mount Parnassus ... crushing vast numbers beneath their weight"

Herodotus, describing the Persian defeat at Delphi

Sanctuary of Apollo

(Delphi, Greece)

Temple at the heart of ancient Greece, dedicated to the revered Delphic oracle Apollo

Apollo's temple-sanctuary complex, in its stunning mountainous setting, is part of the ancient site of Delphi. The sanctuary is one of the four major pan-Hellenic sanctuaries, and the temple represents the heart of ancient Greece—indeed, the Greeks believed that it marked the center of the world. Greek legend relates how two eagles, released from the west and east by the great god Zeus, both flew to the point that would become Delphi. A stone called the *omphalos* (navel) marked the spot and became the centerpiece of a temple to Apollo, the handsome, virile, all-powerful Greek god. An eternal flame burned within the temple and the site became the ancient world's most widely revered oracle, where leaders of Greece's perennially warring city-states came to seek Apollo's advice on momentous decisions.

What remains of Apollo's temple today are foundations, columns, and steps dating from a fourth-century B.C.E. version of the building. The first major temple seems to have been built in the seventh century B.C.E. and burned down in 548 B.C.E.; a second, built in the second half of the sixth century B.C.E., was destroyed in 373 B.C.E. The sanctuary area was a walled rectangular space through which passed the Sacred Way—a path lined with monuments dedicated to Apollo that zigzags its way uphill to the temple. This was a Doric-style building fronted by an impressive altar. At the back of the temple was a small space where the oracle itself was supposedly located.

The ancient Romans captured Delphi in the second century B.C.E. and many of its treasures were looted over the following years. By the end of the fourth century C.E., the rise of Christianity had resulted in the Romans closing Delphi as a religious site and it lay neglected until major excavation work started in the 1890s. It became a World Heritage site in 1987. **AK**

> *"A wall of wood alone shall be uncaptured, a boon to you and your children."*

The Oracle's prophecy that navies would defeat Persia

Bodonitsa Castle

(Mendhenítsa, Greece)

Stronghold defending Pass of Thermopylae

Despite their long and turbulent past and even in their crumbled state, the tumbled ruins of Bodonitsa Castle are still a commanding sight. The castle is partway up the slopes of Mount Kallidromos with sweeping views down through the Pass of Thermopylae, over the village of Mendhenítsa, and for many miles beyond.

The history of the castle dates back to around 1204 when the crusader king of Thessalonika (Boniface of Montferrat) ceded the Bodonitsa region as a fief to Guy Pallavicini, the first margrave of Bodonitsa, shortly after the sacking of Constantinople in 1203–04. Pallavicini was then charged with guarding the strategically important Pass of Thermopylae and, in doing so, protecting Montferrat's territories in Macedonia and Thessaly.

Pallavicini built the castle soon afterward, choosing his location carefully and superbly. The castle overlooks the pass and the land beyond, making it ideal for its strongly defensive role. In 1224, when the Despot of Epirus, Theodore I Komnenos Doukas, conquered Thessalonica, Pallavicini managed to hold out against the assault, and the castle became one of the few strongholds to survive the fall of its capital city and helped prevent Theodore from moving farther south. The marquisate of Bodonitsa went on to flourish during the latter half of the fourteenth century. In 1410, however, the Ottomans attacked the castle, killing the marquis and taking control of the building and area, although the castle was returned to the Italians in 1416 as part of an agreement between the Ottomans and Venice.

Bodonitsa Castle is still an imposing structure today, and it takes only a little imagination to hear the ancient battle cries and clashing of arms drifting up through the Pass of Thermopylae and around the old castle's walls. **TP**

Battlefield of Marathon

(Marathon, Greece)

Site of Athenian victory in the Persian Wars

In 490 B.C.E. the Persian emperor Darius the Great sent an expeditionary force against the Greek city-state of Athens to punish it for supporting the recent Ionian revolt against Persian rule. Between twenty and twenty-five thousand Persian soldiers landed on the beaches of Marathon—just to the north of Athens—in preparation for a march against the city.

An Athenian-led force of around ten thousand infantry marched swiftly to the plain around Marathon. Clearly outnumbered, the Greeks debated their best course of action. One group wanted to wait for Spartan reinforcements; another, led by the Athenian

> *"So, when Persia was dust, all cried, 'To Acropolis!/Run, Pheidippides, one race more!"*
>
> Robert Browning, *Pheidippides* (1879)

general Miltiades, argued for an immediate attack. Miltiades won the argument and led the assault on the Persians. Once they joined the battle, the Greek center wavered in the face of Persian spears and arrows, but the Greeks overwhelmed the enemy line on both flanks, causing disorganization among the Persians, who feared being surrounded. The Persians retreated from the Greek mainland, and although a larger Persian invasion took place in 480 B.C.E., the Greeks had demonstrated their fighting superiority.

As a postscript to the battle of Marathon, a legend grew up that a Greek runner called Pheidippides ran from the battlefield to give the citizens of Athens news of their victory—the distance between the two places being the basis for the modern marathon race, now set at 26.2 miles (42.2 km). **AG**

1896 Olympic Stadium

(Athens, Greece)

The stadium that hosted the 1896 Olympics, built on the site of the ancient Panathinaiko Stadium

One of the world's most historic and ancient cities, Athens is home to two Olympic stadiums. It is a city that has embraced the new and the old alike, and within its glittering midst rise ancient classical monuments alongside shining, modern buildings.

The first documented evidence of the Olympic Games dates back to 776 B.C.E., though they had probably been in existence for many years before that. The games were held every four years until they were abolished by either Emperor Theodosius I, in 394 C.E., or by his grandson Theodosius II, in 435 C.E., on the grounds of paganism. The games were revived in 1896 and the site of the classical Panathinaiko Stadium in Athens, which seated 50,000 spectators, was the location chosen for the new stadium.

Begun in 566 B.C.E., this stadium, built from white marble, had been the scene of the Panathenaic Games, which were modeled on the Olympics. The site was excavated in 1870, and in 1895 the new stadium was built. The massive project was financed by George Averoff and built by the architects Anastasios Metaxas and Ernst Ziller. It followed the layout of the ancient stadium closely, but seated 80,000 people. Although the 1896 Summer Olympics were a success despite a lack of adequate financing, the games would not return to their country of origin until the summer of 2004, when they were again a great success and for which another new stadium was built. The 1896 stadium, however, was the venue for the archery competition during the 2004 Olympics, and is today being used for other sporting events and functions. The 1896 Olympic stadium, built on the site of the ancient Panathinaiko Stadium (also known as Kallimarmaron) is an important historical building, which acts as a bridge between the ancient past of the city of Athens and its modern reincarnation. **TP**

> *""The Olympic Games, with the ancient [Greeks], controlled athletics and promoted peace."*
>
> Baron de Coubertin, founder of modern Olympics

Arch of Hadrian

(Athens, Greece)

En route to the Temple of Olympian Zeus

The monumental Arch of Hadrian in Athens was built across a road leading from the center of the city to a complex of buildings to the southeast of the Acropolis that includes the Temple of Olympian Zeus. The occasion of its construction is uncertain, but may have been the visit of the Emperor Hadrian to Athens to mark the completion of the temple in 131 or 132 C.E.

Construction of the temple began originally c. 515 B.C.E. under the Tyrant of Athens, Peisistratus, but was soon abandoned. Building recommenced under the Hellenistic king Antiochus IV Epiphanes in the third century B.C.E., but the temple was not completed until the second century C.E. by Hadrian. It was the largest temple in the Hellenistic and Roman worlds, measuring 315 x 131 feet (96 x 40 m) with its two levels reaching a height of 59 feet (18 m). In 86 B.C.E. the Roman general Sulla took two columns from the temple for the Temple of Jupiter (the Roman version of Zeus) on the Capitoline hill in Rome.

Like the Temple of Olympian Zeus and the Parthenon, the Arch of Hadrian was built of Pentelic marble, which is renowned for its quality and beauty. The lower level consists of a wall with an arched passageway flanked by Corinthian columns between Corinthian pilasters. The tripartite upper level is divided by columns and pilasters, topped by a triangular pediment. The central opening was originally filled in with a thin block of stone. There is no evidence of sculptural decoration, but various schemes have been proposed, including statues of Theseus and Hadrian in the upper level, matching the two inscriptions on either side of the arch that name them as founders of the city. The form of the arch is reminiscent of a Roman triumphal arch, but the upper level is smaller and less solid, and the lack of decoration makes it a sparser, more elegant construction. **RF**

Parliament Building

(Athens, Greece)

Nineteenth-century Neoclassical palace

The magnificent Neoclassical Old Palace, or Parliament Building, sits at one end of a large square at the eastern limits of Athens. The building was designed in 1836 by the Bavarian architect Gartner and was built originally as a palace for the young Bavarian king Otto. Gartner chose a simple, monumental style that reflects the ancient history of Athens, and the resulting building was an imposing, elegantly Neoclassical square structure with four exterior wings of three floors, and one middle wing of two floors and two courtyards. Each wing was accessible separately and designed to facilitate different functions. The interior of the palace

> *"[Otto] was neither ruthless enough to be feared, nor compassionate enough to be loved . . ."*
>
> Professor Thomas W. Gallant, historian

was decorated with scenes from history and Greek mythology, but few have survived.

Over the checkered next eighty years, the palace became home to George I. It suffered two fires: one in 1884 and another in 1909 that resulted in substantial damage. In 1924 the Greek Republic was established and the dynasty was ousted. State administrative bodies and the air force defense then occupied the building before the decision was made to relocate parliament there. In 1929 the central wing was rebuilt and the interior reorganized to accommodate the building's new function. Parliament took over the building on July 1, 1935, and continues there today.

The Old Palace has retained its effortless, elegant, Neoclassical appearance, and is a fitting place for the country's seat of government. **TP**

Parthenon (Athens, Greece)

Temple dedicated to Athena Parthenos, and symbol of Ancient Greece

> *"Earth proudly wears*
> *the Parthenon*
> *As best gem upon her zone."*

Ralph Waldo Emerson, "The Problem" (1839)

⬆ The Acropolis and Parthenon viewed from the southeast, in a photograph dating from *c.* 1890.

➡ The Parthenon sits atop the Acropolis, with the Odeon of Herods Atticus and the Stoa of Eumenes below.

Ancient Athens's "Golden Age," between the Persian and Peloponnesian wars in the fifth century B.C.E., saw the construction of most of the buildings that survive on the Acropolis, the hill that rises above the city. The Temple of Athena Parthenos, goddess and guardian of Athens—built at the initiative of Pericles, politician and general of Athens—is the grandest and most well known of all these monuments. It is known everywhere—as familiar and identifiable a symbol of Ancient Greece and Athenian democracy as the Statue of Liberty is of the United States.

Financed by contributions from Athens's allies, the Delian League (an association of fifth-century B.C.E. Greek city-states), the Parthenon was Pericles's grand project and became a testament to the greatness of the city, as well as his legacy and a monument to his driving force and will. Pheidias, the great sculptor of his age, was put in charge of the construction of the temple, which began in 447 B.C.E. and was finished in 431 B.C.E. The temple is built in the Doric style, even though Athens was an Ionic city. Pheidias is known to have built a colossal gold and ivory cult statue of Athena that stood inside the building, but this is now lost and known only from copies. In Greek mythology, Athena was born, fully grown, from the head of Zeus, and a pediment at the eastern end of the building depicts this event. The temple also housed a number of other sculptures showing the famous defeat of the giants and centaurs by the Greek gods.

The Parthenon was partly destroyed in 1687 when gunpowder stored there by the Ottoman Turks exploded following a Venetian mortar attack. At the beginning of the nineteenth century, British ambassador Lord Elgin controversially bought some of the temple's sculptures from the Turks and took them back to London. Known as the Elgin Marbles, they can still be seen in the British Museum today. **OR**

 **Propylaia**

(Athens, Greece)

Standing at the end of the Sacred Way, a monumental entrance to the Acropolis

The Propylaia served as the monumental entrance to the Athenian Acropolis, with its complex of temples, treasuries, and other buildings. Construction of the Propylaia started soon after the Parthenon was completed in 437 B.C.E. but was halted in 431 B.C.E. with the outbreak of the Peloponnesian War, and never completed—the east wing was not built and some wall surfaces were left unfinished. The entire Acropolis building program was instigated by Pericles, general of Athens in the mid-fifth century B.C.E. Pheidias was the architect in charge of the project, but it was another architect, Mnesikles, who designed and oversaw the construction of the Propylaia.

Approached by a ramp, the gateway stood at the end of the Sacred Way that led from Eleusis to Athens. At the Propylaia, the ramp narrowed and was flanked by four stone steps leading up to an entrance of six massive Doric columns. This led to a central hall with a row of three Ionic columns on each side, supporting a roof made of marble slabs. The immense weight was relieved by coffering—stepped insets decorated with painted stars. The north wing was described by Pausanias (a traveler who wrote a guide to Greece in the second century C.E.) as a *pinakotheke* (art gallery) on the basis of the paintings he saw of famous Greek battles. The wing may have served as a dining room for ritual meals. The smaller south wing, little more than a facade, was adjacent to the Temple of Athena Nike. Constructed of white Pentelic marble with accents in gray Eleusinian marble, the Propylaia's Doric order reflected that of the Parthenon, and its monumentality was similarly designed to impress.

The Propylaia remained intact long after the Classical period but was badly damaged by a gunpowder explosion in 1656. It still serves as the main entrance to the Acropolis today. **RF**

"There is but one entry to the Acropolis . . . it is unrivalled for the beauty and size of its stones."

Pausanias, *Description of Greece* (c. 160 C.E.)

Theater of Dionysus

(Athens, Greece)

The birthplace of dramatic art

There are two theaters near the Acropolis in Athens. The first is called the Odeon and was built by the Romans; the second—older and more important—is the Theater of Dionysus. Drama, as we know it in the Western world, began in ancient Athens, so a visit to the theater is a must for any follower of dramatic art.

Dionysus was the Greek god of theater and wine; mystery surrounded him, and his female followers—known as Bacchantes and powerfully portrayed in Euripides's play *The Bacchae*—were known as wild women who acted irrationally when possessed by the god. The theater of Dionysus featured performances of plays by the great fifth-century B.C.E. dramatists Aeschylus, Sophocles, Euripides, and Aristophanes—the playwrights known to us today as the founders of Western drama. Since then, the theater has been adapted and extended by Greeks and Romans alike.

The Theater of Dionysus, cut into the southern cliff face of the Acropolis, was the first stone theater ever built. Seating as many as 17,000 people, it was the ideal location for ancient Athens's greatest theatrical competition, the Dionysia, which consisted of plays in three categories: Greek Comedy, Tragedy, and Satyr. Wooden benches would have seated most of the audience until the middle of the fourth century, when stone tiers were brought in to house more people. The stage is laid out in the traditional Greek manner, with the orchestra—the area in which the chorus of the play is performed—in front of the stage. The theater is an amphitheater with an open stage surrounded by a gradually ascending oval area. The design, which provides for excellent acoustics, formed a prototype for theaters throughout ancient Greece. The theater fell into disuse after the fourth century, but there is evidence that the Emperor Nero, himself a keen singer, carried out extensive renovations. **OR**

Tower of the Winds

(Athens, Greece)

Ancient weather vane and timepiece

Designed by the Macedonian astronomer Andronicus of Cyrrhus, the *Horologion* or Tower of the Winds served as a wind vane, sundial, and water clock. Scholars are divided as to whether it was constructed during the Hellenistic period in the second century B.C.E. or during the early days of the Roman empire in the first century B.C.E. The octagonal tower, 42 feet (13 m) high and 26 feet (8 m) in diameter, is located to the east of the Roman *agora* (marketplace).

At the top of the tower stands the wind vane in the form of Triton, the Greek sea god with the head and torso of a man and the tail of a fish; his pointed

---

"Some have held that there are only four winds … more careful investigators tell us there are eight."

Vitruvius, *De Architectura* (*c.* 27 B.C.E.)

---

wand indicated the direction of the wind. Below is a frieze of eight wind deities sculpted in low relief, each representing the wind from the corresponding compass direction. For example, the northeast wind Kaikias has a basket of hailstones, the south wind Notus drops rain from a pot, and the warm west wind, Zephyrus, is a seminaked youth scattering flowers. Below the wind sculptures were nine sundials and inside the tower was a water clock, or *clepsydra*. Like the Parthenon and other notable buildings in Athens, the *Horologion* was built of fine white Pentelic marble.

During the Byzantine period, the tower served as the bell tower of a church, and during the Turkish occupation it was occupied by Dervishes. In the eighteenth century, it inspired the design of the Radcliffe Observatory in Oxford, England. **RF**

Ancient Olympic Stadium

(Elis, Greece)

Original Olympic stadium, place of pilgrimage and sporting competition

The Olympic Games were first held in 776 B.C.E. and from then until 395 C.E. people came from all over the ancient Greek world to Olympia, the permanent setting for the games. The games were held in honor of Zeus, the ruler of the Greek gods, and a visit to Olympia was also a religious pilgrimage—to the sacred grove known as Altis and to the Temple of Zeus, one of the seven ancient wonders of the world. Unlike the modern Olympics, the ancient games combined worship and sporting competition.

Olympia is situated on the Peloponnese peninsula, in a fertile, grassy plain on the north bank of the river Alpheios, near the mountains of Elis. Driving through the dry mountainous area that surrounds the plain, it is hard to see how an ancient pilgrim would have been able to get to the site, but Olympia in those days was well served by the then navigable river and by the many roads that led out of the area.

The Altis grove was the focus of the site because it contained the Temple of Hera and the Temple of Zeus. The latter was finished in 456 B.C.E. and eventually destroyed by an earthquake in the fifth century C.E. For many years Olympia lay derelict and abandoned, a relic of a mysterious and long-passed golden age. The site was not properly excavated until 1829 when the French Expedition Scientifique de Moree began to piece together the layout of the site. There are very few buildings at Olympia that remain largely intact, but the area still holds a persuasive power. Sporting competition as we know it in the West began at Olympia, and an investigation into the Greek search for physical perfection and religious devotion begins here. Only young men took part in the early games, which consisted of up to twenty events, with the victorious athlete being presented with a crown of leaves from the sacred olive tree. **OR**

"On his head is a sculpted wreath of olive sprays. In his right hand he holds a figure of Victory . . ."

Pausanias, of the statue of Zeus at Olympia

Temple of Aphaia

(Aegina, Greece)

Greek temple with Minoan connections

One of the Saronic Islands of Greece, separated from the Peloponnese by the Hydra Gulf, Aegina is home to the Temple of Aphaia, one of the best preserved temples from the Classical world. It stands on top of a small, partially wooded hill in the northeast of the island, and—together with the Parthenon in Athens and the Temple of Poseidon at Sounion—forms the third point on an equilateral triangle of pre-Christian temples.

The temple was initially dedicated to the deity Aphaia, then became associated also with Athena, and it was the focus for a cult, possibly dating back to the second millennium B.C.E. According to Cretan legend, Aphaia (originally named Britomartis) was the daughter of Zeus and Carme. Fleeing from Minos (the mythical king of the island of Crete), who had fallen in love with her, she became entangled in the nets of some fishermen who took her on their boat. Escaping from them, she swam toward the island of Aegina, reaching land and running away to the northeast and hiding in the temple. Her name translates as "vanishing" and was given to her by the fishermen as she disappeared from their view. The surviving temple is the second building on this site, and dates back to around 500 B.C.E., although it was added to in the years that followed. The body of the temple was enclosed by thirty-two Doric columns of which twenty-five still stand, with twelve along each side and six each to the front and rear. The temple was within a perimeter wall that also enclosed the stone altar area to the east of the temple, various edifices for displaying sculpture, a subsidiary building, and the old sanctuary.

The first extensive archeological work on the site was started in 1901, when many Mycenaean artifacts were found. Work resumed in 1966 to the late 1980s, unearthing further artifacts and clues to the long and ancient history of this important site. **TP**

Ancient Corinth

(Corinth, Greece)

Wealthy city-state, visited by the Apostle Paul

Ancient Corinth was one of the wealthiest and most important city-states in Greece, deriving its wealth from trading activity that was facilitated by its position on a narrow isthmus of land in the northeast Peloponnese. From the eighth to mid-sixth century B.C.E., Corinth was a major exporter of pottery, and its characteristic small flasks, decorated with miniature friezes of animals, warriors, and plant motifs, have been found all over the Greek world.

One of the most famous buildings in Ancient Corinth was the Temple of Aphrodite, positioned on the Acrocorinth acropolis, and well known for the

> *"It was on account of these women that the city was crowded with people and grew rich."*
>
> Strabo, describing the sacred prostitutes in Corinth

thousand prostitutes who were employed there. Under Periander—the second Tyrant of Corinth—in the seventh century B.C.E., great technological advances were made, including the development of a third order of classical architecture, the highly decorative Corinthian order. The Romans, under Lucius Mummius, destroyed Corinth in 146 B.C.E. but Julius Caesar refounded the city in 44 B.C.E., which became the seat of government for southern Greece.

The Apostle Paul, a prolific contributor to the New Testament and, along with St. Peter, the most notable of early Christian missionaries, first visited Corinth *c.* 51 C.E. He returned six years later, when he wrote two of his epistles: The First and Second Epistle of Paul the Apostle to the Corinthians, which are included as books in the New Testament. **RF**

🏛 ◉ Lion Gate (Mycenae, Greece)

Monumental entrance to the ancient citadel of Mycenae

In the Homeric epics, Mycenae is the city of Agamemnon, the leader of the Greeks; it is a place "rich in gold," well built, and its streets are wide. Mycenaean civilization lasted for about five hundred years—from the first burial in shaft graves, at Mycenae, in around 1600 B.C.E. to its final disappearance around 1050 B.C.E. The people of the city dominated the lands around them during an era of Greek history now known as the "Mycenaean" period. The crowning achievement of the age was the citadel of Mycenae itself, standing proud above the Argive plain, 56 miles (90 km) southwest of Athens.

The circuit of walls at Mycenae reached 0.6 miles (1 km) in length and had two principal entrances—the North East Postern and the monumental Lion Gate. The citadel contains many structures dating back to the thirteenth century B.C.E. and, of these, the Lion Gate is the most imposing. The gate marks the entrance to the main road leading up to the palace. Its size is remarkable, especially when you consider that it was built almost eight hundred years before the major sites of classical Athens. It was built in the form of a "relieving triangle" to support the weight of the stones. The massive unshaped blocks of limestone, piled on top of each other with close-fitting joints, led later Greeks to refer to the walls at Mycenae as "Cyclopean," after the enormous, mythical, one-eyed creatures that—according to legend—must have helped carry such large boulders. In the middle of the arch, above the doorway, are the two heraldic lions that give the gate its name. Sculpted out of the stone, 10 feet (3 m) high, they remain impressive guardians even though their heads have crumbled away.

The gate was discovered by the Greek archeologist Kyriakos Pittakis in 1841. Since then further excavations have taken place, including that of the Mycenaean acropolis in 1902. **OR**

"And for seven years he ruled over Mycenae, rich in gold, after he slew the son of Atreus . . ."

Homer, *The Odyssey* (*c.* 850 B.C.E.)

Mystras Fortress (Mount Taygetos, Greece)

Impregnable thirteenth-century fortress on a hilltop in the Peloponnese

The rugged and picturesque countryside of the Peloponnese in southern Greece is a landscape of contrasts, from open plains to the impressive mountain range of Taygetos that extends for about 65 miles (100 km). In the foothills of these mountains and near the site of ancient Sparta is one of the best-preserved Byzantine ruins, the ancient town and fortress of Mystras.

The town was built into the side of a hill, with the impressive fortress on the top, from where it had views across the surrounding landscape. The small peak in the foothills of Mount Taygetos was an ideal place for a defensive settlement, and in 1249 William II of Villehardouin, a French duke, started to build the fortress there. Like the other structures in the town, the fortress was built using stone from older demolished buildings. Many additions were made over the following centuries, including a circular tower and cistern in the outer yard, built during the years of Turkish rule. William had plans to use his indomitable fortress as a base to spread French dominance throughout the area, but in 1262 he was forced to turn the fortress over to the Greeks in exchange for his life. Following that date, the French tried, unsuccessfully, to recapture the building on several occasions. The town flourished under Byzantine rule and was greatly expanded, becoming a major city by 1348. By 1460, however, the Turks had taken over and it fell into decline. The city enjoyed a brief renaissance under Venetian rule at the end of the seventeenth century, but was finally sacked and burned by the Egyptians in 1825, from which it never recovered.

There are still many fine examples of Byzantine buildings at the site of Mystras, especially churches with fabulous architecture and artwork. The site has endured a long and arduous history, but the Byzantine city was built to last—and last in great part it has. **TP**

"Mystras, the 'wonder of Morea,' was abandoned … leaving only the breathtaking medieval ruins …"

UNESCO

🏛 ◈ **Sanctuary of Asklepios** (Epidaurus, Greece)

Healing center of the ancient world, dedicated to the Greek god of medicine and healing

To the ancient Greeks and Romans, the god Asclepius was the father of healing and medicine. So revered was he that a widespread cult arose in his name. A major temple-sanctuary complex devoted to him flourished at Epidaurus, close to his supposed birthplace; it was influenced stylistically by the nearby Greek city-state of Argos.

This complex contained temples, a sacred well used for cleansing rites, stadium, banqueting hall, hospital, *tholos* (round building), baths, gymnasium and, perhaps best known of all, a massive theater. This is the best-preserved example of an ancient Greek theater still in existence. Seating at least 12,000 people, it has remarkable acoustics and is now being used for performances once again. Like the theater, most of the other main sights at Epidaurus date from the fourth century B.C.E. The theater is usually attributed to the famous sculptor Polyclitus the Younger. He also designed the site's striking *tholos*, which had beautiful carvings and whose interior columns exerted a great influence on the development of the Corinthian style. The *tholos* was probably the site of major rites; beneath it lay a labyrinth that might have housed sacred serpents.

First and foremost, however, Epidaurus was, at its height, the healing center of the ancient world, and various inscriptions found at the site give details of miraculous cures. It was believed that Asclepius gave his divine guidance in dreams, so hopeful sick people flocked to Epidaurus and to other temples dedicated to him, to sleep within their precincts. Epidaurus flourished well into the Roman Empire and was still a place of pilgrimage for those seeking cures in early Christian times, although earthquake damage in the sixth century C.E. led to its desertion. The site was listed by UNESCO in 1988. **AK**

🏛 ◎ Delos (Delos, Greece)

Aegean island, rich in ancient history and revered as the birthplace of Apollo and Artemis

The Greek island of Delos was selected as a World Heritage site because of the island's rich history, dating as far back as the civilizations of the Aegean world in the third millennia B.C.E. Originally the island was regarded as a holy sanctuary but, with the advent of Olympian Greek mythology in the eighth century B.C.E., it became known as the birthplace of Apollo and Artemis. The association with two such powerful gods transformed Delos into a cultural hub and, by the seventh century B.C.E., it had become a center of religious importance in the region. In the third century B.C.E. Delos developed still further, culturally and politically, when Greek monarchs competed for favor on the island by erecting civic monuments, statues, and pedestals, many of which can be seen today.

Delos became even more powerful in 314 B.C.E. when it achieved independence. This was short-lived, however, and in 166 B.C.E. the Romans handed control of the island to the Athenian city-state. Athenian domination of Delos aided its expansion still further, by declaring the port to be an "international" harbor. The absence of taxes also helped the island to prosper economically. However, from the middle of the first century B.C.E., Delos began to decline and by the second and third centuries C.E. only a small settlement remained, the island losing its importance as Christianity began to replace the older religion. Today Delos is largely a center for archeology and tourism.

The rich architecture and extensive artifacts on Delos combine to make it an exceptional archeological site. The complex structure of both buildings and monuments has been compared to Delphi and Olympia. Those who visit the island today experience a rich array of impressive temples, ancient halls, town squares, and elaborate fountains. Delos was listed as a UNESCO World Heritage site in 1990. **KH**

Akrotiri (Thera, Greece)

Well-preserved Bronze Age town, destroyed in an ancient volcanic eruption

About 49 acres (20 ha) in area, Akrotiri on the Cycladic island of Thera (also known as Santorini) was the site of an impressively constructed and important town during the Bronze Age. Though occupation started during the Late Neolithic period, it developed into a major town from *c.* 2000 B.C.E. The site is perhaps best known for its dramatic destruction by a volcanic eruption, the result of which can be seen in the shape of the island—the center was blown out by the explosion, leaving a crescent form. The date of this event is disputed: Traditional archeological methods date the eruption between 1550 and 1500 B.C.E. However, scientific evidence places the eruption a century earlier, *c.* 1650 to 1600 B.C.E.

Excavations at Akrotiri have revealed streets, squares, houses preserved up to a height of 26 feet (8 m), and an elaborate drainage system. The town plan consisted of blocks of houses and freestanding structures; the buildings were constructed of stone, some with monumental ashlar facings. Evidence of household activities, such as the storage and preparation of food, and of craft production has been found. The material culture of the site (including large quantities of pottery and metal ware) indicates close connections with Crete, the Greek mainland, the Dodecanese, Cyprus, and the Near East. Many of the buildings are decorated with elaborate frescoes. In one, an apparently ritual scene shows women gathering saffron, which is presented to a seated female flanked by a blue monkey and a griffin.

Akrotiri is one of several locations proposed for the fabled lost city of Atlantis, which was first mentioned by the Greek philosopher Plato. While some scholars see his account of the island's demise as a political allegory, others suggest that it may have been inspired by memories of real events. **RF**

🏛 ◎ Cave of the Apocalypse (Pátmos, Greece)

Home to the apostle John while he wrote his Gospels and Apocalypse

On the small and rocky island of Pátmos, the Cave of the Apocalypse can be found deep within a monastery that surrounds and protects it. Rising up out of the crystal-blue Aegean Sea, Pátmos is the most northerly of a group of Greek islands, just off the southwest coast of Turkey. It is believed that St. John the Theologian (identified by early Christian tradition as John the Apostle) lived here, halfway between the island's two main towns of Chorá and Skala.

John the Apostle was exiled to Pátmos by the Roman Emperor Domitian in 95 C.E. and stayed there for two years. During this period he lived in this small cave, where he reputedly dictated his Gospel and Apocalypse (or Revelation) to his disciple Prochorus, who later became Bishop of Nicomedia. The Apocalypse, with its disturbing revelations, has been the focus of controversy ever since, and was the last book of the Bible to be written.

In the tenth century, the cave on Pátmos was enclosed by a Greek Orthodox monastery to protect it physically and to guard its spiritual importance. It has been an important place of Christian pilgrimage ever since. The small area of the cave has hollows in the rock where St. John is thought to have rested his head and hand, and this is now lit with seven silver lights, one of which hangs over the spot where he slept. At the entrance to the cave is a mosaic illustrating the visions received by the apostle while in the cave.

Although the veracity of the cave's history cannot be established conclusively, it is a place that resounds with an intense spirituality and depth of feeling that makes its authenticity seem unshakeable. It forms one of the most historically important sites within the Christian world, and this significance was recognized in 1999 when it was designated as a UNESCO World Heritage site. **TP**

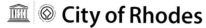 ## City of Rhodes

(Rhodes, Greece)

Walled medieval city, legacy of the Knights Hospitaller, on an island steeped in history

Enclosed by striking turreted battlements rising up against the Aegean sky, the medieval district of the city of Rhodes was essentially created by the Crusader Knights of St. John. This is one of the world's oldest inhabited cities, with a labyrinth of fascinating little streets, as well as numerous cafés and shops. Exploring the cobbled alleyways provides glimpses of ancient remains—evidence of a history dating back to ancient Greek, Hellenistic, and Byzantine empires.

It was in 1309 that the Knights of St. John took over Rhodes, ruling it like an independent state and building a moated, walled fortress town designed to fulfill a medieval ideal. The knights began life in eleventh-century Jerusalem as an order that cared for sick Christian pilgrims. By the time they arrived on Rhodes, they had become a military Crusader order. From their bastion on Rhodes, they spent the next two hundred years aggressively harrying any Muslim shipping that entered eastern Aegean waters. Today, interesting St. John attractions include the Hospital of the Knights (now an archeological museum), the Street of the Knights (Ippotón Street), the Palace of the Grand Master, the knights' castle, and the walls of the city. No trace remains today of the Colossus of Rhodes, one of the seven wonders of the ancient world, that stood in the harbor from 280 to 224 B.C.E.

The sixteenth century saw the Crusader knights driven out of Rhodes by the Ottoman forces of Süleyman the Magnificent. Impressive Turkish baths, mosques, and minarets remain from the centuries of Turkish rule, which ended only when Italy seized the island in 1912. The Italians undertook extensive restoration work (of varying effectiveness) in the old medieval town, which suffered severe bomb damage during World War II. The island was handed over to Greece in the late 1940s. **AK**

> *"Rhodes . . . replete with the remains of dwellings, palaces, and churches once the property of the knights."*

J. W. McGarvey, *Lands of the Bible* (1881)

Hania Town Walls

(Hania, Crete, Greece)

Remnants of Venetian and Turkish city walls

Hania (Chania) is the second-largest town on the Greek island of Crete and lies on the north coast of the island. It is an important economic and commercial center for the island, a position that the ancient town has held for hundreds of years.

Excavations at Hania have revealed that the town is built on the foundations of an older town, that of ancient Kydonia, and that the area has been inhabited since Neolithic times. This lends it an extraordinarily rich and varied history, and many artifacts, especially of the Minoan period, have been discovered. The original city is thought to have been largely destroyed by the Saracens around 828, but the Byzantines reestablished the area from around 951 when they began to fortify the town. In 1204 Crete was given to Boniface of Montferrat, who sold it to the Venetians. The Venetians again began work on building fortifying walls to protect Hania, demolishing the old Roman theater in order to reuse the stone. New walls were built between 1336 and 1356 as well as many Venetian-style buildings. The walls were again modified and strengthened in 1536 under the directive of the famous Italian engineer and architect Michele Sanmicheli, and were worked on until 1568. In 1645, after fierce fighting that lasted for more than two months, the Turks took possession of the city and did more work on the city walls, rebuilding parts and pulling other parts down.

Today there are only fragments left of Hania's battle-scarred walls. The fortifications evolved slowly over the centuries and they form part of a greater picture, telling the story of hundreds of years of human civilization in a single area, making them an important part of Greek history. Hania's museums house a wealth of sculptures, mosaics, and pottery tracing the long and checkered history of the city. **TP**

Palace of Phaistos

(near Mires, Crete, Greece)

Remains of Minoan palace on stunning site

The royal residence complex at Phaistos (Festós) was one of the most splendid examples of the great "palace culture" of the Minoans, whose civilization flourished on and around the island of Crete between *c.* 2000 and 1400 B.C.E. Its site alone is stunning—on a hill commanding wonderful views over the wide Mesara Plain, Crete's most fertile pastureland.

The years between *c.* 1900 and 1400 B.C.E. saw various palaces rise and fall at Phaistos, as well as at other Cretan palace sites such as Knossos. Around 1700 B.C.E. a magnificent new palace was built on the foundations of the old one, and today's remains are

> *"The famous spearman Idomeneus led the Cretans, who held . . . the populous town of Phaestus"*
>
> Homer, *The Iliad* (*c.* 850 B.C.E.)

fascinating because they trace different layers of building over the years. At its height, this new palace was a place of lavish royal apartments and long, open courtyards, positioned to make the most of the spectacular views. There was advanced sanitation and a cleverly complex layout of steps and walkways connecting various different levels and making the palace buildings hug the outlines of the hill. The palace was the center of a vibrant city that was a major hub of culture and trade. The famous Phaistos disk was found here—a clay disk featuring characters that have never been deciphered.

Phaistos city continued to be inhabited through several subsequent eras, but by 200 B.C.E. it was dominated by the nearby city of Gortyn. The palace was excavated in the early 1900s. **AK**

Palace of Knossos (near Heraklion, Crete, Greece)

Largest of the Minoan palaces and legendary home of the half-man, half-bull Minotaur

> *"The whole place seemed to awake awhile to life and movement."*
>
> Sir Arthur Evans, archeologist

The Palace of Knossos, situated 3 miles (5 km) southeast of the Cretan capital of Heraklion, was built in 1700 B.C.E. and inhabited until 1400 B.C.E.—but the site is thought to have had a settlement since 7000 B.C.E. What draws visitors is the suggestion that the palace was once home to the half-man, half-bull Minotaur of Greek legend. According to legend, Daedalus built the Labyrinth (a mazelike structure) for King Minos of Crete to contain the Minotaur, which was eventually slaughtered by Theseus. Although no actual maze has been located, the Knossos complex has a labyrinthine structure with some thirteen hundred interconnecting rooms.

The structure of the palace is in good condition, but this is a curse as well as a blessing, given that early archeological excavations at the site led to a hasty reconstruction that has made it difficult for contemporary archeologists to assess its accuracy. Minos Kalokairinos, a wealthy Cretan merchant, carried out the first extensive excavation in 1878, but the site was overhauled in its entirety by the English archeologist Sir Arthur Evans between 1900 and 1905. Evans's enthusiasm ensured the restoration of the palace, but he used materials such as concrete that have caused problems in determining the authenticity of the original layout and building.

The walls of the palace are decorated with frescoes depicting various Minoan rituals such as bull-leaping—in which a participant holds on to the bull's horns to enable him to vault over its back. (Bulls were the object of veneration in Minoan civilization.) With the frescoes, too, there has been controversy because they were completely redone by the artist Piet de Jong, based on what little remained on the plaster. These works may therefore owe much to the artist's imagination and guesswork regarding what the originals actually depicted. **CK**

Spinalonga Fortress (Kalidon, Crete, Greece)

Impregnable Venetian fortress, more recently used as a leper colony

Just off the northeast coast of Crete, on the small islet of Kalidon, Spinalonga Fortress occupies a strategic position guarding Elounda Bay. The location was probably first used by Christians fleeing the Arabs who occupied Crete from 824 to 960. In the early thirteenth century the island was acquired by Venice and the fortress was constructed on the ruins of an ancient acropolis to help protect Crete from invasion by the Ottoman Empire. The fortress's high walls ensured that ships could not land on the island, and its bastions allowed artillery to command the surrounding waters. Although Venice eventually lost Crete to the Ottomans in 1669, the Venetians were allowed to keep Spinalonga to protect the nearby harbor where their ships stopped to take on provisions. Spinalonga Fortress eventually fell to the Ottomans in 1715, and its military function ceased, but it was then put into service as a prison for members of the Cretan independence movement.

When Crete eventually gained independence in 1898, Ottoman Turkish families sought refuge in the fortress. In 1903, in an attempt to force them out, the Cretan government designated Spinalonga Fortress a leper colony. Lepers—at one time viewed as "unclean" and requiring segregation from society—entered the colony through a tunnel known as Dante's Gate, to live in a simple community where their basic needs, including medical care, were met. The colony was eventually disbanded in 1957 and the island is now uninhabited, though it is a popular tourist destination, reachable by ferry from the nearby resorts of Elounda or Agios Nicolaos. There are still just two entrances to the fortress: the tunnel through which the lepers passed, and a jetty on the seaward side.

Spinalonga Fortress reflects Crete's shifting history, as well as the engineering skills of the Venetians who ruled Crete from 1204 to 1669. **JF**

"The leper who has the disease shall wear torn clothes and let the hair of his head hang loose ..."

Leviticus 13: 45–56

🏛️ ◎ Emperor Diocletian's Palace (Split, Croatia)

Roman fortified residence, destined to become the nucleus of Split

> *"... your emperor ... wouldn't dare suggest I replace the peace and happiness of this place ..."*

Diocletian, refusing a second term in office

Diocletian was a soldier from the Roman province of Dalmatia who rose to become one of the most effective emperors of Rome's later years. At the age of fifty-nine, after a grave illness, he decided to retire to his country home by the sea, a palace he had commissioned some 5 miles (8 km) from his birth town of Salona (now the town of Solin).

The fortified palace, built over 7 acres (3 ha), was part villa, part military camp, with sixteen towers placed around its 23-foot- (7-m-) high walls. A road between the eastern and western gates divided the interior between the military quarters and the emperor's residence, the latter featuring a monumental court, an octagonal mausoleum, three temples, and arcaded apartments adjoining the southern facade that rose directly from the sea. Diocletian lived there, happily growing cabbages, until his death at the age of seventy.

The palace remained in use until the sixth century, when it withstood a battering from invading Avars from Eurasia. The town of Salona was less fortunate and, after a disastrous raid in *c.* 614, the inhabitants fled to the safety of the palace's walls and set up home, effectively founding the town of Spalato—the modern city of Split. Successive generations under regional rulers altered and rebuilt the interior—construction spilling outside the walls as the population grew—and today's palace is an architectural assortment of medieval, Renaissance, and Baroque styles within a recognizably Roman carapace. The palace in central Split was made a UNESCO World Heritage site in 1979 as the most valuable example of Roman architecture on the eastern coast of the Adriatic. More than 9,000 people still inhabit the buildings in and around the walls, and fashionable boutiques, galleries, restaurants, and bars trade daily from within its ancient arcades. **JB**

Pile Gate (Dubrovnik, Croatia)

Defensive portal leading into the beautiful center of Dubrovnik

The Pile Gate is the main entrance to Dubrovnik, the beautiful old town that has been a UNESCO World Heritage site since 1979. For centuries, the Pile Gate has been a feature of the city's defenses and the entryway to the "Pearl of the Adriatic."

The Pile Gate is situated on the route into Dubrovnik from the suburb of Pile. The town fortifications were begun in the eighth century, a reflection of its growing economic importance. Dubrovnik gained independence from the Venetian Republic in 1358, when it became a self-governing city state. Faced with threats from the Venetians, Slavs, and Ottomans, Dubrovnik's senate instituted a significant redevelopment of the city's defenses in the fifteenth and sixteenth centuries. The Pile Gate is actually a complex of two gates—an internal gate dating from the fifteenth century and an external gate dating from 1537. The two gates are linked by a drawbridge over a ditch dug in 1350. It was through the Pile Gate that Napoleonic troops entered Dubrovnik in 1808, ending nearly five centuries of the city's independence.

Inside a niche in the inner gate is a statue of the city's patron, St. Blaise, by the famed religious sculptor Ivan Meštrović. The Pile Gate leads into a plaza that was paved in 1468 and features a grand fountain designed by the Italian Onofrio della Cava. The Pile Gate also gives access to Dubrovnik's city walls, 1.2 miles (2 km) long, which are 82 feet (25 m) high and 20 feet (6 m) thick in some places and offer stunning views of the town and Adriatic.

Dubrovnik's old town was extensively damaged in Croatia's struggle for independence, first against the Yugoslav People's Army and then against the Serbs from Yugoslavia, in 1991 and 1992. Fortunately, the Pile Gate survived the conflicts and today it stands proudly as the gateway to the historic heart of one of Europe's most beautiful cities. **JF**

"By the pleading of St. Blaise, may God relieve you of ailments of the throat and other evils. Amen."

Blessing on St. Blaise's feast day, February 3

Mirogoj Cemetery

(Zagreb, Croatia)

Funerary testament to Croatian culture

The Mirogoj Cemetery, or Gradska Groblja, in Zagreb lies to the north of the city, a short bus ride from the cathedral. A member of the International Association of Significant Cemeteries in Europe, it is more than a resting place for the dead. It is an open-air museum of art, architecture, garden design, and Croatian history.

The cemetery was founded in 1876 on land once owned by Ljudevit Gaj, the linguist, politician, and writer who created the Latin alphabet used to write Croatian, Bosnian, Montenegrin, and Serbian languages (his tomb can be found within). The city's aim was to unify its scattered cemeteries and create a magnificent resting place for the dead. They commissioned Hermann Bollé, a German architect responsible for the restoration of Zagreb Cathedral and the Zagreb Museum of Arts and Crafts, to conceptualize and build the new necropolis.

Bollé's vision was hardly modest. His intention was to create a celestial Jerusalem in neo-Renaissance style, with elegant arcades, avenues, cupola-topped chapels, and a mortuary. Financial problems led to the cemetery being half a century in the making (it was completed after Bollé's death), but it remains true to the architect's plans and is a fitting memorial to a man who devoted fifty years to the Croatian arts.

The cemetery's tombs include those of Stjepan Radić, leader of the Croatian Peasant Party, Franjo Tudjman, the first Croatian president, and Drazen Petrović, one of the country's most celebrated basketball players, who died tragically in a car accident. On All Saints Day, November 1, the old Croatian custom of placing lighted lamps on the graves of loved ones turns the cemetery ablaze, when the citizens of Zagreb cover tombs, memorials, and even entire pathways with tiny colored lights in memory of the dead. **JB**

Petrovaradin Fortress

(Petrovaradin, Serbia)

Serbia's unrivaled fortified system

Petrovaradin Fortress on the banks of the River Danube is Europe's largest surviving complete fortress system, covering 276 acres (112 ha). There has been a fort of some kind on the site since the early Bronze Age (*c.* 3,000 B.C.E.), although research of the area has shown that an earlier settlement on the site dates back to the Paleolithic era (19,000–15,000 B.C.E.).

The first large fortifications were built at Petrovaradin by the Romans. In 1235 King Béla IV of Hungary brought a group of Cistercian monks to the site, who constructed strong walls from 1247 to 1252. On July 27, 1526, the fortress fell to the advancing

> ## *"Nec arte, nec marte" (Neither by force, nor by tricks)*
>
> Inscription at Petrovaradin Fortress

Ottoman forces after a two-week siege, as the area became part of their empire. In 1687, the fortress was captured by the Austrian army, and Emperor Leopold I ordered the old fortress to be torn down and replaced. The new fortress successfully withstood an Ottoman siege in 1694. Major works were added to the fortress from 1753 to 1776, including more than 10 miles (16 km) of underground anti-mine passages. The fortress was used by the Viennese court to store their valuables during Napoleon's advance into Austria. In later years the fortress was employed as a prison.

Petrovaradin is now seen primarily as an unrivaled example of eighteenth-century military engineering and architecture. Large areas of the fortress have been restored, making it appear as formidable now as it was when it was first constructed. **JF**

Belgrade Cathedral

(Belgrade, Serbia)

Orthodox Christian cathedral embodying Serbian culture

In 1573 a priest named Gerlah visited the city of Belgrade. He recorded in his diary his impressions of the church of St. Michael the Archangel: "It is fairly large and is the only church here," he wrote, and went on to describe a marble baptistery, carved wooden candlesticks, and a wooden altar draped with a white cloth. This appears to be the first written record of what is now the Serbian Orthodox Cathedral in Belgrade. The original buildings were destroyed during a Turkish invasion in the early eighteenth century, and a new cathedral was built on the same foundations in the nineteenth century. Work was begun in 1845 and finished in 1847. Unsurprisingly, the architecture demonstrates influences from both the Byzantine and Austrian cultures, two cultures that have exerted strong influences over Serbian history.

Several famous Serbians are buried in the cathedral, including Prince Milos Obrenovic, a former leader of Serbia who led uprisings against the Turks. The graves of two of his sons, Milan and Mihailo, are also in the cathedral. Both princes became rulers of Serbia: Milan died very young, while still in power; Mihailo was assassinated. In addition, there are coffins said to contain the relics of Serbian princes from the fourteenth century, also killed by Turkish invaders. The remains of two popular nineteenth-century Serbian writers are also interred in the cathedral: Vuk Karadzic and Dositej Obradovic.

The cathedral stands at the center of the most important political, business, and commercial regions of old Belgrade, very close to the Kalemegdan Fortress. The churches on this site have struggled to keep their identities as Orthodox churches amid regular invasions from the Muslim Ottoman empire and Catholic Austria, yet despite centuries of unrest, the modern-day cathedral is still Serbian Orthodox. **LH**

"A crowd was pouring down the steps that fall from the [Belgrade] cathedral square."

Rebecca West, *Black Lamb and Grey Falcon* (1945)

Kalemegdan Fortress

(Belgrade, Serbia)

Powerful stronghold and symbol of the city of Belgrade

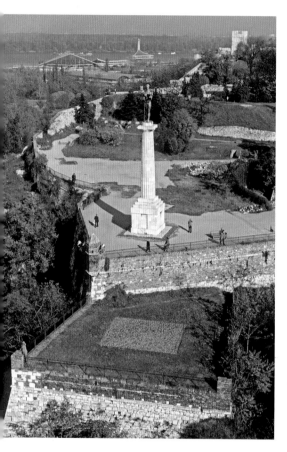

> *"The fortress Kalemegdan has a very long history, going back to the* castrum *of Roman times."*

Andrea Milani Comparetti, author

There has been a fortress or castle on this site since the Roman occupation in the first century, and all have left their historic mark. Mainly dating from the 1740s, the present fortress has origins in the twelfth century, when it was built on the site of previously destroyed buildings; its walls represent the confines of the old city of Belgrade.

Kalemegdan Fortress was built by the Byzantines and was destined to witness the many and varied rulers of a troubled region. After 1521, when the Ottoman empire overthrew the Byzantine rulers, Kalemegdan fell into disrepair. In the early eighteenth century, Austria ruled the region for more than two decades and restored the fortress for its troops. Later, the two World Wars wrought damage, which has since been repaired. Today, Kalemegdan Fortress remains a proud symbol of the city, amazingly still intact despite Belgrade's long history of invasions and, in recent years, NATO bombs. All around the fortress's walls, the scars of battles reveal Belgrade's war-torn past.

Kalemegdan Fortress is built on rocks that, on one side, overlook the confluence of the Sava and Danube rivers. It is now Belgrade's principal tourist attraction. The relics of its varied past include Roman ruins, the grave of a pasha, an observatory, and several museums. The surrounding park is filled with sculptures, including the controversial *The Victor* (1928), an enormous statue of a male nude, atop a tall pedestal, that was made as a celebration of Serbia's liberation from Turkey. When it was first unveiled in central Belgrade, public sensibilities were offended, so the nude was moved to Kalemegdan Park. It now towers above the rivers and the new suburbs of the city. Another striking monument is an enormous bronze statue dedicated to the people of France, in thanks for their assistance during World War I. **LH**

Tito's Mausoleum

(Belgrade, Serbia)

Tomb of Yugoslavia's most famous leader

Marshal Josip Broz Tito, president of Yugoslavia, died on May 4, 1980. His funeral in Belgrade was attended by 122 heads of state from all over the world and a mausoleum was built on the site of his former home, in the wealthy district of Dedinje. Tito, son of a Croatian father and Slovenian mother, was born in 1892 in what was then Austria-Hungary. He spent much of his youth traveling and working in a fast-changing Europe, serving as a soldier in World War I before becoming a communist in 1919. In 1920 he returned to a new country, a joint federation of the Croats, Serbs, and Slovenes, which would become known as Yugoslavia. A committed communist, Tito was nonetheless opposed to Stalin's tyrannical regime; as leader of Yugoslavia during World War II, he was vociferous in his feelings about the Russian leader.

In the 1980s, visitor numbers to Tito's mausoleum were huge, with long lines a constant feature. These numbers have dropped considerably as the peoples of the former Yugoslavia attempt to find their own national identities; many have turned away from what Tito represented. When Yugoslavia descended into civil war during the 1990s, the mausoleum and its museum were closed to the public.

Today, Tito's Mausoleum, also known as the House of Flowers, is open again with large numbers of visitors paying their respects on the date of his death, May 4, and what would have been his birthday, May 25 (also celebrated as the Day of Youth). The mausoleum is a popular tourist attraction, even though it lacks the pomp and circumstance that surrounded it in its heyday—gone are the armed guards, the army of gardeners, and several of the museums. Despite an upsurge of visitors, Tito's last resting place currently resembles a neglected graveyard more than a site of national importance. **LH**

Karageorge Mausoleum

(Topola, Serbia)

Tomb of a founding father of Serbia

Djordje Petrović (1768–1817), known by the anglicized Karageorge—a name meaning "Black George" on account of his dark features—is regarded by Serbians as one of the founding fathers of the modern Serbian state. He was born in the area surrounding Topola in 1752 and rose from a humble farming background to become the leader of the Serbian rebels against Ottoman rule during the First Serbian Uprising (1804–13), after previously distinguishing himself fighting for the Austrians in the Austro-Turkish War (1787–91).

While the Ottoman empire was distracted by a prolonged war with Russia, Karageorge was successful

> ## "Milos [Obrenovic, rival Serbian leader] had the great rebel's head stuffed and sent to Istanbul."
>
> Steven W. Sowards, historian

in overthrowing Turkish governors and liberating several regions, including the area around Belgrade, as well as implementing various national education and justice reforms. In 1813, however, he was confronted with the full might of the Ottomans, after the threat posed by Napoleon had forced Russia to make peace with the empire. The Serbian Uprising was finally defeated and Karageorge was forced to flee the country. He returned in secret in 1817 but was assassinated by the Ottomans, with the assistance of one of his Serbian rivals.

He was later buried in the Mausoleum of St. George (known as the Karageorge Mausoleum), built by his grandson King Peter I on the Oplenac hill just outside his birthplace of Topola. Family members, including King Peter, are also buried there. **AS**

🏛 ⟠ Studenica Monastery (Studenica, Serbia)

Byzantine religious buildings with incomparable fourteenth-century frescoes

Established in the late twelfth century, Studenica Monastery is a remote compound of religious buildings that together form one of the richest storehouses of Byzantine architecture and fresco painting in Eastern Europe. The monastery is made up of two principal buildings, the Church of the Virgin and the King's Church (officially the Church of St. Anne and St. Joachim), surrounded by the smaller Church of St. Nicholas, the foundations of a church dedicated to St. John the Baptist, a bell tower, and a later monastic residence dating from the eighteenth century.

The complex was originally founded by Stevan Nemanja—the father of the medieval Serbian state—shortly before he abdicated his throne in 1196 to become a monk. Nemanja had chanced upon the site while hunting and identified it as perfect for a monastic community. His work on the site was continued by his sons, who completed the Church of the Virgin in the early thirteenth century and the King's Church in the early fourteenth century.

As well as being important as the birthplace of the Serbian Orthodox Church, these buildings are significant artistic treasures in their own right. They represent a unique fusion of Byzantine and Romanesque architectural styles into a separate style known as the Raska School, which was to influence the design of churches throughout the region for several centuries. In addition, they are decorated with extremely well-preserved frescoes; the King's Church contains a fresco cycle of the life of the Virgin painted by Greek artisans brought in to work on the building in the early fourteenth century, whereas the Church of the Virgin contains murals dating from 1209 that rival those of the contemporaneous Florentine masters Cimabue, Duccio, and Giotto. Recognizing the site's extensive historic and artistic legacy, UNESCO made the monastery a World Heritage site in 1986. **AS**

> *"Studenica [has conserved] an array of exceptional monuments inside its circular wall."*
>
> UNESCO

Skull Tower (Niš, Serbia)

Macabre Ottoman monument to victory, and symbol of Serbian nationalism

When the First Serbian Uprising began in 1804, Serbia had been under the control of the Ottoman empire for around 350 years, having been conquered in the mid-fifteenth century. The uprising was put down in 1813, although the Second Serbian Uprising began shortly afterward in 1815. The second Serbian attempt was ultimately successful, leading to the official independence of the country in 1829.

The Skull Tower dates from the first revolt, and was originally an Ottoman monument intended to mark the empire's success in defeating the Serbian rebels close to Niš in May 1809. Wanting to exploit earlier victories and expand their newly captured territory, Serbian forces under a local duke, Stevan Sindjelic, had waited for the Ottomans in newly dug trenches. Thanks to an overly defensive strategy and divisions between Serbian commanders—factors that allowed the Ottomans time to focus their strength against the Serbs—Sindjelic found himself vastly outnumbered. Realizing his situation was hopeless, he blew up his ammunition stores—apparently with a shot from his own pistol—devastating the Ottoman and Serbian forces alike. In the aftermath of the battle, the Turkish commander, Hurshid Pasha, ordered the decapitation of the Serbian bodies and the construction of a monument using the heads as building blocks. When completed, the tower was 10 feet (3 m) high, contained 952 skulls, and was topped with the head of Sindjelic himself. Skulls were gradually removed during the nineteenth century, both for proper burial and as ghoulish souvenirs of the battle, until there were only fifty or sixty left in 1892, when a chapel was built over the monument to preserve what remained.

Built by a victorious occupying power as a warning to the Serbian people, the Skull Tower has since become a symbol of a heroic, albeit tragic, action in the cause of Serbian independence. **AS**

" . . . those brave men whose cut-off heads made the cornerstone of the independence of their homeland."

From a plaque at the Skull Tower chapel

🏛 ◎ Old Bridge (Mostar, Bosnia and Herzegovina)

Suleiman the Magnificent's bridge, that unites the past and the future

"The Old Bridge enhanced the town's development and prosperity. It was its raison d'être."

UNESCO

⬆ The bridge, more than 400 years old, was built to link the Ottoman Empire with target cities to the west.

➡ The reconstructed bridge, completed in 2004, still attracts divers willing to continue a long tradition.

The splendid stone arch that soars across the River Neretva encapsulates the history of Bosnia in a single architectural masterpiece. The Old Bridge (Stari Most) was commissioned by the Ottoman emperor Suleiman the Magnificent after his Balkan campaigns of 1566. An architectural student named Hayruddin was asked to prepare plans and construction began immediately. Rumors of a radical and unworkable design led to Hayruddin preparing his own funeral for the day of the bridge's unveiling and the removal of the supportive scaffolding—the rumors fortunately proved incorrect. The name *Stari Most* and the town's name of Mostar come from the towers constructed at either end of the bridge and the unit of Ottoman soldiers protecting the crossing. Both were known as "Mostari," or Guardians of the Bridge.

The bridge spans 98 feet (30 m) and towers 78 feet (24 m) above the torrent of the River Neretva. The arch soars 39 feet (12 m) high and encloses an elegant roadway of 13 feet (4 m). When commissioned, the bridge was the longest single-span bridge in the world. For Suleiman, its primary function was to provide ease of access for his armies to the rich cities of the Dalmatian coast. It also facilitated trade from the mountainous interior of Bosnia, rich in silver, and allowed rapid transfer of valuable salt to inland communities from the salt pans of Dalmatia.

The bridge was destroyed on November 9, 1993, by Croatian artillery during the vicious civil war that engulfed Yugoslavia in 1991. When news reached Sarajevo of its destruction, the government declared a day of national mourning, despite the siege and destruction of Sarajevo itself. The destruction of the Old Bridge encapsulated the pointless and furious bloodletting of the civil war. After many years of wrangling, the UNESCO-sponsored reconstruction project reopened the bridge in July 2004. **IS**

🏛 ◉ Alexander Nevski Monastery (St. Petersburg, Russia)

Complex of religious buildings and the graves of many great Russians

The Alexander Nevski Monastery was built to house the remains of St. Alexander Nevski, a Russian prince and military commander, and the patron saint of St. Petersburg. The monastery is one of the most significant sites in the Russian Orthodox Church; in 1797 it was raised to the highest rank, *lavra*, by Emperor Paul I.

The monastery was founded in July 1710 by Tsar Peter the Great on the site of a former Swedish fort. The first church on the site was built in wood in 1712, and consecrated a year later. In 1724 a new church, designed by Domenico Trezzini, was built to house the saint's remains. In 1750 the remains were rehoused in a silver shrine by Empress Elizabeth—one and a half tons of solid silver went into its creation. A Neoclassical cathedral, named for the Holy Trinity and designed by Ivan Starov, was built from 1778 to 1790, and the shrine and its contents were moved there from the city of

Vladimir in 1790. In addition to the monastery's religious significance, its two graveyards are the final home of many eminent Russians, including Pyotr Ilyich Tchaikovsky and Fyodor Dostoevsky.

Numerous churches and other structures were added to the site, and by 1900 the complex was home to sixteen churches. Under communist rule the monastery suffered; Nevski's remains were moved from the site, the monastery's treasures were looted, every one of the churches within the complex was closed, and the buildings were used to house a museum, government offices, and storerooms.

Although only five of the sixteen churches of the Alexander Nevski Monastery survived communist rule, there are still two Baroque churches and the original Neoclassical cathedral in the complex. The site remains the final resting place of some of the great figures of Russian culture. **JF**

🏛 ◉ Mariinsky Theater (St. Petersburg, Russia)

Opulent nineteenth-century theater built under the direction of Tsar Alexander II

The palatial, icy-blue edifice of the Mariinsky Theater does not prepare theatergoers for the awe inspired by its grandly eloquent, five-tier, 1,625-seat auditorium. Entering the stalls, visitors are dwarfed by the scale and dazzled by the sumptuous azure, gilt, and crystal hangings set against a famous backdrop—Alexander Golovin's luxurious painted curtains. Fine molded decorations and alabaster sculptures, set off by the light and dark blue tints of the walls, velvet chairs, and curtains, complete the impressive spectacle.

Looking up to the massive three-tiered bronze chandelier with crystal pendants designed by E. Frachioli, their gaze is also likely to catch the painted ceiling depicting dancers around the Muse of Dance. Opposite the stage stands the restored Royal Box—a mini theater within a theater with its own draped curtains, staircase, and foyer. It harks back to an Imperial Russia of tsarist golden eagles and gilded

crown (removed in the 1917 October Revolution along with its sumptuously liveried attendants).

The site now occupied by the theater was previously a circus for riding and parading horses. However, in 1859 the partly stone circus building burned down, and it was quickly reconstructed as a purpose-built theater by Albert Cavos under the direction of Tsar Alexander II. Named Mariinsky after the tsar's wife, it reopened in October 1860 with a performance of Glinka's aptly titled opera, *A Life for the Tsar*. In later years various architects left their marks on the site, notably Victor Shreter, whose renovations in the 1880s increased the theater's capacity.

The cupola atop the large dome, itself topped with a lyre and a crown, is a notable external feature. The lyre was renovated to replace a damaged one; the crown had to be replaced by a new one after a bizarre theft. **JH**

🏛 ◉ Menshikov Palace (St. Petersburg, Russia)

Residence of one of Russia's most powerful and ambitious politicians

Menshikov Palace was constructed as the residence of the first governor of St. Petersburg, Aleksandr Danilovich Menshikov. Menshikov was the right-hand man of Tsar Peter the Great, and was one of the most powerful and influential men in Russia.

The construction of Menshikov Palace involved numerous European architects and artists, and incorporated both traditional Russian design and new ideas imported from the rest of Europe. The interior decoration included marble, contemporary Italian sculpture, and Dutch cobalt tiles. The Menshikov Palace was the cultural center of Russia's new capital. When Peter the Great died in 1725, Menshikov secured the succession for his second wife, Empress Catherine, and during her short reign he was essentially the ruler of Russia. However, he overreached himself when he attempted to marry his daughter to the next emperor, the young Peter II. The Russian nobility ousted Menshikov and forced him into exile in Siberia, where he died. His palace and other property were confiscated and passed into the hands of the state.

Menshikov Palace was used to house the First Cadet Corps, the nation's leading high school. In the 1880s, a museum of the Cadet Corps was established at the palace, and remained open until 1924. During the 1970s the palace was restored to its original appearance, opening its doors to visitors in 1981. The palace was part of the large Hermitage Museum complex, and so could draw on a vast collection made up of confiscated imperial and noble property.

The Menshikov Palace, and the historic center of St. Petersburg of which it is part, is a UNESCO World Heritage site. Now faithfully restored to its former glory, it is a monument to one of the most powerful politicians in Russian history, who rose to near-imperial status before his eventual downfall. **JF**

🏛 ⊚ Pavlovsk Palace (near St. Petersburg, Russia)

Glorious palace and gardens in the English style, commissioned by Catherine the Great

When Catherine the Great ordered a grand garden in the English style at Pavlovsk, wild and forested hunting grounds were transformed into a formal park in the finest English stately home tradition, dotted with Greek temples, classical bridges, and statues. The 1,300-acre (600 ha) sanctuary was the inspired work of Catherine's pet architect, Scotsman Charles Cameron. He outlined the general layout of the park and designed several pavilions, including the Temple of Friendship, a large domed rotunda with Doric columns. However, the Scotsman's signature design was the elegant three-storied rectangular gold and white palace, crowned by a flat dome or cupola on sixty-four columns, in the style of the Pantheon.

Catherine presented the estate to her unloved son Paul on the birth of his first child, and Pavlovsk became his summer palace. Cameron never had the same free hand in the service of Paul I and his wife, Grand Duchess Maria Feodorovna. The latter was a gardening fanatic and had plants shipped over from London's Kew Gardens. Scheming architects, notably Vincenzo Brenna, jostled for royal favor, pushing Cameron aside. The palace's semicircular wing-colonnades are Brenna's work and are reminiscent of Palladian villas.

Maria Feodorovna's influence is also discernible in the exquisitely furnished interiors, such as the Grecian Hall. Together with a succession of architects (including Andrei Voronikhin and Carlo Rossi) as well as painters and sculptors, she created exquisite set pieces comprising paintings, textiles, sculptures, Sèvres porcelain, crystal glass, and chandeliers, all set in marble and colored stucco.

The formation of the Pavlovsk complex took place while Russia was dominant in Europe. The ensemble— which was virtually rebuilt after Nazi occupation— reflects the spirit of the age of absolute monarchs. **JH**

Peter and Paul Fortress (St. Petersburg, Russia)

Island fortification lying at the heart of St. Petersburg

Tsar Peter the Great founded the city of St. Petersburg in 1703 on land that had been captured from Sweden, intending it to be the new capital of Russia. At the time, Russia was at war with Sweden in the Great Northern War (1700–21), so the city's first structure was the Peter and Paul Fortress, built on one of the city's islands. The complex was eventually extended to include a prison and cathedral, and is one of the monuments of Peter the Great's determination to make Russia a modern state.

St. Petersburg was created virtually at the will of Peter the Great. While the city was being built, he sometimes resided in a simple log cabin that in 1703 had been constructed in three days to the east of the site of the Peter and Paul Fortress. The fortress was not actually needed during the war because the Swedish forces never reached St. Petersburg. A grand stone cathedral was built between 1712 and 1733 as part of the complex, and was used as the final resting place for all the tsars of Russia from Peter the Great to the executed Nicholas II. From around 1720 onward, the fortress was used as a garrison and as a jail for political prisoners. During the October Revolution of 1917, the Peter and Paul Fortress played an important role. It was first used to hold imperial officials to protect them from public anger, and eventually it fell into the hands of the Bolsheviks. In 1924 the fortress was converted into a museum.

The Peter and Paul Fortress spans modern Russian history from the days of Peter the Great to Vladimir Lenin. It was the first large-scale structure to be built in the magnificent city of St. Petersburg, and stands as a monument to the absolute power that the tsars of Russia enjoyed before the revolution. The fortress is part of the UNESCO World Heritage site, designated in 1990, which incorporates all the historic center of St. Petersburg surrounding the fortress. **JF**

> *"[It] was the last island of the delta and no ships could enter without passing first by the fortress."*
>
> Knopf Guides, *St. Petersburg* (1995)

Smolny Institute (St. Petersburg, Russia)

A finishing school that hosted a revolution

Inside this pastel-yellow, classical Palladian, country-style mansion on the Neva, Lenin announced the birth of the Bolshevik state to a rapt audience. Yet just a few years earlier the building was a "finishing school" for the debutante daughters of wealthy Russians.

The assembly hall is where Lenin made his speech before leading his sympathizers to the Winter Palace on October 25, 1917. It was also here that the Second All-Russian Congress of Soviets convened—they confirmed Lenin's position, and the building remained his seat of government until March 1918. On display today are Lenin's office with writing desk and chair (used later by Stalin) and other rooms that he occupied. On December 1, 1934, party leader Sergey Kirov was gunned down here (probably on Stalin's orders), thus providing the excuse for a series of purges that led to the infamous gulags. Today the building serves as the office of the governor of St. Petersburg.

Originally the institute was a three-story, south-facing addition to the convent and other buildings that made up the original complex "for noble maidens." It was designed by Giacomo Quarenghi, the foremost practitioner of Palladian architecture in Imperial Russia, who created a traditional rectangular ground plan with two wings; the main facade focuses on a portico with Ionic columns. Today the Imperial eagle is back in its place on the portico, replacing the Soviet hammer and sickle, but a statue of Lenin and a vast portrait of the prominent leader are still found inside. The site is dotted with Palladian-style propylaea (monumental gateways) that were added in 1923 and 1924 under the direction of architects Vladimir Shchuko and Vladimir Gelfreikh.

The Lenin Museum in the Smolny Institute is one of the few still dedicated to the revolutionary in St. Petersburg; most were closed in the anticommunist wave following the breakup of the Soviet Union. **JH**

> "[Lenin] stood there waiting, apparently oblivious to the long-rolling ovation."
>
> Leon Trotsky, *History of the Russian Revolution* (1930)

Pushkin's House (St. Petersburg, Russia)

Museum recreating the poet's final hours

The small first-floor flat where Alexander Pushkin (1799–1837) died is hidden away in a courtyard behind a wooden gate. Russia's preeminent poet, credited with "inventing" the modern Russian language, lived in these rooms with his family for several months and died here after being mortally wounded after a duel over his wife.

The building, which dates from the 1720s, was the palace of Pushkin's friend and fellow revolutionary sympathizer Prince Volkhonsky. Pushkin moved here with his wife, Natalya, their four children, and Natalya's two sisters in October 1836. In January 1837 Pushkin was provoked into the fateful duel by an officer named d'Anthès. This man, chasing Pushkin's wife, goaded Pushkin with letters announcing him a cuckold. In snowbound woodland, Pushkin was wounded; he died two days later, January 29, 1837, in his study—arranged now exactly as it was then, including the couchette on which he bled to death. The study also displays the waistcoat Pushkin was wearing when shot and his death mask. His study desk holds a treasured inkstand of an Ethiopian boy, a reminder of Pushkin's African great-grandfather Abram Hannibal. Bought as a slave in 1706 by the Russian ambassador to Constantinople, he rose to be one of Peter the Great's generals. Pushkin's bookcases, containing 4,500 volumes, dominate the study.

It was in 1925, under the Soviets, that the apartment became a museum. In 1987 the apartment was reconstructed to look as it did on the day Pushkin died, as described in rough sketches drafted by fellow poet Vasily Zhokovsky, who had kept vigil in Pushkin's final hours and closed his eyes after he died. In Pushkin's study there is a lithograph portrait of Zhokovsky, bearing the inscription, "To the victorious student who surpassed his teacher." **JH**

 ◉ **Peterhof** (near St. Petersburg, Russia)

Imperial palace overlooking St. Petersburg's port of Kronstadt on the Gulf of Finland

Peterhof (also known as Petrodvorets) is a series of palaces and gardens begun by Tsar Peter the Great after he moved the capital of Russia from Moscow to St. Petersburg in 1712. It is located near the harbor at Kronstadt, which Peter developed into an important deep-water port to serve the new capital. Peterhof's location also captivated many of the tsars who ruled Russia after Peter, who added to or extended the palace according to their own tastes, creating a magnificent ensemble.

Peterhof overlooks the Gulf of Finland and is situated on a bluff near the coast. Peter designed and built a small wooden palace on the site in 1710, but the first major work was Monplaisir, which he began in 1714. Peter added several other palaces as well as a formal French garden (the Lower Gardens) on the coast, and ornamental fountains. The complex was officially inaugurated on August 15, 1723. The main building in Peterhof is the Grand Palace, which was extended by Empress Elizabeth from 1745 to 1755. The Grand Palace overlooks the Grand Cascade—a monumental water feature with several fountains. It is powered by a 13.6-mile- (22-km-) long system of gravity-fed pumps. At the foot of the Grand Cascade is a sea channel that runs to the Gulf of Finland.

Peterhof was one of the main imperial residences until the Russian Revolution. In 1918 it was made into a state museum. In World War II it was occupied by the Germans from 1941 to 1944, and while retreating they vandalized and destroyed large parts of the complex. However, much of the palace has been restored. In 1990 it became part of a UNESCO World Heritage site that includes historic St. Petersburg and outlying monuments. It is an important and sumptuous legacy of imperial Russia and a testament to the vision of one of Russia's greatest rulers, Peter the Great. **JF**

🏛 ◉ **Winter Palace** (St. Petersburg, Russia)

Residence of tsars and principal building of the present-day Hermitage museum

"You are bankrupt.... Go where you belong from now on—in the garbage-pile of history!"

Leon Trotsky, berating non-Bolshevik socialists

⊡ Originally, the Winter Palace was yellow, white, and gold, in common with other civic buildings.

⊡ Bolshevik troops led by Leon Trotsky attack the Winter Palace on November 7, 1917.

A dazzling Baroque creation now decorated in green and white, the Winter Palace is so named because it became the winter residence of the Russian tsars. It was originally commissioned by Empress Elizabeth I, daughter of Peter the Great, and was built between 1754 and 1762. Elizabeth died before it was completed, but it was used by Catherine the Great and her successors. It remained a royal home until imperial rule was ended by the revolution of 1917.

The palace's Italian architect, Bartolomeo Rastrelli, produced a stunning lesson in lavish Baroque architecture, employing a riot of decorative features across the palace's three stories ranging from Corinthian capitals and numerous sculptures to beautifully curvaceous moldings. Although the whole building exudes an elegant symmetry, each facade has decorative differences that make every view of the palace an artistic surprise. The interior is no less sumptuous, with more than 1,000 luxuriously decorated rooms and halls.

In 1837 the palace burned to the ground, but it was rebuilt two years later to Rastrelli's original design. Since then it has formed a dramatic backdrop to Russian history. The 1905 revolution was sparked when workers who had marched to the palace to present a petition to Tsar Nicholas II were attacked by imperial troops. The palace was later stormed during the 1917 revolution.

Today the Hermitage complex, which includes the palace, is one of the world's leading art museums and galleries, a role begun by Catherine the Great in the 1760s when she hung a great art collection there. Exhibits range from ancient Egyptian artifacts to the work of Leonardo da Vinci, Cézanne, and an enormous selection of Russian art. It is said that if viewers devoted one minute to each exhibit, it would take them eleven years to see the whole collection. **AK**

🏛 ◉ Catherine Palace (near St. Petersburg, Russia)

Tsarist summer residence and site of the famously opulent Amber Room

The Catherine Palace is one of the most ornate and flamboyant buildings in Russia. The summer residence of the Russian emperors for most of the eighteenth century, it was famed for its lavish interiors, especially the Amber Room, a large chamber entirely decorated with panels of amber, mirrors, and gilded ornament. Once known as the eighth wonder of the world, it was stripped in World War II, its contents never to be seen again. However, the room was reconstructed with new amber and opened in 2003.

In 1717 Empress Catherine I commissioned the construction of a summer residence, which was susbequently added to by her niece Empress Anna. This palace was in a sober Baroque style and Anna's daughter, Empress Elizabeth, found it old-fashioned and ordered its rebuilding. A new Rococo palace, designed by court architect Bartolomeo Rastrelli, was unveiled on July 30, 1756. The most ornate part of the palace was a suite of rooms known as the Golden Enfilade, which included the Amber Room. More than 220 pounds (100 kg) of gold were used to gild the stucco facade and ornamental statues. There was also a formal garden, centering on the azure and white Hermitage Pavilion. When Empress Catherine II "The Great" ascended the throne in 1762, she regarded the palace as overelaborate and dated, preferring the Neoclassical style. She commissioned her favorite architect, the Scotsman Charles Cameron, to refurbish a wing, as well as to construct her personal apartments, the Agate Rooms.

In 1944, the retreating German army destroyed most of the palace, leaving behind only a shell. However, much of the palace was reconstructed in time for the tercentenary of St. Petersburg in 2003. Today it testifies to the luxury and splendor enjoyed by Russia's emperors and empresses, and the changing tastes of one of Europe's most powerful dynasties. **JF**

"… the Empress spent much money out of her own pocket on it, without ever counting."

Catherine the Great, on Empress Elizabeth

Dostoevsky's House (Staraya Russa, Russia)

The great writer's refuge, now a museum

In the picturesque provincial town of Staraya Russa, by the banks of the Pererytitsa River, is a shady two-story wooden dacha once owned by the novelist Fyodor Mikhailovich Dostoevsky. He called it his "nest" and for a wandering writer, whose life was as harrowing as his fiction, this was possibly the one place he felt truly at home. He wrote much of his last novel, *The Brothers Karamazov*, here and the fictional settings of the novel are thinly disguised parts of Staraya Russa.

The cottage is open to visitors as a museum: On the second floor are the six rooms where the writer, his young second wife and former stenographer, Anna Grigorievna, and their children had their summer home. Decorations, pictures, heavy furniture, and numerous photographs recreate their warm and cozy setup. Exhibits include a few genuine possessions (top hat and gloves, a medicine bottle with receipt), personal documents, editions of his works in different languages, and paintings, drawings, and sculptures. A lower sitting room plays host to special exhibits and literary events. The museum extends outside to include the large shady grove, kitchen garden, outer sheds, courtyard with bathhouse, and river.

Staraya Russa was a fashionable health resort famed for its salt springs and mud baths. Dostoevsky sought physical respite there for his epilepsy, financial respite for gambling debts, and spiritual healing within the Russian Orthodox Church. The Dostoevskys initially rented the building from a retired lieutenant colonel, A. K. Gribbe; in 1876 they bought it outright.

After the writer's death in 1881, Anna Grigorievna preserved the memory of their life together here. In 1931 a commemorative plaque was mounted and in 1971, for the 150th anniversary of Dostoevsky's birth, an exhibit, which became the basis for a museum, was opened. The F. M. Dostoevsky Memorial House-Museum was officially opened on May 4, 1981. **JH**

"What is hell? I maintain that it is the suffering of being unable to love."

Fyodor Dostoevsky, *The Brothers Karamazov* (1880)

🏛 ◈ Cathedral of St. Sophia (Novgorod, Russia)

Centerpiece of the religious architecture of Russia's former capital city

Novgorod is a hidden gem: It is littered with churches and monasteries, and fine sculptures, most famously the Millennium Monument of 1842, commemorating the first millennium of Russian history with 129 bronze figures, all of them approved by Emperor Alexander II. Novgorod was Russia's first capital, founded in 859, and it became a center for Orthodox spirituality as well as Russian architecture. The latter is epitomized by the distinctively domed Cathedral of St. Sophia, also known in the Orthodox world as the Church of Divine Wisdom. It is one of Russia's earliest stone structures.

Little is given away by the massive monolithic structure: The walls are austere, the buttresses flat and bare, and the windows small and narrow to keep out the biting cold. The outer walls are divided by sharply protruding pilaster strips, which correspond exactly to the divisions of the interior. The masonry consists mostly of large, odd-sized blocks of undressed limestone set in a pinkish mortar of crushed brick and lime, which accentuates the irregular shape and enhances the power and austere beauty of the exterior. The central dome—not onion-shaped like the other four domes—was gilded later in the fifteenth century along with its central cross.

Visitors enter the church through the northern gates. The main (western) gates are opened only on a few special occasions. They protect two very rare bronze doors (crafted in the German city of Magdeburg in the twelfth century and seized as booty from Sigtuna in Sweden) whose detail shows portraits of the craftsmen involved. Frescoes frame this portal. Inside, the frescoes and ancient mural paintings have faded badly. There is, however, an impressive iconostasis (six-tiered icon screen) and other icons, including the famous Virgin of the Sign, returned to the cathedral in 1991. **JH**

🏛 ⊚ Church of the Transfiguration (Kizhi Island, Russia)

Finest example of wooden architecture in Russia

The Church of the Transfiguration is the most outstanding of an extraordinary collection of wooden buildings on Kizhi Island in Russia. Its magnificent onion domes and tiers were constructed entirely of wood; its builders did not even use nails. Kizhi Island has been a UNESCO World Heritage site since 1990.

The Church of the Transfiguration was erected in 1714. The church embodies the gaiety of Russian folk culture as well as sophisticated engineering. Its main body was constructed entirely of pine. The church is pyramidal in profile, formed by three octahedrons of diminishing size placed one on top of the other. The roof is covered by twenty-two onion domes, clad in shingles made of aspen. A system of drains is integrated into the structure of the church to preserve and protect it. Amazingly, the church was constructed using the simplest tools, and most of the work was done with axes. The identity of the individual

carpenters and designers involved is unknown. Legend has it that the church is the work of a single carpenter called Nestor, who, after it was finished, threw his ax into Lake Onega saying, "There never was, nowhere is, and never will be a church like this." There are numerous other churches on Kizhi Island, including the nine-domed Church of the Intercession (1764) and the fourteenth-century Church of St. Lazarus, the oldest surviving wooden church in Russia. Also on the island are examples of eighteenth-century Russian households, and a nature reserve.

The Church of the Transfiguration is one of the jewels of Russian architecture. Its sophistication, grandeur, and elegance is especially striking given it was constructed using only wood, and with only a few simple tools. Indeed, the whole of Kizhi Island is a monument to the beauty of Russian wooden architecture and the ingenuity of the craftsmen. **JF**

🏛 ◎ Trinity–St. Sergius Monastery

(Sergiev-Possad, Russia)

Religious complex with two beautiful cathedrals at its heart

"The number of your monks will be as … the birds, and it will not decrease if they follow your path."

Voice heard by St. Sergius in a miraculous vision

Trinity–St. Sergius was founded as a monastery between 1337 and 1340 by the Russian monk and mystic Sergius of Radonezh. It remains today the spiritual center of Russian Orthodox Christianity, with bearded Sergius monks in their flowing black robes and distinctive "klobuk" headgear milling from church to seminary to refectory. At first sight, the seemingly impregnable 40-foot- (12-m-) high walls punctuated by towers suggest military might rather than peaceful pilgrimage. This is exactly what Ivan the Terrible wanted to achieve when he turned the monastery into a massive fortress in the sixteenth century. It withstood a sixteen-month siege of Polish and Lithuanian troops in the early 1600s.

Trinity–St. Sergius Monastery (also known as the Holy Trinity Lavra) lies some 45 miles (75 km) northeast of Moscow and comprises a hotchpotch of Russian vernacular architecture in its thirty-plus buildings and towers. At its heart stand not one but two beautiful cathedrals. The Cathedral of the Assumption is recognized immediately by its four gorgeous blue onion domes patterned with golden stars. It was commissioned by Ivan the Terrible and took twenty-eight years to complete. The lofty interior was painted in just one hundred days by students of the acclaimed Yaroslavi school of artists led by Dmitriy Griorev in 1684. Their names are inscribed beneath a fresco of the Last Judgment on the west wall. Outside the west door is the grave of Tsar Boris Godunov, the only tsar buried outside Moscow or St. Petersburg (his skull is missing, apparently). The Holy Trinity Cathedral was built in 1422 and the holy relics of St. Sergius were discovered miraculously intact during its construction. The building is distinguished by its gleaming white exterior and gold-topped domes (semicircular or shaped like a cross section of an onion). **JH**

Belozersky Monastery

(near Vologda Oblast, Russia)

A monk's refuge that grew dramatically

This massive and stunningly beautiful monastery-fortress, some 250 miles (400 km) northeast of St. Petersburg, soars impressively more than 100 feet (30 m) above the frozen tundra and icy Lake Siversky. It was founded by St. Kirill, a fourteenth-century monk who was driven by a prophecy to seek solitude far from the bustle of Moscow. With another monk, he chose a hill on the bank of Lake Siversky, dug an earth-house, and lived in it. He named it Belozersky after another nearby lake, Beloye Ozero (the White Lake).

Kirillo-Belozersky grew to occupy 30 acres (12 ha), enclosing several churches, a cathedral, and the labors of some 20,000 peasants. Kirill was buried here and later canonized. His small refuge grew to become one of the biggest and wealthiest monasteries in Europe, second only to Trinity–St. Sergius Monastery.

New stone walls were erected between 1654 and 1680 and Kirillo-Belozersky became a powerful fortress, instrumental in Russia's wars with the Swedes and Poles. These walls can still be seen today, with their towers: The Vologodskaja tower has five fighting levels and an observation cabin; Ferapontovskaja tower is the highest, at 130 feet (40 m); and Svitochnaja tower is named after the monastery servants who washed clothes (*svitoks*). Another feature are several *kiots*—niches in the walls housing holy icons.

Catherine the Great stripped the monastery of its thousands of peasants and lands in 1764—the town jail was placed in the low-level chambers of the fortress walls and the gradual decline of the monastery began. Some reconstruction work was carried out in the late nineteenth century, on the monastery's 500th anniversary, but it was not enough. The fortress was closed in 1924 and turned into a state museum. In 1998 one part of the complex became a monastery once again. **JH**

Bolshoi Theater

(Moscow, Russia)

Moscow's premier theater

On July 1, 2005, the heavy silk and gold curtain of Moscow's Bolshoi Theater came down for the last time before a multimillion-dollar overhaul. Following 300 performances a year for 150 years, the theater was literally sinking and crumbling to the touch. Bombs, Bolsheviks, and botched repairs had all taken their toll.

The Bolshoi Theater opened on August 20, 1856, when its five-tiered, red-velvet, and gilt-edged auditorium routinely accommodated more than 2,200 Muscovites. It symbolized the city's efforts to lose its "country cousin" image in comparison with St. Petersburg and its grand Mariinsky Theater.

> *"Scale is part of the company's identity. It's the effect of its home stage, . . . Bolshoi means 'big'."*
>
> Zoe Anderson, dance critic

The Bolshoi Theater was designed by Osip Bove in an imperial style with an eight-columned classical portico, crowned by a bronze sculpture of Apollo on a chariot carrying the sun. The theater is famed for its acoustics. The interior, measuring 69 feet (21 m) high, 82 feet (25 m) long, and 85 feet (26 m) wide, was trimmed in wood, and has been likened to a musical instrument. The original wood used for the stage, seating, balconies, and surrounds is of such excellent resonance that it has been kept in the reconstruction.

The site has been plagued by fires. In 1805 the Old Petrovskiy Theater burned down. Osip's masterpiece succumbed to flames in 1853 (the walls and facade survived), after which Albert Kavos used Bove's plans to redesign the theater with an additional third story and even more opulent decor. **JH**

🏛 ◎ St. Basil's Cathedral (Moscow, Russia)

Gemlike monument commemorating a military conquest of Ivan the Terrible

> "... a monument whose
> composition has no parallel in the
> entire history of ... architecture."

Great Buildings Online

⬆ Tsar Ivan IV commissioned St. Basil's after his victory over the Tatars and annexation of their territory.

➡ When St. Basil's was first built, it was not multicolored; its scheme was red brick enlivened by white plaster.

St. Basil's Cathedral, famous for its onion-shaped domes in many swirling colors, is probably the best-known building in Moscow. St. Basil's comprises nine individual chapels joined together in a single foundation, all grouped around one central spire.

The cathedral was commissioned by Tsar Ivan IV "The Terrible," and built between 1555 and 1561 to commemorate his conquest of the Tatar Khanate of Kazan. The decisive victory came on the feast day of the Intercession of Mary, the original name of the cathedral. It became known as St. Basil's after a popular saint, Basil Fool for Christ.

The original design of the cathedral featured eight chapels laid out in the shape of a star. Ivan IV's son, Tsar Feodor Ivanovich, added a ninth chapel in 1588 to house the tomb of St. Basil, who had been interred in the cathedral that formerly stood on the site. Legend has it that Ivan IV ordered the architect, Postnik Yakovlev, to be blinded after it was completed to keep him from ever again designing anything that would rival the beauty of St. Basil's. The truth of this is doubtful; Yakovlev went on to design several other structures when his work on St. Basil's was finished.

Compared with the extravagant exterior, the interior of the cathedral is relatively subdued and dimly lit. In the garden outside St. Basil's is a statue of two Russian heroes, Dmitry Pozharsky and Kuzma Minin, who successfully rallied a Russian volunteer army against the invading Poles in the early seventeenth century. The statue, erected in 1818, was originally placed in the center of the Red Square but was moved in 1936 because it was considered an obstruction during parades.

St. Basil's Cathedral has survived centuries of war and political upheaval to become perhaps the most recognized symbol of Moscow, built by one of Russia's most feared and successful rulers. **JF**

 ⊚ **Novodevichy Convent** (Moscow, Russia)

One of Russia's finest and most beautiful religious foundations

Novodevichy Convent is one of the best-known cloisters in Russia. It was founded in the early sixteenth century and was extensively added to throughout the 1680s. The structure has remained virtually unchanged since then.

The Grand Prince of Moscow, Vasili III, founded Novodevichy Convent in 1524 to commemorate his 1514 conquest of Smolensk, in western Russia. The Cathedral of Our Lady of Smolensk was constructed from 1524 to 1525. The foundation was based around the River Moskva, and formed an important part of a chain of monastic ensembles that were integrated into the defense systems of Moscow. Vasili III gave the convent 3,000 rubles and endowed them with land. Tsar Ivan IV "The Terrible" also patronized the convent. Tsarina Eudoxia Lopukhina, first wife of Tsar Peter the Great, made extensive additions to the convent in the 1680s in the Muscovite Baroque style. These included

other churches and a bell tower. The convent sheltered many ladies from the Russian royal family, including Eudoxia Lopukhina after her divorce from Peter the Great, as well as his sister Sophia Alekseyevna. The convent also served as a charitable foundation. From 1724 it housed a military hospital, as well as orphanages and almshouses. In 1812 French soldiers under Napoleon attempted to blow up the convent, but they were stopped by the nuns who lived there.

After the Bolsheviks seized power, the convent was closed in 1922 and converted into a museum. However, from 1994 nuns have been allowed to return to Novodevichy. Numerous prominent Russians are buried in the convent's cemetery, including Anton Chekhov, Sergei Prokofiev, and Nikita Khrushchev.

Novodevichy Convent was designated a UNESCO World Heritage site in 2004. The convent continues as a working nunnery as well as a museum. **JF**

🏛 ◈ Kremlin (Moscow, Russia)

Residence of Russian tsars and hierarchs, and now of the Russian president

Until the early eighteenth century, the Kremlin was the primary residence of the Russian tsars and the hierarchs of the Russian Orthodox Church. The origins of this fortified complex go back to the late eleventh century, although it was not until 1475 that a major building program, instigated by Grand Prince Ivan III, also known as Ivan the Great, gave the Kremlin its present outline.

Situated alongside the River Moskva, the Kremlin developed into a collection of churches, monasteries, palaces, and government offices, surrounded by a high wall. The complex is roughly triangular in plan. Ivan invited Italian architects to help him in his reconstruction work—it later became commonplace for the more ambitious tsars to employ foreigners to help modernize the backward Russian state. It was in the early sixteenth century that Ivan built his famous bell tower that, after further work in 1600, soared above the Kremlin to a height of 266 feet (81 m). Over the centuries different rulers demolished and erected new buildings to suit the fashions of the day, but the Kremlin retained its Russian character, not least in its onion-shaped domes. A crisis point in the Kremlin's history occurred in 1812 when it was occupied for a month by Napoleon's invading forces and was partly destroyed on the French retreat from Moscow.

Fundamental change came after the Russian Revolution of 1917 when the Bolsheviks brought the seat of government back to Moscow. The old churches and monasteries were redeveloped to make way for new institutions such as the communist military school and the Palace of the Congresses. In 1955 parts of the Kremlin were opened up to foreign tourists who were able to visit the site's museums. Since the break-up of the Soviet Union, the Kremlin has become the official residence of the Russian president. **AG**

Lenin's Mausoleum

(Moscow, Russia)

Resting place of the former Bolshevik leader

On the death of Vladimir Ilyich Lenin (1870–1924) there were calls from the communist faithful to be allowed to pay their respects to their hero. In response, the revolutionary's body was embalmed and a mausoleum swiftly constructed from wood. This was later replaced by a larger wooden structure, but when the demand to file past the body showed no signs of diminishing, the communist authorities constructed a permanent memorial. Work started in Red Square in 1929 and was completed the following year. The new stone mausoleum was built as a stepped pyramid, faced with red granite, porphyry, and black labradorite. The inscription "Lenin" was carved above the bronze doors, which were flanked by a guard of honor.

Inside the mausoleum is the memorial hall where the glass sarcophagus containing Lenin's body is held for public view. Lenin's body has been remarkably well preserved, so much so that there have been suspicions that the body has been replaced by a wax model, although the authorities decline to comment on the matter. In 1953 Lenin was joined by the embalmed body of Josef Stalin, although in 1961 the Soviet leader Nikita Khrushchev had Stalin's body removed to a burial place within the Kremlin.

During the period 1924 to 1972 some ten million people filed past Lenin's body, and today it remains both a popular tourist destination and a place of communist pilgrimage. Since the breakup of the Soviet Union, the mausoleum has been downgraded by the state, with upkeep and administration the responsibility of private institutions. Calls for the mausoleum to be closed—by Boris Yeltsin among others—have been resisted by Lenin supporters.

Ironically, all the communist leaders whose bodies have been preserved—Lenin, Mao Zedong, Ho Chi Minh, and Kim Il-sung—wished to be cremated. **AG**

> *"We can guarantee preservation of his body indefinitely, certainly for a century and more."*
>
> Prof. Valery Bykov, Mausoleum Group

Moscow Metro

(Moscow, Russia)

Grandiose Soviet subway system

Work began on an underground railway system for the city of Moscow in the 1930s, and the opening stage was built from 1935 to 1937; the first line stretched from Sokolniki to Park Kultury. The second stage was completed before the Soviet Union entered World War II in 1941, and work on the third stage continued throughout the war, with stations being used as underground shelters from German bombing. The fourth and fifth stages were constructed during the later 1940s and into the 1950s, at the time of the Cold War; consequently, some of the stations were built to withstand a nuclear strike.

The Moscow Metro system consists of a series of eleven radial lines running like spokes from the central hub to the outskirts of the city, plus the Number 5 (Koltseveya), which runs around the city in a 12 mile (20 km) circle, linking the other lines. The Metro is one of the busiest subway networks in the world, and on a normal weekday will carry more than eight million passengers along 173 miles (279 km) of track, visiting 172 stations on route.

The most striking feature of the Metro is the grand and ornate styling of many of its stations, which are decorated to resemble the interiors of tsarist palaces. The tiled walls are inset with inspiring sculptures, mosaics, and paintings of workers, peasants, and soldiers enjoying the fruits of the Soviet system—a deliberate ploy to advance the cause of communism.

The Moscow system has a good reputation for efficiency and features an unusual gender-specific announcement scheme. A male voice reads the announcements for all trains going into the city center, whereas a female voice does the same for outward-bound trains. On line Number 5, a male voice indicates travel in a clockwise direction, a female voice for counterclockwise travel. **AG**

Astrakhan Kremlin

(Astrakhan, Russia)

Center of the Russian presence in Astrakhan

The Astrakhan Kremlin is a walled complex featuring extensive fortifications and battlements, as well as cathedrals and a palace. In 1556 Tsar Ivan IV "The Terrible" conquered Astrakhan, located in southern European Russia, from the Tatars. A wooden fortress was constructed in 1558 on the steep Hare Hill overlooking the Volga River. In 1569 it successfully withstood a siege from the Ottoman Turks. Ivan IV decided to replace the wooden fortress with a stone structure, and sent military engineers from Moscow.

The stone used to build the Astrakhan Kremlin allegedly came from the nearby ruins of the city of

---

"In the whole of my empire, there is not a single cathedral as beautiful as this one."

Tsar Peter the Great, on the Assumption Cathedral

Sarai Batu. The fortifications are triangular in shape, with eight towers along the walls. The largest tower is above the main gate and contains a belfry. Another tower was known as Torture and contained a prison. Later, two cathedrals were added: St. Trinity in 1700 and the Assumption in 1710. The second of the cathedrals, erected between 1698 and 1710, was designed by the serf architect Dorofei Myakishev. During 1705 and 1706, the Astrakhan Kremlin was at the center of a local revolt against the tsar, and rebels stormed the Kremlin, executing the regional governor and around 300 other nobles and officials.

The Astrakhan Kremlin was the country's gateway to Asia from the late sixteenth century and is an important example of Russian military engineering and church building. It is now a museum. **JF**

Vladivostok Station

(Vladivostok, Russia)

Terminus of the Trans-Siberian railway

Vladivostok is so remote that it is closer to China and Japan than Moscow, seven time zones away. That is why it is literally "the end of the line" when it comes to the Trans-Siberian Express, which starts (or finishes) its magical marathon rail trip here at Vladivostok station.

The city's most recognizable landmark is the station's faux-seventeenth-century facade with its odd assortment of turrets and towers. It is a near replica of Yaroslavskyi station in Moscow, 5,771 miles (9,288 km) away; the distance is marked by a milestone just by the station. It resembles a palace fit for a tsar rather than a utilitarian terminus—indeed in 1891 the cornerstone was symbolically laid by Tsarevich (tsar-in-waiting) Nicholas (later Nicholas II). Construction then began following the designs of architect A. Basilevsky.

By 1907 the original structure was too small to serve Vladivostok's booming economy. A new station was built, designed by N. V. Konovalov; he preserved the old towers and part of the walls, and created the handsome châteaux-style building that stands today. Over one entrance arch was a panel of bright mosaic tiles portraying St. George slaying a dragon (the saint being the emblem of Moscow). This and other imperial flourishes were destroyed by the Soviets, who also cut off the heads of the two-headed imperial eagle. From 1958 to 1991 Vladivostok was closed to outsiders. In 1994 the outside of this architectural gem was painstakingly restored, including the cobblestones on the square in front. This was followed two years later by a delicate restoration of the grand interior.

The nearby square is the birthplace of the city, founded 150 years ago. A short walk from the terminus is the central (and first-built) street, Svetlanskaya, where most of the city's historic sites are clustered—including the restored family home of Oscar-winning actor Yul Brynner, a native of Vladivostok. **JH**

Brest Fortress

(Brest, Belarus)

Scene of a heroic defense in World War II

Situated close to the present Polish border, on a strategic site on the confluence of the rivers Bug and Mukhavets, the fortress at Brest was the most impressive military stronghold in Russia. Built from 1836, the project was suggested by a military engineer called Delovan and carried out by three others, Opermann, Maletzki, and Feldmann, between 1836 and 1842. It proved to be a mammoth undertaking, which involved moving most of the town of Brest (then called Brest-Litovsk) a couple of miles to the east. The core of the new fortress was the citadel, a curved, two-story building that could accommodate 12,000

> "... we could hear the Russian soldiers screaming and groaning, but they continued to fight."

General Schlieper, German 45th Division

troops. The fortress was extended and strengthened from 1878 to 1888, and again from 1911 to 1914.

Brest belonged to Poland for much of the early twentieth century, but in 1940 it was back in Russian hands. It saw its most significant action in the following year, during Operation Barbarossa, when Hitler's forces invaded Russia. The defenders held out for weeks, even though they were heavily outnumbered and outgunned. In the 1960s the Soviet authorities decided to turn the scarred remains into a monument to Russian resistance. In 1965 the site was awarded the title of "Hero Fortress" and work began on a memorial complex, which was opened in 1971. Some monumental sculptures were commissioned, most notably a massive figure called *Thirst*, symbolizing "the thirst for life, struggle, and victory." **IZ**

Monastery of the Caves

(Kiev, Ukraine)

Subterranean center of Orthodox Christianity, with later above ground churches

The Kiev Monastery of the Caves is a monastic complex, based around two man-made cave systems, and was established in 1051 by St. Anthony—a Kievan who had spent his early years in a monastery on Mount Athos in Greece and had returned to his homeland to encourage the adoption of monasticism. He had arrived in Kiev and made his home in a cave on a hill just outside the city. His example attracted increasing numbers of followers who began to construct a series of tunnels and monastic cells, now known as the Far Caves and the Near Caves. As well as domestic quarters, the underground part of the complex contained several churches. Aboveground, the Cathedral of the Dormition was built in the second half of the eleventh century, where it was joined by several smaller churches, various theological academies, an encircling defensive wall, and the impressive Great Lavra Bell Tower. This was the highest freestanding bell tower in the world when it was finished in 1745, and is still one of the most distinctive structures on the site and in Kiev as a whole.

By the turn of the twentieth century, the monastery housed around 1,000 monks and ranked as one of the most important religious centers in the Eastern Orthodox Church. In the 1920s, however, the fervently atheistic Soviet regime tried to strip the institution of its religious significance, insisting that it was nothing more than a site of historic cultural interest. In World War II the Dormition Cathedral was mined by the Soviet army in anticipation of the Nazi occupation of Kiev; in the subsequent detonation the cathedral was almost entirely destroyed. The building has since been rebuilt in its eighteenth-century form, and although part of the complex remains under State administration, some control has been returned to the Ukrainian Orthodox Church. **AS**

"This is the only sacred place of such rank in Ukraine. It is called 'the second Jerusalem.'"

Pavel, senior priest of the monastery

Cathedral of St. Sophia

(Kiev, Ukraine)

Kiev's Byzantine cathedral, built to rival Constantinople's Hagia Sophia

Toward the end of the tenth century, Vladimir, the Prince of Kiev—recognizing the threat posed by the Vikings to the west and the other Russian territories to the east—chose to strengthen his ties with the Byzantine Empire by seeking baptism and marrying the sister of the fearsome ruler of Constantinople, Basil II. Vladimir's son, Yaroslav the Wise, consolidated the new alliance by founding Kiev's Cathedral of St. Sophia in 1017 in imitation of, and as a rival to, the Hagia Sophia in Constantinople.

St. Sophia's crowning glory is a central dome surrounded by twelve others, representing Christ with his apostles, and its interior is similarly magnificent, being decorated with 2,800 square feet (260 sq m) of mosaics and 32,300 square feet (3,000 sq m) of wall paintings. These decorations include glorious interpretations of the Annunciation, the Virgin Mary at Prayer, and the Communion of the Apostles, and there are also paintings of secular scenes, such as bear hunts and feasts. St. Sophia soon became one of the most important buildings in the Eastern Orthodox Church, with the artisans spreading the stylistic features of its decoration throughout the surrounding territories. Fortunately, although the cathedral's exterior suffered during several invasions of the city, restoration work undertaken during the seventeenth and eighteenth centuries left the interior almost untouched.

The Soviet authorities confiscated the cathedral and planned to demolish it during the 1920s, but relented and instead transformed it into an architectural and historical monument. There have been discussions about returning the building to the Russian Orthodox Church, but the cathedral is still primarily a monument to Kiev's history, rather than a functioning place of worship. It was designated a UNESCO World Heritage site in 1990. **AS**

> *"... strongly influenced by both the Slavic and the cosmopolitan culture of the Prince of Kiev."*
>
> UNESCO

Potemkin Steps

(Odessa, Ukraine)

Scene of mass slaughter in the Revolution

In 1905, workers in the Black Sea port of Odessa went on strike, rebelling against tsarist oppression in what would become known as "the first Russian revolution"—and prove a pretaste of the 1917 revolution. The battleship *Potemkin Tavrichesky* was ordered to sail into Odessa so the sailors could help the tsar's army put down the insurgents. However, a large number of sailors were in sympathy with the workers and they mutinied, causing rebellion on board ship; they refused to cooperate with the army and led the striking workers in their uprising. The leader of the mutiny was killed in the battle that ensued and his body laid at the base of what were then called the Richelieu Steps. As thousands of people passed by to pay their respects to the corpse, the tsarist troops moved in, slaughtering around 2,000 people. In 1925 moviemaker Sergei Eisenstein depicted the rebellion in his film *Battleship Potemkin*, at the same time immortalizing the steps on celluloid.

The 192 steps were constructed between 1837 and 1841 by the French architect F. Boffo. The staircase is laid out in such a way that it creates an optical illusion: When standing at the top, it appears that there are no steps at all, just a few landings stretching ahead. From the bottom the steps are visible but nothing at the top can be seen until the climber has almost reached the summit.

The name *Potemkin* came from the lover and secret husband of Catherine the Great, Prince Potemkin. He conquered much of the Black Sea coast in the late eighteenth century and founded the Black Sea navy. The steps were given their new name only after the battleship's rebellion. Their original name, the Richelieu Steps, was taken from the Duc de Richelieu, a former governor of Odessa, who had commissioned the steps to be built. **LH**

Livadia Palace

(Livadia, Ukraine)

Venue of the Yalta Conference in 1945

This splendid building was the summerhouse of the Russian tsars, whose era ended with the execution of Tsar Nicholas II in 1917. The estate was originally built for Tsar Alexander II, who purchased the land in 1861. Alexander employed the architect Ippolito Antonovich Monighetti, who had gained fame after designing the Stroganov Institute in Moscow. In addition to a palace, Monighetti built an entire complex at Livadia, including a church, luxurious private houses, and work buildings; eventually the estate comprised more than sixty buildings, which were surrounded by some exquisitely landscaped gardens. The palace was

> *"We could find no words to express our joy … to have this home, exactly as we wanted it to be built."*
>
> Tsar Nicholas II, diary entry

subsequently rebuilt for Nicholas II in 1911 by the architect M. Krasnov.

After the revolution, the palace was turned into a sanatorium. These quiet years would end in 1945 when the Livadia Palace was used as the site of the Yalta Conference, where Franklin D. Roosevelt, Winston Churchill, and Joseph Stalin worked together to redefine the borders of postwar Europe. Stalin would famously break his conference pledge to allow free democratic elections in Eastern Europe.

In the 1970s the park and its estate were turned into a museum; today, Livadia is one of the Crimea's most popular tourist attractions. The 99-acre (40-ha) park around the palace encompasses gardens that were originally laid out by the then-famous team of landscape gardeners Delilger and Pater. **LH**

The world's second-largest continent is where, it is thought, the human race originally developed. Evidence of human occupation at Sterkfontein Caves in South Africa dates back some 3 million years. Sites such as Great Zimbabwe, as well as monumental tombs as far apart as Mali and Ethiopia, testify to empires that still figure in African folklore. However, coastal fortresses of the European slave traders are a grim reminder of how black Africans were traded as a commodity for hundreds of years.

⬅ The Great Sphinx of Giza, carved from sandstone more than 4,500 years ago.

Africa

Tour Hassan (Rabat, Morocco)

Grand minaret of a planned mosque that was never built

The capital of Morocco, on the Atlantic coast, Rabat began as a Phoenician and later Carthaginian and Roman trading port, some traces of which are still left. After the Arab conquest, it became a fortified military camp and was used as a base for campaigns in Spain by the first of the Almohad sultans of Morocco, Abd el Mumene, in the twelfth century. His grandson Yacoub el Mansour ("the Conqueror"), the son of a black slave, came to power in 1184. A dynamic ruler, he pushed farther into Spain and brought back Christian captives to work as slaves on his mighty building projects in Rabat, which he made his capital.

Sections still survive of the town walls that he built, as does his main city gate, the handsome Bab Oudaia, but his mightiest project of all was to be the Mosque el Hassan. Intended to celebrate a victory over the Spaniards at Alarcos, it was to be big enough to hold his entire army, but Yacoub died in 1199, too soon to complete it. The mosque's principal survivor, and now the symbol of the city, is the minaret, or Tour Hassan. Its name, which means "beautiful tower," is justified. The red stone tower stands 140 feet (44 m) high, though it was intended to be almost double that height. Each of the six stories has a single room, and a wide ramp runs up inside the building, up which the sultan had intended to ride his horse. At the other end of the original mosque site is the Mausoleum of King Mohammed V, which was built in the 1960s. **RC**

"Two hundred columns mark out the area where the mosque was to stand."

Tour Hassan Guidebook

🏛 ◉ **Triumphal Arch** (Volubilis, Morocco)

Surviving monument of an outpost of the Roman Empire

Ancient Rome was the biggest city the world had ever known (until 1800, when London overtook it). Sixty percent of its inhabitants' prodigious need for corn was supplied by the Roman colonies in North Africa. After taking Carthage, the Romans moved west into what are now Algeria and Morocco, and in 25 B.C.E. the emperor Augustus installed a young Berber prince, Juba II, as the local ruler. Juba II married the daughter of Mark Antony and Cleopatra, and his capital was probably to the north of present-day Meknes at Volubilis, which was already a prosperous town and from the first to the third century C.E. was the seat of the Roman provincial governor. Protected by its walls, it had a population of perhaps 20,000 at its peak.

After the Romans abandoned it, Volubilis survived as a Christian center until the conquering Arabs arrived in the seventh century. The local Berbers converted to Islam and the town was renamed Oualili, after a

Moroccan flower, but the sultans lived elsewhere and the town was left to molder. It was badly damaged in the 1755 earthquake that devastated Lisbon.

Volubilis today has the finest Roman ruins in Morocco. The site is an exceptionally well-preserved example of a large Roman colonial town on the fringes of the empire. Surviving the earthquake comparatively unscathed was the Triumphal Arch built in honor of the emperor Caracalla in the year of his death. The marble columns and ornamental medallions are impressive, though it has lost the top section of the arch, which would have been dominated by a heroic figure of the emperor in his chariot. It was built at the end of the main central road of the town, the Decumanus Maximus. Other notable sights in Volubilis include the forum, the capitol, and beautiful mosaic floors that can be seen in the House of Venus and the House of the Labors of Hercules. **RC**

Moulay Ismaïl's Mausoleum (Meknes, Morocco)

The magnificent tomb of a monumentally cruel sultan

Moulay Ismaïl, who ruled from 1672 until his death in 1727 at the age of eighty-one, was one of the greatest of the Moroccan sultans, one of the most powerful and effective, and one of the cruelest. He is said to have had more than 500 women in his harem, by whom he had around 800 children. The sultan, who was protected by a special Black Guard of soldiers, built a colossal complex of palaces in his "imperial city" of Meknes as radiations of his glory. He greatly admired his contemporary Louis XIV of France, and suggested that the king become a Muslim. He also asked—unsuccessfully—for one of Louis's daughters as a wife. His palaces were intended to rival Versailles.

Moulay Ismaïl surrounded Meknes with 15 miles (25 km) of huge walls; their magnificent gates included the overpowering Bab el-Mansour (Gate of the Conqueror). His city had mosques, barracks, beautiful gardens, and a zoo. His building works were carried out by a labor force of 2,500 Christian slaves and 30,000 Moroccan rebels and criminals, who were viciously ill treated. Those who died were used as additional building material for the walls.

The mausoleum was begun by Moulay Ismaïl. A succession of courtyards with central fountains and notable tiles and stucco work leads to a chamber containing the sultan's tomb and those of his favorite wife, Lalla Khnouata, and two of his sons, who became sultans after him. The fine French clocks were a present from Louis XIV. The mausoleum was restored in the 1950s by King Mohammed V of Morocco, who decided it should be open to non-Muslim visitors.

The Historic City of Meknes represents, in an exceptionally complete and well-preserved manner, the urban fabric and monumental buildings of a seventeenth-century Maghreb capital city. It combines Islamic and European design and planning in a harmonious fashion. **RC**

> *"Tyrannical sultan Moulay Ismaïl . . . was known as 'the megalomaniac of architecture.'"*
>
> Sue Paterick, journalist

Ali ben Youssef Medersa (Marrakesh, Morocco)

Fourteenth-century theology and law college

Once the capital of Morocco, Marrakesh has as its predominant color the red of the local soil, reflected in the city's building materials. Legend has it that when the Koutoubia Mosque—one of the biggest mosques in Africa and Marrakesh's principal landmark—was built by the Almohad sultans in the twelfth century, it was placed directly into the city's heart, from which so much blood poured that the town's walls and buildings were permanently stained.

The Ali ben Youssef Medersa was built in the fourteenth century as a college for Muslim theology and law students. It was one of the first in the country, and the largest, reputed to have accommodated more than 800 pupils at its peak. In the sixteenth century, it was completely rebuilt by Abdullah el Ghallib of the Saadian dynasty (Arabs from the south of Morocco who claimed descent from the prophet Muhammad). The Saadian dynasty took Marrakesh in 1525 and went on to oust the reigning sultans and decisively defeat the Portuguese, who had mounted a so-called "crusade" against them in 1578.

The medersa was named in honor of a Muslim holy man, Sidi Youssef Ibn Ali. It is admired for its lively Saadian decorations, which were probably created by craftsmen brought over from Spain. The pupils' tiny little rooms are arranged around a central court with a pool, open to the sky, and there is a beautifully proportioned prayer hall. The walls have mosaic tiles, stucco arches, and pinecone designs, and there are quotations from the Koran.

The students were also taught in the nearby Ben Youssef Mosque, rebuilt by the Saadians and then rebuilt again in the nineteenth century. Although the medersa is open to the public, non-Muslims are not allowed into the mosque. The tombs of the Saadian sultans and their ruined El Badi Palace can also be seen in Marrakesh and are open to the public. **RC**

"At last Marrakesh itself appeared to us, in the form of a red wall across a red wilderness."

Edith Wharton, *In Morocco* (1920)

🏛 ◎ Carthage (near Tunis, Tunisia)

Rival power to the Roman Empire and birthplace of Hannibal

According to tradition, Carthage ("new city"), was founded by the Phoenicians in 814 B.C.E., although the date is still debated by historians. Built on a promontory on the Tunisian coast, it was excellently placed to influence and control ships passing between Sicily and the North African coast as they traversed the Mediterranean. Rapidly becoming a thriving port and trading center, it eventually developed into a major Mediterranean power and a rival to Rome.

During the Punic (the term refers to Phoenician) Wars of the third and second centuries B.C.E., the great Carthaginian general Hannibal menaced Rome, but in 146 B.C.E. Carthage fell to a Roman army and was destroyed. Late in the next century, a successful Roman colony was founded on the site, which became an important Christian center. Later it was ruled for a period by Vandal kings, then recovered for the Byzantine Empire in 533, before being conquered by the Arabs in 705. From then on Carthage played second fiddle to the new town of Tunis.

The remains of this long and checkered history, in what is now a prosperous suburb of Tunis, include the Tophet site where thousands of small children were burned to death in sacrifice to the Carthaginian deities and their ashes buried in urns. From the Roman period, the old harbor, an aqueduct, a baths complex, and an amphitheater remain. There are also ruins from the Vandal period, and those of the principal Christian church, which was rebuilt in the sixth century. Part of the Carthaginian town of Hannibal's day has been excavated on Byrsa Hill. Once occupied by the temple of a Carthaginian god and then by the Roman forum, it is now the site of a late nineteenth-century French cathedral dedicated to Louis IX, the crusading French king who died in Tunis in 1270. The nearby museum has fine Carthaginian and Roman collections. **RC**

🏛 ◎ Kerkuane Punic Town (near Cap Bon, Tunisia)

Long-buried settlement founded by Phoenician refugees

The Phoenicians from the Lebanese coast built up a successful seaborne trading empire in the Mediterranean from about 1000 B.C.E., established Carthage and other colonies, and even found the time to create the alphabet. Kerkuane was founded by Phoenician refugees, probably from Tyre after an attack in 574 B.C.E. by King Nebuchadnezzar II of Babylon. The settlement seems to have been abandoned in 256 B.C.E. after it was sacked by the Romans in one of the wars between the rival powers of Carthage and Rome. Forgotten for centuries, its accidental rediscovery beneath the sand in 1952 gave French archeologists access for the first time to an unspoiled Punic (or Phoenician) town. They called it Kerkuane; its original name is unknown.

The town was protected on the landward side by a double wall. There seems to have been no harbor, so fishermen and traders among the 2,000 or so inhabitants presumably simply drew their boats up onto the beach. They made their living by fishing and trading, and their most valuable export was Tyrian purple dye, extracted from rotting shellfish. The town did not grow up randomly, but was efficiently planned with wide streets and uniform houses, mostly with an inner courtyard and a bathroom equipped in many cases with a basin and a sitting-bath.

Finds on the site show that the people traded with other Mediterranean centers, including the Greek colony of Capua in Italy, from which they obtained pottery. They do not seem to have farmed the surrounding countryside, but they buried their dead outside the walls of the town, where four cemeteries have been discovered. There were public baths, and in the center of the town was a sanctuary apparently dedicated to Carthaginian deities—the god Baal and the goddess Tanit. **RC**

Red Castle (Tripoli, Libya)

Sprawling, fortified heart of Tripoli, rebuilt by its Ottoman conquerors

Libya's capital city and principal port began as a Phoenician trading post called Oea, around 500 B.C.E. It became known as Tripoli when the Romans began to refer to the three towns of Oea, Leptis Magna, and Sabratha as the Tripolis, or "three cities." With an excellent natural harbor, it became the gateway to sub-Saharan Africa and the finishing point of many trading caravan routes. The port was later controlled by a succession of foreigners—from the Romans, the Vandals, and the Byzantines to the Arabs, the Norman rulers of Sicily, and the Arabs again—until it was taken by the Spanish in 1510. It was held for a time by the Knights of St. John from Malta before falling to the Ottoman Turks in 1551. Much later on, Tripoli was in Italian hands, from 1911 to 1943, and then under British control until Libya became independent in 1951.

The old walled city beside the harbor is dominated by the Red Castle (Assai al-Hamra). It was built on the site of a Roman fort after the Arab conquest, but was strengthened and enlarged by the Spanish and the Knights of St. John. When the Ottomans descended on Tripoli in 1551, the fortress was betrayed by one of the garrison who informed the besieging Turks of the weak spot in the defenses, enabling them to focus their efforts upon it and break in.

The castle as it stands today dates mainly from the Turkish period and later. It was the residence of a succession of Ottoman local governors, and from 1711 to 1835 it housed the Karamanlis dynasty, founded by an Ottoman officer. The castle residents lived largely by piracy and were twice involved in war with the United States in the early 1800s. Much of the interior, including the harem, dates from this time, and the castle grew into a community with its own houses, shops, and a labyrinth of streets. Part of the castle now houses the exceptional Jamahiriya Museum of Libyan history and heritage. **RC**

> *"The Ottoman Turks had arrived as a major power ... their very name would terrorize the Christian world."*
>
> Chris Butler, journalist

Leptis Magna (near Tripoli, Libya)

Roman city rich in monumental and well-preserved remains

One of the world's most spectacular Roman cities, Leptis Magna was the birthplace of Septimius Severus, Roman emperor from 193 to 211 C.E. and the first non-Italian-born emperor. Many of Leptis Magna's grandest buildings date from his time.

Located on the Mediterranean coast southeast of Tripoli, the city was founded as a Phoenician trading post in the seventh century B.C.E. It was later taken over by the Carthaginians, and its excellent natural harbor made it an important staging point on both the Mediterranean and the cross-Saharan trade routes. In 111 B.C.E. the city recognized where its best interests lay and allied itself with Rome, growing in size and architectural quality as wealthy residents improved and embellished it. A theater was built in 2 C.E. and an amphitheater in 56 C.E.; a superb set of baths was added in the second century C.E., when the city was home to Lucius Apuleius, author of *The Golden Ass*.

Septimius Severus initiated a major building program, with a colonnaded street leading from the Temple of Nymphs in the city center to the harbor. Next to the new forum a colonnaded law court was built that was later converted into a Christian church. An aqueduct 12 miles (19 km) long brought water into the city and the so-called "hunting baths" were built, decorated with painted hunting scenes, including one of a leopard hunt. The city was a unique artistic realization in the domain of urban planning.

In later centuries, with the Roman Empire in decline, Leptis began to deteriorate, too. The Vandals conquered Libya in the fifth century and, although the Byzantines recovered the coastal cities in the sixth century, Leptis was abandoned after the Arab conquest in the seventh century and fell into ruin. The city was plundered by the French consul around 1700, but most of the ruins were covered by sand until they were rediscovered in the twentieth century. **RC**

"A Libyan named Severus, a born administrator and a man of tremendous energy."

Herodian, third century C.E. historian

🏛 ⊚ Jebel Acacus (near Ghat, Libya)

Rock paintings and carvings in the Acacus Mountains

The town of Ghat is a Tuareg settlement in the southwest of Libya, close to the Jebel Acacus (Acacus Mountains) with their rich heritage of Saharan rock art. This art was first made known to the West by Heinrich Barth and Gustav Nachtigal in 1850. There is more art across the border in Algeria in the Tassili N'Ajjer range, and both zones are World Heritage sites.

The Sahara has not always been a barren desert. At times in the past it was a well-watered, fertile area and its inhabitants created thousands of rock paintings and carvings over a stretch of time roughly from 10,000 B.C.E. to 100 C.E. The first European explorers in the nineteenth century thought the art was so impressive that it must have been made by white people, but the Libyan sites have been investigated by a joint Italian-Libyan archeological mission since 1955 and it is clear that this assumption was mistaken. The earliest pictures, which are generally the most admired, were created by people who lived by hunting; they portray Saharan mammals of the time, including elephants, rhinos, giraffes, ostriches, and various species of antelope. The human figures are armed with bows and arrows, clubs, throwing-sticks, and axes, and the pictures may have been intended to lend magical assistance to success in hunting. Among the portraits of hunting there are scenes of humans dancing, music-making, and having sex.

From perhaps about 6,000 B.C.E., the climate became drier. People turned from hunting to farming and herds of cows and goats appear in the art. From about 1,500 B.C.E. the horse was introduced into the region, duly appearing in the artworks, along with domesticated dogs. With the horse came the chariot, and there are pictures of armed charioteers careering along at full gallop. Finally, the camel was introduced and appears in the latest paintings. **RC**

Siwa Oasis (Siwa, Egypt)

Famous and fertile oasis with a legendary oracle

Among the sand dunes and mountains of the northeastern Sahara Desert are occasional fertile oases. The most famous of them is Siwa, 30 miles (48 km) or so from the Libyan border, where the battered mud-brick walls of an old Berber town date back to the thirteenth century. The roll call of visitors runs from Alexander the Great to Field Marshal Erwin Rommel. Possibly occupied since the Stone Age, Siwa was renowned by traders for its dates and olives. It lies on an old caravan route, but it was always an isolated place, and it was not until the 1980s that a modern road was built to it.

How much control over the area the Egyptian pharaohs had is uncertain, but a temple was built here to the god Amun that became famed for its oracle. Alexander the Great managed to reach the oasis in 331 B.C.E., to consult the oracle, which declared that Alexander was himself a god.

Excavations have uncovered a long history of visitors and invaders. Queen Cleopatra may have visited Siwa; the Roman emperor Augustus used it as a place of banishment for political enemies, and there are tombs dating back to the Graeco-Roman period in the Gebel el-Mawta cemetery at the northern end of the town. Attempts by Muslim armies to take the oasis seem to have failed until the twelfth century.

European visitors began arriving from the 1790s onward. It was dangerous territory so the first of them disguised themselves as Arabs and traveled with the date caravans. During World War I, British forces captured Siwa in 1917; almost immediately the oasis began to become a tourist destination and a small hotel was opened. In World War II Siwa changed hands several times between the British—the Long Range Desert Group had its headquarters there—and the German Afrika Korps under Rommel. **RC**

El Alamein War Cemeteries (El Alamein, Egypt)

Poignant World War II grave site

Fighting between British forces of the Eighth Army, with Free French, Polish, and Greek contingents, and those of the Axis powers—Germany and Italy—aiming to seize the Suez Canal, surged across Egypt's Western Desert from 1940. The Axis advance on Alexandria was halted at El Alamein on the Mediterranean coast in July 1942. In an even more decisive battle there in October and November, the Axis troops were driven into a retreat that carried them back across Libya into Tunisia. The Ninth Australian Division, with only 10 percent of the strength of the Eighth Army, played a crucial part in the victory.

> *"There were no winners and losers in this most dreaded of wars. Only dead heroes and grieving widows."*

Samir Raafat, journalist

Afterward came the grim task of finding and identifying the shattered, charred, and decomposing corpses. Today, in the Commonwealth war cemetery, lines of gravestones honor some 7,300 soldiers killed at El Alamein and in other Western Desert actions. The identities of some 800 of the dead are not known. A memorial honors more than 600 men whose remains were cremated and panels list the names of men with no known grave—more than 3,000 airmen and 8,500 soldiers killed in Egypt, Libya, and Tunisia.

The German and Italian dead are also honored. The fortresslike German cemetery, on a hill outside the town, contains the bones of 4,200 Germans. In addition, in galleries in the Italian cemetery there are thousands of tombs, each marked either with the soldier's name or simply *Ignoto* (Unknown). **RC**

Kom Ash Shuqqafa Catacombs (Alexandria, Egypt)

Ancient secret rediscovered in 1900

Alexandria was founded by and named in honor of Alexander the Great, who conquered Egypt in the fourth century B.C.E. The city became the cultural capital of the Graeco-Roman world in the eastern Mediterranean, famed for its magnificent library and its lighthouse (one of the Seven Wonders of the Ancient World), although neither has survived.

One day in 1900, a man was riding his donkey when the animal stumbled in a hole in the path. This accident led to the rediscovery of a labyrinth of catacombs, which may have begun as a private family tomb, but developed into the biggest Graeco-Roman necropolis in the country.

The complex was dug down to a depth of about 115 feet (35 m) with three levels of rooms and tunnels. Bodies were lowered down a shaft, which was encircled by a spiral staircase for visitors, into a passage. This led to a domed central rotunda and a banqueting hall where relatives feasted in memory of, and in close proximity to, their dead. It was thought unlucky to take the dishes away, so they were smashed in situ, hence the Arabic name of the catacombs, which means "mounds of shards." Some corpses were buried in niches and there were also urns containing the ashes of cremated bodies.

The catacombs' decorations are an unusual blend of ancient Egyptian and Graeco-Roman motifs and themes. The Egyptian god Anubis, for instance, who was linked with rituals for the dead, is shown as a Roman legionary in armor, whereas giant serpents and Medusa heads create what has been likened to "a horror movie set." Part of the complex was dedicated to the Greek goddess Nemesis.

The bones of horses have also been uncovered, and it is possible that successful racehorses were buried in the catacombs. **RC**

Al-Azhar Mosque

(Cairo, Egypt)

Reputed to be the oldest teaching mosque in the world

In 969, Egypt was conquered by the Fatimid rulers of Tunisia. The Fatimid were Shia Muslims who claimed descent from the prophet Muhammad through his daughter Fatima. In their purloined territory, they built a new settlement, protected behind walls, to the north of the Egyptian capital. It was named Al-Qahirah (the Subduer), which is the origin of the name *Cairo*.

Within the settlement were luxurious palaces, barracks for troops, and lush gardens, as well as the new Al-Azhar (the Resplendent) mosque. The Fatimid ruler Al-Moizz had a library of 120,000 volumes, the largest in the entire medieval world, and he made the mosque the center of what is said to be the world's oldest surviving university (although this is challenged by the University of Fez in Morocco). It became the Muslim world's most famous seat of learning. Ironically, it later became a bastion of conservative Sunni orthodoxy under the rulers who followed the Fatimid dynasty.

The mosque has been rebuilt many times, with minarets, mausoleums, and schools added. When Napoleon invaded Egypt in 1798, the Al-Azhar clerics proclaimed holy war against him, leading to riots in the streets of Cairo. The French responded in kind by shelling the city for several hours, concentrating their fire on the mosque before charging into it on horseback, to the horror of the Muslim sheikhs, and sacking it—at which point resistance ceased.

Standing opposite is the revered mosque of Sayyidna al-Husayn. The prophet's grandson Husayn was murdered in 680 and according to legend his severed head was brought to Cairo in 1153 and buried there, to keep it safe from the Christian crusaders. Built on the site between 1864 and 1873 by the Khedive Ismail, the mosque is visited by millions of pilgrims every year. **RC**

"[The mosque] rests alone intact like an inviolable island in this milieu of torment and destruction."

Arthur Rhone, Egyptologist, 1882

Bab Zuwayla (Cairo, Egypt)

Historic eleventh-century gate in the walls that protected the Fatimid dynasty

The Fatimid royal area of Cairo, Al-Qahirah, was originally protected by walls of mud-brick, but in the eleventh century these had to be replaced by stone walls to protect an unpopular ruler. When the Nile failed to irrigate its valley for several years in succession, the dry conditions reduced many of the population to starvation, sparking a revolt against the Fatimid ruler al-Mustansir. He called in an Armenian general, Badr al-Jamali, to suppress it, who restored order, rebuilding the walls in stone *c.* 1085.

Stretches of this original boundary have survived, as well as the tremendous gates in the northern, eastern, and southern walls. The southern gate, the Bab Zuwayla, was named after a Berber tribe of soldiers quartered nearby. Rising above it are the towering, ornate minarets of the al-Mu'ayyid Mosque, added around 1420. The gateways were closed by iron-studded doors, which were guarded by troops.

In medieval times, the gates were a hub of miscellaneous activity. Donkeys were available for hire, and people passing through the gates were blessed by Koran chanters. Popular entertainers performed in the square outside, including musicians and dancers, conjurors, fakirs, and snake charmers. Stalls sold sweets and there was a musical instrument market. Yet there were also prostitutes for rent and the square was used for public executions. Some criminals were nailed to the gates' doors, some were impaled, and some were beheaded, with their heads put on spikes. After a mechanical garroting device—a tall brass clockwork doll—was invented, victims were fastened to the device and the doll began to dance wildly until it strangled its partner.

In 1517, the Ottomans took Cairo and the last Mameluke ruler, Ashram Tumanbey, was hanged from the top of the gate. The rope broke twice and the crowd roared as his neck snapped on the third try. **RC**

> *"Guide Thou us on the straight path/The path of those to whom Thou hast been gracious."*

Koranic verse, recited when passing the Bab Zuwayla

🏛 ◎ Beit Suhaymi (Cairo, Egypt)

Luxurious merchant's home in the heart of Cairo

In 1517, after overwhelmingly defeating the Mamelukes in battle, the Ottoman Sultan known as Selim the Grim took Cairo and surrounded his camp with hundreds of severed Mameluke heads on lances. Egypt became a province of the Ottoman Empire, ruled by Turkish pashas appointed in Istanbul and supported by 5,000 crack Ottoman troops, the Janissaries, who were quartered in the Citadel.

Under Selim the Grim, Cairo went into slow decline and stagnation as the provincial government grew steadily more inefficient and corrupt; the great buildings of the city's past were left to become dilapidated, the seasonal irrigation of the Nile valley often failed, and there were outbreaks of plague. What came to the rescue was the new European craze for coffee. Merchants made their fortunes importing Arabian coffee beans through the Yemen to Cairo and distributing them around the Mediterranean.

The home of one of the rich merchant dynasties, or rather two houses of the seventeenth and eighteenth centuries combined into one, in the Gamaliyah district in the heart of the historic old Fatimid quarter of Cairo, shows how families of this kind lived. The building and the nearby houses have been recently restored. The central courtyard, with a fountain splashing and a garden behind, kept the house cool in summer. The master of the household's realm was principally the ground floor. Here he received friends and business contacts in the imposing reception room, where they could eat, smoke, and watch entertainers. The women's realm was upstairs, where they had their own quarters in light, airy rooms and a delightful common sitting room overlooking the courtyard through a screened window and decorated with Damascus tiles. The window seats have welcoming deep cushions and there is a vivid impression of luxury and elegance. **RC**

"Coffee is the common man's gold, and . . . brings to every man the feeling of luxury and nobility."

Sheik Abd-al-Kadir, *In Praise of Coffee* (1587)

🏛 ⊚ **Cairo Citadel** (Cairo, Egypt)

From where Egypt was ruled for six centuries

Egypt was governed from this fortress from the thirteenth to the nineteenth century. It was originally built by Saladin, who ousted the last Fatimid ruler in 1171, but it has been added to and rebuilt many times. In Saladin's time, the fortress housed the royal palaces, the army headquarters, and government offices. From 1250 the early Mameluke sultans replaced many of the buildings with structures in a grander style, but these were later knocked down in their turn, except for the mosque of An-Nasir Muhammad, which was completed in 1335. The harem, with its pavilions and gardens and a population of more than 1,200, was based on the site now occupied by the mosque of Muhammad Ali. In 1400 some 6,000 young boys were kept as slaves in the sultan's palace.

Mosques, gates, and keeps were added in the period after 1517, when Egypt was a province of the Ottoman Empire, ruled by Turkish pashas. They include the Burg al-Muqattam tower, which rises to 80 feet (25 m) above the eastern entrance. By 1650 the citadel had developed into a residential district with streets, private houses, shops, markets, and public baths. Napoleon's French troops occupied it after invading Egypt in 1798, and British troops held it from 1882 until their departure in 1947.

Muhammad Ali Pasha, appointed viceroy of Egypt by the Ottoman emperor in 1805, established a ruling dynasty of his own that lasted until 1953. An efficient modernizer—his new palace in the citadel was lit by gas—he reorganized Cairo, building new streets and replacing old buildings in the citadel with new ones, including a colossal, florid mosque, which was completed in 1848. Muhammad Ali Pasha was later buried at that mosque. The complex today also contains the national police museum and the Egyptian military museum. **RC**

🏛 ⊚ Ibn Tulun Mosque (Cairo, Egypt)

The largest mosque in Cairo, built to accommodate an army

The Arabs invaded Egypt in 639 and established a military base at Cairo in 642, outside the old Roman fortress and the existing settlement. Immigrants soon started to arrive from Arabia, and Cairo grew into a thriving town. Egypt was administered from here by governors, who were appointed by the Umayyad caliphs of Damascus. In 750 the Abbasids took over the caliphate and moved their capital to Baghdad.

In 868 a thirty-three-year-old Turkish general from Baghdad, Ahmad Ibn Tulun, was appointed governor of Egypt. He soon established himself as the independent ruler of Egypt and built himself a luxurious palace in Cairo. It was equipped with a pool of quicksilver where, according to legend, Ibn Tulun floated on cushions pulled to and fro by slave girls. He also built a mosque big enough for his entire army.

Today, the mosque is all that is left of his grand capital and it is still the largest mosque in Cairo. It has a central courtyard covering more than 4 acres (2 ha) and is surrounded by massive double walls. Its wooden *minbar* or pulpit was added in 1296 by Sultan Lagin, who restored the mosque in gratitude after hiding there from enemies. He also rebuilt the minaret, which had been created with an unusual spiral stairway on the outside. An enjoyable story attributes the original design of this staircase to Ibn Tulun. According to legend, Ibn Tulun was idly winding a piece of paper around his finger at a meeting, instead of paying attention to the problems being debated. When asked what he was doing, he hastily replied that he was designing his mosque.

Although the mosque remained in use for several hundred years after Ibn Tulun's death (in 884), by the nineteenth century it was being used as a military hospital, then as a prison. Restoration work began in 1918 and again in 2004. **RC**

Al Rifa'i Mosque (Cairo, Egypt)

Mosque, mausoleum, and burial place of the notorious King Farouk

Cairo's last great mosque, with costly and luxurious interiors of marble and gold, is notable for those buried there. They include Khedive Ismail who, from 1863, modernized Cairo and encouraged the building of the Suez Canal (he was deposed by the Ottomans in 1879 under pressure from the British). The canal was crucial to British imperial interests. In 1882 the British annexed Egypt and controlled it through a succession of Egyptian khedives, sultans, and kings.

Originally the Al Rifa'i mosque was built as a family mausoleum by Ismail's mother, Princess Khushayr. Ismail was buried there after his death in 1895. The mosque was named in honor of Sheikh Ali al-Rifa'i, the founder of a Sufi school of Islamic mysticism, who is believed to have been buried at the site. Although work began in the nineteenth century, it was not actually completed until 1912.

Construction was overseen by the princess's chief eunuch and she herself was buried in the mosque, as were Khedive Ismail's son Sultan Husayn Kamil, who died in 1914, and his son Fu'ad, who was recognized by the British as King of Egypt in 1922. Fu'ad died in 1936 and was succeeded by his baby son, who grew up to be the notorious King Farouk and was forced into exile in 1952 by Egyptian army officers led by General Neguib and Colonel Gamel Abdel Nasser.

When Farouk died in 1965, his body was brought back to Egypt and eventually interred in the mosque. It is also the burial place of the last Shah of Iran, Mohammed Reza Pahlavi. Expelled from Iran in 1979, he died in Egypt in 1980. His first wife, Fawzia, who was Farouk's sister, was also buried in the mosque. **RC**

◪ Three of Ismail's sons succeeded him as Khedive, including Tewfik, pictured here with his father.

◧ The predominant architectural style of the mosque is Mamluk, as shown by the dome and minaret.

Hanging Church (Cairo, Egypt)

Once Egypt's most important Coptic church

The area called Old Cairo (Misr al-Qadimah), close to the Nile in the south of the city, has a remarkable concentration of Coptic and Orthodox churches and burial grounds. The Copts were the principal Christian minority in Muslim Egypt after the Arab conquest. They were Monophysites, who did not accept that Christ had both a divine and a human nature, which distinguished them from the Eastern Orthodox church. They adopted Arabic as the main language of their churches.

The area was a Jewish and Christian enclave before the coming of the Arabs, and the church is on the site of a Roman fortress from the late first century. Part of the fortifications of the fortress survive, including the southern gate. On top of it is the Hanging Church (Al-Muallaqa), dedicated to the Virgin Mary and once believed to contain the stone of an olive she ate. Founded possibly in the seventh century, it was rebuilt many times and boasts a fine pulpit and screen from medieval times. In the thirteenth century it was Egypt's most important Coptic church.

Nearby is the Ben Ezra synagogue and the church of St. Sergius, thought to be Cairo's oldest church and said to have been built above a cave where Jesus, Mary, and Joseph lived when they fled to Egypt from King Herod. The round Orthodox church of St. George, situated in one of the towers of the Roman fortress, was rebuilt in 1909 after a fire. The Coptic Museum, founded in 1908 to preserve Cairo's heritage of Christian art, has a collection of early gnostic books, written on papyrus leaves and some of them bound in leather, the earliest leather-bound books known. **RC**

↗ The Coptic Pope Shenouda III of Alexandria is a frequent visitor at Cairo's Hanging Church.

→ The interior of the church is beautifully decorated with murals, decorative screens, and a marble pulpit.

Northern Cemetery (Cairo, Egypt)

A cemetery for the living and the dead

The rulers of Egypt in the mid-thirteenth century relied on an army composed largely of Turkish slave-soldiers, known as Mamelukes. After repelling an invasion by Christian crusaders in 1250, the Mameluke leaders seized control of the country and established a regime that would last for 250 years. The Mamelukes built fine palaces and mosques, but their most lasting contribution to Cairo's character was the cemetery they established north of the Citadel, as an addition to the earlier one located toward the south.

Cemeteries are often referred to as the cities of the dead, but this one also became a city of the living as people began to move in and make themselves at home. Most of the tombs resemble small houses, with a courtyard and two or three rooms, beneath which the body is buried—lying on its side, unshrouded, and facing toward Mecca. These tombs were the humble successors to the pharaohs' pyramids and the rooms

were intended for visiting family and friends to stay overnight, hold parties, and have picnics close to their dead. By the fourteenth century, many people were choosing to live in the tombs' spare rooms.

The sultans built much grander burial places for themselves and their families, for example the mausoleum of the first Circassian Mameluke sultan, Burquq, who ruled from 1382 until 1389. In the 1470s Sultan Qait Bey erected a splendid funerary complex, including a beautiful mosque, which was financed by his profits from the lucrative spice trade between the Far East and Europe.

Today the cemetery has become a town, with shops and apartment blocks, flea markets, police stations, post offices, and bus stops, even though most of the streets are too narrow for anything bigger than a donkey cart. A flock of sheep is also kept in the Northern Cemetery. **RC**

🏛 ◉ Great Pyramid of Khufu (Giza, Egypt)

The only remaining "wonder" of the Seven Wonders of the Ancient World

The only survivor of the Seven Wonders of the Ancient World has been an object of awe for centuries, the center of numerous scholarly disagreements, and the focus of wild theories. One of those theories is that the pyramid contains an accurate prophecy of the future—a prophecy scholars and theologians have constantly attempted to unravel.

The pyramid was built for Pharaoh Khufu (or Cheops), the son of Pharaoh Snofru. The largest of all the Egyptian pyramids, it was originally covered in white limestone to make it gleam in the sun. The first accurate measurements were taken by Sir Flinders Petrie in the 1880s. The pyramid originally stood 480 feet (146 m) high, contained more than two million blocks of stone, and was built with such precision that the base was almost a perfect square, with each side 755 feet (230 m) long. It may have taken a workforce, perhaps 100,000 strong at its peak, as long as fifty years to build, although scholars' estimates vary enormously, as do the suggested dates.

Not far away is a cedarwood boat, discovered in 1945 in one of five boat pits sunk around Khufu's pyramid; it is now preserved in the Solar Boat Museum. The boat may have been intended to carry the dead king with the sun god on his daily journey across the sky and through the underworld at night. Also close by is the slightly smaller pyramid of Khufu's son, Khafre (or Chephren). A professional strongman turned tomb robber called Giovanni Belzoni blasted his way inside the pyramid in 1818, and then discovered that robbers had been there long before him. The Great Sphinx is close to Chephren's pyramid and there is a third, smaller pyramid built by his son Menkaure (or Mycerinus). Apparently, the huge expenditure of money and labor on pyramid building was by this time on the wane. **RC**

🏛 ◎ **Great Sphinx** (Giza, Egypt)

Representative of the essence of Egypt for thousands of years

The Greeks used the word "sphinx" for a creature of ancient Egyptian mythology that had the face of a human and the body of a lion. Sphinxes in Egyptian belief guarded thresholds and sacred complexes, and were identified with royal power and the sun god. The Greek name was derived from or linked with a verb meaning "to strangle," hence the tale of the female Theban sphinx that strangled people who failed to answer its riddle: what goes first on four feet, then on two, then on three? When Oedipus got the correct answer—man—the sphinx killed itself.

The greatest Egyptian sphinx is the colossal one next to the pyramid of Khafre at Giza, whose face is a portrait of the pharaoh himself. Facing the rising sun, it has seen more than a million sunrises. It may have been carved out of a block of limestone left by the builders of Khafre's pyramid, but there are theories that Khafre's father, Khufu, built it or that it is far older and was there long before the pyramids. The sphinx was covered with sand by the time of Thutmose IV, who saw it in a dream. The dream promised him the throne of Egypt if he restored the sphinx. He did so around 1400 B.C.E., and became pharaoh.

One of the world's oldest and largest monumental statues, the Great Sphinx is 185 feet (57 m) long, 20 feet (6 m) wide, and 65 feet (20 m) high. The Arabs called it Abu ul-Hol (Father of Terror). It was damaged by a fanatical Muslim ruler in 1380 and was subsequently used for target practice by soldiers. Legend spoke of secret passages inside the sphinx's figure and archeologists have discovered three tunnels in it that do not seem to lead anywhere. The sphinx's face is famously missing its nose, but whether this is due to vandalism or to the rigors of weather and time on the limestone is still open to debate. A major restoration project was carried out on the statue in the 1990s. **RC**

"The sand of the desert whereon I am laid has covered me. Save me…"

Inscription on the Sphinx's Dream Stela

⬆ A photograph from *c.* 1885, showing the Sphinx partially free of the sand that had once buried it up to its neck.

➡ The Dream Stela lies between the paws, describing Thutmose IV's restoration of the statue in antiquity.

🏛 ⊚ **Step Pyramid of Zoser** (Saqqara, Egypt)

The greatest work of the world's earliest known architect

> *"This remarkable [Imhotep] . . . left so notable a reputation that his name was never forgotten."*
>
> James Henry Breasted, archeologist

Little is known about the kings of Egypt in the Old Kingdom period, but the pyramids they created were massively impressive statements of their power and wealth, as well as of their immortality. The first of them was the step pyramid designed for Pharaoh Zoser (or Djoser) by the world's first named architect, Imhotep, who is also a key figure in the history of medicine. Imhotep designed the pyramid around the twenty-seventh century B.C.E.

Constructed at a location in the desert outside Zoser's capital city of Memphis, from where it could be seen dominating the skyline, the pyramid was a translation of earlier Egyptian architecture into stone. Its diminishing "step" layers of stone and clay rose to a height of about 200 feet (61 m) and were originally covered in gleaming white limestone. The four faces of the pyramid's square base were oriented to the cardinal points. There were numerous gates, but the one true entrance was between columns and led through to the central courtyard.

The pyramid held statues of the Egyptian gods and of Zoser himself and members of his family, including a life-sized sculpture of him seated on his throne. Beneath the pyramid was an underground structure of unprecedented size and complexity, with galleries and some 400 rooms.

The pyramid stood in a complex of buildings, some of which were apparently dummies, perhaps meant for the king's spirit for a time after death or connected with his jubilee ceremonies. On the south side was the marked-out course that each pharaoh would run around during his coronation ceremony and again at his jubilee. There were also tombs for other members of the ruling house. The wall around the complex was more than 1 mile (1.6 km) long and originally 34 feet (11 m) high. The whole site has been described as "a vast city of the dead." **RC**

The burial place of the sacred Apis bulls

In the early 1850s a young French official named Auguste Mariette was in Egypt to collect Coptic manuscripts for the Louvre museum. Visiting Memphis and the Saqqara area in the desert, he became seduced by its history; he forgot about manuscripts, hired a team of thirty workmen, and began, rather furtively, to dig. Over the course of the next few years he uncovered the huge Serapeum, the burial place of the sacred Apis bulls, and acquired quantities of ancient Egyptian antiquities for the Louvre. The Khedive of Egypt presently appointed him conservator of monuments and Mariette spent the rest of his life excavating and preserving the Egyptian past.

The god Apis was an Egyptian fertility deity who became associated with Ptah, who in the Memphis tradition was the creator god of the primeval mound: He brought all the things in the world into existence simply by speaking their names. There is a theory that the name of a shrine to Ptah in Memphis called Hwt-ka-Ptah, and translated in the Greek language as Aiguptos, is the word from which the name of Egypt originally derived.

Each of the black or black-and-white Apis bulls was selected by the priests as an incarnation of Ptah and oracles were drawn from its behavior. The bull would usually survive for twenty years or more. In early times, when a bull died, it may have been cooked and eaten by the pharaoh and the priests before the remains were buried. In later years, however, the whole carcass of each sacred bull was embalmed and ceremonially buried in a stone sarcophagus, weighing up to 60 to 80 tons. It was buried in an underground tomb, which formed part of a complex of galleries and tunnels; here Mariette also discovered human-headed jars containing the viscera of bulls. The cult of the sacred bulls continued into Christian times, but the Serapeum was finally closed in 398 c.e. **RC**

"I was compelled to spend four years in the desert—four years, however, I can never regret."

Auguste Mariette, *Monuments of Upper Egypt* (1877)

Pyramids of Dahshur (near Memphis, Egypt)

Three remarkable structures, including the world's first "true" pyramid

The three pyramids built for Pharaoh Snofru were an architectural advance from Pharaoh Zoser's step pyramid. The first of Snofru's pyramids, which was built at Meidum, was created as a series of diminishing steps, which were later filled in to create a true pyramid. The second structure, located at Dahshur, called the Bent Pyramid, is thought to have been the first one designed as a true pyramid to begin with, but the angle of the slope was altered halfway up, presumably because the original angle was unstable. The third one, the Red Pyramid, also at Dahshur, was the first true pyramid ever constructed. It remains unknown why the pharaoh needed three pyramids instead of just one; if there were three original purposes, this knowledge has been lost.

The pyramid shape is perhaps representative of the original primeval mound, which in Egyptian mythology appeared from the waters of chaos at the beginning of the world. If that theory is correct, the pyramids linked each buried pharaoh with the theme of order emerging from chaos and with the supreme rule of the sun god, the dominant Egyptian deity, who first brought life into being on the primeval mound.

Snofru was buried in the Bent Pyramid, which has two entrances, one in the north face as is typical, but another in the west face. The reason for having two entrances is not known. Just to the south is a smaller pyramid, which may have been the resting place of Snofru's queen. Close by is the much later pyramid of Pharaoh Unas, who died in 2350 B.C.E., where the interior is inscribed with the earliest known pyramid texts; these were recited during a dead king's funeral ceremony to release his spirit from the earth to join his father, the sun god, in the heavens and become one with him. The tombs of Unas's family, courtiers, and officials are nearby, among later tombs. **RC**

🏛 ◈ St. Catherine's Monastery (Mount Sinai, Egypt)

Holy site revered by Jews, Christians, and Muslims

Mount Sinai, where Moses received the Ten Commandments from God, is revered in Jewish, Christian, and Muslim tradition. The empress Helena, mother of Constantine the Great and a devout Christian, made a pilgrimage to Jerusalem in the fourth century and was believed to have discovered the True Cross, on which Christ was crucified. Before her death in 330 she also apparently ordered a small chapel to be built beside the burning fiery bush at the foot of Mount Sinai, from which God spoke to Moses.

The site became a Greek Orthodox monastery, and in the mid-sixth century the emperor Justinian enlarged it and protected it behind a thick wall. Justinian also added the church dedicated to St. Catherine of Alexandria, who had been martyred on a spiked wheel and beheaded. Tradition had it that angels spirited her body away to the top of the mountain in Sinai now named after her. It was later discovered, taken to the monastery, and placed in a golden casket, which is preserved there. The altar of the church was built over the roots of the burning bush and a descendant of the bush flourishes outside.

The monastery has attracted pilgrims for centuries. Among its treasures are icons and mosaics, and a superb library. Jacob's Well is said to be the spot where Moses first met his future wife, Zipporah, and there is also a small mosque. The charnel house is full of the bones of past generations of monks. **RC**

"Mount Sinai was completely in smoke, because the Lord descended upon it in fire."

Exodus 19:17-18

St. Antony's Monastery (Hurghada, Egypt)

The oldest inhabited Christian monastery in the world

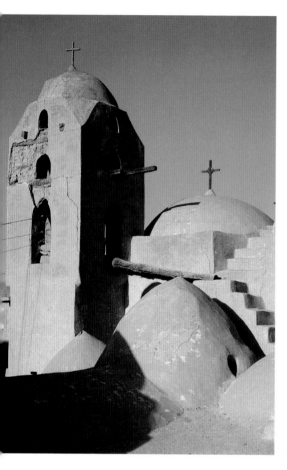

Early Christian hermits retreated into the deserts where they could focus on God away from the busy world of humanity. The famous hermit St. Antony of Egypt lived in a cave on Mount Qalah, close to the Red Sea coast. Icons show him dressed in animal pelts with a white beard and an escort of guardian lions. He experienced strange visions, which later became a theme in Christian art, and he died in 356, reputedly at the age of 105.

St. Antony was one of the earliest exponents of Christian monasticism in the Egyptian desert. After his death, admirers built a chapel to him lower down the mountain. This eventually developed into a Coptic Orthodox monastery, which is the oldest inhabited Christian monastery in the world. The monastery was repeatedly attacked, destroyed, and rebuilt. In the fifteenth century the monks were massacred, yet the monastery was rebuilt once again, this time with fortifications around it for protection.

A village grew up around the monastery, with five churches inside walls more than 1 mile (1.6 km) long. In addition to a church to St. Anthony from the thirteenth century, there is a church dedicated to St. Mark the Evangelist, traditionally the apostle to Egypt, where his relics are preserved. The settlement's water is drawn from a well in which Moses's sister Miriam is believed to have bathed when the Israelites were fleeing Egypt. Higher up the mountain, just over 1 mile (1.6 km) from the monastery, the walls of St. Antony's cave are covered with pious graffiti scrawled by pilgrims since medieval times.

To the southeast is the monastery of St. Paul the Theban (not the St. Paul who had his famous conversion on the road to Damascus), who lived in another cave from the age of sixteen until his death in 348, allegedly aged 120. The cave is inside the church dedicated to the saint, and contains his relics. **RC**

> *"Our life and death are with our neighbour. If we gain our brother we have gained God."*
>
> St. Antony of Egypt

Temple of Hathor (Dendera, Egypt)

Honoring the goddess of love and beauty

After the death of Alexander the Great, in 323 B.C.E., his empire was divided up and Egypt went to one of his Macedonian generals, Ptolemy, whose successors ruled the country until Roman times. Tombs at Dendera go back far earlier than this, however, and include burials of sacred animals, including cows.

One of the forms reputed to have been taken by the goddess Hathor was that of a cow. She suckled each infant pharaoh and was often depicted in human form with a cow's ears and a crown embellished with the disk of the sun between her horns. Hathor was the goddess of love and beauty, and in her capacity as "the mistress of drunkenness," she was linked with dancing and revelry. She gradually merged with the goddess Isis, who was one of the most revered deities in the eastern Mediterranean world.

Hathor's Ptolemaic temple at Dendera replaced an earlier temple and was itself altered and added to, up until the time of the early Roman emperors. A unique feature in Egypt was a sanitorium where the sick could spend the night in hope of experiencing a healing dream sent by the goddess.

The temple is decorated and on one exterior wall is a large relief of Queen Cleopatra, who died in 30 B.C.E., depicted with Caesarion, her son by Julius Caesar. Cleopatra may well have used this image to identify herself with the goddess. A few years after Cleopatra's death, Emperor Augustus built a separate temple to Isis; scenes in the main temple show later emperors making offerings to the goddess.

In the Emperor Tiberius's time—c. 35 C.E.—a hypostyle (columned) hall was added. It has column capitals in the shape of a sistrum—an ancient Egyptian musical instrument connected with the goddess Isis—and a ceiling bearing signs of the zodiac. Part of the building was turned into a Coptic Christian church in the fifth century. **RC**

"Thou art the Mistress of Jubilation, the Queen of the Dance, the Mistress of Music . . ."

Hymn to Hathor

The grave of Egypt's boy king, a site believed by many to be cursed

"*The chamber gradually loomed before me, with its medley of extraordinary and beautiful objects.*"

Howard Carter's diary, November 26, 1922

⬆ Howard Carter and his assistants view the sarcophagus of Tutankhamen for the first time.

➡ The solid gold mask of King Tutankhamen is inlaid with stone and glass, and weighs 22.5 pounds (11kg).

The Valley of the Kings in the desert to the west of Luxor was the burying place of the pharaohs of the New Kingdom period, from the sixteenth century B.C.E., who made Egypt the heart of an empire and the most powerful country in the ancient world. The graves were plundered by tomb robbers, but in 1922 the English archeologist Howard Carter discovered a tomb that was still almost intact and contained astonishing treasures of Egyptian art and craftsmanship. Carter and his financial backer, the Earl of Caernarvon, were the first for thousands of years to enter the grave of the young Pharaoh Tutankhamen (Living Image of Amun) and the world's media made much of the event with the notion that a fatal curse would destroy everyone involved.

The discovery made Tutankhamen the most famous of the pharaohs, even though he died after a reign of only a few years. His fame stems from the fact that his tomb was found intact with its magnificent tomb-treasure, rather than from the historical relevance of his reign. Tutankhamen became pharaoh at the age of nine and political decisions would have been largely taken by advisers such as the vizier, Ay, who became his successor. The treasures continue to draw huge and fascinated crowds every time they are put on show. They include the king's golden coffin and golden mask (with pierced ears), his carved throne, model ships, jewelry, lamps, jars, chariots, boomerangs, and bows and arrows. There were vivid painted scenes on the tomb walls and even long-wilted bunches of flowers left with his corpse.

For years it was suggested that Tutankhamen had been murdered, but a thorough reexamination of his mummy in 2005 did not support the idea; it suggested his leg was so badly broken that it caused a fatal infection. More than sixty other tombs in the Valley of the Kings have been excavated. **RC**

Temple of Luxor (Luxor, Egypt)

Constructed by Pharaoh Amenhotep III, who claimed to be the son of the god Amun

The city that we now know as Luxor was the capital of Egypt for many years, starting around 2100 B.C.E. Many centuries ago it was known by the Greek name of Thebes. In the works of the poet Homer it is called "the city of a hundred gates."

The word "Luxor" comes from the city's Arabic name, el-Uqsur, or "city of palaces." The site reached its zenith under the pharaohs of the New Kingdom period, from the sixteenth century B.C.E., and though it eventually ceased to be the capital city, it was still considered an important place throughout the later centuries B.C.E. and into the Roman period. Later still, some of the city's temples were converted into Christian churches. Napoleon's expedition to Egypt in 1798 inspired intense archeological interest, and when the tour operator Thomas Cook took tourists on his very first expedition to Egypt in 1869, Luxor was included on the itinerary.

Smaller than the gigantic temple at Karnak, the Luxor Temple of Amun was started by Pharaoh Amenhotep III, who claimed to be Amun's son. In one of the chambers the god is shown entering Amenhotep's mother's room disguised as her husband and breathing the child into her nose. Although Amenhotep III's own son, Akhenaten, devoted himself to a monotheistic cult of his own god, Aten, to whom he built a temple, the Amun temple was enlarged by his successors, including Tutankhamen and especially Ramses II, in the thirteenth century B.C.E. There are three colossal statues of Amun at the entrance, where the gateway depicts him victorious in battle.

The god's sacred boat was kept in a special shrine, which Alexander the Great rebuilt in the fourth century B.C.E. Part of the site was converted into a Coptic Christian church in the fourth century C.E. and now part is a mosque, most of which dates from the nineteenth century. **RC**

"Hail to you Amun-Re, Lord of the Thrones of the Two Lands, foremost in Thebes."

Prayer carved on a tablet of stone from Thebes

Temple of Karnak (Karnak, Egypt)

One of the largest religious complexes in the world

After a period of civil war, the pharaohs of the Eleventh Dynasty took a firm grip on Egypt. The city of Thebes (now known as Luxor) became their capital in about 2100 B.C.E.; as a result the revered local god, Amun, achieved widespread fame. Amun's consort, the goddess Mut, and their child Khonsu, the moon god, were honored with him.

For centuries, temples to all three gods were built, altered, and lavishly enlarged by a succession of pharaohs. The huge Karnak temple of the king of the gods, Amun (whose name means "The Hidden One," or "The Unknowable"), is at the heart of a complex that covers more than 10 square miles (25 sq km). Amun was usually portrayed as a man, but depictions also exist that show him as a ram, a goose, and a snake renewing itself by shedding its skin. Amun was later linked with the sun god, Re, and became known as Amun-Re, the supreme deity of all Egypt. The influence and wealth of Amun-Re's priests grew to such an extent that the power of the holy men rivaled that of the pharaohs themselves.

At the temple at Karnak, Amun's holiest statue was hidden inside a cedarwood shrine created in the innermost part of the building. Around the shrine were halls, columns, and gateways (pylons) bearing hieroglyphic inscriptions and representations of gods and pharaohs. Among the buildings is the spectacular hypostyle (columned) hall with its 134 giant columns in the form of papyrus plants, the tallest of which stand 75 feet (23 m) high. Some of them still show traces of their original colors. There is a colossal figure of Pharaoh Ramses II, with his daughter in front of his legs, and an obelisk honoring Hatshepsut, the woman pharaoh of the fifteenth century B.C.E. Avenues of ram-headed sphinxes led to the temple from the Nile and from Luxor, along which the god was carried in his sacred barge. **RC**

"O Amun, great of might! My sacrifice and prayers, are they in vain? . . . Hear thou my cry."

Ancient Egyptian love poem

Temple of Horus (Edfu, Egypt)

Where one of the most popular Egyptian gods was honored in splendor

When the god Horus, "Lord of the Sky," became one of ancient Egypt's major deities, each subsequent pharaoh was identified with him as "the Living Horus," the defender of the right order of things on earth.

Although the legend occasionally varies, Horus was widely worshipped as the son of the gods Isis and Osiris. He is often depicted as a man with the head of a falcon, as an animal with the head of a falcon, or as a falcon itself. A huge granite figure in the principal courtyard of the Edfu temple depicts Horus as a majestic falcon wearing the Egyptian crown.

The Temple of Horus has been described as "the most perfectly preserved monument of the ancient world" and its inscriptions have yielded a wealth of information about rituals and festivals, the priesthood, and Ancient Egyptian mythology. The present temple, which replaced an earlier one, was built by successive rulers of the Ptolemaic dynasty: The Greek Ptolemies adopted the gods and religion of Egypt in order to bolster their royal power. Begun by Ptolemy III in 237 B.C.E., the temple was completed 180 years later by Ptolemy XII. On the entrance gate are huge figures of Horus, other gods, and a pharaoh destroying his enemies; above the gateway the disk of the sun is flanked by serpents. In the temple's inner sanctuary remains a shrine of polished stone in which a golden figure of Horus was concealed.

The temple had an extensive library as well as a perfume laboratory, with inscriptions on the walls detailing recipes for perfumes and incense. Once a year a statue of Horus's mother, the goddess Isis, was brought to Edfu along the Nile in a gilded barge from her temple at Dendera to the north. She passed rejoicing crowds on the riverbanks to give birth to the god symbolically, in revelry and happiness, in "the Feast of the Beautiful Meeting." **RC**

🏛 ⊚ Abu Simbel Temples (Nubia, Egypt)

Ramses II's colossal stone temples—and glorification of himself

Ramses II was one of the most powerful of all ancient Egyptian rulers; he has been identified by several historians as the pharaoh depicted in the Bible's book of Exodus, which describes the Israelites' escape from Egypt. It is thought that he reigned for sixty-six years, from 1279 B.C.E., and was survived by more than a hundred children, by a number of wives and concubines, when he died in 1213 B.C.E.

There are more surviving statues of Ramses II than of any other pharaoh; in addition he created, enlarged, and embellished numerous temples. His temple to the sun god, carved into a mountainside at Abu Simbel in Nubia, is famous for the four colossal figures of the pharaoh wearing his crown and seated on his throne, with tiny figures of members of his family at his feet. Carved out of the rock to dominate the facade and standing more than 65 feet (20 m) tall, the figures have been described as "tremendous egos in stone" and

were intended to impress the local tribes with the pharaoh's superhuman power. On top of the facade, baboons are shown saluting the sun. Inside are statues of the pharaoh and depictions of his triumphs in war.

When it was rediscovered in 1813 by the Swiss Orientalist Johann Ludwig Burckhardt, the temple was almost completely covered in sand. Giovanni Belzoni, an Italian tomb robber, managed to get inside in 1817 and took away everything he could. A second, smaller temple of the love goddess Hathor was built for Ramses II's favorite wife, Nefertari, for "whose sake the very sun does shine."

When the Aswan High Dam was being constructed in the early 1960s, an International Campaign, launched by UNESCO, assembled funds and technical expertise to move the temples at Abu Simbel to higher ground so that they would not be inundated by the waters of Lake Nasser. **RC**

🏛 ◉ Senegambia Stone Circles (The Gambia and Senegal)

World's largest concentration of stone circles

The Gambia is an unusual enough country geographically—a narrow strip of land about 300 miles (500 km) long and only 30 miles (50 km) wide, entirely surrounded by Senegal except where it meets the sea—but it shares with Senegal one of the mysteries of prehistoric Africa in the form of hundreds of stone circles, along with standing stones and burial mounds. These are contained in four large groups— Sine Ngayème, Wanar, Wassu, and Kerbatch—within a large area between the Saloum and Gambia rivers. The stones range in height from about 2.5 feet (750 cm) to 10 feet (3 m) and their circumference ranges from 15 feet (5 m) to 30 feet (10 m). Most of them are single circles, but there are also groups of concentric circles. The reddish-colored laterite stones are generally round and flat-topped, but some are square, some taper to the top, some have a round top with a ball cut in it, and some have a hollow on top.

They seem to have been built between the third century B.C.E. and the sixteenth century C.E.

The circles were evidently burial sites and human bones have been unearthed in the center of them, along with spears, arrows, and other objects. No one knows who constructed them and why, but they were certainly erected over an immensely long period of time, skillfully quarried and shaped, and their creation would have required a prosperous society and a well-organized labor force.

A new museum (the Wassu) was opened in 2000 close to the Gambian circles, which are thought to have been erected from about 750 C.E. There are between ten and twenty-four stones in each circle. Whether they were built around the graves of local rulers is uncertain. Offerings of vegetables, candles, and money are still left on them today, and it is said that some of the stones shine at night. **RC**

🏛 ◉ Tomb of Emperor Askia (Gao, Mali)

Monumental, mud-built, pyramidal tomb complex in the Islamic style

The area alongside the River Niger south of the Sahara Desert was ruled in medieval times by the empire of Mali. Flourishing mainly on trade in gold and Saharan salt, the empire stretched from Nigeria to the Atlantic. The area—whose chief commercial centers were at Timbuktu and Djenne—adopted Islam and became a center of Muslim scholarship. Meanwhile, however, the Songhai people established their city-state of Gao on the Niger in the east of the region and in the fifteenth century they superseded the Mali Empire, dominated Timbuktu, and conquered the Sahel—the "shore" along the border of the Sahara.

The first Songhai emperor, Askia Muhammad I, went on pilgrimage to Mecca in 1495 and brought back with him the earth and wood needed to build his tomb; this was said to have taken thousands of camels to carry. Standing more than 50 feet (17 m) high, roughly pyramidal in shape, with numerous wooden poles protruding from it, the tomb—the region's biggest structure of pre-colonial architecture—has been described as looking like a termite mound. Some of the emperor's successors are buried in the courtyard. The complex includes two mosques, a cemetery, and an assembly ground. The Songhai Empire lasted almost another century after Askia Muhammad's time, but was eventually laid low by the Moroccans, led by Judar Pasha.

In 2004, Emperor Askia's Tomb was chosen as a World Heritage site, as it reflects the way local building traditions, in response to Islamic needs, absorbed influences from North Africa to create a unique architectural style across the West African Sahel. The tomb, as is necessary for the maintenance of mud buildings, has been replastered regularly since it was built. The mosques were enlarged in the 1960s and 1970s, and a wall was built around the site in 1999. **RC**

Church of St. Mary of Zion (Aksum, Ethiopia)

Alleged home of the Ark of the Covenant, and site of coronations of Ethiopian emperors

Christianity reached Aksum, in the northeast of what is now Ethiopia, very early on, and from the fourth century it was the state religion under King Ezana of Axum, whose coins bore the Christian cross. Ezana built a church in Aksum, which may have been the first in Africa, but it was destroyed centuries later, probably in a Muslim attack in 1535. The church's stone altar allegedly came from Mount Zion, near Jerusalem. What is now called the old church of St. Mary of Zion (which is not open to women) was built in 1665, probably on the site of the earlier church. The church was where Ethiopian emperors came to be crowned. A much bigger new church, which has been unkindly described as resembling a public swimming pool, was built nearby in the 1960s.

Between these two churches is a small chapel in which, according to legend, rests the holiest relic in Ethiopia, the Ark of the Covenant. Seldom, if ever, shown to visitors, it is said to have been brought from Jerusalem to Ethiopia in King Solomon's time, in the tenth century B.C.E., by King Menelik I, who was Solomon's son by the Queen of Sheba. The Ark was the portable shrine in which the Israelites carried Jehovah with them on their journey to Palestine and in which were placed the tablets of the Ten Commandments delivered to Moses on Mount Sinai. The Ark could be safely touched only by the Levite priests who carried it. Anyone else who ventured to touch the Ark was likely to be destroyed on the spot by the huge force of divine power inside it, like a gigantic charge of electricity. The most sacred object in every Ethiopian church, normally shrouded from view, is a replica of one of the tablets of the law. The Ark chapel also contains an archeological museum. Aksum is regarded as the holiest place in Ethiopia and is an important destination for pilgrims. **RC**

🏛 ⊚ Aksum Stelae (Aksum, Ethiopia)

Massive stone obelisks marking the graves of Aksum's rulers

According to legend, the Queen of Sheba lived in Aksum in the tenth century B.C.E. and the women of the town still use the queen's bath for washing clothes. What is more certain is that the kingdom of Aksum in Ethiopia and Eritrea, located at the profitable junction of important trading routes and with a port on the Red Sea, was one of the most powerful in the Middle East in the early centuries of the Christian era. Largely destroyed in a Muslim attack in the sixteenth century, Aksum is now just a minor country town, but it is rich in churches, monasteries, and the remains of palaces and tombs left from its great days.

To mark their graves and as monuments to their power and wealth, Aksum's rulers erected standing stones of enormous size, known as stelae, up to 100 feet (33 m) high and covered with carvings and inscriptions. Some of the stelae are carved to look like multistory buildings. Each may originally have had a metal moon disk on top, perhaps engraved with a portrait of the ruler it commemorated. At the bottom of each stela, a stone platform was provided for offerings to the dead to be laid. Also surviving in the area are some impressive royal tombs with granite-lined galleries and chambers, most of which were pillaged long ago by robbers.

The biggest stelae park is to the north of Aksum, with seventy-five or more of these extraordinary monuments. The 500-ton Great Stele, which apparently collapsed while it was being erected, around 330 B.C.E., is said to be the largest single block of stone that human beings have ever attempted to raise. UNESCO designated the ruins of the ancient city of Aksum a World Heritage site in 1980, and signed a contract in 2007 to begin the re-erection of the second-largest obelisk, Stela 2, which was returned to Aksum from Rome in 2005. **RC**

🏛 ⦿ Royal Enclosure (Gondar, Ethiopia)

Former Ethiopian capital, with royal palaces, castles, and churches

During the Middle Ages, Ethiopian rulers moved their court frequently, the emperors traveling about with courtiers and officials, judges, guards, servants, and prostitutes, carried on anything up to 100,000 mules. In the 1630s, however, when Emperor Fassilidas succeeded his father, Susenyos, a Roman Catholic convert, he reverted to the country's Coptic Christian tradition, closed the country to foreigners, and created a permanent capital in Gondar. At the meeting point of three important caravan routes, Gondar became a wealthy commercial center that remained Ethiopia's capital for about 250 years and is so rich in palaces, castles, and churches that—despite being sacked by a dervish army from the Sudan in 1888—it has been called Africa's Camelot.

The oldest building behind the high stone walls of the Royal Enclosure is the castle built by Fassilidas, which has been recently restored. With its domed towers, it seems to reflect Indian, Moorish, and Portuguese influences and may have been designed by an Indian architect. Tunnels and paths lead to buildings added by later rulers, including the library of Yohannes I and the palace of Iyasu I, who ruled until 1706 and is considered the greatest of his line. There are also the cages where the emperor's lions were kept, the squares used for public executions, and the tomb of Walter Plowden, the British consul and a friend of the emperor Tewodros in the mid-nineteenth century. The compound was bombed by the British in 1941 when the Italians had their headquarters there.

Outside the town are the splendidly decorated Debre Berhan Selassie Church and Fassilidas's Bath— the scene of the annual Timket celebration when it is blessed before being opened for bathing. The city contains some impressive Art Deco architecture from the period of Italian occupation (1936–41). **RC**

🏛 ◉ Lalibela Rock Churches (Lalibela, Ethiopia)

Churches carved from the rocks in the mountains of northern Ethiopia

Under its former name of Rotha, the town perched in the Ethiopian mountains was the capital of the Zagwe dynasty in the twelfth and thirteenth centuries. Legend has it that King Lalibela visited Jerusalem and vowed to create a New Jerusalem when he returned home. All eleven of the churches chiseled out of the soft, red rock are attributed to him, though in fact some may have been created by other rulers. Tradition has it that angels worked on their construction during the night when the human workmen were asleep. Many of the town's features have biblical names—including the local river, which is called the Jordan.

The churches are arranged in four groups: In the Northern Group is Bete Medhane Alem (the Saviour of the World), which looks like a Greek temple and is said to be the largest monolithic church in existence. In the church is a solid gold cross, now recovered after being stolen by an antiques dealer in 1997. Three empty

graves in the church are supposed to have been prepared for the bodies of Abraham, Isaac, and Jacob. Tunnels lead to smaller churches, including Bete Maryam, dedicated to the Virgin Mary and decorated with notable frescoes and carvings, and Bete Golgotha, named after the scene of Christ's crucifixion, where King Lalibela is said to be buried. Hermits still live in caves inside the chapel of Bete Meskel. The story attached to Bete Gyorgis—in the Western Group and said to be the best-preserved of the churches—is that St. George appeared to King Lalibela and complained that none of the churches was dedicated to him. The king promptly vowed to build him the most beautiful church of all. Bete Gyorgis is the result and it is said that the hoof prints of the saint's horse can be seen imprinted in stone in the entrance. The Eastern Group includes several other churches, including one linked to a holy bakery. **RC**

 🏛 ⊚ **Harar Town Walls** (Harar, Ethiopia)

Stout walls surrounding the sacred Muslim city of Harar Jugol

In eastern Ethiopia, south of the Chercher Mountains, the fortified town of Harar is home to an astonishing eighty-two mosques and more than 100 shrines to Muslim holy men. However, the town houses, with their exceptional interiors, comprise the most spectacular part of the town. Dating possibly from the twelfth century, the town was ruled from 1525 by Muhammad Gragn the Left-Handed, who waged holy war against the Christians of Ethiopia until he was killed in 1543 in battle against an Ethiopian Christian army. His successor in Harar, Nur Ibn al-Wazir, built stout walls around the town, 16 feet (5 m) thick and still surviving, to defend it from the Galla people who were moving north from Kenya. The wall had five gates, with two more added later.

Harar prospered for the next four centuries as virtually an independent Muslim city-state at the junction of profitable trade routes between the Middle East, Africa, and India, and became a center of Islamic scholarship. The site was forbidden to Christians—the first to visit it was the English explorer Sir Richard Burton in the 1850s, when the town was still engaged in the slave trade. Harar had a checkered history from 1875, occupied by the Egyptians and then taken over by the Ethiopian emperor Menelik II. The French poet Arthur Rimbaud lived there in the 1880s, toward the end of his life, and there is now a museum to him. Ras Makonnen, appointed as governor by the emperor Menelik, was the father of Ras Tafari, the future emperor Haile Selassie, who was governor in his turn from 1911 and whose house is on show. The impact of African and Islamic traditions on the development of the town's building types and layout make for the particular character and uniqueness of Harar. But the town's oddest attraction is the feeding of hyenas at night outside the Sanga Gate. **RC**

Manhyia Palace (Kumasi, Ghana)

Official residence of the Ashanti king in Ghana's second city

The Ashanti—a major ethnic group in Ghana—resisted British colonization in the nineteenth century, though they were finally overcome. Kumasi was the Ashanti capital from the 1690s when, according to tradition, the golden stool that was the throne of the Asantehene, the Ashanti confederation's ruler, descended to him from the sky. By 1750 the Ashanti had seized control of much of modern Ghana, and by 1820 the Ashanti Empire had expanded into what are now the neighboring states of Côte d'Ivoire, Togo, and Burkina Faso.

Human sacrifice was a fundamental feature of Ashanti society. One visitor in 1817 recorded seeing 100 men sacrificed at the yam harvest and their blood poured into the ground; other travelers described Kumasi as "a monstrous golden bowl filled with the blood of human sacrifice." The Ashanti Empire's economy depended heavily on trade in gold, ivory, and slaves, and as the slave trade declined in the nineteenth century, the Asantehene's power declined with it. Even so, the Ashanti army was strong enough to hold off the British in successive wars until the 1890s, but in 1896 the British absorbed the Ashanti kingdom into their Gold Coast colony, and in 1900 an uprising led by Yaa Asantewaa—the Queen Mother of Ejisu, a state in the Asante Confederacy—failed.

The Ashanti king is still an important figure in Ghana and the Manhyia Palace is his official residence, built when the Asantehene of the time was allowed to return from exile. During the Adae festivals every few weeks, the king receives the homage of his lesser chiefs and subjects, with spectacular costumes and drumming. More material related to the Ashanti kings and their people is on show at the National Cultural Centre and at Kumasi Fort, which was completed by the British in 1897. **RC**

🏛 ◈ St. George's Castle (Elmina, Ghana)

Erected by the Portuguese in 1482, the earliest European building in sub-Saharan Africa

Thought to be the oldest surviving European building in Africa south of the Sahara, St. George's Castle (originally known as São Jorge da Mina, or St. George of the Mine Castle) was built by the Portuguese, who began exploring the West African coast for both trading and Christian missionary purposes in the fifteenth century. In 1471 they arrived at a fishing village—which was subsequently called Elmina—from the Portuguese De Costa da el Mina de Ouro (the Coast of Gold Mines). There they established a friendly and profitable relationship with a powerful local chief they called Caramansa. In 1482 Caramansa permitted the Portuguese to build a fort commanding the harbor, which seems to have been intended mainly to protect them against attack from the land side. Remarkably, it was constructed from numbered, prefabricated, granite blocks shipped out from Portugal in a fleet of eleven ships together with 700 soldiers for the garrison. Even more remarkably perhaps, one of those on the expedition was Christopher Columbus, ten years before he set sail on his voyage of discovery of America.

Elmina became the center of Portuguese trade on the Gold Coast in gold and slaves, who were bought from African chiefs and shipped to Brazil and other Portuguese colonies. In the sixteenth century, the Dutch, the British, and the French took an increasing interest in the West African coast, and the Dutch attacked Elmina several times. In 1637 they successfully bombarded the castle into submission, and Elmina then became the main Dutch Gold Coast center until the British replaced them in the early 1870s. The Dutch greatly enlarged and strengthened the Portuguese castle, whose chapel they converted for use in staging slave auctions. The dungeons, where as many as 200 slaves at a time were held before shipment, can still be seen. **RC**

> *"[The castle], with its neat red Dutch bricks reminds the modern visitor of views of Delft by Vermeer."*

William St. Clair, historian

One of the principal shipping posts of the trans-Atlantic slave trade

The castle at Cape Coast is one of the biggest and best-preserved European buildings in West Africa. The original timber building was built in 1653 for the Swedes, who named it Carolusborg after their king, Charles X. The fort was subsequently rebuilt in stone.

The name "Cape Coast" comes from Cabo Corso (Short Cape), which was what the Portuguese called the place when they passed by in 1471. They made their base at Elmina, just along the coast, and when the first British sea captains came exploring in the mid-1550s, Cape Coast was a fishing village of twenty or so houses. One hundred years later the village was controlled for a few years by Swedes, who built the fort in 1653, then by Danes, then by the Dutch, and from 1664 by the British, who over the next century and more turned the fort into a much larger and more powerful castle, well stocked with cannons, which reached its present appearance by about 1795.

Cape Coast was the main British base and administrative center on the Gulf of Guinea, and by the 1690s it was a town of 500 houses, which the local paramount chief made his capital. In the eighteenth century, Cape Coast was one of the principal shipping points for slaves across the Atlantic, and at any one time up to 1,500 Africans were held in the castle dungeons waiting for the next slaving ship. The walls of the dungeons still bear the graffiti scratched by the prisoners. When the British ended the slave trade in 1807, they closed the tunnel through which the male slaves had been marched to the ships. It is now a shrine to local gods.

From 1874 Cape Coast Castle was briefly the seat of government of the British colony of the Gold Coast, but in 1877 the British moved their capital to Accra. In the 1920s the castle was restored by the British; the Ghanaian government restored it again in 1957. Until 1993 part of the castle was used as a prison. **RC**

> *"The screams . . . echo down through the centuries from the scratches they made in the walls."*
>
> Khephra Burns, author

Royal Palaces of Abomey

(Abomey, Benin)

Unique reminders of a vanished kingdom and its way of life

Until 1975, what is now the Republic of Benin was called Dahomey after the African kingdom that once dominated the southern part of the country. A highly militarized society in which boys were trained as soldiers from a young age, Dahomey was famed for its elite Amazon female warriors, the king's guards. Human sacrifice was practiced on an epic scale, with thousands of slaves and prisoners of war beheaded at festivals. Located on the West African "Slave Coast," Dahomey was involved in the slave trade from the sixteenth century. King Gezo, who ruled from 1818 to 1858, raided the Yoruba people in Nigeria to take captives for the trade, but eventually, in 1885, the last Portuguese slaving ship sailed away, and in the 1890s the area was taken over by the French.

The kings of Dahomey used their wealth and power to build impressive palaces, their facades decorated with intricate bas-reliefs. The first palace was built by Wegbaja, who reigned for forty years from about 1645. He threw the corpse of a defeated chief called Da into the foundations—hence the name *Dahomey*, meaning "on Da's belly." With the exception of King Akaba, who had a separate enclosure, each successive ruler built his own palace within the compound at Abomey until, by the nineteenth century, the complex covered about 100 acres (40 ha), within a 2.5-mile- (4-km-) long cob wall. Fleeing from the French in 1892, the last Dahomean ruler ordered Abomey to be destroyed, but some of the palace buildings have survived, with a harem for eight hundred women, ceremonial rooms, and voodoo religious objects. There are carved wooden royal thrones, some with silver and copper decorations; the legs of Gezo's throne are mounted on human skulls. Behind the thrones, banners depict Dahomey's history and the warlike deeds of its kings. **RC**

> *"[They] were awestruck by the splendor of the court and the grandeur of the ceremonies."*
>
> UNESCO, on nineteenth-century visitors to Abomey

Lambaréné Hospital

(Lambaréné, Gabon)

Hospital set up by Albert Schweitzer in 1913

The town of Lambaréné in southern Gabon is located mainly on an island in the Ogooué river, in the Central African rain forest. Visitors today are drawn to see the hospital established by Albert Schweitzer, the German theologian and medical missionary, who was awarded the Nobel Peace Prize in 1952. A successful academic as a young man, Schweitzer was a devout Christian who had a "reverence for life" and vowed to devote his energies to the service of humanity. In his thirties, he and his young wife, Hélène, went to Lambaréné, in what was then French Equatorial Africa. They established a hospital there in 1913 in order to study the major causes of local diseases. The hostilities of World War I, however, made Schweitzer's position as a German in French terrritory difficult.

With the war over, Schweitzer refounded the hospital and recruited more medical staff. Patients, who were charged only what they could afford to pay, were brought from miles around by their families, who often stayed with them. Thus, the hospital doubled as a lively village, with people cheerfully cooking their food outside the huts, and with a population of around six hundred at its peak. Schweitzer was no bleeding heart, but a dominating and determined character. He presided over a Christian service on Sundays but, although he regarded native African religious beliefs as childish, his Christian proselytizing was taken gently. Apart from occasional visits to Europe, Schweitzer lived at the hospital for the rest of his life until his death there in 1965.

The original hospital in Lambaréné has been replaced by a more modern one, but the old operating rooms and laboratories, the nurses' dormitory, Schweitzer's own rooms, with his white apron and parrot's cage, and the living quarters for patients and their families, have been preserved. **RC**

Fort Jesus

(Mombasa, Kenya)

Sixteenth-century Portuguese fort

In the fifteenth century the East African ports enjoyed official connections with the emperor of China. Profitable trade across the Indian Ocean attracted Portuguese attention after Vasco da Gama's epoch-making voyage to India in 1498, and in the following century the Portuguese took control of the East African coast by force. Mombasa, once the principal port on the Indian Ocean, fell to the Portuguese in 1505 and, after Turkish raids in the 1580s, they built Fort Jesus to guard the harbor and the town. It was designed by an Italian architect, Joao Batista Cairato, who had done much work for the Portuguese in Goa.

"The fort is today hailed as one of the best examples of 16th century Portuguese military architecture."

Fort Jesus Museum

Though partly ruined, the fort is highly impressive. The walls were designed to make it impossible to attack a stretch of them without being a target from other parts of the battlements. Inside are cannons, the remains of a church and the fort's well, Omani Arab buildings, and outside latrines.

The fort had a checkered history, frequently changing hands between the Portuguese and the Arabs. In 1698 Arabs from Oman took it after a siege that lasted for close to three years, by which time the Portuguese garrison had been reduced to ten men and a priest. The Portuguese lost Fort Jesus for the last time in 1729. From 1746 Mombasa was ruled by its own independent sultans and later by the sultans of Zanzibar until Kenya came under British control in the 1880s. The fort was then used as a prison. **RC**

Buganda Royal Tombs

(Kasubi, Uganda)

Mausoleum of Buganda kings, built of organic materials, in traditional style

"*The inside is hidden from view by a huge curtain of tree-bark behind which is the 'sacred forest' …*"

UNESCO

The territory from which the state of Uganda was created in the 1890s was dominated by the Bantu-speaking Baganda people under their *kabakas*, or kings. Lying inland, south of the Sudan, it had little contact with outsiders until the middle of the nineteenth century, when Arab slavers penetrated the interior. Kabaka Mutesa I built himself a palace on Kasubi Hill, outside Kampala, in 1881 and was buried there when he died three years later. He was the first of his line to be buried complete with his jawbone, which, in the traditional practice, was put in a separate shrine because it contained the spirit of the deceased.

Also buried on Kasubi Hill were three of Kabaka Mutesa's successors. Mwanga II, who roasted Christian converts alive on a spit and survived a civil war against him by both Muslims and Christians in the 1880s, finally died in exile in 1903. His son, Daudi Chwa II, lasted until 1939; and his son, Edward Mutesa II, in turn, was deposed in 1966 after Uganda had gained independence. He died in London three years later but his remains were brought back for burial on Kasubi Hill in 1971. Other royal family members lie buried behind the principal shrine and there are houses for the remains of widows of the *kabakas*.

The domed and thatched circular building, said to be the biggest African mausoleum of its kind, was built in the traditional Baganda style of reeds and bark cloth, supported on wooden poles and surrounded by reed fences, with a reed gateway. The former *kabakas'* possessions include Mutesa I's pet leopard, which is now stuffed, spears and weapons, fetish objects, drums, and musical instruments. There is a special curtained-off area for royal ceremonies and consultation with the spirit world and the ancestors. The Kasubi Tombs were designated a UNESCO World Heritage site in 2001. **RC**

Church of St. Michael & All Angels (Blantyre, Malawi)

Magnificent church built by African labor

The imposing church of St. Michael and All Angels, with its towers and dome, soaring arches, and stained-glass windows, was built between 1888 and 1891 for the Church of Scotland mission, established in Blantyre in 1876. It was constructed with the simplest of tools by African laborers who could never have seen or built anything remotely like it before.

The missionaries named their settlement Blantyre after the place in Scotland where David Livingstone was born—appropriately enough, because it was the Scottish explorer and missionary who had inspired their presence. By the 1840s the Malawi region, known as Nyasaland from 1907 to 1964, was the target of internal tribal warfare and an Arab-run slave trade in which thousands of Africans were taken by slave raiders and countless others were killed in the raids or died on the march to the coast. Livingstone, who in the 1850s was the first European to cross the continent from west to east, was determined to wipe out the trade, which he believed could be achieved only by the introduction to Africa of what he called "the three Cs"—Christianity, colonization, and commerce.

After Livingstone's death in 1873, various Christian missions from Britain arrived in what is now Malawi, including the one from the Church of Scotland that settled at Blantyre. Though fiercely criticized in its early days for its tyrannical treatment of the natives, from 1881 the mission was run for thirty years by the Reverend Clement Scott, who believed in "Africa for the Africans." It was he who designed the church of St. Michael. This and other missions introduced good schools and new crops and farming methods, and encouraged peaceful relations between the indigenous tribes. Many of the leaders of the subsequent drive for Malawian independence received their education in mission schools. **RC**

Livingstone Statue (Victoria Falls, Zimbabwe)

Monument to the Scottish explorer

The Victoria Falls, twice the size of Niagara and one of the most thrilling and spectacular sights in the world, were "discovered" in 1856 by the Scottish missionary and explorer David Livingstone, but they had of course been known to Africans since time immemorial. In Livingstone's time, the Makololo people of the area called them the Moisatunya Falls, meaning "The Thundering Smoke," because the river makes a huge roaring noise and creates a massive veil of spray.

Livingstone and some two hundred tribesmen under the leadership of the young Makololo chief Sekeletu had set off in a fleet of canoes along the

> *"I determined never to stop until I had come to the end and achieved my purpose."*
>
> David Livingstone

Zambesi River, toward the east coast, when they heard the distant thundering of the falls; from 6 miles (10 km) away they could see the columns of spray rising up. They landed on an island at the edge of the falls and Livingstone lay on his stomach, getting soaked by the spray as he looked down at the incredible sight beneath him. He cut his initials and the date on the bark of a tree on the island, which he later described as the only time he had ever been guilty of such vandalism. He later dedicated "the most wonderful sight" he had seen in Africa to Queen Victoria.

Livingstone's statue, by W. Reid Dick, was erected in 1934 outside the village of Victoria Falls on the Zimbabwe side of the river. It looks out over the Devil's Cataract, which plunges down onto an island in the river in an awesome display of beauty and power. **RC**

🏛 ◎ **Great Zimbabwe** (Masvingo, Zimbabwe)

Ruins of a southern African city, believed to be the work of the Shona people

The ruins of Great Zimbabwe, built from the eleventh to the fifteenth century, form the most impressive pre-European site in Africa south of the Sahara. They were long attributed to the ancient Egyptians, the Phoenicians, and the Greeks, among others, because the native African peoples were considered too backward for such an achievement. It is now accepted, however, that Great Zimbabwe was the creation of the Shona people and the capital of a rich trading empire. The name "Zimbabwe" probably comes from the Shona phrase *dzimba dzembabwe* (houses of stone).

The Shona lived mainly by raising cattle and trading in beef, but the countryside near Great Zimbabwe had lucrative reserves of gold. A village was built in the eleventh century on the highest hill in the area. This was massively expanded in the thirteenth century with various enclosures inside granite walls, built without mortar, incorporating the boulders on the hilltop. The most striking feature of the site, now called the Great Enclosure and possibly a royal fortress-compound, was protected by a wall up to 16 feet (5 m) thick and 36 feet (11 m) high. Inside is the stone, possibly phallic, Conical Tower, 30 feet (10 m) high, whose purpose is unknown. The only representational pieces of art found are soapstone carvings of birds, which may have been regarded as messengers between the ancestors and the living.

The inhabitants of Great Zimbabwe did business with the Far East through the coastal ports, probably trading gold and ivory for imports from Asia: Archeologists have discovered objects from Persia, India, and China. The population of Great Zimbabwe reached a peak of somewhere between 11,000 and perhaps as many as 18,000, but for reasons that remain uncertain the settlement was abandoned late in the sixteenth century. **RC**

Thaba Bosiu (near Maseru, Lesotho)

Impregnable stronghold built by founder of Basutoland

Moshoeshoe I was the virtual creator of modern Lesotho, under its earlier name of Basutoland. Born in about 1786, he rose in rank from being a village headman of the Sotho people to become one of the shrewdest and most powerful rulers in southern Africa in the nineteenth century. He made himself rich in cattle by a mixture of efficient husbandry and ruthless rustling and, by skilled diplomacy, built up alliances with powerful chiefs.

In 1824 Moshoeshoe and his followers found themselves an almost impregnable stronghold on the steep-sided, flat-topped hill of Thaba Bosiu (Mountain of the Night)—so called because, according to legend, one night it swelled from being a mere hill into a mountain. It was often attacked but never taken, and Moshoeshoe brought together under his protection groups of Africans, mainly Sotho speakers, who had fled from slave traders or been attacked by the Zulus

and the Ndebele. He encouraged the work of Christian missionaries, though he did not become a Christian himself, and his reputation for sagacity and open-handedness still endures.

In the 1850s and 1860s, Moshoeshoe's kingdom suffered from attacks by the Boers of the Orange Free State in search of land. They tried several times to storm Thaba Bosiu, but were successfully beaten back. To avoid Boer domination, Moshoeshoe turned to the British and, in 1868, he accepted a British protectorate for Basutoland, which survived to become an independent state as Lesotho in 1965.

Moshoeshoe died at Thaba Boisu in 1870 and was buried on the hilltop, as were his successors, including Moshoeshoe II, who was the first king of independent Lesotho and who died in 1996. The remains of the houses and the defensive fortifications can still be seen at this imposing site. **RC**

Paul Kruger's House

(Pretoria, South Africa)

Restored residence of Transvaal president

The South African statesman Paul Kruger (1825–1904) lived in this house in Pretoria from 1884 as president of the Transvaal, one of two independent republics (the other was the Orange Free State) set up by Boer emigrants from Cape Colony, which had been established by the Dutch East India Company in 1652. From 1880 to 1881, Kruger (himself a Boer emigrant as a boy) was one of the commanders when the Transvaalers successfully fought the British for their independence, and in 1883 he was appointed president of the republic. Profoundly conservative—he is said to have believed that the Earth was flat—Kruger determinedly opposed attempts to create a united, British-dominated South Africa. War broke out again in 1899 and when the British took Pretoria in 1900, Kruger was forced to escape by way of Mozambique to Holland. He eventually settled in Switzerland, where he died in 1904.

Paul Kruger's house in Pretoria was built using milk instead of water to mix the poor-quality cement—ironically, as there was nothing milk-and-watery about "Oom Paul," as he was nicknamed. One of the first Pretoria homes to be lit by electricity, the house has been restored as closely as possible to its condition when Kruger and his wife, Gezina, lived there. Family possessions include a harmonium, a remarkable number of spittoons, and one of Pretoria's first telephones, installed in 1891.

Many famous people visited the Krugers—Cecil Rhodes and Mark Twain among them—and the lions on the veranda were a present from Barney Barnato, the diamond magnate. The flag in front of the house is that of the Transvaal; when the Krugers lived there the flag was hoisted at 6 A.M. every day and struck at sundown. Across the street from the house is the Dutch Reformed Church where they worshipped. **RC**

Doornkloof Farm

(near Pretoria, South Africa)

Home of former prime minister Jan Smuts

Jan Christiaan Smuts (1870–1950), one of the great figures of South African history, was a brilliant guerrilla leader during the Anglo-Boer War, but he later came to believe in the advantages of working with the British instead of against them. Prime minister of South Africa from 1919 to 1924 and again from 1939 to 1948, Field Marshal Smuts had an important role in drafting the 1946 United Nations charter.

In 1908 Smuts bought part of Doornkloof Farm from the Erasmus family, who had owned it for years, and moved a large building of corrugated iron lined with wood (formerly a British officers' mess during the

> *"If a nation does not want a monarchy, change the nation's mind."*
>
> **Jan Smuts**

Boer War) to the farm as a home for himself and his family. It was hot in summer and icy cold in winter—his son and biographer described it as "an ideal refuge for stoics." Wild bees lived in the house, as well as the family, and pets over the years included a leopard and two lions. A more comfortable house was meant to be built higher up the hill, but somehow that never happened. There was plenty of room for visitors and Smuts's thousands of books, and he and his family loved Doornkloof dearly. He lived there for the rest of his life, including his periods in office as prime minister, and the house, much as it was in his time, has been retained as a museum to him. From the house there is a path to a group of rocks on a low hill, which he liked to walk every day and where his ashes were scattered after his death at Doornkloof in 1950. **RC**

Union Buildings

(Pretoria, South Africa)

Seat of the South African government, built in Neoclassical style in early twentieth century

Founded in 1855 and named after the Boer leader who defeated the Zulus at Blood River, Pretoria became the capital of the Boer republic of Transvaal in 1860. It remained the capital under the British and in 1910, when the new Union of South Africa came into existence, Pretoria was named as the administrative capital and the seat of the president and the government. The new Union Buildings were designed by Sir Herbert Baker, who had trained as an architect in England and went to South Africa in his twenties in 1890. He quickly made a favorable impression on Cecil Rhodes, who became his enthusiastic and highly influential patron. Baker designed many fine houses and buildings in South Africa, as well as the Rhodes Memorial in Cape Town. He would go on to help design New Delhi in India and many major buildings after his return to England.

Completed in 1913 after three years' work, the Union Buildings were built on top of a hill called Meintjieskop in the Arcadia district of Pretoria—a location intended to bring the Acropolis of Athens to mind—and were designed in a Neoclassical style as a symbol of South Africa's new unity. The two wings, with their domed towers, stand for the country's two languages, Afrikaans and English, and are joined by a semicircular colonnaded block with a 9,000-seat amphitheater. Terraced gardens on the hillside were stocked entirely with native South African plants and there are statues of notable South African figures, including a dashing equestrian statue of Louis Botha, the Union's first prime minister. There are also war memorials and a garden of remembrance.

In 1994 a crowd of tens of thousands gathered outside the Union Buildings to see Nelson Mandela take the oath of office as president after the country's first free elections took place. **RC**

"My fellow South Africans— the people of South Africa: This is indeed a joyous night."

Nelson Mandela, election victory speech, May 2, 1994

🏛 ◈ Sterkfontein Caves

(near Johannesburg, South Africa)

Archeological site with evidence of human occupation dating back three million years

> "The area contains essential elements that define the origin and evolution of humankind."

UNESCO

Part of the World Heritage Cradle of Humankind site established in 1999, the six linked caves of Sterkfontein have yielded some thrilling finds. The limestone caves—near the town of Krugersdorp, northwest of Johannesburg—were rediscovered in the 1890s by an Italian prospector, and later investigation showed that in the far-distant past the area was populated by sabre-tooth cats, long-legged hyenas, and giant monkeys. More important, the area was also inhabited by hominids—humanlike creatures that were the predecessors of modern humans.

The fossilized remains of hominids have been found in this dark underground labyrinth, which was investigated between 1936 and 1951 by Dr. Robert Bloom of the Transvaal Museum in Pretoria. In 1936 Bloom found fossils of the hominid species now called *Australopithecus africanus*, and in 1947 he discovered most of the skull of an adult female (now thought possibly to be male) australopith, though without the lower jaw and teeth, who lived an estimated 2.5 million years ago. He called her a *Plesianthropus* and she was known familiarly as "Mrs. Ples."

More was to come. In 1995 Dr. R. J. Clarke found four fossilized foot bones of a hominid christened "Little Foot," which had both human and apelike characteristics and could walk upright and climb trees. He was convinced that the rest of the skeleton must be on the site, and in 1997 he and his helpers found not only the skeleton but the complete skull, with its lower and upper jaws and teeth. It was quite a sizable creature and would have weighed 110 pounds (50 kg) or more. It had apparently fallen down a shaft, more than three million years ago, landed facedown with its head resting on its left arm, its right arm by its side, and its legs crossed, and died. Productive excavations continue at Sterkfontein today. **RC**

Big Hole

(Kimberley, South Africa)

South Africa's richest diamond mine

Diamonds had been picked up by farmers in the area near Hope Town since the 1860s and, unsurprisingly, interest in the area was mounting when, in 1871, an African found an 83-carat specimen on a hill owned by two brothers called De Beer. The discovery drew thousands of prospectors to the area and a town developed. Originally called New Rush, the town was renamed Kimberley in 1873 (after the British colonial secretary of the day, John Wodehouse, first Earl of Kimberley). The hill vanished and turned into the Big Hole—the richest diamond mine in South Africa.

The Big Hole is the world's largest hole dug by pick and shovel. It eventually reached a depth of 700 feet (215 m), with a perimeter of almost 1 mile (1.6 km); it yielded close to 3 tons (2,700 kg) of diamonds before it was closed in 1914. From the 1880s it was run by the De Beers Company, founded by Cecil Rhodes, a British-born South African businessman and politician. Africans flocked to work in the mines and, by the end of 1871, Kimberley had a bigger population than Cape Town. A rough frontier town of drinking saloons and dance halls with no law enforcement agencies, its inhabitants lived by "diggers' law." In 1882, however, it was the first town in the southern hemisphere to equip itself with street lighting and, in 1896, the first school of mining in South Africa was opened there, 50 percent financed by De Beers. The town was besieged by the Boers in 1899 to 1900 and food had to be rationed in the town, where the British later built a concentration camp for Boer women and children.

Next to the Big Hole, many of the town's oldest buildings have been preserved or reconstructed in the Kimberley Mine Museum. These include the Digger's Rest bar, the boxing academy opened by the diamond magnate Barney Barnato, and a corrugated-iron ballroom dating from 1901. **RC**

Isandlwana Battlefield

(Isandlwana, South Africa)

Scene of 1879 British defeat by Zulu warriors

The area around Isandlwana has many battlefields dating from 1838 when Boers, invading Zulu territory, achieved victory at Blood River. In the late 1870s, the British challenged Zulu might under their king Cetshwayo and experienced one of the most shattering defeats in all their colonial wars. On January 22, 1879, the 24th Regiment of Foot was overwhelmed by 25,000 Zulu warriors, who remained completely silent in a valley out of sight of the redcoats, who had no idea they were there until a patrol happened across them. The Zulu warriors, armed with spears, hurled themselves into attack over the hill and outflanked

> *"An assegai has been thrust into the nation's belly, there are not enough tears to mourn the dead."*
>
> King Cetshwayo, on the Zulu losses at Isandlwana

their far less numerous opponents. After four hours more than 1,300 British lay dead. As the fighting came to an end, there was an eclipse of the sun.

The battlefield today is largely unchanged. Cairns mark the places where the bodies were buried and the memorials to the slain include a recent one to the Zulu dead. Not far away is Rorke's Drift, celebrated in the movie *Zulu*, where the reverse happened and a mere 110 British soldiers held a small Swedish mission against a twelve-hour assault by 3,000 to 4,000 Zulus who had moved on from Isandlwana. Refusing to surrender, the British defended themselves behind a barricade of biscuit boxes and grain bags until the Zulus withdrew. Eleven Victoria Crosses were won that day, the most ever awarded for a single action. The mission is now an enthralling museum. **RC**

Gandhi Settlement (Bambayi, South Africa)

Settlement where Mahatma Gandhi began campaigning for Indian rights

> *"Victory attained by violence is tantamount to a defeat, for it is momentary."*

Mahatma Gandhi, statesman and spiritual leader

⬆ South African President Thabo Mbeki at the Gandhi Centenary celebrations in Durban in 2006.

➡ Gandhi (seated center) poses with colleagues in front of a window of his law office in Durban.

Mahatma Gandhi studied law in England in his youth before returning to India. Finding work hard to come by in his homeland, in 1893, in his early twenties, he went to South Africa to work as a lawyer for an Indian merchant firm. There was a substantial Indian population of close to 100,000 in South Africa by this time, based mainly in Natal, where Indians had been imported in the 1860s to work on the sugar plantations. Many others had arrived from India and set up successful businesses.

Gandhi soon opened his own law office in Durban. He helped to organize the Natal Indian Congress and in 1903 started a weekly paper, *Indian Opinion*. The following year he founded a community at Phoenix Farm, north of Durban at Bambayi (the Zulu approximation of Bombay). He and his wife, Kasturbai, lived there in a simple wooden house that he called Sarvodaya, "a place for upliftment for all," where he had his newspaper's printing press. The other inhabitants were friends and relatives who built their own houses and started farming. It was at the Phoenix settlement that Gandhi worked out his philosophy of nonviolent civil disobedience for tackling injustices and discrimination, and began campaigning for Indian rights. Frequently imprisoned, he left South Africa in 1914 and spent the rest of his life in India. His son, Manilal, returned to South Africa three years later.

A huge squatter camp grew up close by at Inanda, originally a Zulu settlement founded in 1845, and in 1985 the Phoenix settlement was raided by squatters who looted and destroyed it. Gandhi's house and the Phoenix Settlement were restored and reopened in 2000 at a ceremony attended by President Thabo Mbeki of South Africa and the Zulu king Goodwill Zwelithini. The Phoenix Settlement now includes a clinic, an HIV/Aids center, and other facilities. The development is part of the Inanda Heritage Trail. **RC**

Castle of Good Hope (Cape Town, South Africa)

South Africa's oldest colonial building

> *"It was the world's largest trading company, owning more than half the world's sea-going shipping."*

Dr. Thomas Crump, on the Dutch East India Company

The Cape of Good Hope was named by the Portuguese navigator Bartholomew Diaz when he rounded it in 1487, and the Portuguese, under the command of Antonio de Saldanha, landed in Table Bay, more or less by mistake, in 1503. However, it was not until 1652 that the first permanent European settlement in South Africa was established. The Dutch East India Company sent Jan Van Riebeeck with three ships and ninety men to create a base at the foot of Table Mountain, which would serve as a staging post where ships going to and from the East could put in for supplies and repairs. Van Riebeeck built a small clay and timber fort and laid out a garden for growing vegetables and fruit, which is still there today as a botanical garden. Although the early settlers were nervous about this strange country and its animals—they thought there were unicorns in the interior—the base grew into Cape Town. A more substantial, five-pointed stone castle was built between 1666 and 1679 on Strand Street along the edge of the harbor—though the water has receded a long way since then.

The Castle of Good Hope is South Africa's oldest surviving colonial building and the original bell—weighing just over 660 pounds (300 kg)—still hangs in the entrance tower. As a tribute to the castle's strength, it has never heard a shot fired in anger. The castle originally housed a church, bakery, workshops, living quarters, shops, and cells—graffiti scrawled by prisoners can be seen in the dungeons. Under the British it was the government headquarters and since 1917 it has been used by the South African Defence Force. The Secunde's House is where the Dutch East India Company's deputy governor lived. The imposing battlements command fine views over Table Bay and there is a ceremonial changing of the guard every day. The castle also has a military museum and collections of Dutch furniture and paintings. **RC**

Koopmans-De Wet House (Cape Town, South Africa)

Restored mansion in Cape Dutch style

This house is a delightful example of a grand eighteenth-century Cape Town mansion. The big rooms, benefiting from high ceilings and shutters on the sash windows, were designed to alleviate the fierce summer heat. The house interiors are now restored to the late eighteenth- and early nineteenth-century style. The lantern above the entrance door was a stock feature of houses of this period in Cape Town. Its purpose was to throw a flood of light onto the street at night to deter groups of slaves from gathering outside. A succession of damaging fires in the colony was attributed to slaves, who were blamed for the fires that ravaged Cape Town in 1736 and 1798.

Built for a rich goldsmith called Reyner Smedinga at a time when Cape Town's population was about 2,000 strong, the original house probably had one story and a thatched roof, in Cape Dutch style. It changed hands many times and was substantially enlarged between the 1770s and 1790s. The second story was added when the house was owned by Pieter Malet from Amsterdam, who needed space for his sixteen children. Malet is said to have employed Louis Michel Thibault, the leading Cape Town architect of the time. After studying architecture in France, Thibault had joined the Dutch East India Company, later becoming the principal architect and military engineer in South Africa. He designed many of Cape Town's important public buildings, including the present-day facade of the Slave Lodge.

In 1806 the house was bought by the eminent De Wet family. It was the home of Marie De Wet, who married a German called Johann Koopmans in 1864. Marie Koopmans-De Wet was a leading figure in Cape Town social and political circles until her death in 1906. Her home was opened to the public in 1914, and visitors may view a fine collection of Cape furniture, Dutch Delft, and ceramics from China and Japan. **RC**

"The most impressive feature of the Cape Dutch Homestead is . . . the ornamental gable."

Fransen and Cook, *The Old Houses of the Cape* (1965)

Robben Island

(Cape Town, South Africa)

Once an isolated hellhole, now a monument to the triumph of the human spirit

Nelson Mandela was held prisoner on Robben Island from 1964 to 1982. He was then transferred to a prison in Cape Town, and, in 1988, to a house in the grounds of another prison near Paarl, while he and white politicians conducted secret negotiations. Mandela said it was the first comfortable home he had ever had. In 1990 Mandela was released from the life sentence imposed on him at the "Rivonia Trial" for his anti-apartheid activities as a leader of the African National Congress. In 1993 he shared the Nobel Peace Prize with the South African President F. W. De Klerk for their achievement in dismantling apartheid, and in 1994 he was elected president of South Africa in the country's first election open to black voters.

The story of Robben Island as a prison goes back much further, to 1658, when a local African leader was incarcerated there. He was followed by other political prisoners jailed for opposing the Dutch regime in the East Indies and South Africa. In the nineteenth century, the British used the island for political prisoners and criminals and, from 1846, for a miscellany of minor offenders and lunatics. A leper colony was established on the island and lasted until 1930. The prison was finally closed down in 1996 and designated as a UNESCO World Heritage site in 1999.

Tours of the island, conducted by former prisoners and warders, include what is left of the leper colony, with its graveyard and its church designed by Sir Herbert Baker, and the lime quarry where prisoners worked. In the old prison, the dormitories and isolation cells can be seen. The cell occupied by Nelson Mandela has been left as it was during his incarceration. The buildings of Robben Island bear eloquent testimony to its somber history and symbolize the triumph of the human spirit, of freedom, and of democracy over oppression. **RC**

"During my lifetime I have dedicated myself to this struggle of the African people."

Nelson Mandela, statement at Rivonia Trial, 1964

Slave Lodge

(Cape Town, South Africa)

Built by the Dutch to house slave labor

The early settlers in Cape Colony suffered from a shortage of labor to work on their farms, on building projects, and as servants. The Dutch East India Company put restrictions on conscripting the local Africans—Hottentots, as the Dutch called them—so slaves were imported from the rest of the Dutch Empire, where slavery was an accepted institution, and from other parts of Africa. The first consignments arrived in the 1650s and, during the next 150 years, more than 60,000 slaves were brought from East Africa and the East Indies to the colony.

The Slave Lodge has been altered many times in its long and curious history. Completed in 1679, it is one of the oldest buildings in Cape Town and was built originally by the Dutch East India Company to house its own slaves—a brick building with no windows, where the conditions grew thoroughly filthy and rundown. Almost one thousand slaves were living there in the 1770s and at one time it was the colony's principal brothel. Some of the inhabitants worked in the hospital opposite the lodge. After the British took over Cape Colony in 1806, they decided to convert the building into government offices. At that point there were almost three hundred slaves living in the lodge, many of them elderly. Those who could still work were auctioned off, and the rest were moved elsewhere and freed in 1828. Slavery was abolished altogether in the 1830s after the Slavery Abolition Act gave all slaves in the British Empire their freedom.

The Slave Lodge was used as the Supreme Court for many years and in 1966 the building became the Cultural History Museum. It was renamed in 1998 and converted to tell the story of slavery as part of the social and cultural history of South Africa. A plaque in Spin Street behind the museum marks the place where slaves were bought and sold. **RC**

Rhodes Memorial

(Cape Town, South Africa)

Monument to Cecil Rhodes

After arriving in the Kimberley diamond fields as a young man from England, and making his fortune, Cecil Rhodes (1853–1902) dedicated his money and his energies to the building up of the British Empire in Africa. He projected a Cape to Cairo railway, which was never completed, secured the British hold on what was subsequently named Rhodesia after him, and was prime minister of Cape Colony in the 1890s. Rhodes died in 1902, aged only forty-eight, in Muizenberg.

The first idea for a memorial was to put a colossal figure of Rhodes, modeled on the Statue of Liberty, on Signal Hill in Cape Town, but this idea was dropped

> *"To think of these stars that you see overhead at night . . . I would annex the planets if I could."*
>
> Cecil Rhodes

and he is commemorated in Cape Town today by the impressive monument designed by Sir Herbert Baker and formally opened ten years after Rhodes's death. A cast of G. F. Watts's vigorous statue *Physical Energy*, as a symbol of Rhodes's gift for action, faces northeast—the direction of Cairo—at the foot of broad steps that lead up (between pairs of bronze lions symbolizing calm strength and power held in reserve) to a Classical-style temple with a bust of Rhodes.

The monument is below Devil's Peak in the Groote Schuur estate on the flank of Table Mountain, which Rhodes bought to prevent it from being spoiled, and which he gave to the nation. Not far to the south are the Kirstenbosch National Botanical Gardens, South Africa's oldest and largest gardens, which Rhodes established in 1895. **RC**

The largest continent on earth, stretching from Turkey and Arabia to Japan, produced the great ancient civilizations of Persia, India, and China. Vast empires have clashed as peoples fought for control of fertile lands and rich cities such as Babylon, Constantinople, Jerusalem, Agra, Samarkand, and Beijing. Asia has seen the splendours of the Ottoman sultans and the Mughal emperors, and gave birth to the world's major religions: Hinduism, Buddhism, Judaism, Christianity, and Islam.

← Stone heads at Angkor's Bayon temple may be portraits of King Jayavarman VII.

Asia

Citadel of Raymond de St. Gilles (Tripoli, Lebanon)

Imposing Crusader castle–fortress

Perched on a rocky outcrop above Tripoli in Lebanon, the Citadel of Raymond de St. Gilles is a fortress with a long and complex past. Although Arab soldiers first built a stronghold on the site in 636, it is a Christian Crusader knight, Raymond de St. Gilles, Count of Toulouse, after whom the building is now named.

A powerful military leader in the First Crusade (1096–99) against the Muslim-dominated eastern Mediterranean, Raymond set his sights upon the conquest of Tripoli, a prosperous port and city defended by formidable walls. Unable to take the city by storm, in 1103 he ordered the construction of a new castle on the rocky ridge, which was separated from Tripoli by about 3 miles (4.8 km) of gardens and orchards. Once installed in his castle, which he called Mount Pilgrim, Raymond was able to control land access to the city. The city's Muslim defenders mounted sorties in an attempt to dislodge the Christians from the fortress, during one of which Raymond was fatally wounded. He died in the castle in February 1105. His son Bertrand, however, succeeded in capturing the city in 1109 and was declared Count of Tripoli.

The city remained under Christian rule until 1289, when the Egyptian Mamluks captured and sacked Tripoli as part of their final push to drive the Crusaders out of Lebanon. The Mamluks razed the old port-city and built a new inland town under the walls of the citadel. Much extended and rebuilt, the citadel remained in continuous use as an administrative center under the Mamluks up to 1516 and then under the Ottoman Turks.

The imposing buildings that remain today are the residue of nine centuries of history. The architectural highlight is the entrance, which has three gateways: one Ottoman, one Mamluk, and one Crusader. **RG**

🏛 ◉ Byblos (Jbeil, Lebanon)

One of the world's oldest cities, occupied by numerous world civilizations

Byblos (or Jbeil) is one of the oldest cities in the world, with a history that dates back around 7,000 years. It was a thriving port and a hugely important city in the Phoenician Empire. The Phoenicians (also known as Canaanites) came from what is now Lebanon, and their empire expanded throughout the Middle East and beyond; among the things they gave to the world was the root of the Greek, Etruscan and Western alphabets. Since the Phoenicians, Byblos has been inhabited by representatives of some of the world's great cultures. The city has been claimed by Egyptians, Persians, Ottomans, Arabs, Greeks, Romans, and Byzantines. Consequently, archeological excavations have brought forth a wealth of treasures from all these disparate cultures. In many ways, the study of Byblos can be seen as the study of human civilization.

As each new culture arrived at Byblos, it introduced different rules and religions. Temples were sacked and recreated as a shrine to whichever god the newest settlers worshipped. One of the most stunning ruined temples, littered as it is with a huge number of old obelisks, has been named the Temple of the Obelisks. It must have once been a truly majestic temple; today it is a truly majestic ruin. Other remarkable ruins at the site include the Phoenicians' necropolis, a 4,000-year-old Egyptian temple, a Roman amphitheater, and a twelfth-century crusader's castle.

In 1860 a Frenchman called Ernest Renan began excavating the site of the old city, but the bulk of the work was carried out during the twentieth century, with a number of prominent archeologists sharing the work over five decades of digs that began in the 1920s. Amazingly, Byblos has managed to escape the worst battles of Lebanon's recent war, although it remains at risk from bombs for as long as the people of Lebanon remain in danger. **LH**

🏛 ◉ Temple of Bacchus (Baalbek, Lebanon)

Well-preserved ruins of a spectacular Roman temple

Roman ruins often conjure up majestic visions of imperial splendor, but the temples at Baalbek are in a class of their own. Set high on an ancient hill site, these spectacular ruins rise out of the parched earth of the Bekaa Valley. Of the structures still remaining, the temple dedicated to Bacchus, surrounded by forty-two Corinthian columns each 62 feet (19 m) high, is the best preserved. The site dates back to the third millennium B.C.E. when the area was inhabited by the Phoenicians. They constructed a temple dedicated to the sun god Baal, and gave the city its name.

During the Hellenistic period, Baalbek was known as Heliopolis—the City of the Sun. It became a Roman colony under Julius Caesar, and a building boom followed with a succession of emperors expanding the site. Baalbek was a major center of worship for the Romans, and the three main temples were dedicated to Bacchus (god of wine and fertility), Jupiter, and

Venus. The city thrived until Christianity was legalized in 313 C.E. and became the official religion of the empire. Pagan worship diminished, Heliopolis fell into decline, and temples were closed and often partly destroyed. Considering this damage and the later powerful earthquakes in the area, it is remarkable that so much of the Temple of Bacchus has survived. The decorated frieze and entablature as well as intricate carvings of figures including Mars and Diana wait to be discovered by the visitor. Despite its attribution to Bacchus, iconography has been noted that suggests the temple was dedicated to Mercury, the winged messenger of the gods.

In the seventh century Baalbek was besieged by Muslim armies, and the temples were turned into a fortress. Despite a stormy past, the temple ruins stubbornly remain as a testimony to the creators of this masterpiece more than 2,000 years ago. **KB**

🏛️ 🔘 **Ruins of Anjar** (Bekaa Valley, Lebanon)

Striking remnants of an Umayyad city

These magnificent ruins, standing out like a bare skeleton against the sunlit Lebanese sky, are a thrilling reminder of the region's history. Today, the population of Anjar is composed largely of Armenian immigrants, brought here at the outbreak of World War II by the French. When they arrived, the town was all but deserted and bleak; the refugees lived in tents and large numbers of them died from disease and hunger. Since then, they have made Anjar their home and turned it into a green, agricultural area once more.

Anjar's heyday was during the Umayyad period (660–750). It was built by Caliph Walid I and became a thriving, bustling town and vitally important trading center, boasting more than 6,000 shops. The Umayyads used Anjar as their hunting resort and a retreat in the hottest months of the summer.

The first excavations of the Umayyad city—which was known to its inhabitants as Gerrha—began in 1949 and are still ongoing. There are the ruins of tall pillars and slender archways that formed an elegant arcade of shops. There are the remains of bathhouses, homes, palaces, a mosque, souks, and well-paved streets. The city was heavily fortified, and the imposing gateways and sturdily built watchtowers can still be seen. Anjar was built alongside a stream, and guttering and pipes were put in place to harness the water.

Anjar's architecture is a mixture of vernacular and imported, and fragments of Greek, Roman, and early Christian buildings are frequently found in the masonry of its walls, suggesting that material from earlier structures were recycled and spoils of war were incorporated into the architecture. Large, now headless statues, carved as though richly draped in cloth, stand guard over the deserted ruins. A short distance away are the decimated remains of an even older civilization, a Roman castle. **LH**

🏛 ⊚ Aleppo Citadel

(Aleppo, Syria)

One of the oldest medieval fortresses in the Middle East

This commanding fortress in the heart of the ancient city of Aleppo is one of the oldest citadels still standing in the region. The current fortress was built for Ghazi, who reigned from *c.* 1193 to *c.* 1215, the son of the famed Muslim leader, Saladin. The citadel was created from an earlier citadel, which in turn had been built over previous foundations. Archeological digs suggest that the site on which it was built has been occupied since the tenth century B.C.E.; oral history claims it is even older and that the citadel's hill goes back to the sixteenth century B.C.E.

The citadel is reached by an impressive avenue of steep stone steps and is surrounded by what is now a dry moat. The districts of Aleppo—one of the oldest cities in the world—have grown up around the citadel, keeping the fortress at their center. The beautiful old streets and hidden artisans' quarters all emanate from this high hill, spilling down into the lower areas as Aleppo's population grew. In the twelfth century, the citadel and its troops protected the precious surrounding agricultural land as well as Aleppo's citizens. The citadel was a separate mini city of its own, containing palaces and more humble residences, military quarters and training grounds, a dungeon, an arsenal, public bathhouses, water cisterns, food storage areas, a mosque, and several religious shrines.

Over the subsequent centuries, the citadel was remodeled by a number of leaders, most notably Sayf al-Din Jakam, who was responsible for repairs after a Mongol invasion led by Tamerlane. In the nineteenth century, the buildings were damaged by an earthquake and the process of rebuilding took several decades. In the twentieth century, the citadel was turned into a premier tourist attraction and today there is an amphitheater where members of the public can watch concerts and performances. **LH**

"A virile population, a splendid architecture, the quickening sense of a fine Arab tradition ..."

Gertrude Bell, archeologist and writer, on Aleppo

Qala'at Samaan Basilica

(near Aleppo, Syria)

Ancient church housing relic of famous hermit

This extraordinary ancient Syrian church was actually built as four basilicas, arranged in the shape of a cross around a large, octagonal space, at the center of which stands the remains of a precious relic of early Christianity—a stone pillar on which the fifth-century hermit St. Simeon ended his days.

Seeking an isolated existence close to the heavens, the saint spent around thirty-six years of his life in open countryside on increasingly tall pillars, ultimately living atop one that was 50 feet (15 m) high. Here he eked out an existence exposed to the elements and surviving on paltry food donations. During his life, people flocked here to seek his spiritual guidance. After his death in 459, a great church was built on the site in his memory. At the time it was the world's largest church and it became a major pilgrimage site for Christians.

Of the four basilicas, the eastern one is a little bigger than the others because the most important ceremonies were held here. The site also includes a monastery, a chapel, and a baptistery, the last built slightly later close by the church. Also nearby is a road that leads to Deir Samaan, the ancient site of a monastery where St. Simeon lived at one stage. Although the pillar is now reduced to a boulder about 6.5 feet (2 m) tall, the remains of this church complex are well preserved. The overall shape of the buildings is clear, the principal facade—of Romanesque style—is still intact and the dramatic site, looking out over beautiful countryside bursting with flowers in the spring, is filled with atmosphere. During his life, St. Simeon was said to have been an influential Christian, preaching to large and respectful crowds. The first "stylite"—or pillar-hermit—he inspired many subsequent generations of ascetics, including stylites as late as the 1800s. **AK**

Dura Europos

(near Dayr az-Zawr, Syria)

The Pompeii of the Syrian desert

Located high up on a promontory above the River Euphrates, Dura Europos is a remote Hellenistic–Roman defensive town on the eastern borders of Syria. *Dura* means "fortress" in Old Semitic and Europos was the birthplace of Seleucus Nicator I, a Macedonian general of Alexander the Great in the fourth century B.C.E. First occupied by the Babylonians, Dura Europos was used as a military outpost before being rebuilt as a Hellenistic city by the Seleucids in 303 B.C.E. The city became a frontier fortress of the Parthian Empire in 113 B.C.E. and was later annexed by Rome in 165 C.E. The Sassanids, a Persian dynasty, viewing Dura Europos as

> *"Creeping up the Euphrates as quietly as we could … we found ourselves at Dura."*
>
> James Breasted, archeologist

an obstacle to their western expansion, captured and destroyed the city in 256 C.E.

Dura Europos is the site of the oldest known Christian church and synagogue, dated by Aramaic inscription to 244 C.E. The synagogue's frescoes depicting scenes from the Old Testament are today displayed in the National Museum in Damascus. The church's murals, including an image of Christ, are among the earliest examples of Christian art. The archeological remains at Dura Europos also include temples, palaces, bathhouses, and an amphitheater.

Eventually hidden by shifting sands, the site was rediscovered by a British soldier in 1920. The excellently preserved archeological remains, the site's historical importance, and its striking location make it one of Syria's most important archeological sites. **EP**

🏛 ◈ Crac des Chevaliers (near Homs, Syria)

Uniquely preserved Crusader castle, the finest example in the world

T. E. Lawrence ("Lawrence of Arabia") once described Crac des Chevaliers as "the best preserved and most wholly admirable castle in the world," and few people would disagree. Set on a high, rocky ledge, with commanding views of the surrounding valley, the fortified castle appears impregnable.

Crac des Chevaliers occupied a crucial strategic position. Located in the Homs Gap, close to the Lebanese border, it controlled the main route between Antioch and Beirut, and formed part of a network of castles defending the Crusader states. The importance of the site was historically well known: The Egyptians appear to have held it during their struggle against the Hittites, and the Emir of Homs built a fortress here in 1031. This fell to the Crusaders in 1099 and, after changing hands several times in the early twelfth century, in 1142 it was taken over by the Knights Hospitallers, a Christian military order,

somewhat similar to the the Knights Templar. They were also the chevaliers of the castle's name.

The Hospitallers rebuilt the fortress over a period of time. They partly modeled it on European and Byzantine castles, but Crac is more impressive than such structures. Its defenses were based on two concentric rings: an outer curtain wall with cylindrical towers, and an inner ring protecting the main stronghold. The castle's appearance was sufficiently intimidating to deter most attackers. In the end, the fortress fell to a ruse rather than a siege, when the knights were tricked into surrendering by a forged letter from their commander in 1271.

The castle was a military stronghold long after the Crusaders left. As its usefulness in this respect diminished, a village grew up within its walls. This settlement was removed by the French authorities in 1934 and the site is now a popular tourist attraction. **IZ**

 ◈ **Palmyra** (Palmyra, Syria)

Great ancient city at the crossroads of different civilizations

The sheer extent of the ruins at Palmyra underlines the fact that this was one of the great cities of the ancient world. Its extensive trading links and relations with Rome helped it to prosper, while also developing a distinctive culture. Ultimately, though, it became a victim of its own success, leading to its fall in 273 C.E.

Palmyra's importance stemmed from its location, at an oasis in the heart of the Syrian desert. This site made it an important staging post for the caravans that traveled along the old Silk Road—the trade route carrying luxury items to and from the East. The site was occupied from at least the second millennium B.C.E., when it was mentioned in the archives of Mari (now Tell Hariri). Palmyra's glory days, however, coincided with Rome's heyday. It became a province of the empire, but was a valued ally and retained a considerable degree of independence. During the reign of Queen Zenobia, though, this fine balance was

threatened. Unlike her late husband, Odenathus, who had been a favorite of Rome, Zenobia wanted to expand Palmyra's borders. Her army took territories in Egypt and Asia and when she proclaimed her son Vaballath as emperor, Rome saw it as a direct threat. Palmyra was sacked under Emperor Aurelian's orders, and Zenobia taken to Rome, where she is said to have been paraded through the streets in golden chains.

The art and architecture of Palmyra, standing at the crossroads of several civilizations, married Greco-Roman techniques with local traditions and Persian influences. Most of the remains at Palmyra date from the Roman era. The principal sites are the Temple of Bel, the Great Colonnade, the Baths of Diocletian, and the Tetrapylon. Some of these were later adapted for military use (the Temple of Bel, for example, became an Arab fortress in the twelfth century), but the city never recovered from Aurelian's attack. **IZ**

🏛️ ⓪ Azem Palace (Damascus, Syria)

A masterpiece of eighteenth-century Islamic architecture

The Azem Palace, built between 1749 and 1752 for Assad Pasha al-Azem, the Ottoman governor of Damascus, is the grandest and most lavishly decorated of the Ottoman residences in the Old City of Damascus. The palace adopts the layout typical of the Ottoman style, with three courtyards close together. The *salamlik*, or reception courtyard, is a formal hall with fine marble floors and a central fountain, to keep it cool. A graceful, intricately decorated, open arch leads to an area for summer seating. There is also a summer room with high ceilings and a central fountain, ornately constructed with ten brass snake heads. A warmer winter room, with an exceptionally beautiful marble floor, has a fireplace. The family quarters, or *haramlik*, with its large courtyard and pool surrounded by citrus trees, leads to the private family rooms, including a school, library, armory, marriage room, pilgrimage room, music room, and the bath complex complete with domed roofs. The *khadamlik*, or servants' quarters, lie beyond the *haramlik*.

The palace is built on a grand scale and is a lavish showcase for rare and beautiful materials and exquisite craftsmanship. Several types of stone were used in the building, including limestone, sandstone, basalt, and many types of marble. The governor had Roman columns from Bosra incorporated into the palace, as well as ancient paving stones from Banyas. The walls are thick to keep the house warm during the winter and cool in the summer, and the whole residence conveys a sense of serenity and gracious living.

The palace was badly damaged by fire in 1925 and since that time it has been carefully restored using materials salvaged from contemporary buildings. The palace was bought from the Azem family by the Syrian government in 1951 and opened to the public as one of the country's first museums in 1954. It is now the Museum of Popular Arts and Tradition. **LC**

> *"The reconstitution of the Azem Palace has been an important event in the Islamic world."*
>
> Aga Khan Architecture Award jury

# Great Mosque (Damascus, Syria)

One of the first Islamic monumental buildings on a significant religious site

The city of Damascus has a history spanning thousands of years. The earliest record of the city comes from 1500 B.C.E., when it was conquered by Pharaoh Thutmosis III. The city was at the center of Aramean history, has been involved in battles with the Hebrews, Assyrians, Judeans, and Babylonians, and Alexander the Great sent one of his lieutenants to conquer it. Damascus is mentioned in the Old Testament and famed in the New Testament as the destination to which St. Paul was journeying when he was converted to Christianity. Today, the Great Mosque—or the Ummayad Mosque—stands in the heart of this historic city. There has been a religious building on this site for thousands of years, and the earliest known relics come from an Aramaic temple of *c.* 3000 B.C.E. The Roman occupiers built a temple to Jupiter here, early Christians turned it into a church, and the Great Mosque was constructed in the early years of the eighth century. A fire destroyed much of the mosque in 1893, but it was rebuilt in the twentieth century.

The Great Mosque was one of the first Islamic monumental buildings and its design influenced Islamic architecture throughout the world. The caliph of Damascus at the time of the mosque's building was Walid bin Abd al-Malik, who made the following speech to his citizens about the site: "People of Damascus, four things give you marked superiority over the rest of the world: your climate, water, fruits and baths. To these I add a fifth: this mosque." Inside the mosque is the tomb of one of the most illustrious Muslim leaders, Saladin, who recaptured Jerusalem from the Crusaders.

Today, the Great Mosque in Damascus retains an atmosphere of peace and beauty. The picturesque courtyard with its central fountain , and the vast sense of space inside the mosque engender a feeling of enormous tranquility. **LH**

"Oh Allah, be satisfied with this soul and open to him the gates of paradise."

Inscription above Saladin's tomb

🏛 ◉ Roman Theater and Citadel (Bosra, Syria)

One of the best preserved theaters in the Roman world

The ancient city of Bosra is located 67 miles (108 km) south of Damascus in Syria. First mentioned in the fourteenth century B.C.E. as Burana, it later became the capital of the Nabataean kingdom. Bosra was later conquered in 106 C.E. by the Roman emperor Trajan, who renamed it Neatrajana Bustra and made it the capital of the Roman province of Arabia. Bosra was an important stopover for pilgrims on the ancient caravan route to Mecca and Medina. It served as a key Roman fortress east of the Jordan River. The city achieved the title of metropolis under the third-century Roman emperor Philip, a native of the city. Bosra became a Christian bishopric early in the fourth century and fell into Arab Muslim hands in 634 to 635. The Crusaders attacked Bosra in 1140 and 1183 but failed to hold it; this threat pushed the Ayyubids, Egyptian dynastic rulers, into converting the theater into a fortress in the thirteenth century.

Roman remains on the site include an impressive and well-preserved theater with tall stage buildings, as well as temples, triumphal arches, bathhouses, aqueducts, and water reservoirs. The theater was built in the second century and could seat up to 15,000 people. The stage was 148 feet (45 m) wide and 26 feet (8 m) deep. Later remains include two early Christian churches and several early Islamic mosques, including the seventh-century Omar Mosque. The medieval citadel around the theater was built in several stages. The first walls were built during the Ayyubid period, with further additions, such as towers, built in the mid-eleventh and early twelfth century.

The blending of Roman, Byzantine, and Muslim influences, and the excellent state of preservation of the remains make the citadel one of the major archeological sites in Syria. Bosra was declared a UNESCO World Heritage site in 1980. **EP**

🏛 ◎ **Acre Crusader Capital** (Acre, Israel)

The maritime capital of the Crusaders in the Holy Land

The ancient city of Acre (also known as Akko) is located on the Mediterranean Sea, 14 miles (23 km) north of Haifa. It was originally a Phoenician port established in the third century B.C.E., and it was regarded in the biblical period as one of the most important coastal cities in the eastern Mediterranean.

It became an important trading and military port during the Roman occupation (64–63 B.C.E.) and Emperor Claudius awarded the city the title of Colonia, the first in the country. Acre continued to be an important center during the early Christian and Byzantine periods until 636 C.E. when it was ruled by the Muslim caliphs. In 1104, Acre fell to the armies of the First Crusade and became the main port of the Latin kingdom of Baldwin I of Jerusalem. Acre was an important Crusader city in the twelfth century before being taken by Saladin in 1187. It was recaptured during the Third Crusade by Richard I "Lionheart" of

England and Philip II of France in 1191, becoming the capital of the Latin kingdom. The Crusaders lost control of the city to the Mamluks in 1291 and the city slowly fell into disrepair. Acre was partially rebuilt in the seventeenth and eighteenth centuries under the rule of the Ottoman Empire.

There are numerous Crusader buildings to visit in Acre, including the Hospitaller Castle, an underground town, the Crypt of St. John, the old harbor, and fortified city walls. Later remains include a newly restored Ottoman bathhouse, mosques, caravanserais, and the largest prison during the British Mandate.

Acre was one of the main maritime centers in the eastern Mediterranean and the largest city of the Crusader kingdom. The imposing and well-preserved Crusader city make it one of the most interesting historic sites in Israel, and Acre gained its UNESCO World Heritage site listing in 2001. **EP**

Church of the Annunciation (Nazareth, Israel)

Childhood home of the Virgin Mary

According to Roman Catholic tradition, the Church of the Annunciation is where Mary, mother of Jesus, was visited by the Archangel Gabriel, who told her that she was to give birth to the son of God. It is reputed that this was the childhood home of the Virgin Mary.

A number of churches built on this site have been destroyed. The third to be constructed was erected in the early twelfth century by Tancred, Prince of Galilee, and stood until 1263, when it was destroyed by Baibars, an Egyptian sultan. The Franciscans built a new church on the site in 1730, which was pulled down in 1955 to make way for the modern-day church, which was consecrated in 1969. This latest incarnation of the Church of the Annunciation was designed by Italian architect Giovanni Muzio, who wanted to retain some of the historical elements of the site and to depict the diverse nature of the Roman church. Divided into two levels, the side walls of the building were built on top of surviving walls from the older structure. The main entrance leads to the Grotto of the Annunciation, the only part of the church that Baibars failed to destroy, and the area where the Annunciation itself is thought to have taken place.

Adorned with stained glass windows and long-standing mosaics depicting scenes from the Bible, the church holds the work of many different artists from around the world. It is also a significant archeological site—excavations in 1955 revealed a network of caves, oil presses, dwellings, cisterns, and granaries, some of which can be seen from the church. Under Roman Catholic canon, the Church of the Annunciation enjoys the status of a minor basilica. However, Greek Orthodox tradition has it that Mary was visited by Gabriel while she was drawing water from a well in Nazareth, and therefore commemorates this event with St. Gabriel's Church at this alternate site. **RR**

Sepphoris (near Nazareth, Israel)

Administrative and intellectual capital of Galilee

Historically the most important city in Galilee in the north of Israel, Sepphoris (or Zippori) has been the site of many battles but was ironically known as the "city of peace." In 38 B.C.E., King Herod took control of the city, but it was later captured by the Romans who all but destroyed it. Herod's son, Herod Antipas, later restored the city, which is now a major archeological site. Sepphoris is strategically located high on a hilltop and has incredible views over the surrounding land.

Revered by Jews and Christians, Sepphoris—the administrative and intellectual capital of the Galilee—is believed to be where eminent rabbis and Jewish

> *"[It was named Zippori] because it is perched on the top of a mountain like a bird (tsipor)."*
> Babylonian Talmud

scholars (the Sanhedrin) of the early Common Era finished writing the Mishna, a book of Jewish law, and the Talmud, a collection of interpretations of the Old Testament, which contains a number of references to the city. By the fifth century, the capital of the Galilee had become the seat of a Christian bishopric.

After major excavations in the twentieth century, Sepphoris National Park was opened in 1992. A well-marked trail leads you through remains from the successive cities that were built on the site. These include a Roman theater, a Byzantine house, a fifth-century synagogue, and a Crusader fortress. The city has beautiful mosaics, the most prominent of which illustrates events occurring along the River Nile. The site also houses a church and a watchtower in tribute to the Virgin Mary's parents, Anne and Joachim. **RR**

# Megiddo

(Megiddo, Israel)

One of the foremost biblical sites and an archeological treasure house

Megiddo is one of the most important biblical sites in Israel. Some interpretations of the Bible argue that Megiddo will also be Armageddon, the location of a final encounter between the forces of good and evil at the end of the world. Megiddo was one of the first cities to be founded in the North Canaan region; consequently it illustrates the enormous cultural, political, and historical changes that took place over time. It became one of the most powerful centers in the world from the fourth to the second millennium B.C.E. and today it stands as a remarkable archeological relic and a testament to a bygone era.

Megiddo is recognized for a combination of historical, theological, and geographical reasons. Its geographical location is on a hilltop, standing above twenty or so layers of successive settlements of ancient buildings. The hill is strategically situated at the head of a pass through the Carmel Ridge, which in ancient times was an important trade route between Egypt and Assyria. The city acted as a guard point on the pass. Because of its strategic position, Megiddo was the subject of countless battles over the years and the city changed hands repeatedly.

Today, those who visit Megiddo can enjoy the remains of the settlement, and visit the excellent museum that stands beside it. The museum has a number of interesting exhibits, as well as a video telling the story of Megiddo. The site is marked by ancient artifacts, such as an enormous Canaanite gate dating back to the Late Bronze Age. There is also a grand observation point offering majestic views of the Nazareth Mountains and Mount Bilboa, as well as an ancient mosaic spread across an area of 580 square feet (54 sq m), which was discovered beneath a prison. The site offers rich rewards for visitors who are alive to its historic significance. **RR**

"The kings came and fought, then fought the kings of Canaan in Taanach by the waters of Megiddo."

Judges 5:19

Bahai Shrine (Haifa, Israel)

Center of the Bahai faith

Haifa's most spectacular building was built as a memorial to the Bab, who founded the Bahai religion and foretold the coming of the Bahai prophet, Baha'ullah. The huge gold-domed building dominates the city, and honors the 1850 martyring of the Bab, whose remains were kept hidden until it was possible for him to be buried in the place that Baha'ullah had marked out for him in 1890.

Haifa is the world headquarters for the Bahai faith, and the architecture of the shrine reflects the ethos of a world religion that teaches the unity of all religions. In the Bahai belief, messengers of God, such as Moses, Jesus, and Muhammad, are sent throughout history to

"We desire but the good of the world. ... That all nations should become one in faith."

Baha'ullah, prophet of the Bahai faith

bring a similar message that fits the social needs of the day. As such, the shrine blends Western and Eastern styles, with Roman columns, Greek Corinthian capitals, and Oriental arches.

With a dome constructed from 12,000 gold-leaf tiles, supported by a mausoleum built of Italian-cut Chiampo stone, with columns of Rose Baveno granite, the extravagant decor of the shrine's exterior contrasts strongly with its modest interior. The tomb itself comprises two small rooms—one is a simple carpeted prayer room, the other houses the shrine. Outside the shrine are the magnificent Persian Gardens, planted in 1909, which feature stone peacocks and eagles among the immaculately kept plants. Every year, thousands of followers of the Bahai faith visit Haifa to make a pilgrimage to the shrine. **RR**

Elijah's Cave (Haifa, Israel)

Sacred site for three world religions

Nestled in the foothills of Mount Carmel in northern Israel is one of the few places in the country where you are likely to see Jews, Christians, and Muslims worshipping in the same place. Elijah is traditionally seen as the prophet of wrath who isolated himself in deserts and mountains, and hid in caves. This is the cave where the prophet Elijah allegedly sheltered when hiding from the king and queen of the period, Ahab and Jezebel, because he faced punishment for denouncing their idol worshipping. It is also believed that this is the site where Elijah later established a school for studying religion.

The cave—which was uncovered by excavations in the 1950s—houses a small altar and is overlooked by a Carmelite monastery constructed by the Christian religious order he inspired. Christians also believe that Jesus and his family sheltered in the same cave on their return from Egypt while escaping from King Herod. For Muslims, Elijah is a green prophet, signifying freshness of spirit, and during the British Mandate of Palestine the site was called *waqf el-Hadra* (the green). Jews see Elijah as a "guardian angel," and Jewish legends refer to the prophet appearing in times of trouble. Believing that Elijah did not die but went to heaven in a chariot of fire during Passover, Elijah is still invited into households with a symbolic door opening during the Passover Seder.

Looking out from Elijah's Cave, there is a spectacular view across the mountain range, an opportunity to witness the challenging conditions Elijah would have encountered to reach the cave. Thousands of pilgrims believe the cave has healing powers, and pilgrimages and huge dramatic ceremonies are held here frequently throughout the year. The walls of the cave are covered in thousands of inscriptions made by the numerous pilgrims who visit the site, some dating from the fifth century. **RR**

Caesarea (Caesarea Palaestina, Israel)

Splendid harbor of Palestine and the site of the Jewish revolt

The site of ancient Caesarea is located on the Mediterranean Sea, about midway between Haifa and Tel Aviv. Originally a Phoenician port called Strato's Tower after a Sidonian king, King Herod the Great turned Caesarea into one of the grandest cities of Palestine between the years 22 and 10 B.C.E. and renamed it in honor of the Roman emperor, Augustus Caesar. Renowned for the splendor of its public buildings, Caesarea became the capital of the Roman province of Judaea in 6 C.E. and the capital of Palestine in 70 C.E., when the Romans quelled the Jewish revolt. Control of the city alternated between Crusaders and Muslims from 639 to the thirteenth century. In 1251, during the Sixth Crusade, the French King Louis IX fortified the town. The Crusader city was eventually conquered and destroyed by the Mamluk Sultan Baybars of Egypt in 1265.

A well-preserved, high-level, 13-mile- (20-km-) long aqueduct, a restored Roman theater, a hippodrome (one of the largest in the Roman world), a temple dedicated to Augustus, and a palatial villa are what remains of Roman Caesarea, which covered about 164 acres (66 ha). Herod the Great also built an imposing deep-sea harbor in 21 B.C.E., the largest in the eastern Mediterranean, and named it Sebastos in honor of Emperor Augustus (*Sebaste* being the Greek word for Augustus). The ancient harbor is now several feet below sea level. In the fourth century, Caesarea converted to Christianity and became a major center of the Christian Roman Empire. Later remains include a Byzantine church, a Crusader fortress, and fortified walls dating from the thirteenth century.

Caesarea is one of Israel's principal tourist attractions with Roman, Byzantine, Arab, and Crusader remains. The impressive archeological ruins and the complex history of the location make it one of the most interesting archeological sites in Israel. **EP**

> *"It is almost impossible to imagine the splendor of the city and harbor."*
>
> John J. Rousseau and Rami Arav, historians

🏛 ◎ Masada (Masada, Israel)

Symbol of one of the most dramatic episodes in Jewish history

Located on a high plateau overlooking the Dead Sea, Masada is a fortified palace built in 37 B.C.E. by the Judean king, Herod the Great. Masada had been occupied by a Roman garrison after Herod's death, but became a refuge for Jewish zealots (the Sicarii) who revolted against Roman rule and fled Jerusalem in 66 C.E. The Roman Tenth Legion set out in 73 C.E. to conquer Masada, the last point of Jewish insurrection, which resulted in the death of more than 900 zealots who chose mass suicide over surrender.

Situated on the Dead Sea's western shore, Masada is set at the western end of a plateau—2,000 feet (304 m) long, with a maximum width of 1,000 feet (608 m)—that rises about 1,300 feet (396 m) above the sea. Looking over cliffs, the palace has stunning views toward the Dead Sea and the Judean Desert. Buildings dating back to 100 B.C.E. already existed at Masada when Herod the Great built his palace on the western side of the mountaintop. It was a luxurious residence with three descending terraces at the northern end of the rock, Roman-style bathhouses, storehouses, dwelling houses, fortified walls with defensive towers, and a synagogue (the oldest in Israel). Herod's most remarkable construction project was the advanced water system built to sustain the needs of the fortress. Twelve cisterns, each with a capacity of up to 140,000 cubic feet (4,000 cu m), were cut into the rock.

Today Masada is a popular tourist attraction. Excavations of the site were conducted by the Hebrew University of Jerusalem in the early 1960s. The palace is an Israeli national shrine and was declared a UNESCO World Heritage site in 2001. **EP**

◩ Steep cliffs protected Herod the Great's refuge at Masada from attack from the plateau summit.

◨ The remains of a bathhouse hotroom. The piles raised the floor, allowing hot air from a furnace to circulate.

Ben-Gurion House (Sde Boker, Negev, Israel)

Desert home of the first leader of the State of Israel

The first prime minister of Israel, David Ben-Gurion (1886–1973), was deeply concerned with settling and cultivating the deserts of Israel to make them flourish. On his retirement in 1963, he moved permanently to his home on a kibbutz (a collective community) in the Negev Desert in southern Israel. He remained here until his death in 1973, and is buried next to his wife Paula in the grounds of the kibbutz.

The house now serves as a museum paying tribute to the Zionist leader, who insisted on being treated the same way as everyone else in the kibbutz. Although the kibbutz around the museum has altered considerably over the years, Ben-Gurion's house remains largely the same as it was when he died in 1973. Displays tell the story of his life, from his early years in Russia, through his rise to the Zionist leadership and his key role in the establishment of the state of Israel in 1948. Other exhibits explore the leader's deep feelings about the Negev region. The graves of Ben-Gurion and his wife in the peaceful grounds are marked by simple white slabs within a picturesque garden, situated on the edge of a sheer rock face that provides magnificent views of the surrounding desert landscape.

Ben-Gurion lived out his last years in what was, for him, an ideal setting. In an article in the *New York Times Magazine* in 1954, he wrote: "This life as a simple citizen and laborer has its benefits not only for the person himself but perhaps also for his country. After all, there is room for only one prime minister, but for those who make the desert bloom there is room for hundreds, thousands, and even millions." **EP**

▷ After a remarkable political career, Israel's leader wrote his memoirs in the study of the house at Sde Boker.

▷ Ben-Gurion's house was a modest prefab, as were the other residences on the kibbutz.

Church of St. Mary Magdalene (Jerusalem)

Distinctive Russian Orthodox church

With its Kremlin-style Russian architecture, the Church of St. Mary Magdalene is a distinctive landmark. Commissioned by Tsar Alexander III, the seven sparkling gold onion-shaped domes of the building are conspicuously situated on the Mount of Olives. It was built as a memorial to Tsar Alexander's mother Empress Maria Alexandrovna.

The tsar's sister-in-law, Grand Duchess Elizabeth, commissioned Russian artist Sergei Ivanov to paint a series of murals depicting St. Mary Magdalene's life. The Grand Duchess Elizabeth was widowed in 1905 and became a nun, establishing a convent in Moscow.

> *"Mary Magdalene went to the disciples with the news: 'I have seen the Lord!'"*
>
> John 20:16-18

In 1918 she was thrown into a mine shaft and left to die by the Bolsheviks after the Russian Revolution, and her remains were laid to rest in St. Mary Magdalene Church, along with those of her companion, Sister Barbara. The church also houses the remains of Princess Alice of Greece, mother of Prince Philip, Britain's Duke of Edinburgh, who died in 1969. Her remains were transferred to the crypt below the church in 1988, fulfilling her wish to be buried near the Grand Duchess Elizabeth, who she strove to emulate through charitable work.

The church is situated within the Garden of Gethsemane, where it is believed that Jesus spent his last night on earth before he was crucified. It remains a working church today as the place of daily worship for the women's convent of St. Mary Magdalene. **RR**

Church of the Assumption (Jerusalem)

Tomb of the Virgin Mary

Venerated by Christians and Muslims alike, the Church of the Assumption (also known as the Tomb of the Virgin) nestles in the foothills of the Mount of Olives in the Kidron Valley of Jerusalem. The tomb dates from the first century, and several churches have been built and destroyed on the same site, although the earliest is thought to date to the early fifth century.

A small square chapel marks the supposed site of the Tomb of the Virgin Mary, which has been cut away from the surrounding rock. Other burial places thought to be on the same site are those of Mary's parents, Joachim and Anne, and the tomb of the Crusader Queen Melisande (died 1161), as well as that of Mary's husband Joseph.

The church is populated by tributes from different eras and different countries, including architecture from the Byzantine and Crusader periods, and altars from the Greeks, Armenians, and Ethiopians. The facade of the church is one of the oldest examples of Crusader architecture in Jerusalem, and was built in the eleventh century.

Descending forty steps leads you to the remains of the Byzantine church. A *mihrab* (prayer niche) indicating the direction of Mecca denotes the Islamic significance of this site—Muslims believe that Muhammad saw a light over Mary's tomb on his night journey from Medina to Jerusalem. Each year on August 15—also the date that Roman Catholics mark the Feast of the Assumption of the Blessed Virgin Mary—the Greeks and the Armenians celebrate the Assumption of Mary in the church with a feast.

Although there is some dispute about whether this site is actually where Mary's remains lie, many thousands of visitors believe that this was indeed the mother of Jesus's tomb and it has become a shrine and monument for her assumption into heaven. **RR**

Dome of the Rock

(Jerusalem)

One of Jerusalem's best known landmarks

The Dome of the Rock, Qubbat as-Sakhrah in Arabic, was built during the Umayyad Dynasty, under the patronage of Abd al-Malik bin Marwan—the seventh caliph of the Muslim world—who ruled from 685 to 705. Completed in 691, it is also known as the Mosque of Omar. Although it is not a mosque, it is the first major Muslim monument for public worship.

The location of the site has religious significance for Muslims because, according to the Koran, the prophet Muhammad flew from Mecca to Jerusalem with the archangel Gabriel and went to the Rock to make his ascension to heaven. At the same time, Christians and Jews believe that the Dome is built on the rock where God tested the faith of Abraham by demanding that he sacrifice his son, Isaac. Beside its religious meaning, the site of the Dome has political relevance. The esplanade on which it was built previously contained the Jewish Second Temple of Herod the Great, which was destroyed by the Romans in 70 C.E. By building on the site, the caliph Abd al-Malik therefore symbolically underlined the supremacy of Islam over the other extant monotheistic religions. Inside the octagon and written five times in gold on a blue background, his message is explicit: *la sharika lahu* (God has no companion).

There are four gateways oriented in the four cardinal directions. The techniques and materials used were very elaborate: stucco, tesserae, and carving. The high wooden dome and its drum are covered with lead on a framework of timber. The dome is structured by a double shell of wood placed with metal and has a gilded finishing. The octagonal Syrian–Byzantine plan, the richness of the mosaics, and the dome that contrasts with the Ottoman tile works on the facade are harmoniously arranged. The Dome remains a powerful statement of Muslim ambition. **SJ**

"He sought to build for the Muslims a mosque that should be unique and a wonder to the world."

Shams al-Din al-Maqdisi, medieval Muslim scholar

City of David (Jerusalem)

Remains of the capital of the legendary Israelite king

The City of David (also known as Ophel, meaning a hill) was the earliest part of Jerusalem to be occupied. It is situated on a narrow promontory southeast of the Old City, between the Kidron Valley to the east and the Tyropoeon Valley to the west. As well as good defenses, the location had a fresh water supply, the Gihon Spring, at the foot of the hill on the east.

The earliest evidence of human activity is some early Bronze Age pottery (third millennium B.C.E.). The city later features in the Amarna letters, the clay tablet correspondence dating to the mid-second millennium B.C.E. between the Egyptian pharaoh Akhenaten and the rulers of western Asia. The Book of Samuel describes David as the first Israelite ruler of Ophel, hence the name of the city. King David established his new capital to unify the tribes of the Kingdom of Israel. Acclaimed as a warrior, musician, and poet, David is traditionally seen as the author of the Psalms.

The few remains of the City of David today include fragments of the circumference wall and evidence of terraces of stone and rubble, which allowed houses to be built on the steep slopes of the ridge. Beneath the City of David exciting archeological remains have been uncovered. Most of these—such as Warren's Shaft and Hezekiah's Tunnel—relate to the water supply; a series of tunnels allowed the city's inhabitants safe access to water from the spring, which lay outside the city walls. Other remains include the Ashlar House and the House of Ahiel, Iron Age structures built from a mixture of rough limestone blocks and well-dressed ashlar blocks.

The Babylonians destroyed the City of David *c.* 587 B.C.E., leaving traces of burned wooden beams, some with carved motifs. The site continued to be occupied as part of the much expanded city of Jerusalem after this time, although archeological traces are few. **RF**

"And David dwelt in the castle; therefore they called it the city of David."

1 Chronicles 11:7

Church of the Holy Sepulchre (Jerusalem)

Revered by many Christians as the site of Jesus's crucifixion and burial

This site is one of the major Christian holy sites in the world, located in the northwest quarter of Jerusalem's Old City. Ancient historians describe how the site was covered with earth and a Temple of Venus was built on top, probably as part of Hadrian's reconstruction of Jerusalem. In *c.* 325–26 Emperor Constantine I had the pagan temple destroyed and three connected churches were built: the Martyrium, a basilica; an open-air atrium called the Triportico that was built around the traditional Rock of Calvary; and an open-air rotunda, known as the Anastasis (Resurrection), said to be the burial site of Jesus, which by the fifth century was covered by a dome.

The site has been a major pilgrimage destination since the fourth century. The original church was destroyed by a Persian invasion in 614. An Egyptian ruler destroyed the rebuilt church again in 1009, and the tomb was razed to the bedrock. The Crusaders rebuilt the church, resulting in what is primarily seen standing today. The rotunda and the exterior of the Edicule were rebuilt in 1809–10 in the Ottoman Baroque style. The current dome dates from 1870.

As a religious site venerated by different Christian churches, conflicts can occur among the church's various custodians—primarily the Greek Orthodox, the Armenian Apostolic, and Roman Catholic churches and, to a lesser extent, the Coptic Orthodox, the Ethiopian Orthodox, and the Syriac Orthodox. In 2002 when a Coptic monk, who is based on the roof to express Coptic claims to the Ethiopian territory there, moved his chair from its agreed spot into the shade, a fight broke out and eleven people were hospitalized.

Although the site's authenticity as the burial place of Christ is disputed, this church is the last and most sacred station of the Way of the Cross. As part of Jerusalem, it was inscribed on the UNESCO List of World Heritage in Danger in 1982. **AP**

> *"[Despite uncertainty that this is the burial site] we have no other site that can lay a claim nearly as weighty."*
>
> Dan Bahat, former City Archeologist of Jerusalem

🏛 ◉ Jerusalem Ramparts (Jerusalem)

Impressive fortifications of an ancient city

"A city, the fame of which has gone out from one end of the world to the other."

The Talmud

The Jerusalem ramparts surround the Old City of Jerusalem, an area barely 0.4 square miles (1 sq km) that contains such important historic landmarks as the Western Wall, the Esplanade of the Mosques/Temple Mount, which includes the Dome of the Rock, and the Holy Sepulchre. The current walls of the Old City were constructed by Sultan Suleiman I, the sixteenth-century Ottoman ruler known as "The Magnificent."

The Ottomans took over Jerusalem in 1517 from the Egyptian Mamluks, who had ruled the city since the mid-thirteenth century. The city had been without walls since 1244, when an invading Tatar army destroyed the city's defenses and took the city from its Christian rulers. From 1535 to 1538 Suleiman built new walls around the Old City, occasionally on the site of antique walls that supposedly dated back to the time of King Solomon. The system of walls is 2.5 miles (4 km) long. In addition to the walls, many of the historic gates survive. Five of the eleven entrances date from the time of Suleiman I—the Damascus Gate, the Lion's Gate, the Dung Gate, the Zion Gate, and the Jaffa Gate. The gates are sharply angled, supposedly to deter attackers on horseback charging through them. The oldest surviving entrance is the Golden Gate, constructed by the Romans in the sixth century. Jewish tradition holds that the Messiah will enter Jerusalem through this gate. Allegedly, in an effort to forestall this event, Suleiman I had the gate sealed off in 1541—and it remains so. The most recently added entrance, the New Gate, was constructed in 1887.

Under the rule of Suleiman The Magnificent Jerusalem enjoyed peace and flourished, and the city was tolerant of all religions. The rebuilt walls demonstrate how his rule brought stability to the city. The ramparts surround some of the most historic sites in the world, and are a gateway into the rich, historic past of Old Jerusalem. **JF**

🏛 ◉ Jerusalem Citadel (Jerusalem)

One of Jerusalem's most enduring landmarks

The Jerusalem Citadel has been used as a stronghold for more than 2,000 years. Situated on the western hill, it was the weakest point in the settlement's defenses and successive leaders of the city built on the site. It has played a key part in the history of Jerusalem and it remains a landmark and symbol of the city today.

The citadel is also known as the Tower of David, however, there is no connection between the structure and the biblical King David. It was first built between 960 and 586 B.C.E., during the First Temple period. In the first century B.C.E., work continued under the Hasmonean kings, who fortified the area. Between 37 and 34 B.C.E., Herod the Great developed the citadel; he added three substantial towers, only one of which (the Phasael) still stands, now incorporated into the northwestern ramparts. (Christian pilgrims during the Byzantine period incorrectly identified this tower as the Tower of David.) In 70 C.E., Roman troops took control of the citadel and later still, in the fourth century, it passed to a community of monks. The tower changed hands yet again in 638 and came under the control of a Muslim community, which was eventually supplanted in 1099 by Crusaders. In the sixteenth century, the Ottoman Turks captured Jerusalem from the Egyptian Mamluks and remodeled the citadel into its current form; for the garrison they added a mosque, with a prominent minaret that became known as the Tower of David. Over the years, control of the citadel has passed from one faith to another. After the 1967 Arab–Israeli War, the citadel lost its religious significance and became a cultural heritage center.

Today, the Museum of the History of Jerusalem is housed within the citadel. The exhibition is spread throughout the recently restored citadel, with rooms in various towers each describing a period of Jerusalem's 4,000-year-old, turbulent history. **KH**

"The view of Jerusalem is the history of the world; it is more, it is the history of earth and of heaven."

Benjamin Disraeli, former British prime minister

Dormition Church (Jerusalem)

Place where Mary, the mother of Jesus, "fell asleep"

Marking the place where Roman Catholics believe the Virgin Mary fell asleep for the last time, the Dormition Church was built for German Catholics between 1901 and 1910, and is owned by the German Benedictine Order. The Turkish sultan dedicated the land to Kaiser Wilhelm II upon his visit to Jerusalem in 1898. The prominent landmark is situated on Mount Zion, in the southern part of Jerusalem's Old City.

Built in a Romanesque style, the church resembles a fortress, topped with a towering domed clock tower, a gray conical roof, and four turrets. The design, meant to replicate Charlemagne's Aachen Cathedral in western Germany, was based on plans by Heinrich Renard, the architect for the archdiocese of Cologne. The central attraction of the church is the Chapel of the Dormition, which is home to a life-sized statue of a sleeping Mary. The crypt contains a mosaic in the dome above the statue, of Christ receiving her soul,

surrounded by the biblical women Eve, Sarah, Miriam, Esther, Yael, and Judith.

The mosaics provide some of the most striking features of the church. The mosaic pavement in the main chapel symbolizes the Holy Trinity, depicting three intersecting circles, and is surrounded by further tributes to Christianity including the names of the prophets Daniel, Isaiah, Jeremiah, and Ezekial, and those of the twelve Apostles. This mosaic is surrounded by twelve zodiac signs. The church is bordered by significant Christian sites, including the "Room of the Last Supper" and the tomb of David—although most now argue that he never lay there.

During the 1948 and 1967 battles over Jerusalem, the church was damaged and parts of the building have never been restored. Every two years the church presents the Mount Zion Award to people who have contributed to Christian–Muslim–Jewish dialogue. **RR**

🏛 ◈ **Western Wall** (Jerusalem)

The holiest site for prayer in Judaism

The Western Wall (also called the Wailing Wall) is the sole surviving part of the original Jewish Second Temple, which was destroyed by the soldiers of Emperor Titus in 70 C.E. A retaining wall, it is part of the Esplanade of the Mosques/Temple Mount.

Texts explaining the survival of the wall vary; one suggests that God saved this fragment for the Jewish people; another holds that Titus left it as a painful reminder of the Roman defeat of Judea. Today, it is traditional for Jews to push slips of paper with wishes or prayers on them into the wall's cracks. Some texts hold that the nearby Dome of the Rock covers the area where the Holy of Holies was located during Temple times, and most Jewish teachings state that the gate of heaven is situated directly above it. Jews are forbidden from entering this area by religious law.

There are restrictions on Jewish women praying at the wall. A group called Women of the Wall have, for almost twenty years, been conducting a court battle to secure the right of women to pray out loud at the site, wearing a tallit and reading from the Torah.

The site is also of great importance to Islam, whose followers believe that Muhammad tied the winged horse that brought him from Mecca to Jerusalem to the Western Wall. The story goes that an angel then took him to meet Moses, Jesus, and Elijah, and here he saw the destiny awaiting humans after death. This event is marked by the Dome of the Rock shrine looming above the wall. Indeed, the juxtaposition of the Islamic, Jewish, and Christian monuments partly explains why the Old City of Jerusalem is such a mesmerizing place to visit. Although the Wailing Wall is unspectacular in architectural terms, the sight of religious Jews praying fervently at its foot, in such close proximity to the glistening golden dome of the Muslim shrine above it, is quite beguiling. **AP**

Basilica of the Nativity (Bethlehem, West Bank)

Traditional site of Jesus's birth and the oldest church in the Holy Land

The Basilica of the Nativity marks the spot where Mary and Joseph were obliged to seek shelter in a stable and use a manger for the birth of Jesus, in a scene replicated by thousands of schoolchildren every year.

The Basilica of the Nativity is the oldest church in the Holy Land that is still in use. It has undergone a number of restorations since it was first built in *c.* 326 by St. Helena, mother of the Byzantine emperor Constantine. The foundation of the present building was built during the reign of the Byzantine emperor Justinian, and in the twelfth century the Crusaders added a cloister and a monastery. The simple interior contains four rows of monolithic columns carved from local stone and forty-four white marble pillars. Remaining traces of frescoes of the Apostles and mosaics are evidence of the former striking surroundings of the church. The building houses a number of tributes to the birth of Christ, including an altar commemorating his circumcision and a chapel dedicated to St. Joseph, who was told by an angel to take Mary and baby Jesus to Egypt to flee Herod.

In 1852 the Roman Catholic, Armenian, and Greek Orthodox churches were given shared custody of the church. The three-sided building is encircled by the high walls of three convents representing each of these branches: the Franciscan Monastery and Church of St. Catherine on the northeast side, the Armenian Monastery, and the Greek Orthodox Monastery on the southeast side. The Greeks are responsible for the Grotto of the Nativity, which marks the traditional site of the birth of Jesus. A large fourteen-pointed silver star encased in white marble marks the scene of the nativity. Burning lamps around the star represent each of the three communities. On Christmas Eve, thousands gather in Manger Square, in front of the church, to sing carols before midnight mass. **RR**

Qumran (West Bank)

Secret hiding place of the Dead Sea Scrolls

Qumran, on the northwestern shore of the Dead Sea in the West Bank, is famous for being the settlement closest to the secret hiding place of the Dead Sea Scrolls. The first seven scrolls were discovered accidentally in 1947 by two Bedouin shepherds, who came across the ceramic jars storing them in a cave in the steep cliffs of the dry riverbed valley of Wadi Qumran. Over the next decade, around 900 scrolls were found in nearby caves, suggesting to some researchers that the dry cave system was once used to house the settlement's library. The scrolls were important because the texts in them described the religious beliefs and practices of different Jewish sects and doctrines in ancient Israel.

The intrigue of tracking down the scrolls and analyzing their significance has proved almost as fascinating as the content of the ancient manuscripts themselves. Initially, the scholar E. L. Sukenik acquired three scrolls for the Hebrew University, whereas four scrolls were smuggled to the United States, where they were later offered for sale in a newspaper. Sukenik's son, Yigael Yadin, acquired them and returned them to Israel, where they are kept in closely monitored atmospheric conditions in the Shrine of the Book.

Archeologists estimate that the settlement at Qumran was built between 134 and 104 B.C.E., under the reign of John Hyrcanus. The settlement was occupied at different stages until Emperor Titus destroyed it in 68 C.E. What is left of the site, including the cemeteries, assembly rooms and complex cisterns, suggests that Qumran was the home of the Essene sect. Various scholars disagree, suggesting that it was a Roman fort or a lavish villa; however, the majority of archeologists agree that Qumran was an important religious settlement. **KH**

Hisham's Palace (West Bank)

Splendid palace of the Umayyad dynasty

A legacy of the eighth-century Umayyad dynasty, Hisham's Palace (or Khirbat El-Mafjar) lies 3 miles (5 km) north of Tell es-Sultan, the remains of ancient Jericho. It is believed to have been built by El-Walid ibn el-Yazid, although it is named after his uncle the Caliph el-Hisham ibn Abd el-Malik. Built as a hunting lodge, it boasted ornate architecture and sumptuous decor. However, the palace remained unfinished when el-Yazid, who had assumed the caliphate, was assassinated in 744, a year after coming to power.

The site gives a good impression of how the privileged lived in the eighth century. Modeled on a Roman bathhouse, it contains the remains of a large residence, a bath, a swimming pool, a banqueting hall, and two mosques. There is evidence of a sophisticated network of underground pipes to heat water. The palace was originally a two-storied square building planned around a central courtyard, but was damaged in a major earthquake in the region in 749.

The palace, now being restored with renewed stucco decoration, is an exceptional example of Islamic art and architecture. The stucco, made to imitate marble, was used, for the first time in the region, for ornament as well as practical purposes. Some of the original carved plaster is now in the Jerusalem Museum. The palace's exquisite mosaics have been undergoing restoration in situ. The most famous mosaic, located in a small room in the northwest corner, depicts gazelles grazing underneath a large fruit tree that represents the Tree of Life, while a lion attacks one of the gazelles.

The 98-square-foot (30-sq-m) hall, which used to be the vaulted vestibule of the bath, is paved with mosaics, and is the largest known example of ancient mosaic in the world. Also on view at the site is the carved stone star of Jericho that used to occupy a frame within the palace's monumental entrance. **RR**

Jericho (West Bank)

One of the world's first settlements

Jericho, or Tell es-Sultan, has been called the first city in the world, and although experts may argue about exactly what constitutes a city, the site has been continuously occupied for some 11,000 years. It is also the most excavated site after Jerusalem. Excavations were first carried out in 1868 by Charles Warren, but Jericho was most famously excavated from 1952 to 1958 by Kathleen Kenyon, who established most of what we know of Jericho today.

The earliest traces of occupation on Tell es-Sultan are Mesolithic and include circular dwellings and burials of groups of bodies. In the Neolithic period, Jericho expanded to a walled settlement of about 10

> *"By faith the walls of Jericho fell, after the people had marched around them for seven days."*
>
> Hebrews 11:30

acres (4 ha); its population lived in mud-brick houses with clay floors. It was the erosion of these structures that gradually built up in layers to form the tell, or hill site. Excavations have revealed signs of an unusual funerary rite practiced at Jericho—skulls were disjointed from the rest of the skeletons, covered in plaster, and set with shell eyes.

The only surviving written history of Jericho is the biblical account of the destruction of the heavily fortified city, when its walls reputedly came tumbling down and the Israelites, led by Joshua, conquered the Canaanites. There are archeological remains of collapsed walls at Jericho, which may have been caused by an earthquake. However, experts disagree about whether the biblical chronology tallies with the archeological evidence at Jericho. **RF**

🏛 ◎ Assur (near Qalat Sharqat, Iraq)

Ancient Mesopotamian city on the banks of the River Tigris

The city of Assur lay buried and unknown until it was discovered in 1821 by Claudius Rich, a British traveler. Much of our knowledge of the layout and buildings of the city comes from seventh-century B.C.E. clay tablets, uncovered by early twentieth-century excavations.

Occupying a stony hill 174 miles (280 km) north of Baghdad, Assur overlooks an area thought by its builders to be home to the god Assur. The Assyrians, who were named after both the god and the city, probably originated in Sumeria; they founded Assur around 2,500 B.C.E., although the site had been inhabited during the previous millennium. The city grew as a center for trade with Anatolia, mainly in tin and wool. According to the unearthed tablets, a fortified wall, 2.5 miles (4 km) long, encircled the city. Inside were three royal palaces and thirty-four temples, as well as grand, spacious public areas and houses, and neighborhoods of cramped, poor dwellings.

Although Assur ceased to be the royal residence in the early years of the first millennia B.C.E., it served as a royal burial site until the Medes people destroyed the city in 614 B.C.E. Gradual reoccupation and rebuilding followed, until a second sacking, this time by the Sassanids, in the third century C.E.

The site of Assur continues to be revered by modern Assyrians. Visitors to the city are struck first by the ziggurat, a large, rectangular, stepped-brick structure dedicated to Assur, the principal Assyrian deity. To date, thirty-four temples have been discovered, and a palace has recently been reconstructed. The future of the city is uncertain, however. A proposal to dam the River Tigris to provide much-needed water for northern Mesopotamia would flood the site; although the project is in abeyance, the demand for water remains. Given these concerns, the site has been included on the UNESCO List of World Heritage in Danger. **FR**

"Assur is the most famous and oldest documented trade center."

John Russell, archeologist

🏛 ◉ Petra (Petra, Jordan)

Legendary long-lost city, now famous for its sculpted buildings

"... but rose-red as if the blush of dawn/that first beheld them were not yet withdrawn ..."

John William Burgon, "Petra" (1845)

⬆ Sheltered from wind-blown sand, the treasury is better preserved than many other monuments at Petra.

➡ For hundreds of years, travelers to Petra have been awed by their first dramatic glimpse of the treasury.

Through a narrow gorge in the desert (*al-Siq* or "the shaft"), an ancient trail between spectacular sheer rock walls leads to the city of Petra. Forgotten by the West for centuries, Petra was rediscovered by the Swiss explorer Johann Ludwig Burckhardt in 1812. Its origins are unclear, and its history is better known from around 300 B.C.E., when it thrived as the capital of the Arab Nabataeans, who controlled the caravan routes from Arabia to Syria. Petra fell under Roman control in the mid-first century B.C.E. but remained autonomous until 106 C.E., when it became part of the province of Arabia Petraea. A change of trade routes and a powerful earthquake determined its decline, yet it was the seat of a bishopric during the Byzantine age and was included in the fortified system of the Crusaders.

Petra lies along the Wadi Musa (Valley of Moses), with buildings extending into the open valley from both sides of a central colonnaded street. It boasted a huge theater, imposing temples, and churches of the Christian era; an advanced hydraulic engineering system carried and stored rainwater. However, the fascination of Petra is its rock-cut edifices. Hundreds of monuments are carved in the primeval sandstone rock layers, whose colors, from pale yellows through reds to darker browns, inspired poet John William Burgon's description of Petra as a "rose-red city half as old as time." Remarkable are the monastery (El-Deir) and the royal tombs, but the finest structure is the treasury (El-Khaznat), a Nabataean tomb carved out of the mountain in Hellenistic style. According to legend, a cache of treasure was hidden at the top, and for a long time bedouins fired at its summit in the vain hope of being flooded by a shower of gold.

The carved details of many of the monuments at Petra have suffered from weathering over the centuries, and an artificial sandstone product is being used to preserve surviving details for the future. **MC**

Persepolis (near Shiraz, Iran)

Glorious ancient city of the Persian Empire

Spread out over a massive terrace bounded by a great wall and the bulk of a mountain called the "Mount of Mercy," this splendid palace complex was the ceremonial capital of the mighty Achaemenid Empire. The Achaemenids were a powerful dynasty of kings in ancient Persia (now Iran), and the buildings that they created here are seen as a peak of Achaemenid artistic achievement. Construction of the complex seems to have begun under King Darius I, around the time of his accession (he ruled from 522 to 486 B.C.E.) and continued under his successors Xerxes and Artaxerxes I.

The isolated, mountainous location of Persepolis meant that it became mostly a spring and summer residence, with imperial administration organized from other cities, such as Babylon. However, it was a very important Persian capital, with a major tribute festival being held here each year. Accordingly, considerable care and attention were lavished upon its buildings. These structures drew inspiration from those of the sophisticated ancient Mesopotamians and were built on a huge scale, from dark gray stone hewn from the neighboring mountain. They included magnificent, symmetrically designed palaces, a huge double stairway leading up to the west side of the terrace, a great audience hall, treasury, and harem building. The site is famous for its massive pillars and also for its beautiful relief sculptures. A number of records and inscriptions—on gold and silver plate and stone—have been found that provide information about the extent of the Persian Empire and the building of Persepolis. Near to Persepolis lie various impressive royal tombs.

In 330 B.C.E., Alexander the Great sacked and conquered this royal center, emptying the treasury and burning the palace of Xerxes. The city became a capital for a province of Alexander's Macedonian Empire, but subsequently declined. **AK**

> *"Alexander described it . . . as the most hateful of the cities of Asia, and gave it to his soldiers to plunder."*
>
> Diodorus Siculus, Greek historian

🏛 ◎ Imam Mosque (Esfahan, Iran)

Sublime masterpiece of Persian architecture

Imam Square and the buildings that surround it are the sublime subject of the Persian proverb: "Esfahan is half the world." Commissioned by the powerful Safavid Shah Abbas I and extended and enhanced by his successor Shah Abbas II, Imam Square (or Shah Square as it was known prior to 1979) was the centerpiece of Esfahan. It was designed to reflect both architectural and symbolic perfection, mirroring the spiritual and temporal power of the Safavid dynasty.

The rectangular square is flanked on all four sides by a two-story galleried arcade. On the western side stands the highly decorated Ali Qapu Palace, a light and airy pavilion reflecting the elegance of the Safavid Royal Court. Opposite this palace, sits one of the most stunning examples of Islamic architecture in the world, Sheik Lotfollah Mosque. However, dominating the southern part of the square stands the masterful Imam Mosque, which frames both the square and the city skyline. Constructed over a period of eighteen years and completed in 1629 during the final year of Shah Abbas I's life, only minor later additions to the interior detract from the unity of purpose conceived by the Shah. The seven-colored tile work that covers the four *iwans* (vaulted halls with one side open) framing the main courtyard are spectacular. The architects included slight mismatches in the symmetry of the work, reflecting their humility in the face of God.

The north side of the square is broken by the entrance to a public bazaar that is still one of the main markets for the modern city. The smaller eastern bazaar is primarily dedicated to the many Iranian tourists that flock to the city. Originally designed as a polo pitch (the ornamental goal posts still stand at either end), the square is the public heart of Esfahan and should be experienced at dusk, as the sun drapes the buildings in a magical glow and Iranian families invite visitors to share their picnics. **IS**

"The first step into the cavernous [mosque] is one of those moments for which travelers live and die."

Stephen Kinzer, writer

Naqsh-e Rostam (near Shiraz, Iran)

Rock-cut tombs of the Achaeminid Empire

The enigmatic tombs and rock-cut reliefs at Naqsh-e Rostam get their modern Farsi name from medieval tales of the Persian hero Rostam. Arab armies brought Islam to Persia in the seventh century, when many pagan monuments were destroyed. Later, Persian scholars surmised that the reliefs represented the Islamic hero Rostam and preserved them.

It is now known that the reliefs that surround the rock-cut tombs in the sheer cliff face represent the first and final stages of this monument to kingship. A partially destroyed image of a figure in the left side of the cliff depicts an Elamite priest-king. The Elamites controlled a powerful early state based around southwestern Iran during the late second millennium B.C.E. The second phase of the monument provides the basic structure around which later Sassanian elements developed. The growth of the powerful Achaemenid Empire by Cyrus the Great led his successor Darius I to build his fabulous palace at Persepolis. On discovering the towering cliff etched with ancient memorials dedicated to kingship only a few miles north of his new palace, Darius had four burial tombs carved there. The Achaemenid kings held the Prophet Zoroaster in high regard. Sometime during the dynasty, a curious cubic structure was built at the base of the cliff, later linked to Zoroaster. Its purpose is still unknown.

The expansion of the later Persian-speaking, profoundly Zoroastrian, Sassanian dynasty led to expansion of the site. Seven rock-cut reliefs depict rulers of the dynasty receiving their Royal Insignia from Ahura Mazada, the Zoroastrian herald of good. The earliest investiture scene of Ardeshir I also contains the first recorded use of the name "Iran." With the overthrow of the Persian Sassanian state by the Arab armies of Islam, understanding of the iconography of this magnificent site passed into folklore. **IS**

Masmak Fortress (Riyadh, Saudi Arabia)

National symbol of the founding of the modern Kingdom of Saudi Arabia

At the heart of central Saudi Arabia lies the capital city, Riyadh, meaning "place of garden and trees." It is a small, fertile oasis within the larger, arid terrain of the country, and was originally fed by a number of watercourses that have since run dry. Although Riyadh is now a vast, thriving modern city—a pantheon to contemporary glass, steel, and concrete architecture— the old quarter still remains, and it is here that the substantial Masmak Fortress can be found.

The beautiful fortified structure was built around 1865 in the traditional form, from clay and mud bricks on a stone foundation. The thick and seemingly impenetrable external walls shelter the castle, along with a mosque and well, and have four circular watchtowers along their length. The building is the color of much of Saudi's sweeping lands, a soft pink-orange that radiates luminosity when bathed by the setting sun—the fortress is a structure central to Saudi Arabia's history and has become one of the most revered buildings by its people.

Masmak Fortress had been the residence of the ruling Al Saud family until they were ousted from power by the Al Rashidi, a rival dynasty. On January 15, 1902, the young Ibn Saud managed to heroically storm the fortress with just 40 men and reclaim his family's seat and power. This single historic event sparked the long, bloody sequence of power struggles and battles that eventually led to the Al Saud tribe consolidating authority through the Arabian Peninsula and Ibn Saud proclaiming himself king of Saudi Arabia.

The Masmak Fortress is a symbol of great national importance and pride to Saudi Arabia, and in 1995 the building was converted into a museum, housing collections of traditional dress and crafts. It has been greatly renovated and restored in recent years, and is a place of great cultural interest. **TP**

Murabba Palace (Riyadh, Saudi Arabia)

Elegant royal residence of King Ibn Saud

The original old city of Riyadh was built within fortified mud-brick and clay walls with nine gates leading into the city center. The city's buildings were also constructed of the traditional mud and clay, and lined the winding and narrow streets. Today, the walls and gates have gone and the majority of the original buildings have been replaced with modern structures—Riyadh is one of the fastest growing cities in the world. This huge expansion began slowly after Ibn Saud's heroic taking of the city in 1902, but in 1932—with the creation of the kingdom of Saudi Arabia—the building work escalated.

The extensive and lavish Murabba Palace was constructed in 1936 by King Ibn Saud as his home and seat of government. It was built north of the old city walls, and was allegedly so vast and magnificent that it was often mistaken for the capital city itself. The palace was used by King Ibn Saud until the time of his death in 1953, and, consequently, it occupies an important place within Saudi history.

Recently the Murabba Palace and its surrounding historic structures have been subject to an extensive renovation and restoration program that has turned the area into the King Abdul Aziz Historical Center. This substantial project includes educational, cultural, and religious facilities in the Murabba Palace area, and has also led to some destroyed structures, such as smaller palaces, being reconstructed in their original mud-brick form. Close by is the Riyadh Water Tower—a distinctive landmark in the city—and the al-Hamra Palace, named for its red color, which was built by King Ibn Saud's successor.

The Murabba Palace and other features of the King Abdul Aziz Historical Center are of central importance within the history of Saudi Arabia, and their careful preservation has ensured that this piece of history is one that will not be erased. **TP**

> *"What we saw was no city but the King's new palace . . . then in the course of erection."*
>
> Violet Dickson, wife of colonial administrator (1937)

Old Dir'aiyah (near Riyadh, Saudi Arabia)

Former capital and ancestral home of the ruling Al Saud family

The ghostly ruins of Old Dir'aiyah rise up from the shifting desert landscape of central Saudi Arabia, not far from the pulsating city of Riyadh and along the edge of the Wadi Hanifa, a long valley peppered with lush areas. Here the palm trees flourish and the patches of green provide a welcome respite from the vast, yellow terrain at the heart of the country, and the sharp, stinging desert winds that blow through the uninhabited streets of Dir'aiyah, one of Saudi Arabia's most famous archeological sites.

The town dates to the fifteenth century when Manea' Al-Mereedi of the House of Al Saud moved to the Wadi Hanifa area and began to build a settlement. From these small beginnings rose the town of Dir'aiyah, which continued to grow and prosper with the powerful Al Saud family remaining in residence.

In 1744 Dir'aiyah became the capital of the First Saudi State. During this period Prince Ibn Saud and Sheikh Ibn Abd al Wahhab (who advocated a brand of Muslim fundamentalism which he claimed was a return to the original Islam) formed a concrete alliance and set the precedents by which the Saudi State would rule and rise in power. The city was virtually destroyed in 1818 during battles with the Ottoman leader Ibrahim Pasha, and after this the capital was moved to nearby Riyadh, and Dir'aiyah gradually became a ghost town.

There has been an extensive restoration project at work in Dir'aiyah to preserve the historic buildings, and some excellent examples of traditional mud and adobe architecture have survived, including the huge Saad bin Saud Palace, the Salwa Palace, Imam Mohammed bin Saud Mosque, Saad Mosque, the Guest House, and the Turaif Bath House. This is a place that holds the key to the rise of Saudi Arabia and, as such, is possibly the most fundamentally important site in the country. **TP**

"Reports credit [Ibn Saud] with powers of physical endurance rare even in hard-bitten Arabia."

Gertrude Bell, traveler and writer

Mada'in Saleh (near Al-'Ula, Saudi Arabia)

Unique remains of the Nabataean culture

The extraordinary remains of Mada'in Saleh can be found in the vast and harsh desert lands of northwest Saudi Arabia, approximately 13 miles (22 km) to the northeast from the ancient city of Al-'Ula. Unlike conventional sand desert, here the red-ocher terrain runs into mountains and is peppered with massive rock outcrops. These outcrops house the Nabataean tombs, which make the area so archeologically and historically important.

The origins of the Nabataean culture are unclear, but it is known that they were important ancient traders who lived in and controlled southern Jordan and northern Arabia, with their capital being at Petra. They developed a web of trading routes across this area, along which staging posts such as Mada'in Saleh were built. The Nabataean people are renowned for their architectural skills, their use of inscriptions on their structures, and their highly developed artistic aesthetics. There is evidence that Mada'in Saleh, which was mentioned in the Koran, dated to before the Nabataeans and possibly back to the sixth century B.C.E., but it is the tombs dated to between the second century B.C.E. and the second century C.E. that have survived. The Nabataeans built their tombs, which were monumental, decorative structures, into the sides of the surrounding rocky mountains and spread across a wide area. The 132 existing tombs form the most important surviving representation of the Nabataean culture and are astonishing in their size, the facades of some rising 65 feet (20 m) high.

Beside the tombs and religious buildings, domestic mud-brick dwellings have been excavated as well as evidence of the Nabataeans' highly sophisticated water storage and irrigation systems. The site also boasts a carefully preserved railway station, built in the early 1900s during the Ottoman period, which served the historic Hejaz railway. **TP**

> *"[Nabataeans] are conspicuously lovers of freedom and flee into the desert, using this as a stronghold."*
>
> Diodorus Siculus, Greek historian

Naseef House (Jeddah, Saudi Arabia)

Lavish residence in one of the biggest commercial centers of the Arab world

The history of Jeddah extends back more than 2,500 years when it was first settled as a fishing community. It is located in western Saudi Arabia along the Red Sea coast, and became an important stopping point for traders on routes between India and the Far East, and the Mediterranean. Ships bringing pilgrims traveling to the nearby Holy City of Mecca also frequented its large and beautiful natural harbor. Old Jeddah (or Bala) was walled and fortified, and although the walls have since disappeared, it is here that one of the oldest houses—the Naseef House—can be found. The area is known for its Turkish-style houses.

Omar Naseef, a wealthy local merchant and businessman, built the house in 1872 as a home for his large family. Accordingly, it is a property of substantial dimensions with more than 100 rooms spread across four floors. It was also the tallest building in Jeddah for many years and as a further sign of its prestige was built next to the only tree in the city—although there are more now. The foundations and walls of the house were constructed from coral sequestered from the nearby sea, whereas the interior floors are wood and much of the internal decor consists of intricately carved woodwork. The exterior has the traditional wooden lattice window coverings that can be seen on many of the older buildings. In 1924 Jeddah was taken over by King Ibn Saud and integrated into Saudi Arabia. The king was invited to stay at the Naseef House in 1925 when he visited the area, which adds to the house's historic value.

Jeddah has expanded rapidly over the years, and, to prevent its antique buildings being lost, the Jeddah Historical Area Preservation Department was formed in 1999. The Naseef House was one of the first to be completely restored and has since been turned into a museum; it is one of the best preserved and most important historic buildings in the city. **TP**

"The closest place one can get [to 1,001 Arabian Nights] is Bala ... a part of Old Jeddah."

M. Ahmed Nagoor, travel writer

Hanging Village of Habalah (near Abha, Saudi Arabia)

Remarkable hidden village

To the southwest of Abha in Saudi Arabia is an extraordinary landscape of plunging cliffs, towering mountains, and craggy rock faces that leads, eventually, in an uneven giant staircase of granite down to the sparkling waters of the Red Sea. Scattered across this inhospitable but beautiful terrain are small pockets of fertile growth where brave trees cling to the rock face. Buried deep within this majestic, impenetrable wilderness is a small deserted village, Habalah, or the Hanging Village.

The tiny village is barely perceptible at first, and teeters halfway down a steep mountainside with a sheer rock wall soaring 600 feet (180 m) above and below it. The houses were constructed out of, and from, the rock and stone some 350 years ago by indigenous peoples trying to escape the onslaught of the Ottomans. Originally the village could only be reached by rope ladders (a rough translation of *habal* is "rope ladder"), and was so well hidden that the villagers were able to avoid capture. They built terraces from the rock face and grew crops including coffee and fruit, raised sheep and goats, and lived a self-sufficient existence. Today, remnants of the terraces survive, and surprisingly for the seemingly barren area, they remain somewhat fertile, aided by a natural spring that fed the village with water. Burials were also performed in the village, and the bodies were interred within holes in the rock face that were then filled with stones. Habalah continued to be occupied up until the 1980s, at which time the villagers were moved to a settlement in a more forgiving location.

This extraordinary place can now be reached by cable car, the first one to have been built in Saudi Arabia. Some of the buildings have been partially restored and the essence of the village remains authentic and compelling. **TP**

Muscat Town Walls (Muscat, Oman)

Former stronghold of Portugal's empire

Solid, stone walls, built by the Portuguese, enclose the town of Muscat to the south, protecting it from attack overland. The walls have only three gates: Bab Saghir (small gate) for pedestrians and donkeys; Bab Kabeer (large gate), the main gate for carts and horses; and Bab Mathaib, only used by larger vehicles with permission to travel between Muscat and Muttrah. Different tribes were once responsible for guarding the gates. Muscat imposed a curfew on its inhabitants, and the Bab Kabeer gate was closed after sunset, after a warning drum and three explosions had sounded from Fort Merani twenty minutes beforehand.

> *"Much of Oman's tumultuous history is written in the stone, stucco, and mud-brick of its architecture."*
>
> Lynn Teo Simarski, writer

Muscat was ideal as a strategic command point, with a natural harbor ringed by impenetrable, jagged rocks, traversed only by a few footpaths that could be closely guarded from watchtowers. The first road to Muscat was built in 1929, when a single-lane track was cut through the mountains by the British army.

After the European discovery of India by Vasco da Gama in 1498, the Portuguese gained control of the trading routes between Europe and India. Oman became a stronghold of the Portuguese Empire with Muscat its chief port. Although the Portuguese tended to rule their colonies indirectly, strategic defense could not be left to local control, and fortifications, such as the old town walls of Muscat, remain today as a reminder of sixteenth-century Portuguese domination of the Gulf region. **EH**

Shibam

(near Say'un, Yemen)

Sixteenth-century desert "skyscraper" city

The city of Shibam in Yemen—with its distinctive form of architecture described by early twentieth-century travelers as "The Manhattan of the Desert"—rises from the floor of the vast Wadi Hadramawt in central Yemen like a science fiction city from the *Star Wars* movie saga. The mud-brick tower houses—rising between five and nine stories high—are packed together so tightly that its inhabitants could visit their relations by skywalking from roof to roof.

Shibam's sixteenth-century walls encircle more than 500 dwellings, sheltering a population of around 7,000 people. The walls of the houses taper from 3 feet (1 m) thick at the base to less than 1 foot (0.3 m) thick at the top, and are plastered with mud and chopped straw. The tops and bases are painted with white lime plaster that serves as waterproofing (and as an eyecatching decoration), and a good proportion of the beautifully carved wooden windows and doors remain. Traditionally, the ground and first floors housed animals and food stores, the second floor was for entertaining, and the third floor upward was for the women and children.

The geometric plan of the streets and the height of its towerlike buildings—the tallest of which reaches 97 feet (30 m) above street level—are thought to originate from the scarcity of land after a flood *c.* 1532. From that time dwellings began to be strategically situated and huddled together on the highest ground. Today, date groves surround the walls of the town on three sides and the sandy bed of the Wadi—where the ancient trade caravans used to halt—lies to the south.

Deemed by UNESCO as one of the oldest and best examples of urban planning based on the principle of vertical construction, the old "skyscraper" city of Shibam was named a World Heritage site in 1982. **JB**

"As if a lower cliff had wandered out into the middle valley . . . splashed with white as by a giant paintbrush."

Freya Stark, traveler and writer

Old Marib (Marib, Yemen)

Ancient Sabaean city linked to the fabled Queen of Sheba

The ancient city of Marib was once the capital of the Sabaean Empire (biblical Sheba), the great wealth of which came from the taxes levied on the incense caravans that entered its gates. Inscriptions show the city to have been thriving from the eighth century B.C.E., though it was most likely founded centuries earlier. Today, its attractions are chiefly archeological, for the old city is ruined and its elegant mud-brick towers are crumbling back to earth.

Marib's most famous sites lie on its outskirts to the south and east: two mighty dams (old and new), and the temples of the legendary Queen of Sheba. The original Marib dam, constructed across the Wadi Adhanah around 750 to 600 B.C.E., was vast. More than 2,360 feet (719 m) long, 200 feet (60 m) wide, and 115 feet (35 m) high, it captured sufficient water from monsoon rains to sustain 30,000 to 50,000 people. The mud-walled dam was built in several stages over 500 years by both the Sabaeans and conquering Himyarites. Despite continual maintenance, the dam was frequently breached, its final catastrophic destruction featuring in the Koran. With no supply of water, 50,000 people were forced to leave the region.

More enigmatic are the archeological remains of the Almaqah Temple of Bar'an (known locally as 'Arsh Bilqis, or the Throne of the Queen of Sheba) and the Mahram Bilqis (Temple of the Moon God). The former dates from the tenth century B.C.E. and the latter from the twelfth century B.C.E. Mahram Bilqis, under continuing excavation, is one of the largest and most impressive pre-Islamic sanctuary sites in Arabia. Eight stone columns stand before the temple, whereas behind the peristile hall is a limestone wall bearing inscriptions, many of them still buried below the sands. Bone finds suggest animal sacrifice though, and sadly for local folklore, connections with Sheba's mythical queen have yet to be found. **JB**

> *"[Sheba's] history remains an enigma. She was a woman of power ... a founder of nations."*
>
> Michael Wood, historian

Aden Tanks (Aden, Yemen)

Marvel of engineering in southern Arabia

The Aden Tanks—massive, gypsum, cement-lined hollows hewn from rocks in the mountainous Crater area of the city—are something of a mystery. They were discovered in 1854 by the then assistant resident in Yemen, Lieutenant (later Sir Lambert) Playfair, hidden beneath layers of rubbish and soil from the surrounding hills. Playfair had the site cleared with funding from the British government; today the lower circular tank bears his name.

A series of descending watertight cisterns linked by conduits and accessible by precipitous staircases, the tanks (known locally as the Tawila tanks) were built to store rainwater—a precious commodity in the humid port, where temperatures often exceed 100° F (38° C). Acknowledged as a superb feat of engineering, there are eighteen cisterns in all, with a storage capacity of 20 million gallons (42 million liters) of water. It can only be estimated how much the original fifty-three cisterns might have held.

The tanks are believed, though not known, to have been built in the first century C.E. by the Himyarites, a powerful Semitic tribe who practiced fishing and agriculture and also trade, exporting the coveted tree gums of frankincense and myrrh. Water from the tanks meant they could irrigate their crops despite the sporadic rainfall. The tanks' huge capacity also offered protection from flash floods. However, no inscriptions, decorative features, or other artifacts have so far been found that point to definite origins. Maintained and used by successive generations, the tanks were later abandoned and in spite of the best efforts of the nineteenth-century engineers who cleared them, they could never be used again.

This 2,000-year-old hydrological marvel is situated in a rocky gorge below the peak of the extinct volcano upon which the port of Aden lies. Access is close to the Aden Museum, to the southwest of the town. **JB**

"In peace time few travelers stop at Aden without seeing the Aden Tanks ..."

R. A. B. Hamilton, *Geographical Journal* (March 1943)

Gallipoli (Gallipoli Peninsula, Turkey)

Site of a famous World War I campaign

"*Our last great effort to achieve . . . success against the Turks was the most ghastly and costly fiasco.*"

Ellis Ashmead-Bartlett, British war correspondent

⬆ The Gallipoli battlefields, looking down the narrow ridge known as the Nek toward Anzac Cove.

➡ An Australian soldier carries a wounded comrade toward a field hospital in Anzac Cove.

Early in World War I, a plan was developed to outflank the trench deadlock on the Western Front in Flanders and establish a supply route to Russia: Britain and France determined to attack Austria and Germany's main ally, the Ottoman Empire. The plan was for an assault against Turkish positions along the Dardanelles Straits, in preparation for a march on Istanbul that, it was argued, would knock the Ottomans out of the war. After the initial failure of an Anglo-French naval squadron to fight its way up the Dardanelles, an amphibious landing was proposed to secure the Gallipoli Peninsula.

A large Allied force from Britain, Australia, New Zealand, and France landed at Cape Helles and Gaba Tepe on April 25, 1915, and although a bridgehead was established, Turkish resistance prevented any further progress. In August, landings were made in Suvla Bay but again little headway was made, and the fighting bogged down into a form of brutal trench warfare. General Sir Ian Hamilton, the Allied commander, asked for more men but his request was refused and, in October, he was replaced by General Munro who recommended an evacuation; this was completed on January 9, 1916. Both the Allies and Ottomans suffered heavy casualties, with almost 400,000 men killed, wounded, and missing from the two sides.

The harsh terrain of the Gallipoli Peninsula gives the modern traveler a good idea of the nightmare the Allies faced, with the Turks holding the high ground, looking down on the Allied positions tenuously clinging to the shoreline. The site is popular with Turks—for whom the battle was a great victory—as well as visitors from the Allied countries. The main base of the Australian and New Zealand troops became known as Anzac Cove, and is often visited. As well as a number of military cemeteries, the battle site has a museum and some preserved trenches. **AG**

🏛 ◉ Ruins of Troy (Hissarlik, Turkey)

Legendary city and battle site described in Homer's Iliad

Troy was one of the great cities of the ancient world. It occupied a key position on the trade routes between Europe and Asia, enabling it to become enormously wealthy and powerful. It also played an important role in Greek culture because the Trojan War was the central theme of Homer's masterpiece, the *Iliad*. So, for nineteenth-century archeologists, reared on the classical texts, the search for Troy was the greatest prize of all.

This quest for Troy was eventually won by a German archeologist, Heinrich Schliemann. In 1870 he began excavating a mound at Hissarlik, close to the Dardanelles—just on the Asian side of the border with Europe. This site proved far more complex than expected. Gradually, it became clear that there had been at least nine separate periods of occupation on the spot—in other words, Troy had been destroyed and rebuilt several times. The earliest settlement (now known as Troy I) was a citadel dating back to the Bronze Age (*c.* 3800 B.C.E.); other strongholds followed this until Roman times, when the Troy IX site was finally abandoned.

For historians, the priority was to find Homer's Troy, to discover if the legends of the Trojan War were based on real events. This is still a controversial issue, but most experts believe that Troy VIIa is the likeliest candidate. The date it was destroyed (*c.* 1260 B.C.E.) tallies approximately with the period when the ancient Greeks themselves believed that the conflict took place. More significantly, the city appears to have come to a violent end, with traces of bones found in the streets and in private houses. Unfortunately, this layer was partially damaged by Schliemann himself as he continued to excavate beneath it.

The extensive and complex ruins are open to visitors and there is a museum on the site. There is much potential for future excavations. **IZ**

> *"The day shall come, that great avenging day/Which Troy's proud glories in the dust shall lay."*

Homer, *Iliad* (trans. Alexander Pope, 1720)

Süleymaniye Mosque (Istanbul, Turkey)

Hilltop mosque complex and Istanbul landmark

The Süleymaniye Mosque is a grand structure built on the orders of, and named after, Sultan Suleiman I (Suleiman the Magnificent, 1494–1566). It was designed by Mimar Sinan, one of the great architects of his time, and architect-in-chief to Suleiman for almost 28 years. During its construction, up to 2,000 workers at a time labored on the building. Suleiman I sought to use his new mosque to rival the grandeur of the Byzantine-built Hagia Sophia. The Süleymaniye Mosque is smaller than the Hagia Sophia, but it is arguably a more graceful structure. It measures 194 feet (59 m) long and 190 feet (58 m) wide; the main dome is 174 feet (53 m) high and 89 feet (27 m) in diameter. It has four minarets, and domes descend in tiers from the central dome.

The complex housed many other structures, including a bathhouse, hospital, public kitchen to feed the poor, and several *madrassa* (Koran schools). In the garden behind the mosque, there are two mausoleums, housing the tombs of some important figures, including those of Suleiman I and his wife, Roxelana. It also houses the tombs of Sultan Suleiman II and Sultan Ahmed II.

In 1660 the mosque was damaged by fire and restored by Sultan Mehmed IV in a Baroque style, resulting in considerable damage to the original structure. It was returned to its original style in the nineteenth century, but was damaged again during World War I when its courtyard was used as a weapons depot and ammunition ignited another major fire. The mosque was not restored again until 1956.

It is a grand monument to perhaps the greatest of the Ottoman sultans and a superb example of the grace and sophistication of architecture at the peak of the Ottoman Empire. The mosque became the architectural model for all subsequent mosques built by the sultans in Istanbul. **JF**

"In the course of his lifetime, like the stars, he too created many wonders."

Inscription on Sinan's tomb

🏛 ◉ Hagia Sophia (Istanbul, Turkey)

Beautiful Byzantine building, a former Christian basilica and Muslim mosque

The magnificently domed giant basilica of Hagia Sophia (meaning "divine wisdom") is one of the crowning glories of Byzantine architecture. Its appearance reflects the long story of historical change in this part of the world. The building changed from an early Christian to Eastern Orthodox church before the conquering Ottoman Turks turned it into a major mosque in 1453. It became a museum in the 1930s.

Between the fourth and sixth century, two major churches had already stood, and perished, on this site before the sixth-century Byzantine emperor Justinian I supervised the building of a third—the basis of the current building. The church became a fitting showpiece for his imperial capital, Constantinople, as Istanbul was then known. Over the centuries various problems led to differing degrees of rebuilding work, with the dome collapsing more than once. Although some of these events have been blamed on basic

design errors, nothing can detract from the incredible vision, audacity, and scale of this building. It is often said that the massive central dome, more than 180 feet (55 m) high with a diameter of more than 100 feet (30 m), seems to float above the nave. This effect is achieved partly by numerous small windows at the dome's base, flooding the interior with magical light. The effect is also helped by the dome's ribbed design and by the fact that it sits on four huge stone triangles rather than the conventional rectangle. These triangular structures take the weight before it passes down through enormous stone pillars.

Visitors today see the minarets and inscriptions of Islam as well as the colored marble and lavish mosaics of Christian days. Ongoing restoration work has proved tricky because Muslims covered up the "idolatrous" mosaics and uncovering them risks damage to the work placed over the top. **AK**

⚙ Blue Mosque (Istanbul, Turkey)

Supreme demonstration of Ottoman architectural capabilities

The Blue Mosque is one of the most magnificent structures of the Ottoman Empire, and its six minarets and many domes and semidomes still dominate the skyline of the old part of Istanbul. The building became known as the Blue Mosque for the color of its interior, but it is in fact properly known as the Sultan Ahmed Mosque—named after Sultan Ahmed I, who ordered its construction.

The Blue Mosque was built between 1609 and 1616 in the former center of Istanbul, which was captured by the Ottomans from the Byzantines in 1453. It is directly opposite Hagia Sophia, the grand former Orthodox Church converted to a mosque. Ahmed I chose this location deliberately—he wanted to show that Ottoman architects and builders could match their Christian precursors. Ultimately, the dome of the Blue Mosque was not as large as Hagia Sophia's, but the mosque's architect, Sedefhar Mehmet Aga,

sought to make up for this by the perfect proportions of its structure. The carved marble *minber* (pulpit) is positioned so that the imam can be heard from anywhere in the mosque. The central dome of the mosque is 108 feet (33 m) in diameter, and 141 feet (43 m) high. The interior is lined with more than 20,000 handmade ceramic tiles from Iznik, which are richly decorated with flowers, trees, and abstract patterns. More than 200 stained-glass windows allow daylight to flood in. Ahmed I died shortly after the mosque was completed, and is buried in a mausoleum just outside the walls of the mosque.

The Blue Mosque holds about 10,000 worshippers, and hundreds of Muslims still use it for daily prayers five times a day, many more on Fridays and during Muslim festivals. The way in for nonworshippers is by the north entrance, but the west entrance is the most superbly decorated. **JF**

Sumptuously furnished palace by the Bosphorus

In an attempt to modernize Istanbul, Sultan Abdülmecid II built Istanbul's first European-style palace, the Dolmabahçe Sarayı, between 1842 and 1853 at a cost of five million Ottoman gold pounds— the equivalent of 35 tons of gold. It was on the site of a former wooden Ottoman palace and imperial gardens constructed by the Bosphorus (the name *Dolmabahçe* means "filled-in garden"). The sultan spared no expense in furnishing the palace, even though many of his subjects lacked the basic necessities. The best view of the palace is from the Bosphorus.

The palace is divided into three sections: the Mabeyn-i Hümâyûn or Selamlık (men's quarters), the Muayede Salonu (ceremonial halls), and the Harem-i Hümâyûn (the harem, or the apartments of the sultan's family). There are 285 rooms, 43 halls, 6 hamams or baths (the main one made of pure alabaster), and 68 toilets. Some 14 tons of gold and 6 tons of silver were used in interior decorations. The Crystal Staircase, in the shape of a double horseshoe, is constructed of Baccarat crystal, brass, and mahogany. In the vast ballroom-cum-throne room hangs a Bohemian crystal chandelier weighing more than 4 tons. It was presented by Queen Victoria and hangs from the dome, which is 120 feet (36 m) high. The upper galleries were reserved for orchestras and the diplomatic corps. The palace also contains a large collection of European porcelain and Hereke carpets made for the palace by the Hereke Imperial Factory.

The founder and first president of the Turkish Republic, Mustafa Kemal Atatürk, used to stay in the Dolmabahçe Sarayı when he visited Istanbul, and he died here at 9:05 A.M. on November 10, 1938. Before his body was taken to Ankara, it was laid in state for the public to pay their last respects, and all the clocks in the palace are still stopped, displaying the time of his death. **LL**

"The rules that govern our life and livelihood must change, develop, and be renewed with time."

Mustafa Kemal Atatürk, Turkish statesman

🏛 ◎ **Hippodrome** (Istanbul, Turkey)

Park on the site of a Roman hippodrome, still scattered with historic remains

Built in the third century C.E. during the reign of the Roman emperor Septimius Severus in the provincial town of Byzantium, the Hippodrome—an arena for chariot racing—became the sporting and social center of the Eastern Roman Empire. In 324 C.E. the emperor Constantine moved his capital from Rome to Byzantium, which was renamed Constantinople. One of his major projects was renovating the Hippodrome: The arena was expanded to 1,500 by 425 feet (450 by 130 m), with room for 100,000 spectators. Constantine and his successors then marked the site's importance with works from around the empire, some of which remain; the area is now a park.

On Constantine's orders, the Tripod of Plataea, celebrating the Greek victory over Persia in 479 B.C.E., was brought from the Temple of Apollo at Delphi. A huge column supported a gold cauldron on three serpents' heads; the cauldron disappeared in 1204, during the Fourth Crusade, and only the shorter "Serpentine Column" remains. In 390 C.E. the emperor Theodosius transported an obelisk dating from around 1490 B.C.E. from the Temple of Karnak in Luxor to the Hippodrome, where the top section still stands. The core of another obelisk also survives. It was originally faced with bronze plaques, but these were stolen during the Fourth Crusade, as were the four bronze horses now atop St. Mark's Basilica in Venice.

The Hippodrome remained a focal point throughout the Byzantine period. Huge amounts of money were bet on chariot races, and rivalry often spilled over into politics and religion, leading to riots. After the Sack of Constantinople in 1204, the Hippodrome fell into disrepair. The Ottoman Turks, who captured the city in 1453 and made it their capital, had no interest in chariot racing. However, the site was never built over and the Turkish name, At Meydani, means "horse square." **LL**

"[It] was a locus for monuments whose form embodied ideas appropriate to Constantinople."

Sarah Guberti Bassett, art historian

Topkapı Sarayı

(Istanbul, Turkey)

Intricate and extensive palace of the sultans

At the height of its power in the sixteenth century, the Ottoman Empire stretched from the Danube to the Persian Gulf and from the Caspian Sea to modern Morocco. At its heart lay Istanbul, and at the heart of Istanbul lay Topkapı Sarayı, the sultan's palace and the empire's seat of government.

Mehmet II, who took Constantinople in 1453 and renamed it Istanbul, was responsible for founding Topkapı, although it was refashioned and expanded over the next 400 years. Since 1924 it has been a museum. It is laid out in the Oriental style, around a series of courtyards linked by gateways, each representing a step closer to the seat of power. The first courtyard would have been a hubbub of traders, visitors, and supplicants, but only the favored few penetrated as far as the fourth courtyard with its pavilions and tulip garden. Opening onto the second courtyard is the Divan Salonu, where the sultan's councilors would settle affairs of state. Beyond lay the Throne Room and Treasury. Here some of the fabulous wealth of the Ottoman sultans is now displayed, including casual piles of gold plate and enormous emeralds, one of the world's largest diamonds, and, most famous of all, the bejeweled Topkapı Dagger.

Behind this public face of the sultanate lies the very private harem. At times the harem's women wielded great power from behind the harem grilles. This maze of some 400 rooms was not just the women's quarters but the private residence of the sultan and his extensive family, servants, and guard of eunuchs. In addition to the sumptuous apartments, some areas reflect the harem's darker side: a fountain room to provide privacy from eavesdroppers, and the Cage, for all male relations who might aspire to the throne—Topkapı's reputation for plots and intrigues was well founded. **CB**

> "... irregular, asymmetric, non-axial, and unmonumental proportions."

Description of Topkapı by an early European visitor

Ani

(Ani, Turkey)

Medieval city built by Armenians

Situated on the edge of Turkey, on the border with Armenia, is an intriguing town called Ani. It is a decaying medieval city, long-since deserted, the remains of which are still standing. The history of Ani is much disputed, but two things are clear: Ani was once the capital of a medieval Armenian kingdom but it is now uninhabited and in ruins. At the height of its glory, the metropolis had a population of 100,000 to 200,000 people and stood as a rival to Constantinople, Baghdad, and Cairo. It was once renowned for its splendor and elegance and called the City of 1001 Churches, but today it is largely forgotten.

Ani is first mentioned in the fifth century C.E. in *The Armenian Chronicles*. It is described as a strong fortress, built on a hilltop. Over the years, Ani changed hands many times and experienced different rulers. Historians believe that it was in the reign of King Gagik I, from 989 to 1020, that Ani achieved its heyday. Its gradual decline began in 1236, when the Mongols captured the city and ransacked it, after which Ani declined progressively until the city was abandoned entirely due to an earthquake in 1319. Today the site is under Turkish rule, as a result of the Treaty of Kars. However, a dispute over the real ownership of Ani continues to this day.

Ani is a fascinating site, rich in historic, cultural, and religious interest. Disputes between Turkey and Armenia have threatened the city's remains in the past, but today it is possible to visit Ani freely and enjoy its myriad monuments, including a cathedral, a citadel, churches, mosques, chapels, bathhouses, and the foundations of several palaces. The beauty of these buildings lies in their dogged persistence in the face of time and change. The edifices are widely seen as among the most structurally advanced and creatively wrought in the medieval world. **KH**

Anıtkabir

(Ankara, Turkey)

Mausoleum of Turkey's first president

Anıtkabir is the final resting place of Mustafa Kemal Atatürk (1881–1938), the founder and first president of the Turkish Republic. Built on a hill overlooking the capital city, it stands severe and unadorned except for a vast mosaic courtyard and the mausoleum, the inside of which is covered in gold leaf. Building materials were sourced from many different parts of Turkey to symbolize the unity of the country.

The mausoleum is approached by a flight of stairs, via a succession of allegorical statues and two square kiosks, one of which contains a model of the tomb and photographs of its construction. An avenue flanked by

---

> *"Peace at home is peace in the country. Peace in the country is peace in the world."*
>
> **Mustafa Kemal Atatürk, Turkish statesman**

---

twenty-four stone lions modeled in Hittite style leads into the colonnaded courtyard, 420 feet (130 m) long and 275 feet (84 m) wide, which can accommodate 15,000 people. Gilded inscriptions on the walls are quotations from Atatürk's speech celebrating the tenth anniversary of the republic. Huge bronze doors open onto a hall that contains an immense cenotaph weighing 40 tons and cut from a single piece of marble. Atatürk lies directly beneath this symbolic tombstone. His sarcophagus points toward Mecca.

Anıtkabir is more than just a tomb. A permanent display of memorabilia relating to Atatürk's life, as well as a range of personal effects, is housed in a museum on the eastern side of the courtyard, emphasizing the influence that the father of modern Turkey continues to have on his country. **LL**

🏛 ◉ Hattusha Archeological Site (Bogazköy, Turkey)

Remains of an ancient Hittite city

The Hittites were one of the great powers of the ancient world. They triumphantly conquered Babylon, overshadowed Troy, and built up an empire that rivaled those of the Egyptians and the Assyrians. The visible remains of their civilization are less plentiful than those of some of their neighbors, but the site of their capital at Hattusha (now Bogazköy) gives some idea of their achievements.

Hattusha is located in Anatolia, in modern-day Turkey, around 90 miles (145 km) east of Ankara. The site was first occupied in the third millennium B.C.E., but the arrival of the Hittites appears to date from around 1700 B.C.E. The name of King Hattusili I ("the one from Hattusha"), who ruled *c.* 1650–1620 B.C.E., confirms its importance. It remained the chief stronghold of the Hittites until its destruction *c.* 1190 B.C.E. The site was later occupied by the Phrygians and the Galatians, but it never regained its importance.

Archeologists were aware of the site from the 1830s, but its true significance was not recognized until the twentieth century, after the excavations of two German archeologists, Hugo Winckler (from 1906) and Kurt Bittel (from 1932). These digs revealed the size of the city, which extends over 450 acres (35 ha), and led to the discovery of some 10,000 clay tablets on which valuable information about the Hittites was inscribed, including a peace treaty, one of the oldest known examples. Within the city, archeologists discovered at least seven temples, the largest of which contained shrines to the weather god, Hatti, and the sun goddess, Arinna. The most impressive remains, though, are at the gateways to the city. The Hittites excelled at sculpture and took particular pains over the massive forms of the guardian spirits, which flanked the main entrances. These include huge reliefs of lions, sphinxes, and warriors. **IZ**

🏛 ◎ **Derinkuyu** (Derinkuyu, Turkey)

Complex and self-contained underground city

Concealed beneath the inhospitable plains of Cappadocia, in central Anatolia, are entire towns excavated out of the soft volcanic rock that characterizes the region. Best known of these is Derinkuyu, which, it is estimated, could accommodate 20,000 to 30,000 people.

The first tunnels and caves may have been begun up to 4,000 years ago, and certainly they were well occupied by 700 B.C.E. Settlers coming to cultivate the area's rich volcanic soil would have welcomed the underground protection from the extremes of the weather, and a subterranean life would have become increasingly permanent during the many times when these exposed uplands were the battlegrounds of successive enemies with Hittites against Thracians, and Christians against Muslims.

Derinkuyu, which means "Deep Well," goes down eight and possibly more levels (it is yet to be fully explored). The extensive network of passageways links thousands of excavated "rooms," some cell-like, some cavernous, that provided not just basic living accommodation but a real self-contained community, with churches, schools, communal kitchens, meeting areas, and even stables and winemaking areas. A complex system of ventilation shafts kept the air breathable. Various defenses were incorporated into the city including secret tunnels, escape routes, and large circular "doors" that could be rolled in front of tunnel entrances by means of a pole inserted through a central hole. Once the door was in place, the hole could then serve as an arrow slit.

The way of life provided by Derinkuyu and the other Cappadocian underground cities—more than forty have been found so far—eventually became too restrictive, and the troglodyte communities drifted away to more conventional towns. **CB**

🏛 ◈ Göreme (Göreme, Turkey)

Magical valley of dwellings and churches hollowed out of natural rock formations

To walk into the Göreme valley is rather like entering a land of pixies or a scene from Tolkien. Conical houses topped by stone caps look more like stalagmites crossed with toadstools than any conventional house, but there are doors and windows.

This extraordinary landscape is the result of millennia of erosion. Eruptions from Mount Erciyes (Argeus of classical times) laid down deep strata of tuff, a soft rock formed from compressed volcanic ash. As it weathered, numerous phallic buttes were created where boulders of harder rock, usually basalt, impeded the rate of erosion.

Christianity came early to Anatolia (St. Paul traveled through the region), and Cappadocia's remoteness attracted adherents seeking a hermit's solitude and, later, those fleeing persecution. As communities grew, the basic chambers they scooped out of the soft rock developed into more complex dwellings and places of worship. More than 1,000 rock churches have been found all over Cappadocia, and a concentration of "fairy chimney" houses and churches near Göreme has been designated an open-air museum. Lack of exposure to light and, until recently, visitors have preserved the painted interiors of the rock churches astonishingly well. Some, dating from the Iconoclastic Controversy (726–843), when figurative representation was forbidden, have geometrical designs, mostly in red ocher, whereas those from the tenth and eleventh centuries are lively with saints and biblical scenes. One of the largest, Tokalı Kilise, glows a rich blue, and Karanlık Kilise (the "dark church"), reached by a winding stairway, is especially well preserved. A little way from the main cluster, Saki Kilise has a particular charm. Its biblical characters are depicted, not in the Holy Land but walking in Göreme's own fairy landscape. **CB**

Celsus Library (near Selcuk, Turkey)

Imposing and beautifully restored library and tomb

The magnificent Celsus Library is one of the showpiece buildings among the breathtaking remains of ancient Ephesus (Efes in Turkish). Ephesus played host to a succession of different ancient civilizations. It was a major center of Ionian Greece before the conquering Romans made it part of their vast empire as the capital of Emperor Augustus's province of Asia. The imposing library dates from Roman days and the rule of Emperor Trajan in the second century C.E., famed for his massive building program of monumental structures.

The library was built originally as a combined library and grand tomb for Celsus Polemaeanus—Roman senator, general governor of the province of Asia, and a great booklover—by his son, Julius Aquila. The vault itself lies beneath the ground floor, a lead container within a marble tomb. When the building quickly found use as a library, eminent scholars from all over the ancient world congregated here, studying its 12,000 to 15,000 scrolls. East-facing reading rooms caught the very best of the morning light, and an underground tunnel led to an adjacent building that may have been a drinking den or brothel.

Most arresting is the library's facade, expertly reconstructed from original remains in modern times. Its main entrance is larger than the entrances on either side; this has the effect of making the building appear a great deal larger than it actually is. There is a second level of columns above the first, and there may have been a third level.

The Goth invasion in the third century saw the city begin its decline from the peaks of grandeur it had reached in its Classical past, and, despite being on the map of the Byzantine Empire, that decline was well under way by the late middle ages. Major archeological work took place at Ephesus in the 1800s and today it is a popular tourist attraction. **AK**

Kayseri Citadel (Kayseri, Turkey)

Fortifications of a key ancient city

Looming over the ancient city of Kayseri are the remains of an imposing black basalt citadel originally constructed in the sixth century by the Roman emperor Justinian and later rebuilt by the Seljuk sultan Alaeddin Keykubat I in the thirteenth century, with further repairs made by the Ottoman sultan Mehmet the Conqueror in the fifteenth century. The ruins are all that is left of the city's once formidable defenses, which included an extensive network of walls to protect this major center of learning and commerce.

Kayseri sits in the middle of a vast, flat plain dominated by Mount Erciyes, an extinct volcano permanently capped with snow. The principal city in the region now, its importance extends back to at least the third millennium B.C.E., at the time of the Hittites and Assyrians, with trade routes from the Mediterranean, Aegean, and Black Sea all meeting here. Originally called Mazaka, it was the capital of the kingdom of Cappadocia. When this became a Roman province in 17 C.E., the city was renamed Caesarea Cappadociae.

By the beginning of the fifth century, reports suggest, the inhabitants were living in constant fear of attack by marauders, but it was not until the reign of Justinian that a citadel using black basalt from the volcano was built. What can be seen today is largely the Seljuk reconstruction. The Seljuk Turks conquered Caesarea in 1084, renaming it Kayseri. The city once again became an important center, reaching a peak during the reign of Alaeddin Keykubat I, when frontiers were secured and many roads and bridges built. Having decided to reinforce Justinian's citadel, the sultan built over the Byzantine foundations, adding nineteen towers and erecting inner walls almost 10 feet (3 m) thick. Now, nearly 800 years later but continuing the theme of Kayseri's commercial significance, the citadel is a shopping precinct. **LL**

Apollo Temple (Didim, Turkey)

Ancient Greek oracle

Visitors to the temple and oracle of Apollo at Didyma (modern Didim) made their approach via the statue-lined Sacred Way from Miletos, a Greek city in Ionia on the west coast of modern Turkey. There was apparently a cult based on the sacred spring at the site before the arrival of the Greeks in Ionia, but the earliest temple was constructed in the eighth century B.C.E.; remains from this original structure include a wall, well, and altar. The temple was enlarged in about 560 B.C.E. and attracted wide fame. In 494 B.C.E. it was destroyed by the Persians, and the cult statue of Apollo stolen. The statue was returned in 300 B.C.E. and construction of a new temple commenced. Had it ever been completed,

> *"The temple is adorned with costliest offerings consisting of early works of art."*
>
> Strabo, *Geographica* (23 C.E.)

it would have been the largest in the Greek world: 387 feet by 197 feet (118 m by 60 m).

The new temple was constructed in the Ionic order, surrounded by two files of columns, 120 in total, each a towering 64 feet (19.5 m) high. At the top of the fourteen steps leading to the temple was a veritable forest of stone because the forecourt, or *pronaos*, consisted of three rows of four columns. Inside was the *cella* (inner chamber), and inside this was the *naiskos*, a small temple containing the sacred spring and cult image of Apollo. From here, a staircase led to the oracle's room, where a female priestess breathed in fumes from the water and uttered answers to pilgrims' questions. It is said that Alexander the Great heard that he would defeat the Persians from the oracle at Didyma. **RF**

Mevlana Tekke (Konya, Turkey)

Tomb and headquarters of the whirling dervishes

The tomb of the mystic Sufi philosopher, poet, and theologian Jalal al-Din Mohammad al-Rumi (1207–73), also known as Mevlana, sits at the heart of what were the headquarters of the whirling dervishes, until the sect's abolition in 1925 as part of a massive crackdown on religious extremism by the newly established Turkish Republic. The Mevlana Tekke complex contains a mosque, a ritual hall *(tekke)* where the whirling ceremony or *sema* took place, kitchens where food for the dervishes and their guests was prepared, and accommodation cells, in addition to many other tombs and cemeteries.

The site, which was once a royal Seljuk rose garden to the east of the walled city of Konya, was given in 1228 to Mevlana's father, the theologian Bahaeddin Veled of Balkh, and this is where both men were buried. It was also here, based on Mevlana's teachings, that his successors established and developed the order of whirling dervishes, who sought union with the divine through ritual chanting and dance. The first tomb over Mevlana's grave, a simple domed structure, was built shortly after his death but, in 1397, as the influence of his teachings increased, the dome was replaced with the magnificent sixteen-sided conical crown covered in turquoise tiles that can be seen today. The mosque and ritual hall were added by later Ottoman sultans.

Today an attractive courtyard containing an ablution fountain and a number of smaller tombs leads, via a silver door, to the main tomb chamber. Mevlana's sarcophagus, like that of his father, sits prominently on a raised dais, draped in a velvet shroud embroidered in gold, with a huge symbolic turban at one end. The most important Islamic shrine in Turkey, Mevlana's tomb continues to receive thousands of pilgrims each year, even though the whole complex was reclassified as a museum in 1927. **LL**

> *"Out beyond ideas of wrongdoing and rightdoing, there is a field. I will meet you there."*
>
> Jalal al-Din Mohammad al-Rumi, Sufi mystic

🏛 ⊛ Nemrut Dağ Statues (near Adıyaman, Turkey)

Mausoleum of Antiochus I, featuring statues of Greek and Persian deities

Listed as Nemrut Dağ World Heritage site in 1987, the first-century B.C.E. mausoleum of Antiochus I of Commagene on Nemrut Dağ mountain, in southeastern Anatolia, is one of the most ambitious constructions of the Hellenistic period.

Commagene, a kingdom to the north of Syria and the Euphrates that was founded after the breakup of Alexander the Great's empire, had links with both Persia and Macedonia thanks to its geographical position and the lineage of its rulers (Antiochus counted Darius the Great and Seleucus I Nicator among his ancestors). It is this mix that makes the site so interesting. Antiochus had workmen build a tumulus 160 feet (50 m) high on top of the mountain, between temple compounds on terraces of rock. It is not clear whether this tumulus houses his remains or not. On the eastern terrace, five colossal seated statues some 30 feet (9 m) high have been identified as

Apollo-Mithras, Tyche (the Commagene fertility goddess), Zeus-Oromasdes, Antiochus himself, and Hercules-Artagnes. The statues on the western terrace depict the same Greek and Persian deities and there are also bas-reliefs. The heads of the statues from both terraces have fallen to the ground—the area is prone to earthquakes—but even they are more than 6 feet (2 m) high. On the western terrace, the background of a stone slab depicting a lion shows an arrangement of nineteen stars and the planets Jupiter, Mercury, and Mars that would suggest a date of July 7, 62 B.C.E., which might be when construction began.

Nobody outside the area knew anything about the site until 1881, when an Ottoman survey team came across this remote mountaintop and its statues. Archeological work proper did not begin until 1953, when a German-American team embarked on a scientific investigation. **LL**

Temple of the Sun God (Garni, Armenia)

Reconstructed temple to Mithras on strategic hilltop site

This temple is the best-preserved building on a hilltop site that may have been used as a base by Armenian tribal kings as long ago as the third millennium B.C.E. The temple was built as a shrine to Mithras—an East Mediterranean deity associated with the sun who was enthusiastically adopted by the Romans as the focus of a military religious cult. It is generally thought to date from the first century C.E. and is claimed to have been built by King Tiridates I of Armenia, who traveled to Rome and received both money and political endorsement from Emperor Nero. There is, however, an alternative theory that it was built as the burial place for a different Armenian king and was constructed slightly later than previously thought, around 175 C.E.

Regardless of its original use, it is an excellent example of the way Armenian artisans modified traditional Greco-Roman temple design, using basalt instead of marble and incorporating a wealth of ornamentation traditionally associated with this area of the Roman Empire, such as grapes and pomegranates, and older, pre-Roman motifs of bulls and lions.

The temple is only one part of an extensive complex. There are also the remains of the fortress that was the original raison d'être for the site; this was later turned into a palace. Ruins of Roman-era baths can still be seen, decorated with elaborate mosaics depicting figures from Greek mythology, and there are the remains of several churches that were built soon after Armenia adopted Christianity as the state religion in 301. Sadly, the buildings on the site were almost completely destroyed by an earthquake in 1679, although the temple is in a relatively good state of repair, thanks to a rebuilding program undertaken by Soviet authorities during the 1970s. **AS**

Echmiatsin Cathedral

(Echmiatsin, Armenia)

Center of the Armenian church, built to a design that had great influence on later churches

There has been a place of worship on the site now occupied by Echmiatsin Cathedral since around 500 B.C.E.; during excavations undertaken in the 1950s, the main altar was discovered to have been built over a much older shrine, believed to have been dedicated to the Greek hunter goddess Artemis. The cathedral is the seat of the catholicos—the head of the Armenian Apostolic Church—and was founded by the first catholicos, Gregory the Illuminator, in 303, two years after Armenia became the first nation to adopt Christianity as the official state religion. According to church teachings, Gregory received a divine vision, in which he saw Christ descend from heaven and strike the ground with a golden hammer, indicating where the cathedral was to be built; the cathedral derives its name from this event—Echmiatsin may be translated as "the place where the Only Begotten descended." One of the relics in the church is said to be the lance that pierced the side of Christ on the cross.

The original cathedral was a vaulted basilica but it was rebuilt in the fifth and sixth centuries as a cruciform church, with a central dome supported on four massive pillars. Despite the addition in the eighteenth century of various belfries and four smaller domes, the church looks much as it would have in 618, when the original wooden cupola was replaced with one in stone. This design has proved hugely influential, and all other domed cruciform churches ultimately derive from Echmiatsin.

Under the heading of Cathedral and Churches of Echmiatsin and the Archeological Site of Zvartnots, the cathedral became a UNESCO World Heritage site in 2000, along with some of the surrounding buildings—the Church of St. Hripsimeh (618), the Church of St. Gayaneh (630), and the Zvartnots archeological site. **AS**

> *"I was to build a temple to God on the place where the gold base had been shown to me ..."*
>
> Gregory the Illuminator, relating his vision

Vardzia Cave City

(near Aspindza, Georgia)

City hewn out of a mountainside

In remote Georgian countryside, rearing up magnificently from the banks of the Mtkvari River, lies a honeycomb of intriguing openings hewn from massive cliff faces of the Lesser Caucasus mountains. This is the external evidence of a vast cave-city created here in the twelfth century. The outer view, spectacular in itself, is as nothing compared with the ambition and scale of the city behind its rocky facade.

Close to the Turkish and Armenian borders, Vardzia was conceived as a military stronghold by Giorgi III, Christian king of Georgia, at a time when invasions of Muslim Turks were an ever-present threat. It is said that the name "Vardzia" springs from a phrase that Princess Tamar, Giorgi's daughter, called out to tell people where she was when she became lost in the caves. When Giorgi died in 1184, Tamar took over the project, turning it into a fortified monastery. As queen, she presided over a great era of Georgian power and culture, and Vardzia is a fitting expression of her vision—the best of its kind in a land known for its cave architecture.

At its height, the city was considered a miraculous creation, its thirteen tiers and thousands of rooms capable of housing 50,000 people. Here was a banquet hall, stables, libraries, bakeries, bathing pools, wine cellars, and a grand main church whose northern wall bears a famous fresco of Tamar and her father. A sophisticated irrigation system supplied water and fed terraced areas under cultivation. The late 1200s brought an earthquake that destroyed some of the city and exposed entrances once hidden from view, and the 1500s saw a plundering Persian attack that hastened the city's demise. Over the centuries this relatively inaccessible site went largely unnoticed, but recent efforts at restoration and promotion have raised its profile enormously. **AK**

Stalin's Birthplace

(Gori, Georgia)

Birthplace of former Soviet dictator

Even the briefest glance around the industrial city of Gori will tell the visitor that this was where Joseph Stalin (1879–1953)—Soviet dictator and perhaps the world's most powerful man between the 1920s and 1950s—was born and grew up. Stalin Avenue slices through the heart of Gori to Stalin Square, site of one of the last statues of Stalin still standing in the former Soviet Union. Nearby is the Stalin Museum, and Stalin Park is on the edge of the city center.

Stalin's iron rule dominated the former Soviet Union, of which Georgia was a part, from the early 1920s until his death in 1953. His beginnings, however,

> *"If the opposition disarms, well and good. If it refuses to disarm, we shall disarm it ourselves."*
>
> Joseph Stalin, Soviet dictator

were humble. He was born as Ioseb Dzhugashvili, the son of a poor cobbler, when Georgia was a part of the Russian tsarist empire. The house where he was born and spent his first few years stands today in central Gori, preserved under a stone canopy. Next to the house lies the Stalin Museum, built in the 1950s and containing objects chosen to tell his life story. Outside the museum is a heavily armor-plated railway carriage used exclusively by Stalin from the 1940s onward—he traveled in this to the famous World War II Yalta Conference with Churchill and Roosevelt.

Stalin attended Gori's church school from 1888 to 1894 before leaving to study at Tbilisi Theological Seminary, where he spent his time secretly reading communist texts before being expelled in 1899 and beginning a long and eventful political career. **AK**

🏛 ◉ Svetitskhoveli Cathedral (Mtskheta, Georgia)

Medieval church with a rich history, the most important in Georgia

Svetitskhoveli Cathedral is the seat of the Georgian catholicos (leader of the country's Orthodox Church), and was built from 1010 on the site of an earlier church that was constructed soon after the country adopted Christianity in 317.

According to legend, the cathedral houses the robe that Christ was wearing when he was crucified, which was apparently brought to Georgia by a native who was in Jerusalem at the time of the Crucifixion and purchased the robe from the Roman centurion who had presided over the execution. On bringing the garment to his homeland, the Georgian met his sister, who immediately died on touching the holy cloth. She was grasping it so tightly that it had to be buried with her. A mysterious cedar grew up over her grave, and when King Mirian III was converted to Christianity by St. Nino, he ordered the tree to be cut down and made into seven pillars to form the base for

a new church to be built on the site. The seventh pillar miraculously rose into the air and returned to earth only after St. Nino prayed for an entire night for its return, whereupon it started producing a mysterious liquid that cured any disease; "svetitskhoveli" translates as "life-giving pillar."

The cathedral has been sacked several times by invading armies, including those of the legendary Tamerlane, as Georgia was conquered and reconquered by Persians, Muslim Arabs, Ottoman Turks, and eventually Russians under Catherine the Great. Therefore, the present structure is the result of several centuries of more or less constant restoration. The original architect's presence survives, however, in the form of the sculpture of a disembodied arm and hand holding a chisel on the exterior of the church accompanied by an inscription: "The hand of Arsukisdze, slave of God. May forgiveness be his." **AS**

🏛 ⊚ **Merv** (Merv, Turkmenistan)

Ancient city on the Silk Road

Merv, previously an oasis city in Central Asia, today stands abandoned in the modern state of Turkmenistan. The city was located on the Silk Road, the series of interconnected East–West trade routes linking China with Arabia and Mediterranean Europe. The Silk Road existed from prehistoric times and Merv grew in importance as trade along the route increased. Archeological surveys have established that Merv was undoubtedly in business as far back as the third millennia B.C.E., but the history of the city may reach even further back into the past.

Over the centuries, Merv was ruled by many different leaders of Iranian, Greek, Turkish, and Central Asian descent. Its history is long and complex. There was a brief period, between 813 and 818 C.E., when the Caliph al-Ma'mun held temporary residence in Merv, effectively making it the capital city of the Muslim world. Then, between 1145 and 1153, Merv was considered for a time to have become the largest city in the world, with a population of 200,000. In 1221 the city's population was decimated by attacks from the Mongols and its decline continued from then. In 1794 the entire population, some 100,000 inhabitants, was deported by the emir of Bokhara. The city's degeneration went on and Merv continued to change hands until, in 1883, it was occupied by the Russians.

The Russian occupation of Merv meant that excavations of the ancient site began as early as 1890. Since then, teams of archeologists have performed a number of excavations. The settlement now covers an area of more than 15 square miles (39 sq km). The site also contains an assortment of citadels, mosques, and residential quarters. These relics provide an immense amount of information about the shifting culture, geography, and politics of Merv, a major city at the heart of Central Asia. **KH**

🏛 ⊚ Gur-Emir (Samarkand, Uzbekistan)

Mausoleum of Tamerlane, intricately decorated inside and out

Timur the Lame—known to English speakers by the corruption Tamerlane or Tamburlaine—attempted to recreate the Mongol Empire of Genghis Khan a generation before him, and eventually came to rule over territories stretching from modern-day Turkey in the west to the borders of China in the east before dying during a campaign against the Chinese Ming emperors in 1405. He had begun the Gur-Emir (the Tomb of the King) only two years earlier as a mausoleum for his grandson and heir apparent Muhammed Sultan, but came to be buried there himself alongside Muhammed, a second grandson Ulugh Beg, his sons Shah Rukh and Miran Shah, and his teacher Mir Said Baraka.

The mausoleum is surrounded by the remains of buildings from a slightly earlier religious complex, and its relatively simple layout enriched with ornate decoration influenced later Mughal tombs, including the Taj Mahal. It is the ornamentation that leaves the most lasting impression; thousands of blue and white tiles, arranged in intricate geometric patterns, cover the exterior—matching the intense blue-green of the single dome—whereas elaborate paintings and gilded moldings dominate the interior. In a separate room in the center of the mausoleum sit the tombstones, marking the spot where the bodies lie in a crypt below the floor. Distinct from the marble tombstones of his relatives and teacher, Tamerlane's grave is marked with a slab of dark green jade, which is supposed to have once stood in a Chinese emperor's palace before being looted by the Mongol Golden Horde. The tomb bears an inscription that curses anybody who disturbs Tamerlane's rest; the most recent people to do so were a team of Soviet archeologists who disinterred Tamerlane's body in 1941 to reconstruct his likely appearance during life—Nazi troops invaded Russia a few months later. **AS**

> *"Anyone who violates my stillness … will be subjected to inevitable punishment and misery."*
>
> From the inscription on Tamerlane's tomb

Mazar of Khoja Ahmed Yasawi (Turkestan, Kazakhstan)

Fine example of medieval Islamic architecture created to honor a Sufi poet

The Mazar (Mausoleum) of Yasawi is Kazakhstan's most significant architectural masterpiece. Its massive blue-tiled dome floats above a small complex of buildings that together are the most complete example of the architecture of the medieval Timurid Empire. Built between 1389 and 1405 during the reign of Tamerlane in the ancient town of Yasi (modern Turkestan), it remains unfinished.

The Mausoleum was commissioned by Tamerlane to enhance the grave of Khoja Ahmed Yasawi. A famed Sufi mystic, Yasawi was born in 1103, lived for most of his life in the nearby city of Turkestan, and died around 1166. Yasawi had a gift for translating his profound spiritual message through the medium of poetry; apparently simple words conveyed a deep set of meaning to the attuned listener. Significantly he wrote in the local Turkic dialects and not in Classical Arabic, so that all people could understand his words. Yasawi founded an order of Sufi mystics—the Yasauia—who conveyed his gifts across the medieval Islamic world. The site of his tomb became a significant place of pilgrimage; it was said that three journeys to the Mausoleum equaled one Hajj to Mecca.

It was Yasawi's reputation that led Tamerlane to pull down an earlier simple tomb and replace it with the magnificent and unfinished monument that we see today. The main body of the complex supports the largest dome in Central Asia, covered in exquisite green and golden tiles. The walls are covered in a fabulously complex mixture of heavily stylized text and elegant geometric patterns. The main facade was unfinished by the time of Tamerlane's death and the original supporting scaffolding still protrudes from the walls. Fortunately, later dynasties had neither the resources nor the interest in completing Tamerlane's vision, and it remains a shining example of the architectural legacy of Islamic Central Asia. **IS**

"If you want to know about us, examine our buildings."

Inscription on one of Tamerlane's buildings

Minaret of Jam (Jam, Afghanistan)

Magnificent example of Islamic architecture notable for its ornamentation

> *"Its impact is heightened by its dramatic setting, a deep . . . valley between towering mountains."*
>
> UNESCO

The enigmatic Minaret of Jam stands isolated in the valley of the Hari Rud, in the highlands of central Afghanistan, officially "discovered" in 1957 by French archeologist Andre Maricq. Scholarship at the site has been hampered by the remote location of the minaret and the recent troubled history of Afghanistan. Limited work during the 1960s and 1970s has successfully translated the elegant and complex Kufic script that adorns the entirety of the monument. The minaret is constructed of pale, baked mud brick unadorned by color, except a turquoise and lapis lazuli tile collar of text, two-thirds up its 206-foot (63-m) height. This collar is the key text of the sixty-third Surya (or verse) of the Koran known as the "Miriam Surya." This Surya refers to the status of Mary, the mother of Jesus, and confirms the cosmopolitan nature of the Ghurid builders of the minaret. Debate over the date of the construction of the minaret is hampered by damage to the relevant text on the monument.

The Ghurid dynasty burst out of the mountainous heartlands of Afghanistan during the early twelfth century, and quickly brought together a state that stretched from central Iran to the Bay of Bengal in India. The short-lived empire was devastated by the incursions of the Mongols, and by 1221 the Ghurid state was a minor historical footnote.

Recent archeological work has confirmed that like many modern towns in the Afghan mountains, an urban center could be found in the locality, spread out along the two local river valleys and up the steep slopes of the surrounding mountains. This spread of buildings was protected by a medieval system of towers and walls. Further confirmation was provided by the discovery of a Hebrew cemetery and the associated tombstones of Jewish merchants. The Minaret of Jam was declared Afghanistan's first World Heritage site in 2002. **IS**

🏛 ◎ Taxila (Taxila, Pakistan)

Ancient center of Buddhist learning and capital of the eastern Punjab

Taxila was built by the Gandhara civilization, an ancient kingdom that thrived in what is now Pakistan and Afghanistan. From the fifth century B.C.E. until the second century C.E., this site was a center of Buddhist learning, a renowned place in which to learn about art, philosophy, religion, and culture. Located between two important rivers, the Indus and the Hydaspes, and on several important trading routes, Taxila comprises a number of distinct archeological sites and was added to the UNESCO World Heritage List in 1980.

Taxila bears the traces of Persian, Greek, and Central Asian inhabitants. In the fourth century B.C.E., Alexander the Great arrived here and—according to legend—joined forces with King Ambi against neighboring King Porus. In return for Alexander's help, Ambi provided him with troops and elephants. Alexander defeated Porus in a dramatic victory, although the men later became friends and allies. A century after Alexander's presence, the famous Buddhist king Asoka conquered the region. Asoka, an Indian ruler, had been notorious for his cruelty until his conversion to Buddhism when, according to legend, his behavior changed dramatically and he became a great and virtuous ruler.

Despite this turbulence, Taxila retained its reputation as a place of great learning, and scholars traveled from as far away as the Mediterranean and China to study here. The archeological remains include Buddhist stupas, a monastery, and breathtaking Gandhara sculptures. Taxila's origins are perhaps best glimpsed in its great surviving statues. Among them is a large and commanding Buddha who greets visitors with a firm stare, a departure from the more usual depictions in which he has his eyes closed and a look of serenity on his face. This ancient Buddha has his eyes wide open and appears to be directly challenging the viewer. **LH**

"If the 'Pillared hall' [in Taxila] was indeed a sanctuary, . . . it is the oldest known Hindu shrine."

Jona Lendering, historian

🏛️ 🔶 Lahore Fort (Lahore, Pakistan)

Strategically important fort complex that contains lavish palaces and mosques

In the sixteenth century Lahore was captured by the Mughals and, under Akbar the Great, it became the second city after Agra. The fort constructed here was one of the finest of the Mughal Empire and exercised considerable influence throughout the Indian subcontinent. It is smaller than the famous Red Fort at Agra, but of a similar layout. The design of Lahore Fort was influenced by both local Hindu and Persian architecture. Building work began in the 1580s, but the fort was added to and enlarged over the centuries. The oldest part, constructed during Akbar's reign, was built in red sandstone. Akbar was also responsible for the construction of the now-famous city walls and their twelve gates. He moved his court to Lahore in 1584 and it remained the seat of his government for fourteen years.

The fort is divided into two separate sections: a residential one and an administrative one. These sections comprise private living areas, a grand mosque, administration and military areas, public areas, gardens, and courtyards. The imposing gateway is wide enough to allow a caravan of royal elephants to pass through it with ease.

Later buildings are more ornate than those built by Akbar, using expensive materials such as imported marble and Persian ceramics. The most famous room is the Shish Mahal—known as the Crystal Palace or the Hall of Mirrors, built for Shah Jahan—with its walls and ceiling covered in thousands of small colored mirrors. Nearby is the beautiful marble Naulakha Pavilion; a cool retreat from the midday sun, the pavilion became a favorite place of the harem. In 1841, after the fall of the Mughals, Lahore Fort was besieged and badly damaged. Restoration work began in the twentieth century and the fort was added to UNESCO's World Heritage List in 1981. **LH**

🏛 ◉ Mohenjo-daro (Indus Valley, Pakistan)

These ruins are an early example of efficient town planning

This was one of the most important cities of the ancient Indus Valley civilization—an incredibly sophisticated urban culture that flourished between 2600 and 1900 B.C.E. and only really came to light in the 1920s. Sited in the Indus River delta, Mohenjo-daro (Mound of the Dead—the city is a series of mounds) is probably one of the first properly planned cities. Like other great centers of this civilization, such as Harappa city (located to the north), Mohenjo-daro was devised on a gridlike plan with broad, crisscrossing avenues that created distinct, rectangular blocks. Down smaller side streets were private houses with their own bathrooms and sanitary water supplies, and the whole city enjoyed an advanced drainage system that seems to surpass anything else found around the world at the time.

First excavated in 1922, the remains of the city open to view today give a real feel for life in this metropolis, which may have housed more than 35,000 people. The overall plan is clearly visible, as are defensive towers and fortifications, main roads and high-walled side streets, houses, courtyards, wells, and covered street drains, with unbaked bricks as the principal surviving building material.

Archeological evidence has divided the city into two main areas: the Citadel and Lower City (much of the latter is yet to be excavated). Archeologists believe that the Citadel was the seat of government, and administration and major buildings that have been excavated there include what are thought to be a great public bath, an assembly hall, and a structure said by some to be a granary. Also to be admired, rising majestically above the site, is an impressive Buddhist stupa dating to about 200 C.E.—evidence of habitation long after the Indus Valley civilization had faded. **AK**

Tomb of the Emperor Jahangir (near Lahore, Pakistan)

Lavish monument to an eccentric ruler

In a provincial suburb of Lahore is the grand tomb of the Mughal emperor Jahangir (1569–1627). It is an outstanding piece of architecture that effectively illustrates the power, wealth, and prestige that so many emperors once enjoyed. It was commissioned by Jahangir's son, Shah Jahan, to commemorate the momentous life of his deceased father.

The emperor, originally born Nuruddin Jahangir, was a fascinating man with many twists and turns in his life. By the age of thirty he had already staged a revolt against his own father, and by thirty-six he had superseded his father on the throne. At the start of his reign he was popular among his people, but only a year later he was forced to fend off his own son's claim to the throne. After defending himself successfully, Jahangir decided to imprison his son and later blind him. However, several years later he became conscience-stricken and employed the best physicians to repair his son's eyesight. In addition to this dramatic series of events, Jahangir is remembered for having married twelve times, for being an alcoholic, and for losing his grip on the throne. It therefore seems fitting that an extravagant and theatrical mausoleum commemorates this eccentric ruler.

The mausoleum is situated within an attractive garden surrounded by high walls. These walls are decorated with delicate patterning and interspersed by four enormous 98-foot- (30-m-) high minarets and two massive entry gates made of stone and masonry. The exterior of the tomb is enhanced with a stunning mosaic built on a flower pattern and the Koranic verses, whereas the interior of the mausoleum contains a white marble sarcophagus, the sides of which are intricately bedecked with more mosaics. The detailed features of this tomb make it one of the finest ancient tombs to be still standing. **KH**

Golden Temple (Amritsar, India)

The holiest site in Sikh history

Amritsar is the center of Sikh history and culture, and the Golden Temple is its most important religious site. In the early sixteenth century the first guru, Nanak, founded the new religion here, and under succeeding gurus, especially Arjan, the Sikh holy book, the *Adi Granth*, was compiled and the earliest temple was established to house it. Today the Golden Temple is the main place of pilgrimage for all Sikhs.

The three-story marble temple dates from the eighteenth century and was much influenced by late Mughal architecture. The colonnades, turrets, niches, balconies, parapets, and the central dome, in the

> *"The site has been a meditation retreat for wandering mendicants and sages since deep antiquity."*
>
> **Martin Gray, anthropologist**

shape of an inverted lotus, are all typical of contemporary mosques and palaces. Rather than having one entrance, there are doors and balconies open to all four directions, signifying the importance of acceptance in the Sikh religion. The exterior is gilded with gold leaf on the upper two levels; the interior is decorated with inlaid marble, carved woodwork, ivory mosaics, embossed gold and silver, and murals. Reached by a marble causeway, the temple stands in the middle of a massive rectangular tank, the Amrita Sarovar or Pool of Nectar, around which are offices, storerooms, a dining hall, kitchen, guesthouse, and watchtowers. There is also a prominent clock tower at the northern entrance, and to the west is the Ahal Takht, a domed building that serves as the seat of the supreme Sikh council. **LL**

Jama Masjid

(Mumbai, India)

The largest mosque in India

More than five thousand builders and craftsmen were involved in the construction of the Jama Masjid or "Friday Mosque"—also known as the Masjid-i-Jahanuma or "Mosque Commanding a View of the World." The largest mosque in India and the last great building to be erected by the seventeenth-century Mughal emperor Shah Jahan before he was imprisoned by his son Aurangzeb, it stands on a natural outcrop of rock and dominates the city.

The mosque has three huge gateways, four angle towers, and two minarets 130 feet (39 m) high built of red sandstone inlaid with strips of white marble. The approach to the mosque is via broad flights of steps that lead through gateways into a massive courtyard with a central basin and fountain. The eastern gateway was opened only for the emperor, and later for the governor-general. Massive doors are overlaid with brass arabesques. On the western side, the prayer hall is capped by three domes decorated with alternate stripes of black and white marble, with the top parts covered in gold. These are flanked by minarets. The domes rise above a facade of eleven bays, over which are tablets of white marble inlaid with inscriptions in black marble giving the history of the building and glorifying the reign and virtues of Shah Jahan.

The floor of the prayer hall imitates a Muslim prayer mat in black and white marble, with a thin black border divided into spaces for 899 worshippers. Fittingly, the present imam is a direct descendant of the imam appointed by Shah Jahan to inaugurate the mosque on July 23, 1656. **LL**

↗ A view towards the south, showing the gold-topped domes and one of the mosque's two minarets.

→ Indian Muslims gather for prayers in the mosque's main courtyard, which can hold 25,000 worshippers.

 # Red Fort

(Mumbai, India)

The complex of buildings reflects the creativity and prowess of Mughal architecture

> "A couplet inscribed in the palace reads, 'If there be a paradise on earth, it is here, it is here.'"
>
> UNESCO

Named for its warm, red, sandstone walls, which look almost on fire in the rays of the setting sun, this magnificent complex was built by Shah Jahan, the Mughal emperor with a passion for ambitious building projects. Shah Jahan had also conceived the Taj Mahal, and the Red Fort is another stunning example of Mughal architecture. The idea was that this fort would be the shah's own personal fortified paradise within the new city of Shahjahanabad that he created here. The fort's 1.5 miles (2.4 km) of towering turreted walls sheltered a whole variety of buildings, including luxurious palaces and apartments, royal baths, and richly decorated pavilions where the shah held private audiences or addressed the public, as well as tranquil landscaped gardens where fountains played. A wide moat (now dry) encircled the fort, fed by the nearby Yamuna River.

Today, entrance to the fort is via the massive Lahore Gate, leading into a vaulted souvenir shop arcade called Chatta Chowk, once filled with gossiping court ladies admiring the fine jewels and Persian carpets on sale. From here, there is easy access to the complex's other buildings. Highlights include the marble baths, the pretty marble Pearl Mosque, and the Diwan-i-Khas private pavilion. This pavilion has long lost its legendary Peacock Throne—jewel-encrusted and shaped like two fan-tailed peacocks—but retains some impressive decorative features. Throughout the fort are the lovely scalloped arches and *pietra dura* inlay work that lend such a strong Mughal character. Many of its extravagant treasures have disappeared, but this is still a highly atmospheric place, and one that resonates with history for the Indian people, making it a focal point for annual public events such as the prime minister's Independence Day speech and the Republic Day parade. **AK**

Qutb Minar Complex
(Mumbai, India)

The tallest brick minaret in the world is surrounded by a complex of historic buildings

The intriguing complex of structures known collectively as the Qutb Minar represents the arrival of organized Islam in the subcontinent and a radical change in the direction and form of Indian culture. The main minaret echoes the Minaret of Jam in construction, but stands taller at 240 feet (73 m). It was commissioned by the Turkish slave general, tasked by the Ghurid sultan Ghiyath al-Din, to commemorate his victories against the Hindus. Initially the Indian conquests fueled the rapid expansion of the Ghurid state and enriched its cities with tribute and booty.

The Ghurid sultan entrusted these rich domains, not to relatives who could become rivals for the throne, but to trusted warrior slaves who owed him personal loyalty. Slave soldiers summoned their families from the steppes of the north and a small but powerful Islamic community was created in the region of modern Delhi. The destruction of the Ghurid state during 1221 to 1222 left the slave generals without a master, and they quickly declared themselves sultans of Delhi. They were the first Islamic dynasty of India and laid the foundations for the successful Mughal State that followed.

Qutb Minar continues a practice of incorporating Hindu architecture as subservient pieces to Islamic construction. Here this includes the famed 23-foot- (7-m-) tall Iron Pillar that probably came from a Hindu or Jain temple in Bihar. The most intriguing aspect of this piece is the remarkable purity of the iron involved: 98 percent—once thought impossible to achieve using the technology of the day. The main complex was further enhanced by a variety of structures after its foundation, including royal tombs and *madrassas* (Koran schools) by both the sultans of the slave dynasty and later Mughal rulers keen to identify with the arrival of their Islamic heritage. **IS**

"An unfortunate hint of the factory chimney; white smoke ... would not seem out of place."

John Keay, historian

Jaisalmer Fort (Jaisalmer, India)

Strategically sited on a crucial trade route

The huge fortified city of Jaisalmer in Rajasthan rises from the sands of the Thar Desert (literally "Abode of Death"), which for centuries acted as a natural barrier between the Indus Valley and the fertile plains of the north. Founded by Prince Jaisal in 1156, the city became the new capital of the Bhatti Rajputs, one of the biggest and most feared tribes of Rajputs, after they moved from the more vulnerable Lodhruva. In the Middle Ages, Jaisalmer grew to be a major center for camel trains plying the flourishing trade routes from India to Egypt, Arabia, Persia, Africa, and Europe, while also controlling the way into northern India across the desert.

The fort, which is also known as Sonar Quila or the Golden Fort because of its color, stands on Trikuta Hill, at a height of some 250 feet (76 m). It is enclosed by an impressive crenellated sandstone wall 30 feet (9 m) high and reinforced with ninety-nine bastions (ninety-

two of these were built between 1633 and 1647 for use as gun platforms). From the beginning, a number of wells within the fort ensured a reliable water supply, making it possible for a large population to be maintained; even today a quarter of the old city's residents live inside the fort.

One of the most remote places in India, the city is a blend of Rajput and Islamic styles of architecture, untouched by European influences. Inside the monumental gateways of the fort are royal palaces, some with richly detailed murals and glass mosaics, as well as Jain temples and a number of mansions or *havelis* with delicately carved stone facades and balconies that belonged to noblemen and merchants. The substantial quantity of fine buildings and the superb quality of the workmanship, especially the stone carving, testify to the wealth and power that were concentrated here at one point. **LL**

Tiger Fort (Jaipur, India)

Part of a defensive ring to protect Jaipur

In 1727 Sawai Jai Singh II left his fortress at Amer and founded Jaipur, the fabled pink city of Rajasthan. Seven years later, on a ridge in the rugged Aravali Hills some 4 miles (6 km) to the northwest, he built the majestic Tiger or Nahargarh Fort. This, together with the forts at Amer and Jaigarh, completed a defensive ring to protect his new city.

In fact, the city of Jaipur never faced an attack from either the Mughals or the armies of other Rajput kingdoms, but during the Sepoy Revolt of 1857 the Tiger Fort served as a refuge for Europeans fleeing from the violence perpetrated by mutineers in neighboring states. It was then extended in 1868 before being transformed, in the 1880s, by Sawai Madho Singh into a summer retreat for the royal family. Each of the maharaja's nine wives had a two-story apartment decorated with exquisite frescoes and stucco work, built on three sides of a courtyard.

The maharaja's personal wing was built on the fourth. The style was Indian, with European features. The apartments were arranged so that the maharaja could visit any of his wives without the others knowing.

Legend has it that the site was haunted by the spirit of the long-dead Prince Nahar Singh; during construction, it would appear each day and destroy whatever had just been built. Prayers were offered, and fortunately the spirit was appeased when it was proposed that the fort be named Nahargarh. **LL**.

> *"Amer has a more feminine elegance to it, Nahargarh is steeped in masculine beauty."*

Preeti Sharma, travel writer

Palace of the Winds (Jaipur, India)

The most unusual, intricate, and eye-catching facade in the city

The Palace of the Winds or Hawa Mahal was built for Maharaja Sawai Pratap Singh in 1799 at a time when female members of the royal household observed very strict purdah. An extension of the main palace, it was constructed in such a way as to allow the women to observe everyday life on the streets outside while remaining out of sight.

Standing on a high platform adjoining the city wall, the palace looks like an enormous honeycombed screen with its symmetrical five-story facade, which rises to a height of 50 feet (15 m). It is built of the red and pink sandstone typical of many buildings in Jaipur, and is outlined with white borders and motifs that are painted in a lime wash. The facade contains 935 spectacular small windows arranged on a huge curve. Each of them has a beautifully carved projecting balcony and crowning arched roof with a hanging cornice. The openings are almost like peepholes,

partly blocked by fine plaster latticework, and would have provided a much-needed constant flow of air into the small chambers behind. The top three stories of the building are just a single room wide. There is an arched entrance to the west and this opens onto a courtyard surrounded by a two-story building on three sides; on the fourth, eastern, side the building rises an extra level. Interestingly, there are no stairs to reach the upper floors, only ramps. The lack of ornamentation in the chambers and the open areas of the interior are in striking contrast to the exterior, making it clear that the palace was never intended for residential use.

Sawai Pratap Singh was a great devotee of the Hindu deity Krishna, to whom he dedicated the palace, and it is said that the facade was designed to resemble the crown or *mukut* worn by the god. It is best viewed in the golden glow of sunrise. **LL**

Meherangarh Fort (Jodhpur, India)

A truly formidable fort that dominates its surrounding area

In 1459 Rao Jodha, the fifteenth Rathore ruler of Marwar, decided that he needed to move his capital from Mandore to somewhere that he could defend more easily. Work started right away on the fortifications of a new city 5 miles (9 km) to the south that would be named after him: Jodhpur.

One of the largest forts in India, the Meherangarh Fort stands on a range of sandstone hills 400 feet (122 m) above the inhospitable Thar Desert, dominating the surrounding area. Its imposing walls rise to a height of 120 feet (36 m), are 65 feet (20 m) wide in places, and incorporate 101 bastions. There are seven gates, and the spikes on the first were to deter attacks using elephants. The immense fortifications enclose a number of beautiful palaces that are renowned for their intricately carved stonework, beautiful filigree sandstone windows, and expansive interconnecting courtyards that provide much-

needed shade. The Moti Mahal (Pearl Palace) and Phool Mahal (Flower Palace) in particular have exquisitely painted ceilings and walls, whereas the Sheesh Mahal (Hall of Mirrors) has, as the name suggests, fine inlay and mirror decoration. The last ruler to live in the fort was the nineteenth-century maharaja Takhat Singh. He constructed a magnificent new residence, Takhat Vilas, in a blend of traditional and European styles. The paintings on the walls and the wooden ceiling beams range in subject from religious scenes to the Rathore sport of pig-sticking, and the works are still in good condition.

No one lives in the Meherangarh Fort any longer, but it still belongs to the maharaja of Jodhpur. The palaces now house a number of galleries displaying collections of Mughal artworks, folk musical instruments, turbans, armor, elephant howdahs, miniature paintings, furniture, and costumes. **LL**

Udaipur City Palace

(Udaipur, India)

Largest palace complex in Rajasthan

The beautiful white Udaipur City Palace, standing majestically on a crest overlooking the Pichola Lake, was originally built by Maharana Udai Singh of the Sisodia clan and was extended to its present form by subsequent rulers. It is the impressive centerpiece of what was once the capital of the Rajput kingdom of Mewar Udaipur.

The palace is built from granite and marble and was surrounded by fortified walls, incorporating medieval European and Chinese architecture in its buildings, hanging gardens, octagonal towers, fountains, and balconies with views across the lake toward the Lake Palace—its only real rival for splendor within the city. Most rooms have beautiful paintings, intricate glass work, mirror tiles, and colorful enamel. The main part of the palace houses a museum displaying a large and diverse array of artworks and artifacts, including an armory collection and examples of the infamous two-pronged sword.

The city of Udaipur, hemmed in by the lush hills of the Aravails, is one of the jewels of colorful Rajasthan, and this site is the state's largest palace complex. It is an intensely romantic setting steeped in fascinating history—visitors can go to the eight carved marble arches under which past rulers were weighed against gold and silver, the value of which was then distributed among the poor. According to one intriguing legend, the city's founder, Maharana Udai Singh, was hunting one day when he met and was blessed by a holy man meditating on a hill overlooking the lake, who advised him to build a palace at this spot. Now immortalized in popular Western culture, the city is also visited by James Bond fans because it was the setting for the film *Octopussy*. Like the Taj Mahal, Udaipur is a must-see historic site in the subcontinent. **AP**

Sabarmati Ashram

(Ahmedabad, India)

Center of Gandhi's independence movement

Having returned to India from South Africa six months earlier, Mohandas Gandhi established the Satyagraha Ashram with twenty-five followers on May 25, 1915. In July 1917 the group moved to a new site by the Sabarmati River, and it was there that the nonviolence movement that eventually led to independence from Britain was born.

Gandhi defined an ashram as "group life lived in a religious spirit," using the word "religious" in the broadest sense. Only a few simple rules were enforced: some (to be truthful, nonviolent, and chaste) were universally applicable; others (to undertake physical

> *"Earth provides enough to satisfy every man's need, but not every man's greed."*
>
> Mahatma Gandhi, statesman

work, eradicate untouchability, and practice fearlessness) were specific to Indian society.

On March 12, 1930, Gandhi left Sabarmati on the epic Dandi Salt March: a 240-mile journey (460-km) to protest against the salt tax imposed by Britain. His activities, civil disobedience in the eyes of the authorities, led to periods of imprisonment. Gandhi—now known as Mahatma, or Great Soul—said before the Salt March that he would never return to Sabarmati until India was independent. Sadly, although independence was achieved on August 15, 1947, he was assassinated on January 30, 1948, without seeing the ashram again. At Sabarmati there is now a museum devoted to the Mahatma's life, containing paintings, photographs, books, and letters. The cottage in which he lived, Hriday Kunj, is also preserved. **LL**

Khajuraho Temples

(Khajuraho, India)

Exquisite series of temples, best known for their erotic carvings

The architecture created during the Chandella dynasty (950–1050) is regarded as the pinnacle of Hindu temple building. Several of the temples at Khajuraho are dedicated to Shiva, the Hindu god of destruction and the favored god of the Chandella rulers. The Chandella dynasty was, however, tolerant of different belief systems, including other sects of Hinduism, as well as Jainism and Buddhism. Other gods who had temples built to them at Khajuraho include the Hindu deities Lord Brahma, Lord Vishnu, the sun god Surya Dev, and the goddess Kali, and the first Jain *tirthankara* or saint, Adinatha.

The temples have become famous for their erotic carvings and statues, including an 8-foot- (2.4-m-) high penis and, most controversially, for the scenes depicting sex between humans and animals. The most renowned shrines decorated with erotic sculptures are those known as the Hindu Lakshmana, Kandariya Mahadeva, Duladeo, and Devi Jagadambi, as well as the Jain Parshvanath temples. The *mithunas* or loving couples, and the *nayikas* or heroines, are depicted adopting sensual, yogic, and erotic postures. Religious scholars are divided between those who consider the sculptures to be spiritual and sacred, and those who consider them profane.

These temples were built according to the shastric tradition. They were usually constructed on a plinth and were composed of an entrance porch, hall, great hall, vestibule, and the main tower structure. Within the main tower is the inner sanctum, where an icon was lodged in the shrine or *garbhagriha* (womb chamber). The weather and history have taken their toll on this region, and of the original eighty-five temples constructed at the site, only twenty-two remain standing. In 1986, the Khajuraho Temples were added to the UNESCO World Heritage List. **SJ**

"The temples at Khajuraho … strike a perfect balance between architecture and sculpture."
UNESCO

Man Singh Palace (Gwalior, India)

A splendid palace built to royal excess

"When Man Singh built his palace, he rashly assumed eight wives were going to be sufficient."

Stanley Stewart, journalist

In the fifteenth century, the ruling Rajput clan, the Tomars, built a huge fort at Gwalior, with walls 35 feet (10 m) high and 2 miles (3 km) long. Described as "the pearl among the fortresses of India" by the Mughal emperor Babur, it completely dominates the surrounding area. Inside are numerous monuments, including six palaces, the most impressive of which is the Man Singh.

Known also as the Chit Mandir or Painted Palace for the richness of the ceramic mosaics decorating the outer walls, it was built by Raja Man Singh (who reigned from 1486 to 1516) with two stories above and two below ground. The southern facade has three round towers connected by latticework battlements and is richly ornamented: crocodiles holding lotuses between their heads, while their tails intertwine to form vases, are interspersed with emerald-green panels—men, elephants, tigers, peacocks, and trees are depicted in enameled tiles and mosaics of blue, green, and gold. The eastern facade, comprising a sheer sandstone wall, is punctuated by five round towers crowned by domed cupolas and linked by delicately carved parapets, covered in bright blue tiles. Inside the palace, two courtyards are surrounded by suites of rooms. The interior decoration of these rooms is mainly plain, but some do have elaborate ceilings. Iron rings on the ceilings, doors, and windows were used for hanging children's cots and also the screens behind which women of the palace would listen to Gwalior's musicians. In the circular chambers underground, royal prisoners were tortured and killed: The last sultan of Ahmednagar died here in 1600, as did Murad, brother of Emperor Aurangzeb, in 1661.

Gwalior Fort has had a turbulent and eventful past, changing hands many times. It witnessed fierce fighting in 1857 during the Indian Mutiny and the palace was significantly restored in 1881. **LL**

Fine Mughal fortress and palatial complex

In 1558 the Mughal emperor Akbar moved his headquarters from Delhi to Agra, which became the new capital of the Mughal Empire. He commissioned a great fortress to be built on a strategic bend in the Jumna River, as a symbol of his power; construction began in 1565 and was finished in 1571. The red sandstone used for the construction of the building quickly earned it the nickname of "the red fort." It is a perfect and beautiful example of Mughal architecture and one of the earliest remaining buildings from the Akbari period. During Akbar's time, the powerful fort was predominantly a military building, but by the time of his grandson Shah Jahan's reign it had evolved into a sumptuously regal residence, large enough to house the emperor's extensive court.

The beauty and sheer size of this monumental fortress are deeply impressive. Its walls encompass a number of buildings, including the picturesque Jahangir and Akbari palaces, which replicate the symbolic notion of Islamic paradise, with water sources dividing the courtyards. The fort contained private and public areas, including two stunning mosques, numerous prayer halls, exquisitely decorated rooms, and the *zenana*, a secluded area that housed the women's quarters.

The fort's ground plan was asymmetrical, laid out in a semicircle to complement the curve of the river, and there were three main entrances: the Water, the Akbari, and the Delhi gates. The extensive fortification was provided by a double defensive wall enclosure, which rises up to a height of 66 feet (20 m). The fort's blend of Hindu and Mughal decorations imparts a unique ambience. Mythical creatures, pavilions, Mughal vaulted arches, beams, flat roofs, ramparts, marble decorations, and terraces are all integrated harmoniously within the architecture and make this one of India's most stunning ancient sites. **SJ**

"[Agra is] full of gardens with running water, flowing … into reservoirs of jasper and marble."

Niccolao Manucci, seventeenth-century doctor

Taj Mahal (Agra, India)

India's most famous building was a labor of love by Emperor Shah Jahan

> *"[The Taj Mahal is] like a solitary tear suspended on the cheek of time."*
>
> Rabindranath Tagore, poet

↑ Shah Jahan, the emperor of India, built the Taj Mahal for his favorite wife, Mumtaz Mahal, pictured.

→ Although it belongs to a larger complex, the white mausoleum remains the most famous part of the Taj.

Only the worst cynic could fail to be moved by the beauty of the Taj, despite it being one of the world's most frequently photographed monuments. A 20,000-strong workforce labored for about twenty years to produce what is simultaneously a true wonder of the world, a major expression of Indian culture, and one man's tribute to his favorite wife. This man was the Indian Mughal emperor Shah Jahan. He conceived the lavish Taj Mahal complex as a mausoleum dedicated to his beloved wife of twenty years, Mumtaz Mahal, who died in childbirth.

Visitors approach the building via a monumental red sandstone gateway that hints at the treasures to come—one inscription here welcomes the faithful to paradise. The main domed mausoleum stands at the end of decorative gardens, reflected beautifully in a centrally placed watercourse. A massive vision in fine white marble, it seems to float against the open sky behind it—a deliberate effect.

Blinding white in the daytime heat, the marble glows red at sunset and blue in the moonlight. The four almost identical sides, the giant central dome—about 240 feet (73 m) high—four lesser corner domes, and four surrounding minarets form an essay in harmonious symmetry. The mausoleum's walls shimmer with *pietra dura*—incredibly delicate decoration traced with gems such as lapis lazuli and amethyst—and the special acoustics of its main dome make each musical note echo five times. Inside are the false tombs of the shah and his wife, placed over real ones buried beneath.

Its architecture, decoration, and Arabic calligraphy make this complex the finest example of Mughal art, fusing Indian, Persian, and Islamic influences. Other attractions include twin mosque buildings (placed symmetrically on either side of the mausoleum), lovely gardens, and a museum. **AK**

Emperor Akbar's Mausoleum (near Agra, India)

Dignified monument to the emperor

Akbar (1542–1605) was only fourteen years old when he succeeded his father, Humayun. He was illiterate but he patronized the arts in order to fill this void. He was ambitious, curious, and interested in legends and adventure stories, and spent most of his time hunting.

The emperor continued the *Akbarnama*—a true historical piece of evidence where the everyday life of the emperor at court has been described and illustrated with extremely realistic portraits. The architecture that the emperor commissioned was also represented in these illustrations. The architectural landscape dating from his reign is a mixture of Iranian and Indian elements, with Mughal conventions.

The mausoleum was elaborated by Akbar himself, but his son Jahangir completed the building in 1613. It is composed of two parts; the most impressive one is probably the large gate that leads to the mausoleum. The juxtaposition of the local red sandstone with the white marble is innovative, whereas the four minarets crowning the architecture are typically Islamic. The inner part of the main arch has a *mirhab* form. It is flanked by two other arches that mimic the shape. In the last terrace a cenotaph with the ninety-nine attributes of Allah has been carved out of a single block of marble. Unfortunately, the funerary chamber suffered from profanation in 1761 by the Jats. Although this room is now empty, the monument still represents Akbari wealth and power. **SJ**

> *"A monarch should be ever intent on conquest, lest his neighbours rise in arms against him."*
>
> Emperor Akbar

🏛 ◎ **Fatehpur Sikri** (near Agra, India)

One-time capital of the Mughal Empire and center of religious tolerance

As the name Fatehpur Sikri (City of Victory) indicates, this site commemorates victory in war. It was built to celebrate the triumph of the Mughal emperor Akbar over the sultan of Ahmedabad in Gujarat. Akbar also built the Red Fort at Agra and a royal road was constructed between these two sites. It was while the Red Fort was under construction that Akbar moved to Fatehpur Sikri, where he established his new capital from 1571 to 1585.

Akbar was a Muslim, but he did not insist that his people follow the same religion that he did. A remarkably tolerant ruler, he established in Fatehpur Sikri a place known as the House of Worship. Here, representatives from different religions gathered to discuss and debate theology. Akbar was inspired by this same spirit of tolerance when he planned the monuments of the city, and as a result the architecture at Fatehpur Sikri is a harmonious mixture of Hindu,

Buddhist, Jain, Christian, and Islamic decorations and techniques. The monuments of the complex include the Diwan-i-khas where Akbar used to address the public from the platform of the central pillar, and the largest congregational mosque in India, the lavishly decorated Jama Masjid. The compound boasts two magnificent main entrances: the Badshahi gate and the Buland gate. The latter is the most impressive, crowned by thirteen parapets or *chatris*.

In building Fatehpur Sikri, Akbar wanted to pay homage to Salim Christi, a holy man who had become his adviser. When Salim Christi died in 1572, Akbar ordered a grand mausoleum to be built in the city. Most of the architecture at Fatehpur Sikri is made from the local red sandstone, but Salim Chisti's mausoleum is of white marble to accentuate his holiness and to honor the emperor's spiritual guide. Fatehpur Sikri became a UNESCO World Heritage site in 1986. **SJ**

Vishwanath Temple (Varanasi, India)

Central place of worship in Hindu religion

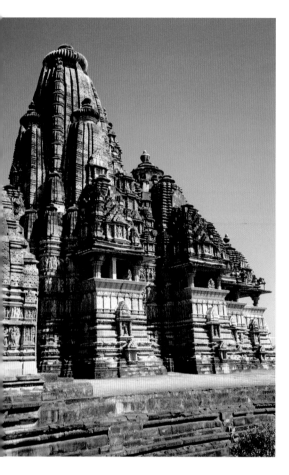

"I am the shark among the fishes and the Ganges among the rivers."

Bhagavad Gita (*c.* third century B.C.E.)

The Vishwanath Temple, which stands on the west bank of the River Ganges in the Hindu holy city of Varanasi, is one of India's most important temples. It is dedicated to Shiva, who has been worshipped here for hundreds of years in the form of Vishwanatha or Vishweshwara, "Ruler of the World." Hindu pilgrims continue to flock to the site to pay homage.

There were several earlier versions of the temple. The first large-scale reconstruction was sanctioned by the Mughal emperor Akbar in 1585, but his grandson Aurangzeb ordered its demolition in 1699 to provide materials for a new mosque that was being erected nearby. The present structure, which is popularly known as the Golden Temple because of the gold used in the plating of its spires and domes, is believed to have been built during the eighteenth century by Maharani Ahilya Bai Holkar of Indore.

The columns, beams, and walls are decorated with finely carved ornamentation. Inside the temple compound, which is hidden behind a wall and accessible only to Hindus, there are numerous smaller lingams (stylized phallic symbols representing the god Shiva) clustered around the principal object of worship—the smooth black stone lingam that stands 2 feet (0.6 m) high, is 3 feet (0.9 m) in circumference, and sits proudly on a silver pedestal. A series of lesser shrines, with more lingams and goddess images, can be found in the courtyard. An open colonnade to the north contains the Jnana Vapi or Wisdom Well, the water of which is commonly believed to be a liquid form of enlightenment.

According to Hindu philosophy, visiting the Vishwanath Temple and bathing in the River Ganges are important stages on the path to liberation or *moksha*; therefore devotees from all over the country make an effort to visit the city of Varanasi at least once in their lifetime. **LL**

Lucknow Residency (Lucknow, India)

The ruined complex is a national monument to the siege of Lucknow

Throughout the colonial period, Britain appointed officials known as residents to act as government representatives within the Indian states. The Lucknow Residency, built by Saadat Ali Khan, the Nawab of Oudh, was to become the focus of the epic siege and relief of Lucknow in 1857, during the series of armed uprisings against British colonial authority that took place between 1857 and 1858.

Oudh was annexed by the British in 1856, causing considerable resentment. In 1857 it was decided to fortify the residency complex at the capital, Lucknow. Chief Commissioner Henry Lawrence had about 1,500 troops, half of them loyal sepoys (Indian private soldiers under British command), and the same number of civilians to protect. A strong rebel force attacked on July 1 and Lawrence died three days later. The defenders held out in appalling conditions against a force five times their number while the hurriedly fortified residency was blasted around them. Every building changed use: The treasury served as an arsenal; the banqueting hall became a hospital; Dr. Fayer's House, a large single-story structure with rooms underground, sheltered the women and children. A relief force under the leadership of Henry Havelock fought its way through on September 25, but was unable to evacuate those inside. Instead, they joined the trapped garrison and waited for help. This came on November 16, when troops led by Colin Campbell stormed the Secundra Bagh, a walled enclosure that barred the way to the residency.

Now a national monument, the once elegant residency serves as a museum commemorating the events of 1857, complete with a model of the original residency, old photographs, paintings, and period weapons. The structure remains in its battle-scarred condition, its ruined tower appearing exactly as it did at the end of the siege. **LL**

"Put on my tomb only this; Here lies Henry Lawrence who tried to do his duty."

Inscription on Henry Lawrence's gravestone

🏛️ ◎ Mahabodhi Temple (Bodh Gaya, India)

One of the four most important sites for Buddhists

Before the Buddha died, he summoned his disciples to remember the four important places where major events took place in his life. Among these places was Bodh Gaya. As with other religions, the topographical element has its place in Buddhism. Indeed, according to a specific time period and geographic coordinates, a site can become a pilgrimage center. This is the case for Bodh Gaya, believed to be where the Buddha Shakyamuni reached enlightenment in the seated position on the diamond throne, with his hands touching the earth beneath the Bo tree, or sacred fig.

The worshipping of the tree is not exclusive to Buddhism; it has been a folk tradition since the Indus Valley civilization. Every consequent event in the Buddha's life occurred in the presence of a different type of tree. The diamond throne and a reconstitution of the sacred tree are found at Bodh Gaya at the west corner of the temple. Although the dating of the Mahabodhi temple is contested, it is believed that it was erected during the fifth or sixth century. In the nineteenth century the British had it rebuilt.

The temple is oriented eastward in the direction of the rising sun. The original railing leading to the temple where pilgrims circumambulate is believed to date from the second-century Shunga dynasty. Initially, the decorations depicting the life of the Buddha were not in anthropomorphic form. Instead, Buddhist symbols such as the stupa, the wheel, the empty throne, or the royal umbrella were used to imply the dedication of the shrine to the Great Lord. Nonetheless, the emergence of the iconic period converted the reliefs into images of the Buddha in his human form and his incarnations were also portrayed. By the sixth century the multiplicity of the Buddha images enshrined in niches and mini stupas had grown tremendously. **SJ**

🏛 ◉ Himalayan Mountain Railway (Darjeeling, India)

A remarkable feat of engineering that opened up mountainous terrain

At a height of 7,000 feet (2,200 m), Darjeeling is renowned for the grandeur of its scenery and the stunning views it provides of the snowcapped eastern Himalayas. In the nineteenth century it was one of the most famous hill stations in India, serving as the summer headquarters of the government of Bengal, but rail connections from Calcutta reached only as far as Siliguri, at the foot of the Himalayas, and from there the journey had to be undertaken by cart road.

In 1878 Franklin Prestage, an agent of the Eastern Bengal Railway Company, proposed to the government that a steam tramway be built from Siliguri to Darjeeling and, after a feasibility study, his proposal was accepted in 1879. Gillander Arbuthnot & Company of Calcutta began construction work the same year and on July 4, 1881, the Darjeeling Himalayan Railway was officially opened. Nicknamed the "Toy Train," the 24-inch (610-cm) narrow-gauge railway initially followed the line of the road, but it soon became apparent that the gradient was too steep in places, so in 1882 four loops and reverses were added. The original carriages were small four-wheeled trolleys with canvas roofs and two wooden benches for seats, but these were later replaced. Likewise, the original engine, capable of pulling loads of only about 7 tons, was replaced to allow loads up to five times as heavy.

Still operational today, despite damage from land slips and earthquakes over the years, this passenger railway is an outstanding example of bold, ingenious engineering solutions to the problem of establishing an effective rail link through rugged, mountainous terrain. The Darjeeling Himalayan Railway, which was previously inscribed on the World Heritage List, is now part of the Mountain Railways of India UNESCO World Heritage site. **LL**

Dakshineswar Kali Temple (Kolkata, India)

Ramakrishna promoted religious harmony

The majestic Dakshineswar Temple sits on the east bank of the Hooghly River, a distributary of the Ganges. The presiding deity is Bhavatarini, an aspect of the goddess Kali, but this is a pilgrimage site for both Hindus and members of other religions, too, largely because of the temple's association with Ramakrishna Paramahansa, who was the priest here for thirty years in the nineteenth century.

According to legend, in 1847 the wealthy widow Rani Rasmani was preparing to go by boat from Calcutta to the sacred city of Banaras in order to worship the Divine Mother. The night before she planned to leave, the Divine Mother appeared to her in a dream as Kali, telling her that there was no need to go to Banaras. Instead, she should erect the goddess's statue in a beautiful temple on the banks of the Ganges and arrange for her worship there. Profoundly affected, Rasmani purchased 25 acres (10 ha) of land and work began immediately. The resulting complex, which is 46 feet (14 m) square and rises to more than 100 feet (30 m), has at its center a nine-spired temple to Kali, but there are also twelve other temples dedicated to Shiva and Radha-Krishna. Rasmani spent a fortune on construction and yet more money on the consecration ceremony, which took place on May 31, 1855. When Ramkumar, the first priest, died within the year, responsibility passed to his younger brother, Ramakrishna Paramahansa.

Convinced of the transitory nature of worldly matters, this important Hindu religious teacher, who was also an influential figure in the nineteenth-century Bengal Renaissance, emphasized the harmony of all religions. The continuing popularity of his ideas means that his room, in the northwestern corner of the courtyard, beyond the last of the Shiva temples, is one of the most visited parts of the temple complex. **LL**

Victoria Memorial (Kolkata, India)

Monument to British rule in India

The Victoria Memorial was conceived by Lord Curzon as a fitting monument to Queen Victoria. He organized funding for the project from within India and commissioned one of the leading British architects of the day. After lengthy construction work, the building was formally opened on December 28, 1921.

A majestic white marble edifice situated in the middle of 64 acres (25 ha) of sprawling gardens, the Victoria Memorial dominates the center of the city. Architecturally, it seems to reflect contemporary British civic classicism, but there are deliberate Eastern references as well. The marble comes from the same

> *"Let us have a building, stately . . . and grand, to which every newcomer in Calcutta will turn."*
>
> Lord Curzon, governor-general of India (1899–1905)

Makrana quarries in Jodhpur that were used for the construction of the Taj Mahal, and the corner domes are faintly Mughal in style. The whole composition is crowned by a bronze statue of Victory that stands 16 feet (4.8 m) high; though not a true weather vane, it rotates when the wind is strong enough. The sides of the memorial are linked by open colonnades and in the south entrance, approached through a triumphal archway commemorating Edward VII, there is a statue of Lord Curzon himself. The entrance hall contains bronze busts and marble statues of royal figures, and the walls are decorated with murals showing scenes from Queen Victoria's life and texts from her imperial proclamations. The interior rooms display important collections of paintings, sculpture, artifacts, books, and manuscripts, all relating to royalty and empire! **LL**

(Konârak, India)

Even in its ruined state the temple is a magnificent representation of the sun god's chariot

Konârak is a thirteenth-century Hindu temple dedicated to the sun god Surya. It is the pinnacle of Hindu Orissan architecture and is unique in terms of its sculptural innovations and the quality of its carvings. According to textual evidence, it is believed that King Narasimha (who reigned between 1238 and 1264) of the Eastern Ganga dynasty commissioned the temple. This is plausible as secular events are also depicted on the reliefs of Konârak. The shrine may have been built to celebrate the military victory of Narasimha over the Muslims. In this way, the king legitimized his right to rule as though appointed by the gods.

The plan of Konârak was composed of three sections in a row: a main shrine is connected to an entrance and prayer hall; in front of this, and separate from it, is a pillared dance hall. Decorating the exterior of the joined shrine and entrance hall are twelve pairs of large wheels—together, the two buildings represent the chariot of Surya. The statues of seven galloping horses used to draw the chariot, but now only one horse remains well preserved. Between the wheels, two friezes with amorous couples, dancing girls, and nymphs separated by pilasters decorate the lower reliefs of the temple. The function of erotic sculptures on a religious temple is unclear; however, one can deduce that the reasons were auspicious and that they were intended to avert evil.

The temple, like many other Hindu examples, is raised off the ground on a plinth to emphasize its holiness. The roof and superstructure of the main sanctuary, which reached a height of 227 feet (69 m), no longer exists; it collapsed in the nineteenth century. The entrance hall retains its pyramidal roof structure, but cannot be entered because the entire building was filled with stone and sand in the nineteenth century to ensure it did not also collapse. **SJ**

"One of the most stupendous buildings ... a pile of overwhelming grandeur even in its decay."

Earl of Ronaldshay, *India: A Bird's-Eye View* (1931)

🏛 ◉ Ajanta Caves (near Jalgaon, India)

The caves contain paintings and sculptures that are masterpieces of Buddhist art

During the first or second century B.C.E., caves began to appear at Ajanta in the district of Maharashtra in western India. The caves were deliberately carved out of the rock and divided into prayer halls, or *chaitya*, and monastic cells, or *vihara*. Already of great significance in the Buddhist world, the caves grew to further prominence between the third and sixth century C.E., when their location became part of an important trade route. Huge numbers of pilgrims, traders, artisans, and craftsmen traveled along the route, and Ajanta became an area where ideas and news were exchanged, thus aiding the spread of Buddhism beyond the Indian subcontinent.

The site of Ajanta was rediscovered in 1819 by two British soldiers on a hunting expedition; the caves had been forgotten for centuries and were amazingly well preserved. Two distinct phases can be seen in the style of the paintings, sculptures, and frescoes of Ajanta. The early phase dates from *c.* 200 B.C.E. and the later phase from the Classical age of the Gupta dynasty (from the fourth to sixth century C.E.). Although Ajanta was patronized by Hindu courts, the site itself remains Mahayana Buddhist and includes a number of giant carved representations of the Buddha and of the Bodhisattva.

Secular and historic events are also depicted in the beautiful wall paintings, and there was a distinct attempt at realism by the artists. The carvings and paintings of people demonstrate Classical Guptan conventions: the linear treatments of the human body, the narrow waists, the long black hair, the idealized shapes of the women, the full lips, the slender nose, and the lotus eyes. Visiting Ajanta is an unforgettable experience: The rock-cut caves are strongly evocative and seem designed to guide visitors along a spiritual, as well as cultural, journey. **SJ**

🏛 ◉ Ellora Caves (near Aurangabad, India)

The complex is an example of the religious tolerance of ancient Indian civilizations

The Ellora caves created in the Deccan Plateau have architectural similarities with other caves in the central Deccan region; they include thirty-four temples and monasteries dedicated to Buddhism, Hinduism, and Jainism. The Buddhist and Jain monasteries tend to be constructed on several stories and are divided into prayer halls and monastic cells. The Buddhist caves are decorated with Buddhas, Bodhisattvas, mother goddesses, musicians, nymphs, guardian figures, and animals sculpted out of the rock. Plaster and natural pigments were used to embellish the icons. One of the most impressive structures (Cave 10) is laid out in a horseshoe shape, and contains a pillared hall leading to a colossal seated Buddha enshrined in a stupa.

During the ninth century, five Jain temples were constructed, including the magnificent Chota Kailash temple (Cave 16), the largest known rock-cut temple in the world. A sculpture of the seated Jain lord Mahavira Tirthankara is preserved in the Assembly Hall of Indra (Cave 32), one of the most stunning examples of Jain architecture in India.

The Hindu caves differ from the Jain and Buddhist caves by having higher ceilings and more variety of decorations and icons. Dating from the eighth century, the Hindu Kailasanatha temple attempts to replicate Mount Kailasha (the abode of Shiva and Parvati). The sixth-century Rameshvara cave-temple displays a relief of the demon Ravana shaking Mount Kailasha in order to annoy Shiva and Parvati. Although the Ellora caves were created for three different religions, the style of the decorations, the structure of the architecture, and the symbolism of these monuments are analogous. The caves functioned as an area of meditation and helped the diffusion of these three religions. Images were, and arguably still are, the best way to communicate ideas. **SJ**

Gateway of India (Mumbai, India)

Mumbai's most famous monument

Situated on the Apollo Bunder overlooking the Arabian Sea, the Gateway of India was designed to commemorate the visit in 1911 of King George V and Queen Mary, who had been en route to the durbar being held in Delhi to celebrate their coronation as emperor and empress of India.

The foundation stone was laid on March 31, 1913, by the governor of Bombay, Sir George Sydenham Clarke, with architect George Wittet's designs finally being approved in August 1914. Between 1915 and 1919 a stretch of land along the harbor front was reclaimed from the sea, and it was here that the gateway and a new sea wall were built. The foundations were completed the following year and construction was finished in 1924. Built of honey-colored basalt, the gateway is a conventional triumphal arch in concept, but architecturally it is Indo-Saracenic in style, modeled on sixteenth-century Gujarati work. This absorption of Mughal influences was consciously done, with a view to suggesting the link with earlier rulers and thus conveying the legitimacy of British colonial rule. Intricate latticework decorates the walls, and four turrets surround an imposing central dome that is 50 feet (15 m) in diameter and rises to 85 feet (26 m) high. Side chambers and halls were added to accommodate civic receptions. The building was opened to the public on December 4, 1924, by the viceroy of India, the Earl of Reading.

Within a generation, this grand symbol of empire also became an epitaph, when the last British regiment to leave India after independence in 1947, the First Battalion of the Somerset Light Infantry, passed through the gateway before finally setting sail for home on February 28, 1948. Today it is one of India's most popular tourist sites. **LL**

Chhatrapati Shivaji Terminus (Mumbai, India)

Indian and British architectural styles are evident in this unique and ornate building

The mighty Chhatrapati Shivaji Terminus in Bombay, now Mumbai, presents many visitors with their first impression of the huge metropolis, yet it is by no means typical of Indian architecture. To understand its colossal scale and ambition, the palatial structure must be read as a centerpiece of what for more than a century was the most important nation in the British Empire. Its English architect, Frederick Williams Stevens, toured Europe for several months looking for inspiration, and similarities with many stations on the continent are not coincidental. However, Italianate Gothic Revival architecture is forcefully blended with traditional Indian domes, turrets, and pointed arches to create a fusion style that accurately represented nineteenth-century Bombay's role as the country's gateway to the West, and it continues to do so as the city westernizes as quickly as any other in this fast-growing, emerging economy. Internally, the ornamental railings, woodcarving, tiles, balustrades, and other ornaments owe much to students of the Bombay School of Art.

Despite the current national policy of replacing place and town names that derive from the British Empire with Indian names, Chhatrapati Shivaji Terminus is still popularly referred to as V. T., short for Victoria Terminus. The station is Mumbai's main commuter hub, and rush hour encapsulates the city's chaotic yet dynamic feel. Travelers cram on to the trains, even sitting on luggage racks, as they are drawn from outer suburbs to jobs downtown. Separate carriages for women and men may seem like an archaic throwback, but the proximity to fellow passengers is far beyond what can be witnessed on the London Underground or Tokyo Metro. Visit the terminus for an architectural snapshot of the British Empire at its grandest. **AP**

Qutb Shahi Tombs

(near Golconda, India)

Royal tombs of almost an entire dynasty

Golconda was a famous fort and commercial center in the thirteenth and fourteenth centuries—it had been described as a flourishing city by Marco Polo as early as 1292—but it was only with the emergence of the Qutb Shahi sultans in the sixteenth century that it became a dynastic capital.

The royal tombs are located in a landscaped garden to the northwest of the fort and the entire dynasty was buried here, apart from two members who died in exile. The construction of each tomb was personally supervised by the sultan during his lifetime. The style of Islamic funerary architecture is distinctive: Each tomb has an onion-shaped dome resting on a cube with decorated minarets at the corners, surrounded by a richly ornamented arcade. Many of the larger tombs are two stories high. Built of local granite and plaster, they stand on a raised platform reached by flights of steps and were originally faced in enamel or glazed green and turquoise tiles that were inscribed with verses from the Koran. The first sultan to be buried here, Ibrahim Quli Qutb Shah (who reigned from 1512 to 1543), was murdered by his son at the age of ninety. His black tombstone is engraved in the finest Persian calligraphy.

The most spectacular tomb, standing more than 180 feet (55 m) high, including its 60-foot- (18-m-) high dome, belongs to Muhammad Quli Qutb Shah, the founder of Hyderabad. The tombs once contained interior decorations of carpets, chandeliers, and velvet canopies on silver poles. Golden spires were fitted on the sarcophagi of the sultans to distinguish them from those of other less important members of the royal family. During the Qutb Shahi period, the numerous royal tombs were held in such great veneration that criminals who took refuge here were automatically granted pardon. **LL**

Charminar

(Hyderabad , India)

Remarkable for its size and beauty

Built in 1591 by Muhammad Quli Qutb Shah, Charminar is an outstanding monument set in the heart of Hyderabad in southern India. It was originally built to commemorate the end of a ferocious plague, but today it has become one of the most important landmarks of the city. Legend has it that the emperor Quli Qutb Shah chose to build Charminar as a result of a promise he made in a prayer. He vowed that if the plague that was then raging through the city were brought to an end, he would build a mosque at the site on which he was standing. When the plague ended, the emperor fulfilled his oath and built the

> *"These minarets may symbolize the first four khalifs of Islam, but I cannot vouch for this."*
>
> Mir Moazzam Husain, historian

mosque. It took the name Charminar as a reference to its four distinctive minarets.

Charminar is a stunning, square monument that is expansive in both width and height. In fact, it is so large that it dominates the surrounding city. It is 65 feet (20 m) wide on each side, and within each of these sides stand giant arches 36 feet (11 m) wide and 65 feet (20 m) tall. The detail of the carving is phenomenal. The granite and lime-mortar has been so delicately wrought that the finish is almost lacelike, and the four minarets, which protrude from the corners of the monument, are prime examples of this. They are utterly beautiful and, at a height of 160 feet (48 m), awe inspiring in their vastness. The architectural specifications and the artful blend of styles, from Cazia to Islamic architecture, are simply breathtaking. **KH**

Church of Bom Jesus
(Old Goa, India)

This excellent example of Baroque architecture houses the remains of St. Francis Xavier

Old Goa, the original capital of the former Portuguese colony of Goa, once rivaled Lisbon in size and splendor, though it is now little more than a village. It was the first Christian colony in the Indies and in 1565 could boast a healthy population of 200,000. However, malaria and cholera epidemics ravaged the city in the seventeenth century and it was then largely abandoned, so that by 1775 the population had fallen to a mere 1,500.

The huge Church of Bom Jesus (Good Jesus) is also known as the Church of St. Francis Xavier because the saint, who was based in Goa from 1542, is buried here. Erected in 1594 and consecrated in 1605, the church is a superb example of Renaissance Baroque architecture in India. Cruciform in plan, it combines Ionic, Doric, Corinthian, and composite styles. Three elegant entrances are surmounted by three large rectangular windows, then three smaller circular windows, culminating in a richly carved central gable. The chapel and tomb of St. Francis Xavier—a pupil of St. Ignatius Loyola, founder of the Jesuits—lie on the south side of the transept. The ornate tomb was a gift from Grand Duke Cosimo III of Tuscany. Carved by Giovanni Battista Foggini, it took ten years to complete and was erected in 1698. The silver casket containing St. Francis's remains is a magnificent hybrid of Italian and Indian art. When the saint's body was transferred here a year after his death it was said to be "as fresh as the day it was buried." St. Francis is credited with miraculous healing powers, and his body is displayed to the faithful on the anniversary of his death, December 2, every ten years (next due in 2014), attracting pilgrims from far and wide.

The Church of Bom Jesus is just one of the group of "Churches and Convents of Goa" listed as a World Heritage site in 1986. **LL**

"Let us work . . . with heartfelt conviction that we are doing nothing, and God everything."

St. Ignatius Loyola, founder of the Jesuits

Vijayanagara

(Hampi, India)

This ruined city was once a prosperous and much-admired Hindu capital

> *"In this city you will find men belonging to every nation, because of the great trade."*
>
> Domingo Paez, sixteenth-century traveler

Between the fourteenth and sixteenth century the now ruined city of Vijayanagara (City of Victory), just south of the Tungabhadra River near Hampi, was the largest and most powerful Hindu capital in the Deccan. Its fabulously rich kings built temples and palaces that were admired far and wide. The Persian ambassador Abdu'r-Razzaq, who visited in 1443, declared that nothing existed to equal it anywhere in the world. Muslims and Europeans were welcomed in this cultured and cosmopolitan environment, and yet within a six-month period in 1565 the city was overrun and pillaged by a force led by the four Muslim sultans of the Deccan, and then abandoned.

The site is spread over 9 square miles (25 sq km) but most of the monuments are grouped in two distinct areas: The Sacred Center, with temples, *gopuras*, and *ghats*, is concentrated around Hampi; to the south, within a ring of massive fortifications, is the Royal Center, with the remains of palaces, pavilions, elephant stables, guard houses, and more temples. Between the two run ancient canals that formed part of the original irrigation system. On the plains to the south of the Royal Center are the city's suburbs, where there is evidence of a system of concentric protective walls. Gateways are located along the roads leading into the urban center.

The historical importance of the monuments, which bear exceptional testimony to the vanished civilization of Vijayanagar, led to Hampi being designated a World Heritage site in 1986. However, it is also considered a sacred site, the location of the monkey god Hanuman's kingdom. This legendary association, which extends to the identification of specific places mentioned in the Sanskrit epic *Ramayana*, would have influenced the people who originally designed and constructed the city. **LL**

Daria Daulat Bagh

(Srirangapatnam, India)

Tipu Sultan's favorite palace

Srirangapatnam, an island in the Cauvery River, was the capital of Mysore under the rule of the eighteenth-century rajas Haidar Ali and his son Tipu Sultan, or Sultan Fateh Ali Tipu, who was also known as the Tiger of Mysore. Between them, they managed to transform the small state of Mysore into a major Muslim power devoted to driving the British out of India.

The Daria Daulat Bagh is a two-story summer palace built by Tipu Sultan beyond the eastern wall of the city's fort in the midst of landscaped gardens stocked with plants from all over India. The Indo–Islamic structure, made largely of teak, stands on a raised platform 5 feet (1.5 m) high, and every inch of the walls, ceilings, and arches is covered in rich arabesque detail. There is a central hall where Tipu Sultan is said to have received ambassadors and guests. The outer walls were painted with battle scenes and portraits, whereas the interior walls were decorated with scrolls of foliage and floral patterns in geometrical designs. An avenue of cypress trees leads from an intricately carved gateway to the Gumbaz mausoleum. Built at the same time as the palace, the mausoleum was the burial place of both Haidar Ali and Tipu Sultan.

After the fall of Srirangapatnam to the British in 1799, the Daria Daulat Bagh palace was occupied by Colonel Arthur Wellesley, later the Duke of Wellington, who ordered its restoration, in particular the repainting of the murals adorning the outer walls. This included a lively—and unflattering—work depicting Haidar Ali's victory over Colonel Baillie at Pollilore in September 1780, which was later whitewashed over. The palace has been converted into a museum housing a small collection of Tipu Sultan's personal belongings, together with European paintings and Persian manuscripts. **LL**

Palace of Mysore

(Mysore, India)

Fairy-tale palace and official royal residence

The city of Mysore in southern India is home to a number of palaces, but when people talk of the Palace of Mysore, they are referring to the jewel in the crown that is the Amba Vilas. The sprawling three-story, gray granite, Indo-Saracenic building is capped by a five-story tower that culminates in a gilded dome, but perhaps what is most surprising to Western eyes is the cows grazing happily among the lush gardens and twelve Hindu temples that also make up the complex. The population of Mysore is predominantly Hindu, and sacred cows can roam freely, even on royal turf. The site's history is closely linked to that of the royal

> ## "You'll be hard-pressed to find an undecorated section of wall or ceiling."
>
> *Frommer's Review*

family of the former kingdom of Mysore, the Wodeyar dynasty. The family ruled the area from 1399, when they first lived in a palace at Mysore, and the city became the kingdom's capital in 1799.

The first recorded mention of a palace on the current site was in 1638. In 1793 Tipu Sultan is said to have knocked down the palace to make way for the new city of Nazarbadh, and he replaced the old building with a wooden structure. But the palace was burned to the ground in 1897 during wedding festivities. The then queen regent commissioned British-Indian architect Henry Irwin to design a new palace, and work was completed in 1912. After India's independence in 1947, the palace fell into state ownership, although part has been given over to the descendants of the former maharajas. **CK**

Brihadisvara Temple

(Tanjore, India)

Outstanding example of the architectural and artistic techniques of the Chola empire

Tanjore or Thanjavur came to prominence under the Chola kings, who ruled in southern India from the ninth to the thirteenth century and established one of their capitals here. The Brihadisvara Temple, a royal foundation inaugurated by Rajaraja I, is widely considered to be the crowning architectural achievement of the period.

This Hindu temple stands in the middle of a large rectangular courtyard containing other smaller shrines. It is entered from the east via two *gopuras*—pyramidal gateways with vaulted roofs. Chola sculptures remain on the upper stories, and carvings on the lower levels illustrate a number of different episodes from the life of Shiva, the principal god worshipped here. The main tower of the temple, the *vimana*, rises in thirteen diminishing stories to an impressive 215 feet (65 m) high. In the middle of the walls on each side are doorways flanked by huge guardian figures bearing clubs. Niches contain images of deities, mostly though not exclusively Shiva. Two massive blocks of granite, together weighing some 80 tons, form an octagonal domelike roof, whereas the walls of the *vimana* are inscribed with information about the origins and construction of the temple, together with details of the endowments made by Rajaraja and his family. The most prominent of the king's gifts was the gilded finial still visible at the very top of the tower. Inside the *vimana* a colossal lingam 12 feet (3.6 m) high, representing Shiva, is raised on a circular pedestal, and sculptures and paintings of the god adorn the walls and ceiling.

The Brihadisvara Temple was inscribed on UNESCO's World Heritage List in 1987, together with the Temple of Gangaikondacholisvaram and the Airavatesvara Temple at Darasuram, under the heading of "Great Living Chola Temples." **LL**

> *"A sculptor's dream, a historian's mine, . . . a sociologist's scoop, a painter's delight, all rolled in one."*
>
> B. Venkataraman, writer

Meenakshi Amman Temple (Madurai, India)

Temple of Meenakshi and Sundareswarar

According to Hindu legend, the god Shiva came to Madurai in the form of Sundareswarar to marry the daughter of the Pandya ruler, Meenakshi, a manifestation of the goddess Parvati. The Meenakshi Amman Temple is dedicated to their union.

The massive temple is enclosed by high walls entered through soaring *gopuras* or towers. Inside are colonnades, columned *mandapas* or halls (some were used for shops, storerooms, and stables), a sacred tank, lesser shrines, and, at the center, the two main shrines to Sundareswarar and Meenakshi. The *gopuras* are some of the most elaborately decorated in India: Brightly painted, they are completely covered with figures of divinities, celestial beings, monster masks, guardians, and animal mounts. The tallest of the twelve, the southern *gopura*, rises to more than 170 feet (50 m). Within the temple complex is the magnificent Aiyaram Kaal Mandapa (Thousand Pillar Hall), which in fact contains 985 columns carved with divinities, female musicians, and attendant figures. The Pottamarai Kulam (Golden Lily Tank), a large pool where devotees can bathe in holy water, is surrounded by a colonnade whose walls are decorated with murals depicting the miracles Shiva performed in Madurai. A doorway in the west wall leads to the Meenakshi shrine. This stands in its own enclosure, within which are several subsidiary shrines, together with the bedchamber, where the image of Sundareswarar is brought every night from its own shrine.

This is a living temple. Every week golden figures of Meenakshi and Sundareswarar are seated on a swing and hymns are sung; at the annual Teppa festival their images are mounted on floats and pulled back and forth over water; and the goddess's wedding festival is celebrated each year for twelve days in the month of Chaitra (April/May). **LL**

Cellular Jail (Port Blair, Andaman Islands, India)

Scene of the torture of political prisoners

Port Blair is named after Lieutenant Archibald Blair of the British East India Company, who unsuccessfully tried to establish a colony here in 1789. It was not until 1858 that the British occupied the site again, this time as a penal colony in the aftermath of the Sepoy Uprising. Indian revolutionaries were deported from the mainland—some 850 miles (1,370 km) to the west—to the Andaman Islands and made to clear land to build their own prison, before being incarcerated there. As the freedom movement in India continued to grow, the British decided it was necessary to build a new jail, and toward the end of the nineteenth century

> "Cellular Jail stood mute witness to the tortures meted out to the freedom fighters."
>
> Onkar Singh, journalist

work began on a large circular building to house the ever-increasing numbers of political prisoners.

The Cellular Jail overlooks the sea from a small hill in the northeast of the town. It originally comprised seven wings of puce-colored brick, three of which remain, the rest having been destroyed by the Japanese during World War II. The wings branched out like the spokes of a wheel from a central turreted tower. Each was three stories high, with cells on the first three floors and a watchtower on the fourth. In total there were 698 cells, and here prisoners could be held in solitary confinement. Frequent executions took place in full view of the cells.

The jail, which continued in operation until 1945, was declared a national monument in 1979. It suffered some structural damage in the tsunami of 2004. **LL**

🏛 ◎ Sacred City of Anuradhapura (Anuradhapura, Sri Lanka)

An ancient capital city, dating back to the fifth century B.C.E.

Founded in the fifth century B.C.E., Anuradhapura went on to become the great capital city of Sri Lanka (formerly Ceylon) for around 1,400 years.

A thriving royal center, Anuradhapura reached a spiritual peak when it became home to what was believed to be a major Buddhist relic. This was supposedly a cutting from the Bo tree at Bodh Gaya (Bihar state, India), beneath which Gautama Buddha was said to have become "enlightened." The cutting was brought to Anuradhapura in the third century B.C.E. by Sanghamitta, a leading Buddhist missionary. Today an ancient fig tree, growing among the remains of the once-thriving city, is said to have grown from that precious cutting.

The kings of ancient Anuradhapura presided over a wonderful era for the arts, commissioning stunning sculptures, palaces, monasteries, temples, beautiful gardens, and massive *dagobas*. These are rounded

stupas—Buddhist shrines often built to house sacred relics. Those at Anuradhapura are made from sun-baked bricks.

Anuradhapura became the center of a sophisticated culture spread over a wide area and developed into a major force in this part of Asia. By the eleventh century, the city had been invaded from southern India, so the capital was moved elsewhere, and Anuradhapura was gradually swallowed up by jungle. In the 1800s the city was rediscovered, after which Buddhist pilgrims began flocking there. Preservation work has been ongoing ever since and today it is the most famous of Sri Lanka's ancient remains. There is a modern city at Anuradhapura, situated on a major arterial road. During the 1900s, some of the newer city was moved in order to help preserve the ancient quarter and today these remains form one of the world's major archeological sites. **AK**

 ◎ **Gal Vihara** (Polonnaruwa, Sri Lanka)

A kingdom that once harbored true religious harmony

The great stone Buddhas of Polonnaruwa, perhaps the finest in Sri Lanka, represent a time when religious harmony was forged from squabbling sects and peace came, at least for a while, to a war-torn kingdom.

Parakrama Bahu, who came to the Sinhalese throne in 1153, spent the first decade of his reign quelling his enemies, but was then able to focus on enriching his capital, Polonnaruwa. Among the range of religious complexes that grew up around the city was Gal Vihara, also called the "Northern Monastery." The temple's brick and timber enclosures are long gone, but its beautiful representations of the Buddha survive, carved into the southern face of a single granite rock 168 feet (51 m) long. A porchlike shrine hewn from the granite shelters the smallest Buddha and to the left of the shrine is a large seated Buddha, attended by Tantric symbols. Most memorable, however, are the carved figures on the right. The

solemn figure standing 23 feet (7 m) tall is the oldest of the group. The unusual crossed-arm pose led archeologists to identify it with Ananda Thera, the Buddha's closest disciple, but it is now believed that all the Gal Vihara carvings represent the Buddha in different stages of life. The final figure, on the far right, is also the largest, stretching 46 feet (14 m). This portrays the reclining Buddha at his most serene as he enters Nirvana.

Beside the standing Buddha, a lengthy carved inscription records Parakrama Bahu's efforts to unite the differing Buddhist sects and the code of conduct he laid down for religious practice. Polonnaruwa flourished under his rule but was later abandoned in favor of safer territory further south. The area was reclaimed by the jungle until British Archeological Commissioner H. C. P. Bell began uncovering Sri Lanka's lost kingdoms in the late nineteenth century. **CB**

🏛️ ⊚ Sigiriya (Sigiriya, Sri Lanka)

Buddhist archeological site with the remains of King Kasyapa's castle

Sigiriya, or Lion Rock, is a stunning archeological site dominated by the cube-shaped rock at its center. The volcanic rock is 1,214 feet (370 m) high, and there is a sheer drop on all its four sides. At the top, its flat surface covers 3.5 acres (1.4 ha).

It is believed that Sigiriya was a Buddhist monastery in the fourth century, and the surrounding complex was a city built by King Kasyapa a century later. The site is separated from the jungle by gardens, which are edged by a mud moat boundary. The top of the rock is home to what remains of a castle built by King Kasyapa as his hilltop stronghold, or perhaps as his pleasure palace; the castle's water cisterns are still visible. After the king's death, the complex reverted to being a monastery once more, but the buildings fell into disuse in the sixteenth century.

A terrace cut into one side of the rock face houses what is known as the Mirror Wall measuring 460 feet (140 m) long and 131 feet (40 m) high. It contains twenty frescoes painted on plaster that depict 500 beautiful women with flowers in their hair. There may have been as many as 500 frescoes in the past, but these have disappeared over time. The multicolored murals have inspired hundreds of people across the centuries to write love poems on the wall.

Above the terrace is a narrow, wrought-iron, spiral staircase that lies between the front paws of a stone lion. The paws are all that remains of the Lion's Gate, which originally included a lion's head as well. Visitors would have gained access to the castle via the lion's gaping mouth. The staircase enables visitors to climb to the summit, and enjoy the view extending miles into the distance, across the surrounding flat plains. The staircase is so narrow that there is space for only one foot on each step—take note if you do not enjoy a tricky climb and heights. **CK**

 🏛 ⊚ **Temple of the Tooth** (Kandy, Sri Lanka)

Shrine housing Sri Lanka's most important Buddhist relic

The Sri Dalada Maligawa, or Temple of the Sacred Tooth Relic, is Sri Lanka's most important Buddhist shrine. Said to house a tooth of the Buddha Siddhartha Gautama, it is a pilgrimage site for Buddhists from around the world. It has, however, also been claimed that the original tooth was burned in 1650 by the Archbishop of Goa, and the one now held in Kandy is a fake. The tooth is housed in a two-story inner shrine in the complex, packed with offerings of flowers, often lotuses; the air is usually thick with the smell of incense. The tooth lies on a solid gold lotus flower within a series of gold and jeweled caskets that sit on a throne, and is rarely on public display. Buddhist worshippers line up every evening to enter the shrine to pay homage to the tooth.

According to legend, when the Buddha died, his body was cremated in Kusinara in India; his left canine tooth was retrieved from the ashes of the sandalwood funeral pyre and given to King Brahmadatte. A tradition emerged that whoever possessed the relic had the divine right to rule that land. Inevitably this led to wars over the relic, and the last Indian king to possess the tooth, King Guhasiva of Kalinga, had it smuggled to Sri Lanka in 371 during the reign of the Sri Lankan king Kirti Sri Megavanna, who built a shrine for it. The relic went on to have various homes around the island before it finally arrived in Kandy.

The temple was built *c.* 1600 during the reign of King Vimaladharmasuriya I, and was rebuilt during the reign of King Kirthi Sri Rajasinghe in the eighteenth century. The complex is also home to the Sri Dalda Museum that contains a collection of documents and photographs relating to the tooth's history, and the Pattiripuwa octagonal tower built in 1803 by King Sri Wickrama Rajasinghe is used as a library to house important palm-leaf manuscripts. **CK**

Lalbagh Fort

(Dhaka, Bangladesh)

An unfinished edifice and sad gravesite

Dhaka is the sprawling capital of Bangladesh and is one of the most densely populated cities in the world. The vibrant and frenetic pace of the city is in sharp contrast to the still, tranquil beauty of one of its treasures, the Lalbagh, or Aurangabad, Fort.

The Lalbagh Fort was never finished and it deteriorated over the years, but careful excavation and restoration has uncovered much of the original layout and preserved that which remains. The lavish complex was begun in 1678 and planned as a large, rectangular compound bounded by high defensive walls, a long fortification wall, and splendid gateways that protected the richly decorated structures inside. It was commissioned by Prince Muhammed Azam, son of Emperor Aurangzeb, in 1688. Work continued on the fort for fifteen months, at which point the prince was summoned from Dhaka to aid the emperor, and Governor Nawab Shaista Khan (Mughal governor of Bengal 1664–88) took over. Shaista Khan's beloved daughter, Bibi Pari, who was betrothed to Muhammed Azam, died suddenly and the fort project was stopped. Later a tomb was built for Bibi Pari, and this remains the best preserved and most impressive of the surviving fort structures. Bibi Pari's tomb is located near two other striking buildings, the Mosque and the Lalbagh Hammam and Audience Hall—a monumental building thought to have been Shaista Khan's palatial residence. Apart from the imposing beauty of the fort buildings, there is a highly sophisticated grid of water works—sewage and drainage pipes that chaneled hot and cold water, served a heating system, and disposed of waste.

The fort, now a museum, is imbued with the colorful history of Dhaka's past and brings together some of the finest buildings in the city—it is a site of great historic and cultural importance. **TP**

Pink Palace

(Dhaka, Bangladesh)

The home of the first Nawab of Dhaka

The exotic city of Dhaka, capital of Bangladesh, was officially founded in 1608 as the seat of the imperial Mughal viceroy of Bengal. It grew along the banks of the Buriganga River, which led to a rapid growth in Dhaka's trading and commercial interests. At its heart is the Pink Palace (Ahsan Manzil), the gardens of which slope down to the waters of the Buriganga.

The Pink Palace is one of the most magnificent buildings in the capital. Businessman Khwaja Alimullah bought it from the French Trading House in 1830 and turned it into his home. His son Khwaja Abdul Ghani completely rebuilt it between 1859 and 1872 to create

> *"Ahsan Manzil, a wedding-cake pink building . . . [that] makes me wish I'd had more time to explore."*
> Michael Palin, *Himalaya* (2004)

its present palatial appearance. Abdul Ghani was a brilliant strategist and philanthropist who, after supporting the British Raj during the Sepoy Uprising of 1857, was made an honorary magistrate. In 1875 he was created Nawab (leader) of Dhaka, a title that was later made hereditary. The Pink Palace became central to political activity through the Nawab's reign, and it was from here that Muslim leadership of East Bengal emerged and the All India Muslim League was founded in 1906. In 1952, after the East Bengal Estate Acquisition Act, the fortunes of the Nawab and the palace turned and the building fell into near ruin.

In 1985 the Bangladesh government began restoration work and the former palace was turned into a museum with twenty-three galleries displaying artifacts from the time of the Nawabs. **TP**

 # Hanuman Dhoka

(Kathmandu, Nepal)

Kathmandu's Old Royal Palace, with buildings and monuments spanning the centuries

The small, mountainous state of Nepal is bordered by India to the south, east, and west, with Tibet to the north. Kathmandu, the capital city, lies within the Kathmandu Valley, the most fertile and urbanized area of the country. It is a place of huge historic importance and home to many ancient buildings and monuments reflecting the country's rich cultural past.

At the heart of Kathmandu city is Hanuman Dhoka (Gate of Hanuman—the monkey god), the eclectic complex of temples, courtyards, and palace buildings that forms the Old Royal Palace of the Malla and Shah kings. It is a fascinating collection of buildings that has been added to throughout the centuries. Sources suggest that a royal palace stood here in the seventh century, but the complex as it appears today was essentially created between the sixteenth and early twentieth century. Within this period it was King Pratap Malla in the seventeenth century who carried out the most extensive building and planning of the palace. Numerous temples, courtyards, and gardens were laid out during this time, including the courtyards Sundari Chowk, Nasal Chowk (where royal coronations were held), and the Bhandarkhal Royal Garden. Pratap Malla also consecrated the image of Vishvaroopa and Hanuman in front of the main entrance and built the temple of Panchamukhi Hanuman in the Nasal Chowk. The royal palace housed the royal family as well as providing administrative areas, ceremonial space, and temples. Documents from 1830 show that the complex included more than thirty-five courtyards, but now, though still spectacular, it is greatly diminished and is under threat from encroaching urban development.

Hanuman Dhoka, together with a number of other monuments and buildings in Kathmandu Valley, was designated a World Heritage site in 1979. **TP**

"That wherever the deeds of Sri Rama are sung ... does Hanuman cry tears of devotion and joy."

Valmiki, *Ramayana* (c. third century B.C.E)

🏛️ ◉ Lumbini (Lumbini, Nepal)

Birthplace of the Buddha, with a temple devoted to his mother, Maya Devi

Lumbini has become Nepal's most popular pilgrimage site. It houses a Buddhist monastery and temples erected by Buddhists from all over the world—including China, Japan, Sri Lanka, Myanmar, and Vietnam—but its ancient ruins are far more evocative.

The word *Lumbini* has long been known as the name of the Buddha's birthplace, but with the passage of time and the changing of political and geographical boundaries, the town was forgotten and for centuries its exact location was uncertain. It was rediscovered toward the end of the nineteenth century, when a German archeologist, Dr. Alois Fuhrer, deciphered the ancient text on a stone column. It declared that this was the birthplace of the Buddha and that it had been visited by the Buddhist emperor Ashoka, who reigned in the third century B.C.E. He had erected the column as a memorial to the Buddha and to commemorate his own visit. Ashoka also decreed that the town of Lumbini was exempt from paying taxes in recognition of the Buddha's greatness.

Not far from the column is a peaceful sacred pool, Puskarni, believed to be the place where the Buddha's mother, Maya Devi, bathed before giving birth and where the baby was given his first wash. Nearby, far into the foundations of the ruins of an ancient temple devoted to the Buddha's mother, is a memorial stone, purportedly marking the exact location where Maya Devi gave birth to her famous son. **LH**

"All that we are is the result of what we have thought. The mind is everything."

Gautama Siddharta Buddha

 🏛 ⊚ **Potala Palace** (Lhasa, Tibet, China)

Hilltop monastery, fortress, and palace—home to the Dalai Lamas

The very first Potala Palace was a magnificent structure built in the seventh century. Wars and weather (including a disastrous lightning strike) laid waste to the old palace, so the fifth Dalai Lama, Ngawang Losang Gyatso, ordered the construction of a new palace on the original palace's foundations. The fifth Dalai Lama and his Gelugpa order became the most important religious power in Tibet and championed several ambitious architectural projects.

Potala Palace is a monastery, a fortress, and a palace, with 1,000 rooms. It was created by more than 7,000 workers, including around 1,500 artisans who created the superb decorations. The palace was built on top of a hill, 430 feet (130 m) above the valley below, partly for reasons of defense and partly to ensure that only true devotees would make their way to such a height. The fifth Dalai Lama and his successors lived at the palace and oversaw the administration of their country from here. The fact that the Dalai Lama established his religious building on the palace of the first king, Songtsen Gampo, was intended to demonstrate that Buddhism superseded political power. In addition, according to Buddhist mythology, the Bodhisattva Avalokiteshvara dwelled in the Potala Mountain. The palace, therefore, bears both religious and secular significance. After the death of the fifth Dalai Lama, the palace was extended substantially to house his mausoleum.

The building was constructed from white stone with black outlined windows, although the newer part of the building, containing the mausoleum, is red and is lavishly decorated with gold and other precious materials. The palace's living quarters are sumptuous and beautiful, a peaceful place for generations of Dalai Lamas to work, study, and relax—if they are ever allowed to return to Tibet. **SJ**

🏛 ◉ **Mogao Caves** (near Dunhuang, China)

Archeological site where rare treasures dating back 1,000 years have been discovered

The Mogao caves, or Caves of the Thousand Buddhas, encapsulate a millennium of Buddhist history. The site, on the ancient Silk Route, is near the Dunhuang oasis, for centuries a popular resting place for travelers, traders, wandering monks, and pilgrims. The caves date back to the fourth century.

It was not only expensive luxury items that were transported via the extensive Silk Route; Buddhism, along with its art and architecture, also made its way from India to China as traders moved across the continent. The caves served as a shelter for travelers, as cells in which to meditate, and as artists' galleries. The iconography of the art discovered inside the Mogao caves was inspired by Indian Buddhism, but the stylistic elements were changed as the religion moved into a new artistic region.

The caves' wealth of artistic treasures include murals, clay sculptures, and priceless manuscripts. The Buddhist community encouraged patronage of the arts, and the emperors of the Tang dynasty (618–906) gave specific financial support to the caves, encouraging artists to work here; two colossal Buddha statues and mural paintings can be dated from that period. As a result of state patronage, the paintings in the caves also depict secular subjects, such as the military exploits of Chinese rulers.

Despite the threat posed by invaders, the caves' cultural legacy has miraculously survived, thanks to monks who hid the manuscripts and Tibetans who protected the site. In 1907, Daoist priest Wang Yuanlu revealed to archeologist Sir Aurel Stein a previously hidden "library cave," which had been sealed a thousand years before. It contained around a thousand well-preserved ancient manuscripts, silk banners, paintings, rare textiles, and secular documents—in total fifty thousand documents in Khotanese, Tibetan, Chinese, Sanskrit, and Uighur. **SJ**

"Religions, languages, arts, fruits, tools, empires, and plagues all crossed Eurasia along the Silk Road."

Sir Aurel Stein, archeologist

Emperor Kangxi's "fleeing the heat mountain villa"

Emperor Kangxi began building his summer resort in 1703 as a cooler alternative to Beijing; the Chinese name *bishu shanzhuang* means "fleeing the heat mountain villa." Kangxi decreed there should be thirty-six beauty spots in Jehol (Chengde's original name) because he spent so much of the year at the resort. His grandson, Emperor Qianlong, also favored the site, decreeing another thirty-six beauty spots and undertaking large extensions. When construction was finished in 1792, the resort was twice the size of Beijing's summer palace.

Because the power resided where the emperor went, Chengde served as a second capital city. Court affairs were handled from here and foreign envoys and tribal leaders met. Official state business was handled in the Hall of Simplicity and Sincerity, constructed from an aromatic Chinese hardwood, *nanmu*. Located behind the hall were the emperor's living quarters. A wall stretching for 6 miles (10 km) surrounds the complex, and the grounds are divided into garden, lake, and flatland sections. In the lake section, the waters are divided by causeways and bridges, reminiscent of scenes from Hangzhou. An expanse of grass on the flatland section is similar to Mongolian terrain and was used for horse riding. To the north and east of the complex are temples. The eight outer temples were built between 1750 and 1780 to symbolize unity with the country's ethnic minorities; they contain elements of each minority's architectural style. Putuozongcheng Temple, the largest, was modeled on Lhasa's Potala Palace.

Although some of the resort's former glory has been damaged by war, much of the complex and its surrounding temples remain intact. It continues to play an important part in the Qing history of China, a favored site of the country's emperors, and the site of politically historic events. **MA**

> *"[It] is a rare historic vestige of the final development of feudal society in China."*
> UNESCO

🏛️ 🔷 Great Wall of China (Shanhai Pass to Lop Nur, China)

The longest man-made structure in the world, the earliest fragments dating from 221 B.C.E.

"*You're not a real man if you haven't climbed the Great Wall.*"

Mao Zedong, revolutionary leader and statesman

⊞ As China's foremost symbol, the Great Wall was a natural stop during President Nixon's 1972 tour.

⊞ The neglected Simatai section of the wall, 80 miles (130 km) north of Beijing, traces spectacular terrain.

The Great Wall of China is one of the world's great structures, though—despite popular myth—it is not really visible from space. The longest man-made structure in the world, it stretches across northern China for approximately 3,945 miles (6,350 km) from Lop Nur in the west to the Shanhai Pass in the east.

When China was first united around 221 B.C.E., the new Qin dynasty emperor ordered the building of a wall to protect his possessions from incursions by the tribal Xiongnu peoples to the north. Little is known of this wall, however, and only a few fragments have survived.

The next and greatest phase of wall building occurred during the Ming dynasty, when, in the latter half of the fifteenth century, the Ming rulers decided to construct a series of walls to keep out their aggressive Mongol neighbors. The construction techniques varied according to the terrain encountered and the availability of materials, but a mixture of brick and stone was the most common. Watchtowers were built at regular intervals along the wall, and a highly sophisticated system of communication ensured that enemy movements could be monitored, whereas the wall itself was wide enough to allow reinforcements to be rushed along it to stem enemy attacks with minimal delay. Larger forts and barracks were also built to house the garrisons that manned the walls.

The wall fell into disrepair with the eventual conquest of China by the Manchus from the north and the formation of the Qing dynasty from 1644 onward. As Qing lands now extended far north of the wall, there was little need for such a protective barrier. Although some parts of the wall have been well-preserved, much of it is now in poor condition, subject to erosion and despoliation by local people who use it as a source of building materials. **AG**

🏛 ◉ Manchu Imperial Palace (Shenyang, China)

Residence of the Manchu emperors

This small-scale forbidden city was built by the Manchu emperors as their seat of government. Construction began in 1624 under the reign of Nurhachi and was completed by his son Abahai. It was from here that the Manchus' power spread out, conquering China and laying the foundations for the Qing dynasty (1644–1911).

The site can be divided into three sections: eastern, middle, and western. Dominating the eastern section is the Hall of Great Affairs where the emperor issued imperial edicts and received victorious generals. The middle section was the center of power, where Abahai held court—the most important place in the palace. Abahai and his concubines slept in Qingning Palace. The Phoenix Tower finishes off the middle section and at three stories high was—when it was built—the highest building in Shengjing (the old name for Shenyang, or Mukden in Manchu).

Emperor Qianlong added the western section during his reign. The main building, the Wensu Pavilion, housed the classic texts and was used as a reading room by emperors. In the pavilion is a stage for performances. Overall the palace contains more than 300 rooms in seventy buildings, in an area covering 645,000 square feet (60,000 sq m). Architecturally the site contains a mixture of Manchu styles and those from other parts of China. Qianlong added Han and Mongol styles to the buildings. Surrounded by a high red-brick wall, the buildings are constructed largely of stone and brick, capped with brightly colored tiles.

After the Manchus founded the Qing dynasty, the capital moved to Beijing. However, the palace still remained important as their ancestral power base and they continued to maintain it. It is the second-best remaining example of a palace in China, and one of the few remaining large ethnic minority buildings. **MA**

🏛️ ⊛ **Ming Tombs** (Beijing, China)

Impressive burial chambers of some of China's greatest emperors

In 1402 Emperor Zhu Di (also known by the imperial name of Yongle) seized the throne from his nephew Zhu Yunwen. In doing so, Zhu Di became the third Ming emperor and moved the capital from Nanjing to his own city, Beijing. When his wife, Empress Xu, died in 1407 Zhu Di sent a diviner to find a suitable location for an imperial burial ground. The chosen area was good for both scenery and military defense as it was surrounded on three sides by Yanshan Mountain. Construction began in 1409 and thirteen of the sixteen Ming emperors were eventually buried here, with the last tomb dating from 1644.

The site of the tombs covers 15 square miles (40 sq km). Although there is variation in the scale and grandeur of the tombs, all follow the same basic layout. Each mausoleum is surrounded by a wall and entered through the Gate of Prominent Favors. This leads to the Hall of Prominent Favors used for the offering of sacrifices and worship by the deceased emperor's descendants. The halls are generally made of nanmu wood, which was favored in the Ming era. Behind the hall is the walled burial mound for the emperor and empress, and in front of this is the Soul Tower. This small building holds a stele bearing the emperor's posthumous title. Surrounding the complex were the quarters of the officials who were in charge of offerings. Bricks used in the construction weighed about 55 pounds (25 kg) and had the word *shou* (longevity) imprinted. The scale of the tombs varied partly according to whether they were built by the emperor himself or by his descendants.

The tombs are approached by a long sacred way lined with statues of animals and officials. Today only three of the tombs are open; of these, Zhu Di's tomb is the most impressive, but in the Dingling tomb it is possible to enter the burial mound. **MA**

🏛 ⊚ **Temple of Heaven** (Beijing, China)

A symbolic representation of the world according to ancient Chinese beliefs

One of the best-known symbols of Beijing, the Temple of Heaven and Earth was built during the reign of Emperor Zhu Di (also known as Yongle), who reigned from 1402 until 1424. Its name was shortened in the sixteenth century, during the reign of Emperor Jiajing. The temple was used to offer sacrifices to heaven.

The site is laid out on a north–south axis. At the south end the site is square shaped, symbolizing the earth; the northern end is semicircular and raised above the south end, representing heaven. Constructed in 1530 and rebuilt in 1740, the circular altar is a white marble, three-layered, terraced structure. Ming and Qing emperors offered sacrifices to heaven here at the winter solstice. Surrounding the entrance to the Imperial Vault of Heaven is the Echo Wall, where a whisper can travel 213 feet (65 m). The vault, built at the same time as the altar, is similar in design to the older Hall of Prayer for Good Harvests

and was used to house memorial tablets dedicated to the emperor's ancestors, which were used in the winter solstice ceremony. Dominating the complex is the Hall of Prayer for Good Harvests, which performed an important ceremonial role. Sitting on a three-tiered marble terrace, the building is supported by twenty-eight pillars. The inner circle of four represents the seasons, the next twelve represents the months of the year, and the remaining twelve represents *shichen* (each day was divided into twelve *shichen*).

Inscribed as a World Heritage site in 1998, the Temple of Heaven is a masterpiece of architecture and landscape design that simply and graphically illustrates a cosmogony of great importance for the evolution of one of the world's great civilizations. The symbolic layout and design of the Temple of Heaven had a profound influence on architecture and planning in the Far East over many centuries. **MA**

🏛 ◎ **Forbidden City** (Beijing, China)

Palace complex of the Ming and Qing dynasties, dating from 1407

Work on the Forbidden City—the imperial palace complex of the Ming and Qing dynasties—began in 1407 and was completed fourteen years later, with as many as 200,000 men laboring on the project. Designed to symbolize imperial power and majesty, it was regarded as the earthly counterpart of the abode of the Celestial Emperor. The name refers to the fact that no one could enter or leave the site without the permission of the emperor.

The rectangular palace complex—with a main gate set in each side—was surrounded by a moat 19 feet (6 m) deep and a wall 32 feet (10 m) high. With an overall size of around 178 acres (72 ha), the Forbidden City contained some 800 buildings with 8,880 rooms, although some sources put the number of rooms at a more poetical 9,999. Among these buildings were five large halls and seventeen palaces. The Forbidden City was divided into two areas: The southern section or Outer Court was where the emperor conducted his day-to-day business, while he and his family lived in the northern section or Inner Court. The buildings were constructed predominantly from wood. The City contains the world's largest collection of ancient wooden structures, their roofs being painted in the traditional royal color of yellow.

The ten emperors of the Qing Dynasty, which replaced the Ming in 1644, used the Forbidden City as their seat of government. In 1912, following the Xinhai Revolution, the last Chinese emperor, Puyi, abdicated and the Forbidden City eventually became a museum, where its many treasures and curiosities were put on display (although some of these artifacts were removed to Taiwan during the Chinese Civil War). Since the relaxation of Chinese communist rule, the Forbidden City has become a major attraction for both Chinese and foreign tourists. **AG**

🏛 ◈ Summer Palace (Beijing, China)

Masterpiece of Chinese landscape garden design

The first stage of construction on the Summer Palace was commissioned in 1750 by the Emperor Qinglong—the fifth emperor of the Manchu Qing Dynasty—as a present to his mother, and also as a summer retreat for the imperial family from the heat and bustle of the Forbidden City.

The Summer Palace and its related buildings were set in hilly woodland and artfully positioned amid three lakes created by damming a stream. A key theme of the designers was the incorporation of architectural and garden styles from different parts of China. The famous West Lake in the Hangzhou area, for example, was reworked as the lake in the south of the Summer Palace gardens. The Garden of Harmonious Interests was based on a typical water town found in south China. Tibetan-style buildings were constructed on the northern side of Longevity Hill, whereas Suzhou Street was lined with shops built in a traditional

Chinese style. The whole palace complex was divided into three zones: the administrative area, where official state business was conducted; the residential area, which housed the emperor and his court; and the scenic area of lakes and gardens. The effect of the harmonious combination of water, land, and buildings was one of tranquil beauty.

The Summer Palace was devastated by invading European forces, first in 1860 and again in 1902. On both occasions the palace was rebuilt by Dowager Empress Cixi, and to many Chinese people the palace became a symbol of national and cultural resistance in the face of foreign barbarism. Following the 1911 revolution and the setting up of the new republic, the Summer Palace was opened to the public, and from 1924 it became a park for the people of Beijing. UNESCO designated the Summer Palace a World Heritage site in 1998. **AG**

Tiananmen (Beijing, China)

One of the entrances to the Forbidden City, and scene of major political events

The Tiananmen or Tian'an Gate (Gate of Heavenly Peace) was one of the four main entrances to Beijing's Forbidden City, and has since given its name to the enormous plaza of Tiananmen Square. This stretches some 2,887 feet (880 m) from north to south and 1,640 feet (500 m) from east to west, making it the largest urban square in the world.

Work on the Tiananmen began in 1417 as part of the Ming Dynasty's development of the Forbidden City, although it was the renovation work in 1699 that gave it the general appearance we know today. Until the twentieth century, the area in front of the Tiananmen was occupied by government offices, and it was only as a result of damage caused during the Boxer Rebellion of 1902 that the area was cleared. In the early 1950s the clearances were extended further south with the removal of the Gate of China and the small streets that had grown up around it. In the Mao

era several major buildings were built around the square, including the Great Hall of the People, the National Museum, and the Mao Zedong Memorial Hall, which holds the embalmed body of the "Great Helmsman," Mao Zedong, who died in 1976.

Tiananmen Square has achieved prominence and even notoriety for the political events that have occurred there. On October 1, 1949, Mao proclaimed the People's Republic of China in the square, which then became the site of the mass pro-government demonstrations and parades that were such a feature of communism. More recently the square has witnessed protest demonstrations, notably from the Democracy Movement. These demonstrations culminated in the protest of 1989, which was eventually crushed with great brutality by the authorities, with one source suggesting that 186 protesters were killed in the fighting. **AG**

🏛 ◎ **Dragon Bone Hill** (Zhoukoudian, China)

Site of the discovery of Peking Man — an early example of Homo erectus

1929年北京猿人第一头盖骨发现处
The first skull-cap of Peking Man was discovered here in 1929

"It excited the curiosity of ordinary people worldwide and made 'Peking Man' a household name."

Sheila Melvin, journalist, on Pei Wenzhong's work

Dragon Bone Hill is the location of one of the most important discoveries of human remains in the twentieth century. In 1921 Johann Gunnar Andersson, a Swedish geologist and archaeologist, working with Otto Zdansky, an Austrian palaeontologist, found two humanlike teeth while working here. In 1926 Andersson announced the discovery of early human teeth, shocking the scientific world, which had not been aware that humans had lived in Asia at such an early date. The discovery was given a new genus and species with the name *Sinanthropus pekinensis*; it was later reclassified as *Homo erectus pekinensis*. In 1929, with the discovery of a nearly complete skull cap by geologist Pei Wenzhong, doubts about the fossils were laid to rest. It also proved that modern man evolved from apes through an erect man stage.

Excavations continued at Dragon Bone Hill up until World War II, yielding a number of skulls. However, in an attempt to send the remains to the United States—during the Japanese occupation of China—all were mysteriously lost and have still not been found. Subsequent excavations yielded little until 1966 when skull fragments were recovered, allowing a skull cap to be reassembled. The cave where the fossils were found was filled with deposits up to a depth of 164 feet (50 m). Scientists divided the depth into seventeen layers, and it seems that Peking Man lived in the cave from layer ten (dated at about 500,000 years ago) until layer three (about 230,000 years ago). Early *Homo sapiens* fossils have also been recovered in excavations of different caves. The sites have yielded many tools and give an insight into the lives of these early humans.

Dragon Bone Hill, listed as a World Heritage site in 1987, is an important location on the evolutionary path of human life. Excavations continue and further fossil remains have been found. **MA**

🏛 ⦿ Mount Taishan Temples (Tai'an, China)

China's most sacred peak, destination of pilgrims and tourists

Mount Taishan is a mountain steeped in legend and culture. According to the creation myth of Pan Gu, it is said that when Pan Gu died, his head became Taishan. Considered one of the five most important Taoist mountains, it is also important in Buddhism. For thousands of years it has been China's most sacred peak and was considered by the emperors of ancient China to be the son of the Emperor of Heaven. One of the first things a new emperor did was ascend the mountain and pray to heaven and earth for his ancestors. When Confucius climbed Taishan in the sixth century B.C.E, he proclaimed: "The world is small." Millennia later, Mao Zedong declared: "The East is Red."

The mountain lies about 5,070 feet (1,546 m) above sea level and contains 22 temples, 97 ruins, 819 stone tablets, and 1,018 cliff-side and stone inscriptions. At the highest point is the Temple of the Jade Emperor, who, in ancient belief, was the ruler of the world. In front of the temple is the Wordless Monument, left blank because the emperor was dissatisfied with the proposed inscriptions. The largest, most complete structure is the Temple of the God of Mount Taishan, which was first built during the Qin Dynasty. Also commonly visited is the Azure Clouds Temple dedicated to Bixia, the Taoist goddess of childbirth and dawn. A stone staircase of 6,660 steps was cut into the mountain in ancient times.

Guo Moruo, the modern Chinese scholar, called Taishan "a partial miniature of Chinese culture." The importance of the mountain in symbolizing ancient Chinese civilizations and beliefs was recognized in its 1987 UNESCO World Heritage List inscription. It now receives thousands of visitors who make the trek in the belief that a successful climb will allow them to live to be a hundred. The mountain is often enveloped in clouds, but many who climb it hope to see the sunrise above the clouds. **MA**

"The Chinese … 'fallen leaves return to the roots' means every ghost will return to Taishan after death."

UNESCO

🏛 ⊚ Confucius Temple (Qufu, China)

Original temple complex dedicated to the influential Chinese philosopher

The original temple in Qufu—legendary birthplace of Kong Fuzi (known in the West as Confucius)—dates back to 478 B.C.E., one year after the philosopher's death. The temple complex grew as Confucius's fame spread, and today it is one of the three largest ancient architectural complexes in China.

Much of what can be seen dates back to Ming and Qing times. Built on a north–south axis, the temple's design was based on that of a royal palace and divided into nine courtyards. The main buildings consist of three halls, one pavilion, one altar, and three ancestral temples. Kuiwen Pavilion (Great Pavilion of the Constellation of Scholars) dates from the Jin dynasty. It is a two-story wooden building whose top floor housed books given by the emperors; on the ground floor items used by the emperors when offering sacrifices were stored. Just beyond the Dacheng Gate is the Apricot Platform from where Confucius taught

his students. The buildings beyond include Dacheng Hall, one of the three largest ancient halls in China, used for sacrifices to Confucius and other scholars. The two other areas are for worship of the family.

As well as the original Confucian temple in Qufu, many others were built. These enjoyed the support of Chinese emperors over two millennia, ensuring that the finest artists and craftsmen were involved in the creation and reconstruction of the buildings and the landscape, all dedicated to Confucius and his deeds.

Confucius's contribution to philosophical and political doctrine in the East, and also in Europe and the West, has been one of the most profound factors in the evolution of modern thought and government. For these reasons the temple, together with the cemetery containing Confucius's tomb and the Kong family mansion, were inscribed by UNESCO as a World Heritage site in 1994. **MA**

🏛 ◉ Mausoleum of the First Qin Emperor (Xi'an, China)

The burial place of the first unifier of China and his vast terracotta army

The first emperor of China, Qin Shi Huangdi (260–210 B.C.E.), unified China into a single political entity. He standardized scripts, weights, measures, and coins throughout the territory, and roads, fortifications, and major defensive walls were built during his reign. However, the most impressive and megalomaniacal architectural project that the emperor ordered was his own extensive burial complex. Since ancient times, the Chinese people have believed in life after death and in the worship of their ancestors. The tombs of emperors and high officials were designed to replicate their life on Earth. Everyday utensils, bronzes for the cult of the ancestors, musical instruments, wives, courtesans, and members of the court were often buried with the deceased to ensure a safe passage.

According to the records of the second-century B.C.E. historian Sima Qian, the mausoleum is a miniature representation of the universe. The 8,000 life-size soldiers (sometimes accompanied by horses) of the famous terracotta army were modeled on human figures and are holding real swords and spears in order to guard the emperor's necropolis. Each soldier has been given a unique facial expression, creating a realistic impression of individuality. To make them appear even more authentic, weapons, clothes, and hairstyles vary from one soldier to the next. This vast terracotta army testifies to the absolute power and great ambitions of the first emperor of China. **SJ**

> *"[The mausoleum is] one of the most universal and beautiful works of art ever created."*
>
> Jonathan Jones, journalist

Big Goose Pagoda (Xi'an, China)

Pagoda close to Da Ci'en Temple, housing Buddhist texts translated by Xuan Zang

"... even in the midst of fierce flames the Golden Lotus may be planted ..."

Wu Cheng'en, *Monkey* (trans. Arthur Waley, 1942)

Buddhism entered China via the Silk Road—an ancient series of trade routes connecting China, through Asia Minor, with the Mediterranean. Ancient Chang'an (Xi'an) marked the eastern terminus of the route and the religion had a big impact on the development of the city. In the seventh century, the monk Xuan Zang had become so dissatisfied with poor translations of the Buddhist works that he decided to travel to India in search of uncorrupted Sanskrit texts from which he could translate new versions. Banned from international travel, he sneaked out of the country in disguise and returned seventeen years later, in 645, with various works.

A few years later, around 648, Emperor Gaozong set about building Da Ci'en Temple (Temple of Great Maternal Grace) and Xuan Zang was made first abbot of the temple. The Big Goose Pagoda was built in the grounds in 652 to house the texts that Xuan Zang translated, with help, into 1,335 volumes. The pagoda was originally five stories high (about 200 feet, 60 m) and made of yellow brick to a simple, Indian-influenced square-cone design. Another two stories were added in 704, bringing the total height to 211 feet (64.5 m). On the walls of the temple are engravings of Buddha by the Chinese painter Yan Liben.

Protected as a significant national relic, the site of the Big Goose Pagoda is well preserved. Today there are three parts to the complex: the pagoda, the temple, and the north square of the pagoda. In front of the temple is a statue of Xuan Zang, who played a pivotal role not only in the history of Buddhism in China but also in literature. His book *Record of the Western Regions* (composed in 646) provided an up-to-date contemporary account of central Asian countries. His story was immortalized later in Wu Cheng'en's part-fictional *Journey to the West* (published in the 1590s)—a work often known in the West as *Monkey*. **MA**

Ming City Wall (Nanjing, China)

Well-preserved city wall, built in the fourteenth century of bricks with an earthen outer wall

Construction of Nanjing city wall began in 1366 to defend rebel Zhu Yuanzhang's power base at the end of the Yuan dynasty. When he defeated the Mongols and established the Ming dynasty in 1368, Nanjing became the capital. The wall was not completed until 1386 and is the world's largest city wall.

Stretching 21 miles (33.7 km) and ranging in height between 46 and 69 feet (14–21 m), the wall contained 13,616 battlements and 200 fortresses. Originally there were two parts to the structure—an inner and an outer wall (the latter was simply made of earth). Solid foundations to the inner wall were provided by laying large slabs of granite or limestone. The wall was then built up using bricks and earth. As with many other ancient Chinese construction projects, each brick carried information about the producer to guarantee good quality. These bricks were transported via the Yangtze River and Grand Canal. Bricks were cemented together using a limewater and glutinous rice paste, and some 200,000 workers labored on the construction of the wall. Unlike earlier walls, such as in Xi'an, the Nanjing wall was not built in a symmetrical shape but instead followed the topography of the land to give better defense. There were originally thirteen gates, of which the largest was Zhonghua Gate (China Gate, also known as Treasure Gate). It dates back to 917 and was strengthened and incorporated into the wall. Only Zhonghua Gate and Heping Gate are still standing.

The wall has seen quite a lot of damage. It was used as a defensive feature during the Taiping Rebellion (1850–64), and the Japanese destroyed parts of the wall during their occupation in the twentieth century. Today about 12 miles (19 km) of the structure are still well preserved. City walls are very much a part of Chinese culture, and the wall of Nanjing is the finest example. **MA**

"Build high walls, stock up rations, and don't be too quick to call yourself a king."

Zhu Sheng, follower of Zhu Yuanzhang

Sun Yatsen Mausoleum (Nanjing, China)

Mausoleum of the "father" of the Republic of China

Dr. Sun Yatsen (1866–1925) is considered the father of modern China by people in both China and Taiwan. An antimonarchist, he spent many of his earlier years in exile after a failed republican uprising in 1895. In 1911 Sun declared China a republic. When he died in 1925 the republic was far from stable, with limited control over the country and increasing problems between the nationalists (Kuomintang) and communists. He requested to be buried in Nanjing but probably did not have in mind the grandeur of the mausoleum built in his honor. More than forty designs were submitted for the site on Purple Mountain. The selected design by Lu Yanzhi was a modern interpretation of classical Chinese tomb design.

Looking like a bell from the air, the design and scale is similar to the tombs of the emperors. A marble memorial archway marks the beginning of the site, which is laid out on a north–south axis. After a path lined with pine and cypress trees, there is a formal three-arched entrance with copper doors. Behind this is a marble pavilion in which there is a 30-foot- (9-m-) high stele. From here a steep staircase leads up the mountain to the large memorial hall, which contains a marble seated statue of Sun with the flag of the republic tiled on the ceiling. To the north is a circular chamber containing the recessed marble sarcophagus complete with a prostrate statue of Sun on the top.

In 2005 Lien Chan, then leader of the opposition Kuomintang party in Taiwan, made a landmark visit to China during which he visited the mausoleum. It is a site that unites both nationalists and communists in their respect for a great leader. **MA**

◩ Dr. Sun Yatsen, here photographed with his second wife, Soong Ching-ling, on a trip to Beijing in 1924.

◩ Once through the mausoleum's Gate Hall, visitors must climb many steps to the larger Main Hall.

🏛 ◎ Giant Buddha of Leshan (Leshan, China)

The world's biggest Buddha statue, where Buddhism was first established in China

At 233 feet (71 m) high, the Leshan Buddha is the biggest Buddha statue in the world. To be precise, it is a Maitreya Buddha—a statue of a future Buddha.

The Buddha is situated at the confluence of the Min, Qingyi, and Dadu rivers, where numerous accidents had occurred. In 713, a monk named Hai Tong decided to carve a Buddha statue to watch over the river, a project that took ninety years to fully complete. The resulting Buddha was immense: Its fingers are 10 feet (3 m) long and the shoulders are 92 feet (28 m) across, the size of a basketball court. At 23 feet (7 m) long, the ears, made of wood covered in mud, were attached to the sculpture in a wonder of ancient engineering. The statue was originally sheltered by a thirteen-story wooden structure but this was destroyed in wars at the start of the Ming dynasty.

The Buddha did stop lives being lost to the rivers, if only because rocks from the construction filled in the riverbed. Today, erosion has taken its toll—plants and fungi are growing on parts of the statue and acid rain has caused the nose to turn black. Repairs are under way, and the local government is making efforts to avoid further deterioration.

Inscribed as a UNESCO World Heritage site in 1996, along with Mount Emei, the site is considered of exceptional cultural significance since it is the place where Buddhism first became established on Chinese territory and from where it spread widely throughout the East. Indeed the first Buddhist temple in China was built in this area in the first century C.E. But it is also an area of natural beauty into which the human element has been integrated. **MA**

⬈ For visitors wishing to examine the upper part of the Buddha there is a stairway to the statue's right.

⬊ Viewed from above, visitors amble about on one of the great stone feet of the Buddha.

Family Home of Mao Zedong (Shaoshan, China)

Birthplace and family home of the first president of the People's Republic of China

> *"We shall support whatever our enemies oppose; and oppose whatever our enemies support."*

Mao Zedong, revolutionary leader and statesman

⊞ Mao's birthplace was a popular pilgrimage site during his life and is no less interesting to the modern Chinese.

⊟ Mao Zedong was unusual in revolutionary leaders in that for many years he oversaw the new regime.

Chairman of the Chinese Communist Party from 1945 until his death in 1976, and first president of the People's Republic of China (established in 1949), Mao Zedong remains a highly significant, though controversial, figure in Chinese history. The story began with his birth on December 26, 1893, in the small village of Shaoshan about 80 miles (130 km) southwest of the provincial capital, Changsha.

Mao's father, Yi-chang, was a hard-working and frugal man. After serving in the army he managed to clear the family's debts and buy some land, where he raised pigs and processed grain into high-quality rice to sell. He could also read and write well enough to do accounts. Soon he became one of the richest men in the village. The family lived in six rooms of one wing of a large, thatched property, with floors and walls of yellow mud bricks. Although Mao was born in Shaoshan, he actually spent most of his early years in his mother's village. When he was eight years old, he returned to Shaoshan to start his schooling, which included the study of the Confucian classics in a tutor's home. He clashed with teachers and went through four schools, at which point his father stopped paying for his education and Mao had to go out to work. At the age of fourteen, he was married off to a woman named Luo. When she died in 1910, Mao demanded to leave Shaoshan. He went to a school near his maternal family's home and then on to the provincial capital Changsha, where he began his political career.

Today, with the village linked by bus and railway to Changsha, it is difficult to imagine how isolated Shaoshan was when Mao was growing up. In those days the thickly forested hills were still home to tigers and leopards. Now the village is a popular destination on the Mao pilgrimage circuit, with his family home open to the public and an exhibition hall where his life and revolutionary activities are memorialized. **MA**

🏛 ⊚ Jongmyo Shrine (Seoul, Republic of Korea)

The oldest Confucian shrine of its kind, where ritual ceremonies continue to be held

The oldest Confucian shrine of its kind in existence, the Jongmyo Shrine in Seoul is exceptional in continuing to hold ritual ceremonies—including music, song, and dance—that were first performed in 1394, when the original shrine was built. Other shrines from the fourteenth century exist, but only those built under the Josean rulers remain fully intact.

The Jongmyo Shrine was built on the order of King Taejo in the late 1300s to provide a temple for the great ancestral tablets of deceased kings and queens. The architects were instructed to avoid the use of excess ornamentation because the building was not intended to overawe visitors. The ancestral tablets of the enshrined royals were to be the most precious part of the building. The grounds were to be open and bare, to enhance the sense of solemnity and dignity. When the shrine was built in 1394, it was thought to be one of the longest buildings in Asia, if not the longest. Despite this, it was extended still farther under the reign of King Sejon. In 1592 the shrine was burned down by Japanese invaders during the Seven Year War (1592–98), but all of the memorial tablets were saved, and by 1601, a new complex had been built to house them.

The recreated shrine is remarkable for its bold structure and impression of simplicity. The buildings are well proportioned and plain, but simple features such as the wide wooden pillars that run around the outer edge of the hall bestow a sense of grandeur and majesty. The interior of the shrine consists of nineteen identical rooms, each of which contains memorial tablets bearing the teachings of members of the former royal family. The Jongmyo Shrine is not only listed as an official national treasure in Korea, but in 1995 it was also inscribed as a UNESCO World Heritage site as the oldest and most authentic of the Confucian royal shrines to have been preserved. **KH**

> *"Reviewing what you have learned and learning anew, you are fit to be a teacher."*
>
> Confucius, philosopher

Konjiki-dō (Hiraizumi, Japan)

Part of an ancient temple, covered completely in gold leaf

During the Heian Period (794–1185), Hiraizumi was the seat of the ruling Fujiwara clan, and rivaled the capital Kyoto culturally, politically, and commercially. Konjiki-dō is one of the two remaining structures of the original Chūson-ji temple complex built in the twelfth century at Hiraizumi in northeastern Japan. Konjiki-dō is a small but special hall among Japanese Buddhist derivatives because it holds a tripartite altar with the mummies of three generations of the Ōshu Fujiwara family—Kiyohira, Motohira, and Hidehira. Mummies were unknown to mainstream Japanese culture until the seventeenth century, and some scholars have argued that Kiyohira is linked to the Emishi culture, which practiced the tradition of mummification. Because of the mixed iconography in the hall, Konjiki-dō has been considered as either an Amida Buddha hall or a mausoleum.

Built over a period of some thirty years, Konjiki-dō is covered completely—except for its pyramidal roof—in gold leaf, inside and out. Where it is not gold, motifs in mother-of-pearl inlay, fine metal, and lacquer work adorn the surface. According to local legend, salmon in the Kitakami River in Hiraizumi were startled by catching the gleam of Konjiki-dō in their eyes, which gave the hall a popular local name, Hikari-dō (Shining Hall). Visiting in 1689, the famous haiku poet Matsuo Bashō composed a haiku about Konjiki-dō, calling it Hikari-dō. Gold, considered a sacred substance within Buddhism, was also the natural resource Hiraizumi once possessed. Konjiki-dō was the manifestation of a Buddhist paradise as well as the symbol of the Ōshu Fujiwaras's wealth.

Konjiki-dō was completely restored under the auspices of the Japanese government between 1962 and 1968 and is now sheltered by a protective concrete structure, which was built in 1965. The hall is a National Treasure of Japan. **FN**

"Even the long rain of May/Has left it untouched—/This Gold Chapel/ Aglow in the sombre shade."

Matsuo Bashō, *Narrow Road to the Deep North* (1689)

🏛 ◎ Mausoleum of Tokugawa Ieyasu (Nikkō, Japan)

Shinto shrine dedicated to the founder of the Tokugawa shōgunate

Surrounded by mountains amid deep forests, the Shinto shrine of Tōshō-gū was erected at Nikkō to deify Tokugawa Ieyasu (1543–1616), the founder of the Tokugawa shōgunate, which ruled Japan for more than 250 years. Ieyasu was given the posthumous title of Tōshō Daigongen, "Great avatar illuminating the east," by the imperial court, doctrinally relating him to the sun goddess Amaterasu, who was the mythical ancestral deity of the imperial family worshipped at the Grand Shrine at Ise.

On the first anniversary of Ieyasu's death, his remains—initially interred at Mount Kunō in Shizuoka—were moved to the Tōshō-gū, which was built in 1617 by his son Hidetada. The current appearance of the Tōshō-gū is attributed to the extensive reconstruction that was undertaken by Ieyasu's grandson, Iemitsu, and completed in 1636 in time for the twentieth anniversary of Ieyasu's death. Iemitsu's project reflected the Shinto ritual of periodic renewal and purification at Ise, where the shrines are rebuilt every twenty years.

The Tōshō-gū complex has a predominantly Shinto character, although it includes some Buddhist elements. The most notable structure is the heavily decorated and colorful Yōmei-mon, "Sun-bright gate," standing at the inner and outer sacred precincts of the shrine. It is also known as Higurashino-mon, "The gate where people can admire until sunset without tiring of it." With more than 500 carvings of mythological creatures, images of Chinese sages and plants fill almost every surface of the gatehouse. The execution of all the paintings was supervised by Kano Tanyū, who directed artists from his own school as well as those from the rival Hasegawa school. Many buildings and artifacts at the Tōshō-gū—listed as a World Heritage site in 1999—are national treasures or important cultural properties of Japan. **FN**

> *"The strong manly ones in life are those who understand the meaning of the word patience."*
>
> Tokugawa Ieyasu, Tokugawa shōgunate founder

Yasukuni-jinja (Tokyo, Japan)

Shrine commemorating all who have died fighting for the Japanese emperor since 1853

At Yasukuni-jinja—as at other Shinto shrines in Japan—rituals are performed to honor the principal deities (*kami*). What distinguishes Yasukuni, however, is that the shrine is dedicated not to the usual Shinto deities, but to the spirits of those who have died fighting for the emperor since 1853. About two and a half million souls are named, including a number of convicted Class A war criminals from World War II who were secretly added to the list in 1979. The shrine—which includes a military museum, opened in 1872, containing many war vehicles, tanks, and weaponry—attracts considerable media attention and protests from neighboring Asian countries whenever it is visited by high-ranking Japanese politicians. Some see the museum as a symbol of Japan's glorious military tradition; others of a brutal and oppressive past.

The shrine was originally built in 1869 on the Kudan Hill in Tokyo, not far from the Imperial Palace, to commemorate the soldiers who had fallen in service to the Meiji Emperor since the 1853 rebellion that led to the Boshin Civil War (1868–69). Initially called the Tokyo Shōkonsha ("Shrine where the divine spirits are invited"), the name was changed to Yasukuni-jinja ("Shrine of the peaceful country") by the Meiji Emperor in 1879. After World War II, the relationship between the shrine and the state was severed by the U.S. occupation authorities, based on a separation of state and religion under the new Japanese Constitution.

Of the buildings within the Yasukuni shrine complex, the Main Sanctuary, the War Museum, and the Chinreisha ("Spirit-pacifying shrine," dedicated to war dead regardless of nationality) are the most significant. Yasukuni-jinja stands as a site not only of ritual but also of personal and collective memory, as well as being a site where ongoing negotiations of the historical meanings and interpretations of Japan's role in several wars take place. **FN**

" . . . the Emperor is merely a symbol . . . he derives his position from the will of the people . . ."

Constitution of Japan

Tsurugaoka Hachiman-gū (Kamakura, Japan)

Kamakura's most important shrine, dedicated to Hachiman, the Shinto god of war

Tsurugaoka Hachiman-gū was the tutelary shrine of the Kamakura shōgunate (1185–1333), which was founded by Minamoto Yoritomo. It is dedicated to Hachiman—a Shinto deity who protects warriors—as well as to the ancient Emperor Ōjin, his mother Empress Jingū, and the goddess Himegami. The shrine was originally founded in 1063 by Minamoto no Yoriyoshi near the Yuigahama coast as a branch shrine of Iwashimizu Hachiman-gū in Kyoto in order to house Hachiman—the guardian deity of the Minamoto family. The shrine was transferred to the current location by the first Kamakura shōgun Yoritomo in 1180. Destroyed by fire in 1191, the shrine was immediately reconstructed and the shrine complex was later expanded. The present main hall of the shrine, which dates from 1828, was built by the eleventh Tokugawa shōgun Ienari and its architecture is representative of that of the Edo period.

Although Tsurugaoka Hachiman-gū is a Shinto shrine, it had a number of Buddhist structures built by the Tokugawa shōgunate. These two religious elements were intimately connected, with some Shinto deities, including Hachiman, considered to be manifestations of Buddhist deities. Tsurugaoka Hachiman-gū had a mixture of Shinto and Buddhist buildings until the Meiji Restoration of 1868, when the government segregated the two religions and made Shinto the state religion. Most of the Buddhist structures were destroyed in the violent anti-Buddhist persecution that followed this segregation policy.

As Kamakura's most important shrine, Tsurugaoka Hachiman-gū hosts a variety of events throughout the year. More than two million visitors visit during the New Year holidays, making it one of the most visited shrines in Japan. Yabusame, archery from horseback, is performed twice a year on the path to the shrine. **FN**

🏛 ◎ **Kinkaku-ji** (Kyoto, Japan)

Villa complex including a replica of the original fourteenth-century Golden Pavilion

Popularly known as Kinkaku-ji for its magnificent Golden Pavilion, Rokuon-ji is one of the finest examples of architecture from the Muromachi period (1338–1573) when the Ashikaga shōgunate reigned. The temple and villa previously owned by the aristocrat Saionji family was renovated by the third Ashikaga shōgun Yoshimitsu as part of the sumptuous villa complex known as Kitayama-dono ("Northern mountain palace"). The villa complex became the center not only of politics but also of the Kitayama culture, which was strongly influenced by Ming Chinese culture. The villa was converted into a Rinzai Zen temple by the fourth Ashikaga shōgun Yoshimochi in 1420 and was called Rokuon (Deer Park) after Yoshimitsu's posthumous name. The temple is a branch temple of Shōkoku-ji, and Musō Soseki is its honorary founder. Much of the building was burned down during the fifteenth-century Ōnin War—a dispute between two powerful families that escalated into a nationwide war (1467–77).

Coated with lacquer and covered with pure gold leaf, the three-story Golden Pavilion is a relic hall built over the spacious Kyōko-chi ("Mirror pond"). Each floor boasts different styles and houses images of the Bodhisattva Kannon and an Amida triad. The Golden Pavilion—the only survivor of the original Yoshimitsu villa complex, spared by U.S. bombers during World War II—was destroyed in 1950 by a fire started accidentally by a young monk. This incident caught the attention of several writers, including Mishima Yukio, whose novel *The Temple of the Golden Pavilion* (1956) was later made into several films. Rebuilt in 1955, the current Golden Pavilion is a near-perfect replica of the original. Kinkaku-ji and the Golden Pavilion are designated World Heritage Historic Monuments of Ancient Kyoto. **FN**

Minami-za (Kyoto, Japan)

Japan's first permanent Kabuki theater, built in 1929

Known for its stylized drama, flamboyant costumes, and makeup, Kabuki is a form of Japanese traditional theater developed during the Edo period (1603–1868), and was the most popular type of entertainment among the commoners at that time. Still popular today, Kabuki continues to be performed regularly in theaters such as Minami-za, the first Kabuki theater in Japan, built at the birthplace of Kabuki.

Kabuki is said to have derived from the dances and skits performed on the banks of Kamogawa River in Kyoto in 1603 by the female itinerant performer Okuni, who may have once been a maiden in the service of the Izumo Shrine. Okuni's troupe and its imitators' suggestive dances, together with the dancers' close link to prostitution, prompted the Tokugawa shōgunate to ban women from Kabuki in 1629 in order to curb immorality. Initially performed only by women, Kabuki has since then—with few

exceptions—been performed only by adult males. The original Kabuki "theaters" were simply raised platforms on riverbanks, enclosed by rudimentary fences. More permanent forms were constructed after the shōgunate began to issue performing licenses. The present Minami-za, designed by Shiranamise in the elaborate style of the Momoyama culture, is a concrete building erected in 1929. It was later extensively renovated in 1991 and is designated as a Tangible Cultural Property of Japan.

The hundred-year-long tradition of the Kaomise Kōgyō ("Face Showing") performances held annually in November to December is the highlight at Minami-za, where popular actors are lined up on the stage. Before the event, the theater is decorated with wooden plates made of cypress called *manaki*, presenting the names of Kabuki actors written in the unique Kanteiryū calligraphic style. **FN**

🏛 ⊚ Nijō-jō (Kyoto, Japan)

Magnificently decorated residence of the Tokugawa shōgunate

Lavishly decorated, Nijō-jō was the symbol of the authority of the Tokugawa shōgunate founded by Tokugawa Ieyasu in the sixteenth century. In 1603, after the victory at the Battle of Sekigahara—a decisive battle that ended more than a century of constant warfare in Japan—Nijō-jō was built as Ieyasu's official Kyoto residence when he received the title of shōgun from the emperor. Although officially called a castle, Nijō-jō was a fortified palace rather than a palatial castle and it served as the headquarters of the shōgunate in western Japan. The ostentatious display of wealth and power embodied in its architecture and ornamentation was a strong political statement, antithetical to the refined tastes of the imperial nobility of Kyoto. When the last Tokugawa shōgun returned sovereignty to the emperor at Nijō-jō in 1867, the castle was also given to the imperial institution and renamed Nijō Detached Palace in 1884.

Expanded to its present size by the third Tokugawa shōgun Iemitsu in 1626, Nijō-jō is a large, elaborate complex consisting of two compounds with separate palaces, Honmaru and Ninomaru, each with a number of buildings and gardens. The original buildings of the Honmaru Palace were destroyed by fire in 1750, and the current structure was transferred from the Kyoto Imperial Palace in 1893. The Ninomaru Palace is laid out in a diagonal configuration along the pond in the Ninomaru Garden, which includes three islands and a three-tiered waterfall. One of the unique features of the palace is the "nightingale floors" in the corridors, constructed so that they would squeak like birds when intruders walked upon them. Many of the sliding doors and walls at Nijō-jō were painted by famous Kanō school artists. Nijō-jō is included on the UNESCO list of World Heritage Historic Monuments of Ancient Kyoto. **FN**

🏛️ ◉ Nishi-Hongan-ji (Kyoto, Japan)

One of two Kyoto temples serving as headquarters of Shin Buddhism

The Hongan-ji temple (officially Jōdo-Shinshū Hongan-ji-ha Hongan-ji) is the headquarters of the Hongan-ji branch of Jōdo-Shinshū (Shin Buddhism), popularly known as Nishi (West) Hongan-ji to distinguish it from its neighbor Higashi (East) Hongan-ji. Shin Buddhism, founded by Shinran in the thirteenth century, is one of the most widely practiced sects of Buddhism. *Hongan-ji* means "temple of the original vow," referring to the vows of Amida Buddha, the manifestation of the Shin Buddhist teachings.

The Hongan-ji is derived from the mausoleum of Shinran built at Ōtani in Kyoto in 1272 by his daughter, Kakushinni. In 1312 it was converted into a temple, initially called Senju-ji, but then changed to Hongan-ji in 1321. After changing its site several times, the Hongan-ji was established at the current site in Kyoto in 1591, thanks to land donated by the feudal ruler Toyotomi Hideyoshi. The Hongan-ji expanded in the fifteenth century, during the time of the eighth chief priest Rennyo. As the uprisings against the feudal system by the followers of Shin Buddhism became serious, the feudal lord Oda Nobunaga tried to destroy the Hongan-ji, then based at Ishiyama in Osaka—the fortress of the followers—resulting in an eleven-year-long siege at the temple. The Hongan-ji was burned down and Nobunaga planned to build a castle at the site where Osaka-jō now stands. In 1602 the Hongan-ji was divided into two by the Tokugawa shōgun Ieyasu—Nishi Hongan-ji and Higashi Hongan-ji.

Most of the wooden buildings at the temple date from the sixteenth to the eighteenth century, notably, the magnificent Founder's Hall and Amida Buddha Hall, which houses an image of the Buddha. The Hongan-ji has the oldest extant sixteenth-century Nō stage in Japan. The site also includes a large tea pavilion and gardens. **FN**

◉ Sanjūsangen-dō (Kyoto, Japan)

Temple housing 1,001 golden statues of Thousand-armed Kannon

Popularly known as Sanjūsangen-dō, the 400-foot-(122-m-) long main hall of Rengeō-in temple is the longest wooden building in Japan, originally built on the order of the retired Emperor Go-Shirakawa in the twelfth century. Sanjūsangen-dō means "a hall with thirty-three bays," which is exactly what it has. Kannon, the Buddhist Deity of Mercy who is worshipped at Sanjūsangen-dō, is said to appear in thirty-three incarnations appropriate to the situation of the person who calls for help. The present hall—a faithful reconstruction of the original hall, which was burned down in 1249—dates from 1266 and is designated as a National Treasure of Japan.

From the end of the eleventh to the early twelfth century, Japan was torn by internal conflicts. The aristocrats of the time built many temples in Kyoto in their attempts to seek peace and some temples served as repositories for Buddhist images.

Sanjūsangen-dō is now the only remaining repository from the period. Inside the hall there is an impressive display of 1,001 golden statues of Thousand-armed Kannon (each Kannon actually has forty arms, but each arm saves twenty-five worlds). The main 6-foot-(1.8-m-) tall Kannon with eleven faces, made by the Kamakura sculptor Tankei, stands in the middle of the hall and is flanked on each side by 500 smaller life-size images of the same deity. Twenty-eight statues of guardian deities stand around the Kannons.

Sanjūsangen-dō is well known for the Tōshiya, an archery contest that has been held annually since the Edo period (1603–1868). Another annual event is the Rite of the Willow, in which participants are touched with a willow branch to prevent or cure headaches. Sanjūsangen-dō belongs to the Myōhō-in Temple of the Tendai school of Buddhism, which had close links with the retired Emperor Go-Shirakawa. **FN**

Osaka-jō (Osaka, Japan)

Rebuilt stronghold of the Toyotomi ruler

The imposing main tower of Osaka-jō that we see today is a twentieth-century restoration of the original sixteenth-century structure, which has again been renovated in the twenty-first century. Over more than 400 years Osaka-jō has undergone a number of transformations, not only architecturally but also politically. Notably, there are two versions of Osaka-jō—Toyotomi Osaka-jō and Tokugawa Osaka-jō.

In 1583, the feudal ruler Toyotomi Hideyoshi began the construction of Osaka-jō, as a symbol of authority, at the site of the former Ishiyama Hongan-ji temple. Modeled after Oda Nobunaga's Azuchi castle, Hideyoshi's Osaka castle was on a grander scale, glittering with gold. The castle served as Hideyoshi's stronghold in his campaign to unify Japan. After Hideyoshi's death, Tokugawa Ieyasu rose in power and established the shōgunate in 1603. Tokugawa-led forces attacked the Toyotomi clan at Osaka in a series

of battles known as the Siege of Osaka, destroying the Toyotomi and their castle. The reconstruction of Osaka-jō began in 1620 under the rule of the second Tokugawa shōgun Hidetada and it surpassed the grandeur of its predecessor. The newly elevated main tower, however, was struck by lightning in 1665 and the castle remained towerless until restorations were undertaken in 1931. The extant stone walls date from the shōgunate and represent the most sophisticated building techniques the shōguns possessed.

Much of the castle was burned down during the civil conflicts that led to the Meiji Restoration in 1868, which ended the Tokugawa era. Later, a weapons factory was built on the east side of Osaka-jō, making it a target for heavy bombing during World War II. The damage has been restored with concrete, and today a museum within the castle documents the life of Toyotomi Hideyoshi and the castle's history. **FN**

🏛️ ⊚ **Daibutsuden** (Nara, Japan)

Temple housing the Great Buddha of Nara

Popularly known as Daibutsuden, the Kon-dō of Tōdai-ji temple was built to house the colossal statue of the Great Buddha (Daibutsu). Nara was the capital of Japan for most of the eighth century, and Tōdai-ji served as the center of state Buddhism. The original timber-frame hall, built in 758, was a structure on a much grander scale than the present Daibutsuden.

Inside the hall stands the bronze statue of Vairocana Buddha, the central deity of the Flower Garland Sutra. This 52-foot- (16-m-) high Buddha is believed to have been the largest bronze casting made in the ancient world. Its construction was the eighth-century emperor Shōmu's conscious attempt to emulate the architectural plans of Empress Wu of Tang China, who had created many Buddhist images. The Eye-Opening Ceremony, the official completion ceremony for the Buddha, was held in 752 under the direction of the Indian monk Bodhisena, with thousands of monks in attendance. The construction of Daibutsuden began after this ceremony.

Burned down in 1180, the original hall was rebuilt in 1185. The new hall was in turn destroyed by fire during civil wars in 1567, and the homeless Buddha's head was blown off in 1610. It was only in 1692 that the statue was repaired and the hall—the third reconstruction to be built on the same site—was rebuilt in 1709. Tōdai-ji was designated a UNESCO World Heritage site in 1998. **FN**

> *"The city's historic monuments provide a vivid picture of life in [Nara] in the eighth century."*
>
> UNESCO

Itsukushima-jinja (Itsukushima Island, Japan)

Shinto shrine dedicated to the worship of nature and three goddesses of the sea

Itsukushima Island (popularly known as Miyajima—shrine island) in the Seto inland sea has been a sacred place of Shintoism since ancient times. A shrine bearing its name, Itsukushima-jinja, is believed to have been founded there originally by Saeki no Kuramoto in 593. The main shrine—which was initially built in 1168 by the powerful warlord Taira no Kiyomori—became the foundation of the present buildings, which were constructed during the thirteenth century. Despite repeated reconstructions and restorations due to wear and damage caused by fires and natural disasters, the shrine has maintained its original design in the shinden-zukuri style of the Heian period (794–1185). The present main sanctuary dates from the sixteenth century and the Nō stage was built in the seventeenth century.

Designed for the worship of nature and three Shinto goddesses of the sea, the shrine stands in the sea against a beautiful natural background of mountains. Although it is a Shinto shrine, the idea of building a shrine over the sea is said to derive either from Ryūgū-jō, the mythical undersea palace of the dragon deity, or as the manifestation of the Pure Land School of Buddhism. The magnificent view of its 52-foot- (16-m-) tall vermilion Ōtorii gate in front of the deep-green virgin forests of Mount Misen on Itsukushima Island is one of the "Three Views of Japan" listed by scholar Hayashi Razan in 1643. (The other two are Matsushima Bay and Amanohashidate.) At high tide, the shrine looks as if it is floating on the sea, adding a dramatic element to the site. The main inner shrine complex has thirty-seven structures and its outer shrine has nineteen onshore buildings.

UNESCO designated the Itsukushima Shinto shrine a World Heritage site in 1996 for its wonderful harmonization of human creativity and natural beauty, a work of incomparable physical beauty. **FN**

> *"The petals of cherry blossoms*
> *Fall in the soup and dishes of*
> *Raw fish under the tree."*

Basho, haiku on Itsukushima-jinja (1815)

A-Bomb Dome (Hiroshima, Japan)

The only structure left standing in Hiroshima after the atomic bomb explosion of 1945

At 8:15 A.M. on August 6, 1945, the U.S. B-29 bomber *Enola Gay* dropped the world's first atomic bomb on the city of Hiroshima. The bomb, called Little Boy, killed about 140,000 people. Hiroshima Peace Memorial—known as Atomic Bomb or Genbaku Dome—stands as a witness of the nuclear devastation as well as a symbol of hope for peace.

The building was originally built in 1915 as the Hiroshima Prefectural Commercial Exhibition Hall. Designed by Czech architect Jan Letzel, it was a three-story brick building in a mixture of Secession and neo-Baroque styles. During World War II, the building was used to house governmental and commercial offices. The hypocenter of the atomic explosion was only about 525 feet (160 m) southeast of this building. The bomb exploded virtually above the building, and because the blast wave traveled straight down through its center, some walls and the steel frames of the structure survived. The ruins of the building came to be known as A-Bomb Dome and have been preserved as they were in the immediate aftermath of the nuclear explosion. After much debate, the city of Hiroshima decided in 1966 to preserve the dome indefinitely, and it is now part of the Hiroshima Peace Memorial Park. The park was designed by Tange Kenzō and has a number of memorials, including the Peace Memorial Museum. Every year on August 6, Hiroshima City holds the Peace Memorial Ceremony in front of the Memorial Cenotaph at the park to remember the victims of the atomic bomb.

Although China and the United States expressed reservations about its inclusion, UNESCO designated the dome a World Heritage site in 1996, describing it as a stark and powerful symbol of the most destructive force ever created by humankind, as well as expressing the hope for world peace and the ultimate elimination of all nuclear weapons. **FN**

"Hiroshima has one intact building . . . in a city which . . . had a population of 310,000."

Wilfred Burchett, first Allied journalist at Hiroshima

🏛 ⊚ Sukhothai Historical Park (near Chiang Mai, Thailand)

Rich in the cultural heritage of the kingdom of Siam

> *"[Sukhothai] became an awesome monumental expression of the strength of Buddhism."*
>
> Elizabeth Harris, journalist

Sukhothai was the first Thai kingdom. Its premier city, also called Sukhothai, was established in 1238 by King Sri Indraditya, after he led the territory to independence from the Khmer occupiers. The city was created to celebrate the victory of the king and his people and to symbolize his vision that they would never again be ruled by the Khmer. Today the remains of that ancient city have been made into a historical park, a huge complex that contains more than 200 venerable buildings.

The architecture at Sukhothai is a blend of styles, mixing Buddhist art with elements of pagan, Khmer, and Sri Lankan architecture. There are a large number of temples and palaces at the site, including the Royal Palace and the equally regal Wat Mahathat, or Temple of the Great Relic, commissioned by Sri Indraditya. The temple was constructed of bricks and Khmer laterite, with decorations in additional local laterite. A colossal seated Buddha with his hands in the traditional *bhumisparsa mudra* position is enshrined in the pillared hall of the Wat Mahathat. The other temples, mostly dedicated to Theravada Buddhism, were built in laterite and covered with stucco. They are typified by "lotus bud" stupas, so-called because of the way they begin with a wide base and taper off to a point.

Sukhothai is one of the most important historic sites in Thailand, not only for its monumental size—which requires two moats and three walls to encompass it—but for its inimitable heritage. This ancient city is the physical memory of the kingdom that became modern-day Thailand, a country with a unique religious, artistic, and social history. A project for an international campaign was adopted by UNESCO in 1977 and a 27-square-mile (70-sq-km) area was declared a historic park in 1988. The Historic Town of Sukhothai and Associated Historic Towns became a UNESCO World Heritage site in 1991. **SJ**

Kanchanaburi War Cemeteries (Kanchanaburi, Thailand)

Monument to the thousands who suffered while building the infamous "Death Railway"

Kanchanaburi lies 80 miles (130 km) west of Bangkok in Thailand's lush countryside, and is most famous for its association with World War II. From 1941 to 1943 the Japanese army built the 258-mile- (415-km-) long "Death Railway." The aim was to connect Bangkok to Rangoon in Burma (now Myanmar) via rail, and decrease the army's reliance on transport by sea. The Japanese used forced labor in the form of 200,000 Asians and 69,000 Allied prisoners of war to lay the track over the jungle-clad mountains. By the time the railway was completed in October 1943, it is estimated that 100,000 conscripted Asians and 16,000 prisoners of war had died while working on the project.

The town is now the site of the Kanchanaburi War Cemetery (also known as the Don-Rak War Cemetery), the Chonk-Kai Cemetery, and the JEATH War Museum. The Kanchanaburi War Cemetery is the burial place of 6,982 British, Australian, and Dutch prisoners of war who lost their lives in brutal and squalid conditions imposed by the Japanese during the construction of the railway. Rows of headstones lie in its tranquil garden. The Chonk-Kai Cemetery is built on the site of one of the prisoner of war camps, and is the smaller but more formal of the two graveyards. The majority of its 1,740 headstones are memorials to the unknown soldiers buried there.

The JEATH War Museum is a replica of the modest bamboo huts the prisoners of war lived in, and takes its name from the initials of the countries involved in building the railway: Japan, England, Australia, Thailand, and Holland. The museum houses items such as spades used in laying the track, and personal memorabilia such as photos, drawings, and clothing that help convey the deprivation of the prisoners of war in a poignant fashion. The town bears the scars of the ruthless intent of the Japanese army to build the railway at any cost. **CK**

"We were overworked, underfed, and subjected to constant physical and mental abuse."

George Duffy, prisoner of war

🏛 ◉ Ayutthaya (near Bangkok, Thailand)

A once-prosperous city of religious tolerance and artistic expression

Ayutthaya became the official capital of what was then Siam during King Ramathibodi's reign in the fourteenth century. Over the ensuing century, the previous capital, Sukhothai, existed as a separate independent province, but was slowly absorbed into the Ayutthaya kingdom. Ayutthaya was at its height between the fourteenth and the eighteenth century, and the city became one of the wealthiest in Asia.

Ramathibodi introduced Theravada Buddhism as his country's official religion, but he remained tolerant toward other faiths and encouraged artistic expression from all regions and religions. Ayutthaya contains a number of examples of Mon and Khmer art and architecture, styles that had been popular in the Sukhothai period, harmoniously blended with newer styles indigenous to the Ayutthaya region. Sri Lankan architecture also influenced the buildings here, such as the Wat Phra Sri Samphet, the three burial structures

of King Ramathibodi II, his elder brother, and his father. The most ancient temple at Ayutthaya is the Wat Bhuddai Svarya.

In the mid-sixteenth century neighboring Burma attacked Ayutthaya and briefly conquered the kingdom. The Burmese were expelled, however, after a dramatic duel fought on elephants in which the Ayutthayan king, Naresuan, fatally wounded Burma's crown prince. In the 1760s Burma attacked Ayutthaya again. The city was sacked in 1767 and a huge number of buildings were destroyed. Archeological remains of the great period still exist, although the full extent of the once-great city cannot be truly fathomed. There are, however, a number of wonderful ruins of temples and palaces to visit. The area was made a national park in the 1970s and added to UNESCO's World Heritage List in 1991 because the site represents an important period of development in Thai art. **SJ**

Grand Palace (Bangkok, Thailand)

This splendidly ornate palace was once the official royal residence

A profusion of stylized, slanting, multilayered roofs—some with *garudas* (the bird-human vehicle of the Hindu god Rama) on the corners, as well as towers and stupas—greets the visitor to the premier tourist spectacle in Bangkok and the major architectural symbol of the Thai royal family.

The Grand Palace is a walled city within a city. It covers an area of 235,000 square feet (21,840 sq m) and is surrounded by four walls totaling 6,230 feet (1,900 m) in length. These walls enclose more than 100 brightly colored buildings, golden spires, and glittering mosaics, dating back to 1782 when Bangkok was founded by Rama I. When you enter the compound, you first see Wat Phra Kaew, the Temple of the Emerald Buddha—Thailand's most sacred temple. Inside lies the tiny Emerald Buddha, which is actually made of jade and is perched so high up inside a glass box that it is not easy to admire in detail.

With the notable exception of the glittering roof, the palace makes a fairly grand nod to colonial and Victorian architecture, especially in the balconies and staircases. Anna, tutor to the son of Rama IV and the main protagonist in *The King and I*, lived here. Among the royal buildings is Boromabiman Hall, built by King Rama VI, where every subsequent king has lived at some point in their reign. Amarin Vinichai Hall is an intriguing blend of European and Thai architecture and has a very spacious European-style reception room (for foreign ambassadors) with a glistening gold throne. Visitors are allowed inside this building, but the others are closed to the public.

The whole place is spotlessly clean and ordered, and, perhaps because of this, it is easy to think you've entered a theme park: The bustling tourists, elephant statues, and starched-uniformed, Raj-style palace guards add to the unreal splendor. **JH**

Luang Prabang (Luang Prabang, Laos)

The town demonstrates a glorious fusion of traditional and European architectural styles

About 265 miles (426 km) north of modern Laos's capital, Vientiane, lies Luang Prabang, the former capital of the independent kingdom of the same name and royal residence until the communist takeover in 1975. When France annexed Laos a century earlier, Luang Prabang was recognized as the royal residence and, in time, the ruler of the town and province became synonymous with the figurehead of the French Protectorate of Laos. When the country achieved its independence, the king became head of state for the kingdom of Laos.

There are dozens of temples and religious sites in Luang Prabang, with the biggest concentration located in the old quarter. Xieng Thong, built in 1560, is probably the most beautiful structure, with lavish decoration in colored glass and gold. Visitors can also take in Haw Kham, the former royal palace and now a museum. A spectacular perspective is offered at the top of Mount Phousi, which lies close to the town center and offers wonderful views of the surrounding temples and hills.

Arriving by boat allows today's visitors the same experience as those who came to trade or engage in battle in previous centuries. As the gold domes of temples poke through the tree canopy, this is also perhaps the most dramatic approach to the site. Encircled by jungle-covered mountains and at the junction of the Mekong and its tributary, the Khan River, Luang Prabang is southeast Asia at its best preserved. Virgin wilderness (tigers still roam the surrounding forests and new species are found with regularity), perfectly preserved buildings, streets that tellingly fuse ancient temples and colonial buildings, and a pace of life that is decidedly not of this century seem all the more unreal given the history of conquest and recapture by clans and rulers. **AP**

Plain of Jars (Xiangkhoang Plateau, Laos)

Archeologists remain puzzled as to the purpose and history of the jars

Why, when, and how Laos's Plain of Jars came into existence are three important questions still very much open to debate. The Plain of Jars covers an immense expanse of land, and the jars in the 400 individual sites vary in size and arrangement. Many archeologists and anthropologists have theorized that the jars were originally used as funerary urns by an ancient Mon-Khmer race and were made between 500 B.C.E. and 800 C.E. These theories are supported by the French archeologist, Madeleine Colani, who performed a very thorough excavation of the region in the 1930s. She discovered caves in close proximity to the jars, within which she found human remains and two enormous chimneys. She concluded that the chimneys were kilns used to cremate human remains, suggesting that the jars were urns for the ashes.

An alternative theory is that the jars were used by travelers for food storage or collecting monsoon rainwater. There is also the legendary Lao theory that the jar region was once inhabited by a race of giants. This race was ruled by King Khun Cheung who, after winning a particularly lengthy battle, decided to celebrate by drinking rice wine from the jars, leaving them behind as reminders of his epic celebrations.

The jars are arranged across an expanse of land stretching from Thailand, through Laos, and into northern India. They appear to be laid in lines, which may have followed an ancient trade route. The jars are mostly made from sandstone and range up to a height of 10 feet (3 m), weighing up to 13 tons. It is still possible to view these phenomenal jars, but not without great caution. The Plain of Jars is covered in many unexploded bombs as a result of the U.S. bombardment in the Secret War (1962–75); if one is lucky enough to visit this historic site, it must be done with an experienced guide. **KH**

The central temple is the pride of the nation and appears on the country's national flag

> "[Angkor Wat] is grander than anything left to us by Greece or Rome."

Henri Mouhot, explorer

⊤ A Khmer army marches to war in one of the intricate friezes at Bayon temple to the north of Angkor Wat.

⊡ Angkor Wat's towers, symbolizing the gods' abode, are reflected in a moat, symbolizing an ocean.

Angkor is renowned as one of the most beautiful temple complexes in the world and visiting it is an experience that never fails to impress. There are over a thousand temples in the area, in varying states of repair, although the most magnificent of them, and certainly the best known, is Angkor Wat.

The Khmer king Yasovarman I began building the Angkor complex around 890. The heart of the complex covers 75 square miles (195 sq km) although it is thought that this central area was surrounded by the largest urban sprawl in the medieval world, approaching an incredible 1,150 square miles (3,000 sq km), roughly the size of modern Los Angeles. The civilization fell into a rapid decline during the thirteenth and fourteenth centuries, and Angkor was eventually sacked by Thai invaders in 1431. The complex was gradually swallowed up by forest and was only rediscovered by French explorers in the late nineteenth century.

The central feature of the complex is undoubtedly Angkor Wat. It was built as a state temple between 1113 and 1150 by Suryavarman II, who dedicated Angkor Wat to his ancestors and to the god Vishnu. The temple is laid out as five tower structures or *prasats* forming a pyramid in three levels. The towers represent the five peaks of the mythical abode of the Hindu gods, Mount Meru, the center of the Hindu universe. The outer gallery is home to an impressive narrative bas-relief that stretches for 2,500 feet (762 m). This prodigious work of art portrays battle scenes from the sacred text the *Mahabharata*; depictions of a popular Hindu myth, the Churning of the Sea of Milk; scenes from Vishnu's victory over demons; and everyday life in the time of Suryavarman II. The pediments of the temple are home to more than 2,000 carved celestial maidens or *apsaras*, who act as guards to ward off evil. **SJ**

Killing Fields Memorial (near Phnom Penh, Cambodia)

Memorial to those ruthlessly killed and unceremoniously buried by the Khmer Rouge

Here, at Choeung Ek—a former orchard—is the Killing Fields Memorial that attracts more than 100,000 visitors annually. They come from around the world to see one of Cambodia's most important sites and to pay their respects to those who died under the Khmer Rouge's brutal regime.

The Khmer Rouge, Cambodian communists who had a new, agrarian vision of how Cambodia should be, came to power in 1975. From then until 1979, when the Vietnamese defeated them, they killed an estimated 1.7 million people. Most victims did not know the name Pol Pot; their oppressor hid behind the name Angka or the "Organization." The Killing Fields was the site where the regime killed and buried its victims. Around 17,000 people were killed at Choeung Ek. Coming off the bumpy road that snakes out of the capital, one is greeted by a three-story-high memorial pagoda. Inside, more than 8,000 skulls are stacked up, divided by age and gender. Victims were interrogated at the "re-education camp," otherwise known as Tuol Sleng, and then brought to Choeung Ek to be killed. Behind the memorial pagoda are the mass graves—pits of bones with grass and dirt thrown over them. The site is surrounded by paddy fields; it is peaceful and quiet but, just like a Nazi concentration camp, it was once a site of unimaginable horror.

Many people in Cambodia, a Buddhist country, believe that the skulls must be taken off display because if the body is not cremated the soul cannot be liberated. The museum remains though, in the belief that it is more important to remember what happened, in order for it never to happen again. **OR**

◩ Skulls found at the Choeung Ek Killing Fields are kept at this memorial stupa as evidence of the genocide.

◰ Photographs of Pol Pot's victims are displayed at Tuol Sleng Genocide Museum at Phnom Penh.

Hoa Lo Prison (Hanoi, Vietnam)

Inmates were housed in poor conditions and frequently tortured

Constructed by Vietnam's French colonial rulers, Hoa Lo Prison was largely used to house political prisoners. Known to the French as Maison Centrale, it was built on a street previously used for the manufacture of portable earthen stoves, known as *hoa lo* (fiery furnace). After North Vietnamese independence, the prison was used to accommodate U.S. prisoners of war (mainly airmen) during the Vietnam War.

The prison was housed in buildings made of thick yellow stone. An imposing black door marking the entrance received the nickname "monster's mouth" from locals. For much of its life, what went on behind the walls was the torture and abuse of prisoners, first at the hands of the French and then the Vietnamese. In 1913 there were 615 prisoners but, by 1953, the number of inmates had increased to more than 2,000. Largely they consisted of Viet Minh resistance members, and the guillotine in the grounds was regularly in use. Do Muoi, former general secretary of the Communist Party, was a former inmate who escaped along with 100 others through the sewer system in 1945. U.S. prisoners of war started arriving in 1964, and the facility was used until 1973. It was nicknamed the "Hanoi Hilton" and perhaps the most famous prisoner was U.S. senator John McCain. Inmates were kept shackled to their beds, and tortured and abused in violation of the Geneva Convention.

In 1993 most of the prison was demolished for Singaporean businessmen to build the Hanoi Tower complex. What remains today is a museum largely focusing on how the Vietnamese suffered at the hands of the French. **MA**

☒ The ugly red arch above the black prison door may have suggested the nickname of "monster's mouth."

☒ Wax figures of prisoners illustrate how inmates were shackled to their beds in the notorious prison.

Mausoleum of Ho Chi Minh (Hanoi, Vietnam)

Simple monument to an iconic political figure

LỊCH SỬ SANG TRANG

Born Nguyen Tat Thanh in 1890, Ho Chi Minh (meaning "he who enlightens") is a legend. Traveler, patriot, revolutionary, soldier, leader; he not only founded the Vietnamese Communist Party but was also a founding member of the French party. Leading resistance to the Japanese in Vietnam during World War II with his Viet Minh group, he capitalized on the power vacuum of the Japanese surrender. To a crowd of half a million in central Hanoi he declared Vietnamese independence in September 1945. The French did not accept this decision and tried to regain control in 1946. This led to war between the Viet Minh and the French, culminating in the division of Vietnam in 1954. Ho became president of North Vietnam and died in 1969 during the Vietnam War.

Recognizing his iconic status, party officials decided to embalm the body and build a mausoleum on the spot where Ho had declared independence. A three-story building made of native Vietnamese materials was designed and built. The body, clothed in a simple tunic and sandals, is held in a glass case in a gray, cubelike, squat building ringed with columns and topped with the words "Chu Tich (President) Ho Chi Minh." Inside the foyer is the inscription: "There is nothing more precious than independence and freedom." The mausoleum stands in front of a large parade ground used for military displays.

Today the mausoleum is the focus of Vietnamese commemorations of Ho. Nearby are the Ho Chi Minh Museum and also the president's former home, a simple wooden stilted house built in the traditional style consisting of only two rooms. **MA**

↖ The mausoleum, built of gray granite and red marble, displays the revolutionary leader's embalmed body.

← Ho Chi Minh, here depicted as a military leader, said "It was patriotism, not communism, that inspired me."

🏛 ◉ Imperial Tombs (near Hué, Vietnam)

A spectacular series of tombs, built to reflect the personality of the emperor

Tombs are very important for the Vietnamese because they believe the layout of the tomb affects the soul's journey into the spirit world. Formal ceremonies to the dead are also believed to affect the fortunes of the living. It is no surprise, therefore, that Vietnam's imperial tombs on the banks of the Perfume (Huong) River outside Hué should be so elaborate, having such an influence on the ongoing success of an imperial dynasty.

The sites fulfilled two functions: as a tomb but also as a secondary royal palace where the emperor could entertain guests. Construction of a tomb therefore began during the reign of the emperor for whom it was intended, and reflected his taste and personality. The tomb of Gia Long, for example, is built in a simple yet magnificent style, whereas one of the most elaborate tombs is that of Tu Duc, which reflects his reputation for being decadent. During his reign, the power of the monarchy declined because of increasing French domination, and toward the end of his rule he spent increasing amounts of time at the tomb. His body and treasure were not buried here but at a secret site. The tomb of Khai Dinh was largely built under French influence using concrete and lacks the harmony of earlier tombs.

The tombs and the Hué Citadel were made a UNESCO World Heritage site in 1993 as part of the Complex of Hué Monuments. As monuments they span an important period of history, including Vietnam's loss of independence to the French in the mid-1800s, when the ruling dynasty became mere figureheads to colonial overlords. **MA**

↗ The tomb of Khai Dinh, who died in 1925, boasts a statuary of court officials, soldiers and horses.

→ Emperor Khai Dinh approved French plans to tax the peasants in Vietnam to pay for his extravagant tomb.

Corregidor Island (Manila Bay, The Philippines)

Site of a strategic victory for the Japanese against U.S. forces

Corregidor was the main fortified island that guarded the entrance to the strategically vital Manila Bay. During the early twentieth century, when the Philippines were under U.S. control, the U.S. Army undertook substantial building works on the tadpole-shaped island, some 2 miles (3.2 km) from the Bataan Peninsula on the main island of Luzon. As well as heavy artillery emplacements, an intricate tunnel network was dug into Corregidor Island, which housed an administrative headquarters, several army barracks, an underground hospital, and storehouses with enough food and water to last 10,000 men for up to six months.

When the Japanese invaded Luzon in December 1941, U.S. and Filipino troops fell back to the Bataan Peninsula. Corregidor came under heavy artillery and aerial bombardment, but the position of the troops became critical only when the defenders on Bataan surrendered on April 9, 1942. The Japanese then turned the full weight of their firepower on Corregidor. The guns on Corregidor had been intended for use against long-range naval targets and, apart from some heavy mortars, they were of limited use against the Japanese land forces on Bataan. The island was battered into submission, and when a Japanese amphibious force landed on the island on May 5, they met little organized opposition. As the Japanese began to enter the tunnel system, the U.S. commander, Lieutenant-General Jonathan Wainwright, felt he had no option but to surrender, thus ending all U.S. resistance on the Philippines.

Corregidor today is a historic monument, with the mangled military installations left as they were after the battle. It has become a popular tourist stop, as well as a place of reflection for surviving veterans who had to endure not only the battle but also more than three years of Japanese captivity. **AG**

> *"We are being subjected to terrific bombardment; it is unreasonable to expect we can hold out for long."*
>
> Lieutenant-General Jonathan Wainwright

Intramuros (Manila, The Philippines)

The oldest district in Manila was developed when the Spanish colonized the islands

For more than three centuries Intramuros was the center of Spanish rule in the Philippines. The walled complex consisted of houses, churches, and schools surrounded by a system of fortifications. The city's name comes from the Latin *intra muros*—meaning "within the walls."

Intramuros occupies a strategically important position on the Pasig River and Manila Bay, and before the imposition of Spanish rule, the city was a center of power for both indigenous chiefs and Malayan Muslims. In 1570, the Spanish arrived in Manila Bay and, after a year of war, made peace with the native rulers. The Spanish governor general, López de Legazpi, declared the town to be the center of Spanish rule in the islands. The walls, begun in 1573 and based on the structure of a medieval castle, covered 158 acres (64 ha) and were 26 feet (8 m) thick and 72 feet (22 m) high. Inside the complex were many important buildings, including the Governor's Palace, Manila Cathedral, and several religious schools and universities. During World War II, Intramuros was used as the base of the Japanese occupation. In the Battle of Manila (1945), almost all of Intramuros was destroyed. The only structure within the walls to survive was San Agustín Church (built 1587–1606). One of the main forts along the walls, Fort Santiago (first erected in 1571), also survived, and is used as a museum of the Spanish administration. It also houses a shrine to José Rizal, the Filipino nationalist hero, who was held at the fort before his execution.

During the 1980s, the Intramuros area was restored and it remains relatively untouched by the modernization of the rest of Manila. Intramuros, unlike most of Manila, still retains aspects of Spanish-era design. In spite of the rapid changes in Manila and throughout the rest of the nation, Intramuros remains as a legacy of Spanish rule in the Philippines. **JF**

"... a reinterpretation of European Baroque by Chinese and Philippine craftsmen."

UNESCO, on the architecture of San Agustín Church

Malacanang Palace

(Manila, The Philippines)

Ex-colonial home of Filipino heads of state

Like many palaces, Malacanang has weathered centuries of dramatic political change to become a potent symbol. Located at the heart of the capital city of the Philippines, it has a long history as a residence of the country's heads of state and is perhaps best known as the former home of the Marcos regime. President from 1965 to 1986, the dictatorial ruler Ferdinand Marcos lived lavishly here with his wife, Imelda. His opponent and successor, Corazon Aquino, symbolically installed herself in the guesthouse rather than in the palace itself.

The main building is a strikingly elegant villa in the Spanish colonial style, stretching picturesquely along the Pasig River's northern bank. It housed first Spanish and then U.S. colonial governors-general in the nineteenth and early twentieth centuries before becoming the official residence to the Filipino presidents who have ruled since the nation gained independence in the 1940s.

Continual expansion and restoration have substantially changed the palace since it was built in the eighteenth century as the private summerhouse of a Spanish aristocrat, Don Luis Rocha. Outside are typically ornate Spanish features such as shady patios, arches, balconies, and window grilles. Inside, spectacular features—many embellished during the Marcos days—include a grand main staircase in burnished woods and a beautiful music room. The Marcos's personal belongings, including the infamous shoe collection that came to international attention when the people stormed the palace in the mid-1980s, are no longer on show. The palace complex includes other buildings, such as the guesthouse and government offices (notably the grand 1920s executive building), and the palace now houses a museum telling the story of past rulers. **AK**

Raffles Hotel

(Singapore)

One of the most famous hotels in the world

When it opened in 1887 this grand old establishment had just ten rooms, but now it boasts 103 suites, eighteen state rooms, eighteen restaurants and bars, along with numerous shops, a theater, and a spa. The hotel has long been a byword for elegance and glamor and, over the years, has attracted a host of celebrities and set the scene for many a movie.

The hotel was founded by four Armenian brothers—Arshak, Aviet, Tigran, and Martin Sarkies. They named it after Sir Stamford Raffles, who had established the British settlement on Singapore in 1819. Originally a converted bungalow, the hotel soon

> *"Providence conducted me . . . to Raffles Hotel, where the food is as excellent as the rooms are bad."*
>
> **Rudyard Kipling, writer**

expanded and a fine, neo-Renaissance building was constructed in 1899. Raffles swiftly earned a reputation for the high quality of its food and cocktails, most notably the Singapore Sling, which was created by one of its barmen *c.* 1910. Joseph Conrad and Rudyard Kipling were the first of many writers to sing the praises of the hotel. The hotel's fame reached a peak in the 1920s and 1930s when Somerset Maugham and Sir Noel Coward became regulars.

In common with any other hotel, Raffles's fortunes have fluctuated over the years. It was forced to close during the Depression, was occupied by the Japanese in World War II, and later became a transit camp for prisoners of war. In spite of these setbacks, the hotel was soon restored to its former glory, particularly after a major refit from 1989 to 1991. **IZ**

Borobudur
(near Magelang, Indonesia)

Well-known Buddhist temple and pilgrimage site

The temple of Borobudur was built over several decades during the Shailandra dynasty, and was created by both Hindus and Buddhists. The original builders were Hindus who began work here in the late eighth century, but by the time the building was finished *c.* 830, the main religion of the region had changed to Buddhism. The temple's structure is organized in nine levels of three tiers, a square base with diminishing platforms in stepped pyramids, and five circular terraces where seventy-two sitting Buddha sculptures are enshrined in perforated stupas. Sculptures illustrating the life of Gautama Buddha were carved on the reliefs of the walls and balustrades.

Like other stupa, the plan of Borobudur is organized around a central axis called the axis mundi, which represents the center of the universe. The main symbolism of Borobudur comes from the tripartite division of its architecture, which represents the three realms of existence in Buddhism. The stupa's base is representative of the world of desire; the mid-section symbolizes the world of the forms; and the upper circular level is indicative of the sacred realm where humans abandon all earthly concerns. The temple rises up to a height of 116 feet (35 m). This height and the design of the temple—which leads visitors on a pilgrimage around and up via a series of airy corridors and sun-filled terraces—are representative of the Buddha's upward journey to Nirvana.

By the eleventh century, Borobudur was all but forgotten and it was not until the nineteenth century that it was rediscovered, by Dutch colonists. The monument was restored with UNESCO's help in the 1970s, and in 1991 it was added to their World Heritage List because Borobudur is a principal monument of Buddhist patrimony and forms a characteristic ensemble of Buddhist art in Java. **SJ**

> *"Borobudur has resumed its old historical role as a place of learning, dedication and training."*

Professor R. Soekmono, archeologist

The Aboriginal peoples arrived in Australia some 40,000 years ago; rock paintings have survived at sites such as Kakadu National Park. In New Zealand, Maori resistance to European settlement is commemorated at Ruapekapeka Pa. Modern Australia was at first a British penal colony, and many of its historic sites are colonial in origin. In the Pacific islands, however, there is evidence of long-disappeared native cultures, such as the artificial islets at Nan Madol and the moai statues of Rapa Nui.

Oceania

◁ Rapa Nui's moai
date from between
1000 and 1500 C.E. and
may represent chiefs.

Perth Mint
(Perth, Australia)

Prolific output of coins and ingots

When Western Australia was still a British colony, its gold sovereigns and half-sovereigns (the most valuable coins in common use) were made at the Royal Mint in London. The gold for these coins came, however, from Western Australia, among other places, so it was decided to open a branch of the mint in Perth to refine the local gold and turn it into gold coinage.

The Perth Mint opened in 1889 and struck more than 106 million gold sovereigns and nearly 735,000 half-sovereigns until the coins were withdrawn from circulation in 1931. In 1940 the mint started to produce Australian silver and copper coins, including the new decimal coinage introduced in 1966, until production finally stopped in 1973. Oddly, the mint remained under British ownership until 1970, when it was passed to the Western Australian government. Today the mint is owned by Australia's Gold Corporation and produces high-quality platinum, gold, and silver coins and proof sets for collectors and investors.

The foundation stone for the mint was laid by Sir John Forrest, the first premier of Western Australia, and the building was opened in 1899. The neo-Romanesque design, by George Temple Pool, the main architect of many other fine buildings in Perth, features a three-story central tower with two two-story wings, linked by splendid colonnades with verandas above. The yellowish limestone of the walls is offset by a red tile roof and white woodwork. The mint includes a museum with coins, gold nuggets and ingots, and a gold mining and refining display, with an hourly "Gold Pour" of molten gold taking place in the Melting House. The world's largest collection of gold bars, some of which have been crafted in unusual shapes, can also be viewed at the site. In 2003 a new manufacturing facility was opened next to the original mint. **SA**

Fremantle Prison
(Fremantle, Australia)

Important site of convict heritage

The British Swan River Colony was founded in 1829 and initially rejected convict labor, preferring to attract free settlers. Some 1,000 settlers had arrived by 1831, but the struggle to survive against the hostile climate and the even more hostile Aboriginals—the two sides fought a large-scale skirmish at Pinjara in 1834—meant that in 1850 the first convicts were shipped out from Britain to support the new colony. Among the first things they did was to replace the earlier Round House by building a prison in Fremantle, now the oldest building still standing in the city. Work began in 1852 and the first convicts were imprisoned in 1855.

"It is believed that 9,501 convicts stepped onto Western Australian soil alive."

Gillian O'Mara, historian

The entrance building to the main cell block is an imposing structure, with an elegant, gabled facade bearing the initials VR (Victoria Regina), a crown, and the date of construction in gold relief. The complex has a large boundary wall, a gatehouse tower, chapel, hospital, and particularly grim cell blocks, some of which have murals painted by inmates. An execution chamber was built in 1888 and became the colony's only legal place of execution. In 1964 the serial killer Eric Edgar Cooke was the last man to be hanged here.

The prison was originally known as the Convict Establishment and then the Imperial Convict Establishment. The convict authorities handed the prison over to the colonial government in 1886, and it continued to hold prisoners until 1991. The building has been restored and is now open to the public. **SA**

⊚ # Kakadu National Park

(Northern Territory, Australia)

Archeological finds record the artworks and lifestyles of ancient civilizations

Kakadu National Park is in the far north of the Northern Territory, 75 miles (120 km) east of Darwin. It is one of four Australian UNESCO World Heritage sites that are listed for both cultural and natural values. The 7,646-square-mile (19,804-sq-km) park was added to the UNESCO list in three stages after 1981. It is jointly managed by the director of National Parks and Bininj/Mungguy, the Aboriginal traditional owners, who lease their land to the government.

There are at least 5,000 Aboriginal art sites in the park—some at least 20,000 years old and of great spiritual significance—with outstanding examples of artwork accessible to visitors. The contemporary Bininj/Mungguy culture can also be experienced through ranger-guided activities and an increasing number of Bininj/Mungguy-owned, culture-based businesses. Kakadu protects six major habitats, from the tidal flats and mangrove forests of the coast, through freshwater floodplains and wetlands, savanna woodlands, and monsoon forest patches, to the stone country of the Arnhem Land plateau and on to the southern hills and ridges. The park also includes the entire catchment of a major tropical river, the South Alligator. A sandstone escarpment from 98 to 980 feet (30 to 300 m) in height extends 124 miles (200 km) through Kakadu, a dramatic boundary between the woodlands and stone country. Gorges and outliers of this escarpment are some of Kakadu's best known natural features.

Kakadu is home to a vast range of flora and fauna, with more than 60 mammal species, 289 bird species—more than one-quarter of all Australian bird species—25 species of frogs, 55 species of freshwater fish, and more than 10,000 species of insects. Kakadu also includes 132 reptile species—probably the most ferocious among them being the estuarine crocodile (*Crocodylus porosus*). **PS**

"This unique archeological and ethnological reserve has been inhabited . . . for 40,000 years."

UNESCO

Broken Hill (Broken Hill, Australia)

The ore deposits mined here were the largest of their kind in the world

"It is an interesting paradox,
I suppose, that art and mining
have come together in Broken Hill."

Bronwen Standley-Woodroffe, artist

⬆ This work is one of twelve sculptors' impressions of Broken Hill that are exhibited to the north of the city.

➡ Broken Hill was a boom town around 1900, attracting many thousands of miners.

Driving across the expansive, red outback of northwest New South Wales, a vast slag heap looms up in the distance. Broken Hill lies to its northeast. The approach is not an attractive introduction to Broken Hill, but it is faithful to the city's origins because this was for many years one of the major and most prosperous mining towns in Australia.

Broken Hill was founded in 1883 when a German-born boundary rider, Charles Rasp, obtained a 40-acre (16-ha) lease on a "broken hill" that he believed contained tin. In fact it was a "line of lode," a 4-mile (7-km) band of lead, silver, and zinc ores. A syndicate of seven men formed Broken Hill Proprietary (BHP), which mined the hill until 1939. Mining continues to this day, although with much reduced output. The worked-out Delprats mine is now a mining museum. Packed into a steel cage with fourteen other people, descending 427 feet (130 m) underground into the hill, the visitor is then expertly guided by former miners along the narrow, low tunnels to inspect the ore faces and see some mining machinery in action.

The city itself is an oasis of green in the outback. Laid out on a grid pattern with wide streets, it is a surprisingly gracious city with many fine municipal buildings. Palace Hotel, a large three-story building with a typical cast-iron, covered balcony wrapped around it, contains many garish murals painted by the owner and is famous for featuring in the movie *The Adventures of Priscilla, Queen of the Desert*. Australia's first mosque, a red, tin building erected by Afghan and Indian camel drivers in 1891, lies on the outskirts. In recent years, the city has reinvented itself as an arts center thanks to the Brushmen of the Bush, a painting school founded by Pro Hart, a former miner. Hart's gallery is one of many art galleries in the city, and a sculpture park has been established on a hill 3.7 miles (6 km) out of town. **SA**

James Craig
(Sydney, Australia)

Excellent example of an iron barque

One glorious sunny day in February 2001, Sydney Harbour witnessed a great sight. For the first time in nearly eighty years, the tall ship the *James Craig* hoisted all her twenty-one sails and showed just what a beautiful ship she was and now is again.

The *James Craig* was originally called the *Clan Macleod* and was launched in Sunderland, England, in 1874. Her maiden voyage was to Peru and for the next twenty-six years she sailed the trade routes of the world, rounding Cape Horn twenty-three times. In 1901 she was purchased by J. J. Craig of Auckland and carried general cargo across the Tasman Sea. Renamed in 1905, she was laid up in 1911 because of increasing competition from steamships. She was then stripped and used as a copra hulk in New Guinea. The loss of many cargo ships during World War I gave her a new lease on life, and she was towed to Sydney for refitting. However, in 1925 she was retired again and became a coal hulk in Recherche Bay, Tasmania. In 1932 she was abandoned and beached after she broke her moorings in a storm. There she remained until 1972, when volunteers from the Sydney Heritage Fleet refloated her and towed her to Hobart for temporary repairs. In 1981 she was towed to Sydney for a full restoration and was relaunched in 1997, becoming fully operational once again in 2001.

The *James Craig* is one of the best examples of the working iron ships that carried cargoes such as coal, salt, cotton goods, and machinery from the U.K. around the Cape of Good Hope to the rapidly developing Australia, returning with wool and raw materials via Cape Horn. She is technically a barque—a three- (or more) masted ship with her two foremasts rigged square and her aft (rear) mast carrying triangular sails rigged fore and aft. Today, this beautiful tall ship carries passengers on cruises most weekends. **SA**

Hyde Park Barracks
(Sydney, Australia)

Evidence of Australia's convict history

The Hyde Park Barracks in Sydney epitomize the history of a country whose origins lie in penal servitude. Designed by a forger and ex-convict and built by convict labor, the barracks were designed to house 600 convicts who had previously been forced to find their own quarters after a long and hard day's work.

Australia is the only country whose currency once paid tribute to a convicted forger because, until recently, Francis Greenway appeared on the $10 bill. Greenway was convicted in England and transported to Australia in 1814. He was appointed civil architect by Governor Lachlan Macquarie in 1816, receiving a full

> *"Never had a colony been founded so far from its parent state or in such ignorance of the land it occupied."*

Robert Hughes, *The Fatal Shore* (1988)

King's Pardon in 1819, and built more than forty buildings. The Hyde Park Barracks is probably his finest work. It sits set back from one of Sydney's most elegant streets, and is enclosed by a perimeter wall and railings. The three-story building is well proportioned and built in Georgian style from local sandstone. The top floor has been reconstructed as convict quarters of the 1820s, complete with replica hammocks. The Greenway Gallery on the first floor holds temporary exhibitions on history and culture, whereas other rooms display objects recovered during archeological digs at the site, as well as pictures, artifacts, and models relating to convict history. Computer terminals allow internet access to information on the convicts' varied backgrounds and unfortunate histories. **SA**

Sydney Harbour Bridge

(Sydney, Australia)

One of the most famous bridges in the world and a beloved icon of Sydney

Without a doubt, Sydney Harbour Bridge is one of the most iconic and striking bridges in the world, dominating the skyline and providing a ready-made symbol for the city and harbor it straddles. Opened in 1932 as a road, rail, and pedestrian link between Sydney city center and the North Shore, it now has another life as a spectacular platform for firework displays, celebrating the new millennium, the 2000 Olympics, and every New Year's Day, as well as its own seventy-fifth birthday on March 18, 2007.

The bridge consists of a single-span steel arch 1,650 feet (503 m) long and 161 feet (49 m) wide and towering 440 feet (134 m) at its apex, although its height can increase by up to 7 inches (180 mm) as the steel expands on hot days. The eight lanes of road—two of them formerly tram tracks—two railway tracks, a footpath, and a cycle track are carried on a deck 161 feet (49 m) above the water at mid-span. Most of the 39,000 tons of steel needed to build the bridge came from Middlesbrough, England, although the entire 1,400 workforce on the bridge were Australian and the project provided much-needed employment when the Great Depression hit the country. The concrete and granite for the two pylons at either end were both sourced locally. The total weight of the bridge is 52,800 tons and it is held together with 6 million hand-driven rivets.

After the bridge was opened, cars had to pay an initial toll of sixpence toward the construction loan. That loan was eventually paid off in 1988 and the toll is now used for maintenance costs and for the cost of the Sydney Harbour Tunnel. As the bridge is made of steel, it needs regular repainting, requiring 6,593 gallons (30,000 liters) of paint for each coat. The bridge is open to the public, although you need a head for heights to walk across the upper arch. **SA**

"[It] will never date, never grow old—a structure of its time has become a structure for all times."

Marie Bashir, governor of New South Wales

Botany Bay (Sydney, Australia)

Historic site where Captain Cook first set foot on Australian soil

In his log entry for May 6, 1770, the English explorer Captain James Cook wrote: "The great quantity of these sort of fish found in this place occasioned my giving it the name of Stingrays Harbour." When later writing his journal based on the log, he changed his mind: "The great quantity of plants . . . found in this place occasioned my giving it the name of Botany Bay." It is by this name that we know the bay where Captain Cook first made landfall in Australia, and where, eighteen years later, Captain Arthur Phillip led the First Fleet to found a penal colony. However, Phillip found the sandy, infertile shores of the bay unsuitable for his purposes and within days sailed north to Port Jackson and Sydney Cove. Despite this move, the first penal colony would for many years be known as Botany Bay.

The historic bay itself lies in the southern suburbs of Sydney. Today it is somewhat dominated by the industry of Sydney (Kingsford Smith) Airport, the high-security prison of Long Bay, the container terminal of Port Botany, an oil refinery, and a sewage outlet. But the remaining quiet sandy beaches, surrounding marshlands, and clear waters give us some idea of what Cook and the crew of HMS *Endeavour* first saw of Australia, and what later greeted the 732 convicts, their 22 children, and 619 soldiers and ships' crew on board the 11-strong First Fleet.

A red buoy in the southeast of Botany Bay near the Kurnell Peninsula marks the spot where Cook first anchored on April 29, 1770. His landing place is marked by a monument at the southern end of Botany Bay National Park, which covers either side of the narrow entrance to the bay from the Pacific Ocean. On the north shore is La Perouse, which is Sydney's oldest Aboriginal settlement and now part of the national park. More than thirty other Aboriginal sites exist in the park. **SA**

"As the symbolic birthplace of modern Australia [Kurnell Peninsula] should be celebrated."

Ian Campbell, politician

Melbourne Cricket Ground (Melbourne, Australia)

The first cricket Test match between Australia and England was played at this ground

Australia is famously a sports-mad nation, and there is no more famous sports ground in the country than the Melbourne Cricket Ground, the MCG as it is affectionately known. Although little remains of its original structure, the ground embodies the history of sport in Australia.

The Melbourne Cricket Club (MCC) was founded in 1838 and was granted the land on which the club now stands in 1853 when it was forced to move from its former site to make way for Australia's first steam train. An 1876 stand—now long gone—was reversible, allowing spectators to watch cricket at the ground in summer or football in the park in winter. Only the historic members' stand now remains because the ground has been consistently redeveloped and expanded over the years, most recently to accommodate the 2006 Commonwealth Games. The ground currently seats more than 100,000 people.

The MCC has played a major role in Australian cricket because it was the first club formed in Victoria and in 1856 hosted the first match between New South Wales and Victoria. In 1862 the MCC hosted the first match against an England team and, most famously, in 1877 the first game of Test cricket between Australia and England, won by Australia by 45 runs. England won the second match by four wickets, thus drawing the series. The club also hosted the first one-day international cricket match in 1971 and the 1992 World Cup cricket final. As well as cricket, the ground is home to many other sports. The MCC was involved in drafting the first set of rules for Australian Rules Football in 1859 and has hosted numerous soccer matches. The stadium was also the centerpiece of the 1956 Melbourne Olympic Games. Pope John Paul II held a mass here when he visited the city in 1986, and numerous rock bands have performed in this hallowed ground. **SA**

"The first ball in England–Australia cricket was bowled by Billy Caffyn, publican of the Parade Hotel."

Garrie Hutchinson, journalist

Old Melbourne Jail

(Melbourne, Australia)

Victoria's oldest surviving prison and scene of numerous executions

Founded in 1835 and named Melbourne after the British prime minister in 1837, the city of Melbourne grew rapidly in size, particularly after gold was discovered at nearby Ballarat in 1851. As the population grew, so did crime, necessitating the construction of a city jail.

The first jail was built in 1839 to 1840 but proved far too small. A new, larger jail was built of sandstone between 1841 and 1844. When this also proved inadequate, a massive new wing, built of bluestone with its own perimeter wall and observation towers and modeled on Pentonville Prison in north London, England, was added in 1852 and completed twelve years later. Between 1880 and 1924, the jail became progressively dilapidated and parts of it were demolished, including the original sandstone building. The stones of the surrounding bluestone walls and the towers were used to build sea-retaining walls at nearby St. Kilda and Hampton. The jail finally closed in 1929, but was later used as police stables and a storage depot, and housed deserters during World War II.

The first of 135 prisoners was executed in the jail in 1845. Among them was the famous bushranger Ned Kelly, whose death mask and the beam from which he was hanged are on display. His mother was in prison at the same time having hit a policeman over the head, and was therefore able to visit her son. Others executed at the site include Martha Knorr, who adopted babies for a modest fee and then killed and buried them in her backyard. The death masks on display in the cells were made in the nineteenth century when phrenology—the study of people's characters relating to the size and shape of their skulls—was believed to hold the clue to criminal behavior. Also on display is the triangle on which prisoners were flogged with a cat-o'-nine-tails. **SA**

"I'm Ned Kelly! I am an outlaw, and my orders must be obeyed. Make no noise. Raise no alarm."

Ned Kelly, orders given during a bank raid

Polly Woodside

(Melbourne, Australia)

Grand lady of the sea

Launched in Belfast, Northern Ireland, in 1884, the *Polly Woodside* is a three-masted, iron-hulled barque. Although launched relatively late for a sailing ship, in a period when steamships were rapidly supplanting the old three-masters, the *Polly Woodside* carried cargoes of coal from Britain to Chile and returned with nitrate or wheat from Argentina. By 1897 she had rounded Cape Horn sixteen times and circumnavigated the world twice between 1901 and 1904. In 1904 she was sold to New Zealand owners and renamed *Rona*, a Maori name; she sailed the Tasman Sea between Australia and New Zealand, as well as making several

> **"Polly Woodside *is not only one of the most important historic vessels, she is an iconic feature …"***
>
> Justin Madden, politician

trips across the Pacific. In 1924 she was sold to the Adelaide Steam Ship Company and became a coal hulk, servicing steamships in the Port of Melbourne, and also carried bulk materials such as timber, cement, and grain. She was then requisitioned by the Royal Australian Navy during World War II to service U.S. and Australian ships in New Guinea before returning to Australian waters again. She finally retired in 1962, by which time she was the only deep-water commercial sailing ship still afloat in Australia.

The campaign to restore this working ship led the National Trust of Australia to purchase her for one cent in 1968. She was then fully restored and opened to the public in 1978. She is now permanently moored at the old Duke and Orr's dry dock on the Yarra River and is part of the Melbourne Maritime Museum. **SA**

Old Parliament House

(Canberra, Australia)

Seat of parliament during troubled times

When the Commonwealth of Australia was created in 1901, the federal government decided to establish a new seat of government for the new nation. In 1908 Canberra was chosen as the preferred site. American architect Walter Burley Griffin won an international competition to design the new structure, and planned an imposing parliament building on Camp Hill. However, the outbreak of World War I caused the postponement of the project, and after the war it was decided to build a temporary building below Griffin's site that would serve as a parliament house for no more than fifty years. The first sod was turned on August 28, 1923, and the building was opened by the Duke of York—later King George VI—on May 9, 1927.

Griffin had planned an ornate, arresting building, but the new architect, the Australian John Smith Murdoch designed a plain structure in the "stripped Classical style" common to many government buildings of the period. Modest and functional, the building is filled with natural light from windows, skylights, and light wells, and has numerous verandas and colonnades. The strong horizontal lines and simple, geometric exterior of the building is matched inside with geometric patterns and plain surfaces. Every element of the building, including all the furniture and fittings, was designed to Murdoch's specifications. The main rooms are the King's Hall, named after the statue of King George V that dominates the room, the House of Representatives Chamber and the Senate Chamber, and the Prime Minister's Suite, built as an extension in 1974.

When the parliament house first opened, it was home to around 300 people. By the 1980s, however, it was struggling to accommodate up to 4,000 people. A new parliament house was thus commissioned and built on the hill it was originally intended to sit on. **SA**

Australian National War Memorial

(Canberra, Australia)

Australia's permanent national shrine to their war dead

Australia's national memorial to members of its armed forces who died fighting for their country is situated in the national capital, Canberra. It lies just outside the Parliamentary Triangle of government buildings and tree-lined roads in the center of the city facing the equally imposing Parliament House. The memorial is also a museum of national military history.

Charles Bean, later Australia's official World War I historian, conceived the idea of a memorial while observing Australian soldiers fighting in France in 1916. Australia had joined Britain in the war against Germany and its troops had suffered proportionally very heavy casualties during the fighting in Gallipoli, Turkey, in 1915. An architectural competition in 1927 for the design of the memorial produced no winner, but the two leading entrants, both Sydney architects, were asked to produce a joint design.

The memorial is approached up Anzac Parade, lined with memorials to every war Australia has fought in. Inside the building, visitors pass the Roll of Honour, bronze panels listing the names of all 102,600 Australians killed in battle. The Pool of Reflection and an eternal flame set the mood; rosemary bushes planted by the pool symbolize remembrance. Steps lead up to the main Hall of Memory, a Byzantine-style hall with a vast, 6-million-piece mosaic in the dome depicting World War II veterans. A blue stained glass window commemorates veterans of World War I and a red marble slab in the floor covers the Tomb of the Unknown Soldier, the official war grave. Galleries to both World Wars sit either side of the main hall.

Many people date the birth of the Australian nation, not to its creation as an independent commonwealth in 1901, but to the carnage of Gallipoli. The country commemorates its war dead every year on April 25, Anzac Day. **SA**

> *"ANZAC stood for reckless valour in a good cause ... and endurance that will never admit defeat."*
>
> Charles Bean, journalist and historian

Cascade Brewery

(Hobart, Australia)

Oldest brewery in operation in the country

Unsurprisingly, as a hot, dry country, Australia has developed a reputation for great beer, with a large and profitable industry to ensure constant supplies. Yet its oldest brewery, dating from 1832, was built on the cooler, offshore island state of Tasmania.

The Cascade Brewery was founded by Peter Degraves, an Englishman of French background educated in engineering, architecture, and the law. Accompanied by his wife and eight children, he left England in 1821 to seek his fortune in Van Diemen's Land, as Tasmania was then known. However, the ship he had chartered was damaged and Degraves was forced to return home to England, where he faced a battle with his creditors and was briefly imprisoned for unpaid debts. He finally reached the island in 1824 and soon established a sawmill. His past rapidly caught up with him, however, and in 1826 he was thrown into prison for not having paid off his debts in England. When he was released in 1831, he was even more determined to succeed.

In 1832 Degraves built a new brewery next to his sawmill. The building is an impressive seven-story, granite tower with the stone pillars of the entrance gates topped with imitation beer casks. Cool water for the brewery flows from nearby Mount Wellington and contributed much to the success of his beers, which were considered far superior to their mainland rivals. Cascade is also unique among Australian breweries and rare among breweries worldwide in that it operates its own maltings, producing malt for its beers from locally grown barley. Malts for its dark and seasonal beers are imported from the mainland. Australia's oldest manufacturing enterprise, the brewery is no longer in family hands. It became a public company in 1883 and is now part of the Foster's Group. Guided tours are available. **SA**

Port Arthur Historic Site

(Port Arthur, Australia)

Harsh penal colony for hardened criminals

Port Arthur was established in 1830 as a prison settlement for convicts from Britain who had seriously reoffended in New South Wales or Van Diemen's Land. These men were viewed as having no redeeming features, and were thus condemned to work like slaves in what was probably the harshest institution of its kind in the British Empire.

The first 150 convicts developed a timber industry in the area, but gradually Port Arthur became a self-supporting industrial complex, with shipbuilding, brick making, shoe making, wheat growing, and milling facilities. The four-story flour mill, the largest

> *"Flogging became a way of life, 100 lashes being the normal punishment for escape attempts."*
>
> Larry Rivera, journalist

building in Australia when it was constructed in 1844, was turned into a prison in the 1850s and housed almost 500 prisoners in its dormitories and cells. Here, up to fifty prisoners were subject to complete isolation and sensory deprivation in the belief it would promote their "moral reform;" these inmates were always referred to by number, not by name. Among the buildings on the site were a hospital, an asylum housing more than 100 mentally ill convicts (which later became a town hall and is now a museum and café), a paupers' mess, and a church, built in 1836 but not consecrated because it was used by all denominations.

Transportation of mainland convicts to Port Arthur ceased in 1853 but the prison remained open until 1877. By this time, more than 12,000 men had passed through it. **SA**

Waitangi Marae (Waitangi, New Zealand)

Meeting place where Maori chiefs signed the Treaty of Waitangi with the British government

New Zealand was discovered in 1769 by Captain James Cook and attracted increasing numbers of settlers from the 1820s onward. In an attempt to protect the indigenous Maori people from British immigrants desperate for land, and to thwart French interests in the region, the British government ordered its representative to conclude a treaty with as many Maori chiefs as possible to formally bring New Zealand within the British Empire. The treaty offered British citizenship and a guarantee that the Maori people would retain ownership of their possessions for as long as they wished, in exchange for the government's exclusive right to purchase land sold by the Maori.

The official signing took place at the Waitangi Marae (meeting place) in the North Island's Bay of Islands in 1840, and was signed by about forty chiefs, before being taken around the country to be signed by others who could not travel to the *marae*. Although

subsequently ignored by colonial governments, the Treaty of Waitangi is now regarded as the founding document of New Zealand, and is frequently referred to by the courts on issues of constitutional importance.

New Zealand's national day (Waitangi Day) is in February, and every year senior representatives from the government travel to the *marae* to take part in commemorations. Although many historical Maori grievances stemming from perceived abuse of the provisions in the treaty have been settled through a series of tribunals, most Waitangi Days see the *marae* become the focus of heated political protest against historical treatment of the Maori people. The situation has become even more complicated in recent years with the right of the Prime Minister Helen Clark to speak on the *marae* challenged by those seeking to uphold Maori protocol, which reserves the right of public speaking for men. **AS**

Ruapekapeka Pa (near Whangarei, New Zealand)

Site of a major challenge to British forces by Maori tribes

For thirty years in the mid-nineteenth century, New Zealand endured a series of wars between the indigenous Maori population and the new colonial government. A rapid influx of settlers led to an increasing demand for land, and Maori tribes found themselves suffering a gradual encroachment on their territories. Ruapekapeka Pa was the site of one of the last engagements in the far north of New Zealand between the local Maori tribe and government forces.

A *pa* is a fortified area, usually associated with a village, traditionally located on high ground and surrounded by wooden palisades. Effective against Maori enemies before the arrival of Europeans, Maori *pa* design faced a major challenge from British firearms and cannons. The local chief, Te Ruki Kawiti, had several months to prepare for the British invasion of his lands and dug a complicated series of trenches, gun pits, and tunnels around the perimeter of the *pa*, the

outlines of which can still be seen today. This allowed his fighters to pour fire down on the attacking force while remaining under cover at all times. In effect, Kawiti had preempted World War I trench warfare by seventy years, and his defensive innovation was copied and developed during the next thirty years of Maori unrest throughout the country. The British commander eventually managed to breach the *pa* walls and circumnavigate the defensive positions, but the defenders escaped into the dense bush surrounding the *pa* clearing. The British soldiers had to be satisfied with burning the *pa*, knowing they would be ambushed if they attempted to follow the Maori.

A peace settlement was subsequently achieved between Kawiti and the British Governor, Sir George Grey. Kawiti is reputed to have said, *"Mehe mea kua mutukoe"* (If you have had enough, I have had enough); Grey replied, *"Kuamutu ahoe"* (I have had enough). **AS**

Mansion House (Kawau Island, New Zealand)

Residence of one of colonial New Zealand's most important public figures

Sir George Grey was one of New Zealand's most influential colonial governors, holding office on two separate occasions between the late 1840s and late 1860s during a time of rapid British settlement and increasing unrest from New Zealand's native Maori population. He was governor in 1862 when he bought Kawau Island, which lies in the Hauraki Gulf just to the north of the then-capital Auckland.

Mansion House was previously the residence of the manager of a copper mine on the island, but Grey engaged leading architect Sir Frederick Thatcher to turn it into the stately home it is today, adding around twenty rooms to the house's original ten. The house still features beautiful native kauri wood paneling and is an impressive building in its own right, restored to represent its appearance when Grey was in residence with sections from its pre-Grey incarnation dating back to 1845. Just as remarkable, however, are the surrounding parklands, which Grey converted into a zoological and botanical reserve. A regular correspondent of Charles Darwin, Grey introduced various exotic plants to the island, including an extensive collection of conifers, as well as wallabies, monkeys, zebra, kookaburras, peacocks, and possums, in an experiment to see how these introduced species would adapt to a foreign climate. Unfortunately, the wallabies and possums who live on the island to this day adapted only too well, becoming major pests to the detriment of the island's native birdlife, which includes New Zealand's unofficial emblem, the kiwi.

Grey sold the estate and, after a period of private ownership, it became public property in 1967. **AS**

◸ Sir George Grey earned acclaim as Governor of New Zealand from 1845 to 1853, and from 1861 to 1868.

◳ Mansion House was Grey's residence during his later political career in New Zealand as MP and premier.

Rotorua (Rotorua, New Zealand)

A major tourist center based on geothermal activity and Maori culture

The first thing you notice about Rotorua is the smell. The area is actively volcanic, and the bubbling mud pools and geysers add a tang of sulphur to the air. The tectonic plates that fuel the Pacific "Ring of Fire" groan just under the earth's crust, creating remarkable tourist attractions while threatening to destroy them at the same time. The most famous example of this were the Pink and White terraces. Known as the "Eighth Wonder of the World," these formations attracted thousands of international visitors but were destroyed overnight in 1886 when the nearby volcano, Tarawera, erupted.

The indigenous Maori population had utilized the geothermal activity in the area long before it was packaged as an attractive spa destination. Indeed the local tribe, Te Arawa, came to resent the increasing numbers of European settlers in the late 1800s, resulting in several skirmishes. Careful mediation has led to the settlement of most historic grievances. The local Maori population now skilfully exploit their heritage for the benefit of modern tourists, while ensuring their rich culture is tastefully preserved. Visitors flock in their thousands to see the beautiful lakes, hot pools, and Maori carvings. However, some tension, bubbling under the surface, remains. This was most famously captured by the writer Alan Duff in his book, (later made into a successful movie), *Once Were Warriors* (1990). Duff grew up in the city, and the setting for his fictional story is "Two Lakes"—the English translation of the placename, Rotorua.

In a young nation, Rotorua is a reminder of New Zealand's rich indigenous history, geology, and incredible natural beauty. **PH**

↗ Traditional Maori carving on a *marae* (meeting house). The stylized figures represent the tribe's ancestors.

→ Charles Blomfield's *The White Terrace* (1885). This terrace was 98 feet (30 m) high, and 787 feet (240 m) wide.

Old St. Paul's Cathedral

(Wellington, New Zealand)

First Anglican cathedral in the city

Construction of the Anglican cathedral began in 1865, the year after Wellington became New Zealand's capital city. The church was consecrated in 1866, but by the late nineteenth century it had already become too small for its congregation. Finally in 1954 construction of a new cathedral began. With the transfer of St. Paul's ecclesiastical function to the new St. Paul's in 1964, the future of the old cathedral became a cause for concern. After a lengthy debate, old St. Paul's escaped demolition and was purchased by the government in 1967.

The structure of the building is made purely of native timbers—rimu, totara, matai, and kauri. It was designed in an early English Gothic style by Reverend Frederick Thatcher, vicar of Thorndon parish from 1861 to 1864. The short spire is a result of the high winds the city of Wellington is noted for. Additions to the original structure include the south transept (1868), the north transept (1874), and the chancel and minor transepts (1876). Interior decorations show Wellington's early history, and the stained-glass windows commemorate former parishioners and depict scenes from the Bible. Flags hanging from the ceiling include the White Ensign of the Royal Navy and the Red Ensign of the New Zealand Merchant Navy, along with the flag of the United States and Second Division Marine Corps. The original organ (1877) and peal of bells (1867) were moved to the new cathedral and have since been replaced.

Now Old St. Paul's is managed by the New Zealand Historic Places Trust, and is supported by the Friends of Old St Paul's Society. Still consecrated, it lies one block away from the new cathedral and is used for weddings and other services as well as concerts and cultural events. It remains a fine example of colonial Gothic Revival architecture. **MA**

Colonial Cottage

(Wellington, New Zealand)

The oldest identified building in Wellington

This carefully preserved building was built in 1858 by William Wallis—a carpenter newly arrived from England—and typifies the colonial building style in Wellington. The cottage is constructed almost entirely from wood, in compliance with a contemporary recommendation to build with timber to minimize injury and loss of life from an earthquake. Only a decade before the cottage was built, a serious earthquake had not only demolished many earlier brick buildings, but had raised a substantial amount of land from the sea. The reliance on wooden construction was also a product of Wellington's

"The house is built mainly of kauri and began as a four-roomed box with a steeply pitched roof."

Ian Bowman, architect and conservator

topography. Many settlers, like Wallis, purchased their land before leaving England on the basis of a survey map that had been drawn up without taking account of Wellington's many hills. Consequently, Wallis would have found his allotment to be on a significant gradient, unsuitable for building in heavier materials. Indeed, this reliance on wood extended beyond private homes to public buildings; the Old Government Buildings is still the largest wooden building in the Southern Hemisphere.

Colonial Cottage is on two stories, with kitchen, nursery, parlor, and main bedroom on the ground floor, with a separate washhouse, and two smaller bedrooms on the upper floor. It is preserved as though the Wallis family were still in residence, with original features—furniture, wallpaper, and fittings in place. **AS**

Katherine Mansfield's Birthplace

(Wellington, New Zealand)

Katherine Mansfield drew much inspiration from her childhood in this house

In October 1888, Katherine Mansfield, one of the most influential Modernist writers of short fiction, was born in the Wellington suburb of Thorndon.

Thorndon was one of the first areas of settlement in the city throughout the 1850s and 1860s, but, thanks to the economic depression of the early 1880s, the home built by the author's father, Harold Beauchamp, is relatively simple; the house is square, with wooden weatherboards and a corrugated iron roof, and wooden carving around the windows to mimic stonework. However, the garden is of particular interest, having been replanted using only plants that would have been available in Wellington in the 1880s and 1890s, to give a sense of how it would have looked when the Beauchamps were living there. According to Mansfield, the garden was "small and square with flower beds on either side. All down one side big clumps of arum lilies aired their rich beauty, on the other side there was nothing but a straggle of what the children called 'grandmother's pincushions.'"

After a series of moves around Wellington, Mansfield permanently left New Zealand in 1908 to pursue a career as a writer in London. But she became increasingly nostalgic for New Zealand, writing to her father, ". . . the longer I live, the more I return to New Zealand. A young country is a real heritage, though it takes one time to remember it. But New Zealand is in my very bones." It is perhaps fitting then that some of her best-known stories are records of her childhood around colonial Wellington. She was never to return to New Zealand, dying in January 1923 in France. **AS**

↗ Katherine Mansfield was born Kathleen Mansfield Beauchamp; she adopted her pseudonym in 1911.

➡ Mansfield's childhood in Wellington was lonely, but her later works often refer to her former home.

Canterbury Cathedral (Christchurch, New Zealand)

The city's famous cathedral was designed by an Englishman and built from local materials

Christchurch was New Zealand's first city, being awarded its Royal Charter, and hence its official status, in July 1856. It is generally regarded as the most English of New Zealand's cities, and was always intended to be a small piece of "home" by the English settlers who arrived at Lyttleton Harbour in 1850. They named their settlement after one of Oxford University's colleges; decided that the city's river would be the Avon, in tribute to Shakespeare; and transplanted the English tradition of building cities around cathedrals to the new colony. Given these strong links with the home country, it is perhaps unsurprising that when they came to planning their cathedral the settlers turned to the preeminent architect of the English neo-Gothic revival, George Gilbert Scott—better known for his contribution to the Houses of Parliament in London. With plans in hand, the cathedral's foundation stone was laid in 1864 only to be promptly abandoned for a decade because of a lack of funds. The novelist Anthony Trollope visited Christchurch in 1872, and while praising the "honest, high-toned idea" of the cathedral, he decided that, ultimately, it had become a "huge record of failure." Gilbert Scott's plans were taken up by Benjamin Mountfort, whose buildings are dotted all over the city, and the nave was finally completed in 1881. However, it took another twenty-three years for the transepts, chancel, and sanctuary to be finished, these areas of the cathedral being opened in 1904.

Inside, the building combines local stone from the Canterbury region, with timber—predominantly matai and totara—sourced from the forests that used to cover the nearby Banks Peninsula. Despite the native building materials, it is impossible to ignore the fact that this cathedral and its surrounding city were built as defiantly English symbols of a burgeoning British Empire. **AS**

> *"Scott Sr. was the Norman Foster of Victorian England; forever busy, an inveterate traveler . . ."*
>
> Jonathan Glancey, journalist

Larnach Castle (Dunedin, New Zealand)

No expense was spared in the construction of New Zealand's only castle

Construction of Larnach Castle began in 1871 and after three years' work by 200 craftsmen the Larnach family moved in. It would, however, take another twelve years' work for the interior to be complete. Born in Australia, William Larnach's banking career started in the goldfields of South Australia before he became manager of the Bank of Otago, based in Dunedin, New Zealand. A great entrepreneur, he also had a great ego. Riding with his son Donald on the high ground of the Otago Peninsula, he searched out the best view for a grand family house.

Larnach Castle was built for his first wife, Eliza, in a mixture of the Gothic revival and colonial styles. No expense was spared on the construction materials and furnishings. Along with craftsmen from around the world came marble from Italy, tiles from England, glass from Venice and France, and slate from Wales. Wood used included both native and exotic species. The nursery was equipped with a 1-ton marble bath, a replica of the one found in the ruins of Herculaneum. In 1886 a ballroom was added to the castle as a twenty-first birthday present for William's favorite daughter, Kate. Unfortunately she died shortly after her birthday and the ballroom is said to be haunted by her ghost. When Larnach became a politician, the castle was used to entertain many of the country's leading figures.

In 1898 William Larnach shot himself in the parliament building. With no valid will, family infighting broke out, eventually leading to the sale of the castle. Through periods of use as a mental asylum and World War II billet, the building fell into a very poor state of repair. In 1967 the Barker family bought the castle and set about restoring it and opening it to the public. It is now one of Dunedin's top tourist attractions, and once again echoes its former heyday as New Zealand's only castle. **MA**

"The ceilings were down in the two top floors, the wiring was gone, and the place leaked like a sieve..."

Margaret Barker, castle owner

Grave of Robert Louis Stevenson (Mt Vaea, Samoa)

The burial site of Stevenson and his wife occupies a scenic spot near his former home

Robert Louis Stevenson (1850–94), the author of *Treasure Island, Kidnapped,* and *The Strange Case of Dr. Jekyll and Mr. Hyde,* was one of Scotland's greatest writers. He was passionate about his native land, but became equally attached to his final home on the other side of the globe. His grave in Samoa is a fitting tribute to his later achievements.

Stevenson left Britain for the last time in 1888, looking for a warmer climate to aid his frail constitution. He eventually settled with his wife on Upolu, the second largest of the Samoan islands, where they built a large home for themselves called Vailima (Five Waters). The author brought reminders from home—a tablecloth given by Queen Victoria, a sugar bowl that had belonged to Sir Walter Scott—but he also took a keen interest in his new environment. In later novels, such as *The Ebb-Tide,* he was highly critical about the damaging effects of European colonialism in the South Seas.

For their part, the Samoans grew equally fond of their Tusitala (teller of tales). When he died suddenly in December 1894, they carried him from his home to his burial site, near the summit of Mount Vaea. They subsequently built the "Road of the Loving Hearts" to facilitate access to this spot. The grave itself is in a picturesque location, overlooking the Pacific and Stevenson's former home. It bears an inscription from one of his poems. His wife, Fanny, is also buried there. She left Samoa to spend her final years in the United States but, after her death in 1914, her ashes were transferred to Upolu. On the tomb, there is a bronze plaque with her Samoan name, Aolele. **IZ**

▣ Stevenson's life as a poet, novelist, and adventurer was dogged from childhood by recurrent ill-health.

◰ Stevenson's epitaph reads: "Here he lies where he longed to be/Home is the sailor, home from sea . . ."

Nan Madol (Pohnpei Island, Micronesia)

Magnificent site of megalithic architectural achievements

The "Venice of the Pacific" is a term often used to describe Nan Madol—an indication of its attraction as a city with a rich political and cultural history. This is an apt comparison, given that Nan Madol and Venice are both based upon a network of canals and waterways. However, unlike Venice, Nan Madol dates back only to the first or second century C.E. Furthermore, Nan Madol is built around a series of islets artificially constructed by the digging of intersecting canals, whereas Venice was originally founded on natural formations. In further contrast to Venice, Nan Madol is no longer inhabited. There may be several reasons for this, but foremost is that the islets' elite occupants depended on their subjects to bring fresh water and food; when conditions changed and the supplies ceased, living there became impossible. Today, Nan Madol is a carefully preserved historic site.

Excavations have revealed artifacts dating back to as early as 200 B.C.E., but the exact date of foundation remains uncertain. Archeological evidence has established that Nan Madol was an eminent political and religious center, particularly under the Saudeler dynasty in the first and second centuries. However, this success was temporary and, after the Saudeler dynasty came to an end, a gradual decline began.

Perhaps the most remarkable parts are the mortuary sector, which is set across a complex network of fifty-eight islets in the northeastern area, and the royal mortuary, in which a colossal tomb is surrounded by walls 16–26 feet (5–8 m) high. Nan Madol covers 7 square miles (18 sq km), and the possibilities for further discoveries are endless. **KH**

↗ One theory holds that Nan Madol was a Versailles of the Pacific where chiefs lived under regal scrutiny.

→ The imposing black basalt walls of the royal mortuary probably date from the twelfth or thirteenth century.

World famous for the unique statues whose purpose continues to puzzle archeologists

> "… a powerful, imaginative, and original tradition of monumental sculpture and architecture."

UNESCO

⊤ With their backs to the sea, a row of seven moai maintain their vigil. Some moai are 1,000 years old.

➡ Half-finished moai lie partially buried at Rano Raraku. Half the island's sculptures are found at this quarry.

Easter Island is one of the most remote archeological sites on earth, with its nearest neighbor (Pitcairn Island) situated more than 1,000 miles (1,600 km) away. This isolation helped to create one of the most unique civilizations known about today—although what we do know amounts to very little, hence the mystery that surrounds this tiny, ancient community. The extraordinary island has long fascinated archeologists and mystery lovers alike.

Also known as Rapa Nui, the small Polynesian island was discovered by Europeans in 1722; a Dutch sailor Jacob Roggeveen landed at the island on Easter Sunday. The Spanish laid claim to the island in 1770, although this was never officially recognized. In 1774 Captain Cook arrived and took back to Europe more stories of this incredible island, encouraging explorers and archeologists to visit and to remove a number of artifacts—these now stand in museums all over the world. Since 1888, Easter Island has been considered part of Chile.

The island has become famous because of its remarkable statues, or *moai*, the earliest of which dates back to *c.* 1000 C.E. It is believed the *moai* were made to commemorate the indigenous people's ancestors and were an important part of religious and traditional rites. In later centuries other religions took over and, with the devastating arrival of Christianity to the island, many of the statues were smashed or at least toppled. When standing, the statues are up to 30 feet (9 m) tall and are impressively broad. How they were created and transported around the island remains a mystery, as does the complete story of the original islanders' arrival, culture, and society, and of the presumed civil war that drastically reduced their population. The exact number of statues is unknown, because many were reduced to rubble, but estimates place the figure at between 800 and 1,000. **LH**

Index of UNESCO World Heritage sites

There are entries on 399 UNESCO World Heritage sites in this book, identified by symbols next to their titles. Listed below are the official UNESCO World Heritage names with the dates of the sites' inscription, each followed by the relevant entries in this book and their page references.

Index of People and Events

Contributors

Simon Adams (SA) was born in Bristol and studied at London and Bristol universities. He worked as an editor of children's reference books before becoming a full-time writer twenty years ago. Since then, he has written more than sixty books, including numerous travel and history books.

Mark Andrews (MA) is an internationally published writer and photographer on topics such as travel, culture, business, and food and drink. He has lived and traveled throughout Asia for many years and currently resides in Shanghai.

Caroline Ball (CB) is a freelance book editor, writer, and occasional translator, on subjects ranging from art, antiques, and design to history, gardens, and health. Extensive travel in Asia and Europe has taken her to many historic sites.

Peter Ball (PB) first knew Lübeck when, after wartime service, he remained in the British Zone and Berlin until 1948. Later postings took him to the Far East and Latin America, and in retirement he worked as a regimental archivist for fifteen years.

Jo Bourne (JB), MA, is an archeologist and journalist from Kent, England. A former deputy editor of *Geographical* magazine (the magazine of the Royal Geographical Society), she has written on travel, tourism, and geopolitics from around the world.

Katherine Boyle (KB) graduated from Bristol University with a first-class degree in the History of Art. Since that time she has worked as Projects Assistant for the World Monuments Fund in Britain.

Lucy Cave (LC) has explored much of Europe, the United States, and parts of the Middle East. She engages with the people, language, culture, and history of the places she visits.

Stephen Cave (SC) has traveled widely through Europe, the United States, and the Middle East and fully intends to explore the world. His passions include reading, rugby, rowing, and sailing.

Richard Cavendish (RC) is a historian of ideas and an authority on Britain's historic heritage. He is the author of *A Guidebook to Prehistoric England*, writes a regular monthly column in *History Today* magazine, and has just completed a book on the kings and queens of Britain. He was for several years editor of *Out of Town* magazine. He has lectured and broadcast in Britain, Denmark, Canada, the United States, and Australia.

Monica Cortiletti (MC) is a medievalist archeologist specializing in building archeology and burial practices in the Middle Ages. She worked as a researcher at the University of Padua, Italy, for two years, and she is now completing her PhD at University College London.

Amanda Elsdon-Dew (AED) is a long-in-the-tooth history and English graduate from York University.She has worked in publishing as a copy editor and editorial services controller, and is currently engaged as assistant editor of her son's school magazine and general homework assistant.

Tim Evans (TE) has worked for newspapers in the Midlands of the UK as well as ITN (Independent Television News). When he is not reviewing films for Skymovies.com, he enjoys exploring the older parts of Spain and Portugal.

Rachel Fentem (RF) is a PhD student at the Institute of Archaeology, University College London. Her research examines the consumption and reception of Near Eastern material culture in the Bronze and Early Iron Age Aegean.

Jacob Field (JF) read history at the University of Oxford. He is currently completing his PhD on the popular reaction to the Great Fire of London at Newcastle University.

Adrian Gilbert (AG) is a writer and editorial consultant specializing in military and historical subjects. He has contributed to a variety of publications, including the *Guardian* and *The Sunday Times*. His most recent book is *POW: Allied Prisoners in Europe, 1939–1945*.

Reg Grant (RG) has written more than twenty books on a wide variety of historical subjects. His works include *The Rise and Fall of the Berlin Wall*; *Flight: 100 Years of Aviation*; *The Visual History of Britain from 1900 to the Present Day*; *Assassinations*; and *Soldier: A Visual History of the Fighting Man*.

Philip Hall (PH) was born in New Zealand, where he earned a Degree in English Literature and a Masters Degree in Law. He currently lives and works in London and writes on a variety of subjects.

James Harrison (JH) has entries on the world's largest countries: Russia and Canada. He visited pre-perestroika Russia unshackled by Intourist (not an easy option at the time). The only tyranny he experienced in Canada (his father's family come from the Saskatchewan prairies) was that of the mind-dulling distances.

Lucinda Hawksley (LH) is an art historian, biographer, public speaker, and award-winning travel writer. She has an MA in Literature and History of Art and is a patron of the Charles Dickens Museum in London. She has written books on the Pre-Raphaelites and is also the world expert on the nineteenth-century artist Kate Perugini.

Linda Haynes (LHay) is married with four children and four grandchildren. She lives with her husband in the Surrey hills where she runs her own administration business. She is fascinated by Romania and visits regularly with a local charity that undertakes building projects for the benefit of Romanian children.

Elizabeth Horne (EH), now a consultant, has worked in educational publishing for nearly thirty years. She has held senior management posts in multi-national publishing groups and has twice set up and developed companies of her own.

Katarina Horrox (KH) is an Anglo-Swedish writer and commentator based in London. Her work has been widely published by websites and magazines such as *Art Review* and *Saatchi Online Magazine*. She has contributed to the *Encyclopaedia of Contemporary Scandinavian Culture* and is currently writing for the Swedish Government.

Sandrine Josefsada (SJ), born in Belgium, graduated with a Bachelor degree in History of Art and Archeology from Soas in 2006. Specializing in the arts of India, she completed her final independent study project "Reactions and Functionalities of Eroticism in Indian Art, From Khajuraho to Bollywood."

Ann Kay (AK) is a freelance writer and editor specializing in arts subjects. She has worked on a wide variety of history, art history, and literature projects for both magazine and book publishers.

Carol King (CK) is a freelance writer and editor who studied English Literature at the University of Sussex and Fine Art at St. Martin's art school in London. She is happy to have been able to share experiences from her travels in this book.

Laura Lankester (LaL) holds an MA in Modern Literature from University College London. She is a script developer for film and television and a freelance journalist. She is writing a historical novel.

Lesley Levene (LL) trained as an archeologist but for the last twenty years has worked freelance as a book editor and writer. She has traveled widely and has spent many months in Turkey and India.

Robin Elam Musumeci (RM) has a degree in English and History, and a Masters degree in English Literature. She loves to read and write about many different subjects, travel to exotic locations, eat good food, and spend time with friends and family.

Salvatore Musumeci (SM) holds a Masters degree from Trinity College,

Hartford, and an MPhil from Queen Mary, University of London. He is completing a PhD at Queen Mary on the culinary and material culture of the monastery of Santa Trinita in fourteenth-century Florence.

Fuyubi Nakamura (FN) is an anthropologist specializing in the visual and material cultures of Japan. She is currently a postdoctoral fellow at the Research School of Humanities at the Australian National University and holds a doctorate from the University of Oxford.

Elisabeth Pamberg (EP) is studying for a PhD on Roman North African archeology at University College London. She has worked for museums in New York, Venice, Paris, and London, and regularly participates in archeological expeditions in North Africa and the Near East.

Ashim Paun (AP) studied in Manchester, Brighton, and at the LSE, and lives in London where he conducts research into companies for ethical investment providers, having worked previously for a conservation NGO and in government. He has written recently for a monthly lifestyle magazine and weekly industry newsletter.

Tamsin Pickeral (TP) studied History of Art before furthering her education in Italy. She has traveled extensively throughout the world, and continues to divide her time between writing about art, history, and horses. Her most recent publications include, *The Horse*, *30,000 Years of the Horse in Art*, *Van Gogh*, *The Impressionists*, *Turner*, *Whistler*, *Monet*, *Secret Britain*, *Charles Rennie Mackintosh*, and contributions to *1001 Paintings*.

Oscar Rickett (OR) is a freelance writer and actor from London. He has written on a variety of subjects, including the history and culture of Argentina, American literature of the twentieth century, and the music of Eastern Europe.

Frank Ritter (FR) is a freelance editor and writer specializing in architecture, gardens, and the visual arts. For this

series, he was recently involved in the editing of *1001 Gardens* and *1001 Buildings*.

Rachel Rouse (RR) is just starting out as a journalist, living in London with her family. She studied politics and international relations at Manchester University, and journalism at City University London.

Tobias Selin (TS) was born in Sweden and studied Mechanical Engineering and the Philosophy of Science. He currently works as an editor in London.

Iain Shearer (IS) is an archeologist working for the Centre for Applied Archaeology at the Institute of Archaeology, University College London. He is a specialist in conflict regions and the Islamic world, having worked extensively in Afghanistan, Bosnia, central Asia, Iran, and Israel/Palestine.

Andrew Smith (AS) is a New Zealander who studied English at the University of Cambridge. He graduated in 2006 with an MPhil in eighteenth-century and Romantic Literature, and currently works in London.

Paul Styles (PS) is Tourism & Visitor Services Manager with Kakadu National Park, Australia.

Iain Zaczek (IZ) is a freelance writer, living in London. He was born in Dundee and educated at Wadham College, Oxford, and the Courtauld Institute of Art. He has contributed to *The Collins Big Book of Art* and *Masterworks*.

Picture Credits

20-21 ©mediacolor's/Alamy **22** ©Natalia Bratslavsky/Alamy **23** ©Museum of History and Industry/CORBIS **25** ©Michael Jenner/Alamy **26** ©Paul A. Souders/CORBIS **29** ©Kelly-Mooney Photography/Corbis **30** ©All Canada Pictures/Photoshot **31** ©AM Corporation/Alamy **32** ©Greg Probst/CORBIS **33** ©Nik Wheeler/CORBIS **34 (t)** ©Digital Vision/Alamy **34 (b)** ©Bettmann/CORBIS **36 (t)** David R. Frazier Photolibrary, Inc./Alamy **36 (b)** ©Bettmann/CORBIS **37 (t)** ©Tom Bean/CORBIS **37 (b)** ©Nik Wheeler/CORBIS **38 (t)** ©Bettmann/CORBIS **38 (b)** ©Don Smetzer/Alamy **39 (t)** ©CORBIS **39 (b)** ©dk/Alamy **40** ©Joseph Sohm/Visions of America/Corbis **42** ©Michael S. Lewis/CORBIS **43** ©Richard A. Cooke/CORBIS **44** ©imagebroker/Alamy **45** ©MONSERRATE SCHWARTZ/Alamy **46 (t)** ©Paul A. Souders/CORBIS **46 (b)** ©Bettmann/CORBIS **48** ©ImageState/Alamy **49** ©Galen Rowell/CORBIS **50** ©SCPhotos/Alamy **51** ©JUPITERIMAGES/ Brand X/Alamy **52** ©Jerry Dennis/Art Directors **53** ©Kelly-Mooney Photography/Corbis **54** ©MERVYN REES/Alamy **55** ©Chuck Pefley/Tips Images **56** ©Steven Vidler/Eurasia Press/Corbis **59** ©John-Marshall Mantel/CORBIS **60** ©Christie's Images/CORBIS **61** ©Bettmann/CORBIS **62** ©Brooklyn Museum/Corbis **63** ©Richard Cummins/Corbis **64 (t)** ©Scottish National Portrait Gallery, Edinburgh, Scotland/ The Bridgeman Art Library **64 (b)** ©AM Corporation/Alamy **65 (t)** ©De Agostini/Photolibrary Group **65 (b)** ©Bildagentur/Tips Images **66** ©Philip Scalia/Alamy **67** ©Mark Sykes/Alamy **68 (t)** ©Liberty Island, New York, USA/ The Bridgeman Art Library **68 (b)** ©CORBIS **69 (t)** ©Mark E. Gibson/CORBIS **69 (b)** ©Getty Images **70** ©The Art Archive/Global Book Publishing **72** ©Photolibrary Group **73** ©Jon Arnold Images/Alamy **74 (t)** ©Rachel Royse/CORBIS **74 (b)** ©Allen Ginsberg/CORBIS **76** ©Catherine Karnow/CORBIS **77** ©Getty Images **78** ©Richard Cummins/CORBIS **79** ©Nik Wheeler/CORBIS **80** ©De Agostini/Photolibrary Group **81** ©Jerzy Dabrowski/dpa/Corbis **82** ©POPPERFOTO/Alamy **83** ©Patrick Eden/Alamy **84 (t)** ©Patti Mc Conville/Tips Images **84 (b)** ©Private Collection/ Peter Newark Western Americana/ The Bridgeman Art Library **85 (t)** ©The Art Archive **85 (b)** ©George H. H. Huey/CORBIS **87** ©Danny Lehman/CORBIS **88** ©Bildagentur/Tips Images **89** ©nagelestock.com/Alamy **90 (t)** ©Jon Arnold Images/Alamy **90 (b)** ©Private Collection/ Peter Newark American Pictures/ The Bridgeman Art Library **92 (t)** ©Bettmann/CORBIS **92 (b)** ©Wm. Baker/GhostWorx Images/Alamy **93 (t)** ©Russell Kord/Alamy **93 (b)** ©Kim Karpeles/Alamy **94** ©Tim Thompson/CORBIS **95** ©Arcaid/Alamy **96 (t)** ©Bettmann/CORBIS **96 (b)** ©Alison Wright/Corbis **97 (t)** ©Time & Life Pictures/Getty Images **97 (b)** ©William Manning/Corbis **98** ©Visions of America, LLC/Alamy **99** ©Bettmann/CORBIS **101 (t)** ©Luis Castaneda/Tips Images **101 (b)** ©CORBIS **102** ©Michael T. Sedam/CORBIS **103** ©Bettmann/CORBIS **104** ©Amritaphotos/Alamy **105** ©Photo Resource Hawaii/Alamy **107** ©Danny Lehman/CORBIS **108** ©Hannah Chen **109** ©The Art Archive/Gianni Dagli Orti **111** ©Danny Lehman/CORBIS **112** ©Gianni Dagli Orti/CORBIS **114** ©Danny Lehman/CORBIS **115** ©SCPhotos/Alamy **116** ©Nik Wheeler/CORBIS **118 (t)** ©Danny Lehman/CORBIS **118 (b)** ©Archivo Iconografico, S.A./CORBIS **120 (t)** ©The Art Archive/Museo de las Culturas Oaxaca/Gianni Dagli Orti **120 (b)** ©Antonio de la Cova **121 (t)** ©Danny Lehman/CORBIS **121 (b)** ©Danny Lehman/CORBIS **122** ©UNESCO/Mauchamp Desbrosses **123** ©M. Timothy O'Keefe/Alamy **124** ©Michele Westmorland/CORBIS **125** ©Craig Lovell/CORBIS **126** ©Keren Su/CORBIS **127** ©Bildarchiv Monheim GmbH/Alamy **128** ©Keith Dannemiller/D70s/Corbis **129** ©Macduff Everton/CORBIS **131** ©Barry Lewis/Corbis **133** ©Colin Brynn/Robert Harding **134** ©Bettmann/CORBIS **135** ©CORBIS **136** ©Danny Lehman/CORBIS **137** ©Danny Lehman/Corbis **138** ©Gerry White/Alamy **140** ©isifa Image Service s.r.o./Alamy **142** ©Photolibrary Group/National Geographic **143** ©WORLDWIDE photo/Alamy **144** ©John Rodriguez/iStockphoto **145** ©Bruce Adams; Eye Ubiquitous/CORBIS **146 (t)** POPPERFOTO/Alamy **146 (b)** ©Philip Gould/CORBIS **147 (t)** ©Photolibrary Group **147 (b)** ©J Marshall - Tribaleye Images/Alamy **148** ©Photolibrary Group **150** ©Diego Lezama Orezzoli/CORBIS **152** ©Wilmar Photography/Alamy **153** ©Wolfgang Kaehler/CORBIS **154** ©Andrew Kemp/Alamy **155** ©Yann Arthus-Bertrand/CORBIS **156** ©Tony Morrison **157** ©Andrew Holt/Alamy **158** ©ImageState/Alamy **159** ©Arco Images/Alamy **160** ©Anna Bailetti **161** ©Julio Donoso/CORBIS SYGMA **162** ©Archivo Iconografico, S.A./CORBIS **163** ©Yann Arthus-Bertrand/CORBIS **164** ©Jim Erickson/CORBIS **165** ©Nevada Wier/CORBIS **166** ©Melvyn Longhurst/Alamy **167** ©Gary Cook/Alamy **168** ©Alison Wright/CORBIS **169** ©Michele Falzone/Alamy **170** ©Bruno Woltzenlogel Paleo **171** ©James Brunker/Alamy **172** ©LOETSCHER CHLAUS/Alamy **173** ©UNESCO **174** ©Lemarco/Alamy **175** ©Tony Morrison **176** ©Yadid Levy/Alamy **178** ©Arco Images/Alamy **180 (t)** ©Brukenthal National Museum, Sibiu, Romania/ The Bridgeman Art Library **180 (b)** ©Alan Howden - Argentina Stock Photography/Alamy **181 (t)** ©POPPERFOTO/Alamy **181 (b)** ©Peter M. Wilson/CORBIS **183** ©Hubert Stadler/CORBIS **184-185** ©Franz-Marc Frei/CORBIS **186** ©Arni Magnusson Institute, Reykjavik, Iceland/The Bridgeman Art Library **187** ©Frans Lemmens/zefa/Corbis **188** ©Joel W. Rogers/CORBIS **189** ©akg-images/Erich Lessing **190** ©Bildarchiv Monheim GmbH/Alamy **191** ©akg-images/Juergen Sorges **192** ©Paul Thompson Images/Alamy **194** ©Stefan Selin **195** ©Mark Harris/Fotolibra **196 (t)** ©Ted Spiegel/CORBIS **196 (b)** ©Werner Forman/CORBIS **197 (t)** ©Barbro Paulsson/fotoLibra **197 (b)** ©akg-images/NordicPhotos **198** ©Photononstop/Tips Images **199** ©CuboImages srl/Alamy **200** ©INTERFOTO Pressebildagentur/Alamy **201** ©Svenja-Foto/zefa/Corbis **202** ©Dave Bartruff/CORBIS **203** ©Bildarchiv Monheim GmbH/Alamy **204** ©Robert Harding Picture Library Ltd/Alamy **205** ©f1 online/Alamy **206** ©Esa Hiltula/Alamy **207** ©INTERFOTO Pressebildagentur/Alamy **208 (t)** Richard Klune/Corbis **208 (b)** ©Wilmar Photography/Alamy **209 (t)** ©Bettmann/CORBIS **209 (b)** nagelestock.com/Alamy **210** ©Yann Arthus-Bertrand/CORBIS **212** ©akg-images/ullstein bild **213** ©UPPA/Photoshot **214** ©Massimo Listri/CORBIS **215** ©Ken Welsh/Alamy **216** ©Michael St. Maur Sheil/CORBIS **217** ©Design Pics Inc./Alamy **218 (t)** ©Adam Woolfitt/CORBIS **218 (b)** Photolibrary Group **220 (t)** akg-images **220 (b)** ©Ian M Butterfield/Alamy **221 (t)** ©Steven Vidler/Eurasia Press/Corbis **221 (b)** ©akg-images/Michael Teller **222** ©James Osmond/Alamy **223** ©Barry Mason/Alamy **224 (t)** ©Russ Merne/Alamy **224 (b)** ©Sean Sexton Collection/CORBIS **226** ©Uwe Stiens/fotoLibra **227** ©Guy Standen/fotoLibra **228** ©isifa Image Service s.r.o./Alamy **229** ©Declan Walsh/fotoLibra **230** ©Navin Mistry/Alamy **231** ©South West Images Scotland/Alamy **232** ©akg-images/Juergen Sorges **233** ©f1 online/Alamy **234 (t)** ©RogerPix/Alamy **234 (b)** ©FORBES Magazine Collection, New York, USA/ The Bridgeman Art Library **235 (t)** ©Doug Houghton/Alamy **235 (b)** ©Hulton-Deutsch Collection/CORBIS **236** ©E.O. Hoppé/CORBIS **237** ©David Robertson/Alamy **238** ©Sheila Taylor/fotoLibra **239** ©nobody/Alamy **240** ©Wojtek Buss/Tips Images **242** ©Arch White/Alamy **243** ©Jeremy Inglis/Alamy **244 (t)** ©ACE STOCK LIMITED/Alamy **244 (b)** ©Philip Mould Ltd, London/The Bridgeman Art Library **245 (t)** ©David Robertson/Alamy **245 (b)** ©akg-images **246 (t)** ©Andrew Bell/Alamy **246 (b)** ©The Print Collector/Alamy **247 (t)** ©Scottish National Portrait Gallery, Edinburgh, Scotland/ The Bridgeman Art Library **247 (b)** ©John Peter Photography/Alamy **248** ©Private Collection/ The Bridgeman Art Library **249** ©Farrell Grehan/CORBIS **250 (t)** ©Michael Jenner/Alamy **250 (b)** ©Wojtek Buss/Tips Images **252** ©Robert Harding Picture Library Ltd/Alamy **253** ©Dennis Cox/Alamy **254** ©Gari Wyn Williams/Alamy **255** ©Angelo Hornak/CORBIS **257 (t)** ©Detail Heritage/Alamy **257 (b)** ©Getty Images **258** ©Chris Pancewicz/Alamy **259** ©Geray Sweeney/CORBIS **260** ©Photolibrary Group **261** ©Glyn Thomas/Alamy 262 (t) ©World Pictures/Alamy **262 (b)** ©The National Trust Photolibrary/Alamy **263 (t)** ©Ashley Cooper/CORBIS **263 (b)** ©Gustavo Tomsich/CORBIS **264** ©Patrick Ward/CORBIS **266** ©AM Corporation/Alamy **267** ©Andy Williams/Loop Images/Corbis **268** ©Dick Makin/Alamy **269** ©Holmes Garden Photos/Alamy **270** ©Glyn Thomas/Alamy **272 (t)** ©Martin Power/fotoLibra **272 (b)** ©akg-images **273 (t)** ©Peter Turnley/CORBIS **273 (b)** ©Bettmann/CORBIS **274** ©Rod Edwards/Alamy **275** ©Adam Woolfitt/Robert Harding World Imagery/Corbis **276** ©Jose Fuste Raga/CORBIS **277** ©akg-images **278 (t)** ©Tom Mackie/Alamy **278 (b)** ©akg-images **280** ©Jan Butchofsky-Houser/CORBIS **281** ©akg-images/Sambraus **282** ©Adam Woolfitt/Robert Harding World Imagery/Corbis **283** ©Philippa Lewis; Edifice/CORBIS **284** ©Adam Woolfitt/CORBIS **285** ©Elaine Robertson/fotoLibra **286** ©Werner Forman/CORBIS **287** ©Eric Nathan/Alamy **288** ©Hulton-Deutsch Collection/CORBIS **290** ©Photolibrary Group **291** ©World Pictures/Photoshot **292** ©akg-images/Richard Booth **293** ©Jacky Parker/Alamy **294 (t)** ©Pawel Libera/Alamy **294 (b)** ©Mary Evans Picture Library/Alamy **295 (t)** ©Andy Keate; Edifice/CORBIS **295 (b)** akg-images **296** ©Skyscan/CORBIS **297** ©Clive Collie/fotoLibra **298** ©Jeremy Horner/CORBIS **299** ©Ian Goodrick/Alamy **300** ©Angelo Hornak/Corbis **301** ©Bettmann/CORBIS **302** ©akg-images/Erich Lessing **304** ©Goodshoot/Corbis **305** ©Robert Harding Picture Library/Photolibrary **306 (t)** ©akg-images **306 (b)** ©Andy Ward/fotoLibra **307 (t)** ©Eric Nathan/Alamy **307 (b)** ©Photolibrary Group **308** ©Carlos Dominguez/Corbis **309** ©Hulton-Deutsch Collection/CORBIS **310** ©Adam Woolfitt/CORBIS **311** ©Robert Preston/Alamy **312 (t)** ©akg-images **312 (b)** ©Photolibrary Group **313 (t)** ©Danita Delimont/Alamy **313 (b)** ©Greenhalf Photography/CORBIS **314** ©Photolibrary Group **316** ©Angelo Hornak/CORBIS **318 (t)** ©Mike Booth/Alamy **318 (b)** ©Photolibrary Group **319 (t)** ©Bettmann/CORBIS **319 (b)** ©Rolf Richardson/Alamy **320** ©Arcaid/Alamy **321** ©Photolibrary Group **322 (t)** ©akg-images **322 (b)** ©The National Trust Photolibrary/Alamy **323 (t)** ©akg-images akg-images/Erich Lessing **323 (b)** ©Nik Wheeler/CORBIS **324** ©Travelshots.com/Alamy **325** ©Mark Hamilton/Alamy **326** ©John Miller/Robert Harding World Imagery/Corbis **328 (t)** ©Wolfgang Kaehler/CORBIS **328 (b)** ©akg-images/ullstein bild **329 (t)** ©Arco Images/Alamy **329 (b)** ©akg-images/Erich Lessing **330** ©Photolibrary Group **331** ©Peter Horree/Alamy **333** ©Rolf Richardson/Robert Harding World Imagery/Corbis **334** ©Martyn Vickery/Alamy **335** ©akg-images **336** ©Arco Images/Alamy **338** ©Mauritius World Pictures/Photoshot **339** ©Karl Johaentges **340** ©imagebroker/Alamy **341** ©Bloomberg News/Landov/Photoshot **342 (t)** ©Fridmar Damm/zefa/Corbis **342 (b)** ©Markus Schweiß **343 (t)** ©De Agostini/Photolibrary **343 (b)** ©f1 online/Alamy **345 (t)** ©Kevin Burke/CORBIS **345 (b)** ©Bettmann/CORBIS **346 (t)** ©Mick Leeming/fotoLibra **346 (b)** ©Ludovic Maisant/CORBIS **347 (t)** ©Bildagentur RM/Tips Images **347 (b)** ©De Agostini/Photolibrary **348** ©f1 online/Alamy **349** ©Photolibrary Group **350** ©VISUM Foto GmbH/Alamy **351** ©Picture Alliance **352** ©Fridmar Damm/zefa/Corbis **353** ©Photolibrary **354 (t)** ©The Art Archive/Corbis **354 (b)** ©World Illustrated/Photoshot **355 (t)** ©tbkmedia.de/Alamy **355 (b)** ©Hulton-Deutsch Collection/CORBIS **357** ©Westend61/Alamy **359 (t)** ©Jan Woitas/dpa/Corbis **359 (b)** ©Bettmann/CORBIS **360** ©Time & Life Pictures/Getty Images **361** ©Vanni Archive/CORBIS **362 (t)** ©Bildarchiv Monheim GmbH/Alamy **362 (b)** ©Neue Pinakothek, Munich, Germany/ The Bridgeman Art Library **363 (t)** ©Albert Knapp/Alamy **363 (b)** ©Albert Knapp/Alamy **364** ©INTERFOTO Pressebildagentur/Alamy **365** ©Bob Krist/CORBIS **366** ©De Agostini/Photolibrary Group **369 (t)** ©Bildarchiv Monheim GmbH/Alamy **369 (b)** ©Maximilian Weinzierl/Alamy **370** ©Bettmann/CORBIS **371** ©Bildarchiv Monheim GmbH/Alamy **373 (t)** Peter Widmann/Alamy **373 (b)** ©Adam Woolfitt/CORBIS **374** ©Photolibrary Group **375** ©De Agostini/PhotoLibrary Group **376** ©The Bridgeman Art Library **377** ©Photolibrary Group **378** ©Reuters/CORBIS **379** ©Photolibrary Group **380** ©World Illustrated/Photoshot **381** ©Bettmann/CORBIS **383** ©Sandro Vannini/CORBIS **384** ©Alinari Archives/Corbis **385** ©Photolibrary Group **386** ©Musee Nat. du Chateau de Malmaison, Rueil-Malmaison, France/ Giraudon/ The Bridgeman Art Library **387** ©Gian Berto Vanni/CORBIS **388** ©akg-images **389** ©Photolibrary Group **390** ©Photolibrary Group **391** ©Hervé Champollion/akg-images **393 (t)** Photolibrary Group **393 (b)** ©Archivo Iconografico, S.A./CORBIS **394** ©Photolibrary Group **395** ©Alfred/epa/Corbis **396** ©Robert Holmes/CORBIS **397** ©Tibor Bognar/Corbis **398** ©Hervé Champollion/akg-images **399** ©Stuart Crump/Alamy **400 (t)** akg-images **400 (b)** ©jan isachsen/imagesfrance.com/Alamy **401 (t)** ©Don Hammond/Design Pics/Corbis **401 (b)** ©Bettmann/CORBIS **402** ©Harald A. Jahn; Harald Jahn/CORBIS **404** ©Sandro Vannini/CORBIS **405** ©Charles & Josette Lenars/CORBIS **406** ©World Pictures/Photoshot **407** ©Tips Images **408** ©Joe Cornish **410** ©Robert Haines/Alamy **411** ©Vanni Archive/CORBIS **412** ©Adam Woolfitt/CORBIS **413** ©Macduff Everton/CORBIS **414 (t)** De Agostini/Photo Library Group **414 (b)** ©Frederic Pitchal/Sygma/Corbis **415 (t)** ©Arthur Thévenart/CORBIS **415 (b)** ©Art Kowalsky/Alamy **416** ©World Pictures/Photoshot **417** ©Tristan Deschamps/Alamy **418** ©Robert Estall/CORBIS **419** ©Bildarchiv Monheim/Arcaid **420** ©Patrick Ward/Alamy **423** ©P. Deliss/Godong/Corbis **424** ©Mark ZYLBER/Alamy **425** ©J Lightfoot/Robert Harding/Photolibrary Group **426** ©World Pictures/Photoshot **427** ©Robert Estall photo agency/Alamy **429** ©akg-images/Schütze/Rodemann **430** ©Art Kowalsky/Alamy **433 (t)** ©Dave G. Houser/Corbis **433 (b)** ©Europress/Sygma/Corbis **434** ©Robert

Acknowledgments

Quintessence would like to thank Alexandra Capello, Gina Doubleday, and Vesna Vujicic-Lugassy at the UNESCO World Heritage Centre for their invaluable guidance and support during the creation of this book.

If you have any enquiries you would like to address to the organization, please contact:

World Heritage Centre
UNESCO
7, Place de Fontenoy
75007 Paris
France

Tel: ++ 33 1 45 68 15 71
Fax: ++ 33 1 45 68 55 70
Email: wh-info@unesco.org
http://whc.unesco.org

Quintessence would also like to thank the following individuals for their assistance in producing the book:

Additional photography: Dr. Antonio de la Cova, Gunnar Envall, Stefan Selin

Editorial consultancy: Ivo Juan Rodríguez Barthe, Andrea Espinosa, Alberto Vascon

Editing: Becky Gee, Carol King, Irene Lyford, Jane Simmonds

Editorial Assistance: Georg Sponholz

Index: Kay Ollerenshaw

Picture research: Helena Baser, Andrea Sadler

Proof-reading: Richard Rosenfeld

Quintessence would also like to thank the following picture libraries, and in particular, the individuals named for their assistance in tracking down the many hundreds of fantastic images to be found in the book:

Alamy
Princy Jose, Nicola Lewis, Mili Elsa, Naadiya Rasheed, Pramod Raveendran, Sajin Salim

AKG Images
Sonia Marion Harder

Arcaid
Gavin Jackson

Art Directors
Helene Rogers

Bridgeman Art Library
Georgina French, Aimee Rendell

Corbis
Giovanni D'Angelico, Ben Ghirardani, John Moelwyn-Hughes, Adriano Palumbo, Marcus Pantazis

Getty
Hayley Newman

Fotolibra
Gwyn Headley, Yvonne Seeley

Nature's Pic Images
Rob Suisted

Photolibrary
Tim Kantoch, Lorel Ward

Photoshot
David Brenes, Selina Chooramun, Colin Finlay, Tim Harris

Picture Desk
Stefanie Dedek

Rex Features
Stephen Atkinson

Robert Harding World Imagery
Andrew Mitchell

Scala Picture Library
Elvira Allocati, Veneta Bullen

Tips Images
Kate Wyras

UNESCO Photobank
Niamh Burke